GREAT POLITICAL THINKERS

Books by
WILLIAM EBENSTEIN

POLITICAL THOUGHT IN PERSPECTIVE

MODERN POLITICAL THOUGHT
The Great Issues

GREAT POLITICAL THINKERS
Plato to the Present (3rd Ed.)

INTRODUCTION TO POLITICAL PHILOSOPHY

TODAY'S ISMS
Communism, Fascism, Capitalism, Socialism (2nd Ed.)

THE GERMAN RECORD
A Political Portrait

THE PURE THEORY OF LAW

THE NAZI STATE

THE LAW OF PUBLIC HOUSING

FASCIST ITALY

GREAT POLITICAL THINKERS

THINKERS
Plato to the

Present   **by** WILLIAM EBENSTEIN

Professor of Politics, Princeton University

Third Edition

HOLT, RINEHART AND WINSTON · NEW YORK

All Rights Reserved
Library of Congress Catalog Card Number: 60-8429

To
RUTH

April, 1962

22052-0510

PREFACE

THE purpose of this book is to present the major turning points of western political thought from Plato to the present. The best way to understand these vital and trail-blazing ideas is to read the great writers themselves rather than works about them. There is room for commentary and critical analysis, but neither can take the place of the original sources. Political philosophy, like all philosophy, is not always easy and unambiguous, and the reproduction of the original statements familiarizes the reader most faithfully with the intention of the writer. Moreover, the great works of political literature have attained the rank of classics not only because they reveal philosophical depth and penetration but because they are perennially fresh and exciting as pieces of literature, providing aesthetic pleasure and enjoyment as well as intellectual challenge and stimulation. The presentation of carefully selected portions from original writings is most likely to attain both objectives.

The original materials from the great political writings are supplemented in this book in two ways. First, each chapter is prefaced by an introductory essay that seeks to place thinkers and issues in the proper historical setting and perspective. Second, the Bibliographical Notes at the end of the book contain explanatory and critical data and comments designed to help the student in his research on a particular author or problem. The customary listing of mere titles for further reading is of little use to the student who desires to broaden the range and scope of his knowledge, and it is hoped that the more detailed Bibliographical Notes in this book will aid him in discovering and exploring the vast territories of political philosophy. In general, the emphasis is on books and articles in English, but consideration is also given to bibliographical resources in other languages.

The problem of selecting important political writers for a book of this sort is not without its difficulties. Some authors are obvious musts, others are less imperative. With regard to American political thought, the field has grown so immensely that I hope to prepare a separate volume on it which will give due scope to its importance. Also, the question arises whether each author should be presented by a comparatively lengthy selection from his major work or by several briefer excerpts from several of his works. Most chapters in this book deal with only one writer, and the selection is usually limited to his single most important work. Such a method makes it possible for the reader to concentrate on fewer authors and to familiarize himself more thoroughly with the outstanding political classics of world literature and philosophy. The purpose of providing portions of great works in the original is to whet the reader's appetite to read them in their entirety, and it is hoped that this book will contribute to that end.

Whether all authors included deserve to be called "great" is open to question. Particularly regarding the more recent writers, history alone will tell how important they are from a long-term viewpoint. In some instances writers have been included, not necessarily because they are great thinkers, but because they have had considerable influence on politics, and because their statements typify an entire school of thought that is of direct and vital concern today. Similarly, not all the authors included fall, strictly speaking, into the domain of traditional political science. But it is hoped that a great economist, like Keynes, or psychologist, like Freud, will awaken in the student of politics the awareness that our political wisdom will grow in proportion to our ability to draw on new sources of knowledge and insight.

WILLIAM EBENSTEIN

Princeton University
Princeton, New Jersey

PREFACE TO THE SECOND EDITION

The friendly and generous reception accorded the first edition by both students and teachers has encouraged publication of a second edition. A new chapter on The Welfare State has been added, emphasizing its philosophical, political, and economic aspects. I hope that the usefulness of the book will thus be considerably enhanced, since the problem of the welfare state is inevitably emerging as one of the major issues of contemporary political thought.

W. E.

PREFACE TO THE THIRD EDITION

In addition to many minor changes, this new edition contains two major ones: Chapter 12 on the Protestant Reformation has been greatly expanded by the inclusion of Luther and Calvin, and the Bibliographical Notes have been completely revised and brought up-to-date.

W. E.

CONTENTS

GREAT POLITICAL THINKERS

CHAPTER 1

PLATO

THE imperishable contribution of the Greeks to western civilization lies in the taming of man and nature through reason. In the pre-Greek world, advanced peoples had learned to live with nature by wresting from it, through patient observation, some of its secrets, and by applying them to gainful purposes. But such practical knowledge never lost its close association with demons and myths, fears and hopes, punishments and rewards; and the pre-Greek conception of nature viewed physical phenomena as essentially individual, unique, and incalculable rather than as general, universal, and predictable. The Greeks were not the first to think about recurrent regularities of inanimate events, but they were the first to develop—going beyond observation and knowledge—the *scientific attitude,* a new approach to the world that constitutes to this day one of the distinctive elements of western life.

In the field of human relations, too, Greek inventiveness and originality lay, not in this or that political theory, but in the discovery of the scientific study of politics. The Greeks were not the first to think about the problem of a well-ordered society. But pre-Greek political thought had been a mixture of legend, myth, theology, and allegory, and if there was an element of independent reasoning, it served as a means to a higher end, usually to be found in the tenets of a nonrational or supernatural system, such as religion. Thus the contribution of Jewish thought to the political heritage of the world has been seminal: the idea of the brotherhood of man, of "one world," is deeply rooted in the conception of monotheism as transmitted through the Bible. By contrast, polytheism made it difficult for the Greeks to see the basic oneness of mankind, and their religious pluralism reflected their inability to transcend, intellectually and institutionally, the confines of the city-state.

From a social viewpoint, the Bible was opposed to slavery on principle—a unique phenomenon in antiquity—established a weekly day of rest (still unknown in some parts of the earth), and contained a host of protective rules in favor of workers, debtors, women, children, and the poor. The concept of "covenant," first appearing in the agreement between God and Abraham, is a frequent theme in the Bible whenever momentous decisions are to be made; it becomes again an inspiration centuries later when the Puritans attempt to build a new religion and civil society, or, still later, when President Wilson, a devout Presbyterian, names the constitution of the League of Nations a "Covenant." But, significant as these contributions to western civilization have been, they never were, nor were they meant to be, political science. They were political and social *ethics* rather than science, and as such constitute one of the three chief tributaries to the mainstream of western civilization, the other two being the Christian principle of *love* and the Greek principle of *rationalism*.

The first work that deserves to be called political science, in that it applies systematic reasoning and critical inquiry to political ideas and institutions, is Plato's *Republic*. After twenty-three hundred years it is still matchless as an introduction to the basic issues that confront human beings as citizens. No other writer on politics has equaled Plato (427–347 B. c.) in combining penetrating and dialectical reasoning with poetic imagery and symbolism.

One of the main (and most revolutionary) assumptions of the *Republic* is that the right kind of government and politics can be the legitimate object of rigorous scientific thinking, rather than the inevitable product of muddling through fear and faith, indolence and improvisation. This Platonic assumption of the applicability of reason to social relations is as hotly debated in the twentieth century as it was in Plato's own time, and it is one of the key elements that go into the making of our political outlook and temperament. To the extent that we believe in the possibility of applying reason and critical analysis to the solution of political and social issues we are all Plato's spiritual heirs, although we may heartily disagree with any or all of his specific teachings. By seeking to disprove Plato on a point of political doctrine or practice, the anti-Platonist has already conceded to Plato the most important single point: that political and social issues can be clarified by argument rather than by force and dogma.

Socrates, Plato's teacher and the chief figure in the *Republic,* has been contemptuously called the "first Social Democrat" by some modern totalitarians; what they hate in him above all is his irritating habit of endlessly searching, through argument, for the reason that lies behind accepted ideas and institutions. Other totalitarians, penetrating less deeply into Plato's thought, have usurped him as their first intellectual ancestor because there is so much in the *Republic* that is explicitly undemocratic, or outright antidemocratic. Yet implicit in Plato's and Socrates' rationalism is the assumption, incompatible with the cult of violence, that man's intellect can discover the nature of the good life and the means of attaining it by philosophical inquiry.

In one basic point, modern political analysis would gain in insight and understanding if it followed Plato more closely: Plato never starts out with the hypothesis of a *homo politicus,* an abstract "political man" unrelated to the richness and complexity of individual selves or of society as a whole. Today Plato's psychology may seem naïve in its analogies and presumed facts, but what is of timeless significance is his conviction that no theory of politics can be sound unless based on the study of man. Modern psychology has taught us enough about neurotic persons to make us realize that a healthy society cannot be composed of men and women who are haunted by fear and insecurity.

Plato's political thought also introduced the concept of the "public" as distinct from the "private." As a Greek, Plato could not be clearly aware of the opposing ideas of the individual and (or, rather, versus) the state, because the city-state was not only a social, economic, and political unity but also a spiritual and religious one. The Jewish and Christian religions separated man's soul from his quality as a citizen and established the notion of an inalienable and indestructible human spirit outside the domain and jurisdiction of government, a philosophy that was unknown and unknowable to Plato. In the polytheistic religions of the city-states, the gods were community gods, and there could be no question of the individual's being in one respect a member of his community, and in another not. Yet if Plato was unaware of the opposition of the individual versus the state—since the seventeenth century the dominant leitmotiv of all western political speculation—he was keenly aware of the *res publica,* the "common thing" in the mutual relations of human beings.

Before Greek experience and analysis, the only major dichotomy known to man, consciously or unconsciously, was that between the "sacred" and the "profane." Its evolution into that of "public" and "private" is part of western secularism that goes back directly to Greek life and thought. Medieval feudalism abandoned the distinction between private and public relations in political and economic institutions; from the king downward there was no clear-cut division between the private and public property or authority of the lords and their vassals. In such a system the color and intensity of personal relations between the ruler and the ruled make rational discussion of political issues and true constitutionalism difficult; this fact can still be observed today in countries in which (as in some parts of Latin America or Asia) impersonal government is an ideal rather than a reality.

Even when the concept of the modern sovereign state first developed in sixteenth-century Italy, *"lo stato"* meant essentially the ruler and the "machine" that he had built up for himself, and it was a long time before "the state" assumed the anonymous and impersonal character with which it was later endowed. In fascist regimes, rulers tend again to mingle inextricably the domains of the public and the private, "borrowing" castles and picture galleries that belong to their own or a conquered state, "acquiring" vast industrial empires for their brothers and nephews, and building up private, and often personal, military forces competing with those of the state. The inevitable growth of corruption in all fascist regimes is the price paid for the dissolution of the clear separation between public and private authority.

One of the hallmarks of genius is that it can enrich each generation anew. In the heyday of laissez faire, Plato's ideal of a highly trained administrative and political class, dedicated to public service without consideration of personal happiness or financial gain, exercised relatively less appeal because society was assumed to be an automatic and self-regulating piece of machinery, and political wisdom could well be summarized in the succinct formula of "the less government, the better." Plato's conception of government as the highest moral and practical task to which men of knowledge and virtue ought to devote themselves seemed out of date in the days in which doing nothing was deemed to be the noblest function of a political association. The force of circumstances, accelerated by wars and depressions, has necessarily enlarged, in recent times, the scope and function of government, and in Plato we rediscover the ideal of public service as second to none. Democrats are bound to reject Plato's own solution of this problem, the rule of those who know over those who do not, regardless of the latter's consent, but they will have to grasp, if democracy is to survive in a tough and dangerous world of competing skills, that there is no substitute for high-minded and efficient government in solving tensions and conflicts within and between nations.

We also increasingly practice Plato's teaching that the road to better government and public service is through an appropriately conceived system of education. In fact, the ultramodern and rapidly growing realization of education as a never-ending process, embracing adults as well as the young, goes back directly to Plato: he clearly saw that education was more than the acquiring of basic facts and ideas in one's childhood and adolescence, and he was the first to propose an elaborate system of adult training and education.

Democrats differ with Plato's system of education on two scores: first, Plato reserved educational opportunities of prolonged duration and intensity for future rulers only, whereas the democrat looks on education as a means to the good life that should be available to all. Second, Plato believed that the selection of rulers could best be made through the prolonged training of men and women, generally those born into the ruling class or picked, in exceptional situations, from the lower classes of the workers, farmers, and merchants. Democrats reject such a scheme and insist that political rulers be selected by popular voting. This democratic theory is valid as long as voters have enough judgment and discrimination to elect the best to public office. When they freely choose to put knaves and fools into high positions of public trust and authority, the democratic theory of selecting rulers is quickly swept away by demagogues and dictators. Whereas democracy will continue to reject Plato's scheme of training an elite of political *rulers,* it will view more sympathetically the possibility and desirability of training *public servants.* On that point, democracies are more and more abandoning the older doctrine that the spoils system, or government by crony, can be a substitute for honest and efficient administration.

One of the main causes of Plato's pervasive and persuasive influence throughout history is that he is the ablest exponent of the aristocratic theory of the state, and the acutest critic of the democratic way of life. In the evolution of mankind the extent of democratic experience is infinitesimally small, compared with its ignorance of democratic living, and putting the one on top of the other is like putting a postage stamp on top of a tall skyscraper. If history has been hitherto largely the history of inequality, it is no wonder that Plato's philosophy of inequality, mellowed by the accretion of prestige and sweetened by the reasonableness of its argument, should have been the most venerated and idealized political philosophy of the ages. Its relative moderation has immensely added to the influence of the *Republic.* Though in general in favor of a hierarchical society that, once set up, is closed rather than open, the *Republic* must seem repugnant to some conservatives on several grounds: the idea of rational inquiry into the foundations of society, that is, going to the roots of social institutions, must seem too radical, because the conservative likes to behold them as a product of natural growth with which one must not willfully, by intelligence or other means, interfere.

In describing the "first city," before the "feverish condition" sets in that necessitates the formation of the two classes of the rulers (guardians) and soldier-administrators (auxiliaries), Plato portrays a pattern of natural growth of social institutions, untampered by conscious reason, that would appeal to the conservative. But the first city, whose sole *raison d'être* lies in the satisfaction of material wants through the principle of the division of labor, is, as Glaucon puts it, a "community of pigs," lacking as yet the conscious direction of a ruling class whose specific excellence is reason. The growth of the simple first city into a condition of fever is caused, according to Plato, by the expansion and refinement of human wants, that is, by luxury. The inability of the community to fill the newly developing luxurious needs out of the existing resources (land, labor, skills) is the cause of war, either aggressive or defensive war.

The feverish condition is, however, not limited to the threat of external war but also implies the possibility of the disruption or dissolution of the health and balance of the first city through internal unrest. In order to safeguard or, rather, restore the original balance of the community, a special class of fighters is needed. Yet, if the new fighting class is not to degenerate into a class of praetorians, drunk with power and quarreling continuously among themselves and with the members of the producing class, it must receive a training that will make its members "gentle to their own people and dangerous only to enemies," instill them with courage to defend the city against internal and external enemies, and at the same time imbue them with an understanding of the principles that make the city worth defending.

The class of the fighters (auxiliaries) thus makes the existence of a still higher class necessary, the guardians, or rulers, who pick and train the auxiliaries as well as the future guardians. The characteristic quality of the rulers is *wisdom*, just as *courage* (tempered by understanding) is the characteristic quality of the fighters, and *appetite* (or the desire to satisfy material wants) is the distinctive trait of the working population (workers, farmers, merchants, doctors, nurses, actors). Just as the first city was the product of unconscious growth, the "second," or "ideal," city of the *Republic* is the product of rational direction.

The Platonic community is the first example of a planned state; but it must be borne in mind that the planned sector of this state applies only to the guardians and auxiliaries, whereas the producing class is left to itself as far as its economic activities go. Plato was an aristocrat who exhibited the bias against labor and business so characteristic of aristocrats in all ages, and the lack of regulations of the economic order of the producing class in the *Republic* indicates the contempt of the nobleman for the prosaic existence of those who must work for a living.

The life of the guardians and auxiliaries excludes individual interests, whether in property, love, or the family, but this community of absolute sharing is not socialism. The outlook of socialism is hedonistic: its objective is the increase of human happiness through the abolition of want and misery. The goal of socialism is not the realization of a preconceived just ideal of society but the attainment of maximum *happiness* for the maximum number of people *here and now*. The sharing of the guardians and auxiliaries in the *Republic* is based on a principle that is almost diametrically opposed to that of socialism: the principle of *austerity*, which puts little, if any, value on material wants and their satisfaction. Not happiness of human beings with varying and unique personalities, but the realization of a predetermined social ideal of justice is the purpose of the political community as described in the *Republic*.

Though the analogy to the communal life of the guardians and auxiliaries is not to be found in the socialist state (in which all citizens share in the amenities of life) nor in socialist communities within a nonsocialist state, it can be found in armies, monastic orders, and the clergy of churches who are denied marriage or private property. In all such groups the ruling class shares with the Platonic guardians the certainty of knowing what is best for the ruled, without asking for their consent, as well as the relative disregard for property, sex, family, or other forms of personal happiness. Plato's "socialism" of the guardians was authoritarian service rather than the sharing of happiness and enjoyment, and as such the exact antithesis of western socialism. Frederick the Great has often been called by German writers the first German socialist, because in serving the state he was as ruthless against himself as against others. Similarly, the Japanese system of "military socialism" denoted an authoritarian regime of unflinching service and sacrifice: what was shared was the readiness to die, not to enjoy life. Modern western socialism affirms, by contrast, life, not death.

The *Republic* is opposed to democracy on two levels of argument: a more obvious explicit level and a less obvious implicit level. The explicit opposition of the *Republic* to democracy rests on the threefold division of the population into rulers, fighters, and producers (farmers, artisans, traders). A numerically small aristocracy of rulers, in command of a well-trained body of soldiers and administrators, governs the third class, or producers, which constitutes four fifths or more of the total population. Plato claims that the threefold class division of the second city is but an extension of the principle of the division of labor, characteristic of the first city. Ruling or defending a state, Plato argues, is just as much a *specialized craft* as shoemaking; and if the principle of the division of labor forbids the shoemaker from making furniture, he is equally excluded from ruling, or defending and administering, the city—functions that constitute special, and specialized, crafts.

There is one objection to Plato's reasoning here (and this objection is fundamental to the whole edifice of the *Republic*): if the nature of ruling and administering a state is a specialized craft no different from shoemaking or farming, it is difficult to see why he does not simply add the two new crafts of the second city to the already existing number of crafts of the first city. In it, we may recall, there were no special crafts of ruling and administering, because the harmony of society was maintained naturally, growing out of the division of labor and without conscious guidance or rule. If, for example, the number of crafts in the first city was one hundred, the addition of two new crafts of ruling and fighting in the second city should produce one hundred and two crafts, if the second city were still based, as before, on the principle of division of labor. Instead, Plato presents us with the concept of *three classes* in the second city: first, the class of rulers (guardians in the narrower sense); second, the class of military and civilian executive aides (auxiliaries); third, the class of producers or handworkers. This last class composed, in the first city, the entire population, organized on the principle of division of labor; now, in the second city, the working part makes up only from eighty to ninety per cent.

The principle of the division of labor can produce only more and more specialized crafts, as the needs and skills of society proliferate, but it can never lead to a class system based on hierarchical values. If Plato nevertheless introduces the concept of the threefold class division into the second city, a new principle, different from that of the division of labor, must be found to distinguish the functions of ruling and administering the state from all other crafts. The main difference between the ruler-philosophers and the producers in the *Republic* is the difference between *political wisdom* and *technical knowledge*. Only the philosophers have insight into *human* problems, insight that is more than highly specialized learning. The craftsman, by contrast, has no all-comprehensive understanding of the phenomena of nature and society of which he is a part, only *limited* knowledge of a *technical* nature. Even where such knowledge, as in medicine, applies to human beings, it is still only technical knowledge and not higher philosophical understanding and insight, because the physician is interested in human beings as parts of the psychophysical world, and not of the world of values and ideas.

The Platonic craftsman is thus inferior, in two ways, to the philosopher: first, his material is limited and finite, and subject to causal or aesthetical laws the knowledge of which is relatively easy, compared with the material of the philosopher—mankind and the cosmos, the laws of which are most difficult to discover and grasp. Second, the knowledge of the craftsman never attains the height of wisdom and understanding that the philosopher reaches in his study of ultimate values, intrinsic forms, and cosmic laws. The knowledge of the craftsman is only an intermediary stage, raw material that goes into the process of learning and acquiring wisdom to which the philosopher is subjected in the *Republic*.

The democratic theory of politics challenges Plato not only in his basic assumption that the capacity to govern is possessed by only a small class, but that such capacity can be transmitted, in general (Plato admits occasional exceptions), by selective breeding. This Platonic concept of a hereditary aristocratic ruling class, not too hermetically closed to talent from below, is rejected by the democratic theory of man and the state on grounds of historical evidence and rational reflection. The democratic view of man is less pessimistic than Plato's and assumes hopefully that wisdom and understanding may be found in the most unexpected places, in log cabins as well as in stately mansions —in fact, that it is more likely to be found in log cabins.

If the explicit opposition of the *Republic* to the democratic way of life is serious enough, the implicit opposition is even more fundamental and irreconcilable. Plato assumes (in the *Republic* as in his other writings) that Truth (with a capital "T") is something eternal, unchanging and unchangeable, and that it can be made accessible to a select few through an ingeniously devised training reserved for the future fighters and rulers. The preparation of the rulers begins before they are born, as the very pairing of the parents is arranged by a preconceived plan that is to insure the highest physical and mental qualities of the offspring to be bred. Nothing is left to personal whim or accident from infancy on, and the process of education, both theoretical and practical, continues until the age of fifty. Literature, music, physical and military instruction, elementary and advanced mathematics, philosophy and metaphysics, and subordinate military and civilian-service assignments are the stages of the planned program of training philosopher-rulers: "Then when they are fifty, those who have come safely through and proved the best in all points in action and in study must be brought at last to the goal. They must lift up the eye of the soul to gaze on that which sheds light on all things; and when they have seen the Good itself, take it as a pattern for the right ordering of the state and the individual, themselves included. For the rest of their lives, most of their time will be spent in study; but they will all take their turn at the troublesome duties of public life and act as Rulers for their country's sake, not regarding it as a distinction but as an unavoidable task." Plato thus regarded the training in literary, mathematical, and philosophical knowledge as a mere preparation for the "ascent to the vision of Goodness," the "highest object of knowledge," which final stage cannot be mastered by mere rational instruction or comprehension, but partakes of the nature of *revelation,* a mystical and socially incommunicable experience. Even more explicitly than in the *Republic,* Plato stated his position in his *Seventh Letter:* "The truths of philosophy cannot be expressed in words as other subjects can, but after personal assistance in these studies from a guide, after living for some time with that guide, suddenly a flash of understanding, as it were, is kindled by a spark that leaps across, and once it has come into being within the soul it proceeds to nourish itself."

Plato nowhere defines the nature of the Good in verifiable or rational terms; it is a secret, "something beyond truth and knowledge, and, precious as these both are, of still higher worth," as he says in the *Republic.* The only approach to it is through vision and revelation, and few are blessed with the capacity to "climb the ascent" to such visions. The Platonic philosopher-ruler thus bases his rule over the people, not on superior character and rational knowledge alone, as it might appear from a hasty reading of the *Republic,* but on a personal and unique innermost experience that is mystical and incommunicable in rational terms. To know is to "contemplate the realities themselves as they are for ever in the same unchanging state," and because the ruler *knows,* as the result of his vision of the Good, he has the right to rule the people; they can never hope to attain similar summits of insight and vision, and can only *believe* in, but not rationally understand, a social order built on intuitions that are, in the ultimate, mysterious and inaccessible to common-sense experience.

The nature and scope of the authority of the rulers in the *Republic* are intimately related to its foundation. Just as the knowledge of the rulers that gives them title to rule is directed to the absolute, so is their authority, which is morally based on their training and wisdom, absolute and unconditional. The rulers have the moral right to constrain the ruled if they show any sign of defection from the established order. Plato assumes that, in general, such compulsion will not be necessary. The people will be brought up to believe in the existing class system by means of myths and allegories, because they are incapable of rigorous scientific and philosophical thinking.

But if the use of force in the *Republic* raises serious critical considerations, the recommended use of censorship and the "medicinal lie" for the upbringing of the ruling and military-executive classes is no less alarming. Plato often compares the rulers to doctors, and the ruled to patients, and he says that "for a private person to mislead the Rulers we shall declare to be a worse offence than for a patient to mislead his doctor"; and he goes on to attack such crimes as "fatal" and "subversive" in a state. Though the ruled are under no circumstances permitted to deviate from truth, particularly in their relations with the rulers, the latter may lie "in the way of a medicine." Just as a medicine may be handled only by a doctor, "if anyone, then, is to practice deception, either on the country's enemies or on its citizens, it must be the Rulers of the commonwealth, acting for its benefit; no one else may meddle with this privilege."

An illustration of such a "medicinal lie" is the fable of the origins of the class system, according to which God put gold into those who are fit to rule, silver into the auxiliaries, and iron and brass into the farmers and craftsmen. "I shall try to convince," Socrates says, "first the Rulers and the soldiers, and then the whole community," and if they accept this fable, all three classes will think of each other as "brothers born of the same soil" and will be ready to defend their land, which they will eventually think of as "mother and nurse." It is significant that Plato's example of a "medicinal lie" relates, not to a matter of subordinate expediency and convenience, but to the root of his ideal political community, namely, the inequality of the threefold class system.

As to censorship, Plato frequently expresses in the *Republic* hostility toward artists. His hostility arises from his apprehension that art appeals to feeling and passion rather than to reason and intellect. Specifically, poets must write in a way that will further the objectives of the future rulers' training (it may be recalled that only the rulers and the military-executive, but not the ruled population, are to be educated). Negatively, the poet must not, for example, present the gods in an unattractive and "all-too-human" light; if he does, "we shall be angry and refuse him the means to produce his play." Positively, the poets will be told by the rulers what elements to stress in their stories and "the limits beyond which they must not be allowed to go." The main, perhaps only, value of art is moral education, particularly self-control: "And for the mass of mankind that chiefly means obeying their governors, and themselves governing their appetite for the pleasure of eating and drinking and sex."

Plato finds Homer, Hesiod, and the other masters of Greek literature opprobrious and corrupting. Toward the end of the *Republic* the conclusion is presented that "all poetry, from Homer onwards, consists in representing a semblance of its subject, whatever it may be, including any kind of human excellence, with no grasp of the reality." In fact, the artist is assigned a place below the shoemaker or smith, because the latter have at least a limited *direct* knowledge of reality, that of their craft, whereas the artist "knows nothing worth mentioning, about the subjects he represents"; art, therefore, "is a form of play, not to be taken seriously." Because the poet, by appealing to sentiment rather than reason, "sets up a vicious form of government" in the individual soul, "we shall be justified in not admitting him into a well-ordered commonwealth."

In accepting the "medicinal lie" and the regulation, positive and negative, of the arts, Plato started a line of thought that has been enthusiastically accepted by those who base their right to rule on superior and exclusive knowledge rather than on the freely expressed consent of the ruled. Those who adhere to the creed of certainty are eventually driven to use, as a means of governing, medicinal lies, censorship, thought control, and physical compulsion.

The Platonic conception of Truth is challenged by the modern view of truth (with a small "t") as something much more tentative, hypothetical, fluid and changeable, and subject to constant checking and verifying. Further, modern philosophers insist that truth is intimately related to experience, that it can never be fully grasped, that it is an *endless process* of testing new hypotheses against new experiences, that it is not something that exists prior to man, but that it is constantly made and remade in *doing*, rather than discovered in intellectual speculation or in a flash of mystical insight. Plato's concept of Truth is more *absolute* and *individual-aristocratic*: Truth is eternally the same and unchangeable, and it can be perceived by the use of the speculative and intuitive faculties of the philosophical person, who therefore has the right to rule those who do not possess these capacities. The modern view of truth is more *relative*, *empirical*, and *social-cooperative*: truth is not eternally the same, is changeable and changing, is never attainable more than in a proximate and practical way, and—what is perhaps most important of all—it is not the product of brilliant individual intellects but of the cooperative effort of many individuals and social groups.

To take a practical illustration: whereas according to Plato, the concept of social justice is one that can be discovered and defined through illuminated reasoning, the more modern empirical and relative view holds that social justice is not a pre-existing reality logically or intuitively *discovered* by speculation or revelation, but that *temporary approximations* to justice can be worked out in a socially satisfactory fashion through negotiation and bargaining of interested groups and classes. This *dynamic* concept of truth is more modest than the *static* one of Plato, inasmuch as it appreciates the limitations of human capacity and disinterestedness in the face of a constantly changing world of circumstances; but at the same time it is also more optimistic than Plato's concept, because it holds that the process of working out approximations to truth is *open to all*, and that, in fact, such approximations are likely to be more accurate if related to the widest possible range of ascertainable experience. By contrast, Plato's view of the possibility of finding truth is more pessimistic in the sense that it is con-

ceived as a form of intellectual insight that is open, because of its final and absolute value, to only a *few select* minds. If antidemocratic and authoritarian political systems throughout history have looked back sympathetically to Plato, the
reason has been less the explicit opposition of the *Republic* to democracy than
the implicit view of a world in which truth—social, philosophical, metaphysical,
religious—is the prerogative of a small elect class, endowed with special and
exclusive capacities to apprehend it in a regime of formal training, and enabled
to translate it into reality in a preconceived framework of society in which the
few govern and the many obey and conform.

The *Republic* is not a utopia but the work of a thinker passionately interested in practical politics. Rejecting the doctrine that man must fatally and
inextricably remain a prisoner of natural or social circumstances, Plato has faith
in man's ability to create a community that will correspond to the ideal of
knowledge and, therefore, justice. If philosophy and the vision of the Good are
the highest forms of human activity, "there can be no rest from troubles" for
states or for all mankind, "unless either philosophers become kings in their
countries or those who are now called kings and rulers come to be sufficiently
inspired with a genuine desire for wisdom; unless, that is to say, political power
and philosophy meet together." This passage, probably the most famous in the
Republic, summarizes Plato's conception of a society in which the best rule, and
it makes little difference to him whether this rule is monarchy ("when there is
one man who stands out above the rest of the rulers") or aristocracy ("when
there are more than one"). The plan of such a perfect constitution and of a
"perfect man" might be difficult, "but not impossible."

Nevertheless, Plato anticipated the eventual decline of the best state and
its degeneration into progressively lower types of constitution. The first of these
forms of state is timocracy, based on ambition and love of honor and war, as
represented by Crete and Sparta, "so commonly admired." The second is oligarchy or plutocracy, the rule of the wealthy; the third is democracy, the rule
of the people; the fourth, and most imperfect, is despotism, which develops inevitably out of the anarchy of the democratic state. In each instance, Plato cor-
relates a type of human character with the form of government in which it is
most commonly reflected: "Constitutions cannot come out of sticks and stones;
they must result from the preponderance of certain characters which draw the
rest of the community in their wake."

This penetrating insight of Plato's, that government is more than a piece of
machinery, that its essence is ultimately determined by the quality of the men
and women who compose it, is still not fully grasped today. The twentieth century, in particular, is strewn with the wreckage of constitutions that failed dis-
mally, not because they were imperfect in themselves, but because they were not
suited to the "preponderant characters" in the societies for which they were devised.

In his classification of forms of state, Plato considered democracy the second
worst type of government. His description of life in a democratic society may be
overdrawn, but it remains to this day the most incisive critique of democracy.
Unless democrats assume that democracy is an exception to all human creations,

and thus free from imperfections, they must be aware of its intrinsic as well as its incidental weaknesses. If Plato maintains that democracy is "an agreeable form of anarchy with plenty and variety and an equality of a peculiar kind for equals and unequals alike," who can say that his thesis is completely wrong? The buoyant diversity and creative pluralism of the democratic society are its glory, but they are often the path to dissolution and disintegration when its members forget that they are not merely individuals with rights and liberties but also social beings with duties and obligations. Similarly, the unwillingness of democratic citizens to be led is one of the mainsprings of democratic vitality; but if carried too far, if the honest and able leaders are prevented from governing, the dishonest demagogues will take their place.

The fate of democracies in the twentieth century, in particular, has demonstrated that Plato's critique of democracy and the democratic man, far from being an unrealistic caricature of democratic life, is full of sound warnings that no democrat should miss. Nazi, fascist, and communist criticisms of democracy are relatively ephemeral and superficial, compared with the enduring and fundamental objections that Plato raises. The answer to Plato's apprehensions about the possibility of democracy lies, not in the arguments of democrats, but in their lives. The experience of history is harder to disprove than a theoretical argument. If Plato makes democrats more keenly conscious how difficult the life of freedom and fellowship is, he has, perhaps unwittingly, performed a major service to the cause of democracy.

The literary form of the *Republic* is the dialogue, in which Socrates is both the narrator and chief figure. In fact, as the dialogue proceeds, it becomes virtually a monologue, for the other participants increasingly confine their dialectical contributions to nods, monosyllabic expressions of consent, and brief rhetorical assertions that merely give Socrates a cue to go on with his argument. The conversation starts in the house of Cephalus, a retired wealthy businessman. The company includes Cephalus' son, Polemarchus, Plato's two elder brothers, Glaucon and Adeimantus, and a sophist, Thrasymachus, who is represented as a cynic. The discussion soon turns to the central question in the *Republic*, What is justice? In the discussion of justice, all elements of Plato's political philosophy are contained. In his theory of justice the relations of man to nature, to the *polis*, and to his fellow men form an architectonic whole.

Cephalus states the view, based on a long life of practical experience, that justice means honesty and rendering what is due to gods and men. Socrates sees some merit in this approach but is not satisfied with it. Polemarchus next suggests that justice means helping one's friends and harming one's enemies. Socrates is again not satisfied, as such a definition befits more the moral standards of a despot than those of a just man. At this point Thrasymachus breaks into the discussion and puts forward the view that "just" or "right" means nothing but "what is to the interest of the stronger party."

PLATO

The Republic *

1. Justice as the Interest of the Stronger

All this time Thrasymachus had been trying more than once to break in upon our conversation; but his neighbours had restrained him, wishing to hear the argument to the end. In the pause after my last words he could keep quiet no longer; but gathering himself up like a wild beast he sprang at us as if he would tear us in pieces. Polemarchus and I were frightened out of our wits, when he burst out to the whole company:

What is the matter with you two, Socrates? Why do you go on in this imbecile way, politely deferring to each other's nonsense? If you really want to know what justice means, stop asking questions and scoring off the answers you get. You know very well it is easier to ask questions than to answer them. Answer yourself, and tell us what you think justice means. I won't have you telling us it is the same as what is obligatory or useful or advantageous or profitable or expedient; I want a clear and precise statement; I won't put up with that sort of verbiage.

I was amazed by this onslaught and looked at him in terror. If I had not seen this wolf before he saw me, I really believe I should have been struck dumb; [1] but fortunately I had looked at him earlier, when he was beginning to get exasperated with our argument; so I was able to reply, though rather tremulously:

Don't be hard on us, Thrasymachus. If Polemarchus and I have gone astray in our search, you may be quite sure the mistake was not intentional. If we had been looking for a piece of gold, we should never have deliberately allowed politeness to spoil our chance of finding it; and now when we are looking for justice, a thing much more precious than gold, you cannot imagine we should defer to each other in that foolish way and not do our best to bring it to light. You must believe we are in earnest, my friend; but I am afraid the task is beyond our powers, and we might expect a man of your ability to pity us instead of being so severe.

Thrasymachus replied with a burst of sardonic laughter.

Good Lord, he said; Socrates at his old trick of shamming ignorance! I knew it; I told the others you would refuse to commit yourself and do anything sooner than answer a question.

Yes, Thrasymachus, I replied; because you are clever enough to know that if you asked someone what are the factors of the number twelve, and at the same time warned him: "Look here, you are not to tell me that 12 is twice 6, or 3 times 4, or 6 times 2, or 4 times 3; I won't put up with any such nonsense"—you must surely see that no one would answer a question put like that. He would say: "What do you

---

* From *The Republic of Plato* (trans. F. M. Cornford, Oxford University Press, 1945). By permission.

[1] A popular superstition, that if a wolf sees you first, you become dumb.

mean, Thrasymachus? Am I forbidden to give any of these answers, even if one happens to be right? Do you want me to give a wrong one?" What would you say to that?

Humph! said he. As if that were a fair analogy!

I don't see why it is not, said I; but in any case, do you suppose our barring a certain answer would prevent the man from giving it, if he thought it was the truth?

Do you mean that you are going to give me one of those answers I barred?

I should not be surprised, if it seemed to me true, on reflection.

And what if I give you another definition of justice, better than any of those? What penalty are you prepared to pay? [2]

The penalty deserved by ignorance, which must surely be to receive instruction from the wise. So I would suggest that as a suitable punishment.

I like your notion of a penalty! he said; but you must pay the costs as well.

I will, when I have any money.

That will be all right, said Glaucon; we will all subscribe for Socrates. So let us have your definition, Thrasymachus.

Oh yes, he said; so that Socrates may play the old game of questioning and refuting someone else, instead of giving an answer himself!

But really, I protested, what can you expect from a man who does not know the answer or profess to know it, and, besides that, has been forbidden by no mean authority to put forward any notions he may have? Surely the definition should naturally come from you, who say you do know the answer and can tell it us. Please do not disappoint us. I should take it as a kindness, and I hope you will not be chary of giving Glaucon and the rest of us the advantage of your instruction.

Glaucon and the others added their en-

treaties to mine. Thrasymachus was evidently longing to win credit, for he was sure he had an admirable answer ready, though he made a show of insisting that I should be the one to reply. In the end he gave way and exclaimed:

So this is what Socrates' wisdom comes to! He refuses to teach, and goes about learning from others without offering so much as thanks in return.

I do learn from others, Thrasymachus; that is quite true; but you are wrong to call me ungrateful. I give in return all I can—praise; for I have no money. And how ready I am to applaud any idea that seems to me sound, you will see in a moment, when you have stated your own; for I am sure that will be sound.

Listen then, Thrasymachus began. What I say is that "just" or "right" means nothing but what is to the interest of the stronger party. Well, where is your applause? You don't mean to give it me.

I will, as soon as I understand, I said. I don't see yet what you mean by right being the interest of the stronger party. For instance, Polydamas, the athlete, is stronger than we are, and it is to his interest to eat beef for the sake of his muscles; but surely you don't mean that the same diet would be good for weaker men and therefore be right for us?

You are trying to be funny, Socrates. It's a low trick to take my words in the sense you think will be most damaging.

No, no, I protested; but you must explain.

Don't you know, then, that a state may be ruled by a despot, or a democracy, or an aristocracy?

Of course.

And that the ruling element is always the strongest?

Yes.

Well then, in every case the laws are made by the ruling party in its own interest; a democracy makes democratic laws, a despot autocratic ones, and so on. By making these laws they define as "right"

---

[2] In certain lawsuits the defendant, if found guilty, was allowed to propose a penalty alternative to that demanded by the prosecution. The judges then decided which should be inflicted. The "costs" here means the fee which the sophist, unlike Socrates, expected from his pupils.

for their subjects whatever is for their own interest, and they call anyone who breaks them a "wrongdoer" and punish him accordingly. That is what I mean: in all states alike "right" has the same meaning, namely what is for the interest of the party established in power, and that is the strongest. So the sound conclusion is that what is "right" is the same everywhere: the interest of the stronger party.

Now I see what you mean, said I; whether it is true or not, I must try to make out. When you define right in terms of interest, you are yourself giving one of those answers you forbade to me; though, to be sure, you add "to the stronger party."

An insignificant addition, perhaps!

Its importance is not clear yet; what is clear is that we must find out whether your definition is true. I agree myself that right is in a sense a matter of interest; but when you add "to the stronger party," I don't know about that. I must consider.

Go ahead, then.

I will. Tell me this. No doubt you also think it is right to obey the men in power?

I do.

Are they infallible in every type of state, or can they sometimes make a mistake?

Of course they can make a mistake.

In framing laws, then, they may do their work well or badly?

No doubt.

Well, that is to say, when the laws they make are to their own interest; badly, when they are not?

Yes.

But the subjects are to obey any law they lay down, and they will then be doing right?

Of course.

If so, by your account, it will be right to do what is not to the interest of the stronger party, as well as what is so.

What's that you are saying?

Just what you said, I believe; but let us look again. Haven't you admitted that the rulers, when they enjoin certain acts on their subjects, sometimes mistake their own best interests, and at the same time

that it is right for the subjects to obey, whatever they may enjoin?

Yes, I suppose so.

Well, that amounts to admitting that it is right to do what is not to the interest of the rulers or the stronger party. They may unwittingly enjoin what is to their own disadvantage; and you say it is right for the others to do as they are told. In that case, their duty must be the opposite of what you said, because the weaker will have been ordered to do what is against the interest of the stronger. You with your intelligence must see how that follows.

Yes, Socrates, said Polemarchus, that is undeniable.

No doubt, Cleitophon broke in, if you are to be a witness on Socrates' side.

No witness is needed, replied Polemarchus; Thrasymachus himself admits that rulers sometimes ordain acts that are to their own disadvantage, and that it is the subjects' duty to do them.

That is because Thrasymachus said it was right to do what you are told by the men in power.

Yes, but he also said that what is to the interest of the stronger party is right; and, after making both these assertions, he admitted that the stronger sometimes command the weaker subjects to act against their interests. From all which it follows that what is in the stronger's interest is no more right than what is not.

No, said Cleitophon; he meant whatever the stronger *believes* to be in his own interest. That is what the subject must do, and what Thrasymachus meant to define as right.

That was not what he said, rejoined Polemarchus.

No matter, Polemarchus, said I; if Thrasymachus says so now, let us take him in that sense. Now, Thrasymachus, tell me, was that what you intended to say —that right means what the stronger thinks is to his interest, whether it really is so or not?

Most certainly not, he replied. Do you suppose I should speak of a man as "stronger" or "superior" at the very moment when he is making a mistake?

I did think you said as much when you admitted that rulers are not always infallible.

That is because you are a quibbler, Socrates. Would you say a man deserves to be called a physician at the moment when he makes a mistake in treating his patient and just in respect of that mistake; or a mathematician, when he does a sum wrong and just in so far as he gets a wrong result? Of course we do commonly speak of a physician or a mathematician or a scholar having made a mistake; but really none of these, I should say, is ever mistaken, in so far as he is worthy of the name we give him. So strictly speaking—and you are all for being precise—no one who practises a craft makes mistakes. A man is mistaken when his knowledge fails him; and at that moment he is no craftsman. And what is true of craftsmanship or any sort of skill is true of the ruler: he is never mistaken so long as he is acting as a ruler; though anyone might speak of a ruler making a mistake, just as he might of a physician. You must understand that I was talking in that loose way when I answered your question just now; but the precise statement is this. The ruler, in so far as he is acting as a ruler, makes no mistakes and consequently enjoins what is best for himself; and that is what the subject is to do. So, as I said at first, "right" means doing what is to the interest of the stronger.

Very well, Thrasymachus, said I. So you think I am quibbling?

I am sure you are.

You believe my questions were maliciously designed to damage your position?

I know it. But you will gain nothing by that. You cannot outwit me by cunning, and you are not the man to crush me in the open.

Bless your soul, I answered, I should not think of trying. But, to prevent any more misunderstanding, when you speak of that ruler or stronger party whose interest the weaker ought to serve, please make it clear whether you are using the words in the ordinary way or in that strict sense you have just defined.

I mean a ruler in the strictest possible sense. Now quibble away and be as malicious as you can. I want no mercy. But you are no match for me.

Do you think me mad enough to beard a lion or try to outwit a Thrasymachus?

You did try just now, he retorted, but it wasn't a success.

2. Ruling as an Art

Enough of this, said I. Now tell me about the physician in that strict sense you spoke of: is it his business to earn money or to treat his patients? Remember, I mean your physician who is worthy of the name.

To treat his patients.

And what of the ship's captain in the true sense? Is he a mere seaman or the commander of the crew?

The commander.

Yes, we shall not speak of him as a seaman just because he is on board a ship. That is not the point. He is called captain because of his skill and authority over the crew.

Quite true.

And each of these people has some special interest? [1]

No doubt.

And the craft in question exists for the very purpose of discovering that interest and providing for it?

Yes.

Can it equally be said of any craft that it has an interest, other than its own greatest possible perfection?

What do you mean by that?

Here is an illustration. If you ask me

---

[1] All the persons mentioned have some interest. The craftsman *qua* craftsman has an interest in doing his work as well as possible, which is the same thing as serving the interest of the subjects on whom his craft is exercised; and the subjects have their interest, which the craftsman is there to promote.

whether it is sufficient for the human body just to be itself, with no need of help from without, I should say, Certainly not; it has weaknesses and defects, and its condition is not all that it might be. That is precisely why the art of medicine was invented: it was designed to help the body and provide for its interests. Would not that be true?

It would.

But now take the art of medicine itself. Has that any defects or weaknesses? Does any art stand in need of some further perfection, as the eye would be imperfect without the power of vision or the ear without hearing, so that in their case an art is required that will study their interests and provide for their carrying out those functions? Has the art itself any corresponding need of some further art to remedy its defects and look after its interests; and will that further art require yet another, and so on for ever? Or will every art look after its own interests? Or, finally, is it not true that no art needs to have its weaknesses remedied or its interests studied either by another art or by itself, because no art has in itself any weakness or fault, and the only interest it is required to serve is that of its subject-matter? In itself, an art is sound and flawless, so long as it is entirely true to its own nature as an art in the strictest sense—and it is the strict sense that I want you to keep in view. Is not that true?

So it appears.

Then, said I, the art of medicine does not study its own interest, but the needs of the body, just as a groom shows his skill by caring for horses, not for the art of grooming. And so every art seeks, not its own advantage—for it has no deficiencies—but the interest of the subject on which it is exercised.

It appears so.

But surely, Thrasymachus, every art has authority and superior power over its subject.

To this he agreed, though very reluctantly.

So far as arts are concerned, then, no art ever studies or enjoins the interest of the superior or stronger party, but always that of the weaker over which it has authority.

Thrasymachus assented to this at last, though he tried to put up a fight. I then went on:

So the physician, as such, studies only the patient's interest, not his own. For as we agreed, the business of the physician, in the strict sense, is not to make money for himself, but to exercise his power over the patient's body; and the ship's captain, again, considered strictly as no mere sailor, but in command of the crew, will study and enjoin the interest of his subordinates, not his own.

He agreed reluctantly.

And so with government of any kind: no ruler, in so far as he is acting as ruler, will study or enjoin what is for his own interest. All that he says and does will be said and done with a view to what is good and proper for the subject for whom he practises his art.

At this point, when everyone could see that Thrasymachus' definition of justice had been turned inside out, instead of making any reply, he said:

Socrates, have you a nurse?

Why do you ask such a question as that? I said. Wouldn't it be better to answer mine?

Because she lets you go about sniffling like a child whose nose wants wiping. She hasn't even taught you to know a shepherd when you see one, or his sheep either.

What makes you say that?

Why, you imagine that a herdsman studies the interests of his flocks or cattle, tending and fattening them up with some other end in view than his master's profit or his own; and so you don't see that, in politics, the genuine ruler regards his subjects exactly like sheep, and thinks of nothing else, night and day, but the good he can get out of them for himself. You are so far out in your notions of right and wrong, justice and injustice, as not to know that "right" actually means what is good for someone else, and to be "just" means serving the interest of the stronger who rules, at the cost of the subject who obeys; whereas injustice is just the reverse, asserting its authority over those innocents who are called just, so that they minister solely to their master's advantage and happiness, and not in the least degree to their own. Innocent as you are yourself, Socrates, you must see that a just man always has the worst of it. Take a private business: when a partnership is wound up, you will never find that the more honest of two partners comes off with the larger share; and in their relations to the state, when there are taxes to be paid, the honest man will pay more than the other on the same amount of property; or if there is money to be distributed, the dishonest will get it all. When either of them hold some public office, even if the just man loses in no other way, his private affairs at any rate will suffer from neglect, while his principles will not allow him to help himself from the public funds; not to mention the offence he will give to his friends and relations by refusing to sacrifice those principles to do them a good turn. Injustice has all the opposite advantages. I am speaking of the type I described just now, the man who can get the better of other people on a large scale: you must fix your eye on him, if you want to judge how much it is to one's own interest not to be just. You can see that best in the most consummate form of injustice, which rewards wrongdoing with supreme welfare and happiness and reduces its victims, if they won't retaliate in kind, to misery. That form is despotism, which uses force or fraud to plunder the goods of others, public or private, sacred or profane, and to do it in a wholesale way. If you are caught committing any one of these crimes on a small scale, you are punished and disgraced; they call it sacrilege, kidnapping, burglary, theft and brigandage. But if, besides taking their property, you turn all your countrymen into slaves, you will hear no more of those ugly names;

your countrymen themselves will call you the happiest of men and bless your name, and so will everyone who hears of such a complete triumph of injustice; for when people denounce injustice, it is because they are afraid of suffering wrong, not of doing it. So true is it, Socrates, that injustice, on a grand enough scale, is superior to justice in strength and freedom and autocratic power; and "right," as I said at first, means simply what serves the interest of the stronger party; "wrong" means what is for the interest and profit of oneself.

Having deluged our ears with this torrent of words, as the man at the baths might empty a bucket over one's head, Thrasymachus meant to take himself off; but the company obliged him to stay and defend his position. I was specially urgent in my entreaties.

My good Thrasymachus, said I, do you propose to fling a doctrine like that at our heads and then go away without explaining it properly or letting us point out to you whether it is true or not? Is it so small a matter in your eyes to determine the whole course of conduct which every one of us must follow to get the best of life?

Don't I realize it is a serious matter? he retorted.

Apparently not, said I; or else you have no consideration for us, and do not care whether we shall lead better or worse lives for being ignorant of this truth you profess to know. Do take the trouble to let us into your secret; if you treat us handsomely, you may be sure it will be a good investment; there are so many of us to show our gratitude. I will make no secret of my own conviction, which is that injustice is not more profitable than justice, even when left free to work its will unchecked. No; let your unjust man have full power to do wrong, whether by successful violence or by escaping detection; all the same he will not convince me that he will gain more than he would by being just. There may be others here who feel as I do, and set justice above injustice. It is for you to convince us that we are not well advised.

How can I? he replied. If you are not convinced by what I have just said, what more can I do for you? Do you want to be fed with my ideas out of a spoon?

God forbid! I exclaimed; not that. But I do want you to stand by your own words; or, if you shift your ground, shift it openly and stop trying to hoodwink us as you are doing now. You see, Thrasymachus, to go back to your earlier argument, in speaking of the shepherd you did not think it necessary to keep to that strict sense you laid down when you defined the genuine physician. You represent him, in his character of shepherd, as feeding up his flock, not for their own sake but for the table or the market, as if he were out to make money as a caterer or a cattle-dealer, rather than a shepherd. Surely the sole concern of the shepherd's art is to do the best for the charges put under its care; its own best interest is sufficiently provided for, so long as it does not fall short of all that shepherd ing should imply. On that principle it followed, I thought, that any kind of authority, in the state or in private life, must, in its character of authority, consider solely what is best for those under its care. Now what is your opinion? Do you think that the men who govern states—I mean rulers in the strict sense—have no reluctance to hold office?

I don't think so, he replied; I know it.

Well, but haven't you noticed, Thrasymachus, that in other positions of authority no one is willing to act unless he is paid wages, which he demands on the assumption that all the benefit of his action will go to his charges? Tell me: Don't we always distinguish one form of skill from another by its power to effect some particular result? Do say what you really think, so that we may get on.

Yes, that is the distinction.

And also each brings us some benefit that is peculiar to it: medicine gives health, for example; the art of navigation, safety at sea; and so on.

Yes.

And wage-earning brings us wages; that is its distinctive product. Now, speaking with that precision which you proposed, you would not say that the art of navigation is the same as the art of medicine, merely on the ground that a ship's captain regained his health on a voyage, because the sea air was good for him. No more would you identify the practice of medicine with wage-earning because a man may keep his health while earning wages, or a physician attending a case may receive a fee.

No.

And, since we agreed that the benefit obtained by each form of skill is peculiar to it, any common benefit enjoyed alike by all these practitioners must come from some further practice common to them all?

It would seem so.

Yes, we must say that if they all earn wages, they get that benefit in so far as they are engaged in wage-earning as well as in practising their several arts.

He agreed reluctantly.

This benefit, then—the receipt of wages—does not come to a man from his special art. If we are to speak strictly, the physician, as such, produces health; the builder, a house; and then each, in his further capacity of wage-earner, gets his pay. Thus every art has its own function and benefits its proper subject. But suppose the practitioner is not paid; does he then get any benefit from his art?

Clearly not.

And is he doing no good to anyone either, when he works for nothing?

No, I suppose he does some good.

Well then, Thrasymachus, it is now clear that no form of skill or authority provides for its own benefit. As we were saying some time ago, it always studies and prescribes what is good for its subject—the interest of the weaker party, not of the stronger. And that, my friend, is why I said that no one is willing to be in a position of authority and undertake to set straight other men's troubles, without demanding to be paid; because, if he is to do his work well, he will never, in his capacity of ruler, do, or command others to do, what is best for himself, but only what is best for the subject. For that reason, if he is to consent, he must have his recompense, in the shape of money or honour, or of punishment in case of refusal.

What do you mean, Socrates? asked Glaucon. I recognize two of your three kinds of reward; but I don't understand what you mean by speaking of punishment as a recompense.

Then you don't understand the recompense required by the best type of men, or their motive for accepting authority when they do consent. You surely know that a passion for honours or for money is rightly regarded as something to be ashamed of.

Yes, I do.

For that reason, I said, good men are unwilling to rule, either for money's sake or for honour. They have no wish to be called mercenary for demanding to be paid, or thieves for making a secret profit out of their office; nor yet will honours tempt them, for they are not ambitious. So they must be forced to consent under threat of penalty; that may be why a readiness to accept power under no such constraint is thought discreditable. And the heaviest penalty for declining to rule is to be ruled by someone inferior to yourself. That is the fear, I believe, that makes decent people accept power; and when they do, they face the prospect of authority with no idea that they are coming into the enjoyment of a comfortable berth; it is forced upon them because they can find no one better than themselves, or even as good, to be entrusted with power. If there could ever be a society of perfect men, there might well be as much competition to evade office as there now is to gain it; and it would then be clearly seen that the genuine ruler's nature is to seek only the advantage of the subject, with the consequence that any man of understanding would sooner have another to do the best for him than be at the pains to do the best for that other himself. On this point, then, I entirely disagree with Thrasymachus' doctrine that right means what is to the interest of the stronger.

3. The Rudiments of Social Organization

I was delighted with these speeches from Glaucon and Adeimantus, whose gifts I had always admired. How right, I exclaimed, was Glaucon's lover to begin that poem of his on your exploits at the battle of Megara by describing you two as the

sons divine
of Ariston's noble line!

Like father, like sons: there must indeed be some divine quality in your nature, if you can plead the cause of injustice so eloquently and still not be convinced yourselves that it is better than justice. That you are not really convinced I am sure from all I know of your dispositions, though your words might well have left me in doubt. But the more I trust you, the harder I find it to reply. How can I come to the rescue? I have no faith in my own powers, when I remember that you were not satisfied with the proof I thought I had given to Thrasymachus that it is better to be just. And yet I cannot stand by and hear justice reviled without lifting a finger. I am afraid to commit a sin by holding aloof while I have breath and strength to say a word in its defence. So there is nothing for it but to do the best I can.

Glaucon and the others begged me to step into the breach and carry through our inquiry into the real nature of justice and injustice, and the truth about their respective advantages. So I told them what I thought. This is a very obscure question, I said, and we shall need keen sight to see our way. Now, as we are not remarkably clever, I will make a suggestion as to how we should proceed. Imagine a rather short-sighted person told to read an inscription in small letters from some way off. He would think it a godsend if someone pointed out that the same inscription was written up elsewhere on a bigger scale, so that he could first read the larger characters and then make out whether the smaller ones were the same.

No doubt, said Adeimantus; but what analogy do you see in that to our inquiry?

I will tell you. We think of justice as a quality that may exist in a whole community as well as in an individual, and the community is the bigger of the two. Possibly, then, we may find justice there in larger proportions, easier to make out. So I suggest that we should begin by inquiring what justice means in a state. Then we can go on to look for its counterpart on a smaller scale in the individual.

That seems a good plan, he agreed.

Well then, I continued, suppose we imagine a state coming into being before our eyes. We might then be able to watch the growth of justice or of injustice within it. When that is done, we may hope it will be easier to find what we are looking for.

Much easier.

Shall we try, then, to carry out this scheme? I fancy it will be no light undertaking; so you had better think twice.

No need for that, said Adeimantus. Don't waste any more time.

My notion is, said I, that a state comes into existence because no individual is self-sufficing; we all have many needs. But perhaps you can suggest some different origin for the foundation of a community?

No, I agree with you.

So, having all these needs, we call in one another's help to satisfy our various requirements; and when we have collected a number of helpers and associates to live together in one place, we call that settlement a state.

Yes.

So if one man gives another what he has to give in exchange for what he can get, it is because each finds that to do so is for his own advantage.

Certainly.

Very well, said I. Now let us build up our imaginary state from the beginning. Apparently, it will owe its existence to our needs, the first and greatest need being the provision of food to keep us alive. Next we shall want a house; and thirdly, such things as clothing.

True.

How will our state be able to supply all these demands? We shall need at least one man to be a farmer, another a builder, and a third a weaver. Will that do, or shall we add a shoemaker and one or two more to provide for our personal wants?

By all means.

The minimum state, then, will consist of four or five men.

Apparently.

Now here is a further point. Is each one of them to bring the product of his work into a common stock? Should our one farmer, for example, provide food enough for four people and spend the whole of his working time in producing corn, so as to share with the rest; or should he take no notice of them and spend only a quarter of his time on growing just enough corn for himself, and divide the other three-quarters between building his house, weaving his clothes, and making his shoes, so as to save the trouble of sharing with others and attend himself to all his own concerns?

The first plan might be the easier, replied Adeimantus.

That may very well be so, said I; for, as you spoke, it occurred to me, for one thing, that no two people are born exactly alike. There are innate differences which fit them for different occupations.

I agree.

And will a man do better working at many trades, or keeping to one only?

Keeping to one.

And there is another point: obviously work may be ruined, if you let the right time go by. The workman must wait upon the work; it will not wait upon his leisure and allow itself to be done in a spare moment. So the conclusion is that more things will be produced and the work be more easily and better done, when every man is set free from all other occupations to do, at the right time, the one thing for which he is naturally fitted.

That is certainly true.

We shall need more than four citizens,

then, to supply all those necessaries we mentioned. You see, Adeimantus, if the farmer is to have a good plough and spade and other tools, he will not make them himself. No more will the builder and weaver and shoemaker make all the many implements they need. So quite a number of carpenters and smiths and other craftsmen must be enlisted. Our miniature state is beginning to grow.

It is.

Still, it will not be very large, even when we have added cowherds and shepherds to provide the farmers with oxen for the plough, and the builders as well as the farmers with draught-animals, and the weavers and shoemakers with wool and leather.

No; but it will not be so very small either.

And yet, again, it will be next to impossible to plant our city in a territory where it will need no imports. So there will have to be still another set of people, to fetch what it needs from other countries.

There will.

Moreover, if these agents take with them nothing that those other countries require in exchange, they will return as empty-handed as they went. So, besides everything wanted for consumption at home, we must produce enough goods of the right kind for the foreigners whom we depend on to supply us. That will mean increasing the number of farmers and craftsmen.

Yes.

And then, there are these agents who are to import and export all kinds of goods—merchants, as we call them. We must have them; and if they are to do business overseas, we shall need quite a number of shipowners and others who know about that branch of trading.

We shall.

Again, in the city itself how are the various sets of producers to exchange their products? That was our object, you will remember, in forming a community and so laying the foundation of our state.

Obviously, they must buy and sell.

That will mean having a market-place, and a currency to serve as a token for purposes of exchange.

Certainly.

Now suppose a farmer, or an artisan, brings some of his produce to market at a time when no one is there who wants to exchange with him. Is he to sit there idle, when he might be at work?

No, he replied; there are people who have seen an opening here for their services. In well-ordered communities they are generally men not strong enough to be of use in any other occupation. They have to stay where they are in the market-place and take goods for money from those who want to sell, and money for goods from those who want to buy.

That, then, is the reason why our city must include a class of shopkeepers—so we call these people who sit still in the market-place to buy and sell, in contrast with merchants who travel to other countries.

Quite so.

There are also the services of yet another class, who have the physical strength for heavy work, though on intellectual grounds they are hardly worth including in our society—hired labourers, as we call them, because they sell the use of their strength for wages. They will go to make up our population.

Yes.

Well, Adeimantus, has our state now grown to its full size?

Perhaps.

Then, where in it shall we find justice or injustice? If they have come in with one of the elements we have been considering, can you say with which one?

I have no idea, Socrates; unless it be somewhere in their dealings with one another.

You may be right, I answered. Anyhow, it is a question which we shall have to face.

4. The Luxurious State

Let us begin, then, with a picture of our citizens' manner of life, with the provision we have made for them. They will be producing corn and wine, and making clothes and shoes. When they have built their houses, they will mostly work without their coats or shoes in summer, and in winter be well shod and clothed. For their food, they will prepare flour and barley-meal for kneading and baking, and set out a grand spread of loaves and cakes on rushes or fresh leaves. Then they will lie on beds of myrtle-boughs and byrony and make merry with their children, drinking their wine after the feast with garlands on their heads and singing the praises of the gods. So they will live pleasantly together; and a prudent fear of poverty or war will keep them from begetting children beyond their means.

Here Glaucon interrupted me: You seem to expect your citizens to feast on dry bread.

True, I said; I forgot that they will have something to give it a relish, salt, no doubt, and olives, and cheese, and country stews of roots and vegetables. And for dessert we will give them figs and peas and beans; and they shall roast myrtle-berries and acorns at the fire, while they sip their wine. Leading such a healthy life in peace, they will naturally come to a good old age, and leave their children to live after them in the same manner.

That is just the sort of provender you would supply, Socrates, if you were founding a community of pigs.

Well, how are they to live, then, Glaucon?

With the ordinary comforts. Let them lie on couches and dine off tables on such dishes and sweets as we have nowadays.

Ah, I see, said I; we are to study the growth, not just of a state, but of a luxurious one. Well, there may be no harm in that; the consideration of luxury may help us to discover how justice and injustice take root in society. The community I have described seems to me the ideal one, in sound health as it were: but if you want to see one suffering from inflammation, there is nothing to hinder us. So some

people, it seems, will not be satisfied to live in this simple way; they must have couches and tables and furniture of all sorts; and delicacies too, perfumes, unguents, courtesans, sweetmeats, all in plentiful variety. And besides, we must not limit ourselves now to those bare necessaries of house and clothes and shoes; we shall have to set going the arts of embroidery and painting, and collect rich materials, like gold and ivory.

Yes.

Then we must once more enlarge our community. The healthy one will not be big enough now; it must be swollen up with a whole multitude of callings not ministering to any bare necessity: hunters and fishermen, for instance; artists in sculpture, painting, and music; poets with their attendant train of professional reciters, actors, dancers, producers; and makers of all sorts of household gear, including everything for women's adornment. And we shall want more servants: children's nurses and attendants, lady's maids, barbers, cooks and confectioners. And then swineherds—there was no need for them in our original state, but we shall want them now; and a great quantity of sheep and cattle too, if people are going to live on meat.

Of course.

And with this manner of life physicians will be in much greater request.

No doubt.

The country, too, which was large enough to support the original inhabitants, will now be too small. If we are to have enough pasture and plough land, we shall have to cut off a slice of our neighbours' territory; and if they too are not content with necessaries, but give themselves up to getting unlimited wealth, they will want a slice of ours.

That is inevitable, Socrates.

So the next thing will be, Glaucon, that we shall be at war.

No doubt.

We need not say yet whether war does good or harm, but only that we have discovered its origin in desires which are the most fruitful source of evils both to individuals and to states.[1]

Quite true.

This will mean a considerable addition to our community—à whole army, to go out to battle with any invader, in defence of all this property and of the citizens we have been describing.

Why so? Can't they defend themselves?

Not if the principle was right, which we all accepted in framing our society. You remember we agreed that no one man can practise many trades or arts satisfactorily.

True.

Well, is not the conduct of war an art, quite as important as shoemaking?

Yes.

But we would not allow our shoemaker to try to be also a farmer or weaver or builder, because we wanted our shoes well made. We gave each man one trade, for which he was naturally fitted; he would do good work, if he confined himself to that all his life, never letting the right moment slip by. Now in no form of work is efficiency so important as in war; and fighting is not so easy a business that a man can follow another trade, such as farming or shoemaking, and also be an efficient soldier. Why, even a game like draughts or dice must be studied from childhood; no one can become a fine player in his spare moments. Just taking up a shield or other weapon will not make a man capable of fighting that very day in any sort of warfare, any more than taking up a tool or implement of some kind will make a man a craftsman or an athlete, if he does not understand its use and has never been properly trained to handle it.

No; if that were so, tools would indeed be worth having.

These guardians of our state, then, inasmuch as their work is the most important of all, will need the most complete freedom from other occupations and the greatest amount of skill and practice.

I quite agree.

[1] "All wars are made for the sake of getting money," *Phaedo* 66 c.

And also a native aptitude for their calling.

Certainly.

So it is our business to define, if we can, the natural gifts that fit men to be guardians of a commonwealth, and to select them accordingly. It will certainly be a formidable task; but we must grapple with it to the best of our power.

Yes.

5. The Guardians' Temperament

Don't you think then, said I, that, for the purpose of keeping guard, a young man should have much the same temperament and qualities as a well-bred watch-dog? I mean, for instance, that both must have quick sense to detect an enemy, swiftness in pursuing him, and strength, if they have to fight when they have caught him.

Yes, they will need all those qualities.

And also courage, if they are to fight well.

Of course.

And courage, in dog or horse or any other creature, implies a spirited disposition. You must have noticed that a high spirit is unconquerable. Every soul possessed of it is fearless and indomitable in the face of any danger.

Yes, I have noticed that.

So now we know what physical qualities our Guardian must have, and also that he must be of a spirited temper.

Yes.

Then, Glaucon, how are men of that natural disposition to be kept from behaving pugnaciously to one another and to the rest of their countrymen?

It is not at all easy to see.

And yet they must be gentle to their own people and dangerous only to enemies; otherwise they will destroy themselves without waiting till others destroy them.

True.

What are we to do, then? If gentleness and a high temper are contraries, where shall we find a character to combine them?

Both are necessary to make a good Guardian, but it seems they are incompatible. So we shall never have a good Guardian.

It looks like it.

Here I was perplexed, but on thinking over what we had been saying, I remarked that we deserved to be puzzled, because we had not followed up the comparison we had just drawn.

What do you mean? he asked.

We never noticed that, after all, there are natures in which these contraries are combined. They are to be found in animals, and not least in the kind we compared to our Guardian. Well-bred dogs, as you know, are by instinct perfectly gentle to people whom they know and are accustomed to, and fierce to strangers. So the combination of qualities we require for our Guardian is, after all, possible and not against nature.

Evidently.

Do you further agree that, besides this spirited temper, he must have a philosophical element in his nature?

I don't see what you mean.

This is another trait you will see in the dog. It is really remarkable how the creature gets angry at the mere sight of a stranger and welcomes anyone he knows, though he may never have been treated unkindly by the one or kindly by the other. Did that never strike you as curious?

I had not thought of it before; but that certainly is how a dog behaves.

Well, but that shows a fine instinct, which is philosophic in the true sense.

How so?

Because the only mark by which he distinguishes a friendly and an unfriendly face is that he knows the one and does not know the other; and if a creature makes that the test of what it finds congenial or otherwise, how can you deny that it has a passion for knowledge and understanding?

Of course, I cannot.

And that passion is the same thing as philosophy—the love of wisdom.[1]

Yes.

Shall we boldly say, then, that the same is true of human beings? If a man is to be gentle towards his own people whom he knows, he must have an instinctive love of wisdom and understanding.

Agreed.

So the nature required to make a really noble Guardian of our commonwealth will be swift and strong, spirited, and philosophic.

Quite so.

Given those natural qualities, then, how are these Guardians to be brought up and educated? First, will the answer to that question help the purpose of our whole inquiry, which is to make out how justice and injustice grow up in a state? We want to be thorough, but not to draw out this discussion to a needless length.

Glaucon's brother answered: I certainly think it will help.

If so, I said, we must not think of dropping it, though it may be rather a long business.

I agree.

Come on then. We will take our time and educate our imaginary citizens.

Yes, let us do so.

6. Primary Education of the Guardians: Censorship of Literature

What is this education to be, then? Perhaps we shall hardly invent a system better than the one which long experience has worked out, with its two branches for the cultivation of the mind and of the body. And I suppose we shall begin with the mind, before we start physical training.

Naturally.

[1] The ascription of a philosophic element to dogs is not seriously meant. We might regard man's love of knowledge as rooted in an instinct of curiosity to be found in animals; but curiosity has no connexion with gentleness, and for Plato reason is an independent faculty, existing only in man and not developed from any animal instinct.

Under that head will come stories;[1] and of these there are two kinds: some are true, others fictitious. Both must come in, but we shall begin our education with the fictitious kind.

I don't understand, he said.

Don't you understand, I replied, that we begin by telling children stories, which, taken as a whole, are fiction, though they contain some truth? Such story-telling begins at an earlier age than physical training; that is why I said we should start with the mind.

You are right.

And the beginning, as you know, is always the most important part, especially in dealing with anything young and tender. That is the time when the character is being moulded and easily takes any impress one may wish to stamp on it.

Quite true.

Then shall we simply allow our children to listen to any stories that anyone happens to make up, and so receive into their minds ideas often the very opposite of those we shall think they ought to have when they are grown up?

No, certainly not.

It seems, then, our first business will be to supervise the making of fables and legends, rejecting all which are unsatisfactory; and we shall induce nurses and mothers to tell their children only those which we have approved, and to think more of moulding their souls with these stories than they now do of rubbing their limbs to make them strong and shapely. Most of the stories now in use must be discarded.

What kind do you mean?

If we take the great ones, we shall see in them the pattern of all the rest, which are bound to be of the same stamp and to have the same effect.

No doubt; but which do you mean by the great ones?

The stories in Hesiod and Homer and the poets in general, who have at all times composed fictitious tales and told them to mankind.

Which kind are you thinking of, and what fault do you find in them?

The worst of all faults, especially if the story is ugly and immoral as well as false —misrepresenting the nature of gods and heroes, like an artist whose picture is utterly unlike the object he sets out to draw.

That is certainly a serious fault; but give me an example.

A signal instance of false invention about the highest matters is that foul story, which Hesiod repeats, of the deeds of Uranus and the vengeance of Cronos;[2] and then there is the tale of Cronos's doings and of his son's treatment of him. Even if such tales were true, I should not have supposed they should be lightly told to thoughtless young people. If they cannot be altogether suppressed, they should only be revealed in a mystery, to which access should be as far as possible restricted by requiring the sacrifice, not of a pig, but of some victim such as very few could afford.[3]

It is true: those stories are objectionable.

Yes, and not to be repeated in our commonwealth, Adeimantus. We shall not tell a child that, if he commits the foulest crimes or goes to any length in punishing his father's misdeeds, he will be doing nothing out of the way, but only what the first and greatest of the gods have done before him.

I agree; such stories are not fit to be repeated.

Nor yet any tales of warfare and intrigues and battles of gods against gods, which are equally untrue. If our future

---

[1] In a wide sense, tales, legends, myths, narratives in poetry or prose.

[2] Hesiod, *Theogony*, 154 ff. A primitive myth of the forcing apart of Sky (Uranus) and Earth (Gaia) by their son Cronos, who mutilated his father. Zeus, again, took vengeance on his father Cronos for trying to destroy his children. These stories were sometimes cited to justify ill-treatment of parents.

[3] The usual sacrifice at the Eleusinian Mysteries was a pig, which was cheap. In a mystery unedifying legends might be given an allegorical interpretation, a method which had been applied to Homer since the end of the sixth century B. C.

Guardians are to think it a disgrace to quarrel lightly with one another, we shall not let them embroider robes with the Battle of the Giants [4] or tell them of all the other feuds of gods and heroes with their kith and kin. If by any means we can make them believe that no one has ever had a quarrel with a fellow citizen and it is a sin to have one, that is the sort of thing our old men and women should tell children from the first; and as they grow older, we must make the poets write for them in the same strain. Stories like those of Hera being bound by her son, or of Hephaestus flung from heaven by his father for taking his mother's part when she was beaten, and all those battles of the gods in Homer, must not be admitted into our state, whether they be allegorical or not. A child cannot distinguish the allegorical sense from the literal, and the ideas he takes in at that age are likely to become indelibly fixed; hence the great importance of seeing that the first stories he hears shall be designed to produce the best possible effect on his character.

Yes, that is reasonable. But if we were asked which of these stories in particular are of the right quality, what should we answer?

I replied: You and I, Adeimantus, are not, for the moment, poets, but founders of a commonwealth. As such, it is not our business to invent stories ourselves, but only to be clear as to the main outlines to be followed by the poets in making their stories and the limits beyond which they must not be allowed to go.

True; but what are these outlines for any account they may give of the gods?

Of this sort, said I. A poet, whether he is writing epic, lyric, or drama, surely ought always to represent the divine nature as it really is. And the truth is that that nature is good and must be described as such.

Unquestionably.

Well, nothing that is good can be harm-

ful; and if it cannot do harm, it can do no evil; and so it cannot be responsible for any evil.

I agree.

Again, goodness is beneficent, and hence the cause of well-being.

Yes.

Goodness, then, is not responsible for everything, but only for what is as it should be. It is not responsible for evil.

Quite true.

It follows, then, that the divine, being good, is not, as most people say, responsible for everything that happens to mankind, but only for a small part; for the good things in human life are far fewer than the evil, and, whereas the good must be ascribed to heaven only, we must look elsewhere for the cause of evils.

I think that is perfectly true.

So we shall condemn as a foolish error Homer's description of Zeus as the "dispenser of both good and ill." We shall disapprove when Pandarus' violation of oaths and treaties is said to be the work of Zeus and Athena, or when Themis and Zeus are said to have caused strife among the gods. Nor must we allow our young people to be told by Aeschylus that "Heaven implants guilt in man, when his will is to destroy a house utterly." If a poet writes of the sorrows of Niobe or the calamities of the house of Pelops or of the Trojan war, either he must not speak of them as the work of a god, or, if he does so, he must devise some such explanation as we are now requiring: he must say that what the god did was just and good, and the sufferers were the better for being chastised. One who pays a just penalty must not be called miserable, and his misery then laid at heaven's door. The poet will only be allowed to say that the wicked were miserable because they needed chastisement, and the punishment of heaven did them good. If our commonwealth is to be well-ordered, we must fight to the last against any member of it being suffered to speak of the divine, which is good, being responsible for evil. Neither young nor

---

[4] Such a robe was woven by maidens for the statue of Athena at the Great Panathenaea.

old must listen to such tales, in prose or verse. Such doctrine would be impious, self-contradictory, and disastrous to our commonwealth.

I agree, he said, and I would vote for a law to that effect.

Well then, that shall be one of our laws about religion. The first principle to which all must conform in speech or writing is that heaven is not responsible for everything, but only for what is good.

I am quite satisfied.

If anyone, then, is to practise deception, either on the country's enemies or on its citizens, it must be the Rulers of the commonwealth, acting for its benefit; no one else may meddle with this privilege. For a private person to mislead such Rulers we shall declare to be a worse offence than for a patient to mislead his doctor or an athlete his trainer about his bodily condition, or for a seaman to misinform his captain about the state of the ship or of the crew. So, if anyone else in our commonwealth "of all that practise crafts, physician, seer, or carpenter," is caught not telling the truth, the Rulers will punish him for introducing a practice as fatal and subversive in a state as it would be in a ship.

7. Selection of Rulers: The Guardians' Manner of Living

Good, said I; and what is the next point to be settled? Is it not the question, which of these Guardians are to be rulers and which are to obey?

No doubt.

Well, it is obvious that the elder must have authority over the young, and that the rulers must be the best.

Yes.

And as among farmers the best are those with a natural turn for farming, so, if we want the best among our Guardians, we must take those naturally fitted to watch over a commonwealth. They must have the right sort of intelligence and ability; and also they must look upon the commonwealth as their special concern—the sort of concern that is felt for something so closely bound up with oneself that its interests and fortunes, for good or ill, are held to be identical with one's own.

Exactly.

So the kind of men we must choose from among the Guardians will be those who, when we look at the whole course of their lives, are found to be full of zeal to do whatever they believe is for the good of the commonwealth and never willing to act against its interest.

Yes, they will be the men we want.

We must watch them, I think, at every age and see whether they are capable of preserving this conviction that they must do what is best for the community, never forgetting it or allowing themselves to be either forced or bewitched into throwing it over.

How does this throwing over come about?

I will explain. When a belief passes out of the mind, a man may be willing to part with it, if it is false and he has learnt better, or unwilling, if it is true.

I see how he might be willing to let it go; but you must explain how he can be unwilling.

Where is your difficulty? Don't you agree that men are unwilling to be deprived of good, though ready enough to part with evil? Or that to be deceived about the truth is evil, to possess it good? Or don't you think that possessing truth means thinking of things as they really are?

You are right. I do agree that men are unwilling to be robbed of a true belief.

When that happens to them, then, it must be by theft, or violence, or bewitchment.

Again I do not understand.

Perhaps my metaphors are too high-flown. I call it theft when one is persuaded out of one's belief or forgets it. Argument in the one case, and time in the other, steal it away without one's knowing what is happening. You understand now?

Yes.

And by violence I mean being driven to change one's mind by pain or suffering.

That too I understand, and you are right.

And bewitchment, as I think you would agree, occurs when a man is beguiled out of his opinion by the allurements of pleasure or scared out of it under the spell of panic.

Yes, all delusions are like a sort of bewitchment.

As I said just now, then, we must find out who are the best guardians of this inward conviction that they must always do what they believe to be best for the commonwealth. We shall have to watch them from earliest childhood and set them tasks in which they would be most likely to forget or to be beguiled out of this duty. We shall then choose only those whose memory holds firm and who are proof against delusion.

Yes.

We must also subject them to ordeals of toil and pain and watch for the same qualities there. And we must observe them when exposed to the test of yet a third kind of bewitchment. As people lead colts up to alarming noises to see whether they are timid, so these young men must be brought into terrifying situations and then into scenes of pleasure, which will put them to severer proof than gold tried in the furnace. If we find one bearing himself well in all these trials and resisting every enchantment, a true guardian of himself, preserving always that perfect rhythm and harmony of being which he has acquired from his training in music and poetry, such a one will be of the greatest service to the commonwealth as well as to himself. Whenever we find one who has come unscathed through every test in childhood, youth, and manhood, we shall set him as a Ruler to watch over the commonwealth; he will be honoured in life, and after death receive the highest tribute of funeral rites and other memorials. All who do not reach this standard we must reject. And that, I think, my dear Glaucon, may be taken as an outline of the way in which we shall select Guardians to be set in authority as Rulers.

I am very much of your mind.

These, then, may properly be called Guardians in the fullest sense, who will ensure that neither foes without shall have the power, nor friends within the wish, to do harm. Those young men whom up to now we have been speaking of as Guardians, will be better described as Auxiliaries, who will enforce the decisions of the Rulers.

I agree.

Now, said I, can we devise something in the way of those convenient fictions we spoke of earlier, a single bold flight of invention,[1] which we may induce the community in general, and if possible the Rulers themselves, to accept?

What kind of fiction?

Nothing new; something like an Eastern tale of what, according to the poets, has happened before now in more than one part of the world. The poets have been believed; but the thing has not happened in our day, and it would be hard to persuade anyone that it could ever happen again.

You seem rather shy of telling this story of yours.

With good reason, as you will see when I have told it.

Out with it; don't be afraid.

Well, here it is; though I hardly know how to find the courage or the words to express it. I shall try to convince, first the Rulers and the soldiers,[2] and then the whole community, that all that nurture and education which we gave them was only something they seemed to experience as it were in a dream. In reality they were the whole time down inside the earth, being moulded

---

[1] This phrase is commonly rendered by "noble lie," a self-contradictory expression no more applicable to Plato's harmless allegory than to a New Testament parable or the Pilgrim's Progress, and liable to suggest that he would countenance the lies, for the most part ignoble, now called propaganda.

[2] Note that the Guardians themselves are to accept this allegory, if possible. It is not "propaganda" foisted on the masses by the Rulers.

and fostered while their arms and all their equipment were being fashioned also; and at last, when they were complete, the earth sent them up from her womb into the light of day. So now they must think of the land they dwell in as a mother and nurse, whom they must take thought for and defend against any attack, and of their fellow citizens as brothers born of the same soil.

You might well be bashful about coming out with your fiction.

No doubt; but still you must hear the rest of the story. It is true, we shall tell our people in this fable, that all of you in this land are brothers; but the god who fashioned you mixed gold in the composition of those among you who are fit to rule, so that they are of the most precious quality; and he put silver in the Auxiliaries, and iron and brass in the farmers and craftsmen. Now, since you are all of one stock, although your children will generally be like their parents, sometimes a golden parent may have a silver child or a silver parent a golden one, and so on with all the other combinations. So the first and chief injunction laid by heaven upon the Rulers is that, among all the things of which they must show themselves good guardians, there is none that needs to be so carefully watched as the mixture of metals in the souls of the children. If a child of their own is born with an alloy of iron or brass, they must, without the smallest pity, assign him the station proper to his nature and thrust him out among the craftsmen or the farmers. If, on the contrary, these classes produce a child with gold or silver in his composition, they will promote him, according to his value, to be a Guardian or an Auxiliary. They will appeal to a prophecy that ruin will come upon the state when it passes into the keeping of a man of iron or brass. Such is the story; can you think of any device to make them believe it?

Not in the first generation; but their sons and descendants might believe it, and finally the rest of mankind.[3]

Well, said I, even so it might have a good effect in making them care more for the commonwealth and for one another; for I think I see what you mean.

So, I continued, we will leave the success of our story to the care of popular tradition; and now let us arm these sons of Earth and lead them, under the command of their Rulers, to the site of our city. There let them look round for the best place to fix their camp, from which they will be able to control any rebellion against the laws from within and to beat off enemies who may come from without like wolves to attack the fold. When they have pitched their camp and offered sacrifice to the proper divinities, they must arrange their sleeping quarters; and these must be sufficient to shelter them from winter cold and summer heat.

Naturally. You mean they are going to live there?

Yes, said I; but live like soldiers, not like men of business.

What is the difference?

I will try to explain. It would be very strange if a shepherd were to disgrace himself by keeping, for the protection of his flock, dogs who were so ill-bred and badly trained that hunger or unruliness or some bad habit or other would set them worrying the sheep and behaving no better than wolves. We must take every precaution against our Auxiliaries treating the citizens in any such way and, because they are stronger, turning into savage tyrants instead of friendly allies; and they will have been furnished with the best of safeguards, if they have really been educated in the right way.

But surely there is nothing wrong with their education.

We must not be too positive about that, my dear Glaucon; but we can be sure of what we said not long ago, that if they are to have the best chance of being gentle

---

[3] Just as the tradition that the Athenians were "autochthonous" in a literal sense was popularly believed, though Plato would suppose it to have been originally invented by some myth-making poet.

and humane to one another and to their charges, they must have the right education, whatever that may be.

We were certainly right there.

Then besides that education, it is only common sense to say that the dwellings and other belongings provided for them must be such as will neither make them less perfect Guardians nor encourage them to maltreat their fellow citizens.

True.

With that end in view, let us consider how they should live and be housed. First, none of them must possess any private property beyond the barest necessaries. Next, no one is to have any dwelling or store-house that is not open for all to enter at will. Their food, in the quantities required by men of temperance and courage who are in training for war, they will receive from the other citizens as the wages of their guardianship, fixed so that there shall be just enough for the year with nothing over; and they will have meals in common and all live together like soldiers in a camp. Gold and silver, we shall tell them, they will not need, having the divine counterparts of those metals always in their souls as a god-given possession, whose purity it is not lawful to sully by the acquisition of that mortal dross, current among mankind, which has been the occasion of so many unholy deeds. They alone of all the citizens are forbidden to touch and handle silver or gold, or to come under the same roof with them, or wear them as ornaments, or drink from vessels made of them. This manner of life will be their salvation and make them the saviours of the commonwealth. If ever they should come to possess land of their own and houses and money, they will give up their guardianship for the management of their farms and households and become tyrants at enmity with their fellow citizens instead of allies. And so they will pass all their lives in hating and being hated, plotting and being plotted against, in much greater fear of their enemies at home than of any foreign foe, and fast heading for the destruction that will soon overwhelm their country with themselves. For all these reasons let us say that this is how our Guardians are to be housed and otherwise provided for, and let us make laws accordingly.

By all means, said Glaucon.

Here Adeimantus interposed. Socrates, he said, how would you meet the objection that you are not making these people particularly happy? It is their own fault too, if they are not; for they are really masters of the state, and yet they get no good out of it as other rulers do, who own lands, build themselves fine houses with handsome furniture, offer private sacrifices to the gods, and entertain visitors from abroad; who possess, in fact, that gold and silver you spoke of, with everything else that is usually thought necessary for happiness. These people seem like nothing so much as a garrison of mercenaries posted in the city and perpetually mounting guard.

Yes, I said, and what is more they will serve for their food only without getting a mercenary's pay, so that they will not be able to travel on their own account or to make presents to a mistress or to spend as they please in other ways, like the people who are commonly thought happy. You have forgotten to include these counts in your indictment, and many more to the same effect.

Well, take them as included now.

And you want to hear the answer?

Yes.

We shall find one, I think, by keeping to the line we have followed so far. We shall say that, though it would not be surprising if even these people were perfectly happy under such conditions, our aim in founding the commonwealth was not to make any one class specially happy, but to secure the greatest possible happiness for the community as a whole. We thought we should have the best chance of finding justice in a state so constituted, just as we should find injustice where the constitution was of the worst possible type; we could then decide the question which has been before us all this time. For the moment, we are constructing, as we believe, the state which will be happy as a whole, not trying to secure the well-being of a select few; we shall study a state of the opposite kind presently. It is as if we were colouring a statue and someone came up and blamed us for not putting the most beautiful colours on the noblest parts of the figure; the eyes, for instance, should be painted crimson, but we had made them black. We should think it a fair answer to say: Really, you must not expect us to paint eyes so handsome as not to look like eyes at all. This applies to all the parts: the question is whether, by giving each its proper colour, we make the whole beautiful. So too, in the present case, you must not press us to endow our Guardians with a happiness that will make them anything rather than guardians. We could quite easily clothe our farmers in gorgeous robes, crown them with gold, and invite them to till the soil at their pleasure; or we might set our potters to lie on couches by their fire, passing round the wine and making merry, with their wheel at hand to work at whenever they felt so inclined. We could make all the rest happy in the same sort of way, and so spread this well-being through the whole community. But you must not put that idea into our heads; if we take your advice, the farmer will be no farmer, the potter no longer a potter; none of the elements that make up the community will keep its character. In many cases this does not matter so much: if a cobbler goes to the bad and pretends to be what he is not, he is not a danger to the state; but, as you must surely see, men who make only a vain show of being guardians of the laws and of the commonwealth bring the whole state to utter ruin, just as, on the other hand, its good government and well-being depend entirely on them. We, in fact, are making genuine Guardians who will be the last to bring harm upon the commonwealth; if our critic aims rather at producing a happiness like that of a party of peasants feasting at a fair, what he has

in mind is something other than a civic community. So we must consider whether our aim in establishing Guardians is to secure the greatest possible happiness for them, or happiness is something of which we should watch the development in the whole commonwealth. If so, we must compel these Guardians and Auxiliaries of ours to second our efforts; and they, and all the rest with them, must be induced to make themselves perfect masters each of his own craft. In that way, as the community grows into a well-ordered whole, the several classes may be allowed such measure of happiness as their nature will compass.

I think that is an admirable reply.

8. The Virtues in the State

So now at last, son of Ariston, said I, your commonwealth is established. The next thing is to bring to bear upon it all the light you can get from any quarter, with the help of your brother and Polemarchus and all the rest, in the hope that we may see where justice is to be found in it and where injustice, how they differ, and which of the two will bring happiness to its possessor, no matter whether gods and men see that he has it or not.

Nonsense, said Glaucon; you promised to conduct the search yourself, because it would be a sin not to uphold justice by every means in your power.

That is true; I must do as you say, but you must all help.

We will.

I suspect, then, we may find what we are looking for in this way. I take it that our state, having been founded and built up on the right lines, is good in the complete sense of the word.

It must be.

Obviously, then, it is wise, brave, temperate, and just.

Obviously.

Then if we find some of these qualities in it, the remainder will be the one we have not found. It is as if we were looking somewhere for one of any four things: if we detected that one immediately, we should be satisfied; whereas if we recognized the other three first, that would be enough to indicate the thing we wanted; it could only be the remaining one. So here we have four qualities. Had we not better follow that method in looking for the one we want?

Surely.

To begin then: the first quality to come into view in our state seems to be its wisdom; and there appears to be something odd about this quality.[1]

What is there odd about it?

I think the state we have described really has wisdom; for it will be prudent in counsel, won't it?

Yes.

And prudence in counsel is clearly a form of knowledge; good counsel cannot be due to ignorance and stupidity.

Clearly.

But there are many and various kinds of knowledge in our commonwealth. There is the knowledge possessed by the carpenters or the smiths, and the knowledge how to raise crops. Are we to call the state wise and prudent on the strength of these forms of skill?

No; they would only make it good at furniture-making or working in copper or agriculture.

Well then, is there any form of knowledge, possessed by some among the citizens of our new-founded commonwealth, which will enable it to take thought, not for some particular interest, but for the best possible conduct of the state as a whole in its internal and external relations?

Yes, there is.

What is it, and where does it reside?

It is precisely that art of guardianship which resides in those Rulers whom we just called Guardians in the full sense.

And what would you call the state on the strength of that knowledge?

Prudent and truly wise.

And do you think there will be more or fewer of these genuine Guardians in our state than there will be smiths?

Far fewer.

Fewer, in fact, than any of those other groups who are called after the kind of skill they possess?

Much fewer.

So, if a state is constituted on natural principles, the wisdom it possesses as a whole will be due to the knowledge residing in the smallest part, the one which takes the lead and governs the rest. Such knowledge is the only kind that deserves the name of wisdom, and it appears to be ordained by nature that the class privileged to possess it should be the smallest of all.

Quite true.

Here then we have more or less made out one of our four qualities and its seat in the structure of the commonwealth.

To my satisfaction, at any rate.

Next there is courage. It is not hard to discern that quality or the part of the community in which it resides so as to entitle the whole to be called brave.

Why do you say so?

Because anyone who speaks of a state as either brave or cowardly can only be thinking of that part of it which takes the field and fights in its defence; the reason being, I imagine, that the character of the state is not determined by the bravery or cowardice of the other parts.

No.

Courage, then, is another quality which a community owes to a certain part of itself. And its being brave will mean that, in this part, it possesses the power of preserving, in all circumstances, a conviction about the sort of things that it is right to be afraid of—the conviction implanted by the education which the law-giver has established. Is not that what you mean by courage?

I do not quite understand. Will you say it again?

[1] Because the wisdom of the whole resides in the smallest part, as explained below.

I am saying that courage means preserving something.

Yes, but what?

The conviction, inculcated by lawfully established education, about the sort of things which may rightly be feared. When I added "in all circumstances," I meant preserving it always and never abandoning it, whether under the influence of pain or of pleasure, of desire or of fear. If you like, I will give an illustration.

Please do.

You know how dyers who want wool to take a purple dye, first select the white wool from among all the other colours, next treat it very carefully to make it take the dye in its full brilliance, and only then dip it in the vat. Dyed in that way, wool gets a fast colour, which no washing, even with soap, will rob of its brilliance; whereas if they choose wool of any colour but white, or if they neglect to prepare it, you know what happens.

Yes, it looks washed-out and ridiculous.

That illustrates the result we were doing our best to achieve when we were choosing our fighting men and training their minds and bodies. Our only purpose was to contrive influences whereby they might take the colour of our institutions like a dye, so that, in virtue of having both the right temperament and the right education, their convictions about what ought to be feared and on all other subjects might be indelibly fixed, never to be washed out by pleasure and pain, desire and fear, solvents more terribly effective than all the soap and fuller's earth in the world. Such a power of constantly preserving, in accordance with our institutions, the right conviction about the things which ought, or ought not, to be feared, is what I call courage. That is my position, unless you have some objection to make.

None at all, he replied; if the belief were such as might be found in a slave or an animal—correct, but not produced by education—you would hardly describe it as in accordance with our institutions, and you would give it some other name than courage.

Quite true.

Then I accept your account of courage. You will do well to accept it, at any rate as applying to the courage of the ordinary citizen; [2] if you like we will go into it more fully some other time. At present we are in search of justice, rather than of courage; and for that purpose we have said enough.

I quite agree.

Two qualities, I went on, still remain to be made out in our state, temperance and the object of our whole inquiry, justice. Can we discover justice without troubling ourselves further about temperance?

I do not know, and I would rather not have justice come to light first, if that means that we should not go on to consider temperance. So if you want to please me, take temperance first.

Of course I have every wish to please you. Do go on then.

I will. At first sight, temperance seems more like some sort of concord or harmony than the other qualities did.

How so?

Temperance surely means a kind of orderliness, a control of certain pleasures and appetites. People use the expression, "master of oneself," whatever that means, and various other phrases that point the same way.

Quite true.

Is not "master of oneself" an absurd expression? A man who was master of himself would presumably be also subject to himself, and the subject would be master; for all these terms apply to the same person.

No doubt.

I think, however, the phrase means that within the man himself, in his soul, there is a better part and a worse; and that he is his own master when the part which is better by nature has the worse under its control. It is certainly a term of praise; whereas it is considered a disgrace, when,

---

[2] As distinct from the perfect courage of the philosophic Ruler, based on immediate knowledge of values.

through bad breeding or bad company, the better part is overwhelmed by the worse, like a small force outnumbered by a multitude. A man in that condition is called a slave to himself and intemperate.

Probably that is what is meant.

Then now look at our newly founded state and you will find one of these two conditions realized there. You will agree that it deserves to be called master of itself, if temperance and self-mastery exist where the better part rules the worse.

Yes, I can see that is true.

It is also true that the great mass of multifarious appetites and pleasures and pains will be found to occur chiefly in children and women and slaves, and, among free men so called, in the inferior multitude; whereas the simple and moderate desires which, with the aid of reason and right belief, are guided by reflection, you will find only in a few, and those with the best inborn dispositions and the best educated

Yes, certainly.

Do you see that this state of things will exist in your commonwealth, where the desires of the inferior multitude will be controlled by the desires and wisdom of the superior few? Hence, if any society can be called master of itself and in control of pleasures and desires, it will be ours.

Quite so.

On all these grounds, then, we may describe it as temperate. Furthermore, in our state, if anywhere, the governors and the governed will share the same conviction on the question who ought to rule. Don't you think so?

I am quite sure of it.

Then, if that is their state of mind, in which of the two classes of citizens will temperance reside—in the governors or in the governed?

In both, I suppose.

So we were not wrong in divining a resemblance between temperance and some kind of harmony. Temperance is not like courage and wisdom, which made the state wise and brave by residing each in one particular part. Temperance works in a

different way; it extends throughout the whole gamut of the state, producing a consonance of all its elements from the weakest to the strongest as measured by any standard you like to take—wisdom, bodily strength, numbers, or wealth. So we are entirely justified in identifying with temperance this unanimity or harmonious agreement between the naturally superior and inferior elements on the question which of the two should govern, whether in the state or in the individual.

I fully agree.

Good, said I. We have discovered in our commonwealth three out of our four qualities, to the best of our present judgment. What is the remaining one, required to make up its full complement of goodness? For clearly this will be justice.

Clearly.

Now is the moment, then, Glaucon, for us to keep the closest watch, like huntsmen standing round a covert, to make sure that justice does not slip through and vanish undetected. It must certainly be somewhere hereabouts; so keep your eyes open for a view of the quarry, and if you see it first, give me the alert.

I wish I could, he answered; but you will do better to give me a lead and not count on me for more than eyes to see what you show me.

Pray for luck, then, and follow me.

I will, if you will lead on.

The thicket looks rather impenetrable, said I; too dark for it to be easy to start up the game. However, we must push on.

Of course we must.

Here I gave the view halloo. Glaucon, I exclaimed, I believe we are on the track and the quarry is not going to escape us altogether.

That is good news.

Really, I said, we have been extremely stupid. All this time the thing has been under our very noses from the start, and we never saw it. We have been as absurd as a person who hunts for something he has all the time got in his hand. Instead of looking at the thing, we have been staring into the distance. No doubt that is why it escaped us.

What do you mean?

I believe we have been talking about the thing all this while without ever understanding that we were giving some sort of account of it.

Do come to the point. I am all ears.

Listen, then, and judge whether I am right. You remember how, when we first began to establish our commonwealth and several times since, we have laid down, as a universal principle, that everyone ought to perform the one function in the community for which his nature best suited him. Well, I believe that that principle, or some form of it, is justice.

We certainly laid that down.

Yes, and surely we have often heard people say that justice means minding one's own business and not meddling with other men's concerns; and we have often said so ourselves.

We have.

Well, my friend, it may be that this minding of one's own business, when it takes a certain form, is actually the same thing as justice. Do you know what makes me think so?

No, tell me.

I think that this quality which makes it possible for the three we have already considered, wisdom, courage, and temperance, to take their place in the commonwealth, and so long as it remains present secures their continuance, must be the remaining one. And we said that, when three of the four were found, the one left over would be justice.

It must be so.

Well now, if we had to decide which of these qualities will contribute most to the excellence of our commonwealth, it would be hard to say whether it was the unanimity of rulers and subjects, or the soldier's fidelity to the established conviction about what is, or is not, to be feared, or the watchful intelligence of the Rulers; or whether its excellence were not above all due to the observance by everyone, child or woman, slave or freeman or artisan, ruler or ruled, of this principle that each one should do his own proper work without interfering with others.

It would be hard to decide, no doubt.

It seems, then, that this principle can at any rate claim to rival wisdom, temperance, and courage as conducing to the excellence of a state. And would you not say that the only possible competitor of these qualities must be justice?

Yes, undoubtedly.

Here is another thing which points to the same conclusion. The judging of lawsuits is a duty that you will lay upon your Rulers, isn't it?

Of course.

And the chief aim of their decisions will be that neither party shall have what belongs to another or be deprived of what is his own.

Yes.

Because that is just?

Yes.

So here again justice admittedly means that a man should possess and concern himself with what properly belongs to him.

True.

Again, do you agree with me that no great harm would be done to the community by a general interchange of most forms of work, the carpenter and the cobbler exchanging their positions and their tools and taking on each other's jobs, or even the same man undertaking both?

Yes, there would not be much harm in that.

But I think you will also agree that another kind of interchange would be disastrous. Suppose, for instance, someone whom nature designed to be an artisan or tradesman should be emboldened by some advantage, such as wealth or command of votes or bodily strength, to try to enter the order of fighting men; or some member of that order should aspire, beyond his merits, to a seat in the council-chamber of the Guardians. Such interference and exchange of social positions and tools, or the attempt to combine all these forms of work in the same person, would be fatal to the commonwealth.

Most certainly.

Where there are three orders, then, any plurality of functions or shifting from one order to another is not merely utterly harmful to the community, but one might fairly call it the extreme of wrongdoing. And you will agree that to do the greatest of wrongs to one's own community is injustice.

Surely.

This, then, is injustice. And, conversely, let us repeat that when each order—tradesman, Auxiliary, Guardian—keeps to its own proper business in the commonwealth and does its own work, that is justice and what makes a just society.

I entirely agree.

9. The Three Parts of the Soul

We must not be too positive yet, said I. If we find that this same quality when it exists in the individual can equally be identified with justice, then we can at once give our assent; there will be no more to be said; otherwise, we shall have to look further. For the moment, we had better finish the inquiry which we began with the idea that it would be easier to make out the nature of justice in the individual if we first tried to study it in something on a larger scale. That larger thing we took to be a state, and so we set about constructing the best one we could, being sure of finding justice in a state that was good. The discovery we made there must now be applied to the individual. If it is confirmed, all will be well; but if we find that justice in the individual is something different, we must go back to the state and test our new result. Perhaps if we brought the two cases into contact like flint and steel, we might strike out between them the spark of justice, and in its light confirm the conception in our own minds.

A good method. Let us follow it.

Now, I continued, if two things, one large, the other small, are called by the same name, they will be alike in that respect to which the common name applies. Accordingly, in so far as the quality of justice is concerned, there will be no difference between a just man and a just society.

No.

Well, but we decided that a society was just when each of the three types of human character it contained performed its own function; and again, it was temperate and brave and wise by virtue of certain other affections and states of mind of those same types.

True.

Accordingly, my friend, if we are to be justified in attributing those same virtues to the individual, we shall expect to find that the individual soul contains the same three elements and that they are affected in the same way as are the corresponding types in society.

That follows.

Here, then, we have stumbled upon another little problem: Does the soul contain these three elements or not?

Not such a very little one, I think. It may be a true saying, Socrates, that what is worth while is seldom easy.

Apparently; and let me tell you, Glaucon, it is my belief that we shall never reach the exact truth in this matter by following our present methods of discussion; the road leading to that goal is longer and more laborious. However, perhaps we can find an answer that will be up to the standard we have so far maintained in our speculations.

Is not that enough? I should be satisfied for the moment.

Well, it will more than satisfy me, I replied.

Don't be disheartened, then, but go on.

Surely, I began, we must admit that the same elements and characters that appear in the state must exist in every one of us; where else could they have come from? It would be absurd to imagine that among peoples with a reputation for a high-spirited character, like the Thracians and Scythians and northerners generally, the states have not derived that character from their individual members; or that it is otherwise with the love of knowledge, which would be ascribed chiefly to our own part of the world, or with the love of money, which one would specially connect with Phoenicia and Egypt.

Certainly.

So far, then, we have a fact which is easily recognized. But here the difficulty begins. Are we using the same part of ourselves in all these three experiences, or a different part in each? Do we gain knowledge with one part, feel anger with another, and with yet a third desire the pleasures of food, sex, and so on? Or is the whole soul at work in every impulse and in all these forms of behaviour? The difficulty is to answer that question satisfactorily.

I quite agree.

Let us approach the problem whether these elements are distinct or identical in this way. It is clear that the same thing cannot act in two opposite ways or be in two opposite states at the same time, with respect to the same part of itself, and in relation to the same object. So if we find such contradictory actions or states among the elements concerned, we shall know that more than one must have been involved.

Very well.

Consider this proposition of mine, then. Can the same thing, at the same time and with respect to the same part of itself, be at rest and in motion?

Certainly not.

We had better state this principle in still more precise terms, to guard against misunderstanding later on. Suppose a man is standing still, but moving his head and arms. We should not allow anyone to say that the same man was both at rest and in motion at the same time, but only that part of him was at rest, part in motion. Isn't that so?

Yes.

An ingenious objector might refine still further and argue that a peg-top, spinning with its peg fixed at the same spot, or indeed any body that revolves in the same place, is both at rest and in motion as a whole. But we should not agree, because the parts in respect of which such a body is moving and at rest are not the same. It contains an axis and a circumference; and in respect of the axis it is at rest inasmuch as the axis is not inclined in any direction, while in respect of the circumference it revolves; and if, while it is spinning, the axis does lean out of the perpendicular in all directions, then it is in no way at rest.

That is true.

No objection of that sort, then, will disconcert us or make us believe that the same thing can ever act or be acted upon in two opposite ways, or be two opposite things, at the same time, in respect of the same part of itself, and in relation to the same object.

I can answer for myself at any rate.

Well, anyhow, as we do not want to spend time in reviewing all such objections to make sure that they are unsound, let us proceed on this assumption, with the understanding that, if we ever come to think otherwise, all the consequences based upon it will fall to the ground.

Yes, that is a good plan.

Now, would you class such things as assent and dissent, striving after something and refusing it, attraction and repulsion, as pairs of opposite actions or states of mind —no matter which?

Yes, they are opposites.

And would you not class all appetites such as hunger and thirst, and again willing and wishing, with the affirmative members of those pairs I have just mentioned? For instance, you would say that the soul of a man who desires something is striving after it, or trying to draw to itself the thing it wishes to possess, or again, in so far as it is willing to have its want satisfied, it is giving its assent to its own longing, as if to an inward question.

Yes.

And, on the other hand, disinclination, unwillingness, and dislike, we should class on the negative side with acts of rejection or repulsion.

Of course.

That being so, shall we say that appetites form one class, the most conspicuous being those we call thirst and hunger?

Yes.

Thirst being desire for drink, hunger for food?

Yes.

Now, is thirst, just in so far as it is thirst, a desire in the soul for anything more than simply drink? Is it, for instance, thirst for hot drink or for cold, for much drink or for little, or in a word for drink of any particular kind? Is it not rather true that you will have a desire for cold drink only if you are feeling hot as well as thirsty, and for hot drink only if you are feeling cold; and if you want much drink or little, that will be because your thirst is a great thirst or a little one? But, just in itself, thirst or hunger is a desire for nothing more than its natural object, drink or food, pure and simple.

Yes, he agreed, each desire, just in itself, is simply for its own natural object. When the object is of such and such a particular kind, the desire will be correspondingly qualified.[1]

We must be careful here, or we might be troubled by the objection that no one desires mere food and drink, but always wholesome food and drink. We shall be told that what we desire is always something that is good; so if thirst is a desire, its object must be, like that of any other desire, something—drink or whatever it may be—that will be good for one.[2]

[1] The object of the following subtle argument about relative terms is to distinguish thirst as a mere blind craving for drink from a more complex desire whose object includes the pleasure or health expected to result from drinking. We thus forestall the objection that all desires have "the good" (apparent or real) for their object and include an intellectual or rational element, so that the conflict of motives might be reduced to an intellectual debate, in the same "part" of the soul, on the comparative values of two incompatible ends.

[2] If this objection were admitted, it would follow that the desire would always be correspond-

Yes, there might seem to be something in that objection.

But surely, wherever you have two correlative terms, if one is qualified, the other must always be qualified too; whereas if one is unqualified, so is the other.

I don't understand.

Well, "greater" is a relative term; and the greater is greater than the less; if it is much greater, then the less is much less; if it is greater at some moment, past or future, then the less is less at that same moment. The same principle applies to all such correlatives, like "more" and "fewer," "double" and "half"; and again to terms like "heavier" and "lighter," "quicker" and "slower," and to things like hot and cold.

Yes.

Or take the various branches of knowledge: is it not the same there? The object of knowledge pure and simple is the knowable—if that is the right word—without any qualification; whereas a particular kind of knowledge has an object of a particular kind. For example, as soon as men learnt how to build houses, their craft was distinguished from others under the name of architecture, because it had a unique character, which was itself due to the character of its object; and all other branches of craft and knowledge were distinguished in the same way.

True.

This, then, if you understand me now, is what I meant by saying that, where there are two correlatives, the one is qualified if, and only if, the other is so. I am not saying that the one must have the same quality as the other—that the science of health and disease is itself healthy and diseased, or the knowledge of good and evil is itself good and evil—but only that, as soon as you have a knowledge that is restricted to a particular kind of object, namely health and disease, the knowledge itself becomes a particular kind of knowledge. Hence we no

ingly qualified. It is necessary to insist that we do experience blind cravings which can be isolated from any judgment about the goodness of their object.

longer call it merely knowledge, which would have for its object whatever can be known, but we add the qualification and call it medical science.

I understand now and I agree.

Now, to go back to thirst: is not that one of these relative terms? It is essentially thirst for something.

Yes, for drink.

And if the drink desired is of a certain kind, the thirst will be correspondingly qualified. But thirst which is just simply thirst is not for drink of any particular sort —much or little, good or bad—but for drink pure and simple.

Quite so.

We conclude, then, that the soul of a thirsty man, just in so far as he is thirsty, has no other wish than to drink. That is the object of its craving, and towards that it is impelled.

That is clear.

Now if there is ever something which at the same time pulls it the opposite way, that something must be an element in the soul other than the one which is thirsting and driving it like a beast to drink; in accordance with our principle that the same thing cannot behave in two opposite ways at the same time and towards the same object with the same part of itself. It is like an archer drawing the bow: it is not accurate to say that his hands are at the same time both pushing and pulling it. One hand does the pushing, the other the pulling.

Exactly.

Now, is it sometimes true that people are thirsty and yet unwilling to drink?

Yes, often.

What, then, can one say of them, if not that their soul contains something which urges them to drink and something which holds them back, and that this latter is a distinct thing and overpowers the other?

I agree.

And is it not true that the intervention of this inhibiting principle in such cases always has its origin in reflection; whereas the impulses driving and dragging the soul are engendered by external influences and abnormal conditions? [3]

Evidently.

We shall have good reason, then, to assert that they are two distinct principles. We may call that part of the soul whereby it reflects, rational; and the other, with which it feels hunger and thirst and is distracted by sexual passion and all the other desires, we will call irrational appetite, associated with pleasure in the replenishment of certain wants.

Yes, there is good ground for that view.

Let us take it, then, that we have now distinguished two elements in the soul. What of that passionate element which makes us feel angry and indignant? Is that a third, or identical in nature with one of those two?

It might perhaps be identified with appetite.

I am more inclined to put my faith in a story I once heard about Leontius, son of Aglaion. On his way up from the Piraeus outside the north wall, he noticed the bodies of some criminals lying on the ground, with the executioner standing by them. He wanted to go and look at them, but at the same time he was disgusted and tried to turn away. He struggled for some time and covered his eyes, but at last the desire was too much for him. Opening his eyes wide, he ran up to the bodies and cried, "There you are, curse you; feast yourselves on this lovely sight!"

Yes, I have heard that story too.

The point of it surely is that anger is sometimes in conflict with appetite, as if they were two distinct principles. Do we not often find a man whose desires would force him to go against his reason, reviling himself and indignant with this part of his nature which is trying to put constraint on him? It is like a struggle between two factions, in which indignation takes the side of reason. But I believe you have never ob-

---

[3] Some of the most intense bodily desires are due to morbid conditions, e.g. thirst in fever, and even milder desires are caused by a departure from the normal state, which demands "replenishment."

served, in yourself or anyone else, indignation make common cause with appetite in behaviour which reason decides to be wrong.

No, I am sure I have not.

Again, take a man who feels he is in the wrong. The more generous his nature, the less can he be indignant at any suffering, such as hunger and cold, inflicted by the man he has injured. He recognizes such treatment as just, and, as I say, his spirit refuses to be roused against it.

That is true.

But now contrast one who thinks it is he that is being wronged. His spirit boils with resentment and sides with the right as he conceives it. Persevering all the more for the hunger and cold and other pains he suffers, it triumphs and will not give in until its gallant struggle has ended in success or death; or until the restraining voice of reason, like a shepherd calling off his dog, makes it relent.

An apt comparison, he said; and in fact it fits the relation of our Auxiliaries to the Rulers: they were to be like watch-dogs obeying the shepherds of the commonwealth.

Yes, you understand very well what I have in mind. But do you see how we have changed our view? A moment ago we were supposing this spirited element to be something of the nature of appetite; but now it appears that, when the soul is divided into factions, it is far more ready to be up in arms on the side of reason.

Quite true.

Is it, then, distinct from the rational element or only a particular form of it, so that the soul will contain no more than two elements, reason and appetite? Or is the soul like the state, which had three orders to hold it together, traders, Auxiliaries, and counsellors? Does the spirited element make a third, the natural auxiliary of reason, when not corrupted by bad upbringing?

It must be a third.

Yes, I said, provided it can be shown to be distinct from reason, as we saw it was from appetite.

That is easily proved. You can see that much in children: they are full of passionate feelings from their birth; but some, I should say, never become rational, and most of them only late in life.

A very sound observation, said I, the truth of which may also be seen in animals. And besides, there is the witness of Homer in that line I quoted before: "He smote his breast and spoke, chiding his heart." The poet is plainly thinking of the two elements as distinct, when he makes the one which has chosen the better course after reflection rebuke the other for its unreasoning passion.

I entirely agree.

10. The Virtues in the Individual

And so, after a stormy passage, we have reached the land. We are fairly agreed that the same three elements exist alike in the state and in the individual soul.

That is so.

Does it not follow at once that state and individual will be wise or brave by virtue of the same element in each and in the same way? Both will possess in the same manner any quality that makes for excellence.

That must be true.

Then it applies to justice: we shall conclude that a man is just in the same way that a state was just. And we have surely not forgotten that justice in the state meant that each of the three orders in it was doing its own proper work. So we may henceforth bear in mind that each one of us likewise will be a just person, fulfilling his proper function, only if the several parts of our nature fulfil theirs.

Certainly.

And it will be the business of reason to rule with wisdom and forethought on behalf of the entire soul; while the spirited element ought to act as its subordinate and ally. The two will be brought into accord, as we said earlier, by that combination of mental and bodily training which will tune up one string of the instrument and relax the other, nourishing the reasoning part on the study of noble literature and allaying the other's wildness by harmony and rhythm. When both have been thus nurtured and trained to know their own true functions, they must be set in command over the appetites, which form the greater part of each man's soul and are by nature insatiably covetous. They must keep watch lest this part, by battening on the pleasures that are called bodily, should grow so great and powerful that it will no longer keep to its own work, but will try to enslave the others and usurp a dominion to which it has no right, thus turning the whole of life upside down. At the same time, those two together will be the best of guardians for the entire soul and for the body against all enemies from without: the one will take counsel, while the other will do battle, following its ruler's commands and by its own bravery giving effect to the ruler's designs.

Yes, that is all true.

And so we call an individual brave in virtue of this spirited part of his nature, when, in spite of pain or pleasure, it holds fast to the injunctions of reason about what he ought or ought not to be afraid of.

True.

And wise in virtue of that small part which rules and issues these injunctions, possessing as it does the knowledge of what is good for each of the three elements and for all of them in common.

Certainly.

And, again, temperate by reason of the unanimity and concord of all three, when there is no internal conflict between the ruling element and its two subjects, but all are agreed that reason should be ruler.

Yes, that is an exact account of temperance, whether in the state or in the individual.

Finally, a man will be just by observing the principle we have so often stated.

Necessarily.

Now is there any indistinctness in our vision of justice, that might make it seem somehow different from what we found it to be in the state?

I don't think so.

Because, if we have any lingering doubt, we might make sure by comparing it with some commonplace notions. Suppose, for instance, that a sum of money were entrusted to our state or to an individual of corresponding character and training, would anyone imagine that such a person would be specially likely to embezzle it?

No.

And would he not be incapable of sacrilege and theft, or of treachery to friend or country; never false to an oath or any other compact; the last to be guilty of adultery or of neglecting parents or the due service of the gods?

Yes.

And the reason for all this is that each part of his nature is exercising its proper function, of ruling or of being ruled.

Yes, exactly.

Are you satisfied, then, that justice is the power which produces states or individuals of whom that is true, or must we look further?

There is no need; I am quite satisfied.

And so our dream has come true—I mean the inkling we had that, by some happy chance, we had lighted upon a rudimentary form of justice from the very moment when we set about founding our commonwealth. Our principle that the born shoemaker or carpenter had better stick to his trade turns out to have been an adumbration of justice; and that is why it has helped us. But in reality justice, though evidently analogous to this principle, is not a matter of external behaviour, but of the inward self and of attending to all that is, in the fullest sense, a man's proper concern. The just man does not allow the several elements in his soul to usurp one another's functions; he is indeed one who sets his house in order, by self-mastery and discipline coming to be at peace with himself, and bringing into tune those three parts, like the terms in the proportion of a musical scale, the highest and lowest notes and the mean between them, with all the intermediate intervals. Only when he has linked these parts together in well-tempered harmony and has made himself one man instead of many, will he be ready to go about whatever he may have to do, whether it be making money and satisfying bodily wants, or business transactions, or the affairs of state. In all these fields when he speaks of just and honourable conduct, he will mean the behaviour that helps to produce and to preserve this habit of mind; and by wisdom he will mean the knowledge which presides over such conduct. Any action which tends to break down this habit will be for him unjust; and the notions governing it he will call ignorance and folly.

That is perfectly true, Socrates.

Good, said I. I believe we should not be thought altogether mistaken, if we claimed to have discovered the just man and the just state, and wherein their justice consists.

Indeed we should not.

Shall we make that claim, then?

Yes, we will.

So be it, said I. Next, I suppose, we have to consider injustice.

Evidently.

This must surely be a sort of civil strife among the three elements, whereby they usurp and encroach upon one another's functions and some one part of the soul rises up in rebellion against the whole, claiming a supremacy to which it has no right because its nature fits it only to be the servant of the ruling principle. Such turmoil and aberration we shall, I think, identify with injustice, intemperance, cowardice, ignorance, and in a word with all wickedness.

Exactly.

And now that we know the nature of justice and injustice, we can be equally clear about what is meant by acting justly and again by unjust action and wrongdoing.

How do you mean?

Plainly, they are exactly analogous to those wholesome and unwholesome activ-

ities which respectively produce a healthy or unhealthy condition in the body; in the same way just and unjust conduct produce a just or unjust character. Justice is produced in the soul, like health in the body, by establishing the elements concerned in their natural relations of control and subordination, whereas injustice is like disease and means that this natural order is inverted.

Quite so.

It appears, then, that virtue is as it were the health and comeliness and well-being of the soul, as wickedness is disease, deformity, and weakness.

True.

And also that virtue and wickedness are brought about by one's way of life, honourable or disgraceful.

That follows.

So now it only remains to consider which is the more profitable course: to do right and live honourably and be just, whether or not anyone knows what manner of man you are, or to do wrong and be unjust, provided that you can escape the chastisement which might make you a better man.

But really, Socrates, it seems to me ridiculous to ask that question now that the nature of justice and injustice has been brought to light. People think that all the luxury and wealth and power in the world cannot make life worth living when the bodily constitution is going to rack and ruin; and are we to believe that, when the very principle whereby we live is deranged and corrupted, life will be worth living so long as a man can do as he will, and wills to do anything rather than to free himself from vice and wrongdoing and to win justice and virtue?

Yes, I replied, it is a ridiculous question.

11. Equality of Women

We must go back, then, to a subject which ought, perhaps, to have been treated earlier in its proper place; though, after all, it may be suitable that the women should have their turn on the stage when the men have quite finished their performance, especially since you are so insistent. In my judgment, then, the question under what conditions people born and educated as we have described should possess wives and children, and how they should treat them, can be rightly settled only by keeping to the course on which we started them at the outset. We undertook to put these men in the position of watch-dogs guarding a flock. Suppose we follow up the analogy and imagine them bred and reared in the same sort of way. We can then see if that plan will suit our purpose.

How will that be?

In this way. Which do we think right for watch-dogs: should the females guard the flock and hunt with the males and take a share in all they do, or should they be kept within doors as fit for no more than bearing and feeding their puppies, while all the hard work of looking after the flock is left to the males?

They are expected to take their full share, except that we treat them as not quite so strong.

Can you employ any creature for the same work as another, if you do not give them both the same upbringing and education?

No.

Then, if we are to set women to the same tasks as men, we must teach them the same things. They must have the same two branches of training for mind and body and also be taught the art of war, and they must receive the same treatment.

That seems to follow.

Possibly, if these proposals were carried out, they might be ridiculed as involving a good many breaches of custom.

They might indeed.

The most ridiculous—don't you think?— being the notion of women exercising naked along with the men in the wrestling-schools; some of them elderly women too, like the old men who still have a passion for exercise when they are wrinkled and not very agreeable to look at.

Yes, that would be thought laughable, according to our present notions.

Now we have started on this subject, we must not be frightened of the many witticisms that might be aimed at such a revolution, not only in the matter of bodily exercise but in the training of women's minds, and not least when it comes to their bearing arms and riding on horseback. Having begun upon these rules, we must not draw back from the harsher provisions. The wits may be asked to stop being witty and try to be serious; and we may remind them that it is not so long since the Greeks, like most foreign nations of the present day, thought it ridiculous and shameful for men to be seen naked. When gymnastic exercises were first introduced in Crete and later at Sparta, the humorists had their chance to make fun of them; but when experience had shown that nakedness is better uncovered than muffled up, the laughter died down and a practice which the reason approved ceased to look ridiculous to the eye. This shows how idle it is to think anything ludicrous but what is base. One who tries to raise a laugh at any spectacle save that of baseness and folly will also, in his serious moments, set before himself some other standard than goodness of what deserves to be held in honour.

Most assuredly.

The first thing to be settled, then, is whether these proposals are feasible; and it must be open to anyone, whether a humorist or serious-minded, to raise the question whether, in the case of mankind, the feminine nature is capable of taking part with the other sex in all occupations, or in none at all, or in some only; and in particular under which of these heads this business of military service falls. Well begun is half done, and would not this be the best way to begin?

Yes.

Shall we take the other side in this debate and argue against ourselves? We do not want the adversary's position to be taken by storm for lack of defenders.

I have no objection.

Let us state his case for him. "Socrates and Glaucon," he will say, "there is no need for others to dispute your position; you yourselves, at the very outset of founding your commonwealth, agreed that everyone should do the one work for which nature fits him." Yes, of course; I suppose we did. "And isn't there a very great difference in nature between man and woman?" Yes, surely. "Does not that natural difference imply a corresponding difference in the work to be given to each?" Yes. "But if so, surely you must be mistaken now and contradicting yourselves when you say that men and women, having such widely divergent natures, should do the same things?" What is your answer to that, my ingenious friend?

It is not easy to find one at the moment. I can only appeal to you to state the case on our own side, whatever it may be.

This, Glaucon, is one of many alarming objections which I foresaw some time ago. That is why I shrank from touching upon these laws concerning the possession of wives and the rearing of children.

It looks like anything but an easy problem.

True, I said; but whether a man tumbles into a swimming-pool or into mid-ocean, he has to swim all the time. So must we, and try if we can reach the shore, hoping for some Arion's dolphin or other miraculous deliverance to bring us safe to land.[1]

I suppose so.

Come then, let us see if we can find the way out. We did agree that different natures should have different occupations, and that the natures of man and woman are different; and yet we are now saying that these different natures are to have the same occupations. Is that the charge against us?

[1] The musician Arion, to escape the treachery of Corinthian sailors, leapt into the sea and was carried ashore at Taenarum by a dolphin, Herod. i. 24.

Exactly.

It is extraordinary, Glaucon, what an effect the practice of debating has upon people.

Why do you say that?

Because they often seem to fall unconsciously into mere disputes which they mistake for reasonable argument, through being unable to draw the distinctions proper to their subject; and so, instead of a philosophical exchange of ideas, they go off in chase of contradictions which are purely verbal.

I know that happens to many people; but does it apply to us at this moment?

Absolutely. At least I am afraid we are slipping unconsciously into a dispute about words. We have been strenuously insisting on the letter of our principle that different natures should not have the same occupations, as if we were scoring a point in a debate; but we have altogether neglected to consider what sort of sameness or difference we meant and in what respect these natures and occupations were to be defined as different or the same. Consequently, we might very well be asking one another whether there is not an opposition in nature between bald and long-haired men, and, when that was admitted, forbid one set to be shoemakers, if the other were following that trade.

That would be absurd.

Yes, but only because we never meant any and every sort of sameness or difference in nature, but the sort that was relevant to the occupations in question. We meant, for instance, that a man and a woman have the same nature if both have a talent for medicine; whereas two men have different natures if one is a born physician, the other a born carpenter.

Yes, of course.

If, then, we find that either the male sex or the female is specially qualified for any particular form of occupation, then that occupation, we shall say, ought to be assigned to one sex or the other. But if the only difference appears to be that the male begets and the female brings forth, we shall conclude that no difference between man and woman has yet been produced that is relevant to our purpose. We shall continue to think it proper for our Guardians and their wives to share in the same pursuits.

And quite rightly.

The next thing will be to ask our opponent to name any profession or occupation in civic life for the purposes of which woman's nature is different from man's.

That is a fair question.

He might reply, as you did just now, that it is not easy to find a satisfactory answer on the spur of the moment, but that there would be no difficulty after a little reflection.

Perhaps.

Suppose, then, we invite him to follow us and see if we can convince him that there is no occupation concerned with the management of social affairs that is peculiar to women. We will confront him with a question: When you speak of a man having a natural talent for something, do you mean that he finds it easy to learn, and after a little instruction can find out much more for himself; whereas a man who is not so gifted learns with difficulty and no amount of instruction and practice will make him even remember what he has been taught? Is the talented man one whose bodily powers are readily at the service of his mind, instead of being a hindrance? Are not these the marks by which you distinguish the presence of a natural gift for any pursuit?

Yes, precisely.

Now do you know any human occupation in which the male sex is not superior to the female in all these respects? Need I waste time over exceptions like weaving and watching over saucepans and batches of cakes, though women are supposed to be good at such things and get laughed at when a man does them better?

It is true, he replied, in almost everything one sex is easily beaten by the other. No doubt many women are better at many things than many men; but taking the sexes as a whole, it is as you say.

To conclude, then, there is no occupation concerned with the management of social affairs which belongs either to woman or to man, as such. Natural gifts are to be found here and there in both creatures alike; and every occupation is open to both, so far as their natures are concerned, though woman is for all purposes the weaker.

Certainly.

Is that a reason for making over all occupations to men only?

Of course not.

No, because one woman may have a natural gift for medicine or for music, another may not.

Surely.

Is it not also true that a woman may, or may not, be warlike or athletic?

I think so.

And again, one may love knowledge, another hate it; one may be high-spirited, another spiritless?

True again.

It follows that one woman will be fitted by nature to be a Guardian, another will not; because these were the qualities for which we selected our men Guardians. So for the purpose of keeping watch over the commonwealth, woman has the same nature as man, save in so far as she is weaker.

So it appears.

It follows that women of this type must be selected to share the life and duties of Guardians with men of the same type, since they are competent and of a like nature, and the same natures must be allowed the same pursuits.

Yes.

We come round, then, to our former position, that there is nothing contrary to nature in giving our Guardians' wives the same training for mind and body. The practice we proposed to establish was not impossible or visionary, since it was in accordance with nature. Rather, the contrary practice which now prevails turns out to be unnatural.

So it appears.

Well, we set out to inquire whether the plan we proposed was feasible and also the best. That it is feasible is now agreed; we must next settle whether it is the best. Obviously.

Now, for the purpose of producing a woman fit to be a Guardian, we shall not have one education for men and another for women, precisely because the nature to be taken in hand is the same.

True.

What is your opinion on the question of one man being better than another? Do you think there is no such difference?

Certainly I do not.

And in this commonwealth of ours which will prove the better men—the Guardians who have received the education we described, or the shoemakers who have been trained to make shoes?

It is absurd to ask such a question.

Very well. So these Guardians will be the best of all the citizens?

By far.

And these women the best of all the women?

Yes.

Can anything be better for a commonwealth than to produce in it men and women of the best possible type?

No.

And that result will be brought about by such a system of mental and bodily training as we have described?

Surely.

We may conclude that the institution we proposed was not only practicable, but also the best for the commonwealth.

Yes.

The wives of our Guardians, then, must strip for exercise, since they will be clothed with virtue, and they must take their share in war and in the other social duties of guardianship. They are to have no other occupation; and in these duties the lighter part must fall to the women, because of the weakness of their sex. The man who laughs at naked women, exercising their bodies for the best of reasons, is like one that "gathers fruit unripe," for he does not know what it is that he is laughing at or what he is doing. There will never be a finer saying than the one which declares that whatever does good should be held in honour, and the only shame is in doing harm.

That is perfectly true.

12. Abolition of the Family for the Guardians

So far, then, in regulating the position of women, we may claim to have come safely through with one hazardous proposal, that male and female Guardians shall have all occupations in common. The consistency of the argument is an assurance that the plan is a good one and also feasible. We are like swimmers who have breasted the first wave without being swallowed up.

Not such a small wave either.

You will not call it large when you see the next.

Let me have a look at the next one, then.

Here it is: a law which follows from that principle and all that has gone before, namely that, of these Guardians, no one man and one woman are to set up house together privately: wives are to be held in common by all; so too are the children, and no parent is to know his own child, nor any child his parent.

It will be much harder to convince people that that is either a feasible plan or a good one.

As to its being a good plan, I imagine no one would deny the immense advantage of wives and children being held in common, provided it can be done. I should expect dispute to arise chiefly over the question whether it is possible.

There may well be a good deal of dispute over both points.

You mean, I must meet attacks on two fronts. I was hoping to escape one by running away: if you agreed it was a good plan, then I should only have had to inquire whether it was feasible.

No, we have seen through that manœuvre. You will have to defend both positions.

Well, I must pay the penalty for my cowardice. But grant me one favour. Let me indulge my fancy, like one who entertains himself with idle day-dreams on a solitary walk. Before he has any notion how his desires can be realized, he will set aside that question, to save himself the trouble of reckoning what may or may not be possible. He will assume that his wish has come true, and amuse himself with settling all the details of what he means to do then. So a lazy mind encourages itself to be lazier than ever; and I am giving way to the same weakness myself. I want to put off till later that question, how the thing can be done. For the moment, with your leave, I shall assume it to be possible, and ask how the Rulers will work out the details in practice; and I shall argue that the plan, once carried into effect, would be the best thing in the world for our commonwealth and for its Guardians. That is what I shall now try to make out with your help, if you will allow me to postpone the other question.

Very good; I have no objection.

Well, if our Rulers are worthy of the name, and their Auxiliaries likewise, these latter will be ready to do what they are told, and the Rulers, in giving their commands, will themselves obey our laws and will be faithful to their spirit in any details we leave to their discretion.

No doubt.

It is for you, then, as their lawgiver, who have already selected the men, to select for association with them women who are so far as possible of the same natural capacity. Now since none of them will have any private home of his own, but they will share the same dwelling and eat at common tables, the two sexes will be together; and meeting without restriction for exercise and all through their upbringing, they will surely be drawn towards union with one another by a necessity of their nature—necessity is not too strong a word, I think?

Not too strong for the constraint of love, which for the mass of mankind is more persuasive and compelling than even the necessity of mathematical proof.

Exactly. But in the next place, Glaucon, anything like unregulated unions would be a profanation in a state whose citizens lead the good life. The Rulers will not allow such a thing.

No, it would not be right.

Clearly, then, we must have marriages, as sacred as we can make them; and this sanctity will attach to those which yield the best results.

Certainly.

How are we to get the best results? You must tell me, Glaucon, because I see you keep sporting dogs and a great many game birds at your house; and there is something about their mating and breeding that you must have noticed.

What is that?

In the first place, though they may all be of good stock, are there not some that turn out to be better than the rest?

There are.

And do you breed from all indiscriminately? Are you not careful to breed from the best so far as you can?

Yes.

And from those in their prime, rather than the very young or the very old?

Yes.

Otherwise, the stock of your birds or dogs would deteriorate very much, wouldn't it?

It would.

And the same is true of horses or of any animal?

It would be very strange if it were not.

Dear me, said I; we shall need consummate skill in our Rulers, if it is also true of the human race.

Well, it is true. But why must they be so skilful?

Because they will have to administer a large dose of that medicine we spoke of earlier. An ordinary doctor is thought good enough for a patient who will submit to be dieted and can do without medicine; but he must be much more of a man if drugs are required.

True, but how does that apply?

It applies to our Rulers: it seems they will have to give their subjects a considerable dose of imposition and deception for their good. We said, if you remember, that such expedients would be useful as a sort of medicine.

Yes, a very sound principle.

Well, it looks as if this sound principle will play no small part in this matter of marriage and child-bearing.

How so?

It follows from what we have just said that, if we are to keep our flock at the highest pitch of excellence, there should be as many unions of the best of both sexes, and as few of the inferior, as possible, and that only the offspring of the better unions should be kept.[1] And again, no one but the Rulers must know how all this is being effected; otherwise our herd of Guardians may become rebellious.

Quite true.

We must, then, institute certain festivals at which we shall bring together the brides and bridegrooms. There will be sacrifices, and our poets will write songs befitting the occasion. The number of marriages we shall leave to the Rulers' discretion. They will aim at keeping the number of the citizens as constant as possible, having regard to losses caused by war, epidemics, and so on; and they must do their best to see that our state does not become either great or small.[2]

Very good.

I think they will have to invent some ingenious system of drawing lots, so that, at each pairing off, the inferior candidate may blame his luck rather than the Rulers.

Yes, certainly.

Moreover, young men who acquit themselves well in war and other duties, should be given, among other rewards and privileges, more liberal opportunities to sleep with a wife,[3] for the further purpose that, with good excuse, as many as possible of the children may be begotten of such fathers.

Yes.

As soon as children are born, they will be taken in charge by officers appointed for the purpose, who may be men or women or both, since offices are to be shared by both sexes. The children of the better parents they will carry to the crèche to be reared in the care of nurses living apart in a certain quarter of the city. Those of the inferior parents and any children of the rest that are born defective will be hidden away, in some appropriate manner that must be kept secret.[4]

They must be, if the breed of our Guardians is to be kept pure.

---

[1] That is, "kept *as Guardians*." The inferior children of Guardians were to be "thrust out among the craftsmen and farmers." A breeder of race-horses would *keep* the best foals, but not kill the rest.

[2] Plato seems to forget that these rules apply only to Guardians. If the much larger third class is to breed without restriction, a substantial rise in their numbers might entail suspension of all childbirth among Guardians, with a dysgenic effect. Plato, however, feared a decline, rather than a rise, in the birth-rate. (The state described in the *Laws* is always to have 5,040 citizens, each holding one inalienable lot of land.)

The "number of marriages" may include both the number of candidates admitted at each festival and the frequency of the festivals. But it is perhaps likely that the festivals are to be annual, so that women who had borne children since the last festival would be re-marriageable. If so, at each festival a fresh group will be called up, consisting of all who have reached the age of 25 for men or 20 for women since the previous festival. Some or all of these will be paired with one another or with members of older groups. The couples will cohabit during the festival, which might last (say) for a month. The marriages will then be dissolved and the partners remain celibate until the next festival at earliest. This follows from the statement that the resulting batch of children will all be born between 7 and 10 months after the festival.

[3] Not to have several wives at once, but to be admitted at more frequent intervals to the periodic marriage festivals, not necessarily with a different wife each time.

[4] Infanticide of defective children was practised at Sparta; but the vague expression used does not imply that all children of inferior Guardians are to be destroyed. Those not defective would be relegated to the third class. Promotion of children from that class was provided for above (p. 30).

These officers will also superintend the nursing of the children. They will bring the mothers to the crèche when their breasts are full, while taking every precaution that no mother shall know her own child; and if the mothers have not enough milk, they will provide wet-nurses. They will limit the time during which the mothers will suckle their children, and hand over all the hard work and sitting up at night to nurses and attendants.

That will make child-bearing an easy business for the Guardians' wives.

So it should be. To go on with our scheme: we said that children should be born from parents in the prime of life. Do you agree that this lasts about twenty years for a woman, and thirty for a man? A woman should bear children for the commonwealth from her twentieth to her fortieth year; a man should begin to beget them when he has passed "the racer's prime in swiftness," and continue till he is fifty-five.

Those are certainly the years in which both the bodily and the mental powers of man and woman are at their best.

If a man either above or below this age meddles with the begetting of children for the commonwealth, we shall hold it an offence against divine and human law. He will be begetting for his country a child conceived in darkness and dire incontinence, whose birth, if it escape detection, will not have been sanctioned by the sacrifices and prayers offered at each marriage festival, when priests and priestesses join with the whole community in praying that the children to be born may be even better and more useful citizens than their parents.

You are right.

The same law will apply to any man within the prescribed limits who touches a woman also of marriageable age when the Ruler has not paired them. We shall say that he is foisting on the commonwealth a bastard, unsanctioned by law or by religion.

Perfectly right.

As soon, however, as the men and the women have passed the age prescribed for producing children, we shall leave them free to form a connexion with whom they will, except that a man shall not take his daughter or daughter's daughter or mother or mother's mother, nor a woman her son or father or her son's son or father's father; and all this only after we have exhorted them to see that no child, if any be conceived, shall be brought to light, or, if they cannot prevent its birth, to dispose of it on the understanding that no such child can be reared.[5]

That too is reasonable. But how are they to distinguish fathers and daughters and those other relations you mentioned?

They will not, said I. But, reckoning from the day when he becomes a bridegroom, a man will call all children born in the tenth or the seventh month sons and daughters, and they will call him father. Their children he will call grandchildren, and they will call his group grandfathers and grandmothers; and all who are born within the period during which their mothers and fathers were having children will be called bothers and sisters. This will provide for those restrictions on unions that we mentioned; but the law will allow brothers and sisters to live together, if the lot so falls out and the Delphic oracle also approves.[6]

---

[5] The unofficial unions might be permanent. The only unions barred as incestuous are between parents and children, or grandparents and grandchildren (all such are included, since, if a woman cannot marry her father's father, a man cannot marry his son's daughter). It seems to follow that Plato did not regard the much more probable connexions of brothers and sisters as incestuous; and if so, he would see no reason against legal marriage of real brothers and sisters, who would not know they were so related. Such unions were regular in Egypt; and some modern authorities deny that they are dysgenic. Greek law allowed marriage between brother and half-sister by a different mother.

[6] This last speech deals with two distinct questions: (1) avoidance of incestuous unions as above defined; (2) legal marriage of brothers and sisters.

(1) Since the elderly people forming unofficial unions are not to know who are their parents or children, they must avoid all persons who could possibly be so related to them. This is easy, if

Very good.

This, then, Glaucon, is the manner in which the Guardians of your commonwealth are to hold their wives and children in common. Must we not next find arguments to establish that it is consistent with our other institutions and also by far the best plan?

Yes, surely.

---

cohabitation in legal marriage is confined to the duration of a marriage festival and the children of any parent must therefore belong to a batch born in the seventh or tenth month after any festival at which that parent has been married. (Most ancient authorities denied that a child could be born in the eighth month.) If a register was kept, a man could be told all the dates in question without being told who were his real children.

(2) After explaining how incestuous unions can be avoided by a man treating certain whole groups as his parents or children or grandparents or grandchildren, Plato adds that all persons "born within the period during which their mothers and fathers (not *his* father and mother) were having children" will be called "brothers" and "sisters." If unions of real brothers and sisters are not incestuous, this clause has nothing to do with avoidance of incest. It only adds to the definition of nominal parents and children and grandparents and grandchildren, a definition of those who will call one another "brothers" and "sisters," whether they are really so related or not. Probably, it is meant that these will be all the Guardians born in the same generation (in a vague sense). Since there is no question of incest, these persons will never need to inquire about dates of marriage and birth, if they wish to form a union.

The last sentence refers to both topics of the previous one: (1) avoidance of incestuous unions, (2) legal marriage of real brothers and sisters. It has been held that Plato regarded such marriages as incestuous and that the Oracle was to guard against them. But either the Rulers knew how all Guardians were related or they did not. If (as seems likely) they did know, they could avoid arranging such marriages without invoking an oracle to negative their own proposals. If they did not (though it would be folly to keep no registers if *any* incest was to be avoided), then how could the Oracle know? Granted that Plato did not hold marriage of brothers and sisters to be incestuous, the Rulers could sometimes knowingly arrange such marriages. The Oracle might be asked once for all to approve the whole scheme of marriage laws, or it might be formally invoked at each festival. If it raised no objection, the Rulers would be protected from any charge of violating religious law.

We had better begin by asking what is the greatest good at which the lawgiver should aim in laying down the constitution of a state, and what is the worst evil. We can then consider whether our proposals are in keeping with that good and irreconcilable with the evil.

By all means.

Does not the worst evil for a state arise from anything that tends to rend it asunder and destroy its unity, while nothing does it more good than whatever tends to bind it together and make it one?

That is true.

And are not citizens bound together by sharing in the same pleasures and pains, all feeling glad or grieved on the same casions of gain or loss; whereas the is broken when such feelings are no universal, but any event of public or sonal concern fills some with joy and othe with distress?

Certainly.

And this disunion comes about when the words "mine" and "not mine," "another's" and "not another's" are not applied to the same things throughout the community. The best ordered state will be the one in which the largest number of persons use these terms in the same sense, and which accordingly most nearly resembles a single person. When one of us hurts his finger, the whole extent of those bodily connexions which are gathered up in the soul and unified by its ruling element is made aware and it all shares as a whole in the pain of the suffering part; hence we say that the man has a pain in his finger. The same thing is true of the pain or pleasure felt when any other part of the person suffers or is relieved.

Yes; I agree that the best organized community comes nearest to that condition.

And so it will recognize as a part of itself the individual citizen to whom good or evil happens, and will share as a whole in his joy or sorrow.

It must, if the constitution is sound.

It is time now to go back to our own commonwealth and see whether these conclusions apply to it more than to any other type of state. In all alike there are rulers and common people, all of whom will call one another fellow citizens.

Yes.

But in other states the people have another name as well for their rulers, haven't they?

Yes; in most they call them masters; in democracies, simply the government.

And in ours?

The people will look upon their rulers as preservers and protectors.

And how will our rulers regard the people?

As those who maintain them and pay their wages.

And elsewhere?

As slaves.

And what do rulers elsewhere call one another?

Colleagues.

And ours?

Fellow Guardians.

And in other states may not a ruler regard one colleague as a friend in whom he has an interest, and another as a stranger with whom he has nothing in common?

Yes, that often happens.

But that could not be so with your Guardians? None of them could ever treat a fellow Guardian as a stranger.

Certainly not. He must regard everyone whom he meets as brother or sister, father or mother, son or daughter, grandchild or grandparent.

Very good; but here is a further point. Will you not require them, not merely to use these family terms, but to behave as a real family? Must they not show towards all whom they call "father" the customary reverence, care, and obedience due to a parent, if they look for any favour from gods or men, since to act otherwise is contrary to divine and human law? Should not all the citizens constantly reiterate in the hearing of the children from their earliest years such traditional maxims of conduct towards those whom they are taught to call father and their other kindred?

They should. It would be absurd that terms of kinship should be on their lips without any action to correspond.

In our community, then, above all others, when things go well or ill with any individual everyone will use that word "mine" in the same sense and say that all is going well or ill with him and his.

Quite true.

And, as we said, this way of speaking and thinking goes with fellow-feeling; so that our citizens, sharing as they do in a common interest which each will call his own, will have all their feelings of pleasure or pain in common.

Assuredly.

A result that will be due to our institutions, and in particular to our Guardians' holding their wives and children in common.

Very much so.

But you will remember how, when we compared a well-ordered community to the body which shares in the pleasures and pains of any member, we saw in this unity the greatest good that a state can enjoy. So the conclusion is that our commonwealth owes to this sharing of wives and children by its protectors its enjoyment of the greatest of all goods.

Yes, that follows.

Moreover, this agrees with our principle that they were not to have houses or lands or any property of their own, but to receive sustenance from the other citizens, as wages for their guardianship, and to consume it in common. Only so will they keep to their true character; and our present proposals will do still more to make them genuine Guardians. They will not rend the community asunder by each applying that word "mine" to different things and dragging off whatever he can get for himself into a private home, where he will have his separate family, forming a centre of exclusive joys and sorrows. Rather they will all, so far as may be, feel together and aim at the same ends, because they are convinced that all their interests are identical.

Quite so.

Again, if a man's person is his only private possession, lawsuits and prosecutions will all but vanish, and they will be free of those quarrels that arise from ownership of property and from having family ties. Nor would they be justified even in bringing actions for assault and outrage; for we shall pronounce it right and honourable for a man to defend himself against an assailant of his own age, and in that way they will be compelled to keep themselves fit.

That would be a sound law.

And it would also have the advantage that, if a man's anger can be satisfied in this way, a fit of passion is less likely to grow into a serious quarrel.

True.

But an older man will be given authority over all younger persons and power to correct them; whereas the younger will, naturally, not dare to strike the elder or do him any violence, except by command of a Ruler. He will not show him any sort of disrespect. Two guardian spirits, fear and reverence, will be enough to restrain him— reverence forbidding him to lay hands on a parent, and fear of all those others who as sons or brothers or fathers would come to the rescue.

Yes, that will be the result.

So our laws will secure that these men will live in complete peace with one another; and if they never quarrel among themselves, there is no fear of the rest of the community being divided either against them or against itself.

No.

There are other evils they will escape, so mean and petty that I hardly like to mention them: the poor man's flattery of the rich, and all the embarrassments and vexations of rearing a family and earning just enough to maintain a household; now borrowing and now refusing to repay, and by any and every means scraping together money to be handed over to wife and servants to spend. These sordid troubles are familiar and not worth describing.

Only too familiar.

Rid of all these cares, they will live a more enviable life than the Olympic victor, who is counted happy on the strength of far fewer blessings than our Guardians will enjoy. Their victory is the nobler, since by their success the whole commonwealth is preserved; and their reward of maintenance at the public cost is more complete, since their prize is to have every need of life supplied for themselves and for their children; their country honours them while they live, and when they die they receive a worthy burial.

Yes, they will be nobly rewarded.

Do you remember, then, how someone who shall be nameless reproached us for not making our Guardians happy: they were to possess nothing, though all the wealth of their fellow citizens was within their grasp? We replied, I believe, that we would consider that objection later, if it came in our way: for the moment we were bent on making our Guardians real guardians, and moulding our commonwealth with a view to the greatest happiness, not of one section of it, but of the whole.

Yes, I remember.

Well, it appears now that these protectors of our state will have a life better and more honourable than that of any Olympic victor; and we can hardly rank it on a level with the life of a shoemaker or other artisan or of a farmer.

I should think not.

However, it is right to repeat what I said at the time: if ever a Guardian tries to make himself happy in such a way that he will be a guardian no longer; if, not content with the moderation and security of this way of living which we think the best, he becomes possessed with some silly and childish notion of happiness, impelling him to make his power a means to appropriate all the citizens' wealth, then he will learn the wisdom of Hesiod's saying that the half is more than the whole.

My advice would certainly be that he should keep to his own way of living.

You do agree, then, that women are to take their full share with men in education, in the care of children, and in the guardianship of the other citizens; whether they stay at home or go out to war, they will be like watch-dogs which take their part either in guarding the fold or in hunting and share in every task so far as their strength allows. Such conduct will not be unwomanly, but all for the best and in accordance with the natural partnership of the sexes.

Yes, I agree.

13. The Paradox: Philosophers Must Be Kings

But really, Socrates, Glaucon continued, if you are allowed to go on like this, I am afraid you will forget all about the question you thrust aside some time ago: whether a society so constituted can ever come into existence, and if so, how. No doubt, if it did exist, all manner of good things would come about. I can even add some that you have passed over. Men who acknowledged one another as fathers, sons, or brothers and always used those names among themselves would never desert one another; so they would fight with unequalled bravery. And if their womenfolk went out with them to war, either in the ranks or drawn up in the rear to intimidate the enemy and act as a reserve in case of need, I am sure all this would make them invincible. At home, too, I can see many advantages you have not mentioned. But, since I admit that our commonwealth would have all these merits and any number more, if once it came into existence, you need not describe it in further detail. All we have now to do is to convince ourselves that it can be brought into being and how.

This is a very sudden onslaught, said I; you have no mercy on my shilly-shallying. Perhaps you do not realize that, after I have barely escaped the first two waves, the third, which you are now bringing down upon me, is the most formidable of all.

When you have seen what it is like and heard my reply, you will be ready to excuse the very natural fears which made me shrink from putting forward such a paradox for discussion.

The more you talk like that, he said, the less we shall be willing to let you off from telling us how this constitution can come into existence; so you had better waste no more time.

Well, said I, let me begin by reminding you that what brought us to this point was our inquiry into the nature of justice and injustice.

True; but what of that?

Merely this: suppose we do find out what justice is, are we going to demand that a man who is just shall have a character which exactly corresponds in every respect to the ideal of justice? Or shall we be satisfied if he comes as near to the ideal as possible and has in him a larger measure of that quality than the rest of the world?

That will satisfy me.

If so, when we set out to discover the essential nature of justice and injustice and what a perfectly just and a perfectly unjust man would be like, supposing them to exist, our purpose was to use them as ideal patterns: we were to observe the degree of happiness or unhappiness that each exhibited, and to draw the necessary inference that our own destiny would be like that of the one we most resembled. We did not set out to show that these ideals could exist in fact.

That is true.

Then suppose a painter had drawn an ideally beautiful figure complete to the last touch, would you think any the worse of him, if he could not show that a person as beautiful as that could exist?

No, I should not.

Well, we have been constructing in discourse the pattern of an ideal state. Is our theory any the worse, if we cannot prove it possible that a state so organized should be actually founded?

Surely not.

That, then, is the truth of the matter.

But if, for your satisfaction, I am to do my best to show under what conditions our ideal would have the best chance of being realized, I must ask you once more, to admit that the same principle applies here. Can theory ever be fully realized in practice? Is it not in the nature of things that action should come less close to truth than thought? People may not think so; but do you agree or not?

I do.

Then you must not insist upon my showing that this construction we have traced in thought could be reproduced in fact down to the last detail. You must admit that we shall have found a way to meet your demand for realization, if we can discover how a state might be constituted in the closest accordance with our description. Will not that content you? It would be enough for me.

And for me too.

Then our next attempt, it seems, must be to point out what defect in the working of existing states prevents them from being so organized, and what is the least change that would effect a transformation into this type of government—a single change if possible, or perhaps two; at any rate let us make the changes as few and insignificant as may be.

By all means.

Well, there is one change which, as I believe we can show, would bring about this revolution—not a small change, certainly, nor an easy one, but possible.

What is it?

I have now to confront what we called the third and greatest wave. But I must state my paradox, even though the wave should break in laughter over my head and drown me in ignominy. Now mark what I am going to say.

Go on.

Unless either philosophers become kings in their countries or those who are now called kings and rulers come to be sufficiently inspired with a genuine desire for wisdom; unless, that is to say, political

power and philosophy meet together, while the many natures who now go their several ways in the one or the other direction are forcibly debarred from doing so, there can be no rest from troubles, my dear Glaucon, for states, nor yet, as I believe, for all mankind; nor can this commonwealth which we have imagined ever till then see the light of day and grow to its full stature. This it was that I have so long hung back from saying; I knew what a paradox it would be, because it is hard to see that there is no other way of happiness either for the state or for the individual.

Socrates, exclaimed Glaucon, after delivering yourself of such a pronouncement as that, you must expect a whole multitude of by no means contemptible assailants to fling off their coats, snatch up the handiest weapon, and make a rush at you, breathing fire and slaughter. If you cannot find arguments to beat them off and make your escape, you will learn what it means to be the target of scorn and derision.

Well, it was you who got me into this trouble.

Yes, and a good thing too. However, I will not leave you in the lurch. You shall have my friendly encouragement for what it is worth; and perhaps you may find me more complaisant than some would be in answering your questions. With such backing you must try to convince the unbelievers.

I will, now that I have such a powerful ally.

14. The Allegory of the Cave

Next, said I, here is a parable to illustrate the degrees in which our nature may be enlightened or unenlightened. Imagine the condition of men living in a sort of cavernous chamber underground, with an entrance open to the light and a long passage all down the cave.[1] Here they have been from

---

[1] The *length* of the "way in" (*eisodos*) to the chamber where the prisoners sit is an essential feature, explaining why no daylight reaches them.

childhood, chained by the leg and also by the neck, so that they cannot move and can see only what is in front of them, because the chains will not let them turn their heads. At some distance higher up is the light of a fire burning behind them; and between the prisoners and the fire is a track [2] with a parapet built along it, like the screen at a puppet-show, which hides the performers while they show their puppets over the top.

I see, said he.

Now behind this parapet imagine persons carrying along various artificial objects, including figures of men and animals in wood or stone or other materials, which project above the parapet. Naturally, some of these persons will be talking, others silent.[3]

It is a strange picture, he said, and a strange sort of prisoners.

Like ourselves, I replied; for in the first place prisoners so confined would have seen nothing of themselves or of one another, except the shadows thrown by the fire-light on the wall of the Cave facing them, would they?

Not if all their lives they had been prevented from moving their heads.

And they would have seen as little of the objects carried past.

Of course.

Now, if they could talk to one another, would they not suppose that their words referred only to those passing shadows which they saw? [4]

Necessarily.

---

[2] The track crosses the passage into the cave at right angles, and is *above* the parapet built along it.

[3] A modern Plato would compare his Cave to an underground cinema, where the audience watch the play of shadows thrown by the film passing before a light at their backs. The film itself is only an image of "real" things and events in the world outside the cinema. For the film Plato has to substitute the clumsier apparatus of a procession of artificial objects carried on their heads by persons who are merely part of the machinery, providing for the movement of the objects and the sounds whose echo the prisoners hear. The parapet prevents these persons' shadows from being cast on the wall of the Cave.

And suppose their prison had an echo from the wall facing them? When one of the people crossing behind them spoke, they could only suppose that the sound came from the shadow passing before their eyes.

No doubt.

In every way, then, such prisoners would recognize as reality nothing but the shadows of those artificial objects.

Inevitably.

Now consider what would happen if their release from the chains and the healing of their unwisdom should come about in this way. Suppose one of them set free and forced suddenly to stand up, turn his head, and walk with eyes lifted to the light; all these movements would be painful, and he would be too dazzled to make out the objects whose shadows he had been used to see. What do you think he would say, if someone told him that what he had formerly seen was meaningless illusion, but now, being somewhat nearer to reality and turned towards more real objects, he was getting a truer view? Suppose further that he were shown the various objects being carried by and were made to say, in reply to questions, what each of them was. Would he not be perplexed and believe the objects now shown him to be not so real as what he formerly saw?

Yes, not nearly so real.

And if he were forced to look at the fire-light itself, would not his eyes ache, so that he would try to escape and turn back to the things which he could see distinctly, convinced that they really were clearer than these other objects now being shown to him?

Yes.

And suppose someone were to drag him away forcibly up the steep and rugged ascent and not let him go until he had hauled him out into the sunlight, would he not suffer pain and vexation at such treatment,

---

[4] Adam's text and interpretation. The prisoners, having seen nothing but shadows, cannot think their words refer to the objects carried past behind their backs. For them shadows (images) are the only realities.

and, when he had come out into the light, find his eyes so full of its radiance that he could not see a single one of the things that he was now told were real?

Certainly he would not see them all at once.

He would need, then, to grow accustomed before he could see things in that upper world. At first it would be easiest to make out shadows, and then the images of men and things reflected in water, and later on the things themselves. After that, it would be easier to watch the heavenly bodies and the sky itself by night, looking at the light of the moon and stars rather than the Sun and the Sun's light in the day-time.

Yes, surely.

Last of all, he would be able to look at the Sun and contemplate its nature, not as it appears when reflected in water or any alien medium, but as it is in itself in its own domain.

No doubt.

And now he would begin to draw the conclusion that it is the Sun that produces the seasons and the course of the year and controls everything in the visible world, and moreover is in a way the cause of all that he and his companions used to see.

Clearly he would come at last to that conclusion.

Then if he called to mind his fellow prisoners and what passed for wisdom in his former dwelling-place, he would surely think himself happy in the change and be sorry for them. They may have had a practice of honouring and commending one another, with prizes for the man who had the keenest eye for the passing shadows and the best memory for the order in which they followed or accompanied one another, so that he could make a good guess as to which was going to come next.[5] Would our released prisoner be likely to covet those prizes or to envy the men exalted to honour and power in the Cave? Would he not feel like Homer's Achilles, that he would far sooner "be on earth as a hired servant in the house of a landless man" or endure anything rather than go back to his old beliefs and live in the old way?

Yes, he would prefer any fate to such a life.

Now imagine what would happen if he went down again to take his former seat in the Cave. Coming suddenly out of the sunlight, his eyes would be filled with darkness. He might be required once more to deliver his opinion on those shadows, in competition with the prisoners who had never been released, while his eyesight was still dim and unsteady; and it might take some time to become used to the darkness. They would laugh at him and say that he had gone up only to come back with his sight ruined; it was worth no one's while even to attempt the ascent. If they could lay hands on the man who was trying to set them free and lead them up, they would kill him.[6]

Yes, they would.

Every feature in this parable, my dear Glaucon, is meant to fit our earlier analysis. The prison dwelling corresponds to the region revealed to us through the sense of sight, and the fire-light within it to the power of the Sun. The ascent to see the things in the upper world you may take as standing for the upward journey of the soul into the region of the intelligible; then you will be in possession of what I surmise, since that is what you wish to be told. Heaven knows whether it is true; but this, at any rate, is how it appears to me. In the world of knowledge, the last thing to be perceived and only with great difficulty is the essential Form of Goodness. Once it is perceived, the conclusion must follow that, for all things, this is the cause of whatever is right and good; in the visible world it gives birth to light and to the lord of light, while it is itself sovereign in the intelligible world and the parent of intelligence and truth. Without

---

[5] The empirical politician, with no philosophic insight, but only a "knack of remembering what usually happens" (*Gorg.* 501 A). He has *eikasia* = conjecture as to what is likely (*eikos*).

[6] An allusion to the fate of Socrates.

having had a vision of this Form no one can act with wisdom, either in his own life or in matters of state.

So far as I can understand, I share your belief.

Then you may also agree that it is no wonder if those who have reached this height are reluctant to manage the affairs of men. Their souls long to spend all their time in that upper world—naturally enough, if here once more our parable holds true. Nor, again, is it at all strange that one who comes from the contemplation of divine things to the miseries of human life should appear awkward and ridiculous when, with eyes still dazed and not yet accustomed to the darkness, he is compelled, in a law-court or elsewhere, to dispute about the shadows of justice or the images that cast those shadows, and to wrangle over the notions of what is right in the minds of men who have never beheld Justice itself.

It is not at all strange.

No; a sensible man will remember that the eyes may be confused in two ways—by a change from light to darkness or from darkness to light; and he will recognize that the same thing happens to the soul. When he sees it troubled and unable to discern anything clearly, instead of laughing thoughtlessly, he will ask whether, coming from a brighter existence, its unaccustomed vision is obscured by the darkness, in which case he will think its condition enviable and its life a happy one; or whether, emerging from the depths of ignorance, it is dazzled by excess of light. If so, he will rather feel sorry for it; or, if he were inclined to laugh, that would be less ridiculous than to laugh at the soul which has come down from the light.

That is a fair statement.

If this is true, then, we must conclude that education is not what it is said to be by some, who profess to put knowledge into a soul which does not possess it, as if they could put sight into blind eyes. On the contrary, our own account signifies that the soul of every man does possess the power of learning the truth and the organ to see

it with; and that, just as one might have to turn the whole body round in order that the eye should see light instead of darkness, so the entire soul must be turned away from this changing world, until its eye can bear to contemplate reality and that supreme splendour which we have called the Good. Hence there may well be an art whose aim would be to effect this very thing, the conversion of the soul, in the readiest way; not to put the power of sight into the soul's eye, which already has it, but to ensure that, instead of looking in the wrong direction, it is turned the way it ought to be.

Yes, it may well be so.

It looks, then, as though wisdom were different from those ordinary virtues, as they are called, which are not far removed from bodily qualities, in that they can be produced by habituation and exercise in a soul which has not possessed them from the first. Wisdom, it seems, is certainly the virtue of some diviner faculty, which never loses its power, though its use for good or harm depends on the direction towards which it is turned. You must have noticed in dishonest men with a reputation for sagacity the shrewd glance of a narrow intelligence piercing the objects to which it is directed. There is nothing wrong with their power of vision, but it has been forced into the service of evil, so that the keener its sight, the more harm it works.

Quite true.

And yet if the growth of a nature like this had been pruned from earliest childhood, cleared of those clinging overgrowths which come of gluttony and all luxurious pleasure and, like leaden weights charged with affinity to this mortal world, hang upon the soul, bending its vision downwards; if, freed from these, the soul were turned round towards true reality, then this same power in these very men would see the truth as keenly as the objects it is turned to now.

Yes, very likely.

Is it not also likely, or indeed certain after what has been said, that a state can never be properly governed either by the uneducated who know nothing of truth or by men who are allowed to spend all their days in the pursuit of culture? The ignorant have no single mark before their eyes at which they must aim in all the conduct of their own lives and of affairs of state; and the others will not engage in action if they can help it, dreaming that, while still alive, they have been translated to the Islands of the Blest.

Quite true.

It is for us, then, as founders of a commonwealth, to bring compulsion to bear on the noblest natures. They must be made to climb the ascent to the vision of Goodness, which we called the highest object of knowledge; and, when they have looked upon it long enough, they must not be allowed, as they now are, to remain on the heights, refusing to come down again to the prisoners or to take any part in their labours and rewards, however much or little these may be worth.

Shall we not be doing them an injustice, if we force on them a worse life than they might have?

You have forgotten again, my friend, that the law is not concerned to make any one class specially happy, but to ensure the welfare of the commonwealth as a whole. By persuasion or constraint it will unite the citizens in harmony, making them share whatever benefits each class can contribute to the common good; and its purpose in forming men of that spirit was not that each should be left to go his own way, but that they should be instrumental in binding the community into one.

True, I had forgotten.

You will see, then, Glaucon, that there will be no real injustice in compelling our philosophers to watch over and care for the other citizens. We can fairly tell them that their compeers in other states may quite reasonably refuse to collaborate: there they have sprung up, like a self-sown plant, in despite of their country's institutions; no one has fostered their growth, and they cannot be expected to show gratitude for a care they have never received. "But,"

we shall say, "it is not so with you. We have brought you into existence for your country's sake as well as for your own, to be like leaders and king-bees in a hive; you have been better and more thoroughly educated than those others and hence you are more capable of playing your part both as men of thought and as men of action. You must go down, then, each in his turn, to live with the rest and let your eyes grow accustomed to the darkness. You will then see a thousand times better than those who live there always; you will recognize every image for what it is and know what it represents, because you have seen justice, beauty, and goodness in their reality; and so you and we shall find life in our commonwealth no mere dream, as it is in most existing states, where men live fighting one another about shadows and quarrelling for power, as if that were a great prize; whereas in truth government can be at its best and free from dissension only where the destined rulers are least desirous of holding office."

Quite true.

Then will our pupils refuse to listen and to take their turns at sharing in the work of the community, though they may live together for most of their time in a purer air?

No; it is a fair demand, and they are fair-minded men. No doubt, unlike any ruler of the present day, they will think of holding power as an unavoidable necessity.

Yes, my friend; for the truth is that you can have a well-governed society only if you can discover for your future rulers a better way of life than being in office; then only will power be in the hands of men who are rich, not in gold, but in the wealth that brings happiness, a good and wise life. All goes wrong when, starved for lack of anything good in their own lives, men turn to public affairs hoping to snatch from thence the happiness they hunger for. They set about fighting for power, and this internecine conflict ruins them and their country. The life of true philosophy is the only one that looks down upon offices of state; and access to power must be confined to men who are not in love with it; otherwise rivals will start fighting. So whom else can you compel to undertake the guardianship of the commonwealth, if not those who, besides understanding best the principles of government, enjoy a nobler life than the politician's and look for rewards of a different kind?

There is indeed no other choice.

15. Democracy and the Democratic Man

Democracy, I suppose, should come next. A study of its rise and character should help us to recognize the democratic type of man and set him beside the others for judgment.

Certainly that course would fit in with our plan.

If the aim of life in an oligarchy is to become as rich as possible, that insatiable craving would bring about the transition to democracy. In this way: since the power of the ruling class is due to its wealth, they will not want to have laws restraining prodigal young men from ruining themselves by extravagance. They will hope to lend these spendthrifts money on their property and buy it up, so as to become richer and more influential than ever. We can see at once that a society cannot hold wealth in honour and at the same time establish a proper self-control in its citizens. One or the other must be sacrificed.

Yes, that is fairly obvious.

In an oligarchy, then, this neglect to curb riotous living sometimes reduces to poverty men of a not ungenerous nature. They settle down in idleness, some of them burdened with debt, some disfranchised, some both at once; and these drones are armed and can sting. Hating the men who have acquired their property and conspiring against them and the rest of society, they long for a revolution. Meanwhile the usurers, intent upon their own business, seem unaware of their existence; they are too busy planting their own stings into any fresh victim who offers them an opening to inject the poison of their money; and while they multiply their capital by usury, they are also multiplying the drones and the paupers. When the danger threatens to break out, they will do nothing to quench the flames, either in the way we mentioned, by forbidding a man to do what he likes with his own, or by the next best remedy, which would be a law enforcing a respect for right conduct. If it were enacted that, in general, voluntary contracts for a loan should be made at the lender's risk, there would be less of this shameless pursuit of wealth and a scantier crop of those evils I have just described.

Quite true.

But, as things are, this is the plight to which the rulers of an oligarchy, for all these reasons, reduce their subjects. As for themselves, luxurious indolence of body and mind makes their young men too lazy and effeminate to resist pleasure or to endure pain; and the fathers, neglecting everything but money, have no higher ideals in life than the poor. Such being the condition of rulers and subjects, what will happen when they are thrown together, perhaps as fellow-travellers by sea or land to some festival or on a campaign, and can observe one another's demeanour in a moment of danger? The rich will have no chance to feel superior to the poor. On the contrary, the poor man, lean and sunburnt, may find himself posted in battle beside one who, thanks to his wealth and indoor life, is panting under his burden of fat and showing every mark of distress. "Such men," he will think, "are rich because we are cowards"; and when he and his friends meet in private, the word will go round: "These men are no good: they are at our mercy."

Yes, that is sure to happen.

This state, then, is in the same precarious condition as a person so unhealthy that the least shock from outside will upset the balance or, even without that, internal disorder will break out. It falls sick and is at war with itself on the slightest occasion, as soon as one party or the other calls in allies from a neighbouring oligarchy or democracy; and sometimes civil war begins with no help from without.

Quite true.

And when the poor win, the result is a democracy. They kill some of the opposite party, banish others, and grant the rest an equal share in civil rights and government, officials being usually appointed by lot.

Yes, that is how a democracy comes to be established, whether by force of arms or because the other party is terrorized into giving way.

Now what is the character of this new régime? Obviously the way they govern themselves will throw light on the democratic type of man.

No doubt.

First of all, they are free. Liberty and free speech are rife everywhere; anyone is allowed to do what he likes.

Yes, so we are told.

That being so, every man will arrange his own manner of life to suit his pleasure. The result will be a greater variety of individuals than under any other constitution. So it may be the finest of all, with its variegated pattern of all sorts of characters. Many people may think it the best, just as women and children might admire a mixture of colours of every shade in the pattern of a dress. At any rate if we are in search of a constitution, here is a good place to look for one. A democracy is so free that it contains a sample of every kind; and perhaps anyone who intends to found a state, as we have been doing, ought first to visit this emporium of constitutions and choose the model he likes best.

He will find plenty to choose from.

Here, too, you are not obliged to be in authority, however competent you may be, or to submit to authority, if you do not like it; you need not fight when your fellow citizens are at war, nor remain at peace when they do, unless you want peace; and though you may have no legal right to hold office or sit on juries, you will do so all the same if the fancy takes you. A wonder-

fully pleasant life, surely, for the moment.

For the moment, no doubt.

There is a charm, too, in the forgiving spirit shown by some who have been sentenced by the courts. In a democracy you must have seen how men condemned to death or exile stay on and go about in public, and no one takes any more notice than he would of a spirit that walked invisible. There is so much tolerance and superiority to petty considerations; such a contempt for all those fine principles we laid down in founding our commonwealth, as when we said that only a very exceptional nature could turn out a good man, if he had not played as a child among things of beauty and given himself only to creditable pursuits. A democracy tramples all such notions under foot; with a magnificent indifference to the sort of life a man has led before he enters politics, it will promote to honour anyone who merely calls himself the people's friend.

Magnificent indeed.

These then, and such as these, are the features of a democracy, an agreeable form of anarchy with plenty of variety and an equality of a peculiar kind for equals and unequals alike.

All that is notoriously true.

Now consider the corresponding individual character. Or shall we take his origin first, as we did in the case of the constitution?

Yes.

I imagine him as the son of our miserly oligarch, brought up under his father's eye and in his father's ways. So he too will enforce a firm control over all such pleasures as lead to expense rather than profit—unnecessary pleasures, as they have been called. But, before going farther, shall we draw the distinction between necessary and unnecessary appetites, so as not to argue in the dark? [1]

---

[1] A classification of appetites is needed because oligarchy, democracy, and despotism are based on the supremacy of three sorts of appetite: (1) the necessary, (2) the unnecessary and spendthrift, and (3) the lawless.

Please do so.

There are appetites which cannot be got rid of, and there are all those which it does us good to fulfil. Our nature cannot help seeking to satisfy both these kinds; so they may fairly be described as necessary. On the other hand, "unnecessary" would be the right name for all appetites which can be got rid of by early training and which do us no good and in some cases do harm. Let us take an example of each kind, so as to form a general idea of them. The desire to eat enough plain food—just bread and meat —to keep in health and good condition may be called necessary. In the case of bread the necessity is twofold, since it not only does us good but is indispensable to life; whereas meat is only necessary in so far as it helps to keep us in good condition. Beyond these simple needs the desire for a whole variety of luxuries is unnecessary. Most people can get rid of it by early discipline and education; and it is as prejudicial to intelligence and self-control as it is to bodily health. Further, these unnecessary appetites might be called expensive, whereas the necessary ones are rather profitable, as helping a man to do his work. The same distinctions could be drawn in the case of sexual appetite and all the rest.

Yes.

Now, when we were speaking just now of drones, we meant the sort of man who is under the sway of a host of unnecessary pleasures and appetites, in contrast with our miserly oligarch, over whom the necessary desires are in control. Accordingly, we can now go back to describe how the democratic type develops from the oligarchical. I imagine it usually happens in this way. When a young man, bred, as we were saying, in a stingy and uncultivated home, has once tasted the honey of the drones and keeps company with those dangerous and cunning creatures, who know how to purvey pleasures in all their multitudinous variety, then the oligarchical constitution of his soul begins to turn into a democracy. The corresponding revolution was effected in the state by one of the two factions calling in the help of partisans from outside. In the same way one of the conflicting sets of desires in the soul of this youth will be reinforced from without by a group of kindred passions; and if the resistance of the oligarchical faction in him is strengthened by remonstrances and reproaches coming from his father, perhaps, or his friends, the opposing parties will soon be battling within him. In some cases the democratic interest yields to the oligarchical: a sense of shame gains a footing in the young man's soul, and some appetites are crushed, others banished, until order is restored.

Yes, that happens sometimes.

But then again, perhaps, owing to the father's having no idea how to bring up his son, another brood of desires, akin to those which were banished, are secretly nursed up until they become numerous and strong. These draw the young man back into clandestine commerce with his old associates, and between them they breed a whole multitude. In the end, they seize the citadel of the young man's soul, finding it unguarded by the trusty sentinels which keep watch over the minds of men favoured by heaven. Knowledge, right principles, true thoughts, are not at their post; and the place lies open to the assault of false and presumptuous notions. So he turns again to those lotus-eaters and now throws in his lot with them openly. If his family send reinforcements to the support of his thrifty instincts, the impostors who have seized the royal fortress shut the gates upon them, and will not even come to parley with the fatherly counsels of individual friends. In the internal conflict they gain the day; modesty and self-control, dishonoured and insulted as the weaknesses of an unmanly fool, are thrust out into exile; and the whole crew of unprofitable desires take a hand in banishing moderation and frugality, which, as they will have it, are nothing but churlish meanness. So they take possession of the soul which they have swept clean, as if purified for initiation into higher mysteries; and nothing remains but to marshal the great procession bringing home Insolence, Anarchy, Waste, and Impudence, those resplendent divinities crowned with garlands, whose praises they sing under flattering names: Insolence they call good breeding, Anarchy freedom, Waste magnificence, and Impudence a manly spirit. Is not that a fair account of the revolution which gives free rein to unnecessary and harmful pleasures in a young man brought up in the satisfaction only of the necessary desires?

Yes, it is a vivid description.

In his life thenceforward he spends as much time and pains and money on his superfluous pleasures as on the necessary ones. If he is lucky enough not to be carried beyond all bounds, the tumult may begin to subside as he grows older. Then perhaps he may recall some of the banished virtues and cease to give himself up entirely to the passions which ousted them; and now he will set all his pleasures on a footing of equality, denying to none its equal rights and maintenance, and allowing each in turn, as it presents itself, to succeed, as if by the chance of the lot, to the government of his soul until it is satisfied. When he is told that some pleasures should be sought and valued as arising from desires of a higher order, others chastised and enslaved because the

desires are base, he will shut the gates of the citadel against the messengers of truth, shaking his head and declaring that one appetite is as good as another and all must have their equal rights. So he spends his days indulging the pleasure of the moment, now intoxicated with wine and music, and then taking to a spare diet and drinking nothing but water; one day in hard training, the next doing nothing at all, the third apparently immersed in study. Every now and then he takes a part in politics, leaping to his feet to say or do whatever comes into his head. Or he will set out to rival someone he admires, a soldier it may be, or, if the fancy takes him, a man of business. His life is subject to no order or restraint, and he has no wish to change an existence which he calls pleasant, free, and happy.

That well describes the life of one whose motto is liberty and equality.

Yes, and his character contains the same fine variety of pattern that we found in the democratic state; it is as multifarious as that epitome of all types of constitution. Many a man, and many a woman too, will find in it something to envy. So we may see in him the counterpart of democracy, and call him the democratic man.

CHAPTER 2

ARISTOTLE

PLATO'S strength and weakness lay in his gift to confront social reality with what *ought* to be. If that is utopian, every critic and reformer is a utopian. The *Republic* is not a work of abstract contemplation by an aloof philosopher addressed to no one in particular, but the impassioned plea of an Athenian old-family aristocrat. Opposing popular government, Plato recommended to his fellow citizens a constitution and way of life that in many respects, though not in all, resembled those of Sparta, a military and aristocratic state whose distinctive marks were discipline, unity, and complete subordination of the individual to the state. Deeply concerned about practical affairs as he was, Plato nevertheless often went beyond the analysis of what does happen, or is likely to happen, and let himself be carried off into the realm of the Ought. Looking into what may or ought to develop in the future, one is more likely to think in terms of the absolute and perfect, because the imagination of the future is pure idea, unmodified by that relentless relativist and compromiser—experience.

Plato found the corrective to his thinking in his own student, Aristotle (384–322 B. C.), not an Athenian, but a native of Stagira, a Greek colonial town on the Macedonian coast. Reared on the fringe of Greek civilization, Aristotle early acquired some of the worldly wisdom, detachment, and tolerance that were generally characteristic of colonial Greeks in constant touch with other peoples and cultures. Unlike Plato, Aristotle came from an upper-middle-class family, his father being a physician. At the age of seventeen, Aristotle went to Athens, the intellectual center of Greece, entered Plato's Academy, and studied under Plato for twenty years, until his master's death. During the subsequent twelve years, he traveled widely and spent several years at the Court of Philip of Macedon as tutor to his son, Alexander.

In 335 B. C. Aristotle returned to Athens and set up a school of his own, the Lyceum, whose teaching and research program included every branch of knowledge. In 323 B. C. Alexander suddenly died, and the national-democratic forces in Athens quickly rose against the Macedonian overlordship and its lieutenants and spokesmen in Greece. Aristotle, widely known for his intimate associations with the Macedonian monarchy and Alexander, was suspected of pro-Macedonian sentiments and indicted. However, Aristotle preferred exile to a court trial and possible sentence; he died the following year (322 B. C.) in Chalcis, a stronghold of Macedonian influence that gave him generous refuge during the last months of his life.

In the history of political philosophy no one has surpassed Aristotle in encyclopedic interest and accomplishment. From his father he inherited a flair for medical and biological subjects, and he may have practiced medicine for a time. This interest drew him into zoology, physics, and the natural sciences in general, and fostered in him the habit of observing and weighing data before expressing any general formulas and hypotheses. In philosophy proper, logic and metaphysics were his two main branches of study and writing; he also contributed to aesthetics and rhetoric and wrote the first book on psychology; and his *Ethics* and *Politics* are the first systematic treatises in their respective fields. The *Politics* lacks the fire and poetic imagery of the *Republic*, but it is more systematic and analytical, and after twenty-three hundred years it is still an introductory textbook to the entire field of political science. It cannot easily be surpassed in clarity of thought, sobriety of expression, range of topics, and undogmatic openness of mind, for Aristotle prefers being occasionally self-contradictory to being always right.

Aristotle opens the *Politics* with two important ideas: (1) that the state is a community, and (2) that it is the highest of all communities, "which embraces all the rest, aims at good in a greater degree than any other, and at the highest good." The first thesis came naturally to a Greek of the classical period: his *polis* was a city-state with a small area and population; lacking the impersonal anonymity of ancient empires or modern national states, it combined within itself the active citizenship of an early New England or modern Swiss community and the warmth and fellowship of a religious congregation, all deepened by a joint sharing in the arts and pleasures of life.

Aristotle may not have been the first to consider the state a community, but he was the first to define it clearly as such, and thus he laid the foundation for the *organic* conception of the state, one of the two major types into which all political theories of the state may roughly be divided. According to him, the state is a natural community, an organism with all the attributes of a living being. The other major type views the state as an instrument, a mechanism, a piece of machinery to be used for purposes and ends higher than itself. This type, called the *instrumentalist* view of the state, is actually older, having been propounded by the Sophists a century before Aristotle; however, it was rejected by Plato and revived only in modern times by Hobbes, Locke, and John Dewey.

Aristotle conceives of the state as "natural" in two ways. First, he briefly delineates the evolution of social institutions from the family through the village to the city-state; in this historical sense, the state is the natural and final stage in the growth of human relations. However, the state is also considered by Aristotle to be natural in a logical and philosophical sense: "The state is by nature clearly prior to the family and the individual, since the whole is of necessity prior to the part." Similarly, Aristotle says that "man is by nature a political animal," and that only gods or beasts can exist without the confines of the sheltering city.

But Aristotle maintains not only that the state is a community but that it is the *highest community* aiming at the highest good. The family is the first form of association, lowest in the chain of social evolution, and lowest on the rung of values, because it is established by nature "for the supply of men's everyday wants." The village is the second form of association, genetically more complex than the family, and aiming "at something more than the supply of daily needs," meeting at least some rudimentary and primitive cultural wants that the family cannot satisfy. The third and highest form of association is the city-state, highest in terms of social evolution and highest in terms of value and purpose: whereas family and village exist essentially for the preservation of life and the comforts of companionship, the "state exists for the sake of a good life, and not for the sake of life only," and "political society exists for the sake of noble actions, and not of mere companionship."

Unlike Plato, who conceives of reality in terms of unchanging and unchangeable static essences and Ideas, Aristotle identifies the nature of a thing with the end toward which it is developing; at each unfinished stage, the thing is partly realizing its own nature and is fully itself when its end is wholly realized. Aristotle's biological, scientific, and historical interests enabled him to view the philosophical problem of reality from a more dynamic and relative standpoint than Plato's, and Aristotle's conception of the state therefore encompasses a wider range of forms of state, varying blends of idea and circumstance, of the perfect and the imperfect.

The state is the highest form of association, not only in terms of the social and institutional, or objective, values, but in terms of man's own nature. In the family, man reproduces himself; in the village, he satisfies elementary wants of human companionship; in the state alone, he realizes his entire self, and particularly the highest part of himself. Man thus represents a compound of qualities that are reflected in corresponding forms of association: his *material* appetites and biological urges, the lowest on the scale of values, are reflected in the family; his *social* sentiment, his desire for companionship and community, is expressed in the village; his *moral* nature, the quality that makes him most specifically human, is fulfilled in the state.

In modern thought, especially in the social sciences, a sharper distinction is drawn between the individual, social groups and associations, and, finally, the state. Aristotle sees all three as organically connected with one another. Man cannot be conceived as being apart from, or superior to, the state because, as was explained earlier, Aristotle considers that "the whole is of necessity prior to the part." Only a "beast or a god" is unable to live in society, or has no need for it. Man can realize himself, that which is most human in him, in society alone. Similarly, Aristotle recognizes no basic difference between social and political associations. To him, all associations are political, inasmuch as they aim at a common good through joint action; the state differs from other associations in that it aims at the highest good, the general advantage of all.

Since the seventeenth century the state has been sharply distinguished from all other organizations because it alone possesses sovereignty, or the highest authority in a politically organized community, and the legal monopoly of enforcing such authority in its territory. Aristotle knows not of the conceptual distinction, or contrast, between individual and society, nor can he visualize the later conflict between society (conceived as the sphere of unhindered and spontaneous activity) and the state (conceived as the sphere of regulated and compelled behavior). If Aristotle were to think at all of the state as sovereign, he would think of the *highest purpose* of the state rather than of its supreme authority over its citizens. His is a conception of *moral sovereignty* rather than of *legal sovereignty*. Nurtured in the tradition of the small city-state, Aristotle could still say that "the will to live together is friendship," and he would have abhorred the conception that the state is held together, not by personal bonds of fellowship and friendship, but by impersonal and anonymous rules of law, uniformly applying to vast territories and populations, as in modern states and empires.

In his organic view of the state Aristotle expresses more clearly what is implicit, and to some extent explicit, in Plato, but he is unwilling to go as far as his teacher. Unity became for Plato an ideal to which almost anything else was to be sacrificed, the happiness of the rulers as well as the ruled. By contrast, Aristotle warns against the dangers of excessive unity in the state; even if it could be attained, it ought to be rejected, "for it would be the destruction of the state." Moreover, Aristotle is doubtful whether such perfect unity is attainable, and he likens the guardian-rulers of the *Republic* to a "mere occupying garrison," with the result that Plato's ideally united state actually contains "two states in one, each hostile to the other."

Whereas Plato saw only a few basic differences of men, such as the differences between members of the three classes of the ideal state, Aristotle is aware of many more differences, and he expresses a truth that is as provocative today as ever, that "a state is not made up only of so many men, but of different kinds of men," and that "the nature of a state is to be a plurality." The danger of all organic theories of the state is that they tend to stress communal unity over individual differences and to subordinate the individual to the state. Plato's conception of the state carried the idea of unity, implicit in all organic theories, to the excess of self-destruction; Aristotle found the counterweight to such an extreme and perfectionist view in the elements of his thinking that pointed toward relativism and pluralism.

Aristotle's organic conception of the state has been used more eagerly and more frequently by conservatives and antidemocrats than by democratic political writers. Yet as time goes on, the awareness is growing even among the heirs of eighteenth- and nineteenth-century liberalism that the state is more than an instrument or piece of machinery, that the democratic state in particular must aim at becoming a community, not only of law, but of fellowship. Underlying the modern development of the welfare state is the notion that society must have no outcasts, that its inequalities must be reduced, and that the basic amenities of civilized life must be accessible to all.

The second basic doctrine of Aristotle, that the state is the highest community, is less likely to be accepted by democrats. Two objections can be raised: first, democrats are unwilling to concede that any institution *per se* is entitled to claim primary and exclusive loyalty. Man feels attached to various, and often conflicting, religious, social, economic, and political groups, and his conscience has to decide in each instance of conflict which loyalty comes first. In one instance he may put his church above his country, in another his country above his economic interest, but there is no way of telling a priori that any institution is entitled to first allegiance under all circumstances. As a Greek, Aristotle would have felt little sympathy for such a conception of the state, which is implicit in all democratic political doctrines, because the small city-state with its intimate social life was church and state at the same time, and no sharp distinction was felt between social-economic and political institutions.

The second objection against the conception of the state as the highest community can be made by democrats on the ground, originally stated by the Sophists and later re-emphasized by the Stoics, that man's loyalty is to mankind as a whole rather than to any particular fraction. This faith was given added force by the Jewish-Christian religious tradition, in which the oneness of God inspires the belief in the oneness of mankind.

By studying virtually all then-known constitutions and political systems, Aristotle laid the foundations of an important branch of political science: *comparative government and politics*. Of one hundred and fifty-eight such studies made by him, only one survives, the *Constitution of Athens,* discovered in 1890. The study of comparative political institutions is of interest to the political scientist as well as to the practicing statesman, who must know the varieties of political experience if he is to be able to remedy the defects of existing constitutions.

In considering the general problem of the various forms of government, Aristotle says, in an obvious reference to Plato, that "there are some who would have none but the most perfect." The knowledge of the best state may have some value as a norm and standard, but, on the other hand, "the best is often unattainable, and therefore the true legislator and statesman ought to be acquainted, not only with (1) that which is best in the abstract, but also with (2) that which is best relatively to circumstances." Where the attention of Plato, in the *Republic* at least, is centered on the desirable kind of state, Aristotle holds that we "should consider, not only what form of government is best, but also what is possible and what is easily attainable by all."

In classifying the forms of state, Aristotle distinguishes governments that are carried on "with a view to the common interest" from those that serve private interests, whether of one, of few, or of many. Of true governments, there are three: kingship, aristocracy, and constitutional government. Each form has its perversion, of which there are also three: tyranny, oligarchy, and democracy (the rule of the poor).

Of the three true forms, Aristotle holds monarchy to be the most ideal kind of government. If a man "pre-eminent in virtue" can be found, who surpasses in virtue and political capacity "all the rest," he cannot be regarded as a part of the state, subject to the law like everybody else: "Such an one may truly be deemed a God among men." Since there is no law for men of pre-eminent virtue, monarchs "are themselves a law." Their superior virtue and political capacity give them the right to "practise compulsion and still live in harmony with their cities, if their own government is for the interest of the state."

Like Plato, Aristotle puts virtue of the rulers above consent of the ruled, although both would prefer to have the ruled submit voluntarily to their rulers, to avoid the necessity of compulsion. If a man of pre-eminent virtue be the monarch, Aristotle argues, "all should joyfully obey such a ruler, according to what seems to be the order of nature." Monarchy can be justified, however, by another consideration: that "a king is the resource of the better classes against the people," and that "the idea of a king is to be a protector of the rich against unjust treatment, of the people against insult and oppression."

Aristotle's deep sympathy for monarchy, as expressed in the *Politics* in so many passages, is to be understood in the light of his relations with the rising Macedonian monarchy. His father had been the royal physician at the Macedonian court, and Aristotle himself the tutor of Alexander. Both Philip and Alexander sought to conquer Greece intellectually as well as politically and militarily; just as in the struggle between Sparta and Athens class loyalties often came before patriotism, and each city had its (antidemocratic) Spartan and (prodemocratic) Athenian party, so the Macedonian effort to annex Greece to its rule was accompanied by the growth of pro-Macedonian groups in the major Greek city-states. In Athens, the national and democratic movement was led by Demosthenes, to whom all monarchy, good or bad, was "un-Athenian"; the conservative classes, anxious above all to maintain their privileged social-economic position, received their intellectual support from Aristotle's school of philosophy and Plato's Academy, and they were therefore generally pro-Macedonian.

Aristocracy is nowhere described in the *Politics* systematically, perhaps because the problem of aristocracy and democracy (particularly in relation to Athenian self-government) was not of such practical importance as that of monarchy (particularly in relation to the Macedonian kingdom). Aristotle defines aristocracy as a "government formed of the best men absolutely," and not merely of men who are good relatively, that is, in relation to changing circumstances and constitutions. But Aristotle admits that, in addition to such a pure form of aristocracy, which is based on merit and virtue only, there is a type of aristocracy that also takes into account the elements of wealth. Generally, however, Aristotle speaks of monarchy and aristocracy as "the perfect state," the government of the best, both forms aiming at the general good; the main difference between the two consists in the fact that in monarchy virtue is centered in one "pre-eminent" man, whereas in aristocracy virtue is diffused among several men. The deteriorated form of aristocracy is oligarchy, in which government by the wealthy is carried on for their own benefit rather than for that of the whole state. Whereas merit and virtue are the distinctive qualities to be considered in selecting the rulers in an aristocracy, wealth is the basis of selection in an oligarchy.

The third of the true forms of state is constitutional government ("polity").

Aristotle defines it as the state that the citizens at large administer for the common interest. Constitutional government is a compromise between the two principles of freedom and wealth, the attempt to "unite the freedom of the poor and the wealth of the rich," without giving either principle exclusive predominance. Aristotle concedes that the doctrine of the multitude being supreme rather than the few best, "though not free from difficulty, yet seems to contain an element of truth." When many ordinary persons meet together, their collective wisdom and experience may be superior to that of the few good, "just as a feast to which many contribute is better than a dinner provided out of a single purse." Aristotle suggests the general analogy of the user of a thing being a better judge than its producer, and that, returning to culinary similes, "the guest will judge better of a feast than the cook."

Thinking realistically of the stability of the state, Aristotle holds that the freedom of the poor must be given some consideration, "for a state in which many poor men are excluded from office will necessarily be full of enemies." Aristotle never abandons the ideal state (monarchy or aristocracy, that is, the rule of the best) as an "aspiration," but he realizes that it assumes a standard of virtue "which is above ordinary persons"; in practice, therefore, constitutional government, based on limited suffrage, turns out to be "the best constitution for most states, and the best life for most men."

By relating forms of political organization to the social milieu that conditions them, Aristotle anticipated some of the main doctrines of Montesquieu and, still more recently, the sociological approach to the study of politics. He saw the danger that would arise if any principle singly and exclusively dominated the constitution, and he therefore advocated, for reasons of stability and practicability, *mixed constitutions*, such as "polity" (constitutional government), based on the two principles of wealth and numbers. However, he realized that a mixed political system could exist in the long run only if backed by a stable society without extremes of wealth and poverty.

Although many persons in the twentieth century find the cause of revolution in conspiracies of evil men, and its remedy in intimidation by investigatory committees or in repression by antirevolutionary legislation, Aristotle states that "poverty is the parent of revolution and crime," and that "when there is no middle class, and the poor greatly exceed in number, troubles arise, and the state soon comes to an end." Because he realized that political stability depends on an equitable social and economic order, he was opposed to selfish class rule by either an excessively wealthy plutocracy (called by him "oligarchy") or by a propertyless proletariat (called by him "democracy"): "Thus it is manifest that the best political community is formed by citizens of the middle class, and that those states are likely to be well-administered, in which the middle class is large, and stronger if possible than both the other classes, or at any rate than either singly." The middle classes thus provided for Aristotle the balance and equilibrium without which no constitution can endure.

The degenerate form of constitutional government (or "polity") is called by Aristotle "democracy," and defined as a system in which "the poor rule." It is government by the poor, and for the poor only, just as tyranny is government by one for his own benefit, and oligarchy government by the wealthy few for their class benefit. But of the degenerate forms, government of the poor for the benefit of the poor ("democracy") is "the most tolerable of the three." Aristotle names popular sovereignty and individual liberty the two characteristic principles of democracy, and he condemns them, in language similar to that of Plato, as incompatible with the stability of the existing moral and political order: "Men think that what is just is equal; and that equality is the supremacy of the popular will; and that freedom means the doing what a man likes. In such democracies every one lives as he pleases."

Though Aristotle was more appreciative than Plato of the common sense and collective wisdom of the people, he was nevertheless afraid of government in which the democratic principle of popular sovereignty was allowed to operate without the modifying influence of other principles, particularly wealth. In this fear of the sovereignty of the majority, Aristotle is conservative rather than antidemocratic, and the godfather of all conservatives in history who have tried to harmonize respect for constitutional government with social and economic inequality. In such a combination, Aristotle resembles more the Whig of the seventeenth century than the Liberal of the nineteenth and twentieth centuries.

Aristotle's conservative viewpoint is also clearly expressed in his conception of *citizenship*. He defines a citizen as follows: "he who has the power to take part in the deliberative or judicial administration of any state." Representative government was unknown to Aristotle because the Greek city-state was governed directly by its citizens, with but few representative elements. Aristotle could not have foreseen the modern concept of the citizen whose main (and often sole) political act is to vote (and frequently he neglects to do that) every few years in an election, and otherwise to leave the actual functions of government to professional legislators, judges, and civil servants. Within the small city-state, all slaves and the majority of the free were excluded from citizenship; to be a citizen meant to participate directly in the legislative and executive functions of government.

Aristotle's idea of citizenship is that of the economically independent gentleman who has enough experience, education, and leisure to devote himself to *active* citizenship, for "citizens must not lead the life of mechanics or tradesmen, for such life is ignoble, and inimical to virtue. Neither must they be husbandmen, since leisure is necessary both for the development of virtue and the performance of political duties." Stressing even more clearly the relation between property and virtue, Aristotle maintains that "the ruling class should be the owners of property, for they are citizens, and the citizens of a state should be in good circumstances; whereas mechanics or any other class which is not a producer of virtue have no share in the state."

Aristotle makes an important distinction between the "parts" of the state and its "necessary conditions." Only those who actively share, or have the means and leisure to share, in the government of the state are its component or integral parts. All the others are merely the "necessary condition" who provide the material environment within which the active citizens, freed from menial tasks, can function. Aristotle finds it "no more absurd" to exclude "the lower class" from citizenship than to exclude "slaves and freedmen," none of whom are resident aliens or foreigners; what the "lower class" has in common with slaves and freedmen is the fact that all its members are "necessary to the existence of the state" but not parts of the state. Aristotle even notes that in ancient times, the "artisan class *were* slaves or foreigners, and therefore the majority of them are so now." Although mechanics and laborers are not legally aliens, morally and politically they are, because "he who is excluded from the honours of the state is no better than an alien."

In comparing the propertied citizens with the propertyless mechanics and laborers, Aristotle draws the analogy between ends and means, the latter existing for the sake of the former. Aristotle was unaware of the idea, expressed in religious terms by the Jewish-Christian teachings in antiquity, and in philosophical terms by Immanuel Kant in modern times, that every man is, by virtue of being human, an end in himself, and must not be reduced to a means.

If free artisans and laborers are to be treated as means rather than ends, it is none too difficult for Aristotle to defend the institution of *slavery*. Whereas artisans and laborers are to be viewed as means in relation to the state only, slaves are means in every aspect of their existence; they belong "wholly" to their masters. Aristotle assumes that nature is universally ruled by the contrast of the superior and inferior: man is superior to the animals, the male to the female, the soul to the body, reason to passion. In all these divisions, it is just that the superior rule over the inferior, and such a rule is to the advantage of both. Among men, there are those "whose business is to use their body, and who can do nothing better," and they are by nature slaves. Just as it is fair to hunt against wild animals, so it is "against men who, though intended by nature to be governed, will not submit." Because the question of who is intended by nature to govern, or to be governed, is likely to be decided by the conquerors of a defeated nation rather than by an impartial, third-party court of appeal, Aristotle—in his doctrine of just wars of conquest and enslavement—anticipates Hegel's dictum that "world history is the world court."

Aristotle concedes to slaves the mental ability of apprehending the rational actions and orders of their masters but denies them the ability of acting rationally on their own initiative. The slave is a possession, a live tool; comparing slaves to tame animals, Aristotle notes the difference that the latter cannot even apprehend reason, whereas slaves do, but "the use made of slaves and of tame animals is not very different; for both with their bodies minister to the needs of life." Untouched by the monotheistic doctrine of the divinity and uniqueness of every human soul, Aristotle expresses the pagan view that "from the hour of their birth, some are marked out for subjection, others for rule."

Aristotle was realistic enough to see that many were slaves by law rather than nature, particularly those who were reduced to slavery by conquest, a custom widely practiced in the wars of antiquity. Feeling strongly about the cultural unity (and superiority) of the Greeks, Aristotle was particularly disturbed by slavery in Greece, and said that "Hellenes do not like to call Hellenes slaves, but confine the term to barbarians." Just as Plato had urged that Greeks conduct war against one another with a higher set of standards than against "barbarians," Aristotle looked on the mastery-slavery relation as not fitting superior Greeks, because "some are slaves everywhere, others nowhere."

This difference, however, was not a fact to be observed, but a wish to be expressed, because Greeks did enslave one another, and some of those who were slaves were by nature (and often, by birth) free. Aristotle did not resolve the dilemma between his general theory of slavery, which was based on moral and rational superiority, and the slavery of his time, which was based on force, custom, and utility, and had little to do with moral superiority.

All in all, Aristotle's view of slavery was not too extreme for his time. By reminding the master that his rule over the slave must be based on moral excellence and that abuse of his authority was injurious to both, by allowing the possibility of friendship between them, by conceding to slaves the faculty of apprehending reason, Aristotle prepared the ground for more searching ideas. Yet his general acceptance of slavery shows how even a wise and great philosopher is captive of the institutions of his time, and of the prejudices that rationalize them.

Aristotle's views on *property* are developed in direct reference to Plato, but they are of more general bearing and constitute to this day the ablest defense of private property. In his polemic against Plato, Aristotle attributes to him the advocacy of a communist property scheme in the *Republic*. In fact, Plato proposed nothing of the sort: the workers, artisans, and farmers in the *Republic* live in a system of private ownership and management of property; as to the rulers, they own no means of production of any kind, and their only economic activity consists in consuming what they derive from the farming and working population as tribute befitting an austere yet noble style of living. Although Plato did not advocate economic communism, he nevertheless outlawed private property for the rulers as a possible menace to their sense of unity and their devotion to the state.

By contrast, Aristotle denies that private property is, in itself, a threat to moral perfection, and he defends his view on four grounds. First, he adduces the *incentive and progress* argument: when "every one has a distinct interest, men will not complain of one another, and they will make more progress, because every one will be attending to his own business." Thus Aristotle links the idea of self-interest with that of social progress through greater individual effort and competence, whereas under a communist system, "those who labour much and get little will necessarily complain of those who labour little and receive or consume much."

Aristotle's second argument in support of private property is the *pleasure* that the ownership of property gives, "for all, or almost all, men love money and other such objects in a measure." Aristotle sharply distinguishes such love of property from selfishness and miserliness, and considers it rather from the viewpoint of self-respect and material self-realization.

The third argument is that of *liberality*. Under communism, no one can afford to practice generosity and liberality because of the excessive equalization of property; it takes a system of private property, with at least some wealth and inequality, to "set an example of liberality or do any liberal action; for liberality consists in the use which is made of property."

Aristotle's fourth argument has a distinctly Burkean flavor: there must be something deeply and enduringly human in the idea of private property, if it has *existed* for such a *long time,* and "we should not disregard the experience of ages." As to communist practices, "in the multitude of years these things, if they were good, would certainly not have been unknown."

Aristotle is aware of the evils that befall men in a system of private property, but he says that they "are due to a very different cause—the wickedness of human nature." The cure for social imperfections is not equality of property but the moral improvement of man, and "the beginning of reform is not so much to equalize property as to train the nobler sort of natures not to desire more, and to prevent the lower from getting more; that is to say, they must be kept down, but not ill-treated." As a matter of public policy, the legislator ought to aim at equitable, rather than equal, distribution of property; what seems most important to Aristotle is *not who owns property but how property is used,* and that is an essentially moral question, not one of political economy.

Aristotle nevertheless realizes that excessive inequalities of wealth are dangerous to the balance and harmony of the state, and for this reason he praises with deep feeling the advantages of a society in which the middle classes are strongest. By contrast, where "some possess much, and the others nothing," constitutional government is impossible to maintain, and the state will be ruled by one of two extremes: either a plutocratic regime (oligarchy) for the exclusive benefit of the wealthy, or a proletarian regime (democracy) for the benefit of the urban poor, and "a tyranny may grow out of either extreme."

Unlike Plato, who searched for perfect justice, Aristotle understood that the basic issue is between the *rule of law* and the *rule of men.* Conceding that man-made law can never attain perfect justice, Aristotle nevertheless stresses that "the rule of the law is preferable to that of any individual," and that magistrates should regulate only matters on which the law is silent, because a general rule or principle cannot embrace all particulars. Whereas government based on law cannot be perfectly just, it is at least the lesser evil, when contrasted with the arbitrariness and passion inherent in government based on the rule of men.

The Aristotelian concept of the rule of law became one of the dominant political ideas of the Middle Ages, during which political relations were largely based on custom. In modern times the concept of the rule of law has become one of the pillars of the constitutional edifice of the United States. In Germany the doctrine of the *Rechtsstaat,* that is, the state based on the rule of law, was one of the most civilizing and liberalizing political influences in the nineteenth century. In England, A. V. Dicey's formulation of the rule of law and its specific relations to the British political system has become a vital contribution to the understanding of constitutional government. The concept of the rule of law, of the constitutional state, is perhaps the most important legacy Aristotle has bequeathed to posterity.

Aristotle's specific ideas, beliefs, and proposals are generally conservative, even for his own time. But running through all his works, and implicit in his temper and personality, is a spirit that is wise and gentle, moderate, broad in outlook, open to new ideas, averse to dogmatism, conscious of the intricacy and complexity of human affairs, and imbued with sympathy that illuminates and enriches philosophical enquiry. Though explicitly conservative, Aristotle's thinking was suffused with qualities that characterize the liberal temper, the open mind. In the twentieth century we have had the opportunity to learn again that there is perhaps no force so destructive, so deadly, to civilized life as fanaticism: it starts out with unbending certainty and reckless intransigence, and ends up, in the name of high ideals, with savage murder. Aristotle was not a fanatic.

ARISTOTLE

Politics*

1. Nature and Origin of the State

Every state is a community of some kind, and every community is established with a view to some good; for mankind always act in order to obtain that which they think good. But, if all communities aim at some good, the state or political community, which is the highest of all, and which embraces all the rest, aims at good in a greater degree than any other, and at the highest good.

Some people think that the qualifications of a statesman, king, householder, and master are the same, and that they differ, not in kind, but only in the number of their subjects. For example, the ruler over a few is called a master; over more, the manager of a household; over a still larger number, a statesman or king, as if there were no difference between a great household and a small state. The distinction which is made between the king and the statesman is as

*From Aristotle, *Politics* (trans. Benjamin Jowett, Oxford University Press). By permission.

follows: When the government is personal, the ruler is a king; when, according to the rules of the political science, the citizens rule and are ruled in turn, then he is called a statesman.

But all this is a mistake; for governments differ in kind, as will be evident to any one who considers the matter according to the method which has hitherto guided us. As in other departments of science, so in politics, the compound should always be resolved into the simple elements or least parts of the whole. We must therefore look at the elements of which the state is composed, in order that we may see in what the different kinds of rule differ from one another, and whether any scientific result can be attained about each one of them.

He who thus considers things in their first growth and origin, whether a state or anything else, will obtain the clearest view of them. In the first place there must be a union of those who cannot exist without each other; namely, of male and female, that the race may continue (and this is a union which is formed, not of deliberate purpose, but because, in common with other animals and with plants, mankind have a natural desire to leave behind them an image of themselves), and of natural ruler and subject, that both may be preserved. For that which can foresee by the exercise of mind is by nature intended to be lord and master, and that which can with its body give effect to such foresight is a subject, and by nature a slave; hence master and slave have the same interest. Now nature has distinguished between the female and the slave. For she is not niggardly, like the smith who fashions the Delphian knife for many uses; she makes each thing for a single use, and every instrument is best made when intended for one and not for many uses. But among barbarians no distinction is made between women and slaves, because there is no natural ruler among them: they are a community of slaves, male and female. Wherefore the poets say—

It is meet that Hellenes should rule over barbarians;

as if they thought that the barbarian and the slave were by nature one.

Out of these two relationships between man and woman, master and slave, the first thing to arise is the family, and Hesiod is right when he says—

First house and wife and an ox for the plough,

for the ox is the poor man's slave. The family is the association established by nature for the supply of men's everyday wants, and the members of it are called by Charondas "companions of the cupboard", and by Epimenides the Cretan, "companions of the manger." But when several families are united, and the association aims at something more than the supply of daily needs, the first society to be formed is the village. And the most natural form of the village appears to be that of a colony from the family, composed of the children and grandchildren, who are said to be suckled "with

the same milk". And this is the reason why Hellenic states were originally governed by kings; because the Hellenes were under royal rule before they came together, as the barbarians still are. Every family is ruled by the eldest, and therefore in the colonies of the family the kingly form of government prevailed because they were of the same blood. As Homer says:

Each one gives law to his children and to his wives.

For they lived dispersedly, as was the manner in ancient times. Wherefore men say that the Gods have a king, because they themselves either are or were in ancient times under the rule of a king. For they imagine, not only the forms of the Gods, but their ways of life to be like their own.

When several villages are united in a single complete community, large enough to be nearly or quite self-sufficing, the state comes into existence, originating in the bare needs of life, and continuing in existence for the sake of a good life. And therefore, if the earlier forms of society are natural, so is the state, for it is the end of them, and the nature of a thing is its end. For what each thing is when fully developed, we call its nature, whether we are speaking of a man, a horse, or a family. Besides, the final cause and end of a thing is the best, and to be self-sufficing is the end and the best.

Hence it is evident that the state is a creation of nature, and that man is by nature a political animal. And he who by nature and not by mere accident is without a state, is either a bad man or above humanity; he is like the

Tribeless, lawless, heartless one,

whom Homer denounces—the natural outcast is forthwith a lover of war; he may be compared to an isolated piece at draughts.

Now, that man is more of a political animal than bees or any other gregarious animals is evident. Nature, as we often say, makes nothing in vain, and man is the only animal whom she has endowed with the gift of speech. And whereas mere voice is but an indication of pleasure or pain, and is therefore found in other animals (for their nature attains to the perception of pleasure and pain and the intimation of them to one another, and no further), the power of speech is intended to set forth the expedient and inexpedient, and therefore likewise the just and the unjust. And it is a characteristic of man that he alone has any sense of good and evil, of just and unjust, and the like, and the association of living beings who have this sense makes a family and a state.

Further, the state is by nature clearly prior to the family and to the individual, since the whole is of necessity prior to the part; for example, if the whole body be destroyed, there will be no foot or hand, except in an equivocal sense, as we might speak of a stone hand; for when destroyed the hand will be no better than that. But things are defined by their working and power; and we ought not to say that they are the same when they no longer have their proper quality, but only that they have the same name. The proof that the state is a creation of nature and prior to the individual is that the individual, when isolated, is not self-sufficing; and therefore he is like a part in relation to the whole. But he who is unable to live in society, or who has no need because he is sufficient for himself, must be either a beast or a god: he is no part of a state. A social instinct is implanted in all men by nature, and yet he who first founded the state was the greatest of benefactors. For man, when perfected, is the best of animals, but, when separated from law and justice, he is the worst of all; since armed injustice is the more dangerous, and he is equipped at birth with arms, meant to be used by intelligence and virtue, which he may use for the worst ends. Wherefore, if he have not virtue, he is the most unholy and the most savage of animals, and the most full of lust and gluttony. But justice is the bond of men in states, for the administration of justice, which is the determination of what is just, is the principle of order in political society.

2. Slavery

But is there any one thus intended by nature to be a slave, and for whom such a condition is expedient and right, or rather is not all slavery a violation of nature?

There is no difficulty in answering this question, on grounds both of reason and of fact. For that some should rule and others be ruled is a thing not only necessary, but expedient; from the hour of their birth, some are marked out for subjection, others for rule.

And there are many kinds both of rulers and subjects (and that rule is the better which is exercised over better subjects—for example, to rule over men is better than to rule over wild beasts; for the work is better which is executed by better workmen, and where one man rules and another is ruled, they may be said to have a work); for in all things which form a composite whole and which are made up of parts, whether continuous or discrete, a distinction between the ruling and the subject element comes to light. Such a duality exists in living creatures, but not in them only; it originates in the constitution of the universe; even in things which have no life there is a ruling principle, as in a musical mode. But we are wandering from the subject. We will therefore restrict ourselves to the living creature, which, in the first place, consists of soul and body: and of these two, the one is by nature the ruler, and the other the subject. But then we must look for the intentions of nature in things which retain their nature, and not in things which are corrupted. And therefore we must study the man who is in the most perfect state both of body and soul, for in him we shall see the true relation of the two; although in bad or corrupted natures the body will often appear to rule over the soul, because they are in an evil and unnatural condition. At all events we may firstly observe in living creatures both a despotical and a constitutional rule; for the soul rules the body with a despotical rule, whereas the intellect rules the appetites with a constitutional and royal rule. And it is clear that the rule of the soul over the body, and of the mind and the rational element over the passionate, is natural and expedient; whereas the equality of the two or the rule of the inferior is always hurtful. The same holds good of animals in relation to men; for tame animals have a better nature than wild, and all tame animals are better off when they are ruled by man; for then they are preserved. Again, the male is by nature superior, and the female inferior; and the one rules, and the other is ruled; this principle, of necessity, extends to all mankind. Where then there is such a difference as that between soul and body, or between men and animals (as in the case of those whose business is to use their body, and who can do nothing better), the lower sort are by nature slaves, and it is better for them as for all inferiors that they should be under the rule of a master. For he who can be, and therefore is, another's, and he who participates in rational principle enough to apprehend, but not to have, such a principle, is a slave by nature. Whereas the lower animals cannot even apprehend a principle; they obey their instincts. And indeed the use made of slaves and of tame animals is not very different; for both with their bodies minister to the needs of life. Nature would like to distinguish between the bodies of freemen and slaves, making the one strong for servile labour, the other upright, and although useless for such services, useful for political life in the arts both of war and peace. But the opposite often happens—that some have the souls and others have the bodies of freemen. And doubtless if men differed from one another in the mere forms of their bodies as much as the statues of the Gods do from men, all would acknowledge that the inferior class should be slaves of the superior. And if this is true of the body, how much more just that a similar distinction should exist in the soul? but the beauty of the body is seen, whereas the beauty of the soul is not seen. It is clear, then, that some men are by nature free,

and others slaves, and that for these latter slavery is both expedient and right.

But that those who take the opposite view have in a certain way right on their side, may be easily seen. For the words slavery and slave are used in two senses. There is a slave or slavery by law as well as by nature. The law of which I speak is a sort of convention—the law by which whatever is taken in war is supposed to belong to the victors. But this right many jurists impeach, as they would an orator who brought forward an unconstitutional measure: they detest the notion that, because one man has the power of doing violence and is superior in brute strength, another shall be his slave and subject. Even among philosophers there is a difference of opinion. The origin of the dispute, and what makes the views invade each other's territory, is as follows: in some sense virtue, when furnished with means, has actually the greatest power of exercising force: and as superior power is only found where there is superior excellence of some kind, power seems to imply virtue, and the dispute to be simply one about justice (for it is due to one party identifying justice with goodwill, while the other identifies it with the mere rule of the stronger). If these views are thus set out separately, the other views have no force or plausibility against the view that the superior in virtue ought to rule, or be master. Others, clinging, as they think, simply to a principle of justice (for law and custom are a sort of justice), assume that slavery in accordance with the custom of war is justified by law, but at the same moment they deny this. For what if the cause of the war be unjust? And again, no one would ever say that he is a slave who is unworthy to be a slave. Were this the case, men of the highest rank would be slaves and the children of slaves if they or their parents chance to have been taken captive and sold. Wherefore Hellenes do not like to call Hellenes slaves, but confine the term to barbarians. Yet, in using this language, they really mean the natural slave of whom we spoke at first; for it must be admitted that some are slaves everywhere, others nowhere. The same principle applies to nobility. Hellenes regard themselves as noble everywhere, and not only in their own country, but they deem the barbarians noble only when at home, thereby implying that there are two sorts of nobility and freedom, the one absolute, the other relative. The Helen of Theodectes says:

Who would presume to call me servant who am on both sides sprung from the stem of the Gods?

What does this mean but that they distinguish freedom and slavery, noble and humble birth, by the two principles of good and evil? They think that as men and animals beget men and animals, so from good men a good man springs. But this is what nature, though she may intend it, cannot always accomplish.

We see then that there is some foundation for this difference of opinion, and that all are not either slaves by nature or freemen by nature, and also that there is in some cases a marked distinction between the two classes, rendering it expedient and right for the one to be slaves and the others to be masters: the one practising obedience, the others exercising the authority and lordship which nature intended them to have. The abuse of this authority is injurious to both; for the interests of part and whole, of body and soul, are the same, and the slave is a part of the master, a living but separated part of his bodily frame. Hence, where the relation of master and slave between them is natural they are friends and have a common interest, but where it rests merely on law and force the reverse is true.

3. Critique of Plato's Republic

Our purpose is to consider what form of political community is best of all for those who are most able to realize their ideal of life. We must therefore examine not only this but other constitutions, both such as actually exist in well-governed states, and any theoretical forms which are held in esteem; that what is good and useful may be brought to light. And let no one suppose that in seeking for something beyond them we are anxious to make a sophistical display at any cost; we only undertake this inquiry because all the constitutions with which we are acquainted are faulty.

We will begin with the natural beginning of the subject. Three alternatives are conceivable: The members of a state must either have (1) all things or (2) nothing in common, or (3) some things in common and some not. That they should have nothing in common is clearly impossible, for the constitution is a community, and must at any rate have a common place—one city will be in one place, and the citizens are those who share in that one city. But should a well-ordered state have all things, as far as may be, in common, or some only and not others? For the citizens might conceivably have wives and children and property in common, as Socrates proposes in the Republic of Plato. Which is better, our present condition, or the proposed new order of society?

There are many difficulties in the community of women. And the principle on which Socrates rests the necessity of such an institution evidently is not established by his arguments. Further, as a means to the end which he ascribes to the state, the scheme, taken literally, is impracticable, and how we are to interpret it is nowhere precisely stated. I am speaking of the premiss from which the argument of Socrates proceeds, "that the greater the unity of the state the better." Is it not obvious that a state may at length attain such a degree of unity as to be no longer a state? —since the nature of a state is to be a plurality, and in tending to greater unity, from being a state, it becomes a family, and from being a family, an individual; for the family may be said to be more than the state, and the individual than the family.

So that we ought not to attain this greatest unity even if we could, for it would be the destruction of the state. Again, a state is not made up only of so many men, but of different kinds of men; for similars do not constitute a state. It is not like a military alliance. The usefulness of the latter depends upon its quantity even where there is no difference in quality (for mutual protection is the end aimed at), just as a greater weight of anything is more useful than a less (in like manner, a state differs from a nation, when the nation has not its population organized in villages, but lives an Arcadian sort of life); but the elements out of which a unity is to be formed differ in kind. Wherefore the principle of compensation, as I have already remarked in the *Ethics*, is the salvation of states. Even among freemen and equals this is a principle which must be maintained, for they cannot all rule together, but must change at the end of a year or some other period of time or in some order of succession. The result is that upon this plan they all govern; just as if shoemakers and carpenters were to exchange their occupations, and the same persons did not always continue shoemakers and carpenters. And since it is better that this should be so in politics as well, it is clear that while there should be continuance of the same persons in power where this is possible, yet where this is not possible by reason of the natural equality of the citizens, and at the same time it is just that all should share in the government (whether to govern be a good thing or a bad), an approximation to this is that equals should in turn retire from office and should, apart from official position, be treated alike. Thus the one party rule and the others are ruled in turn, as if they were no longer the same persons. In like manner when they hold office there is a variety in the offices held. Hence it is evident that a city is not by nature one in that sense which some persons affirm; and that what is said to be the greatest good of cities is in reality their destruction; but surely the good of things must be that which preserves them. Again,

in another point of view, this extreme unification of the state is clearly not good; for a family is more self-sufficing than an individual, and a city than a family, and a city only comes into being when the community is large enough to be self-sufficing. If then self-sufficiency is to be desired, the lesser degree of unity is more desirable than the greater.

4. Property: Equality or Inequality?

Next let us consider what should be our arrangements about property: should the citizens of the perfect state have their possessions in common or not? This question may be discussed separately from the enactments about women and children. Even supposing that the women and children belong to individuals, according to the custom which is at present universal, may there not be an advantage in having and using possessions in common? Three cases are possible: (1) the soil may be appropriated, but the produce may be thrown for consumption into the common stock; and this is the practice of some nations. Or (2), the soil may be common, and may be cultivated in common, but the produce divided among individuals for their private use; this is a form of common property which is said to exist among certain barbarians. Or (3), the soil and the produce may be alike common.

When the husbandmen are not the owners, the case will be different and easier to deal with; but when they till the ground for themselves the question of ownership will give a world of trouble. If they do not share equally in enjoyments and toils, those who labour much and get little will necessarily complain of those who labour little and receive or consume much. But indeed there is always a difficulty in men living together and having all human relations in common, but especially in their having common property. The partnerships of fellow-travelers are an example to the point; for they generally fall out over everyday matters and quarrel about any trifle which turns up. So with servants: we are most liable to take offense at those with whom we most frequently come into contact in daily life.

These are only some of the disadvantages which attend the community of property; the present arrangement, if improved as it might be by good customs and laws, would be far better, and would have the advantages of both systems. Property should be in a certain sense common, but, as a general rule, private; for, when every one has a distinct interest, men will not complain of one another, and they will make more progress, because every one will be attending to his own business. And yet by reason of goodness, and in respect of use, "Friends," as the proverb says, "will have all things common." Even now there are traces of such a principle, showing that it is not impracticable, but, in well-ordered states, exists already to a certain extent and may be carried further. For, although every man has his own property, some things he will place at the disposal of his friends, while of others he shares the use with them. The Lacedaemonians, for example, use one another's slaves, and horses, and dogs, as if they were their own; and when they lack provisions on a journey, they appropriate what they find in the fields throughout the country. It is clearly better that property should be private, but the use of it common; and the special business of the legislator is to create in men this benevolent disposition. Again, how immeasurably greater is the pleasure, when a man feels a thing to be his own; for surely the love of self is a feeling implanted by nature and not given in vain, although selfishness is rightly censured; this, however, is not the mere love of self, but the love of self in excess, like the miser's love of money; for all, or almost all, men love money and other such objects in a measure. And further, there is the greatest pleasure in doing a kindness or service to friends or guests or companions, which can only be rendered when a man has private property. These advantages are lost by excessive unification of the state. The exhibition of two virtues, besides, is visibly annihilated in such a state: first, temperance towards women (for it is an honourable action to abstain from another's wife for temperance sake); secondly, liberality in the matter of property. No one, when men have all things in common, will any longer set an example of liberality or do any liberal action; for liberality consists in the use which is made of property.

Such legislation may have a specious appearance of benevolence; men readily listen to it, and are easily induced to believe that in some wonderful manner everybody will become everybody's friend, especially when some one is heard denouncing the evils now existing in states, suits about contracts, convictions for perjury, flatteries of rich men and the like, which are said to arise out of the possession of private property. These evils, however, are due to a very different cause—the wickedness of human nature. Indeed, we see that there is much more quarrelling among those who have all things in common, though there are not many of them when compared with the vast numbers who have private property.

Again, we ought to reckon, not only the evils from which the citizens will be saved, but also the advantages which they will lose. The life which they are to lead appears to be quite impracticable. The error of Socrates must be attributed to the false notion of unity from which he starts. Unity there should be, both of the family and of the state, but in some respects only. For there is a point at which a state may attain such a degree of unity as to be no longer a state, or at which, without actually ceasing to exist, it will become an inferior state, like harmony passing into unison, or rhythm which has been reduced to a single foot. The state, as I was saying, is a plurality, which should be united and made into a community by education; and it is strange that the author of a system of education which he thinks will make the state virtuous, should expect to improve his citizens by regulations of this sort, and not by philosophy or by customs and laws, like those which prevail at Sparta and Crete respecting common meals, whereby the legislator has made property common. Let us remember that we should not disregard the experience of ages; in the multitude of years these things, if they were good, would certainly not have been unknown; for almost everything has been found out, although sometimes they are not put together; in other cases men do not use the knowledge which they have. Great light would be thrown on this subject if we could see such a form of government in the actual process of construction; for the legislator could not form a state at all without distributing and dividing its constituents into associations for common meals, and into phratries and tribes. But all this legislation ends only in forbidding agriculture to the guardians, a prohibition which the Lacedaemonians try to enforce already.

But, indeed, Socrates has not said, nor is it easy to decide, what in such a community will be the general form of the state. The citizens who are not guardians are the majority, and about them nothing has been determined: are the husbandmen, too, to have their property in common? Or is each individual to have his own? and are the wives and children to be individual or common? If, like the guardians, they are to have all things in common, in what do they differ from them, or what will they gain by submitting to their government? Or, upon what principle would they submit, unless indeed the governing class adopt the ingenious policy of the Cretans, who give their slaves the same institutions as their own, but forbid them gymnastic exercises and the possession of arms. If, on the other hand, the inferior classes are to be like other cities in respect of marriage and property, what will be the form of the community? Must it not contain two states in one, each hostile to the other? He makes the guardians into a mere occupying garrison, while the husbandmen and artisans and the rest are the real citizens. But if so the suits and quarrels, and all the evils which Socrates affirms to exist in other states, will exist equally among them. He says indeed that, having so good an education, the citizens will not need many laws, for example laws about the city or about the markets; but then he confines his education to the guardians. Again, he makes the husbandmen owners of the property upon condition of their paying a tribute. But in that case they are likely to be much more unmanageable and conceited than the Helots, or Penestae, or slaves in general. And whether community of wives and property be necessary for the lower equally with the higher class or not, and the questions akin to this, what will be the education, form of government, laws of the lower class, Socrates has nowhere determined: neither is it easy to discover this, nor is their character of small importance if the common life of the guardians is to be maintained.

Again, if Socrates makes the women common, and retains private property, the men will see to the fields, but who will see to the house? And who will do so if the agricultural class have both their property and their wives in common? Once more: it is absurd to argue, from the analogy of the animals, that men and women should follow the same pursuits, for animals have not to manage a household. The government, too, as constituted by Socrates, contains elements of danger; for he makes the same persons always rule. And if this is often a cause of disturbance among the meaner sort, how much more among high-spirited warriors? But that the persons whom he makes rulers must be the same is evident; for the gold which the God mingles in the souls of men is not at one time given to one, at another time to another, but always to the same: as he says, "God mingles gold in some, and silver in others, from their very birth; but brass and iron in those who are meant to be artisans and husbandmen." Again, he deprives the guardians even of happiness, and says that the legislator ought to make the whole state happy. But the whole cannot be happy unless most, or all, or some of its parts enjoy happiness. In this respect happiness is not like the even principle in numbers, which may exist only in the whole, but in neither of the parts; not so happiness. And if the guardians are not happy, who are? Surely not the artisans, or the common people. The Republic of which Socrates discourses has all these difficulties, and others quite as great.

There is another point: Should not the amount of property be defined in some way which differs from this by being clearer? For Socrates says that a man should have so much property as will enable him to live temperately, which is only a way of saying "to live well"; this is too general a conception. Further, a man may live temperately and yet miserably. A better definition would be that a man must have so much property as will enable him to live not only temperately but liberally; if the two are parted, liberality will combine with luxury; temperance will be associated with toil. For liberality and temperance are the only eligible qualities which have to do with the use of property. A man cannot use property with mildness or courage, but temperately and liberally he may; and therefore the practice of these virtues is inseparable from property. There is an inconsistency, too, in equalizing the property and not regulating the number of the citizens; the population is to remain unlimited, and he thinks that it will be sufficiently equalized by a certain number of marriages being unfruitful, however many are born to others, because he finds this to be the case in existing states. But greater care will be required than now; for among ourselves, whatever may be the number of citizens, the property is always distributed among them, and therefore no one is in want; but, if the property were incapable of division as in the *Laws*, the supernumeraries, whether few or many, would get nothing. One would have thought that it was even more necessary to limit population than property; and that the limit should be fixed by calculating the chances of mortality in the children, and of sterility in married persons. The neglect of

this subject, which in existing states is so common, is a never-failing cause of poverty among the citizens; and poverty is the parent of revolution and crime. Pheidon the Corinthian, who was one of the most ancient legislators, thought that the families and the number of citizens ought to remain the same, although originally all the lots may have been of different sizes: but in the *Laws* the opposite principle is maintained. What in our opinion is the right arrangement will have to be explained hereafter.

Other constitutions have been proposed; some by private persons, others by philosophers and statesmen, which all come nearer to established or existing ones than either of Plato's. No one else has introduced such novelties as the community of women and children, or public tables for women: other legislators begin with what is necessary. In the opinion of some, the regulation of property is the chief point of all, that being the question upon which all revolutions turn. This danger was recognized by Phaleas of Chalcedon, who was the first to affirm that the citizens of a state ought to have equal possessions. He thought that in a new colony the equalization might be accomplished without difficulty, not so easily when a state was already established; and that then the shortest way of compassing the desired end would be for the rich to give and not to receive marriage portions, and for the poor not to give but to receive them.

Plato in the *Laws* was of opinion that, to a certain extent, accumulation should be allowed, forbidding, as I have already observed, any citizen to possess more than five times the minimum qualification. But those who make such laws should remember what they are apt to forget—that the legislator who fixes the amount of property should also fix the number of children; for, if the children are too many for the property, the law must be broken. And, besides the violation of the law, it is a bad thing that many from being rich should become poor; for men of ruined fortunes are sure to stir up revolutions. That the equalization of property exercises an influence on political society was clearly understood even by some of the old legislators. Laws were made by Solon and others prohibiting an individual from possessing as much land as he pleased; and there are other laws in states which forbid the sale of property: among the Locrians, for example, there is a law that a man is not to sell his property unless he can prove unmistakably that some misfortune has befallen him. Again, there have been laws which enjoin the preservation of the original lots. Such a law existed in the island of Leucas, and the abrogation of it made the constitution too democratic, for the rulers no longer had the prescribed qualification. Again, where there is equality of property, the amount may be either too large or too small, and the possessor may be living either in luxury or penury. Clearly, then, the legislator ought not only to aim at the equalization of properties, but at moderation in their amount. Further, if he prescribe this moderate amount equally to all, he will be no nearer the mark; for it is not the possessions but the desires of mankind which require to be equalized, and this is impossible, unless a sufficient education is provided by the laws. But Phaleas will probably reply that this is precisely what he means; and that, in his opinion, there ought to be in states, not only equal property, but equal education. Still he should tell precisely what he means; and what, in his opinion, there ought to be in having one and the same for all, if it is of a sort that predisposes men to avarice, or ambition, or both. Moreover, civil troubles arise, not only out of the inequality of property, but out of the inequality of honour, though in opposite ways. For the common people quarrel about the inequality of property, the higher class about the equality of honour; as the poet says—

The bad and good alike in honour share.

There are crimes of which the motive is want; and for these Phaleas expects to find a cure in the equalization of property, which will take away from a man the temptation to be a highwayman, because he is hungry or cold. But want is not the sole incentive to crime; men also wish to enjoy themselves and not to be in a state of desire—they wish to cure some desire, going beyond the necessities of life, which preys upon them; nay, this is not the only reason—they may desire superfluities in order to enjoy pleasures unaccompanied with pain, and therefore they commit crimes.

Now what is the cure of these three disorders? Of the first, moderate possessions and occupation; of the second, habits of temperance; as to the third, if any desire pleasures which depend on themselves, they will find the satisfaction of their desires nowhere but in philosophy; for all other pleasures we are dependent on others. The fact is that the greatest crimes are caused by excess and not by necessity. Men do not become tyrants in order that they may not suffer cold; and hence great is the honour bestowed, not on him who kills a thief, but on him who kills a tyrant. Thus we see that the institutions of Phaleas avail only against petty crimes.

There is another objection to them. They are chiefly designed to promote the internal welfare of the state. But the legislator should consider also its relation to neighbouring nations, and to all who are outside of it. The government must be organized with a view to military strength; and of this he has said not a word. And so with respect to property: there should not only be enough to supply the internal wants of the state, but also to meet dangers coming from without. The property of the state should not be so large that more powerful neighbours may be tempted by it, while the owners are unable to repel the invaders; nor yet so small that the state is unable to maintain a war even against states of equal power, and of the same character. Phaleas has not laid down any rule; but we should bear in mind that abundance of wealth is an advantage. The best limit will probably be, that a more powerful neighbour must have no inducement to go to war with you by reason of the excess of your wealth, but only such as he would have had if you had possessed less. There is a story that Eubulus, when Autophradates was going to besiege Atarneus, told him to consider how long the operation would take, and then reckon up the cost which would be incurred in the time. "For," said he, "I am willing for a smaller sum than that to leave Atarneus at once." These words of Eubulus made an impression on Autophradates, and he desisted from the siege.

The equalization of property is one of the things that tend to prevent the citizens from quarrelling. Not that the gain in this direction is very great. For the nobles will be dissatisfied because they think themselves worthy of more than an equal share of honours; and this is often found to be a cause of sedition and revolution. And the avarice of mankind is insatiable; at one time two obols was pay enough; but now, when this sum has become customary, men always want more and more without end; for it is of the nature of desire not to be satisfied, and most men live only for the gratification of it. The beginning of reform is not so much to equalize property as to train the nobler sort of natures not to desire more, and to prevent the lower from getting more; that is to say, they must be kept down, but not ill-treated. Besides, the equalization proposed by Phaleas is imperfect; for he only equalizes land, whereas a man may be rich also in slaves, and cattle, and money, and in the abundance of what are called his movables. Now either all these things must be equalized, or some limit must be imposed on them, or they must all be let alone. It would appear that Phaleas is legislating for a small city only, if, as he supposes, all the artisans are to be public slaves and not to form a supplementary part of the body of citizens. But if there is a law that artisans are to be public slaves, it should only apply to those engaged on public works, as at Epidamnus, or at Athens on the plan which Diophantus once introduced.

From these observations any one may judge how far Phaleas was wrong or right in his ideas.

5. Citizenship

He who would inquire into the essence and attributes of various kinds of governments must first of all determine "What is a state?" At present this is a disputed question. Some say that the state has done a certain act; others, no, not the state, but the oligarchy or the tyrant. And the legislator or statesman is concerned entirely with the state; a constitution or government being an arrangement of the inhabitants of a state. But a state is composite, like any other whole made up of many parts;— these are the citizens, who compose it. It is evident, therefore, that we must begin by asking, "Who is the citizen," and what is the meaning of the term? For here again there may be a difference of opinion. He who is a citizen in a democracy will often not be a citizen in an oligarchy. Leaving out of consideration those who have been made citizens, or who have obtained the name of citizen in any other accidental manner, we may say, first, that a citizen is not a citizen because he lives in a certain place, for resident aliens and slaves share in the place; nor is he a citizen who has no legal right except that of suing and being sued; for this right may be enjoyed under the provisions of a treaty. Nay, resident aliens in many places do not possess even such rights completely, for they are obliged to have a patron, so that they do but imperfectly participate in citizenship, and we call them citizens only in a qualified sense, as we might apply the term to children who are too young to be on the register, or to old men who have been relieved from state duties. Of these we do not say quite simply that they are citizens, but add in the one case that they are not of age, and in the other, that they are past the age, or something of that sort; the precise expression is immaterial, for our meaning is clear. Similar difficulties to those which I have mentioned may be raised and answered about deprived citizens and about exiles. But the citizen whom we are seeking to define is a citizen in the strictest sense, against whom no such exception can be taken, and his special characteristic is that he shares in the administration of justice, and in offices. Now of offices some are discontinuous, and the same persons are not allowed to hold them twice, or can only hold them after a fixed interval; others have no limit of time—for example, the office of dicast or ecclesiast.[1] It may, indeed, be argued that these are not magistrates at all, and that their functions give them no share in the government. But surely it is ridiculous to say that those who have the supreme power do not govern. Let us not dwell further upon this, which is a purely verbal question; what we want is a common term including both dicast and ecclesiast. Let us, for the take of distinction, call it "indefinite office," and we will assume that those who share in such office are citizens. This is the most comprehensive definition of a citizen, and best suits all those who are generally so called.

But we must not forget that things of which the underlying principles differ in kind, one of them being first, another second, another third, have, when regarded in this relation, nothing, or hardly anything, worth mentioning in common. Now we see that governments differ in kind, and that some of them are prior and that others are posterior; those which are faulty or perverted are necessarily posterior to those which are perfect. (What we mean by perversion will be hereafter explained.) The citizen then of necessity differs under each form of government; and our definition is best adapted to the citizen of a democracy; but not necessarily to other states. For in some states the people are not acknowledged, nor have they any regular assembly, but only extraordinary ones; and suits are distributed by sections among the magistrates. At Lacedaemon, for instance, the Ephors determine suits about contracts, which they distribute among themselves, while the elders are judges of homicide, and other causes are decided by other magistrates. A similar principle prevails at Carthage; there certain magistrates decide all causes. We may, indeed, modify our definition of the citizen so as to include these states. In them it is the holder of a definite, not of an indefinite office, who legislates and judges, and to some or all such holders of definite offices is reserved the right of deliberating or judging about some things or about all things. The conception of the citizen now begins to clear up.

He who has the power to take part in the deliberative or judicial administration of any state is said by us to be a citizen of that state; and, speaking generally, a state is a body of citizens sufficing for the purposes of life.

There is a point nearly allied to the preceding: Whether the virtue of a good man and a good citizen is the same or not. But, before entering on this discussion, we must certainly first obtain some general notion of the virtue of the citizen. Like the sailor, the citizen is a member of a community. Now, sailors have different functions, for one of them is a rower, another a pilot, and a third a look-out man, a fourth is described by some similar term; and while the precise definition of each individual's virtue applies exclusively to him, there is, at the same time, a common definition applicable to them all. For they have all of them a common object, which is safety in navigation. Similarly, one citizen differs from another, but the salvation of the community is the common business of them all. This community is the constitution; the virtue of the citizen must therefore be relative to the constitution of which he is a member. If, then, there are many forms of government, it is evident that there is not one single virtue of the good citizen which is perfect virtue. But we say that the good man is he who has one single virtue which is perfect virtue. Hence it is evident that the good citizen need not of necessity possess the virtue which makes a good man.

The same question may also be approached by another road, from a considera-

---

[1] "Dicast" = juryman and judge in one: "ecclesiast" = member of the ecclesia or assembly of the citizens.

tion of the best constitution. If the state cannot be entirely composed of good men, and yet each citizen is expected to do his own business well, and must therefore have virtue, still, inasmuch as all the citizens cannot be alike, the virtue of the citizen and of the good man cannot coincide. All must have the virtue of the good citizen—thus, and thus only, can the state be perfect; but they will not have the virtue of a good man, unless we assume that in the good state all the citizens must be good.

Again, the state, as composed of unlikes, may be compared to the living being: as the first elements into which a living being is resolved are soul and body, as soul is made up of rational principle and appetite, the family of husband and wife, property of master and slave, so of all these, as well as other dissimilar elements, the state is composed; and, therefore, the virtue of all the citizens cannot possibly be the same, any more than the excellence of the leader of a chorus is the same as that of the performer who stands by his side. I have said enough to show why the two kinds of virtue cannot be absolutely and always the same.

But will there then be no case in which the virtue of the good citizen and the virtue of the good man coincide? To this we answer that the good *ruler* is a good and wise man, and that he who would be a statesman must be a wise man. And some persons say that even the education of the ruler should be of a special kind; for are not the children of kings instructed in riding and military exercises? As Euripides says:

No subtle arts for me, but what the state requires.

As though there were a special education needed by a ruler. If then the virtue of a good ruler is the same as that of a good man, and we assume further that the subject is a citizen as well as the ruler, the virtue of the good citizen and the virtue of the good man cannot be absolutely the same, although in some cases they may; for the virtue of a ruler differs from that of a citizen. It was the sense of this difference which made Jason say that "he felt hungry when he was not a tyrant," meaning that he could not endure to live in a private station. But, on the other hand, it may be argued that men are praised for knowing both how to rule and how to obey, and he is said to be a citizen of approved virtue who is able to do both. Now if we suppose the virtue of a good man to be that which rules, and the virtue of the citizen to include ruling and obeying, it cannot be said that they are equally worthy of praise. Since, then, it is sometimes thought that the ruler and the ruled must learn different things and not the same, but that the citizen must know and share in them both, the inference is obvious. There is, indeed, the rule of a master, which is concerned with menial offices—the master need not know how to perform these, but may employ others in the execution of them: the other would be degrading; and by the other I mean the power actually to do menial duties, which vary much in character and are executed by various classes of slaves, such, for example, as handicraftsmen, who, as their name signifies, live by the labour of their hands:—under these the mechanic is included. Hence in ancient times, and among some nations, the working classes had no share in the government—a privilege which they only acquired under the extreme democracy. Certainly the good man and the statesman and the good citizen ought not to learn the crafts of inferiors except for their own occasional use; if they habitually practice them, there will cease to be a distinction between master and slave.

This is not the rule of which we are speaking; but there is a rule of another kind, which is exercised over freemen and equals by birth—a constitutional rule, which the ruler must learn by obeying, as he would learn the duties of a general of cavalry by being under the orders of a general of cavalry, or the duties of a general of infantry by being under the orders of a general of infantry, and by having had the command of a regiment and of a company. It has been well said that "he who has never learned to obey cannot be a good commander." The two are not the same, but the good citizen ought to be capable of both; he should know how to govern like a freeman, and how to obey like a freeman— these are the virtues of a citizen. And, although the temperance and justice of a ruler are distinct from those of a subject, the virtue of a good man will include both; for the virtue of the good man who is free and also a subject, e. g. his justice, will not be one but will comprise distinct kinds, the one qualifying him to rule, the other to obey, and differing as the temperance and courage of men and women differ. For a man would be thought a coward if he had no more courage than a courageous woman, and a woman would be thought loquacious if she imposed no more restraint on her conversation than the good man; and indeed their part in the management of the household is different, for the duty of the one is to acquire, and of the other to preserve. Practical wisdom only is characteristic of the ruler: it would seem that all other virtues must equally belong to ruler and subject. The virtue of the subject is certainly not wisdom, but only true opinion; he may be compared to the maker of the flute, while his master is like the flute-player or user of the flute.

From these considerations may be gathered the answer to the question, whether the virtue of the good man is the same as that of the good citizen, or different, and how far the same, and how far different.

There still remains one more question about the citizen: Is he only a true citizen who has a share of office, or is the mechanic to be included? If they who hold no office are to be deemed citizens, not every citizen can have this virtue of ruling and obeying; for this man is a citizen. And if none of the lower class are citizens, in which part of the state are they to be placed? For they are not resident aliens, and they are not foreigners. May we not reply, that as far as this objection goes there is no more absurdity in excluding them than in excluding slaves and freedmen from any of the above-mentioned classes? It must be admitted that we cannot consider all those to be citizens who are necessary to the existence of the state; for example, children are not citizens equally with grown-up men, who are citizens absolutely, but children, not being grown up, are only citizens on a certain assumption. Nay, in ancient times, and among some nations, the artisan class *were* slaves or foreigners, and therefore the majority of them are so now. The best form of state will not admit them to citizenship; but if they are admitted, then our definition of the virtue of a citizen will not apply to every citizen, not to every free man as such, but only to those who are freed from necessary services. The necessary people are either slaves who minister to the wants of individuals, or mechanics and labourers who are the servants of the community. These reflections carried a little further will explain their position; and indeed what has been said already is of itself, when understood, explanation enough.

Since there are many forms of government there must be many varieties of citizens, and especially of citizens who are subjects; so that under some governments the mechanic and the labourer will be citizens, but not in others, as, for example, in aristocracy or the so-called government of the best (if there be such an one), in which honours are given according to virtue and merit; for no man can practise virtue who is living the life of a mechanic or labourer. In oligarchies the qualification for office is high, and therefore no labourer can ever be a citizen; but a mechanic may, for an actual majority of them are rich. At Thebes there was a law that no man could hold office who had not retired from business for ten years. But in many states the law goes to the length of admitting aliens; for in some democracies a man is a citizen though his mother only be a citizen; and a similar principle is applied to illegitimate children; the law is relaxed when there is a dearth of population. But when the number of citizens increases, first the children of a male or a female slave are excluded; then those whose mothers only are citizens; and at last the right of citizenship is confined to those whose fathers and mothers are both citizens.

Hence, as is evident, there are different kinds of citizens; and he is a citizen in the highest sense who shares in the honours of the state. Compare Homer's words "like some dishonoured stranger"; he who is excluded from the honours of the state is no better than an alien. But when this exclusion is concealed, then the object is that the privileged class may deceive their fellow inhabitants.

As to the question whether the virtue of the good man is the same as that of the good citizen, the considerations already adduced prove that in some states the good man and the good citizen are the same, and in others different. When they are the same it is not every citizen who is a good man, but only the statesman and those who have or may have, alone or in conjunction with others, the conduct of public affairs.

As in other natural compounds the conditions of a composite whole are not necessarily organic parts of it, so in a state or in any other combination forming a unity not everything is a part, which is a necessary condition. The members of an association have necessarily some one thing the same and common to all, in which they share equally or unequally; for example, food or land or any other thing. But where there are two things of which one is a means and the other an end, they have nothing in common except that the one receives what the other produces. Such, for example, is the relation in which workmen and tools stand to their work; the house and the builder have nothing in common, but the art of the builder is for the sake of the house. And so states require property, but property, even though living beings are included in it, is no part of a state; for a state is not a community of living beings only, but a community of equals, aiming at the best life possible. Now, whereas happiness is the highest good, being a realization and perfect practice of virtue,

which some can attain, while others have little or none of it, the various qualities of men are clearly the reason why there are various kinds of states and many forms of government; for different men seek after happiness in different ways and by different means, and so make for themselves different modes of life and forms of government. We must see also how many things are indispensable to the existence of a state, for what we call the parts of a state will be found among the indispensables. Let us then enumerate the functions of a state, and we shall easily elicit what we want:

First, there must be food; secondly, arts, for life requires many instruments; thirdly, there must be arms, for the members of a community have need of them, and in their own hands, too, in order to maintain authority both against disobedient subjects and against external assailants; fourthly, there must be a certain amount of revenue, both for internal needs, and for the purposes of war; fifthly, or rather first, there must be a care of religion, which is commonly called worship; sixthly, and most necessary of all, there must be a power of deciding what is for the public interest, and what is just in men's dealings with one another.

These are the services which every state may be said to need. For a state is not a mere aggregate of persons, but a union of them sufficing for the purposes of life; and if any of these things be wanting, it is as we maintain impossible that the community can be absolutely self-sufficing. A state then should be framed with a view to the fulfilment of these functions. There must be husbandmen to procure food, and artisans, and a warlike and a wealthy class, and priests, and judges to decide what is necessary and expedient.

Having determined these points, we have in the next place to consider whether all ought to share in every sort of occupation. Shall every man be at once husbandman, artisan, councillor, judge, or shall we suppose the several occupations just mentioned assigned to different persons? or, thirdly, shall some employments be assigned to individuals and others common to all? The same arrangement, however, does not occur in every constitution; as we were saying, all may be shared by all, or not all by all, but only by some; and hence arise the differences of constitutions, for in democracies all share in all, in oligarchies the opposite practice prevails. Now, since we are here speaking of the best form of government, i. e. that under which the state will be most happy and happiness, as has been already said, cannot exist without virtue), it clearly follows that in the state which is best governed and possesses men who are just absolutely, and not merely relatively to the principle of the constitution, the citizens must not lead the life of mechanics or tradesmen, for such a life is ignoble, and inimical to virtue. Neither must they be husbandmen, since leisure is necessary both for the development of virtue and the performance of political duties.

Again, there is in a state a class of warriors, and another of councillors, who advise about the expedient and determine matters of law, and these seem in an especial manner parts of a state. Now, should these two classes be distinguished, or are both functions to be assigned to the same persons? Here again there is no difficulty in seeing that both functions will in one way belong to the same, in another, to different persons. To different persons in so far as these employments are suited to different primes of life, for the one requires wisdom and the other strength. But on the other hand, since it is an impossible thing that those who are able to use or to resist force should be willing to remain always in subjection, from this point of view the persons are the same; for those who carry arms can always determine the fate of the constitution. It remains therefore that both functions should be entrusted by the ideal constitution to the same persons, not, however, at the same time, but in the order prescribed by nature, who has given to young men strength and to older men wisdom. Such a distribution of duties will be expedient and also just, and is founded upon a principle of conformity

to merit. Besides, the ruling class should be the owners of property, for they are citizens, and the citizens of a state should be in good circumstances; whereas mechanics or any other class which is not a producer of virtue have no share in the state. This follows from our first principle, for happiness cannot exist without virtue, and a city is not to be termed happy in regard to a portion of the citizens, but in regard to them all. And clearly property should be in their hands, since the husbandmen will of necessity be slaves or barbarian Perioeci.

Of the classes enumerated there remain only the priests, and the manner in which their office is to be regulated is obvious. No husbandman or mechanic should be appointed to it; for the Gods should receive honour from the citizens only. Now since the body of the citizens is divided into two classes, the warriors and the councillors, and it is beseeming that the worship of the Gods should be duly performed, and also a rest provided in their service for those who from age have given up active life, to the old men of these two classes should be assigned the duties of the priesthood.

We have shown what are the necessary conditions, and what the parts of a state: husbandmen, craftsmen, and labourers of all kinds are necessary to the existence of states, but the parts of the state are the warriors and councillors. And these are distinguished severally from one another, the distinction being in some cases permanent, in others not.

Since every political society is composed of rulers and subjects let us consider whether the relations of one to the other should interchange or be permanent. For the education of the citizens will necessarily vary with the answer given to this question. Now, if some men excelled others in the same degree in which gods and heroes are supposed to excel mankind in general (having in the first place a great advantage even in their bodies, and secondly in their minds), so that the superiority of the governors was undisputed and patent to their subjects, it would clearly be better that once for all the one class should rule and the others serve. But since this is unattainable, and kings have no marked superiority over their subjects, such as Scylax affirms to be found among the Indians, it is obviously necessary on many grounds that all the citizens alike should take their turn of governing and being governed. Equality consists in the same treatment of similar persons, and no government can stand which is not founded upon justice. For if the government be unjust every one in the country unites with the governed in the desire to have a revolution, and it is an impossibility that the members of the government can be so numerous as to be stronger than all their enemies put together. Yet that governors should excel their subjects is undeniable. How all this is to be effected, and in what way they will respectively share in the government, the legislator has to consider. The subject has been already mentioned. Nature herself has provided the distinction when she made a difference between old and young within the same species, of whom she fitted the one to govern and the other to be governed. No one takes offence at being governed when he is young, nor does he think himself better than his governors, especially if he will enjoy the same privilege when he reaches the required age.

We conclude that from one point of view governors and governed are identical, and from another different. And therefore their education must be the same and also different. For he who would learn to command well must, as men say, first of all learn to obey. As I observed in the first part of this treatise, there is one rule which is for the sake of the rulers and another rule which is for the sake of the ruled; the former is a despotic, the latter a free government. Some commands differ not in the thing commanded, but in the intention with which they are imposed. Wherefore, many apparently menial offices are an honour to the free youth by whom they are performed; for actions do not differ as honourable or dishonourable in themselves so much as in the end and intention of them. But since we say that the virtue of the citizen and ruler is the same as that of the good man, and that the same person must first be a subject and then a ruler, the legislator has to see that they become good men, and by what means this may be accomplished, and what is the end of the perfect life.

Now the soul of man is divided into two parts, one of which has a rational principle in itself, and the other, not having a rational principle in itself, is able to obey such a principle. And we call a man in any way good because he has the virtues of these two parts. In which of them the end is more likely to be found is no matter of doubt to those who adopt our division; for in the world both of nature and of art the inferior always exists for the sake of the better or superior, and the better or superior is that which has a rational principle. This principle, too, in our ordinary way of speaking, is divided into two kinds, for there is a practical and a speculative principle. This part, then, must evidently be similarly divided. And there must be a corresponding division of actions; the actions of the naturally better part are to be preferred by those who have it in their power to attain to two out of the three or to all, for that is always to every one the most eligible which is the highest attainable by him. The whole of life is further divided into two parts, business and leisure, war and peace, and of actions some aim at what is necessary and useful, and some at what is honourable. And the preference given to one or the other class of actions must necessarily be like the preference given to one or other part of the soul and its actions over the other; there must be war for the sake of peace, business for the sake of leisure, things useful and necessary for the sake of things honourable. All these points the statesman should keep in view when he frames his laws; he should consider the parts of the soul and their functions, and above all the better and the end; he should also remember the diversities of human lives and actions. For men must be able to engage in business and go to war, but leisure and peace are better; they must do what is necessary and indeed what is useful, but what is honourable is better. On such principles children and persons of every age which requires education should be trained. Whereas even the Hellenes of the present day who are reputed to be best governed, and the legislators who gave them their constitutions, do not appear to have framed their governments with a regard to the best end, or to have given them laws and education with a view to all the virtues, but in a vulgar spirit have fallen back on those which promised to be more useful and profitable. Many modern writers have taken a similar view: they commend the Lacedaemonian constitution, and praise the legislator for making conquest and war his sole aim, a doctrine which may be refuted by argument and has long ago been refuted by facts. For most men desire empire in the hope of accumulating the goods of fortune; and on this ground Thibron and all those who have written about the Lacedaemonian constitution have praised their legislator, because the Lacedaemonians, by being trained to meet dangers, gained great power. But surely they are not a happy people now that their empire has passed away, nor was their legislator right. How ridiculous is the result, if, while they are continuing in the observance of his laws and no one interferes with them, they have lost the better part of life! These writers further err about the sort of government which the legislator should approve, for the government of freemen is nobler and implies more virtue than despotic government. Neither is a city to be deemed happy or a legislator to be praised because he trains his citizens to conquer and obtain dominion over their neighbours, for there is great evil in this. On a similar principle any citizen who could, should obviously try to obtain the power in his own state—the crime which the Lacedaemonians accuse king Pausanias of attempting, although he had so great honour already. No such principle and no law having this object is either

statesmanlike or useful or right. For the same things are best both for individuals and for states, and these are the things which the legislator ought to implant in the minds of his citizens. Neither should men study war with a view to the enslavement of those who do not deserve to be enslaved; but first of all they should provide against their own enslavement, and in the second place obtain empire for the good of the governed, and not for the sake of exercising a general despotism, and in the third place they should seek to be masters only over those who deserve to be slaves. Facts, as well as arguments, prove that the legislator should direct all his military and other measures to the provision of leisure and the establishment of peace. For most of these military states are safe only while they are at war, but fall when they have acquired their empire; like unused iron they lose their temper in time of peace. And for this the legislator is to blame, he never having taught them how to lead the life of peace.

6. Political Systems

Having determined these questions, we have next to consider whether there is only one form of government or many, and if many, what they are, and how many, and what are the differences between them.

A constitution is the arrangement of magistracies in a state, especially of the highest of all. The government is everywhere sovereign in the state, and the constitution is in fact the government. For example, in democracies the people are supreme, but in oligarchies, the few; and, therefore, we say that these two forms of government also are different: and so in other cases.

First, let us consider what is the purpose of a state, and how many forms of government there are by which human society is regulated. We have already said, in the first part of this treatise, when discussing household management and the rule of a master, that man is by nature a political animal. And therefore, men, even when they do not require one another's help, desire to live together; not but that they are also brought together by their common interests in proportion as they severally attain to any measure of well-being. This is certainly the chief end, both of individuals and of states. And also for the sake of mere life (in which there is possibly some noble element so long as the evils of existence do not greatly overbalance the good) mankind meet together and maintain the political community. And we all see that men cling to life even at the cost of enduring great misfortune, seeming to find in life a natural sweetness and happiness.

There is no difficulty in distinguishing the various kinds of authority; they have been often defined already in discussions outside the school. The rule of a master, although the slave by nature and the master by nature have in reality the same interests, is nevertheless exercised primarily with a view to the interest of the master, but accidentally considers the slave, since, if the slave perish, the rule of the master perishes with him. On the other hand, the government of a wife and children and of a household, which we have called household management, is exercised in the first instance for the good of the governed or for the common good of both parties, but essentially for the good of the governed, as we see to be the case in medicine, gymnastic, and the arts in general, which are only accidentally concerned with the good of the artists themselves. For there is no reason why the trainer may not sometimes practise gymnastics, and the helmsman is always one of the crew. The trainer or the helmsman considers the good of those committed to his care. But, when he is one of the persons taken care of, he accidentally participates in the advantage, for the helmsman is also a sailor, and the trainer becomes one of those in training. And so in politics: when the state is framed upon the principle of equality and likeness, the citizens think that they ought to hold office by turns. Formerly, as is natural, every one would take his turn of service; and then again, somebody else would look after his interest, just as he, while in office, had looked after theirs. But nowadays, for the sake of the advantage which is to be gained from the public revenues and from office, men want to be always in office. One might imagine that the rulers, being sickly, were only kept in health while they continued in office; in that case we may be sure that they would be hunting after places. The conclusion is evident: that governments which have a regard to the common interest are constituted in accordance with strict principles of justice, and are therefore true forms; but those which regard only the interest of the rulers are all defective and perverted forms, for they are despotic, whereas a state is a community of freemen.

Having determined these points, we have next to consider how many forms of government there are, and what they are; and in the first place what are the true forms, for when they are determined the perversions of them will at once be apparent. The words constitution and government have the same meaning, and the government, which is the supreme authority in states, must be in the hands of one, or of a few, or of the many. The true forms of government, therefore, are those in which the one, or the few, or the many, govern with a view to the common interest; but governments which rule with a view to the private interest, whether of the one, or of the few, or of the many, are perversions. For the members of a state, if they are truly citizens, ought to participate in its advantages. Of forms of government in which one rules, we call that which regards the common interests, kingship or royalty; that in which more than one, but not many, rule, aristocracy; and it is so called, either because the rulers are the best men, or because they have at heart the best interests of the state and of the citizens. But when the citizens at large administer the state for the common interest, the government is called by the generic name—a constitution. And there is a reason for this use of language. One man or a few may excel in virtue; but as the number increases it becomes more difficult for them to attain perfection in every kind of virtue, though they may in military virtue, for this is found in the masses. Hence in a constitutional government the fighting-men have the supreme power, and those who possess arms are the citizens.

Of the above-mentioned forms, the perversions are as follows:—of royalty, tyranny; of aristocracy, oligarchy; of constitutional government, democracy. For tyranny is a kind of monarchy which has in view the interest of the monarch only; oligarchy has in view the interest of the wealthy; democracy, of the needy: none of them the common good of all.

7. Democracy and Oligarchy

Let us begin by considering the common definitions of oligarchy and democracy, and what is justice oligarchical and democratical. For all men cling to justice of some kind, but their conceptions are imperfect and they do not express the whole idea. For example, justice is thought by them to be, and is, equality, not, however, for all, but only for equals. And inequality is thought to be, and is, justice; neither is this for all, but only for unequals. When the persons are omitted, then men judge erroneously. The reason is that they are passing judgment on themselves, and most people are bad judges in their own case. And whereas justice implies a relation to persons as well as to things, and a just distribution, as I have already said in the *Ethics,* implies the same ratio between the persons and between the things, they agree about the equality of the things, but dispute about the equality of the persons, chiefly for the reason which I have just given—because they are bad judges in their

own affairs; and secondly, because both the parties to the argument are speaking of a limited and partial justice, but imagine themselves to be speaking of absolute justice. For the one party, if they are unequal in one respect, for example wealth, consider themselves to be unequal in all; and the other party, if they are equal in one respect, for example free birth, consider themselves to be equal in all. But they leave out the capital point. For if men met and associated out of regard to wealth only, their share in the state would be proportioned to their property, and the oligarchical doctrine would then seem to carry the day. It would not be just that he who paid one mina should have the same share of a hundred minae, whether of the principal or of the profits, as he who paid the remaining ninety-nine. But a state exists for the sake of a good life, and not for the sake of life only: if life only were the object, slaves and brute animals might form a state, but they cannot, for they have no share in happiness or in a life of free choice. Nor does a state exist for the sake of alliance and security from injustice, nor yet for the sake of exchange and mutual intercourse; for then the Tyrrhenians and the Carthaginians, and all who have commercial treaties with one another, would be the citizens of one state. True, they have agreements about imports, and engagements that they will do no wrong to one another, and written articles of alliance. But there are no magistracies common to the contracting parties who will enforce their engagements; different states have each their own magistracies. Nor does one state take care that the citizens of the other are such as they ought to be, nor see that those who come under the terms of the treaty do no wrong or wickedness at all, but only that they do no injustice to one another. Whereas, those who care for good government take into consideration virtue and vice in states. Whence it may be further inferred that virtue must be the care of a state which is truly so called, and not merely enjoys the name: for without this end the community becomes a mere alliance which differs only in place from alliances of which the members live apart; and law is only a convention, "a surety to one another of justice," as the sophist Lycophron says, and has no real power to make the citizens good and just.

This is obvious; for suppose distinct places, such as Corinth and Megara, to be brought together so that their walls touched, still they would not be one city, not even if the citizens had the right to intermarry, which is one of the rights peculiarly characteristic of states. Again, if men dwelt at a distance from one another, but not so far off as to have no intercourse, and there were laws among them that they should not wrong each other in their exchanges, neither would this be a state. Let us suppose that one man is a carpenter, another a husbandman, another a shoemaker, and so on, and that their number is ten thousand: nevertheless, if they have nothing in common but exchange, alliance, and the like, that would not constitute a state. Why is this? Surely not because they are at a distance from one another: for even supposing that such a community were to meet in one place, but that each man had a house of his own, which was in a manner his state, and that they made alliance with one another, but only against evil-doers; still an accurate thinker would not deem this to be a state, if their intercourse with one another was of the same character after as before their union. It is clear then that a state is not a mere society, having a common place, established for the prevention of mutual crime and for the sake of exchange. These are conditions without which a state cannot exist; but all of them together do not constitute a state, which is a community of families and aggregations of families in well-being, for the sake of a perfect and self-sufficing life. Such a community can only be established among those who live in the same place and intermarry. Hence arise in cities family connexions, brotherhoods, common sacrifices, amusements which draw men together. But these are created by friendship, for the will to live together is friendship. The end of the state is the good life, and these are the means towards it. And the state is the union of families and villages in a perfect and self-sufficing life, by which we mean a happy and honourable life.

Our conclusion, then, is that political society exists for the sake of noble actions, and not of mere companionship. Hence they who contribute most to such a society have a greater share in it than those who have the same or a greater freedom or nobility of birth but are inferior to them in political virtue; or than those who exceed them in wealth but are surpassed by them in virtue.

From what has been said it will be clearly seen that all the partisans of different forms of government speak of a part of justice only.

There is also a doubt as to what is to be the supreme power in the state:—Is it the multitude? Or the wealthy? Or the good? Or the one best man? Or a tyrant? Any of these alternatives seems to involve disagreeable consequences. If the poor, for example, because they are more in number, divide among themselves the property of the rich—is not this unjust? No, by heaven (will be the reply), for the supreme authority justly willed it. But if this is not injustice, pray what is? Again, when in the first division all has been taken, and the majority divide anew the property of the minority, is it not evident, if this goes on, that they will ruin the state? Yet surely, virtue is not the ruin of those who possess her, nor is justice destructive of a state; and therefore this law of confiscation clearly cannot be just. If it were, all the acts of a tyrant must of necessity be just; for he only coerces other men by superior power, just as the multitude coerce the rich. But is it just then that the few and the wealthy should be the rulers? And what if they, in like manner, rob and plunder the people— is this just? If so, the other case will likewise be just. But there can be no doubt that all these things are wrong and unjust.

Then ought the good to rule and have

supreme power? But in that case everybody else, being excluded from power, will be dishonoured. For the offices of a state are posts of honour; and if one set of men always hold them, the rest must be deprived of them. Then will it be well that the one best man should rule? Nay, that is still more oligarchical, for the number of those who are dishonoured is thereby increased. Some one may say that it is bad in any case for a man, subject as he is to all the accidents of human passion, to have the supreme power, rather than the law. But what if the law itself be democratical or oligarchical, how will that help us out of our difficulties? Not at all; the same consequences will follow.

Most of these questions may be reserved for another occasion. The principle that the multitude ought to be supreme rather than the few best is one that is maintained, and, though not free from difficulty, yet seems to contain an element of truth. For the many, of whom each individual is but an ordinary person, when they meet together may very likely be better than the few good, if regarded not individually but collectively, just as a feast to which many contribute is better than a dinner provided out of a single purse. For each individual among the many has a share of virtue and prudence, and when they meet together, they become in a manner one man, who has many feet, and hands, and senses; that is a figure of their mind and disposition. Hence the many are better judges than a single man of music and poetry; for some understand one part, and some another, and among them they understand the whole. There is a similar combination of qualities in good men, who differ from any individual of the many, as the beautiful are said to differ from those who are not beautiful, and works of art from realities, because in them the scattered elements are combined, although, if taken separately, the eye of one person or some other feature in another person would be fairer than in the picture. Whether this principle can apply to every democracy, and to all bodies of men, is not clear. Or rather, by heaven, in some cases it is impossible of application; for the argument would equally hold about brutes; and wherein, it will be asked, do some men differ from brutes? But there may be bodies of men about whom our statement is nevertheless true. And if so, the difficulty which has been already raised, and also another which is akin to it—viz. what power should be assigned to the mass of freemen and citizens, who are not rich and have no personal merit—are both solved. There is still a danger in allowing them to share the great offices of state, for their folly will lead them into error, and their dishonesty into crime. But there is a danger also in not letting them share, for a state in which many poor men are excluded from office will necessarily be full of enemies. The only way of escape is to assign to them some deliberative and judicial functions. For this reason Solon and certain other legislators give them the power of electing to offices, and of calling the magistrates to account, but they do not allow them to hold office singly. When they meet together their perceptions are quite good enough, and combined with the better class they are useful to the state (just as impure food when mixed with what is pure sometimes makes the entire mass more wholesome than a small quantity of the pure would be), but each individual, left to himself, forms an imperfect judgment. On the other hand, the popular form of government involves certain difficulties. In the first place, it might be objected that he who can judge of the healing of a sick man would be one who could himself heal his disease, and make him whole—that is, in other words, the physician; and so in all professions and arts. As, then, the physician ought to be called to account by physicians, so ought men in general to be called to account by their peers. But physicians are of three kinds:—there is the ordinary practitioner, and there is the physician of the higher class, and thirdly the intelligent man who has studied the art: in all arts there is such a class; and we attribute the power of judging to them quite as much as to professors of the art. Secondly, does not the same principle apply to elections? For a right election can only be made by those who have knowledge; those who know geometry, for example, will choose a geometrician rightly, and those who know how to steer, a pilot; and, even if there be some occupations and arts in which private persons share in the ability to choose, they certainly cannot choose better than those who know. So that, according to this argument, neither the election of magistrates, nor the calling of them to account, should be entrusted to the many. Yet possibly these objections are to a great extent met by our old answer, that if the people are not utterly degraded, although individually they may be worse judges than those who have special knowledge—as a body they are as good or better. Moreover, there are some arts whose products are not judged of solely, or best, by the artists themselves, namely those arts whose products are recognized even by those who do not possess the art; for example, the knowledge of the house is not limited to the builder only; the user, or, in other words, the master, of the house will be even a better judge than the builder, just as the pilot will judge better of a rudder than the carpenter, and the guest will judge better of a feast than the cook.

This difficulty seems now to be sufficiently answered, but there is another akin to it. That inferior persons should have authority in greater matters than the good would appear to be a strange thing, yet the election and calling to account of the magistrates is the greatest of all. And these, as I was saying, are functions which in some states are assigned to the people, for the assembly is supreme in all such matters. Yet persons of any age, and having but a small property qualification, sit in the assembly and deliberate and judge, although for the great officers of state, such as treasurers and generals, a high qualification is required. This difficulty may be solved in the same manner as the preceding, and the present practice of democracies may be really defensible. For the power does not reside in the dicast, or senator, or ecclesiast, but in the court, and the senate, and the assembly, of which individual senators, or ecclesiasts, or dicasts, are only parts or members. And for this reason the many may claim to have a higher authority than the few; for the people, and the senate, and the courts consist of many persons, and their property collectively is greater than the property of one or of a few individuals holding great offices. But enough of this.

The discussion of the first question shows nothing so clearly as that laws, when good, should be supreme; and that the magistrate or magistrates should regulate those matters only on which the laws are unable to speak with precision owing to the difficulty of any general principle embracing all particulars. But what are good laws has not yet been clearly explained; the old difficulty remains. The goodness or badness, justice or injustice, of laws varies of necessity with the constitutions of states. This, however, is clear, that the laws must be adapted to the constitutions. But if so, true forms of government will of necessity have just laws, and perverted forms of government will have unjust laws.

8. Monarchy

If, however, there be some one person, or more than one, although not enough to make up the full complement of a state, whose virtue is so pre-eminent that the virtues or the political capacity of all the rest admit of no comparison with his or theirs, he or they can be no longer regarded as part of a state; for justice will not be done to the superior, if he is reckoned only as the equal of those who are so far inferior to him in virtue and in political capacity. Such an one may truly be deemed a God among men. Hence we see that legislation is necessarily concerned only with those who are equal in birth and in capacity; and that for men of pre-eminent virtue there is no law—they are themselves a law. Any one would be ridiculous who attempted to make laws for them: they would probably retort what, in the fable of Antisthenes, the lions said to the hares, when in the council of the beasts the latter began haranguing and claiming equality for all. And for this reason democratic states have instituted ostracism; equality is above all things their aim, and therefore they ostracized and banished from the city for a time those who seemed to predominate too much through their wealth, or the number of their friends, or through any other political influence. Mythology tells us that the Argonauts left Heracles behind for a similar reason; the ship Argo would not take him because she feared that he would have been too much for the rest of the crew. Wherefore those who denounce tyranny and blame the counsel which Periander gave to Thrasybulus cannot be held altogether just in their censure. The story is that Periander, when the herald was sent to ask counsel of him, said nothing, but only cut off the tallest ears of corn till he had brought the field to a level. The herald did not know the meaning of the action, but came and reported what he had seen to Thrasybulus, who understood that he was to cut off the principal men in the state; and this is a policy not only expedient for tyrants or in practice confined to them, but equally necessary in oligarchies and democracies. Ostracism is a measure of the same kind, which acts by disabling and banishing the most prominent citizens. Great powers do the same to whole cities and nations, as the Athenians did to the Samians, Chians, and Lesbians; no sooner had they obtained a firm grasp of the empire, than they humbled their allies contrary to treaty; and the Persian king has repeatedly crushed the Medes, Babylonians, and other nations, when their spirit has been stirred by the recollection of their former greatness.

The problem is a universal one, and equally concerns all forms of government, true as well as false; for, although perverted forms with a view to their own interests may adopt this policy, those which seek the common interest do so likewise. The same thing may be observed in the arts and sciences; for the painter will not allow the figure to have a foot which, however beautiful, is not in proportion, nor will the ship-builder allow the stern or any other part of the vessel to be unduly large, any more than the chorus-master will allow any one who sings louder or better than all the rest to sing in the choir. Monarchs, too, may practise compulsion and still live in harmony with their cities, if their own government is for the interest of the state. Hence where there is an acknowledged superiority the argument in favor of ostracism is based upon a kind of political justice. It would certainly be better that the legislator should from the first so order his state as to have no need of such a remedy. But if the need arises, the next best thing is that he should endeavour to correct the evil by this or some similar measure. The principle, however, has not been fairly applied in states; for, instead of looking to the good of their own constitution, they have used ostracism for factious purposes. It is true that under perverted forms of government, and from their special point of view, such a measure is just and expedient, but it is also clear that it is not absolutely just. In the perfect state there would be great doubts about the use of it, not when applied to excess in strength, wealth, popularity, or the like, but when used against some one who is pre-eminent in virtue—what is to be done with him? Mankind will not say that such an one is to be expelled and exiled; on the other hand, he ought not to be a subject—that would be as if mankind should claim to rule over Zeus, dividing his offices among them. The only alternative is that all should joyfully obey such a ruler, according to what seems to be the order of nature, and that men like him should be kings in their state for life.

9. Liberty and Equality

The basis of a democratic state is liberty; which, according to the common opinion of men, can only be enjoyed in such a state;—this they affirm to be the great end of every democracy. One principle of liberty is for all to rule and be ruled in turn, and indeed democratic justice is the application of numerical not proportionate equality; whence it follows that the majority must be supreme, and that whatever the majority approve must be the end and the just. Every citizen, it is said, must have equality, and therefore in a democracy the poor have more power than the rich, because there are more of them, and the will of the majority is supreme. This, then, is one note of liberty which all democrats affirm to be the principle of their state. Another is that a man should live as he likes. This, they say, is the privilege of a freeman, since, on the other hand, not to live as a man likes is the mark of a slave. This is the second characteristic of democracy, whence has arisen the claim of men to be ruled by none, if possible, or, if this is impossible, to rule and be ruled in turns; and so it contributes to the freedom based upon equality.

Such being our foundation and such the principle from which we start, the characteristics of democracy are as follows:—the election of officers by all out of all; and that all should rule over each, and each in his turn over all; that the appointment to all offices, or to all but those which require experience and skill, should be made by lot; that no property qualification should be required for offices, or only a very low one; that a man should not hold the same office twice, or not often, or in the case of few except military offices: that the tenure of all offices, or of as many as possible, should be brief; that all men should sit in judgment, or that judges selected out of all should judge, in all matters, or in most and in the greatest and most important—such as the scrutiny of accounts, the constitution, and private contracts; that the assembly should be supreme over all causes, or at any rate over the most important, and the magistrates over none or only over a very few. Of all magistracies, a council is the most democratic when there is not the means of paying all the citizens, but when they are paid even this is robbed of its power; for the people then draw all cases to themselves, as I said in the previous discussion. The next characteristic of democracy is payment for services; assembly, law-courts, magistrates, everybody receives pay, when it is to be had; or when it is not to be had for all, then it is given to the law-courts and to the stated assemblies, to the council and to the magistrates, or at least to any of them who are compelled to have their meals together. And whereas oligarchy is characterized by birth, wealth, and education, the notes of democracy appear to be the opposite of these—low birth, poverty, mean employment. Another note is that no magistracy is perpetual, but if any such have survived some ancient change in the constitution it should be stripped of its power, and the holders should be elected by lot and no longer by vote. These are the points common to all democracies; but democracy and demos in their truest form are based upon the recognized principle of democratic justice, that all should count equally; for equality implies that the poor should have no more share in the government than the rich, and should not be the only rulers, but that all should rule equally according to their numbers. And in this way men think that they will secure equality and freedom in their state.

Next comes the question, how is this equality to be obtained? Are we to assign to a thousand poor men the property qualifications of five hundred rich men? and shall we give the thousand a power equal to that of the five hundred? or, if this is not to be the mode, ought we, still retaining the same ratio, to take equal numbers from each and give them the control of the elections and of the courts?—Which, according to the democratical notion, is the juster form of the constitution—this or one based on numbers only? Democrats say that justice is that to which the majority agree, oligarchs that to which the wealthier class; in their opinion the decision should be given according to the amount of property. In both principles there is some inequality and injustice. For if justice is the will of the few, any one person who has more wealth than all the rest of the rich put together, ought, upon the oligarchical principle, to have the sole power—but this would be tyranny; or if justice is the will of the majority, as I was before saying, they will unjustly confiscate the property of the wealthy minority. To find a principle of equality in which they both agree we must inquire into their respective ideas of justice.

Now they agree in saying that whatever is decided by the majority of the citizens is to be deemed law. Granted:—but not without some reserve; since there are two classes out of which a state is composed—the poor and the rich—that is to be deemed law, on which both or the greater part of both agree; and if they disagree, that which is approved by the greater number, and by those who have the higher qualification. For example, suppose that there are ten rich and twenty poor, and some measure is approved by six of the rich and is disapproved by fifteen of the poor, and the remaining four of the rich join with the party of the poor, and the remaining five of the poor with that of the rich; in such a case the will of those whose qualifications, when both sides are added up, are the greatest, should prevail. If they turn out to be equal, there is no greater difficulty than at present, when, if the assembly or the courts are divided, recourse is had to the lot, or to some similar expedient. But, although it may be difficult in theory to know what is just and equal, the practical difficulty of inducing those to forbear who can, if they like, encroach, is far greater, for the weaker are always asking for equality and justice, but the stronger care for none of these things.

10. The Rule of Law

At this place in the discussion there impends the inquiry respecting the king who acts solely according to his own will; he has now to be considered. The so-called limited monarchy, or kingship according to law, as I have already remarked, is not a distinct form of government, for under all governments, as, for example, in a democracy or aristocracy, there may be a general holding office for life, and one person is often made supreme over the administration of a state. A magistracy of this kind exists at Epidamnus, and also at Opus, but in the latter city has a more limited power. Now, absolute monarchy, or the arbitrary rule of a sovereign over all the citizens, in a city which consists of equals, is thought by some to be quite contrary to nature; it is argued that those who are by nature equals must have the same natural right and worth, and that for unequals to have an equal share, or for equals to have an uneven share, in the offices of state, is as bad as for different bodily constitutions to have the same food and clothing. Wherefore it is thought to be just that among equals every one be ruled as well as rule, and therefore that all should have their turn. We thus arrive at law; for an order of succession implies law. And the rule of the law, it is argued, is preferable to that of any individual. On the same principle, even if it be better for certain individuals to govern, they should be made only guardians and ministers of the law. For magistrates there must be—this is admitted; but then men say that to give authority to any one man when all are equal is unjust. Nay, there may indeed be cases which the law seems unable to determine, but in such cases can a man? Nay, it will be replied, the law trains officers for this express purpose, and appoints them to determine matters which are left undecided by it, to the best of their judgment. Further, it permits them to make any amendment of the existing laws which experience suggests. Therefore he who bids the law rule may be deemed to bid God and Reason alone rule, but he who bids man rule adds an element of the beast; for desire is a wild beast, and passion perverts the minds of rulers, even when they are the best of men. The law is reason unaffected by desire. We are told that a patient should call in a physician; he will not get better if he is doctored out of a book. But the parallel of the arts is clearly not in point; for the physician does nothing contrary to rule from motives of friendship; he only cures a patient and takes a fee; whereas magistrates do many things from spite and partiality. And, indeed, if a man suspected the physician of being in league with his enemies to destroy him for a bribe, he would rather have recourse to the book. But certainly physicians, when they are sick, call in other physicians, and training-masters, when they are in training, other training-masters, as if they could not judge truly about their own case and might be influenced by their feelings. Hence it is evident that in seeking for justice men seek for the mean or neutral, for the law is the mean. Again, customary laws have more weight, and relate to more important matters, than written laws, and a man may be a safer ruler than the written law, but not safer than the customary law.

Again, it is by no means easy for one man to superintend many things; he will have to appoint a number of subordinates, and what difference does it make whether these subordinates always existed or were appointed by him because he needed them? If, as I said before, the good man has a right to rule because he is better, still two good men are better than one: this is the old saying—

two going together,

and the prayer of Agamemnon—

would that I had ten such counsellors!

And at this day there are magistrates, for example judges, who have authority to decide some matters which the law is unable to determine, since no one doubts that the law would command and decide in the best manner whatever it could. But some things can, and other things cannot, be comprehended under the law, and this is the origin of the vexed question whether the best law or the best man should rule. For matters of detail about which men deliberate cannot be included in legislation. Nor does any one deny that the decision of such matters must be left to man, but it is argued that there should be many judges, and not one only. For every ruler who has been trained by the law judges well; and it would surely seem strange that a person should see better with two eyes, or hear better with two ears, or act better with two hands or feet, than many with many; indeed, it is already the practice of kings to make to themselves many eyes and ears and hands and feet. For they make colleagues of those who are the friends of themselves and their governments. They must be friends of the monarch and of his government; if not his friends, they will not do what he wants; but friendship implies likeness and equality; and, therefore, if he thinks that his friends ought to rule, he must think that those who are equal to himself and like himself ought to rule equally with himself. These are the principal controversies relating to monarchy.

11. Constitutional Government

Polity or constitutional government may be described generally as a fusion of oligarchy and democracy; but the term is usually applied to those forms of government which incline towards democracy, and the term aristocracy to those which incline towards oligarchy, because birth and education are commonly the accompaniments of wealth. Moreover, the rich already possess the external advantages the want of which is a temptation to crime, and hence they are called noblemen and gentlemen. And inasmuch as aristocracy seeks to give predominance to the best of the citizens, people say also of oligarchies that they are composed of noblemen and gentlemen. Now it appears to be an impossible thing that the state which is governed not by the best citizens but by the worst should be well-governed, and equally impossible that the state which is ill-governed should be governed by the best. But we must remember that good laws, if they are not obeyed, do not constitute good government. Hence there are two parts of good government; one is the actual obedience of citizens to the laws, the other part is the goodness of the laws which they obey; they may obey bad laws as well as good. And there may be a further subdivision; they may obey either the best laws which are attainable to them, or the best absolutely.

The distribution of offices according to merit is a special characteristic of aristocracy, for the principle of an aristocracy is virtue, as wealth is of an oligarchy, and freedom of a democracy. In all of them there of course exists the right of the majority, and whatever seems good to the majority of those who share in the government has authority. Now in most states the form called polity exists, for the fusion goes no further than the attempt to unite the freedom of the poor and the wealth of the rich, who commonly take the place of the noble. But as there are three grounds on which men claim an equal share in the government, freedom, wealth, and virtue (for the fourth or good birth is the result of the two last, being only ancient wealth and virtue), it is clear that the admixture of the two elements, that is to say, of the rich and poor, is to be called a polity or constitutional government; and the union of the three is to be called aristocracy or the government of the best, and more than any other form of government, except the true and ideal, has a right to this name.

Thus far I have shown the existence of forms of states other than monarchy, democracy, and oligarchy, and what they are, and in what aristocracies differ from one another, and polities from aristocracies—that the two latter are not very unlike is obvious.

Next we have to consider how by the side of oligarchy and democracy the so-called polity or constitutional government springs up, and how it should be organized. The nature of it will be at once understood from a comparison of oligarchy and democracy; we must ascertain their different characteristics, and taking a portion from each, put the two together, like the parts of an indenture. Now there are three modes in which fusions of government may be affected. In the first mode we must combine the laws made by both governments, say concerning the administration of justice. In oligarchies they impose a fine on the rich if they do not serve as judges, and to the poor they give no pay; but in democracies they give pay to the poor and do not fine the rich. Now (1) the union of these two modes is a common or middle term between them, and is therefore characteristic of a constitutional government, for it is a combination of both. This is one mode of uniting the two elements. Or (2) a mean may be taken between the enactments of the two: thus democracies require no property qualification, or only a small one, from members of the assembly, oligarchies a high one; here neither of these is the common term, but a mean between them. (3) There is a third mode, in which something is borrowed from the oligarchical and something from the democratical principle. For example, the appointment of magistrates by lot is thought to be democratical, and the election of them oligarchical; democratical again when there is no property qualification, oligarchical when there is. In the aristocratical or constitutional state, one element will be taken from each—from oligarchy the principle of electing to offices, from democracy the disregard of qualification. Such are the various modes of combination.

There is a true union of oligarchy and democracy when the same state may be termed either a democracy or an oligarchy; those who use both names evidently feel that the fusion is complete. Such a fusion there is also in the mean; for both extremes appear in it. The Lacedaemonian constitution, for example, is often described as a democracy, because it has many democratical features. In the first place the youth receive a democratical education. For the sons of the poor are brought up with the sons of the rich, who are educated in such a manner as to make it possible for the sons of the poor to be educated like them. A similar equality prevails in the following period of life, and when the citizens are grown up to manhood the same rule is observed; there is no distinction between the rich and poor. In like manner they all have the same food at their public tables, and the rich wear only such clothing as any poor man can afford. Again, the people elect to one of the two greatest offices of state, and in the other they share; for they elect the Senators and share in the Ephoralty. By others the Spartan constitution is said to be an oligarchy, because it has many oligarchical elements. That all offices are filled by election and none by lot, is one of these oligarchical characteristics; that the power of inflicting death or banishment rests with a few persons is another; and there are others. In a well attempered polity there should appear to be both elements and yet neither; also the government should rely on itself, and not on foreign aid, and on itself not through the good will of a majority—they might be equally well-disposed when there is a vicious form of government —but through the general willingness of all classes in the state to maintain the constitution.

Enough of the manner in which a constitutional government, and in which the so-called aristocracies ought to be framed.

12. The Best State

In all arts and sciences which embrace the whole of any subject, and do not come into being in a fragmentary way, it is the province of a single art or science to consider all that appertains to a single subject. For example, the art of gymnastic considers not only the suitableness of different modes of training to different bodies (2) but what sort is absolutely the best (1); (for the absolutely best must suit that which is by nature best and best furnished with the means of life), and also what common form of training is adapted to the great majority of men (4). And if a man does not desire the best habit of body, or the greatest skill in gymnastics, which might be attained by him, still the trainer or the teacher of gymnastic should be able to impart any lower degree of either (3). The same principle equally holds in medicine and ship-building, and the making of clothes, and in the arts generally.

Hence it is obvious that government too is the subject of a single science, which has to consider what government is best and of what sort it must be, to be most in accordance with our aspirations, if there were no external impediment, and also what kind of government is adapted to particular states. For the best is often unattainable, and therefore the true legislators and statesman ought to be acquainted, not only with (1) that which is best in the abstract, but also with (2) that which is best relatively to circumstances. We should be able further to say how a state may be constituted under any given conditions (3); both how it is originally formed and, when formed, how it may be longest preserved; the supposed state being so far from having the best constitution that it is unprovided even with the conditions necessary for the best; neither is it the best under the circumstances, but of an inferior type.

He ought, moreover, to know (4) the form of government which is best suited to states in general; for political writers, although they have excellent ideas, are often unpractical. We should consider, not only what form of government is best, but also what is possible and what is easily attainable by all. There are some who would have none but the most perfect; for this many natural advantages are required. Others, again, speak of a more attainable form, and, although they reject the constitution under which they are living, they extol some one in particular, for example the Lacedaemonian. Any change of government which has to be introduced should be one which men, starting from their existing constitutions, will be both willing and able to adopt, since there is quite as much trouble in the reformation of an old constitution as in the establishment of a new one, just as to unlearn is as hard as to learn. And therefore, in addition to the qualifications of the statesman already mentioned, he should be able to find remedies for the defects of existing constitutions, as has been said before. This he cannot do unless he knows how many forms of government there are. It is often supposed that there is only one kind of democracy and one of oligarchy. But this is a mistake; and, in order to avoid such mistakes, we must ascertain what differences there are in the constitutions of states, and in how many ways they are combined. The same political insight will enable a man to know which laws are the best, and which are suited to different constitutions; for the laws are, and ought to be, relative to the constitution, and not the constitution to the laws. A constitution is the organization of offices in a state, and determines what is to be the governing body, and what is the end of each community. But laws are not to be confounded with the principles of the constitution; they are the rules according to which the magistrates should administer the state, and proceed against offenders. So that we must know the varieties, and the number of varieties, of each form of government, if only with a view to making laws. For the same laws cannot be equally suited to all oligarchies or to all democracies, since there is certainly more than one form both of democracy and of oligarchy.

13. Political Moderation and Stability: The Middle Classes

We have now to inquire what is the best constitution for most states, and the best life for most men, neither assuming a standard of virtue which is above ordinary persons, nor an education which is exceptionally favoured by nature and circumstances, nor yet an ideal state which is an aspiration only, but having regard to the life in which the majority are able to share, and to the form of government which states in general can attain. As to those aristocracies, as they are called, of which we were just now speaking, they either lie beyond the possibilities of the greater number of states, or they approximate to the so-called constitutional government, and therefore need no separate discussion. And in fact the conclusion at which we arrive respecting all these forms rests upon the same grounds. For if what was said in the *Ethics* is true, that the happy life is the life according to virtue lived without impediment, and that virtue is a mean, then the life which is in a mean, and in a mean attainable by every one, must be the best. And the same principles of virtue and vice are characteristic of cities and of constitutions; for the constitution is in a figure the life of the city.

Now in all states there are three elements: one class is very rich, another very poor, and a third in a mean. It is admitted that moderation and the mean are best, and therefore it will clearly be best to possess the gifts of fortune in moderation; for in that condition of life men are most ready to follow rational principle. But he who greatly excels in beauty, strength, birth, or wealth, or on the other hand who is very poor, or very weak, or very much disgraced, finds it difficult to follow rational principle. Of these two the one sort grow into violent and great criminals, the others into rogues and petty rascals. And two sorts of offences correspond to them, the one committed from violence, the other from roguery. Again, the middle class is least likely to shrink from rule, or to be over-ambitious for it; both of which are injuries to the state. Again, those who have too much of the goods of fortune, strength, wealth, friends, and the like, are neither willing nor able to submit to authority. The evil begins at home; for when they are boys, by reason of the luxury in which they are brought up, they never learn, even at school, the habit of obedience. On the other hand, the very poor, who are in the opposite extreme, are too degraded. So that the one class cannot obey, and can only rule despotically; the other knows not how to command and must be ruled like slaves. Thus arises a city, not of freemen, but of masters and slaves, the one despising, the other envying; and nothing can be more fatal to friendship and good fellowship in states than this: for good fellowship springs from friendship; when men are at enmity with one another, they would rather not even share the same path. But a city ought to be composed, as far as possible, of equals and similars; and these are generally the middle classes. Wherefore the city which is composed of middle-class citizens is necessarily best constituted in respect of the elements of which we say the fabric of the state naturally consists. And this is the class of citizens which is most secure in a state, for they do not, like the poor, covet their neighbours' goods; nor do others covet theirs, as the poor covet the goods of the rich; and as they neither plot against others, nor are themselves plotted against, they pass through life safely. Wisely then did Phocylides pray—"Many things are best in the mean; I desire to be of a middle condition in my city."

Thus it is manifest that the best political community is formed by citizens of the middle class, and that those states are likely to be well-administered, in which the middle class is large, and stronger if possible than both the other classes, or at any rate than either singly; for the addition of the middle class turns the scale, and prevents either of the extremes from being dominant. Great then is the good fortune of a state in which the citizens have a moderate and sufficient property; for where some possess much, and the others nothing, there may arise an extreme democracy, or a pure oligarchy; or a tyranny may grow out of either extreme—either out of the most rampant democracy, or out of an oligarchy; but it

is not so likely to arise out of the middle constitutions and those akin to them. I will explain the reason of this hereafter, when I speak of the revolutions of states. The mean condition of states is clearly best, for no other is free from faction; and where the middle class is large, there are least likely to be factions and dissensions. For a similar reason large states are less liable to faction than small ones, because in them the middle class is large; whereas in small states it is easy to divide all the citizens into two classes who are either rich or poor, and to leave nothing in the middle. And democracies are safer and more permanent than oligarchies, because they have a middle class which is more numerous and has a greater share in the government; for when there is no middle class, and the poor greatly exceed in number, troubles arise, and the state soon comes to an end. A proof of the superiority of the middle class is that the best legislators have been of a middle condition; for example, Solon, as his own verses testify; and Lycurgus, for he was not a king; and Charondas, and almost all legislators.

These considerations will help us to understand why most governments are either democratical or oligarchical. The reason is that the middle class is seldom numerous in them, and whichever party, whether the rich or the common people, transgresses the mean and predominates, draws the constitution its own way, and thus arises either oligarchy or democracy. There is another reason—the poor and the rich quarrel with one another, and whichever side gets the better, instead of establishing a just or popular government, regards political supremacy as the prize of victory, and the one party sets up a democracy and the other an oligarchy. Further, both the parties which had the supremacy in Hellas looked only to the interest of their own form of government, and established in states, the one, democracies, and the other, oligarchies; they thought of their own advantage, of the public not at all. For these reasons the middle form of government has rarely, if ever, existed, and among a very few only. One man alone of all who ever ruled in Hellas was induced to give this middle constitution to states. But it has now become a habit among the citizens of states, not even to care about equality; all men are seeking for dominion, or, if conquered, are willing to submit.

What then is the best form of government, and what makes it the best, is evident; and of other constitutions, since we say that there are many kinds of democracy and many of oligarchy, it is not difficult to see which has the first and which the second or any other place in the order of excellence, now that we have determined which is the best. For that which is nearest to the best must of necessity be better, and that which is furthest from it worse, if we are judging absolutely and not relatively to given conditions: I say "relatively to given conditions," since a particular government may be preferable, but another form may be better for some people.

14. Causes of Revolution

In considering how dissensions and political revolutions arise, we must first of all ascertain the beginnings and causes of them which affect constitutions generally. They may be said to be three in number; and we have now to give an outline of each. We want to know (1) what is the feeling? (2) what are the motives of those who make them? (3) whence arise political disturbances and quarrels? The universal and chief cause of this revolutionary feeling has been already mentioned; viz. the desire of equality, when men think that they are equal to others who have more than themselves; or, again, the desire of inequality and superiority, when conceiving themselves to be superior they think that they have not more but the same or less than their inferiors; pretensions which may and may not be just. Inferiors revolt in order that they may be equal, and equals that they may be superior. Such is the state of mind which

creates revolutions. The motives for making them are the desire of gain and honour, or the fear of dishonour and loss; the authors of them want to divert punishment or dishonour from themselves or their friends. The causes and reasons of revolutions, whereby men are themselves affected in the way described, and about the things which I have mentioned, viewed in one way may be regarded as seven, and in another as more than seven. Two of them have been already noticed; but they act in a different manner, for men are excited against one another by the love of gain and honour—not, as in the case which I have just supposed, in order to obtain them for themselves, but at seeing others, justly or unjustly, engrossing them. Other causes are insolence, fear, excessive predominance, contempt, disproportionate increase in some part of the state; causes of another sort are election intrigues, carelessness, neglect about trifles, dissimilarity of elements.

15. How to Prevent Revolution

We have next to consider what means there are of preserving constitutions in general, and in particular cases. In the first place it is evident that if we know the causes which destroy constitutions, we also know the causes which preserve them; for opposites produce opposites, and destruction is the opposite of preservation.

In all well-attempered governments there is nothing which should be more jealously maintained than the spirit of obedience to law, more especially in small matters; for transgression creeps in unperceived and at last ruins the state, just as the constant recurrence of small expenses in time eats up a fortune. The expense does not take place all at once, and therefore is not observed; the mind is deceived, as in the fallacy which says that "if each part is little, then the whole is little." And this is true in one way, but not in another, for the whole and the all are not little, although they are made up of littles.

In the first place, then, men should guard against the beginnings of change, and in the second place they should not rely upon the political devices of which I have already spoken invented only to deceive the people, for they are proved by experience to be useless. Further, we note that oligarchies as well as aristocracies may last, not from any inherent stability in such forms of government, but because the rulers are on good terms both with the unenfranchised and with the governing classes, not maltreating any who are excluded from the government, but introducing into it the leading spirits among them. They should never wrong the ambitious in a matter of honour, or the common people in a matter of money; and they should treat one another and their fellow-citizens in a spirit of equality. The equality which the friends of democracy seek to establish for the multitude is not only just but likewise expedient among equals. Hence, if the governing class are numerous, many democratic institutions are useful; for example, the restriction of the tenure of offices to six months, that all those who are of equal rank may share in them. Indeed, equals or peers when they are numerous become a kind of democracy, and therefore demagogues are very likely to arise among them, as I have already remarked. The short tenure of office prevents oligarchies and aristocracies from falling into the hands of families; it is not easy for a person to do any great harm when his tenure of office is short, whereas long possession begets tyranny in oligarchies and democracies. For the aspirants to tyranny are either the principal men of the state, who in democracies are demagogues and in oligarchies members of ruling houses, or those who hold great offices, and have a long tenure of them.

Constitutions are preserved when their destroyers are at a distance, and sometimes also because they are near, for the fear of them makes the government keep in hand the constitution. Wherefore the ruler who has a care of the constitution should invent terrors, and bring distant dangers near, in order that the citizens may be on their guard, and, like sentinels in a night-watch, never relax their attention. He should endeavour too by help of the laws to control the contentions and quarrels of the notables, and to prevent those who have not hitherto taken part in them from catching the spirit of contention. No ordinary man can discern the beginning of evil, but only the true statesman.

As to the change produced in oligarchies and constitutional governments by the alteration of the qualification, when this arises, not out of any variation in the qualification but only out of the increase of money, it is well to compare the general valuation of property with that of past years, annually in those cities in which the census is taken annually, and in larger cities every third or fifth year. If the whole is many times greater or many times less than when the ratings recognized by the constitution were fixed, there should be power given by law to raise or lower the qualification as the amount is greater or less. Where this is not done a constitutional government passes into an oligarchy, and an oligarchy is narrowed to a rule of families; or in the opposite case constitutional government becomes democracy, and oligarchy either constitutional government or democracy.

It is a principle common to democracy, oligarchy, and every other form of government not to allow the disproportionate increase of any citizen, but to give moderate honour for a long time rather than great honour for a short time. For men are easily spoilt; not every one can bear prosperity. But if this rule is not observed, at any rate the honours which are given all at once should be taken away by degrees and not all at once. Especially should the laws provide against any one having too much power, whether derived from friends or money; if he has, he should be sent clean out of the country. And since innovations creep in through the private life of individuals also, there ought to be a magistracy which will have an eye to those whose life is not in harmony with the government, whether oligarchy or democracy or any other. And for a like reason an increase of prosperity in any part of the state should be carefully watched. The proper remedy for this evil is always to give the management of affairs and offices of state to opposite elements; such opposites are the virtuous and the many, or the rich and the poor. Another way is to combine the poor and the rich in one body, or to increase the middle class: thus an end will be put to the revolutions which arise from inequality.

But above all every state should be so administered and so regulated by law that its magistrates cannot possibly make money. In oligarchies special precautions should be used against this evil. For the people do not take any great offence at being kept out of the government—indeed they are rather pleased than otherwise at having leisure for their private business—but what irritates them is to think that their rulers are stealing the public money; then they are doubly annoyed; for they lose both honour and profit. If office brought no profit, then and then only could democracy and aristocracy be combined; for both notables and people might have their wishes gratified. All would be able to hold office, which is the aim of democracy, and the notables would be magistrates, which is the aim of aristocracy. And this result may be accomplished when there is no possibility of making money out of the offices; for the poor will not want to have them when there is nothing to be gained from them—they would rather be attending to their own concerns; and the rich, who do not want money from the public treasury, will be able to take them; and so the poor will keep to their work and grow rich, and the notables will not be governed by the lower class. In order to avoid peculation of the public money, the transfer of the revenue should be made at a general assembly of the citizens, and duplicates of the accounts deposited with the different brotherhoods, companies, and tribes. And honours should be given by law to magistrates who have the reputation of being incorruptible. In democracies the rich should be spared; not only should their property not be divided, but their incomes also, which in some states are taken from them imperceptibly, should be protected. It is a good thing to prevent the wealthy citizens, even if they are willing, from undertaking expensive and useless public services, such as the giving of choruses, torch-races, and the like. In an oligarchy, on the other hand, great care should be taken of the poor, and lucrative offices should go to them; if any of the wealthy classes insult them, the offender should be punished more severely than if he had wronged one of his own class. Provision should be made that estates pass by inheritance and not by gift, and no person should have more than one inheritance; for in this way properties will be equalized, and more of the poor rise to competency. It is also expedient both in a democracy and in an oligarchy to assign to those who have less share in the government (i. e. to the rich in a democracy and to the poor in an oligarchy) an equality or preference in all but the principal offices of state. The latter should be entrusted chiefly or only to members of the governing class.

CHAPTER 3

POLYBIUS

WHEN Greece was politically and militarily subjugated by the Macedonian monarchy, Greek civilization continued to dominate the new and larger horizons of empire; Aristotle's tutoring of Alexander symbolically represented the fact that Greece was still the mistress of the world in the realm of thought, though deprived of independence in the realm of political action. But so difficult was the adaptation of Greeks to the new dimensions of political organization that Aristotle still discussed the city-state as the only imaginable form of state at the very time when it was rapidly becoming a thing of the past. The Greek city-state was never to recover its vitality; the only change during the two centuries following Aristotle was the substitution of Rome for Macedon.

Some Greek statesmen tried to maintain a precarious neutrality in the struggle of Rome and Macedon, but with no success. Shortly after the conquest of Macedon by Rome, one thousand distinguished Greeks were deported to Rome as political prisoners, to await trial against them; no trial was ever held, and after seventeen years the surviving three hundred exiles were finally released.

Among the deported was Polybius (204–122 B. C.), a promising young statesman who had rendered illustrious public service to the Achaean League, a confederation of city-states, and the chief political power in Greece at that time. In Rome, Polybius became acquainted with the leading families; in this and other ways he was able to observe the inner workings of Roman politics at home and abroad. Personal ties of friendship with top political figures, intellectual curiosity concerning the growth of Rome from a small city to the dominant world power, and admiration for Roman civil and military statesmanship turned him into a friend and ally of Rome. He traveled widely in military and diplomatic missions, in Europe as well as in Asia and Africa. His rich practical and scholarly experience is reflected in his *Histories,* written in forty books, of which the first five are fully preserved, and the remaining thirty-five in fragments.

Next to Herodotus and Thucydides, Polybius is recognized as the greatest Greek historian. His work is the first universal history written by a student of politics, for he had the Greek intellectual background of keen observation and philosophical analysis, as well as firsthand experience of world affairs which at that time only long and intimate association with Roman politics and statesmanship could give. His work centers on a relatively short period, the fifty-three years from the Second Punic War (219 B. c.) to the conquest of Macedon by Rome (167 B. c.), but it is the critical period of the rise of Rome from a small state to world hegemony.

Polybius was the first to apply the institutional method to the study of politics and, more particularly, to relate foreign policy to domestic policies and practices. The more he studied the nature and evolution of Roman political institutions, the more he became convinced that Rome's rise to world supremacy was the work, not of a few heroic individuals or of great military leaders, but of the less visible and less dramatic force of high political standards and practices. Whereas Plato and Aristotle had studied political institutions in relation to the good life of the community and the individual—assuming a Greek world in which small, self-sufficient city-states existed side by side without a great deal of mutual interference—Polybius was the first to examine the institutional fabric of a state as the chief determining factor in the formation of national strength.

Polybius thought that the secret of Roman political health lay in the principle of the *mixed constitution*. Aristotle had clearly suggested this principle, but in a more social and economic sense: the mixture was one of social and economic groups and classes, and not of branches of government, and his system of constitutional government (polity) was based on the principles of the wealth of the few and freedom of the many (poor). By contrast, Polybius' idea of the mixed constitution implies a blend of different principles of government authority. Following Aristotle, Polybius saw in monarchy, aristocracy, and democracy the three chief forms of government, and, even more keenly than Aristotle, he was aware that each form carried within itself the seed of its own degeneration, if it were allowed to operate without checks and balances provided by its opposing principles. Monarchy could easily become tyranny, aristocracy sink into oligarchy, and democracy turn into mob rule of force and violence. In the Roman constitution Polybius believed he found the near-perfect balance between these three principles: the consuls represented the monarchical principle; the senate, the aristocratic one; and the popular assemblies, the democratic.

Polybius describes in detail how the natural tendency of each of the three basic powers of government is to check and balance the two others, so that "none of the three is absolute, but the purpose of one can be counterworked and thwarted by the others," and "any aggressive impulse is sure to be checked."

This system of checks and balances must have appeared to many contemporaries of Polybius—friends and enemies of Roman power—to have an inevitably divisive effect on the internal unity of the state and its capacity to act. Polybius says that, on the contrary, the method of checks and balances "is adequate to all emergencies, so that it is impossible to find a better political system than this." Whenever the menace of a common danger from abroad compels the various branches of government "to act in concord and support each other, so great does the strength of the state become, that nothing which is requisite can be neglected, as all are zealously competing in devising means of meeting the need of the hour, nor can any decision arrived at fail to be executed promptly, as all are cooperating both in public and in private to the accomplishment of the task they have set themselves; and consequently this peculiar form of constitution possesses an irresistible power of attaining every object upon which it is resolved." Dictators have lost many wars against constitutionally governed states because they find it difficult, accustomed as they are to the fetish of unity and uniformity, to comprehend the inner reservoirs of strength that lie behind the apparent divisions and quarrels of free peoples.

Polybius knows, however, that no political system can in itself guarantee the growth and vitality of the state, and that ultimately the quality of the people, particularly its leaders and officials, will determine the issue of strength and survival. He compares the lax standards of value in Carthage, where "nothing which results in profit is regarded as disgraceful," with Roman standards, which condemn "unscrupulous gain from forbidden sources." More specifically, "at Carthage candidates for office practise open bribery, whereas at Rome death is the penalty for it." Polybius idealizes perhaps the political morals of his Roman conquerors, but the general principle he states is as valid today as in his own time.

Polybius' influence on Cicero assured him of a popular audience in antiquity, and later on, too, because Cicero was for a long time one of the most widely read ancient authors. In the Middle Ages, Polybius' main ideas are traceable in thinkers as diverse as Marsilio of Padua and St. Thomas of Aquinas, and in the modern era Locke and Montesquieu added new weight to the doctrine of the balance of powers. In the history of the United States, in particular, Polybius played an important intellectual role in the drafting of the Constitution. The political leaders of that formative era, Jefferson, Adams, and many others, were thoroughly familiar with Polybius, and they used his ideas in framing a Constitution based on the principle of checks and balances, of liberty through limited government.

POLYBIUS

The Histories *

1. The Forms of State

In the case of those Greek states which have often risen to greatness and have often experienced a complete change of fortune, it is an easy matter both to describe their past and to pronounce as to their future. For there is no difficulty in reporting the known facts, and it is not hard to foretell the future by inference from the past. But about the Roman state it is neither at all easy to explain the present situation owing to the complicated character of the constitution, nor to foretell the future owing to our ignorance of the peculiar features of public and private life at Rome in the past. Particular attention and study are therefore required if one wishes to attain a clear general view of the distinctive qualities of their constitution.

Most of those whose object it has been to instruct us methodically concerning such matters, distinguish three kinds of constitutions, which they call kingship, aristocracy, and democracy. Now we should, I think, be quite justified in asking them to enlighten us as to whether they represent these three to be the sole varieties or rather to be the best; for in either case my opinion is that they are wrong. For it is evident that we must regard as the best constitution a combination of all these three varieties, since we have had proof of this not only theoreti-

cally but by actual experience, Lycurgus having been the first to draw up a constitution—that of Sparta—on this principle. Nor on the other hand can we admit that these are the only three varieties; for we have witnessed monarchical and tyrannical governments, which while they differ very widely from kingship, yet bear a certain resemblance to it, this being the reason why monarchs in general falsely assume and use, as far as they can, the regal title. There have also been several oligarchical constitutions which seem to bear some likeness to aristocratic ones, though the divergence is, generally, as wide as possible. The same holds good about democracies. The truth of what I say is evident from the following considerations. It is by no means every monarchy which we can call straight off a kingship, but only that which is voluntarily accepted by the subjects and where they are governed rather by an appeal to their reason than by fear and force. Nor again can we style every oligarchy an aristocracy, but only that where the government is in the hands of a selected body of the justest and wisest men. Similarly that is no true democracy in which the whole crowd of citizens is free to do whatever they wish or purpose, but when, in a community where it is traditional and customary to reverence the gods, to honour our parents, to respect our elders, and to obey the laws, the will of the greater number prevails, this is to be called a democracy. We should therefore assert that there are six kinds of governments, the three

* From Polybius, *The Histories* (trans. W. R. Paton, Loeb Classical Library, Harvard University Press, 1923), Vol. III. By permission.

above mentioned which are in everyone's mouth and the three which are naturally allied to them, I mean monarchy, oligarchy, and mob-rule. Now the first of these to come into being is monarchy, its growth being natural and unaided; and next arises kingship derived from monarchy by the aid of art and by the correction of defects. Monarchy first changes into its vicious allied form, tyranny; and next, the abolishment of both gives birth to aristocracy. Aristocracy by its very nature degenerates into oligarchy; and when the commons inflamed by anger take vengeance on this government for its unjust rule, democracy comes into being; and in due course the licence and lawlessness of this form of government produces mob-rule to complete the series. The truth of what I have just said will be quite clear to anyone who pays due attention to such beginnings, origins, and changes as are in each case natural. For he alone who has seen how each form naturally arises and develops, will be able to see when, how, and where the growth, perfection, change and end of each are likely to occur again. And it is to the Roman constitution above all that this method, I think, may be successfully applied, since from the outset its formation and growth have been due to natural causes.

2. The Causes of Political Change

Perhaps this theory of the natural transformations into each other of the different forms of government is more elaborately set forth by Plato and certain other philosophers; but as the arguments are subtle and are stated at great length, they are beyond the reach of all but a few. I therefore will attempt to give a short summary of the theory, as far as I consider it to apply to the actual history of facts and to appeal to the common intelligence of mankind. For if there appear to be certain omissions in my general exposition of it, the detailed discussion which follows will afford the reader ample compensation for any difficulties now left unsolved.

What then are the beginnings I speak of and what is the first origin of political societies? When owing to floods, famines, failure of crops or other such causes there occurs such a destruction of the human race as tradition tells us has more than once happened, and as we must believe will often happen again, all arts and crafts perishing at the same time, then in the course of time, when springing from the survivors as from seeds men have again increased in numbers and just like other animals form herds— it being a matter of course that they too should herd together with those of their kind owing to their natural weakness—it is a necessary consequence that the man who excels in bodily strength and in courage will lead and rule over the rest. We observe and should regard as a most genuine work of nature this very phenomenon in the case of the other animals which act purely by instinct and among whom the strongest are always indisputably the masters—I speak of bulls, boars, cocks, and the like. It is probable then that at the beginning men lived thus, herding together like animals and following the lead of the strongest and bravest, the ruler's strength being here the sole limit to his power and the name we should give his rule being monarchy.

But when in time feelings of sociability and companionship begin to grow in such gatherings of men, then kingship has struck root; and the notions of goodness, justice, and their opposites begin to arise in men. The manner in which these notions come into being is as follows. Men being all naturally inclined to sexual intercourse, and the consequence of this being the birth of children, whenever one of those who have been reared does not on growing up show gratitude to those who reared him or defend them, but on the contrary takes to speaking ill of them or ill treating them, it is evident that he will displease and offend those who have been familiar with his parents and have witnessed the care and pains they spent on attending to and feeding their children. For seeing that men are distinguished from the other animals by possessing the faculty of reason, it is obviously improbable that such a difference of conduct should escape them, as it escapes the other animals: they will notice the thing and be displeased at what is going on, looking to the future and reflecting that they may all meet with the same treatment. Again when a man who has been helped or succoured when in danger by another does not show gratitude to his preserver, but even goes to the length of attempting to do him injury, it is clear that those who become aware of it will naturally be displeased and offended by such conduct, sharing the resentment of their injured neighbour and imagining themselves in the same situation. From all this there arises in everyone a notion of the meaning and theory of duty, which is the beginning and end of justice. Similarly, again, when any man is foremost in defending his fellows from danger, and braves and awaits the onslaught of the most powerful beasts, it is natural that he should receive marks of favour and honour from the people, while the man who acts in the opposite manner will meet with reprobation and dislike. From this again some idea of what is base and what is noble and of what constitutes the difference is likely to arise among the people; and noble conduct will be admired and imitated because it is advantageous, while base conduct will be avoided. Now when the leading and most powerful man among the people always throws the weight of his authority on the side of the notions on such matters which generally prevail, and when in the opinion of his subjects he apportions rewards and penalties according to desert, they yield obedience to him no longer because they fear his force, but rather because their judgement approves him; and they join in maintaining his rule even if he is quite enfeebled by age, defending him with one consent and battling against those who conspire to overthrow his rule. Thus by insensible degrees the monarch becomes a king, ferocity and force having yielded the supremacy to reason.

Thus is formed naturally among men the first notion of goodness and justice, and their opposites; this is the beginning and birth of true kingship. For the people maintain the supreme power not only in the hands of these men themselves, but in those of their descendants, from the conviction that those born from and reared by such men will also have principles like to theirs. And if they ever are displeased with the descendants, they now choose their kings and rulers no longer for their bodily strength and brute courage, but for the excellency of their judgement and reasoning powers, as they have gained experience from actual facts of the difference between the one class of qualities and the other. In old times, then, those who had once been chosen to the royal office continued to hold it until they grew old, fortifying and enclosing fine strongholds with walls and acquiring lands, in the one case for the sake of the security of their subjects and in the other to provide them with abundance of the necessities of life. And while pursuing these aims, they were exempt from all vituperation or jealousy, as neither in their dress nor in their food and drink did they make any great distinction, but lived very much like everyone else, not keeping apart from the people. But when they received the office by hereditary succession and found their safety now provided for, and more than sufficient provision of food, they gave way to their appetites owing to this superabundance, and came to think that the rulers must be distinguished from their subjects by a peculiar dress, that there should be a peculiar luxury and variety in the dressing and serving of their viands, and that they should meet with no denial in the pursuit of their amours, however lawless. These habits having given rise in the one case to envy and offence and in the other to an outburst of hatred and passionate resentment, the kingship changed into a tyranny; the first steps towards its overthrow were taken by the subjects, and conspiracies began to be formed. These conspiracies were not the work of the worst men, but of the noblest, most high-spirited, and most courageous, because such men are least able to brook the insolence of princes. The people now having got leaders, would combine with them against the ruling powers for the reasons I stated above; kingship and monarchy would be utterly abolished, and in their place aristocracy would begin to grow. For the commons, as if bound to pay at once their debt of gratitude to the abolishers of monarchy, would make them their leaders and entrust their destinies to them. At first these chiefs gladly assumed this charge and regarded nothing as of greater importance than the common interest, administering the private and public affairs of the people with paternal solicitude. But here again when children inherited this position of authority from their fathers, having no experience of misfortune and none at all of civil equality and liberty of speech, and having been brought up from the cradle amid the evidences of the power and high position of their fathers, they abandoned themselves some to greed of gain and unscrupulous money-making, others to indulgence in wine and the convivial excess which accompanies it, and others again to the violation of women and the rape of boys; and thus converting the aristocracy into an oligarchy aroused in the people feelings similar to those of which I just spoke, and in consequence met with the same disastrous end as the tyrant. For whenever anyone who has noticed the jealousy and hatred with which they are regarded by the citizens, has the courage to speak or act against the chiefs of the state he has the whole mass of the people ready to back him. Next, when they have either killed or banished the oligarchs, they no longer venture to set a king over them, as they still remember with terror the injustice they suffered from the former ones, nor can they entrust the government with confidence to a select few, with the evidence before them of their recent error in doing so. Thus the only hope still surviving unimpaired is in themselves, and to this they resort, making the state a democracy instead of an oligarchy and assuming the responsibility for the conduct of affairs. Then as long as some of those survive who experienced the evils of oligarchical dominion, they are well pleased with the present form of government, and set a high value on equality and freedom of speech. But when a new generation arises and the democracy falls into the hands of the grandchildren of its founders, they have become so accustomed to freedom and equality that they no longer value them, and begin to aim at pre-eminence; and it is chiefly those of ample fortune who fall into this error. So when they begin to lust for power and cannot attain it through themselves or their own good qualities, they ruin their estates, tempting and corrupting the people in every possible way. And hence when by their foolish thirst for reputation they have created among the masses an appetite for gifts and the habit of receiving them, democracy in its turn is abolished and changes into a rule of force and violence. For the people, having grown accustomed to feed at the expense of others and to depend for their livelihood on the property of others, as soon as they find a leader who is enterprising but is excluded from the honours of office by his penury, institute the rule of violence; and now uniting their forces massacre, banish, and plunder, until they degenerate again into perfect savages and find once more a master and monarch.

Such is the cycle of political revolution, the course appointed by nature in which constitutions change, disappear, and finally return to the point from which they started. Anyone who clearly perceives this may indeed in speaking of the future of any state be wrong in his estimate of the time the process will take, but if his judgement is not tainted by animosity or jealousy, he will very seldom be mistaken as to the stage of growth or decline it has reached, and as to the form into which it will change. And especially in the case of the Roman state will this method enable us to arrive at a knowledge of its formation, growth, and greatest perfection, and likewise of the change for the worse which is sure to follow some day. For, as I said, this state, more than any other, has been formed and has grown naturally, and will undergo a natural decline and change to its contrary.

At present I will give a brief account of the legislation of Lycurgus, a matter not alien to my present purpose. Lycurgus had perfectly well understood that all the above changes take place necessarily and naturally, and had taken into consideration that every variety of constitution which is simple and formed on one principle is precarious, as it is soon perverted into the corrupt form which is proper to it and naturally follows on it. For just as rust in the case of iron and wood-worms and ship-worms in the case of timber are inbred pests, and these substances, even though they escape all external injury, fall a prey to the evils engendered in them, so each constitution has a vice engendered in it and inseparable from it. In kingship it is despotism, in aristocracy oligarchy, and in democracy the savage rule of violence; and it is impossible, as I said above, that each of these should not in course of time change into this vicious form. Lycurgus, then, foreseeing this, did not make his constitution simple and uniform, but united in it all the good and distinctive features of the best governments, so that none of the principles should grow unduly and be perverted into its allied evil, but that, the force of each being neutralized by that of the others, neither of them should prevail and outbalance another, but that the constitution should remain for long in a state of equilibrium like a well-trimmed boat, kingship being guarded from arrogance by the fear of the commons, who were given a sufficient share in the government, and the commons on the other hand not venturing to treat the kings with contempt from fear of the elders, who being selected from the best citizens would be sure all of them to be always on the side of justice; so that that part of the state which was weakest owing to its subservience to traditional custom, acquired power and weight by the support and influence of the elders. The consequence was that by drawing up his constitution thus he preserved liberty at Sparta for a longer period than is recorded elsewhere.

Lycurgus then, foreseeing, by a process of reasoning, whence and how events naturally happen, constructed his constitution untaught by adversity, but the Romans while they have arrived at the same final result as regards their form of government, have not reached it by any process of reasoning, but by the discipline of many struggles and troubles, and always choosing the best by the light of the experience gained in disaster have thus reached the same result as Lycurgus, that is to say, the best of all existing constitutions.

3. Advantages of a Mixed Constitution

The three kinds of government that I spoke of above all shared in the control of the Roman state. And such fairness and propriety in all respects was shown in the use of these three elements for drawing up the constitution and in its subsequent administration that it was impossible even for a native to pronounce with certainty whether the whole system was aristocratic, democratic, or monarchical. This was indeed only natural. For if one fixed one's eyes on the power of the consuls, the constitution seemed completely monarchical and royal; if on that of the senate, it seemed again to be aristocratic; and when one looked at the power of the masses, it seemed clearly to be a democracy. The parts of the state falling under the control of each element were and with a few modifications still are as follows.

The consuls, previous to leading out their legions, exercise authority in Rome over all public affairs, since all the other magistrates except the tribunes are under them and bound to obey them, and it is they who introduce embassies to the senate. Besides this it is they who consult the senate on matters of urgency, they who carry out in detail the provisions of its decrees. Again as concerns all affairs of state administered by the people it is their duty to take these under their charge, to summon assemblies, to introduce measures, and to preside over the execution of the popular decrees. As for preparation for war and the general conduct of operations in the field, here their power is almost uncontrolled; for they are empowered to make what demands they choose on the allies, to appoint military tribunes, to levy soldiers and select those who are fittest for service. They also have the right of inflicting, when on active service, punishment on anyone under their command; and they are authorized to spend any sum they decide upon from the public funds, being accompanied by a quaestor who faithfully executes their instructions. So that if one looks at this part of the administration alone, one may reasonably pronounce the constitution to be a pure monarchy or kingship. I may remark that any changes in these matters or in others of which I am about to speak that may be made in present or future times do not in any way affect the truth of the views I here state.

To pass to the senate. In the first place it has the control of the treasury, all revenue and expenditure being regulated by it. For with the exception of payments made to the consuls, the quaestors are not allowed to disburse for any particular object without a decree of the senate. And even the item of expenditure which is far heavier and more important than any other—the outlay every five years by the censors on public works, whether constructions or repairs—is under the control of the senate, which makes a grant to the censors for the purpose. Similarly crimes committed in Italy which require a public investigation, such as treason, conspiracy, poisoning, and assassination, are under the jurisdiction of the senate. Also if any private person or community in Italy is in need of arbitration or indeed claims damages or requires succour or protection, the senate attends to all such matters. It also occupies itself with the dispatch of all embassies sent to countries outside of Italy for the purpose either of settling differences, or of offering friendly advice, or indeed of imposing demands, or of receiving submission, or of declaring war; and in like manner with respect to embassies arriving in Rome it decides what reception and what answer should be given to them. All these matters are in the hands of the senate, nor have the people anything whatever to do with them. So that again to one residing in Rome during the absence of the consuls the constitution appears to be entirely aristocratic; and this is the conviction of many Greek states and many of the kings, as the senate manages all business connected with them.

After this we are naturally inclined to ask what part in the constitution is left for the people, considering that the senate controls all the particular matters I mentioned, and, what is most important, manages all matters of revenue and expenditure, and considering that the consuls again have uncontrolled authority as regards armaments and operations in the field. But nevertheless there is a part and a very important part left for the people. For it is the people which alone has the right to confer honours and inflict punishment, the only bonds by which kingdoms and states and in a word human society in general are held together. For where the distinction between these is overlooked or is observed but ill applied, no affairs can be properly administered. How indeed is this possible when good and evil men are held in equal estimation? It is by the people, then, in many cases that offences punishable by a fine are tried when the accused have held the highest office; and they are the only court which may try on capital charges. As regards the latter they have a practice which is praiseworthy and should be mentioned. Their usage allows those on trial for their lives when found guilty liberty to depart openly, thus inflicting voluntary exile on themselves, if even only one of the tribes that pronounce the verdict has not yet voted. Such exiles enjoy safety in the territories of Naples, Praeneste, Tibur, and other *civitates foederatae*. Again it is the people who bestow office on the deserving, the noblest reward of virtue in a state; the people have the power of approving or rejecting laws, and what is most important of all, they deliberate on the question of war and peace. Further in the case of alliances, terms of peace, and treaties, it is the people who ratify all these or the reverse. Thus here again one might plausibly say that the people's share in the government is the greatest, and that the constitution is a democratic one.

Having stated how political power is distributed among the different parts of the state, I will now explain how each of the three parts is enabled, if they wish, to counteract or co-operate with the others. The consul, when he leaves with his army invested with the powers I mentioned, appears indeed to have absolute authority in all matters necessary for carrying out his purpose; but in fact he requires the support of the people and the senate, and is not able to bring his operations to a conclusion without them. For it is obvious that the legions require constant supplies, and without the consent of the senate, neither corn, clothing, nor pay can be provided; so that the commander's plans come to nothing, if the senate chooses to be deliberately negligent and obstructive. It also depends on the senate whether or not a general can carry out completely his conceptions and designs, since it has the right of either superseding him when his year's term of office has expired or of retaining him in command. Again it is in its power to celebrate with pomp and to magnify the successes of a general or on the other hand to obscure and belittle them. For the processions they call triumphs, in which the generals bring the actual spectacle of their achievements before the eyes of their fellow-citizens, cannot be properly organized and sometimes even cannot be held at all, unless the senate consents and provides the requisite funds. As for the people it is most indispensable for the consuls to conciliate them, however far away from

home they may be; for, as I said, it is the people which ratifies or annuls terms of peace and treaties, and what is most important, on laying down office the consuls are obliged to account for their actions to the people. So that in no respect is it safe for the consuls to neglect keeping in favour with both the senate and the people.

The senate again, which possesses such great power, is obliged in the first place to pay attention to the commons in public affairs and respect the wishes of the people, and it cannot carry out inquiries into the most grave and important offences against the state, punishable with death, and their correction, unless the *senatus consultum* is confirmed by the people. The same is the case in matters which directly affect the senate itself. For if anyone introduces a law meant to deprive the senate of some of its traditional authority, or to abolish the precedence and other distinctions of the senators or even to curtail them of their private fortunes, it is the people alone which has the power of passing or rejecting any such measure. And what is most important is that if a single one of the tribunes interposes, the senate is unable to decide finally about any matter, and cannot even meet and hold sittings; and here it is to be observed that the tribunes are always obliged to act as the people decree and to pay every attention to their wishes. Therefore for all these reasons the senate is afraid of the masses and must pay due attention to the popular will.

Similarly, again, the people must be submissive to the senate and respect its members both in public and in private. Through the whole of Italy a vast number of contracts, which it would not be easy to enumerate, are given out by the censors for the construction and repair of public buildings, and besides this there are many things which are farmed, such as navigable rivers, harbours, gardens, mines, lands, in fact everything that forms part of the Roman dominion. Now all these matters are undertaken by the people, and one may almost say that everyone is interested in these contracts and the work they involve. For certain people are the actual purchasers from the censors of the contracts, others are the partners of these first, others stand surety for them, others pledge their own fortunes to the state for this purpose. Now in all these matters the senate is supreme. It can grant extension of time; it can relieve the contractor if any accident occurs; and if the work proves to be absolutely impossible to carry out it can liberate him from his contract. There are in fact many ways in which the senate can either benefit or injure those who manage public property, as all these matters are referred to it. What is even more important is that the judges in most civil trials, whether public or private, are appointed from its members, where the action involves large interests. So that all citizens being at the mercy of the senate, and looking forward with alarm to the uncertainty of litigation, are very shy of obstructing or resisting its decisions. Similarly everyone is reluctant to oppose the projects of the consuls as all are generally and individually under their authority when in the field.

Such being the power that each part has of hampering the others or co-operating with them, their union is adequate to all emergencies, so that it is impossible to find a better political system than this. For whenever the menace of some common danger from abroad compels them to act in concord and support each other, so great does the strength of the state become, that nothing which is requisite can be neglected, as all are zealously competing in devising means of meeting the need of the hour, nor can any decision arrived at fail to be executed promptly, as all are co-operating both in public and in private to the accomplishment of the task they have set themselves; and consequently this peculiar form of constitution possesses an irresistible power of attaining every object upon which it is resolved. When again they are freed from external menace, and reap the harvest of good fortune and affluence which is the result of their success, and in the enjoyment of this

prosperity are corrupted by flattery and idleness and wax insolent and overbearing, as indeed happens often enough, it is then especially that we see the state providing itself a remedy for the evil from which it suffers. For when one part having grown out of proportion to the others aims at supremacy and tends to become too predominant, it is evident that, as for the reasons above given none of the three is absolute, but the purpose of the one can be counterworked and thwarted by the others, none of them will excessively outgrow the others or treat them with contempt. All in fact remains *in statu quo*, on the one hand, because any aggressive impulse is sure to be checked and from the outset each estate stands in dread of being interfered with by the others.

4. Integrity in Public Affairs

The laws and customs relating to the acquisition of wealth are better in Rome than at Carthage. At Carthage nothing which results in profit is regarded as disgraceful; at Rome nothing is considered more so than to accept bribes and seek gain from improper channels. For no less strong than their approval of money-making by respectable means is their condemnation of unscrupulous gain from forbidden sources. A proof of this is that at Carthage candidates for office practise open bribery, whereas at Rome death is the penalty for it. Therefore as the rewards offered to merit are the opposite in the two cases, it is natural that the steps taken to gain them should also be dissimilar.

But the quality in which the Roman commonwealth is most distinctly superior is in my opinion the nature of their religious convictions. I believe that it is the very thing which among other peoples is an object of reproach, I mean superstition, which maintains the cohesion of the Roman State. These matters are clothed in such pomp and introduced to such an extent into their public and private life that nothing could exceed it, a fact which will surprise many. My own opinion at least is that they have adopted this course for the sake of the common people. It is a course which perhaps would not have been necessary had it been possible to form a state composed of wise men, but as every multitude is fickle, full of lawless desires, unreasoned passion, and violent anger, the multitude must be held in by invisible terrors and suchlike pageantry. For this reason I think, not that the ancients acted rashly and at haphazard in introducing among the people notions concerning the gods and beliefs in the terrors of hell, but that the moderns are most rash and foolish in banishing such beliefs. The consequence is that among the Greeks, apart from other things, members of the government, if they are entrusted with no more than a talent, though they have ten copyists and as many seals and twice as many witnesses, cannot keep their faith; whereas among the Romans those who as magistrates and legates are dealing with large sums of money maintain correct conduct just because they have pledged their faith by oath. Whereas elsewhere it is a rare thing to find a man who keeps his hands off public money, and whose record is clean in this respect, among the Romans one rarely comes across a man who has been detected in such conduct.

5. The Decay of Political Glory

That all existing things are subject to decay and change is a truth that scarcely needs proof; for the course of nature is sufficient to force this conviction on us.

There being two agencies by which every kind of state is liable to decay, the one external and the other a growth of the state itself, we can lay down no fixed rule about the former, but the latter is a regular process. I have already stated what kind of state is the first to come into being, and what the next, and how the one is transformed into the other; so that those who are capable of connecting the opening propositions of this inquiry with its conclusion will now be able to foretell the future unaided. And what will happen is, I think, evident. When a state has weathered many great perils and subsequently attains to supremacy and uncontested sovereignty, it is evident that under the influence of long established prosperity, life will become more extravagant and the citizens more fierce in their rivalry regarding office and other objects than they ought to be. As these defects go on increasing, the beginning of the change for the worse will be due to love of office and the disgrace entailed by obscurity, as well as to extravagance and purse-proud display; and for this change the populace will be responsible when on the one hand they think they have a grievance against certain people who have shown themselves grasping, and when, on the other hand, they are puffed up by the flattery of others who aspire to office. For now, stirred to fury and swayed by passion in all their counsels, they will no longer consent to obey or even to be the equals of the ruling caste, but will demand the lion's share for themselves. When this happens, the state will change its name to the finest sounding of all, freedom and democracy, but will change its nature to the worst thing of all, mob-rule.

CHAPTER 4

CICERO

BECAUSE Roman political thought was not expressed in systematic philosophical works, it has been wrongly assumed by many not to have existed
at all. Of political *theory*, expressed in formal treatises by professional thinkers
and publicists, there is not much in Roman literature that compares with the
brilliant masterpieces of Greek philosophers. But political theory is only one of
the sources of political *thought*, its obvious and most directly accessible expression, but not necessarily its most creative one. The political ideas of a nation or
an era may, in some instances, have to be culled from less formal and direct
sources than systematic treatises by philosophers and political writers. Law, lore,
and literature may be important sources for the study of political thinking,
though one will find in them more its indirect reflection than its direct statement.
But what such sources lack in easy availability and overt presentation, they gain
in variety, authenticity, and richness.

This approach to Roman political thought is perhaps not quite so unique
as may appear at first sight. If one were to look for the most enduring expressions
of American political thought in the first half of the twentieth century, one would
probably profit more from an examination, say, of the judicial opinions of jurists
like Holmes, Hughes, Sutherland, Brandeis, Cardozo, and Black than from the
mass of formal theory produced by professional political writers and publicists.

Law and administration are the two great contributions of Rome to the
conceptions and practices of government and politics in the western world. The
Roman law, constantly adapting itself to changing environments, is still the law
of a goodly portion of the globe; its existence to this day as the predominant
system on the European Continent, in Latin America, in parts of North America,
and in Asia and Africa is proof of a vitality that, enduring for over two thousand
years, has been nourished by sources more spiritual than those imposition by
armed conquest could have supplied. The flexibility of Roman law, its capacity
to adjust itself to changing social and economic conditions, its ability to grow
from the law of a city into that of a world empire, its willingness to admit the

121

stranger different in speech and religion into the world-wide community in which the *pax romana* reigned supreme—all this could hardly have been the result of "muddling through"; it was, in fact, the reflection of political wisdom of the highest order. Rome eagerly accepted the universalistic heritage of Hellenic civilization and passed it on to the western world through institutions rather than through ideas. The marriage between Greek speculative and Roman institutional genius has brought forth much that has become an integral part of the political inheritance of the world.

The only Roman political writer who has exercised enduring influence throughout the ages is Cicero (106–43 B. C.). Characteristically, he was not a professional philosopher and leader of a school or academy of his own, but a lawyer and statesman whose works are reflections on politics rather than on political theory. Like other educated Romans of his class, he owed his philosophical outlook as much to Plato and Aristotle as to Stoicism.

Cicero studied law in Rome, and philosophy in Athens and other Greek centers of learning, and he early acquired wide contacts with other peoples and civilizations. He became the leading lawyer of his time and also rose to the highest offices of state, both in Rome and in the provinces. Yet his life was not free from sadness; only five years after he had held the highest office in Rome, the consulate, he found himself in exile for a year, and his political fortunes never reached their previous summit.

Rome, unable to solve the growing social and imperial problems in the framework of the traditional institutions of the Republic, incessantly moved toward monarchical government. Cicero thought primarily of political and administrative remedies for the decay of the ancient republican spirit, and he had little understanding of the profound economic issues and cleavages that the rise of a propertyless proletariat in Rome and the other large cities had produced. Instead of looking into the future and accepting as permanent the new social and economic forces in Roman life, he looked back into a past in which these forces had not existed. When confronted with a sweeping popular movement of the poorer classes against the rich, led by Catiline, Cicero suppressed it ruthlessly, and had its leaders executed under circumstances that were hardly legal. Because the aristocrats and wealthy businessmen, Cicero's political friends, understood the revolutionary implications of these social and economic transformations no better than he did, monarchical government, based on considerable popular support, supplanted the proud Republic in which freedom had been nursed to greatness in so many generations.

Cicero fervently believed in moderation, concord, and constitutionalism; such a political faith flourishes best in a time of social stability. When this stability has become seriously undermined by intolerable rifts in society, constitutionalism as a purely political faith offers no solution, unless supplemented by basic social and economic reforms. And when men of moderation and good will fail, demagogues and dictators will take their place and often carry through, albeit in a perverted and distorted fashion, the reforms that, if applied by the conservatives in time, might have saved the traditional fabric of the state.

Realizing the danger too late, Cicero nevertheless showed considerable personal courage in opposing the drift toward dictatorship based on popular support. Caesar was assassinated in 44 B. C., and a year later, in 43 B. C., Cicero was murdered by the henchmen of Antony, a member of the triumvirate set up after Caesar's death. In an age of social revolution, the plea for honest government is not enough.

Cicero's two main works on government are his *Republic* and *Laws*, written in obvious reference to Plato's two works of the same titles. Superficially there is a great deal in Cicero's two works that appears to be a close imitation of Plato and Aristotle. Yet when it comes to the inner meaning of Cicero's political views, his temper and outlook, there is a remarkable freshness and difference. Most important of all, perhaps, Cicero had a *sense of the world*, whereas Plato and Aristotle were never able to go beyond the conception of the *city-state* as the ultimate in political organization. Both Plato and Aristotle had no place for mankind in their political theories; the world was divided in Greeks and others, who were barbarians and—as Aristotle clearly avowed—inferior to cultured Greeks, who had the right to enslave them. By contrast, Cicero had a more universal outlook, fostered by his political and administrative experience in Rome and the empire, and also fed by the springs of Hellenic Stoicism, which had spread throughout the Mediterranean basin.

Cicero believed in the mission of the Roman empire, but he understood that imperial unity could be attained only through liberty and self-government of the constituent parts, and there was an element of truth in his statement that the Romans "by defending their allies have gained dominion over the whole world." Though every empire profits, in the last analysis, its founders more than its dependent beneficiaries, the Roman empire spread throughout the then-known world and lasted for centuries because the gap between promise and fulfillment was rarely felt to be offensive and intolerable. Cicero believed that the whole universe is "one commonwealth of which both gods and men are members," and that there is a law "valid for all nations and all times." Whereas the general Greek view, as typically expressed by Aristotle, held that some people were superior to others, Cicero said that "there is no human being of any race who, if he finds a guide, cannot attain to virtue."

One of the characteristic assumptions of both Plato's *Republic* and Aristotle's *Politics* is the implicit faith that, once general principles of government are laid down, the process of government can be safely entrusted to the rulers. Philosophy, not law, is the queen of both Plato's and Aristotle's masterpieces. By contrast, Cicero—the Roman, the practicing lawyer, the experienced administrator, the fighting statesman—always speaks of law whenever he discusses the state: in one of his briefest definitions, the state is a "community of law" (*iuris societas*). The *rule of law* is important to him, and he says that although "we cannot agree to equalize men's wealth, and equality of innate ability is impossible, the legal rights at least of those who are citizens of the same commonwealth ought to be equal."

Cicero derived his faith in law as the basis of civilized life not only from his Roman background and legal training but from his personal creed. The very idea of existence was linked to that of law and government, "without which existence is impossible for a household, a city, a nation, the human race, physical nature, and the universe itself." But Cicero refused to think of law only in terms of formal authority and compulsion: "True law is right reason in agreement with nature." The task of justice is therefore to discover the "nature of things" in a given situation rather than to impose upon it a preconceived solution, supplied either by revelatory insights or logical deductions. By maintaining that man is the only living creature endowed with the faculty of thinking and reasoning, Cicero emphasizes again the oneness of mankind. All men have this faculty in common, and "those who have reason in common must also have right reason in common," that is, common conceptions of law and justice.

There is another note, too, in Cicero that points forward, toward Christianity, rather than backward, to Plato and Aristotle: Cicero's consciousness of *love* as a mighty social bond. Both Plato and Aristotle were more than pure rationalists, and the *Republic* as well as the *Politics* starts out with the hypothesis that man is by nature a social animal, and that the state is the ultimate development of man's need of society. Plato and Aristotle agree that man's social needs and sympathies are the source and starting point of political associations culminating in the state. But the sentiments and instincts of man are, for Plato and Aristotle, no more than the raw material out of which creative reason molds social and political institutions, and it is by their concordance with reason that these institutions can be measured. Affection was, for Plato and Aristotle, a genetic source of the growth of political association, the state, but not a standard by which it could be tested. Cicero sees, by contrast, the foundation of law in "our natural inclination to love our fellow-men."

This aspect of Cicero exercised a profound influence on the early fathers of the church. At the beginning of the Middle Ages he was perhaps more widely read and quoted than other ancient political writers, as he seemed to pass on a great deal of the best in classical Greek thinking, combined with a new attitude that harmonized with the teachings of Christianity.

In his reflections on the various forms of state, Cicero follows the Aristotelian principle that the distinguishing criterion is the *end* of the state; when its purpose is justice, it makes little difference whether the form is kingship, aristocracy, or democracy. More skeptical than Aristotle, however, Cicero did not advocate any of the three desirable forms of state, because he feared that kingship might develop too easily into tyranny, aristocracy into plutocracy, and democracy into anarchical mob rule. Cicero therefore considered a "balanced combination" between kingship, aristocracy, and democracy the best constitution; his belief in the virtues of the mixed constitution went back to Aristotle, but it was also a lesson of Roman political history that an astute observer like Cicero could hardly have missed.

Where Cicero goes further than Aristotle is in his stress on popular consent as the foundation of legitimate government, and on liberty: "Liberty has no dwelling-place in any state except that in which the people's power is the greatest, and surely nothing can be sweeter than liberty; but if it is not the same for all, it does not deserve the name of liberty." The principle of popular consent as a source of the law was a commonplace to a Roman lawyer; the conception

of the people (*populus*) as a political and legal force in the process of government acquired in Roman constitutional history connotations and undertones
similar to those the word "people" has acquired again in modern times in the
world-wide struggles for democracy and popular self-government. Plato and
Aristotle know of the *polis,* the city-state, and of social classes, but not of the
people. The conception of the "people" in western political thinking is a contribution, not of Roman philosophy, but of Roman public law.

CICERO

The Republic and The Laws *

1. Civic Responsibility: Its Duties and Rewards

[Without active patriotism] [1] . . . could
[never] have delivered [our native land]
from attack; nor could Gaius Duelius,
Aulus Atilius, or Lucius Metellus have
freed [Rome] from her fear of Carthage;
nor could the two Scipios [2] have extinguished with their blood the rising flames
of the Second Punic War; nor, when it
broke forth again with greater fury, could
Quintus Maximus [3] have reduced it to impotence or Marcus Marcelus have crushed
it; nor could Publius Africanus [4] have torn
it from the gates of this city and driven it
within the enemy's walls.

Marcus Cato again, unknown and of obscure birth—by whom, as by a pattern for

our emulation, all of us who are devoted to
the same pursuits are drawn to diligence
and valour—might surely have remained at
Tusculum in the enjoyment of the leisurely
life of that healthful spot so near to Rome.
But he, a madman as our friends [5] maintain,
preferred, though no necessity constrained
him, to be tossed by the billows and storms
of our public life even to an extreme old
age, rather than to live a life of complete
happiness in the calm and ease of such retirement. I will not speak of the men, countless in number, who have each been the
salvation of this republic; and as their lives
do not much antedate the remembrance of
the present generation, I will refrain from
mentioning their names, lest someone complain of the omission of himself or some
member of his family. I will content myself with asserting that Nature has implanted in the human race so great a need
of virtue and so great a desire to defend the
common safety that the strength thereof
has conquered all the allurements of pleasure and ease.

---

* From Cicero, *De re publica, De legibus* (trans.
Clinton Walker Keyes, Loeb Classical Library,
Harvard University Press, 1928). By permission.

[1] Conjectural restorations of the sense in fragmentary passages are enclosed in brackets.

[2] Publius Cornelius Scipio (consul 218) and his
brother Gnaeus Cornelius Scipio Calvus (consul
222).

[3] Quintus Fabius Maximus Cunctator.

[4] Publius Cornelius Scipio Africanus Minor.

[5] The Epicureans, whose ideal of a quiet life free
from pain made them discountenance participation
in politics.

But it is not enough to possess virtue, as if it were an art of some sort, unless you make use of it. Though it is true that an art, even if you never use it, can still remain in your possession by the very fact of your knowledge of it, yet the existence of virtue depends entirely upon its use; and its noblest use is the government of the State, and the realization in fact, not in words, of those very things that the philosophers, in their corners, are continually dinning in our ears. For there is no principle enunciated by the philosophers—at least none that is just and honourable—that has not been discovered and established by those who have drawn up codes of law for States. For whence comes our sense of duty? From whom do we obtain the principles of religion? Whence comes the law of nations, or even that law of ours which is called "civil"? Whence justice, honour, fair-dealing? Whence decency, self-restraint, fear of disgrace, eagerness for praise and honour? Whence comes endurance amid toils and dangers? I say, from those men who, when these things had been inculcated by a system of training, either confirmed them by custom or else enforced them by statutes. Indeed Xenocrates, one of the most eminent of philosophers, when asked what his disciples learned, is said to have replied: "To do of their own accord what they are compelled to do by the law." Therefore the citizen who compels all men, by the authority of magistrates and the penalties imposed by law, to follow rules of whose validity philosophers find it hard to convince even a few by their admonitions, must be considered superior even to the teachers who enunciate these principles. For what speech of theirs is excellent enough to be preferred to a State well provided with law and custom? Indeed, just as I think that "cities great and dominant," as Ennius calls them, are to be ranked above small villages and strongholds, so I believe that those who rule such cities by wise counsel and authority are to be deemed far superior, even in wisdom, to those who take no part at all in the business of government. And

since we feel a mighty urge to increase the resources of mankind, since we desire to make human life safer and richer by our thought and effort, and are goaded on to the fulfilment of this desire by Nature herself, let us hold to the course which has ever been that of all excellent men, turning deaf ears to those who, in the hope of even recalling those who have already gone ahead, are sounding the retreat.

As their first objection to these arguments, so well founded and so obviously sound, those who attack them plead the severity of the labour that must be performed in the defence of the State—surely a trifling obstacle to the watchful and diligent man, and one that merits only scorn, not merely with reference to matters of such moment, but even in the case of things of only moderate importance, such as a man's studies, or duties, or even his business affairs. Then too they allege the danger to which life is exposed, and confront brave men with a dishonourable fear of death; yet such men are wont to regard it a greater misfortune to be consumed by the processes of Nature and old age, than to be granted the opportunity of surrendering for their country's sake, in preference to all else, that life which in any event must be surrendered to Nature. On this point, however, the objectors wax wordy and, as they imagine, eloquent, going on to cite the misfortunes of eminent men and the wrongs they have suffered at the hands of their ungrateful fellow-citizens. For at this point they enumerate, first the famous illustrations taken from Greek history—the story of Miltiades, vanquisher and conqueror of the Persians, who, before the wounds had yet healed which he had received full in the front on the occasion of his glorious victory, was cast into chains by his own fellow-countrymen, and at their hands lost the life which the enemy's weapons had spared; and that of Themistocles, who when driven in terror from his country, the land which he had set free, took refuge, not in the harbours of Greece, saved by his prowess, but in the recesses of the barbarian land which he had laid prostrate. Indeed there is no lack of instances of the fickleness and cruelty of Athens toward her most eminent citizens; and this vice, originating and spreading there, has, they say, overflowed even into our own powerful republic. For we are reminded of the exile of Camillus, the disgrace suffered by Ahala, the hatred directed against Nasica, the exile of Laenas, the condemnation of Opimius, the flight of Metellus, the bitter disaster to Gaius Marius, and, a little later, the slaughter and ruin of so many eminent men. In fact they now include my name also, and presumably because they think it was through my counsel and at my risk that their own peaceful life has been preserved to them, they complain even more bitterly and with greater kindness of the treatment I have received. But I find it difficult to say why, when these very men cross the seas merely to gain knowledge and to visit other countries, [they should expect us to be deterred by considerations of danger from the much more important task of defending our native land. For if the philosophers are repaid for the dangers of travel by the knowledge they gain thereby, statesmen surely win a much greater reward in the gratitude of their fellow-citizens. Few may have imagined, in view of all I had suffered, that when,] as I retired from the consulship, I took my oath before an assembly of the people, and the Roman people took the same oath, that the republic was safe [as a result of my efforts alone,] I was amply repaid thereby for all the anxiety and vexation that resulted from the injustice done to me. And yet my sufferings brought me more honour than trouble, more glory than vexation, and the joy I found in the affectionate longing felt for me by good citizens was greater than my grief at the exultation of the wicked. But, as I said before, if it had happened otherwise, how could I complain? For none of the misfortunes that fell to my lot in consequence of my great services was unexpected by me or more serious than I had foreseen. For such was my nature that, although, on account

of the manifold pleasures I found in the studies which had engaged me from boyhood, it would have been possible for me, on the one hand, to reap greater profit from a quiet life than other men, or, on the other hand, if any disaster should happen to us all, to suffer no more than my fair share of the common misfortune, yet I could not hesitate to expose myself to the severest storms, and, I might almost say, even to thunderbolts, for the sake of the safety of my fellow-citizens, and to secure, at the cost of my own personal danger, a quiet life for all the rest. For, in truth, our country has not given us birth and education without expecting to receive some sustenance, as it were, from us in return; nor has it been merely to serve our convenience that she has granted to our leisure a safe refuge and for our moments of repose a calm retreat; on the contrary, she has given us these advantages so that she may appropriate to her own use the greater and more important part of our courage, our talents, and our wisdom, leaving to us for our own private uses only so much as may be left after her needs have been satisfied.

Moreover we ought certainly not to listen to the other excuses to which these men resort, that they may be more free to enjoy the quiet life. They say, for example, that it is mostly worthless men who take part in politics, men with whom it is degrading to be compared, while to have conflict with them, especially when the mob is aroused, is a wretched and dangerous task. Therefore, they maintain, a wise man should not attempt to take the reins, as he cannot restrain the insane and untamed fury of the common herd; nor is it proper for a freeman, by contending with vile and wicked opponents, to submit to the scourgings of abuse or expose himself to wrongs which are intolerable to the wise—as if, in the view of good, brave, and high-minded men, there could be any nobler motive for entering public life than the resolution not to be ruled by wicked men and not to allow the republic to be destroyed by them, seeing that the philosophers themselves, even if they should desire to help, would be impotent.

And who in the world can approve of the single exception they make, when they say that no wise man will take any part in public affairs unless some emergency compels him to do so? As if any greater emergency could come upon anyone than that with which I was confronted; and what could I have done in that crisis unless I had been consul at the time? And how could I have been consul unless I had held to a manner of life from my boyhood which led me to the highest office of State in spite of my equestrian birth? Hence it is clear that the opportunity of serving the State, however great by the dangers with which it is threatened, does not come suddenly, or when we wish it, unless we are in such a position that it is possible for us to take action. It has always seemed to me that the most amazing of the teachings of learned men is that they deny their own ability to steer when the sea is calm, having never learned the art nor cared to know it, while at the same time they assure us that, when the waves dash highest, they will take the helm. For it is their habit to proclaim openly, and even to make it their great boast, that they have neither learned nor do they teach anything about the principles of the State, either to establish it or to safeguard it, and that they consider the knowledge of such things unsuited to learned or wise men, but better to be left to those who have trained themselves in that business. How can it be reasonable, therefore, for them to promise to aid the State in case they are compelled by an emergency to do so, when they do not know how to rule the State when no emergency threatens it, though this is a much easier task than the other? Indeed, if it be true that the wise man does not, as a general thing, willingly descend from his lofty heights to statecraft, but does not decline the duty if conditions force him to assume it, yet I should think he ought by no means to neglect this science of politics, because it is his duty to acquire in advance all the knowledge that, for aught he knows, it may

be necessary for him to use at some future time.

I have treated these matters at considerable length because I have planned and undertaken in this work a discussion of the State; hence, in order that this discussion might not be valueless, I had, in the first place, to remove all grounds for hesitation about taking part in public affairs. Yet if there be any who are influenced by the authority of philosophers, let them for a few moments listen and attend to those whose authority and reputation stand highest among learned men; for even if these have not governed the State themselves, nevertheless, since they have dealt with the State in many investigations and treatises, I consider that they have performed a certain function of their own in the State. And in fact I note that nearly every one of those Seven whom the Greeks called "wise" took an important part in the affairs of government. For there is really no other occupation in which human virtue approaches more closely the august function of the gods than that of founding new States or preserving those already in existence.

2. The Main Types of State

Scipio. Well, then, a commonwealth is the property of a people.[1] But a people is not any collection of human being brought together in any sort of way, but an assemblage of people in large numbers associated in an agreement with respect to justice and a partnership for the common good. The first cause of such an association is not so much the weakness of the individual as a certain social spirit which nature has implanted in man. For man is not a solitary or unsocial creature, but born with such a nature that not even under conditions of great prosperity of every sort [is he willing to be isolated from his fellow men.] . . .

---

[1] *I.e., res publica* (public thing or property) is the same as *res populi* (thing or property of a people).

[About fifteen lines are lost. The following fragment may be part of the missing passage.]

. . . In a short time a scattered and wandering multitude had become a body of citizens by mutual agreement. . . .

. . . . certain seeds, as we may call them, for [otherwise] no source for the other virtues nor for the State itself could be discovered. Such an assemblage of men, therefore, originating for the reason I have mentioned, established itself in a definite place, at first in order to provide dwellings; and this place being fortified by its natural situation and by their labours, they called such a collection of dwellings a town or city, and provided it with shrines and gathering places which were common property. Therefore every people, which is such a gathering of large numbers as I have described, every city, which is an orderly settlement of a people, every commonwealth, which, as I said, is "the property of a people," must be governed by some deliberative body if it is to be permanent. And this deliberative body must, in the first place, always owe its beginning to the same cause as that which produced the State itself. In the second place, this function must either be granted to one man, or to certain selected citizens, or must be assumed by the whole body of citizens. And so when the supreme authority is in the hands of one man, we call him a king, and the form of this State a kingship. When selected citizens hold this power, we say that the State is ruled by an aristocracy. But a popular government (for so it is called) exists when all the power is in the hands of the people. And any one of these three forms of government (if only the bond which originally joined the citizens together in the partnership of the State holds fast), though not perfect or in my opinion the best, is tolerable, though one of them may be superior to another. For either a just and wise king, or a select number of leading citizens, or even the people itself, though this is the least commendable type, can nevertheless, as it seems, form a government that is not unstable, provided that

no elements of injustice or greed are mingled with it.

But in kingships the subjects have too small a share in the administration of justice and in deliberation; and in aristocracies the masses can hardly have their share of liberty, since they are entirely excluded from deliberation for the common weal and from power; and when all the power is in the people's hands, even though they exercise it with justice and moderation, yet the resulting equality itself is inequitable, since it allows no distinctions in rank. Therefore, even though the Persian Cyrus was the most just and wisest of kings, that form of government does not seem to me the most desirable, since "the property of the people" (for that is what a commonwealth is, as I have said) is administered at the nod and caprice of one man; even though the Massilians, now under our protection, are ruled with the greatest justice by a select number of their leading citizens, such a situation is nevertheless to some extent like slavery for a people; and even though the Athenians at certain periods, after they had deprived the Areopagus of its power, succeeded in carrying on all their public business by the resolutions and decrees of the people, their State, because it had no definite distinctions in rank, could not maintain its fair renown.

I am now speaking of these three forms of government, not when they are confused and mingled with one another, but when they retain their appropriate character. All of them are, in the first place, subject each to the faults I have mentioned, and they suffer from other dangerous faults in addition: for before every one of them lies a slippery and precipitous path leading to a certain depraved form that is a close neighbour to it. For underneath the tolerable, or, if you like, the lovable King Cyrus (to cite him as a pre-eminent example) lies the utterly cruel Phalaris, impelling him to an arbitrary change of character; for the absolute rule of one man will easily and quickly degenerate into a tyranny like his. And a close neighbour to the excellent Massilian government, conducted by a few leading citizens, is such a partisan combination of thirty men as once ruled Athens. And as for the absolute power of the Athenian people—not to seek other examples of popular government—when it changed into the fury and licence of a mob . . .

[About fifteen lines are lost. The first two lines of what follows appear to be corrupt, and cannot be translated.]

. . . and likewise some other form usually arises from those I have mentioned, and remarkable indeed are the periodical revolutions and circular courses followed by the constant changes and sequences in governmental forms. A wise man should be acquainted with these changes, but it calls for great citizens and for a man of almost divine powers to foresee them when they threaten, and, while holding the reins of government, to direct their courses and keep them under his control. Therefore I consider a fourth form of government the most commendable—that form which is a well-regulated mixture of the three which I mentioned at first.

Laelius. I know that is your opinion, Africanus, for I have often heard you say so. Nevertheless, if it will not give you too much trouble, I should like to know which you consider the best of the three forms of government of which you have been speaking. For it might help us somewhat to understand . . .

[About fifteen lines are lost. In what follows Scipio is evidently stating the common opinion that liberty is impossible in a monarchy or an aristocracy.]

Scipio. . . . and every State is such as its ruler's character and will make it. Hence liberty has no dwelling-place in any State except that in which the people's power is the greatest, and surely nothing can be sweeter than liberty; but if it is not the same for all, it does not deserve the name of liberty. And how can it be the same for all, I will not say in a kingdom, where there is no obscurity or doubt about the slavery of the subject, but even in States where everyone is ostensibly free? I mean States in which the people vote, elect commanders and officials, are canvassed for their votes, and have bills proposed to them, but really grant only what they would have to grant even if they were unwilling to do so, and are asked to give to others what they do not possess themselves. For they have no share in the governing power, in the deliberative function, or in the courts, over which selected judges preside, for those privileges are granted on the basis of birth or wealth. But in a free nation, such as the Rhodians or the Athenians, there is not one of the citizens who [may not hold the offices of State and take an active part in the government.] . . .

[About fifteen lines are lost. In what follows Scipio evidently continues his summing up of the common arguments in favour of democratic government.]

. . . [Our authorities] say [that] when one person or a few stand out from the crowd as richer and more prosperous, then, as a result of the haughty and arrogant behaviour of these, there arises [a government of one or a few], the cowardly and weak giving way and bowing down to the pride of wealth. But if the people would maintain their rights, they say that no form of government would be superior, either in liberty or happiness, for they themselves would be masters of the laws and the courts, of war and peace, of international agreements, and of every citizen's life and property; this government alone, they believe, can rightly be called a commonwealth, that is, "the property of the people." And it is for that reason, they say, that "the property of the people" is often liberated from the domination of kings or senators, while free peoples do not seek kings or the power and wealth of aristocracies. And indeed they claim that this free popular government ought not to be entirely rejected on account of the excesses of an unbridled mob, for, according to them, when a sovereign people is pervaded by a spirit of harmony and tests every measure by the standard of their own safety and liberty, no form of government is less subject to change or more stable. And they insist that harmony is very easily obtainable in a State where the interests of all are the same, for discord arises from conflicting interests, where different measures are advantageous to different citizens. Therefore they maintain that when a senate has been supreme, the State has never had a stable government, and that such stability is less attainable by far in kingdoms, in which, as Ennius says,

No sacred partnership or honour is.

Therefore, since law is the bond which unites the civic association, and the justice enforced by law is the same for all, by what justice can an association of citizens be held together when there is no equality among the citizens? For if we cannot agree to equalize men's wealth, and equality of innate ability is impossible, the legal rights at least of those who are citizens of the same commonwealth ought to be equal. For what is a State except an association or partnership in justice? . . .

[About fifteen lines are lost. There is no change of topic.]

. . . Indeed they think that States of the other kinds have no right at all to the names which they arrogate to themselves. For why should I give the name of king, the title of Jupiter the Best, to a man who is greedy for personal power and absolute authority, a man who lords it over an oppressed people? Should I not rather call him tyrant? For tyrants may be merciful as well as oppressive; so that the only difference between the nations governed by these rulers is that between the slaves of a kind and those of a cruel master; for in any case the subjects must be slaves. And how could Sparta, at the time when the mode of life inculcated by her constitution was considered so excellent, be assured of always having good and just kings, when a person of any sort, if he was born of the royal family, had to be accepted as king? As to aristocrats, who could tolerate men

that have claimed the title without the people's acquiescence, but merely by their own will? For how is a man adjudged to be "the best"? On the basis of knowledge, skill, learning, [and similar qualities surely, not because of his own desire to possess the title!]

[About thirty lines are lost. At the end of the gap, Scipio is criticizing the arguments for democracy, and stating those for aristocracy.]

. . . If [the State] leaves [the selection of its rulers] to chance,[2] it will be as quickly overturned as a ship whose pilot should be chosen by lot from among the passengers. But if a free people chooses the men to whom it is to entrust its fortunes, and, since it desires its own safety, chooses the best men, then certainly the safety of the State depends upon the wisdom of its best men, especially since Nature has provided not only that those men who are superior in virtue and in spirit should rule the weaker, but also that the weaker should be willing to obey the stronger.

But they claim that this ideal form of State has been rejected on account of the false notions of men, who, through their ignorance of virtue—for just as virtue is possessed by only a few, so it can be distinguished and perceived by only a few—think that the best men are those who are rich, prosperous, or born of famous families. For when, on account of this mistaken notion of the common people, the State begins to be ruled by the riches, instead of the virtue, of a few men, these rulers tenaciously retain the title, though they do not possess the character, of the "best." For riches, names, and power, when they lack wisdom and the knowledge of how to live and to rule over others, are full of dishonour and insolent pride, nor is there any more depraved type of State than that in which the richest are accounted the best. But what can be nobler than the government of the State by virtue? For then the man

---

[2] *I.e.*, chooses its rulers by lot, as had been done in Athens.

who rules others is not himself a slave to any passion, but has already acquired for himself all those qualities to which he is training and summoning his fellows. Such a man imposes no laws upon the people that he does not obey himself, but puts his own life before his fellow-citizens as their law. If a single individual of this character could order all things properly in a State, there would be no need of more than one ruler; or if the citizens as a body could see what was best and agree upon it, no one would desire a selected group of rulers. It has been the difficulty of formulating policies that has transferred the power from a king to a larger number; and the perversity and rashness of popular assemblies that have transferred it from the many to the few. Thus, between the weakness of a single ruler and the rashness of the many, aristocracies have occupied that intermediate position which represents the utmost moderation; and in a State ruled by its best men, the citizens must necessarily enjoy the greatest happiness, being freed from all cares and worries, when once they have entrusted the preservation of their tranquillity to others, whose duty it is to guard it vigilantly and never to allow the people to think that their interests are being neglected by their rulers. For that equality of legal rights of which free peoples are so fond cannot be maintained (for the people themselves, though free and unrestrained, give very many special powers to many individuals, and create great distinctions among men and the honours granted to them), and what is called equality is really most inequitable. For when equal honour is given to the highest and the lowest—for men of both types must exist in every nation—then this very "fairness" is most unfair; but this cannot happen in States ruled by their best citizens. These arguments and others like them, Laelius, are approximately those which are advanced by men who consider this form of government the best.

Laelius. But what about yourself, Scipio? Which of these three forms do you consider the best?

Scipio. You are right to ask which I consider the best of the three, for I do not approve of any of them when employed by itself, and consider the form which is a combination of all them superior to any single one of them. But if I were compelled to approve one single unmixed form, [I might choose] the kingship . . . the name of king seems like that of father to us, since the king provides for the citizens as if they were his own children, and is more eager to protect them than . . . to be sustained by the care of one man who is the most virtuous and most eminent. But here are the aristocrats, with the claim that they can do this more effectively, and that there will be more wisdom in the counsels of several than in those of one man, and an equal amount of fairness and scrupulousness. And here also are the people, shouting with a loud voice that they are willing to obey neither one nor a few, that nothing is sweeter than liberty even to wild beasts, and that all who are slaves, whether to a king or to an aristocracy, are deprived of liberty. Thus kings attract us by our affection for them, aristocracies by their wisdom, and popular governments by their freedom, so that in comparing them it is difficult to say which one prefers.

3. The Best Constitution

. . . [I consider] the best constitution for a State to be that which is a balanced combination of the three forms mentioned, kingship, aristocracy, and democracy, and does not irritate by punishment a rude and savage heart . . .

. . . sixty-five years older, for it was founded in the thirty-ninth year before the first Olympiad. And Lycurgus, who lived in very ancient times, had almost the same idea. This equalized system, this combination of three constitutions, is in my opinion common to those nations and to ours. But the unique characteristic of our own commonwealth—the most splendid conceivable

—I shall describe more completely and accurately, if I can, because nothing like it is to be found in any other State. For those elements which I have mentioned were combined in our State as it was then, and in those of the Spartans and Carthaginians, in such a way that there was no balance among them whatever. For in a State where there is one official who holds office for life, particularly if he be a king, even if there is a senate, such as existed at Rome under the monarchy and at Sparta under the code of Lycurgus, and even if the people possess some power, as they did under our kings—in spite of these facts the royal power is bound to be supreme, and such a government is inevitably a monarchy and will inevitably be so called. And this form of government is the most liable of all to change, because one man's vices can overthrow it and turn it easily toward utter destruction. For not only is the kingship in itself not at all reprehensible, but I am inclined to consider it by far the best of the simple forms of government—if I could approve any of the simple forms—but only so long as it retains its true character. But it does that only when the safety, equal rights, and tranquillity of the citizens are guarded by the life-long authority, the justice, and the perfect wisdom of a single ruler. To be sure a nation ruled by a king is deprived of many things, and particularly of liberty, which does not consist in serving a just master, but in [serving] no [master at all]. . . .

4. Natural Law and the Unity of Mankind

True law is right reason in agreement with nature; it is of universal application, unchanging and everlasting; it summons to duty by its commands, and averts from wrongdoing by its prohibitions. And it does not lay its commands or prohibitions upon good men in vain, though neither have any effect on the wicked. It is a sin to try to alter this law, nor is it allowable to attempt to repeal any part of it, and it is impossible to abolish it entirely. We cannot be freed from its obligations by senate or people, and we need not look outside ourselves for an expounder or interpreter of it. And there will not be different laws at Rome and at Athens, or different laws now and in the future, but one eternal and unchangeable law will be valid for all nations and all times, and there will be one master and ruler, that is, God, over us all, for he is the author of this law, its promulgator, and its enforcing judge. Whoever is disobedient is fleeing from himself and denying his human nature, and by reason of this very fact he will suffer the worst penalties, even if he escapes what is commonly considered punishment.

That animal which we call man, endowed with foresight and quick intelligence, complex, keen, possessing memory, full of reason and prudence, has been given a certain distinguished status by the supreme God who created him; for he is the only one among so many different kinds and varieties of living beings who has a share in reason and thought, while all the rest are deprived of it. But what is more divine, I will not say in man only, but in all heaven and earth, than reason? And reason, when it is full grown and perfected, is rightly called wisdom. Therefore, since there is nothing better than reason, and since it exists both in man and God, the first common possession of man and God is reason. But those who have reason in common must also have right reason in common. And since right reason is Law, we must believe that men have Law also in common with the gods. Further, those who share Law must also share Justice; and those who share these are to be regarded as members of the same commonwealth. If indeed they obey the same authorities and powers, this is true in a far greater degree; but as a matter of fact they do obey this celestial system, the divine mind, and the God of transcendent power. Hence we must now conceive of this whole universe as one commonwealth of which both gods and men are members.

Out of all the material of the philosophers' discussions, surely there comes nothing more valuable than the full realization that we are born for Justice, and that right is based, not upon men's opinions, but upon Nature. This fact will immediately be plain if you once get a clear conception of man's fellowship and union with his fellow-men. For no single thing is so like another, so exactly its counterpart, as all of us are to one another. Nay, if bad habits and false beliefs did not twist the weaker minds and turn them in whatever direction they are inclined, no one would be so like his own self as all men would be like all others. And so, however we may define man, a single definition will apply to all. This is a sufficient proof that there is no difference in kind between man and man; for if there were, one definition could not be applicable to all men; and indeed reason, which alone raises us above the level of the beasts and enables us to draw inferences, to prove and disprove, to discuss and solve problems, and to come to conclusions, is certainly common to us all, and, though varying in what it learns, at least in the capacity to learn it is invariable. For the same things are invariably perceived by the senses, and those things which stimulate the senses, stimulate them in the same way in all men; and those rudimentary beginnings of intelligence to which I have referred, which are imprinted on our minds, are imprinted on all minds alike; and speech, the mind's interpreter, though differing in the choice of words, agrees in the sentiments expressed. In fact, there is no human being of any race who, if he finds a guide, cannot attain to virtue.

But the most foolish notion of all is the belief that everything is just which is found in the customs or laws of nations. Would that be true, even if these laws had been enacted by tyrants? If the well-known Thirty had desired to enact a set of laws at Athens, or if the Athenians without exception were delighted by the tyrants' laws, that would not entitle such laws to be re-garded as just, would it? No more, in my opinion, should that law be considered just which a Roman interrex proposed, to the effect that a dictator might put to death with impunity any citizen he wished, even without a trial. For Justice is one; it binds all human society, and is based on one Law, which is right reason applied to command and prohibition. Whoever knows not this Law, whether it has been recorded in writing anywhere or not, is without Justice.

But if Justice is conformity to written laws and national customs, and if, as the same persons claim, everything is to be tested by the standard of utility, then anyone who thinks it will be profitable to him will, if he is able, disregard and violate the laws. It follows that Justice does not exist at all, if it does not exist in Nature, and if that form of it which is based on utility can be overthrown by that very utility itself. And if Nature is not to be considered the foundation of Justice, that will mean the destruction [of the virtues on which human society depends]. For where then will there be a place for generosity, or love of country, or loyalty, or the inclination to be of service to others or to show gratitude for favours received? For these virtues originate in our natural inclination to love our fellow-men, and this is the foundation of Justice. Otherwise not merely consideration for men but also rites and pious observances in honour of the gods are done away with; for I think that these ought to be maintained, not through fear, but on account of the close relationship which exists between man and God. But if the principles of Justice were founded on the decrees of peoples, the edicts of princes, or the decisions of judges, then Justice would sanction robbery and adultery and forgery of wills, in case these acts were approved by the votes or decrees of the populace. But if so great a power belongs to the decisions and decrees of fools that the laws of Nature can be changed by their votes, then why do they not ordain that what is bad and baneful shall be considered good and salutary? Or, if a law can make Justice out of Injustice, can it not also make good out of bad? But in fact we can perceive the difference between good laws and bad by referring them to no other standard than Nature; indeed, it is not merely Justice and Injustice which are distinguished by Nature, but also and without exception things which are honourable and dishonourable. For since an intelligence common to us all makes things known to us and formulates them in our minds, honourable actions are ascribed by us to virtue, and dishonourable actions to vice; and only a madman would conclude that these judgments are matters of opinion, and not fixed by Nature.

What of the many deadly, the many pestilential statutes which nations put in force? These no more deserve to be called laws than the rules a band of robbers might pass in their assembly. For if ignorant and unskilful men have prescribed deadly poisons instead of healing drugs, these cannot possibly be called physicians' prescriptions; neither in a nation can a statute of any sort be called a law, even though the nation, in spite of its being a ruinous regulation, has accepted it. Therefore Law is the distinction between things just and unjust, made in agreement with that primal and most ancient of all things, Nature; and in conformity to Nature's standard are framed those human laws which inflict punishment upon the wicked but defend and protect the good.

The function of a magistrate is to govern, and to give commands which are just and beneficial and in conformity with the law. For as the laws govern the magistrate, so the magistrate governs the people, and it can truly be said that the magistrate is a speaking law, and the law a silent magistrate. Nothing, moreover, is so completely in accordance with the principles of justice and the demands of Nature (and when I use these expressions, I wish it understood that I mean Law) as is government, without which existence is impossible for a household, a city, a nation, the human race, physical nature, and the universe itself. For the universe obeys God; seas and lands obey the universe, and human life is subject to the decrees of supreme Law.

As one and the same Nature holds together and supports the universe, all of whose parts are in harmony with one another, so men are united by Nature; but by reason of their depravity they quarrel, not realizing that they are of one blood and subject to one and the same protecting power. If this fact were understood, surely man would live the life of the gods!

CHAPTER 5

SLAVE AND EMPEROR: TWO STOIC PHILOSOPHERS

PLATO and Aristotle failed in one vital point: neither clearly perceived that the division of Greece into independent sovereign city-states would finally lead to its political end. Both philosophers took the city-state of their age as much for granted as twentieth-century political writers tend to consider the national state the ultimate in political wisdom. When the Greeks were subjugated, first by Macedon and later by Rome, the teachings of Plato and Aristotle, based on their belief that the Greek city-state was superior to the outside "barbarians," seemed inadequate for the new age of empire. The citizen of formerly self-governing small political communities was reduced from an active citizen-ruler to a passive imperial subject.

What was needed was a philosophy of man as an individual in relation to himself and to the world at large. In the small and highly integrated society of the city-state, human relations were essentially aspects of citizenship, as there was no sharp delimitation between individual and community. On the one hand, the individual was rarely faced with fundamental challenges affecting him as a person, and, on the other, he was seldom drawn into a collectivity so large as to make his individuality disappear altogether. The fall of the city-state and the rise of the Macedonian and Roman empires were political revolutions that called for a new philosophy expressing changed psychological realities. In the new world of empire the old traditional ties of intimate fellowship of the city-state were dissolved; an impersonal and anonymous machinery of government whose object was smooth administrative functioning, and not the good life, took their place.

Deprived of the city-state, the spiritual habitat that had nourished him so long, the individual now found himself tossed between two extremes of existence to which he had to adapt himself. First, he was thrown back on his own inner resources as a person who somehow had to survive in the collapse of traditional political forms and organizations. As his habitual sources of collective support and comfort dwindled, he had to stand on his own feet, derive strength from himself, and learn the lesson that social and political organizations come and go but that individual human beings have to keep on living. This painful discovery of loneliness after centuries of rich communal life must have been a real shock to the inhabitant of the former city-state, whose traditional values and goals did not seem to fit into the new world.

If the vastness and anonymity of empire forced the citizen to become more consciously aware of himself as an individual, depriving him as they did of the traditional sources of satisfaction that are to be derived from a small society, he was also forced to broaden immensely the range of his outlook and to think in terms of the world. In the new political reality of world empire, the city-state was little more than a small unit of local administration, and the individual had to grow accustomed to the fact that he was part of a motley realm, full of strange and unknown peoples, customs, and ideas. Compared with the citizen of the old city-state, the subject of the new empires had to undergo the double strain of being more intensely *individual* and at the same time more *universal* in outlook than he had ever been before.

Such was the intellectual vitality of Greece even after the loss of her political independence that she continued to lead the world in the realm of intellect and philosophy, as she had done in the heyday of Plato and Aristotle; Alexander himself, when he conquered the ancient empires and states of the East, spread the Greek language throughout the new Greco-oriental, or "Hellenistic," world. Although from the viewpoint of narrow Greek patriotism, the Hellenization of "barbarians" might have appeared a falsification and dilution of "pure" Greek culture, from the broader vantage point of world history, Hellenization was the process of transmitting basic values of Greek life and thought to universal civilization. The dilution of tribal purity in the larger stream of hybrid humanity was a relatively small price.

The five centuries from about 300 B. C. to A. D. 200 were predominantly centuries of Hellenistic cultural influence, with Greece proper never failing to play an important part of her own. Even at the peak of Roman political and economic power there was more Hellenization of the Latin world than Romanization of the Hellenistic world. Romanization and Latinization became permanent successes only in areas in which they did not compete with Hellenistic culture. History has never witnessed again such a long hegemony of one civilization; the nearest parallel to it, French cultural leadership in the seventeenth and eighteenth centuries, lasted for about two hundred years, but it was not nearly so expansive and creative, in the sense of entirely transforming existing national societies into an alien pattern of language, art, philosophy, science, and thought.

The Hellenistic period was characterized, however, not only by the impact of Greece on the outside world but also by the continuous entry of non-Greeks into Greek life. Gradually Greece ceased to be the source and instead became the universal clearinghouse of new ideas. In the garb of Greek language and forms, non-Greeks thought, new ideas would be more likely to receive a universal hearing and perhaps acceptance; consequently individual persons and entire families Hellenized their names, adopted the Greek language, studied in Greece or one of the new centers of learning, such as Alexandria, and identified themselves with Hellenistic culture.

The most representative and influential philosophical school of the five centuries from about 300 B. C. to A. D. 200 was *Stoicism*. It was founded by Zeno around 300 B. c., and derived its name from the Painted Porch (or "Stoa") in Athens, in which Zeno used to teach. Zeno was a native of Cyprus, of Hellenized Phoenician origin, and a stranger to Athens. Similarly, nearly all the early leaders of Stoic thought were non-Greeks who came from the fringe of Greek settlements or well beyond them. The geographic variety of Stoicism was matched by its social latitude; it is perhaps symbolic of the personal and universal message of Stoicism that its two most representative figures were a Greek slave from Asia Minor and a Roman emperor.

Epictetus (about A. D. 50–120) was a Phrygian slave who came to Rome at an early age. His master permitted him to study philosophy and later freed him. Epictetus then set up his own school in Rome; in A. D. 89 Emperor Domitian banished philosophers from Rome, and Epictetus went to Greece to teach philosophy there. Like Socrates, Epictetus never wrote a book; a disciple of his, Flavius Arrian, who was a Roman official, recorded Epictetus' lectures and informal conversations in the *Discourses* and a brief *Manual*, or summary, of his basic ideas.

Epictetus was of poor health and became lame early in life. His master, a freedman at Nero's court, once twisted Epictetus' leg. Epictetus serenely smiled: "You will break it." His master continued, and when the leg was broken, Epictetus merely said: "I told you so." This anecdote vividly reflects one of the qualities that popular imagination has come to regard as particularly characteristic of Stoicism: fortitude of mind under all circumstances, the triumph of mind and will over matter and pain.

The most illustrious philosophical successor to Epictetus was Marcus Aurelius (A. D. 121–180), Roman emperor from A. D. 161–180. Marcus Aurelius was born in Rome of a family that was originally Spanish; he was the nephew of his predecessor on the throne and thus acquainted with public affairs from an early age. He is one of the half-dozen philosopher-kings in history, like those of whom Plato had dreamed in the *Republic,* and he was perhaps more in his element as a philosopher than as the ruler of the Roman empire. Like Epictetus, Marcus Aurelius wrote no books. His *Meditations* are not a book, and were not planned as such by him, but are more in the nature of a journal (as the title has often been rendered), informal notes and observations addressed to himself rather than to the public.

The author, though a Roman emperor, wrote in Greek, which he mastered from early youth. The only other famous ruler who wrote in a foreign language was Frederick the Great of Prussia, who preferred French to German, declaring his own tongue "fit for horses." During the period of Marcus Aurelius it was not uncommon for non-Greeks to write in Greek, the language of prestige and universal currency, just as during the seventeenth and eighteenth centuries French had no rival among the educated.

Marcus Aurelius was well aware of his general debt to Stoic predecessors in philosophy, but he felt himself under a particular obligation to Epictetus, whom he deeply venerated and whose sayings he often quoted word by word. By identifying himself so closely with a lowly slave, Marcus Aurelius thus practiced the Stoic faith in the equality of all men, regardless of their nationality and station in life.

The Stoics did not think of themselves primarily as political theorists, and Stoicism is not a theory of the state. This fact, however, did not preclude Stoic thought from exercising a considerable influence on government and politics, partly because so many kings and high officials of the Hellenistic and Roman periods were professing, though not always practicing, Stoics. Stoicism appeals to the individual as an individual rather than as a member of an organized community, and in this characteristic lies its strength and weakness. The moral appeal to the individual is not, as in the closely knit city-state of Plato and Aristotle, to idolize and worship the laws and morals of one's community but to live in accordance with nature.

The Stoic concept of nature was different from the earlier view, which presented numerous demons and gods reveling in unpredictable adventures, as it was distinct from the later view, which conceived of nature as a machine, operating according to physical laws. The Stoic conception of nature was less demonistic and less mechanistic than either: nature includes both the process of growth and the goal and principle toward which this process is moving and to which it seeks to give life. Nature, the whole cosmos, is thus pervaded by goal and purpose, and to live according to nature means to work with it toward the harmony and orderliness that is inherent in it. The "one principle of action that governs all things" is to *be at one with oneself,* to know oneself, and to act in conformity with one's purposes and rational principles.

Like nature, human beings also are subject to an all-pervading harmonious and rational ordering, and just as cosmic peace is the expression of such law and harmony, so tranquillity of the individual "is nothing else than the good ordering of the mind." According to this Stoic view, man and nature are not opposites; both partake of reason and harmony, which are more important than accidental differences. *The "true self" of man* is therefore, not his "flesh or bones or sinews, but the faculty which uses them," that is, *reason,* the part of man that characterizes him as human, through which he shares in what gives life and purpose to the world as a whole.

Once he has recognized his rational faculty as his true nature, man can attain complete *selfhood,* in other words, if he learns to guide his life in accordance with what is essential, his reason, and if he is not overly impressed by external events that in themselves are neither good nor bad, productive of neither pain nor pleasure, because what "disturbs men's minds is not events, but their judgments on events." If man can preserve the inner freedom that he possesses as a rational being, no external evil or threat of evil, not even death, can be potent enough to break his freedom, his self, his quality as a rational being. External things, then, are not good or evil in themselves; they are merely "materials for the will, in dealing with which it will find its own good or evil."

Epictetus, in particular, deals with the question of how the isolated individual can preserve himself against the tyrant who is surrounded by sycophantic adulation and who commands irresistible force. The tyrant has power over individuals only to the extent that they fear him, that is, to the extent that they treasure their accidental possessions of property and health, their life, more than their inner freedom, their reason, over which no one else can have authority. What maintains a tyrant, therefore, is not his command over external means of compulsion, police and prisons, but the failure of men to preserve their true natures in the face of such external pressures. In other words, it is the control over men's minds rather than their bodies that gives a tyrant his parasitical power; if men began to live in accordance with their natures, their reason and freedom of will, tyrannical power could not long persist.

Epictetus and Marcus Aurelius express an important idea in saying that "no man can rob us of our free will," and that even death is not frightening, as it involves only the return of the material parts of the body to the elements of which it was made up. Moreover, they say, one should be content with death, because it is one of the things that nature wills; one should wait for it as "one of the operations of nature." The Stoic therefore learns to detach himself from events that are beyond his control, because whatever is "beyond the control of my will, is nothing to me."

Epictetus was aware of the charge that his doctrine of an inalienable rational self, which no tyrant could subjugate, might teach men to "despise the laws." His argument in reply to this charge is ingenious. Stoicism, far from teaching political disobedience, actually makes us obedient to the laws, he says, because it teaches us to give way in regard to "our poor body," property, parents, and children, to "give up everything, resign everything; only our judgments it reserves, and these Zeus willed should be each man's special property."

To the interjection that a man's judgments are "the greatest matters of all," Epictetus retorts in this way: as long as the main concern of rulers is how to live in palaces, enjoy the services of slaves and freedmen, the pleasures of feasts and plays, the power supplied by armies and police forces, and other external matters, men of reason and integrity will cheerfully acknowledge the superiority of their rulers. But how insignificant are such matters when compared with moral selfhood, which cannot be conquered by external force. To influence men's judgment and reason, the rulers ought to busy themselves less with external things, Epictetus says; they should concern themselves more with their own rational selves, if they want to understand those of others. The Stoic is thus willing to give way to the king or tyrant in matters of external force, because there the ruler is superior; "where, on the other hand, I am the better man, it is for you to give way to me, for I have made this my concern, and you have not."

The Stoic doctrine is not free from self-contradiction. If the value of life, property, family, offices, health, and freedom is denigrated, the citizen is more readily inclined to obey the ruler's commands, as long as the latter has the physical means to enforce their compliance. In this sense, Stoicism has had a *conservative* influence throughout the ages, encouraging the individual to submit completely to the powers that be and to realize himself as a person in other realms of thought and action. On the other hand, there is no doubt that the Stoic doctrine of complete individual *moral integrity*, which must not be compromised even at the price of death, has *revolutionary* implications. Some rulers may be satisfied with external, formal obedience. Others will insist on inner adherence and voluntary acceptance, and here Stoicism, fully aware that these are "the greatest matters of all" in human relations, has a distinctly revolutionary flavor. What opposes tyrants and dictators, after all, is not this or that party program but the moral courage of individual human beings, whose integrity and faith in themselves and others, in reason and justice, cannot be broken by any external pressure.

No philosophy before Stoicism, and perhaps none after, has centered its teachings so emphatically on individual responsibility and integrity, and done so without threatening penalties or promising rewards, as religions are wont to do. The Stoics did not even hold out the immortality of the soul as an ultimate goal to which mortals could hopefully look forward. A philosophical or moral creed has rarely demanded so much of men, and promised so little; as a consequence, Stoicism has never appealed to masses and groups but to individuals in whom the "categorical imperative" (as Immanuel Kant later put it) was a living and indomitable force.

Stoicism thus attracted two opposing types of men: first, the more reflective, saintly ascetic, who attains full peace of mind and soul by withdrawing from the world completely, to whom love and friendship, pain and pleasure, property and office, mean nothing. He finds his self-realization in contemplation and meditation, which bring him closer to that merging with the Whole of which he is an infinitesimally small part. The second type of Stoic, by contrast, is more active; he seeks his communion with the Whole, not by contemplating it, but by working toward its high purposes and goals, which also encompass his own life.

Epictetus himself, usually considered the more reflective kind of Stoic, nevertheless observes that "it is not arguments that are wanting nowadays," but "the man who will apply his arguments, and bear witness to them by action." Similarly, Marcus Aurelius, who spent a lifetime of hard work in governing a far-flung empire, said: "Not in passivity, but in activity lie the evil and the good of the rational social animal, just as his virtue and his vice lie not in passivity, but in activity." In the beginning of the *Meditations*, in which he analyzes the sources of his moral heritage, Marcus Aurelius also expresses gratitude to his brother who had early taught him a "disposition to do good, and to give to others readily, and to cherish good hopes, and to believe that I am loved by my friends." The ethical ideal of Stoicism was most vividly expressed in a Latin phrase, translated by Pliny from a Greek Stoic: "God is man's helping of man" (*Deus est mortali iuvare mortalem*).

There is a certain degree of contradiction between the two main Stoic types, based as they are on two not fully reconcilable philosophical conceptions. On the one hand, the world is thought of in terms of Reason, Law, and Harmony, and things and events are predetermined within this realm of cosmic necessity. On the other hand, there are freedom of will and the moral duty to work for that rational ordering of the world toward which it is perpetually moving, and moving more rapidly with the aid of human goodness and reason. This contradiction between the two main types of Stoics is characteristic of most philosophies and religions that try to combine natural law with individual freedom, or the predetermined harmony of the world with its manifest phenomena of discord.

The refusal to promise absolutes prevented Stoicism from becoming a popularly accepted creed; unable to satisfy the quest for certainty that gives mass movements their emotional appeal, Stoicism was taken up by strong personalities who felt themselves equal to its austere demands. According to the Stoic view, no human activity can claim ultimate validity. All that human beings can do is to live and work in accordance with nature, that is, bring every activity and thing to the highest level of perfection of which it is capable.

Viewed from the outside, such activities may perhaps appear unimportant in relation to eternal and absolute values. Stoics therefore often compare life to a play: "Remember that you are an actor in a play, and the Playwright chooses the manner of it: if he wants it short, it is short; if long, it is long. If he wants you to act a poor man you must act the part with all your powers; and so if your part be a cripple or a magistrate or a plain man. For your business is to act the character that is given you and act it well; the choice of the cast is Another's." The important thing is therefore, as for an actor in a play, to perform one's task well, regardless of its ultimate value and purpose. Without the promise of heaven and the threat of hell, the Stoic is satisfied with having tried hard, having played his role well, just as the actor is concerned more about the acting of his part than about the character he personifies, or about the success or failure of his doings in the play. The Stoic symbolism of life as a play reflects the contradiction between the two strands in Stoicism that alternatively stress reflection and action, necessity and freedom, predetermined perfection and striving toward perfection. Yet these contradictions in Stoicism possibly reflect, not avoidable imperfections of faulty logic or philosophy, but life itself.

As was pointed out earlier, the decline of the city-state and the rise of empire not only made the individual more conscious of himself as an individual but enlarged his horizon. Here, again, the Stoic philosophy attempted to provide philosophical answers to needs and challenges of restless and changing societies. Zeno, the Hellenized Phoenician, founder of Stoicism, wrote an anti-Platonic *Republic* in which he taught that the ideal state must be a world-state, and that an end should be put to the many individual states, each with its own laws and conceptions of justice. Citizenship would be universal for all men, and there would be one system of law, based on universally accepted reason rather than on local customs and conventions. Zeno also opposed institutions that seemed to him artificial, such as temples, law courts, money, and marriage, and he vigorously condemned the inequality of women, not, as Plato had done, of women who belonged to the ruling class, but of all women. Unlike Aristotle, who assumed that some human beings are by nature slaves, Zeno and the early Stoics insisted that slavery was contrary to natural law, that it was no more than an arbitrary convention based on force and expediency, and that there were no nations or ethnic groups naturally inferior, fit only to serve those who claimed to be superior.

Because the earlier Stoics were Hellenized non-Greeks, they were able to appraise Greek life with a fresh eye. They took nothing for granted, bowed to no sacrosanct taboos, and exposed even the most solidly entrenched practices and prejudices to critical examination. Later on, such radical attacks were toned down, particularly when Rome became the center of Stoicism.

Practical-minded, the Roman Stoics abandoned some of the early denunciations of all conventions and institutions, but they retained the basic Stoic doctrine of *one world*. According to the pantheistic and panrationalistic view of Stoicism, the universe is God, and God is Reason. In this "frame of things," governed by universal reason, "men and God are united," and from this unity, Epictetus says, "come the seeds from which are begotten not only my own father or grandfather, but all things that are begotten and that grow upon earth, and rational creatures in particular—for these alone are by nature fitted to share in the society of God, being connected with Him by the bond of reason—why should he not call himself a citizen of the universe and a son of God?" Epictetus also expresses, in an amazing parallel to Jewish-Christian monotheism, the doctrine of the brotherhood of mankind, inasmuch as all men have "God as maker and father and kinsman."

Marcus Aurelius formulates the idea of universal political and legal unity even more clearly. Because all human beings have mind in common, "the reason also, in respect of which we are rational beings, is common: if this is so, common also is the reason which commands us what to do, and what not to do; if this is so, there is a common law also; if this is so, we are fellow-citizens; if this is so, we are members of some political community; if this is so, the world is in a manner of a state." Marcus Aurelius sees himself both as the emperor of Rome and as a man, a citizen of the world: "But my nature is rational and social; and my city and country, so far as I am Antoninus,[1] is Rome, but so far as I am a man, it is the world. The things then which are useful to these cities are alone useful to me."

The Stoics thus consider the faculty to reason the most human quality, one that is shared by all men. The laws of reason prevail independently of, and are above, legal and political rules that owe their acceptance to convenience and expediency rather than to inherent truth. Stressing what unites men rather than what separates them, the Stoics not only attacked narrow tribalism and chauvinism but also pleaded for greater equality of women and slaves, a revolutionary doctrine at that time, and a far from complete realization today.

Once the Stoics clearly understood the unity of mankind (and they were among the first in history to attain this conception on a rational, secular basis), differences of sex, class, social status, and political constitution seemed relatively insignificant. The unity of man was in itself part of a larger world held together by the law of nature, a law whose validity rested on its intrinsic rationality

---

[1] The full name of the emperor was Marcus Aelius Aurelius Antoninus.

rather than on the fiats of kings and emperors. The Stoic concept of natural law found its practical application in the Roman philosophical idea of *ius naturale* (natural law), as well as in the Roman legal system of *ius gentium* (law of nations) ; thus it laid the foundations for the later development of international law.

In theory, there was a sharp distinction between the law of nations and natural law; for example, slavery was considered by Roman lawyers to be contrary to natural law but a recognized institution of the law of nations. Yet the sharp theoretical distinction between the law of nations as a set of *rules of positive law* and the law of nature as a *philosophical system* of what the *law ought to be* was gradually abandoned under the impact of Stoic ideas, and the two were increasingly identified. Because, as explained earlier, Stoicism stresses what human institutions have in common rather than what separates them—the first being their essence and the second what is accidental, local, and arbitrary in them—natural law and the law of nations became merged into one philosophical conception, according to which, as defined in the *Institutes* of Emperor Justinian's *Corpus Juris Civilis*, "the law that natural reason has prescribed for all men, is equally observed by all nations, and is called the law of nations, because all nations make use of it" (1. 2. 1). Thus, wherever the Roman law expanded— and it usually stayed once it had taken root—it carried with it an openness and universality that it owed to the Stoic sense of all men living in "one world."

The Stoic influence on Christianity was no less profound than that on Roman law. When St. Paul stated that there was "neither Jew nor Greek, neither bond nor free," he gave voice to an ideal that was in complete harmony with the Stoic legacy.

Thrice in modern times have Stoic doctrines played a vitalizing part. First, the development of a new international law from the sixteenth century on was strengthened by the revival of natural law, based on secular or religious foundations. The process is not yet finished, and the Stoic vision of universal government through universal law and justice still awaits its realization. The second impact of Stoic ideas occurred in eighteenth-century France, when the makers of the French Revolution, fired by ideals of liberty, equality, and fraternity, sought to build a new world on purely rational principles, without the burdensome conventions of traditional religion, privilege, or class. Finally, the Stoic idea of a "law above the law" became the fundamental principle of the American constitutional system, jealously guarded by the judiciary and profoundly revered by the American people, who have been unwilling to accept the view that laws of fallible men, exposed to the temptations of passion and interest, are binding under all circumstances.

Every revolution appeals to natural law for justification. Every country, therefore, that has experienced popular revolutions has incorporated some natural law into its heritage. Unlike most other countries, the United States remembers its major revolution, not as one among many phases of its historical experience, but as the source and origin of its very existence. As a result, the tradition of thinking according to natural law, a tradition that goes back directly to Stoic principles, is particularly strong in the United States.

I. EPICTETUS

The Discourses and The Manual *

1. We Are All God's Kinsmen

If these statements of the philosophers are true, that God and men are akin, there is but one course open to men, to do as Socrates did: never to reply to one who asks his country, "I am an Athenian," or "I am a Corinthian," but "I am a citizen of the universe." For why do you say that you are an Athenian, instead of merely a native of the little spot on which your bit of a body was cast forth at birth? Plainly you call yourself Athenian or Corinthian after that more sovereign region which includes not only the very spot where you were born, and all your household, but also generally that region from which the race of your forbears has come down to you. When a man therefore has learnt to understand the government of the universe and has realized that there is nothing so great or sovereign or all-inclusive as this frame of things wherein men and God are united, and that from it come the seeds from which are sprung not only my own father or grandfather, but all things that are begotten and that grow upon earth, and rational creatures in particular—for these alone are by nature fitted to share in the society of God, being connected with Him by the bond of reason—why should he not call himself a citizen of the universe and a son of God? Why should he fear anything that can happen to him among men? When kinship

with Caesar or any other of those who are powerful in Rome is sufficient to make men live in security, above all scorn and free from every fear, shall not the fact that we have God as maker and father and kinsman relieve us from pains and fears?

"And where am I to find food to eat, if I have nothing?" says one.

Well, what do slaves do when they leave their masters, or what do they rely on? Do they rely on fields, or servants, or silver plate? No, on nothing but themselves; nevertheless sustenance does not fail them. And shall our philosopher in his wanderings have to rest his confidence in others, instead of taking care of himself? Is he to be baser and more cowardly than the unreasoning beasts? For each one of them is content with itself, and lacks not its proper sustenance nor the way of life that is naturally suited to it.

I think that the old man who sits here to teach you ought to devote his skill not to save you from being low-minded, and from reasoning about yourselves in a low and ignoble spirit, but rather to prevent young men from arising of the type who, discovering their kinship with the gods, and seeing that we have these fetters attached to us in the shape of the body and its possessions and all that we find necessary for the course and management of our life by reason of the body, may desire to fling all these away as vexatious and useless burdens and so depart to the gods their kindred.

And so your teacher and instructor, if he were a true teacher, should engage in this conflict of argument:

* From Epictetus, *The Discourses and Manual* (trans. P. E. Matheson, Oxford University Press, 1916). By permission.

You come saying, "Epictetus, we can bear no longer to be bound with the fetters of this wretched body, giving it meat and drink and rest and purgation, and by reason of the body having to adapt ourselves to this or that set of circumstances. Are not these things indifferent and as nothing to us, and death no evil thing? Are we not kinsmen of the gods, from whom we have come hither? Suffer us to depart to the place whence we have come, suffer us to be released from these bonds that are fastened to us and weigh us down. Here are robbers and thieves and law-courts and so-called kings, who by reason of our poor body and its possessions are accounted to have authority over us. Suffer us to show them that they have authority over nothing."

Hereupon I answer: "Men as you are, wait upon God. When He gives the signal and releases you from this service, then you shall depart to Him; but for the present be content to dwell in this country wherein He appointed you to dwell. Short indeed is the time of your dwelling here, and easy for them whose spirit is thus disposed. What manner of tyrant or what thief or what law-courts have any fears for those who have thus set at nought the body and its possessions? Stay where you are, and depart not without reason." Such should be the answer of the teacher to his gifted pupils. How different is what we see! There is no life in your master, and no life in you. When you have had your fill to-day, you sit groaning about the morrow, and how you are to find food. Slave, if you get food, you will have it; if not, you will depart: the door is open. Why do you whine? What room is there for tears any more? What occasion for flattery any more? Why should one envy another? Why should he gaze with wonder on them that are rich or powerful, especially if they be strong and quick to anger? For what will they do with us? We will pay no heed to what they have power to do, what we really care for they cannot touch. Who, I ask you, will be master over one who is of this spirit?

How did Socrates approach these matters? Surely as one should who is convinced of his kinship with the gods. "If you tell me," he says, " 'We acquit you on condition that you discourse no longer as you have done hitherto, and that you do not annoy young or old among us,' " I shall answer, "It is absurd for you to suppose that, while I am bound to maintain and guard any post to which your general appointed me, and should rather die ten thousand times than abandon it, yet if God has appointed us to a certain place and way of life we ought to abandon that." [Plato, *Apology*, 29c, 28e] Here you see a man who is a kinsman of the gods in very truth. But as for us—we think of ourselves as if we were all belly and flesh and animal desire; such are our fears, such our passions; those that can help us to these ends we flatter, and at the same time fear.

Some one has asked me to write for him to Rome, one who, as the world thought, had had misfortunes; he had once been famous and rich, and had now lost everything and was living here. So I wrote for him in a humble tone. And he read my letter and gave it me back and said, "I wanted your help, not your pity." So, too, Rufus, to try me, used to say, "Your master will do this or that to you"; and when I answered him, "This is the lot of man," "Why then," said he, "do I appeal to your master when I can get everything from you?" for, indeed, it is true that what a man has of himself it is idle and futile for him to receive from another. Am I then, who can get from myself the gift of a noble and lofty spirit, to get from you a field or money or office? Heaven forbid! I will not be so blind to my true possessions. But when a man is mean and cowardly, for him one must needs write letters as for one that is dead. "Make us a present of the corpse of so and so and his miserable quart of blood." For indeed such a one is a mere corpse and a quart of blood and nothing more. If he were anything more, he would have realized that one man cannot make another miserable.

2. How to Behave toward Tyrants

If a man possesses some advantage, or thinks he does though he does not, he is bound, if he be uneducated, to be puffed up because of it. The tyrant, for instance, says, "I am mightiest of all men."

Well, and what can you give me? Can you enable me to get what I will to get? How can you? Can you avoid what you will to avoid, independent of circumstances? Is your impulse free from error? How can you claim any such power?

Tell me, on shipboard, do you put confidence in yourself or in the man who knows? And in a chariot? Surely in him who knows. How is it in other arts? Exactly the same. What does your power come to then?

"All men pay me attention."

Yes, and I pay attention to my platter and work it and polish it and I fix up a peg for my oil-flask. Does that mean that these are superior to me? No, but they do me some service, and for this reason I pay them attention. Again: do I not pay attention to my ass? Do I not wash his feet? Do I not curry him? Do you not know that every man pays regard to himself, and to you only as to his ass? For who pays regard to you as a man? Show me. Who wishes to become like you? Who regards you as one like Socrates to admire and follow?

"But I can behead you."

Well said. I forgot, of course, one ought to pay you worship as if you were fever or cholera, and raise an altar to you, like the altar to Fever in Rome.

What is it then which disturbs and confounds the multitude? Is it the tyrant and his guards? Nay, God forbid! It is impossible for that which is free by nature to be disturbed or hindered by anything but itself. It as a man's own judgements which disturb him. For when the tyrant says to a man, "I will chain your leg," he that values his leg says, "Nay, have mercy," but he that values his will says, "If it seems more profitable to you, chain it."

"Do you pay no heed?"

No, I pay no heed.

"I will show you that I am master."

How can you? Zeus gave me my freedom. Or do you think that he was likely to let his own son be enslaved? You are master of my dead body, take it.

"Do you mean that when you approach me, you pay no respect to me?"

No, I only pay respect to myself: if you wish me to say that I pay respect to you too, I tell you that I do so, but only as I pay respect to my water-pot.

This is not mere self-love: for it is natural to man, as to other creatures, to do everything for his own sake; for even the sun does everything for its own sake, and in a word so does Zeus himself. But when he would be called "The Rain-giver" and "Fruit-giver" and "Father of men and gods," you see that he cannot win these names or do these works unless he does some good to the world at large: and in general he has so created the nature of the rational animal, that he can attain nothing good for himself, unless he contributes some service to the community. So it turns out that to do everything for his own sake is not unsocial. For what do you expect? Do you expect a man to hold aloof from himself and his own interest? No: we cannot ignore the one principle of action which governs all things—to be at unity with themselves.

What follows? When men's minds harbour wrong opinions on things beyond the will, counting them good and evil, they are bound to pay regard to tyrants. Would that it were only tyrants, and not chamberlains too! How can a man possibly grow wise of a sudden, when Caesar appoints him to the charge of the privy? How is it we straightway say, "Felicio has spoken wisely to me"? I would fain have him deposed from the dung-heap, that he may seem foolish to you again. Epaphroditus had a shoemaker, whom he sold because he was useless: then by some chance he was bought by one of Caesar's officials, and became Caesar's shoemaker. If you could have seen how Epaphroditus honoured him. "How is my good Felicio, I pray you?" Then if some one asked us, "What is your master doing?" the answer was, "He is consulting Felicio about something." What, had he not sold him for useless? Who has suddenly made a wise man of him? This is what comes of honouring anything outside one's will.

He has been honoured with a tribuneship. All who meet him congratulate him; one kisses his eyes, another his neck, his slaves kiss his hands. He comes into his house and finds lamps being lighted. He goes up to the Capitol and offers sacrifice. Who, I ask you, ever offered sacrifice in gratitude for right direction of the will or for impulse in accordance with nature? For we give thanks to the gods for what we think our good!

To-day one spoke to me about the priesthood of Augustus. I told him, "Fellow, leave the thing alone; you will spend a great deal on nothing."

"Well, but those who draw up contracts will record my name."

Can you be there when men read it and say to them, "That is my name," and even supposing you can be there now, what will you do if you die?

"My name will remain."

Write it in a stone and it will remain. But who will remember you outside Nicopolis?

"But I shall wear a golden crown."

If you desire a crown at all, take a crown of roses and wear that: you will look smarter in that.

3. On Constancy

The essence of good and of evil lies in an attitude of the will.

What are external things then?

They are materials for the will, in dealing with which it will find its own good or evil.

How will it find its good?

If it does not value over much the things that it deals with. For its judgements on matters presented to it, if they be right,

make the will good, and if crooked and perverse make it bad. This law God has ordained and says, "If you want anything good, get it from yourself."

You say, "Not so, but from another."

I say, No, from yourself. So when the tyrant threatens and does not invite me, I say, "What does he threaten?" If he says, "I will bind you," I say, "He threatens my hands and my feet." If he says, "I will behead you," I say, "He threatens my neck." If he says, "I will put you in prison," I say, "He threatens all my poor flesh," and if he threatens banishment, the same.

"Does he then not threaten you at all?"

Not at all, if I feel that these things are nothing to me: but if I fear any of them, he does threaten me. Who is there left for me to fear, and over what has he control? Over what is in my power? No one controls that. Over what is not in my power? I have no concern in that.

"Do you philosophers then teach us to despise kings?"

Heaven forbid! Which of us teaches men to resist them in the matters over which they have authority? Take my bit of a body, take my property, take my good name, take my companions. If I try to persuade any of them to resist, I give him leave to accuse me indeed.

"Yes, but I want to command your judgements."

Who has given you this authority? How can you conquer another's judgement?

"I will conquer him," he says, "by bringing fear to bear on him."

You are not aware that it was the judgement that conquered itself, it was not conquered by another. The will may conquer itself, but nothing else can conquer it. That is the reason too why the noblest and most just law of God is this: "Let the better always be victorious over the worse."

"Ten," you say, "are better than one."

Better for what? To bind, to slay, to carry off where they will, to take away property. Ten conquer one therefore only in so far as they are better.

"In what then are they worse?"

They are worse if the one has right judgements, and the ten have not. I ask you, can they conquer him in this? How can they? If we weigh them in the balance, must not the heavier pull down the scale?

"This is your outcome then, that Socrates should suffer the fate he did at the hands of the Athenians?"

Slave, why do you say, "Socrates"? State the fact as it really is, That Socrates' vile body should be arrested and haled to prison by those who are stronger, and that some one should give hemlock to Socrates' vile body and it should die of chill—does this seem to you marvellous, does this seem unjust, is it for this you accuse God? Did Socrates then get nothing in exchange? In what did his true good consist? Which are we to attend to? To you or to him? Nay, what does Socrates say? "Anytus or Meletus can slay me, but they cannot harm me" [Plato, *Apology*, 30c]: and again, "If God so will, so be it." [Plato, *Crito*, 43d] Prove, I say, that one who has worse judgements gains the mastery over him who is his superior in judgements. You will not prove it: far from it. For the law of nature and of God is this, "Let the better always come out victor over the worse." Victorious in what? In that wherein it is better. One body is stronger than another, the majority are stronger than one, the thief stronger than he who is not a thief. That is why I too lost my lamp, because in the matter of vigilance the thief was a stronger man than I. But he bought his lamp for this price: for a lamp he became a thief, for a lamp he broke his faith, for a lamp he became a brute. This seemed to his judgement to be profitable.

Very well: but now some one has laid hold on my cloak, and drags me into the market, then others raise a clamour against me, "Philosopher, what good have your judgements done you? for, see, you are haled to prison, see, you are about to be beheaded."

And what sort of Introduction to philosophy could I have studied, that would save me from being haled off, if a stronger man seizes my cloak, or, if ten men drag me about and cast me into prison, will save me from being cast there? Have I then learnt nothing else? I have learnt to see that everything that happens, if it is beyond the control of my will, is nothing to me. Have you not gained benefit then in this respect? Why do you seek benefit elsewhere than where you learnt that it is to be found?

I sit on then in prison and say, "This person who clamours at me has no ear for the true meaning of things, he does not understand what is said, in a word he has taken no pains to know what philosophers do or say. Let him be."

But the answer comes, "Come out of your prison."

If you have no more need of me in prison, I come out: if you need me again, I will come in. For how long? For as long as reason requires that I should abide by my vile body; but when reason demands it no longer, take it from me and good health to you! Only let me not cast it off without reason or from a faint heart, or for a casual pretext. For again God wills it not: for He has need of a world like this, and of such creatures as ourselves to move upon the earth. But if He give the signal of retreat, as He gave it to Socrates, one must obey His signal as that of the general in command.

"What then? must I say these things to the multitude?"

Why should you? Is it not sufficient to believe them yourself? For when children come up to us and clap their hands and say, "A good Saturnalia to you to-day!" do we say "These things are not good"? Not at all, we clap with them ourselves. So, when you cannot change a man's opinion, recognize that he is a child, clap with him, and if you do not wish to do this, you have only to hold your peace.

These things we must remember, and when called to face a crisis that is to test us we must realize that the moment is come to show whether we have learnt our lesson. For a young man going straight from his studies to face a crisis may be compared to one who has practised the analysis of syllogisms. If some one offers him one that is easy to analyse, he says, "Nay, propound me one which is cunningly involved, that I may get proper exercise." And so wrestlers are discontented if put to wrestle with young men of light weight: "He cannot lift me," one says. Here is a young man of parts, yet when the crisis calls he must needs weep and say, "I would fain go on learning."

Learning what? If you did not learn your lesson to display it in action, what did you learn it for?

I imagine one of those who are sitting here crying out in the travail of his heart, "Why does not a crisis come to me such as has come to him? Am I to wear my life out idly in a corner, when I might win a crown at Olympia? When will some one bring me news of a contest like that?" Such ought to be the attitude of you all. Why, among Caesar's gladiators there are some who are vexed that no one brings them out or matches them in fight, and they pray to God and go to the managers and implore them to let them fight; and shall no one of you display a like spirit? That is exactly why I should like to take ship for Rome to see how my wrestler puts his lesson into practice.

"I do not want," says he, "an exercise of this sort."

What? is it in your power to take the task you choose? No, a body is given you of such a kind, parents of such a kind, brothers of such a kind, a country of such a kind, a position in it of such a kind: and yet you come to me and say, "Change the task set me." What! have you not resources to deal with what is given you? Instead of saying, "It is yours to set the task, and mine to study it well," you say, "Do not put before me such a syllogism, but such an one: do not impose on me such a conclusion, but such an one." A time will soon come when tragic actors will imagine that they are merely mask and shoes and robe, and nothing else. Man, you have these things given you as your subject and task. Speak your part, that we may know whether you are a

tragic actor or a buffoon: for except their speech they have all else in common. Does the tragic actor disappear, if you take away his shoes and mask and bring him on the stage in the bare guise of a ghost, or is he there still? If he has a voice he is there still.

So it is in life: "Take a post of command"; I take it, and taking it show how a philosopher behaves.

"Lay aside the senator's dress, and put on rags and appear in that character." Very well: is it not given me still to display a noble voice?

In what part then do you appear now?

As a witness called by God: "Come and bear witness for me, for I count you worthy to come forward as my witness. Is anything good or evil which lies outside the range of the will? Do I harm any one? Do I put each man's advantage elsewhere than in himself?"

What is the witness you now bear to God?

"I am in danger, O Lord, and in misfortune; no man heeds me, no man gives me anything, all blame me and speak evil of me."

Is this the witness you are going to bear, and so dishonour the calling that he has given you, in that he honoured you thus and counted you worthy to be brought forward to bear such weighty witness?

But suppose that he who has authority pronounces, "I judge you to be godless and unholy," how does this affect you?

"I am judged to be godless and unholy."

Nothing more?

"Nothing."

If he had been giving judgement on a hypothetical proposition and had declared, "I judge the proposition 'if it be day, there is light' to be false," how would it have affected the proposition? Who is judged here? Who is condemned? The proposition or the man who is deluded about it? Who in the world then is this who has authority to pronounce upon you? Does he know what godliness or ungodliness is? Has he made a study of it? Has he learnt it? Where and with what master?

If a musician pays no heed to him when he pronounces that the lowest note is the highest, nor a geometrician when he decides that the lines from the centre of a circle to the circumference are not equal, shall he who is educated in true philosophy pay any heed to an uneducated man when he gives judgement on what is holy and unholy, just and unjust? What a great wrong for philosophers to be guilty of! Is this what you have learnt by coming to school?

Leave other people, persons of no endurance, to argue on these matters to little purpose. Let them sit in a corner and take their paltry fees, or murmur that no one offers them anything, and come forward yourself and practise what you have learnt. For it is not arguments that are wanting nowadays: no, the books of the Stoics are full of them. What then is the one thing wanting? We want the man who will apply his arguments, and bear witness to them by action. This is the character I would have you take up, that we may no longer make use of old examples in the school, but may be able to show an example from our own day.

Whose business then is it to take cognizance of these questions? It is for him that has studied at school; for man is a creature with a faculty of taking cognizance, but it is shameful for him to exercise it in the spirit of runaway slaves. No: one must sit undistracted and listen in turn to tragic actor or harp-player, and not do as the runaways do. At the very moment one of them is attending and praising the actor, he gives a glance all round, and then if some one utters the word "master" he is fluttered and confounded in a moment. It is shameful that philosophers should take cognizance of the works of nature in this spirit. For what does "master" mean? No man is master of another man; his masters are only death and life, pleasure and pain. For, apart from them, you may bring me face to face with Caesar and you shall see what constancy I show. But when he comes in thunder and lightning with these in his train, and I show fear of them, I am only recognizing my master as the runaway does. But so long as I have respite from them I am just like the runaway watching in the theatre: I wash, drink, sing, but do everything in fear and misery. But if I once free myself from my masters, that is from those feelings which make masters formidable, my trouble is past, and I have a master no more.

"Should I then proclaim this to all men?"

No! One should study the weakness of the uninstructed and say to them, "This man advises me what he thinks good for himself, and I excuse him." For Socrates too excused the gaoler who wept when he was going to drink the poison, and said, "How nobly he has wept for us!" Does he say to the gaoler, "That is why we dismissed the women"? No, he says that to his intimate friends, who were fit to hear it, but the gaoler he treats considerately like a child. [Plato, *Phaedo*, 116d]

4. *Freedom from Fear*

What makes the Emperor an object of fear?

The guards, one says, with their swords, and the chamberlains and those who close the door against those who enter.

Why is it then that, if you bring a child to him when his guards are with him, the child is not afraid? Is it because the child is not aware of them? Now if a man is aware of the guards and their swords, but comes for that very purpose, because his misfortunes make him wish to die and he is anxious to die easily by some one else's hand, does he fear the guards?

"No, for he wishes for the very thing which makes men fear them."

If then a man whose will is not set on dying or living, but who is content with what is given him, comes before the Tyrant, what prevents him from coming without fear?

"Nothing."

Now suppose a man is of the same mind in regard to property as this man in regard to his body: suppose he feels the same about wife and children: suppose, in a word, he is so distracted and desperate that he regards it as indifferent whether he has these things or not: just as children playing with potsherds are anxious about the game, but do not care for the potsherds in themselves, so he has not set his heart on material things, but accepts the game cheerfully, and enjoys handling them—how can any tyrant, how can any guards or swords inspire fear in such a one?

Yet if madness can produce this attitude of mind, if even habit can produce it in the Galilaeans, can reason and demonstration teach no one that God has made all things in the world, and the world itself as a whole to have its own end without hindrance, but its individual parts to subserve the whole? Now all other things are without the capacity of understanding His governance, but the rational creature has faculties that enable him to reflect on all these things, to realize that he is a part, and what part he is, and that it is well for the parts to give way to the whole. And further, being by nature noble and generous and free, he sees that he has some of the things about him unhindered and in his own control, and some again subject to hindrance and dependent on others, the acts of his will unhindered, and things beyond his will subject to hindrance. And therefore if he makes up his mind that his good and his interest lie in the former alone, in things that are unhindered and depend upon himself, he will be free, tranquil, happy, unharmed, highminded, reverent, giving thanks for everything to God, on no occasion blaming or accusing any one for what happens; but if he finds his good in things outside and beyond his will, he is bound to be hindered and hampered, and to be the slave of those who have authority over those things on which his admiration and his fear are centred, he is bound to be irreverent because he thinks that God is injuring him, and unfair, always seeking to win for himself more than his share; he is bound to be of a mean and paltry spirit.

If a man understands this, there is nothing to prevent him from living with an easy and obedient spirit, content with his past lot and awaiting with a gentle spirit all that may yet befall him.

"Would you give me poverty?" Give it me and you shall learn what poverty is when a good actor plays the part. "Would you give me office?" Give it me, and troubles with it. "Exile?" Wherever I go, it will be well with me: for even here it was not the place that made me well off, but my judgements, and these I shall carry away with me, for no one can rob me of them; these alone are my own and cannot be taken away, with these I am content wherever I am and whatever I do. "But now the time is come to die." What do you mean by "die"? Do not use fine words, but state the facts as they are. "Now is the time for your material part to be restored to the elements of which it was composed." What is there dreadful in that? What loss to the universe will this mean, what strange or irrational event? Is this a thing to make one fear the tyrant? Is this what makes the swords of the guards seem long and sharp? Let others look to that; I have considered the whole matter, and no one has authority over me. God has set me free, I have learnt to understand His commands, no one can make a slave of me any more, my judges and he who claims my freedom are as they should be.

"Am I not master of your body?"

What does that concern *me*?

"Am I not master of your property?"

Well, how does that concern *me*?

"Am I not master of exile and imprisonment?"

Again, I resign all, yes, and my body itself for you to deal with, when you will. Only try your authority and you will learn how far it extends. What then can I fear any more? The chamberlains? What should I fear their doing? Fear their shutting me out? If they find me wanting to enter, let them shut me out!

"Why then do you come to the king's door?"

Because I think it is fitting for me to join in the game while it lasts.

"How then do you escape being shut out?"

If I am not received, it is not my will to enter; my will is always to prefer what comes to pass, for I consider what God wills better than what I will. I will attach myself to Him as His minister and servant, my impulses and my wishes are one with His, in a word my will is His will. There can be no exclusion for me, but only for those who try to press in.

Why then do I not press in?

Because I know that nothing good is given within to those who have entered. But when I hear a man called happy because he is honoured by Caesar I say, "What is his portion?" "A province or a procuratorship." Does he also get a judgement, such as a governor should have? Does he get the skill to use a procuratorship? Why should I push my way in any more? Some one flings a shower of figs and nuts: the children try to seize them, and fight with one another for them; grown men do not, for they count it a small matter. If one fling potsherds even children do not try to catch them. Governorships are being given to this man and that: the children shall see to them! A praetorship, a consulship: let the children scramble for them: let them be shut out and beaten, let them kiss the hands of the giver and his slaves; for me they are figs and nuts. But what if a fig chance to fall into my lap when he is throwing? Take and eat it, for one may value a fig so far. But if I stoop for it and upset my neighbour or am upset by him, if I flatter those who enter, the fig is not worth while, nor is any other of the good things which the philosophers have persuaded me not to believe to be good.

Show me the swords of the guards.

"See how large and how sharp they are."

Well, what do these large, sharp swords do?

"They kill."

What does fever do?

"The same."

What does a tile do?

"The same."

Would you have me then stand in awe of all these things, and pay them reverence, and go about as the slave of all?

God forbid! No, if I have once learnt that what is born must needs also be destroyed in order that the world may not stand still or be hindered, it makes no difference to me whether a fever is to destroy it or a falling tile or a soldier, but if I must compare them I know that the soldier will do the thing quicker and with less pain. Seeing then that I neither fear anything that he can do to me nor desire anything that he can provide, why do I stand in awe and amazement before him any more? Why do I fear the guards? Why do I rejoice if he speaks to me in a friendly way and gives me a welcome? Why do I tell other people how he talked to me? Is he a Socrates or a Diogenes, that his praise of me should be a proof of what I am? Do I admire his character? No, it is to keep up the game that I come to him and serve him, so long as he commands me to do nothing stupid or unseemly. But if he says to me, "Go and fetch Leon of Salamis," I say to him, "Look for some one else, I will play no longer."

"Away with him."

I follow; it is in the game.

"But you lose your neck."

Well! does the Emperor himself, and you who obey him, keep his neck for ever?

"But you will be flung abroad unburied."

I shall be, if I and the dead body are one, but if I am not the same as the dead body, state the facts with more discrimination, and do not try to frighten me. These are things to frighten children and fools. But if a man has once entered a philosopher's lecture-room and does not know what his true self is, he deserves to fear and to flatter what he flattered afterwards: I mean, if he has not yet learnt that he is not flesh or bones or sinews, but the faculty which uses them, and which also governs the impressions and understands them.

"Yes, but these arguments make men despise the laws."

Nay, these arguments of all others make those who adopt them obedient to the laws. Law is not what any fool can do. Yet see how these arguments make us behave rightly even towards our critics, since they teach us to claim nothing against them, in which they can surpass us. They teach us to give way in regard to our poor body, to give way in regard to property, children, parents, brothers, to give up everything, resign everything: only our judgements they reserve, and these Zeus willed should be each man's special property. How can you call this lawlessness, how can you call it stupidity? I give way to you in that wherein you are better and stronger than I: where, on the other hand, I am the better man, it is for you to give way to me, for I have made this my concern, and you have not. You make it your concern, how to live in a palace, how slaves and freedmen are to serve you, how you are to wear conspicuous raiment, how you are to have a multitude of huntsmen, minstrels, players. Do I lay claim to any of these? But you, for your part, have you concerned yourself with judge-ments? Have you concerned yourself with your own rational self? Do you know what are its constituents, what is its principle of union, how it is articulated, what are its faculties and of what nature? Why are you vexed then, if another who has made these things his study has the advantage of you here?

"But these are the greatest matters of all."

Who, I ask, prevents you from busying yourself with these and devoting your attention to these? Who has a larger equipment of books, of leisure, of masters who will do you good? Only incline your mind to these things, bestow a little time, if no more, on your own Governing Principle, consider what this possession is and whence it has come to you, this faculty which uses all the rest, which proves all the rest, selecting and rejecting. So long as you busy yourself with external things, no one will succeed with them so well as you, but this faculty of reason will be, what your own choice makes it, mouldy and neglected.

II. MARCUS AURELIUS

Meditations *

1. My Spiritual Heritage

1. From my grandfather Verus I learned good morals and the government of my temper.

2. From the reputation and remembrance of my father, modesty and a manly character.

---

* From Marcus Aurelius Antoninus, *Meditations* (trans. George Long, 1862).

3. From my mother, piety and beneficence, and abstinence, not only from evil deeds, but even from evil thoughts; and further, simplicity in my way of living, far removed from the habits of the rich.

4. From my great-grandfather, not to have frequented public schools, and to have had good teachers at home, and to know that on such things a man should spend liberally.

5. From my governor, to be neither of the green nor of the blue party at the games in the Circus, nor a partizan either of the Parmularius or the Scutarius at the gladiators' fights; from him too I learned endurance of labour, and to want little, and to work with my own hands, and not to meddle with other people's affairs, and not to be ready to listen to slander.

6. From Diognetus, not to busy myself about trifling things, and not to give credit to what was said by miracle-workers and jugglers about incantations and the driving away of daemons and such things; and not to breed quails for fighting, nor to give myself up passionately to such things; and to endure freedom of speech; and to have become intimate with philosophy; and to have been a hearer, first of Bacchius, then of Tandasis and Marcianus; and to have written dialogues in my youth; and to have desired a plank bed and skin, and whatever else of the kind belongs to the Grecian discipline.

7. From Rusticus I received the impression that my character required improvement and discipline; and from him I learned not to be led astray to sophistic emulation, nor to writing on speculative matters, nor to delivering little hortatory orations, nor to showing myself off as a man who practises much discipline, or does benevolent acts in order to make a display; and to abstain from rhetoric, and poetry, and fine writing; and not to walk about in the house in my outdoor dress, nor to do other things of the kind; and to write my letters with simplicity, like the letter which Rusticus wrote from Sinuessa to my mother; and with respect to those who have offended me by words, or done me wrong, to be easily disposed to be pacified and reconciled, as soon as they have shown a readiness to be reconciled; and to read carefully, and not to be satisfied with a superficial understanding of a book; nor hastily to give my assent to those who talk overmuch; and I am indebted to him for being acquainted with the discourses of Epictetus, which he

communicated to me out of his own collection.

8. From Apollonius I learned freedom of will and undeviating steadiness of purpose; and to look to nothing else, not even for a moment, except to reason; and to be always the same, in sharp pains, on the occasion of the loss of a child, and in long illness; and to see clearly in a living example that the same man can be both most resolute and yielding, and not peevish in giving his instruction; and to have had before my eyes a man who clearly considered his experience and his skill in expounding philosophical principles as the smallest of his merits; and from him I learned how to receive from friends what are esteemed favours, without being either humbled by them or letting them pass unnoticed.

9. From Sextus, a benevolent disposition, and the example of a family governed in a fatherly manner, and the idea of living comformably to nature; and gravity without affectation, and to look carefully after the interests of friends, and to tolerate ignorant persons, and those who form opinions without consideration: he had the power of readily accommodating himself to all, so that intercourse with him was more agreeable than any flattery; and at the same time he was most highly venerated by those who associated with him: and he had the faculty both of discovering and ordering, in an intelligent and methodical way, the principles necessary for life; and he never showed anger or any other passion, but was entirely free from passion, and also most affectionate; and he could express approbation without noisy display, and he possessed much knowledge without ostentation.

10. From Alexander the grammarian, to refrain from fault-finding, and not in a reproachful way to chide those who uttered any barbarous or solecistic or strange-sounding expression; but dexterously to introduce the very expression which ought to have been used, and in the way of answer or giving confirmation, or joining in an inquiry about the thing itself, not about the word, or by some other fit suggestion.

11. From Fronto I learned to observe what envy, and duplicity, and hypocrisy are in a tyrant, and that generally those among us who are called Patricians are rather deficient in paternal affection.

12. From Alexander the Platonic, not frequently nor without necessity to say to any one, or to write in a letter, that I have no leisure; nor continually to excuse the neglect of duties required by our relation to those with whom we live, by alleging urgent occupations.

13. From Catulus, not to be indifferent when a friend finds fault, even if he should find fault without reason, but to try to restore him to his usual disposition; and to be ready to speak well of teachers, as it is reported of Domitius and Athenodotus; and to love my children truly.

14. From my brother Severus, to love my kin, and to love truth, and to love justice; and through him I learned to know Thrasea, Helvidius, Cato, Dion, Brutus; and from him I received the idea of a polity in which there is the same law for all, a polity administered with regard to equal rights and equal freedom of speech, and the idea of a kingly government which respects most of all the freedom of the governed; I learned from him also consistency and undeviating steadiness in my regard for philosophy; and a disposition to do good, and to give to others readily, and to cherish good hopes, and to believe that I am loved by my friends; and in him I observed no concealment of his opinions with respect to those whom he condemned, and that his friends had no need to conjecture what he wished or did not wish, but it was quite plain.

15. From Maximus I learned self-government, and not to be led aside by anything; and cheerfulness in all circumstances, as well as in illness; and a just admixture in the moral character of sweetness and dignity, and to do what was set before me without complaining. I observed that everybody believed that he thought as he spoke, and that in all that he did he never had any bad intention; and he never showed amazement and surprise, and was never in a hurry, and never put off doing a thing, nor was perplexed nor dejected, nor did he ever laugh to disguise his vexation, nor, on the other hand, was he ever passionate or suspicious. He was accustomed to do acts of beneficence, and was ready to forgive, and was free from all falsehood; and he presented the appearance of a man who could not be diverted from right rather than of a man who had been improved. I observed, too, that no man could ever think that he was despised by Maximus, or ever venture to think himself a better man. He had also the art of being humorous in an agreeable way.

16. In my father I observed mildness of temper, and unchangeable resolution in the things which he had determined after due deliberation; and no vainglory in those things which men call honours; and a love of labour and perseverance; and a readiness to listen to those who had anything to propose for the common weal; and undeviating firmness in giving to every man according to his deserts; and a knowledge derived from experience of the occasions for vigorous action and for remission. And I observed that he had overcome all passion for boys; and he considered himself no more than any other citizen; and he released his friends from all obligation to sup with him or to attend him of necessity when he went abroad, and those who had failed to accompany him, by reason of any urgent circumstances, always found him the same. I observed too his habit of careful inquiry in all matters of deliberation, and his persistency, and that he never stopped his investigation through being satisfied with appearances which first present themselves; and that his disposition was to keep his friends, and not to be soon tired of them, nor yet to be extravagant in his affection; and to be satisfied on all occasions, and cheerful; and to foresee things a long way off, and to provide for the smallest without display; and to check immediately popular applause and all flattery; and to be ever watchful over the things which were necessary for

the administration of the empire, and to be a good manager of the expenditure, and patiently to endure the blame which he got for such conduct; and he was neither superstitious with respect to the gods, nor did he court men by gifts or by trying to please them, or by flattering the populace; but he showed sobriety in all things and firmness, and never any mean thoughts or action, nor love of novelty. And the things which conduce in any way to the commodity of life, and of which fortune gives an abundant supply, he used without arrogance and without excusing himself; so that when he had them, he enjoyed them without affectation, and when he had them not, he did not want them. No one could ever say of him that he was either a sophist or a home-bred flippant slave or a pedant; but every one acknowledged him to be a man ripe, perfect, above flattery, able to manage his own and other men's affairs. Besides this, he honoured those who were true philosophers, and he did not reproach those who pretended to be philosophers, nor yet was he easily led by them. He was also easy in conversation, and he made himself agreeable without any offensive affection. He took a reasonable care of his body's health, not as one who was greatly attached to life, nor out of regard to personal appearance, nor yet in a careless way, but so that, through his own attention, he very seldom stood in need of the physician's art or of medicine or external applications. He was most ready to give way without envy to those who possessed any particular faculty, such as that of eloquence or knowledge of the law or of morals, or of anything else; and he gave them his help, that each might enjoy reputation according to his deserts; and he always acted conformably to the institutions of his country, without showing any affectation of doing so. Further, he was not fond of change nor unsteady, but he loved to stay in the same places, and to employ himself about the same things; and after his paroxysms of headache he came immediately fresh and vigorous to his usual occupations. His secrets were not many, but

very few and very rare, and these only about public matters; and he showed prudence and economy in the exhibition of the public spectacles and the construction of public buildings, his donations to the people, and in such things, for he was a man who looked to what ought to be done, not to the reputation which is got by a man's acts. He did not take the bath at unseasonable hours; he was not fond of building houses, nor curious about what he ate, nor about the texture and colour of his clothes, nor about the beauty of his slaves. His dress came from Lorium, his villa on the coast, and from Lanuvium generally. We know how he behaved to the toll-collector at Tusculum who asked his pardon; and such was all his behaviour. There was in him nothing harsh, nor implacable, nor violent, nor, as one may say, anything carried to the sweating point; but he examined all things severally, as if he had abundance of time, and without confusion, in an orderly way, vigorously and consistently. And that might be applied to him which is recorded of Socrates, that he was able to abstain from, and to enjoy, those things which many are too weak to abstain from, and cannot enjoy without excess. But to be strong enough both to bear the one and to be sober in the other is the mark of a man who has a perfect and invincible soul, such as he showed in the illness of Maximus.

17. To the gods I am indebted for having good grandfathers, good parents, a good sister, good teachers, good associates, good kinsmen and friends, nearly everything good. Further, I owe it to the gods that I was not hurried into any offence against any of them, though I had a disposition which, if opportunity had offered, might have led me to do something of this kind; but, through their favour, there never was such a concurrence of circumstances as put me to the trial. Further, I am thankful to the gods that I was not longer brought up with my grandfather's concubine, and that I preserved the flower of my youth, and that I did not make proof of my virility before the proper season, but even deferred the

time; that I was subjected to a ruler and a father who was able to take away all pride from me, and to bring me to the knowledge that it is possible for a man to live in a palace without wanting either guards or embroidered dresses, or torches and statues, and suchlike show; but that it is in such a man's power to bring himself very near to the fashion of a private person, without being for this reason either meaner in thought, or more remiss in action, with respect to the things which must be done for the public interest in a manner that befits a ruler. I thank the gods for giving me such a brother, who was able by his moral character to rouse me to vigilance over myself, and who, at the same time, pleased me by his respect and affection; that my children have not been stupid nor deformed in body; that I did not make more proficiency in rhetoric, poetry, and the other studies, in which I should perhaps have been completely engaged, if I had seen that I was making progress in them; that I made haste to place those who brought me up in the station of honour, which they seemed to desire, without putting them off with hope of my doing it some time after, because they were then still young; that I knew Apollonius, Rusticus, Maximus; that I received clear and frequent impressions about living according to nature, and what kind of a life that is, so that, so far as depended on the gods, and their gifts, and help, and inspirations, nothing hindered me from forthwith living according to nature, though I still fall short of it through my own fault, and through not observing the admonitions of the gods, and, I may almost say, their direct instructions; that my body has held out so long in such a kind of life; that I never touched either Benedicta or Theodotus, and that, after having fallen into amatory passions, I was cured; and, though I was often out of humour with Rusticus, I never did anything of which I had occasion to repent; that, though it was my mother's fate to die young, she spent the last years of her life with me; that, whenever I wished to help any man in his need,

or on any other occasion, I was never told that I had not the means of doing it; and that to myself the same necessity never happened, to receive anything from another; that I have such a wife, so obedient, and so affectionate, and so simple; that I had abundance of good masters for my children; and that remedies have been shown to me by dreams, both others, and against bloodspitting and giddiness; and that, when I had an inclination to philosophy, I did not fall into the hands of any sophist, and that I did not waste my time on writers of histories, or in the resolution of syllogisms, or occupy myself about the investigation of appearances in the heavens; for all these things require the help of the gods and fortune.

2. Human Reason and One World

1. That which rules within, when it is according to nature, is so affected with respect to the events which happen, that it always easily adapts itself to that which is possible and is presented to it. For it requires no definite material, but it moves towards its purpose, under certain conditions however; and it makes a material for itself out of that which opposes it, as fire lays hold of what falls into it, by which a small light would have been extinguished: but when the fire is strong, it soon appropriates to itself the matter which is heaped on it, and consumes it, and rises higher by means of this very material.

2. Let no act be done without a purpose, nor otherwise than according to the perfect principles of art.

3. Men seek retreats for themselves, houses in the country, sea-shores, and mountains; and thou too art wont to desire such things very much. But this is altogether a mark of the most common sort of men, for it is in thy power whenever thou shalt choose to retire into thyself. For nowhere either with more quiet or more freedom from trouble does a man retire than into his

own soul, particularly when he has within him such thoughts that by looking into them he is immediately in perfect tranquillity; and I affirm that tranquillity is nothing else than the good ordering of the mind. Constantly then give to thyself this retreat, and renew thyself; and let thy principles be brief and fundamental, which, as soon as thou shalt recur to them, will be sufficient to cleanse the soul completely, and to send thee back free from all discontent with the things to which thou returnest. For with what art thou discontented? With the badness of men? Recall to thy mind this conclusion, that rational animals exist for one another, and that to endure is a part of justice, and that men do wrong involuntarily; and consider how many already, after mutual enmity, suspicion, hatred, and fighting, have been stretched dead, reduced to ashes; and be quiet at last.—But perhaps thou art dissatisfied with that which is assigned to thee out of the universe.—Recall to thy recollection this alternative; either there is providence or atoms, fortuitous concurrence of things; or remember the arguments by which it has been proved that the world is a kind of political community, and be quiet at last.—But perhaps corporeal things will still fasten upon thee.—Consider then further that the mind mingles not with the breath, whether moving gently or violently, when it has once drawn itself apart and discovered its own power, and think also of all that thou hast heard and assented to about pain and pleasure, and be quiet at last.—But perhaps the desire of the thing called fame will torment thee.—See how soon everything is forgotten, and look at the chaos of infinite time on each side of the present, and the emptiness of applause, and the changeableness and want of judgement in those who pretend to give praise, and the narrowness of the space within which it is circumscribed, and be quiet at last. For the whole earth is a point, and how small a nook in it is this thy dwelling, and how few are there in it, and what kind of people are they who will praise thee.

This then remains: Remember to retire into this little territory of thy own, and above all do not distract or strain thyself, but be free, and look at things as a man, as a human being, as a citizen, as a mortal. But among the things readiest to thy hand to which thou shalt turn, let there be these, which are two. One is that things do not touch the soul, for they are external and remain immovable; but our perturbations come only from the opinion which is within. The other is that all these things, which thou seest, change immediately and will no longer be; and constantly bear in mind how many of these changes thou hast already witnessed. The universe is transformation: life is opinion.

4. If our intellectual part is common, the reason also, in respect of which we are rational beings, is common: if this is so, common also is the reason which commands us what to do, and what not to do; if this is so, there is a common law also; if this is so, we are fellow-citizens; if this is so, we are members of some political community; if this is so, the world is in a manner a state. For of what other common political community will any one say that the whole human race are members? And from thence, from this common political community comes also our very intellectual faculty and reasoning faculty and our capacity for law; or whence do they come? For as my earthly part is a portion given to me from certain earth, and that which is watery from another element, and that which is hot and fiery from some peculiar source (for nothing comes out of that which is nothing, as nothing also returns to non-existence), so also the intellectual part comes from some source.

5. Death is such as generation is, a mystery of nature; a composition out of the same elements, and a decomposition into the same; and altogether not a thing of which any man should be ashamed, for it is not contrary to the nature of a reasonable animal, and not contrary to the reason of our constitution.

6. It is natural that these things should

be done by such persons, it is a matter of necessity; and if a man will not have it so, he will not allow the fig-tree to have juice. But by all means bear this in mind, that within a very short time both thou and he will be dead; and soon not even your names will be left behind.

7. Take away thy opinion, and then there is taken away the complaint, "I have been harmed." Take away the complaint, "I have been harmed," and the harm is taken away."

8. That which does not make a man worse than he was, also does not make his life worse, nor does it harm him either from without or from within.

9. The nature of that which is universally useful has been compelled to do this.

10. Consider that everything which happens, happens justly, and if thou observest carefully, thou wilt find it to be so. I do not say only with respect to the continuity of the series of things, but with respect to what is just, and as if it were done by one who assigns to each thing its value. Observe then as thou hast begun; and whatever thou doest, do it in conjunction with this, the being good, and in the sense in which a man is properly understood to be good. Keep to this in every action.

11. Do not have such an opinion of things as he has who does thee wrong, or such as he wishes thee to have, but look at them as they are in truth.

12. A man should always have these two rules in readiness; the one, to do only whatever the reason of the ruling and legislating faculty may suggest for the use of men; the other, to change thy opinion, if there is any one at hand who sets thee right and moves thee from any opinion. But this change of opinion must proceed only from a certain persuasion, as of what is just or of common advantage, and the like, not because it appears pleasant or brings reputation.

13. Hast thou reason? I have.—Why then dost not thou use it? For if this does its own work, what else dost thou wish?

3. Elements of Stoicism

1. He who acts unjustly acts impiously. For since the universal nature has made rational animals for the sake of one another to help one another according to their deserts, but in no way to injure one another, he who transgresses her will, is clearly guilty of impiety towards the highest divinity. And he too who lies is guilty of impiety to the same divinity; for the universal nature is the nature of things that are; and things that are have a relation to all things that come into existence. And further, this universal nature is named truth, and is the prime cause of all things that are true. He then who lies intentionally is guilty of impiety inasmuch as he acts unjustly by deceiving; and he also who lies unintentionally, inasmuch as he is at variance with the universal nature, and inasmuch as he disturbs the order by fighting against the nature of the world; for he fights against it, who is moved of himself to that which is contrary to truth, for he had received powers from nature through the neglect of which he is not able now to distinguish falsehood from truth. And indeed he who pursues pleasure as good, and avoids pain as evil, is guilty of impiety. For of necessity such a man must often find fault with the universal nature, alleging that it assigns things to the bad and the good contrary to their deserts, because frequently the bad are in the enjoyment of pleasure and possess the things which procure pleasure, but the good have pain for their share and the things which cause pain. And further, he who is afraid of pain will sometimes also be afraid of some of the things which will happen in the world, and even this is impiety. And he who pursues pleasure will not abstain from injustice, and this is plainly impiety. Now with respect to the things towards which the universal nature is equally affected—for it would not have made both, unless it was equally affected towards both—towards these they who wish to follow nature should be of the same mind with it, and equally

affected. With respect to pain, then, and pleasure, or death and life, or honour and dishonour, which the universal nature employs equally, whoever is not equally affected is manifestly acting impiously. And I say that the universal nature employs them equally, instead of saying that they happen alike to those who are produced in continuous series and to those who come after them by virtue of a certain original movement of Providence, according to which it moved from a certain beginning to this ordering of things, having conceived certain principles of the things which were to be, and having determined powers productive of beings and of changes and of such like successions.

2. It would be a man's happiest lot to depart from mankind without having had any taste of lying and hypocrisy and luxury and pride. However to breathe out one's life when a man has had enough of these things is the next best voyage, as the saying is. Hast thou determined to abide with vice, and has not experience yet induced thee to fly from this pestilence? For the destruction of the understanding is a pestilence, much more indeed than any such corruption and change of this atmosphere which surrounds us. For this corruption is a pestilence of animals so far as they are animals; but the other is a pestilence of men so far as they are men.

3. Do not despise death, but be well content with it, since this too is one of those things which nature wills. For such as it is to be young and to grow old, and to increase and to reach maturity, and to have teeth and beard and grey hairs, and to beget, and to be pregnant and to bring forth, and all the other natural operations which the seasons of thy life bring, such also is dissolution. This, then, is consistent with the character of a reflecting man, to be neither careless nor impatient nor contemptuous with respect to death, but to wait for it as one of the operations of nature. As thou now waitest for the time when the child shall come out of thy wife's womb, so be ready

for the time when thy soul shall fall out of this envelope. But if thou requirest also a vulgar kind of comfort which shall reach thy heart, thou wilt be made best reconciled to death by observing the objects from which thou art going to be removed, and the morals of those with whom they soul will no longer be mingled. For it is no way right to be offended with men, but it is thy duty to care for them and to bear with them gently; and yet to remember that thy departure will be not from men who have the same principles as thyself. For this is the only thing, if there be any, which could draw us the contrary way and attach us to life, to be permitted to live with those who have the same principles as ourselves. But now thou seest how great is the trouble arising from the discordance of those who live together, so that thou mayest say, Come quick, O death, lest perchance I, too, should forget myself.

4 He who does wrong does wrong against himself. He who acts unjustly acts unjustly to himself, because he makes himself bad.

5. He often acts unjustly who does not do a certain thing; not only he who does a certain thing.

6. Thy present opinion founded on understanding, and thy present conduct directed to social good, and thy present disposition of contentment with everything which happens—that is enough.

7. Wipe out imagination: check desire: extinguish appetite: keep the ruling faculty in its own power.

8. Among the animals which have not reason one life is distributed; but among reasonable animals one intelligent soul is distributed: just as there is one earth of all things which are of an earthy nature, and we see by one light, and breathe one air, all of us that have the faculty of vision and all that have life.

9. All things which participate in anything which is common to them all move towards that which is of the same kind with themselves. Everything which is earthy turns towards the earth, everything which

is liquid flows together, and everything which is of an aërial kind does the same, so that they require something to keep them asunder, and the application of force. Fire indeed moves upwards on account of the elemental fire, but it is so ready to be kindled together with all the fire which is here, that even every substance which is somewhat dry, is easily ignited, because there is less mingled with it of that which is a hindrance to ignition. Accordingly then everything also which participates in the common intelligent nature moves in like manner towards that which is of the same kind with itself, or moves even more. For so much as it is superior in comparison with all other things, in the same degree also is it more ready to mingle with and to be fused with that which is akin to it. Accordingly among animals devoid of reason we find swarms of bees, and herds of cattle, and the nurture of young birds, and in a manner, loves; for even in animals there are souls, and that power which brings them together is seen to exert itself in the superior degree, and in such a way as never has been observed in plants nor in stones nor in trees. But in rational animals there are political communities and friendships, and families and meetings of people; and in wars, treaties and armistices. But in the things which are still superior, even though they are separated from one another, unity in a manner exists, as in the stars. Thus the ascent to the higher degree is able to produce a sympathy even in things which are separated. See, then, what now takes place. For only intelligent animals have now forgotten this mutual desire and inclination, and in them alone the property of flowing together is not seen. But still though men strive to avoid this union, they are caught and held by it, for their nature is too strong for them; and thou wilt see what I say, if thou only observest. Sooner, then, will one find anything earthy which comes in contact with no earthy thing than a man altogether separated from other men.

10. Both man and God and the universe produce fruit; at the proper seasons each produces it. But if usage has especially fixed these terms to the vine and like things, this is nothing. Reason produces fruit both for all and for itself, and there are produced from it other things of the same kind as reason itself.

11. If thou art able, correct by teaching those who do wrong; but if thou canst not, remember that indulgence is given to thee for this purpose. And the gods, too, are indulgent to such persons; and for some purposes they even help them to get health, wealth, reputation; so kind they are. And it is in thy power also; or say, who hinders thee?

12. Labour not as one who is wretched, nor yet as one who would be pitied or admired: but direct thy will to one thing only, to put thyself in motion and to check thyself, as the social reason requires.

13. To-day I have got out of all trouble, or rather I have cast out all trouble, for it was not outside, but within and in my opinions.

14. All things are the same, familiar in experience, and ephemeral in time, and worthless in the matter. Everything now is just as it was in the time of those whom we have buried.

15. Things stand outside of us, themselves by themselves, neither knowing aught of themselves, nor expressing any judgement. What is it, then, which does judge about them? The ruling faculty.

16. Not in passivity, but in activity lie the evil and the good of the rational social animal, just as his virtue and his vice lie not in passivity, but in activity.

17. For the stone which has been thrown up it is no evil to come down, nor indeed any good to have been carried up.

18. Penetrate inwards into men's leading principles, and thou wilt see what judges thou art afraid of, and what kind of judges they are of themselves.

19. All things are changing: and thou thyself art in continuous mutation and in a manner in continuous destruction, and the whole universe too.

20. It is thy duty to leave another man's wrongful act there where it is.

21. Termination of activity, cessation from movement and opinion, and in a sense their death, is no evil. Turn thy thoughts now to the consideration of thy life, thy life as a child, as a youth, thy manhood, thy old age, for in these also every change was a death. Is this anything to fear? Turn thy thoughts now to thy life under thy grandfather, then to thy life under thy mother, then to thy life under thy father; and as thou findest many other differences and changes and terminations, ask thyself, Is this anything to fear? In like manner, then, neither are the termination and cessation and change of thy whole life a thing to be afraid of.

22. Hasten to examine thy own ruling faculty and that of the universe and that of thy neighbour: thy own that thou mayest make it just: and that of the universe, that thou mayest remember of what thou art a part; and that of thy neighbour, that thou mayest know whether he has acted ignorantly or with knowledge, and that thou mayest also consider that his ruling faculty is akin to thine.

23. As thou thyself art a component part of a social system, so let every act of thine be a component part of social life. Whatever act of thine then has no reference either immediately or remotely to a social end, this tears asunder thy life, and does not allow it to be one, and it is of the nature of a mutiny, just as when in a popular assembly a man acting by himself stands apart from the general agreement.

24. Quarrels of little children and their sports, and poor spirits carrying about dead bodies, such is everything; and so what is exhibited in the representation of the mansions of the dead strikes our eyes more clearly.

25. Examine into the quality of the form of an object, and detach it altogether from its material part, and then contemplate it; then determine the time, the longest which a thing of this peculiar form is naturally made to endure.

26. Thou hast endured infinite troubles through not being contented with thy ruling faculty, when it does the things which it is constituted by nature to do. But enough of this.

27. When another blames thee or hates thee, or when men say about thee anything injurious, approach their poor souls, penetrate within, and see what kind of men they are. Thou wilt discover that there is no reason to take any trouble that these men may have this or that opinion about thee. However thou must be well disposed towards them, for by nature they are friends. And the gods too aid them in all ways, by dreams, by signs, towards the attainment of those things on which they set a value.

28. The periodic movements of the universe are the same, up and down from age to age. And either the universal intelligence puts itself in motion for every separate effect, and if this is so, be thou content with that which is the result of its activity; or it puts itself in motion once, and everything else comes by way of sequence in a manner; or indivisible elements are the origin of all things.—In a word, if there is a god, all is well; and if chance rules, do not thou also be governed by it.

Soon will the earth cover us all: then the earth, too, will change, and the things also which result from change will continue to change for ever, and these again for ever. For if a man reflects on the changes and transformations which follow one another like wave after wave and their rapidity, he will despise everything which is perishable.

29. The universal cause is like a winter torrent: it carries everything along with it. But how worthless are all these poor people who are engaged in matters political, and, as they suppose, are playing the philosopher! All drivellers. Well then, man: do what nature now requires. Set thyself in motion, if it is in they power, and do not look about thee to see if any one will observe it; nor yet expect Plato's *Republic:* but be content if the smallest thing goes on well, and consider such an event to be no small matter. For who can change men's opinions?

And without a change of opinions what else is there than the slavery of men who groan while they pretend to obey? Come now and tell me of Alexander and Philip and Demetrius of Phalerum. They themselves shall judge whether they discovered what the common nature required, and trained themselves accordingly. But if they acted like tragedy heroes, no one has condemned me to imitate them. Simple and modest is the work of philosophy. Draw me not aside to indolence and pride.

30. Look down from above on the countless herds of men and their countless solemnities, and the infinitely varied voyagings in storms and calms, and the differences among those who are born, who live together, and die. And consider, too, the life lived by others in olden time, and the life of those who will live after thee, and the life now lived among barbarous nations, and how many know not even thy name, and how many will soon forget it, and how they who perhaps now are praising thee will very soon blame thee, and that neither a posthumous name is of any value, nor reputation, nor anything else.

31. Let there be freedom from perturbations with respect to the things which come from the external cause; and let there be justice in the things done by virtue of the internal cause, that is, let there be movement and action terminating in this, in social acts, for this is according to thy nature.

32. Thou canst remove out of the way many useless things among those which disturb thee, for they lie entirely in thy opinion; and thou wilt then gain for thyself ample space by comprehending the whole universe in thy mind, and by contemplating the eternity of time, and observing the rapid change of every several thing, how short is the time from birth to dissolution, and the illimitable time before birth as well as the equally boundless time after dissolution.

33. All that thou seest will quickly perish, and those who have been spectators of its dissolution will very soon perish too.

And he who dies at the extremest old age will be brought into the same condition with him who died prematurely.

34. What are these men's leading principles, and about what kind of things are they busy, and for what kind of reasons do they love and honour? Imagine that thou seest their poor souls laid bare. When they think that they do harm by their blame or good by their praise, what an idea!

35. Loss is nothing else than change. But the universal nature delights in change, and in obedience to her all things are now done well, and from eternity have been done in like form, and will be such to time without end. What, then, dost thou say? That all things have been and all things always will be bad, and that no power has ever been found in so many gods to rectify these things, but the world has been condemned to be bound in never ceasing evil?

36. The rottenness of the matter which is the foundation of everything! Water, dust, bones, filth: or again, marble rocks, the callosities of the earth; and gold and silver, the sediments; and garments, only bits of hair; and purple dye, blood; and everything else is of the same kind. And that which is of the nature of breath is also another thing of the same kind, changing from this to that.

37. Enough of this wretched life and murmuring and apish tricks. Why art thou disturbed? What is there new in this? What unsettles thee? Is it the form of the thing? Look at it. Or is it the matter? Look at it. But besides these there is nothing. Towards the gods, then, now become at last more simple and better. It is the same whether we examine these things for a hundred years or three.

38. If any man has done wrong, the harm is his own. But perhaps he has not done wrong.

39. Either all things proceed from one intelligent source and come together as in one body, and the part ought not to find fault with what is done for the benefit of the whole; or there are only atoms, and nothing else than mixture and dispersion.

Why, then, art thou disturbed? Say to the ruling faculty, Art thou dead, art thou corrupted, art thou playing the hypocrite, art thou become a beast, dost thou herd and feed with the rest?

40. Either the gods have no power or they have power. If then, they have no power, why dost thou pray to them? But if they have power, why dost thou not pray for them to give thee the faculty of not fearing any of the things which thou fearest, or of not desiring any of the things which thou desirest, or not being pained at anything, rather than pray that any of these things should not happen or happen? for certainly if they can co-operate with men, they can co-operate for these purposes. But perhaps thou wilt say, the gods have placed them in thy power. Well, then, is it not better to use what is in thy power like a free man than to desire in a slavish and abject way what is not in thy power? And who has told thee that the gods do not aid us even in the things which are in our power? Begin, then, to pray for such things, and thou wilt see. One man prays thus: How shall I be able to lie with that woman? Do thou pray thus: How shall I not desire to lie with her? Another prays thus: How shall I be released from this? Another prays: How shall I not desire to be released? Another thus: How shall I not lose my little son? Thou thus: How shall I not be afraid to lose him? In fine, turn thy prayers this way, and see what comes.

41. Epicurus says, In my sickness my conversation was not about my bodily sufferings, nor, says he, did I talk on such subjects to those who visited me; but I continued to discourse on the nature of things as before, keeping to this main point, how the mind, while participating in such movements as go on in the poor flesh, shall be free from perturbations and maintain its proper good. Nor did I, he says, give the physicians an opportunity of putting on solemn looks, as if they were doing something great, but my life went on well and happily. Do, then, the same that he did both in sickness, if thou art sick, and in any other circumstances; for never to desert philosophy in any events that may befall us, nor to hold trifling talk either with an ignorant man or with one unacquainted with nature, is a principle of all schools of philosophy; but to be intent only on that which thou art now doing and on the instrument by which thou doest it.

42. When thou art offended with any man's shameless conduct, immediately ask thyself, Is it possible, then, that shameless men should not be in the world? It is not possible. Do not, then, require what is impossible. For this man also is one of those shameless men who must of necessity be in the world. Let the same considerations be present to thy mind in the case of the knave, and the faithless man, and of every man who does wrong in any way. For at the same time that thou dost remind thyself that it is impossible that such kind of men should not exist, thou wilt become more kindly disposed towards every one individually. It is useful to perceive this, too, immediately when the occasion arises, what virtue nature has given to man to oppose to every wrongful act. For she has given to man, as an antidote against the stupid man, mildness, and against another kind of man some other power. And in all cases it is possible for thee to correct by teaching the man who is gone astray; for every man who errs misses his object and is gone astray. Besides wherein hast thou been injured? For thou wilt find that no one among those against whom thou art irritated has done anything by which thy mind could be made worse; but that which is evil to thee and harmful has its foundation only in the mind. And what harm is done or what is there strange, if the man who has not been instructed does the acts of an uninstructed man? Consider whether thou shouldst not rather blame thyself, because thou didst not expect such a man to err in such a way. For thou hadst means given thee by thy reason to suppose that it was likely that he would commit this error, and yet thou hast forgotten and art amazed that he has erred. But most of all when thou blamest a man as faithless

or ungrateful, turn to thyself. For the fault is manifestly thy own, whether thou didst trust that a man who had such a disposition would keep his promise, or when conferring thy kindness thou didst not confer it absolutely, nor yet in such way as to have received from thy very act all the profit. For what more dost thou want when thou hast done a man a service? Art thou not content that thou hast done something conformable to thy nature, and dost thou seek to be paid for it? Just as if the eye demanded a recompense for seeing, or the feet for walking. For as these members are formed for a particular purpose, and by working according to their several constitutions obtain what is their own; so also as man is formed by nature to acts of benevolence, when he has done anything benevolent or in any other way conducive to the common interest, he has acted conformably to his constitution, and he gets what is his own.

CHAPTER 6

ST. AUGUSTINE

THE destruction of Roman power in the fifth century was more than a political revolution. The Germanic conquerors from the North swept away an empire that seemed eternal and universal to its inhabitants, and wiped out a civilization and way of life that seemed imperishable. Yet the military helplessness of Rome was not so much the deeper cause of her fall as a symptom of her general decline and disintegration. Military defeat was the end, and not the beginning, of rot and decay.

Rome's decline can be said to have started in the growing betrayal of her pristine civic virtues and in her abandonment of republicanism in favor of despotic, monarchical imperialism. Amid immense material wealth there had been disturbing signs of failure of nerve and loss of faith; above all, unwillingness or inability to solve the social conflicts born of poverty, slavery, and serfdom had contributed to the weakening of the Roman empire and to its final conquest by barbarians emerging from a cultural nowhere—from the dark forests and endless plains beyond the confines of civilization.

The Gothic, Vandal, and Hun warriors could only destroy; they had no civilization of their own that they could substitute for, or mingle with, that of the Roman world. The recorded history of the West knows of no similar catastrophe, when a way of life was so thoroughly destroyed that men forgot what their ancestors had known for centuries, and had to start all over again groping toward a new existence.

It was a long and painful experience, and the process of gradual recovery from a near-mortal illness, the medieval period, fills the ten centuries between the fall of the Roman empire in the fifth century and the revival of ancient thought and learning in the fifteenth. Interest in this period has not been intense until recently, because it was assumed that nothing could henceforth stop the march of progress and scientific development, and that history was an unceasing process of liberty unfolding itself all over the world. This optimism, so typical of the eighteenth and nineteenth centuries, has been rudely shaken in our own by World Wars I and II, which, had the free nations been defeated, might have inaugurated a new dark age. The atomic and hydrogen bombs, if used in a new war, may produce a destruction of civilization more final than that of fifteen hundred years ago, and of such dimensions that no convalescence will be physically possible. The study of the Middle Ages is therefore of special interest to the contemporary of the second half of the twentieth century, who lives in fear and anxiety at a turning point in history, and who is not sure whether enough spiritual and material resources will be at hand after a war of mutual and perhaps total annihilation. The lesson of the fifth century is that an entire civilization can be razed from the earth, and mankind barbarianized and decivilized. Whether such sickness is, in view of present-day weapons, mortal or not, cannot be ascertained from the example of the Middle Ages.

When Rome was sacked by the Visigoths in A. D. 410, a popular explanation was that it was the fault of the Christians. Christianity had been officially tolerated in the Roman empire from A. D. 313, and eighty years later it became the official religion of state, paganism being proscribed and prohibited. Because the fall of Rome in A. D. 410 occurred so soon after the triumph of Christianity, many pagans and perhaps even some Christians were inclined to see a connection between the rise of Christianity—so long considered officially a subversive movement—and the weakening of Roman power. From the traditional, pagan, upper-class Roman viewpoint, the Christian qualities of otherworldliness, meekness, pacifism, disregard for public affairs, and contempt for revered national deities had been persistently sapping the strength of Rome. Above all, the Christian refusal to recognize loyalty to Rome as the first loyalty, the dogged perseverance in putting a foreign religion above family, community, and state, must have appeared as a flagrant demonstration of "un-Roman" disloyalty.

Political-minded Romans of the old school were not deeply interested in religions as such, and as long as members of any creed were willing to make a formal gesture of obeisance to the ultimate authority of Rome and its personified imperial divinity, there was no cause for discord and conflict. Few empires and civilizations have, in fact, been as free from religious bigotry and persecution as Rome was, partly because of the moderation and political wisdom of its ruling classes and partly because religion was not taken seriously enough to turn men into tormentors and killers. The very polytheism of paganism ensured a basically tolerant attitude, as all pluralistic viewpoints tend to do. When Rome sought to extirpate Christianity by force in the second half of the third century, the charge was not against Christianity as a religion but against its alleged attempt to build up a state within the state, its boring from within every social class, and its gradual absorption of the Roman empire by infiltration and ideological appeals without overt acts of force.

Neither contempt nor ostracism, nor outright persecution, stopped the march of Christianity. In fact, in the fourth and fifth centuries, when Christianity became the religion of state, the roles were reversed, and paganism was put on the defensive and finally outlawed. The victory of Christianity appeared inevitable and providential to the Christian, because it was the only true religion; but to many pagans the effective extirpation of paganism by Christianity proved

only that Christianity was more ruthless than its rival in the contest of persecution, and that the Roman emperors had made the mistake of treating the subversive Christians too leniently, wasting generosity on fanatics who would brook
no compromise themselves if put in a position of authority.

When Rome was ravaged in 410, a wave of shock and horror swept through
the world. For eight centuries Rome had proudly remained inviolate, growing
from a small municipality into the center of a vast empire. The ease and speed
with which this empire was broken up took everyone by surprise. The pagans,
as we have said, ascribed the catastrophe to the betrayal of the old Roman deities
under which Rome had risen to the position of the dominant world power, but
Christians, too, were perplexed: it was hard to understand how Rome could be
so shamed just after Christianity had become the religion of state, and many
Christians began to wonder whether the official alliance of church and empire
was such an advantage after all. If Rome was not strong enough to safeguard
its own existence against heathen tribes, how could it be the source of worldly
power that the church needed in spreading Christianity?

Some Christians who were particularly perturbed about what seemed the
end of the world were recent converts; and yet, the strongest reaffirmation of
Christian idealism was the work of a convert, St. Augustine (A. D. 354–430), a
native and lifelong inhabitant of Roman North Africa. St. Augustine's parents
were North Africans; his mother was a devout Christian, but his father never
embraced the Christian faith. St. Augustine was baptized in Italy in A. D. 387,
after many years of active and more than gay living, led in complete contradiction
to Christian standards of morals and belief. But once he was baptized, he rose
quickly in the hierarchy of the church; he was made Biship of Hippo (the modern port of Buna, in Algeria) in 395, where he stayed until his death in 430.

St. Augustine was moved especially by the pagan attacks that attributed
the fall of Rome to the victory of Christianity. He started the *City of God* (*De
Civitate Dei*) in 413, and finished the voluminous work, consisting of twenty-two
books, in 426. He set out to answer two main questions. The first concerns the
pagan challenge to Christianity. Although from a purely theological viewpoint
the issue of paganism is not so intense and controversial in the twentieth century
as it was in the fifth, St. Augustine's critique is always vital and timely, if one
substitutes for paganism the qualities with which he identified it: contempt for
spiritual values, smugness, pride, and injustice.

The rebuttal of paganism, however, is only the more negative part of the
City of God. Having demonstrated the hollowness and inconsistency of paganism,
materialism, and worldly success, Augustine proceeds to his more constructive
task: the vision of the heavenly city, as contrasted with the earthly city (*civitas
terrena*). St. Augustine's use of the word *civitas*, however, should not be interpreted in a political sense; St. Augustine was not a constitutional lawyer or political theorist but a theologian. He was interested in God, Faith, and Salvation,
and not so much in the organization of the state and its political-juridical relations to the church. His heavenly city, or City of God, is therefore not identical
with the church, and the earthly city is not the state.

As a theologian and passionate Christian who took his faith seriously, St.

Augustine was primarily concerned with *ways of life* and *not* with *organizations of life*. The great struggle in the universe is, then, not between church and state (as later writers mistakenly interpreted St. Augustine for sectarian purposes), but between two opposing ways of life: in the earthly city, the love of self, the lust of power predominate, whereas in the heavenly city the love of God, "even to the contempt of self," is the foundation of order. St. Augustine therefore divides the human race into two parts, "the one consisting of those who live according to man, the other of those who live according to God. And these we also mystically call the two cities, or the two communities of men, of which the one is predestined to reign eternally with God, and the other to suffer eternal punishment with the devil." St. Augustine himself thus emphasizes that the two communities of the heavenly and earthly cities can be called cities only in a mystical or allegorical sense.

Even more explicitly, St. Augustine often speaks of the heavenly city as the eternal kingdom of God that includes the angels preceding the creation of man and the saintly elect (*communio sanctorum*); by contrast, the earthly city is the "society of the impious" (*societas impiorum*), which includes fallen angels as well as human beings who "live after the flesh." Eternal reign with God is the destiny of the heavenly city, whereas eternal punishment with the devil is the doom awaiting the earthly city.

The basic conflict between Good and Evil rages not only in mankind as a whole but in every individual. Just as Plato had stated that the problem of the just society was that of the just individual "writ large," so St. Augustine notes that the struggle between Good and Evil in the world is closely related to, and a reflection of, the conflicts within the individual human being: "For in each individual there is first of all that which is reprobate, that from which we must begin, but in which we need not necessarily remain; afterwards is that which is well approved, to which we may by advancing attain, and in which, when we have reached it, we may abide." In fact, Plato had anticipated the idea of the complex structure of the individual human soul by viewing it as a composite of the three rivaling elements of appetite, courage, and reason, representing three types of men and three ways of living. Justice, or righteousness, is the central concept in Plato's *Republic*: an individual is just if the elements of his own soul are rightly ordered and arranged, and consequently he will also act justly in his relations with others by staying in his own station, by living the kind of life he was meant to live. St. Augustine transforms this secular conception of justice into a religious one: the essence of *justice* is the *relation between man and God*, from which right relations between man and man will inevitably follow.

If man is to become worthy of entry into the eternal kingdom of heaven, the City of God, there must be some agency on earth, St. Augustine realizes, that leads in the right direction. Although the central meaning of "heavenly city" is a way of life dedicated to the service of God, St. Augustine also uses this term "mystically," that is, symbolically, for the *church*. It is the part of the heavenly city that "sojourns on earth and lives by faith," and it "lives like a captive and stranger in the earthly city." In inspiring words that recall the Stoic message of universal unity and brotherhood, St. Augustine says that the heavenly city, "while it sojourns on earth, calls citizens out of all nations, and gathers together a society of pilgrims in all languages, not scrupling about diversities in the manners, laws, and institutions whereby earthly peace is secured and maintained," and that these diversities of men ought to be preserved, as long as men are united in God's service.

Yet St. Augustine nowhere clearly defines the church; in one place he calls it the Invisible Church of God's Elect (including some as yet to be converted), and in another, the Visible Church, made up of true believers and of those whose Christianity is little more than formal membership in the church. Because he failed to distinguish sharply the Invisible from the Visible Church, he claimed rights for the one that he would not have claimed for the other, particularly in relation to the state. As a result, his arguments were used later by adherents of papalist doctrines as well as by those who affirmed the sovereignty of mundane rulers over the church.

Just as the heavenly city symbolically represents, but is not identical with, the church, so the earthly city is symbolically reflected in the state. Strictly speaking, the *earthly city* is not identical with any empirical social or political organization but is the *community of the unrighteous,* including sinful members of the church and excluding righteous citizens of the state. Whereas the earthly city, as the incarnation of sin and lust, is the antithesis of any value whatsoever, the state, by contrast, has positive value, though it is not the absolute value inherent in the heavenly city.

The Greco-Roman background of St. Augustine comes out in his assumption that "the life of the wise man must be social," and that there is no man who "does not wish to have peace." The state, therefore, by providing social peace, "has its good in this world"; and St. Augustine recalls Greco-Roman ideas in saying that the state is, "in its own kind, better than all other human good. For it desires earthly peace for the sake of enjoying earthly goods."

At this point St. Augustine parts company with Plato and Cicero, who so strongly influenced him. The peace that the state provides is, according to St. Augustine, not an end in itself, but only a means, a condition that makes the service to God possible. The peace of the state is the temporary tranquillity that enables man to work for the heavenly city, which is "peace never-ending."

Peace is therefore conceived by St. Augustine in terms of justice (that is, the right relation of man and God); it is not merely the absence of social strife and conflict. Without justice there can be no peace, and this moral and religious conception is behind St. Augustine's famous statement: "Justice being taken away, then, what are kingdoms but great robberies?" St. Augustine goes on to say that, viewed from the standpoint of formal, effective authority, robberies (that is, bands of robbers) are but little kingdoms themselves; the difference, therefore, between a state and a band of robbers is qualitative and not quantitative.

St. Augustine thus Christianizes the classical approach to the theory of the state by imbuing the Platonic concept of justice and the Aristotelian notion of the good life with the ideals of Christianity, and his doctrine is firmly anchored in the Greco-Roman and Biblical conceptions of the state in terms of moral purpose rather than formal authority, the monopoly to use force, or sovereignty.

The strong influence of Greco-Roman conceptions and preconceptions on St. Augustine can also be seen in his attitude toward slavery. In essence, it is a Christianized version of Aristotle's rationalization of slavery. Man was created in God's image, to be master of irrational creatures, beasts, but not of fellow men. Slavery is therefore not the result of man's nature, as originally intended by God, but the "result of sin." It is both punishment and remedy for sin, as for Aristotle slavery is the just relation between those who possess virtue and those who do not.

St. Augustine specifically opposes the law of the Old Testament according to which all servitude was to be ended every seventh year, and states that bad slaves are made into good by the example of Christ, and that slaves should not refuse to serve wicked masters. St. Augustine appeals to the slaves to serve their masters "heartily and with good will, so that, if they cannot be freed by their masters, they may themselves make their slavery in some sort free, by serving not in crafty fear, but in faithful love, until all righteousness pass away, and all principality and every human power be brought to nothing, and God be in all." Like Aristotle, St. Augustine also appeals to the masters to act benevolently and responsibly; they "ought to feel their position of authority a greater burden than servants their service."

Yet St. Augustine never examined his theory in the light of empirical evidence: was it really true that slaves were worse sinners than the free? Although he occasionally notes that there are "many wicked masters who have religious men as their slaves," this observation leads him, not to a re-examination of his basic assumption that slavery is the punishment and remedy for sin, but to the more startling conclusion that even such slavery is legitimate because "it is a happier thing to be the slave of a man than of a lust." Weighed carefully, therefore, St. Augustine's theory of slavery, like that of the church in general, probably seemed more reasonable to masters than to slaves, although the institution of slavery was mitigated, in actual use, by the influence of Christianity. After all, the Christian conception of the uniqueness and dignity of the human soul was incompatible, in the long run, with such practice.

St. Augustine, the greatest of the church fathers, stood at the turning point of two worlds, that of antiquity and Christianity. The impact of Plato in particular, but also that of Aristotle, Cicero, and the Stoics, is clearly evident in his work, and he helped to transmit the ancient heritage to the new world that was being born. While the Roman empire was breaking up before his eyes, he sought to construe, as a Christian, the vision of a timeless empire in which peace and justice would forever reign: the City of God.

ST. AUGUSTINE

The City of God *

1. Justice—the Foundation of the State

Justice being taken away, then, what are kingdoms but great robberies? For what are robberies themselves, but little kingdoms? The band itself is made up of men; it is ruled by the authority of a prince, it is knit together by the pact of the confederacy; the booty is divided by the law agreed on. If, by the admittance of abandoned men, this evil increases to such a degree that it holds places, fixes abodes, takes possession of cities, and subdues peoples, it assumes the more plainly the name of a kingdom, because the reality is now manifestly conferred on it, not by the removal of covetousness, but by the addition of impunity. Indeed, that was an apt and true reply which was given to Alexander the Great by a pirate who had been seized. For when that king had asked the man what he meant by keeping hostile possession of the sea, he answered with bold pride, "What thou meanest by seizing the whole earth; but because I do it with a petty ship, I am called a robber, whilst thou who dost it with a great fleet art styled emperor." [1]

2. The True Happiness of the Ruler

For neither do we say that certain Christian emperors were therefore happy because

they ruled a long time, or, dying a peaceful death, left their sons to succeed them in the empire, or subdued the enemies of the republic, or were able both to guard against and to suppress the attempt of hostile citizens rising against them. These and other gifts or comforts of this sorrowful life even certain worshippers of demons have merited to receive, who do not belong to the kingdom of God to which these belong; and this is to be traced to the mercy of God, who would not have those who believe in Him desire such things as the highest good. But we say that they are happy if they rule justly; if they are not lifted up amid the praises of those who pay them sublime honors, and the obsequiousness of those who salute them with an excessive humility, but remember that they are men; if they make their power the handmaid of His majesty by using it for the greatest possible extension of His worship; if they fear, love, worship God; if more than their own they love that kingdom in which they are not afraid to have partners; if they are slow to punish, ready to pardon; if they apply that punishment as necessary to government and defence of the republic, and not in order to gratify their own enmity; if they grant pardon, not that iniquity may go unpunished, but with the hope that the transgressor may amend his ways; if they compensate with the lenity of mercy and the liberality of benevolence for whatever severity they may be compelled to decree; if their luxury is as much restrained as it might have been unrestrained; if they prefer to govern depraved desires rather than any nation whatever; and if they do all these

---

* From St. Augustine, *The City of God* (trans. Marcus Dods, in Vol. II of *A Select Library of the Nicene and Post-Nicene Fathers of the Christian Church*, ed. Philip Schaff, Buffalo, 1887).

[1] Cicero, *De Republica*, III.

things, not through ardent desire of empty glory, but through love of eternal felicity, not neglecting to offer to the true God, who is their God, for their sins, the sacrifices of humility, contrition, and prayer. Such Christian emperors, we say, are happy in the present time by hope, and are destined to be so in the enjoyment of the reality itself, when that which we wait for shall have arrived.

3. The Earthly and the Heavenly City

Accordingly, two cities have been formed by two loves: the earthly by the love of self, even to the contempt of God; the heavenly by the love of God, even to the contempt of self. The former, in a word, glories in itself, the latter in the Lord. For the one seeks glory from men; but the greatest glory of the other is God, the witness of conscience. The one lifts up its head in its own glory; the other says to its God, "Thou art my glory, and the lifter up of mine head." [1] In the one, the princes and the nations it subdues are ruled by the love of ruling; in the other, the princes and the subjects serve one another in love, the latter obeying, while the former take thought for all. The one delights in its own strength, represented in the persons of its rulers; the other says to its God, "I will love Thee, O Lord, my strength." [2] And therefore the wise men of the one city, living according to man, have sought for profit to their own bodies or souls, or both, and those who have known God "glorified Him not as God, neither were thankful, but became vain in their imaginations, and their foolish heart was darkened; professing themselves to be wise"—that is, glorying in their own wisdom, and being possessed by pride—"they became fools, and changed the glory of the incorruptible God into an image made like to corruptible man, and to birds, and four-footed beasts,

and creeping things." For they were either leaders or followers of the people in adoring images, "and worshipped and served the creature more than the Creator, who is blessed for ever." [3] But in the other city there is no human wisdom, but only godliness, which offers due worship to the true God, and looks for its reward in the society of the saints, of holy angels as well as holy men, that God may be all in all. [4]

4. The Two Types of Man

Of the bliss of Paradise, of Paradise itself, and of the life of our first parents there, and of their sin and punishment, many have thought much, spoken much, written much. We ourselves, too, have spoken of these things in the foregoing books, and have written either what we read in the Holy Scriptures, or what we could reasonably deduce from them. And were we to enter into a more detailed investigation of these matters, an endless number of endless questions would arise, which would involve us in a larger work than the present occasion admits. We cannot be expected to find room for replying to every question that may be started by unoccupied and captious men, who are ever more ready to ask questions than capable of understanding the answer. Yet I trust we have already done justice to these great and difficult questions regarding the beginning of the world, or of the soul, or of the human race itself. This race we have distributed into two parts, the one consisting of those who live according to man, the other of those who live according to God. And these we also mystically call the two cities, or the two communities of men, of which the one is predestined to reign eternally with God, and the other to suffer eternal punishment with the devil. This, however, is their end, and of it we are to speak afterwards. At present, as we have said enough

---

[1] Ps. iii. 3.
[2] Ps. xviii. 1.

[3] Rom. i. 21–25.
[4] I Cor. xv. 28.

about their origin, whether among the angels, whose numbers we know not, or in the two first human beings, it seems suitable to attempt an account of their career, from the time when our two first parents began to propagate the race until all human generation shall cease. For this whole time or world-age, in which the dying give place and those who are born succeed, is the career of these two cities concerning which we treat.

Of these two first parents of the human race, then, Cain was the first-born, and he belonged to the city of men; after him was born Abel, who belonged to the city of God. For as in the individual the truth of the apostle's statement is discerned, "that is not first which is spiritual, but that which is natural, and afterward that which is spiritual," [1] whence it comes to pass that each man, being derived from a condemned stock, is first of all born of Adam evil and carnal, and becomes good and spiritual only afterwards, when he is grafted into Christ by regeneration: so was it in the human race as a whole. When these two cities began to run their course by a series of deaths and births, the citizen of this world was the first-born, and after him the stranger in this world, the citizen of the city of God, predestinated by grace, elected by grace, by grace a stranger below, and by grace a citizen above. By grace—for so far as regards himself he is sprung from the same mass, all of which is condemned in its origin: but God, like a potter (for this comparison is introduced by the apostle judiciously, and not without thought) of the same lump made one vessel to honor, another to dishonour. [2] But first the vessel to dishonor was made, and after it another to honor. For in each individual, as I have already said, there is first of all that which is reprobate, that from which we must begin, but in which we need not necessarily remain; afterwards is that which is well-approved, to which we may by advancing attain, and in which, when we have reached it, we may

abide. Not, indeed, that every wicked man shall be good, but that no one will be good who was not first of all wicked; but the sooner any one becomes a good man, the more speedily does he receive this title, and abolish the old name in the new. Accordingly, it is recorded of Cain that he built a city, [3] but Abel, being a sojourner, built none. For the city of the saints is above, although here below it begets citizens, in whom it sojourns till the time of its reign arrives, when it shall gather together all in the day of the resurrection; and then shall the promised kingdom be given to them, in which they shall reign with their Prince, the King of the ages, time without end.

5. Conflict and Peace in the Earthly City

But the earthly city, which shall not be everlasting (for it will no longer be a city when it has been committed to the extreme penalty), has its good in this world, and rejoices in it with such joy as such things can afford. But as this is not a good which can discharge its devotees of all distresses, this city is often divided against itself by litigations, wars, quarrels, and such victories as are either life-destroying or short-lived. For each part of it that arms against another part of it seeks to triumph over the nations though itself in bondage to vice. If, when it has conquered, it is inflated with pride, its victory is life-destroying; but if it turns its thoughts upon the common casualties of our mortal condition, and is rather anxious concerning the disasters that may befall it than elated with the successes already achieved, this victory, though of a higher kind, is still only short-lived; for it cannot abidingly rule over those whom it has victoriously subjugated. But the things which this city desires cannot justly be said to be evil, for it is itself, in its own kind, better than all other human good. For it desires earthly peace for the sake of en-

[1] I Cor. xv. 46.
[2] Rom. ix. 21.
[3] Gen. iv. 17.

joying earthly goods, and it makes war in order to attain to this peace; since, if it has conquered, and there remains no one to resist it, it enjoys a peace which it had not while there were opposing parties who contested for the enjoyment of those things which were too small to satisfy both. This peace is purchased by toilsome wars; it is obtained by what they style a glorious victory. Now, when victory remains with the party which had the juster cause, who hesitates to congratulate the victor, and style it a desirable peace? These things, then, are good things, and without doubt the gifts of God. But if they neglect the better things of the heavenly city, which are secured by eternal victory and peace neverending, and so inordinately covet these present good things that they believe them to be the only desirable things, or love them better than those things which are believed to be better—if this be so, then it is necessary that misery follow and ever increase.

6. The Lust for Power in the Earthly City

Thus the founder of the earthly city was a fratricide. Overcome with envy, he slew his own brother, a citizen of the eternal city, and a sojourner on earth. So that we cannot be surprised that this first specimen, or, as the Greeks say, archetype of crime, should, long afterwards, find a corresponding crime at the foundation of that city which was destined to reign over so many nations, and be the head of this earthly city of which we speak. For of that city also, as one of their poets has mentioned, "the first walls were stained with a brother's blood," [1] or, as Roman history records, Remus was slain by his brother Romulus. And thus there is no difference between the foundation of this city and of the earthly city, unless it be that Romulus and Remus were both citizens of the earthly city. Both desired to have the glory of founding the Roman republic, but both could not have as much glory as if one only claimed it; for he who wished to have the glory of ruling would certainly rule less if his power were shared by a living consort. In order, therefore, that the whole glory might be enjoyed by one, his consort was removed; and by this crime the empire was made larger indeed, but inferior, while otherwise it would have been less, but better. Now these brothers, Cain and Abel, were not both animated by the same earthly desires, nor did the murderer envy the other because he feared that, by both ruling, his own dominion would be curtailed—for Abel was not solicitous to rule in that city which his brother built—he was moved by that diabolical, envious hatred with which the evil regard the good, for no other reason than because they are good while themselves are evil. For the possession of goodness is by no means diminished by being shared with a partner either permanent or temporarily assumed; on the contrary, the possession of goodness is increased in proportion to the concord and charity of each of those who share it. In short, he who is unwilling to share this possession cannot have it; and he who is most willing to admit others to a share of it will have the greatest abundance to himself. The quarrel, then, between Romulus and Remus shows how the earthly city is divided against itself; that which fell out between Cain and Abel illustrated the hatred that subsists between the two cities, that of God and that of men. The wicked war with the wicked; the good also war with the wicked. But with the good, good men, or at least perfectly good men, cannot war; though, while only going on towards perfection, they war to this extent, that every good man resists others in those points in which he resists himself. And in each individual "the flesh lusteth against the spirit, and the spirit against the flesh." [2] This spiritual lusting, therefore, can be at war with the carnal lust of another man; or carnal lust may

---

1 Lucan, *Phar.* i. 95.

2 Gal. v. 17.

be at war with the spiritual desires of an-other, in some such way as good and wicked men are at war; or, still more certainly, the carnal lusts of two men, good but not yet perfect, contend together, just as the wicked contend with the wicked, until the health of those who are under the treatment of grace attains final victory.

7. Limitations of Social Life

We give a much more unlimited approval to their idea that the life of the wise man must be social. For how could the city of God either take a beginning or be developed, or attain its proper destiny, if the life of the saints were not a social life? But who can enumerate all the great grievances with which human society abounds in the misery of this mortal state? Who can weigh them? Hear how one of their comic writers makes one of his characters express the common feelings of all men in this matter: "I am married; this is one misery. Children are born to me; they are additional cares." [1] What shall I say of the miseries of love which Terence also recounts—"slights, suspicions, quarrels, war to-day, peace to-morrow?" [2] Is not human life full of such things? Do they not often occur even in honorable friendships? On all hands we experience these slights, suspicions, quarrels, war, all of which are undoubted evils; while, on the other hand, peace is a doubtful good, because we do not know the heart of our friend, and though we did know it to-day, we should be as ignorant of what it might be to-morrow. Who ought to be, or who are more friendly than those who live in the same family? And yet who can rely even upon this friendship, seeing that secret treachery has often broken it up, and produced enmity as bitter as the amity was sweet, or seemed sweet by the most perfect dissimulation? It is on this account that the words of Cicero so move the heart of every

one, and provoke a sigh: "There are no snares more dangerous than those which lurk under the guise of duty or the name of relationship. For the man who is your declared foe you can easily baffle by precaution; but this hidden, intestine, and domestic danger not merely exists, but overwhelms you before you can foresee and examine it." [3] It is also to this that allusion is made by the divine saying, "A man's foes are those of his own household" [4]—words which one cannot hear without pain; for though a man have sufficient fortitude to endure it with equanimity, and sufficient sagacity to baffle the malice of a pretended friend, yet if he himself is a good man, he cannot but be greatly pained at the discovery of the perfidy of wicked men, whether they have always been wicked and merely feigned goodness, or have fallen from a better to a malicious disposition. If, then, home, the natural refuge from the ills of life, is itself not safe, what shall we say of the city, which, as it is larger, is so much the more filled with lawsuits civil and criminal, and is never free from the fear, if sometimes from the actual outbreak, of disturbing and bloody insurrections and civil wars?

8. Shortcomings of Human Justice

What shall I say of these judgments which men pronounce on men, and which are necessary in communities, whatever outward peace they enjoy? Melancholy and lamentable judgments they are, since the judges are men who cannot discern the consciences of those at their bar, and are therefore frequently compelled to put innocent witnesses to the torture to ascertain the truth regarding the crimes of other men. What shall I say of torture applied to the accused himself? He is tortured to discover whether he is guilty, so that, though innocent, he suffers most undoubted punishment for crime that is still doubtful,

---

[1] Terent. Adelph. v. 4.
[2] Eunuch, i. 1.

[3] In Verrem, ii. 1. 15.
[4] Matt. x. 36.

not because it is proved that he committed it, but because it is not ascertained that he did not commit it. Thus the ignorance of the judge frequently involves an innocent person in suffering. And what is still more unendurable—a thing, indeed, to be bewailed, and, if that were possible, watered with fountains of tears—is this, that when the judge puts the accused to the question, that he may not unwittingly put an innocent man to death, the result of this lamentable ignorance is that this very person, whom he tortured that he might not condemn him if innocent, is condemned to death both tortured and innocent. For if he has chosen, in obedience to the philosophical instructions to the wise man, to quit this life rather than endure any longer such tortures, he declares that he has committed the crime which in fact he has not committed. And when he has been condemned and put to death, the judge is still in ignorance whether he has put to death an innocent or a guilty person, though he put the accused to the torture for the very purpose of saving himself from condemning the innocent; and consequently he has both tortured an innocent man to discover his innocence, and has put him to death without discovering it. If such darkness shrouds social life, will a wise judge take his seat on the bench or no? Beyond question he will. For human society, which he thinks it a wickedness to abandon, constrains him and compels him to this duty. And he thinks it no wickedness that innocent witnesses are tortured regarding the crimes of which other men are accused; or that the accused are put to the torture, so that they are often overcome with anguish, and, though innocent, make false confessions regarding themselves, and are punished; or that, though they be not condemned to die, they often die during, or in consequence of, the torture; or that sometimes the accusers, who perhaps have been prompted by a desire to benefit society by bringing criminals to justice, are themselves condemned through the ignorance of the judge, because they are unable to prove the truth of their accusations though they are true, and because the witnesses lie, and the accused endures the torture without being moved to confession. These numerous and important evils he does not consider sins; for the wise judge does these things, not with any intention of doing harm, but because his ignorance compels him, and because human society claims him as a judge. But though we therefore acquit the judge of malice, we must none the less condemn human life as miserable. And if he is compelled to torture and punish the innocent because his office and his ignorance constrain him, is he a happy as well as a guiltless man? Surely it were proof of more profound considerateness and finer feeling were he to recognize the misery of these necessities, and shrink from his own implication in that misery; and had he any piety about him, he would cry to God "From my necessities deliver Thou me." [1]

9. The Misery of War

After the state or city comes the world, the third circle of human society—the first being the house, and the second the city. And the world, as it is larger, so it is fuller of dangers, as the greater sea is the more dangerous. And here, in the first place, man is separated from man by the difference of languages. For if two men, each ignorant of the other's language, meet, and are not compelled to pass, but, on the contrary, to remain in company, dumb animals, though of different species, would more easily hold intercourse than they, humans though they be. For their common nature is no help to friendliness when they are prevented by diversity of language from conveying their sentiments to one another; so that a man would more readily hold intercourse with his dog than with a foreigner. But the imperial city has endeavored to impose on subject nations not only her yoke, but her language, as a bond of peace,

1 Ps. xxv. 17.

so that interpreters, far from being scarce, are numberless. This is true; but how many great wars, how much slaughter and bloodshed, have provided this unity! And though these are past, the end of these miseries has not yet come. For though there have never been wanting, nor are yet wanting, hostile nations beyond the empire, against whom wars have been and are waged, yet, supposing there were no such nations, the very extent of the empire itself has produced wars of a more obnoxious description—social and civil wars—and with these the whole race has been agitated, either by the actual conflict or the fear of a renewed outbreak. If I attempted to give an adequate description of these manifold disasters, these stern and lasting necessities, though I am quite unequal to the task, what limit could I set? But, say they, the wise man will wage just wars. As if he would not all the rather lament the necessity of just wars, if he remembers that he is a man; for if they were not just he would not wage them, and would therefore be delivered from all wars. For it is the wrong-doing of the opposing party which compels the wise man to wage just wars; and this wrong-doing, even though it gave rise to no war, would still be matter of grief to man because it is man's wrong-doing. Let every one, then, who thinks with pain on all these great evils, so horrible, so ruthless, acknowledge that this is misery. And if any one either endures or thinks of them without mental pain, this is a more miserable plight still, for he thinks himself happy because he has lost human feeling.

10. The Objective of War: Peace

Whoever gives even moderate attention to human affairs and to our common nature, will recognize that if there is no man who does not wish to be joyful, neither is there any one who does not wish to have peace. For even they who make war desire nothing but victory—desire, that is to say, to attain to peace with glory. For what else is victory than the conquest of those who resist us? and when this is done there is peace. It is therefore with the desire for peace that wars are waged, even by those who take pleasure in exercising their warlike nature in command and battle. And hence it is obvious that peace is the end sought for by war. For every man seeks peace by waging war, but no man seeks war by making peace. For even they who intentionally interrupt the peace in which they are living have no hatred of peace, but only wish it changed into a peace that suits them better. They do not, therefore, wish to have no peace, but only one more to their mind. And in the case of sedition, when men have separated themselves from the community, they yet do not effect what they wish, unless they maintain some kind of peace with their fellow-conspirators. And therefore even robbers take care to maintain peace with their comrades, that they may with greater effect and greater safety invade the peace of other men. And if an individual happen to be of such unrivalled strength, and to be so jealous of partnership, that he trusts himself with no comrades, but makes his own plots, and commits depredations and murders on his own account, yet he maintains some shadow of peace with such persons as he is unable to kill, and from whom he wishes to conceal his deeds. In his own home, too, he makes it his aim to be at peace with his wife and children, and any other members of his household; for unquestionably their prompt obedience to his every look is a source of pleasure to him. And if this be not rendered, he is angry, he chides and punishes; and even by this storm he secures the calm peace of his own home, as occasion demands. For he sees that peace cannot be maintained unless all the members of the same domestic circle be subject to one head, such as he himself is in his own house. And therefore if a city or nation offered to submit itself to him, to serve him in the same style as he had made his household serve him, he would no longer lurk in brigand's hiding-places, but lift his head in open day as a king, though the same coveteousness and wickedness should remain in him. And thus all men desire to have peace with their own circle whom they wish to govern as suits themselves. For even those whom they make war against they wish to make their own, and impose on them the laws of their own peace.

But let us suppose a man such as poetry and mythology speak of—a man so insociable and savage as to be called rather a semi-man than a man.[1] Although, then, his kingdom was the solitude of a dreary cave, and he himself was so singularly bad-hearted that he was named Κακός, which is the Greek word for *bad;* though he had no wife to soothe him with endearing talk, no children to play with, no sons to do his bidding, no friend to enliven him with intercourse, not even his father Vulcan (though in one respect he was happier than his father, not having begotten a monster like himself); although he gave to no man, but took as he wished whatever he could, from whomsoever he could, when he could; yet in that solitary den, the floor of which, as Virgil [2] says, was always reeking with recent slaughter, there was nothing else than peace sought, a peace in which no one should molest him, or disquiet him with any assault or alarm. With his own body he desired to be at peace, and he was satisfied only in proportion as he had this peace. For he ruled his members, and they obeyed him; and for the sake of pacifying his mortal nature, which rebelled when it needed anything, and of allaying the sedition of hunger which threatened to banish the soul from the body, he made forays, slew, and devoured, but used the ferocity and savageness he displayed in these actions only for the preservation of his own life's peace. So that, had he been willing to make with other men the same peace which he made with himself in his own cave, he would neither have been called bad, nor a monster, nor a semi-man. Or if the appearance of his body

and his vomiting smoky fires frightened men from having any dealings with him, perhaps his fierce ways arose not from a desire to do mischief, but from the necessity of finding a living. But he may have had no existence, or, at least, he was not such as the poets fancifully describe him, for they had to exalt Hercules, and did so at the expense of Cacus. It is better, then, to believe that such a man or semi-man never existed, and that this, in common with many other fancies of the poets, is mere fiction. For the most savage animals (and he is said to have been almost a wild beast) encompass their own species with a ring of protecting peace. They cohabit, beget, produce, suckle, and bring up their young, though very many of them are not gregarious, but solitary—not like sheep, deer, pigeons, starlings, bees, but such as lions, foxes, eagles, bats. For what tigress does not gently purr over her cubs, and lay aside her ferocity to fondle them? What kite, solitary as he is when circling over his prey, does not seek a mate, build a nest, hatch the eggs, bring up the young birds, and maintain with the mother of his family as peaceful a domestic alliance as he can? How much more powerfully do the laws of man's nature move him to hold fellowship and maintain peace with all men so far as in him lies, since even wicked men wage war to maintain the peace of their own circle, and wish that, if possible, all men belonged to them, that all men and things might serve but one head, and might, either through love or fear, yield themselves to peace with him! It is thus that pride in its perversity apes God. It abhors equality with other men under Him; but, instead of His rule, it seeks to impose a rule of its own upon its equals. It abhors, that is to say, the just peace of God, and loves its own unjust peace; but it cannot help loving peace of one kind or other. For there is no vice so clean contrary to nature that it obliterates even the faintest traces of nature.

He, then, who prefers what is right to what is wrong, and what is well-ordered to what is perverted, sees that the peace of

---

[1] He refers to the giant Cacus.
[2] *Aeneid*, viii. 195.

unjust men is not worthy to be called peace in comparison with the peace of the just. And yet even what is perverted must of necessity be in harmony with, and in dependence on, and in some part of the order of things, for otherwise it would have no existence at all. Suppose a man hangs with his head downwards, this is certainly a perverted attitude of body and arrangement of its members; for that which nature requires to be above is beneath, and *vice versa*. This perversity disturbs the peace of the body, and is therefore painful. Nevertheless the spirit is at peace with its body, and labors for its preservation, and hence the suffering; but if it is banished from the body by its pains, then, so long as the bodily framework holds together, there is in the remains a kind of peace among the members, and hence the body remains suspended. And inasmuch as the earthly body tends towards the earth, and rests on the bond by which it is suspended, it tends thus to its natural peace, and the voice of its own weight demands a place for it to rest; and though now lifeless and without feeling, it does not fall from the peace that is natural to its place in creation, whether it already has it, or is tending towards it. For if you apply embalming preparations to prevent the bodily frame from mouldering and dissolving, a kind of peace still unites part to part, and keeps the whole body in a suitable place on the earth—in other words, in a place that is at peace with the body. If, on the other hand, the body receive no such care, but be left to the natural course, it is disturbed by exhalations that do not harmonize with one another, and that offend our senses; for it is this which is perceived in putrefaction until it is assimilated to the elements of the world, and particle by particle enters into peace with them. Yet throughout this process the laws of the most high Creator and Governor are strictly observed, for it is by Him the peace of the universe is administered. For although minute animals are produced from the carcass of a larger animal, all these little atoms, by the law of the same Creator, serve the animals they belong to in peace. And although the flesh of dead animals be eaten by others, no matter where it be carried, nor what it be brought into contact with, nor what it be converted and changed into, it still is ruled by the same laws which pervade all things for the conservation of every mortal race, and which bring things that fit one another into harmony.

11. The Tranquillity of Order in the Universe

The peace of the body then consists in the duly proportioned arrangement of its parts. The peace of the irrational soul is the harmonious repose of the appetites, and that of the rational soul the harmony of knowledge and action. The peace of body and soul is the well-ordered and harmonious life and health of the living creature. Peace between man and God is the well-ordered obedience of faith to eternal law. Peace between man and man is well-ordered concord. Domestic peace is the well-ordered concord between those of the family who rule and those who obey. Civil peace is a similar concord among the citizens. The peace of the celestial city is the perfectly ordered and harmonious enjoyment of God, and of one another in God. The peace of all things is the tranquillity of order. Order is the distribution which allots things equal and unequal, each to its own place. And hence, though the miserable, in so far as they are such, do certainly not enjoy peace, but are severed from that tranquillity of order in which there is no disturbance, nevertheless, inasmuch as they are deservedly and justly miserable, they are by their very misery connected with order. They are not, indeed, conjoined with the blessed, but they are disjoined from them by the law of order. And though they are disquieted, their circumstances are notwithstanding adjusted to them, and consequently they have some tranquillity of order, and therefore some peace. But they are wretched because, although not wholly miserable, they are not in that place where any mixture of misery is impossible. They would, however, be more wretched if they had not that peace which arises from being in harmony with the natural order of things. When they suffer, their peace is in so far disturbed; but their peace continues in so far as they do not suffer, and in so far as their nature continues to exist. As, then, there may be life without pain, while there cannot be pain without some kind of life, so there may be peace without war, but there cannot be war without some kind of peace, because war supposes the existence of some natures to wage it, and these natures cannot exist without peace of one kind or other.

And therefore there is a nature in which evil does not or even cannot exist; but there cannot be a nature in which there is no good. Hence not even the nature of the devil himself is evil, in so far as it is nature, but it was made evil by being perverted. Thus he did not abide in the truth,[1] but could not escape the judgment of the Truth; he did not abide in the tranquillity of order, but did not therefore escape the power of the Ordainer. The good imparted by God to his nature did not screen him from the justice of God by which order was preserved in his punishment; neither did God punish the good which He had created, but the evil which the devil had committed. God did not take back all He had imparted to his nature, but something He took and something He left, that there might remain enough to be sensible of the loss of what was taken. And this very sensibility to pain is evidence of the good which has been taken away and the good which has been left. For, were nothing good left, there could be no pain on account of the good which had been lost. For he who sins is still worse if he rejoices in his loss of righteousness. But he who is in pain, if he derives no benefit from it, mourns at least the loss of health. And as righteousness and health are both good things, and as the loss

of any good thing is matter of grief, not of joy—if, at least, there is no compensation, as spiritual righteousness may compensate for the loss of bodily health—certainly it is more suitable for a wicked man to grieve in punishment than to rejoice in his fault. As, then, the joy of a sinner who has abandoned what is good is evidence of a bad will, so his grief for the good he has lost when he is punished is evidence of a good nature. For he who laments the peace his nature has lost is stirred to do so by some relics of peace which make his nature friendly to itself. And it is very just that in the final punishment the wicked and godless should in anguish bewail the loss of the natural advantages they enjoyed, and should perceive that they were most justly taken from them by that God whose benign liberality they had despised. God, then, the most wise Creator and most just Ordainer of all natures, who placed the human race upon earth as its greatest ornament, imparted to men some good things adapted to this life, to wit, temporal peace, such as we can enjoy in this life from health and safety and human fellowship, and all things needful for the preservation and recovery of this peace, such as the objects which are accommodated to our outward senses, light, night, the air, and waters suitable for us, and everything the body requires to sustain, shelter, heal, or beautify it: and all under this most equitable condition, that every man who made a good use of these advantages suited to the peace of this mortal condition, should receive ampler and better blessings, namely, the peace of immortality, accompanied by glory and honor in an endless life made fit for the enjoyment of God and of one another in God; but that he who used the present blessings badly should both lose them and should not receive the others.

12. Rulers as Servants of the Ruled

The whole use, then, of things temporal has a reference to this result of earthly

---

[1] John viii. 44.

peace in the earthly community, while in the city of God it is connected with eternal peace. And therefore, if we were irrational animals, we should desire nothing beyond the proper arrangement of the parts of the body and the satisfaction of the appetites— nothing, therefore, but bodily comfort and abundance of pleasures, that the peace of the body might contribute to the peace of the soul. For if bodily peace be wanting, a bar is put to the peace even of the irrational soul, since it cannot obtain the gratifica- tion of its appetites. And these two together help out the mutual peace of soul and body, the peace of harmonious life and health. For as animals, by shunning pain, show that they love bodily peace, and, by pursuing pleasure to gratify their appetites, show that they love peace of soul, so their shrink- ing from death is a sufficient indication of their intense love of that peace which binds soul and body in close alliance. But, as man has a rational soul, he subordinates all this which he has in common with the beasts to the peace of his rational soul, that his in- tellect may have free play and may regu- late his actions, and that he may thus en- joy the well-ordered harmony of knowledge and action which constitutes, as we have said, the peace of the rational soul. And for this purpose he must desire to be neither molested by pain, nor disturbed by desire, nor extinguished by death, that he may ar- rive at some useful knowledge by which he may regulate his life and manners. But, owing to the liability of the human mind to fall into mistakes, this very pursuit of knowledge may be a snare to him unless he has a divine Master, whom he may obey without misgiving, and who may at the same time give him such help as to preserve his own freedom. And because, so long as he is in this mortal body, he is stranger to God, he walks by faith, not by sight; and he therefore refers all peace, bodily or spiritual or both, to that peace which mortal man has with the immortal God, so that he exhibits the well-ordered obedience of faith to eter- nal law. But as this divine Master inculcates two precepts—the love of God and the love

of our neighbor—and as in these precepts a man finds three things he has to love—God, himself, and his neighbor—and that he who loves God loves himself thereby, it follows that he must endeavor to get his neighbor to love God, since he is ordered to love his neighbor as himself. He ought to make this endeavor in behalf of his wife, his children, his household, all within his reach, even as he would wish his neighbor to do the same for him if he needed it; and consequently he will be at peace, or in well-ordered con- cord, with all men, as far as in him lies. And this is the order of this concord, that a man, in the first place, injure no one, and, in the second, do good to every one he can reach. Primarily, therefore, his own house- hold are his care, for the law of nature and of society gives him readier access to them and greater opportunity of serving them. And hence the apostle says, "Now, if any provide not for his own, and specially for those of his own house, he hath denied the faith, and is worse than an infidel." [1] This is the origin of domestic peace, or the well- ordered concord of those in the family who rule and those who obey. For they who care for the rest rule—the husband the wife, the parents the children, the masters the servants; and they who are cared for obey— the women their husbands, the children their parents, the servants their masters. But in the family of the just man who lives by faith and is as yet a pilgrim journeying on to the celestial city, even those who rule serve those whom they seem to command; for they rule not from a love of power, but from a sense of the duty they owe to others —not because they are proud of authority, but because they love mercy.

13. Liberty and Slavery

This is prescribed by the order of nature: it is thus that God has created man. For "let them," He says, "have dominion over the fish of the sea, and over the fowl of the air, and over every creeping thing which

[1] I Tim. v. 8.

creepeth on the earth." [1] He did not intend that His rational creature, who was made in His image, should have dominion over anything but the irrational creation—not man over man, but man over the beasts. And hence the righteous men in primitive times were made shepherds of cattle rather than kings of men, God intending thus to teach us what the relative position of the creatures is, and what the desert of sin; for it is with justice, we believe, that the condition of slavery is the result of sin. And this is why we do not find the word "slave" in any part of Scripture until righteous Noah branded the sin of his son with this name. It is a name, therefore, introduced by sin and not by nature. The origin of the Latin word for slave is supposed to be found in the circumstance that those who by the law of war were liable to be killed were sometimes preserved by their victors, and were hence called servants. And these circumstances could never have arisen save through sin. For even when we wage a just war, our adversaries must be sinning; and every victory, even though gained by wicked men, is a result of the first judgment of God, who humbles the vanquished either for the sake of removing or of punishing their sins. Witness that man of God, Daniel, who, when he was in captivity, confessed to God his own sins and the sins of his people, and declared with pious grief that these were the cause of the captivity.[2] The prime cause, then, of slavery is sin, which brings man under the dominion of his fellow—that which does not happen save by the judgment of God, with whom is no unrighteousness, and who knows how to award fit punishments to every variety of offence. But our Master in heaven says, "Every one who doeth sin is the servant of sin." [3] And thus there are many wicked masters who have religious men as their slaves, and who are yet themselves in bondage; "for of whom a man is overcome, of the same is he brought

in bondage." [4] And beyond question it is a happier thing to be the slave of a man than of a lust; for even this very lust of ruling, to mention no others, lays waste men's hearts with the most ruthless dominion. Moreover, when men are subjected to one another in a peaceful order, the lowly position does as much good to the servant as the proud position does harm to the master. But by nature, as God first created us, no one is the slave either of man or of sin. This servitude is, however, penal, and is appointed by that law which enjoins the preservation of the natural order and forbids its disturbance; for if nothing had been done in violation of that law, there would have been nothing to restrain by penal servitude. And therefore the apostle admonishes slaves to be subject to their masters, and to serve them heartily and with good-will, so that, if they cannot be freed by their masters, they may themselves make their slavery in some sort free, by serving not in crafty fear, but in faithful love, until all unrighteousness pass away, and all principality and every human power be brought to nothing, and God be all in all.

14. Equitable Rule

And therefore, although our righteous fathers [1] had slaves, and administered their domestic affairs so as to distinguish between the condition of slaves and the heirship of sons in regard to the blessings of this life, yet in regard to the worship of God, in whom we hope for eternal blessings, they took an equally loving oversight of all the members of their household. And this is so much in accordance with the natural order, that the head of the household was called *paterfamilias;* and this name has been so generally accepted, that even those whose rule is unrighteous are glad to apply it to themselves. But those who are true fathers of their households desire and endeavor that

---

[1] Gen. i. 26.
[2] Dan. ix.
[3] John viii. 34.

[4] II Pet. ii. 19.
[1] The patriarchs.

all the members of their household, equally with their own children, should worship and win God, and should come to that heavenly home in which the duty of ruling men is no longer necessary, because the duty of caring for their everlasting happiness has also ceased; but, until they reach that home, masters ought to feel their position of authority a greater burden than servants their service. And if any member of the family interrupts the domestic peace by disobedience, he is corrected either by word or blow, or some kind of just and legitimate punishment, such as society permits, that he may himself be the better for it, and be readjusted to the family harmony from which he had dislocated himself. For as it is not benevolent to give a man help at the expense of some greater benefit he might receive, so it is not innocent to spare a man at the risk of his falling into graver sin. To be innocent, we must not only do harm to no man, but also restrain him from sin or punish his sin, so that either the man himself who is punished may profit by his experience, or others be warned by his example. Since, then, the house ought to be the beginning or element of the city, and every beginning bears reference to some end of its own kind, and every element to the integrity of the whole of which it is an element, it follows plainly enough that domestic peace has a relation to civic peace—in other words, that the well-ordered concord of domestic obedience and domestic rule has a relation to the well-ordered concord of civic obedience and civic rule. And therefore it follows, further, that the father of the family ought to frame his domestic rule in accordance with the law of the city, so that the household may be in harmony with the civic order.

15. The Supranational Character of the Heavenly City on Earth

But the families which do not live by faith seek their peace in the earthly advantages of this life; while the families which live by faith look for those eternal blessing which are promised, and use as pilgrims such advantages of time and of earth as do not fascinate and divert them from God, but rather aid them to endure with greater ease, and to keep down the number of those burdens of the corruptible body which weigh upon the soul. Thus the things necessary for this mortal life are used by both kinds of men and families alike, but each has its own peculiar and widely different aim in using them. The earthly city, which does not live by faith, seeks an earthly peace, and the end it proposes, in the well-ordered concord of civic obedience and rule, is the combination of men's wills to attain the things which are helpful to this life. The heavenly city, or rather the part of it which sojourns on earth and lives by faith, makes use of this peace only because it must, until this mortal condition which necessitates it shall pass away. Consequently, so long as it lives like a captive and a stranger in the earthly city, though it has already received the promise of redemption, and the gift of the Spirit as the earnest of it, it makes no scruple to obey the laws of the earthly city, whereby the things necessary for the maintenance of this mortal life are administered; and thus, as this life is common to both cities, so there is a harmony between them in regard to what belongs to it. But, as the earthly city has had some philosophers whose doctrine is condemned by the divine teaching, and who, being deceived either by their own conjectures or by demons, supposed that many gods must be invited to take an interest in human affairs, and assigned to each a separate function and a separate department—to one the body, to another the soul; and in the body itself, to one the head, to another the neck, and each of the other members to one of the gods; and in like manner, in the soul, to one god the natural capacity was assigned, to another education, to another anger, to another lust; and so the various affairs of life were assigned—cattle to one, corn to another, wine to another, oil to another, the woods to another, money to another, navigation to another, wars and victories to another, marriages to another, births and fecundity to another, and other things to other gods: and as the celestial city, on the other hand, knew that one God only was to be worshipped, and that to Him alone was due that service which the Greeks call *latreia*, and which can be given only to a god, it has come to pass that the two cities could not have common laws of religion, and that the heavenly city has been compelled in this matter to dissent, and to become obnoxious to those who think differently, and to stand the brunt of their anger and hatred and persecutions, except in so far as the minds of their enemies have been alarmed by the multitude of the Christians, and quelled by the manifest protection of God accorded to them. This heavenly city, then, while it sojourns on earth, calls citizens out of all nations, and gathers together a society of pilgrims of all languages, not scrupling about diversities in the manners, laws, and institutions whereby earthly peace is secured and maintained, but recognizing that, however various these are, they all tend to one and the same end of earthly peace. It therefore is so far from rescinding and

abolishing these diversities, that it even preserves and adopts them, so long only as no hindrance to the worship of the one supreme and true God is thus introduced. Even the heavenly city, therefore, while in its state of pilgrimage, avails itself of the peace of earth, and, so far as it can without injuring faith and godliness, desires and maintains a common agreement among men regarding the acquisition of the necessaries of life, and makes this earthly peace bear upon the peace of heaven; for this alone can be truly called and esteemed the peace of the reasonable creatures, consisting as it does in the perfectly ordered and harmonious enjoyment of God and of one another in God. When we shall have reached that peace, this mortal life shall give place to one that is eternal, and our body shall be no more this animal body which by its corruption weighs down the soul, but a spiritual body feeling no want, and in all its members subjected to the will. In its pilgrim state the heavenly city possesses this peace by faith; and by this faith it lives righteously when it refers to the attainment of that peace every good action towards God and man; for the life of the city is a social life.

CHAPTER 7

JOHN OF SALISBURY

CHRISTIANITY introduced a revolutionary principle into communal life by destroying the previous equation of personality and citizenship, and by postulating autonomy of a spiritual sphere independent of, and even superior to, political authority. Thus for a time Christianity was on the defensive, and the needs of institutional survival naturally overshadowed the need for theoretical formulas. But after Christianity became the official religion of state in the fourth century, and the only permitted creed in the fifth, interest in the theory of the relation of church and state developed more rapidly.

St. Augustine was so deeply concerned with the theological defense of Christianity against paganism and heresy that he did not elaborate a political theory clearly defining the boundaries between political and ecclesiastical power, but toward the close of the fifth century, Pope Gelasius defined the relation between the two authorities (or "two swords," as they were later called). Christ himself was king and priest, but knowing the sinfulness and weakness of human nature, he divided, according to Gelasius, the two offices, assigning to ecclesiastical authority the spiritual and religious welfare of men, and to political authority the care and administration of temporal matters. Both ecclesiastical and political powers derive their authority from God; each is independent, and therefore supreme, in its own sphere, the church in religious matters and the state in political affairs. Yet this independence also implies mutual dependence: because the state is supreme only in its own sphere, the political, it must bow to the supremacy of the church in religious issues. Similarly, the church, because it is supreme only in religious matters, must recognize the authority of the state in mundane government and administration.

Gelasius did not raise, or answer, the question of who is to decide whether a specific issue is predominantly religious or political. In his dualistic conception of authority he assumed that church and state would cooperate in practical tasks rather than engage in bitter jurisdictional disputes: the church needs the state for temporal purposes, and the state needs the church for the attainment of spiritual salvation. The clergy should therefore not interfere with the government's secular business, and the political rulers should keep clear of spiritual matters.

Had Gelasius pressed the issue to its logical conclusions and gone into the question of who is to decide authoritatively, in a given situation, whether the ecclesiastical or temporal interest is predominant, he would have discovered that his dualistic theory was not wholly satisfactory. Under his dualistic doctrine of two coordinate authorities, whoever has the right or power to decide whether a matter at issue is primarily ecclesiastical or temporal, will, in effect, be the first, or, to use a more modern phrase, sovereign authority. But the formulation of socially significant questions is not a matter of mere logic, and Gelasius may have felt that the cause of peace and the long-term interests of the church would best be served by a doctrine that stressed the possibility of equilibrium rather than of strife. The dualism of ecclesiastical and temporal authority was not conceived to be final: God is the source of both, and in serving God both authorities find their reason for existence.

Nevertheless, Gelasius weighed his doctrine somewhat in favor of the church by mentioning that its burden is heavier than that of the state, because the priest is answerable for the souls of all—subjects, lords, and kings. In Gelasius' own mind, this special position of the church merely involved special responsibilities, inasmuch as the heaviest task of all, spiritual salvation, was assigned to it. Yet the doctrine of the heavier burden—originally a moral ideal of fuller dedication to selfless service—became, from the ninth century on, a positive claim for more dignity and authority in relation to mundane government.

As the conflict between church and empire grew, particularly from the tenth to the twelfth centuries, each side tended to give up the older Gelasian doctrine of two authorities poised in equilibrium. The papalists claimed supreme authority for the church as the representative of the spiritual principle in society and insisted that all authority, ecclesiastical and secular, was originally given to the church; that, retaining the title and exercise of spiritual power, the church then transferred the exercise of secular authority to the state, without, however, abandoning the original title to it. According to the basic papalist theory, the church held its authority directly from God, whereas the state exercised its authority indirectly, having received it from the church as the intermediary between God and society.

In the age of feudalism, social rights and institutions were less well defined and clear-cut than in premedieval or modern times. Thus landed property was not attached to a single owner who had absolute dominion over it, but was broken up into its component elements, so that one person might be the legal owner, whereas many others might share in its uses. Or the owner might retain for himself some forms of the use of his property, and grant other forms of use to his vassals. The papalist doctrine claiming that secular authority was held only as a "fief" (in tenure) by the state, true title resting with the church, was no stranger in construction than was the medieval (and still valid) legal doctrine of "eminent domain" under which the king retains the ultimate title to all property in the land.

In pre- and postfeudal eras the argument of the medieval papalists might logically lead to theocracy, a government in which the priests rule in both ecclesiastical and secular matters. The specific environment of feudalism permitted the formulation of a theory in which even the papalists merely claimed the original title to secular authority but left its exercise to the state. What the papalists demanded was not so much that the pope actually rule and administer the empire but that he control the emperor's action from the viewpoint of Christian values, that he protect the subjects against rulers who strayed from the path of righteousness, and that he have the right to censure and admonish the emperor, and, if necessary, excommunicate and depose him.

By contrast, the representatives of the imperialist position made, in theory at least, more moderate claims. They were willing to concede that neither power was supreme over the other as far as its source and title were concerned, for both powers were handed down directly from God to church and state. Thus, in essence, the moderate imperialist writers were satisfied to restate the Gelasian doctrine of equality and equilibrium between secular and spiritual authorities. As the contest between the papalists and the imperialists sharpened, particularly from the eleventh century on, extreme antipapalists suggested that the office of the king or emperor was, in itself, higher than that of bishop and pope, and that secular authority was supreme in worldly and spiritual matters.

The struggle between papalist and antipapalist doctrines was not only, or even chiefly, an issue of theological disagreement but the expression of vital conflicts of power and control. In particular, the contest was by no means as universal as the phrase "church and empire" would imply. In the first place, the Holy Roman Empire (which originated in the coronation of Charlemagne in Rome in 800 and ended in the abdication of the Habsburg emperor Francis II in 1806) was little more than a German empire, including a great part of Italy but excluding the all-important political areas of England, France, and Spain. Similarly, the church could at no time in the Middle Ages speak in the name of all Christendom, but only of those who, especially in the West, were under the jurisdiction of Rome. To this day the Roman Catholic Church has preserved, in Italy, the flavor of a specifically Italian institution, inasmuch as the popes and the majority of the cardinals have in general been Italian.

But contestants in any dispute seek to buttress their case by identifying their partial interest with a more general, and possibly universal, one. It was therefore not unnatural for the Roman Catholic Church to represent itself as the guardian of all Christendom, just as it was in the interest of German expansionist monarchs to hug the cloak of the Holy Roman Empire and thus acquire more respectability and universality. Although the Roman empire had been defeated militarily in the fifth century by Germanic invaders streaming into Italy and her possessions from all directions, such was the indestructible heritage of Roman political experience and genius that the Roman popes continued, during the Middle Ages, the struggle with expanding German power—a power that the political and military leaders of the empire had been unable to stem by force. It is to be noted that the papacy also collided with French and English kings, but the principal adversary was the German monarchy, which threatened Italy and the Roman church most directly.

The second aspect of the conflict between church and state was intimately tied to the feudal system. Bishops were, on the one hand, charged with the administration of the church and the care of souls, but at the same time they were feudal holders of land and as such vassals of the king. The feudal link of authority, unlike that of the modern state, was of a highly personal kind, and loyalty of the vassal to the lord was more profound and absorbing than is implied in the modern concept of obeying an impersonal law. The church has always been, and still is, an owner of large landed properties, but the modern concept of ownership is more absolute and does not involve a special kind of allegiance to the government, as was the situation in the feudal era in which landed property was the determining element in the machinery of government.

Another source of conflict lay in the fact that, as the clergy in the Middle Ages for a long time enjoyed a monopoly of literacy and learning, they were entrusted with important administrative positions in the courts and chancelleries of Europe. In theory, perhaps, a bishop could be a faithful representative of the church in spiritual matters and a loyal vassal of the king in economic and political affairs; but this theory was based on the assumption that church and state did not disagree on major policies. When there was disagreement, bishops and priests had to choose which was their first loyalty. The papalists advised them that the church was higher in dignity and authority. The antipapalists insisted that, in secular matters at least, and perhaps in spiritual, too, royal authority was supreme.

The first great conflict between church and empire occurred in the latter part of the eleventh century, when, in 1076, Emperor Henry IV deposed Pope Gregory VII; shortly thereafter, the pope not only deposed the emperor but also excommunicated him and relieved his subjects from their oath of allegiance. From that time until the end of the thirteenth century the conflict between ecclesiastical and secular power dominated the theory as well as the practice of politics.

The most incisive presentation of the papalist viewpoint is the work of an Englishman, John of Salisbury (about 1120-1180). He is considered by many to be the most typical medieval political writer before the discovery and spread of Aristotelianism in the thirteenth century, which gave rise to such divergent and overtowering figures as St. Thomas Aquinas and Marsilio of Padua.

John of Salisbury spent twelve years of his schooling in France, mostly in Paris, then the world center of philosophy and theology, and in Chartres, an important center of humanistic studies. Like other great English political writers later on (Locke, Burke, John Stuart Mill), John of Salisbury had wide practical experience in public affairs. At an early age, as the secretary of Archbishop Theobald of Canterbury, he acquired intimate knowledge of government and politics in England, as well as inside penetration into the character and management of the church. He frequently traveled to the papal court in Rome, and was an intimate friend of Adrian IV, the only English pope in history. He also became a friend of Thomas Becket; when the latter succeeded Theobald as Archbishop of Canterbury, John of Salisbury continued as secretary to the new archbishop.

The conflict between ecclesiastical and temporal power in England developed rapidly during this period, and in 1164 John of Salisbury was exiled to France, shortly to be followed by Thomas Becket. Six years later they returned to England, and John of Salisbury was probably with Thomas Becket on the day the latter was murdered in his own cathedral at Canterbury by the henchmen of Henry II, king of England. In 1176 John of Salisbury was asked by the French king, Louis VII, to become bishop of Chartres. John gladly accepted the invitation to return to the city in which he had been introduced, as a youth, to humanistic learning, and in Chartres, where he felt so much at home, he died in 1180.

John of Salisbury's most important work is his *Statesman's Book (Policraticus)*. There is perhaps no single doctrine that he can claim to have discovered first; yet his book is one of the most influential medieval political statements because of the originality with which he combines existing isolated ideas into a new pattern, and because of his style, which has freshness, integrity, and a sense of humor—the latter a particularly rare quality in a medieval writer on politics.

John is best known for his championing of the supremacy of the ecclesiastical over the temporal power. From the ninth century on, this struggle between the two powers had not ceased. The Gelasian doctrine of equilibrium and cooperation between church and state was constantly modified by the conflicts of power between the popes and the German emperors, and the developing interpretations of church-state relations reflected the strains and tensions of the struggle for hegemony. In the twelfth century, an era of increasing strife between ecclesiastical and mundane authority, the papalists were particularly fortunate in finding John of Salisbury for one of their first spokesmen; he was undisputedly their most effective.

There are no ifs and buts in his argument: he clearly states that both swords, the material and the spiritual, belong to the church, and that the *prince receives his sword*, or authority, *from the church*, that he is a "minister of the priestly power, and one who exercises that side of the sacred offices which seems unworthy of the hands of the priesthood." As the original and true owner of the temporal sword, the church has the right to depose the prince if he violates the law of God and disregards the precepts of the church, for "he who can lawfully bestow can lawfully take away."

The human body is another symbolic analogy that John of Salisbury employs for proving the superiority of the ecclesiastical over the secular power. John compares the commonwealth to a body, each organ, group, and class representing symbolically parts of the body. Thus farmers and workers correspond to the feet, public-finance officers to the stomach and intestines, officials and soldiers to the hands, and the senate to the heart, while the prince occupies the place of the head. But the church and clergy occupy the highest place of all, as they are likened to the soul in the body, and "the soul is, as it were, the prince of the body, and has rulership over the whole thereof." The secular ruler is therefore subject to God and "to those who exercise His office and represent Him on earth." John of Salisbury was not familiar with Aristotle's *Politics* and its organic conception of the political community; for John, in contrast to Aristotle, the organic theory meant that each organ of state and society had its unchangeable place.

John of Salisbury does not propose that the church actually take over the temporal government and administer it through priests, nor does he recommend that a prince submit every law for prior approval to a supreme court of priests. Yet he makes the extreme claim that "a statute or ordinance (*constitutio*) of the prince is a thing of nought if not in conformity with the teaching (*disciplina*) of the Church." Without proposing the administrative absorption of the state into the church, and unable to think—as a medieval writer—in terms of clearly defined concepts of legal sovereignty, John of Salisbury nevertheless made such an overwhelming case for the moral sovereignty of the church over the secular ruler that later protagonists of the papal cause found it none too difficult to go beyond him and plead for legal supremacy as well.

In his supporting sources, John of Salisbury, like most medieval papalist writers and pamphleteers except St. Augustine, leaned heavily on the Old Testament with its firm bias against temporal rulers, and he quotes frequently from the Hebrew prophets and their struggle against kings and princes. The New Testament emphasized more positively that "the powers that be are ordained of God" (*Rom.*, 13:1), and made it possible to interpret the Christian acceptance of mundane power in a manner that would maintain the supremacy of the church. But it was easier to go back to the Old Testament in which the hostility against secular rulers was consistent and unequivocal. Nearly five centuries after John of Salisbury, the English Puritans reverted, in their struggle against secular authority, to the Old Testament as a main source of fighting inspiration.

From the modern secularist viewpoint, the church ought to stay in its place and not contend with the state for temporal power. But John of Salisbury and the papal apologists, in seeking to curb the authoritarian claims of kings and princes, or to gain at least equal authority for the church, were (knowingly or unknowingly) fighting a cause that was larger than their own: the whole issue of human liberty was at stake, and it was a more important issue than the rivalry for power and supremacy that raged between popes and emperors. And though John of Salisbury and the medievalists did not solve this larger issue, neither have the secularists: Is the state, even the democratic state, to have absolute and complete authority, or must there be some competing principles of allegiance that will make it difficult, or impossible, for the state to become an all-absorbing Leviathan? The church can no longer, as in the Middle Ages, play the part of a competing major source of loyalty and authority, but thus far no institution or idea is in sight that can be relied on to do the job. The democratic state—precisely because of its popular source of support—has by no means abolished the possibility of tyranny and repression, as was so prophetically foreseen by Alexis de Tocqueville and John Stuart Mill a century ago.

John of Salisbury's second main political doctrine, the distinction between king and tyrant and the justification of tyrannicide, is as provocative today as it was in his own time. The distinction between king and tyrant goes back to Aristotle: the king rules in the interest of the ruled, the tyrant in his own. John of Salisbury states, by contrast, that the *king rules in accordance with the laws,* whereas the *tyrant rules by force.* This distinction is directly related to the Christian and typically medieval respect for law, and it is closer to the modern distinction between legitimate and illegitimate government than is Aristotle's emphasis on interest.

By violating the rule of law, John of Salisbury says, the tyrant assails the grace of God, and "it is God himself who in a sense is challenged to battle." The prince fights for the laws and liberties of the people, and "as the likeness of the Deity is to be loved, worshipped and cherished; the tyrant, the likeness of wickedness, is generally to be even killed." In one passage John does qualify his general position on tyrannicide by expressing his hope that the most useful and safest way of destroying tyrants is for the oppressed to pray devoutly "that the scourge wherewith they are afflicted may be turned aside from them." But such occasional qualification does not detract from his general view that *tyrants may be lawfully slain.*

In fact, John of Salisbury goes further and asserts that it is not only lawful but even right and just to kill the tyrant, for he who takes the sword shall perish by the sword. The ruler has a special responsibility to obey the law and protect justice. The tyrant usurps power, oppresses justice, and enslaves the law to his arbitrary whims. Of all forms of treason, "none is more deadly than that which is aimed against the very body of justice." In resisting and killing the tyrant, no violation of the law is being committed, as it is the tyrant "who disarms the laws," and it is therefore fitting that "justice arm herself against him." He who does not prosecute and attack the tyrant, sins against himself and against the whole community.

Thus, completely abandoning the Augustinian tradition, John of Salisbury expressed the doctrine of tyrannicide more forcefully and challengingly than anyone else in the Middle Ages; not until the sixteenth century did resistance to tyrants, and assassination, become again a major theme of political speculation. John Locke expressed the doctrine of revolution and resistance to tyrants in words that bear a striking resemblance to John of Salisbury's. According to Locke, absolute government "is no form of civil government at all," and the absolute prince is in a state of nature, outside the realm of law and justice. The true rebels are the arbitrary and oppressive rulers who violate the law, and resistance to such rulers is the first step toward restoring the law. John of Salisbury thus was one of the first writers to establish the doctrine that obedience to authority is not absolute but conditional, that political authority is ultimately based on justice, and that resistance is a right and duty when peaceful change of a tyrannical regime is impossible.

What made John of Salisbury so convincing as a political writer and papal protagonist was his sense of proportion and his ability to see things in grey rather than black and white. One of the most revealing passages of *The States-man's Book* is his account of a conversation with Pope Adrian IV on what people thought of the church and of the pope. As John explains, he was "entirely frank" with the pope; he recited a scathing catalogue of sins and vices attributed by many persons to the church and the clergy. He stressed particularly the love of money prevalent among the priests: "They give judgment not for the truth but for money. For money you can get anything done today, and without waiting; but you will not get it done even tomorrow if you do not pay a price."

Next to avarice, John charges the church and priesthood with duplicity and the lust for power, and says they have no compassion for the suffering and misery of the afflicted. Though he was speaking to a pope, John said: "Even the Roman pontiff himself is a grievous and almost intolerable burden to all; the complaint is everywhere made that while the churches which were built by the devotion of the fathers are falling into ruin and collapsing, he has built for himself palaces, and walks abroad not merely in purple but in gold. The palaces of priests dazzle the eye, and meanwhile in their hands the Church of Christ is defiled."

The pope—an Englishman, a friend of John, and a person with a sense of humor—laughed after John had finished, congratulated him for having spoken so frankly, and asked him to report in the future anything unfavorable about the church.

Toward the end of his book, John of Salisbury returns to the subject of ecclesiastical vices and abuses, and attacks, above all, the struggle for power and office within the church; he is shocked by the lack of scruples—even when it comes to murder—among contenders for the papal office: "It is alleged by some, and it is indeed the truth, that the office of Roman pontiff has sometimes, nay rather has often, been contested by ambitious men, and not without the shedding of fraternal blood has the pontiff entered the Holy of Holies." One of the concluding observations of John's is therefore that, as between the temporal and ecclesiastical tyrant, the latter is the worse.

It is precisely because of John of Salisbury's capacity to criticize ruthlessly the abuses of his church that his defense of ecclesiastical supremacy over the temporal power proved so effective. His *Statesman's Book* is not only an important medieval political treatise but also a thoroughly enjoyable piece of literature, modern in its wit, urbanity, learning, balance, and perspective. His papalist viewpoint was not commonly accepted by his countrymen in his own day, and it is less well received today. But his thought and personality point to those qualities in English political philosophy that later assured it a unique position of influence in the world.

JOHN OF SALISBURY

The Statesman's Book *

1. The Nature and Source of Royal Authority

Between a tyrant and a prince there is this single or chief difference, that the latter obeys the law and rules the people by its dictates, accounting himself as but their servant. It is by virtue of the law that he makes good his claim to the foremost and chief place in the management of the affairs of the commonwealth and in the bearing of its burdens; and his elevation over others consists in this, that whereas private men are held responsible only for their private affairs, on the prince fall the burdens of the whole community. Wherefore deservedly there is conferred on him, and gathered together in his hands, the power of all his subjects, to the end that he may be sufficient unto himself in seeking and bringing about the advantage of each individually, and of all; and to the end that the state of the human commonwealth may be ordered in the best possible manner, seeing that each and all are members one of another. Wherein we indeed but follow nature, the best guide of life; for nature has gathered together all the senses of her microcosm or little world, which is man, into the head, and has subjected all the members in obedience to it in such wise that they will all function properly so long as they follow the guidance of the head, and the head remains sane. Therefore the prince stands

* From John of Salisbury, *The Statesman's Book* (trans. John Dickinson, 1927). Copyright by Appleton-Century-Crofts. By permission.

on a pinnacle which is exalted and made splendid with all the great and high privileges which he deems necessary for himself. And rightly so, because nothing is more advantageous to the people than that the needs of the prince should be fully satisfied; since it is impossible that his will should be found opposed to justice. Therefore, according to the usual definition, the prince is the public power, and a kind of likeness on earth of the divine majesty. Beyond doubt a large share of the divine power is shown to be in princes by the fact that at their nod men bow their necks and for the most part offer up their heads to the axe to be struck off, and, as by a divine impulse, the prince is feared by each of those over whom he is set as an object of fear. And this I do not think could be, except as a result of the will of God. For all power is from the Lord God, and has been with Him always, and is from everlasting. The power which the prince has is therefore from God, for the power of God is never lost, nor severed from Him, but He merely exercises it through a subordinate hand, making all things teach His mercy or justice. "Who, therefore, resists the ruling power, resists the ordinance of God," [1] in whose hand is the authority of conferring that power, and when He so desires, of withdrawing it again, or diminishing it. For it is not the ruler's own act when his will is turned to cruelty against his subjects, but it is rather the dispensation of God for His good pleasure

[1] Rom. xiii, 2.

to punish or chasten them. Thus during the Hunnish persecution, Attila, on being asked by the reverend bishop of a certain city who he was, replied, "I am Attila, the scourge of God." Whereupon it is written that the bishop adored him as representing the divine majesty. "Welcome," he said, "is the minister of God," and "Blessed is he that cometh in the name of the Lord," and with sighs and groans he unfastened the barred doors of the church, and admitted the persecutor through whom he attained straightway to the palm of martyrdom. For he dared not shut out the scourge of God, knowing that His beloved Son was scourged, and that the power of this scourge which had come upon himself was as nought except it came from God. If good men thus regard power as worthy of veneration even when it comes as a plague upon the elect, who should not venerate that power which is instituted by God for the punishment of evil-doers and for the reward of good men, and which is promptest in devotion and obedience to the laws? To quote the words of the Emperor, "it is indeed a saying worthy of the majesty of royalty that the prince acknowledges himself bound by the Laws." [2] For the authority of the prince depends upon the authority of justice and law; and truly it is a greater thing than imperial power for the prince to place his government under the laws, so as to deem himself entitled to do nought which is at variance with the equity of justice.

2. The Relation of the Prince to the Law

Princes should not deem that it detracts from their princely dignity to believe that the enactments of their own justice are not to be preferred to the justice of God, whose justice is an everlasting justice, and His law is equity. Now equity, as the learned jurists define it, is a certain fitness of things which compares all things rationally, and seeks to apply like rules of right and wrong to like cases, being impartially disposed toward all persons, and allotting to each that which belongs to him. Of this equity the interpreter is the law, to which the will and intention of equity and justice are known. Therefore Crisippus asserted that the power of the law extends over all things, both divine and human, and that it accordingly presides over all goods and ills, and is the ruler and guide of material things as well as of human beings. To which Papinian, a man most learned in the law, and Demosthenes, the great orator, seem to assent, subjecting all men to its obedience because all law is, as it were, a discovery, and a gift from God, a precept of wise men, the corrector of excesses of the will, the bond which knits together the fabric of the state, and the banisher of crime; [1] and it is therefore fitting that all men should live according to it who lead their lives in a corporate political body. All are accordingly bound by the necessity of keeping the law, unless perchance there is any who can be thought to have been given the license of wrong-doing. However, it is said that the prince is absolved from the obligations of the law; but this is not true in the sense that it is lawful for him to do unjust acts, but only in the sense that his character should be such as to cause him to practice equity not through fear of the penalties of the law but through love of justice; and should also be such as to cause him from the same motive to promote the advantage of the commonwealth, and in all things to prefer the good of others before his own private will. Who, indeed, in respect of public matters can properly speak of the will of the prince at all, since therein he may not lawfully have any will of his own apart from that which the law or equity enjoins, or the calculation of the common interest requires? For in these matters his will is to have the force of a judgment; and most properly that which pleases him therein has the force of law, because his decision may not be at variance with the intention of

---

equity. "From thy countenance," says the Lord, "let my judgment go forth, let thine eyes look upon equity"; [2] for the uncorrupted judge is one whose decision, from assiduous contemplation of equity, is the very likeness thereof. The prince accordingly is the minister of the common interest and the bond-servant of equity, and he bears the public person in the sense that he punishes the wrongs and injuries of all, and all crimes, with even-handed equity. His rod and staff also, administered with wise moderation, restore irregularities and false departures to the straight path of equity, so that deservedly may the Spirit congratulate the power of the prince with the words, "Thy rod and thy staff, they have comforted me." [3] His shield, too, is strong, but it is a shield for the protection of the weak, and one which wards off powerfully the darts of the wicked from the innocent. Those who derive the greatest advantage from his performance of the duties of his office are those who can do least for themselves, and his power is chiefly exercised against those who desire to do harm. Therefore not without reason he bears a sword, wherewith he sheds blood blamelessly, without becoming thereby a man of blood, and frequently puts men to death without incurring the name or guilt of homicide. For if we believe the great Augustine, David was called a man of blood not because of his wars, but because of Uria. And Samuel is nowhere described as a man of blood or a homicide, although he slew Agag, the fat king of Amalech. Truly the sword of princely power is as the sword of a dove, which contends without gall, smites without wrath, and when it fights, yet conceives no bitterness at all. For as the law pursues guilt without any hatred of persons, so the prince most justly punishes offenders from no motive of wrath but at the behest, and in accordance with the decision, of the passionless law. For although we see that the prince has lictors of his own, we must yet think of him as in reality himself the sole or chief lictor, to whom is granted by the law the privilege of striking by a subordinate hand. If we adopt the opinion of the Stoics, who diligently trace down the reason for particular words, "lictor" means "legis ictor," or "hammer of the law," because the duty of his office is to strike those who the law adjudges shall be struck. Wherefore anciently, when the sword hung over the head of the convicted criminal, the command was wont to be given to the officials by whose hand the judge punishes evil-doers, "Execute the sentence of the law," or "Obey the law," to the end that the misery of the victim might be mitigated by the calm reasonableness of the words.

3. The Prince Subordinate to the Priests

This sword, then, the prince receives from the hand of the Church, although she herself has no sword of blood at all. Nevertheless she has this sword, but she uses it by the hand of the prince, upon whom she confers the power of bodily coercion, retaining to herself authority over spiritual things in the person of the pontiffs. The prince is, then, as it were, a minister of the priestly power, and one who exercises that side of the sacred offices which seems unworthy of the hands of the priesthood. For every office existing under, and concerned with the execution of, the sacred laws is really a religious office, but that is inferior which consists in punishing crimes, and which therefore seems to be typified in the person of the hangman. Wherefore Constantine, most faithful emperor of the Romans, when he had convoked the council of priests at Nicaea, neither dared to take the chief place for himself nor even to sit among the presbyters, but chose the hindmost seat. Moreover, the decrees which he heard approved by them he reverenced as if he had seen them emanate from the judgment-seat of the divine majesty. Even the rolls of petitions containing accusations against priests

2 Ps. xvii, 2.
3 Ps. xxiii, 4

which they brought to him in a steady stream he took and placed in his bosom without opening them. And after recalling them to charity and harmony, he said that it was not permissible for him, as a man, and one who was subject to the judgment of priests, to examine cases touching gods, who cannot be judged save by God alone. And the petitions which he had received he put into the fire without even looking at them, fearing to give publicity to accusations and censures against the fathers, and thereby incur the curse of Cham, the undutiful son, who did not hide his father's shame. Wherefore he said, as is narrated in the writings of Nicholas the Roman pontiff, "Verily if with mine own eyes I had seen a priest of God, or any of those who wear the monastic garb, sinning, I would spread my cloak and hide him, that he might not be seen of any." Also Theodosius, the great emperor, for a merited fault, though not so grave a one, was suspended by the priest of Milan from the exercise of his regal powers and from the insignia of his imperial office, and patiently and solemnly he performed the penance for homicide which was laid upon him. Again, according to the testimony of the teacher of the gentiles, greater is he who blesses man than he who is blessed; [1] and so he in whose hands is the authority to confer a dignity excels in honor and the privileges of honor him upon whom the dignity itself is conferred. Further, by the reasoning of the law it is his right to refuse who has the power to grant, and he who can lawfully bestow can lawfully take away.[2] Did not Samuel pass sentence of deposition against Saul by reason of his disobedience, and supersede him on the pinnacle of kingly rule with the lowly son of Ysai? [3] But if one who has been appointed prince has performed duly and faithfully the ministry which he has undertaken, as great honor and reverence are to be shown to him as the head excels in honor all the members of the

[1] Heb. vii, 7.
[2] Dig. I. 17, § 3.
[3] I.e. Jesse

body. Now he performs his ministry faithfully when he is mindful of his true status, and remembers that he bears the person of the *universitas* of those subject to him; and when he is fully conscious that he owes his life not to himself and his own private ends, but to others, and allots it to them accordingly, with duly ordered charity and affection. Therefore he owes the whole of himself to God, most of himself to his country, much to his relatives and friends, very little to foreigners, but still somewhat. He has duties to the very wise and the very foolish, to little children and to the aged. Supervision over these classes of persons is common to all in authority, both those who have care over spiritual things and those who exercise temporal jurisdiction.

4. Justice and Mercy

It should hold true of the prince, as it should hold true of all men, that no one should seek his own interest but that of others. Yet the measure of the affection with which he should embrace his subjects like brethren in the arms of charity must be kept within the bounds of moderation. For his love of his brethren should not prevent him from correcting their errors with proper medicine; he acknowledges the ties of flesh and blood to the end that he may subdue these to the rule of the spirit. It is the practice of physicians when they cannot heal a disease with poultices and mild medicines to apply stronger remedies such as fire or steel. But they never employ these unless they despair of restoring health by milder means, and so the ruling power when it cannot avail by mild measures to heal the vices of its subjects, rightly resorts, though with grief, to the infliction of sharp punishments, and with pious cruelty vents its rage against wrong-doers to the end that good men may be preserved uninjured. But who was ever strong enough to amputate the members of his own body without grief and pain? Therefore the prince grieves when called upon to inflict the punishment which guilt demands, and yet administers it with reluctant right hand. For the prince has no left hand, and in subjecting to pain the members of the body of which he is the head, he obeys the law in sadness and with groans. Philip once heard that a certain Phicias, who was a good fighting man, had become alienated from him because in his poverty he found difficulty in supporting his three daughters and yet received no aid from the king. When his friends advised him accordingly to beware of the man, "What," said Philip, "if a part of my body were sick, would I cut it off rather than seek to heal it?" Then he sought out this Phicias privately in a friendly way, and provided him with sufficient money which he accepted for the necessities of his private difficulties. And thereby the king made this man better disposed toward him and more faithful than he had been before he supposed himself offended. Accordingly, as Lucius says: "A prince should have an old man's habit of mind, who follows moderate counsels, and should play the part of a physician, who heals diseases sometimes by reducing the diet of the overfed, and again by increasing that of the under-nourished, who allays pain at times by cautery, and at other times by poultices." In addition, he should be affable of speech, and generous in conferring benefits, and in his manners he should preserve the dignity of his authority unimpaired. A pleasant address and a gracious tongue will win for him the reputation of benignity. Kindness will compel the most faithful and constant love from even the sternest, and will increase and confirm the love which it has produced. And the reverence of subjects is the fit reward of dignity of manners.

Excellently did Trajan, the best of the pagan emperors, answer his friends when they reproached him with making himself too common toward all men and more so, they thought, than was becoming for an emperor; for he said that he desired to be toward private citizens such an emperor as he had desired to have over him when he was a private citizen himself. And in accordance with this principle, acting on the report of the younger Pliny who at that time with other judges was designated to persecute the Church, he recalled the sword of persecution from the slaughter of the martyrs and moderated his edict. And perchance he would have dealt more gently still with the faithful, had not the laws and examples of his predecessors, and the advice of men who were considered wise counsellors, and the authority of his judges, all urged him to destroy a sect regarded by public opinion as superstitious, and as enemies of true religion. I do not unreservedly and in all respects commend the judgment of a man who knew not Christ, yet I do extenuate the fault of him who broke loose from the pressure of others and followed the instinct of his own natural piety toward kindness and pity, a man whose nature it was to be merciful toward all, though stern toward the few whom it would be sinful to spare; so that in the course of his whole reign only one of the senators or nobles of the city was condemned, although a great number could have been found who had offended grievously against him. And this man was condemned by the Senate without the knowledge of Trajan himself. For it was his habit to say that a man is insane who, having inflamed eyes, prefers to dig them out rather than to cure them. So again he said that the nails, if they are too sharp, should be trimmed and not plucked out. For if a cithern player and other performers on stringed instruments can by diligence find a way to correct the fault of a string which is out of tune and bring it again into accord with the other strings, and so out of discord make the sweetest harmony, not by breaking the strings but by making them tense or slack in due proportions; with how much care should the prince moderate his acts, now with the strictness of justice, and now with the leniency of mercy, to the end that he may make his subjects all be of one mind in one house, and thus as it were out of discordant dispositions bring to pass one great perfect harmony in the service of peace and in the works of charity? This, however, is certain, that it is safer for the cords to be relaxed than to be stretched too tautly. For the tension of slack cords can be corrected by the skill of the artificer so that they will again give forth the proper sweetness of tone; but a string that has once been broken, no artificer can repair.

5. The State as an Organism

A commonwealth, according to Plutarch, is a certain body which is endowed with life by the benefit of divine favor, which acts at the prompting of the highest equity, and is ruled by what may be called the moderating power of reason. Those things which establish and implant in us the practice of religion, and transmit to us the worship of God (here I do not follow Plutarch, who says "of the Gods") fill the place of the soul in the body of the commonwealth. And therefore those who preside over the practice of religion should be looked up to and venerated as the soul of the body. For who doubts that the ministers of God's holiness are His representatives? Furthermore, since the soul is, as it were, the prince of the body, and has rulership over the whole thereof, so those whom our author calls the prefects of religion preside over the entire body. Augustus Cæsar was to such a degree subject to the priestly power of the pontiffs that in order to set himself free from this subjection and have no one at all over him, he caused himself to be created a pontiff of Vesta, and thereafter had himself promoted to be one of the gods during his own life-time. The place of the head in the body of the commonwealth is filled by the prince, who is subject only to God and to those who exercise His office and represent Him on earth, even as in the human body the head is quickened and governed by the soul. The place of the heart is filled by the senate, from which proceeds the initiation of good works and ill. The duties of eyes, ears, and tongue are claimed by the judges and the governors of provinces. Officials and soldiers correspond to the hands. Those who always attend upon the prince are likened to the sides. Financial officers and keepers (I speak now not of those who are in charge of the prisons, but of those who are keepers of the privy chest) may be compared with the stomach and intestines, which, if they become congested through excessive avidity, and retain too tenaciously their accumulations, generate innumerable and incurable diseases, so that through their ailment the whole body is threatened with destruction. The husbandmen correspond to the feet, which always cleave to the soil, and need the more especially the care and foresight of the head, since while they walk upon the earth doing service with their bodies, they meet the more often with stones of stumbling, and therefore deserve aid and protection all the more justly since it is they who raise, sustain, and move forward the weight of the entire body. Take away the support of the feet from the strongest body, and it cannot move forward by its own power, but must creep painfully and shamefully on its hands, or else be moved by means of brute animals.

6. The "Feet" of the Commonwealth

Those are called the feet who discharge the humbler offices, and by whose services the members of the whole commonwealth walk upon solid earth. Among these are to be counted the husbandmen, who always cleave to the soil, busied about their ploughlands or vineyards or pastures or flowergardens. To these must be added the many species of cloth-making, and the mechanic arts, which work in wood, iron, bronze and the different metals; also the menial occupations, and the manifold forms of getting a livelihood and sustaining life, or increasing household property, all of which, while they do not pertain to the authority of the governing power, are yet in the highest degree useful and profitable to the corporate whole of the commonwealth. All these different occupations are so numerous that the commonwealth in the number of its feet exceeds not only the eight-footed crab but even the centipede, and because of their very multitude they cannot be enumerated; for while they are not infinite by nature, they are yet of so many different varieties that no writer on the subject of offices or duties has ever laid down particular precepts for each special variety. But it applies generally to each and all of them that in their exercise they should not transgress the limits of the law, and should in all things observe constant reference to the public utility. For inferiors owe it to their superiors to provide them with service, just as the superiors in their turn owe it to their inferiors to provide them with all things needful for their protection and succor. Therefore Plutarch says that that course is to be pursued in all things which is of advantage to the humbler classes, that is to say to the multitude; for small numbers always yield to great. Indeed the reason for the institution of magistrates was to the end that subjects might be protected from wrongs, and that the commonwealth itself might be "shod," so to speak, by means of their services. For it is as it were "unshod" when it is exposed to wrongs,— than which there can be no more disgraceful pass of affairs to those who fill the magistracies. For an afflicted people is a sign and proof of the goutiness, so to speak, of the prince. Then and then only will the health of the commonwealth be sound and flourishing when the higher members shield the lower, and the lower respond faithfully and fully in like measure to the just demands of their superiors, so that each and all are as it were members one of another by a sort of reciprocity, and each regards his own interest as best served by that which he knows to be most advantageous for the others.

7. The Love of Liberty and Free Speech

Liberty means judging everything freely in accordance with one's individual judgment, and does not hesitate to reprove what it sees opposed to good morals. Nothing but virtue is more splendid than liberty, if indeed liberty can ever properly be severed from virtue. For to all right-thinking men it is clear that true liberty issues from no other source. Wherefore, since all agree that virtue is the highest good in life, and that it alone can strike off the heavy and hateful yoke of slavery, it has been the opinion of philosophers that men should die, if need arose, for the sake of virtue, which is the only reason for living. But virtue can never be fully attained without liberty, and the absence of liberty proves that virtue in its full perfection is wanting. Therefore a man is free in proportion to the measure of his virtues, and the extent to which he is free determines what his virtues can accomplish; while, on the other hand, it is the vices alone which bring about slavery, and subject a man to persons and things in unmeet obedience; and though slavery of the person may seem at times the more to be pitied, in reality slavery to the vices is ever far the more wretched. And so what is more lovely than liberty? And what more agreeable to a man who has any reverence for virtue? We read that it has been the impelling motive of all good princes; and that none ever trod liberty under foot save the open foes of virtue. The jurists know what good laws were introduced for the sake of liberty, and the testimony of historians has made famous the great deeds done for love of it. Cato drank poison, pierced himself with his sword, and that no delay might prolong life on terms which he deemed ignoble, he thrust in his hand to widen the wound, and poured out his noble blood, that he might not see Cæsar reigning. Brutus set on foot civil wars to save the city from slavery; and that seat of empire perferred rather to bear the wretched afflictions of perpetual war than to endure a lord, though of the mildest character. I pass on to the weaker sex. The wives of the Teutons, because of the value they set upon their chastity, besought Marius after his victory that they might be presented as a gift to the Vestal Virgins, promising that they would abstain from all unchastity; and when their prayers were not heeded, on the following night they ended their lives by strangling themselves in order not to become slaves or suffer loss of their chastity. If I wished to recall individual instances of this kind, time would run out before the examples were exhausted. The practice of liberty is a notable thing and displeasing only to those who have the character of slaves.

Things which are done or spoken freely avoid the fault of timidity on the one hand and of rashness on the other, and so long as the straight and narrow path is followed, merit praise and win affection. But when under the pretext of liberty rashness unleashes the violence of its spirit, it properly incurs reproach, although, as a thing more pleasing in the ears of the vulgar than convincing to the mind of the wise man, it often finds in the indulgence of others the safety which it does not owe to its own prudence. Nevertheless, it is the part of a good and wise man to give a free rein to the liberty of others and to accept with patience the words of free speaking, whatever they may be. Nor does he oppose himself to its works so long as these do not involve the casting away of virtue. For since each virtue shines by its own proper light, the merit of tolerance is resplendent with a very special glory.

Once a certain man of Privernum, when asked how the captives from his city would keep the peace if they were granted amnesty, replied to the Roman consul: "If you grant them an advantageous peace, they will keep it forever; if a disadvantageous one, they will not keep it long." By these bold words, freely spoken, it came to pass that the citizens of Privernum obtained not only pardon for their rebellion, but the benefits of Roman citizenship besides, because one

man of them had dared to speak out thus boldly in the Senate.

8. The Difference between a Tyrant and a True Prince

Wherein the prince differs from the tyrant has already been set forth above when we were reviewing Plutarch's "Instruction of Trajan"; and the duties of the prince and of the different members of the commonwealth were also carefully explained at that point. Wherefore it will be easier to make known here, and in fewer words, the opposite characteristics of the tyrant. A tyrant, then, as the philosophers have described him, is one who oppresses the people by rulership based upon force, while he who rules in accordance with the laws is a prince. Law is the gift of god, the model of equity, a standard of justice, a likeness of the divine will, the guardian of well-being, a bond of union and solidarity between peoples, a rule defining duties, a barrier against the vices and the destroyer thereof, a punishment of violence and all wrong-doing. The law is assailed by force or by fraud, and, as it were, either wrecked by the fury of the lion or undermined by the wiles of the serpent. In whatever way this comes to pass, it is plain that it is the grace of God which is being assailed, and that it is God himself who in a sense is challenged to battle. The prince fights for the laws and the liberty of the people; the tyrant thinks nothing done unless he brings the laws to nought and reduces the people to slavery. Hence the prince is a kind of likeness of divinity; and the tyrant, on the contrary, a likeness of the boldness of the Adversary, even of the wickedness of Lucifer, imitating him that sought to build his throne to the north and make himself like unto the Most High,[1] with the exception of His goodness. For had he desired to be like unto Him in goodness, he would never have striven to tear from Him the glory of

[1] Isa. xiv, 12–14.

His power and wisdom. What he more likely did aspire to was to be equal with him in authority to dispense rewards. The prince, as the likeness of the Deity, is to be loved, worshipped and cherished; the tyrant, the likeness of wickedness, is generally to be even killed. The origin of tyranny is iniquity, and springing from a poisonous root, it is a tree which grows and sprouts into a baleful pestilent growth, and to which the axe must by all means be laid.

9. Tyrannicide

It would be a long and tedious task if I wished to bring down to our own times the series of gentile tyrants; a man with only one life will hardly be able to recall the list, for it eludes the mind and overpowers the tongue. My opinions on the subject of tyrants are, however, set forth more fully in my little work entitled "Of the Ends of Tyrants," [1] a brief manual wherein I have carefully sought to avoid the tedium of prolixity and the obscurity of too great compression. But lest the authority of Roman history be held in small account because it has for the most part been written by infidels concerning infidels, let its lesson be confirmed by examples drawn from sacred and Christian history. For it is everywhere obvious that, in the words of Valerius, only that power is secure in the long run which places bounds to its own exercise. And surely nought is so splendid or so magnificent that it does not need to be tempered by moderation. The earliest tyrant whom the divine page brings before us is Nembroth, the mighty hunter before the Lord (who is also called Ninus in some histories, although this does not agree with the proper reckoning of dates); and I have already said above that he was a reprobate. For verily he desired to be lord in his own right and not under God, and it was in his time that the attempt to raise a tower to

---

[1] This work of John of Salisbury is not known to be extant.

Heaven was made by frail mortality, destined in their blindness to be overthrown and scattered in confusion. Let us, therefore, advance to him who was set over the people by the divine choice, which deserted him when he gave himself up to a wicked desire of ruling rather than of reigning, and in the end he was so utterly overthrown that in the anguish of his suffering he was compelled to put an end to himself. For a right and wholesome assumption of the royal office is of no avail, or only of very little, if the later life of the ruler is at variance therewith, nor does a judge look wholly to the origin of things, but makes his judgment to depend upon their outcome and ending.

The historics teach, however, that none should undertake the death of a tyrant who is bound to him by an oath or by the obligation of fealty. For we read that Sedechias, because he disregarded the sacred obligation of fealty, was led into captivity; and that in the case of another of the kings of Juda whose name escapes my memory, his eyes were plucked out because, falling into faithlessness, he did not keep before his sight God, to whom the oath is taken; since sureties for good behavior are justly given even to a tyrant.

But as for the use of poison, although I see it sometimes wrongfully adopted by infidels, I do not read that it is ever permitted by any law. Not that I do not believe that tyrants ought to be removed from our midst, but it should be done without loss of religion and honor. For David, the best of all kings that I have read of, and who, save in the incident of Urias Etheus, walked blamelessly in all things, although he had to endure the most grievous tyrant, and although he often had an opportunity of destroying him, yet preferred to spare him, trusting in the mercy of God, within whose power it was to set him free without sin. He therefore determined to abide in patience until the tyrant should either suffer a change of heart and be visited by God with return of charity, or else should fall in battle, or otherwise meet his end by the just judgment of God. How great was his patience can be discerned from the fact that when he had cut off the edge of Saul's robe in the cave, and again when, having entered the camp by night, he rebuked the negligence of the sentinels, in both cases he compelled the king to confess that David was acting the juster part. And surely the method of destroying tyrants which is the most useful and the safest, is for those who are oppressed to take refuge humbly in the protection of God's mercy, and lifting up undefiled hands to the Lord, to pray devoutly that the scourge wherewith they are afflicted may be turned aside from them. For the sins of transgressors are the strength of tyrants.

Thus the end of tyrants is confusion, leading to destruction if they persist in malice, to pardon if they return into the way of righteousness. For there is prepared a great fire wherewith to consume the scourge after the Father has employed it for the correction of His children. And it is written, "Acab has humbled himself before my face; therefore will I not bring evil in his days." [2] But Jezebel, who persisted in cruelty, paid the penalty therefore in the merited cruelty of her end, giving her blood to be lapped up by dogs in the place where dogs had lapped up the blood of innocent Naboth. But if the blood of innocent Naboth was thus required at her hands, will not the blood of so many other innocent victims also be required? Her unrighteousness coveted the vineyard of a just man, and as the price thereof she lost her rights to a whole kingdom. Thus wickedness is always punished by the Lord; but sometimes it is His own, and at others it is a human hand, which He employs as a weapon wherewith to administer punishment to the unrighteous.

The emperor Julian, the vile and filthy apostate, persecuted the Christians rather by guile than by the open use of force, yet

2 I Kings xxi, 29.

he did not refrain from force. For under him arose the most grievous persecution of the Christians, and he sought by his impious attempt to blot out the very name of the Galilean, as he called Him. But while he was leading an ill-fated expedition against the Parthians, and on his return was offering up the slaughter of the Christians as a sacrifice to idols, God took pity upon the prayers of the great Basil and others of the saints, and appointed as his instrument the martyr Mercurius, who, at the command of the Blessed Virgin, pierced the tyrant in his camp with a lance, and compelled the impious wretch as he was dying to confess that the Galilean, namely Christ, whom he persecuted, was victor and had triumphed over him. For when the aforesaid bishop had gathered together the faithful of Cæsarea, in the church of the ever Virgin, the Mother of God, to watch out the night in prayer, on that same night the saint recognized the Blessed Virgin herself in a vision and received consolation in this wise: "Call to me," said she, "Mercurius, and he shall depart to slay Julian, who proudly blasphemes against my Son and God."

10. Ecclesiastical Tyrants

But grant that it is permissible for men of the flesh to contend for the primacy, still I think that on no account is this ever permissible for churchmen. Yet from the example of men of the flesh, impiety creeps forward under the guise of religion, and priestly power is now not merely contended for, but actually fought for. Of old time men were dragged unwillingly to the seats of honor in the Church although they were eager for martyrdom; but they fled from the chief seats more earnestly than from the prison and the cross. Today priests speak openly to the opposite effect and say that the proverb is a thing of nought. "We do not wish to be martyrs," they say, "but we will not give to another the glory of our thrones." Verily a poor and miserable speech in the mouth of a priest who thus confesses Christ in such wise that he openly admits his unwillingness to follow Him. Can it be doubted whether one dies a true confessor who is not at all times ready to bow his neck to the persecutor should need arise? For Ciprian says, "If a bishop be afraid, all hope for him is gone." But grant him leave to be afraid even; for him not to stand fast in time of need is a thing which is not permissible. A deserter is noxious, infamous.

Yet there is one thing wherein they seem to imitate the steadfastness of martyrs, namely if it becomes needful to fight for their thrones. It is alleged by some, and it is indeed the truth, that the office of Roman pontiff has sometimes, nay rather has often, been contested by ambitious men, and not without the shedding of fraternal blood has the pontiff entered the Holy of Holies. Once more there have been kindled wars more than civil, and priestly conflict has excused Cæsar and Pompey and all the presumption and impious work at Philippi, Leucas, Mutina, or in Egypt or Spain. Are men Christians who thus procure the shedding of blood to the end that they rather than others may be advanced to the office of laying down their lives for their flock, which is the duty of a shepherd? Do they rend the Church asunder and profane the sanctuary, to the end that there may be somewhat to build again and sanctify? Perhaps they wrack the nations with extortion, harry kingdoms, plunder the resources of churches, only to the end that they may create for themselves the opportunity and means of deserving well, only to the end that they may set all things in order and that they may snatch from their competitors the necessity of ministering to and providing for the poor. But if, on the contrary, their object is to procure but a wider license and larger impunity for themselves, to heap up money, to favor, aggrandize and corrupt their flesh and blood, to ennoble their family, if in short they seek their own glory in the Church, lording it haughtily over their flocks rather than being an example unto them, then although with their lips they pretend to assume the pastoral office, they are more rightly to be numbered among tyrants than among princes. The philosophers say, and I think truly, that there is nothing in human affairs better nor more useful than man, and among men themselves nothing better nor more useful than a prince, whether ecclesiastical or temporal; on the contrary there is nothing more hurtful to man than man, and among them the temporal or ecclesiastical tyrant is more hurtful than any other. But certainly of the two kinds, the ecclesiastical is worse than the temporal.

I remember that I once journeyed to Apulia to visit the pontiff, Lord Adrian the Fourth, who had admitted me to his closest friendship, and I sojourned with him at Beneventum for almost three months. We often conversed in the way of friends concerning many things, and he asked me confidentially and earnestly how men felt concerning himself and the Roman Church. I was entirely frank with him, and explained without reserve the abuses which I had heard of in the different provinces. For it was said by many that the Roman Church, which is the mother of all the churches, shows herself to be not so much a mother to the rest as a very stepmother. Scribes and Pharisees sit in her seats, and place on the shoulders of men unbearable burdens which they themselves do not deign to touch with even the tip of their finger. They lord it over the clergy instead of making their own lives an example to lead the flock to life by the straight and narrow path; they pile up costly furniture, they load their tables with gold and silver, sparing themselves overmuch even out of their own avarice. A poor man is seldom or never admitted to their number, and then rather as a result of his own vainglorious ambition than for the love of Christ. They oppress the churches with extortion, stir up strife, bring the clergy and people into conflict, never take compassion on the sufferings and misery of the afflicted, rejoice in the spoils of churches, and count all gain as godliness.

They give judgment not for the truth but for money. For money you can get anything done today, and without waiting; but you will not get it done even tomorrow if you do not pay a price. Too often they commit injury, and imitate the demons in thinking that they are doing good when they merely refrain from doing evil; except a few of them who fulfil the name and duties of a shepherd. Even the Roman pontiff himself is a grievous and almost intolerable burden to all; the complaint is everywhere made that while the churches which were built by the devotion of the fathers are falling into ruin and collapsing, he has built for himself palaces, and walks abroad not merely in purple but in gold. The palaces of priests dazzle the eye, and meanwhile in their hands the Church of Christ is defiled. They rend apart the spoils of the provinces as if they strove to refill the treasuries of Cresus. But the Most High deals justly with them, for they are delivered into the hands of others, and often the vilest of men, to be plundered in their own turn. And while they thus wander in the wilderness, the scourge of God will, I think, never fail to scourge them. Truly the mouth of God has promised that by what judgment they have judged, they shall themselves be judged, and that with their own good measure it shall be meted out to them again. The Ancient of Days cannot lie.

"These are the things, father, which the people are saying," I told him, "since you wish me to bring their opinions to your knowledge." "And you, yourself," he asked, "what do you think?" "There are difficulties," I answered, "about anything that I might say. I fear that I shall be branded with the reproach of falsehood or flattery if I venture by myself alone to contradict the people; but on the other hand, if I do not, then I fear that I shall be charged with lèse majesté, and, like one who has set his mouth against Heaven, shall seem to deserve a cross. Nevertheless, since Guido Dens, the cardinal presbyter of St. Potentiana, adds his testimony to that of the people, I shall not presume so far as to con-

tradict him. For he asserts that in the Roman Church there inheres a certain root of duplicity and stimulant of avarice which is the source and root of all evils. Nor did he speak this in a corner, but, while all his brethren sat round about and Holy Eugenius was presiding, he made this public charge when at Florence he blazed out gratuitously against my own innocence. But one thing I will boldly affirm with my conscience as my witness, and this is that I have never anywhere seen more honest clerics than in the Roman Church, or ones who hold avarice in greater abhorrence. Who can help admiring Bernard of Redon, cardinal deacon of Saints Cosmas and Damian, for his self-restraint and utter scorn of lucre? The man is not born from whom he accepted a gift, but what was offered for a pure and honest reason by the fellowship of his brethren he was sometimes persuaded to accept. Who does not marvel at the bishop of Praeneste, who, fearing the scruple of conscience, abstained even from sharing in the common goods? Of many others so great is the modesty, so great the austerity, that they will be found not inferior to Fabricius, whom they excel in all respects for the added reason that they know the way of salvation. But since you urge and press and command me, and since it is certain that it is not lawful to lie to the Holy Spirit, I admit that what you enjoin must be done, although not all of you are to be imitated in all your works. For whoever dissents from the teaching of you of the Roman Church is either a heretic or schismatic. But, thanks to the favor of God, there are some who do not imitate the works of all of you. For the contamination of a few sullies the pure with a stain, and brings infamy upon the Church Universal; and in my opinion the reason why they die so fast is to prevent their corrupting the entire Church. But sometimes the good are likewise snatched away, to the end that they may not be infected with wickedness and turned to evil, and because corrupt Rome is found unworthy of them in the sight of God. Do you, therefore, since it is a part of the duty of your office, seek out and bring in to you men who are humble and despisers of vainglory and money. But I fear lest if you go on asking what you wish, you will hear from an imprudent friend things which you do not wish. What is it, father, to criticize the life of others and not probe searchingly into your own? All men applaud you, you are called father and lord of all, and upon your head is poured all the oil of the sinner.[1] If, therefore, you are father, why do you extort gifts and payments from your children? If you are lord why do you not strike terror into your Romans, and repressing their insolence, call them back to the way of loyalty? But you may answer that you wish to preserve the city to the Church by means of the gifts which you receive. Did Silvester originally acquire it by means of gifts? Father, you are wandering in the trackless wilderness and have strayed from the true way. It must be preserved by means of the same gifts by which it was acquired. What you received without a price, see that you bestow without a price. Justice is the queen of the virtues and blushes to be bartered for a price. If she is to be gracious, she must be gratuitous. It is vain to seek to prostitute for a price her who cannot be corrupted; for she is pure and ever incorrupt. While you oppress others, you will yourself be even more grievously oppressed."

The pontiff laughed and congratulated me upon having spoken with such frankness, enjoining me as often as anything unfavorable concerning him came to my ears, to inform him thereof without delay. And, after urging many things in his favor as well as much against himself by way of reply, he finally put before me an apology after this kind: Once upon a time all the members of the body conspired together against the stomach, as against that which by its greediness devoured utterly the labors of all the rest. The eye is never sated with seeing, the ear with hearing, the hands go on laboring, the feet become callous from walking, and the tongue itself alternates advantageously between speech and silence. In fine, all the members provide watchfully for the common advantage of all; and in the midst of such care and toil on the part of all, only the stomach is idle, yet it alone devours and consumes all the fruits of their manifold labors. What remains to be said? They swore to abstain from work and to starve that idle public enemy. Thus passed one day; that which followed was more irksome. The third was so fatal that almost all commenced to be faint. Then, under the pressure of necessity, the brothers again gathered together to take action concerning their own welfare and the state of the public enemy. When all were present, the eyes were found to be dim, the foot failed to sustain the weight of the body, the arms were numb, and the tongue itself, cleaving to the feeble palate, did not make bold to state the common cause. Accordingly all took refuge in the counsel of the heart and after deliberation there, it became plain that these ills were all due to that which had before been denounced as the public enemy. Because the tribute which they paid it was cut off, like a public rationer it withdrew the sustenance of all. And since no one can perform military service without wages, when the wages are no longer forthcoming the soldier becomes faint and weak. Nor could the blame be cast back upon the rationer, since what he had not received he could not pay out to others. Far more beneficial would it be that he should be supplied with somewhat to distribute than that through his starvation all the other members should go hungry. And so it was done; persuaded by reason, they filled the stomach, the members were revived, and the peace of all was restored. And so the stomach was acquitted, which, although it is voracious and greedy of that which does not belong to it, yet seeks not for itself but for the others, who cannot be nourished if it is empty. "And so it is, brother," he said, "if you will but observe closely, in the body of the commonwealth, wherein, though the magistrates are most grasping, yet they ac-

---

[1] Ps. cxl, 5.

cumulate not so much for themselves as for others. For if they are starved, there is nought to be distributed among the members. For the stomach in the body and the prince in the commonwealth perform the same office, according to the well-known passage of Quintus Serenus:

Those who contend that the stomach is king of the whole body,
Seem to have truth and reason with them in their claim;
For upon its soundness depends the strength of all the members
And, contrariwise, all are enfeebled if it be sick;
Nay rather, if care is not taken, it is said to harm
The brain and pervert the senses from their soundness.[2]

Do not therefore seek to measure our oppressiveness or that of temporal princes, but attend rather to the common utility of all."

[2] Q. Serenus, *Lib. Medecin.* ll. 300–305.

CHAPTER 8

ST. THOMAS AQUINAS

O NE of the most paradoxical aspects of medieval life is the contradiction between the extreme pluralism of its institutions and the deep yearning for unity in its religious and philosophical ideas. The typical institution of the Middle Ages, the feudal system, represents the hallmark of diversity and decentralization that the western world has experienced. By contrast, medieval thinking on religious and secular matters took the *principle of unity* for granted: the oneness of God, of divine law and reason, permeated the whole universe, the heavens, nature, and society. Mankind was conceived as one community, subject to one eternal law and government. Diversities and pluralities were held to exist in the world of fact, but their reason for existence was related to a higher Whole possessing a unity to which they were subordinate.

The duality of man's body and soul was reflected in the two orders of the spiritual and mundane powers, church and empire, each claiming, in theory at least, universal jurisdiction. Both the papalist and imperialist parties were reluctant, in typical medieval fashion, to accept the dualism of church and empire as final. They agreed that there had to be a unifying principle within which the diversity of ecclesiastical and secular powers could be harmonized. The disagreement between papalists and imperialists arose over the nature of the unifying principle and the method of incorporating it into the solution of practical issues. Partisans of the church as well as of the empire also agreed on another major premise: that the *monarchical form of government in church and empire* was the necessary result of the unitary principle, which finds its highest embodiment in God's rule of the universe.

In the realm of thought, the medieval mind drew its nourishment and vitality from two sources: the religious inspiration of Christianity and the intellectual heritage of antiquity. The task of reconciling these two sources, Christian faith and pre-Christian philosophy, was relatively easy in the early medieval period: first, the classical heritage of thought was mainly kept alive in isolated islands of learning in churches and monasteries, and the *major ideological conflicts* in the *early Middle Ages* were *between church and heresy,* and not between theology and philosophy. Second, the relative quietude in this earlier period lay in the fact that, of the great classical philosophers, *Plato* was the *dominant influence,* whereas Aristotle, known only by a few writings on logic, played a minor part.

Plato's doctrine of vision as the ultimate form of knowing the Good, his concept of God, his tendency toward mysticism, his contempt of matter and idealization of spirit, his conception of Ideas as the essence of reality, his scheme of an ideal society in which the spiritual element would rule—all these Platonic strands could be easily woven into the texture of early Christian life and thought. As long as Christianity was still primarily faith and revelation, idea rather than institution, a fraternal community of love rather than an hierarchical organization endowed with the sword of law, Plato seemed to fit the mood and temper of Christian speculation. Of the two giants of the Christian tradition, St. Augustine and St. Thomas Aquinas, the first, St. Augustine, was thoroughly imbued with Platonic ideas; he was a Platonist not only on intellectual grounds, but also in personality, character, and style. And that he was clearly aware of his affinity is evidenced in *The City of God,* where he says that Plato was "justly preferred to all the other philosophers" of paganism, and that "it is evident that none come nearer to us than the Platonists."

But as the church became more and more a political organization struggling for world hegemony, possessing the best-trained bureaucracy of the Great Powers and utilizing diplomacy in peace and armies in war, its entire outlook changed. The original Augustinian conception of the Christian community as a community of the Elect and the conception of the direct participation of the Christian individual in divine grace and salvation were relegated to the background. When papal power reached its peak in the thirteenth century, the intellectual need of the institutionalized church was not so much mystic visions of a highly individual and personal kind but systematic and realistic elaboration of all thought in the light of collective traditions and newly emerging forces pointing to the future.

Particularly as humanistic studies spread in the eleventh and twelfth centuries in Bologna, Paris, Chartres, and Oxford, and classical knowledge became more easily accessible, the labors of publicists, philosophers, and theologians were increasingly devoted to the construction of a unified system of thought in which faith and reason, theology and philosophy, Christianity and pagan antiquity would be reconciled in harmony and lasting accord. The rising universities in Italy, France, England, and Germany—perhaps the most important single contribution of the Middle Ages to western civilization—provided an opportunity for general study and analysis. Originally intended for the training of the young in a single craft (medicine, law, theology), and therein resembling the medieval trade guilds, the universities soon followed the example set by the University of Paris, which was the first to include, early in the thirteenth century, the four faculties of theology, arts, law, and medicine. Henceforth the ideal of unity of knowledge remained the driving force of European universities; the application of the ideal changed with the outlook of the times.

Medieval scholasticism was the first great attempt, after the fall of the Roman empire, to unite in one body knowledge and revelation, philosophy and theology. The principle of unity was the *primacy of religion over philosophy*, of revelation over empirical verification, of faith over knowledge, of dogma over science. The scholastic philosophers did not invent the doctrine of the primacy of religion over philosophy but refined it in accordance with the needs of the time.

Tertullian, one of the early church fathers (A. D. 160–220), and like St. Augustine, a North African, had stated an extreme position by declaring that Christianity and philosophy were utterly irreconcilable, that heresies are the result of philosophy, and that there was the danger of a "mottled Christianity" of Platonic, Aristotelian, and Stoic elements. Sensing acutely that attempts to buttress religion by philosophy would eventually lead to the decline of faith, Tertullian sought to return to the primitive doctrine that religious belief should be based on simplicity of heart and not on subtlety of intellect.

St. Augustine was less extreme than Tertullian; he was not opposed to philosophy as such. According to St. Augustine, the possibility of reasoning originates in the act of faith. The road to truth begins with faith and revelation: "Seek not to understand that you may believe, but believe that you may understand." The Augustinian doctrine is thus an advance over the earlier church fathers because it is not hostile to understanding, provided that the basis and starting point of understanding are the acceptance of nonrational premises: faith and dogma. Yet in effect St. Augustine's method resulted in the enthronement of theology, and both his philosophy and his political thought are essentially theological speculation in content, expression, and symbolism.

From the fifth to the eighth century the main issue confronting western thought was not the struggle of one school against another but the very survival of traditional values and ideas in the aftermath of material and spiritual devastation on an unprecedented scale. Only in monasteries and churches was the connection between the tradition of civilization and the newly emerging medieval world always continued, and the link may have appeared at times to be tenuous indeed. But by the ninth century, physical recovery and consolidation had been attained to a considerable extent, and a more independent and typically medieval intellectual trend began to emerge: *scholasticism*. It was, in fact, as typical of the intellectual character of the Middle Ages as was feudalism of their typical social and economic system. From the ninth to the thirteenth century, scholasticism was the predominant pattern of thought.

The ecclesiastical domination of scholastic philosophy was assured in more than one way. Most philosophical writers and teachers were clerics, nurtured on church doctrine and subject to church discipline, and the one principle underlying their speculations was that reason should never contradict faith. Thus before the argument starts, the writer knows the answer. It is to be found in faith and belief, as stated by authoritative ecclesiastical sources.

In this respect, in scholastic philosophy the search for truth loses the dynamic and evolutionary quality of Greek philosophy, for among the exciting traits of Greek philosophy is that one never knows at the outset where the argument will lead, what the results of reasoning will be. Less influenced by experimental science than is modern thought, Greek philosophy, unhampered by ecclesiastical discipline, developed into greatness because it refused to take anything for granted. Whatever one may think of the conclusions arrived at by the various schools of Greek philosophy, one is always astounded anew by its exhilarating and bold spirit that challenges everything, that allows no argument to hide behind the protective cloak of authority, whatever its source may be.

The authoritative sources of the scholastic philosophers were the Bible, on which they relied heavily, the church fathers, and the relatively few known works of Greek and Roman antiquity. Aristotle, for example, was not adopted by the church until the thirteenth century; thereafter it became impious to attack him, although he had not been a Christian, and he was generally referred to as "the philosopher." Writers in ancient times relied far less on authority, and the literary technique of copious references and quotations in support of one's argument is largely an invention of these scholastic philosophers of the Middle Ages.

Another link between theology and philosophy in scholasticism was forged in the choice of issues. For example, the problem of free will was discussed in relation to the activities of God and the angels, from the spiritual nature of which deductions were made about analogous human problems. Revealed doctrine was the main source of chosen topics, and dogma was the method of regulation and control of philosophical writing. Finally, the influence of the Inquisition was also a limitation of untrammeled research and inquiry; the prospect of being burned alive probably tended to discourage unorthodox thinkers from going too far in the exploration of new ideas.

Scholastic philosophy reached its "golden age" in the thirteenth century, which was also the peak of papal power. The evolution of the church as an institution of universal aspirations demanded a universal, comprehensive, and systematic philosophy. The synthesis of theological doctrine, as elaborated and refined over a thousand years, provided one cornerstone of the new edifice. The rediscovery of Aristotle provided the other.

In the East the tradition of Aristotelian learning had never been abandoned; Constantinople in particular had long been a center of Greek scholarship. From Constantinople Greek studies spread to the Near East and were then carried by Arab and Jewish scholars to Spain. In the West, however, only a few of the logical writings of Aristotle were known before the middle of the twelfth century. From then on, and especially in the thirteenth century, the spread of Aristotelian studies was the outstanding intellectual event of the age. It began in Spain with translations of Arab and Hebrew versions of Aristotle into Latin. Toledo was one of the first centers of the Aristotelian revival, and it spread from there to Paris and Oxford, the two liveliest clearinghouses of new philosophical ideas in the thirteenth century. Gradually most of Aristotle's works were translated directly from Greek into Latin, and his metaphysics, physics, biology, psychology, politics, and ethics, in addition to his logical writings already known, became the common property of the western world. At first the church was concerned about the spread of the new doctrines and sought to stem the tide of Aristotelianism by prohibition. But gradually the attitude of the church changed, and Aristotle moved from toleration into official acceptance.

The triumph of Aristotle in the thirteenth century was the work of many men, schools, and universities, but above all it was due to the influence of St. Thomas Aquinas (1226–1274). He was born near Naples of a family that belonged to the highest Italian aristocracy, related to European kings and emperors. From an early age he was brought up by ecclesiastics, and he joined the mendicant order of the Dominicans at the age of sixteen, against the vehement opposition of his family. He studied in Naples, Cologne, and Paris; in Paris he became well known, first as an outstanding student, and then as a teacher of theology and philosophy.

Although St. Thomas Aquinas died before he was forty-eight, his literary output, about seventy works of all kinds and sizes, was truly encyclopedic. It marks the crowning achievement and summation of scholastic philosophy, his lasting accomplishment being the incorporation of Aristotelianism into Christian thought. With St. Augustine, St. Thomas Aquinas is one of the two leaders in the development of church doctrine. *Augustinianism* is the fusion of *Plato* and *Christianity. Thomism* is the synthesis of *Aristotle* and Christianity.

In the first few centuries of its existence, the strong mystical and idealistic tendency in Christianity found philosophical kinship and affinity in Plato; as St. Augustine himself said, Plato came near to Christian knowledge and revelation, and in a sense Christianity was Platonic from the beginning. By the thirteenth century, the nature of the Christian idea and church had changed considerably, and Platonism could no longer serve as the philosophical and metaphysical foundation of an institution in which the accent had changed from individual inspiration and illumination to institutional stability and sobriety. By accepting Thomism over Augustinianism as its official doctrinal system, the church signified its preference of Aristotle to Plato. St. Augustine, the North African in whom the fires of faith burned with the intensity of his native sun, sought to reaffirm the spirit of the first Christians, for whom Christianity was faith and love, devoid of philosophy, argument, and law. The victory of Thomism over Augustinianism is the final commitment of the church to the long-term institutional, rational, legal viewpoint.

This victory is remarkable for two reasons. In the first place, it shows that the most decisive issue in the philosophical evolution of the church was in effect a repetition of the dialogue between Plato and Aristotle, adapted to the Christian world and its theology. Until the seventeenth century at least, it seemed that Plato and Aristotle had laid down for all time the two possible basic philosophical systems; with all its hostility to pre-Christian pagan philosophy, medieval scholasticism nevertheless was completely under the spell of Plato and Aristotle.

The second remarkable aspect of the victory of Thomism is the light it throws on the adaptability and high survival capacity of the church. As time went by, particularly from the eleventh century on, it became evident that theology was not enough, and that the challenge of budding humanism and secularism had to be met on its own ground. The adoption of Aristotle by the church, through St. Thomas, indicated its tremendous intellectual vitality and flexibility. In Aristotle the church found a systematic and encyclopedic body of thought, encompassing many disciplines and forming a coherent whole; it was moderate in temper and outlook, adaptable to changing circumstances, full of common sense, and therefore altogether human, supranational, and timeless. Though it lacked the spark and brilliance of Plato's philosophy, it was rich in solidity and endurance, characteristics that are prosaic but that wear well under all conditions. To be born, the church needed Plato. To last, it needed Aristotle.

Aristotle himself, as is true of any great disciple of any great teacher, never ceased to be a Platonist in a profound sense; the victory of Thomism over Augustinianism did not mean the elimination of the latter, or of Platonism, from the intellectual heritage of the church, but the relative stress of the Aristotelian over the Platonic system. Augustinian mysticism and emphasis on faith and individual illumination and grace, when politely relegated to a subordinate position in the official church theology, fled into the developing sects and creeds that sought to revive the original character of Christianity in the late Middle Ages. Their Augustinianism was later championed by the Protestant reformers, who were generally opposed to Thomism, in which they saw too much cold logic and too little personal inspiration. Martin Luther, himself an Augustinian monk, declared that he had not found any book that taught him as much of the meaning of God, Christ, man, and the world as he had learned from the Bible and St. Augustine, and that Aristotle is to theology what darkness is to light: "Only without Aristotle can we become theologians." Protestantism was thus a return to the beginnings of Christianity not only because of its stress on the earlier religious sources over the later, but because of its preference of St. Augustine to St. Thomas Aquinas, of Plato to Aristotle.

St. Thomas Aquinas' approach to the problem of faith and reason denoted as great a concession to rationalism in relation to the Augustinian solution, as the Augustinian solution had been an advance in relation to the antirationalism of Tertullian. St. Thomas conceived of faith and knowledge as divine in origin; therefore conflict between them could never be real, only apparent. He thought that the previous trouble had been due largely to the fact that theologians introduced theological criteria into philosophy, and philosophers attempted to philosophize in theology. However, once it is assumed that knowledge and faith are not opposing but supplementary modes of understanding God and the world, there is no reason to reconcile conflict where there is no conflict.

Faith is not contrary to reason but *above reason,* and the results of faith are no less certain than those of reason; they are, in fact, more certain because faith is based on direct revelation of God and therefore closer to the source of all truth than philosophy, which is based on human insight. If articles of faith could be rationally proved, they would become philosophy, and theology as a separate branch of thought would become unnecessary and disappear: the articles of faith, because of their very nature, however, cannot be intellectually proved;

they have to be accepted by an act of *will*. Rational evidence can only support further rational propositions; it can never lead to the foundations of faith, which have to be accepted, not because they correspond to rational evidence, but because they are revealed by God as true. What man can therefore believe, he cannot know, and what he can know, he cannot believe.

If theological truth cannot be proved true by philosophy, neither can it be disproved. Conflict is thus impossible. Where it is apparent, St. Thomas categorically states that faith is higher than knowledge in the hierarchy of truth, and that something must be wrong with philosophy if it seems to contradict revelation: philosophy is only relatively certain, whereas theology is absolutely certain, inasmuch as it is based on divine authority. St. Thomas thus conceives of faith and knowledge as autonomous in their respective spheres, yet does not separate them in tight compartments. Although faith does not interfere with the ordinary operations of reason, it keeps an over-all watch over it, and gives it guidance and purpose.

No one in the history of the church has equaled St. Thomas Aquinas in blending the religious and rational motifs in one vast and rich pattern of thought in which there seems to be room, as in the work of Aristotle, for almost all forms of knowledge and insight. St. Thomas represents the high point of equilibrium that was compatible with the long-term interests of the church, and his position is an enormous concession to rationalism, compared with Tertullian's and St. Augustine's. After St. Thomas, and as early as the fourteenth century, the balance begins to move in the direction of rationalism; the fifteenth century, the cradle of the Renaissance, sees the rebirth of classical humanism, in which knowledge breaks with faith and claims supremacy over it.

The method of argument in St. Thomas' main treatise, the *Summa Theologica*, is characteristic of scholasticism. The entire work (three parts in twenty volumes) is arranged uniformly. Each major subject begins with a question and is subdivided into articles. Each article's heading is again a question, for example, "Whether the Angels Exist in Any Great Number?" The text of the article starts out with a series of "objections" presenting the incorrect doctrinal view (in this particular, that the number of angels is not great). Immediately following the incorrect arguments presented in the objections, the correct doctrine is given, almost invariably in the form of a direct quotation from an authoritative source. Concerning the problem of the number of angels, St. Thomas quotes (*Dan.* 7:10): "Thousands of thousands ministered to Him, and ten thousand times a hundred thousand stood before Him." After thus establishing the large number of angels as incontrovertible, St. Thomas then adduces a number of reasons in support of the true doctrine stated in the quotation. Finally he replies specifically to each objection, demolishing them one by one.

A sense of complete certainty pervades the work. There is no slow and groping search toward the discovery of truth, and there are no questions (among the many thousand discussed) that must be kept open for further thought and inquiry. An element of dialectical reasoning in the method gives it its strength: the erroneous views are given a fair and full hearing. However, the end of the dialectical process, the truth, is not derived from the process of reasoning itself but from an authoritative source that reveals the true doctrine. After the true position is made known, reason then finds the supporting arguments. The medieval conception of *philosophy* as the *handmaiden of theology* is thus exemplified in the substance of scholasticism as well as in its method of argument.

St. Thomas Aquinas did not think of himself principally as a philosopher, and much less as a political philosopher, but as a theologian, a "catholic doctor" fervently devoted to Holy Doctrine. His political views may be best culled from two of his works, the short fragment, *On Kingship* (*De regno*), and *The Sum of Theology* (*Summa Theologica*), his chief work.

The pre-Thomistic medieval theory of the state, unfamiliar with Aristotle's *Politics* and *Ethics,* viewed the origin of political association, of government, as the result of sin and evil, of the distortion of man's natural and original impulses. St. Augustine had been a typical exponent of this Christian-Stoic conception of the state: God did not intend that man, "His rational creature, who was made in His image, should have dominion over anything but the irrational creation—not man over man, but man over the beasts." St. Thomas meets the Augustinian argument by interpreting the concept of "dominion" in two ways: if dominion refers to slavery, St. Thomas is willing to concede (with the Stoics and Roman lawyers) that there was no slavery in the state of nature. But if dominion refers to the "office of governing and directing free men," it is not incompatible with the state of innocence.

St. Thomas suggests two reasons for the necessity of government even in the state of innocence, before the occurrence of sin and evil: first, "Man is naturally a social being and so in the state of innocence he would have led a social life." Because there must be some organization of social life, government emerges as the specific organ of looking after the common good. Second, if one man surpasses others in knowledge and justice, it would be wrong to disregard such superiority for the benefit of all. St. Thomas thus bases the *need for government* on *man's social nature,* and the *organization of government* on the *superior wisdom and morality of the ruler for the benefit of the ruled.* In both views, his kinship to Aristotle is evident, and it constitutes a sharp break with the typical conceptions of state that had been prevalent until Aristotle's *Politics* became known again in the thirteenth century.

St. Thomas agrees with Aristotle that man's social impulse is the origin of the state, and the good life its purpose. But from here on, St. Thomas, the Christian theologian, goes beyond Aristotle. For the Greek, bound to this world, the good life of the community—though nowhere clearly defined—included practical and spiritual ends that could be attained by joint communal effort *here and now.* St. Thomas cannot be satisfied with the community as the ultimate point of reference and the creative source of spiritual values. His Christian, *other-worldly* concern leads him to the view that the Aristotelian doctrine of the good life is still one step short of the ultimate purpose of existence, because "through virtuous living man is further ordained to a higher end, which consists in the enjoyment of God." Whereas Aristotle, whose philosophy and ethics were humanistic and this-worldly, saw the end of man in values that exist within himself, St. Thomas sees, in addition to such man-centered values, an "extrinsic" good that does not exist in man himself and that is yet the supreme value, namely, "final beatitude which is looked for after death in the enjoyment of God."

Because society has the same end as the individual, the ultimate purpose of social life is not merely virtuous living, "but through virtuous living to attain to the possession of God." If man and society could attain this supreme end by human power, the king (as the supreme representative of human power) could guide them in the right direction. However, St. Thomas argues, the possession of God can be attained only by divine power, and human government is unable to guide men toward this end. The ministry of the kingdom of God is not in the hands of earthly kings, but of priests, and—above all—"the chief priest, the successor of St. Peter, the Vicar of Christ, the Roman Pontiff," to whom all kings are to be subject as to Christ himself.

St. Thomas always looks on the world in hierarchical terms, and his system of values is hierarchical, too. From the viewpoint of human and practical needs, the purposes of secular government are legitimate ends. But those ends are themselves means if viewed in relation to a still higher end, the highest of all: the possession of God. Applying the Aristotelian principle that "the one to whom it pertains to achieve the final end commands those who execute the things that are ordained to that end," St. Thomas arrives at the conclusion that *secular government is subject to the church* because the former is concerned with intermediate ends, whereas the latter is concerned with the ultimate end, the salvation of souls.

The question of toleration of heretics illustrates St. Thomas Aquinas' conception of the relation of state and church and also shows how seriously he took his religion. St. Thomas defines heretics as persons who profess the Christian faith "but corrupt its dogmas." The church treats heretics patiently, because it admonishes them twice before it takes drastic action. If the heretic remains stubborn, his crime is graver than other offenses; if forgers of money and other evildoers are put to death, "much more reason is there for heretics, as soon as they are convicted of heresy, to be not only excommunicated but even put to death." Excommunication separates the heretic from the church. In its mercy, the church, because it abhors the shedding of blood by its own organs, "delivers him to the secular tribunal to be exterminated thereby from the world by death." The church thus uses only spiritual weapons, whereas the state, as a temporal power, uses temporal weapons. Yet this separation of ecclesiastical and secular authorities is not final, because church and state cooperate in the highest task of all—the salvation of souls. The church possesses indirect power over secular authorities, employing them for its purposes whenever the defense of the faith so requires.

The death penalty in this world is mild compared with the punishment that awaits the sinner in hell. Of all crimes, the offenses against God are the most serious, and heresy ranks among them. The punishment for such crimes is eternal; first, the souls are punished by the real fire of hell; after the resurrection of the bodies, they, too, are burned in the fire of hell, but miraculously the bodies are never consumed by the fire. The degree of fire depends on the gravity of the sin committed, and heretics will be assigned to the hottest mansions in hell. Another miraculous provision prevents the dulling of the senses or loss of consciousness of the damned who are exposed to eternal hell-fire. The eternity of the penalty ensures that the degree of suffering is constant throughout and that there is no lessening of the pain through habit. The blessed in heaven will watch the sufferings of the damned in hell, in order that "the happiness of the saints may be more delightful to them"; they will rejoice not out of cruelty and hatred, but because they will recognize in these sufferings "the order of divine justice and their own deliverance, which will fill them with joy."

St. Thomas was a man of kindness, charity, humility, moderation, and saintliness. His views on heresy, the treatment to be meted out to heretics in this world, and the eternal damnation awaiting them in the hottest chambers of hell are in stark contrast to St. Thomas the man; they reflect the nature of scholasticism at its peak. That dogmatic certainty is likely to lead to persecution of dissenters and eventually to death has been proved time and again in history, regardless of whether the dogmas are religious or political. Scholasticism must have been particularly certain of its premises and conclusions if a saintly and kindly man like St. Thomas Aquinas could hold such extreme views, however inextricably they were bound up with the theological and philosophical system he accepted as valid. Yet he could not go the whole way. He conceded that under certain circumstances heresy be tolerated: when heretics and unbelievers are numerous, the church may tolerate them in order to avoid disturbances of the peace.

As to the nature and form of political authority, St. Thomas Aquinas starts with the premise that government is related to the divine order. Therefore, because the commandments of God include the duty of obedience to superiors, "disobedience to the commands of a superior is a mortal sin." St. Thomas follows Aristotle in classifying the forms of government into good types, in which the interest of the governed is served, and bad types, in which the interest of the ruler or rulers prevails. But, whereas Aristotle, with some hesitation and only under qualified circumstances, preferred monarchy as the best form of government, St. Thomas is much more unequivocal in his choice of *monarchy*.

Aristotle preferred monarchy because he believed that it was not likely that superior moral and intellectual qualities could be found in more than one man; his hesitation in committing himself absolutely can be attributed to his doubt that the right man can be found. St. Thomas, on the other hand, derives his preference for the monarchial form of government from his religious view of the world. He notices that "in the whole universe there is one God, Maker and Ruler of all things." In the multitude of bodily members, the heart rules all the others; among the bees, there is one king bee, and generally "every natural government is government by one." The governing element represents, in a multiplicity of things, their purpose and guiding principle. In political society, the main practical task and purpose is the unity of peace. St. Thomas identifies unity with peace; he is therefore led to the conclusion that one ruler is most likely to maintain the peace that goes with complete unity, whereas a government made up of several persons might endanger social peace and stability through disagreement.

But St. Thomas seeks to delimit monarchy so that it will not degenerate into tyranny. First, he prefers elective to hereditary kingship: both papacy and empire were ruled by elective heads, as contrasted with the national dynasties in England and France that tended to become hereditary. Second, he suggests that the king's power "be so tempered that he cannot easily fall into tyranny." Without indicating in detail how this tempering is to be accomplished, St. Thomas in one passage stresses the important concept that "all should take some share in the government," and he also views sympathetically the idea of the *mixed constitution* in which monarchy is supplemented by aristocratic and popular elements of participation in government.

St. Thomas is aware that even a limited, or constitutional, monarchy, is no cure-all in itself and that it, too, may degenerate into tyranny. But he distinguishes minor tyranny from excessive tyranny. Regarding the first, he warns that hasty action against the tyrant may unleash unforeseen consequences worse than the evil to be remedied. He also says that *revolutionary resistance to minor tyranny,* if successful, is likely to lead to *even worse tyranny,* because the leader of the victorious revolution, "fearing to suffer from another what he did to his predecessor, oppresses the subjects with an even more grievous slavery." St. Thomas is thus perhaps the first writer on the problem of revolution who understands its inner dynamic, which cannot be halted at will once it is set in motion. He feared that revolution is nearly always a higher price than the evil it seeks to remedy; Edmund Burke was later to apply this Thomistic doctrine to the analysis and condemnation of the French Revolution.

Regarding *excessive tyranny* that becomes unbearable, St. Thomas does not endorse John of Salisbury's justification of *tyrannicide;* it is not up to private persons to decide that the king is a tyrant and then slay him. Such assumption of authority by subjects would be dangerous to the rulers as well as to the people, particularly because wicked men find the rule of a good king no less burdensome than that of a tyrant. If any action is to be taken against tyrants, it can be done only through public authority. Thus, if the people have the right to elect their king, they may lawfully depose him or restrict his power should he abuse it. But if the prince has been appointed by a higher sovereign, only that sovereign may depose him. In the event there is no human remedy, God alone can bring relief, for "it lies in his power to turn the cruel heart of the tyrant to mildness." St. Thomas relates the tyranny of the ruler to the sins of the ruled; tyrants rule by divine permission, as a punishment for the sins of the subjects. If God is to help them against the tyrant, the people must desist from sin.

The part of St. Thomas' political theory that is not primarily Aristotelian is his philosophy of law as developed in the *Summa Theologica*. The great contribution of the Middle Ages to the store of civilization is the conception of the *supremacy of law* based on the *custom of the community*. The origins of this conception are partly to be found in the Jewish-Christian doctrine of a (divine) law above the (human) law, and partly in the Stoic-Roman consciousness of the rational ordering of the world and its reflection in human society. The feudal system itself was largely a product of custom, and the relations between feudal lord and vassal were determined by custom, or law based on custom. The concept of sovereignty was not alien to the Middle Ages; but it was a sovereignty of the *law*, whereas in antiquity and in modern times the idea of sovereignty is attached to the *lawgiver*—a monarch or an aristocracy in the nondemocratic form of sovereignty, and the people in the democratic application of sovereignty. The medieval preference of communal custom to deliberate decision as the basis of the law was not mere philosophical predilection but the ideological reflection of a social reality in which status rather than contract was predominant, in which mobility was relatively low, and political authority greatly decentralized.

In his analysis of law, St. Thomas distinguishes four forms: eternal law, natural law, divine law, and human law. *Eternal law* is identical with the divine reason that governs the universe, and St. Thomas calls it eternal, because God's reason, God's rule of the world, "is not subject to time but is eternal."

As to *natural law*, St. Thomas says that all things, irrational animals and rational man, are subject to divine reason, to eternal law. But only man, as a rational creature, participates in divine providence and reason in a special way, for he provides for himself and for others, whereas all other creations of God, irrational animals and inanimate things, reflect divine reason only by receiving from it the inclinations to their proper acts and ends. Natural law is therefore man's active and transpersonal rationality, his "participation of the eternal law."

More specifically, St. Thomas divides natural law into three species: first, there is the good that man pursues in accordance with the nature he has in common with all substances, such as self-preservation. Next, there is the inclination he has toward certain forms of conduct that he shares with animals, such as "sexual intercourse, education of offspring and so forth." Third, there is the inclination in him that is specifically human, such as the desire to know God, live in society, and avoid offending those with whom one lives.

Divine law is related by St. Thomas to the fact that man's reason is neither the sole nor the most reliable guide to his apprehension of truth and justice. Divine law is communicated to man through revelation in the Old and New Testaments, and it is in no way contradictory to natural law apprehended by reason. St. Thomas' general doctrine that "grace does not abolish nature but perfects it" also applies to divine law, which is revealed by God as an act of grace.

The fourth, and lowest, form of law is *human law;* it is defined by St. Thomas as an "ordinance of reason for the common good, made by him who has care of the community, and promulgated." The need for human law arises out of two difficulties: first, the impossibility of perfectly apprehending, through the human mind, the dictates of divine reason; second, the difficulty of properly applying general principles of natural law to specific situations and circumstances.

There is little room for arbitrariness in St. Thomas' conception of human law, because it must meet several critical tests. First, for a command to have the nature of law, "it needs to be in accord with some rule of reason." Imperfect as the connection between a specific rule of law and first principles of reason may be, some link between the two must exist. The second major characteristic of law is, according to St. Thomas, that it be just and in harmony with the common good; otherwise it is "devoid of the nature of law." The third essential characteristic of the law is legitimacy: it must derive either from the people or from someone who has been entrusted by the people with the office of governing them. Though St. Thomas preferred monarchy to other forms of state, he sharply distinguished it from tyranny, which is illegitimate government. Finally, St. Thomas held that law, to be valid, must be duly promulgated. Unlike the precepts of reason and natural law, which can be grasped by logical deduction, human laws are not endowed with unerring finality; they apply to specific circumstances and therefore must be clearly and publicly promulgated. St. Thomas' insistence on publicity in the legal system is an important contribution to a principle that is one of the primary services the law renders to social life: security.

About fifty years after his death St. Thomas Aquinas was canonized, and it was officially held by the church that his doctrine could not have come into existence without a miracle of God, and that it had done more to illuminate the church than the teachings of all other writers, teachers, and doctors together. From then on, the acceptance of Thomism as the official doctrine of the church has been steady. A large number of popes in the Middle Ages and in the modern period have declared Thomism to be the authoritative guide to doctrine and faith. Leo XIII issued the Encyclical *Aeterni Patris* on August 4, 1879, in which he ordered that the doctrines of St. Thomas, "the pre-eminent guardian and glory of the Catholic Church," be henceforth taught in its academies and schools. In later official pronouncements, Pope Leo XIII decreed that if other writers and theologians disagree with St. Thomas, the "former must be sacrificed to the latter."

The *Summa Theologica* was prescribed as the text of theology in Catholic universities and academies authorized to grant academic degrees and doctorates in philosophy, and all Catholic universities, colleges, and schools were put under the patronage of St. Thomas Aquinas. Pope Pius X declared in his pronouncement of June 29, 1914, that the "capital theses in the philosophy of St. Thomas are not to be placed in the category of opinions capable of being debated one way or another," and he warned all teachers of philosophy and theology that "if they deviated so much as a step, in metaphysics especially, from Aquinas, they exposed themselves to grave risk." The Code of Canon Law, promulgated on May 27, 1917, ordered teachers in Catholic schools to "deal in every particular with the studies of mental philosophy and theology and the education of pupils in such sciences according to the method, doctrine and principles of the Angelic Doctor and religiously to adhere thereto."

Since that time Thomism has been reaffirmed as the official doctrine of the Roman Catholic Church; in addition to conservative Catholic philosophers who are completely committed to the Thomistic line of thought, outstanding liberal Catholic thinkers like Jacques Maritain have also enthusiastically contributed to the renaissance of Thomism. This fact in itself demonstrates the vitality and flexibility of St. Thomas Aquinas' ideas.

How St. Thomas himself would react to the movement of setting him up as the authoritative source of doctrine is difficult to envision. He lived in a turbulent intellectual age that experimented with new sources and materials, and he refashioned the traditional approaches to basic philosophical problems. A profound believer, he nevertheless did not hesitate to reconstruct belief on new foundations. He might have felt that he was not a "Thomist" but a student and teacher seeking to reconcile faith and reason, and he might have doubted, in his modesty and humility, that his views commanded timeless authority.

ST. THOMAS AQUINAS

I. On Kingship *

1. Definition of Kingship

The first step in our undertaking must be to set forth what is to be understood by the term *king*.

In all things which are ordered towards an end, wherein this or that course may be adopted, some directive principle is needed through which the due end may be reached by the most direct route. A ship, for example, which moves in different directions according to the impulse of the changing winds, would never reach its destination were it not brought to port by the skill of the pilot. Now, man has an end to which his whole life and all his actions are ordered; for man is an intelligent agent, and it is clearly the part of an intelligent agent to act in view of an end. Men also adopt different methods in proceeding towards their proposed end, as the diversity of men's pursuits and actions clearly indicates. Conse-

quently man needs some directive principle to guide him towards his end.

To be sure, the light of reason is placed by nature in every man, to guide him in his acts towards his end. Wherefore, if man were intended to live alone, as many animals do, he would require no other guide to his end. Each man would be a king unto himself, under God, the highest King, inasmuch as he would direct himself in his acts by the light of reason given him from on high. Yet it is natural for man, more than for any other animal, to be a social and political animal, to live in a group.

This is clearly a necessity of man's nature. For all other animals, nature has prepared food, hair as a covering, teeth, horns, claws as means of defence or at least speed in flight, while man alone was made without any natural provisions for these things. Instead of all these, man was endowed with reason, by the use of which he could procure all these things for himself by the work of his hands. Now, one man alone is not able to procure them all for himself, for one man could not sufficiently provide

* From St. Thomas Aquinas, *On Kingship* (trans. Gerald B. Phelan, rev., with introduction and notes, by I. T. Eschmann; copyright, 1949, by The Pontifical Institute of Medieval Studies, Toronto). By permission.

for life, unassisted. It is therefore natural that man should live in the society of many.

Moreover, all other animals are able to discern, by inborn skill, what is useful and what is injurious, even as the sheep naturally regards the wolf as his enemy. Some animals also recognize by natural skill certain medicinal herbs and other things necessary for their life. Man, on the contrary, has a natural knowledge of the things which are essential for his life only in a general fashion, inasmuch as he is able to attain knowledge of the particular things necessary for human life by reasoning from natural principles. But it is not possible for one man to arrive at a knowledge of all these things by his own individual reason. It is therefore necessary for man to live in a multitude so that each one may assist his fellows, and different men may be occupied in seeking, by their reason, to make different discoveries—one, for example, in medicine, one in this and another in that.

This point is further and most plainly evidenced by the fact that the use of speech is a prerogative proper to man. By this means, one man is able fully to express his conceptions to others. Other animals, it is true, express their feelings to one another in a general way, as a dog may express anger by barking and other animals give vent to other feelings in various fashions. But man communicates with his kind more completely than any other animal known to be gregarious, such as the crane, the ant or the bee.—With this in mind, Solomon says: "It is better that there be two than one; for they have the advantage of their company."

If, then, it is natural for man to live in the society of many, it is necessary that there exist among men some means by which the group may be governed. For where there are many men together and each one is looking after his own interest, the multitude would be broken up and scattered unless there were also an agency to take care of what appertains to the commonweal. In like manner, the body of a man or any other animal would disintegrate un-

less there were a general ruling force within the body which watches over the common good of all members.—With this in mind, Solomon says: "Where there is no governor, the people shall fall."

Indeed it is reasonable that this should happen, for what is proper and what is common are not identical. Things differ by what is proper to each: they are united by what they have in common. But diversity of effects is due to diversity of causes. Consequently, there must exist something which impels towards the common good of the many, over and above that which impels towards the particular good of each individual. Wherefore also in all things that are ordained towards one end, one thing is found to rule the rest. Thus in the corporeal universe, by the first body, *i.e.* the celestial body, the other bodies are regulated according to the order of Divine Providence; and all bodies are ruled by a rational creature. So, too, in the individual man, the soul rules the body; and among the parts of the soul, the irascible and the concupiscible parts are ruled by reason. Likewise, among the members of a body, one, such as the heart or the head, is the principal and moves all the others. Therefore in every multitude there must be some governing power.

Now it happens in certain things which are ordained towards an end that one may proceed in a right way and also in a wrong way. So, too, in the government of a multitude there is a distinction between right and wrong. A thing is rightly directed when it is led towards a befitting end; wrongly when it is led towards an unbefitting end. Now the end which befits a multitude of free men is different from that which befits a multitude of slaves, for the free man is one who exists for his own sake, while the slave, as such, exists for the sake of another. If, therefore, a multitude of free men is ordered by the ruler towards the common good of the multitude, that rulership will be right and just, as is suitable to free men. If, on the other hand, a rulership aims, not at the common good of the multitude, but at the private good of the ruler, it will be an unjust and perverted rulership. The Lord, therefore, threatens such rulers, saying by the mouth of Ezechiel: "Woe to the shepherds that feed themselves (seeking, that is, their own interest): should not the flocks be fed by the shepherd?" Shepherds indeed should seek the good of their flocks, and every ruler, the good of the multitude subject to him.

If an unjust government is carried on by one man alone, who seeks his own benefit from his rule and not the good of the multitude subject to him, such a ruler is called a *tyrant*—a word derived from *strength*—because he oppresses by might instead of ruling by justice. Thus among the ancients all powerful men were called tyrants. If an unjust government is carried on, not by one but by several, and if they be few, it is called an *oligarchy,* that is, the rule of a few. This occurs when a few, who differ from the tyrant only by the fact that they are more than one, oppress the people by means of their wealth. If, finally, the bad government is carried on by the multitude, it is called a *democracy,* *i.e.* control by the populace, which comes about when the plebeian people by force of numbers oppress the rich. In this way the whole people will be as one tyrant.

In like manner we must divide just governments. If the government is administered by many, it is given the name common to all forms of government, *viz. polity,* as for instance when a group of warriors exercise dominion over a city or province. If it is administered by a few men of virtue, this kind of government is called an *aristocracy, i.e.* noble governance, or governance by noble men, who for this reason are called the *Optimates.* And if a just government is in the hands of one man alone, he is properly called a *king.* Wherefore the Lord says by the mouth of Ezechiel: "My servant, David, shall be king over them and all of them shall have one shepherd."

From this it is clearly shown that the idea of king implies that he be one man who is chief and that he be a shepherd seeking the common good of the multitude and not his own.

Now since man must live in a group, because he is not sufficient unto himself to procure the necessities of life were he to remain solitary, it follows that a society will be the more perfect the more it is sufficient unto itself to procure the necessities of life. There is, to some extent, sufficiency for life in one *family of one household,* namely, insofar as pertains to the natural acts of nourishment and the begetting of offspring and other things of this kind. Self-sufficiency exists, furthermore, in one *street* with regard to those things which belong to the trade of one guild. In a *city,* which is the perfect community, it exists with regard to all the necessities of life. Still more self-sufficiency is found in a *province* because of the need of fighting together and of mutual help against enemies. Hence the man ruling a perfect community, *i.e.* a city or a province, is antonomastically called *the* king. The ruler of a household is called father, not king, although he bears a certain resemblance to the king, for which reason kings are sometimes called the fathers of their peoples.

It is plain, therefore, from what has been said, that a king is one who rules the people of one city or province, and rules them for the common good. Wherefore Solomon says: "The king ruleth over all the land subject to him."

2. Rule by One or by Many?

Having set forth these preliminary points we must now inquire what is better for a province or a city: whether to be ruled by one man or by many.

This question may be considered first from the viewpoint of the purpose of government. The aim of any ruler should be directed towards securing the welfare of that which he undertakes to rule. The duty of the pilot, for instance, is to preserve his ship amidst the perils of the sea and to bring it unharmed to the port of safety. Now the welfare and safety of a multitude formed into a society lies in the preservation of its unity, which is called peace. If this is removed, the benefit of social life is lost and, moreover, the multitude in its disagreement becomes a burden to itself. The chief concern of the ruler of a multitude, therefore, is to procure the unity of peace. It is not even legitimate for him to deliberate whether he shall establish peace in the multitude subject to him, just as a physician does not deliberate whether he shall heal the sick man encharged to him, for no one should deliberate about an end which he is obliged to seek, but only about the means to attain that end. Wherefore the Apostle, having commended the unity of the faithful people, says: "Be ye careful to keep the unity of the spirit in the bond of peace." Thus, the more efficacious a government is in keeping the unity of peace, the more useful it will be. For we call that more useful which leads more directly to the end. Now it is manifest that what is itself one can more efficaciously bring about unity than several—just as the most efficacious cause of heat is that which is by its nature hot. Therefore the rule of one man is more useful than the rule of many.

Furthermore, it is evident that several persons could by no means preserve the stability of the community if they totally disagreed. For union is necessary among them if they are to rule at all: several men, for instance, could not pull a ship in one direction unless joined together in some fashion. Now several are said to be united according as they come closer to being one. So one man rules better than several who come near being one.

Again, whatever is in accord with nature is best, for in all things nature does what is best. Now, every natural governance is governance by one. In the multitude of bodily members there is one which is the principal mover, namely, the heart; and among the powers of the soul one power presides as chief, namely, the reason. Among bees there is one king bee and in the whole universe there is One God, Maker and Ruler of all things. And there is a reason for this. Every multitude is derived from unity. Wherefore, if artificial things are an imitation of natural things and a work of art is better according as it attains a closer likeness to what is in nature, it follows that it is best for a human multitude to be ruled by one person.

This is also evident from experience. For provinces or cities which are not ruled by one person are torn with dissensions and tossed about without peace, so that the complaint seems to be fulfilled which the Lord uttered through the Prophet: "Many pastors have destroyed my vineyard." On the other hand, provinces and cities which are ruled under one king enjoy peace, flourish in justice, and delight in prosperity. Hence, the Lord by His prophets promises to His people as a great reward that He will give them one head and that "one Prince will be in the midst of them."

3. Resistance to Tyrants

Therefore, since the rule of one man, which is the best, is to be preferred, and since it may happen that it be changed into a tyranny, which is the worst (all this is clear from what has been said), a scheme should be carefully worked out which would prevent the multitude ruled by a king from falling into the hands of a tyrant.

First, it is necessary that the man who is raised up to be king by those whom it concerns should be of such condition that it is improbable that he should become a tyrant. Wherefore Daniel, commending the providence of God with respect to the institution of the king says: "The Lord hath sought him a man according to his own heart, and the Lord hath appointed him to be prince over his people." Then, once the king is established, the government of the kingdom must be so arranged that opportunity to tyrannize is removed. At the same time his power should be so tempered that he cannot easily fall into tyranny. How these things may be done we must consider in what follows.

Finally, provision must be made for facing the situation should the king stray into tyranny.

Indeed, if there be not an excess of tyranny it is more expedient to tolerate the milder tyranny for a while than, by acting against the tyrant, to become involved in many perils more grievous than the tyranny itself. For it may happen that those who act against the tyrant are unable to prevail and the tyrant then will rage the more. But should one be able to prevail against the tyrant, from this fact itself very grave dissensions among the people frequently ensue: the multitude may be broken up into factions either during their revolt against the tyrant, or in process of the organization of the government, after the tyrant has been overthrown. Moreover, it sometimes happens that while the multitude is driving out the tyrant by the help of some man, the latter, having received the power, thereupon seizes the tyranny. Then, fearing to suffer from another what he did to his predecessor, he oppresses his subjects with an even more grievous slavery. This is wont to happen in tyranny, namely, that the second becomes more grievous than the one preceding, inasmuch as, without abandoning the previous oppressions, he himself thinks up fresh ones from the malice of his heart. Whence in Syracuse, at a time when everyone desired the death of Dionysius, a certain old woman kept constantly praying that he might be unharmed and that he might survive her. When the tyrant learned this he asked why she did it. Then she said: "When I was a girl we had a harsh tyrant and I wished for his death; when he was killed, there succeeded him one who was a little harsher. I was very eager to see the end of his dominion also, and we began to have a third ruler still more harsh—that was you. So if you should be taken away, a worse would succeed in your place."

If the excess of tyranny is unbearable, some have been of the opinion that it would be an act of virtue for strong men to slay the tyrant and to expose themselves to the danger of death in order to set the multitude free. An example of this occurs even in the Old Testament, for a certain Aioth slew Eglon, King of Moab, who was oppressing the people of God under harsh slavery, thrusting a dagger into his thigh; and he was made a judge of the people.

But this opinion is not in accord with apostolic teaching. For Peter admonishes us to be reverently subject to our masters, not only to the good and gentle but also the froward: "For if one who suffers unjustly bear his trouble for conscience's sake, this is grace." Wherefore, when many emperors of the Romans tyrannically persecuted the faith of Christ, a great number both of the nobility and the common people were converted to the faith and were praised for patiently bearing death for Christ. They did not resist although they were armed, and this is plainly manifested in the case of the holy Theban legion. Aioth, then, must be considered rather as having slain a foe than assassinated a ruler, however tyrannical, of the people. Hence in the Old Testament we also read that they who killed Joas, the king of Juda, who had fallen away from the worship of God, were slain and their children spared according to the precept of the law.

Should private persons attempt on their own private presumption to kill the rulers, even though tyrants, this would be dangerous for the multitude as well as for their rulers. This is because the wicked usually expose themselves to dangers of this kind more than the good, for the rule of a king, no less than that of a tyrant, is burdensome to them since, according to the words of Solomon: "A wise king scattereth the wicked." Consequently, by presumption of this kind, danger to the people from the loss of a good king would be more probable than relief through the removal of a tyrant.

Furthermore, it seems that to proceed against the cruelty of tyrants is an action to be undertaken, not through the private presumption of a few, but rather by public authority.

If to provide itself with a king belongs to the right of a given multitude, it is not unjust that the king be deposed or have his power restricted by that same multitude if, becoming a tyrant, he abuses the royal power. It must not be thought that such a multitude is acting unfaithfully in deposing the tyrant, even though it had previously subjected itself to him in perpetuity, because he himself has deserved that the covenant with his subjects should not be kept, since, in ruling the multitude, he did not act faithfully as the office of a king demands. Thus did the Romans, who had accepted Tarquin the Proud as their king, cast him out from the kingship on account of his tyranny and the tyranny of his sons; and they set up in their place a lesser power, namely, the consular power. Similarly Domitian, who had succeeded those most moderate emperors, Vespasian, his father, and Titus, his brother, was slain by the Roman senate when he exercised tyranny, and all his wicked deeds were justly and profitably declared null and void by a decree of the senate. Thus it came about that Blessed John the Evangelist, the beloved disciple of God, who had been exiled to the island of Patmos by that very Domitian, was sent back to Ephesus by a decree of the senate.

If, on the other hand, it pertains to the right of a higher authority to provide a king for a certain multitude, a remedy against the wickedness of a tyrant is to be looked for from him. Thus when Archelaus, who had already begun to reign in Judaea in the place of Herod his father, was imitating his father's wickedness, a complaint against him having been laid before Caesar Augustus by the Jews, his power was at first diminished by depriving him of his title of king and by dividing one-half of his kingdom between his two brothers. Later, since he was not restrained from tyranny even by this means, Tiberius Caesar sent him into exile to Lugdunum, a city in Gaul.

Should no human aid whatsoever against a tyrant by forthcoming, recourse must be had to God, the King of all, Who is a helper in due time in tribulation. For it lies in his power to turn the cruel heart of the tyrant to mildness. According to Solomon: "The heart of the king is in the hand of the Lord, whithersoever He will He shall turn it." He it was who turned into mildness the cruelty of King Assuerus, who was preparing death for the Jews. He it was who so filled the cruel king Nabuchodonosor with piety that he became a proclaimer of the divine power. "Therefore," he said, "I, Nabuchodonosor do now praise and magnify and glorify the King of Heaven; because all His works are true and His ways judgments, and they that walk in pride He is able to abase." Those tyrants, however, whom he deems unworthy of conversion, he is able to put out of the way or to degrade, according to the words of the Wise Man: "God hath overturned the thrones of proud princes and hath set up the meek in their stead." He it was who, seeing the affliction of his people in Egypt and hearing their cry, hurled Pharaoh, a tyrant over God's people, with all his army into the sea. He it was who not only banished from his kingly throne the above-mentioned Nabuchodonosor because of his former pride, but also cast him from the fellowship of men and changed him into the likeness of a beast. Indeed, his hand is not shortened that He cannot free His people from tyrants. For by Isaias He promised to give his people rest from their labours and lashings and harsh slavery in which they had formerly served; and by Ezechiel He says: "I will deliver my flock from their mouth," *i.e.* from the mouth of shepherds who feed themselves.

But to deserve to secure this benefit from God, the people must desist from sin, for it is by divine permission that wicked men receive power to rule as a punishment for sin, as the Lord says by the Prophet Osee: "I will give thee a king in my wrath" and it is said in *Job* that he "maketh a man that is a hypocrite to reign for the sins of the people." Sin must therefore be done away with in order that the scourge of tyrants may cease.

4. Kings Are Subject to Priests

Just as the founding of a city or kingdom may suitably be learned from the way in which the world was created, so too the way to govern may be learned from the divine government of the world.

Before going into that, however, we should consider that to govern is to lead the thing governed in a suitable way towards its proper end. Thus a ship is said to be governed when, through the skill of the pilot, it is brought unharmed and by a direct route to harbour. Consequently, if a thing be directed to an end outside itself (as a ship to the harbour), it is the governor's duty, not only to preserve the thing unharmed, but further to guide it towards this end. If, on the contrary, there be a thing whose end is not outside itself, then the governor's endeavours will merely tend to preserve the thing undamaged in its proper perfection.

Nothing of this kind is to be found in reality, except God Himself, Who is the end of all. However, as concerns the thing which is directed to an end outside itself, care is exercised by different providers in different ways. One might have the task of preserving a thing in its being, another of bringing it to a further perfection. Such is clearly the case in the example of the ship; (the first meaning of the word *gubernator* [governor] is *pilot*). It is the carpenter's business to repair anything which might be broken, while the pilot bears the responsibility of bringing the ship to port. It is the same with man. The doctor sees to it that a man's life is preserved; the tradesman supplies the necessities of life; the teacher takes care that man may learn the truth; and the tutor sees that he lives according to reason.

Now if man were not ordained to another end outside himself, the above-mentioned cares would be sufficient for him. But as long as man's mortal life endures there is an extrinsic good for him, namely, final beatitude which is looked for after death in the enjoyment of God, for as the Apostle says: "As long as we are in the body we are far from the Lord." Consequently the Christian man, for whom that beatitude has been purchased by the blood of Christ, and who, in order to attain it, has received the earnest of the Holy Ghost, needs another and spiritual care to direct him to the harbour of eternal salvation, and this care is provided for the faithful by the ministers of the church of Christ.

Now the same judgment is to be formed about the end of society as a whole as about the end of one man. If, therefore, the ultimate end of man were some good that existed in himself, then the ultimate end of the multitude to be governed would likewise be for the multitude to acquire such good, and persevere in its possession. If such an ultimate end either of an individual man or a multitude were a corporeal one, namely, life and health of body, to govern would then be a physician's charge. If that ultimate end were an abundance of wealth, then knowledge of economics would have the last word in the community's government. If the good of the knowledge of truth were of such a kind that the multitude might attain to it, the king would have to be a teacher. It is, however, clear that the end of a multitude gathered together is to live virtuously. For men form a group for the purpose of *living well* together, a thing which the individual man living alone could not attain, and *good life* is virtuous life. Therefore, virtuous life is the end for which men gather together. The evidence for this lies in the fact that only those who render mutual assistance to one another in living well form a genuine part of an assembled multitude. If men assembled merely to live, then animals and slaves would form a part of the civil community. Or, if men assembled only to accrue wealth, then all those who traded together would belong to one city. Yet we see that only such are regarded as forming one multitude as are directed by the same laws and the same government to live well.

Yet through virtuous living man is further ordained to a higher end, which consists in the enjoyment of God, as we have said above. Consequently, since society must have the same end as the individual man, it is not the ultimate end of an assembled multitude to live virtuously, but through virtuous living to attain to the possession of God.

If this end could be attained by the power of human nature, then the duty of a king would have to include the direction of men to it. We are supposing, of course, that he is called king to whom the supreme power of governing in human affairs is entrusted. Now the higher the end to which a government is ordained, the loftier that government is. Indeed, we always find that the one to whom it pertains to achieve the final end commands those who execute the things that are ordained to that end. For example, the captain, whose business it is to regulate navigation, tells the shipbuilder what kind of ship he must construct to be suitable for navigation; and the ruler of a city, who makes use of arms, tells the blacksmith what kind of arms to make. But because a man does not attain his end, which is the possession of God, by human power but by divine—according to the words of the Apostle: "By the grace of God life everlasting"—, therefore the task of leading him to that last end does not pertain to human but to divine government.

Consequently, government of this kind pertains to that king who is not only a man, but also God, namely, our Lord Jesus Christ, Who by making men sons of God brought them to the glory of Heaven. This then is the government which has been delivered to Him and which "shall not be destroyed," on account of which He is called, in Holy Writ, not Priest only, but King. As Jeremias says: "The king shall reign and he shall be wise." Hence a royal priesthood is derived from Him, and what is more, all those who believe in Christ, insofar as they are His members, are called kings and priests.

Thus, in order that spiritual things might be distinguished from earthly things, the ministry of this kingdom has been entrusted not to earthly kings but to priests, and most

of all to the chief priest, the successor of St. Peter, the Vicar of Christ, the Roman Pontiff. To him all the kings of the Christian People are to be subject as to our Lord Jesus Christ Himself. For those to whom pertains the care of intermediate ends should be subject to him to whom pertains the care of the ultimate end, and be directed by his rule.

Because the priesthood of the gentiles and the whole worship of their gods existed merely for the acquisition of temporal goods (which were all ordained to the common good of the multitude, whose care devolved upon the king), the priests of the gentiles were very properly subject to the kings. Similarly, since in the old law earthly goods were promised to the religious people (not indeed by demons but by the true God), the priests of the old law, we read, were also subject to the kings. But in the new law there is a higher priesthood by which men are guided to heavenly goods. Consequently, in the law of Christ, kings must be subject to priests.

It was therefore also a marvellous disposition of Divine Providence that, in the city of Rome, which God had foreseen would be the principal seat of the Christian priesthood, the custom was gradually established that the rulers of the city should be subject to the priests, for as Valerius Maximus relates: "Our city has always considered that everything should yield precedence to religion, even those things in which it aimed to display the splendour of supreme majesty. We therefore unhesitatingly made the imperial dignity minister to religion, considering that the empire would thus hold control of human affairs if faithfully and constantly it were submissive to the divine power."

And because it was to come to pass that the religion of the Christian priesthood should especially thrive in France, God provided that among the Gauls too their tribal priests, called Druids, should lay down the law of all Gaul, as Julius Caesar relates in the book which he wrote about the Gallic war.

ST. THOMAS AQUINAS

II. Summa Theologica *

1. Whether Law Is Something Pertaining to Reason?

Objection 1. It seems that law is not something pertaining to reason. For the Apostle says (Rom. vii. 23): *I see another law in my members,* etc. But nothing pertaining to reason is in the members; since the reason does not make use of a bodily organ. Therefore law is not something pertaining to reason.

Obj. 2. Further, in the reason there is nothing else but power, habit, and act. But law is not the power itself of reason. In like manner, neither is it a habit of reason: because the habits of reason are the intellectual virtues of which we have spoken. Nor again is it an act of reason: because then law would cease, when the act of reason ceases, for instance, while we are asleep. Therefore law is nothing pertaining to reason.

Obj. 3. Further, the law moves those who are subject to it to act aright. But it belongs properly to the will to move to act, as is evident from what has been said. Therefore law pertains, not to the reason, but to the will; according to the words of the Jurist (*Lib. i. ff., De Const. Prin.*): *Whatsoever pleaseth the sovereign, has force of law.*

On the contrary, it belongs to the law to command and to forbid. But it belongs to reason to command. Therefore law is something pertaining to reason.

I answer that, law is a rule and measure of acts, whereby man is induced to act or is restrained from acting: for *lex* (law) is derived from *ligare* (to bind), because it binds one to act. Now the rule and measure of human acts is the reason, which is the first principle of human acts, as is evident from what has been stated above; since it belongs to the reason to direct to the end, which is the first principle in all matters of action, according to the Philosopher (*Phys. ii.*). Now that which is the principle in any genus, is the rule and measure of that genus: for instance, unity in the genus of numbers, and the first movement in the genus of movements. Consequently it follows that law is something pertaining to reason.

Reply Obj. 1. Since law is a kind of rule and measure, it may be in something in two ways. First, as in that which measures and rules: and since this is proper to reason, it follows that, in this way, law is in the reason alone.—Secondly, as in that which is measured and ruled. In this way, law is in all those things that are inclined to something by reason of some law: so that any inclination arising from a law, may be called a law, not essentially but by participation as it were. And thus the inclination of the members to concupiscence is called *the law of the members.*

Reply Obj. 2. Just as, in external action, we may consider the work and the work done, for instance the work of building and the house built; so in the acts of reason,

---

* From St. Thomas Aquinas, *Summa Theologica* (trans. the Fathers of the English Dominican Province. Copyright by Benziger Bros., Inc., New York, 1947). By permission.

we may consider the act itself of reason, *i.e.,* to understand and to reason, and something produced by this act. With regard to the speculative reason, this is first of all the definition; secondly, the proposition; thirdly, the syllogism or argument. And since also the practical reason makes use of a syllogism in respect of the work to be done, as stated above and as the Philosopher teaches (*Ethic.* vii.); hence we find in the practical reason something that holds the same position in regard to operations, as, in the speculative intellect, the proposition holds in regard to conclusions. Suchlike universal propositions of the practical intellect that are directed to actions have the nature of law. And these propositions are sometimes under our actual consideration, while sometimes they are retained in the reason by means of a habit.

Reply Obj. 3. Reason has its power of moving from the will: for it is due to the fact that one wills the end, that the reason issues its commands as regards things ordained to the end. But in order that the volition of what is commanded may have the nature of law, it needs to be in accord with some rule of reason. And in this sense is to be understood the saying that the will of the sovereign has the force of law; otherwise the sovereign's will would savour of lawlessness rather than of law.

2. Whether the Law Is Always Directed to the Common Good?

Objection 1. It seems that the law is not always directed to the common good as to its end. For it belongs to law to command and to forbid. But commands are directed to certain individual goods. Therefore the end of the law is not always the common good.

Obj. 2. Further, the law directs man in his actions. But human actions are concerned with particular matters. Therefore the law is directed to some particular good.

Obj. 3. Further, Isidore says (*Etym.* ii.): *If the law is based on reason, whatever is based on reason will be a law.* But reason is the foundation not only of what is ordained to the common good, but also of that which is directed to private good. Therefore the law is not only directed to the good of all, but also to the private good of an individual.

On the contrary, Isidore says (*Etym.* v.) that *laws are enacted for no private profit, but for the common benefit of the citizens.*

I answer that the law belongs to that which is a principle of human acts, because it is their rule and measure. Now as reason is a principle of human acts, so in reason itself there is something which is the principle in respect of all the rest: wherefore to this principle chiefly and mainly law must needs be referred.—Now the first principle in practical matters, which are the object of the practical reason, is the last end: and the last end of human life is bliss or happiness. Consequently the law must needs regard principally the relationship to happiness. Moreover, since every part is ordained to the whole, as imperfect to perfect; and since one man is a part of the perfect community, the law must needs regard properly the relationship to universal happiness. Wherefore the Philosopher, in the above definition of legal matters mentions both happiness and the body politic: for he says (*Ethic.* v.) that we call those legal matters *just, which are adapted to produce and preserve happiness and its parts for the body politic:* since the state is a perfect community, as he says in *Polit.* i.

Now in every genus, that which belongs to it chiefly is the principle of the others, and the others belong to that genus in subordination to that thing: thus fire, which is chief among hot things, is the cause of heat in mixed bodies, and these are said to be hot in so far as they have a share of fire. Consequently, since the law is chiefly ordained to the common good, any other precept in regard to some individual work, must needs be devoid of the nature of a law, save in so far as it regards the common good. Therefore every law is ordained to the common good.

Reply Obj. 1. A command denotes an application of a law to matters regulated by the law. Now the order to the common good, at which the law aims, is applicable to particular ends. And in this way commands are given even concerning particular matters.

Reply Obj. 2. Actions are indeed concerned with particular matters: but those particular matters are referable to the common good, not as to a common genus or species, but as to a common final cause, according as the common good is said to be the common end.

Reply Obj. 3. Just as nothing stands firm with regard to the speculative reason except that which is traced back to the first indemonstrable principles, so nothing stands firm with regard to the practical reason, unless it be directed to the last end which is the common good: and whatever stands to reason in this sense, has the nature of a law.

3. *Whether the Reason of Any Man Is Competent to Make Laws?*

Objection 1. It seems that the reason of any man is competent to make laws. For the Apostle says (Rom. ii 14) that *when the Gentiles, who have not the law, do by nature those things that are of the law, . . . they are a law to themselves.* Now he says this of all in general. Therefore anyone can make a law for himself.

Obj. 2. Further, as the Philosopher says (*Ethic.* ii), *the intention of the lawgiver is to lead men to virtue.* But every man can lead another to virtue. Therefore the reason of any man is competent to make laws.

Obj. 3. Further, just as the sovereign of a state governs the state, so every father of a family governs his household. But the sovereign of a state can make laws for the state. Therefore every father of a family can make laws for his household.

On the contrary, Isidore says (*Etym.* v.; and the passage is quoted in *Decretals, Dist.* 2): *A law is an ordinance of the people, whereby something is sanctioned by the Elders together with the Commonalty.*

I answer that, a law, properly speaking, regards first and foremost the order to the common good. Now to order anything to the common good, belongs either to the whole people, or to someone who is the vicegerent of the whole people. And therefore the making of a law belongs either to the whole people or to a public personage who has care of the whole people: since in all other matters the directing of anything to the end concerns him to whom the end belongs.

Reply Obj. 1. As stated above, a law is in a person not only as in one that rules, but also by participation as in one that is ruled. In the latter way each one is a law to himself, in so far as he shares the direction that he receives from one who rules him. Hence the same text goes on: *Who show the work of the law written in their hearts.*

Reply Obj. 2. A private person cannot lead another to virtue efficaciously: for he can only advise, and if his advice be not taken, it has no coercive power, such as the law should have, in order to prove an efficacious inducement to virtue, as the Philosopher says (*Ethic.* x.). But this coercive power is vested in the whole people or in some public personage, to whom it belongs to inflict penalties. Wherefore the framing of laws belongs to him alone.

Reply Obj. 3. As one man is a part of the household, so a household is a part of the state: and the state is a perfect community, according to *Polit.* i. And therefore, as the good of one man is not the last end, but is ordained to the common good; so too the good of one household is ordained to the good of a single state, which is a perfect community. Consequently he that governs a family, can indeed make certain commands or ordinances, but not such as to have properly the force of law.

4. *Whether Promulgation Is Essential to the Law?*

Objection 1. It seems that promulgation is not essential to a law. For the natural law above all has the character of law. But the natural law needs no promulgation. Therefore it is not essential to a law that it be promulgated.

Obj. 2. Further, it belongs properly to a law to bind one to do or not to do something. But the obligation of fulfilling a law touches not only those in whose presence it is promulgated, but also others. Therefore promulgation is not essential to a law.

Obj. 3. Further, the binding force of a law extends even to the future, since *laws are binding in matters of the future,* as the jurists say (*Cod.* i., tit. *De lege et constit.*). But promulgation concerns those who are present. Therefore it is not essential to a law.

On the contrary, It is laid down in the *Decretals* (*Append. Grat.*) that *laws are established when they are promulgated.*

I answer that a law is imposed on others by way of a rule and measure. Now a rule or measure is imposed by being applied to those who are to be ruled and measured by it. Wherefore, in order that a law obtain the binding force which is proper to a law, it must needs be applied to the men who have to be ruled by it. Such application is made by its being notified to them by promulgation. Wherefore promulgation is necessary for the law to obtain its force.

Thus from the four preceding articles, the definition of law may be gathered; and it is nothing else than an ordinance of reason for the common good, made by him who has care of the community, and promulgated.

Reply Obj. 1. The natural law is promulgated by the very fact that God instilled it into man's mind so as to be known by him naturally.

Reply Obj. 2. Those who are not present when a law is promulgated, are bound to observe the law, in so far as it is notified or can be notified to them by others, after it has been promulgated.

Reply Obj. 3. The promulgation that takes place now, extends to future time by reason of the durability of written characters, by which means it is continually promulgated. Hence Isidore says (*Etym.* ii.)

that *lex* (law) *is derived from legere* (to read) *because it is written.*

5. *Whether the Natural Law Is the Same in All Men?*

Objection 1. It seems that the natural law is not the same in all. For it is stated in the *Decretals* (*Dist.* i.) that *the natural law is that which is contained in the Law and the Gospel.* But this is not common to all men; because, as it is written (Rom. x. 16), *all do not obey the Gospel.* Therefore the natural law is not the same in all men.

Obj. 2. Further, *Things which are according to the law are said to be just,* as stated in *Ethic.* v. But it is stated in the same book that nothing is so universally just as not to be subject to change in regard to some men. Therefore even the natural law is not the same in all men.

Obj. 3. Further, to the natural law belongs everything to which a man is inclined according to his nature. Now different men are naturally inclined to different things; some to the desire of pleasures, others to the desire of honours, and other men to other things. Therefore there is not one natural law for all.

On the contrary, Isidore says (*Etym.* v.): *The natural law is common to all nations.*

I answer that to the natural law belong those things to which a man is inclined naturally: and among these it is proper to man to be inclined to act according to reason. Now the process of reason is from the common to the proper, as stated in *Phys.* i. The speculative reason, however, is differently situated in this matter, from the practical reason. For, since the speculative reason is busied chiefly with necessary things, which cannot be otherwise than they are, its proper conclusions, like the universal principles, contain the truth without fail. The practical reason, on the other hand, is busied with contingent matters, about which human actions are concerned: and consequently, although there is necessity in the general principles, the more we descend to matters of detail, the more frequently we encounter defects. Accordingly then in speculative matters truth is the same in all men, both as to principles and as to conclusions: although the truth is not known to all as regards the conclusions, but only as regards the principles which are called common notions. But in matters of action, truth or practical rectitude is not the same for all, as to matters of detail, but only as to the general principles: and where there is the same rectitude in matters of detail, it is not equally known to all.

It is therefore evident that, as regards the general principles whether of speculative or of practical reason, truth or rectitude is the same for all, and is equally known by all. As to the proper conclusions of the speculative reason, the truth is the same for all, but is not equally known to all: thus it is true for all that the three angles of a triangle are together equal to two right angles, although it is not known to all. But as to the proper conclusions of the practical reason, neither is the truth or rectitude the same for all, nor, where it is the same, is it equally known by all. Thus it is right and true for all to act according to reason: and from this principle it follows as a proper conclusion, that goods entrusted to another should be restored to their owner. Now this is true for the majority of cases: but it may happen in a particular case that it would be injurious, and therefore unreasonable, to restore goods held in trust; for instance if they are claimed for the purpose of fighting against one's country. And this principle will be found to fail the more, according as we descend further into detail, e.g., if one were to say that goods held in trust should be restored with such and such a guarantee, or in such and such a way; because the greater the number of conditions added, the greater the number of ways in which the principle may fail, so that it be not right to restore or not to restore.

Consequently we must say that the natural law, as to general principles, is the same

for all, both as to rectitude and as to knowledge. But as to certain matters of detail, which are conclusions, as it were, of those general principles, it is the same for all in the majority of cases, both as to rectitude and as to knowledge; and yet in some few cases it may fail, both as to rectitude, by reason of certain obstacles (just as natures subject to generation and corruption fail in some few cases on account of some obstacle), and as to knowledge, since in some the reason is perverted by passion, or evil habit, or an evil disposition of nature; thus formerly, theft, although it is expressly contrary to the natural law, was not considered wrong among the Germans, as Julius Caesar relates (*De Bello Gall.* vi.).

Reply Obj. 1. The meaning of the sentence quoted is not that whatever is contained in the Law and the Gospel belongs to the natural law, since they contain many things that are above nature; but that whatever belongs to the natural law is fully contained in them. Wherefore Gratian, after saying that *the natural law is what is contained in the Law and the Gospel,* adds at once, by way of example, *by which everyone is commanded to do to others as he would be done by.*

Reply Obj. 2. The saying of the Philosopher is to be understood of things that are naturally just, not as general principles, but as conclusions drawn from them, having rectitude in the majority of cases, but failing in a few.

Reply Obj. 3. As, in man, reason rules and commands the other powers, so all the natural inclinations belonging to the other powers must needs be directed according to reason. Wherefore it is universally right for all men, that all their inclinations should be directed according to reason.

6. *Whether Every Human Law Is Derived from the Natural Law?*

Objection 1. It seems that not every human law is derived from the natural law. For the Philosopher says (*Ethic.* v.) that *the legal just is that which originally was c matter of indifference.* But those things which arise from the natural law are not matters of indifference. Therefore the enactments of human laws are not all derived from the natural law.

Obj. 2. Further, positive law is contrasted with natural law, as stated by Isidore (*Etym.* v.) and the Philosopher (*Ethic.* v.). But those things which flow as conclusions from the general principles of the natural law belong to the natural law. Therefore that which is established by human law does not belong to the natural law.

Obj. 3. Further, the law of nature is the same for all; since the Philosopher says (*Ethic.* v.) that *the natural just is that which is equally valid everywhere.* If therefore human laws were derived from the natural law, it would follow that they too are the same for all: which is clearly false.

Obj. 4. Further, it is possible to give a reason for things which are derived from the natural law. But *it is not possible to give the reason for all the legal enactments of the lawgivers* (*Pandect. Justin.* Lib. I., Tit. III., Art. V., *De legibus*, etc.). Therefore not all human laws are derived from the natural law.

On the contrary, Tully says (*Rhetor.* ii.): *Things which emanated from nature and were approved by custom, were sanctioned by fear and reverence for the laws.*

I answer that, as Augustine says (*De Lib. Arb.* i.), *that which is not just seems to be no law at all:* wherefore the force of a law depends on the extent of its justice. Now in human affairs a thing is said to be just, from being right, according to the rule of reason. But the first rule of reason is the law of nature, as is clear from what has been stated. Consequently every human law has just so much of the nature of law, as it is derived from the law of nature. But if in any point it deflects from the law of nature, it is no longer a law but a perversion of law.

But it must be noted that something may be derived from the natural law in two ways: first, as a conclusion from premises, secondly, by way of determination of certain generalities. The first way is like to that by which, in sciences, demonstrated conclusions are drawn from the principles: while the second mode is likened to that whereby, in the arts, general forms are particularized as to details: thus the craftsman needs to determine the general form of a house to some particular shape. Some things are therefore derived from the general principles of the natural law, by way of conclusions; *e.g.,* that *one must not kill* may be derived as a conclusion from the principle that *one should do harm to no man:* while some are derived therefrom by way of determination; *e.g.,* the law of nature has it that the evil-doer should be punished: but that he be punished in this or that way, is a determination of the law of nature.

Accordingly both modes of derivation are found in the human law. But those things which are derived in the first way, are contained in human law not as emanating therefrom exclusively, but have some force from the natural law also. But those things which are derived in the second way, have no other force than that of human law.

Reply Obj. 1. The Philosopher is speaking of those enactments which are by way of determination or specification of the precepts of the natural law.

Reply Obj. 2. This argument avails for those things that are derived from the natural law, by way of conclusions.

Reply Obj. 3. The general principles of the natural law cannot be applied to all men in the same way on account of the great variety of human affairs: and hence arises the diversity of positive laws among various people.

Reply Obj. 4. These words of the Jurist are to be understood as referring to decisions of rulers in determining particular points of the natural law: on which determinations the judgment of expert and prudent men is based as on its principles; in so far, to wit, as they see at once what is the best thing to decide.

Hence the Philosopher says (*Ethic.* vi.) that in such matters, *we ought to pay as*

much attention to the undemonstrated say-
ings and opinions of persons who surpass us
in experience, age and prudence, as to their
demonstrations.

7. *Whether Human Law Binds a Man in Conscience?*

Objection 1. It seems that human law does not bind a man in conscience. For an inferior power has no jurisdiction in a court of higher power. But the power of man, which frames human law, is beneath the Divine power. Therefore human law cannot impose its precept in a Divine court, such as is the court of conscience.

Obj. 2. Further, the judgment of conscience depends chiefly on the commandments of God. But sometimes God's commandments are made void by human laws, according to Matth. xv. 6: *You have made void the commandment of God for your tradition.* Therefore human law does not bind a man in conscience.

Obj. 3. Further, human laws often bring loss of character and injury on man, according to Isa. x. 1 *et seq.: Woe to them that make wicked laws, and when they write, write injustice; to oppress the poor in judgment, and do violence to the cause of the humble of My people.* But it is lawful for anyone to avoid oppression and violence. Therefore human laws do not bind man in conscience.

On the contrary, it is written (I Pet. ii. 19.): *This is thanksworthy, if for conscience . . . a man endure sorrow, suffering wrongfully.*

I answer that, laws framed by man are either just or unjust. If they be just, they have the power of binding in conscience, from the eternal law whence they are derived, according to Prov. viii. 15: *By Me kings reign, and lawgivers decree just things.* Now laws are said to be just, both from the end, when, to wit, they are ordained to the common good,—and from their author, that is to say, when the law

that is made does not exceed the power of the lawgiver,—and from their form, when, to wit, burdens are laid on the subjects, according to an equality of proportion and with a view to the common good. For, since one man is a part of the community, each man, in all that he is and has, belongs to the community; just as a part, in all that it is, belongs to the whole; wherefore nature inflicts a loss on the part, in order to save the whole: so that on this account, such laws as these, which impose proportionate burdens, are just and binding in conscience, and are legal laws.

On the other hand laws may be unjust in two ways: first, by being contrary to human good, through being opposed to the things mentioned above:—either in respect of the end, as when an authority imposes on his subjects burdensome laws, conducive, not to the common good, but rather to his own cupidity or vainglory;—or in respect of the author, as when a man makes a law that goes beyond the power committed to him;—or in respect of the form, as when burdens are imposed unequally on the community, although with a view to the common good. The like are acts of violence rather than laws; because, as Augustine says (*De Lib. Arb. i.*), *a law that is not just, seems to be no law at all.* Wherefore such laws do not bind in conscience, except perhaps in order to avoid scandal or disturbance, for which cause a man should even yield his right, according to Matth. v. 40, 41: *If a man . . . take away thy coat, let go thy cloak also unto him; and whosoever will force thee one mile, go with him other two.*

Secondly, laws may be unjust through being opposed to the Divine good: such are the laws of tyrants inducing to idolatry, or to anything else contrary to the Divine law: and laws of this kind must nowise be observed, because, as stated in Acts v. 29, *we ought to obey God rather than men.*

Reply Obj. 1. As the Apostle says (Rom. xiii. 1, 2), all human power is from God *. . . therefore he that resisteth the power,* in matters that are within its scope, *re-*

sisteth the ordinance of God: so that he becomes guilty according to his conscience.

Reply Obj. 2. This argument is true of laws that are contrary to the commandments of God, and which go beyond the scope of (human) power. Wherefore in such matters human law should not be obeyed.

Reply Obj. 3. This argument is true of a law that inflicts unjust hurt on its subjects. The power that man holds from God does not extend to this: wherefore neither in such matters is man bound to obey the law, provided he avoid giving scandal or inflicting a more grievous hurt.

8. Whether Human Law Should Always be Changed, Whenever Something Better Occurs?

Objection 1. It seems that human law should be changed, whenever something better occurs. Because human laws are devised by human reason, like other arts. But in the other arts, the tenets of former times give place to others, if something better occurs. Therefore the same should apply to human laws.

Obj. 2. Further, by taking note of the past we can provide for the future. Now unless human laws had been changed when it was found possible to improve them, considerable inconvenience would have ensued; because the laws of old were crude in many points. Therefore it seems that laws should be changed, whenever anything better occurs to be enacted.

Obj. 3. Further, human laws are enacted about single acts of man. But we cannot acquire perfect knowledge in singular matters, except by experience, which *requires time,* as stated in *Ethic.* ii. Therefore it seems that as time goes on it is possible for something better to occur for legislation.

On the contrary, it is stated in the *Decretals (Dist.* xii.): *It is absurd, and a detestable shame, that we should suffer those traditions to be changed which we have received from the fathers of old.*

I answer that human law is rightly changed, in so far as such change is conducive to the common weal. But, to a certain extent, the mere change of law is of itself prejudicial to the common good: because custom avails much for the observance of laws, seeing that what is done contrary to general custom, even in slight matters, is looked upon as grave. Consequently, when a law is changed, the binding power of the law is diminished, in so far as custom is abolished. Wherefore human law should never be changed, unless, in some way or other, the common weal be compensated according to the extent of the harm done in this respect. Such compensation may arise either from some very great and very evident benefit conferred by the new enactment; or from the extreme urgency of the case, due to the fact that either the existing law is clearly unjust, or its observance extremely harmful. Wherefore the Jurist says, (*Pandect. Justin.* i.) that *in establishing new laws, there should be evidence of the benefit to be derived, before departing from a law which has long been considered just.*

Reply Obj. 1. Rules of art derive their force from reason alone: and therefore whenever something better occurs, the rule followed hitherto should be changed. But *laws derive very great force from custom,* as the Philosopher states (*Polit.* ii.): consequently they should not be quickly changed.

Reply Obj. 2. This argument proves that laws ought to be changed: not in view of any improvement, but for the sake of a great benefit or in a case of great urgency. This answer applies also to the Third Objection.

CHAPTER 9

DANTE

ROMAN civilization reached its fullest flowering in the great urban centers; in fact, "city" and "civilization" come from the same Latin word, *civis*. The countryside, according to the Romans, was good enough as a source of agricultural supplies and a place of occasional refuge and retreat from the cares of the world, but the amenities of civilized living were to be found only in the cities. Unfortunately, many of these amenities were soon to be denied the Romans, for one of the main effects of the invasions that swept over Europe in the early Middle Ages, first of the Germanic tribes, and then of the Arabs and Magyars, was the progressive relapse of Europe into a primitive agrarian way of life. Cities shrank in physical size and, more important, declined as centers of political, economic, and intellectual activity. The city of Rome, which had about a million inhabitants in the first century A. D., dropped to less than half a million in the fourth century and shrank to a small town of seventeen thousand in the census of 1377.

The appearance of feudalism was the outward expression of the disintegration of urban civilization in western Europe. The complex international economy based on trade and transport was replaced, to a considerable extent, by the self-sufficient estate. Actually, the large estates had existed before the coming of medieval feudalism; what was new in the feudal estate was that it no longer produced for an exchange economy but for its own needs. With the decline of the towns and the virtual disappearance of professional merchants, land increasingly defined, from the highest prince and potentate to the lowest serf and slave, a person's wealth, social status, and political position. In politics, too, feudalism connoted a shrinkage of effective range of operation. The prefeudal concept of state and empire, of administration on a large scale, was replaced (in practice at least, though not in theory) by the conception that authority was in the hands of those who possessed land.

The church had a favored position in the feudal system both economically and culturally. As a large owner of land, in some countries the single largest landlord, it directly benefited from a way of life in which land was the measure of all social power and prestige. Culturally, the destruction of urban civilization in the barbarian invasions gave the churches and monasteries a unique position of influence: for centuries they were the only centers of intellectual activity and continuity, saving for posterity the tradition and heritage of art and philosophy that the martial conquerors little understood. Moreover, the general ignorance and illiteracy of laymen compelled emperors and kings to employ clerics in all levels of government, because literacy—not to speak of more advanced accomplishments—was for several centuries confined to priests and ecclesiastics.

The growth of cities from the eleventh century on produced new centers of economic and intellectual life that the church viewed with anxiety and hostility. As a powerful landowner, the church shared the prejudices and fears of all landowners in the face of a new commercial, capitalist economy whose dynamic vitality and immense productivity threatened to overshadow the static, agrarian economy of feudalism. In addition, the church saw in the rise of towns and cities a serious menace to its intellectual predominance. The restless spirit of the urban populations challenged the existing order in which church and aristocracy divided all power between themselves: the existing order recommended itself to church and aristocracy, they argued, not because they were its main beneficiaries, but because it seemed to be in harmony with religion, morals, and custom.

By contrast, the rising bourgeoisie saw in the existing social system unjustifiable privilege and ecclesiastical domination. The legal status of city inhabitants implied freedom and mobility, whereas those who lived and worked on the manorial estates were in complete or partial serfdom. Immigrants from estates into towns shook off the bonds of servitude by mere residence of a year or so, and the medieval saying, "City air makes free," expressed a fact of revolutionary impact in the growth of cities.

The church soon lost its monopoly of learning and technical knowledge in the arts and crafts, and the newly developing cities increasingly assumed the role of intellectual leadership, first apart from the churches and monasteries, and later in direct opposition to them. The accumulation of wealth permitted the growth of a new class of artists, writers, and teachers who were laymen. In nearly every respect the traditional civilization based on church dogma and landed power was challenged, altered, and replaced by a new way of life that was more productive in economics, more equalitarian in government, and more secular in general outlook.

A new elite was thus added to the existing two ruling groups of the clergy and aristocracy: men of wealth, whose claim to greatness ("magnates") and influence was based on financial power. In the beginning this class was primarily concerned about its own privileges in the struggle against the old landed aristocracy and the church, but as time went on, the shared experiences, sorrows, and joys of all townfolk created a new sense of urban solidarity.

The revival of urban life was particularly vigorous in Italy from the twelfth to the fourteenth centuries, and Italian leadership in this rebirth was followed by pre-eminence in the revival of ancient Greek and Roman thought that culminated in the Renaissance. Among Italian cities, Florence, Genoa, and Venice were the most important centers of international trade and finance, not only in Italy but in all Europe. Italians discovered the methods and techniques of banking and credit on domestic and international lines, and Italian terms in banking and finance survive to this day.

The capitalist system did not start with the Industrial Revolution in eighteenth-century England but with these bold commercial and financial enterprises in thirteenth-century Italy; in outlook and impact this early phase of capitalism, which lasted until the middle of the eighteenth century, was perhaps as revolutionary as the later phase of industrial capitalism. The early Italian international traders and financiers clearly exhibited the main impulses and methods of capitalism: pursuit of profit for the sake of accumulating wealth, long-distance operations, and long-term planning. *Contract* and *exchange* became the basic economic patterns in lieu of precapitalist *status* and *servitude,* and ruthless competition was condoned as the inevitable result of acquisitiveness. Faith in an all-pervading rationality permeated all activities of life, translated them into market transactions, and infused them with utilitarian standards of business ethics.

The hold of the church was weaker over the towns than over the countryside from the beginning, and the secular, or lay, outlook of the later Middle Ages is the product of the new urban, commercial civilization. The most important antipapalist, imperialist tract of the Middle Ages, *De monarchia (On Monarchy,* about 1310), is the work of a Florentine, Dante Alighieri (1265–1321), one of the first learned medieval laymen and the greatest poet of the medieval period. By his use of the vernacular in *The Divine Comedy* and other works he helped to create a national Italian language and at the same time to break the monopoly of Latin as the only means of literary communication. To this day the Roman Catholic Church has not permitted the printing of the Bible, without authorization, in any language except Latin, and the use of the vernacular by Dante was, in more than a literary way, an act of revolt against traditional thought and expression.

As an artist, Dante clearly announces the dawn of the Renaissance; he is "modern"—from the twentieth-century viewpoint, at least. His versatility is also of the classical Renaissance style. As a poet, he belongs to the half-dozen immortals, for he moves away from the stereotypes of feeling and expression of the Middle Ages and discovers the intensely personal and individual qualities of man that transcend nationality, religion, class, and caste. But Dante was also, with varying success, a diplomat, soldier, politician, pamphleteer, philologist, theologian, and philosopher. Although he was forced to spend the last third of his life in exile, forbidden to return to Florence under the threat of being burned alive, he made use of his wanderings to enrich his experience and enlarge his horizon.

As a member of the lower nobility, Dante personally abhorred the new business classes, the *nouveaux riches* and their manner of living, and he felt bitter about what seemed to him the vulgarity and coarseness of the new society. Yet such was the force of his environment that his political philosophy, a curious mixture of backward- and forward-looking ideas, of theological scholasticism and pungent antipapalism, was nevertheless a typical product of his age.

In his chief political work, *De monarchia*, Dante raises three questions. The first is whether a *world government, ruled by a monarch,* is necessary for the welfare of the human race. In actuality, two issues are involved in this question: first, the issue of universal government, and, second, the monarchical form of such a world state. Dante derives the need for world government from a philosophical a priori as well as from his conception of man's nature and goals. Philosophically, Dante relates essence and reality to unity, and holds that true being is expressed in the greatest unity, and "where Unity is greatest, there Good is also greatest; and in proportion as anything is far from Being in its highest form, it is far from Unity, and therefore from the Good." Because the distinguishing quality of man is his faculty of reasoning and understanding, he cannot develop what is most specifically human in isolation, particularly if his speculative faculties are to be extended into action. Just as the individual can become perfect in wisdom and prudence only by rest and quiet, so the entire human race develops most freely and applies itself best to its proper work, which is "almost divine," if it can do so in the calm and tranquillity of peace. Of all things designed to secure blessings to man, individually and collectively, "peace is the best."

Dante also stresses an argument in support of world government that has a distinctly practical and modern flavor: the need for *settlement of disputes between states without war:* "Wherever there is controversy, there ought to be judgment," and there can be judgment only if the decision of some authority is recognized as final. In the most recent and contemporary thinking about the possibilities of world order it is generally recognized, as was realized by Dante over six centuries ago, that the first institutional development toward world government is likely to occur in the field of judicial settlement of specific disputes rather than in the legislative enactment and executive enforcement of universal laws. Judicial decisions deal with *individual* issues of the *past,* legislative acts with *general* issues of the *future.* The acceptance of universal arbitration and adjudication on the part of states therefore involves a lesser commitment than the submission to universal legislation.

Concerning the necessity of *monarchical* world government, Dante starts again with a philosophical a priori: that "when a number of things are arranged to attain an end, it behooves one of them to regulate or govern the others, and the others to submit." Within the individual, reason governs all other faculties in pursuing happiness. Within associations—from the household, the village, the city, to the kingdom—one individual must rule if unity and peace are to be preserved for the benefit of all. The end of the human race is the fullest development of its potential capacities: "There must, therefore, be one to guide and govern, and the proper title for this office is Monarch or Emperor. And so it is plain that Monarchy or the Empire is necessary for the welfare of the world."

Dante also refers, in Thomistic fashion, to the example of God as the monarchical ruler of the universe. Mankind is a part of the universe, and all created things should represent God as much as possible. The human race is most like God when it is one and united, and it is most one "when it is united wholly in one body, and it is evident that this cannot be, except when it is subject to one prince."

Dante is far from advocating universal tyranny, however, and he stresses the values of *justice* and freedom. The greatest enemy of justice, he says, is greed and avarice, the inability to be *disinterested* and content. He therefore holds that justice would be strongest in a world government headed by a monarch; there is nothing left for him to desire, "for the passions cannot exist if their objects are destroyed." Even kings are corrupted by the springs of injustice—cupidity and ambition—inasmuch as they seek to enlarge their territory and wealth. Dante stresses the Aristotelian idea that the *rule of law* is to be preferred to the personal judgment of men, because such judgment is likely to be perverted by personal interests, whereas the monarchical head of a world state would be in the best position to dispense justice in accordance with general rules of law, because, having no personal interests at stake, he would care for all men in the world. Lacking avarice and cupidity, the monarch would even go beyond justice and dispense charity, in order to strengthen the bonds of solidarity and peace among men.

Freedom, too, is best realized, according to Dante, in world monarchy. Dante calls freedom "the greatest gift bestowed by God on mankind," but the attainment of liberty is difficult in perverted forms of government in which the ruled exist for the sake of the rulers, rather than the rulers for the ruled. By contrast, good states "aim at liberty, that in them men may live for themselves." Because the monarch of the world state is "the servant of all," mankind will be freer under such a government than under any regime of local or national monarchies in which the ruler can at best identify himself with only a part of humanity.

With all his enthusiasm for a universal state under a monarchical ruler, Dante does not believe in uniformity for its own sake. He recognizes that although a world state would unify mankind with respect to law and government, many ethnic, cultural, and linguistic groups and nations would continue to exist, each with its own traditions and needs dictated by history and external circumstances, such as climate. Trifling matters would therefore not be brought to the attention of the monarch of the world state but would be regulated by municipal and national laws and authorities. Only *matters that affect all mankind* require a *common rule of law* and a *common authority*. Dante is thus one of the first writers on the problem of world government to separate the issue of *political sovereignty*, which must be vested in the central organ of world government, from the issue of *cultural autonomy*, which the individual nations and nationalities will fully preserve in a political world community, "for nations and kingdoms and states have, each of them, certain peculiarities which must be regulated by different laws."

The second main question Dante proposes to answer in *De monarchia* is whether the *Roman people* acquired *world domination* by right. One of Dante's chief authorities in this argument is Virgil, "our divine poet"; his completely natural and uninhibited acceptance of pagans as highest authorities marks Dante off and draws him closer to the Renaissance. Dante betrays Italian national pride in his belief that the Roman people were the noblest and therefore the most fitting to be preferred by God for the government of the world. He notices that the record of the Roman achievement is full of miracles, and that the Roman empire was helped "to its perfection by miracles; therefore it was willed by God and consequently was and is by right."

Although Dante was orthodox in his religious faith, it is apparent from the above statements that he has none of the hostility toward pagan Rome that was so typical of the earlier Middle Ages, as expressed by St. Augustine. Dante says that in bringing the whole world into subjection the Romans aimed at the universal good, renouncing all selfishness, and "that sacred, pious, and glorious people are seen to have neglected their own private interests that they might follow public objects for the good of all mankind." Dante also bases his case on the record of history: Babylonians, Assyrians, Persians, and Egyptians had unsuccessfully tried to subject the whole world, and Alexander the Great came nearest to the prize of world dominion. Only the Romans succeeded in setting up a world empire, and therefore "it was by the judgment of God that it prevailed." In medieval fashion Dante compares the victory of Rome to victory in a duel: according to medieval legal principles what is acquired by duel is "gained by right." Dante anticipates Hegel's famous dictum that "world history is the world court."

Dante never discusses specifically the problem of who the Roman people in the thirteenth century were, because he takes for granted the continuity of the Roman empire and the Holy Roman empire of the German monarchs. Dante was free from political nationalism in the modern sense, and therefore he did not advocate an Italian kingdom on the French or English models. His conception of world monarchy was entirely medieval, though—as an Italian—he thought of Rome as the natural capital of a world monarchy, and of Italy as the preferred "province," which would include the Italian-speaking communes and regions. In this way he hoped that universal monarchy would also bring peace to an Italy whose city-states were rent by civil and foreign wars. But his political thought was focused on world, not nationality, problems, although he was keenly aware of Italy as a cultural and linguistic nation: "To me the world is my country, as the sea is to the fish."

The third main question of *De monarchia* is whether the *authority of the emperor* derives *directly from God* or from some minister or vicar of God, that is, the pope. Dante conceives man as dual in nature, his two essential parts being his body and soul. Following the Aristotelian idea that "every nature is ordained to gain some final end," Dante deduces from man's dual nature two ends: the first is the blessedness of *earthly life,* and the second is the blessedness of *heavenly paradise.* The two ends of man being different, the means to their attainment must be different, too. The blessings of earthly life can be ascertained, Dante says, through the lessons of *reason and philosophy,* whereas we can arrive at the blessings of heavenly paradise by the spiritual lessons, transcending human reason, of *theology, faith, hope,* and *charity.* The truths of philosophy are made manifest by reason and the writings of philosophers, and the supernatural truths of theology are made known in the revelations of the Scriptures. All these considerations lead Dante to this decisive conclusion: "Therefore man had need of two guides for his life, as he had a twofold end in life; whereof one is the Supreme Pontiff, to lead mankind to eternal life, according to the things revealed to us; and the other is the Emperor, to guide mankind to happiness in this world, in accordance with the teaching of philosophy."

Dante's second main argument in support of his antipapalist position is that the Roman empire possessed power and authority before the church even existed. Therefore, Dante holds, the church cannot possibly be the cause of the power or authority of the empire. The authority of the emperor "comes down, with no intermediary will, from the fountain of universal authority; and this fountain, one in its unity, flows through many channels out of the abundance of the goodness of God."

The medieval man in Dante, however, could not be satisfied with a solution under which both church and empire are supreme in their respective spheres of activity. The yearning for ultimate unity, in which the *coordinate powers of pope and emperor* can be brought together again, finds expression in the thought that above the relative superiorities of pope and emperor there is the one absolute superiority in which all others are united: the *unity and supremacy of God*.

Behind Dante's scholastic method of argument, his strictly orthodox religious beliefs, his use of characteristically medieval symbols, allegories, and quotations, lies considerable originality of thought. The Christian conception of the state appeared in two versions in the Middle Ages: according to the earlier view of St. Augustine and the church fathers the origin of government lies in human frailty and sinfulness, and the state is set up by divine providence as the penalty and remedy of sin. The later Thomistic view, developed under the influence of Aristotle, holds, by contrast, that the state is the natural expression of man's social impulses. Dante is the first writer in the Middle Ages who ingeniously combines Augustinian and Thomistic elements in a new synthesis that surpasses, and is contradictory to, the political theories of both St. Augustine and St. Thomas Aquinas. In approaching the general problem of political life, Dante follows the Aristotelian-Thomistic tradition that man needs collective associations, governmental institutions, the state, for the full development of his natural capacities and the satisfaction of his physical and intellectual wants. However, the natural forms of political organization—communes, city-states, principalities, kingdoms—are particularistic and inadequate because the sins of greed and avarice pervert their natures and purposes. The remedy for these sins —and here Dante skillfully utilizes Augustinian elements for his own theory— is the institution of *universal government* by divine providence, so that man may partake of the blessings of earthly peace, justice, and freedom, just as he may partake of the universal church that God has provided for the attainment of the blessings in heaven.

St. Augustine himself thought of the *church* as the *only universal community* of mankind; not identical with the City of God, the church nevertheless approximates and "mystically" reflects it on earth. As for the earthly city, St. Augustine says that as a way of life, in which the love of self rather than of God prevails, it is a universal phenomenon, but he speaks nowhere of a symbolical or "mystical" reflection of the earthly city in a universal temporal organization, but only of *states*. Even the Roman empire could hardly appear to St. Augustine as a universal temporal community of mankind, first, because of its predominantly pagan background, and, secondly, because of its ruin and disintegration before his own eyes.

Similarly, St. Thomas Aquinas reserves the concept of a universal community for the church, headed by the *pope*, but speaks of *princes*, and not of the emperor, when discussing the issue of government in its most general aspects. According to its own view, the church was the only universal community, exercising universal spiritual authority directly, and universal temporal authority indirectly through a variety of kings and princes. The church therefore discouraged the concept of "emperor," and encouraged instead the local rulers who defended their independence against the encroachments of the Holy Roman Empire. The latter became in effect a German-Italian empire and lost all claim to universality because of its internal decay and its humiliation by the papacy in the twelfth and thirteenth centuries. The more independent the small states and local kingdoms were, the easier it was for the church to exercise control over them, and St. Thomas therefore expressed the customary views of the canonists and papalist advocates when he juxtaposed to the church, princes, and not an emperor claiming universal jurisdiction. Dante's concept of a universal temporal community, a world government headed by a monarch with world-wide authority, contradicts and transcends both the Augustinian and Thomistic roots of medieval philosophy.

What makes Dante's secularization of the religious idea of universal community even more revolutionary is his claim that the authority of the monarchical ruler of the world derives directly from God, without any intermediary, minister, vicar, or pope. The concept of man's two "beatitudes," the blessings of earthly life and the blessings of heavenly paradise, was taken over by Dante from traditional Christian doctrines. St. Thomas Aquinas represented the orthodox view in stating that the attainment of earthly blessings, such as peace, was no more than a means to the final end, the blessing of enjoying God after death. Dante's revolutionary break with this medieval conception consists in his refusal to assign a subordinate role to political life, and his insistence that it, too, was a final goal, and that of the two universal orders, church and world-state, each was supreme in its own sphere, equal in relation to the other, and neither subordinate to the other.

Instead of the traditional medieval hierarchy, in which earthly ends are subordinated to heavenly ends, and consequently temporal authority to the church, Dante construes two coordinate authorities, church and universal empire, each reflecting and realizing a different goal of man. Instead of the previous hierarchy, there is a double supremacy, in this world at least. The pope has no superior—as pope; the universal monarch has no superior—as monarch. Both have a point of hierarchical reference, but it is not of this world: God. To him both pope and emperor are subordinate and responsible.

By strictly separating church and empire, and setting them up as virtually "closed systems," Dante does much more than diminish the temporal authority of the church. He notes that the different ends of church and universal government imply different means: reason and philosophy guide the temporal ruler in the attainment of earthly happiness for mankind, whereas theology, faith, and revelation are the means by which the church seeks to secure for its members the blessings of heavenly paradise. By severing the temporal authority of government from the ecclesiastical authority of the church, Dante thus declares the *independence of philosophy from theology:* if their masters are independent of each other, so are they, as the means of the masters.

Dante's separation of philosophy from theology is more important, from the long-term viewpoint, than his separation of church and empire. St. Thomas Aquinas marks the culmination of the scholastic doctrine that philosophy was the "handmaiden" (*ancilla*) of theology. Dante affirms the revolutionary tenet of separation of philosophy and theology on a basis of equality and independence. His challenge is the transition to the next revolutionary transformation, the growing subordination of theology to philosophy in Humanism and Renaissance.

The church was fully aware of the dangerous ideas contained in *De monarchia*. It was burned as heretical by order of Pope John XXII in 1329 and put on the *Index of Forbidden Books* in 1554, before it was printed (it was first printed in Basle in 1559). *De monarchia* stayed on the *Index* until half a century ago, when it was finally removed as being no longer dangerous.

DANTE

De Monarchía *

1. *The End of Political Organization: Universal Peace*

The proper work of the human race, taken as a whole, is to set in action the whole capacity of that understanding which is capable of development: first in the way of speculation, and then, by its extension, in the way of action. And seeing that what is true of a part is true also of the whole, and that it is by rest and quiet that the individual man becomes perfect in wisdom and prudence; so the human race, by living in the calm and tranquillity of peace, applies itself most freely and easily to its proper work; a work which, according to the saying; "Thou hast made him a little lower

* From Dante, *De Monarchia* (trans. F. C. Church, in R. W. Church, *Dante: An Essay,* London, 1878).

than the angels," is almost divine. Whence it is manifest that of all things that are ordered to secure blessings to men, peace is the best. And hence the word which sounded to the shepherds from above was not riches, nor pleasure, nor honour, nor length of life, nor health, nor strength, nor beauty; but peace. For the heavenly host said: "Glory to God in the highest, and on earth, peace to men of good will." Therefore also, "Peace be with you," was the salutation of the Saviour of mankind. For it behoved Him, who was the greatest of saviours, to utter in His greeting the greatest of saving blessings. And this custom His disciples too chose to preserve; and Paul also did the same in his greetings, as may appear manifest to all.

Now that we have declared these matters, it is plain what is the better, nay the best, way in which mankind may attain to do its proper work. And consequently we have seen the readiest means by which to arrive at the point, for which all our works are ordered, as their ultimate end; namely, the universal peace, which is to be assumed as the first principle for our deductions. As we said, this assumption was necessary, for it is as a sign-post to us, that into it we may resolve all that has to be proved, as into a most manifest truth.

2. World Peace through World Empire

As therefore we have already said, there are three doubts, and these doubts suggest three questions, concerning Temporal Monarchy, which in more common speech is called the Empire; and our purpose is, as we explained, to inquire concerning these questions in their given order, and starting from the first principle which we have just laid down. The first question, then, is whether Temporal Monarchy is necessary for the welfare of the world; and that it is necessary can, I think, be shown by the strongest and most manifest arguments; for nothing, either of reason or of authority, opposes me. Let us first take the authority of the Philosopher in his *Politics*. There, on his venerable authority, it is said that where a number of things are arranged to attain an end, it behoves one of them to regulate or govern the others, and the others to submit. And it is not only the authority of his illustrious name which makes this worthy of belief, but also reason, instancing particulars.

If we take the case of a single man, we shall see the same rule manifested in him: all his powers are ordered to gain happiness; but his understanding is what regulates and governs all the others; and otherwise he would never attain to happiness. Again, take a single household: its end is to fit the members thereof to live well; but there must be one to regulate and rule it, who is called the father of the family, or, it may be, one

who holds his office. As the Philosopher says: "Every house is ruled by the oldest." And, as Homer says, it is his duty to make rules and laws for the rest. Hence the proverbial curse: "Mayst thou have an equal at home." Take a single village: its end is suitable assistance as regards persons and goods, but one in it must be the ruler of the rest, either set over them by another, or with their consent, the head man amongst them. If it be not so, not only do its inhabitants fail of this mutual assistance, but the whole neighbourhood is sometimes wholly ruined by the ambition of many, who each of them wish to rule. If, again, we take a single city: its end is to secure a good and sufficient life to the citizens; but one man must be ruler in imperfect as well as in good forms of the state. If it is otherwise, not only is the end of civil life lost, but the city too ceases to be what it was. Lastly, if we take any one kingdom, of which the end is the same as that of a city, only with greater security for its tranquillity, there must be one king to rule and govern. For if this is not so, not only do his subjects miss their end, but the kingdom itself falls to destruction, according to that word of the infallible truth: "Every kingdom divided against itself shall be brought to desolation." If then this holds good in these cases, and in each individual thing which is ordered to one certain end, what we have laid down is true.

Now it is plain that the whole human race is ordered to gain some end, as has been before shown. There must, therefore, be one to guide and govern, and the proper title for this office is Monarch or Emperor. And so it is plain that Monarchy or the Empire is necessary for the welfare of the world.

3. Monarchy as the Form of World Government

Further, the whole human race is a whole with reference to certain parts, and, with reference to another whole, it is a part. For it is a whole with reference to particular kingdoms and nations, as we have shown; and it is a part with reference to the whole universe, as is manifest without argument. Therefore, as the lower portions of the whole system of humanity are well adapted to that whole, so that whole is said to be well adapted to the whole which is above it. It is only under the rule of one prince that the parts of humanity are well adapted to their whole, as may easily be collected from what we have said; therefore it is only by being under one Princedom, or the rule of a single Prince, that humanity as a whole is well adapted to the Universe, or its Prince, who is the One God. And it therefore follows that Monarchy is necessary for the welfare of the world.

4. The Oneness of Mankind and the Oneness of God

And all is well and at its best which exists according to the will of the first agent, who is God. This is self-evident, except to those who deny that the divine goodness attains to absolute perfection. Now, it is the intention of God that all created things should represent the likeness of God, so far as their proper nature will admit. Therefore was it said: "Let us make man in our image, after our likeness." And though it could not be said that the lower part of creation was made in the image of God, yet all things may be said to be after His likeness, for what is the whole universe but the footprint of the divine goodness? The human race, therefore, is well, nay at its best state, when, so far as can be, it is made like unto God. But the human race is then most made like unto God when most it is one; for the true principle of oneness is in Him alone. Wherefore it is written: "Hear, O Israel; the Lord thy God is one God." But the race of man is most one when it is united wholly in one body, and it is evident that this cannot be, except when it is subject to one prince. Therefore in this subjection man-

kind is most made like unto God, and, in consequence, such a subjection is in accordance with the divine intention, and it is indeed well and best for man when this is so, as we showed at the beginning of this chapter.

5. The Need for Authoritative Settlement of Disputes between States

Wherever there is controversy, there ought to be judgment, otherwise there would be imperfection without its proper remedy, which is impossible; for God and Nature, in things necessary, do not fail in their provisions. But it is manifest that there may be controversy between any two princes, where the one is not subject to the other, either from the fault of themselves, or even of their subjects. Therefore between them there should be means of judgment. And since, when one is not subject to the other, he cannot be judged by the other (for there is no rule of equals over equals), there must be a third prince of wider jurisdiction, within the circle of whose laws both may come. Either he will or he will not be a Monarch. If he is, we have what we sought; if not, then this one again will have an equal, who is not subject to his jurisdiction, and then again we have need of a third. And so we must either go on to infinity, which is impossible, or we must come to that judge who is first and highest; by whose judgment all controversies shall be either directly or indirectly decided; and he will be Monarch or Emperor. Monarchy is therefore necessary to the world, and this the Philosopher saw when he said: "The world is not intended to be disposed in evil order; 'in a multitude of rulers there is evil, therefore let there be one prince.'"

6. Freedom under Monarchy

Again, the human race is ordered best when it is most free. This will be manifest if we see what is the principle of freedom. It must be understood that the first principle of our freedom is freedom of will, which many have in their mouth, but few indeed understand. For they come so far as to say that the freedom of the will means a free judgment concerning will. And this is true. But what is meant by the words is far from them: and they do just as our logicians do all day long with certain propositions which are set as examples in the books of logic, as that, "the three angles of a triangle are equal to two right angles."

Therefore I say that Judgment is between Apprehension and Appetite. First, a man apprehends a thing; when he judges it to be good or bad; then he pursues or avoids it accordingly. If therefore the Judgment guides the Appetite wholly, and in no way is forestalled by the Appetite, then is the Judgment free. But if the Appetite in any way at all forestalls the Judgment and guides it, then the Judgment cannot be free: it is not its own: it is captive to another power. Therefore the brute beasts cannot have freedom of Judgment; for in them the Appetite always forestalls the Judgment. Therefore, too, it is that intellectual beings whose wills are unchangeable, and souls which are separate from the body, which have gone hence in peace, do not lose the freedom of their wills, because their wishes cannot change; nay, it is in full strength and completeness that their wills are free.

It is therefore again manifest that this liberty, or this principle of all our liberty, is the greatest gift bestowed by God on mankind: by it alone we gain happiness as men: by it alone we gain happiness elsewhere as gods. But if this is so, who will say that human kind is not in its best state, when it can most use this principle? But he who lives under a Monarchy is most free. Therefore let it be understood that he is free who exists not for another's sake but for his own, as the Philosopher, in his Treatise of simple Being, thought. For everything which exists for the sake of some other thing, is necessitated by that other thing, as a

road has to run to its ordained end. Men exist for themselves, and not at the pleasure of others, only if a Monarch rules; for then only are the perverted forms of government set right, while democracies, oligarchies, and tyrannies, drive mankind into slavery, as is obvious to any who goes about among them all; and public power is in the hands of kings and aristocracies, which they call the rule of the best, and champions of popular liberty. And because the Monarch loves his subjects much, as we have seen, he wishes all men to be good, which cannot be the case in perverted forms of government: therefore the Philosopher says, in his *Politics:* "In the bad state the good man is a bad citizen, but in a good state the two coincide." Good states in this way aim at liberty, that in them men may live for themselves. The citizens exist not for the good of consuls, nor the nation for the good of its king; but the consuls for the good of the citizens, and the king for the good of his nation. For as the laws are made to suit the state, and not the state to suit the laws, so those who live under the laws are not ordered for the legislator, but he for them; as also the Philosopher holds, in what he has left us on the present subject. Hence, too, it is clear that although the king or the consul rule over the other citizens in respect of the means of government, yet in respect of the end of government they are the servants of the citizens, and especially the Monarch, who, without doubt, must be held the servant of all. Thus it becomes clear that the Monarch is bound by the end appointed to himself in making his laws. Therefore mankind is best off under a Monarchy, and hence it follows that Monarchy is necessary for the welfare of the world.

7. *The* Pax Romana

To all these reasons alleged above, a memorable experience adds its confirmation. I mean that condition of mankind which the Son of God, when, for the salvation of man, He was about to put on man, either waited for, or, at the moment when He willed, Himself so ordered. For if, from the fall of our first parents, which was the turning point at which all our going astray began, we carry our thoughts over the distribution of the human race and the order of its times, we shall find that never but under the divine Augustus, who was sole ruler, and under whom a perfect Monarchy existed, was the world everywhere quiet. And that then the human race was happy in the tranquillity of universal peace, this is the witness of all writers of history; this is the witness of famous poets; this, too, he who wrote the story of the "meekness and gentleness of Christ" has thought fit to attest. And last of all, Paul has called that most blessed condition "the fullness of the times." For then, indeed, time was full, and all of the things of time; because no office belonging to our felicity wanted its minister. But how the world has fared since that "seamless robe" has suffered rending by the talons of ambition, we may read in books; would that we might not see it with our eyes. Oh, race of mankind! what storms must toss thee, what losses must thou endure, what shipwrecks must buffet thee, as long as thou, a beast of many heads, strivest after contrary things. Thou art sick in both thy faculties of understanding; thou art sick in thine affections. Unanswerable reasons fail to heal thy higher understanding; the very sight of experience convinces not thy lower understanding; not even the sweetness of divine persuasion charms thy affections, when it breathes into thee through the music of the Holy Ghost: "Behold, how good and how pleasant a thing it is, brethren, to dwell together in unity."

8. The Vocation of the Romans for World Rule

What nature has ordained is maintained of right. For nature in its providence does not come short of men's providence; for if it were to come short, the effect would excel the cause in goodness, which is impossi-

ble. But we see that when public bodies are founded, not only are the relations of the members to each other considered, but also their capacities for exercising offices; and this is to consider the end of right in the society or order which is founded, for right is not extended beyond what is possible. Nature then, in her ordinances, does not come short in this foresight. Therefore it is clear that nature, in ordaining a thing, has regard to its capacities; and this regard is the fundamental principle of right which nature lays down. From this it follows that the natural order of things cannot be maintained without right; for this fundamental principle of right is inseparably joined to the natural order of things. It is necessary, therefore, that it is of right that this order is preserved.

The Roman people was ordained for empire, by nature, and this may be shown as follows: The man would come short of perfection in his art, who aimed only to produce his ultimate form, and neglected the means of reaching it; in the same way, if nature only aimed at reproducing in the world the universal form of the divine likeness, and neglected the means of doing so, she would be imperfect. But nature, which is the work of the divine intelligence, is wholly perfect; she therefore aims at all the means by which her final end is arrived at.

Since then mankind has a certain end, and since there is a certain means necessary for the universal end of nature, it necessarily follows that nature aims at obtaining that means. And therefore the Philosopher, in the second book of *Natural Learning,* well shows that nature always acts for the end. And since nature cannot reach this end through one man, because that there are many actions necessary to it, which need many to act, therefore nature must produce many men and set them to act. And besides the higher influence, the powers and properties of inferior spheres contribute much to this. And therefore we see not only that individual men, but also that certain races are born to govern, and certain others to be governed and to serve, as the Philosopher argues in the *Politics;* and for the latter, as he himself says, subjection is not only expedient, but just, even though they be forced into subjection.

And if this is so, it cannot be doubted that nature ordained in the world a country and a nation for universal sovereignty; if this were not so, she would have been untrue to herself, which is impossible. But as to where that country is, and which is that nation, it is sufficiently manifest, both from what we have said and from we shall say, that it was Rome and her citizens or people; and this our poet very skilfully touches on in the sixth *Aeneid,* where he introduces Anchises prophesying to Aeneas, the ancestor of the Romans: "Others may mould the breathing bronze more delicately—I doubt it not; they may chisel from marble the living countenance; they may surpass thee in pleading causes; they may track the course of the heavens with the rod, and tell when the stars will rise; but thou, Roman, remember to rule the nations with thy sway. These shall be thy endowments —to make peace to be the custom of the world; to spare thy foes when they submit, and to crush the proud." And again, Virgil skilfully notes the appointment of the *place,* in the fourth *Aeneid,* when he brings in Jupiter speaking to Mercury concerning Aeneas: "His fair mother did not promise him to us to be such as this: it was not for this that twice she rescues him from Grecian arms; but that there should be one to rule over Italy, teeming with empires, tempestuous with wars." It has, therefore, sufficiently been shown that the Roman people was by nature ordained to empire. Therefore it was of right that they gained empire, by subduing to themselves the world.

9. The Source of Temporal Power

"He hath shut the lions' mouths and they have not hurt me, forasmuch as before Him justice was found in me." At the beginning of this work I proposed to examine into three questions, according as the subject-matter would permit me. Concerning the two first questions our inquiry, as I think, has been sufficiently accomplished in the preceding books. It remains to treat of the third question; and, perchance, it may arouse a certain amount of indignation against me, for the truth of it cannot appear without causing shame to certain men. But seeing that truth from its changeless throne appeals to me—that Solomon too, entering on the forest of his proverbs, teaches me in his own person "to meditate on truth, to hate the wicked"; seeing that the Philosopher, my instructor in morals, bids me, for the sake of truth, to put aside what is dearest; I will, therefore, take confidence from the words of Daniel in which the power of God, the shield of the defenders of truth, is set forth, and, according to the exhortation of St. Paul, "putting on the breastplate of faith," and in the heat of that coal which one of seraphim had taken from off the altar, and laid on the lips of Isaiah, I will enter on the present contest, and, by the arm of Him who delivered us by His blood from the powers of darkness, drive out from the lists the wicked and the liar, in the sight of all the world. Why should I fear, when the Spirit, which is co-eternal with the Father and the Son, saith by the mouth of David: "The righteous shall be had in everlasting remembrance, he shall not be afraid of evil tidings"?

The present question, then, concerning which we have to inquire, is between two great luminaries, the Roman Pontiff and the Roman Prince: and the question is, does the authority of the Roman Monarch, who, as we have proved, is the monarch of the world, depend immediately on God, or on some minister or vicar of God; by whom I understand the successor of Peter, who truly has the keys of the kingdom of heaven?

10. The Foundations of Church Authority

At the outset we must note in reference to this third question, that the truth of the first question had to be made manifest rather to remove ignorance than to end a dispute. In the second question we sought equally to remove ignorance and to end a dispute. For there are many things of which we are ignorant, but concerning which we do not quarrel. In geometry we know not how to square the circle, but we do not quarrel on that point. The theologian does not know the number of the angels, but he does not quarrel about the number. The Egyptian is ignorant of the political system of the Scythians, but he does not therefore quarrel concerning it. But the truth in this third question provokes so much quarrelling that, whereas in other matters ignorance is commonly the cause of quarrelling, here quarrelling is the cause of ignorance. For this always happens where men are hurried by their wishes past what they see by their reason; in this evil bias they lay aside the light of reason, and being dragged on blindly by their desires, they obstinately deny that they are blind. And, therefore, it often follows not only that falsehood has its own inheritance, but that many men issue forth from their own bounds and stray through the foreign camp, where they understand nothing, and no man understands them; and so they provoke some to anger, and some to scorn, and not a few to laughter.

Now three classes of men chiefly strive against the truth which we are trying to prove.

First, the Chief Pontiff, Vicar of our Lord Jesus Christ and the successor of Peter, to whom we owe, not indeed all that we owe to Christ, but all that we owe to Peter, contradicts this truth, urged it may be by zeal for the keys; and also other pastors of the Christian sheepfolds, and others whom I believe to be only led by zeal for our mother, the Church. These all, perchance from zeal and not from pride, withstand the truth which I am about to prove.

But there are certain others in whom obstinate greed has extinguished the light of reason, who are of their father the devil, and yet pretend to be sons of the Church. They not only stir up quarrels in this question, but they hate the name of the most sacred office of Prince, and would shamelessly deny the principles which we have laid down for this and the previous questions.

There is also a third class called Decretalists, utterly without knowledge or skill in philosophy or theology, who, relying entirely on their Decretals (which doubtless, I think, should be venerated), and hoping, I believe, that these Decretals will prevail, disparage the power of the Empire. And no wonder, for I have heard one of them, speaking of these Decretals, assert shamelessly that the traditions of the Church are the foundation of the faith. May this wickedness be taken away from the thoughts of men by those who, antecedently to the traditions of the Church, have believed in Christ the Son of God, whether to come, or present, or as having already suffered; and who from their faith have hoped, and from their hope have kindled into love, and who, burning with love, will, the world doubts not, be made co-heirs with Him.

And that such arguers may be excluded once for all from the present debate, it must be noted that part of Scripture was *before* the Church, that part of it came *with* the Church, and part *after* the Church.

Before the Church were the Old and the New Testament—the covenant which the Psalmist says was "commanded for ever," of which the Church speaks to her Bridegroom, saying: "Draw me after thee."

With the Church came those venerable chief Councils, with which no faithful Christian doubts but that Christ was present. For we have His own words to His disciples when He was about to ascend into heaven: "Lo, I am with you always, even unto the end of the world," to which Matthew testifies. There are also the writings of the doctors, Augustine and others, of whom, if any doubt that they were aided by the Holy Spirit, either he has never beheld their fruit, or if he has beheld, he has never tasted thereof.

After the Church are the traditions which

they call Decretals, which, although they are to be venerated for their apostolical authority, yet we must not doubt that they are to be held inferior to fundamental Scripture, seeing that Christ rebuked the Pharisees for this very thing; for when they asked: "Why do thy disciples transgress the tradition of the elders?" (for they neglected the washing of hands), He answered them, as Matthew testifies: "Why do ye also transgress the commandment of God by your tradition?" Thus he intimates plainly that tradition was to have a lower place.

But if the traditions of the Church are *after* the Church, it follows that the Church had not its authority from traditions, but rather traditions from the Church; and, therefore, the men of whom we speak, seeing that they have nought but traditions, must be excluded from the debate. For those who seek after this truth must proceed in their inquiry from those things from which flows the authority of the Church.

Further, we must exclude others who boast themselves to be white sheep in the flock of the Lord, when they have the plumage of crows. These are the children of wickedness, who, that they may be able to follow their evil ways, put shame on their mother, drive out their brethren, and when they have done all will allow none to judge them. Why should we seek to reason with these, when they are led astray by their evil desires, and so cannot see even our first principle?

Therefore there remains the controversy only with the other sort of men who are influenced by a certain kind of zeal for their mother the Church, and yet know not the truth which is sought for. With these men, therefore—strong in the reverence which a dutiful son owes to his father, which a dutiful son owes to his mother, dutiful to Christ, dutiful to the Church, dutiful to the Chief Shepherd, dutiful to all who profess the religion of Christ—I begin in this book the contest for the maintenance of the truth.

11. Church and Empire

Certain persons say further that the Emperor Constantine, having been cleansed from leprosy by the intercession of Sylvester, then the Supreme Pontiff, gave unto the Church the seat of Empire which was Rome, together with many other dignities belonging to the Empire. Hence they argue that no man can take unto himself these dignities unless he receive them from the Church, whose they are said to be. From this it would rightly follow, that one authority depends on the other, as they maintain.

The arguments which seemed to have their roots in the Divine words, have been stated and disproved. It remains to state and disprove those which are grounded on Roman history and in the reason of mankind. The first of these is the one which we have mentioned, in which the syllogism runs as follows: No one has a right to those things which belong to the Church, unless he has them from the Church; and this we grant. The government of Rome belongs to the Church; therefore no one has a right to it unless it be given him by the Church. The minor premiss is proved by the facts concerning Constantine, which we have touched on.

This minor premiss then will I destroy; and as for their proof, I say that it proves nothing. For the dignity of the Empire was what Constantine could not alienate, nor the Church receive. And when they insist, I prove my words as follows: No man on the strength of the office which is committed to him, may do aught that is contrary to that office; for so one and the same man, viewed as one man, would be contrary to himself, which is impossible. But to divide the Empire is contrary to the office committed to the Emperor; for his office is to hold mankind in all things subject to one will. Therefore it is not permitted to the Emperor to divide the Empire. If, therefore, as they say, any dignities had been alienated by Constantine, and had passed to the Church, the "coat without seam"—

which even they, who pierced Christ, the true God, with a spear, dared not rend—would have been rent.

Further, just as the Church has its foundation, so has the Empire its foundation. The foundation of the Church is Christ, as Paul says in his first Epistle to the Corinthians: "For other foundation can no man lay than that which is laid, which is Jesus Christ." He is the rock on which the Church is built; but the foundation of the Empire is human right. Now I say that, as the Church may not go contrary to its foundation—but must always rest on its foundation, as the words of the Canticles say: "Who is she that cometh up from the desert, abounding in delights, leaning on her beloved?"—in the same way I say that the Empire may not do aught that transgresses human right. But were the Empire to destroy itself, it would so transgress human right. Therefore the Empire may not destroy itself. Since then to divide the Empire would be to destroy it, because the Empire consists in one single universal Monarchy, it is manifest that he who exercises the authority of the Empire may not destroy it, and from what we have said before, it is manifest that to destroy the Empire is contrary to human right.

Moreover, all jurisdiction is prior in time to the judge who has it; for it is the judge who is ordained for the jurisdiction, not the jurisdiction for the judge. But the Empire is a jurisdiction, comprehending within itself all temporal jurisdiction: therefore it is prior to the judge who has it, who is the Emperor. For it is the Emperor who is ordained for the Empire, and not contrariwise. Therefore it is clear that the Emperor, in so far as he is Emperor, cannot alter the Empire; for it is to the Empire that he owes his being. I say then that he who is said to have conferred on the Church the authority in question either was Emperor, or he was not. If he was not, it is plain that he had no power to give away any part of the Empire. Nor could he, if he was Emperor, in so far as he was Emperor, for such a gift would be a diminishing of his jurisdiction.

Further, if one Emperor were able to cut off a certain portion of the jurisdiction of the Empire, so could another; and since temporal jurisdiction is finite, and since all that is finite is taken away by finite diminutions, it would follow that it is possible for the first of all jurisdictions to be annihilated, which is absurd.

Further, since he that gives is in the position of an agent, and he to whom a thing is given in that of a patient, as the Philosopher holds in the fourth book to Nicomachus, therefore, that a gift may be given, we require not only the fit qualification of the giver, but also of the receiver; for the acts of the agent are completed in a patient who is qualified. But the Church was altogether unqualified to receive temporal things; for there is an express command, forbidding her so to do, which Matthew gives thus: "Provide neither gold, nor silver, nor brass in your purses." For though we find in Luke a relaxation of the command in regard to certain matters, yet I have not anywhere been able to find that the Church after that prohibition had license given her to possess gold and silver. If therefore the Church was unable to receive temporal power, even granting that Constantine was able to give it, yet the gift was impossible; for the receiver was disqualified. It is therefore plain that neither could the Church receive in the way of possession, nor could Constantine give in the way of alienation; though it is true that the Emperor, as protector of the Church, could allot to the Church a patrimony and other things, if he did not impair his supreme lordship, the unity of which does not allow division. And the Vicar of God could receive such things, not to possess them, but as a steward to dispense the fruits of them to the poor of Christ, on behalf of the Church, as we know the Apostles did.

12. The True Relations between Temporal and Ecclesiastical Authority

Although it has been proved that the authority of the Empire has not its cause in the authority of the Supreme Pontiff; for we have shown that this argument led to absurd results; yet it has not been entirely shown that the authority of the Empire depends directly upon God, except as a result from our argument. For it is a consequence that, if the authority comes not from the vicar of God, it must come from God Himself. And therefore, for the complete determination of the question proposed, we have to prove directly that the emperor or monarch of the world stands in an immediate relation to the King of the universe, who is God.

For the better comprehending of this, it must be recognized that man alone, of all created things, holds a position midway between things corruptible and things incorruptible; and therefore philosophers rightly liken him to a dividing line between two hemispheres. For man consists of two essential parts, namely, the soul and the body. If he be considered in relation to his body only, he is corruptible; but if he be considered in relation to his soul only, he is incorruptible. And therefore the Philosopher spoke well concerning the incorruptible soul when he said in the second book "of the Soul:" "It is this alone which may be separated, as being eternal, from the corruptible."

If, therefore, man holds this position midway between the corruptible and the incorruptible, since every middle nature partakes of both extremes, man must share something of each nature. And since every nature is ordained to gain some final end, it follows that for man there is a double end. For as he alone of all beings participates both in the corruptible and the incorruptible, so he alone of all beings is ordained to gain two ends, whereby one is his end in so far as he is corruptible, and the other in so far as he is incorruptible.

Two ends, therefore, have been laid down by the ineffable providence of God for man to aim at: the blessedness of this life, which consists in the exercise of his natural powers, and which is prefigured in the earthly Paradise; and next, the blessedness of the life eternal, which consists in the fruition of the sight of God's countenance, and to which man by his own natural powers cannot rise, if he be not aided by the divine light; and this blessedness is understood by the heavenly Paradise.

But to these different kinds of blessedness, as to different conclusions, we must come by different means. For at the first we may arrive by the lessons of philosophy, if only we will follow them, by acting in accordance with the moral and intellectual virtues. But at the second we can only arrive by spiritual lessons, transcending human reason, so that we follow them in accordance with the theological virtues, faith, hope, and charity. The truth of the first of these conclusions and of these means is made manifest by human reason, which by the philosophers has been all laid open to us. The other conclusions and means are made manifest by the Holy Spirit, who by the mouth of the Prophets and holy writers, and by Jesus Christ, the co-eternal Son of God, and His disciples, has revealed to us supernatural truth of which we have great need. Nevertheless human passion would cast them all behind its back, unless, that men, going astray like the beasts that perish, were restrained in their course by bit and bridle, like horses and mules.

Therefore man had need of two guides for his life, as he had a twofold end in life; whereof one is the Supreme Pontiff, to lead mankind to eternal life, according to the things revealed to us; and the other is the Emperor, to guide mankind to happiness in this world, in accordance with the teaching of philosophy. And since none, or but a few only, and even they with sore difficulty, could arrive at this harbour of happiness, unless the waves and blandishments of human desires were set at rest, and the human race were free to live in peace and quiet, this therefore is the mark at which he who is to care for the world, and whom we call the Roman Prince, must most chiefly aim at: I mean, that in this little plot of earth belonging to mortal men, life may pass in freedom and with peace. And since the order of this world follows the order of the heavens, as they run their course, it is necessary, to the end that the learning which brings liberty and peace may be duly applied by this guardian of the world in fitting season and place, that this power should be dispensed by Him who is ever present to behold the whole order of the heavens. And this is He who alone has pre-ordained this, that by it in His providence He might bind all things together, each in their own order.

But if this is so, God alone elects, God alone confirms: for there is none higher than God. And hence there is the further conclusion, that neither those who now are, nor any other who may, in whatsoever way, have been called, "Electors," ought to have that name; rather they are to be held as declarers and announcers of the providence of God. And, therefore, it is that they to whom is granted the privilege of announcing God's will sometimes fall into disagreement; because that, all of them or some of them have been blinded by their evil desires, and have not discerned the face of God's appointment.

It is therefore clear that the authority of temporal Monarchy comes down, with no intermediate will, from the fountain of uni-versal authority; and this fountain, one in its unity, flows through many channels out of the abundance of the goodness of God.

And now, methinks, I have reached the goal which I set before me. I have un-ravelled the truth of the questions which I asked: whether the office of Monarchy was necessary to the welfare of the world; whether it was by right that the Roman people assumed to themselves the office of Monarchy; and, further, that last question, whether the authority of the Monarch springs immediately from God, or from some other. Yet the truth of this latter ques-tion must not be received so narrowly as to deny that in certain matters the Roman Prince is subject to the Roman Pontiff. For that happiness, which is subject to mortal-ity, in a sense is ordered with a view to the happiness which shall not taste of death. Let, therefore, Caesar be reverent to Peter, as the first-born son should be reverent to his father, that he may be illuminated with the light of his father's grace, and so may be stronger to lighten the world over which he has been placed by Him alone, who is the ruler of all things spiritual as well as tem-poral.

CHAPTER 10

MARSILIO OF PADUA

THE struggle between the papacy and the German emperors seemed to be settled with the victory of the church in the middle of the thirteenth century. The German imperial dynasty, the Hohenstaufen, was destroyed, never to rise again. The authority of the popes was supreme; they made and unmade kings and emperors, their wealth was second to none, and the papalist doctrine of the supremacy of ecclesiastical over temporal power (in contradiction to the older Gelasian doctrine of equilibrium) seemed to have been successfully translated into the reality of a new world order. Yet, as so often happens, absolute and limitless power is its own worst enemy, and less than fifty years after the papacy attained its peak, it was humiliated as never before, and perhaps never since.

Pope Boniface VIII (1294–1303) marks the turning point in the history of church-state relations: he is the last pope to make claims of world rule and the first to descend from the summit of glory to humiliation, even degradation. In defeating the German emperors, the popes had learned to rely heavily on the French monarchs; yet France was the country destined to explode, forever, the papal claim of world hegemony.

The conflict arose over money. The church, like every ambitious Great Power, needed more and more money, and its financial needs came into conflict with those of the new national monarchies, particularly France and England, which were gradually building up an efficient but costly central administrative machine to replace the old feudal system of extreme decentralization. In 1296, Boniface declared (in the bull *Clericis Laicos*) that laymen have no jurisdiction over the clergy, "over both the persons and goods of ecclesiastics," without prior papal permission, and that no mundane authority was permitted to levy taxes on church property, nor the clergy permitted to pay them; the imposition or paying of such taxes without papal approval was put under the sanction of ex-communication from the church.

Both England and France, for whom the papal bull was especially meant, refused to recognize a financial state within the state; first, because political sovereignty without tax sovereignty was meaningless, and second, because church property was so vast that neither monarchy could afford to exempt it from tax-ation. In England, King Edward I threatened that the king's peace could not be had for nothing, and that if the clergy were to refuse taxes he would consider them outcasts and treat them as such. Boniface had to give in, and the basic principle was never raised again. In France, King Philip IV firmly rejected Boniface's interference in French finances, and the pope was powerless to en-force his doctrine.

The year 1300 was celebrated in Rome as the first Christian Jubilee. Hun-dreds of thousands of visitors journeyed from all over Europe to the Eternal City, where a complete indulgence of their sins, hitherto available only to cru-saders, awaited them, as well as magnificent spectacles and public ceremonials. Pope Boniface himself, at the height of his power and prestige, appeared in public in the garb of pope and emperor, wearing the imperial scepter and crown, displaying two swords, and proclaiming himself Pontiff, Caesar, and Emperor. Though the Jubilee added large sums of money to the coffers of the Holy See, it did not allay the conflict between Rome and the new national states.

In 1302 Boniface issued the bull *Unam Sanctam*, one of the two or three most important church documents in history. It affirmed no new doctrine but merely expressed, more clearly and irreconcilably than ever before, the extreme and intransigent papalist viewpoint: there is "neither salvation nor remission of sins" outside the "holy catholic and apostolic church"; this "one and only church" had one body and one head, "not two heads as if it were a monster"; there are two swords, a spiritual and a temporal, and "both swords are in the power of the church, the one by the hand of the priest, the other by the hand of kings and knights, but at the will and sufferance of the priest." The key idea in *Unam Sanctam* is contained in the following sentence: "One sword, moreover, ought to be under the other, and the temporal authority to be subjected to the spiritual." *Unam Sanctam* also decreed that each power be judged by its superior authority; if the highest earthly power, the emperor or king, err, he will be judged by the spiritual authority, the priests. But if the highest priest, the pope, err, he can be judged by God alone, not by man: "A spiritual man judges all things, but he himself is judged by no one," because his authority is divine. The last sentence of the bull runs as follows: "We therefore declare, say, define, and pronounce that it is altogether a necessity of salvation for every human creature to be subject to the Roman Pontiff."

Philip IV accepted the challenge thrust at him by papal diplomacy and decree. Although Boniface excommunicated Philip and freed his subjects from allegiance, Philip planned to bring Boniface before a General Council of the church to be held in France, and to have him deposed for heresy, murder, sexual immorality, trafficking in church offices (simony), magic, idol worship—to men-tion but a few of the twenty-nine charges of his indictment. Significantly, the royal council that approved of such grave charges against the pope included the higher clergy in France; the national support for Philip was overwhelming, because the attitude of the universities, intellectuals, urban middle classes, royal bureaucracy, and nobility was hardly in doubt from the beginning.

While the fulminations were being hurled from pope to monarch and back, Philip proceeded to solve the issue by a *coup*. One of his closest advisers, Nogaret (a man of heretical and bourgeois background), went to Italy, where he organized a small force with the intention of capturing the pope and taking him to France before a General Council of the church that would try, condemn, and depose him. Nogaret's men (about sixteen hundred on horse and foot) broke into Anagni, the papal court southeast of Rome, early in September, 1303, overpowered the small papal guard, and seized Boniface. Before the French could bring Boniface to France, however, he was saved by a local revulsion of feeling against the plot and brought back to Rome. There he died within a few weeks as a result of the shock and strain that the outrage at Anagni had caused him.

Scarcely less remarkable than the *coup* of Anagni was the scant attention it attracted. The victory of Philip over Boniface, of France over Roman ecclesiastical imperialism, was not the outcome of a mere daring act of violence. The French were in a better position than the papacy in at least two major respects: first, the feud had manifestly originated in a quarrel over money—hardly an inspiring issue for the side that claims to represent the highest spiritual values on earth; second, the French monarch was in a morally strong position because he asked for supreme jurisdiction only in his own house, France, whereas Boniface asked for authority, spiritual and temporal, over the entire world.

In 1076, Pope Gregory VII and (the German) Emperor Henry IV had been engaged in as dramatic a conflict as Boniface's and Philip's in 1303. The emperor deposed the pope, on which the pope excommunicated and deposed the emperor. In the ensuing struggle the emperor had to surrender unconditionally to the pope in the famous scene at the mountain fortress of Canossa, in northern Italy. Clothed in penitential garb, the emperor stood barefoot at the gate of the snowbound fortress, to which the pope had come. For three days the emperor had to wait until the pope was willing to see him. The emperor repented, pledged complete submission for the future, and was pardoned. The Holy Roman Empire of the German Nation still lingered on for centuries, but the idea of a universal empire was dead henceforth.

Paradoxically, when the temporal authority (of the German emperors) claimed, like the papacy, universal jurisdiction, it failed; when it sought, with strong domestic support, limited jurisdiction in a national state (as in France) against the papal claims of universal authority, it won. In fighting with the German emperors for supremacy, the popes were colliding with the past; in the struggle with the French monarchy, they were up against the strongest single political institution of the next six centuries: the *sovereign national state*. By destroying the prestige and power of the Holy Roman Empire and its German rulers, the papacy had unknowingly undermined the belief in universal authority as such, and thus had aided in the growth of separatist nationalism. In particular, the papacy had strongly drawn on French support in its conflict with the (German) empire and thereby had contributed to making France the first European power. Having helped the papacy to eliminate the temporal claimant to universal authority, the French monarchy completed the job by eliminating the papacy itself as a pretender to world hegemony in spiritual and secular affairs.

Boniface was succeeded by Pope Benedict XI, also an Italian. Benedict reestablished concord between the Holy See and the Kingdom of France by annulling all excommunications, bulls, and decrees of his predecessor against Philip and his counselors, except Nogaret, the author of the "outrage of Anagni." Before having further opportunities to serve the French monarchy, Benedict XI died—after only eight months in office (1304).

In the following year, a French subject, the archbishop of Bordeaux, was elected pope, and he assumed the name of Clement V. Nogaret and other antipapalists who were not satisfied with the death of Boniface sought to assassinate his memory, too, by having him tried, *post mortem,* for various crimes, particularly heresy. Clement, who was anxious to avoid the scandal of having one of his predecessors condemned as an heretic, promised to have the issue examined by a commission of cardinals. In the end the pope annulled again all pronouncements of Boniface against Philip and his advisers, and this time he included Nogaret in the general absolution. Moreover, Philip was now praised by Clement for his zeal in defending the faith against Boniface, and Clement also gave orders to erase from Boniface's register the bulls and offensive pronouncements against Philip.

Clement did not go to Rome but set up his court in Avignon, in southern France, where he and his six successors, all French, resided more or less continuously in what has been called the "Babylonian captivity" of the papacy (1305–1378). The French era of the Avignon papacy was followed by the Great Schism (1378–1417), during which there were usually two popes, one at Avignon, one at Rome, and at times a third pretender. After the Great Schism, the Protestant Reformation drastically diminished the range of papal jurisdiction by reducing the Roman Catholic Church to one among many.

In the East, the rivalry between Constantinople and Rome went back to the fifth century. After the fall of Constantinople in 1453, Russia predominated in the eastern church; in 1589 a new patriarch was created with a claim of universal leadership, and Moscow was hailed as the "Third Rome."

The principal revolutionary changes in the late Middle Ages were the growing vehemence of anticlerical feeling and the decisive defeat of the papacy, the secularization of life, the rise of the bourgeoisie, and the formation of national states. These new developments are most systematically reflected in Marsilio of Padua's *Defensor Pacis,* or *The Defender of Peace* (1324). Marsilio (1275–1343) was a physician by occupation, and a student of philosophy, law, and theology. During his lifetime the Italian republican city-states were a unique phenomenon, and Padua was particularly known for its spirit of liberty and independence in defending itself against the local clergy and the Roman Curia.

Marsilio was of middle-class origin, and his mold of thought, skeptical, realistic, and empirical, is characteristic of the inhabitant of a free Italian city-republic with ancient secular traditions. His practice of medicine during many years added to his outlook a more critical and scientific cast. Marsilio quotes Aristotle's *Politics* more than all other classical authors put together, and in this respect he is typically medieval. But to most other medieval writers Aristotle was little more than a source of authority and verbal incantation; the two main assumptions of medieval political speculation—the supremacy of theology over philosophy, and the universality of theological-political rule in papacy and empire—were the exact opposite of Aristotle's two main ideals—empirical observation in philosophy, and the city-state in politics. Marsilio's use of Aristotle is more than verbal: he, too, has the background of an urban, secular civilization, and like Aristotle (who also practiced medicine for some time) he tries to use common sense and empirical verification rather than abstract speculation and authoritative dogma.

Next in importance in Marsilio's background is his intellectual experience in France. He spent a considerable portion of his formative years as a student and teacher at the University of Paris, of which he was Rector for a short period in 1312. Paris was then the world's leading university, particularly in philosophy, art, and letters, and the defeat of the papacy by France made Paris the center of secularist groups and ideas. In this lively political and intellectual atmosphere Marsilio received his formal education, and part of the authorship of *The Defender of Peace* is attributed by some to John of Jandun, a leading French scholar and Marsilio's close friend and collaborator during many years.

Taken individually, most of Marsilio's ideas can be traced to the flourishing and fertile school of publicists, pamphleteers, and politicians who congregated in Paris and established there a new kind of political literature and journalism soon to be copied all over Europe. Yet Marsilio was the first to develop a full-fledged doctrine from current isolated arguments and to discern in contemporary events the shape of a future world.

Like Dante, Marsilio is a link in the transition from the medieval to the modern age. But, whereas Dante was still essentially medieval in the formulation and solution of his main problems, Marsilio is essentially modern, though still encumbered by medieval forms of thought and argument. In fact, he is regarded by some as the most original medieval political writer, precisely because he seeks so consciously to break the fetters of his age and because he rejects vigorously and unequivocally any clerical control of thought or government.

Marsilio's irony and skepticism contrast with the deadly seriousness and dogmatic certainty of most medieval political writing. He occasionally admits that he is not sure, that a position he defends may be wrong—concessions that are more modern than medieval in spirit. Where there is complete certainty based on divine knowledge and revelation, there is no room for probabilities and possibilities, attributes of human, not divine, knowledge.

In his discussion of the forms of state, Marsilio merely repeats the Aristotelian division of the three good types (monarchy, aristocracy, constitutionalism) and the three diseased kinds (tyranny, oligarchy, mob dictatorship). He also says that the criterion of distinction is, following Aristotle, whether a government serves the rulers or the ruled. So far, Marsilio offers few surprises. But he differs radically from Aristotle (without, perhaps, being fully aware of it) by adding that in the good forms of government the ruler governs for the common benefit *in accordance with the will of the people.* Conversely, the diseased forms of government are for the benefit of the rulers *without the consent of the people.* This is not a minor addition to Aristotle but a fundamental revision and transformation. It could be argued, logically, that the postulate of government for the benefit of the ruled implies some measure of consent, but Aristotle himself did not see this logic in its full implication, perhaps because of his belief that some men are born to rule and others to obey.

In one passage Marsilio departs from Aristotle even more drastically by abandoning entirely the criterion of the *object of government* (the common benefit), and by replacing it with that of the *method of government,* according to which political rule is "over either voluntary or involuntary subjects." Similarly, recent and contemporary political theory emphasizes that democracy in government is primarily a question of method, the results and consequences of which can be good or bad. It is an assumption of modern democratic thought, as of Marsilio, that the proper method of government, that is, consent, is more likely (though by no means certain) to produce goods ends than are undemocratic methods, though the latter, too, may be employed for the pursuit of the common benefit. The consciousness of the *dynamic relations between means and ends* is one of the main contributions of modern philosophy, and Marsilio points in this direction by stressing that the problem of government is one of means as much as of ends.

Marsilio's break with Aristotle and the Middle Ages becomes especially clear in his conception of law as the manifestation of political authority. The general tendency of medieval writers is to assume that law is intimately related to reason and the common good; because they sincerely believed that such a relation is essential, they often stated, in the words of St. Thomas Aquinas, that law is "an ordinance of reason for the common good." Marsilio defines *law* in a less substantive and more formal way as a *coercive command* of the legislator *enforceable in the courts.* Marsilio hopes that human law will ordinarily be in harmony with divine and natural law, but he concedes the possibility that "sometimes false conceptions of the just and the beneficial become laws, when there is given a command to observe them."

This *positivist conception of law* is a significant deviation from the medieval tradition of natural law, and it reminds one of modern antimetaphysical views. Thus Holmes, perhaps the greatest of many great American jurists, defined the law as "the prophecies of what the courts will do in fact, and nothing more pretentious"; another leading jurist, Hans Kelsen, sees in the threat of coercion an essential element of the law.

Marsilio is aware that human law is, in dignity, below divine and natural law. However, he denudes this concession to his medieval environment of any practical effect by stating that the divine law is binding on the conscience, but that punishment for transgressing it is reserved for the next world. It is also important that Marsilio restricts the divine law to its revelation in the Bible but will have nothing to do with canon law, which to him is a set of statutes and rules of a human organization, the church, and no more. Because of his refusal to identify human law with divine authority or reason, Marsilio is driven to look for another source of validating human law. This source he finds in human society itself. Marsilio did not know the concept of *sovereignty*, although he was groping toward it and clearly described its substance. He says that "the legislator, or the primary and proper efficient cause of the law, is the people or the whole body of citizens, or the weightier part thereof," and that the "weightier part" of the citizens is to be understood in terms of quantity and quality.

Marsilio's use of the Latin word *legislator* is a source of confusion if the translation is simply rendered as "legislator" in English. Marsilio's legislator (whether it be understood as the whole body of citizens, the numerical majority, or the qualitatively weightier part) may mean two different things. The first is the *political sovereign*, the *constituent power* in the state, which alone has the authority to make the constitution; Marsilio comes somewhat closer to the concept of the sovereign, or constituent power, by calling it, in this context, a "primary" or "absolute" legislator.

The second meaning of legislator as used by Marsilio approximates more closely the modern *legislative function*, and here Marsilio distinguishes again two possibilities: either the people in assembly make the laws, are the legislator (as would be possible in small communities), or the people entrust the legislative function to "some person or persons, who are not and cannot be the legislator in the absolute sense, but only in a relative sense and for a particular time and in accordance with the authority of the primary legislator." Even if the political sovereign is made up of the whole people, the concept of citizenship is still not all-inclusive, for children, slaves, women, and foreigners are excluded from active participation in public life.

The people as the source of political authority was a basic conception in Roman jurisprudence and in its revived form during the Middle Ages, and medieval society itself evolved the idea that the community is the source of the law. Marsilio's originality consists, not so much in having discovered the idea of the people as the source of law, but in having shorn the conception of all its encumbrances and ornamentations so that it could evolve from a juridical fiction into a call for action.

As to his complex conception of the "weightier part" of the citizens, which in some instances may take the place of the entire body of citizens as the political sovereign, it should first be noted that Marsilio says that both the quantity *and* quality should be taken into account. He nowhere holds a brief for the idea of an elite; he merely says that the quantitative element alone is not sufficient, and that the qualitative factor should also be considered. He is undogmatic enough to know that qualitative standards cannot be described in detail in advance; they are the result of varying "honorable customs" in different political communities. In his own day Marsilio undoubtedly saw that even in the free city-republics of northern Italy there was no equality of groups and individuals, and yet there was a strong sense that the assembly of the people, the *arengo* or *parlamento,* was the ultimate source of sovereignty.

The problem of Marsilio's "weightier part" of the citizenry may be seen in a more persistent perspective with the aid of two illustrations, one historical and the other contemporary. The Glorious Revolution of 1688 and the Settlement of 1689 established in England the principle of *parliamentary supremacy* rather than *popular sovereignty* in the sense of universal suffrage. Yet the recognition of parliamentary supremacy, under which only the "weightier part" of the citizens (and a small part in numbers) governed the country, made full democratic sovereignty, as developed in the nineteenth and twentieth centuries, a practical possibility. The principle of "one man, one vote" was finally attained only as late as 1948, when the Representation of the People Act abolished the last remnants of plural voting: the business and university votes.

Similarly, Marsilio's concept of the *legislator* certainly implied *constitutional supremacy* and, to a considerable extent, legislative parliamentary supremacy, though hardly popular sovereignty in the strictly democratic sense that each man counts for one vote. In the United States, too, the element of quantity in politics is modified, first, by the deliberate overrepresentation of less populous states in the senate; this deviation from arithmetic implies the value judgment that in some instances historical or geographical considerations override the democratic argument of pure numbers. In addition, social power, prestige, and influence count, in the United States as in other democracies, when it comes to the making of crucial political decisions.

In effect, therefore, the political impact of the individual citizen depends on whether he belongs to the "weightier part" of society, or whether he is a mere quantitative unit whose political influence is confined to the periodical gesture of voting. Moreover, it should be remembered that Marsilio wrote in the fourteenth century, in which social and economic inequality was taken for granted, and that he cannot be fairly measured by advanced twentieth-century standards.

Whereas Marsilio does not describe in detail how the qualitatively weightier part of the body politic is to be ascertained in practice, he enthusiastically defends the basically democratic doctrine of the *common sense of the people* against the theory that a superior elite alone is possessed of political wisdom. Marsilio argues that a defect in a proposed law can be better detected by a large number than by a small fraction of the community, because every whole "is greater in mass and virtue than any part of it taken separately." From the viewpoint of expediency, too, Marsilio says, the utility of a proposed law will be better judged by the whole people, "because no one knowingly harms himself." By contrast, Marsilio thinks that if the law were made by only one or a few, they would be more likely to consider their own private profit than that of society as a whole.

From a psychological viewpoint, too, popular consent is an advantage: the law has a better chance of being observed by all if everybody has an opportunity to comment freely on its merits. Marsilio introduces again a formal, procedural criterion in discussing freedom and despotism, as he has done in defining the law. Abandoning the substantive definitions of representative medieval writers, Marsilio sees *freedom* primarily as the procedure and method of *self-government,* whereas despotism is the lack of self-government, regardless how good the law of the despot is. Conversely, even if the law is bad, citizens will feel a moral obligation to observe it if they have given their consent to it. Marsilio states the heart of the democratic creed as follows: "Those matters, therefore, which can affect the benefit and harm of all ought to be known and heard by all, who thus may attain the beneficial and repel the opposite."

Marsilio is aware of the argument, made then as now, that the majority of men are vicious, undiscerning, and stupid, and that the few who are wise, learned, and virtuous should therefore rule. Marsilio agrees that the vicious and undiscerning should not make the law, but he denies that most citizens are vicious and undiscerning most of the time: "All or most of them are of sound reason and have a right desire for the polity and for the things necessary for it to endure." A minimum of optimism about human nature is a basic condition, in Marsilio as in other political thinkers, for any faith in democracy, modest and limited as it may be. Marsilio concedes that only few have the ability to make wise laws, yet *every citizen can be a proper judge of the law* because "by induction we can see that many men judge rightly about the quality of a picture, a house, a ship, and other works of art, even though they would have been unable to discover or produce them." Marsilio quotes Aristotle's statement that man is not always the best judge of something he makes himself, and he might have quoted the further Aristotelian dictum that "the guest will judge better of a feast than the cook."

Since the active citizens who form the political sovereign (or *legislator*) cannot themselves carry on the work of legislation, government, and administration, there must be a group of persons who act in the name of the citizenry. Marsilio distinguishes clearly, perhaps more than any writer before him, the *state* as the *source of sovereignty* from the *personnel and process of government* as the *instrumentality of sovereignty*. Marsilio calls the instrumentality of sovereignty the ruling part (*pars principans*) of the state, a decidedly different concept from that of the modern executive, and much broader than the latter. The function of the ruling part, Marsilio says, is "to regulate, in accordance with the law, the political or civil acts of men." He stresses that "the elected kind of government is superior to the non-elected," and in monarchy, too, he strongly prefers the elective ruler. Governments established by force or fraud are, by contrast, "diseased."

According to the traditional medieval view, the ruler holds his office by divine sanction, and he is supposed to be superior in virtue and wisdom. Marsilio deals with this question in a more empirical and democratic, and less metaphysical, manner. The authority of the ruler derives its validity and existence from the observable fact of election, and a person becomes a ruler because he is elected, "and not by his knowledge of the laws, his prudence, or moral virtue, although these are qualities of the perfect ruler." Marsilio also mentions that many men may possess these qualities of ruling, yet, lacking the formal and empirical authority by election, they are not rulers.

Just as Marsilio derives the law from an empirical source, the will of the community, rather than from divine providence or natural reason, so he bases the *authority of the rulers* on the *will of the community* as expressed in *election*.

He therefore also stresses the nature of political office as an instrumentality of the *legislator*. The rulers must be guided and controlled by respect for the law, and the armed forces at their disposal should be kept at a level that is at once high enough to maintain order and yet not so high that it will give the rulers despotic power.

If the ruler or rulers violate the trust of office, the *legislator*—which sets them up—has the right to correct and punish them. If their offense is serious, they may even be removed from office. The *legislator* suspends the offending ruler while the proceedings against him are on, because there must never be two competing authorities and also "because he is corrected not as a ruler but as a subject who has transgressed the law." Marsilio's conception of the accountability of the ruler to the people is not new and is typical of the Middle Ages; but, whereas most medieval writers looked for divine punishment or, in more extreme instances, for tyrannicide as a remedy, Marsilio gropes toward an institutionalized method of keeping the ruler responsible to the entire community, should he exceed his authority.

Marsilio's conception of law and government as social regulation owing its coercive authority to the will of the politically organized community (*legislator* or *legislator humanus*) was pointed at lay and clerical despotism. Whereas in the past two hundred years interest in Marsilio's political theory has been steadily growing, in his own time and in the subsequent three centuries his views on the church were more influential. His most revolutionary doctrine in his analysis of the church, and one that was to leave its mark on Protestantism, is the idea of *congregational authority in the church*. The church is a community of believers (*universitas fidelium*), and, as in the political community (*universitas civium*), the only source of authority is the body of its members.

Marsilio does not attack the institution of the papacy as such, but he insists that if the Roman bishop (that is, the pope) has any special authority "it belongs to him through human appointment or election." The papacy started out as a simple headship of prestige and honor in view of the strategic position of Rome, but by a gradual and consistent process of usurpation it finally claimed full and universal jurisdiction over clergy and civil government. Selecting Boniface as one of the chief culprits, Marsilio says that the doctrine of papal plenitude of power was expressed by Boniface "in language as insolent as it is harmful and contrary to the meaning of Scripture, and based upon metaphysical demonstrations."

With regard to the right of appointing bishops and priests, Marsilio holds that it belongs to neither Caesar nor pope, "but rather to the whole body of believers," or to an agency set up by this body for the purpose. As to the rank and status of priests, "all bishops are of equal authority immediately through Christ, nor can it be proved by divine law that there is any superiority or subjection among them in spiritual or temporal affairs." The functions of the priesthood in the church, and it has none outside the church, are administration, teaching, and worship; but—and this is one of the main principles of Marsilio's political theory—the priests, the *church*, have *no coercive authority*, spiritual or temporal, over either clergy or laymen.

Marsilio adds the bold thought that the church has even no coercive authority over heretics. If heresy be a sin, it can—like all violations of divine law—be judged and punished on the day of judgment in the next world; if heresy be a civil offense, it must first be so declared by the secular government, and in this event the purpose is not to save souls but to protect secular interests, such as the unity of the state. If there are to be any penalties for heresy, they are to be fixed by secular authorities and meted out by them. However, Marsilio is not certain that heresy is really a moral offense, but he does not examine the matter in any great detail. He is primarily concerned with destroying the claim of the church to coercive authority, and he deliberately picks an extreme instance to illustrate his argument.

For practical purposes the church becomes, according to Marsilio, a department of the state, and he goes so far as to say that only the civil government has the authority to regulate the number of churches and temples, priests, and ministers. Because teaching has always been claimed by the church as its own domain, Marsilio specifically emphasizes that no license for the public teaching or practice of any art or discipline can be granted by bishops collectively or individually; only the civil government has this authority. Marsilio also recalls that Christ himself had no ambition for secular rule or property, and he therefore admonishes the church, in the Franciscan and Dantean tradition, to return to the original ways of Christianity. Existent church property should be used only for the maintenance of priests and "other gospel ministers," for divine worship, and for the aid of the needy and helpless poor. Whatever church property remains over and above such uses may be appropriated by the state "for the common or public welfare and protection."

Marsilio calls his treatise *The Defender of Peace* because he sees the task of civil government primarily as one of peace. In addition to the older causes of social unrest and discord known to Aristotle and other masters of political thought there is a new element, not known to Aristotle, that produces civil discord and intranquillity, and this new cause "is the belief, desire, and undertaking whereby the Roman bishop and his clerical coterie, in particular, are aiming to seize secular rulerships and to possess excessive temporal wealth." The indictment of the church on these two major grounds was to become one of the driving forces that led, first, to reform movements within the church and, later, to schism and separation in the Protestant Reformation.

In matters of religious faith and doctrine generally, Marsilio believes only in the truth of divine Scriptures, not in the additions and accretions of papal decrees and pronouncements. If the divine law is open to different interpretations, such interpretations may be made only by the general council of the believers, and "no partial group or particular individual, whatever his status, has the authority to make such definitions." Marsilio's insistence on the return to the Scriptures as the sole source of religious faith and divine law, his ruthless demolition of the edifice of dogma and power built up by the church over centuries of institutional growth, is one of the early winds that finally gather in the hurricane of the Protestant Reformation.

Despite his intense concern with church problems, Marsilio is essentially skeptical in matters of faith and religion. His doctrine leads, not to the Protestant state of Luther or Calvin, but to the secular, national, lay state of Machiavelli. Unlike Dante, whose political conceptions centered on the typically medieval image of universal empire, Marsilio shows no great interest in the issue of world government. He briefly notes that mankind is divided into different societies with diverse languages, religions, manners, and customs, and that—in the light of the needs of his time—separate governments suffice for the quiet living together of men in this world. When the conception of the secular national state as the largest sovereign unit displaces the idea of universal papal and imperial authority, the Middle Ages come to a close.

MARSILIO OF PADUA

The Defender of Peace *

1. Forms of Government

There are two genera of ruling parts or governments, one well-tempered, the other diseased. With Aristotle in the *Politics*, Book III, Chapter 5, I call that genus *well-tempered* in which the ruler governs for the common benefit, in accordance with the will of the subjects; while the *diseased* genus is that which is deficient in this respect. Each of these genera, again, is divided into three species: the temperate into kingly monarchy, aristocracy, and polity; the diseased into the three opposite species of tyrannical monarchy, oligarchy, and democracy. And each of these again has subspecies, the detailed discussion of which is not part of our present task.

To obtain a fuller conception of these species of government, which is necessary for the clear understanding of what follows, let us define each species in accordance with

* From Marsilio of Padua, *The Defender of Peace* (1324; trans. Alan Gewirth, Columbia University Press, 1952). By permission.

the view of Aristotle. A *kingly monarchy* then, is a temperate government wherein there is a single ruler who aims at the common benefit, and in accordance with the will or consent of the subjects. *Tyranny*, its opposite, is a diseased government wherein there is a single ruler who aims at his own benefit apart from the will of his subjects. *Aristocracy* is a temperate government in which the honorable class [*honorabilitas*] alone rules in accordance with the will or consent of the subjects and for the common benefit. *Oligarchy*, its opposite, is a diseased government in which some of the wealthier or more powerful rule for their own benefit apart from the will of the subjects. A *polity*, although in one sense it is something common to every genus or species of regime or government, means in another sense a certain species of temperate government, in which every citizen participates in some way in the government or in the deliberative function in turn according to his rank and ability or condition, for the common benefit and with the will or consent of the citizens.

Democracy, its opposite, is a government in which the masses [*vulgus*] or the multitude of the needy establish the government and rule alone, apart from the will or consent of the other citizens and not entirely for the common benefit according to proper proportion.

As to which of the temperate governments is best or which of the diseased governments is worst, and the relative goodness or badness of the other species, the discussion of these points is not part of our present concern. Let it suffice to have said this much about the division of governments into their species and the definition of each.

To make clearer these concepts of Aristotle, and to summarize all the methods of establishing the other kinds of government, we shall say that every government is over either voluntary or involuntary subjects. The first is the genus of well-tempered governments, the second of diseased governments. Each of these genera is divided into three species or kinds. And since one of the species of well-tempered government, and perhaps the more perfect, is kingly monarchy, let us resume our previous statements about its various kinds or methods, by saying that the king or monarch either is named by the election of the inhabitants or citizens, or duly obtains the rulership without their election. If without the election of the citizens, this is either because he or his ancestors first inhabited the region, or because he bought the land and jurisdiction, or acquired it by a just war, or by some other lawful method, such as by gift made to him for some great service. Each of these kinds of monarchy participates so much the more in true kingship, the more it is over voluntary subjects and according to law made for the common benefit of the subjects; and it savors so much the more of tyranny the more it departs from these features, i.e., the consent of the subjects and law established for their common benefit. Hence it is written in the *Politics,* Book IV, Chapter 8: "These monarchies were kingly because they were according to law, and

ruled voluntary subjects; but they were tyrannical because they ruled despotically and in accordance with their [i.e., the monarchs'] own judgment." These two features, then, distinguish temperate from diseased government, as is apparent from the clear statement of Aristotle, but absolutely or in greater degree it is the consent of the subjects which is the distinguishing criterion. Now if the ruling monarch is elected by the inhabitants, it is either with all his posterity succeeding him or not. If the latter, this may be in several ways, as be named either for his own lifetime alone, or for his own lifetime and that of one or more of his successors, or not for the whole lifetime either of himself or of any of his successors but only for some determinate period, such as one or two years, more or less. Again, he is named to exercise either every judicial office, or only one office such as leading the army.

The elected and the non-elected kingly monarchs agree in that each rules voluntary subjects. They differ, however, in that the non-elected kings rule less voluntary subjects, and by laws which are less politic for the common benefit, as we said before in the case of the barbarians. The elected kings, on the other hand, rule more willing subjects, and by laws which are more politic, in that they are made for the common benefit.

From these considerations it is clear, and will be even more apparent in the sequel, that the elected kind of government is superior to the non-elected. This is also the view of Aristotle in that passage of the *Politics,* Book III, Chapter 8, which we cited above with reference to those who were made rulers in the heroic days. Again, this method of establishing governments is more permanent in perfect communities. For at some time or other it becomes necessary to have recourse to this from among all the other methods of establishing governments, but not conversely. For example, if hereditary succession fails, or if for some reason the multitude cannot bear the excessive malice of that family's rule, they must then turn to the method of election, which can never fail so long as the generation of men does not fail. Moreover, by the method of election alone is the best ruler obtained. For it is expedient that the ruler be the best man in the polity, since he must regulate the civil acts of all the rest.

The method of establishing the other species of temperate government is usually election; in some cases the ruler is chosen by lot, without subsequent hereditary succession. Diseased governments, on the other hand, are usually established by fraud or force or both.

2. Authority Based on Election

We must next discuss that efficient cause of the laws which is capable of being demonstrated. For I do not intend to deal here with that method of establishing laws which can be effected by the immediate act or oracle of God apart from the human will, or which has been so effected in the past. It was by this method, as we have said, that the Mosaic law was established; but I shall not deal with it here even insofar as it contains commands with regard to civil acts for the status of the present world. I shall discuss the establishment of only those laws and governments which emerge immediately from the decision of the human mind.

Let us say, to begin with, that it can pertain to any citizen to discover the law taken materially and in its third sense, as the science of civil justice and benefit. Such inquiry, however, can be carried on more appropriately and be completed better by those men who are able to have leisure, who are older and experienced in practical affairs, and who are called "prudent men," than by the mechanics who must bend all their efforts to acquiring the necessities of life. But it must be remembered that the true knowledge or discovery of the just and the beneficial, and of their opposites, is not law taken in its last and most proper sense, whereby it is the measure of human civil acts, unless there is given a coercive command as to its observance, or it is made by way of such a command, by someone through whose authority its transgressors must and can be punished. Hence, we must now say who has the authority to make such a command and to punish its transgressors. This, indeed, is to inquire into the legislator or the maker of the law.

Let us say, then, in accordance with the truth and the counsel of Aristotle in the *Politics,* Book III, Chapter 6, that the legislator, or the primary and proper efficient cause of the law, is the people or the whole body of citizens, or the weightier part thereof, through its election or will expressed by words in the general assembly of the citizens, commanding or determining that something be done or omitted with regard to civil human acts under threat of temporal punishment. By the *weightier part* I mean to take into consideration the quantity and the quality of the persons in that community over which the law is made. The aforesaid whole body of citizens or the weightier part thereof is the legislator regardless of whether it makes the law directly by itself or entrusts the making of it to some person or persons, who are not and cannot be the legislator in the absolute sense, but only in a relative sense and for a particular time and in accordance with the authority of the primary legislator. And I say further that the laws and anything else established through election must receive their necessary approval by that same primary authority and no other, whatever be the case with regard to certain ceremonies or solemnities, which are required not for the being of the matters elected but for their well-being, since the election would be no less valid even if these ceremonies were not performed. Moreover, by the same authority must the laws and other things established through election undergo addition, subtraction, complete change, interpretation, or suspension, insofar as the exigencies of time or place or other circumstances make any such action opportune for the common benefit. And by the same authority, also, must the laws be promulgated or proclaimed after their enactment, so that no citizen or foreigner who is delinquent in observing them may be excused because of ignorance.

A citizen I define in accordance with Aristotle in the *Politics,* Book III, Chapters 1, 3, and 7, as one who participates in the civil community in the government or the deliberative or judicial function according to his rank. By this definition, children, slaves, foreigners, and women are distinguished from citizens, although in different ways. For the sons of citizens are citizens in proximate potentiality, lacking only in years. The weightier part of the citizens should be viewed in accordance with the honorable custom of politics or else should be determined in accordance with the doctrine of Aristotle in the *Politics,* Book VI, Chapter 2.

Having thus defined the citizen and the weightier part of the citizens, let us return to our proposed objective, namely, to demonstrate that the human authority to make laws belongs only to the whole body of the citizens or to the weightier part thereof. Our first proof is as follows. The absolutely primary human authority to make or establish human laws belongs only to those men from whom alone the best laws can emerge. But these are the whole body of the citizens, or the weightier part thereof, which represents that whole body; since it is difficult or impossible for all persons to agree upon one decision, because some men have a deformed nature, disagreeing with the common decision through singular malice or ignorance. The common benefit should not, however, be impeded or neglected because of the unreasonable protest or opposition of these men. The authority to make or establish laws, therefore, belongs only to the whole body of the citizens or to the weightier part thereof.

The first proposition of this demonstration is very nearly self-evident, although its force and its ultimate certainty can be grasped from what has been said earlier. The second proposition, that is, that the best law is made only through the hearing and command of the entire multitude, I prove by assuming with Aristotle in the *Politics,* Book III, Chapter 7, that the best law is that which is made for the common benefit of the citizens. As Aristotle said: "That is presumably right [i.e., in the laws] which is for the common benefit of the state and the citizens." But that this is best achieved only by the whole body of the citizens or by the weightier part thereof, which is assumed to be the same thing, I show as follows: that at which the entire body of the citizens aims intellectually and emotionally is more certainly judged as to its truth and more diligently considered as to its common utility. For a defect in some proposed law can be better noted by the greater number than by any part thereof, since every whole, or at least every corporeal whole, is greater in mass and in virtue than any part of it taken separately. Moreover, the common utility of a law is better considered by the entire multitude, because no one knowingly harms himself. Anyone can look to see whether a proposed law leans toward the benefit of one or a few persons more than of the others or of the community, and can protest against it. Such, however, would not be the case were the law made by one or a few persons, considering their own private benefit rather than that of the community.

Another argument to the principal conclusion is as follows. The authority to make the law belongs only to those men whose making of it will cause the law to be better observed or observed at all. Only the whole body of the citizens are such men. To them, therefore, belongs the authority to make the law. The first proposition of this demonstration is very nearly self-evident, for a law would be useless unless it were observed. Hence Aristotle said in the *Politics,* Book IV, Chapter 6: "Laws are not well ordered when they are well made but not obeyed." He also said in Book VI, Chapter 5: "Nothing is accomplished by forming opinions about justice and not carrying them into effect." The second proposition I prove as follows. That law is better observed by every citizen which each one seems to have imposed upon himself. But such is the law which is made through the hearing and command of the entire multitude of the citizens. The first proposition of this prosyllogism is almost self-evident: "for since the state is a community of free men," as is written in the *Politics*, Book III, Chapter 4, every citizen must be free, and not undergo someone else's despotism, i.e., slavish dominion. But this would not be the case if one or a few of the citizens by their own authority made the law over the whole body of citizens. For those who thus made the law would be despots over the others, and hence such a law, however good it was, would be endured only with reluctance, or not at all, by the rest of the citizens, the more ample part. Having suffered contempt, they would protest against it, and not having been called upon to make it, they would not observe it. On the other hand, a law made by the hearing or consent of the whole multitude, even though it were less useful, would be willingly observed and endured by every one of the citizens, because then each would seem to have set the law upon himself, and hence would have no protest against it, but would rather tolerate it with equanimity. The second proposition of the first syllogism I also prove in this way: the power to cause the law to be observed belongs only to those men to whom belongs coercive force over the transgressors of the law. But these men are the whole body of citizens, or the weightier part thereof. Therefore, to them alone belongs the authority to make the law.

The principal conclusion is also proved in this way. That practical matter whose proper establishment is of greatest importance for the common sufficiency of the citizens in this life, and whose poor establishment threatens harm for the community, must be established by the whole body of the citizens. But such a matter is the law. Therefore, the establishment of the law pertains to the whole body of the citizens. The major proposition of this demonstration is almost self-evident. For men came

together to the civil community in order to attain what was beneficial for sufficiency of life, and to avoid the opposite. Those matters, therefore, which can affect the benefit and harm of all ought to be known and heard by all, in order that they may attain the beneficial and repel the opposite. Such matters are the laws, as was assumed in the minor proposition. For in the laws being rightly made consists a large part of the whole common sufficiency of men, whereas under bad laws there arise unbearable slavery, oppression, and misery of the citizens, the final result of which is that the state is destroyed.

Again, and this is an abbreviation and summary of the previous demonstrations: the authority to make laws belongs only to the whole body of the citizens, as we have said, or else it belongs to one or a few men. But it cannot belong to one man alone, for through ignorance or malice or both, this one man could make a bad law, looking more to his own private benefit than to that of the community, so that the law would be tyrannical. For the same reason, the authority to make laws cannot belong to a few; for they too could sin, as before, in making the law for the benefit of a certain few and not for the common benefit, as can be seen in oligarchies. The authority to make the laws belongs, therefore, to the whole body of citizens or to the weightier part thereof, for precisely the opposite reason. For since all the citizens must be measured by the law in due proportion, and no one knowingly harms or wishes injustice to himself, it follows that all or most wish a law conducing to the common benefit of the citizens.

From these same demonstrations it can also be proved, merely by changing the minor term, that the approval, interpretation, and suspension of the laws pertain to the authority of the legislator alone. And the same must be thought of everything else which is established by election. For the authority to approve or disapprove rests with those who have the primary authority to elect, or with those to whom they have granted this authority of election. For otherwise, if the part could dissolve, by its own authority, what had been established by the whole, the part would be greater than the whole, or at least equal to it.

3. Is the Multitude Fit to Rule?

Objections will be made to our above statements, to the effect that the authority to make or establish laws does not belong to the whole body of the citizens. The first objection is that those who are vicious and undiscerning in most cases should not make the law. For these two sins, malice and ignorance, must be excluded from the legislator, and it was to avoid them in civil judgments that we upheld the necessity of law. But the people or the whole body of citizens have these sins; for men in most cases seem to be vicious and stupid: "The number of the stupid is infinite," as is said in the first chapter of *Ecclesiastes*. Another objection is that it is very difficult, or impossible, to harmonize the views of many vicious and unintelligent persons; but such is not the case with the few and virtuous. It is more useful, therefore, that the law be made by the few than by the whole body of the citizens or the overwhelming majority of them. Again, in every civil community the wise and learned are few in comparison with the multitude of the unlearned. Since, therefore, the law is more usefully made by the wise and learned than by the unlearned and uncultivated, it seems that the authority to make laws belongs to the few, not to the many or to all. Furthermore, that which can be done by fewer persons is needlessly done by more. Since, therefore, the law can be made by the wise, who are few, as has been said, the entire multitude or the greater part of it would needlessly be occupied therein. The authority to make laws does not belong, therefore, to the whole body of the citizens or the weightier part thereof.

As for the first objection, that the au-

thority to make laws does not belong to those who in most cases are vicious and undiscerning, this we grant. But when it is added that the whole body of citizens is such, this must be denied. For most of the citizens are neither vicious nor undiscerning most of the time; all or most of them are of sound mind and reason and have a right desire for the polity and for the things necessary for it to endure, like laws and other statutes or customs. For although not every citizen nor the greater number of the citizens be discoverers of the laws, yet every citizen can judge of what has been discovered and proposed to him by someone else, and can discern what must be added, subtracted, or changed. Hence in the major premiss' reference to the *undiscerning,* if what is meant is that those who cannot, in most of their parts or members, discover the law by themselves, ought not to establish the law, this must be denied as manifestly false, as is borne out by sense induction and by Aristotle in the *Politics,* Book III, Chapter 6. By induction we can see that many men judge rightly about the quality of a picture, a house, a ship, and other works of art, even though they would have been unable to discover or produce them. Aristotle also attests to this in the place just cited, answering the proposed objection with these words: "About some things the man who made them is not the only or the best judge." He proves this in many species of arts, and indicates that the same is true for all the others.

Nor is this position invalidated by those who say that *the wise who are few can discern what should be enacted with regard to practical matters better than can the rest of the multitude.* For even if this be true, it still does not follow that the wise can discern what should be enacted better than can the whole multitude, in which the wise are included together with the less learned. For *every whole is greater than its part* both in acting and in discerning.

The second objection carries little weight, for even though it be easier to harmonize the views of fewer persons than of many, it does not follow that the views of the few, or of the part, are superior to those of the whole multitude, of which the few are a part. For the few would not discern or wish the common benefit equally as well as would the entire multitude of the citizens. Indeed, it would be insecure, as we have already shown, to entrust lawmaking to the will of the few. For they would consult therein their own private benefit, as individuals or as a group, rather than the common benefit.

The third objection can be easily refuted from what we have already said: for although the laws can be better made by the wise than by the less learned, it is not therefore to be concluded that they are better made by the wise alone than by the entire multitude of citizens, in which the wise are included. For the assembled multitude of all of these can better discern and desire the common justice and benefit than any part of it taken separately, however prudent that part may be.

Hence those do not speak the truth who hold that the less learned multitude hinders the election and approval of the true or common good; rather, the multitude is of help in this function when it is joined to those who are more learned and more experienced. For although the multitude cannot by itself discover true and useful measures, it can nevertheless discern and judge the measures discovered and proposed to it by others, as to whether they should be added to, or subtracted from, or completely changed, or rejected. For many things which a man would have been unable to initiate or discover by himself, he can comprehend and bring to completion after they have been explained to him by someone else.

It is hence appropriate and highly useful that the whole body of citizens entrust to those who are prudent and experienced the investigation, discovery, and examination of the standards, the future laws or statutes, bearing upon civil justice and benefit, common difficulties or burdens, and other similar matters. Either some of these prudent and experienced men may be elected by each of the primary parts of the state, according to the proportion of each part; or else all these men may be elected by all the citizens assembled together. And this will be an appropriate and useful method whereby to come together to discover the laws without detriment to the rest of the multitude, i.e., the less learned, who would be of little help in the investigation of such standards, and would be disturbed in their performance of the other functions necessary both to themselves and to others, which would be troublesome both to each individual and to the community.

After such standards, the future laws, have been discovered and diligently examined, they must be laid before the assembled whole body of citizens for their approval or disapproval, so that if any citizen thinks that something should be added, subtracted, changed, or completely rejected, he can say so, since in this way the law will be more usefully ordained. For as we have said, the less learned citizens can sometimes perceive something which must be corrected in a proposed law even though they could not have discovered the law itself. Also, the laws thus made by the hearing and consent of the entire multitude will be better observed, nor will anyone have any protest to make against them.

These standards, the future laws, will thus have been made public, and in the general assembly of the citizens those citizens will have been heard who have wanted to make some reasonable statements with regard to them. Then there must again be elected men of the qualities and by the method indicated above, or else the aforesaid men must be confirmed; and they, representing the position and authority of the whole body of the citizens, will approve or disapprove in whole or in part the aforementioned standards which had been investigated and proposed, or else, if it so wishes, the whole body of the citizens or the weightier part thereof will do this same thing. After this approval, the aforesaid standards are laws and deserve to be so called, not before; and after their publication or proclamation, they alone among human commands make transgressors liable to civil guilt and punishment.

We think we have adequately shown, then, that the authority to make or establish laws, and to give a command with regard to their observance, belongs only to the whole body of the citizens or to the weightier part thereof as efficient cause, or else to the person or persons to whom the aforesaid whole body has granted this authority.

4. The Accountability of Rulers

We have previously stated that it pertains to the legislator to correct governments or to change them completely, just as to establish them. In this connection, someone may well wonder whether it is expedient that rulers be corrected by coercive judgment and force; and if it is expedient, whether they should be corrected for every kind of excess, or only for some and not for others; also who should make such judgments against the rulers, and execute them by coercive force—for it was said above that it pertains to the rulers alone to issue civil sentences and to punish transgressors of the laws by coercive force.

Let us say that the ruler through his action in accordance with the law and the authority given to him is the standard and measure of every civil act, like the heart in an animal. Now if the ruler received no other form beside the law, and the authority and the desire to act in accordance with it, he would never perform any action which was wrong or corrigible or measurable by someone else. And therefore he and his action would be the measure of every civil act of men other than himself, in such manner that he would never be measured by others, like the well-formed heart in an animal. For since the heart receives no form that inclines it to an action contrary to the action which has to emerge from its natural virtue and heat, it always does naturally the appropriate action and never the contrary. Hence it regulates and measures, through its influence or action, the other parts of the animal, in such manner that it is not regulated by them nor does it receive any influence from them.

But since the ruler is a human being, he has understanding and desire, which may receive other forms, like false opinion or perverted desire or both, as a result of which he comes to do the contraries of the things determined by the law. Because of these actions, the ruler is rendered measurable by someone else who has the authority to measure or regulate him, or his unlawful actions, in accordance with the law. For otherwise every government would become despotic, and the life of the citizens servile and insufficient. This is an evil to be avoided.

Now the judgment, command, and execution of any correction of the ruler, in accordance with his demerit or transgression, must be done by the legislator, or by a person or persons appointed for this purpose by the authority of the legislator. And it is well to suspend for some time the office of the ruler who is to be corrected, especially in relation to the person or persons who must judge of his transgression, because otherwise there would then be a plurality of governments in the community, from which would result schism, agitation, and fighting; and also because he is corrected not as a ruler but as a subject who has transgressed the law.

Coming now to the questions which were raised above, let us say that the ruler's excess is either grave or slight; it may occur frequently or only rarely; and, it is among the things determined by law or it is not. If the ruler's excess be grave, such as against the commonwealth or against a notable or any other person, from failure to correct which there could likely arise scandal or agitation among the people, then whether the excess be one which occurs frequently or rarely, the ruler must be corrected for it. For if the excess is not avenged, agitation might arise among the people, and upheaval and destruction of the polity. If the excess is determined by law, it must be corrected according to the law; but if not, then it must be corrected according to the sentence of the legislator; and it must be determined by law as much as possible.

If the ruler's excess be small, then its occurrence and its commission by the ruler may be either rare or frequent. If it is rarely committed or rarely capable of being committed by the ruler, then it must be allowed to pass and be glossed over rather than having the ruler corrected for it. For if the ruler is corrected for every small and infrequent excess, he will be made an object of contempt; which will result in no slight harm to the community, since the citizens then exhibit less respect and obedience for the law and the ruler. Again, since the ruler is unwilling to undergo correction for every slight offense, because he will regard this as bringing him into low repute, there will be a possibility of grave scandal. But such a condition must not be stirred up in communities when no evident utility can emerge therefrom, but rather harm.

Such was clearly the view of Aristotle on this question, in the *Politics*, Book II, Chapter 4, where he said: "It is manifest that some errors of both legislators and rulers should be allowed to pass. For he will do less good by making changes than he will do harm by becoming accustomed to rebelling against the rulers." By *legislator* Aristotle meant an established law; and he says that if men have become accustomed to observing it, then it must not be changed in order to make a slight correction in it, but must rather be allowed to pass. For frequent changing of the laws saps their strength, which is the custom of obeying and observing what the laws command. As Aristotle said in the same book and chapter: "The law has no power for persuasion except that of custom," *i.e.*, for the law to be observed by the subjects, the most important factor is custom. And the case is very similar with regard to respecting and obeying the ruler.

But if the ruler's excess, while slight in extent, be capable of frequent occurrence, then it must be determined by law, and the ruler who frequently commits the offense must be given the appropriate punishment. For an offense, however slight, would be of notable harm to the polity if it were frequently committed, just as small expenses frequently incurred consume a fortune, *i.e.*, in riches. "For the whole sum is not small, although it is made up of small sums," as is written in the *Politics,* Book V, Chapter 4.

Such then are our conclusions concerning the correction of rulers, by whom it should be done, and for what reasons.

5. The Church and Coercive Authority

In this way, then, have the Roman bishops entered upon these affairs: First, under the guise of seeking peace among the Christian believers, they have excommunicated certain men who are unwilling to obey their decree. Then they impose on them penalties both real and personal, more harshly against those who are less able to resist their power, such as communities and individuals among the Italians, whose state, divided and wounded in almost all its parts, can more easily be oppressed, but more mildly against those, like kings and rulers, whose resistance and coercive power they fear. On these latter, however, they are gradually creeping up in the attempt to usurp their jurisdictions, not daring to invade them all at once. Hence their stealthy double-dealing has hitherto been concealed even from the Roman rulers and the peoples subject to them. For the Roman bishops have gradually seized one jurisdiction after another, especially when the imperial seat was vacant; so that now they finally say that they have total coercive temporal jurisdiction over the Roman ruler. Most recently and most obviously, the present bishop has written that he has supreme jurisdiction over the ruler of the Romans, both in the Italian and the German provinces, and also over all the lesser rulers, communities, groups, and individuals of the aforesaid provinces, of whatever dignity and condition they may be, and over all their fiefs and other temporalities. This bishop openly ascribes to himself the power to give and transfer their governments, as all can clearly see from certain writings of this bishop, which he calls *edicts* or *sentences*.

This wrong opinion of certain Roman bishops, and also perhaps their perverted desire for rulership, which they assert is owed to them because of the plenitude of power given to them, as they say, by Christ —this is that singular cause which we have said produces the intranquillity or discord of the city or state. For it is prone to creep up on all states, as was said in our introductory remarks, and by its hateful action it has for a long time distressed the Italian state, and has kept and still keeps it from tranquillity or peace, by preventing with all its force the appointment or institution of the ruler, the Roman emperor, and his

functioning in the said empire. From lack of this function, which is the just regulation of civil acts, there readily emerge injuries and contentions, and these, if not measured by the standard of justice or law because of the absence of the measurer, cause battles, whence there have resulted the separation of the citizens and finally the destruction of the Italian polities or cities, as we have said. With this opinion, therefore, and perhaps also with what we have called a desire for ruling, the Roman bishop strives to make the Roman ruler subject to him in coercive or temporal jurisdiction, whereas that ruler neither rightly ought to be, nor wishes to be subject to him in such judgment. From this there has arisen so much strife and discord that it cannot be extinguished without great effort of souls and bodies and expenditure of wealth. For the office of coercive rulership over any individual, of whatever condition he may be, or over any community or group, does not belong to the Roman or any other bishop, priest, or spiritual minister, as such.

CHAPTER 11

MACHIAVELLI

O NLY in fifth-century Athens has the world seen the dazzling artistic brilliance and fabulous intellectual vitality that characterized the Renaissance. The rebirth and rediscovery of antiquity were both cause and effect: on the one hand, the Renaissance helped to revive the rational, this-worldly, secular, scientific spirit that had lain dormant through many centuries of medieval encasement; on the other hand, the Renaissance was itself the effect of man's growing restlessness as well as of changing social and technological conditions. In particular, printing destroyed the monopoly of knowledge that the clergy had enjoyed for a thousand years, and gunpowder destroyed the military monopoly of the nobility. Like travelers who return from their journey with their prejudices confirmed and strengthened, the men of the Renaissance, in traveling to the remote centuries of classical Greece and Rome, found what they looked for—an exciting world, the image of which had guided them on their voyage.

The most important discovery of the Renaissance—more significant than any single work of art or any one genius—was the *discovery of man*. In antiquity the sense of tribal kinship had not favored the growth of individualism, of isolation from the community. Stoicism and Christianity had been the first to contribute new and lasting elements to a conception of individuality: Stoicism, by stressing the idea of moral selfhood and responsibility, and Christianity, by insisting that man's innermost reality, his soul, was outside the sphere and jurisdiction of mundane authority, and that his salvation depended ultimately on his own decisions, his own works. But the social system of the Middle Ages, built on status and custom, discouraged the mobility and change that favor individualistic attitudes; it emphasized instead the class or group to which a person belonged. The Renaissance goes beyond the moral selfhood of Stoicism, the spiritual uniqueness of Christianity, the aesthetic individuality of the ancient Greeks, and views man in his totality, in his flesh and blood as well as in his mind and spirit—man in relation to himself, to society, to the world. Displacing God, *man* becomes the *center of the universe;* the values of this new solar

278

system are inevitably different from those of the God-centered universe.
The Renaissance was the confluence of many streams and tributaries, yet
the Italian share was predominant from beginning to end. Italy had never lost
living contacts with its ancient past: the country was full of splendid cities
founded in antiquity, it abounded in relics and monuments of past glories, and
the language was still the language (with some minor changes) of Caesar and
Cicero. The dead hand of uniformity had never lain as heavily on Italy as on
other European countries in the Middle Ages, and the feudal system never permeated it as it did, for example, France, England, and Germany. Italy remained
the only major area in which a vigorous communal life had weathered the storms
of wars and invasions, and its city-states were for a long time islands of individualistic republicanism in a sea of European monarchical loyalties. The virtual destruction of the German empire as a world power by the papacy in the
thirteenth century, and the later enslavement of the papacy to the French monarchy in the fourteenth century, gave the independent Italian city-states new
opportunities for self-affirmation and increased self-confidence. Leadership in
international trade, business, and finance made numerous Italian cities wealthy
and prosperous, and provided the economic means for the literary, artistic, and
scholarly activities of a new elite.

Among the centers of the Renaissance, Florence was always first, reaching
its climax in Leonardo da Vinci (1452–1519), who most perfectly represented,
and lived, the Renaissance ideal of *universal man,* creative in painting and the
arts, inventive in science and engineering, and accomplished in philosophy and
letters. In the study of politics, the New Learning finds its clearest expression
in Niccolò Machiavelli (1469–1527).

At the age of twenty-nine Machiavelli entered the public service of his city,
and there he remained for fourteen years. Although not employed on the highest
levels of policy making, he was close enough to the inner circles of the administration to acquire firsthand knowledge of the mechanics of politics. Florence was
at that time an independent republic, and Machiavelli was frequently sent on
diplomatic missions to other Italian states and to great foreign powers like
France and Germany. In 1412 he lost his job when the republican government,
based on French support, was replaced by the absolutist regime of the Medici,
who had been restored to power with papal help. Machiavelli was accused of
serious crimes and tortured, but he was found innocent and banished to his small
farm near Florence.

It was in such enforced leisure that he wrote *The Prince* (1513). The book
was dedicated to Lorenzo di Medici, and Machiavelli fulsomely praised the
dynasty that stood for the exact opposite of his erstwhile republican sentiments.
He even hoped to have his political conversion rewarded by an opportunity to
serve the new antirepublican regime, but in this expectation he failed. The further imposed idleness gave him enough time to work on his most elaborate political book, *The Discourses on the First Ten Books of Titus Livius* (1521). Taking
Roman history as a starting point, *The Discourses* attempts to dissect the anatomy of the body politic, and on a much more philosophical and historical foundation than that of *The Prince. The Discourses* is interesting because Machiavelli

affirms in it his republican sentiment; yet this personal preference does not alter his basic views on the process of politics, regardless of the form of its constitution, republican or despotic.

For all its breadth and elaborateness, and frequent depth and penetration, *The Discourses* is of interest primarily to students of political philosophy, whereas *The Prince,* pithy, shocking, persuasive, provocative, hard-hitting, is destined to remain one of the half-dozen political writings that have entered the general body of world literature. It is a reflection not only of man's political ambitions and passions but of man himself. If Machiavelli had painted, in medieval fashion, the devils who inhabit hell, his impact would have been much less intense on his contemporaries and on posterity. What Machiavelli did, however, was to portray something worse, real human beings; the shock of recognition has created around his work an aura of mixed horror and fascination, and it is hard to tell which is the stronger.

The most revolutionary aspect of *The Prince* is not so much what it says as what it ignores. Before Machiavelli, all political writing—from Plato and Aristotle through the Middle Ages to the Renaissance—had one central question: the *end of the state.* Political power was assumed to be a means only—a means in the service of higher ends, such as justice, the good life, freedom, or God. Machiavelli ignores the issue of the end of the state in extrapolitical (ethical, religious, cultural) terms. He assumes that *power* is *an end in itself,* and he confines his inquiries into the *means* that are best suited to *acquire, retain,* and *expand power.* Machiavelli thus separates power from morality, ethics, religion, and metaphysics, and sets up the *state* as an *autonomous system of values* independent of any other source.

If he follows the value system of the state, the statesman may violate other value systems, such as religion, ethics, or morality. Machiavelli thus develops the idea of the *reason of state,* under which many acts are permissive, even obligatory, that would be considered heinous crimes if judged in the court of religion or morality. Machiavelli does not assert that ethics and morality as such are inferior to the precepts of power, the reason of state; from a general, theoretical viewpoint, the canons of power and the tenets of morality are independent of each other. When it comes to practical collisions, it depends on who faces the alternatives. The moralist will recognize the supremacy of his moral code over competing systems of values. The ecclesiastic will not admit a rival to his religious code. Similarly, the statesman will be guided solely by the precepts of his code, whose end—the acquisition, retention, and expansion of power—is different from other codes, and whose means are therefore different, too.

In the actions of rulers "the end justifies the means. Let a prince therefore aim at conquering and maintaining the state, and the means will always be judged honorable and praised by every one." In *The Discourses,* Machiavelli defines the reason of state even more clearly: "For where the very safety of the country depends upon the resolution to be taken, no consideration of justice or injustice, humanity or cruelty, nor of glory or of shame, should be allowed to prevail. But putting all other considerations aside, the only question should be: what course will save the life and liberty of the country?"

Machiavelli never praises immorality for its own sake; his basic attitude is not one of nihilism: he neither assumes that there are no values in this world, nor wishes to create a world in which all values would be destroyed. Machiavelli is aware that civilization implies some sort of values. His *amorality* implies therefore, not the denial of moral values in all situations, but the affirmation that, in the specific situation of the statesman, the rules of power have priority over those of ethics and morality.

Machiavelli did not invent political murder, treachery, and fraud. But before his time such crimes were committed *de facto,* and no attempt was made to integrate them into a moral world of their own. The traditional reaction to political immorality had been either one of polite neglect, half-hearted excuse, or, at best, severe censure of individual violations of ethics and morality. The sanctity and inviolability of the moral code seemed, before Machiavelli, in no way impaired by the regrettable exceptions to the rule, regardless of how frequent they were. In Machiavelli, the traditional attitude of polite neglect and hypocritical, or sincere, regret is replaced by the positive affirmation that the reason of state is for the statesman the determining code of conduct, and that statecraft constitutes a value system of its own which is different from that of ethics and religion. What is evil from the viewpoint of morality and religion may therefore be good from the viewpoint of the reason of state, if it serves to acquire, retain, or expand power.

Good and *evil* are thus reduced from absolute to *relative* categories, and it depends on the basic assumption of a system of values whether a particular action is good or bad. If the basic assumption and objective of conduct is friendship, service, fellowship, justice, or God, the individual action will be judged good or bad to the extent that it agrees with, or deviates from, such assumptions and goals. If, as for the ruler, the basic assumption is power, the decision as to whether a particular action is good or bad will depend on the extent to which it furthers the gain, retention, and growth of power. In this sense the use of poison may be called "good" if it does a good job in eliminating a political opponent, perhaps by acting slowly and imperceptibly so that the author of the crime cannot be easily detected. The attribution of "goodness" to poison in a specific case of political necessity does not imply a general justification for the use of poison. Assuming *power* as the *end of politics, goodness* thus *coincides with efficiency:* an efficient means of acquiring, consolidating, and expanding power is good; an inefficient means, bad.

Efficiency in politics is thus analogous to virtue in morals or religion, and inefficiency replaces the concept of sin. Machiavelli himself still uses the term "virtue" (*virtù*) for the successful ruler, but he means the ambitious, ruthless, crafty, successful ruler, and not the ruler who is a regular churchgoer, mindful of other men's wives, and generally a practicing moralist. In typical Renaissance style, Machiavelli even sees "grandeur" in elegant and magnificent crimes; this concept of an elegant or beautiful crime would have been unthinkable before the collapse of traditional standards of ethics.

Machiavelli's attitude to the Borgias is a revealing illustration of his more abstract concepts. Cardinal Rodrigo Borgia had four living children, three sons and one daughter, when he became pope in 1492 and assumed the name of Alexander VI. He appointed two of his sons as cardinals, and when he was away from Rome in 1501, he left his daughter, Lucrezia, in charge of the Vatican. Alexander VI had his personal hangman and poisoner. The latter, in particular, was constantly busy, and his victims included several cardinals. Alexander VI was one of the men whom Machiavelli most admired, and he writes of him as follows: "Alexander VI did nothing else but deceive men, he thought of nothing else, and found the occasion for it; no man was ever more able to give assurances, or affirmed things with stronger oaths, and no man observed them less; however, he always succeeded in his deceptions, as he well knew this aspect of things."

If Machiavelli admired Alexander VI, he idolized his son, Caesar Borgia. Caesar assassinated his older brother and murdered the husband of his sister Lucrezia—hardly a typical family idyll of the Renaissance. The number of his other assassinations is legion, and his cruelty was matched only by his treachery and debauchery. Machiavelli knew Caesar Borgia personally and was fully aware of his criminal record. Yet it is generally believed that Caesar Borgia was Machiavelli's model in writing *The Prince;* certainly he is held up "as an example to be imitated by all who by fortune and with the arms of others have risen to power," and "one can find no better example than the actions of this man." Machiavelli had only one fault to find with Caesar Borgia: that he allowed, after the death of his father, Alexander VI, the election of Julian II as pope, because Julian was an enemy of the Borgias. What Machiavelli criticized in the career of his most admired hero was his one failure and not his life of crime.

Machiavelli's views on morals and religion illustrate his belief in the supremacy of power over other social values. He has no sense of religion as a deep personal experience, and the mystical element in religion—its supranatural and suprarational character—is alien to his outlook. Yet he has a positive attitude toward religion; albeit his *religion* becomes a *tool of influence and control* in the hands of the ruler over the ruled. Machiavelli sees in religion the poor man's reason, ethics, and morality put together, and "where religion exists it is easy to introduce armies and discipline." From his reading of history, however, Machiavelli is led to the generalization that "as the observance of divine institutions is the cause of the greatness of republics, so the disregard of them produces their ruin." The fear of the prince, Machiavelli adds, may temporarily supplant the fear of God, but the life of even an efficient ruler is short.

The role of religion as a mere instrument of political domination, cohesion, and unity becomes even clearer in Machiavelli's advice that the ruler support and spread religious doctrines and beliefs in miracles *that he knows to be false.* The main value of religion to the ruler lies in the fact that it helps him to keep the people "well conducted and united," and from this viewpoint of utility it makes no difference whether he spreads among them true or false religious ideas and beliefs.

Machiavelli's interest in Christianity is not philosophical or theological, but purely pragmatic and political. He is critical of Christianity because "it glorifies more the humble and contemplative men than the men of action," whereas the Roman pagan religion "deified only men who had achieved great glory, such as commanders of republics and chiefs of republics." Christianity idealizes, Machiavelli charges, "humility, lowliness, and a contempt for worldly objects," as contrasted with the pagan qualities of grandeur of soul, strength of body, and other qualities that "render men formidable." The only kind of strength that Christianity teaches is fortitude of soul in suffering; it does not teach the strength that goes into the achievement of great deeds.

Concerning the church, Machiavelli preferred two main charges. First, he states that the Italians have become "irreligious and bad" because of the "evil example of the court of Rome." The second and more serious accusation is that the church "has kept and still keeps our country divided." He goes on to say that the sole cause of Italian political disunity is the church. Having acquired jurisdiction over a considerable portion of Italy, "she has never had sufficient power or courage to enable her to make herself sole sovereign of all Italy." Though Machiavelli hated the papacy, he nevertheless would have been happy to see the papacy govern all Italy if her unity could not be attained by any other means. What Machiavelli primarily reproaches the papacy for is not its record of crime and iniquity but its political failure to rule the whole country.

The clue to Machiavelli is his *pessimism*. The pessimist sees man as essentially unchangeable, incapable of progressive perfectibility, and he denies that reason can cope with the hard and limiting facts of nature and history. By contrast, the optimist (politically a democrat, liberal, individualist, socialist, or anarchist) believes that man is perfectible, that progress is possible, and that the chains of nature and history can be relaxed by the liberating and uplifting force of reason. Whereas the pessimist tends to look into the *past* and is primarily conscious of what *has* happened, the optimist looks into the *future* and wonders what *might* happen.

Machiavelli's pessimism is reflected in his conviction that moral considerations may be laudable in themselves (and in this he is less of a nihilist than the later nihilists and Machiavellians), but that the statesman cannot afford the luxury of practicing morality: "For how we live is so far removed from how we ought to live, that he who abandons what is done for what ought to be done, will rather learn to bring about his own ruin than his preservation." In the struggle between rulers, Machiavelli says, "there are two methods of fighting, the one by law, the other by force: the first method is that of men, the second of beasts; but as the first method is often insufficient, one must have recourse to the second. It is therefore necessary for a prince to know well how to use both the beast and the man."

Specifically, the *ruler must imitate the fox and the lion,* "for the lion cannot protect himself from the traps, and the fox cannot defend himself from wolves."

Should a ruler keep faith? This is Machiavelli's most famous question, and his answer to it is the best-known passage in *The Prince*. He admits that everybody knows how "laudable" it is for a ruler to keep faith. However, in the world of actual politics such laudable intentions may be irreconcilable with expediency and interest: "Therefore, a prudent ruler ought not to keep faith when by doing so it would be against his interest, and when the reasons which made him bind himself no longer exist. If men were all good, this precept would not be a good one; but as they are bad, and would not observe their faith with you, so you are not bound to keep faith with them."

Machiavelli thus takes a radically pessimistic view of human nature, and his psychological outlook is intimately related to his political philosophy. The theological conception of man's depravity, one of the central doctrines of the Reformation, must also have influenced Machiavelli and his contemporaries. Indeed, the political methods of the Renaissance were not known for their humanitarian mellowness. Death by poison and the silent dagger was a mere technical detail in the efficient execution of a political program, and there was little difference between kings and popes, princes and bishops. As a result, it was perhaps not unnatural for Machiavelli, as for many of his contemporaries, to take a dim view of human nature in general, and of human nature in the struggle for power in particular. Such skepticism easily developed into pessimism and outright cynicism.

Unlike later Machiavellians, Machiavelli himself was saved from extremism by prudence and moderation. In both *The Prince* and *The Discourses* there are numerous passages in which Machiavelli counsels rulers to be temperate, not to be uselessly cruel or arrogant, "for to incur hatred without any advantage is the greatest temerity and imprudence." The ruler should not use threats or insults, because neither diminishes the strength of the enemy but makes him only more cautious and disposed to hate. Machiavelli's rational skepticism, his horror of panaceas and cure-alls, his moderation and relativism, are apparent in his warning that no state should believe "that it can always follow a safe policy, rather let it think that all are doubtful. This is found in the nature of things, that one never tries to avoid one difficulty without running into another, but prudence consists in being able to know the nature of the difficulties, and taking the least harmful as good."

Machiavelli's fine *sense of the possible* makes his thought utilitarian, experimental, and relativistic. This basic quality—if not scientific in a strict sense—nevertheless partakes of one important aspect of science: empiricism, or the refusal to accept any solution as final.

Where Machiavelli is least scientific is where he thinks himself most scientific: in his belief that his analysis of power is based on solid facts of historical experience, that the record of man's behavior proves him a depraved and wily creature, and that a realistic theory of power must be based on such a pessimistic view of man. If Machiavelli's pessimism is the clue to his political philosophy, the weakness of his theory must be sought in his psychological conceptions. In detail a moderate, Machiavelli is an extremist when it comes to the whole. His doctrine of the badness of man is just as much an unscientific oversimplification as is the opposite exteme of the goodness of man. Man is somewhere between *angel and beast;* but Machiavelli says that the ruler is somewhere between *man and beast,* and that he "must know how to use both natures, and that the one without the other is not durable."

It would not be difficult to prove that human history has as much evidence of human goodness as of wickedness. It is a matter of ultimate—unprovable—personal philosophy of history whether one is more impressed by man's goodness than by his badness. But it is not sound philosophy of history, and still less is it sound science of politics, to reduce all history to one common denominator, be it goodness or badness.

Like other "realists" after him, Machiavelli identifies all too readily naked power politics with the whole of political reality, and he thus fails to grasp that ideas and ideals, if properly mobilized, can become potent facts, even decisive weapons, in the struggle for political survival. History is a vast graveyard filled with the corpses of self-styled "realists" like Napoleon, William II, Hitler, and Mussolini. They all underestimated the important imponderables in the equation of power but missed, in particular, the one component that in the end proved decisive: the will of man to be free, to put freedom above all other goods, even above life itself.

Machiavellian "realists" are usually realistic and rational in the choice of means with which they carry out their schemes of aggrandizement and expansion. But of what use is realism of means, if the ends themselves are utterly megalomaniac and unrealistic? Because Machiavelli was interested only in the means of acquiring, retaining, and expanding power, and not in the end of the state, he remained unaware of the *relations between means and ends*. Ends lead no existence apart from means but are continuously shaped by them. In the short run this inner connection may be concealed, but in the long run no great end can be accomplished by small means. The question, therefore, whether the political techniques and methods in *The Prince* are realistic even from the viewpoint of power cannot be separated from the still more basic issue of the end of power, inasmuch as the nature of the end determines the means most suited to it.

As one examines the references to rulers in *The Prince* more closely, one finds that Machiavelli was not interested in all forms of state, nor in all forms of power. What fascinated him above all was the *dynamics of illegitimate power*; he was little interested in states whose authority was legitimate, as in hereditary monarchies, but was primarily concerned with "new dominions both as to prince and state." He realized that "there is nothing more difficult to carry out, nor more doubtful of success, nor more dangerous to handle, than to initiate a new order of things." His primary concern with founders of new governments and states illuminates his attitude on the use of unethical means in politics. The "founders" of new states are, in effect, revolutionaries, and it is inevitable that in *reducing politics to war and revolution*, one arrives at an outlook in which the extraordinary becomes the ordinary, the abnormal the normal.

Because of his admiration for the outstanding man (and only outstanding men can successfully found "new dominions"), Machiavelli was little interested in the *institutional* framework of politics. He realized that in a period of institutional stability there is less need for the adventurer. In fact, as Machiavelli clearly sees, democrats hate war and revolution: the normal restraints and decencies are then imperiled by the necessity for sheer physical survival, and the habits of institutional stability are more easily subverted than in normal peacetime. The democratic theory of politics therefore tends to stress more the institutional framework of power than unique leader personalities, peace rather than war and revolution. Democrats have learned from long and painful experience that kindliness and decency flourish best in peaceful societies in which stable and just institutions make it difficult for lawless adventurers to thrive.

To the extent that democracies succeed in creating such societies, Machiavelli is wrong. To the extent that they fail, he is right. The ultimate commentary on *The Prince* is not in logic or morality, but in experience and history. Machiavelli laid bare the springs of human motivation with consummate and ruthless insight. It is hard to tell, in reading him, whether we shudder more when he tells the truth about human conduct, or more when he distorts the truth. He has, unwittingly perhaps, rendered a service to mankind by pointing out the abysmal depth of demoralization and bestiality into which men will sink for the sake of power. The twentieth century, in particular, has witnessed crimes of mass murder and genocide on a scale of which even Machiavelli, with all his interest in necessary, skillful, even elegant crimes, could never have dreamed. Our age is not one of facile optimism, and a balance will have to be struck between Machiavelli's pessimism about human nature and overconfident optimism, if an adequate approach to the theory and practice of politics is to be discovered.

MACHIAVELLI

The Prince *

1. Constant Readiness for War

A prince should therefore have no other aim or thought, nor take up any other thing for his study, but war and its organisation and discipline, for that is the only art that is necessary to one who commands, and it is of such virtue that it not only maintains those who are born princes, but often enables men of private fortune to attain to that rank. And one sees, on the other hand, that when princes think more of luxury than of arms, they lose their state. The chief cause of the loss of states, is the contempt of this art, and the way to acquire them is to be well versed in the same.

* From Niccolò Machiavelli, *The Prince* (1513). Modern Library Edition. By permission of Random House, Inc.

Francesco Sforza, through being well armed, became, from private status, Duke of Milan; his sons, through wishing to avoid the fatigue and hardship of war, from dukes became private persons. For among other evils caused by being disarmed, it renders you contemptible; which is one of those disgraceful things which a prince must guard against, as will be explained later. Because there is no comparison whatever between an armed and a disarmed man; it is not reasonable to suppose that one who is armed will obey willingly one who is unarmed; or that any unarmed man will remain safe among armed servants. For one being disdainful and the other suspicious, it is not possible for them to act well together. And therefore a prince who is ignorant of military matters, besides the other misfortunes already mentioned, cannot be esteemed by his soldiers, nor have confidence in them.

He ought, therefore, never to let his thoughts stray from the exercise of war; and in peace he ought to practise it more than in war, which he can do in two ways: by action and by study. As to action, he must, besides keeping his men well disciplined and exercised, engage continually in hunting, and thus accustom his body to hardships; and meanwhile learn the nature of the land, how steep the mountains are, how the valleys debouch, where the plains lie, and understand the nature of rivers and swamps. To all this he should devote great attention. This knowledge is useful in two ways. In the first place, one learns to know one's country, and can the better see how to defend it. Then by means of the knowledge and experience gained in one locality, one can easily understand any other that it may be necessary to observe; for the hills and valleys, plains and rivers of Tuscany, for instance, have a certain resemblance to those of other provinces, so that from a knowledge of the country in one province one can easily arrive at a knowledge of others. And that prince who is lacking in this skill is wanting in the first essentials of a leader; for it is this which teaches how to find the enemy, take up quarters, lead armies, plan battles and lay siege to towns with advantage.

Philopœmen, prince of the Achaei, among other praises bestowed on him by writers, is lauded because in times of peace he thought of nothing but the methods of warfare, and when he was in the country with his friends, he often stopped and asked them: If the enemy were on that hill and we found ourselves here with our army, which of us would have the advantage? How could we safely approach him maintaining our order? If we wished to retire, what ought we to do? If they retired, how should we follow them? And he put before them as they went along all the contingencies that might happen to an army, heard their opinion, gave his own, fortifying it by argument; so that thanks to these con-

stant reflections there could never happen any incident when actually leading his armies for which he was not prepared.

But as to exercise for the mind, the prince ought to read history and study the actions of eminent men, see how they acted in warfare, examine the causes of their victories and defeats in order to imitate the former and avoid the latter, and above all, do as some men have done in the past, who have imitated some one, who has been much praised and glorified, and have always kept his deeds and actions before them, as they say Alexander the Great imitated Achilles, Cæsar Alexander, and Scipio Cyrus. And whoever reads the life of Cyrus written by Xenophon, will perceive in the life of Scipio how gloriously he imitated the former, and how, in chastity, affability, humanity, and liberality Scipio conformed to those qualities of Cyrus as described by Xenophon.

A wise prince should follow similar methods and never remain idle in peaceful times, but industriously make good use of them, so that when fortune changes she may find him prepared to resist her blows, and to prevail in adversity.

2. Why Princes Are Praised or Blamed

It now remains to be seen what are the methods and rules for a prince as regards his subjects and friends. And as I know that many have written of this, I fear that my writing about it may be deemed presumptuous, differing as I do, especially in this matter, from the opinions of others. But my intention being to write something of use to those who understand, it appears to me more proper to go to the real truth of the matter than to its imagination; and many have imagined republics and principalities which have never been seen or known to exist in reality; for how we live is so far removed from how we ought to live, that he who abandons what is done for what ought to be done, will rather learn to bring about his own ruin than his preservation. A man who wishes to make a profession of goodness in everything must necessarily come to grief among so many who are not good. Therefore it is necessary for a prince, who wishes to maintain himself, to learn how not to be good, and to use this knowledge and not use it, according to the necessity of the case.

Leaving on one side, then, those things which concern only an imaginary prince, and speaking of those that are real, I state that all men, and especially princes, who are placed at a greater height, are reputed for certain qualities which bring them either praise or blame. Thus one is considered liberal, another *misero* or miserly (using a Tuscan term, seeing that *avaro* with us still means one who is rapaciously acquisitive and *misero* one who makes grudging use of his own); one a free giver, another rapacious; one cruel, another merciful; one a breaker of his word, another trustworthy; one effeminate and pusillanimous, another fierce and high-spirited; one humane, another haughty; one lascivious, another chaste; one frank, another astute; one hard, another easy; one serious, another frivolous; one religious, another an unbeliever, and so on. I know that every one will admit that it would be highly praiseworthy in a prince to possess all the above-named qualities that are reputed good, but as they cannot all be possessed or observed, human conditions not permitting of it, it is necessary that he should be prudent enough to avoid scandal of those vices which would lose him the state, and guard himself if possible against those which will not lose it him, but if not able to, he can indulge them with less scruple. And yet he must not mind incurring the scandal of those vices, without which it would be difficult to save the state, for if one considers well, it will be found that some things which seem virtues would, if followed, lead to one's ruin, and some others which appear vices result in one's greater security and well-being.

3. Liberality and Niggardliness

Beginning now with the first qualities above named, I say that it would be well to be considered liberal; nevertheless liberality such as the world understands it will injure you, because if used virtuously and in the proper way, it will not be known, and you will incur the disgrace of the contrary vice. But one who wishes to obtain the reputation of liberality among men, must not omit every kind of sumptuous display, and to such an extent that a prince of this character will consume by such means all his resources, and will be at last compelled, if he wishes to maintain his name for liberality, to impose heavy taxes on his people, become extortionate, and do everything possible to obtain money. This will make his subjects begin to hate him, and he will be little esteemed being poor, so that having by this liberality injured many and benefited but few, he will feel the first little disturbance and be endangered by every peril. If he recognises this and wishes to change his system, he incurs at once the charge of niggardliness.

A prince, therefore, not being able to exercise this virtue of liberality without risk if it be known, must not, if he be prudent, object to be called miserly. In course of time he will be thought more liberal, when it is seen that by his parsimony his revenue is sufficient, that he can defend himself against those who make war on him, and undertake enterprises without burdening his people, so that he is really liberal to all those from whom he does not take, who are infinite in number, and niggardly to all to whom he does not give, who are few. In our times we have seen nothing great done except by those who have been esteemed niggardly; the others have all been ruined. Pope Julius II, although he had made use of a reputation for liberality in order to attain the papacy, did not seek to retain it afterwards, so that he might be able to wage war. The present King of Fránce has carried on so many wars without imposing an extraordinary tax, because his extra expenses were covered by the parsimony he had so long practised. The present King of Spain, if he had been thought liberal, would not have engaged in and been successful in so many enterprises.

For these reasons a prince must care little for the reputation of being a miser, if he wishes to avoid robbing his subjects, if he wishes to be able to defend himself, to avoid becoming poor and contemptible, and not to be forced to become rapacious; this niggardliness is one of those vices which enable him to reign. If it is said that Cæsar attained the empire through liberality, and that many others have reached the highest positions through being liberal or being thought so, I would reply that you are either a prince already or else on the way to become one. In the first case, this liberality is harmful; in the second, it is certainly necessary to be considered liberal. Cæsar was one of those who wished to attain the mastery over Rome, but if after attaining it he had lived and had not moderated his expenses, he would have destroyed that empire. And should any one reply that there have been many princes, who have done great things with their armies, who have been thought extremely liberal, I would answer by saying that the prince may either spend his own wealth and that of his subjects or the wealth of others. In the first case he must be sparing, but for the rest he must not neglect to be very liberal. The liberality is very necessary to a prince who marches with his armies, and lives by plunder, sack and ransom, and is dealing with the wealth of others, for without it he would not be followed by his soldiers. And you may be very generous indeed with what is not the property of yourself or your subjects, as were Cyrus, Cæsar, and Alexander; for spending the wealth of others will not diminish your reputation, but increase it, only spending your own resources will injure you. There is nothing which destroys itself so much as liberality, for by using it you lose the power of using it, and become either poor and despicable, or, to escape poverty, rapacious and hated. And of all things that a prince must guard against, the most important are being despicable or hated, and liberality will lead you to one or other of these conditions. It is, therefore, wiser to have the name of a miser, which produces disgrace without hatred, than to incur of necessity the name of being rapacious, which produces both disgrace and hatred.

4. Cruelty and Clemency: Is It Better to Be Loved or Feared?

Proceeding to the other qualities before named, I say that every prince must desire to be considered merciful and not cruel. He must, however, take care not to misuse this mercifulness. Cesare Borgia was considered cruel, but his cruelty had brought order to the Romagna, united it, and reduced it to peace and fealty. If this is considered well, it will be seen that he was really much more merciful than the Florentine people, who, to avoid the name of cruelty, allowed Pistoia to be destroyed. A prince, therefore, must not mind incurring the charge of cruelty for the purpose of keeping his subjects united and faithful; for, with a very few examples, he will be more merciful than those who, from excess of tenderness, allow disorders to arise, from whence spring bloodshed and rapine; for these as a rule injure the whole community, while the executions carried out by the prince injure only individuals. And of all princes, it is impossible for a new prince to escape the reputation of cruelty, new states being always full of dangers. Wherefore Virgil through the mouth of Dido says:

Res dura, et regni novitas me talia cogunt
Moliri, et late fines custode tueri.

Nevertheless, he must be cautious in believing and acting, and must not be afraid of his own shadow, and must proceed in a temperate manner with prudence and humanity, so that too much confidence does not render him incautious, and too much diffidence does not render him intolerant.

From this arises the question whether it is better to be loved more than feared, or feared more than loved. The reply is, that one ought to be both feared and loved, but as it is difficult for the two to go together, it is much safer to be feared than loved, if one of the two has to be wanting. For it may be said of men in general that they are ungrateful, voluble, dissemblers, anxious to avoid danger, and covetous of gain; as long as you benefit them, they are entirely yours; they offer you their blood, their goods, their life, and their children, as I have before said, when the necessity is remote; but when it approaches, they revolt. And the prince who has relied solely on their words, without making other preparations, is ruined; for the friendship which is gained by purchase and not through grandeur and nobility of spirit is bought but not secured, and at a pinch is not to be expended in your service. And men have less scruple in offending one who makes himself loved than one who makes himself feared; for love is held by a chain of obligation which, men being selfish, is broken whenever it serves their purpose; but fear is maintained by a dread of punishment which never fails.

Still, a prince should make himself feared in such a way that if he does not gain love, he at any rate avoids hatred; for fear and the absence of hatred may well go together, and will be always attained by one who abstains from interfering with the property of his citizens and subjects or with their women. And when he is obliged to take the life of any one, let him do so when there is a proper justification and manifest reason for it; but above all he must abstain from taking the property of others, for men forget more easily the death of their father than the loss of their patrimony. Then also pretexts for seizing property are never wanting, and one who begins to live by rapine will always find some reason for taking the goods of others, whereas causes for taking life are rarer and more fleeting.

But when the prince is with his army and has a large number of soldiers under his control, then it is extremely necessary that he should not mind being thought cruel; for without this reputation he could not keep an army united or disposed to any duty. Among the noteworthy actions of Hannibal is numbered this, that although he had an enormous army, composed of men of all nations and fighting in foreign countries, there never arose any dissension either among them or against the prince, either in good fortune or in bad. This could not be due to anything but his inhuman cruelty, which together with his infinite other virtues, made him always venerated and terrible in the sight of his soldiers, and without it his other virtues would not have sufficed to produce that effect. Thoughtless writers admire on the one hand his actions, and on the other blame the principal cause of them.

And that it is true that his other virtues would not have sufficed may be seen from the case of Scipio (famous not only in regard to his own times, but all times of which memory remains), whose armies rebelled against him in Spain, which arose from nothing but his excessive kindness, which allowed more licence to the soldiers than was consonant with military discipline. He was reproached with this in the senate by Fabius Maximus, who called him a corrupter of the Roman militia. Locri having been destroyed by one of Scipio's officers was not revenged by him, nor was the insolence of that officer punished, simply by reason of his easy nature; so much so, that some one wishing to excuse him in the senate, said that there were many men who knew rather how not to err, than how to correct the errors of others. This disposition would in time have tarnished the fame and glory of Scipio had he persevered in it under the empire, but living under the rule of the senate this harmful quality was not only concealed but became a glory to him.

I conclude, therefore, with regard to being feared and loved, that men love at their own free will, but fear at the will of the prince, and that a wise prince must rely on what is in his power and not on what is in the power of others, and he must only contrive to avoid incurring hatred, as has been explained.

5. In What Way Princes Must Keep Faith

How laudable it is for a prince to keep good faith and live with integrity, and not with astuteness, every one knows. Still the experience of our times shows those princes to have done great things who have had little regard for good faith, and have been able by astuteness to confuse men's brains, and who have ultimately overcome those who have made loyalty their foundation.

You must know, then, that there are two methods of fighting, the one by law, the other by force: the first method is that of men, the second of beasts; but as the first method is often insufficient, one must have recourse to the second. It is therefore necessary for a prince to know well how to use both the beast and the man. This was covertly taught to rulers by ancient writers, who relate how Achilles and many others of those ancient princes were given to Chiron the centaur to be brought up and educated under his discipline. The parable of this semi-animal, semi-human teacher is meant to indicate that a prince must know how to use both natures, and that the one without the other is not durable.

A prince being thus obliged to know well how to act as a beast must imitate the fox and the lion, for the lion cannot protect himself from traps, and the fox cannot defend himself from wolves. One must therefore be a fox to recognise traps, and a lion to frighten wolves. Those that wish to be only lions do not understand this. Therefore, a prudent ruler ought not to keep faith when by so doing it would be against his interest, and when the reasons which made him bind himself no longer exist. If men were all good, this precept would not be a good one;

but as they are bad, and would not observe their faith with you, so you are not bound to keep faith with them. Nor have legitimate grounds ever failed a prince who wished to show colourable excuse for the non-fulfilment of his promise. Of this one could furnish an infinite number of modern examples, and show how many times peace has been broken, and how many promises rendered worthless, by the faithlessness of princes, and those that have been best able to imitate the fox have succeeded best. But it is necessary to be able to disguise this character well, and to be a great feigner and dissembler; and men are so simple and so ready to obey present necessities, that one who deceives will always find those who allow themselves to be deceived.

I will only mention one modern instance. Alexander VI did nothing else but deceive men, he thought of nothing else, and found the occasion for it; no man was ever more able to give assurances, or affirmed things with stronger oaths, and no man observed them less; however, he always succeeded in his deceptions, as he well knew this aspect of things.

It is not, therefore, necessary for a prince to have all the above-named qualities, but it is very necessary to seem to have them. I would even be bold to say that to possess them and always to observe them is dangerous, but to appear to possess them is useful. Thus it is well to seem merciful, faithful, humane, sincere, religious, and also to be so; but you must have the mind so disposed that when it is needful to be otherwise you may be able to change to the opposite qualities. And it must be understood that a prince, and especially a new prince, cannot observe all those things which are considered good in men, being often obliged, in order to maintain the state, to act against faith, against charity, against humanity, and against religion. And, therefore, he must have a mind disposed to adapt itself according to the wind, and as the variations of fortune dictate, and, as I said before, not deviate from what is good, if possible, but be able to do evil if constrained.

A prince must take great care that nothing goes out of his mouth which is not full of the above-named five qualities, and, to see and hear him, he should seem to be all mercy, faith, integrity, humanity, and religion. And nothing is more necessary than to seem to have this last quality, for men in general judge more by the eyes than by the hands, for every one can see, but very few have to feel. Everybody sees what you appear to be, few feel what you are, and those few will not dare to oppose themselves to the many, who have the majesty of the state to defend them; and in the actions of men, and especially of princes, from which there is no appeal, the end justifies the means. Let a prince therefore aim at conquering and maintaining the state, and the means will always be judged honourable and praised by every one, for the vulgar is always taken by appearances and the issue of the event; and the world consists only of the vulgar, and the few who are not vulgar are isolated when the many have a rallying point in the prince. A certain prince of the present time, whom it is well not to name, never does anything but preach peace and good faith, but he is really a great enemy to both, and either of them, had he observed them, would have lost him state or reputation on many occasions.

6. Princes Must Avoid Being Despised or Hated

But as I have now spoken of the most important of the qualities in question, I will now deal briefly and generally with the rest. The prince must, as already stated, avoid those things which will make him hated or despised; and whenever he succeeds in this, he will have done his part, and will find no danger in other vices. He will chiefly become hated, as I said, by being rapacious, and usurping the property and women of his subjects, which he must abstain from doing, and whenever one does not attack the property or honour of the generality of men, they will live contented;

and one will only have to combat the ambition of a few, who can be easily held in check in many ways. He is rendered despicable by being thought changeable, frivolous, effeminate, timid, and irresolute; which a prince must guard against as a rock of danger, and so contrive that his actions show grandeur, spirit, gravity, and fortitude; and as to the government of his subjects, let his sentence be irrevocable, and let him adhere to his decisions so that no one may think of deceiving or cozening him.

The prince who creates such an opinion of himself gets a great reputation, and it is very difficult to conspire against one who has a great reputation, and he will not easily be attacked, so long as it is known that he is capable and reverenced by his subjects. For a prince must have two kinds of fear: one internal as regards his subjects, one external as regards foreign powers. From the latter he can defend himself with good arms and good friends, and he will always have good friends if he has good arms; and internal matters will always remain quiet, if they are not perturbed by conspiracy and there is no disturbance from without; and even if external powers sought to attack him, if he has ruled and lived as I have described, he will always if he stands firm, be able to sustain every shock, as I have shown that Nabis the Spartan did. But with regard to the subjects, if not acted on from outside, it is still to be feared lest they conspire in secret, from which the prince may guard himself well by avoiding hatred and contempt, and keeping the people satisfied with him, which it is necessary to accomplish, as has been related at length. And one of the most potent remedies that a prince has against conspiracies, is that of not being hated by the mass of the people; for whoever conspires always believes that he will satisfy the people by the death of their prince; but if he thought to offend them by doing this, he would fear to engage in such an undertaking, for the difficulties that conspirators have to meet are infinite. Experience shows that there have been very many conspiracies, but few have turned out well, for whoever conspires cannot act alone, and cannot find companions except among those who are discontented; and as soon as you have disclosed your intention to a malcontent, you give him the means of satisfying himself, for by revealing it he can hope to secure everything he wants; to such an extent that seeing a certain gain by doing this, and seeing on the other hand only a doubtful one and full of danger, he must either be a rare friend to you or else a very bitter enemy to the prince if he keeps faith with you. And to express the matter in a few words, I say, that on the side of the conspirator there is nothing but fear, jealousy, suspicion, and dread of punishment which frightens him; and on the side of the prince there is the majesty of government, the laws, the protection of friends and of the state which guard him. When to these things is added the goodwill of the people, it is impossible that any one should have the temerity to conspire. For whereas generally a conspirator has to fear before the execution of his plot, in this case, having the people for an enemy, he must also fear after his crime is accomplished, and thus he is not able to hope for any refuge.

Numberless instances might be given of this, but I will content myself with one which took place within the memory of our fathers. Messer Annibale Bentivogli, Prince of Bologna, ancestor of the present Messer Annibale, was killed by the Canneschi, who conspired against him. He left no relations but Messer Giovanni, who was then an infant, but after the murder the people rose up and killed all the Canneschi. This arose from the popular goodwill that the house of Bentivogli enjoyed at that time, which was so great that, as there was nobody left after the death of Annibale who could govern the state, the Bolognese hearing that there was one of the Bentivogli family in Florence, who had till then been thought the son of a blacksmith, came to fetch him and gave him the government of the city, and it was governed by him until Messer Giovanni was old enough to assume the government.

I conclude, therefore, that a prince need trouble little about conspiracies when the people are well disposed, but when they are hostile and hold him in hatred, then he must fear everything and everybody. Well-ordered states and wise princes have studied diligently not to drive the nobles to desperation, and to satisfy the populace and keep it contented, for this is one of the most important matters that a prince has to deal with.

Among the kingdoms that are well ordered and governed in our time is France, and there we find numberless good institutions on which depend the liberty and security of the king; of these the chief is the parliament and its authority, because he who established that kingdom, knowing the ambition and insolence of the great nobles, deemed it necessary to have a bit in their mouths to check them. And knowing on the other hand the hatred of the mass of the people against the great, based on fear, and wishing to secure them, he did not wish to make this the special care of the king, to relieve him of the dissatisfaction that he might incur among the nobles by favouring the people, and among the people by favouring the nobles. He therefore established a third judge that, without direct charge of the king, kept in check the great and favoured the lesser people. Nor could any better or more prudent measure have been adopted, nor better precaution for the safety of the king and the kingdom. From which another notable rule can be drawn, that princes should let the carrying out of unpopular duties devolve on others, and bestow favours themselves. I conclude again by saying that a prince must esteem his nobles, but not make himself hated by the populace.

7. The Usefulness of Fortresses

Some princes, in order to hold their possessions securely, have disarmed their citizens, some others have kept their subject lands divided into parts, others have fomented enmities against themselves, others have endeavoured to win over those whom they suspected at the commencement of their rule: some have constructed fortresses, others have cast them down and destroyed them. And although one cannot pronounce a definite judgment as to these things without going into the particulars of the state to which such a deliberation is to be applied, still I will speak in such a general way as the matter will permit.

A new prince has never been known to disarm his subjects, on the contrary, when he has found them disarmed he has always armed them, for by arming them these arms become your own, those that you suspected become faithful and those that were faithful remain so, and from being merely subjects become your partisans. And since all the subjects cannot be armed, when you give the privilege of arms to some, you can deal more safely with the others; and this different treatment that they recognise renders your men more obliged to you. The others will excuse you, judging that those have necessarily greater merit who have greater danger and heavier duties. But when you disarm them, you commence to offend them and show that you distrust them either through cowardice or lack of confidence, and both of these opinions generate hatred against you. And as you cannot remain unarmed, you are obliged to resort to a mercenary militia, of which we have already stated the value; and even if it were good it cannot be sufficient in number to defend you against powerful enemies and suspected subjects. Therefore, as I have said, a new prince in a new dominion always has his subjects armed. History is full of such examples.

But when a prince acquires a new state as an addition to his old one, then it is necessary to disarm that state, except those who in acquiring it have sided with you; and even these one must, when time and opportunity serve, render weak and effeminate, and arrange things so that all the arms of the new state are in the hands of your soldiers who live near you in your old state.

Our forefathers and those who were esteemed wise used to say that it was necessary to hold Pistoia by means of factions and Pisa with fortresses, and for this purpose they fomented differences in some of their subject towns in order to possess them more easily. In those days when there was a balance of power in Italy, this was doubtless well done, but does not seem to me to be a good precept for the present time, for I do not believe that the divisions thus created ever do any good; on the contrary it is certain that when the enemy approaches, the cities thus divided will be at once lost, for the weaker faction will always side with the enemy and the other will not be able to stand.

The Venetians, actuated, I believe, by the aforesaid motives, fomented the Guelf and Ghibelline factions in the cities subject to them, and although they never allowed them to come to bloodshed, they yet encouraged these differences among them, so that the citizens, being occupied in their own quarrels, might not act against them. This, however, did not avail them anything, as was seen when, after the defeat of Vailà, a part of those subjects immediately took courage and seized the whole state. Such methods, besides, argue weakness in a prince, for in a strong government such dissensions will never be permitted. They are profitable only in time of peace, as by such means it is easy to manage one's subjects, but when it comes to war, the fallacy of such a policy is at once shown.

Without doubt princes become great when they overcome difficulties and opposition, and therefore fortune, especially when it wants to render a new prince great, who has greater need of gaining a great reputation than a hereditary prince, raises up enemies and compels him to undertake wars against them, so that he may have cause to overcome them, and thus climb up higher by means of that ladder which his enemies have brought him. There are many who think therefore that a wise prince ought, when he has the chance, to foment astutely some enmity, so that by suppressing it he will augment his greatness.

Princes, and especially new ones, have found more faith and more usefulness in those men, whom at the beginning of their power they regarded with suspicion, than in those they at first confided in. Pandolfo Petrucci, Prince of Siena, governed his state more by those whom he suspected than by others. But of this we cannot speak at large, as it strays from the subject; I will merely say that these men who at the beginning of a new government were enemies, if they are of a kind to need support to maintain their position, can be very easily gained by the prince, and they are the more compelled to serve him faithfully as they know they must by their deeds cancel the bad opinion previously held of them, and thus the prince will always derive greater help from them than from those who, serving him with greater security, neglect his interests.

And as the matter requires it, I will not omit to remind a prince who has newly taken a state with the secret help of its inhabitants, that he must consider well the motives that have induced those who have favoured him to do so, and if it is not natural affection for him, but only because they were not contented with the state as it was, he will have great trouble and difficulty in maintaining their friendship, because it will be impossible for him to content them. And on well examining the cause of this in the examples drawn from ancient and modern times it will be seen that it is much easier to gain the friendship of those men who were contented with the previous condition and were therefore at first enemies, than that those who not being contented, became his friends and helped him to occupy it.

It has been the custom of princes in order to be able to hold their state securely, to erect fortresses, as a bridle and bit to those who have designs against them, and in order to have a secure refuge against a sudden assault. I approve this method, because it was anciently used. Nevertheless, Messer Niccolò Vitelli has been seen in our own time to destroy two fortresses in Città di Castello in order to keep that state.

Guid'Ubaldo, Duke of Urbino, on returning to his dominions from which he had been driven by Cesare Borgia, razed to their foundations all the fortresses of that province, and considered that without them it would be more difficult for him to lose the state again. The Bentivogli, in returning to Bologna, took similar measures. Therefore fortresses may or may not be useful according to the times; if they do good in one way, they do harm in another. The question may be discussed thus: a prince who fears his own people more than foreigners ought to build fortresses, but he who has greater fear of foreigners than of his own people ought to do without them. The castle of Milan built by Francesco Sforza has given and will give more trouble to the house of Sforza than any other disorder in that state. Therefore the best fortress is to be found in the love of the people, for although you may have fortresses they will not save you if you are hated by the people. When once the people have taken arms against you, there will never be lacking foreigners to assist them. In our times we do not see that they have profited any ruler, except the Countess of Forlì on the death of her consort Count Girolamo, for she was thus enabled to escape the popular rising and await help from Milan and recover the state; the circumstances being then such that no foreigner could assist the people. But afterwards they were of little use to her when Cesare Borgia attacked her and the people being hostile to her allied themselves with the foreigner. So that then and before it would have been safer for her not to have been hated by the people than to have had the fortresses. Having considered these things I would therefore praise the one who erects fortresses and the one who does not, and would blame any one who, trusting in them, recks little of being hated by his people.

8. *How Princes Gain Reputation*

Nothing causes a prince to be so much esteemed as great enterprises and giving proof of prowess. We have in our own day Ferdinand, King of Aragon, the present King of Spain. He may almost be termed a new prince, because from a weak king he has become for fame and glory the first king in Christendom, and if you regard his actions you will find them all very great and some of them extraordinary. At the beginning of his reign he assailed Granada, and that enterprise was the foundation of his state. At first he did it at his leisure and without fear of being interfered with; he kept the minds of the barons of Castile occupied in this enterprise, so that thinking only of that war they did not think of making innovations, and he thus acquired reputation and power over them without their being aware of it. He was able with the money of the Church and the people to maintain his armies, and by that long war to lay the foundations of his military power, which afterwards has made him famous. Besides this, to be able to undertake greater enterprises, and always under the pretext of religion, he had recourse to a pious cruelty, driving out the Moors from his kingdom and despoiling them. No more miserable or unusual example can be found. He also attacked Africa under the same pretext, undertook his Italian enterprise, and has lately attacked France; so that he has continually contrived great things, which have kept his subjects' minds uncertain and astonished, and occupied in watching their result. And these actions have arisen one out of the other, so that they have left no time for men to settle down and act against him.

It is also very profitable for a prince to give some outstanding example of his greatness in the internal administration, like those related of Messer Bernabò of Milan. When it happens that some one does something extraordinary, either good or evil, in civil life, he must find such means of rewarding or punishing him which will be much talked about. And above all a prince must endeavour in every action to obtain fame for being great and excellent.

A prince is further esteemed when he is a true friend or a true enemy, when, that is, he declares himself without reserve in favour of some one or against another. This policy is always more useful than remaining neutral. For if two neighbouring powers come to blows, they are either such that if one wins, you will have to fear the victor, or else not. In either of these two cases it will be better for you to declare yourself openly and make war, because in the first case if you do not declare yourself, you will fall a prey to the victor, to the pleasure and satisfaction of the one who has been defeated, and you will have no reason nor anything to defend you and nobody to receive you. For, whoever wins will not desire friends whom he suspects and who do not help him when in trouble, and whoever loses will not receive you as you did not take up arms to venture yourself in his cause.

Antiochus went to Greece, being sent by the Ætolians to expel the Romans. He sent orators to the Achaeians who were friends of the Romans to encourage them to remain neutral; on the other hand the Romans persuaded them to take up arms on their side. The matter was brought before the council of the Achaeians for deliberation, where the ambassador of Antiochus sought to persuade them to remain neutral, to which the Roman ambassador replied: "As to what is said that it is best and most useful for your state not to meddle in our war, nothing is further from the truth; for if you do not meddle in it you will become, without any favour or any reputation, the prize of the victor."

And it will always happen that the one who is not your friend will want you to remain neutral, and the one who is your friend will require you to declare yourself by taking arms. Irresolute princes, to avoid present dangers, usually follow the way of neutrality and are mostly ruined by it. But when the prince declares himself frankly in favour of one side, if the one to whom you adhere conquers, even if he is powerful and you remain at his discretion, he is under an obligation to you and friendship has been established, and men are never so dishonest as to oppress you with such a patent ingratitude. Moreover, victories are never so prosperous that the victor does not need to have some scruples, especially as to justice. But if your ally loses, you are sheltered by him, and so long as he can, he will assist you; you become the companion of a fortune which may rise again. In the second case, when those who fight are such that you have nothing to fear from the victor, it is still more prudent on your part to adhere to one; for you go to the ruin of one with the help of him who ought to save him if he were wise, and if he conquers he rests at your discretion, and it is impossible that he should not conquer with your help.

And here it should be noted that a prince ought never to make common cause with one more powerful than himself to injure another, unless necessity forces him to it, as before said; for if he wins you rest in his power, and princes must avoid as much as possible being under the will and pleasure of others. The Venetians united with France against the Duke of Milan, although they could have avoided that alliance, and from it resulted their own ruin. But when one cannot avoid it, as happened in the case of the Florentines when the Pope and Spain went with their armies to attack Lombardy, then the prince ought to join for the above reasons. Let no state believe that it can always follow a safe policy, rather let it think that all are doubtful. This is found in the nature of things, that one never tries to avoid one difficulty without running into another, but prudence consists in being able to know the nature of the difficulties, and taking the least harmful as good.

A prince must also show himself a lover of merit, give preferment to the able, and honour those who excel in every art. Moreover he must encourage his citizens to follow their callings quietly, whether in commerce, or agriculture, or any other trade that men follow, so that this one shall not refrain from improving his possessions through fear that they may be taken from him, and that one from starting a trade for fear of taxes; but he should offer rewards to whoever does these things, and to whoever seeks in any way to improve his city or state. Besides this, he ought, at convenient seasons of the year, to keep the people occupied with festivals and shows; and as every city is divided either into guilds or into classes, he ought to pay attention to all these groups, mingle with them from time to time, and give them an example of his humanity and munificence, always upholding, however, the majesty of his dignity, which must never be allowed to fail in anything whatever.

CHAPTER 12

THE PROTESTANT REFORMATION

RENAISSANCE and Reformation are inextricably interwoven with the birth and growth of the modern national state. In the field of secular thought and experience, the Renaissance brought about the rediscovery of the ancient world and witnessed the immense broadening of man's horizon through the discovery of the New World. In the field of religious thought and experience, the Renaissance opened the gates to a new religious world through the Protestant Reformation.

The first leaders of the Reformation denied any revolutionary intentions and merely claimed to return to the early sources of Christianity, faith and the Scriptures. In this sense, Protestantism was a part of the general process of rebirth, the religious aspect of the Renaissance. In the fifteenth century, the conciliar movement had attempted to reform the church from within but failed. Yet in its very failure it had revived the important conception of the congregational character of church authority, with its corollary that office was in the nature of a trusteeship rather than an inalienable power. When reform from within failed, revolution from without took its place.

Prior to the thirteenth century, as long as the church had to withstand the attacks of critics who did not take any religion seriously, it was able to win easily, either by disregarding its critics, by trying to persuade them, or by burning them alive on the stake. The strength of reform movements from the thirteenth century on lay in the fact that the critics of Rome were passionately religious. They assailed the papacy for having lost the original ideals of the Christian faith and for having become corrupted by the worldly ambitions of lust, wealth, and power. For three centuries, therefore, the reform movements within the church had to be held down by all sorts of compulsion and kept in isolation; in the end, the pressure for unity within the church proved stronger than the forces for reform.

In the sixteenth century, however, the reformist tendencies—now driven into revolution by the obstinacy of the church—were more successful because they were allied with other social forces of the time. In particular, wherever Protestant Reform, as in Northern Germany, England, Scandinavia, was associated with monarchy, the strongest power of the age, its victory was never in question. Where, on the other hand, Protestantism was not favored by royal encouragement, as in France, it was unlikely to succeed. Nowhere was the issue purely religious; in all countries it was mixed with political, dynastic, economic, and diplomatic considerations. Although the age of the Reformation itself was truly religious, religion was readily used by unscrupulous persons to cloak less lofty aspirations.

From the viewpoint of the expansion of political liberty, the first Protestant church, Lutheranism, had little effect, either in Germany or elsewhere. Martin Luther (1483–1546) stressed the inner aspects of religious experience, faith rather than good works: "Faith alone is the righteousness of a Christian and the fulfilling of all the commandments" (*Treatise on Christian Liberty*, 1520). Luther argued that liberty is in the conscience and spirit of man, and has no relation to his political or social condition, for "that is making Christian liberty an utterly carnal thing." His ideas on government and the relations of rulers and ruled were most clearly and systematically expressed in his *Secular Authority: To What Extent It Should Be Obeyed* (1523). Luther emphasized that government is ordained by God, and that the subjects must obey their rulers, even though their rule be unjust or cruel. His profound pessimism about men in all stations—rulers or ruled—was reflected in his statement that "the world is too wicked, and does not deserve to have many wise and pious princes. Frogs need storks."

In his assertion of the equality of all Christians as Christians he was of revolutionary import, and his doctrine of the priesthood of all Christians contained possibilities that were more fully exploited later on in England, Scotland, and North America. Though he defended the highly unorthodox view that belief or unbelief is a matter of one's conscience, that faith is an act and expression of freedom, and that it cannot be imposed by force, the bold break with Rome was not accompanied in Luther or Lutheranism by any parallel social or political philosophy. On the contrary, Luther's religious radicalism was matched by extreme conservatism in social and political affairs. Supported by the absolutist princes of Northern Germany, Luther stressed the duty of the subject to obey the commands of his king.

Shortly after Luther published his revolutionary religious theses, German peasants—driven by social and political oppression, and translating too quickly the Lutheran ideals of Christian equality from theological into practical terms—began to rebel. This rebellion of 1525 was the only genuine popular revolution in German history, and the subsequent history of the German people might have been different if the rebellion had succeeded at least in part. Luther instigated the princes to take the sternest measures, including wholesale bloodshed, against the "mad dogs," "scoundrels," and "swine"—as he called the rebelling peasants.

Thus for practical purposes Lutheranism evolved into a faithful ally of political absolutism. Its most serious effect on the German people was to strengthen their fatal habit of nourishing ideals of freedom in the realm of the spirit but of submitting without question to the authority of the state in practical affairs. Luther himself was fully aware that princes are "usually the greatest fools or scoundrels on earth"; yet he insisted on the duty of subjects to obey such impious princes, because, he said, the rest of the world is wicked, too, and does not deserve virtuous rulers. Luther added to his strong respect for the state an equally passionate feeling of German nationalism and even racialism; thus he became—the only Protestant leader to have such progeny—one of the spiritual ancestors of Prussian statism and German Nazism.

After Luther's death, the Religious Peace of Augsburg (1555) settled the problem of religious division in the German states by the principle of *cuius regio eius religio,* according to which the ruler of the country determined the religion of its inhabitants. This principle was more liberal than the medieval method of imposing uniformity of belief from which there was no escape, because under the policy of the Peace of Augsburg, religious dissidents were free to adhere to their religion, provided they emigrated.

No doubt emigration was less harsh than the stake; yet by accepting such a principle Germany lost a vital opportunity of learning toleration. In Holland, England, and North America toleration of religious minorities preceded that of political opposition, and the tradition of liberalism in the English-speaking countries in particular cannot be understood apart from the tradition of religious nonconformity. Frederick the Great referred to himself in his *Political Testament* as the "Pope of the Lutherans," and until 1918 the rulers of Protestant states in Germany were simultaneously the supreme bishops of their state churches. Thus, instead of one religious authoritarianism, Germany had two after the Reformation. Yet by the fact of establishing itself as the first Reform church independent of Rome, Lutheranism encouraged the formation of independent churches elsewhere. As more churches came into existence, increased mutual toleration was inevitable; the relative power of each religion or sect declined in proportion to the growing number of all.

As long as Protestantism was mainly Lutheran, it made little headway in France. But there was a vigorous tradition of anticlericalism and antipapalism in France from the Middle Ages on, and the sense of urgent change grew stronger in the sixteenth century. Protestantism became a national force in France, with an intellectual character of its own, after the appearance of a French leader, John Calvin (1509–1564). In 1534 Calvin, forced to leave France for religious reasons, went to Switzerland, where Protestantism had spread rapidly. In 1536 he wrote the *Institutes of the Christian Religion,* his principal work and still the chief source of Calvinist doctrine. With only a few short interruptions, he stayed in Switzerland for the rest of his life; he governed Geneva from 1536 to 1538, and again from 1541 to 1564, the year of his death. His regime was one of ruthless terror. Though Calvin's theological doctrines did not differ substantially from those of Luther, his impact on history did. Calvinism spread to France, Holland, Scotland, and the English colonies in North America.

Unlike Luther, Calvin admitted—in exceptional cases only, to be sure— the right of resistance to tyrannical rulers, provided that resistance was in the hands of magistrates and organized estates, rather than lawless mobs, or in the hands of a secular savior selected by God to deliver the people from tyranny. In the total doctrine of Calvin, the stress was more on obedience than on resistance. Yet the circumstances of persecution in France and Holland in particular drove Calvinists into active resistance. In Holland, Calvinism was allied with the national movement of liberation from Spain, and in the end it won over the majority of the nation. In France, the monarchy needed the friendship of the papacy against the Habsburgs in the struggle for Italy, and, domestically, the strongly centralizing tendencies of the newly developing national state were opposed to the Calvinist demands for local autonomy. Calvinism was thus put in a position in which it could be easily attacked by its opponents as antinational. A considerable proportion of the French aristocracy, perhaps one third, sympathized with the Protestant cause, and regional, provincial issues were also dragged into religious controversy.

Passion ran high on both sides. Shortly after the "War of Religion" had broken out in France (it lasted, with interruptions, from 1562 to 1593), the Huguenots invited German and English troops to aid them in the civil war. Foreign intervention in civil war is particularly odious if unsuccessful—and the Huguenots lost. On its side, the royalist, nationalist, Catholic party acted with more ruthlessness against its opponents than was customary in French life, and it is doubtful whether the Revolution of 1789, another "war of religion," witnessed as much brutality as the War of Religion in the sixteenth century.

The anti-Protestant frenzy, carefully nursed, with the blessing of Rome, by the royalist-Catholic party, came to a climax in the Massacre of St. Bartholomew (August 24, 1572), in which thirty thousand Huguenots lost their lives. The head of Admiral Coligny, the military and political leader of the Huguenots, was sent to Pope Gregory XIII in Rome, who had also received Coligny's assassin. The happy outcome of the massacre was celebrated by the pope in a public procession and solemn mass of thanksgiving, attended by thirty-three cardinals and many other high ecclesiastic dignitaries. On September 11, 1572, Gregory praised the French king for his punishment of heretics and expressed the hope that the enterprise of suppressing Protestantism, so auspiciously begun on St. Bartholomew's day, would be carried on to the end.

Deprived of their leaders, hacked into a small minority, the Huguenots produced, in the decade following the massacre, a mass of tracts that belong to the most provocative political literature inspired by the Reformation. The best known of these Huguenot pamphlets and books is *A Defense of Liberty against Tyrants (Vindiciae contra tyrannos)*, published in Latin under the pseudonym Stephen Junius Brutus in 1579 and translated into French in 1581. Both editions were printed in Switzerland, then—as earlier and later—an island of freedom in

Europe. Many of the Huguenot pamphlets were published anonymously, for obvious reasons, and their authors were generally exiles; Switzerland, Holland, England, and Germany were among the favorite places of refuge.

The authorship of the *Vindiciae* is not completely certain; according to the longest tradition and best modern judgment, the author was Hubert Languet (1519–1581), a French scholar, lawyer, traveler, and diplomat, who spent many years in Germany. Those who dispute Languet's authorship attribute the book partly or wholly to Philippe Duplessis-Mornay (1549–1623), a young friend of Languet who probably had some connection with the *Vindiciae*, either in aiding Languet in the preparation of the original Latin manuscript or in translating the Latin text into French.

The *Vindiciae* proposes to deal with four main questions: first, whether subjects are bound to obey princes if they command what is against the law of God; second, whether it is lawful to resist a prince who infringes the law of God or ruins the church, and by whom resistance is to be offered, how, and to what extent; third, whether it is lawful to resist a prince who oppresses or ruins the commonwealth, by whom and how far such resistance is to be offered, and by what right it is permitted; fourth, whether neighboring princes or states may lawfully help, or are bound to help, the subjects of other princes who are afflicted for the cause of true religion or oppressed by manifest tyranny. As can be seen from these four questions, the purpose of the *Vindiciae* is not to give a general theory of the state but to inquire into one of its pivotal issues: the problem of *obedience*.

The substance of the answers to the four chief questions raised in the *Vindiciae* lies in the notion of contract. In fact, the argument is based on the theory of *two contracts*: the first is made between God on the one side, and the king and people jointly on the other, "that the people might be the people of God." The second contract is between the king and the people, in which the people promise to obey the king faithfully, provided that he rule justly. Both covenants in the *Vindiciae* are derived from the Old Testament; the Calvinists, like the Puritans a century later, lean heavily on the Old Testament for the idea of the covenant as the foundation of all authority.

The importance of the first covenant, that between God on one side, and king and people on the other, lies in the fact that the king's responsibility does not come to an end if he violates his promises, because the people are bound to see that the covenant, which they, too, have entered into, is fulfilled. If the king violates his share of the joint obligation, the people are entitled, nay, bound, to resist or depose him for the sake of the obligation to God. Similarly, from the second covenant between king and people follows the right of the people to resist or depose the king if he violates his obligations.

The second key idea in the *Vindiciae* is that of *trusteeship*. Speaking in terms of the Bible and Roman law, the *Vindiciae* refers to the king as a "guardian" or "tutor." The nature of trusteeship lies in the fact that whatever authority is given to the trustee, he holds, not for his own benefit, but for that of the person or persons in whose behalf he acts. Kings are made by the people, and they "hold their power and sovereignty from the people." Although God elects the king, the people establish him. No one is ever born with a crown on his head and a scepter in his hand, and no man can be a king without people, whereas people can get along without a king; kings are therefore the creations of the people, even in hereditary monarchies. The right of free election "seems in a sort buried" in hereditary monarchies, but actually it is not dead in them, because new kings receive afresh the symbols of their authority from the hands of the peers and officers of the crown, who represent the people.

The author of the *Vindiciae* anticipates one of the chief ideas of Locke by emphasizing that the purpose of setting up government is to decide civil disputes by *third-party judgments,* particularly disputes about *property*. The king is conceived as a judge rather than a legislator, and the superiority of the law over the king is asserted throughout the *Vindiciae*. The king is but an organ of the law, and it is "more profitable and convenient to obey the law, then the king who is but one man." Taking over the Calvinistic concept of the "priesthood" of all believers, the *Vindiciae* denies that the king's subjects are his "slaves or bondmen," because, considered in one body, "they are lords," and the king should therefore govern his subjects as brethren.

The third key idea of the *Vindiciae* is *resistance to tyranny*. Two kinds of tyranny are distinguished: first, that of the ruler who gains a kingdom by violence; and second, that of the ruler who, lawfully invested with his office, violates his promises and duties by the practice of tyranny. The usurper who rules justly is preferable to the legitimate monarch who rules unjustly: "Certainly I had rather that a thief should feed me, than a shepherd devour me: I had rather receive justice from a robber, than outrage from a judge: I had better be healed by an empiric, than poisoned by a doctor in physic." As to the ruler who is doubly a tyrant, because he has illegally usurped power and because he exercises it unjustly, "the meanest private man may resist and lawfully oppose such an intruding tyrant." Even tyrannicide is lawful when the ruler is a "double" tyrant. When tyrants hold office by law but exercise it unjustly, it is the right and duty of the magistrates and Estates to resist the king and, if necessary, depose and kill him.

Because the tyrant with a legitimate title to rule has been established in his office by the community as a whole, private individuals "may not unsheathe the sword against tyrants by practice." The *Vindiciae* makes it clear in numerous passages that the term "the people" is not to be taken too literally; it means the magistrates and assembly of the Estates. The presbyterian character of early Calvinist church government was aristocratic rather than democratic, and though the position of the *Vindiciae* on the right of resistance is antiauthoritarian and liberal, the liberalism is of the predemocratic age, as it existed from the sixteenth to the eighteenth centuries. The main purpose of the *Vindiciae* was to vindicate the right of conscience in religious matters, yet the general principle involved holds good for any issue of conscience.

The *Vindiciae* quickly established itself as a widely read book and inspired religious, political, and national movements of liberation. Although it was considered dangerous enough to be publicly burned by Cambridge University in 1620 (and by Oxford University, too, but much later, in 1683), an English translation appeared in 1648 under the Cromwellian regime, shortly before Charles I was executed; it was reprinted in 1689, another eventful date in the history of English liberty, when parliamentary supremacy and the right to religious non-conformity became firmly established. The main concepts of the *Vindiciae*, the contractual nature of government, popular sovereignty, political rule as trusteeship, protection of property, and, finally, the right of resistance against unjust rulers, dominated political thought until the appearance of Rousseau in the eighteenth century.

The most powerful impact of the *Vindiciae* has been on Dutch and English thought. Locke's *Two Treatises of Government* was begun in Holland, where Locke, like the author of the *Vindiciae*, lived as a refugee; it was published in 1690 in England, one year after the reprinting of the English translation of the *Vindiciae*. Locke's work had more prestige and influence not only because it was a more systematic treatment of the general theory of the state but also because the *Two Treatises of Government* was published with the self-confidence that is born of victory, whereas the *Vindiciae* showed the marks of bitterness born of defeat. What the Huguenots wanted for France, the Bloodless Revolution achieved for England in 1688.

Democracy is more than a system of government, and the democratic conception of man is based on the hypothesis that there is some area in man's conscience that cannot be subdued from the outside but must be won from within by free assent. The *Vindiciae* belongs to the family of books—not too numerous in the history of thought—that stress freedom rather than authority, consent rather than compulsion, and obedience to the inner voice of conscience rather than to the external force of the state.

I. LUTHER

Secular Authority: To What Extent It Should Be Obeyed[*]

1. Secular Authority Derives from God

We must firmly establish secular law and the sword, that no one may doubt that it is in the world by God's will and ordinance.

The passages which establish this are the following: Romans xiii, "Let every soul be

* From Martin Luther, *Secular Authority: To What Extent It Should Be Obeyed* (1523, transl. J. J. Schindel, Muhlenberg Press, 1930). By permission.

subject to power and authority, for there is no power but from God. The power that is everywhere is ordained of God. He then who resists the power resists God's ordinance. But he who resists God's ordinance shall bring himself under condemnation." Likewise, I Peter ii, "Be subject to every kind of human ordinance, whether to the king as supreme, or to the governors, as to those sent of Him for the punishing of the evil and for the reward of the good."

This penal law existed from the beginning of the world. For when Cain slew his brother he was in such great terror of being in turn killed that God specially forbade it and suspended the sword for his sake,— and no one was to slay him. He would not have had this fear if he had not seen and heard from Adam that murderers should be slain. Moreover God re-established and confirmed it after the Flood in unmistakable terms when He said, "Whoso sheds man's blood, his blood shall be shed again by man." This cannot be understood as a plague and punishment of God upon murderers; for many murderers who repent or are pardoned continue to live, and die by other means than the sword. But it is said of the right of the sword, that a murderer is guilty of death and should in justice be slain by the sword. Though justice be hindered or the sword be tardy, so that the murderer dies a natural death, the Scripture is not on that account false when it says, "Whoso sheddeth man's blood, by man shall his blood be shed." For it is men's fault or merit that this law commanded of God is not carried out; even as other commandments of God are broken.

Afterward it was also confirmed by the law of Moses, Exodus xxi, "If a man presumptuously kill thou shalt take him from My altar that he may die." And again, in the same place, "A life for a life, an eye for an eye, a tooth for a tooth, a foot for a foot, a hand for a hand, a wound for a wound, a bruise for a bruise." Christ also confirms it when He says to Peter in the garden, "He that taketh the sword shall perish by the sword," which is to be interpreted like Genesis ix, "Whoso sheddeth man's blood," etc. Doubtless Christ refers in these words to that passage and incorporates and confirms it in them. John Baptist teaches the same. When the soldiers asked him what they should do, he answered, "Do injustice or violence to no one, and be content with your wages." If the sword were not divinely appointed he should have commanded them to cease being soldiers, since he was to perfect the people and direct them in a proper Christian way. Hence it is sufficiently clear and certain that it is God's will that the sword and secular law be used for the punishment of the wicked and the protection of the upright.

2. Non-Resistance

There seems to be a powerful argument on the other side. Christ says, Matthew v, "Ye have heard that it was said to them of old: An eye for an eye, a tooth for a tooth. But I say unto you, That a man shall not resist evil, but if any one strikes thee upon the right cheek, turn to him the other also; and whoever will go to law with thee to take thy coat, let him have the cloak also, and whoever forces thee a mile, with him go two miles." Likewise Paul, Romans xii, "Dearly beloved, defend not yourselves, but give place to God's wrath, for it is written, Vengeance is mine, I will repay saith the Lord." Likewise Matthew v, "Love your enemies, do good to them that hate you." And I Peter iii, "Let no one repay evil with evil, nor railing with railing," etc. These and the like passages truly would make it appear as though in the New Testament there should be no secular sword among Christians.

Hence the sophists also say that Christ has abolished Moses' law; of such commandments they make counsels for the perfect, and divide Christian teaching and Christians into two classes. One part they call the perfect, and assign to it such counsels. To the other, the imperfect, they assign the commandments. This they do out of sheer perversity and caprice, without any scriptural basis. They do not see that in the same passage Christ lays such stress on His teaching that He is unwilling to have the least word of it set aside, and condemns to hell those who do not love their enemies. Therefore we must interpret these passages differently, so that Christ's words may apply to all alike whether they be "perfect" or "imperfect." For perfection and imperfection consist not in works and do not establish a distinct external order among Christians; but they exist in the heart, in faith and love, so that they who believe and love the most are the perfect ones, whether outwardly they be male or female, prince or peasant, monk or layman. For love and faith produce no sects or outward differences.

3. The Two Kingdoms

We must divide all the children of Adam into two classes; the first belong to the kingdom of God, the second to the kingdom of the world. Those belonging to the kingdom of God are all true believers in Christ and are subject to Christ. For Christ is the King and Lord in the kingdom of God, as the second Psalm and all the Scriptures say. For this reason He came into the world, that He might begin God's kingdom and establish it in the world. Therefore He says before Pilate, "My kingdom is not of the world, but whoever is of the truth hears My voice"; and continually in the Gospel He refers to the kingdom of God and says, "Amend your ways, the kingdom of God is at hand." Likewise, "Seek first the kingdom of God and His righteousness." He also calls the Gospel, a Gospel of the kingdom, for the reason that it teaches, governs, and contains God's kingdom.

Now observe, these people need no secular sword or law. And if all the world were composed of real Christians, that is, true believers, no prince, king, lord, sword, or law would be needed. For what were the use of them, since Christians have in their hearts the Holy Spirit, who instructs them and causes them to wrong no one, to love every one, willingly and cheerfully to suffer injustice and even death from every one. Where every wrong is suffered and every right is done, no quarrel, strife, trial, judge, penalty, law or sword is needed. Therefore, it is not possible for the secular sword and law to find any work to do among Christians, since of themselves they do much more than its laws and doctrines can demand. Just as Paul says in I Timothy i, "The law is not given for the righteous, but for the unrighteous."

Why is this? Because the righteous does of himself all and more than all that all the laws demand. But the unrighteous do nothing that the law demands, therefore they need the law to instruct, constrain, and compel them to do what is good. A good tree does not need any teaching or law to bear good fruit, its nature causes it to bear according to its kind without any law and teaching. A man would be a fool to make a book of laws and statutes telling an apple tree how to bear apples and not thorns, when it is able by its own nature to do this better than man with all his books can define and direct. Just so, by the Spirit and by faith all Christians are throughout inclined to do well and keep the law, much more than any one can teach them with all the laws, and need so far as they are concerned no commandments nor law.

You ask, Why then did God give to all men so many commandments, and why did Christ teach in the Gospel so many things to be done? To put it as briefly as possible here, Paul says that the law is given for the sake of the unrighteous, that is, that those who are not Christians may through the law be externally restrained from evil deeds, as we shall hear later. Since, however, no one is by nature Christian or pious, but every one sinful and evil, God places the restraints of the law upon them all, so that they may not dare give rein to their desires and commit outward, wicked deeds. In addition, St.

Paul gives the law another function in Romans vii and Galatians iii. It is to teach men to recognize sin, that they may be made humble unto grace and unto faith in Christ. Christ also does this here, when He teaches in Matthew v that we should not resist evil, and thereby glorifies the law and teaches how a real Christian ought to be and must be disposed, as we shall hear further on.

All who are not Christians belong to the kingdom of the world and are under the law. Since few believe and still fewer live a Christian life, do not resist the evil, and themselves do no evil, God has provided for non-Christians a different government outside the Christian estate and God's kingdom, and has subjected them to the sword, so that, even though they would do so, they cannot practice their wickedness, and that, if they do, they may not do it without fear nor in peace and prosperity. Even so a wild, savage beast is fastened with chains and bands, so that it cannot bite and tear as is its wont, although it gladly would do so; whereas a tame and gentle beast does not require this, but without any chains and bands is nevertheless harmless. If it were not so, seeing that the whole world is evil and that among thousands there is scarcely one true Christian, men would devour one another, and no one could preserve wife and child, support himself and serve God; and thus the world would be reduced to chaos. For this reason God has ordained the two governments; the spiritual, which by the Holy Spirit under Christ makes Christians and pious people, and the secular, which restrains the unchristian and wicked so that they must needs keep the peace outwardly, even against their will. So Paul interprets the secular sword, Romans xiii, and says it is not a terror to good works, but to the evil. And Peter says it is for the punishment of evil doers.

If any one attempted to rule the world by the Gospel, and put aside all secular law and the secular sword, on the plea that all are baptised and Christian, and that according to the Gospel, there is to be among them neither law nor sword, nor necessity for either, pray, what would happen? He would loose the bands and chains of the wild and savage beasts, and let them tear and mangle every one, and at the same time say they were quite tame and gentle creatures; but I would have the proof in my wounds. Just so would the wicked under the name of Christian abuse this freedom of the Gospel, carry on their knavery, and say that they were Christians subject neither to law nor sword, as some are already raving and ranting.

To such a one we must say, It is indeed true that Christians, so far as they themselves are concerned, are subject to neither law nor sword and need neither; but first take heed and fill the world with real Christians before ruling it in a Christian and evangelical manner. This you will never accomplish; for the world and the masses are and always will be unchristian, although they are all baptised and are nominally Christian. Christians, however, are few and far between, as the saying is. Therefore it is out of the question that there should be a common Christian government over the whole world, nay even over one land or company of people, since the wicked always outnumber the good. Hence a man who would venture to govern an entire country or the world with the Gospel would be like a shepherd who should place in one fold wolves, lions, eagles, and sheep together and let them freely mingle with one another and say, Help yourselves, and be good and peaceful among yourselves; the fold is open, there is plenty of food; have no fear of dogs and clubs. The sheep, forsooth, would keep the peace and would allow themselves to be fed and governed in peace, but they would not live long; nor would any beast keep from molesting another.

For this reason these two kingdoms must be sharply distinguished, and both be permitted to remain; the one to produce piety, the other to bring about external peace and prevent evil deeds; neither is sufficient in the world without the other. For no one can become pious before God by means of the secular government, without Christ's spiritual rule. Hence Christ's rule does not extend over all, but Christians are always in the minority and are in the midst of non-Christians. Where there is only secular rule or law, there, of necessity, is sheer hypocrisy, though the commandments be God's very own. Without the Holy Spirit in the heart no one becomes really pious, he may do as fine works as he will. Where, on the other hand, the spiritual government rules alone over land and people, there evil is given free rein and the door is opened for every kind of knavery; for the natural world cannot receive or comprehend spiritual things.

You see the purpose of Christ's words which we quoted above from Matthew v. They mean that Christians shall not go to law nor use the secular sword among themselves. In reality He says it only to His dear Christians. They alone also accept it and act accordingly, nor do they make counsels of it, as the sophists do, but are so inclined in their heart, through the Spirit, that they do evil to no one and willingly endure evil at every one's hands. If the whole world were Christian, all these words would apply to it and it would keep them. Since, however, it is unchristian the words do not apply to it, nor does it keep them, but is under another rule in which those who are not Christians are under external constraint and are forced to keep the peace and do what is good.

For this reason Christ did not wield the sword nor give it a place in His kingdom; for He is a King over Christians and rules by His Holy Spirit alone, without law. And although He acknowledged the sword, He nevertheless did not use it; for it is of no use in His kingdom, in which are none but the pious. Hence David of old dared not build the temple, because he had shed much blood and had borne the sword; not that he had done wrong thereby, but because he could not be a type of Christ, who without the sword was to have a kingdom of peace. It must be built by Solomon, whose name means "Frederick" or "peaceful," who had a peaceful kingdom, by which the truly peaceful kingdom of Christ, the real Frederick and Solomon, could be represented. In like manner, during the entire building of the temple not the sound of a tool was heard, as the text says; all for this reason, that Christ, without constraint and force, without law and the sword, was to have a people who serve Him freely.

This is what the prophets mean in Psalm cx, "Thy people shall be willing"; and in Isaiah xi, "They shall not hurt nor destroy in all my holy mountain"; and in Isaiah ii, "They shall beat their swords into plowshares and their spears into pruning hooks, and no one shall lift up the sword against another, neither shall they busy themselves in war anymore," etc. Whoever would apply these and similar passages wherever Christ's name is professed, would entirely pervert the Scriptures; for they are spoken only of true Christians, who really do this among themselves.

4. Obedience to Secular Authority

But perhaps you will say, Since Christians do not need the secular sword and the law, why does Paul say to all Christians, in Romans xiii, "Let all souls be subject to power and authority"? And St. Peter says, "Be subject to every human ordinance," etc., as quoted above. I answer, as I have said, that Christians, among themselves and by and for themselves, need no law or sword, since it is neither necessary nor profitable for them. Since, however, a true Christian lives and labors on earth not for himself, but for his neighbor, therefore the whole spirit of his life impels him to do even that which he need not do, but which is profitable and necessary for his neighbor. Because the sword is a very great benefit and necessary to the whole world, to preserve peace, to punish sin and to prevent evil, he submits most willingly to the rule of the sword, pays tax, honors those in authority, serves, helps, and does all he can to further the government, that it may be sustained and held in honor and fear. Although he needs none of these things for himself and it is not necessary for him to do them, yet he considers what is for the good and profit of others, as Paul teaches in Ephesians v.

He serves the State as he performs all other works of love, which he himself does not need. He visits the sick, not that he may be made well; feeds no one because he himself needs food: so he also serves the State not because he needs it, but because others need it,—that they may be protected and that the wicked may not become worse. He loses nothing by this, and such service in no way harms him, and yet it is of great profit to the world. If he did not do it, he would be acting not as a Christian but contrary even to love, and would also be setting a bad example to others, who like him would not submit to authority, though they were no Christians. In this way the Gospel would be brought into disrepute, as though it taught rebellion and made self-willed people, unwilling to benefit or serve any one, when in reality it makes a Christian the servant of every one. Thus in Matthew xviii, Christ gave the tribute money that He might not offend them, although He did not need to do it.

Thus you observe in the words of Christ quoted above from Matthew v that He indeed teaches that Christians among themselves should have no secular sword nor law. He does not, however, forbid one to serve and obey those who have the secular sword and the law; much rather, since you have no need of them and are not to have them, are you to serve those who have not progressed so far as you and still need them. Although you do not need to have your enemy punished, your weak neighbor does. You should help him, that he may have peace and that his enemy may be curbed; which is not possible unless power and authority are honored and feared. Christ does not say, "Thou shalt not serve the State or be subject to it," but "Thou shalt not resist evil." As though He said, "Take heed that you bear everything, so that you may

not need the State to help and serve you and be of profit to you, but that you may on the other hand, help, serve, and be of profit and use to it. I would have you to be far too exalted and noble to have any need of it, but it should have need of you."

5. Christians May Bear the Sword

You ask whether a Christian, also, may bear the secular sword and punish the wicked, since Christ's words, "Thou shalt not resist the evil," are so clear and definite that the sophists have had to make a counsel of them. I answer, You have now heard two propositions. The one is, that the sword can have no place among Christians, therefore you cannot bear it among and against Christians, who do not need it. The question, therefore, must be directed to the other side, to the non-Christians, whether as a Christian you may there bear it. Here the other proposition applies, that you are under obligation to serve and further the sword by whatever means you can, with body, soul, honor or goods. For it is nothing that you need, but something quite useful and profitable for the whole world and for your neighbor. Therefore, should you see that there is a lack of hangmen, beadles, judges, lords, or princes, and find that you are qualified, you should offer your services and seek the place, that necessary government may by no means be despised and become inefficient or perish. For the world cannot and dare not dispense with it.

You ask, Why did not Christ and the apostles bear the sword? Tell me, Why did He not also take a wife, or become a cobbler or a tailor? If an occupation or office is not good because Christ Himself did not occupy it, what would become of all occupations and offices, with the exception of the ministry which alone He exercised? Christ fulfilled His own office and vocation, but thereby did not reject any other. It was not meet that He should bear the sword, for He was to bear only that office by which

His kingdom is governed and which properly serves His kingdom. Now it does not concern His kingdom that He should be a married man, a cobbler, a tailor, a farmer, a prince, a hangman or a beadle, neither is the sword or secular law of any concern, but only God's Word and Spirit, by which His people are inwardly governed. This office which He exercised then, and still exercises, always bestows God's Word and Spirit; and in this office the apostles and all spiritual rulers must needs follow Him. For they are kept so busily employed with the spiritual sword, the Word of God, in fulfilling this their calling, that they must indeed neglect the worldly sword, and leave it to those who do not have to preach; although it is not contrary to their calling to use it, as I have said. For every one must attend to his own calling and work.

Therefore, even though Christ did not bear the sword nor prescribe it, it is sufficient that He did not forbid or abolish it, but rather endorsed it; just as it is sufficient that He did not abolish the state of matrimony, but endorsed it, though He Himself took no wife and gave no commandment concerning it. He had to identify Himself throughout with the occupation and work which properly and entirely served the furtherance of His kingdom, so that no occasion and binding example might be made of it, to teach and believe that the kingdom of God cannot exist without matrimony and the sword and such externals (since Christ's examples are binding), when it is only by God's Word and Spirit that it does exist. This was and had to be Christ's peculiar work as the supreme King in this kingdom. Since, however, not all Christians have this same office, though innately it belongs to them, it is meet that they should have some other, external one, by which God may also be served.

From all this we see what is the true meaning of Christ's words in Matthew v, "Resist not evil," etc. It is this, that a Christian should be so disposed that he will suffer every evil and injustice, not avenge himself nor bring suit in court, and in nothing make use of secular power and law for himself. For others, however, he may and should seek vengeance, justice, protection and help, and do what he can toward this. Likewise, the State should, either of itself or through the instigation of others, help and protect him without complaint, application or instigation on his part. When the State does not do this, he ought to permit himself to be robbed and despoiled, and not resist the evil, as Christ's words say.

6. The Extent of Secular Authority

We come now to the main part of this treatise. For as we have learned that there must be temporal authority on earth, and how it is to be employed in a Christian and salutary way, we must now learn how far its arm extends and how far its hand reaches, lest it extend too far and encroach upon God's kingdom and rule. And it is very necessary to know this, since where it is given too wide a scope, intolerable and terrible injury follows; and, on the other hand, it cannot be too much restricted without working injury. In the latter case the punishment is too light; in the former, too severe. It is more tolerable, however, to err on the latter side and punish too little; since it always is better to let a knave live than to kill a good man, for the world will still have knaves, and must have them, but of good men there are few.

In the first place, it must be noted that the two classes of Adam's children, the one in God's kingdom under Christ, the other in the kingdom of the world under the State, have two kinds of laws, as was said above. Every kingdom must have its own laws and regulations, and without law no kingdom or government can exist, as daily experience sufficiently proves. Worldly government has laws which extend no farther than to life and property and what is external upon earth. For over the soul God can and will let no one rule but Himself. Therefore, where temporal power presumes to prescribe laws for the soul, it encroaches upon God's government and only misleads and destroys the souls. We desire to make this so clear that every one shall grasp it, and that our junkers, the princes and bishops, may see what fools they are when they seek to coerce the people with their laws and commandments into believing one thing or another.

When a man-made law is imposed upon the soul, in order to make it believe this or that, as that man prescribes, there is certainly no word of God for it. If there is no word of God for it, it is uncertain whether God will have it so, for we cannot be certain that what He does not command pleases Him. Nay, we are sure that it does not please Him, for He desires that our faith be grounded simply and entirely on His divine Word, as He says in Matthew xvi, "On this rock will I build my church"; and in John x, "My sheep hear my voice and know me; but the voice of strangers they hear not, but flee from them." It follows from this that the secular power forces souls to eternal death with such an outrageous law, for it compels them to believe as right and certainly pleasing to God what is nevertheless uncertain, nay, what is certainly displeasing to Him, since there is no clear word of God for it. For whoever believes that to be right which is wrong or uncertain denies the truth, which is God Himself, and believes in lies and errors and counts that right which is wrong.

Hence it is the height of folly when they command that one shall believe the Church, the fathers, the councils, though there be no word of God for it. The devil's apostles command such things, not the Church; for the Church commands nothing unless it is sure it is God's Word, as St. Peter says, "If any man speak let him speak as the oracles of God." It will be a very long time, however, before they prove that the statements of the councils are God's Word. Still more foolish is it when they assert that kings and princes and the mass of men believe thus and so. If you please, we are not baptised unto kings, princes, or even unto the mass of men, but unto Christ and unto God himself; neither are we called kings, princes or common folk, but Christians. No one shall and can command the soul, unless he can show it the way to heaven; but this no man can do, only God. Therefore in matters which concern the salvation of souls nothing but God's Word shall be taught and accepted.

Again, consummate fools though they are, they must confess that they have no power over souls. For no human being can kill a soul or make it alive, conduct it to heaven or hell. And if they will not believe us in this, Christ indeed will certify strongly enough to it, since He says in Matthew x, "Fear not them which kill the body and after that have power to do naught; but rather fear Him Who after He has killed the body has power to condemn to hell." I consider that here it is sufficiently clear that the soul is taken out of all human hands and is placed under the power of God alone. Now tell me, how much wit is there in the head of him who imposes commandments where he has no power at all? Who would not regard one as insane if he commanded the moon to shine when he desired it? How fitting it would be if the Leipzigers would impose laws on us Wittenbergers, or again, if we in Wittenberg would lay laws on those in Leipzig. They would certainly send the law-makers a thank-offering of hellebore to clear the brain and cure the snuffles. Nevertheless, our emperors and wise princes continue to permit pope, bishops and sophists to lead them on, one blind man leading the other, to command their subjects to believe, without God's Word, whatever they please, and still would be known as Christian princes. God help us!

Besides, we can understand how any authority shall and may act only where it can see, know, judge, change and convert. For what kind of judge would he be who should blindly judge matters which he neither heard nor saw? Tell me, how can a man see, know, judge, condemn and change hearts? This is reserved for God alone, as Psalm vii says, "God trieth the heart and reins"; likewise, "The Lord shall judge the people"; and Acts xv, "God knoweth the hearts"; and, Jeremiah xvii, "Wicked and unsearchable is the human heart; who can know it? I the Lord, who search the heart and reins." A court ought and must be quite certain and clear about everything, if it is to pass sentence. But the thoughts and intents of the heart can be known to no one but God; therefore it is useless and impossible to command or compel any one by force to believe one thing or another. It must be taken hold of in a different way; force cannot accomplish it. And I am surprised at the great fools, since they themselves all say, *De occultis non judicat ecclesia,*—the Church does not judge secret things. If the spiritual rule of the Church governs only public matters, how dare the senseless secular power judge and control such a secret, spiritual, hidden matter as faith?

Furthermore, every man is responsible for his own faith, and he must see to it for himself that he believes rightly. As little as another can go to hell or heaven for me, so little can he believe or disbelieve for me; and as little as he can open or shut heaven or hell for me, so little can he drive me to faith or unbelief. Since, then, belief or unbelief is a matter of every one's conscience, and since this is no lessening of the secular power, the latter should be content and attend to its own affairs and permit men to believe one thing or another, as they are able and willing, and constrain no one by force. For faith is a free work, to which no one can be forced. Nay, it is a divine work, done in the Spirit, certainly not a matter which outward authority should compel or create. Hence arises the well-known saying, found also in Augustine, "No one can or ought be constrained to believe."

Besides, the blind, wretched folk do not see how utterly hopeless and impossible a thing they are attempting. For no matter how much they fret and fume, they cannot do more than make the people obey them by word and deed; the heart they cannot constrain, though they wear themselves out trying. For the proverb is true, "Thoughts

are free." Why then would they constrain people to believe from the heart, when they see that it is impossible? In this way they compel weak consciences to lie, to deny, and to say what they do not believe in their hearts, and they load themselves down with dreadful alien sins. For all the lies and false confessions which such weak consciences utter fall back upon him who compels them. It were far better, if their subjects erred, simply to let them err, than that they should constrain them to lie and to say what is not in their hearts; neither is it right to defend evil with what is worse.

Would you like to know why God ordains that the temporal princes must offend so frightfully? I will tell you. God has given them over to a perverse mind and will make an end of them, as well as of the spiritual nobles. For my ungracious lords, the pope and the bishops, should be bishops and preach God's Word; this they leave undone and are become temporal princes, and govern with laws which concern only life and property. How thoroughly they have turned things upside down! Inwardly they ought to be ruling souls by God's Word; hence outwardly they rule castles, cities, land and people and torture souls with unspeakable outrages. Similarly, the temporal lords should rule land and people outwardly; this they do not do. All they can do is to flay and scrape, put tax on tax, tribute on tribute, let loose now a bear, now a wolf. Besides this, there is no justice, fidelity or truth to be found among them; what they do would be beneath robbers and knaves, and their temporal rule has sunk quite as low as that of the spiritual tyrants. Hence God also perverts their minds, that they rush on in their senselessness and would establish a spiritual rule over souls, as the others would establish a temporal rule, in order that they may contentedly burden themselves with alien sins, and with God's and all men's hate, until they go under with bishops, priests and monks, one knave with the other. Then they lay all the blame on the Gospel, and instead of doing penance, blaspheme God and say that our preaching has brought about what their perverse wickedness has merited and still unceasingly merits, as the Romans did when they were destroyed. Here then you have God's decree regarding the high and mighty. But they are not to believe it, lest this severe decree of God be hindered by their repentance.

You reply, But Paul said in Romans xiii, "Every soul shall be subject to power and authority," and Peter says, "We should be subject to every ordinance of man." I answer, That is just what I want! These sayings are in my favor. St. Paul speaks of authority and power. Now, you have just heard that no one but God can have authority over souls. Hence Paul cannot be speaking of any obedience except where there can be corresponding authority. From this it follows that he does not speak of faith, and does not say that secular authority should have the right to command faith, but he is speaking of external goods, and that these are to be set in order and controlled on earth. This his words also clearly indicate, when he prescribes the limits to both authority and obedience, and says, "Render to every one his dues, tribute to whom tribute is due, custom to whom custom; honor to whom honor; fear to whom fear." You see, temporal obedience and power apply only externally to tribute, custom, honor and fear. Likewise when he says, "The power is not a terror to good, but to evil works," he again limits the power, so that it is to have the mastery not over faith or the Word of God, but over evil works.

This is what St. Peter also desires, when he says, "Ordinance of man." Human ordinance cannot possibly extend its authority to heaven and over souls, but belongs only to earth, to the external intercourse of men with each other, where men can see, know, judge, sentence, punish and acquit. Christ Himself made this nice distinction and summed it all up briefly when He said, "Give unto Cæsar the things that are Cæsar's, and unto God the things that are God's." If, then, imperial power extended to God's kingdom and power, and were not something by itself, He would not thus have

made it a separate thing. For, as was said, the soul is not under Cæsar's power; he can neither teach nor guide it, neither kill it nor make it alive, neither bind it nor loose it, neither judge it nor condemn it, neither hold it nor release it, which he must do had he power to command it and impose laws upon it; but over life, goods and honor he indeed has this right, for such things are under his authority.

David, too, stated this long ago in one of his short sayings when he says in Psalm cxv, "The heavens hath he given to the Lord of heaven; but the earth hath he given to the children of men." That is, over what is on earth and belongs to the temporal, earthly kingdom, man has authority from God, but that which belongs to the heavenly eternal kingdom is entirely under the heavenly Lord. Nor does Moses forget this when he says in Genesis i, "God said, Let us make man to rule over the beasts of the earth, over the fish in the waters, over the birds in the air." There only external rule is ascribed to men. And, in short, this is the meaning, as St. Peter says, Acts v, "We must obey God rather than men." Thereby he clearly sets a limit to worldly government, for if we had to do all that worldly government demands it would be to no purpose to say, "We must obey God rather than men."

If then your prince or temporal lord commands you to hold with the pope, to believe this or that, or commands you to give up certain books, you should say, It does not befit Lucifer to sit by the side of God. Dear Lord, I owe you obedience with life and goods; command me within the limits of your power on earth, and I will obey. But if you command me to believe, and to put away books, I will not obey; for in this case you are a tyrant and overreach yourself, and command where you have neither right nor power, etc. Should he take your property for this, and punish such disobedience, blessed are you. Thank God that you are worthy to suffer for the sake of the divine Word, and let him rave, fool that he is. He will meet his judge. For I tell you, if you do not resist him but give him his way, and let him take your faith or your books, you have really denied God.

Let me illustrate. In Meissen, Bavaria, in the Mark, and other places, the tyrants have issued an order that the New Testaments be delivered to the courts everywhere. In this case their subjects ought not deliver a page or a letter, at risk of their salvation. For whoever does so, delivers Christ into Herod's hands, since they act as murderers of Christ, like Herod. But if their houses are ordered searched and books or goods taken by force, they should suffer it to be done. Outrage is not to be resisted, but endured, yet they should not sanction it, nor serve or obey or follow by moving foot or finger. For such tyrants act as wordly princes should act,—"wordly" princes they are; but the world is God's enemy. Therefore they must also do what is opposed to God, and in accord with the world, that they may by no means lose all honor, but remain worldly princes. Hence do not wonder that they rage and mock at the Gospel; they must live up to their name and title.

You must know that from the beginning of the world a wise prince is a rare bird indeed; still more so a pious prince. They are usually the greatest fools or the worst knaves on earth; therefore one must constantly expect the worst from them and look for little good from them, especially in divine matters, which concern the salvation of souls. They are God's jailers and hangmen, and His divine wrath needs them to punish the wicked and preserve outward peace. Our God is a great Lord, and therefore must have such noble, honorable and rich hangmen and beadles, and desires that they shall have riches, honor and fear, in full and plenty, from every one. It pleases His divine will that we call His hangmen gracious lords, fall at their feet and be subject to them in all humility, so long as they do not ply their trade too far and desire to become shepherds instead of hangmen. If a prince becomes wise, pious or a Christian, it is one of the great wonders, and one of the most precious tokens of divine grace

upon that land. For the usual course is according to the saying in Isaiah iii, "I will give children to be their princes and babes shall rule over them," and in Hosea xiii, "I will give thee a king in my anger and take him away in my wrath." The world is too wicked, and does not deserve to have many wise and pious princes. Frogs need storks.

Again you say, Temporal power does not force men to believe, but simply prevents them from being misled by false doctrine; otherwise how could heretics be prevented from preaching? I answer, This the bishops should do, to whom, and not to the princes, such duty is entrusted. Heresy can never be prevented by force. That must be taken hold of in a different way, and must be opposed and dealt with otherwise than with the sword. Here God's Word must strive; if that does not accomplish the end it will remain unaccomplished through secular power, though it fill the world with blood. Heresy is a spiritual matter, which no iron can strike, no fire burn, no water drown. God's Word alone avails here, as Paul says, II Corinthians x, "Our weapons are not carnal, but mighty through God to destroy every counsel and high thing that exalteth itself against the knowledge of God, and to bring into captivity every thought to the obedience of Christ."

Moreover, faith and heresy are never so strong as when men oppose them by sheer force, without God's Word. For men count it certain that such force is for a wrong cause and is directed against the right, since it proceeds without God's Word, and does not know how to further its cause except by force, just as the brute beasts do. For even in secular affairs force can be used only after the wrong has been legally condemned. How much less possible is it to act with force, without justice and God's Word, in these high, spiritual matters! See, therefore, what fine, shrewd nobles they are. They would drive out heresy, and set about it in such a way that they only strengthen the opposition, make themselves suspected, and justify the heretics. Friend, would you drive out heresy, then you must find a plan to tear it first of all from the heart and altogether to turn men's wills away from it; force will not accomplish this, but only strengthen the heresy. What avails it to strengthen heresy in the heart and to weaken only its outward expression, and to force the tongue to lie? God's Word, however, enlightens the hearts; and so all heresies and errors perish of themselves from the heart.

Such overpowering of heresy the prophet Isaiah proclaimed in his eleventh chapter when he said, "He shall smite the earth with the rod of His mouth, and slay the wicked with the breath of His lips." You see, if the wicked is to be smitten and converted, it is accomplished by the mouth. In short, such princes and tyrants do not know that to fight against heresy is to fight against the devil, who fills men's hearts with error, as Paul says in Ephesians vi, "We fight not with flesh and blood, but with spiritual wickedness, with the rulers of the darkness of this world." Therefore, as long as the devil is not repelled and driven from the heart, it matters as little to him that I destroy his vessels with fire or sword, as it would if I fought lightning with a straw. Job bore abundant witness to this, when in his forty-first chapter he said that the devil esteemeth iron as straw and fears no power on earth. We learn it also from experience, for although all the Jews and heretics were burned, yet no one has been or will be convinced and converted thereby.

Nevertheless such a world as this deserves such princes, none of whom do their duty. The bishops are to leave the Word of God alone and not rule souls by it, but command the worldly princes to rule them with the sword. The worldly princes, in their turn, are to permit usury, theft, adultery, murder, and other evil works, and themselves do them; and then allow the bishops to punish with the ban. Thus they turn things topsy-turvy, and rule souls with iron and the body with bans, so that worldly princes rule in a spiritual, and spiritual princes in a wordly way. What else does the devil have to do on earth than thus to play the fool and hold carnival with his folk? These are our Christian princes, who defend the faith and devour the Turk. Fine fellows, to be sure, whom we may well trust to accomplish something by such refined wisdom, namely, break their necks and plunge land and people into suffering and want.

I would, however, in all fidelity advise the blinded folk to take heed to the short saying in Psalm cvii, *"Effundit contemptum super principes"* ("He poureth contempt upon princes"). I swear unto you by God that, if through your fault this little text becomes effective against you, you are lost, though every one of you be as mighty as the Turk; and your snorting and raving will help you nothing. A large part has already come true. For there are very few princes that are not reckoned fools or knaves. That is because they show themselves to be such; the common man is learning to think, and the prince's scourge, which God calls *contemptum*, is gathering force among the mob and with the common man. I fear there is no way to stop it, unless the princes conduct themselves in a princely manner and begin again to rule reasonably and thoroughly. Men ought not, men cannot, men will not suffer your tyranny and presumption much longer. Dear princes and lords, be wise and guide yourselves accordingly. God will no longer tolerate it. The world is no longer what it was when you hunted and drove the people like so much game. Therefore drop your outrage and force, and remember to deal justly and let God's Word have its course, as it will and must and shall, nor will you prevent it. If there is heresy abroad, let it be overcome, as is proper, with God's Word. But if you will keep on brandishing the sword, take heed lest there come one who shall bid you sheath it, and that not in God's name.

But should you ask, Since there is to be no secular sword among Christians, how are they to be ruled outwardly? There certainly must be authority also among Christians. I answer, Among Christians there shall and can be no authority; but all are alike subject to one another, as Paul says in Romans xii, "Each shall count the other his superior," and Peter in I Peter v, "All of you be subject one to another." This is also what Christ means in Luke xiv, "When you are bidden to a wedding sit down in the lowest room." There is no superior among Christians, but Christ Himself and Christ alone. And what kind of authority can there be where all are equal and have the same right, power, possession, and honor, and no one desires to be the other's superior, but each the other's inferior? One could not establish authority where there are such people, even if one would, since their character and nature will not permit them to have superiors, for no one is willing or able to be the superior. But where there are no such people, there are no real Christians.

What, then, are the priests and bishops? I answer, Their government is not one of authority or power, but a service and an office; for they are neither higher nor better than other Christians. Therefore they should not impose any law or decree on others without their will and consent; their rule consists in nothing else than in dealing with God's Word, leading Christians by it and overcoming heresy by its means. For, as was said, Christians can be ruled by nothing but by God's Word. For Christians must be ruled in faith, not by outward works. Faith, however, can come through no word of man, but only through the Word of God, as Paul says in Romans x, "Faith cometh by hearing, and hearing by the Word of God." Those who do not believe are not Christians, do not belong to Christ's kingdom, but to the worldly kingdom, and are constrained and ruled by the sword and by outward rule. Christians do of themselves, without constraint, every good thing, and find God's Word alone sufficient for them.

II. CALVIN

Institutes of the Christian Religion*

1. Spiritual and Political Government

Man is under two kinds of government: one spiritual, by which the conscience is formed to piety and the service of God; the other political, by which a man is instructed in the duties of humanity and civility, which are to be observed in an intercourse with mankind. They are generally, and not improperly, denominated the spiritual and the temporal jurisdiction, indicating that the former species of government pertains to the life of the soul, and that the latter relates to the concerns of the present state, not only to the provision of food and clothing, but to the enactment of laws to regulate a man's life among his neighbors by the rules of holiness, integrity, and sobriety. For the former has its seat in the interior of the mind, whilst the latter only directs the external conduct: one may be termed a spiritual kingdom, and the other a political one. But these two, as we have distinguished them, always require to

* From Jean Calvin, *Institutes of the Christian Religion* (1536, trans. John Allen, 1813).

be considered separately; and while the one is under discussion, the mind must be abstracted from all consideration of the other. For man contains, as it were, two worlds, capable of being governed by various rulers and various laws. This distinction will prevent what the Gospel inculcates concerning spiritual liberty from being misapplied to political regulations, as though Christians were less subject to the external government of human laws because their consciences have been set at liberty before God, as though their freedom of spirit necessarily exempted them from all carnal servitude. Again, because even in those constitutions which seem to pertain to the spiritual kingdom, there may possibly be some deception, it is necessary to discriminate between these also—which are to be accounted legitimate, as according with the Divine word, and which, on the contrary, ought not to be received among believers.

The question which, as I have observed, is in itself not very obscure or intricate, greatly perplexes many because they do not distinguish with sufficient precision between the external jurisdiction and the court of conscience. The difficulty is increased by Paul's injunction to obey magistrates "not only for wrath, but also for conscience' sake," [1] from which it should follow that the conscience also is bound by political laws. But if this were true, it would supersede all that we have already said, or are now about to say, respecting spiritual government. For the solution of this difficulty it will be of use, first, to know what conscience is. And the definition of it must be derived from the etymology of the word. For as, when men apprehend the knowledge of things in the mind and understanding, they are thence said *scire,* "to know," whence is derived the word *scientia,* "science" or "knowledge," so when they have a sense of Divine justice, as an additional witness, which permits them not to conceal their sins or to elude accusation at the tribunal of the supreme Judge, this sense is termed *conscientia,* "conscience." For it is a kind of medium be-

tween God and man, because it does not suffer a man to suppress what he knows within himself, but pursues him till it brings him to conviction. This is what Paul means by "their conscience also bearing witness, and their thoughts accusing, or else excusing, one another." [2] Simple knowledge might remain, as it were, confined within a man. This sentiment, therefore, which places man before the Divine tribunal is appointed, as it were, to watch over man, to observe and examine all his secrets, that nothing may remain enveloped in darkness. Hence the old proverb, "Conscience is as a thousand witnesses." For the same reason Peter speaks of "the answer of a good conscience toward God," [3] to express our tranquility of mind when, persuaded of the favor of Christ, we present ourselves with boldness in the presence of God. And the author of the Epistle to the Hebrews expresses absolution or freedom from every future charge of sin, by "having no more conscience of sin." [4]

2. The Discipline of the Church:
No One Exempted

The discipline of the Church depends chiefly on the power of the keys and the spiritual jurisdiction. To make this more easily understood, let us divide the Church into two principal orders—the clergy and the people. I use the word *clergy* as the common, though improper appelation of those who execute the public ministry in the Church. We shall, first, speak of the common discipline to which all ought to be subject; and then we shall proceed to the clergy, who, besides this common discipline, have a discipline peculiar to themselves. But as some have such a hatred of discipline, as to abhor the very name, they should consider the following: that if no society, and even no house, though contain-

---

[1] Rom. 8:1, 5.

[2] Rom. 2:15.
[3] I Pet. 3:21.
[4] Heb. 10:2.

ing only a small family, can be preserved in a proper state without discipline, this is far more necessary in the Church, the state of which ought to be the most orderly of all. As the saving doctrine of Christ is the soul of the Church, so discipline forms the ligaments which connect the members together, and keep each other in its proper place. Whoever, therefore, either desire the abolition of all discipline, or obstruct its restoration, whether they act from design or inadvertency, they certainly promote the entire dissolution of the Church. For what will be the consequence if every man be at liberty to follow his own inclinations? But such would be the case, unless the preaching of the doctrine were accompanied with private admonitions, reproofs, and other means to enforce the doctrine, and prevent it from being altogether ineffectual. Discipline, therefore, serves as a bridle to curb and restrain the refractory who resist the doctrine of Christ; or as a spur to stimulate the inactive; and sometimes as a father's rod, with which those who have grievously fallen may be chastised in mercy, and with the gentleness of the Spirit of Christ. When we see the approach of certain beginnings of a dreadful desolation in the Church, since there is no solicitude or means to keep the people in obedience to our Lord, necessity itself proclaims the want of a remedy; and this is the only remedy which has been commanded by Christ, or which has ever been adopted among believers.

From this discipline none were exempted; so that princes and plebeians yielded the same submission to it; and that with the greatest propriety, since it is evidently the discipline of Christ, to whom it is reasonable that all the sceptres and diadems of kings should be subject. Thus Theodosius, when Ambrose excluded him from the privilege of communion on account of a massacre perpetrated at Thessalonica, laid aside the ensigns of royalty with which he was invested, publicly in the Church bewailed his sin, which the deceitful suggestions of others had tempted him to commit, and implored pardon with groans and tears. For great kings ought not to think it any dishonor to prostrate themselves as suppliants before Christ the King of kings, nor ought they to be displeased at being judged by the Church. As they hear scarcely anything in their courts but mere flatteries, it is the more highly necessary for them to receive correction from the Lord by the mouth of his *ministers;* they ought even to wish not to be spared by the *pastors,* that they may be spared by the Lord. The legitimate process in excommunicating an offender, as is pointed out by Paul, requires it to be done, not by the elders alone, but with the knowledge and approbation of the Church: in such a manner, however, that the multitude of the people may not direct the proceeding, but may watch over it as witnesses and guardians, that nothing may be done by a few persons from any improper motive. Beside the invocation of the name of God, the whole of the proceeding ought to be conducted with a gravity declarative of the presence of Christ, so that there be no doubt of his presiding over the sentence.

3. On Civil Government

Having already stated that man is the subject of two kinds of government, and having sufficiently discussed that which is situated in the soul, or the inner man, and relates to eternal life, we shall now say something of the other kind which relates to civil justice and the regulation of the external conduct. For, though the nature of this argument seems to have no connection with the spiritual doctrine of faith which I have undertaken to discuss, the sequel will show that I have sufficient reason for connecting them together, and, indeed, that necessity obliges me to it, especially since, on the one hand, infatuated and barbarous men madly endeavor to subvert this ordinance established by God, and, on the other hand, the flatterers of princes, extolling their power beyond all just bounds, hesitate not to oppose it to the authority of God himself. Unless both these errors be resisted, the purity of the faith will be destroyed. Besides, it is of no small importance for us to know what benevolent provision God has made for mankind in this instance, that we may be stimulated by a greater degree of pious zeal to testify our gratitude. In the first place, before we enter on the subject itself, it is necessary for us to recur to the distinction which we have already established, lest we fall into an error very common in the world, and injudiciously confound together these two things the nature of which is altogether different.

For some men, when they hear that the Gospel promises a liberty which acknowledges no king or magistrate among them, but submits to Christ alone, think they can enjoy no advantage of their liberty while they see any power exalted above them. They imagine, therefore, that nothing will prosper unless the whole world be modeled in a new form, without any tribunals or laws, or magistrates, or anything of a similar kind which they consider injurious to their liberty. But he who knows how to distinguish between the body and the soul, between this present transitory life and the future eternal one, will find no difficulty in understanding that the spiritual kingdom of Christ and civil government are things very different and remote from each other. Since it is a Jewish folly, therefore, to seek and include the kingdom of Christ under the elements of this world, let us, on the contrary, considering what the Scripture clearly inculcates, that the benefit which is received from the grace of Christ is spiritual—let us, I say, remember to confine within its proper limits all this liberty which is promised and offered to us in him. For why is it that the same apostle who, in one place, exhorts to "stand fast in the liberty wherewith Christ hath made us free and be not entangled again with the yoke of bondage,"[5] in another enjoins servants to "care not for" their servile condition,[6] except that spiritual liberty may very well consist

with civil servitude? In this sense we are likewise to understand him in these passages: "There is neither Jew nor Greek, there is neither bond nor free, there is neither male nor female."[7] Again: "There is neither Greek nor Jew, circumcision nor uncircumcision, Barbarian, Scythian, bond nor free: but Christ is all, and in all,"[8] in which he signifies that it is of no importance what is our condition among men or under the laws of what nation we live, as the kingdom of Christ consists not in these things.

Yet this distinction does not lead us to consider the whole system of civil government as a polluted thing which has nothing to do with Christian men. Some fanatics who are pleased with nothing but liberty, or rather licentiousness without any restraint, do indeed boast and vociferate, That since we are dead with Christ to the elements of this world and, being translated into the kingdom of God, sit among the celestials, it is a degradation to us and far beneath our dignity to be occupied with those secular and impure cares which relate to things altogether uninteresting to a Christian man. Of what use, they ask, are laws without judgments and tribunals? But what have judgments to do with a Christian man? And if it be unlawful to kill, of what use are laws and judgments to us? But as we have just suggested that this kind of government is distinct from that spiritual and internal reign of Christ, so it ought to be known that they are in no respect at variance with each other. For that spiritual reign, even now upon earth, commences within us some preludes of the heavenly kingdom, and in this mortal and transitory life affords us some prelibations of immortal and incorruptible blessedness; but this civil government is designed, as long as we live in this world, to cherish and support the external worship of God, to preserve the pure doctrine of religion, to defend the constitution of the Church, to regulate our lives in a manner requisite for the society of men, to form our manners to civil justice, to promote our

[5] Gal. 5:1.
[6] I Cor. 7:21.
[7] Gal. 3:28.
[8] Col. 3:11.

concord with each other, and to establish general peace and tranquility—all of which I confess to be superfluous if the kingdom of God, as it now exists in us, extinguishes the present life. But if it is the will of God that while we are aspiring toward our true country, we be pilgrims on the earth, and if such aids are necessary to our pilgrimage, they who take them from man deprive him of his human nature. They plead that there should be so much perfection in the Church of God that its order would suffice to supply the place of all laws; but they foolishly imagine a perfection which can never be found in any community of men. For since the insolence of the wicked is so great, and their iniquity so obstinate, that it can scarcely be restrained by all the severity of the laws, what may we expect they would do if they found themselves at liberty to perpetuate crimes with impunity whose outrages even the arm of power cannot altogether prevent?

But for speaking of the exercise of civil polity, there will be another place more suitable. At present we only wish it to be understood that to entertain a thought of its extermination is inhuman barbarism; it is equally as necessary to mankind as bread and water, light and air, and far more excellent. For it not only tends to secure the accommodations arising from all these things, that men may breathe, eat, drink, and be sustained in life, though it comprehends all these things while it causes them to live together, yet I say this is not its only tendency; its objects also are that idolatry, sacrileges against the name of God, blasphemies against his truth, and other offenses against religion may not openly appear and be disseminated among the people; that the public tranquility may not be disturbed; that every person may enjoy his property without molestation; that men may transact their business together without fraud or injustice; that integrity and modesty may be cultivated among them; in short, that there may be a public form of religion among Christians, and that humanity may be maintained among men. Nor let anyone think it strange that I now refer to human polity the charge of the due maintenance of religion, which I may appear to have placed beyond the jurisdiction of men. For I do not allow men to make laws respecting religion and the worship of God now any more than I did before, though I approve of civil government which provides that the true religion contained in the law of God be not violated and polluted by public blasphemies with impunity. But the perspicuity of order will assist the readers to attain a clearer understanding of what sentiments ought to be entertained respecting the whole system of civil administration, if we enter on a discussion of each branch of it. These are three: The magistrate, who is the guardian and conservator of the laws; the laws according to which he governs; the people, who are governed by the laws and obey the magistrate. Let us, therefore, examine, first, the function of a magistrate, whether it be a legitimate calling and approved by God, the nature of the duty, and the extent of the power; secondly, by what laws Christian government ought to be regulated; and lastly, what advantage the people derive from the laws, and what obedience they owe to the magistrate.

4. The Duty of Political Rulers

Here it is necessary to state in a brief manner the nature of the office of magistracy, as described in the word of God, and wherein it consists. If the Scripture did not teach that this office extends to both tables of the law, we might learn it from heathen writers; for not one of them has treated of the office of magistrates, of legislation, and civil government, without beginning with religion and Divine worship. And thus they have all confessed that no government can be happily constituted unless its first object be the promotion of piety, and that all laws are preposterous which neglect the claims of God and merely provide for the interests of men. Therefore, as religion holds the first place among all the philosophers, and as this has always been regarded by the universal consent of all nations, Christian princes and magistrates ought to be ashamed of their indolence if they do not make it the object of their most serious care. We have already shown that this duty is particularly enjoined upon them by God; for it is reasonable that they should employ their utmost efforts in asserting and defending the honor of Him whose vicegerents they are and by whose favor they govern. And the principal commendations given in the Scripture to the good kings are for having restored the worship of God when it had been corrupted or abolished, or for having devoted their attention to religion, that it might flourish in purity and safety under their reigns. On the contrary, the sacred history represents it as one of the evils arising from anarchy, or a want of good government, that when "there was no king in Israel, every man did that which was right in his own eyes." [9] These things evince the folly of those who would wish magistrates to neglect all thoughts of God, and to confine themselves entirely to the administration of justice among men, as though God appointed governors in his name to decide secular controversies, and disregarded that which is of far greater importance—the pure worship of himself according to the rule of his law. But a rage for universal innovation, and a desire to escape with impunity, instigate men of turbulent spirits to wish that all the avengers of violated piety were removed out of the world. With respect to the second table, Jeremiah admonishes kings in the following manner: "Execute ye judgment and righteousness, and deliver the spoiled out of the hand of the oppressor; and do no wrong, do no violence to the stranger, the fatherless, nor the widow, neither shed innocent blood." [10] To the same purpose is the exhortation in the eighty-second psalm: "Defend the poor and fatherless: do justice to the afflicted and needy: deliver the poor and needy: rid them

out of the hand of the wicked." [11] And Moses "charged the judges" whom he appointed to supply his place, saying—

Hear the causes between your brethren, and judge righteously between every man and his brother, and the stranger that is with him: ye shall not respect persons in judgment; but ye shall hear the small as well as the great; ye shall not be afraid of the face of man; for the judgment is God's. [12]

I forbear to remark the directions given by him in another place respecting their future kings: "He shall not multiply horses to himself; neither shall he greatly multiply to himself silver and gold; his heart shall not be lifted up above his brethren; he shall read in the law all the days of his life"; [13] also that judges show no partiality nor take bribes, with similar injunctions, which abound in the Scriptures; because, in describing the office of magistrates in this treatise, my design is not so much to instruct magistrates themselves, as to show to others what magistrates are and for what end God has appointed them. We see, therefore, that they are constituted the protectors and vindicators of the public innocence, modesty, probity, and tranquility, whose sole object it ought to be to promote the common peace and security of all. Of these virtues, David declares that he will be an example when he shall be exalted to the royal throne.

I will set no wicked thing before mine eyes. I will not know a wicked person. Whoso privily slandereth his neighbour, him will I cut off: him that hath a high look and a proud heart will I not suffer. Mine eyes shall be upon the faithful of the land, that they may dwell with me: he that walketh in a perfect way, he shall serve me. [14]

But as they cannot do this unless they defend good men from the injuries of the wicked and aid the oppressed by their re-

---

[9] Judg. 21:25.
[10] Jer. 22:3.
[11] Ps. 82:3–4.
[12] Deut. 1:16–17.
[13] Deut. 17:16–17, 19–20.
[14] Ps. 101:3–6.

lief and protection, they are likewise armed with power for the suppression of crimes, and the severe punishment of malefactors whose wickedness disturbs the public peace. For experience fully verifies the observation of Solon: "That all states are supported by reward and punishment; and that when these two things are removed, all the discipline of human societies is broken and destroyed." For the minds of many lose their regard for equity and justice unless virtue be rewarded with due honor; nor can the violence of the wicked be restrained unless crimes are followed by severe punishments. And these two parts are included in the injunction of the prophet to kings and other governors to "execute judgment and righteousness." [15] "Righteousness" means the care, patronage, defense, vindication, and liberation of the innocent; "judgment" imports the repression of the audacity, the coercion of the violence, and the punishment of the crime of the impious.

5. The Duty of Subjects

The first duty of subjects toward their magistrates is to entertain the most honorable sentiments of their function, which they know to be a jurisdiction delegated to them from God, and on that account to esteem and reverence them as God's ministers and vicegerents. For there are some persons to be found who show themselves very obedient to their magistrates and have not the least wish that there were no magistrates for them to obey, because they know them to be so necessary to the public good, but who, nevertheless, consider the magistrates themselves as no other than necessary evils. But something more than this is required of us by Peter when he commands us to "honor the king"; [16] and by Solomon, when he says,

"Fear thou the Lord and the king"; [17] for Peter, under the term "honor," comprehends a sincere and candid esteem; and Solomon, by connecting the king with the Lord, attributes to him a kind of sacred veneration and dignity. It is also a remarkable commendation of magistrates which is given by Paul, when he says that we "must needs be subject, not only for wrath, but also for conscience' sake"; [18] by which he means that subjects ought to be induced to submit to princes and governors, not merely from a dread of their power, as persons are accustomed to yield to an armed enemy, who they know will immediately take vengeance upon them if they resist; but because the obedience which is rendered to princes and magistrates is rendered to God, from whom they have received their authority. I am not speaking of the persons as if the mask of dignity ought to palliate or excuse folly, ignorance, or cruelty, and conduct the most nefarious and flagitious, and so to acquire for vices the praise due to virtues; but I affirm that the station itself is worthy of honor and reverence, so that, whoever our governors are, they ought to possess our esteem and veneration on account of the office which they fill.

Now, as we have hitherto described a magistrate who truly answers to his title— who is the father of his country and, as the poet calls him, the pastor of his people, the guardian of peace, the protector of justice, the avenger of innocence; he would justly be deemed insane who disapproved of such a government. But, as it has happened, in almost all ages, that some princes, regardless of everything to which they ought to have directed their attention and provision, give themselves up to their pleasures in indolent exemption from every care; others, absorbed in their own interest, expose to sale all laws, privileges, rights, and judgments; others plunder the public wealth which they afterwards lavish in mad prodigality; others commit flagrant outrages, pillaging houses, violating virgins

---

[15] Jer. 22:3.
[16] I Pet. 2:17.

[17] Prov. 24:21.
[18] Rom. 13:5.

and matrons, and murdering infants; many persons cannot be persuaded that such ought to be acknowledged as princes whom, as far as possible, they ought to obey. For in such enormities and actions so completely incompatible, not only with the office of a magistrate, but with the duty of every man, they discover no appearance of the image of God, which ought to be conspicuous in a magistrate; while they perceive no vestige of that minister of God who is "not a terror to good works, but to the evil," who is sent "for the punishment of evildoers, and for the praise of them that do well"; nor recognize that governor whose dignity and authority the Scripture recommends to us. And certainly the minds of men have always been naturally disposed to hate and execrate tyrants as much as to love and reverence legitimate kings.

But, if we direct our attention to the word of God, it will carry us much farther, even to submit to the government, not only of those princes who discharge their duty to us with becoming integrity and fidelity, but of all who possess the sovereignty, even though they perform none of the duties of their function. For, though the Lord testifies that the magistrate is an eminent gift of his liberality to preserve the safety of men, and prescribes to magistrates themselves the extent of their duty, yet he at the same time declares that whatever be their characters, they have their government only from him; that those who govern for the public good are true specimens and mirrors of his beneficence; and that those who rule in an unjust and tyrannical manner are raised up by him to punish the iniquity of the people; that all equally possess that sacred majesty with which he has invested legitimate authority. I will not proceed any further till I have subjoined a few testimonies in proof of this point. It is unnecessary, however, to labor much to evince an impious king to be a judgment of God's wrath upon the world, as I have no expectation that any-one will deny it; and in this we say no

more of a king than of any other robber who plunders our property, or adulterer who violates our bed, or assassin who attempts to murder us; since the Scripture enumerates all these calamities among the curses inflicted by God. But let us rather insist on the proof of that which the minds of men do not so easily admit—that a man of the worst character, and most undeserving of all honor, who holds the sovereign power, really possesses that eminent and Divine authority which the Lord has given by his word to the ministers of his justice and judgment; and, therefore, that he ought to be regarded by his subjects, as far as pertains to public obedience, with the same reverence and esteem which they would show to the best of kings, if such a one were granted to them.

I request my readers to observe and consider with attention what is so frequently and justly mentioned in the Scriptures—the providence and peculiar dispensation of God in distributing kingdoms and appointing whom he pleases to be kings. Daniel says, "God changes the times and the seasons: he removes kings and sets up kings." Again: "That the living may know that the Most High rules in the kingdom of men, and gives it to whomsoever he will." Passages of this kind abound in the Scriptures, but particularly in this prophecy. Now, the character of Nebuchadnezzar, who conquered Jerusalem, is sufficiently known, that he was an invader and depopulator of the territories of others. Yet by the mouth of Ezekiel the Lord declares that he had given him the land of Egypt as a reward for the service which he had performed in devastating Tyre. And Daniel said to him: "Thou, O king, art a king of kings; for the God of heaven has given thee a kingdom, power, strength, and glory; and wheresoever the children of men dwell, the beasts of the field, and the fowls of the heaven, has he given into thine hand, and has made thee ruler over all."

In vain will any one object that this was a special command to the Israelites. For we must observe the reason upon which the Lord founds it. He says: "I have given these lands to Nebuchadnezzar; therefore serve him and live." To whomsoever, therefore, a kingdom shall evidently be given, we have no room to doubt that subjection is due to him. And as soon as he exalts any person to royal dignity, he gives us a declaration of his pleasure that he shall reign. The Scripture contains general testimonies on this subject. Salomon says: "For the transgression of a land, many are the princes thereof." Job says, "He looses the bonds of kings," or divests them of their power, "and girds their loin with a girdle," or restores them to their former dignity. This being admitted, nothing remains for us but to serve and live.

We owe these sentiments of affection and reverence to all our rulers, whatever their characters may be; which I the more frequently repeat that we may learn not to scrutinize the persons themselves, but may be satisfied with knowing that they are invested by the will of the Lord with that function, upon which he has impressed an inviolable majesty. But it will be said that rulers owe mutual duties to their subjects. That I have already admitted. But he who infers from this that obedience ought to be rendered to none but just rulers, is a very bad reasoner. For husbands owe mutual duties to their wives, and parents to their children. Now, if husbands and parents violate their obligations; if parents conduct themselves with discouraging severity and fastidious moroseness towards their children, whom they are forbidden to provoke to wrath; if husbands despise and vex their wives, whom they are commanded to love and to spare as the weaker vessels; does it follow that children should be less obedient to their parents, or wives to their husbands? They are still subject, even to those who are wicked and unkind. As it is incumbent on all not to inquire into the duties of one another, but to confine their attention respectively to their own, this consideration ought particularly to be regarded by those who are subject to the authority of others. Wherefore, if we are inhumanly harassed by a cruel prince; if we are rapaciously plundered by an avaricious or luxurious one; if we are neglected by an indolent one; or if we are persecuted, on account of piety, by an impious and sacrilegious one—let us first call to mind our transgressions against God, which he undoubtedly chastises by these scourges. Thus our impatience will be restrained by humility. Let us, in the next place, consider that it is not in our province to remedy these evils, and that nothing remains for us but to implore the aid of the Lord, in whose hands are the hearts of kings and the revolutions of kingdoms.

6. Resistance to Tyranny

And here is displayed God's wonderful goodness and power and providence; for sometimes he raises up some of his servants as public avengers and arms them with his commission to punish unrighteous domination, and to deliver from their distressing calamities a people who have been unjustly oppressed; sometimes he accomplishes this end by the fury of men who meditate and attempt something altogether different. Thus he liberated the people of Israel from the tyranny of Pharaoh by Moses; from the oppression of Chusan by Othniel; and from other yokes by other kings and judges. Thus he subdued the pride of Tyre by the Egyptians; the insolence of the Egyptians by the Assyrians; the haughtiness of the Assyrians by the Chaldeans; the confidence of Babylon by the Medes and Persians, after Cyrus had subjugated the Medes. The ingratitude of the kings of Israel and Judah and their impious rebellion, nothwithstanding his numerous favors, he repressed and punished sometimes by the Assyrians, sometimes by the Babylonians. These were all the executioners of his vengeance, but not all in the same manner. The former, when they were called forth to the performance of such acts by a legitimate commission from God, in taking arms against kings, were not chargeable with the least violation of that majesty with which kings are invested by the ordination of God; but, being armed with authority from Heaven, they punished an inferior power by a superior one, as it is lawful for kings to punish their inferior officers. The latter, though they were guided by the hand of God in such directions as he pleased, and performed his work without being conscious of it, nevertheless contemplated in their hearts nothing but evil.

But whatever opinion be formed of the acts of men, yet the Lord equally executed his work by them when he broke the sanguinary scepters of insolent kings and overturned tyrannical governments. Let princes hear and fear. But, in the meanwhile, it behooves us to use the greatest caution, that we do not despise or violate that authority of magistrates which is entitled to the greatest veneration, which God has established by the most solemn commands, even though it reside in those who are most unworthy of it, and who, as far as in them lies, pollute it by their iniquity. For though the correction of tyrannical domination is the vengeance of God, we are not, therefore, to conclude that it is committed to us who have received no other command than to obey and suffer. This observation I always apply to private persons. For if there be, in the present day, any magistrates appointed for the protection of the people and the moderation of the power of kings, such as were, in ancient times, the Ephori, who were a check upon the kings among the Lacedaemonians, or the popular tribunes upon the consuls among the Romans, or the Demarchi upon the senate among the Athenians; or with power such as perhaps is now possessed by the three estates in every kingdom when they are assembled; I am so far from prohibiting them, in the discharge of their duty, to oppose the violence or cruelty of kings that I affirm that if they connive at kings in their oppression of their people, such forbearance involves the most nefarious perfidy because they fraudulently betray the liberty of the people, of which they know that they have been appointed protectors by the ordination of God.

But in the obedience which we have shown to be due to the authority of governors, it is always necessary to make one exception, and that is entitled to our first attention—that it do not seduce us from obedience to him to whose will the desires of all kings ought to be subject, to whose decrees all their commands ought to yield, to whose majesty all their scepters ought to submit. And, indeed, how preposterous it would be for us, with a view to satisfy men, to incur the displeasure of him on whose account we yield obedience to men! The Lord, therefore, is the King of kings; who, when he has opened his sacred mouth, is to be heard alone, above all, for all, and before all; in the next place, we are subject to those men who preside over us, but no otherwise than in him. If they command anything against him, it ought not to have the least attention, nor, in this case, ought we to pay any regard to all that dignity attached to magistrates, to which no injury is done when it is subjected to the unrivaled and supreme power of God. On this principle Daniel denied that he had committed any crime against the king in disobeying his impious decree; [19] because the king had exceeded the limits of his office, and had not only done an injury to men, but, by raising his arm against God, had degraded his own authority. On the other hand, the Israelites are condemned for having been too submissive to the impious edict of their king. For when Jeroboam had made his golden calves, in compliance with his will, they deserted the temple of God and revolted to new superstitions. Their posterity conformed to the decrees of their idolatrous kings with the same facility. The prophet severely condemns them for having "willingly walked after the commandment"; [20] so far is any praise from being due to the pretext of humility with which courtly flatterers excuse themselves

[19] Dan. 6:22.
[20] Hos. 5:11.

and deceive the unwary, when they deny that it is lawful for them to refuse compliance with any command of their kings, as if God had resigned his right to mortal men when he made them rulers of mankind, or as if earthly power were diminished by being subordinated to its author before whom even the principalities of heaven tremble with awe. I know what great and present danger awaits this constancy, for kings cannot bear to be disregarded without the greatest indignation; and "the wrath of a king," says Solomon, "is as messengers of death." [21] But since this edict

[21] Prov. 16:14.

has been proclaimed by that celestial herald, Peter, "We ought to obey God rather than men," [22]—let us console ourselves with this thought, that we truly perform the obedience which God requires of us when we suffer anything rather than deviate from piety. And that our hearts may not fail us, Paul stimulates us with another consideration—that Christ has redeemed us at the immense price which our redemption cost him, that we may not be submissive to the corrupt desires of men, much less be slaves to their impiety.[23]

[22] Acts 5:29.
[23] I Cor. 7:23.

III. STEPHEN JUNIUS BRUTUS

A Defense of Liberty against Tyrants *

1. Obedience to Princes or to God?

This question happily may seem at the first view to be altogether superfluous and unprofitable, for that it seems to make a doubt of an axiom always held infallible among Christians, confirmed by many testimonies in Holy Scripture, divers examples of the histories of all ages, and by the death of all the holy martyrs. For it may be well demanded wherefore Christians have endured so many afflictions, but that they were always persuaded that God must be obeyed simply and absolutely, and kings with this exception, that they command not that which is repugnant to the law of God. Otherways wherefore should the apostles have answered, that God must rather be obeyed

* From Stephen Junius Brutus, *A Defense of Liberty against Tyrants* (1579; trans. anon., 1648). Spelling and punctuation have been modernized for this selection.

than men, and also seeing that the only will of God is always just, and that of men may be, and is, oftentimes unjust, who can doubt but that we must always obey God's commandments without any exception, and men's ever with limitation?

There are no estates which ought to be esteemed firm and stable, but those in whom the temple of God is built, and which are indeed the temple itself, and these we may truly call kings, which reign with God, seeing that it is by him only that kings reign: On the contrary, what beastly foolishness it is to think that the state and kingdom cannot subsist if God Almighty be not excluded, and his temple demolished. From hence proceed so many tyrannous enterprises, unhappy and tragic death of kings, and ruins of people. If these syncophants knew what difference there is between God and Caesar, between the King of Kings and a simple king, between the lord and the vassal, and what tributes this lord requires of his subjects, and what authority he gives to kings over those his subjects, certainly so many princes would not strive to trouble the kingdom of God, and we should not see some of them precipitated from their thrones by the just instigation of the Almighty, revenging himself of them, in the midst of their greatest strength, and the people should not be sacked and pillaged and trodden down.

It then belongs to princes to know how far they may extend their authority, and to subjects in what they may obey them, lest the one encroaching on that jurisdiction, which no way belongs to them, and the others obeying him which commands further than he ought, they be both chastised, when they shall give an account thereof before another judge. Now the end and scope of the question propounded, whereof the Holy Scripture shall principally give the resolution, is that which follows. The question is, if subjects be bound to obey kings, in case they command that which is against the law of God: that is to say, to which of the two (God or king) must we rather obey, when the question shall be resolved concerning the king, to whom is attributed absolute power, that concerning other magistrates shall be also determined.

First, the Holy Scripture does teach that God reigns by his own proper authority, and kings by derivation, God from himself, kings from God, that God has a jurisdiction proper, kings are his delegates. It follows then, that the jurisdiction of God has no limits, that of kings bounded, that the power of God is infinite, that of kings confined, that the kingdom of God extends itself to all places, that of kings is restrained within the confines of certain countries. In like manner God has created of nothing both heaven and earth; wherefore by good right He is lord, and true proprietor, both of the one and the other. All the inhabitants of the earth hold of Him that which they have, and are but His tenants and farmers; all the princes and governors of the world are His stipendiaries and vassals, and are bound to take and acknowledge their investitures from Him. Briefly, God alone is the owner and lord, and all men of what degree or quality soever they be, are His servants, farmers, officers and vassals, and owe account and acknowledgment to Him, according to that which He has committed to their dispensation; the higher their place is, the greater their account must be, and according to the ranks whereunto God has raised them, must they make their reckoning before His divine majesty, which the Holy Scriptures teach in infinite places, and all the faithful, yea, and the wisest among the heathen have ever acknowledged.

Now if we consider what is the duty of vassals, we shall find that what may be said of them, agrees properly to kings. The vassal receives his fee of his lord with right of justice, and charge to serve him in his wars. The king is established by the Lord God, the King of Kings, to the end he should administer justice to his people and defend them against all their enemies. The vassal receives laws and conditions from his sovereign. God commands the king to observe his laws and to have them always before his eyes, promising that he and his successors shall possess long the kingdom, if they be obedient, and on the contrary, that their reign shall be of small continuance, if they prove rebellious to their sovereign king. The vassal obliges himself by oath unto his lord, and swears that he will be faithful and obedient. In like manner the king promises solemnly to command, according to the express law of God. Briefly, the vassal loses his fee, if he commit a felony, and by law forfeits all his privileges. In the like case the king loses his right, and many times his realm also, if he despise God, if he complot with his enemies, and if he commit felony against that royal majesty. This will appear more clearly by the consideration of the covenant which is contracted between God and the king, for God does that honor to His servants to call them His confederates. Now we read of two sorts of covenants at the inaugurating of kings, the first between

God, the king, and the people, that the people might be the people of God. The second, between the king and the people, that the people shall obey faithfully, and the king command justly.

Briefly, even as those rebellious vassals who endeavor to possess themselves of the kingdom, do commit felony by the testimony of all laws, and deserve to be extirpated; in like manner those are as really guilty which will not observe the divine law, whereunto all men without exception owe their obedience, or who persecute those who desire to conform themselves thereunto, without hearing them in their just defences: now for that we see that God invests kings into their kingdoms, almost in the same manner that vassals are invested into their fees by their sovereign, we must needs conclude that kings are the vassals of God, and deserve to be deprived of the benefit they receive from their lord if they commit felony, in the same fashion as rebellious vassals are of their estates. These premises being allowed, this question may be easily resolved; for if God hold the place of sovereign Lord, and the king as vassal, who dare deny but that we must rather obey the sovereign than the vassal? If God commands one thing, and the king commands the contrary, what is that proud man that would term him a rebel who refuses to obey the king, when else he must disobey God? But, on the contrary, he should rather be condemned, and held for truly rebellious, who omits to obey God, or who will obey the king, when he forbids him to yield obedience to God.

Briefly, if God calls us on the one side to enrol us in His service, and the king on the other, is any man so void of reason that he will not say we must leave the king, and apply ourselves to God's service: so far be it from us to believe, that we are bound to obey a king, commanding anything contrary to the law of God, that, contrarily, in obeying him we become rebels to God; no more nor less than we would esteem a countryman a rebel who, for the love he bears

to some rich and ancient inferior lord, would bear arms against the sovereign prince, or who had rather obey the writs of an inferior judge than of a superior, the commandments of a lieutenant of a province, than of a prince; to be brief, the directions of an officer rather than the express ordinances of the king himself. In doing this we justly incur the malediction of the prophet Micah, who does detest and curse, in the name of God, all those who obey the wicked and perverse ordinances of kings. By the law of God we understand the two tables given to Moses, in the which, as in unremovable bounds, the authority of all princes ought to be fixed. The first comprehends that which we owe to God, the second that which we must do to our neighbors; briefly, they contain piety and justice conjoined with charity, from which the preaching of the gospel does not derogate, but rather authorize and confirm. The first table is esteemed the principal, as well in order as in dignity. If the prince commands to cut the throat of an innocent, to pillage and commit extortion, there is no man (provided he has some feeling of conscience) who would execute such a commandment.

2. Lawful Resistance to Princes in Defense of Divine Law

This question seems at the first view to be of a high and difficult nature, for so much as there being small occasion to speak to princes that fear God. On the contrary, there will be much danger to trouble the ears of those who acknowledge no other sovereign but themselves, for which reason few or none have meddled with it, and if any have at all touched it, it has been but as it were in passing by. The question is, if it be lawful to resist a prince violating the law of God, or ruinating the church, or hindering the restoring of it? If we hold ourselves to the tenure of the Holy Scripture it will resolve us. For, if in this case it had been lawful to the Jewish people (which may be easily gathered from the books of the Old Testament), yea, if it had been enjoined them, I believe it will not be denied, that the same must be allowed to the whole people of any Christian kingdom or country whatsoever.

But who may punish the king (for here is question of corporal and temporal punishment) if it be not the whole body of the people to whom the king swears and obliges himself, no more nor less, than the people do to the king? We read also that king Josias, being of the age of twenty-and-five years, together with the whole people, makes a covenant with the Lord, the king and the people promising to keep the laws and ordinances of God; and even then for the better accomplishing of the tenure of this agreement, the idolatry of Baal was presently destroyed. If any will more exactly turn over the Holy Bible, he may well find other testimonies to this purpose.

But I see well, here will be an objection made. What will you say? That a whole people, that beast of many heads, must they run in a mutinous disorder, to order the business of the commonwealth? What address or direction is there in an unruly and unbridled multitude? What counsel or wisdom, to manage the affairs of state?

When we speak of all the people, we understand by that, only those who hold their authority from the people, to wit, the magistrates, who are inferior to the king, and whom the people have substituted, or established, as it were, consorts in the empire, and with a kind of tribunitial authority, to restrain the encroachments of sovereignty, and to represent the whole body of the people. We understand also, the assembly of the estates, which is nothing else but an epitome, or brief collection of the kingdom, to whom all public affairs have special and absolute reference; such were the seventy ancients in the kingdom of Israel, amongst whom the high priest was as it were president, and they judged all matters of greatest importance, those seventy

being first chosen by six out of each tribe, which came out of the land of Egypt, then the heads or governors of provinces. In like manner the judges and provosts of towns, the captains of thousands, the centurions and others who commanded over families, the most valiant, noble, and otherwise notable personages, of whom was composed the body of the states, assembled divers times as it plainly appears by the word of the holy scripture. At the election of the first king, who was Saul, all the ancients of Israel assembled together at Kama. In like manner all Israel was assembled, or all Judah and Benjamin, etc. Now, it is no way probable, that all the people, one by one, met together there. Of this rank there are in every well governed kingdom, the princes, the officers of the crown, the peers, the greatest and most notable lords, the deputies of provinces, of whom the ordinary body of the estate is composed, or the parliament or the diet, or other assembly, according to the different names used in divers countries of the world; in which assemblies, the principal care is had both for the preventing and reforming either of disorder or detriment in church or commonwealth.

For as the councils of Basle and Constance have decreed (and well decreed) that the universal council is in authority above the bishop of Rome, so in like manner, the whole chapter may overrule the bishop, the University the rector, the court the president. Briefly, he, whosoever he is, who has received authority from a company, is inferior to that whole company, although he be superior to any of the particular members of it.

A combination or conjuration is good or ill, according as the end whereunto it is addressed is good or ill; and perhaps also according as they are affected who are the managers of it. We say then, that the princes of Judah have done well, and that in following any other course they had failed of the right way. For even as the guardian ought to take charge and care that the goods of his pupil fall not into loss and detriment, and if he omit his duty therein, he may be compelled to give an account thereof, in like manner, those to whose custody and tuition the people have committed themselves, and whom they have constituted their tutors and defenders ought to maintain them safe and entire in all their rights and privileges. To be short, as it is lawful for a whole people to resist and oppose tyranny, so likewise the principal persons of the kingdom may as heads, and for the good of the whole body, confederate and associate themselves together; and as in a public state, that which is done by the greatest part is esteemed and taken as the act of all, so in like manner must it be said to be done, which the better part of the most principal have acted, briefly, that all the people had their hand in it.

3. Kings Made by the People

We have shown before that it is God that does appoint kings, who chooses them, who gives the kingdom to them: now we say that the people establish kings, put the scepter into their hands, and who with their suffrages, approve the election. God would have it done in this manner, to the end that the kings should acknowledge, that after God they hold their power and sovereignty from the people, and that it might the rather induce them to apply and address the utmost of their care and thoughts for the profit of the people, without being puffed with any vain imagination, that they were formed of any matter more excellent than other men, for which they were raised so high above others; as if they were to command our flocks of sheep, or herds of cattle. But let them remember and know, that they are of the same mold and condition as others, raised from the earth by the voice and acclamations, now as it were upon the shoulders of the people unto their thrones, that they might afterward bear on their own shoulders the greatest burdens of the commonwealth. Divers ages before

that, the people of Israel demanded a king. God gave and appointed the law of royal government contained in the seventeenth chapter, verse fourteen of Deuteronomy, when says Moses, "thou art come unto the land which the Lord thy God giveth thee, and shall possess it, and shalt dwell therein, and shalt say, I will set a king over me like as all the nations that are about me, thou shalt in any wise set him whom the Lord thy God shall choose from amongst thy brethren, etc." You see here, that the election of the king is attributed to God, the establishment to the people; now when the practice of this law came in use, see in what manner they proceeded.

The elders of Israel, who presented the whole body of the people (under this name of elders are comprehended the captains, the centurions, commanders over fifties and tens, judges, provosts, but principally the chiefs of tribes) came to meet Samuel in Ramah, and not being willing longer to endure the government of the sons of Samuel, whose ill carriage had justly drawn on them the people's dislike, and withal persuading themselves that they had found the means to make their wars hereafter with more advantage, they demanded a king of Samuel, who asking counsel of the Lord, he made known that He had chosen Saul for the governor of His people. Then Samuel anointed Saul, and performed all those rights which belong to the election of a king required by the people. Now this might, perhaps, have seemed sufficient, if Samuel had presented to the people the king who was chosen by God, and had admonished them all to become good and obedient subjects. Notwithstanding, to the end that the king might know that he was established by the people, Samuel appointed the estates to meet at Mizpah, where being assembled as if the business were but then to begin, and nothing had already been done, to be brief, as if the election of Saul were then only to be treated of, the lot is cast and falls on the tribe of Benjamin, after on the family of Matri, and lastly on Saul, born of that family, who was the same whom God had chosen. Then by the consent of all the people Saul was declared king. Finally, that Saul nor any other might attribute the aforesaid business to chance or lot, after that Saul had made some proof of his valor in raising the siege of the Ammonites in Jabish Gilead, some of the people pressing the business, he was again confirmed king in a full assembly at Gilgal. You see that he whom God had chosen, and the lot had separated from all the rest, is established king by the suffrages of the people.

Briefly, for so much as none were ever born with crowns on their heads, and scepters in their hands, and that no man can be a king by himself, nor reign without people, whereas on the contrary, the people may subsist of themselves, and were, long before they had any kings, it must of necessity follow that kings were at the first constituted by the people; and although the sons and dependants of such kings, inheriting their fathers' virtues, may in a sort seem to have rendered their kingdoms hereditary to their offsprings, and that in some kingdoms and countries the right of free election seems in a sort buried; yet, notwithstanding, in all well-ordered kingdoms, this custom is yet remaining. The sons do not succeed the fathers, before the people have first, as it were, anew established them by their new approbation: neither were they acknowledged in quality, as inheriting it from the dead; but approved and accounted kings then only, when they were invested with the kingdom, by receiving the scepter and diadem from the hands of those who represent the majesty of the people. One may see most evident marks of this in Christian kingdoms, which are at this day esteemed hereditary; for the French king, he of Spain and England, and others, are commonly sacred, and, as it were, put into possession of their authority by the peers, lords of the kingdom, and officers of the crown, who represent the body of the people.

4. The People above the King

Now, seeing that the people choose and establish their kings, it follows that the whole body of the people is above the king; for it is a thing most evident, that he who is established by another, is accounted under him who has established him, and he who receives his authority from another, is less than he from whom he derives his power. Potiphar the Egyptian sets Joseph over all his house; Nebuchadnezar, Daniel over the province of Babylon; Darius, the six score governors over the kingdom. It is commonly said that masters establish their servants, kings their officers. In like manner, also, the people establish the king as administrator of the commonwealth. Good kings have not disdained this title; yea, the bad ones themselves have affected it; insomuch, as for the space of divers ages, no Roman emperor (if it were not some absolute tyrant, as Nero, Domitian, Caligula) would suffer himself to be called lord. Furthermore, it must necessarily be that kings were instituted for the people's sake, neither can it be that for the pleasure of some hundreds of men, and without doubt more foolish and worse than many of the other, all the rest were made, but much rather that these hundred were made for the use and service of all the other, and reason requires that he be preferred above the other, who was made only to and for his occasion: so it is, that for the ship's sail, the owner appoints a pilot over her, who sits at the helm, and looks that she keep her course, nor run not upon any dangerous shelf; the pilot doing his duty, is obeyed by the mariners; yea, and of himself who is owner of the vessel, notwithstanding, the pilot is a servant as well as the least in the ship, from whom he only differs in this, that he serves in a better place than they do.

In a commonwealth, commonly compared to a ship, the king holds the place of pilot, the people in general are owners of the vessel, obeying the pilot, while he is careful of the public good; as though this pilot neither

is nor ought to be esteemed other than servant to the public; as a judge or general in
war differs little from other officers, but that
he is bound to bear greater burdens, and expose himself to more dangers. By the same
reason also which the king gains by ac-
quist of arms, be it that he possesses himself of frontier places in warring on the
enemy, or that which he gets by escheats
or confiscations, he gets it to the kingdom,
and not to himself, to wit, to the people,
of whom the kingdom is composed, no more
nor less than the servant does for his master; neither may one contract or oblige
themselves to him, but by and with reference to the authority derived from the
people. Furthermore, there is an infinite
sort of people who live without a king, but
we cannot imagine a king without people.
And those who have been raised to the royal
dignity were not advanced because they excelled other men in beauty and comeliness,
nor in some excellency of nature to govern
them as shepherds do their flocks, but rather
being made out of the same mass with the
rest of the people, they would acknowledge
that for them, they, as it were, borrow
their power and authority.

The ancient custom of the French represents that exceeding well, for they used to
lift up on a buckler, and salute him king
whom they had chosen. And wherefore is it
said, "I pray you, that kings have an infinite number of eyes, a million of ears,
with extreme long hands and feet exceeding
swift"? Is it because they are like to Argos,
Gerien, Midas, and divers others so celebrated by the poets? No, truly, but it is
said in regard to all the people, whom the
business principally concerns, who lend to
the king for the good of the commonwealth,
their eyes, their ears, their means, their
faculties. Let the people forsake the king,
he presently falls to the ground, although
before, his hearing and sight seemed most
excellent, and that he was strong and in
the best disposition that might be; yea, that
he seemed to triumph in all magnificence,
yet in an instant he will become most vile
and contemptible: to be brief, instead of

those divine honours wherewith all men
adore him, he shall be compelled to become
a pedant, and whip children in the school
at Corinth. Take away but the basis to
this giant, and like the Rhodian Colossus
he presently tumbles on the ground and
falls into pieces. Seeing then that the king
is established in this degree by the people,
and for their sake, and that he cannot subsist without them, who can think it strange,
then, for us to conclude that the people are
above the king?

Now that which we speak of all the people universally, ought also to be understood
of those who in every kingdom or town do
lawfully represent the body of the people,
and who ordinarily are (or at least should
be) called the officers of the kingdom, or
crown, and not of the king; for the officers
of the king, it is he who places and displaces them at his pleasure, yea, after his
death they have no more power, and are
accounted as dead. On the contrary, the
officers of the kingdom receive their authority from the people in the general assembly of the states (or, at the least were
accustomed so anciently to have done) and
cannot be disauthorized but by them, so
then the one depends of the king, the other
of the kingdom, those of the sovereign
officer of the kingdom, who is the king
himself, those of the sovereignty itself, that
is of the people, of which sovereignty both
the king and all his officers of the kingdom
ought to depend, the charge of the one has
proper relation to the care of the king's
person; that of the other, to look that the
commonwealth receive no damage; the first
ought to serve and assist the king, as all
domestic servants are bound to do to their
masters; the other to preserve the rights
and privileges of the people, and to carefully hinder the prince, that he neither omit
the things that may advantage the state,
nor commit anything that may damage the
public.

Briefly, the one are servants and domestics of the king, and received into their
places to obey his person; the other, on the
contrary, are as associates to the king, in

the administration of justice, participating of the royal power and authority, being bound to the utmost of their power to be assisting in the managing of the affairs of state, as well as the king, who is, as it were, president amongst them, and principal only in order and degree.

5. Why Kings Were Created

Now, seeing that kings have been ever established by the people, and that they have had associates joined with them, to contain them within the limits of their duties, the which associates considered in particular one by one, are under the king, and altogether in one entire body are above him: We must consequently see wherefore first kings were established, and what is principally their duty. We usually esteem a thing just and good when it attains to the proper end for which it is ordained.

In the first place every one consents, that men by nature loving liberty, and hating servitude, born rather to command, than obey, have not willingly admitted to be governed by another, and renounced as it were the privilege of nature, by submitting themselves to the commands of others, but for some special and great profit that they expected from it. For as Aesop says, "That the horse being before accustomed to wander at his pleasure, would never have received the bit into his mouth, nor the rider on his back, but that he hoped by that means to overmatch the bull." Neither let us imagine, that kings were chosen to apply to their own proper use the goods that are gotten by the sweat of their subjects; for every man loves and cherishes his own. They have not received the power and authority of the people to make it serve as a pander to their pleasures: for ordinarily, the inferiors hate, or at least envy, their superiors.

Let us then conclude, that they are established in this place to maintain by justice, and to defend by force of arms, both the public state, and particular persons from all damages and outrages, wherefore Saint Augustine said, "Those are properly called lords and masters who provide for the good and profit of others, as the husband for the wife, fathers for their children." They must therefore obey them who provide for them; although, indeed, to speak truly, those who govern in this manner may in a sort be said to serve those whom they command over.

For, as says the same doctor, they command not for the desire of dominion, but for the duty they owe to provide for the good of those who are subjected to them: not affecting any lordlike domineering, but with charity and singular affection, desiring the welfare of those who are committed to them.

Seneca in the eighty-first epistle says, "That in the golden age, wise men only governed kingdoms; they kept themselves within the bounds of moderation, and preserved the meanest from the oppression of the greatest. They persuaded and dissuaded, according as it advantaged or disadvantaged the public profit; by their wisdom, they furnished the public with plenty of all necessaries, and by their discretion prevented scarcity, by their valor and courage they expelled dangers, by their many benefits they increased and enriched their subjects; they pleaded not their duty in making pompous shows, but in well governing their people. No man made trial what he was able to do against them, because every one received what he was capable of from them," etc.

Therefore then, to govern is nothing else but to provide for. These proper ends of commanding, being for the people's commodity, the only duty of kings and emperors is to provide for the people's good. The kingly dignity to speak properly, is not a title of honor, but a weighty and burdensome office. It is not a discharge or vacation from affairs to run a licentious course of liberty, but a charge and vocation to all industrious employments, for the service of the commonwealth; the which has some glimpse of honor with it, because in those first and golden ages, no man would have tasted of such continual troubles, if they had not been sweetened with some relish of honor; insomuch as there was nothing more true than that which was commonly said in those times, "If every man knew with what turmoils and troubles the royal wreath was wrapt withal, no man would take it up, although it lay at his feet."

When, therefore, that these words of "mine" and "thine" entered into the world, and that differences fell amongst fellow citizens, touching the propriety of goods, and wars amongst neighboring people about the right of their confines, the people bethought themselves to have recourse to some one who both could and should take order that the poor were not oppressed by the rich, nor the patriots wronged by strangers.

Nor as wars and suits increased, they chose someone, in whose wisdom and valor they reposed most confidence. See, then, wherefore kings were created in the first ages; to wit, to administer justice at home, and to be leaders in the wars abroad, and not only to repulse the incursions of the enemy, but also to repress and hinder the devastation and spoiling of the subjects and their goods at home; but above all, to expel and drive away all devices and debauchments far from their dominions.

6. Are Kings above the Law?

We must here yet proceed a little further: for it is demanded whether the king who presides in the administration of justice has power to resolve and determine business according to his own will and pleasure. Must the kings be subject to the law, or does the law depend upon the king? The law (says an ancient) is respected by those who otherways contemn virtue, for it enforces obedience, and ministers' conduct in warfaring, and gives vigor and luster to justice and equity. Pausanias the Spartan will answer in a word, that it becomes laws to direct, and men to yield obedience to their authority. Agesilaus, king of Sparta, says that all commanders must obey the commandments of the laws. But it shall not be amiss to carry this matter a little higher. When people began to seek for justice to determine their differences, if they met with any private man that did justly appoint them, they were satisfied with it. Now for so much as such men were rarely and with much difficulty met withal, and for that the judgments of kings received as laws were oftentimes found contrary and difficult, then the magistrates and others of great wisdom invented laws, which might speak to all men in one and the same voice.

This being done, it was expressly enjoined to kings that they should be the guardians and administrators, and sometimes also, for so much as the laws could not foresee the particularities of actions to resolve exactly, it was permitted the king to supply this defect by the same natural equity by which the laws were drawn; and for fear lest they should go against law, the people appointed them from time to time associates, counselors, of whom we have formerly made mention, wherefore there is nothing which exempts the king from obedience which he owes to the law, which he ought to acknowledge as his lady and mistress, esteeming nothing can become him worse than that feminine of which Juvenal speaks: *Sic volo, sic jubeo, sic pro ratione voluntas.* I will, I command, my will shall serve instead of reason. Neither should they think their authority the less because they are confined to laws, for seeing the law is a divine gift coming from above, which human societies are happily governed and addressed to their best and blessedest end; those kings are as ridiculous and worthy of contempt, who repute it a dishonor to conform themselves to law, as those surveyors who think themselves disgraced by using of a rule, a compass, a chain or other instruments, which men understanding the art of surveying are accustomed to do, or a pilot who had rather fail, according to his fantasy and imagination, than steer his course by his needle and sea-card. Who can doubt, but that it is a thing more profitable and convenient to obey the law, than the king who is but one man? The law is the soul of a good king, it gives him motion, sense and life. The king is the organ and as it were the body by which the law displays her forces, exercises her function, and expresses her conceptions. Now it is a thing much more reasonable to obey the soul, than the body; the law is the wisdom of diverse sages, recollected in few words, but many see more clear and further than one alone. It is much better to follow the law than any one man's opinion, be he never so acute. The law is reason and wisdom itself, free from all perturbation, not subject to be moved with choler, ambition, hate, or acceptances of persons.

For, if the welfare of the kingdom depends on the observation of the laws, and the laws are enthralled to the pleasure of one man, is it not most certain, that there can be no permanent stability in that government? Must it not then necessarily come to pass, that if the king (as some have been) be infected with lunacy, either continually, or by intervals, that the whole state fall inevitably to ruin? But if the laws be superior to the king, as we have already proved, and that the king be tied in the same respect of obedience to the laws as the servant is to his master, who will be so senseless, who will not rather obey the law than the king or will not readily yield his best assistance against those who seek to violate or infringe them?

7. Subjects Not the King's Slaves

For truly neither are the subjects, as it is commonly said, the king's slaves, or bondmen: being neither prisoners taken in the wars, nor bought for money. But as considered in one entire body they are lords, as we have formerly proved; so each of them in particular ought to be held as the king's brothers and kinsmen. And to the end that we think not this strange, let us hear what God Himself says when He prescribes a law to kings: That they lift not their heart above their brethern from amongst whom they were chosen. Whereupon Bartolus, a famous lawyer, who lived in an age that bred many tyrants, did yet draw this conclusion from that law, that subjects were to be held and used in the quality and condition of the king's brethren, and not of his slaves. Also king David was not ashamed to call his subjects his brethren. The ancient kings were called Abimelech, an Hebrew word which signifies, my father the king. The almighty and all good God, of whose great gentleness and mercy we are daily partakers, and very seldom feel His severity, although we justly deserve it, yet is it always mercifully mixed with compassion; whereby He teaches princes, His lieutenants, that subjects ought rather to be held in obedience by love, than by fear.

But, lest they should except against me, as if I sought to entrench too much upon the royal authority, I verily believe it is so much the greater, by how much it is likely to be of longer continuance. For, says one, servile fear is a bad guardian, for that authority we desire should continue; for those in subjection hate them they fear, and whom we hate, we naturally wish their destruction. On the contrary, there is nothing more proper to maintain their authority than the affection of their subjects, on whose love they may safely and with most security lay the foundation of their greatness. And therefore that prince who governs his subjects as brethren, may confidently assure himself to live securely in the midst of dangers: whereas he who uses them like slaves, must needs live in much anxiety and fear, and may well be resembled to the condition of that master who remains alone in some desert in the midst of a great troop of slaves; for look how many slaves any has, he must make account of so many enemies, which almost all tyrants who have been killed by their subjects have experienced. Whereas, on the contrary, the subjects of good kings are ever as solicitously careful of their safety, as of their own welfare.

8. Authority Based on Contract

We have shown already that in the establishing of the king there were two alliances or covenants contracted: the first between God, the king, and the people, of which we have formerly treated; the second, between the king and the people, of which we must now say somewhat. After that Saul was established king, the royal law was given him, according to which he ought to govern. David made a covenant in Hebron before the Lord, that is to say, taking God for witness, with all the ancients of Israel, who represented the whole body of the people, and even then he was made king. Joas also by the mouth of Johoiada the high priest, entered into covenant with the whole people of the land in the house of the Lord. And when the crown was set on his head, together with it was the law of the testimony put into his hand, which most expounds to be the law of God; likewise Josias promises to observe and keep the commandments, testimonies, and statutes comprised in the book of the covenant: under which words are contained all which belongs to the duties both of the first and second table of the law of God. In all the before-remembered places of the holy story, it is ever said, "that a covenant was made with all the people, with all the multitude, with all the elders, with all the men of Judah": to the end that we might know, as it is also fully expressed, that not only the principals of the tribes, but also all the milleniers, centurions, and subaltern magistrates should meet together, each of them in the name, and for their towns and communalties, to covenant and contract with the king. In this assembly was the creating of the king determined of, for it was the people who made the king, and not the king the people.

It is certain, then, that the people by way or stipulation require a performance of covenants. The king promises it. Now the condition of a stipulator is in terms of law more worthy than of a promiser. The people ask the king, whether he will govern justly and according to the laws? He promises he will. Then the people answer, and not before, that while he governs uprightly, they will obey faithfully. The king therefore promises simply and absolutely, the people upon condition: the which failing to be accomplished, the people rest according to equity and reason quit from their promise.

In the first covenant or contract there is only an obligation to piety: in the second, to justice. In that, the king promises to serve God religiously: in this, to rule the people justly. By the one he is obliged with the utmost of his endeavors to procure the glory of God: by the other, the profit of the people. In the first, there is a condition expressed, "if thou keep my commandments": in the second, "if thou distribute justice equally to every man." God is the proper revenger of deficiency in the former, and the whole people the lawful punisher of delinquency in the latter, or the estates, the representative body thereof who have assumed to themselves the protection of the people. This has been always practiced in all well-governed estates.

I would ask here, wherefore a man does swear, if it be not to declare that what he delivers he sincerely intends from his heart? Can anything be judged more near to the law of nature, than to observe that which we approve? Furthermore, what is the reason the king swears first, and at the instance, and required by the people, but to accept a condition either tacit or expressed? Wherefore is there a condition opposed to the contract, if it be not that in failing to perform the condition, the contract, according to law, remains void? And if for want of satisfying the condition by right, the contract is of no force, who shall dare to call that people perjured, which refuses to obey a king who makes no account of his promise, which he might and ought to have kept, and willfully breaks those laws which he did swear to observe? On the contrary, may we not rather esteem such a king perfidious, perjured, and unworthy of his place? For if the law free the vassal from his lord, who dealt feloniously with him, although that to speak properly, the lord swears not fealty to his vassal, but he to him: if the law of the twelve tables does detest and hold in execration the protector who defrauds him that is under his tuition: if the civil law permit an enfranchised servant to bring his action against his patron, for any grievous usage: if in such cases the same law delivers the slave from the power of his master, although the obligation be natural only, and not civil: is it not much more reasonable that the people be loosed from that oath of allegiance which they have taken, if the king (who may be not unfitly resembled by an attorney, sworn to look to his client's cause) first break his oath solemnly taken? And what if all these ceremonies, solemn oaths, nay, sacramental promises, had never been taken? Does not nature herself sufficiently teach that kings were on this condition ordained by the people, that they should govern well: judges, that they should distribute justice uprightly; captains in the war, that they should lead their armies against their enemies? If, on the contrary, they themselves forage and spoil their subjects, and instead of governors become enemies, as they leave indeed the true and essential qualities of a king, so neither ought the people to acknowledge them for lawful princes. But what if a people (you will reply) subdued by force, be compelled by the king to take an oath of servitude? And what if a robber, pirate, or tyrant (I will answer) with whom no bond of human society can be effectual, holding his dagger to your throat, constrain you presently to become bound in a great sum of money? Is it not an unquestionable maxim in law, that a promise exacted by violence cannot bind, especially if anything be promised against

common reason, or the law of nature? Is there anything more repugnant to nature and reason, than that a people should manacle and fetter themselves; and to be obliged by promise to the prince, with their own hands and weapons to be their own executioners? There is, therefore, a mutual obligation between the king and the people, which, whether it be civil or natural only, whether tacit or expressed in words, it cannot by any means be annihilated, or by any law be obrogated, much less by force made void. And this obligation is of such power that the prince who willfully violates it, is a tyrant. And the people who purposely break it, may be justly termed seditious.

9. Resistance to Tyrants

Hitherto we have treated of a king. It now rests we do somewhat more fully describe a tyrant. We have shown that he is a king, who lawfully governs a kingdom, either derived to him by succession, or committed to him by election. It follows, therefore, that he is reputed a tyrant, which, as opposite to a king, either gains a kingdom by violence or indirect means, or being invested therewith by lawful election, or succession, governs it not according to law and equity, or neglects those contracts and agreements, to the observation whereof he was strictly obliged at his reception. All which may very well occur in one and the same person. The first is commonly called a tyrant without title: the second a tyrant by practice. Now, it may well so come to pass, that he who possesses himself of a kingdom by force, to govern justly, and he on whom it descends by a lawful title, to rule unjustly. But for so much as a kingdom is rather a right than an inheritance, and an office than a possession, he seems rather worthy the name of a tyrant, who unworthily acquits himself of his charge, than he who entered into his place by a wrong door. In the same sense is the pope called an intruder who entered by indirect means into the papacy: and he an abuser who governs ill in it.

Pythagoras says "that a worthy stranger is to be preferred before an unworthy citizen, yea, though he be a kinsman." Let it be lawful also for us to say, that a prince who gained his principality by indirect courses, provided he govern according to law, and administer justice equally, is much to be preferred before him, who carries himself tyrannously, although he were legally invested into his government with all the ceremonies and rites thereunto appertaining.

For seeing that kings were instituted to feed, to judge, to cure the diseases of the people: Certainly I had rather that a thief should feed me, than a shepherd devour me: I had rather receive justice from a robber, than outrage from a judge: I had better be healed by an empiric, than poisoned by a doctor in physic. It were much more profitable for me to have my estate carefully managed by an intruding guardian, than to have it wasted and dissipated by one legally appointed.

Now, at the last we are come as it were by degrees to the chief and principal point of the question. We have seen how that kings have been chosen by God, either with relation to their families or their persons only, and after installed by the people. In like manner what is the duty of the king, and of the officers of the kingdom, how far the authority, power, and duty both of the one and the other extends, and what and how sacred are the covenants and contracts which are made at the inauguration of kings, and what conditions are intermixed, both tacit and expressed; finally, who is a tyrant without title, and who by practice, seeing it is a thing unquestionable that we are bound to obey a lawful king, which both to God and people carries himself according to those covenants whereunto he stands obliged, as it were to God Himself, seeing in a sort he represents his divine Majesty? It now follows that we treat, how, and by whom a tyrant may be lawfully resisted, and who are the persons who ought to be chiefly actors therein, and what course is to be held, that the action may be managed according to right and reason. We must first speak of him who is commonly called a tyrant without title. Let us suppose then that some Ninus, having neither received outrage nor offence, invades a people over whom he has no color of pretension: that Caesar seeks to oppress his country, and the Roman commonwealth: that Popiclus endeavors by murders and treasons to make the elective kingdom of Polonia to become hereditary to him and his posterity: or some Bruniehilde draws to herself and her Protadius the absolute government of France, or Ebronius, taking advantage of Theoderick's weakness and idleness, gains the entire administration of the state, and oppresses the people, what shall be our lawful refuge herein?

First, the law of nature teaches and commands us to maintain and defend our lives and liberties, without which life is scant worth the enjoying, against all injury and violence. Nature has imprinted this by instinct in dogs against wolves, in bulls against lions, betwixt pigeons and sparrow hawks, betwixt pullen and kites, and yet much more in man against man himself, if man become a beast: and therefore he who questions the lawfulness of defending oneself, does, as much as in him lies, question the law of nature. To this must be added the law of nations, which distinguishes possessions and dominions, fixes limits, and makes out confines, which every man is bound to defend against all invaders. And, therefore, it is no less lawful to resist Alexander the Great, if without any right or being justly provoked, he invades a country with a mighty navy, as well as Diomedes the pirate who scours the seas in a small vessel. For in this case Alexander's right is no more than Diomedes' but only he has more power to do wrong, and not so easily to be compelled to reason as the other. Briefly, one may as well oppose Alexander in pillaging a country, as a thief in purloining a cloak; as well him when he seeks to batter down the walls of a city, as a robber who offers to break into a private house.

There is, besides this, the civil law, or municipal laws of several countries which govern the societies of men, by certain rules, some in one manner, some in another; some submit themselves to the government of one man, some to more; others are ruled by a whole commonalty, some absolutely exclude women from the royal throne, others admit them; these here choose their king descended of such a family, those there make election of whom they please, besides other customs practiced among several nations. If, therefore, any offer either by fraud or force to violate this law, we are all bound to resist him, because he wrongs that society to which we owe all that we have, and would ruin our country, to the preservation whereof all men by nature, by law and by solemn oath, are strictly obliged: insomuch that fear or negligence, or had purposes, make us omit this duty, we may justly be accounted breakers of the laws, betrayers of our country, and contemners of religion. Now as the laws of nature, of nations, and the Civil commands us to take arms against such tyrants; so, is there not any manner of reason that should persuade us to the contrary; neither is there any oath, covenant, or obligation, public or private, of power justly to restrain us; therefore the meanest private man may resist and lawfully oppose such an intruding tyrant. The law Julia, which condemns to death those who raise rebellion against their country or prince, has here no place; for he is no prince, who, without any lawful title invades the commonwealth or confines of another; nor he a rebel, who by arms defends his country; but rather to this had relation the oath which all the youth of Athens were accustomed to take in the temple of Aglaura, "I will fight for religion, for the laws, for the altars, and for our possessions, either alone, or with others; and will do the utmost of my endeavor to leave to posterity our country, at the least, in as good estate as I found it." To as little

purpose can the laws made against seditious persons be alleged here; for he is seditious who undertakes to defend the people, in opposition of order and public discipline; but he is no raiser, but a suppressor of sedition, who restrains within the limits of reason the subverter of his country's welfare, and public discipline.

On the contrary, to this has proper relation the law of tyrannicide, which honors the living with great and memorable recompenses, and the dead with worthy epitaphs, and glorious statues, that have been their country's liberators from tyrants; as Harmodius and Aristogiton at Athens, Brutus and Cassius in Rome, and Aratus of Sycione.

We must remember that all princes are born men, and therefore reason and passion are as hardly to be separated in them, as the soul is from the body while the man lives. We must not then expect princes absolute in perfection, but rather repute ourselves happy if those who govern us be indifferently good. And therefore, although the prince observe not exact mediocrity in state affairs; if sometimes passion overrule his reason, if some careless omission make him neglect the public utility; or if he do not always carefully execute justice with equality, or repulse not with ready valor an invading enemy; he must not therefore be presently declared a tyrant. And certainly, seeing he rules not as a god over men, nor as men over beasts, but is a man composed of the same matter, and of the same nature with the rest: as we would questionless judge that prince unreasonably insolent, who should insult over and abuse his subjects, as if they were brute beasts; so those people are doubtless as much void of reason, who imagine a prince should be complete in perfection, or expect divine abilities in a nature so frail and subject to imperfections. But if a prince purposely ruin the commonwealth, if he presumptuously pervert and resist legal proceedings or lawful rights, if he make no reckoning of faith, covenants, justice nor piety, if he prosecute his subjects as enemies; briefly, if he express all or the chiefest of those wicked practices we have formerly spoken of; then we may certainly declare him a tyrant, who is as much an enemy both to God and men. We do not therefore speak of a prince less good, but of one absolutely bad; not of one less wise, but of one malicious and treacherous; not of one less able judiciously to discuss legal differences, but of one perversely bent to pervert justice and equity; not of an unwarlike, but of one furiously disposed to ruin the people, and ransack the state.

For the wisdom of a senate, the integrity of a judge, the valor of a captain, may peradventure enable a weak prince to govern well. But a tyrant could be content that all the nobility, the counselors of state, the commanders for the wars, had but one head that he might take it off at one blow: those being the proper objects of his distrust and fear, and by consequence the principal subjects on whom he desires to execute his malice and cruelty. A foolish prince, although (to speak according to right and equity) he ought to be deposed, yet may he perhaps in some sort be borne withal. But a tyrant, the more he is tolerated, the more he becomes intolerable.

Furthermore, as the princes' pleasure is not always law, so many times it is not expedient that the people do all that which may lawfully be done; for it may oftentimes chance that the medicine proves more dangerous than the disease. Therefore it becomes wise men to try all ways before they come to blows, to use all other remedies before they suffer the sword to decide the controversy. If then those who represent the body of the people foresee any innovation or machination against the state, or that it be already embarked into a course of perdition; their duty is, first to admonish the prince, and not to attend that the disease by accession of time and accidents becomes unrecoverable. For tyranny may be properly resembled unto a fever hectic, the which at the first is easy to be cured, but with much difficulty to be known; but after it is sufficiently known, it becomes incur-

able. Therefore small beginnings are to be carefully observed, and by those whom it concerns diligently prevented.

If the prince therefore persist in his violent courses, and contemn frequent admonitions, addressing his designs only to that end, that he may oppress at his pleasure, and effect his own desires without fear or restraint; he then doubtless makes himself liable to that detested crime of tyranny: and whatsoever either the law, or lawful authority permits against a tyrant, may be lawfully practiced against him. Tyranny is not only a will, but the chief, and as it were the complement and abstract of vices. A tyrant subverts the state, pillages the people, lays stratagems to entrap their lives, breaks promise with all, scoffs at the sacred obligations of a solemn oath, and therefore is he so much more vile than the vilest of usual malefactors. By how much offences committed against a generality, are worthy of greater punishment than those which concern only particular and private persons. If thieves and those who commit sacrilege be declared infamous; nay, if they justly suffer corporal punishment by death, can we invent any that may be worthily equivalent for so outrageous a crime.

Furthermore, we have already proved that all kings receive their royal authority from the people, that the whole people considered in one body is above and greater than the king; and that the king and emperor are only the prime and supreme governors and ministers of the kingdom and empire; but the people the absolute lord and owner thereof. It therefore necessarily follows that a tyrant is in the same manner guilty of rebellion against the majesty of the people as the lord of a fee, who feloniously transgresses the conditions of his investitures, and is liable to the same punishment, yea, and certainly deserves a much greater one than the equity of those laws inflicts on the delinquents. Therefore as Bartolus says, "He may either be deposed by those who are lords in sovereignty over him, or else justly punished according to the law Julia, which condemns those who offer violence to the public." The body of the people must needs be the sovereign of those who represent it, which in some places are the electors, palatines, peers; in other, the assembly of the general estates. And, if the tyranny have gotten such sure footing, as there is no other means but force to remove him, then it is lawful for them to call the people to arms, to enroll and raise forces, and to employ the utmost of their power, and use against him all advantages and stratagems of war, as against the enemy of the commonwealth, and the disturber of the public peace. Briefly, the same sentence may be justly pronounced against him, as was against Manlius Capitolinus at Rome. "Thou wast to me, Manlius, when thou didst tumble down the Gaules that scaled the capital: but since thou art now become an enemy, like one of them, thou shalt be precipitated down from the same place from whence thou formerly tumbled those enemies."

The officers of the kingdom cannot for this be rightly taxed of sedition; for in a sedition there must necessarily concur but two parts, or sides, the which peremptorily contest together, so that it is necessary that the one be in the right, and the other in the wrong. That part undoubtedly has the right on their side, which defends the laws, and strives to advance the public profit of the kingdom. And those, on the contrary, are questionless in the wrong, who break the laws, and protect those who violate justice, and oppress the commonwealth. Those are certainly in the right way, as said Bartolus, "who endeavor to suppress tyrannical government, and those in the wrong, who oppose lawful authority." And that must ever be accounted just, which is intended only for the public benefit, and that unjust, which aims chiefly at private commodity. Wherefore Thomas Aquinas says, "That a tyrannical rule, having no proper address for the public welfare, but only to satisfy a private will, with increase of particular profit to the ruler, cannot in any reasonable construction be accounted lawful, and therefore the disturbance of such

a government cannot be esteemed seditious, much less traitorous"; for that offence has proper relation only to a lawful prince, who indeed is an inanimated or speaking law; therefore, seeing that he who employs the utmost of his means and power to annihilate the laws, and quell their virtue and vigor, can no ways be justly intituled therewith. So neither, likewise, can those who oppose and take arms against him, be branded with so notorious a crime. Also this offence is committed against the commonwealth; but for so much as the commonwealth is there only where the laws are in force, and not where a tyrant devours the state at his own pleasure and liking, he certainly is quit of that crime which ruins the majesty of the public state, and those questionless are worthily protectors and preservers of the commonwealth, who, confident in the lawfulness of their authority, and summoned thereunto by their duty, do courageously resist the unjust proceedings of the tyrant.

And in this their action, we must not esteem them as private men and subjects, but as the representative body of the people, yea, and as the sovereignty itself, which demands of his minister an account of his administration. Neither can we in any good reason account the officers of the kingdom disloyal, who in this manner acquit themselves of their charge.

There is ever, and in all places, a mutual and reciprocal obligation between the people and the prince; the one promises to be a good and wise prince, the other to obey faithfully, provided he govern justly. The people therefore are obliged to the prince under condition, the prince to the people simply and purely. Therefore, if the prince fail in his promise, the people are exempt from obedience, the contract is made void, the right of obligation of no force. Then the king if he govern unjustly is perjured, and the people likewise forsworn if they obey not his lawful commands. But that people are truly acquit from all perfidiousness, who publicly renounce the unjust dominion of a tyrant, or he, striving unjustly by strong hand to continue the possession, do constantly endeavor to expulse him by force of arms.

It is therefore permitted the officers of a kingdom, either all, or some good number of them, to suppress a tyrant; and it is not only lawful for them to do it, but their duty expressly requires it; and, if they do it not, they can by no excuse color their baseness. For the electors, palatines, peers, and other officers of state, must not think they were established only to make pompous paradoes and shows, when they are at the coronation of the king, habited in their robes of state, as if there were some masque or interlude to be represented; or as if they were that day to act the parts of Roland, Oliver, or Renaldo, and such other personages on a stage, or to counterfeit and revive the memory of the knights of the round table; and after the dismissing of that day's assembly, to suppose they have sufficiently acquitted themselves of their duty, until a recess of the like solemnity. Those solemn rites and ceremonies were not instituted for vain ostentation, nor to pass, as in a dumb show, to please the spectators, nor in children's sports, as it is with Horace, to create a king in jest; but those grandees must know that as well for office and duty, as for honor, they are called to the performance of those rites, and that in them, the commonwealth is committed and recommended to the king, as to her supreme and principal tutor and protector, and to them as coadjutors and assistants to him: and therefore, as the tutors or guardians (yea, even those who are appointed by way of honor) are chosen to have care of and observe the actions and importments of him who holds the principal rank in the tutorship, and to look how he carries himself in the administration of the goods of his pupil. So likewise are the former ordained to have an eye to the courses of the king, for, with an equivalent authority, as the others for the pupil, so are they to hinder and prevent the damage and detriment of the people, the king being properly reputed as the prime guardian, and they his coadjutors.

In like manner, as the faults of the principal tutor who manages the affairs are justly imputed to the coadjoints in the tutorship, if when they ought and might, they did not discover his errors, and cause him to be despoiled, especially failing in the main points of his charge, to wit, in not communicating unto them the affairs of his administration, in dealing unfaithfully in his place, in doing anything to the dishonor of detriment of his pupil, in embezzling of his goods or estate, or if he be an enemy to his pupil: briefly, if either in regard of the worthlessness of his person, or weakness of his judgment, he be unable well to discharge so weighty a charge, so also, are the peers and principal officers of the kingdom accountable for the government thereof, and must both prevent, and if occasion require, suppress the tyranny of the prince, as also supply with their care and diligence, his inability and weakness.

Princes are chosen by God, and established by the people. As all particulars considered one by one, are inferior to the prince; so the whole body of the people and officers of state, who represent that body, are the princes' superiors. In the receiving and inauguration of a prince, there are covenants and contracts passed between him and the people, which are tacit and expressed, natural or civil; to wit, to obey him faithfully while he commands justly, that he serving the commonwealth, all men shall serve him, that while he governs according to law, all shall be submitted to his government, etc. The officers of the kingdom are the guardians and protectors of these covenants and contracts. He who maliciously or willfully violates these conditions, is questionless a tyrant by practice. And therefore the officers of state may judge him according to the laws. And if he support his tyranny by strong hands, their duty binds them, when by no other means it can be effected by force of arms to suppress him.

Of these officers there be two kinds, those who have generally undertaken the protection of the kingdom; as the constable, marshals, peers, palatines, and the rest, every one of whom, although all the rest do either connive or consort with the tyranny, are bound to oppose and repress the tyrant; and those who have undertaken the government of any province, city, or part of the kingdom, as dukes, marquesses, earls, consuls, mayors, sheriffs, etc., they may according to right expel and drive tyranny and tyrants from their cities, confines, and governments.

But particular and private persons may not unsheathe the sword against tyrants by practice, because they were not established by particulars, but by the whole body of the people. But for tyrants who without title intrude themselves, for so much as there is no contract or agreement between them and the people, it is indifferently permitted all to oppose and depose them; and in this rank of tyrants may those be ranged, who, abusing the weakness and sloth of a lawful prince, tyrannously insult over his subjects.

Finally, as there have ever been tyrants distressed here and there, so also all histories testify that there have been neighboring princes to oppose tyranny, and maintain the people in their right. The princes of these times by imitating so worthy examples, should suppress the tyrants both of bodies and souls, and restrain the oppressors both of the commonwealth, and of the church of Christ: otherwise, they themselves, may most deservedly be branded with that infamous title of tyrant.

And to conclude this discourse in a word, piety commands that the law and church of God be maintained. Justice requires that tyrants and destroyers of the commonwealth be compelled to reason. Charity challenges the right of relieving and restoring the oppressed. Those who make no account of these things, do as much as in them lies to drive piety, justice, and charity out of this world, that they may never more be heard of.

CHAPTER 13

BODIN

T HE national state is the central concept of modern political thought, its tacit assumption, just as the city-state was that of antiquity, and universal empire that of the Middle Ages, Machiavelli came close to the idea of the state; he was the first to coin the term "state" (*lo stato*), but, as he was primarily interested in power and the rulers who struggled for it, but not in institutions, his use of the word "state" is strongly permeated with the meaning of "government," the state being essentially the ruler and his political, military, and administrative machine—all still viewed from a personal angle.

A clear formulation of the concepts of state and state sovereignty could occur only in a nation that was actually developing the appropriate judicial, administrative, and legislative institutions. Such institutions had been evolving in France since the late Middle Ages, and a strong sentiment of nationalism and sense of national sovereignty could be seen in the struggle between King Philip IV and Pope Boniface VIII at the end of the thirteenth century. But the appreciation of these changes was slow, and it is not until the sixteenth century that the first systematic and clear conception of *sovereignty* was worked out in *The Six Books on the State* (*Les six livres de la République,* 1576), by Jean Bodin (1530–1596).

Bodin was a native of Angers, and studied law at Toulouse, where he also taught for some time. Toulouse was an important formative phase in Bodin's life, because its university was outstanding in jurisprudence and also because its population included a considerable number of Protestants. Bodin was of middle-class origin and represented the Third Estate in the Estates-General in 1576. He became closely attached to the brother of King Henry III and served in the legal branch of the royal administration. His vast erudition (of which he put too much into his *Six Books on the State,* thus depriving it of many readers, who find its length forbidding) was thus supplemented by public experience in both the legislative and administrative parts of government.

Bodin lived at a time when the unity of France, though finally accomplished territorially, was seriously threatened by religious conflict. Calvinist Protestantism made incessant progress in France during the sixteenth century, and the attempt to eradicate it by force was met by resistance. The "War of Religion" started in 1562 and went on intermittently for over a generation. In the Massacre of St. Bartholomew (August 24, 1572) religious conflict degenerated into murder, and the spirit of intransigence grew on both sides. The religious divisions engendered by the Reformation were intertwined with deep-seated social and economic issues, which made reconciliation even more difficult. What France needed for its preservation was more moderation and compromise, and less fanaticism and radicalism; it needed citizens who preferred the prosaic stability of France in the present to the poetic bliss of heaven in the future.

From the sixties on, a group of administrators, lawyers, and publicists sought to stem the tide of fanaticism that was ruining the nation. They were called *Politiques*. At first the name was meant to be opprobrious, inasmuch as the *Politiques* were charged with putting practical politics above pure principles, and the charge was true as far as it went. The *Politiques* were Catholic, but they were unwilling to sacrifice the interests of the French state and nation to those of the Roman Catholic Church. Their attitude of toleration was generally not based on philosophy but on expediency. Michel de l'Hôpital, Chancellor of France, and an outstanding leader of the *Politiques*, had urged as early as 1560 to get rid "of these devilish words, these names of party, of faction, of sedition— Lutheran, Huguenot, Papist," and had asserted that "a man does not cease to be a citizen for being excommunicated."

If possible, the *Politiques* preferred religious unity, because they felt that political unity would thereby be furthered. Hence they were not opposed to a little persecution at the beginning of a new religious creed, provided that such dissent could be eliminated quickly and without much violence or bloodshed. But when a new faith has been embraced by a substantial portion of the community, as was true of the Huguenots, the *Politiques* were willing to accept the fact of Protestantism, because they believed that the unity of France could not stand the strain of wholesale massacre and permanent civil war.

In the history of France the *Politiques* are the first organized and conscious expression of a "Third Force" in the face of two rivaling extremes. After World War II, when communism and Gaullism seemed to divide France into two irreconcilable camps, the "Third Force" (consisting of such heterogenous elements as moderate Catholics, democratic socialists, and anticlerical free-enterprisers) represented the tradition of the *Politiques*, whereas communism and Gaullism played the twentieth-century parts of the extremist religious factions.

Bodin is the best-known theorist of the *Politiques*, and his *Six Books on the State* expresses the desire for strong government that makes contented and secure citizenship possible. Bodin defines sovereignty—he was the first to use this word —as "the absolute and perpetual power of the state, that is, the greatest power to command." Bodin distinguishes the government from the state, in other words, the exercise of sovereign functions, which may be for a limited time, from sovereignty itself, which is unlimited in time—*perpetual*. Sovereignty exists as long as the state, regardless of its changing forms of government. The *absolute* quality of sovereignty consists in the fact that the sovereign state tolerates no rival legal authority above it: "Only he is absolutely sovereign who, after God, acknowledges no one greater than himself."

Sovereignty is here markedly pointed at two sources that threatened it: universal church and empire. Both were henceforth denied any interference in the ecclesiastical and temporal affairs of the developing national states. Politically the kings looked on themselves as "emperors" in their realms, and ecclesiastically they either became the official heads of their national churches, as in Protestant states, or controlled, according to the theory of "Gallicanism," the clergy in predominantly Catholic states.

The doctrine of sovereignty, however, is directed above all against forces threatening the state from within. Bodin saw more clearly than anyone before him that the essence of sovereignty consists in the *making of general laws.* During the Middle Ages the law was something that was found by judges, not made by legislators; the process of the creation of law was thought of as a slow and imperceptible synthesis of the immemorial custom of the land, the law of nature, and the will of God. The concept of making the law marks a revolutionary break with the medieval tradition, and Bodin specifically refers to local customs and local parliaments; the feudal system of diffusion and decentralization of authority gave way to an authority that was one and indivisible. The nobility, in particular, was the target of the new doctrine of sovereignty. Bodin, like most writers of the *Politiques,* belonged to the Third Estate, and the bourgeoisie also provided the new class of administrators and judges for the constantly expanding activities of the state.

Bodin's attribution of absoluteness to the sovereign is to be understood only in relation to human laws. Still close to the medieval sentiment that the ruler is under a moral obligation to the community and God, Bodin says that the sovereign prince has no authority to violate the laws of God and nature: "In doing so a prince would become guilty of high treason against God." By defining sovereignty at the outset of his treatise as "lawful government," Bodin seeks to distinguish it from the order that bands of robbers and pirates maintain among themselves. Bodin also distinguishes between the sovereign's right to break his laws and his right to break his contracts. The sovereign ruler is not bound by his predecessors' laws or his own, because the authority of lawmaking is unilateral, deriving from the sole authority of the sovereign. But when a contract is made by the prince with his subjects or other rulers, the obligation is mutual and cannot be broken by him at will. Natural law prescribes that agreements be kept (*pacta sunt servanda*), and the prince may not free himself from this obligation by unilateral action any more than the subject may.

Bodin does not discuss in detail how the precepts of divine and natural law limit sovereignty, and in what manner a ruler's violation of divine and natural law is to be ascertained and punished. He cites murder as a case in point. If the sovereign forbids to kill, he is even more bound by it than his subjects, because "such a law is not his, but the law of God and nature."

In addition to divine and natural law, Bodin mentions limitations of sovereignty that derive from human law. First, the sovereign ruler does not have the legal authority to alter the rules of succession to the French crown; second, he has no right to alienate the public domain; third, he may not levy taxes without the consent of the Estates or deprive a subject of his property without "just cause." In the first two instances, Bodin implies that the monarch, though not bound by ordinary statutory law, is bound by the fundamental laws of the realm (*leges imperii*) governing succession and the public domain, because such fundamental laws are the legal basis of the very authority of the sovereign. As for property, Bodin felt that in violating the rights of property without due process the sovereign destroys one of the main purposes of the state, which is the protection of property and the family.

Unlike later protagonists of the doctrine of sovereignty, Bodin was unwilling to deduce limitless *power* of the monarch from his *supreme legal authority*. Parliament is legally supreme as the lawmaking body in Great Britain, yet this fact does not mean that it is able, in actuality, to pass any law whatsoever. Although there are no legal curbs on Parliament as the highest legal authority, there are extralegal and nonlegal forces, such as the electorate, parties, public opinion, trade-unions, churches, and business organizations, that effectively limit and direct its power. The British monarch is even more illustrative of the difference between sovereign authority and political power. Though he has the legal authority to refuse his assent to bills passed by both Houses of Parliament, he has not done so since 1707.

In the field of external relations, too, Bodin felt that sovereignty must be understood as a concept of legal status, and not of political power. A state is sovereign if it is not legally subject to the authority of another state and if its relations with other states are carried on in accordance with international, rather than municipal, law. This definition does not necessarily imply *factual* independence. Small states are often dependent on large states militarily, economically, and politically, but as long as their dependence is one of fact rather than of law, they are sovereign. Bodin himself occasionally blurred the distinction between the highest legal authority of the sovereign and political omnipotence. Yet his line of thought is, in general, unmistakable, and he is saved from confusing legal sovereignty with political despotism by his acute legal learning as well as by his strong sense of the rule of law, which he conceives as the confluence of constitutional, natural, and divine law.

Bodin prefers monarchy to aristocracy and democracy because the unity and indivisibility of authority seem best safeguarded in one man. But in his account of monarchical government he sharply distinguishes between *legitimate* and *illegitimate* monarchy. Royal descent or conquest in lawful war supplies the title of legitimate monarchy, whereas the tyrant, the illegitimate monarch, sets himself up as sovereign prince without rightful claim of election, descent, or lawful war. If the monarch is legitimate, the subjects have no right to encroach, acting individually or jointly, on "the honor or life of the monarch by judicial or other means, though he may have committed all the wicked, impious and cruel misdeeds one can think of." Even less have subjects the right to proceed against the prince by force. As for the tyrant, it is lawful to kill him without formal proceedings because he has put himself outside the law by seizing power illegally; if the tyrant surrenders himself into the hands of the people, thereby recognizing their sovereignty, he may be tried in court. Bodin adds the important observation that it makes no difference whether the tyrant is virtuous or villainous; he may be put to death, regardless of his personal goodness, because he has invaded sovereignty.

Whereas most of the *Politiques* tolerated religious dissent primarily on grounds of expediency, Bodin accepts religious diversity on philosophical grounds. He advises the ruler of a country divided into various churches and religions not to impose forcibly his own religion, because "the more the will of men is forced, the more it becomes obstinate." In a later book, *Colloquium heptaplomeres* (written in 1588, but not printed before 1841), Bodin, presenting seven spokesmen (therefore the title) of various Christian and non-Christian creeds in the world, arrives at a theistic position of rational belief in God, above any particular church or organized religion. Bodin's view on slavery is in harmony with his liberal outlook. Despite his admiration for Aristotle, he felt that slavery was unjust, and that it was not supported by facts, as Aristotle had said, inasmuch as good men may be kept as slaves by masters who are wicked.

Bodin's bourgeois outlook is clearly expressed in his views on property and war. He held that the prince cannot impose taxation without the consent of the Estates, and that he cannot deprive a subject of his property "without just cause." Although recognizing that no cause of revolution is more important than "excessive wealth of the few and extreme poverty of the many," he is strongly opposed to equality of property; the foundation of the state is good faith, and the equalization of property subverts the state by destroying legitimate expectations and conventions. Bodin's views on war are as different from those of Machiavelli as a sixteenth-century French bourgeois from an Ital'an *condottiere* of the Renaissance. Bodin abhors war because it is destructive of the very purpose of human associations, be it material ease or spiritual elevation. He justifies war only to repel aggression.

Bodin's state is strong but not aggressive; monarchical but not tyrannical. It became the model for the new national state in which the interests of the monarchy were allied with those of the rising merchant and middle classes against church and aristocracy. In this new state the bourgeoisie was willing to accept a strong government under kingly command, provided that it was allowed to make money and enjoy reasonable legal and political security. This alliance was to last over two hundred years, until the French Revolution raised the fundamental issue whether sovereignty should be vested in the king or in the people.

BODIN

Six Books on the State *

1. The State

The state is a lawful government, with sovereign power, of different households and their common affairs. We put this definition at the outset because in all things, it is necessary to look first for the chief end, and then for the means of attaining it. A definition is nothing else than the end of a problem that is being considered, and unless it is well founded, whatever is based upon it will soon collapse.

Let us now examine each part of the definition of the state. In the first place, we speak of the state as "lawful government" in order to distinguish it from bands of robbers and pirates, with whom it can have no part, commerce, or alliance. In all well-ordered states, therefore, robbers and pirates have always been excluded from recognition, whether it be a question of making a pledge in negotiating peace, calling off war, setting up offensive or defensive alliances, defining boundaries, or settling disputes between kings and territorial rulers. The law of mankind sharply differentiates between wartime enemies who maintain lawful government in their states, and brigands and pirates who seek to subvert and destroy them.

2. Sovereignty

Sovereignty is the absolute and perpetual power of the state, that is, the greatest

* From Jean Bodin, *Six Books on the State* (1576; trans. William Ebenstein).

power to command. It is necessary to arrive at a definition of sovereignty because neither jurists nor political philosophers have so far defined it, although it is the principal and most urgent point for an understanding of the nature of the state. Having said before that the state is a lawful government, with sovereign power, of many households and their common affairs, the meaning of sovereign power must now be explained. I have said that this power is perpetual, for absolute power may be given to one or several for a certain time only, at the end of which they are subjects again. While they are in authority they still cannot call themselves sovereign rulers, inasmuch as they are only custodians and keepers of sovereign power until it shall please the people or the prince to recall it, just as those who have lent or pawned their goods to others remain the true owners and possessors. Likewise, those who give to others the power and authority to judge and command for a defined period of time, or to be recalled at pleasure, retain power and authority that the others exercise but in the nature of a temporary lease or loan. The governor of a country or the lieutenant of a prince surrenders his power at the expiration of his term, being but the depository and keeper for someone else. It makes no difference whether the official is of high or low rank. If the absolute power granted to the lieutenant of the prince were sovereign, it could be used against the prince himself, who would be left with nothing but an empty title, and the subject would command his lord, the servant his master—

which would be absurd. Whatever power and authority the sovereign prince confers upon others, his own person remains excepted. He always retains more authority than he gives away, and he is never divested of his right to command and examine his officials by way of prevention, concurrence, or challenge, to withdraw their authority altogether, or to permit it to go on to the extent, and as long as, it shall please him.

If the people grant annually absolute power to one or several citizens, without control or appeal, shall we say that they possess sovereignty? Only he is absolutely sovereign who, after God, acknowledges no one greater than himself. These citizens elected to highest office therefore do not possess sovereignty, as they are but trustees of the power lent to them for a given time. The people do not deprive themselves of sovereignty when they entrust absolute authority to one or several rulers, either for a limited time set in advance or to be revoked at their pleasure. In both instances the holders of power remain accountable to those from whom they have received the power to command. This is not true of the sovereign prince, who is accountable to God alone.

But suppose such absolute power be given to a king's lieutenant for life. Is that not sovereign and perpetual power? Otherwise, if we should call perpetual power only that which never came to an end, sovereignty could exist only in aristocratic and popular governments that do not die. Or if the word "perpetual" would apply to a monarch and his heirs, there would be few sovereign monarchs, in view of the fact that only very few monarchies are hereditary, and in view of the fact those who arrive on the throne by the right of election would not be sovereign. "Perpetual" therefore means the lifetime of him who has the power. If the sovereign magistrate, elected for a year or for a defined time limit, continues to exercise the power that has been entrusted to him, he must do so either with

the acquiescence of the governed or by force. If by force, the tyrant is sovereign, just as the violent possession of the thief is genuine possession in nature, although contrary to law, and they who had possession before, no longer have it. But if the magistrate continues his sovereign power with the acquiescence of the people, he is not a sovereign prince, as he exercises it only on sufferance; he is even less sovereign if his term is not defined in advance, as he then holds whatever authority is his as a temporary trust and loan to be revoked at pleasure by the people.

Let us now examine the second part of our definition, and ascertain what the words "absolute power" mean. The people or the aristocracy in a commonwealth may purely and simply give someone the sovereign and perpetual power to dispose of their property and persons, and of all the state, as it may please him, and afterward leave all to whomever he may choose; just as an owner may give away his goods purely and simply, without any cause other than his liberality. Such a gift is a true one, with no conditions asked or received, once the donation is transacted and accomplished, whereas gifts that are granted under charges and conditions are not true gifts. Likewise, the transfer of sovereignty to a prince with charges and conditions does not result in true sovereign authority or absolute power, except when the conditions thus attached to the creation of the sovereign are of divine or natural law.

A prince is not bound by the laws of his predecessors, and much less by his own laws and ordinances. It is possible to receive a law from someone else, but it is impossible, in the nature of things, to give to oneself a law that depends on one's own will, as is stated in the legal maxim: *Nulla obligatio consistere potest, quae a voluntate promittentis statum capit* ("There can be no obligation that derives its validity from the will of him who makes the promise"). This necessary reason evidently proves that the prince cannot be subject to his own laws. As the Pope never ties his hands, according to the canonists, so the sovereign prince cannot tie his hands, even if he desires to do so. Therefore we see at the end of laws and ordinances the words "Because it has so pleased Us," in order to indicate that the laws of the sovereign prince, though they may be based on good and valid reasons, depend nevertheless on nothing but his pure and free will.

As for the laws of God and nature, all princes in the world are bound by them, and they have no authority to violate them. In so doing, a prince would become guilty of high treason against God and of making war on him, under whose greatness all the rulers on earth must bear their yoke and bow their heads in fear and reverence. The absolute power of princes and lords in no way extends, therefore, to the laws of God and nature, and the Pope who has best understood the nature of absolute power and who has brought kings and emperors under his control said that a sovereign can abrogate ordinary law but not divine or natural law.

But is a prince not subject to the laws of his country, which he has sworn to keep? A distinction has to be made here between two possible situations: if the prince has sworn to himself that he will abide by his laws, he is no more bound by them than by any oath made to himself, just as private citizens are not bound by oaths on agreements that the law does not consider binding, however honorable and reasonable they be. If the sovereign prince promises, however, to another ruler to keep the laws that he or his predecessors have made, he is obliged to abide by them, if the other prince has an interest therein, although no oath was included in the promise. But when the ruler, to whom the promise has been made, has no interest in the matter, neither the promise nor the oath is binding.

The same holds true if the promise has been made by the prince to his subjects, either before or after ascending the throne. Not that the prince is bound by his own laws or those of his predecessors, but anyone, ruler or subject, is obliged to keep his just covenants and promises, whether made under oath or not. Similarly, as a private citizen may be relieved of an unjust and unreasonable promise that grieves him too much and into which he has been beguiled by trickery, fraud, error, force, or fear, so as to cause him major damage, the prince, too, may be released from promises that affect the diminution of his majesty, if he is a sovereign prince. Our general rule thus remains, that the prince is not bound by his own laws or those of his predecessors but is obliged to keep his just and reasonable agreements, in the observance of which his subjects in general, or a particular private person, may have an interest.

Law and contracts must not be confused. Law depends on him who possesses sovereignty, and who can bind all his subjects but cannot bind himself. By contrast, a contract is a mutual obligation between prince and subjects that binds them reciprocally, and it cannot be altered except by mutual consent. In this situation, the prince is in no way above the subject, except that, when the justice of the law he has sworn to maintain has ceased to exist, he is no longer bound by his word; this the subjects cannot do, in their private agreements, unless they be relieved by the prince.

The sovereignty of the monarch is in no way altered or diminished by the calling together and deliberations of the estates. On the contrary, seeing all his people recognize him as their sovereign, he finds his majesty thereby enhanced and more illustrious. In such representative assemblies the princes are not unwilling to grant their subjects concessions and favors that they would not otherwise yield, as they are overcome by the requests, petitions, and just grievances of the people, suffering most often without the knowledge of the prince, who sees and hears but through the eyes, ears, and reports of others. We thus conclude that the principal aspect of sovereign rule and absolute power consists in making general laws for the subjects without their consent. Without looking at other countries, we have often seen in our own realm that general customs have been abolished by the edicts of our kings, without hearing the estates, when the injustice of common law and custom was clearly to be seen.

But what if the prince forbids to kill, under the sanction of the death penalty, is he then bound by his own law? I say that such a law is not his, but the law of God and nature. In fact, he is more strictly bound by it than are his subjects, and cannot be freed from its obligation by the people or the senate, being held responsible by the judgment of God, as King Solomon said. Marcus Aurelius said that the magistrates are the judges of private individuals, the princes of magistrates, and God of the princes. Such were the views of two rulers who have been held among the wisest. I shall conclude with that of Antigon, king of Asia, who, on being told by a flatterer that all things were lawful to kings, said: "Yes, to barbarian and tyrannical kings."

The first characteristic of the sovereign prince is the power to make general and special laws, but—and this qualification is important—without the consent of superiors, equals, or inferiors. If the prince requires the consent of superiors, then he is a subject himself; if that of equals, he shares his authority with others; if that of his subjects, senate or people, he is not sovereign. The names of notables that one sees affixed to laws are not put there to endow them with authority but to serve as testimony and additional weight.

3. Legitimate and Despotic Monarchies

Monarchy is based on conquest, legitimate descent, or tyranny. This diversity of government does not signify a similar diversity of state, because state and government are different things. Government is actual policy and administration, as distinguished from the framework of the state. The state may be a monarchy, and yet popularly governed, if the representative assemblies, magistrates, offices, and grants are open to all, without distinctions of birth, wealth, or virtue. A monarchy is aristocratically governed if political representation and public offices are reserved by the king to the noble, the virtuous, or the rich. The aristocratic state may also be governed popularly, when honors and offices are distributed equally among all subjects, or aristocratically, if reserved exclusively for the noble and the rich. This variety of government has confused those who have deduced therefrom a like variety of states, overlooking the fact that the basic constitution of a state is different from its government and administration.

The royal, or legitimate, monarchy is that in which the subjects obey the laws of the monarch, and the monarch the laws of nature, the subjects retaining their natural liberty and property. The monarchy based on conquest is that in which the prince has made himself lord over persons and property by the force of arms in lawful war, ruling over his subjects as the head of the family over his slaves. The tyrannical monarchy is that in which the monarch, in contempt of the laws of nature, abuses free citizens as slaves and treats their property as his own. The same difference between legitimate rule and tyranny is also to be found in aristocracies and democracies; specifically, tyranny may also appear in the democratic state of a frenzied people, as Cicero has so well pointed out.

I have said in the definition of monarchy that the subjects owe obedience to the legitimate king, the sole source of sovereign majesty, and that the king must obey the law of nature, that is to say, govern his subjects and guide his actions by natural justice, which can be seen and perceived as clearly and brightly as the splendor of the sun. It is the true sign of legitimate monarchy when the king obeys and follows the laws of nature as he would like his subjects to do with respect to his own laws. He will accomplish this by fearing God and being merciful toward the afflicted, prudent in his enterprises, bold in his deeds, modest in prosperity, steadfast in adversity, loyal to his given word, wise in counsel, helpful to friends, mindful of his subjects, terrible to enemies, courteous to the good, awe-inspiring to the evil, and just toward all. If the subjects obey the laws of the king, and the king the laws of nature, justice will be mistress or, as Pindar said, queen. Mutual friendship between ruler and people will ensue, as well as harmony of subjects among one another, and of all with the king.

The greatest difference between a king and a tyrant is that the former conducts himself according to the laws of nature, whereas the latter treads them under his feet. The one adheres to piety, justice and faith; the other has no God, no faith, no law. The one does all to serve the public good and the protection of his subjects; the other acts only for his personal profit, vengeance, or pleasure. The one endeavors to enrich his subjects by all means he can think of; the other builds his castle on the ruin of his subjects. The one revenges the injuries inflicted on the people and easily pardons those done to him; the other revenges cruelly the injuries done to him and pardons those of others. The one spares the honor of virtuous women; the other rejoices in their shame. The one takes pleasure in receiving warnings freely expressed and reproof wisely broached; the other hates nothing more than the man who is serious, free, and virtuous. The one endeavors to keep his subjects in peace and unity; the other sows division among them so that they ruin one another, and then enriches himself by confiscating their property. The one takes pleasure in being seen and heard by his subjects; the other hides from them as from his enemies. The one puts his faith in the love of his people; the

other, in their fear. The one fears for nothing more than for his subjects; the other fears nothing more than his subjects. The one imposes upon his subjects as light financial charges as possible, and only for the public good; the other drinks his subjects' blood, gnaws their bones, and sucks the very marrow out of them, in order to weaken them. The one appoints to public office men of integrity; the other employs only thieves and the worst rascals.

4. Just Tyrannicide and Unjust Regicide

We have said that he is a tyrant who by his own authority sets himself up as sovereign prince, without election, right to succession, lot, just war, or by special divine summons. Both the ancient writings and laws agree that the tyrant may be put to death and that his assassins even receive rich awards: titles of nobility, prowess, chivalry, statues and crowns, and the property of the tyrant, as is due to real liberators of home and country. The ancients made no distinction between the tyrannical ruler who is good and virtuous or wicked and villainous, because no man has the right to invade sovereignty and set himself up as master over his fellow citizens under the guise of justice and virtue. In law, he is guilty of death who assumes the marks reserved for sovereignty. If therefore the subject attempts, by whatever means, to steal from the king his rank and status, or—in the popular or aristocratic state—seeks to make himself from an equal into a lord, he deserves death.

One may ask the question whether the tyrant may be slain who, having seized sovereignty by force or fraud, has himself elected by the representatives of the people, for it seems that the solemn act of election is a genuine ratification of his tyranny, agreed to by the people. I say nevertheless that it is lawful to kill him without any trial or formal proceedings, unless the tyrant has surrendered his authority into the hands of the people in order to be judged in court.

Where the prince is a legitimate absolute sovereign, as are the true monarchs of France, Spain, England, Scotland, Ethiopia, Turkey, Persia, Muscovy, his authority is neither shared nor challenged by anyone. In this case, subjects may not, acting individually or jointly, encroach upon the honor or life of the monarch by judicial or other means, though he may have committed all the wicked, impious, and cruel misdeeds one can think of. As to proceeding against the monarch by judicial means, the subjects have no jurisdiction over their prince, upon whom all power and authority to command depend, and who may not only revoke all the power of his magistrates but in whose very presence the power and jurisdiction of magistrates, corporations, colleges, estates, and communities cease to exist. It is not lawful for the subject to bring his prince to trial, for the vassal his lord, nor for the servant his master. In short, if it is not lawful to proceed against the king by judicial means, how could it be lawful to do so by force? The question at issue here is not who is the strongest, but whether the subject has the lawful authority to condemn his sovereign prince.

5. Religion and Social Peace

I do not wish to go into the question of which religion is the best (though there is only one religion, one truth, one divine law revealed by the mouth of God). But the prince who has complete certainty of the true religion and desires to attract to it his subjects divided into sects and factions should not be driven into the use of force, because the more the will of men is forced, the more it becomes obstinate. On the other hand, if the prince follows the true religion without sham or make-believe, he will be able to turn the hearts of his subjects to his religion, without using violence or punishments. In so doing he will avoid hard feelings, troubles and civil war, while leading the subjects who had gone astray into the haven of salvation.

6. The Social Causes of Revolution

Among all the causes of sedition and basic changes of the state, none is more important than excessive wealth of the few and extreme poverty of the many. The record of history is full of examples. Those who have advanced several causes of discontent against the state have taken advantage of the first opportunity that presented itself to them to despoil the rich of their fortunes. These revolutionary changes were more frequent in ancient times than at present because of the infinite number of slaves, who were thirty or forty times more numerous than those who were free. The greatest reward for their services was to be freed, even though they would obtain no other benefit. Many were able to buy liberty only by sacrificing their life-long savings or by borrowing, apart from the servitudes that they owed to their former masters. Despite these wretched conditions, they had an infinite number of children, as usually happens to those who labor most and live most frugally; being free, but oppressed by poverty, they were forced, in order to subsist, to borrow and pay their creditors in cash, crops, or services. The longer they lived, the more heavily they became indebted and the less able to meet their obligations; the Hebrews called usury a biting, because it gnaws the debtor to the very bone and sucks his blood and the marrow of his bones. Swollen in numbers and starved, the poor finally arose against the rich, drove them out of their houses and mansions, or had to be fed at their expense.

This is why Plato called wealth and poverty the ancient pests of states, not only on the ground of the material want that oppresses the starving, but also because of their abjection, which is a very evil and dangerous pestilence. To prevent it, men have searched for equality, which has been praised by many as the nourishing source of peace and friendship among citizens, as contrasted with the effects of inequality, namely, enmities, factions, hatreds, and prejudices. For he who possesses more than another and sees himself richer in property also desires more honors, delights, pleasures, food, and clothes. He wishes to be revered by the poor, whom he despises and tramples under his feet. On their part, the poor feel extreme envy and jealousy; though considering themselves as worthy as the rich, or even more so, they find themselves oppressed by poverty, hunger, misery, and disgrace.

For this reason, several ancient legislators divided the goods equally among all subjects; within recent memory, Thomas More, Chancellor of England, said in his book on the state that the public welfare can be attained only if men live in a community of goods, and that public welfare is impossible where private property exists. When Plato had the power, by the consent of the citizens who sent their ambassadors to him, to set up a new commonwealth, the colony of the Thebans and Phocians, he left without accomplishing anything because the rich were unwilling to share any of their wealth with the poor. Lycurgus endangered his life when, having banned the use of gold and silver, he also equally divided all estates. If Solon was unable to do the same, it was not because of lack of will, for he granted an annulment of bonds and a general abolition of debts.

On the other hand, it may be affirmed that equality of property is very harmful to the state, which has no safer support and foundation than good faith, without which neither justice nor any form of society can endure. Faith inheres in promises of legitimate conventions; if obligations are broken, contracts annulled, debt abolished, what can one then expect but the complete subversion of the state? There will be no

trust whatsoever in one another. Moreover, such general abolitions of debts often harm and even ruin the poor, because poor widows, orphans, and little people who have nothing but a small annuity are lost when debts are generally abolished. By contrast, the usurers take their precaution in time and profit from such abolitions of debts, as happened under Solon and Agis: the usurers, having had advance information about the cancellation of all debts, borrowed money from all sides to defraud their creditors. In addition, the hope of such general abolition of debts encourages the spendthrifts to borrow at any rate of interest; later they join the ranks of the malcontent and desperate poor, and stir up sedition among them, whereas, had there been no expectation of the cancellation of debts at the time of contracting them, everybody would seek to husband his property wisely and live in peace.

If the evil effects of such abolitions are great, they are still worse in the case of the equal division of land and other goods that had been lawfully acquired and held in possession. With regard to debts, there is the pretense of usury and the sterility of money, arguments that cannot be used with respect to lawful estates, so that one is led to conclude that such division of the property of others is nothing but theft under the cloak of equality. And to say that equality nourishes friendship is to abuse the ignorant; for it is certain that there is no greater hatred, no fiercer enmity than among equals, and the jealousy among equals is the source of turmoil, sedition, and civil war. By contrast, the poor, small, and weak willingly submit to, and obey, the great, rich, and powerful for the aid and profit that they hope to receive from them.

7. War

Should citizens be prepared and trained in the military arts? Should the state seek war rather than peace? There is no doubt on these issues. We firmly hold that commonwealth to be happy in which the king obeys the laws of God and nature, in which the magistrates obey the king, the subjects the magistrates, the children their parents, servants their masters, and whose subjects are bound by friendship to one other, and all with the prince, so as to enjoy the sweetness of peace and the true calmness of spirit. War is contrary to all this, and warlike men are the sworn enemies of this kind of life. Also, it is impossible to see a commonwealth flourish in religion, justice, charity, integrity, and, in short, in all the liberal sciences and mechanical arts unless the citizens enjoy a firm and assured peace—which is the ruin of warriors, who, like their equipment, are useless in time of good peace. And who is more hostile to a peaceable man than the furious soldier; to the mild farmer, than the bloodthirsty warrior; to the philosopher, than the captain; to the wise, than fools? For the greatest pleasure of warriors is to forage the open country, rob the peasants, burn the villages, besiege, batter, force, and pillage the towns, massacre the good and bad, the young and old, all ages and sexes, rape the virgins, wash in the blood of their victims, desecrate holy objects, raze temples, blaspheme the name of God, and trample under their feet all divine and human laws. Such are the fruits of war, pleasant and agreeable to warriors, abominable to good men, and detestable to God.

It is unnecessary to amplify in words what one sees happen in so many places, for the memory of these happenings alone fills one with horror. One must therefore beware of raising a warlike spirit among the subjects, guiding them toward such an execrable life, nor seek war under any circumstances, except when it is a matter of repelling violence in an extreme emergency. For those who make use of the slightest occasion to make war, resemble the flies who cannot stay on a well polished mirror, but prefer rough places. They who seek war to aggrandize themselves out of the ruin of others will be in perpetual torment, leading a life of misery, because greed has no limits, though in appearances one may promise oneself to have enough after the conquest of a kingdom. They resemble a slave who first only demands to be unchained; free of his shackles, he desires freedom; emancipated, he wishes to have the status of a citizen; given citizenship rights, he would like to be a public official; having reached the highest ranks of office, he aspires to be king; being king, he seeks to be the sole monarch; and, finally, he wants to be God.

How much happier then is a small prince or a small commonwealth (though there is nothing small in contentment), enjoying the assurance of tranquillity and peace without enemies, without war or envy? The boundary of a well ordered commonwealth is justice, as Pompey said to the king of the Parthians, and not the point of the sword, as King Agesilaus said.

CHAPTER 14

HOBBES

THE modern age, conceived in the Renaissance and Reformation, was born in the crucible of civil and international war in the seventeenth century. A host of old and new issues—social, economic, constitutional—produced intense passions transformed by religion into irreconcilable hatreds. The Thirty Years' War (1618–1648) started with a Protestant revolt in Bohemia. The conflict soon broadened into a major conflagration, until most European states were finally involved; civil wars and revolutions sprang up in half a dozen countries, from Italy to England. Germany, the principal theater of military operations, was depopulated, impoverished, and ruined by the war. Neither Protestantism nor Catholicism won a conclusive victory, and men began to ask themselves whether moral and physical devastation could be justified by theological differences.

Until the age of discovery, that is, as long as the Mediterranean held the pivotal position in commerce and civilization, England lived on the rim of the world's center. But when geographical discovery and overseas expansion shifted the world's focal area from the Mediterranean basin—the "middle of the earth" —to the Atlantic shores of western Europe, England became the center of a new oceanic world largely of her own making, and her rising commercial and industrial wealth quickly put her in the front rank of European nations. Moreover, in the seventeenth century the foundations were laid for the future greatness of England in science, medicine, navigation, philosophy, and political thought. The nineteenth is often called the "English century" because Engalnd then attained the peak of her visible power and world-wide influence. Yet the seventeenth is probably the most exciting and creative century in English history, and the success of the nineteenth century was built on the greatness of the seventeenth.

The turning point was marked by the Puritan Revolution and two civil wars (1642–1649), fought over fundamental issues that could not be resolved peaceably. First, there was the issue of *religious* liberty: the Church of England was criticized for being a state church, and its episcopal organization as well as its liturgy was rejected by many as being too close to Roman Catholicism. A sizable body of respectable Protestants favored presbyterianism as an alternative, and —on the theological left—the independent congregationalist sects began to press their demands. The slogan of King James I, "No Bishop, no King," made compromise with the Puritans difficult, and with the congregationalist sectarians impossible. The second main issue of the civil war was *constitutional*: who was sovereign, Parliament or the King? The third issue, cutting across religion and politics, was *social* and *economic*: to what extent should the merchants, financiers, lawyers, and tradesmen be included in the governing classes of the nation?

The class lines were by no means neatly drawn. The most prominent generals on the parliamentary side came from distinguished aristocratic or landowning families. Conversely, many urban elements, particularly in the North and West, supported the royalist side in the war. Yet on the whole the middle classes, tradesmen and yeoman farmers, supported the parliamentary party; and, though they were not agreed on the form of church government they wanted, they all abhorred the High Anglicanism and episcopalianism of the royalists, which seemed little different from Roman Catholicism—and Romanism meant Spain and France, the two national enemies of England. The parliamentary party was the more nationalistic; nationalism was of less import to those who upheld the doctrine of the divine right of kings.

The parliamentary party won because it commanded superior economic and financial resources, because the fleet was on its side, and because the New Model Army fought with invincible faith in its cause. King Charles I was publicly beheaded in London on January 30, 1649. The first middle-class revolution in history thus asserted itself successfully with decisive and unheard-of audacity. With the head of Charles I, the doctrine of the divine rights of kings rolled to the ground. His fate warned all rulers that political authority is closer to the earth and the people than to God and heaven.

The turbulent first half of the seventeenth century in England provides the background for the political philosophy of a lonely and complex figure, Thomas Hobbes (1588–1679). Hobbes' father was an impecunious vicar and something of a "character." Once, after a Saturday night of playing cards, he dozed in the pulpit and surprised the congregation by awakening with the cry of "Clubs is trumps." He got into a brawl with another parson and was forced to get away, abandoning his wife and three children. His brother, a well-to-do glover, who took charge of the deserted children, became particularly interested in young Thomas, who read and wrote at four, learned Greek and Latin at six, and went to Oxford at fifteen. Hobbes stayed at Oxford for five years but was not too happy about the course of studies, which seemed to him arid and old-fashioned.

On receiving his degree, Hobbes was recommended to Lord Cavendish (afterward the first Earl of Devonshire) for the post of companion and tutor of his eldest son, who was about the same age as Hobbes. The association with the Cavendish family lasted, with some interruptions, until Hobbes' death. Through his close connection with this family, one of the most aristocratic in England, he met men of affairs as well as outstanding scientists of the day, such as Bacon, Harvey, Descartes, and Galileo. Hobbes also traveled widely, and spent—in company with his Cavendish charges or on his own—about twenty years on the

Continent, mostly in Paris; there he came in touch with the new philosophical and scientific developments of the time.

In 1640, when Parliament began to assert its authority, Hobbes fled to France, "the first of all that fled," as he later said of himself. He feared that his intimate associations with royalist circles might endanger his safety; in addition, his writings up to his flight to France had been clearly antiparliamentarian and antidemocratic. During his stay in Paris he instructed, from 1646 to 1648, Charles II, the son of the executed monarch, in mathematics. In 1651, Hobbes went back to England, because he "would not trust his safety with the French clergy," as he later explained. He declared his submission to the new republican regime and stayed in England until his death in 1679.

Hobbes' greatest work, the *Leviathan*, appeared in 1651, shortly before his return to England. The civil war provided some of the atmosphere of the book but little more. Hobbes' main views were formed long before the actual conflict broke out, although there had been no real peace in England since the ascension to the throne of James I in 1603. The *Leviathan* is not an apology for the Stuart monarchy, nor a grammar of despotic government, but the first general theory of politics in the English language.

Unlike most defenders of absolute government, who start out with the gospel of inequality, Hobbes argues that men are naturally equal in mind and body. As to strength of body, the weakest has enough strength to kill the strongest, either by slaying him secretly or by allying himself with others for the purpose. With regard to mental faculties, Hobbes finds an even greater natural equality. Prudence is a matter of time and experience that can be acquired by everybody. Most persons think that they have more wisdom than their fellow men, but this in itself, Hobbes remarks sardonically, is proof that men are equal rather than unequal.

This *basic equality of men* is a principal source of trouble and misery. Men have, in general, equal faculties; they also cherish like hopes and desires. If two men desire the same thing, which they cannot both obtain, they become enemies and seek to destroy each other. In the *state of nature*, therefore, men are in a *condition of war*, of "every man against every man," and Hobbes adds that the nature of the war consists, not in actual fighting, "but in the known disposition thereto." Force and fraud, the two cardinal virtues of war, flourish in this atmosphere of perpetual fear and strife, fed by three psychological causes: competition, diffidence, and glory. In such a condition, there is no place for industry, agriculture, navigation, trade; there are no arts or letters; no society; no amenities of civilized living, and, worst of all, there is "continual fear and danger of violent death; and the life of man, solitary, poor, nasty, brutish, and short."

Hobbes does not extensively discuss the question whether men have actually ever lived in such a state of nature. He notes that the "savage people in many places of America" have no government and live in the brutish manner described. Yet, even if the state of nature has never existed generally all over the world, one could envisage the kind of life men would lead if there were no government. His argument of the *state of nature* is, in other words, *philosophical* and *not historical*. On the basis of the anthropological data that we possess today but that were not accessible to Hobbes, we know that life is actually more regulated in the so-called primitive group than in the community of the more advanced stage. As a thoroughgoing individualist and rationalist, Hobbes was unaware that the family or clan, and not the individual, is the basic social unit in primitive society, and custom or social pressure, and not law, its mechanism of enforcing conformity.

Pessimistic as Hobbes may seem, he is not despondent about man's ability to overcome the predicament in which he finds himself in the state of nature. The *fear of death* is the passion that inclines men to peace: the attractions of power and glory give way to the desire for securing, as a minimum, life, and—if possible —the means of a commodious existence. Hobbes is a strong rationalist, but reason is for him not a *deus ex machina* that appears from nowhere to work miracles, but an integral part of man, his essential faculty that distinguishes him from animals. Once man realizes that his fear of death is primarily due to brutal competition, resulting in perpetual war of all against all, reason shows the way out: to accept the principle of not doing that to another "which thou thinkest unreasonable to be done by another to yourself."

However, on the basis of Hobbes' analysis of the nature of man, a contract among men not to do to one another what they would not wish to have done to themselves would not be sufficient. Though man has the capacity to learn prudence and moderation from his fear of death, his desire for power and glory may tempt him to break his pledge unless there is a restraining power strong enough to keep him to his promise, because "covenants, without the sword, are but words, and of no strength to secure a man at all." If men were peaceable enough, Hobbes notes, to observe covenants without a superior authority for their enforcement, there would be no need for government in the first place, because there would be peace without compulsion. To make the counsel of prudence, born of the fear of death, issue in effective peace, a sovereign authority—one man or an assembly of men—must be created to whom all power is transferred.

The *social contract* of Hobbes is made *between subjects and subjects, not between subjects and sovereign.* The sovereign is not a party to the contract, but its creation. In this conception of the social contract, the sovereign cannot commit any breach of covenant, because he is not a party to it. By participating in the creation of the sovereign, the subject is author of all the ruler does and must therefore not complain of any of the ruler's actions, because thus he would be deliberately doing injury to himself. Hobbes concedes that the sovereign may commit iniquity but not "injustice or injury in the proper signification," because he cannot, by definition, act illegally: he determines what is just and unjust, and his action is law.

The question of the best form of state is not one of logic, according to Hobbes, but of convenience, that is, of the aptitude of the state to produce the security and peace of the people for which a government is instituted. However, on purely practical grounds Hobbes considers monarchy the best form of state because it suffers less from competition for office and power than do aristocracies and democracies; also, it is easier for one than for many to act resolutely and consistently.

Sovereign power is "incommunicable and inseparable," and Hobbes attacks any institution, town or private corporation, that may weaken the omnipotence of the state. He is vehemently opposed to division of powers or mixed government, and he goes so far as to say that there would have been no civil war in England if it had not been for the widespread opinion that sovereignty was divided between King, Lords, and Commons. There is particular danger in the liberty of the subject to challenge the wisdom or legality of the sovereign's actions, the "poisonous doctrine" that "every private man is judge of good and evil actions," and that "whatsoever a man does against his conscience, is sin." Against such "seditious doctrines" Hobbes demands the unqualified obedience of the subject.

To keep the authority of the state strong, Hobbes advises the sovereign not to allow the growth of groups and institutions that intervene between state and individual. Hobbes is particularly anxious to prevent churches from interfering in any way with the activities of the state, and in his doctrine the church becomes, in effect, a department of the state. He reminds the clergy that it is not essential to the commonwealth, and that the safety of the church depends on the state rather than the state on the safety of the church.

Hobbes had no religion. He defines religion in general, together with true religion and superstition, as follows: *"Fear of power invisible, feigned by the mind, or imagined from tales publicly allowed, religion;* not allowed, *superstition.* And when the power imagined is truly such as we imagine, *true religion."* These definitions are included, not in a discussion of theology or metaphysics, but in a catalogue of human passions and their forms of expression. His approach to religion is by way of psychology and public policy, and not by way of theology or philosophy. His definitions of religion, superstition, and true religion are placed between "curiosity" and "panic terror," and there is perhaps some connection in this sequence.

From a strictly political viewpoint Hobbes saw in religions and churches the most serious danger of civil disobedience and disunity, and in the conflict of secular and divine commandments the most frequent pretext of sedition and civil war. He is skeptical about the origin of many commands that claim divine provenance, because it is difficult to know whether a command comes from God or from someone who abuses His name for private ends. But if there is a bona fide conflict between secular and divine laws, the subject should obey the civil sovereign, if compliance does not involve forfeiture of life eternal; if it does, the subject may prefer death of the body to eternal damnation of the soul.

Hobbes' advice to subjects to become martyrs for their consciences' sake, or obey the sovereign, is tantamount to establishing—for most people—the duty of unlimited obedience. Not feeling any deep sympathy for religion, Hobbes invites believers to prove their faith by their willingness to die for it. In his personal attitude, Hobbes preferred the "episcopacy" of the Anglican state church because it was the official church, and "the most commodious that a Christian King can use for the governing of Christ's flock." By contrast, Presbyterians and Puritans encroach on civil authority and encourage men to set themselves up as their own judges—a bad habit easily carried over into secular affairs.

Hobbes' heaviest assaults are directed against the Roman Catholic Church. Hobbes remembered—and the memory is maintained in England to this day by annual public ceremonies—the Catholic conspiracy of the Gunpowder Plot in 1605. The conspirators managed to introduce barrels of gunpowder into the cellars of Parliament just before it was to be opened by King James I, with the aim of blowing up King, Lords, and Commons in one big explosion. The plot failed, and the conspirators were executed, including the Provincial of the Jesuits in England. In 1610, while Hobbes was in Paris with young Cavendish on their first grand tour, King Henry IV of France, at first a Huguenot and later a convert to Catholicism, a conciliatory and temperate ruler, was stabbed to death by François Ravaillac, a Catholic fanatic. The murder made a lifelong impression on Hobbes, and he saw in the Roman Catholic Church the true exemplification of the kingdom of darkness: "For from the time that the Bishop of Rome had gotten to be acknowledged for bishop universal, by pretense of succession to St. Peter, their whole hierarchy, or kingdom of darkness, may be compared not unfitly to the *kingdom of fairies;* that is, to the old wives' *fables* in England concerning *ghosts* and *spirits,* and the feats they play in the night. And if a man consider the original of this ecclesiastical dominion, he will easily perceive that the Papacy is no other than the *ghost* of the deceased *Roman empire,* sitting crowned upon the grave thereof."

Called "father of atheists" even in the entourage of Charles II, Hobbes had to leave France in 1651 because he was afraid of the French clergy, not of politicians. After Charles II returned to England in 1660, Hobbes got into difficulties because of his alleged atheism, and the *Leviathan* could not be reprinted for several years, owing to the opposition of the bishops. In 1666 Hobbes—fearful of official proceedings against him—wrote an essay on heresy to prove why he could not be legally burned for his opinions. The first collected edition of his works in 1688 was published not in England, but in Holland.

In his treatment of the problem of *natural law* Hobbes reveals his novel doctrine. Since the Stoics, the conception has never died out in the West that civil (or positive) law is derived from, and inferior to, a higher law, a "law behind the law"—the law of nature. In the Bible, too, the law of kings and princes is held to be subordinate to the law of God. This Stoic-Jewish-Christian tradition has had a civilizing effect on the western world because it has always reminded rulers that above their edicts and commands there is a higher law, founded on natural reason or divine revelation. Hobbes rejects this approach to the problem of the validity of law on the ground that it places validity beyond the formal source of the legal sovereign. According to Hobbes, there can be no unjust law—the cardinal issue of legal philosophy—because laws are the "rules of just and unjust." As to the relations between civil law and natural law, Hobbes maintains that they "contain each other." In fact, the law of nature is not law at all, but only "qualities that dispose men to peace and obedience."

Hobbes lists equity, justice, gratitude, and "other moral virtues" as the laws of nature. However, these qualities are not true laws, because, before the state is established, there is no authority to decide finally which idea of the law is binding. In practice, therefore, the law of nature is nothing but a set of general principles of the civil law; the main formal difference lies in the fact that the civil law is written, whereas the natural law is unwritten. Thus Hobbes sought to sweep away the doctrine of natural law from the theory of the state. With penetrating insight he foresaw the revolutionary implications of natural-law ideas as they became manifest only a century later in the American and French revolutions. Locke, too, admitted the revolutionary possibilities of the doctrine of natural law, but, unlike Hobbes, he was not overly frightened by the prospect.

On the whole, the practical effect of Hobbes has been to strengthen the *doctrine of the absolute state.* Yet the complex character of his ideas has puzzled his political friends and opponents. Conservatives who believe in legitimate monarchy criticize Hobbes first for being little interested in the divine right of monarchs and in monarchy as a moral institution. Hobbes was solely concerned with the pragmatic question of *effective* government, and legitimacy did not interest him at all. Thus, when he returned to England in 1651, he sent his submission to the Council of State. Though he was a lifelong supporter of the royalist cause, he was willing to submit to Cromwell's regime, because at the time it was the effective government that maintained law and order in England. In 1656, Hobbes boasted of the influence of the *Leviathan* on "the minds of a thousand gentlemen to a conscientious obedience to the present government [of Cromwell], which otherwise would have wavered in that point." After King Charles II returned to England in 1660, and the monarchy was restored, Hobbes explained that the "gentlemen" had appeased Cromwell so as to protect their property and influence for serving the king better later on. This may be realism, but it cannot appeal to a conservative who bases loyalty on moral sentiment.

Moreover, monarchists could never be satisfied with Hobbes' preference for monarchy as the best form of government. No theory of monarchy can be construed without some element of mysticism to make its authority acceptable. Hobbes' preference was entirely devoid of mysticism; his approach was utilitarian and pragmatic. The Hobbesian monarch cannot hide his ineffectiveness behind the cloak of divine or traditional authority. He must "deliver the goods," if he is to retain his regal office. Religious conservatives have charged Hobbes with atheism because he treats the church as he treats other associations, that is, subordinates it to the state, as he subordinates theology to philosophy. For a long time, atheism and agnosticism were branded as Hobbism, and Hobbes' enemies, lay and clerical, have seen in him a combination of Machiavelli's atheism and reason of state, and George Bernard Shaw's satirical impishness and frivolous longevity.

Hobbes' main opponents have been the adherents of parliamentary government and limited powers; because this doctrine has become the dominant tradition in the English-speaking countries, there has been no Hobbesian school in British and American political thought. By contrast, Hobbes has markedly influenced various countries with traditions of absolute, despotic government.

Yet to call Hobbes one of the spiritual fathers of totalitarian fascism or communism is more untenable than would appear from a cursory glance at several key phrases in the *Leviathan.* First, government is set up, according to Hobbes, by a covenant that transfers all power and authority to the sovereign.

This *contractual foundation of government* is anathema to the modern totalitarians: in the political mythology of the Nazis, the origin of the state is to be sought in the *Volksgeist*, the people's spirit, rather than in deliberate creation. Fascists attack the contractual theory of the state because contract implies mutuality of some sort, and, still more important, because there can be no contract without consent. Democracy is government by consent. The communist totalitarians also reject the contractual approach to the origin of the state: the state is the product, not of a rational compact, but of conflict, exploitation, and violence, and in violence it must disappear.

Second, Hobbes assigns to the state a prosaic business: to maintain *order and security for the benefit of the citizens*. By contrast, the aim of the modern totalitarian state is anti-individualistic and antihedonistic: the goal of public policy is dictated, not by the longing of citizens for happiness, but by a collective purpose, such as the glory of the master race in Nazi Germany, the revival of the Roman empire in Fascist Italy, and the triumph of the proletariat in Soviet Russia. Race, Empire, and Class are the modern totalitarian substitutes for Hobbes' bourgeois ideals of Thrift, Industry, and "Commodious Living."

Third, the Hobbesian state is *authoritarian*, not totalitarian. Above all, Hobbes pleads for equality before the law, so that the "rich and mighty" have no legal advantage over "poor and obscure persons." Hobbes' authoritarianism thus lacks one of the most characteristic features of the modern totalitarian state: inequality before the law, and the resulting sense of personal insecurity. Authority in the Hobbesian state is concentrated in the political sphere, and in it alone. The sovereign will normally permit his subjects "the liberty to buy and sell and otherwise to contract with one another, to choose their own abode, their own diet, their own trade of life, and institute their children as they themselves see fit; and the like." The Hobbesian belief in economic laissez faire is the exact opposite of the fascist pattern of a rigidly planned war economy, and the antithesis of the Soviet type of totalitarian economic planning. Similarly, the Hobbesian freedom of bringing up one's children is totally incompatible with the regimenting and drilling of children in modern totalitarian regimes (Nazi-Fascist or Soviet-Communist), in which the state seeks to replace the home and the school in rearing a breed of uniform (and uniformed) robots.

Fourth, Hobbes holds that the sovereign may be one man or an assembly of men, whereas modern totalitarianism—in fact, if not always in theory—is addicted to the leadership principle. Hobbes preferred monarchy for practical reasons, but he was free from the mysticism that endows totalitarian leaders with alleged charismatic and prophetic gifts. The Hobbesian sovereign is a *supreme administrator and lawgiver* but not a top rabble rouser, spellbinder, propagandist, or showman.

Fifth, Hobbes recognizes that war is one of the two main forces (the other being the danger of internal disorder) that drive men to set up a state. But whenever he speaks of war, it is *defensive war*, and there is no glorification of war, let alone of aggressive war, in the *Leviathan*. By contrast, totalitarian, imperialist fascists look on war as something highly *desirable*, and on imperialist war as the highest form of national life; communists—while rejecting, in theory, war between nations—accept the inevitability of war between classes, and the liquidation of the bourgeoisie by violent means.

Sixth, the totalitarian state insists on outer as well as inner conformity; in fact, it considers ideas more dangerous than actions. By contrast, the Hobbesian sovereign desires merely—for purposes of maintaining the peace—*outer conformity* of the subjects to the law. The subject is bound to obey the law, but "not bound to believe it," and human governors can take no notice of his "belief and interior cogitations." What Hobbes is concerned about is social peace, not Truth, whereas the totalitarians of all times are willing to destroy man for the sake of preserving Truth, if a choice has to be made.

Seventh, and finally, the Hobbesian state does not completely swallow the individual: "A man cannot lay down the right of resisting them that assault him by force to take away his life." Since the purpose of civil society is the preservation and protection of man's life, Hobbes recognizes the inalienable *right of the individual to resist* when his life is at stake, because "man by nature chooses the lesser evil, which is danger of death in resisting, rather than the greater, which is certain and present death in not resisting." For a long time this cautionary qualification seemed unimportant, because the sanctity of human life, as a principle at least, was universally accepted. But when, in World War II, millions of people were murdered in gas chambers and concentration camps in pursuance of deliberate state policy, the Hobbesian stress on the inalienability of human life as the irreducible minimum of the state's purpose acquired new meaning.

The fact that Hobbes was not—intellectually or emotionally—of the totalitarian cast should not create the impression that he was a democrat in disguise. He was not. The Hobbesian state finds its realization in neither the modern democratic state nor the totalitarian dictatorship of the Nazi-Fascist or Soviet-Communist brand. In modern times, political Hobbism is to be found in countries that possess social and economic conditions similar to those of seventeenth-century England—some nations in Latin America and Asia. The dictatorships in Latin America in the nineteenth and twentieth centuries, such as that of General Porfirio Diaz in Mexico, closely approximated the Hobbesian state: society was still in a precapitalist or, at best, early capitalist stage. Economic laissez faire was mingled, in such countries, with strong political authority, usually in the form of an open or concealed dictatorship. But the dictatorship was authoritarian, not totalitarian. In cultural, religious, educational, social, and economic affairs it was often very lenient. Compared with an advanced democracy, the Hobbesian state may appear dismal enough. Compared with twentieth-century totalitarianism, it is a vision of refined political civilization.

The Hobbesian theory of politics rests largely on a hypothesis—the solitary, combative, competitive character of man—that is only a half-truth. It is difficult to see how the brutes who lead a life of nasty savagery in the Hobbesian state of nature should suddenly display the prudent reasoning and cooperative effort that go into the making of the social contract creating the sovereign. A group that knows the institution of the contract is well beyond the state of nature, and it would perhaps be truer to say that contract is the product of society rather than society the product of contract. Yet these difficulties rest, not on varying sets of historical facts, but on different interpretations of human nature. If one rejects Hobbes' psychological assumptions as too pessimistic and mechanistic, one will be unable to accept, to that extent, the political ideas derived from them.

The truth of Hobbes' psychological tenets will ultimately be tested by the facts of social life rather than by philosophical arguments. In the area of domestic political organization, the state of nature with its horrors and barbarisms has disappeared. In the area of international relations, Hobbes noted in 1651, independent sovereign states live in the state of nature, "are in continual jealousies, and in the state and posture of gladiators; having their weapons pointing, and their eyes fixed, on one another; that is, their forts, garrisons, and guns upon the frontiers of their kingdoms, and continual spies upon their neighbors; which is a posture of war. But because they uphold thereby the industry of their subjects, there does not follow from it that misery which accompanies the liberty of particular men." As long as the sovereign states of the world continue to exist in the state of nature, a condition of brutish savagery, the Hobbesian view of man will continue to be true of the behavior of states toward one another.

Hobbes is no apologist for war between nations any more than for war within nations. But he thought—three hundred years ago—that war would go on as long as forts and guns at the frontiers could protect the wealth and industry behind the lines of combat. War was then a means of safeguarding "commodious living." In the second half of the twentieth century, however, forts and guns at the frontier of a country have ceased to give the protection they afforded in the seventeenth century, and the prospect of international war in the age of atomic and hydrogen bombs creates a fear of death infinitely more stark and real than ever prevailed in the Hobbesian state of nature. For a long time it was thought that the problem of international peace consists, above all, in finding the "moral equivalent" of war. If that fails, the last chance of mankind to survive may be the more modest motive of the Hobbesian fear of death.

HOBBES

Leviathan *

1. The State of Nature

Nature has made men so equal in the faculties of the body and mind, as that

* From Thomas Hobbes, *Leviathan* (1651). Spelling and punctuation have been modernized for this selection.

though there be found one man sometimes manifestly stronger in body, or of quicker mind than another, yet when all is reckoned together, the difference between man and man is not so considerable, as that one man can thereupon claim to himself any benefit to which another man may not pretend as well as he. For as to the strength of body, the weakest has strength enough to kill the strongest, either by secret machinations, or by confederacy with others that are in the same danger with himself.

And as to the faculties of the mind, setting aside the arts grounded upon words, and especially that skill of proceeding upon general and infallible rules, called science, which very few have, and but in few things, as being not a native faculty, born with us, nor attained, as prudence, while we look after somewhat else, I find yet a greater equality among men than that of strength. For prudence is but experience, which equal time equally bestows on all men in those things they equally apply themselves unto. That which may perhaps make such equality incredible is but a vain conceit of one's own wisdom, which almost all men think they have in a greater degree than the vulgar; that is, than all men but themselves, and a few others, whom by fame, or for concurring with themselves, they approve. For such is the nature of men, that howsoever they may acknowledge many others to be more witty, or more eloquent, or more learned, yet they will hardly believe there be many so wise as themselves; for they see their own wit at hand, and other men's at a distance. But this proves rather that men are in that point equal, than unequal. For there is not ordinarily a greater sign of the equal distribution of anything than that every man is contented with his share.

From this equality or ability arises equality of hope in the attaining of our ends. And therefore if any two men desire the same thing, which nevertheless they cannot both enjoy, they become enemies; and in the way to their end, which is principally their own conservation, and sometimes their delectation only, endeavour to destroy or subdue one another. And from hence it comes to pass that where an invader has no more to fear than another man's single power, if one plant, sow, build, or possess a convenient seat, others may probably be expected to come prepared with forces united, to dispossess and deprive him, not only of the fruit of his labour, but also of his life or liberty. And the invader again is in the like danger of another.

And from this diffidence of one another, there is no way for any man to secure himself, so reasonable, as anticipation; that is, by force, or wiles, to master the persons of all men he can, so long till he see no other power great enough to endanger him; and this is no more than his own conservation requires, and is generally allowed. Also because there be some that, taking pleasure in contemplating their own power in the acts of conquest, which they pursue farther than their security requires, if others, that otherwise would be glad to be at ease within modest bounds, should not by invasion increase their power, they would not be able, long time, by standing only on their defence, to subsist. And by consequence, such augmentation of dominion over men being necessary to a man's conservation, it ought to be allowed him.

Again, men have no pleasure, but on the contrary a great deal of grief, in keeping company where there is no power able to over-awe them all. For every man looks that his companion should value him at the same rate he sets upon himself; and upon all signs of contempt, or undervaluing, naturally endeavours, as far as he dares (which, among them that have no common power to keep them in quiet, is far enough to make them destroy each other), to extort a greater value from his contemners, by damage; and from others, by the example.

So that in the nature of man, we find three principal causes of quarrel. First, competition; secondly, diffidence; thirdly, glory.

The first makes men invade for gain; the second, for safety; and the third, for reputation. The first use violence, to make themselves masters of other men's persons, wives, children, and cattle; the second, to defend them; the third, for trifles, as a word, a smile, a different opinion, and any other sign of undervalue, either direct in their persons, or by reflection in their kindred, their friends, their nation, their profession, or other name.

Hereby it is manifest that, during the time men live without a common power to keep them all in awe, they are in that condition which is called war; and such a war as is of every man against every man. For *war* consists not in battle only, or the act of fighting, but in a tract of time, wherein the will to contend by battle is sufficiently known; and therefore the notion of *time* is to be considered in the nature of war, as it is in the nature of weather. For as the nature of foul weather lies not in a shower or two or rain, but in an inclination thereto of many days together, so the nature of war consists not in actual fighting, but in the known disposition thereto, during all the time there is no assurance to the contrary. All other time is *peace*.

Whatsoever therefore is consequent to a time of war, where every man is enemy to every man, the same is consequent to the time wherein men live without other security than what their own strength, and their own invention, shall furnish them withal. In such condition, there is no place for industry, because the fruit thereof is uncertain; and consequently no culture of the earth; no navigation, nor use of the commodities that may be imported by sea; no commodious building; no instruments of moving, and removing, such things as require much force; no knowledge of the face of the earth; no account of time; no arts; no letters; no society and, which is the worst of all, continual fear, and danger of violent death; and the life of man, solitary, poor, nasty, brutish, and short.

It may seem strange to some man that has not well weighted these things that nature should thus dissociate, and render men apt to invade and destroy one another; and he may therefore, not trusting to this inference, made from the passions, desire perhaps to have the same confirmed by experience. Let him therefore consider with himself: when taking a journey, he arms himself, and seeks to go well accompanied; when going to sleep, he locks his doors; when even in his house he locks his chests; and this when he knows there be laws, and public officers, armed, to revenge all injuries shall be done him; what opinion he has of his fellow-subjects, when he rides armed; of his fellow citizens, when he locks his doors; and of his children and servants, when he locks his chests. Does he not there as much accuse mankind by his actions as I do by my words? But neither of us accuse man's nature in it. The desire, and other passions of man, are in themselves no sin. No more are the actions that proceed from those passions, till they know a law that forbids them, which till laws be made they cannot know, nor can any law be made till they have agreed upon the person that shall make it.

It may peradventure be thought there was never such a time, nor condition of war, as this; and I believe it was never generally so over all the world; but there are many places where they live so now. For the savage people in many places of America, except the government of small families, the concord whereof depends on natural lust, have no government at all, and live at this day in that brutish manner, as I said before. Howsoever, it may be perceived what manner of life there would be, where there were no common power to fear, by the manner of life which men that have formerly lived under a peaceful government used to degenerate into in civil war.

But though there had never been any time wherein particular men were in a condition of war one against another, yet in all times kings and persons of sovereign authority, because of their independency, are in continual jealousies and in the state and posture of gladiators, having their weapons pointing and their eyes fixed on one another; that is, their forts, garrisons and guns upon the frontiers of their kingdoms, and continual spies upon their neighbours, which is a posture of war. But because they uphold thereby the industry of their subjects, there does not follow from it that misery which accompanies the liberty of particular men.

To this war of every man against every man this also is consequent: that nothing can be unjust. The notions of right and wrong, justice and injustice, have there no place. Where there is no common power, there is no law: where no law, no injustice. Force and fraud are in war the two cardinal virtues. Justice and injustice are none of the faculties neither of the body nor mind. If they were, they might be in a man that were alone in the world, as well as his senses and passions. They are qualities that relate to men in society, not in solitude. It is consequent also to the same condition that there be no propriety, no dominion, no *mine* and *thine* distinct, but only that to be every man's that he can get, and for so long as he can keep it. And thus much for the ill condition which man by mere nature is actually placed in, though with a possibility to come out of it, consisting partly in the passions, partly in his reason.

The passions that incline men to peace are fear of death, desire of such things as are necessary to commodious living, and a hope by their industry to obtain them. And reason suggests convenient articles of peace, upon which men may be drawn to agreement. These articles are they which otherwise are called the laws of nature.

2. The Social Contract

The *right of nature*, which writers commonly call *jus naturale*, is the liberty each man has to use his own power, as he will himself, for the preservation of his own nature, that is to say, of his own life, and consequently of doing anything which in his own judgment and reason he shall conceive to be the aptest means thereunto.

By *liberty* is understood, according to the proper signification of the word, the absence of external impediments, which impediments may oft take away part of a man's power to do what he would, but cannot hinder him from using the power left him, according as his judgment and reason shall dictate to him.

A law of nature, *lex naturalis*, is a precept or general rule, found out by reason, by which a man is forbidden to do that which is destructive of his life or takes away the means of preserving the same, and to omit that by which he thinks it may be best preserved. For though they that speak of this subject use to confound *jus* and *lex, right* and *law,* yet they ought to be distinguished, because right consists in liberty to do or to forbear, whereas law determines and binds to one of them, so that law and right differ as much as obligation and liberty, which in one and the same matter are inconsistent.

And because the condition of man, as has been declared in the precedent chapter, is a condition of war of every one against every one, in which case every one is governed by his own reason, and there is nothing he can make use of that may not be a help unto him in preserving his life against his enemies; it follows that in such a condition every man has a right to every thing, even to one another's body. And therefore, as long as this natural right of every man to every thing endures, there can be no security to any man, how strong or wise soever he be, of living out the time which nature ordinarily allows men to live. And consequently it is a precept, or general rule of reason, *that every man ought to endeavour peace as far as he has hope of obtaining it, and when he cannot obtain it, that he may seek, and use, all helps and advantages of war.* The first branch of which rule contains the first, and fundamental, law of nature: which is, *to seek peace and follow it.* The second, the sum of the right of nature: which is, *by all means we can to defend ourselves.*

From this fundamental law of nature, by which men are commanded to endeavour peace, is derived this second law: *that a man be willing, when others are so too, as far-forth as for peace and defence of himself he shall think it necessary, to lay down this right to all things, and be contented with so much liberty against other men as he would allow other men against himself.*

For as long as every man holds this right of doing any thing he likes, so long are all men in the condition of war. But if other men will not lay down their right as well as he, then there is no reason for any one to divest himself of his, for that were to expose himself to prey, which no man is bound to, rather than to dispose himself to peace. This is that law of the Gospel: *whatsoever you require that others should do to you, that do ye to them*. And that law of all men: *quod tibi fieri non vis, alteri ne feceris*.

To *lay down* a man's *right* to any thing is to *divest* himself of the *liberty* of hindering another of the benefit of his own right to the same. For he that renounces or passes away his right, gives not to any other man a right which he had not before, because there is nothing to which every man had not right by nature, but only stands out of his way that he may enjoy his own original right without hindrance from him, not without hindrance from another. So that the effect which redounds to one man by another man's defect of right, is but so much diminution of impediments to the use of his own right original. Right is laid aside either by simply renouncing it or by transferring it to another. By *simply* renouncing: when he cares not to whom the benefit thereof redounds. By transferring: when he intends the benefit thereof to some certain person or persons. And when a man has in either manner abandoned or granted away his right, then he is said to be obliged, or bound, not to hinder those to whom such right is granted or abandoned from the benefit of it, and that he *ought*, and it is his duty, not to make void that voluntary act of his own, and that such hindrance is injustice and injury, as being *sine jure*, the right being before being renounced or transferred. So that *injury*, or *injustice*, in the controversies of the world is somewhat like to that which in the disputations of scholars is called *absurdity*. For as it is there called an absurdity to contradict what one maintained in the beginning, so in the world it is called injustice and injury voluntarily

to undo that which from the beginning he had voluntarily done. The way by which a man either simply renounces or transfers his right, is a declaration, or signification, by some voluntary and sufficient sign, or signs, that he does so renounce or transfer, or has so renounced or transferred the same to him that accepts it. And these signs are either words only, or actions only, or—as it happens most often—both words and actions. And the same are the bonds by which men are bound and obliged: bonds that have their strength, not from their own nature, for nothing is more easily broken than a man's word, but from fear of some evil consequence upon the rupture.

Whensoever a man transfers his right or renounces it, it is either in consideration of some right reciprocally transferred to himself, or for some other good he hopes for thereby. For it is a voluntary act: and of the voluntary acts of every man the object is some *good to himself*. And therefore there be some rights which no man can be understood by any words, or other signs, to have abandoned or transferred. As first a man cannot lay down the right of resisting them that assault him by force to take away his life, because he cannot be understood to aim thereby at any good to himself. The same may be said of wounds, and chains, and imprisonment: both because there is no benefit consequent to such patience, as there is to the patience of suffering another to be wounded or imprisoned, as also because a man cannot tell, when he sees men proceed against him by violence, whether they intend his death or not. And lastly, the motive and end for which this renouncing and transferring of right is introduced, is nothing else but the security of a man's person in his life and in the means of so preserving life as not to be weary of it. And therefore if a man by words, or other signs, seems to despoil himself of the end for which those signs were intended, he is not to be understood as if he meant it or that it was his will, but that he was ignorant of how such words and actions were to be interpreted. The mutual transferring of right is that which men call *contract*.

A covenant not to defend myself from force, by force, is always void. For, as I have showed before, no man can transfer, or lay down, his right to save himself from death, wounds, and imprisonment, the avoiding whereof is the only end of laying down any right; and therefore the promise of not resisting force in no covenant transfers any right nor is obliging. For though a man may covenant thus, *unless I do so or so, kill me,* he cannot covenant thus, *unless I do so or so, I will not resist you when you come to kill me.* For man by nature chooses the lesser evil, which is danger of death in resisting, rather than the greater, which is certain and present death in not resisting. And this is granted to be true by all men, in that they lead criminals to execution and prison with armed men, notwithstanding that such criminals have consented to the law by which they are condemned.

A covenant to accuse oneself, without assurance of pardon, is likewise invalid. For in the condition of nature, where every man is judge, there is no place for accusation, and in the civil state the accusation is followed with punishment which, being force, a man is not obliged not to resist. The same is also true of the accusation of those, by whose condemnation a man falls into misery, as of a father, wife, or benefactor. For the testimony of such an accuser, if it be not willingly given, is presumed to be corrupted by nature, and therefore not to be received: and where a man's testimony is not to be credited, he is not bound to give it. Also accusations upon torture are not to be reputed as testimonies. For torture is to be used but as means of conjecture and light in the further examination and search of truth; and what is in that case confessed, tends to the ease of him that is tortured, not to the informing of the torturers, and therefore ought not to have the credit of a sufficient testimony: for whether he deliver himself by true or false accusation,

he does it by the right of preserving his own life.

3. The Commonwealth

The final cause, end, or design of men who naturally love liberty and dominion over others, in the introduction of that restraint upon themselves in which we see them live in commonwealths, is the foresight of their own preservation and of a more contented life thereby; that is to say, of getting themselves out from that miserable condition of war which is necessarily consequent, as has been shown, to the natural passions of men, when there is no visible power to keep them in awe, and tie them by fear of punishment to the performance of their covenants and observation of the laws of nature.

For the laws of nature, as *justice, equity, modesty, mercy,* and, in sum, *doing to others, as we would be done to,* of themselves, without the terror of some power to cause them to be observed, are contrary to our natural passions that carry us to partiality, pride, revenge, and the like. And covenants, without the sword, are but words, and of no strength to secure a man at all. Therefore notwithstanding the laws of nature (which everyone has then kept, when he has the will to keep them, when he can do it safely), if there be no power erected, or not great enough for our security, every man will, and may, lawfully rely on his own strength and art for caution against all other men. And in all places where men have lived by small families, to rob and spoil one another has been a trade, and so far from being reputed against the law of nature, that the greater spoils they gained, the greater was their honour; and men observed no other laws therein, but the laws of honour, that is, to abstain from cruelty, leaving to men their lives and instruments of husbandry.

The only way to erect such a common power, as may be able to defend them from the invasion of foreigners and the injuries of one another, and thereby to secure them in such sort as that by their own industry and by the fruits of the earth they may nourish themselves and live contentedly, is to confer all their power and strength upon one man, or upon one assembly of men, that may reduce all their wills, by plurality of voices, unto one will: which is as much as to say, to appoint one man, or assembly of men, to bear their persons, and every one to own and acknowledge himself to be author of whatsoever he that so bears their person shall act, or cause to be acted, in those things which concern the common peace and safety, and therein to submit their wills, every one to his will, and their judgments to his judgment. This is more than consent, or concord; it is a real unity of them all, in one and the same person, made by covenant of every man with every man, in such manner as if every man should say to every man, *I authorize and give up my right of governing myself, to this man, or to this assembly of men, on this condition, that thou give up thy right right to him, and authorize all his actions in like manner.* This done, the multitude so united in one person is called a Commonwealth, in Latin, *civitas.* This is the generation of that great *Leviathan,* or rather, to speak more reverently, of that *mortal god* to which we owe, under the *immortal God,* our peace and defence. For by this authority, given him by every particular man in the commonwealth, he has the use of so much power and strength conferred on him that by terror thereof he is enabled to form the wills of them all, to peace at home, and mutual aid against their enemies abroad. And in him consists the essence of the commonwealth; which, to define it, is *one person, of whose acts a great multitude, by mutual covenants one with another, have made themselves every one the author, to the end he may use the strength and means of them all, as he shall think expedient, for their peace and common defence.*

And he that carries this person is called Sovereign, and said to have *sovereign power;* and every one besides, his subject.

The attaining to this sovereign power is by two ways. One, by natural force, as when a man makes his children to submit themselves and their children to his government, as being able to destroy them if they refuse, or by war subdues his enemies to his will, giving them their lives on that condition. The other is when men agree among themselves to submit to some man, or assembly of men, voluntarily, on confidence to be protected by him against all others. This latter may be called a political commonwealth, or commonwealth by *institution;* and the former, a commonwealth by *acquisition.*

4. Rights of the Sovereign

A *commonwealth* is said to be *instituted* when a *multitude* of men do agree and *covenant, every one with every one,* that to whatsoever *man,* or *assembly of men,* shall be given by the major part the *right* to *present* the person of them all, that is to say, to be their *representative,* every one— as well he that *voted for it,* as he that *voted against it,* shall *authorize* all the actions and judgments of that man, or assembly of men, in the same manner as if they were his own, to the end, to live peaceably amongst themselves, and be protected against other men.

From this institution of a commonwealth are derived all the *rights* and *faculties* of him, or them, on whom the sovereign power is conferred by the consent of the people assembled.

First, because they covenant, it is to be understood, they are not obliged by former covenant to any thing repugnant hereunto. And consequently they that have already instituted a commonwealth, being thereby bound by covenant to own the actions and judgments of one, cannot lawfully make a new covenant, among themselves, to be obedient to any other, in any thing whatsoever, without his permission. And therefore, they that are subjects to a monarch cannot without his leave cast off monarchy, and return to the confusion of a disunited multitude, nor transfer their person from him that bears it to another man, or other assembly of men: for they are bound, every man to every man, to own and be reputed author of all that he that already is their sovereign, shall do and judge fit to be done; so that any one man dissenting, all the rest should break their covenant made to that man, which is injustice, and they have also every man given the sovereignty to him that bears their person, and therefore if they depose him, they take from him that which is his own, and so again it is injustice. Besides, if he that attempts to depose his sovereign be killed, or punished by him for such attempt, he is author of his own punishment, as being by the institution author of all his sovereign shall do; and because it is injustice for a man to do any thing for which he may be punished by his own authority, he is also, upon that title, unjust. And whereas some men have pretended for their disobedience to their sovereign a new covenant made, not with men, but with God, this also is unjust, for there is no covenant with God but by mediation of somebody that represents God's person, which none does but God's lieutenant, who has the sovereignty under God. But this pretence of covenant with God is so evident a lie, even in the pretender's own consciences, that it is not only an act of an unjust, but also of a vile and unmanly disposition.

Secondly, because the right of bearing the person of them all is given to him they make sovereign, by covenant only of one to another, and not of him to any of them, there can happen no breach of covenant on the part of the sovereign, and consequently none of his subjects, by any pretence of forfeiture, can be freed from his subjection. That he which is made sovereign makes no covenant with his subjects beforehand, is manifest, because either he must make it with the whole multitude, as one party to the covenant, or he must make a several covenant with every man. With the whole, as one party, it is impossible, because as yet they are not one person; and if he make so many covenants as there be men, those covenants after he has the sovereignty are void, because what act soever can be pretended by any one of them for breach thereof, is the act both of himself and of all the rest, because done in the person and by the right of every one of them in particular. Besides, if any one, or more of them, pretend a breach of the covenant made by the sovereign at his institution, and others, or one other of his subjects, or himself alone, pretend there was no such breach, there is in this case no judge to decide the controversy. It returns therefore to the sword again, and every man recovers the right of protecting himself by his own strength, contrary to the design they had in the institution. It is therefore in vain to grant sovereignty by way of precedent covenant. The opinion that any monarch receives his power by covenant, that is to say, on condition, proceeds from want of understanding this easy truth: that covenants, being but words and breath, have no force to oblige, contain, constrain, or protect any man, but what it has from the public sword, that is, from the united hands of that man, or assembly of men, that has the sovereignty, and whose actions are avouched by them all and performed by the strength of them all, in him united. But when an assembly of men is made sovereign, then no man imagines any such covenant to have passed in the institution, for no man is so dull as to say for example, the people of Rome made a covenant with the Romans to hold the sovereignty on such or such conditions which, not performed, the Romans might lawfully depose the Roman people. That men see not the reason to be alike in a monarchy and in a popular government, proceeds from the ambition of some that are kinder to the government of an assembly, whereof they may hope to participate, than of monarchy, which they despair to enjoy.

Thirdly, because the major part has by

consenting voices declared a sovereign, he that dissented must now consent with the rest, that is, be contented to avow all the actions he shall do, or else justly be destroyed by the rest. For if he voluntarily entered into the congregation of them that were assembled, he sufficiently declared thereby his will, and therefore tacitly covenanted, to stand to what the major part should ordain; and therefore if he refuse to stand thereto, or make protestation against any of their decrees, he does contrary to his covenant, and therefore unjustly. And whether he be of the congregation or not, and whether his consent be asked or not, he must either submit to their decrees, or be left in the condition of war he was in before; wherein he might without injustice be destroyed by any man whatsoever.

Fourthly, because every subject is by this institution author of all the actions and judgments of the sovereign instituted, it follows that whatsoever he does, it can be no injury to any of his subjects, nor ought he to be by any of them accused of injustice. For he that does anything by authority from another, does therein no injury to him by whose authority he acts, but by this institution of a commonwealth every particular man is author of all the sovereign does, and consequently he that complains of injury from his sovereign, complains of that whereof he himself is author, and therefore ought not to accuse any man but himself; no, nor himself of injury, because to do injury to one's self is impossible. It is true that they that have sovereign power may commit iniquity, but not injustice, or injury, in the proper signification.

Fifthly, and consequently to that which was said last, no man that has sovereign power can justly be put to death, or otherwise in any manner by his subjects punished. For seeing every subject is author of the actions of his sovereign, he punishes another for the actions committed by himself.

And because the end of this institution is the peace and defence of them all, and whosoever has right to the end has right to the means, it belongs of right to whatsoever man or assembly that has the sovereignty, to be judge both of the means of peace and defence and also of the hindrances and disturbances of the same, and to do whatsoever he shall think necessary to be done, both beforehand for the preserving of peace and security, by prevention of discord at home and hostility from abroad, and, when peace and security are lost, for the recovery of the same. And therefore:

Sixthly, it is annexed to the sovereignty to be judge of what opinions and doctrines are averse, and what conducing to peace, and consequently on what occasions, how far, and what men are to be trusted withal, in speaking to multitudes of people, and who shall examine the doctrines of all books before they be published. For the actions of men proceed from their opinions, and in the well-governing of opinions consists the well-governing of men's actions, in order to their peace and concord. And though in matter of doctrine nothing ought to be regarded but the truth, yet this is not repugnant to regulating the same by peace. For doctrine repugnant to peace can no more be true than peace and concord can be against the law of nature. It is true that in a commonwealth where by the negligence or unskilfulness of governors and teachers false doctrines are by time generally received, the contrary truths may be generally offensive. Yet the most sudden and rough bustling in of a new truth that can be, does never break the peace, but only sometimes awake the war. For those men that are so remissly governed that they dare take up arms to defend or introduce an opinion, are still in war, and their condition not peace, but only a cessation of arms for fear of one another; and they live, as it were, in the precincts of battle continually. It belongs therefore to him that has the sovereign power to be judge, or constitute all judges of opinions and doctrines as a thing necessary to peace, thereby to prevent discord and civil war.

Seventhly, is annexed to the sovereignty

the whole power of prescribing the rules whereby every man may know what goods he may enjoy, and what actions he may do, without being molested by any of his fellow-subjects; and this is it men call *propriety*. For before constitution of sovereign power, as has already been shown, all men had right to all things, which necessarily causes war: and therefore this propriety. being necessary to peace and depending on sovereign power, is the act of that power, in order to the public peace. These rules of propriety, or *meum* and *tuum*, and of *good*, *evil*, *lawful* and *unlawful* in the actions of subjects, are the civil laws, that is to say, the laws of each commonwealth in particular, though the name of civil law be now restrained to the ancient civil laws of the city of Rome which being the head of a great part of the world, her laws at that time were in these parts the civil law.

Eighthly, is annexed to the sovereignty the right of judicature, that is to say, of hearing and deciding all controversies which may arise concerning law, either civil or natural, or concerning fact. For without the decision of controversies, there is no protection of one subject against the injuries of another; the laws concerning *meum* and *tuum* are in vain; and to every man remains, from the natural and necessary appetite of his own conservation, the right of protecting himself by his private strength, which is the condition of war and contrary to the end for which every commonwealth is instituted.

These are the rights which make the essence of sovereignty, and which are the marks whereby a man may discern in what man, or assembly of men, the sovereign power is placed and resides. For these are incommunicable and inseparable. The power to coin money, to dispose of the estate and persons of infant heirs, to have preemption in markets, and all other statute prerogatives may be transferred by the sovereign, and yet the power to protect his subjects be retained. But if he transfer the *militia*, he retains the judicature in vain, for want of execution of the laws; or if he grant away the power of raising money, the *militia* is in vain; or if he give away the government of doctrines, men will be frightened into rebellion with the fear of spirits. And so if we consider any one of the said rights, we shall presently see that the holding of all the rest will produce no effect in the conservation of peace and justice, the end for which all commonwealths are instituted. And this division is it, whereof it is said, *a kingdom divided in itself cannot stand:* for unless this division precede, division into opposite armies can never happen. If there had not first been an opinion received of the greatest part of England that these powers were divided between the King and the Lords and the House of Commons, the people had never been divided and fallen into this civil war; first between those that disagreed in politics; and after between the dissenters about the liberty of religion; which have so instructed men in this point of sovereign right that there be few now in England that do not see that these rights are inseparable, and will be so generally acknowledged at the next return of peace, and so continue till their miseries are forgotten, and no longer, except the vulgar be better taught than they have hitherto been.

But a man may here object that the condition of subjects is very miserable, as being obnoxious to the lusts and other irregular passions of him or them that have so unlimited a power in their hands. And commonly they that live under a monarch, think it the fault of monarchy; and they that live under the government of democracy or other sovereign assembly, attribute all the inconvenience to that form of commonwealth; whereas the power in all forms, if they be perfect enough to protect them, is the same: not considering that the state of man can never be without some incommodity or other, and that the greatest that in any form of government can possibly happen to the people in general is scarce sensible in respect of the miseries and horrible calamities that accompany a civil war or that dissolute condition of masterless men, without subjection to laws and a coercive power to tie their hands from rapine and revenge: nor considering that the greatest pressure of sovereign governors proceeds not from any delight or profit they can expect in the damage or weakening of their subjects, in whose vigour consists their own strength and glory, but in the restiveness of themselves that, unwillingly contributing to their own defence, make it necessary for their governors to draw from them what they can in time of peace, that they may have means on any emergent occasion, or sudden need, to resist, or take advantage on their enemies. For all men are by nature provided of notable multiplying glasses, that is their passions and self-love, through which every little payment appears a great grievance, but are destitute of those prospective glasses, namely moral and civil science, to see afar off the miseries that hang over them, and cannot without such payments be avoided.

5. Liberty of the Subject

But as men, for the attaining of peace and conservation of themselves thereby, have made an artificial man, which we call a commonwealth, so also have they made artificial chains, called *civil laws,* which they themselves, by mutual covenants, have fastened at one end to the lips of that man, or assembly, to whom they have given the sovereign power, and at the other end to their own ears. These bonds, in their own nature but weak, may nevertheless be made to hold by the danger, though not by the difficulty, of breaking them.

In relation to these bonds only it is that I am to speak now of the *liberty* of *subjects.* For seeing there is no commonwealth in the world, wherein there be rules enough set down for the regulating of all the actions and words of men, as being a thing impossible, it follows necessarily that in all kinds of actions by the laws praetermitted, men have the liberty of doing what their own reasons shall suggest, for the most profitable to themselves. For if we take liberty in the proper sense for corporal liberty, that is to say, freedom from chains and prison, it were very absurd for men to clamour, as they do, for the liberty they so manifestly enjoy. Again, if we take liberty for an exemption from laws, it is no less absurd for men to demand, as they do, that liberty by which all other men may be masters of their lives. And yet, as absurd as it is, this is it they demand, not knowing that the laws are of no power to protect them without a sword in the hands of a man, or men, to cause those laws to be put in execution. The liberty of a subject lies therefore only in those things which, in regulating their actions, the sovereign has praetermitted: such as is the liberty to buy, and sell, and otherwise contract with one another; to choose their own abode, their own diet, their own trade of life, and institute their children as they themselves think fit; and the like.

Nevertheless we are not to understand that by such liberty the sovereign power of life and death is either abolished or limited. For it has been already shown that nothing the sovereign representative can do to a subject, on what pretence soever, can properly be called injustice or injury, because every subject is author of every act the sovereign does, so that he never wants right to any thing, otherwise than as he is himself the subject of God, and bound thereby to observe the laws of nature. And therefore it may, and does often, happen in commonwealths that a subject may be put to death by the command of the sovereign power, and yet neither do the other wrong: as when Jephtha caused his daughter to be sacrificed, in which—and the like cases— he that so dies, had liberty to do the action for which he is nevertheless without injury put to death. And the same holds also in a sovereign prince that puts to death an innocent subject. For though the action be against the law of nature as being contrary to equity, as was the killing of Uriah by David, yet it was not an injury to Uriah, but to God. Not to Uriah, because the right to do what he pleased was given him by Uriah himself: and yet to God, because David was God's subject and prohibited all iniquity by the law of nature, which distinction David himself, when he repented the fact, evidently confirmed saying, *To thee only have I sinned*. In the same manner, the people of Athens, when they banished the most potent of their commonwealth for ten years, thought they committed no injustice; and yet they never questioned what crime he had done, but what hurt he would do: nay, they commanded the banishment of they knew not whom; and every citizen bringing his oystershell into the market place, written with the name of him he desired should be banished, without actually accusing him, sometimes banished an Aristides for his reputation of justice, and sometimes a scurrilous jester, as Hyperbolus, to make a jest of it. And yet a man cannot say the sovereign people of Athens wanted right to banish them, or an Athenian the liberty to jest, or to be just.

The liberty whereof there is so frequent and honourable mention in the histories and philosophy of the ancient Greeks and Romans, and in the writings and discourse of those that from them have received all their learning in the politics, is not the liberty of particular men, but the liberty of the commonwealth: which is the same with that which every man then should have, if there were no civil laws, nor commonwealth at all. And the effects of it also be the same. For as among masterless men there is perpetual war of every man against his neighbour; no inheritance to transmit to the son, nor to expect from the father; no propriety of goods or lands; no security; but a full and absolute liberty in every particular man: so in states and commonwealths not dependent on one another, every commonwealth, not every man, has an absolute liberty to do what it shall judge, that is to say, what that man, or assembly that represents it, shall judge most conducing

to their benefit. But withal, they live in the condition of a perpetual war and upon the confines of battle, with their frontiers armed and cannons planted against their neighbours round about. The Athenians and Romans were free, that is, free commonwealths: not that any particular men had the liberty to resist their own representative, but that their representative had the liberty to resist or invade other people. There is written on the turrets of the city of Lucca in great characters at this day the word "Libertas"; yet no man can thence infer that a particular man has more liberty or immunity from the service of the commonwealth there than in Constantinople. Whether a commonwealth be monarchical, or popular, the freedom is still the same.

But it is an easy thing for men to be deceived by the specious name of liberty, and for want of judgment to distinguish, mistake that for their private inheritance and birth-right which is the right of the public only. And when the same error is confirmed by the authority of men in reputation for their writings on this subject, it is no wonder if it produce sedition and change of government. In these western parts of the world, we are made to receive our opinions concerning the institution and rights of commonwealths from Aristotle, Cicero, and other men, Greeks and Romans, that, living under popular states, derived those rights, not from the principles of nature, but transcribed them into their books out of the practice of their own commonwealths which were popular; as the grammarians describe the rules of language out of the practice of the time, or the rules of poetry out of the poems of Homer and Virgil. And because the Athenians were taught, to keep them from desire of changing their government, that they were freemen, and all that lived under monarchy were slaves, therefore Aristotle puts it down in his *Politics* (*lib*. 6, *cap*. ii): "In democracy, liberty is to be supposed: for it is commonly held that no man is free in any other government." And as Aristotle, so Cicero and other writers have grounded their civil doctrine on the opinions of the Romans, who were taught to hate monarchy, at first, by them that, having deposed their sovereign, shared among them the sovereignty of Rome, and afterwards by their successors. And by reading of these Greek and Latin authors, men from their childhood have gotten a habit, under a false show of liberty, of favouring tumults and of licentious controlling the actions of their sovereigns, and again of controlling those controllers; with the effusion of so much blood, as I think I may truly say, there was never any thing so dearly bought as these western parts have bought the learning of the Greek and Latin tongues.

To come now to the particulars of the true liberty of a subject; that is to say, what are the things which, though commanded by the sovereign, he may nevertheless, without injustice, refuse to do; we are to consider what rights we pass away when we make a commonwealth, or, which is all one, what liberty we deny ourselves by owning all the actions, without exception, of the man, or assembly, we make our sovereign. For in the act of our *submission* consists both our *obligation* and our *liberty*, which must therefore be inferred by arguments taken from thence, there being no obligation on any man which arises not from some act of his own, for all men equally are by nature free. And because such arguments must either be drawn from the express words, *I authorize all his actions*, or from the intention of him that submits himself to his power, which intention is to be understood by the end for which he so submits, the obligation and liberty of the subject is to be derived either from those words or others equivalent, or else from the end of the institution of sovereignty, namely, the peace of the subjects within themselves, and their defence against a common enemy.

First therefore, seeing sovereignty by institution is by covenant of every one to every one, and sovereignty by acquisition, by covenants of the vanquished to the victor, or the child to the parent, it is manifest that every subject has liberty in all those things, the right whereof cannot by covenant be transferred. I have shown before that covenants not to defend a man's own body are void. Therefore, if the sovereign command a man, though justly condemned, to kill, wound, or maim himself, or not to resist those that assault him, or to abstain from the use of food, air, medicine, or any other thing without which he cannot live, yet has that man the liberty to disobey.

If a man be interrogated by the sovereign, or his authority, concerning a crime done by himself, he is not bound, without assurance of pardon, to confess it, because no man can be obliged by covenant to accuse himself.

Again, the consent of a subject to sovereign power is contained in these words, *I authorize, or take upon me, all his actions;* in which there is no restriction at all of his former natural liberty: for by allowing him to *kill* me, I am not bound to kill myself when he commands me. It is one thing to say, *kill me, or my fellow, if you please;* another thing to say, *I will kill myself, or my fellow.* It follows therefore that no man is bound by the words themselves either to kill himself, or any other man, and consequently, that the obligation a man may sometimes have, upon the command of the sovereign to execute any dangerous or dishonourable office, depends not on the words of our submission, but on the intention which is to be understood by the end thereof. When therefore our refusal to obey frustates the end for which the sovereignty was ordained, then there is no liberty to refuse: otherwise there is.

The obligation of subjects to the sovereign is understood to last as long, and no longer, than the power lasts by which he is able to protect them. For the right men have by nature to protect themselves when none else can protect them, can by no covenant be relinquished. The sovereignty is the soul of the commonwealth which, once departed from the body, the members do no more receive their motion from it. The end of obedience is protection which, wheresoever a man sees it either in his own or in another's sword, nature applies his obedience to it, and his endeavour to maintain it. And though sovereignty, in the intention of them that make it, be immortal, yet is it in its own nature, not only subject to violent death by foreign war, but also through the ignorance and passions of men, it has in it—from the very institution— many seeds of a natural mortality by intestine discord.

6. Civil Law and Natural Law

By civil laws I understand the laws that men are therefore bound to observe because they are members, not of this or that commonwealth in particular, but of a commonwealth. For the knowledge of particular laws belongs to them that profess the study of the laws of their several countries; but the knowledge of civil law in general, to any man. The ancient law of Rome was called their *civil law,* from the word *civitas,* which signifies a commonwealth: and those countries which, having been under the Roman empire and governed by that law, retain still such part thereof as they think fit, call that part the civil law, to distinguish it from the rest of their own civil laws. But that is not it I intend to speak of here; my design being not to show what is law here and there, but what is law, as Plato, Aristotle, Cicero and divers others have done, without taking upon them the profession of the study of the law.

And first it is manifest that law in general is not counsel, but command; nor a command of any man to any man, but only of him whose command is addressed to one formerly obliged to obey him. And as for civil law, it adds only the name of the person commanding, which is *persona civitatis,* the person of the commonwealth.

Which considered, I define civil law in this manner. Civil law *is to every subject those rules which the commonwealth has commanded him, by word, writing, or other sufficient sign of the will, to make use of, for the distinction of right and wrong; that is to say, of what is contrary, and what is not contrary to the rule.*

In which definition, there is nothing that is not at first sight evident. For every man sees that some laws are addressed to all the subjects in general, some to particular provinces; some to particular vocations; and some to particular men; and are therefore laws to every of those to whom the command is directed, and to none else. As also, that laws are the rules of just and unjust; nothing being reputed unjust that is not contrary to some law. Likewise, that none can make laws but the commonwealth, because our subjection is to the commonwealth only, and that commands are to be signified by sufficient signs, because a man knows not otherwise how to obey them. And therefore, whatsoever can from this definition by necessary consequence be deduced, ought to be acknowledged for truth. Now I deduce from it this that follows.

The legislator in all commonwealths is only the sovereign, be he one man, as in a monarchy, or one assembly of men, as in a democracy or aristocracy. For the legislator is he that makes the law. And the commonwealth only prescribes and commands the observation of those rules which we call law: therefore the commonwealth is the legislator. But the commonwealth is no person, nor has capacity to do any thing, but by the representative, that is, the sovereign; and therefore the sovereign is the sole legislator. For the same reason, none can abrogate a law made, but the sovereign; because a law is not abrogated, but by another law that forbids it to be put in execution.

The sovereign of a commonwealth, be it an assembly, or one man, is not subject to the civil laws. For having power to make and repeal laws, he may, when he pleases, free himself from that subjection by repealing those laws that trouble him, and making of new; and consequently he was free before. For he is free that can be free when he will: nor is it possible for any person to be bound to himself, because he that can bind can release; and therefore he that is bound to himself only, is not bound.

When long use obtains the authority of a law, it is not the length of time that makes the authority, but the will of the sovereign signified by his silence, for silence is sometimes an argument of consent; and it is no longer law than the sovereign shall be silent therein. And therefore if the sovereign shall have a question of right grounded, not upon his present will, but upon the laws formerly made, the length of time shall bring no prejudice to his right, but the question shall be judged by equity. For many unjust actions and unjust sentences go uncontrolled a longer time than any man can remember. And our lawyers account no customs law, but such as are reasonable, and that evil customs are to be abolished. But the judgment of what is reasonable, and of what is to be abolished, belongs to him that makes the law, which is the sovereign assembly, or monarch.

The law of nature and the civil law contain each other, and are of equal extent. For the laws of nature, which consist in equity, justice, gratitude and other moral virtues on these depending in the condition of mere nature, as I have said before, are not properly laws, but qualities that dispose men to peace and obedience. When a commonwealth is once settled, then are they actually laws, and not before, as being then the commands of the commonwealth, and therefore also civil laws: for it is the sovereign power that obliges men to obey them. For in the differences of private men to declare what is equity, what is justice, and what is moral virtue, and to make them binding, there is need of the ordinances of sovereign power, and punishments to be ordained for such as shall break them, which ordinances are therefore part of the civil law. The law of nature therefore is a part of the civil law in all commonwealths of the world. Reciprocally also, the civil law is a part of the dictates of nature. For jus-

tice, that is to say, performance of covenant, and giving to every man his own, is a dictate of the law of nature. But every subject in a commonwealth has covenanted to obey the civil law, either one with another, as when they assemble to make a common representative, or with the representative itself one by one, when subdued by the sword they promise obedience that they may receive life; and therefore obedience to the civil law is part also of the law of nature. Civil and natural law are not different kinds, but different parts of law, whereof one part, being written, is called civil, the other, unwritten, natural. But the right of nature, that is, the natural liberty of man, may by the civil law be abridged and restrained: nay, the end of making laws is no other but such restraint, without the which there cannot possibly be any peace. And law was brought into the world for nothing else but to limit the natural liberty of particular men in such manner, as they might not hurt, but assist one another and join together against a common enemy.

That law can never be against reason, our lawyers are agreed; and that not the letter, that is, every construction of it, but that which is according to the intention of the legislator, is the law. And it is true: but the doubt is of whose reason it is that shall be received for law. It is not meant of any private reason; for then there would be as much contradiction in the laws, as there is in the Schools, nor yet, as Sir Edward Coke makes it, *an artificial perfection of reason, gotten by long study, observation, and experience,* as his was. For it is possible long study may increase and confirm erroneous sentences: and when men build on false grounds, the more they build, the greater is the ruin: and of those that study and observe with equal time and diligence, the reasons and resolutions are, and must remain, discordant: and therefore it is not that *juris prudentia,* or wisdom of subordinate judges, but the reason of this our artificial man the commonwealth, and his command, that makes law: and the commonwealth being in their representative but one person, there cannot easily arise any contradiction in the laws; and when there does, the same reason is able, by interpretation, or alteration, to take it away. In all courts of justice, the sovereign, which is the person of the commonwealth, is he that judges: the subordinate judge ought to have regard to the reason which moved his sovereign to make such law, that his sentence may be according thereunto; which then is his sovereign's sentence; otherwise it is his own, and an unjust one.

The interpretation of the laws of nature, in a commonwealth, depends not on the books of moral philosophy. The authority of writers, without the authority of the commonwealth, makes not their opinions law, be they never so true. That which I have written in this treatise concerning the moral virtues, and of their necessity for the procuring and maintaining peace, though it be evident truth, is not therefore presently law; but because in all commonwealths in the world it is part of the civil law. For though it be naturally reasonable, yet it is by the sovereign power that it is law: otherwise it were a great error to call the laws of nature unwritten laws; whereof we see so many volumes published, and in them so many contradictions of one another, and of themselves.

The interpretation of the law of nature is the sentence of the judge constituted by the sovereign authority, to hear and determine such controversies, as depend thereon, and consists in the application of the law to the present case. For in the act of judicature, the judge does no more but consider whether the demand of the party be consonant to natural reason and equity, and the sentence he gives is therefore the interpretation of the law of nature; which interpretation is authentic, not because it is his private sentence, but because he gives it by authority of the sovereign, whereby it becomes the sovereign's sentence; which is law for that time, to the parties pleading.

7. Subversive Political Doctrines

Though nothing can be immortal which mortals make, yet, if men had the use of reason they pretend to, their commonwealths might be secured at least from perishing by internal diseases. For by the nature of their institution they are designed to live as long as mankind, or as the laws of nature, or as justice itself which gives them life. Therefore when they come to be dissolved, not by external violence, but intestine disorder, the fault is not in men as they are the *matter,* but as they are the *makers* and orderers of them. For men, as they become at last weary of irregular jostling and hewing one another, and desire with all their hearts to conform themselves into one firm and lasting edifice, so for want both of the art of making fit laws to square their actions by, and also of humility and patience to suffer the rude and cumbersome points of their present greatness to be taken off, they cannot without the help of a very able architect be compiled into any other than a crazy building, such as hardly lasting out their own time, must assuredly fall upon the heads of their posterity.

Among the *infirmities* therefore of a commonwealth, I will reckon in the first place those that arise from an imperfect institution, and resemble the diseases of a natural body which proceed from a defectuous procreation.

Of which this is one, *that a man, to obtain a kingdom, is sometimes content with less power than to the peace and defence of the commonwealth is necessarily required.* From whence it comes to pass that when the exercise of the power laid by is for the public safety to be resumed, it has the resemblance of an unjust act, which disposes great numbers of men, when occasion is presented, to rebel, in the same manner as the bodies of children, gotten by diseased parents, are subject either to untimely death or, to purge the ill quality derived from their vicious conception, by breaking out into biles and scabs. And when kings deny themselves some such necessary power, it is not always, though sometimes, out of ignorance of what is necessary to the office they undertake, but many times out of a hope to recover the same again at their pleasure. Wherein they reason not well, because such as will hold them to their promises shall be maintained against them by foreign commonwealths, who in order to the good of their own subjects let slip few occasions to *weaken* the estate of their neighbours. So was Thomas Becket, archbishop of Canterbury, supported against Henry the Second by the Pope, the subjection of ecclesiastics to the commonwealth having been dispensed with by William the Conqueror at his reception, when he took an oath not to infringe the liberty of the church. And so were the barons, whose power was by William Rufus, to have their help in transferring the succession from his elder brother to himself, increased to a degree inconsistent with the sovereign power, maintained in their rebellion against king John, by the French.

Nor does this happen in monarchy only. For whereas the style of the ancient Roman commonwealth was *The Senate and People of Rome,* neither senate nor people pretended to the whole power, which first caused the seditions of Tiberius Gracchus, Caius Gracchus, Lucius Saturninus, and others, and afterwards the wars between the senate and the people, under Marius and Sylla; and again under Pompey and Caesar, to the extinction of their democracy, and the setting up of monarchy.

The people of Athens bound themselves but from one only action, which was that no man on pain of death should propound the renewing of the war for the island of Salamis; and yet thereby, if Solon had not caused to be given out he was mad, and afterwards in gesture and habit of a madman, and in verse, propounded it to the people that flocked about him, they had had an enemy perpetually in readiness, even at the gates of their city; such damage, or shifts, are all commonwealths forced to that have their power never so little limited.

In the second place, I observe the *dis-eases* of a commonwealth that proceed from the poison of seditious doctrines, whereof one is *that every private man is judge of good and evil actions.* This is true in the condition of mere nature, where there are no civil laws, and also under civil government in such cases as are not determined by the law. But otherwise, it is manifest that the measure of good and evil actions is the civil law, and the judge the legislator who is always representative of the commonwealth. From this false doctrine, men are disposed to debate with themselves and dispute the commands of the commonwealth, and afterwards to obey or disobey them, as in their private judgments they shall think fit; whereby the commonwealth is distracted and *weakened.*

Another doctrine repugnant to civil society is that *whatsoever a man does against his conscience is sin,* and it depends on the presumption of making himself judge of good and evil. For a man's conscience and his judgment is the same thing, and as the judgment, so also the conscience may be erroneous. Therefore, though he that is subject to no civil law sins in all he does against his conscience, because he has no other rule to follow but his own reason, yet it is not so with him that lives in a commonwealth, because the law is the public conscience, by which he has already undertaken to be guided. Otherwise in such diversity as there is of private consciences, which are but private opinions, the commonwealth must needs be distracted, and no man dare to obey the sovereign power further than it shall seem good in his own eyes.

It has been also commonly taught *that faith and sanctity are not to be attained by study and reason, but by supernatural inspiration or infusion.* Which granted, I see not why any man should render a reason of his faith; or why every Christian should not be also a prophet; or why any man should take the law of his country, rather than his own inspiration, for the rule of his action. And thus we fall again in the fault of taking upon us to judge of good and evil, or to make judges of it such private men as pretend to be supernaturally inspired, to the dissolution of all civil government. Faith comes by hearing, and hearing by those accidents which guide us into the presence of them that speak to us; which accidents are all contrived by God Almighty, and yet are not supernatural, but only, for the great number of them that concur to every effect, unobservable. Faith and sanctity are indeed not very frequent; but yet they are not miracles, but brought to pass by education, discipline, correction, and other natural ways by which God works them in his elect, at such times as he thinks fit. And these three opinions, pernicious to peace and government, have in this part of the world proceeded chiefly from the tongues and pens of unlearned divines who, joining the words of Holy Scripture together otherwise than is agreeable to reason, do what they can to make men think that sanctity and natural reason cannot stand together.

A fourth opinion, repugnant to the nature of commonwealth, is this, *that he that has the sovereign power is subject to the civil laws*. It is true that sovereigns are all subject to the laws of nature, because such laws be divine and cannot by any man, or commonwealth be abrogated. But to those laws which the sovereign himself, that is, which the commonwealth makes, he is not subject. For to be subject to laws is to be subject to the commonwealth, that is, to the sovereign representative, that is to himself; which is not subjection, but freedom from the laws. Which error, because it sets the laws above the sovereign, sets also a

judge above him, and a power to punish him; which is to make a new sovereign; and again for the same reason a third, to punish the second; and so continually without end, to the confusion and dissolution of the commonwealth.

A fifth doctrine, that tends to the dissolution of the commonwealth, is *that every private man has an absolute propriety in his goods, such as excludes the right of the sovereign*. Every man has indeed a propriety that excludes the right of every other subject; and he has it only from the sovereign power, without the protection whereof every other man should have equal right to the same. But if the right of the sovereign also be excluded, he cannot perform the office they have put him into, which is to defend them both from foreign enemies and from the injuries of one another; and consequently there is no longer a commonwealth.

And if the propriety of subjects exclude not the right of the sovereign representative to their goods, much less to their offices of judicature, or execution, in which they represent the sovereign himself.

There is a sixth doctrine, plainly and directly against the essence of a commonwealth; and it is this, *that the sovereign power may be divided*. For what is it to divide the power of a commonwealth, but to dissolve it; for powers divided mutually destroy each other. And for these doctrines men are chiefly beholding to some of those that, making profession of the laws, endeavour to make them depend upon their own learning and not upon the legislative power.

CHAPTER 15

LOCKE

REVOLUTIONARY Puritanism ruled England until 1660 but was unable to establish itself permanently. Cromwell died in 1658, and in less than two years Charles II was restored to the throne. After civil war and dictatorship the return to monarchy seemed the best prospect of peace. In bringing Charles II back no clear delimitation between royal and parliamentary authority was made. It was hoped that a practical equilibrium could be obtained without formal constitutional charters, if the King would avoid the arbitrary government of his executed father, and if Parliament would be satisfied with less than absolute supremacy, such as it had exercised in the years 1642–1649, the period of civil war. Yet Charles II lacked the wisdom, or even desire, to contribute his share to the growth of a balanced constitution. His reign lasted from 1660–1685, during which years he increasingly antagonized his subjects on the two key issues of religion and Parliament. A crypto-Catholic, he sought to strengthen the influence of Catholics and fatally returned to the ways of his father by ruling without summoning Parliament for several years.

Charles II was succeeded by his brother, James II, who was an open Catholic and more authoritarian than Charles. James II sought to convert England to Catholicism by prerogative and force, and he methodically subverted the authority of Parliament either by exempting individuals from the law or by suspending laws altogether. He appointed and dismissed judges arbitrarily and built up a standing army to buttress his autocracy. By identifying despotism with Roman Catholicism he outraged not only his subjects' religion and liberty but their very patriotism.

France and Spain were England's chief opponents in the struggle for hegemony, and James II sealed his position as a traitor to the nation when it became known that he, like Charles II and many politicians, was secretly receiving money from Louis XIV of France. In 1688, Whig and Tory leaders invited Prince William of Orange to come to England and deliver her from Romanism and absolutism. William arrived in England in November, and there was great jubilation and almost no resistance. James II saw himself abandoned by Parliament, church, and army, and on December 22, 1688, stealthily sailed for France, never to return. Royal absolutism in England was dead.

Prince William summoned a "Convention Parliament" that met in January of 1689. The first business was to fill the vacant throne. James II was declared to have subverted the Constitution of the Kingdom by breaking the "original contract" between King and people and to have violated the fundamental laws "by the advice of Jesuits and other wicked persons," and to have, by his flight and misdeeds, abdicated the throne. Parliament then invited Prince William and his wife Mary to become King and Queen of England. But the Crown was not given to them without condition. The "Declaration of Right" (passed later in the year as the Bill of Rights) was the instrument that conferred the Crown on William and Mary.

The Bill of Rights begins with a recital of the iniquities and illegalities of James II. The first of the twelve charges accuses him of having assumed and exercised the power to dispense with and suspend laws, and to execute laws, without consent of Parliament. This was the crux of the "Glorious" or "Bloodless" Revolution of 1688: who is to be supreme, king or Parliament? The clear and unmistakable words of the Bill of Rights settled the question once and for all. By denying the king the right to levy money without grant of Parliament, and by prohibiting the raising or keeping of a standing army in time of peace without the consent of Parliament, the Bill of Rights deprived the king of the fiscal and military means of governing without the active consent of Parliament.

Another important condition was attached by Parliament to the British monarchy: no person who professes the Roman Catholic religion or is married to a Roman Catholic may inherit or hold the throne. The work of the Glorious Revolution went further. Judges were made irremovable during good behavior; they could no longer be removed by the arbitrary will of the king, as James II had removed judges who interpreted the law contrary to his wishes. To make the change of the times even more marked, judges were henceforth to be removable only on the address of both Houses of Parliament. The abolition of censorship made for free expression of thought in religious and political matters, and toleration was legally granted to Protestant dissenters; thus the road was opened for the general principle of separating religious faith from political loyalty.

The Glorious Revolution established the first constitutional monarchy in a major European country, and its general character remained unchanged until the reform of parliamentary representation in 1832. The bloodless revolution of 1832, transferring political power from the gentry to the middle classes, would have been impossible without the Bloodless Revolution of 1688. At that time the liberal foundations of British government were judiciously laid, and the British system of today is the direct descendant of the Revolution of 1688. The peaceful revolution of 1945, by which the British working class became the principal political element in the state, is the twentieth-century version of the Reform Act of 1832, and both go back to 1688–1689. *Revolution by consent* sounds like a contradiction in itself, yet the examples of 1688, 1832, and 1945 prove that it is possible to effect fundamental political and social change without bloodshed. As long as Britain will adhere to her liberal and parliamentary tradition, the Revolution of 1688 and the Settlement of 1689 will continue to be the basis of her national life.

The spirit of this rational liberalism is best reflected in the work of John Locke (1632–1704), specifically, in his *Two Treatises of Government* (1690). Locke was born of a middle-class Puritan family; his father had fought in the civil war on the side of the Parliamentary party. He went to Oxford in 1652, and stayed on after graduation as a senior student and tutor. His connection with the university lasted until 1684, when he was deprived of his appointment for political reasons. His interests were at first concentrated on philosophy, then on science, and he became a fellow of the Royal Society, England's first scientific society, shortly after its incorporation. Locke also studied, and occasionally practiced, medicine.

Locke's knowledge of medicine led to a chance meeting with Lord Ashley in 1666. Lord Ashley was the leader of the Whig party and one of the central figures in public life. Locke, who saved the statesman's life by a skillful operation, became attached to his career and household for the next fifteen years. He assisted him in political and commercial affairs, and helped him draw up the *Fundamental Constitutions of Carolina* (1669), of which colony Lord Ashley was one of the founders and chief owners. The Carolina constitution guaranteed religious toleration but accepted Negro slavery as a form of rightful property. In 1672 Lord Ashley was raised to the peerage as Earl of Shaftesbury, and shortly thereafter he was appointed Lord High Chancellor of England. Locke followed Shaftesbury into the government and retained his position until 1675, when Shaftesbury fell in disgrace.

Locke then went to France, where he spent four years, mostly in Montpellier and Paris. On his return to England in 1679 he found political unrest growing. Shaftesbury became the principal leader of the opposition against the court, and he was finally forced to flee to Holland, where he died in 1683. Later in the same year Locke himself, fearful for his safety in England, fled to Holland, where he stayed until early in 1689. He left Holland on the same boat that carried Princess Mary of Orange to England.

Locke's exile in Holland was not free from harassment and uncertainty; yet he always looked back on it with nostalgia. He was captivated by the spirit of freedom and manliness he saw in Holland, and he envied the country that had become the center of political and religious refugees from all Europe, including the British Isles. Locke's liberalism was formed in its fundamentals before he set foot on Dutch soil, but his experience there showed him that liberalism in religion and politics could work, and it reinforced his determination to help rid England of the illiberal government of Charles II, and—later—the despotic obscurantism of James II. The first of Locke's four *Letters Concerning Toleration* was composed and first published in Holland, and an abstract of Locke's chief philosophical work, the *Essay Concerning Human Understanding,* the foundation of modern empiricism, was also first published there.

On his arrival in England the new government offered Locke an ambassadorship in Vienna or Berlin, but, as he preferred to remain in England, he accepted instead an appointment as Commissioner of Appeals, which enabled him to stay away from London much of the time, his health having begun to fail him. In 1696 he was made Commissioner of Trade and Plantations, the forerunner of the later Board of Trade and Colonial Office. Whereas Hobbes had little or no practical acquaintance with government, Locke had wide administrative and political experience both before and after his exile. Hobbes had spent his years of exile in absolutist France, Locke in liberal Holland.

Locke's *Two Treatises of Government* is often dismissed as a mere apology for the victorious Whigs in the Revolution of 1688. Locke himself lends some weight to this interpretation, because he says, in the Preface to the *Two Treatises,* that its purpose is "to establish the throne of our great restorer, our present King William," and "to justify to the world the people of England whose love of their just and natural rights, with their resolution to preserve them, saved the nation when it was on the very brink of slavery and ruin." Every piece of significant political writing is a fragment of the autobiography of its age; yet it becomes great only if, in addition to its vital connection with the period from which it springs, it possesses a universal appeal because of its general human interest. A political treatise that is wholly submerged in the issues of its own age can never rise above the level of a partisan pamphlet. On the other hand, a political work that is isolated from its own age is bound to be arid and abstract. The *Two Treatises* could not have been written by a man without the practical experience and interest of Locke; yet without Locke's philosophical rationalism, luminous common sense, and liberality of spirit it could never have become the Bible of modern liberalism.

Like Hobbes, Locke starts out with the concept of the *state of nature.* Yet from this starting point on, Locke travels a different road and arrives at a different destination. Unlike Hobbes, whose state of nature is little different from the jungle in which force and fraud reign supreme, Locke takes an optimistic view. In Hobbes' state of nature there is no natural law, only natural right, each individual doing as he sees fit for his preservation and enhancement of power. By contrast, Locke's conception of man in the state of nature is not noticeably different from man in organized society. Locke cannot conceive of human beings living together without some sort of law and order, and in the state of nature it is the *law of nature* that rules: "The state of nature has a law of nature to govern it, which obliges every one; and reason, which is that law, teaches all mankind who will but consult it, that, being all equal and independent, no one ought to harm another in his life, health, liberty, or possessions."

The law of nature, through the instrument of reason, defines what is right and wrong; if a violation of the law occurs, the execution of the penalty is, in the state of nature, "put into every man's hands, whereby every one has a right to punish the transgressors of that law to such a degree, as may hinder its violation." Locke penetratingly notes that without some agency of enforcement there can be no law, and that in the law of nature the injured party is authorized to be judge in his own case and to execute the judgment against the culprit.

In actuality, the legal situation that Locke describes as the state of nature still exists (as it did in Locke's time) in two areas. First, within the so-called primitive community there is a body of law that is generally known to its members. In the event of transgression, the injured party (or his family) pursues the malefactor, punishes him, or takes reparation from him. The kin of the murdered victim, who slays the assassin, does not commit murder in the eyes of the primitive community, but re-establishes thereby the sanctity of the law: he is the authorized agent of the law to defend it against the assassin, because as yet there are no third-party judges and specialized law-enforcement agencies. Second, the state of nature still exists between so-called advanced nations. To be sure, there is a body of law, international law, that is binding and recognized as such: yet, when a violation of international law occurs and there is no international judicature and enforcement agency, the injured state is authorized to punish the transgressor. Such penalties or reprisals are not considered contrary to international law but are viewed as acts in behalf of its defense and re-establishment.

The law of the state of nature is thus deficient in three important points. First, it is not sufficiently clear. If all men were guided by pure reason they would all see the same law. But men are biased by their interests and mistake their interest for general rules of law. Second, there is no third-party judge who has no personal stake in disputes. Men who judge their own conflicts are apt to be carried away by passion and revenge. Third, in the state of nature the injured party is not always strong enough to execute the just sentence of the law: "Thus mankind, notwithstanding all the privileges of the state of nature, but being in an ill condition while they remain in it, are quickly driven into society." The purpose of the social contract is to establish organized law and order so that the uncertainties of the state of nature will be replaced by the predictability of known laws and impartial institutions.

After society is set up by contract, government is established, not by a contract, but by a *fiduciary trust*. The legislature is "the supreme power" to which all other powers, particularly the executive, "must be subordinate." Yet the legislature is only relatively supreme among organs of government. Above the legislature there is still something higher: the people. Locke conceives of the institution of the legislature as a "fiduciary power." Ordinarily there are three parties to a trust. The trustor, who creates the trust; the trustee, who is charged with the administration of the trust; and the beneficiary, in whose interest the trust is created. According to Locke's view of government, there are only two parties to the trust: the people, who is both trustor and beneficiary, and the legislature, who is trustee.

The principal characteristic of a trust is the fact that the trustee assumes primarily obligations rather than rights. The purpose of the trust is determined by the interest of the beneficiary and not by the will of the trustee. The trustee is little more than a servant of both trustor and beneficiary, and he may be recalled by the trustor in the event of neglect of duty. Because the legislature is no more than a trustee, "there remains still in the people a supreme power to remove or alter the legislative when they find the legislative act contrary to the trust reposed in them; for all power given with trust for the attaining an end, being limited by that end, whenever that end is manifestly neglected or opposed, the trust must necessarily be forfeited, and the power devolve into the hands of those that gave it, who may place it anew where they shall think best for their safety and security."

Locke thus goes further than the makers of the Glorious Revolution who accused James II of having violated the "original contract between King and people." The contractual conception of kingship was a tremendous attack on the theory of kingship by divine right, according to which the king—and the king only—received his right to govern from God. In the doctrine of contract, people and king were put on the same plane as equals. Locke completes this progression by his conception of government as trust: only the people as trustor (and beneficiary) have rights; the government as trustee has only duties, which are defined by the interests of the trustor and beneficiary, and not by those of the trustee. In the theory of divine right, only the ruler has rights; in the theory of contract, both people and government have rights; in Locke's conception of *government as trust, only the people have rights*.

When Hobbes described the establishment of society and government, he carefully confined the act of covenant to the subjects; they set up the sovereign, transferring to him all power. There was no contract between subjects and sovereign, only between subjects and subjects, because Hobbes was anxious to avoid a conception of government that had duties, under a contract, toward the governed. Similarly, Locke confines the act of covenant to the setting up of society but not of government; yet his aim is exactly the opposite of Hobbes's. Locke's government is not a party to any contract with the people, because he does not wish to give the state any rights against the people. Locke's state never becomes the Hobbesian sovereign but always remains an instrument of the purposes that society sets for it. As a strong believer in natural law, Locke assigned to government the task of *finding the law* rather than of making it in the Hobbesian manner. *Law precedes the state* in Locke, but follows it in Hobbes.

Among the rights which precede government Locke stresses that of *property*. The principal purpose of government, the reason why men give up the state of nature for civil society, is "for the mutual preservation of their lives, liberties, and estates, which I call by the general name, property." This broad Lockean concept of property exceeds man's purely economic needs and interests and encompasses almost the whole orbit of his "life, liberty, and pursuit of happiness." When Locke speaks of property, he thinks of a wider range of action and opportunity than is implied in ordinary language. Of the three elements he lists, economic property is probably considered by him to be the most important; but it must be remembered that Locke thought of property as liberating its owner rather than as enslaving others.

Locke's theory of property starts with the inquiry of how private property can be justified at all. Because every man has a property in his own person, the "labor of his body and the work of his hands we may say are properly his." *Labor creates property:* the human effort that is "mixed" with natural resources is the determining criterion which alone justifies private property. Thus Locke avoids justifying property on the ground that "the law" protects it, and instead goes back to the law behind the law, the law of nature, according to which man's property in his own body also extends to its labor.

But labor does more than create property. It also *determines the value of property*. "It is labor indeed," Locke says, "that puts the difference of value on everything." In fact, he stresses the proportion of labor in value highly enough to say that "of the products of the earth useful to the life of man nine-tenths are the effects of labor."

This Lockean theory of property was later used in defense of capitalism; but in the hands of pre-Marxian socialists it became a powerful weapon of attacking capitalism. When Locke defended property on the ground of individual effort and initiative, he protected the productive capacities of a new system of commercial and industrial capitalism against the restrictive traditions of a repressive state. By making labor the title to property and the source of value, Locke translated the rise of a new class to power into terms of a new political economy. Although himself a mercantilist, Locke's economic philosophy helped to liberate the ingenious and industrious entrepreneur from paralyzing force and custom. The socialists used—a century and a half after Locke—his labor theory of property to demand communal control or ownership of the basic means of production; they did not thereby prove that they were more progressive than Locke, but that economic facts had changed since 1690, resulting in the concentration of property and control in industry and finance.

Locke did not work out a consistently clear theory as to *how much property* a person may fairly claim for himself. In general, he acknowledges that the right to property is limited: "As much as anyone can make use of to any advantage of life before it spoils, so much he may by his labor fix a property in; whatever is beyond this, is more than his share, and belongs to others. Nothing was made by God for man to spoil or destroy." This relative equality of property, based on man's limited capacity to consume, would have lasted forever, "had not the invention of money, and by tacit agreement of men to put a value on it, introduced (by consent) larger possessions and a right to them."

The criterion which Locke here applies is that of waste. Before money was invented, man had no moral right to hoard the products of the earth and allow them to rot and spoil. His ability to use perishable goods determined the amount of property he could rightfully own. In a later phase, man would exchange perishable fruit (like plums) for durable ones (like nuts). By disposing of the plums he had done his duty toward society, for he had prevented them from wasting in his possession. From durable nuts to even more durable gold, or "a sparkling pebble or diamond," was only a small and logical step. And if he kept on hoarding these durable goods (like gold and diamonds and money) "all his life, he invaded not the right of others."

Thus Locke arrives at defining money "as some lasting thing that men might keep without spoiling, and that, by mutual consent, men would take in exchange for the truly useful but perishable supports of life." In his doctrine of property Locke makes no serious attempt to reconcile the teaching of natural law, which postulates a reasonable equality of property, with the inequality of property that stems, by consent among men, from the use of money.

Property precedes government and is the "great and chief end" for which men unite into political society. It follows that the state "cannot take from any man any part of his property without his own consent." Even if a commonwealth is based on freely elected representative institutions, it cannot "dispose of the estates of the subjects arbitrarily." The Fourteenth Amendment to the Constitution of the United States embodies this Lockean idea, that no State shall "deprive any person of life, liberty, or property, without due process of law"

Locke felt—understandably enough in the light of Stuart despotism—a profound distrust of executive power; he had more confidence in the legislature, as representing the will of the people or at least the majority of the electorate. The executive power "is visibly subordinate and accountable" to the legislature, "and may be at pleasure changed and displaced." The legislature is supreme, but not absolutely; it is supreme only in relation to other organs of government, and the limitations of the legislature are the end of government, that is, the protection of life, liberty and property of men.

Specifically, Locke lists four major limitations on the powers of the legislature: first, the law must apply equally to all, rich and poor, favorite at court and countryman at plough; second, the law must not be arbitrary and oppressive, but must be designed for the good of the people; third, the legislature must not raise taxes without the consent of the people or their representatives; fourth, the legislature must not transfer its lawmaking power to anybody else. In this fourth limitation Locke expresses his opposition to government by administrative decree instead of by legislative assembly. Executive power always harbors the peril of uncertainty and arbitrariness, whereas government by legislature means certainty and the Rule of Law.

This part of Locke's political philosophy has retained more vitality in the United States than in England. There the development of cabinet government since the eighteenth century has controverted some of Locke's misgivings about the inherent evil of a strong and effective executive. Despite Locke's fears, England has not become a despotism, although her legislature has been overshadowed by the executive (itself, however, a committee of the legislature). In the United States, on the other hand, the Lockean sanctification of the legislature as contrasted with the devil theory of the executive has not lost its vote-getting magic.

Hobbes was so strongly impressed with the need for compulsion to maintain social cohesion that he could not envisage society without government. The dissolution of government meant for him the end of all order and restraint, the cessation of civilized living, and the return to the barbarous state of nature. Locke enunciates one of the principal doctrines of classical liberalism by drawing a *sharp distinction between state and society*. Of the two, society is by far the more important and enduring. The dissolution of government does not entail that of society, whereas if society "is dissolved, it is certain that the government of that society cannot remain." Locke mentions that the destruction of society usually occurs by external force, by conquerors' swords that "mangle society to pieces." But when government is dissolved from within, Locke does not anticipate chaos— as did Hobbes—but trusts that society will set up a new government to serve its ends and purposes. In general, government dissolves from within if it violates the trust given to it by the people, who then set up a new government.

Absolute monarchy is, according to Locke, *no form of civil government* at all, and, in fact, worse than the state of nature. In the latter, everybody is judge in his own case, whereas in absolute monarchy there is only one person who has that liberty: the king. In civil society, government approaches dissolution whenever the legislators "endeavor to take away and destroy the property of the people, or to reduce them to slavery under arbitrary power." Similarly, government may be destroyed from within by the chief executive if he overrides the laws of the legislature by his own arbitrary will, hinders the legislative assembly from meeting or acting freely, prevents free elections, or delivers the people into the subjection of a foreign power: "In these, and the like cases, when the government is dissolved, the people are at liberty to provide for themselves by erecting a new legislature differing from the other by the change of persons, or form, or both, as they shall find it most for their safety and good."

Before Locke, theories of disobedience usually contained an element of apology when it came to justifying resistance to authority. Locke reversed the position by declaring the arbitrary ruler an outcast and rebel against the law, whereas the people defend the law by revolting against such despots: "In all states and conditions the true remedy of force without authority is to oppose force to it," and the ruler who uses force without authority should be treated like an aggressor in war. Locke qualifies his theory of resistance in two ways; first, force is to be used by the people only against unjust and unlawful force; second, the right of disobedience may not be exercised by one man or a small group of citizens who feel themselves oppressed, but only by the majority of the people when they have suffered from mischief and oppression.

Locke's insistence that there is a higher law above the law of the state has led to the conception, so deeply ingrained in the traditions of democratic nations, that obedience to the law is a high, but not the highest, civic virtue. Opponents of democratic government have charged that making political rule dependent on consent of the ruled "lays a ferment for frequent rebellion," as Locke puts it. Locke does not deny the charge, but asserts that his hypothesis invites *anarchy and rebellion* no more than any other. First, when the people are made miserable, they will rebel under any form of government, let the governors be "sacred and divine, descended or authorized from heaven, give them out for whom or what you please, the same will happen." Second, Locke emphasizes that men do not revolt "upon every little mismanagement in public affairs" (or "for light and transient causes," as the Declaration of Independence puts it). Third, and here Locke moves from the defensive to the offensive, government by consent coupled with the right of the people to rebel is "the best fence against rebellion." The more the channels of free communication and consent are maintained in a society, the less the need for revolution.

What was an argument in 1690 has since become a matter of experience. The most effective reply to the charge that democracy contains within itself the seeds of anarchy and rebellion is to be found in the political history of the last three centuries. The British and American systems of government, based on the Lockean recognition of the right to rebel, have proved themselves the stablest and most successful political societies the world has seen, and the same could be said of countries (smaller in size but great in the glory of freedom) like Holland, Switzerland, and the Scandinavian nations. By contrast, where the right to revolution has been rejected in the name of order and stability, the political results have been *coups d'état,* blood purges, plots and counterplots, conspiracies, and violent swings from one extreme to another—the political record, specifically, of militaristic dictatorships and totalitarian regimes.

By committing themselves to Locke's theories of government the British supplied the case for the American Revolution (and for the later—peaceful—independence of other colonies and India). The text of the Declaration of Independence is pure Locke, and the main elements of the American political system —inviolability of property, limited government, and the inalienable rights of individuals—are all directly traceable to Locke. Writing in an expanding commercial society, his ideas fitted also the needs of a dynamic pioneer country.

Above all, Locke's defense of the right to rebel seemed to the makers of the American Revolution eminently reasonable. Thomas Jefferson, in many respects a Lockean rationalist and lover of freedom and toleration, expressed the American version of Locke's theory of rebellion in the classical phrase that the "tree of liberty must be refreshed from time to time with the blood of patriots and tyrants." Whatever the social or economic system that may exist at a particular time— be it a pioneering frontier country or an old established society, vigorous, self-confident capitalism or mature, skeptical industrialism, welfare New Dealism or experimental democratic socialism—the right to rebel remains the great, perhaps the greatest, tradition of British and American politics. Rebelliousness, too, can, paradoxically, grow into tradition: the tradition of the dignity of man and of his unbreakable spirit.

LOCKE

Two Treatises of Government *

1. The State of Nature

To understand political power aright, and derive it from its original, we must consider, what state all men are naturally in,

* From John Locke, *Two Treatises of Government* (1690).

and that is, a state of perfect freedom to order their actions, and dispose of their possessions and persons, as they think fit, within the bounds of the law of nature, without asking leave, or depending upon the will of any other man.

A state also of equality, wherein all the

power and jurisdiction is reciprocal, no one having more than another; there being nothing more evident, than that creatures of the same species and rank, promiscuously born to all the same advantages of nature, and the use of the same faculties, should also be equal one amongst another without subordination or subjection, unless the lord and master of them all should, by any manifest declaration of his will, set one above another, and confer on him, by an evident and clear appointment, an undoubted right to dominion and sovereignty.

This equality of men by nature, the judicious Hooker looks upon as so evident in itself, and beyond all question, that he makes it the foundation of that obligation to mutual love amongst men, on which he builds the duties they owe one another, and from whence he derives the great maxims of justice and charity. His words are:

The like natural inducement hath brought men to know that it is no less their duty, to love others than themselves; for seeing those things which are equal, must needs all have one measure; if I cannot but wish to receive good, even as much at every man's hands, as any man can wish unto his own soul, how should I look to have any part of my desire herein satisfied, unless myself be careful to satisfy the like desire, which is undoubtedly in other men. We all being of one and the same nature; to have any thing offered them repugnant to this desire, must needs in all respects grieve them as much as me; so that if I do harm, I must look to suffer, there being no reason that others should shew greater measure of love to me, than they have by me shewed unto them; my desire therefore to be loved of my equals in nature, as much as possible may be, imposeth upon me a natural duty of bearing to themward fully the like affection; from which relation of equality between ourselves and them that are as ourselves, what several rules and canons natural reason hath drawn, for direction of life, no man is ignorant. *Eccl. Pol.*, lib. i.

But though this be a state of liberty, yet it is not a state of licence: though man in

that state have an uncontrollable liberty to dispose of his person or possessions, yet he has not liberty to destroy himself, or so much as any creature in his possession, but where some nobler use than its bare preservation calls for it. The state of nature has a law of nature to govern it, which obliges every one, and reason, which is that law, teaches all mankind, who will but consult it, that being all equal and independent, no one ought to harm another in his life, health, liberty, or possessions: for men being all the workmanship of one omnipotent, and infinitely wise maker; all the servants of one sovereign master, sent into the world by his order, and about his business; they are his property, whose workmanship they are, made to last during his, not one another's pleasure: and being furnished with like faculties, sharing all in one community of nature, there cannot be supposed any such subordination among us, that may authorize us to destroy one another, as if we were made for one another's uses, as the inferior ranks of creatures are for ours. Every one, as he is bound to preserve himself, and not to quit his station wilfully, so by the like reason, when his own preservation comes not in competition, ought he as much as he can to preserve the rest of mankind, and not unless it be to do justice on an offender, take away, or impair the life, or what tends to the preservation of the life, the liberty, health, limb or goods of another.

And that all men may be restrained from invading others rights, and from doing hurt to one another, and the law of nature be observed, which willeth the peace and preservation of all mankind, the execution of the law of nature is, in that state, put into every man's hands, whereby every one has a right to punish the transgressors of that law to such a degree, as may hinder its violation. For the law of nature would, as all other laws that concern men in this world, be in vain, if there were nobody that in the state of nature had a power to execute that law, and thereby preserve the innocent and restrain offenders. And if any one in the state of nature may punish another for any evil he has done, every one may do so: for in that state of perfect equality where naturally there is no superiority or jurisdiction of one over another, what any may do in prosecution of that law, every one must needs have a right to do.

And thus, in the state of nature, one man comes by a power over another; but yet no absolute or arbitrary power, to use a criminal, when he has got him in his hands, according to the passionate heats, or boundless extravagancy of his own will; but only to retribute to him, so far as calm reason and conscience dictates, what is proportionate to his transgression, which is so much as may serve for reparation and restraint: for these two are the only reasons why one man may lawfully do harm to another, which is that we call punishment. In transgressing the law of nature, the offender declares himself to live by another rule than that of reason and common equity, which is that measure God has set to the actions of men for their mutual security, and so he becomes dangerous to mankind, the tie, which is to secure them from injury and violence, being slighted and broken by him, which being a trespass against the whole species, and the peace and safety of it, provided for by the law of nature, every man upon this score, by the right he hath to preserve mankind in general, may restrain, or where it is necessary, destroy things noxious to them, and so may bring such evil on any one, who hath transgressed that law, as may make him repent the doing of it, and thereby deter him, and, by his example others, from doing the like mischief. And in this case, and upon this ground, every man hath a right to punish the offender, and be executioner of the law of nature.

I doubt not but this will seem a very strange doctrine to some men; but before they condemn it, I desire them to resolve me, by what right any prince or state can put to death, or punish an alien, for any crime he commits in their country. 'Tis certain their laws, by virtue of any sanction they receive from the promulgated will of the legislative, reach not a stranger: they speak not to him, nor, if they did, is he bound to hearken to them. The legislative authority, by which they are in force over the subjects of that commonwealth, hath no power over him. Those who have the supreme power of making laws in England, France or Holland, are to an Indian, but like the rest of the world, men without authority: and therefore, if by the law of nature every man hath not a power to punish offences against it, as he soberly judges the case to require, I see not how the magistrates of any community can punish an alien of another country; since, in reference to him, they can have no more power than what every man naturally may have over another.

Besides the crime which consists in violating the law, and varying from the right rule of reason, whereby a man so far becomes degenerate, and declares himself to quit the principles of human nature and to be a noxious creature, there is commonly injury done, and some person or other, some other man receives damage by his transgression; in which case he who hath received any damage, has, besides the right of punishment common to him with other men, a particular right to seek reparation from him that has done it: and any other person, who finds it just, may also join with him that is injured, and assist him in recovering from the offender so much as may make satisfaction for the harm he has suffered.

From these two distinct rights, the one of punishing the crime for restraint, and preventing the like offence, which right of punishing is in everybody; the other of taking reparation, which belongs only to the injured party, comes it to pass that the magistrate, who by being magistrate hath the common right of punishing put into his hands, can often, where the public good demands not the execution of the law, remit the punishment of criminal offences by his own authority, but yet cannot remit the satisfaction due to any private man for the damage he has received. That, he who has suffered the damage has a right to demand in his own name, and he alone can remit: the damnified person has this power of appropriating to himself the goods or service of the offender, by right of self-preservation, as every man has a power to punish the crime, to prevent its being committed again, by the right he has of preserving all mankind, and doing all reasonable things he can in order to that end: and thus it is, that every man, in the state of nature, has a power to kill a murderer, both to deter others from doing the like injury, which no reparation can compensate, by the example of the punishment that attends it from every body, and also to secure men from the attempts of a criminal, who having renounced reason, the common rule and measure God hath given to mankind, hath, by the unjust violence and slaughter he hath committed upon one, declared war against all mankind, and therefore may be destroyed as a lion or a tiger, one of those wild savage beasts, with whom men can have no society nor security: and upon this is grounded that great law of nature, *Whoso sheddeth man's blood, by man shall his blood be shed.* And Cain was so fully convinced, that every one had a right to destroy such a criminal, that after the murder of his brother, he cries out, *Every one that findeth me shall slay me;* so plain was it writ in the hearts of all mankind.

By the same reason may a man in the state of nature punish the lesser breaches of that law. It will perhaps be demanded, with death? I answer, each transgression may be punished to that degree, and with so much severity, as will suffice to make it an ill bargain to the offender, give him cause to repent, and terrify others from doing the like. Every offence, that can be committed in the state of nature, may in the state of nature be also punished equally, and as far forth as it may, in a commonwealth: for though it would be besides my present purpose, to enter here into the particulars of the law of nature, or its measures of punishment; yet, it is certain there is such a law, and that too as intelligible and plain to a rational creature, and a studier of that law, as the positive laws of commonwealths:

nay, possibly plainer; as much as reason is easier to be understood, than the fancies and intricate contrivances of men, following contrary and hidden interests put into words; for so truly are a great part of the municipal laws of countries, which are only so far right, as they are founded on the law of nature, by which they are to be regulated and interpreted.

To this strange doctrine, *viz.,* that in the state of nature every one has the executive power of the law of nature, I doubt not but it will be objected, that it is unreasonable for men to be judges in their own cases, that self-love will make men partial to themselves and their friends: and on the other side, ill-nature, passion and revenge will carry them too far in punishing others; and hence nothing but confusion and disorder will follow; and that therefore God hath certainly appointed government to restrain the partiality and violence of men. I easily grant that civil government is the proper remedy for the inconveniences of the state of nature, which must certainly be great where men may be judges in their own case, since 'tis easy to be imagined, that he who was so unjust as to do his brother an injury, will scarce be so just as to condemn himself for it; but I shall desire those who make this objection, to remember, that absolute monarchs are but men; and if government is to be the remedy of those evils, which necessarily follow from men's being judges in their own cases, and the state of nature is therefore not to be endured, I desire to know what kind of government that is, and how much better it is than the state of nature, where one man commanding a multitude, has the liberty to be judge in his own case, and may do to all his subjects whatever he pleases, without the least question or control of those who execute his pleasure? and in whatsoever he doth, whether led by reason, mistake or passion, must be submitted to? which men in the state of nature are not bound to do one to another. And if he that judges, judges amiss in his own, or any other case, he is answerable for it to the rest of mankind.

'Tis often asked as a mighty objection, where are, or ever were there any men in such a state of nature? To which it may suffice as an answer at present, that since all princes and rulers of *independent* governments all through the world, are in a state of nature, 'tis plain the world never was, nor never will be, without numbers of men in that state. I have named all governors of *independent* communities, whether they are, or are not, in league with others: for 'tis not every compact that puts an end to the state of nature between men, but only this one of agreeing together mutually to enter into one community, and make one body politic; other promises, and compacts, men may make one with another, and yet still be in the state of nature. The promises and bargains for truck, etc. between the two men in the desert island, mentioned by Garcilasso de la Vega, in his history of Peru; or between a Swiss and an Indian, in the woods of America, are binding to them, though they are perfectly in a state of nature, in reference to one another: for truth and keeping of faith belongs to men as men, and not as members of society.

To those that say, there were never any men in the state of nature, I will not only oppose the authority of the judicious Hooker, *Eccl. Pol.* lib. i. *sect.* 10, where he says,

the laws which have been hitherto mentioned, *i.e.*, the laws of nature, do bind men absolutely, even as they are men, although they have never any settled fellowship, never any solemn agreement amongst themselves what to do, or not to do: but forasmuch as we are not by ourselves sufficient to furnish ourselves with competent store of things, needful for such a life as our nature doth desire, a life fit for the dignity of man; therefore to supply those defects and imperfections which are in us, as living singly and solely by ourselves, we are naturally induced to seek communion and fellowship with others: this was the cause of men uniting themselves at first in politic societies.

But I moreover affirm, that all men are naturally in that state, and remain so, till by their own consents they make themselves members of some politic society; and I doubt not in the sequel of this discourse, to make it very clear.

2. The State of War

The state of war is a state of enmity and destruction; and therefore declaring by word or action, not a passionate and hasty, but sedate, settled design upon another man's life, puts him in a state of war with him against whom he has declared such an intention, and so has exposed his life to the other's power to be taken away by him, or any one that joins with him in his defence, and espouses his quarrel, it being reasonable and just I should have a right to destroy that which threatens me with destruction; for by the fundamental law of nature, man being to be preserved, as much as possible, when all cannot be preserved, the safety of the innocent is to be preferred; and one may destroy a man who makes war upon him, or has discovered an enmity to his being, for the same reason that he may kill a wolf or a lion, because such men are not under the ties of the common law of reason, have no other rule but that of force and violence, and so may be treated as beasts of prey, those dangerous and noxious creatures that will be sure to destroy him whenever he falls into their power.

And hence it is that he who attempts to get another man into his absolute power does thereby put himself into a state of war with him; it being to be understood as a declaration of a design upon his life. For I have reason to conclude that he who would get me into his power without my consent would use me as he pleased when he had got me there, and destroy me too when he had a fancy to it, for nobody can desire to have me in his absolute power unless it be to compel me by force to that which is against the right of my freedom —*i.e.* make me a slave. To be free from such force is the only security of my preservation, and reason bids me look on him as an enemy to my preservation who would take away that freedom which is the fence to it; so that he who makes an attempt to enslave me thereby puts himself into a state of war with me. He that in the state of nature would take away the freedom that belongs to any one in that state must necessarily be supposed to have a design to take away everything else, that freedom being the foundation of all the rest; as he that in the state of society would take away the freedom belonging to those of that society or commonwealth must be supposed to design to take away from them everything else, and so be looked on as in a state of war.

This makes it lawful for a man to kill a thief who has not in the least hurt him, nor declared any design upon his life, any farther than by the use of force, so to get him in his power as to take away his money, or what he pleases, from him; because using force, where he has no right to get me into his power, let his pretence be what it will, I have no reason to suppose that he who would take away my liberty would not, when he had me in his power, take away everything else. And therefore it is lawful for me to treat him as one who has put himself into a state of war with me—*i.e.*, kill him if I can; for to that hazard does he justly expose himself whoever introduces a state of war, and is aggressor in it.

And here we have the plain difference between the state of nature and the state of war, which however some men have confounded, are as far distant as a state of peace, goodwill, mutual assistance, and preservation; and a state of enmity, malice, violence and mutual destruction are one from another. Men living together according to reason without a common superior on earth, with authority to judge between them, are properly in the state of nature. But force, or a declared design of force upon the person of another, where there is no common superior on earth to appeal to for relief, is the state of war; and 'tis the want of such an appeal gives a man the right of war even against an aggressor, though he be in society and a fellow-subject. Thus, a thief whom I cannot harm, but by appeal to the law, for having stolen all that I am worth, I may kill when he sets on me to rob me but of my horse or coat, because the law, which was made for my preservation, where it cannot interpose to secure my life from present force, which if lost is capable of no reparation, permits me my own defence and the right of war, a liberty to kill the aggressor, because the aggressor allows not time to appeal to our common judge, nor the decision of the law, for remedy in a case where the mischief may be irreparable. Want of a common judge with authority puts all men in a state of nature; force without right upon a man's person makes a state of war both where there is, and is not, a common judge.

But when the actual force is over, the state of war ceases between those that are in society and are equally on both sides subjected to the fair determination of the law; because then there lies open the remedy of appeal for the past injury, and to prevent future harm; but where no such appeal is, as in the state of nature, for want of positive laws, and judges with authority to appeal to, the state of war, once begun, continues with a right to the innocent party to destroy the other whenever he can, until the aggressor offers peace, and desires reconciliation on such terms as may repair any wrongs he has already done, and secure the innocent for the future; nay, where an appeal to the law and constituted judges lies open, but the remedy is denied by a manifest perverting of justice, and a barefaced wresting of the laws to protect or indemnify the violence or injuries of some men or party of men, there it is hard to imagine any thing but a state of war: for wherever violence is used, and injury done, though by hands appointed to administer justice, it is still violence and injury, however coloured with the name, pretences, or forms of law, the end whereof being to protect and redress the innocent, by an unbiassed application of it, to all who are under it; wherever that is not *bona fide* done, war is made upon the sufferers, who having no appeal on earth to right them, they are left to the only remedy in such cases, an appeal to heaven.

To avoid this state of war (wherein there is no appeal but to heaven, and wherein every the least difference is apt to end, where there is no authority to decide between the contenders) is one great reason of men's putting themselves into society, and quitting the state of nature. For where there is an authority, a power on earth from which relief can be had by appeal, there the continuance of the state of war is excluded, and the controversy is decided by that power.

3. Slavery

The natural liberty of man is to be free from any superior power on earth, and not to be under the will or legislative authority of man, but to have only the law of nature for his rule. The liberty of man in society is to be under no other legislative power but that established by consent in the commonwealth, nor under the dominion of any will, or restraint of any law, but what the legislative shall enact according to the trust put in it. Freedom, then, is not what Sir Robert Filmer tells us, *O.A. 55. A liberty for every one to do what he lists, to live as he pleases, and not to be tied by any laws* · but freedom of men under government is to have a standing rule to live by, common to every one of that society, and made by the legislative power erected in it. A liberty to follow my own will in all things where the rule prescribes not, not to be subject to the inconstant, uncertain, unknown, arbitrary will of another man, as freedom of nature is to be under no other restraint but the law of nature.

This freedom from absolute, arbitrary power is so necessary to, and closely joined with, a man's preservation, that he cannot part with it but by what forfeits his preservation and life together. For a man, not

having the power of his own life, cannot, by compact or his own consent, enslave himself to any one, nor put himself under the absolute, arbitrary power of another to take away his life when he pleases. Nobody can give more power than he has himself, and he that cannot take away his own life cannot give another power over it. Indeed, having by his fault forfeited his own life by some act that deserves death, he to whom he has forfeited it may, when he has him in his power, delay to take it, and make use of him to his own service; and he does him no injury by it. For, whenever he finds the hardship of his slavery outweigh the value of his life, 'tis in his power, by resisting the will of his master, to draw on himself the death he desires.

4. Property

God, who hath given the world to men in common, hath also given them reason to make use of it to the best advantage of life and convenience. The earth and all that is therein is given to men for the support and comfort of their being. And though all the fruits it naturally produces, and beasts it feeds, belong to mankind in common, as they are produced by the spontaneous hand of nature, and no body has originally a private dominion exclusive of the rest of mankind in any of them, as they are thus in their natural state, yet being given for the use of men, there must of necessity be a means to appropriate them some way or other before they can be of any use, or at all beneficial, to any particular man. The fruit or venison which nourishes the wild Indian, who knows no enclosure, and is still a tenant in common, must be his, and so his—*i.e.*, a part of him, that another can no longer have any right to it before it can do him any good for the support f his life.

Though the earth and all inferior creatures be common to all men, yet every man has a *property* in his own *person*. This nobody has any right to but himself. The *la-*

bour of his body and the *work* of his hands, we may say, are properly his. Whatsoever, then, he removes out of the state that nature hath provided and left it in, he hath mixed his labour with it, and joined to it something that is his own, and thereby makes it his property. It being by him removed from the common state nature placed it in, it hath by this labour something annexed to it that excludes the common right of other men. For this labour being the unquestionable property of the labourer, no man but he can have a right to what that is once joined to, at least where there is enough, and as good left in common for others.

He that is nourished by the acorns he picked up under an oak, or the apples he gathered from the trees in the wood, has certainly appropriated them to himself. Nobody can deny but the nourishment is his. I ask, then, when did they begin to be his? when he digested? or when he ate? or when he boiled? or when he brought them home? or when he picked them up? And 'tis plain, if the first gathering made them not his, nothing else could. That labour put a distinction between them and common. That added something to them more than Nature, the common mother of all, had done, and so they became his private right. And will any one say he had no right to those acorns or apples he thus appropriated because he had not the consent of all mankind to make them his? Was it a robbery thus to assume to himself what belonged to all in common? If such a consent as that was necessary, man had starved, notwithstanding the plenty God had given him. We see in commons, which remain so by compact, that 'tis the taking any part of what is common, and removing it out of the state Nature leaves it in, which begins the property, without which the common is of no use. And the taking of this or that part does not depend on the express consent of all the commoners. Thus, the grass my horse has bit, the turfs my servant has cut, and the ore I have digged in any place, where I have a right to them in common with others,

become my property without the assignation or consent of any body. The labour that was mine, removing them out of that common state they were in, hath fixed my property in them.

It will perhaps be objected to this, that if gathering the acorns or other fruits of the earth, etc., makes a right to them, then any one may engross as much as he will. To which I answer, Not so. The same law of nature that does by this means give us property, does also bound that property too. *God has given us all things richly,* 1 *Tim.* vi. 12. Is the voice of reason confirmed by inspiration? But how far has he given it us, *to enjoy?* As much as any one can make use of to any advantage of life before it spoils, so much he may by his labour fix a property in. Whatever is beyond this is more than his share, and belongs to others. Nothing was made by God for man to spoil or destroy. And thus considering the plenty of natural provisions there was a long time in the world, and the few spenders, and to how small a part of that provision the industry of one man could extend itself and engross it to the prejudice of others, especially keeping within the bonds set by reason of what might serve for his use, there could be then little room for quarrels or contentions about property so established.

But the chief matter of property being now not the fruits of the earth and the beasts that subsist on it, but the earth itself, as that which takes in and carries with it all the rest, I think it is plain that property in that too is acquired as the former. As much land as a man tills, plants, improves, cultivates, and can use the product of, so much is his property. He by his labour does, as it were, enclose it from the common. Nor will it invalidate his right to say, Every body else has an equal title to it, and therefore he cannot appropriate, he cannot enclose, without the consent of all his fellow-commoners, all mankind. God, when he gave the world in common to all mankind, commanded man also to labour, and the penury of his condition required it of him. God and his reason commanded him to subdue the earth—*i.e.*, improve it for the benefit of life and therein lay out something upon it that was his own, his labour. He that, in obedience to this command of God, subdued, tilled, and sowed any part of it, thereby annexed to it something that was his property, which another had no title to, nor could without injury take from him.

Nor was this appropriation of any parcel of land, by improving it, any prejudice to any other man, since there was still enough and as good left, and more than the yet unprovided could use. So that, in effect, there was never the less left for others because of his enclosure for himself. For he that leaves as much as another can make use of does as good as take nothing at all. No body could think himself injured by the drinking of another man, though he took a good draught, who had a whole river of the same water left him to quench his thirst. And the case of land and water, where there is enough of both, is perfectly the same.

God gave the world to men in common, but since he gave it them for their benefit and the greatest conveniences of life they were capable to draw from it, it cannot be supposed he meant it should always remain common and uncultivated. He gave it to the use of the industrious and rational (and labour was to be his title to it); not to the fancy or covetousness of the quarrelsome and contentious. He that had as good left for his improvement as was already taken up needed not complain, ought not to meddle with what was already improved by another's labour; if he did 'tis plain he desired the benefit of another's pains, which he had no right to, and not the ground which God had given him, in common with others, to labour on, and whereof there was as good left as that already possessed, and more than he knew what to do with, or his industry could reach to.

Nor is it so strange as perhaps before consideration, it may appear, that the property

of labour should be able to overbalance the community of land, for 'tis labour indeed that puts the difference of value on every thing; and let any one consider what the difference is between an acre of land planted with tobacco or sugar, sown with wheat or barley, and an acre of the same land lying in common without any husbandry upon it, and he will find that the improvement of labour makes the far greater part of the value. I think it will be but a very modest computation to say, that of the products of the earth useful to the life of man, nine-tenths are the effects of labour: nay, if we will rightly estimate things as they come to our use, and cast up the several expenses about them, what in them is purely owing to nature and what to labour, we shall find that in most of them ninety-nine hundredths are wholly to be put on the account of labour.

There cannot be a clearer demonstration of any thing than several nations of the Americans are of this, who are rich in land and poor in all the comforts of life; whom nature, having furnished as liberally as any other people with the materials of plenty, *i.e.*, a fruitful soil, apt to produce in abundance what might serve for food, raiment, and delight; yet, for want of improving it by labour, have not one hundredth part of the conveniencies we enjoy. And a king of a large and fruitful territory there feeds, lodges, and is clad worse than a day labourer in England.

From all which it is evident, that though the things of nature are given in common, man (by being master of himself, and proprietor of his own person, and the actions or labour of it) had still in himself the great foundation of property; and that which made up the great part of what he applied to the support or comfort of his being, when invention and arts had improved the conveniencies of life, was perfectly his own, and did not belong in common to others.

Thus labour, in the beginning, gave a right of property, wherever any one was pleased to employ it, upon what was common, which remained a long while, the far greater part, and is yet more than mankind makes use of. Men at first, for the most part, contented themselves with what unassisted nature offered to their necessities; and though afterwards, in some parts of the world, where the increase of people and stock, with the use of money, had made land scarce, and so of some value, the several communities settled the bounds of their distinct territories, and, by laws, within themselves, regulated the properties of the private men of their society, and so, by compact and agreement, settled the property which labour and industry began; and the leagues that have been made between several states and kingdoms, either expressly or tacitly disowning all claim and right to the land in the other's possession, have, by common consent, given up their pretences to their natural common right, which originally they had to those countries; and so have, by positive agreement, settled a property amongst themselves, in distinct parts of the world; yet there are still great tracts of ground to be found, which the inhabitants thereof, not having joined with the rest of mankind in the consent of the use of their common money, lie waste, and are more than the people who dwell on it, do, or can make use of, and so still lie in common; though this can scarce happen amongst that part of mankind that have consented to the use of money.

The greatest part of things really useful to the life of man, and such as the necessity of subsisting made the first commoners of the world look after, as it doth the Americans now, are generally things of short duration, such as, if they are not consumed by use, will decay and perish of themselves. Gold, silver, and diamonds are things that fancy or agreement hath put the value on, more than real use and the necessary support of life. Now of those good things which nature hath provided in common, every one had a right (as hath been said) to as much as he could use, and had a property in all that he could effect with his labour; all

that his industry could extend to, to alter from the state nature had put it in, was his. He that gathered a hundred bushels of acorns or apples had thereby a property in them, they were his goods as soon as gathered. He was only to look that he used them before they spoiled, else he took more than his share, and robbed others. And, indeed, it was a foolish thing, as well as dishonest, to hoard up more than he could make use of. If he gave away a part to any body else, so that it perished not uselessly in his possession, these he also made use of. And if he also bartered away plums that would have rotted in a week, for nuts that would last good for his eating a whole year, he did no injury; he wasted not the common stock; destroyed no part of the portion of goods that belonged to others, so long as nothing perished uselessly in his hands. Again, if he would give his nuts for a piece of metal, pleased with its colour, or exchange his sheep for shells, or wool for a sparkling pebble or a diamond, and keep those by him all his life, he invaded not the right of others; he might heap up as much of these durable things as he pleased; the exceeding of the bounds of his just property not lying in the largeness of his possession, but the perishing of anything uselessly in it.

And thus came in the use of money, some lasting thing that men might keep without spoiling, and that, by mutual consent, men would take in exchange for the truly useful but perishable supports of life.

And as different degrees of industry were apt to give men possessions in different proportions, so this invention of money gave them the opportunity to continue and enlarge them. For supposing an island, separate from all possible commerce with the rest of the world, wherein there were but a hundred families, but there were sheep, horses, and cows, with other useful animals, wholesome fruits, and land enough for corn for a hundred thousand times as many, but nothing in the island, either because of its commonness or perishableness, fit to supply the place of money. What reason could any one have there to enlarge his possessions beyond the use of his family, and a plentiful supply to its consumption, either in what their own industry produced, or they could barter for like perishable, useful commodities with others? Where there is not something both lasting and scarce, and so valuable to be hoarded up, there men will not be apt to enlarge their possessions of land, were it never so rich, never so free for them to take. For I ask, what would a man value ten thousand or an hundred thousand acres of excellent land, ready cultivated and well stocked, too, with cattle, in the middle of the inland parts of America, where he had no hopes of commerce with other parts of the world, to draw money to him by the sale of the product? It would not be worth the enclosing, and we should see him give up again to the wild common of nature whatever was more than would supply the conveniencies of life, to be had there for him and his family.

Thus, in the beginning, all the world was America, and more so than that is now; for no such thing as money was any where known. Find out something that hath the use and value of money amongst his neighbours, you shall see the same man will begin presently to enlarge his possessions.

But since gold and silver, being little useful to the life of man, in proportion to food, raiment, and carriage, has its value only from the consent of men, whereof labour yet makes in great part the measure, it is plain that the consent of men have ageed to a disproportionate and unequal possession of the earth, I mean out of the bounds of society and compact; for in governments the laws regulate it; they having, by consent, found out and agreed in a way how a man may rightfully, and without injury, possess more than he himself can make use of by receiving gold and silver, which may continue long in a man's possession without decaying for the overplus, and agreeing those metals should have a value.

5. Political Society

Man being born, as has been proved, with a title to perfect freedom and an uncontrolled enjoyment of all the rights and privileges of the law of nature, equally with any other man, or number of men in the world, hath by nature a power not only to preserve his property, that is, his life, liberty, and estate, against the injuries and attempts of other men, but to judge of and punish the breaches of that law in others, as he is persuaded the offence deserves, even with death itself, in crimes where the heinousness of the fact, in his opinion, requires it. But because no political society can be, nor subsist, without having in itself the power to preserve the property, and in order thereunto punish the offences of all those of that society: there, and there only, is political society, where every one of the members hath quitted this natural power, resigned it up into the hands of the community in all cases that exclude him not from appealing for protection to the law established by it. And thus all private judgement of every particular member being excluded, the community comes to be umpire, by settled standing rules; indifferent, and the same to all parties: And by men having authority from the community for the execution of those rules, decides all the differences that may happen between any members of that society concerning any matter of right, and punishes those offences which any member hath committed against the society with such penalties as the law has established; whereby it is easy to discern who are, and who are not, in political society together. Those who are united into one body, and have a common established law and judicature to appeal to, with authority to decide controversies between them and punish offenders, are in civil society one with another; but those who have no such common appeal, I mean on earth, are still in the state of nature, each being, where there is no other, judge for himself and executioner; which is, as I have before showed it, the perfect state of nature.

And thus the commonwealth comes by a power to set down what punishment shall belong to the several transgressions they think worthy of it, committed amongst the members of that society (which is the power of making laws) as well as it has the power to punish any injury done unto any of its members by anyone that is not of it (which is the power of war and peace); and all this for the preservation of the property of all the members of that society, as far as is possible. But though every man entered into society has quitted his power to punish offences against the law of nature in prosecution of his own private judgement, yet with the judgement of offences which he has given up to the legislative in all cases where he can appeal to the magistrate, he has given up a right to the commonwealth to employ his force for the execution of the judgements of the commonwealth whenever he shall be called to it, which, indeed, are his own judgements, they being made by himself or his representative. And herein we have the original of the legislative and executive power of civil society, which is to judge by standing laws how far offences are to be punished when committed within the commonwealth; and also by occasional judgements founded on the present circumstances of the fact, how far injuries from without are to be vindicated, and in both these to employ all the force of all the members when there shall be need.

Wherever therefore any number of men are so united into one society as to quit every one his executive power of the law of nature, and to resign it to the public, there and there only is a political or civil society. And this is done wherever any number of men, in the state of nature, enter into society to make one people, one body politic under one supreme government: or else when anyone joins himself to and incorporates with any government already made. For hereby he authorizes the society, or which is all one, the legislative

thereof, to make laws for him as the public good of the society shall require, to the execution whereof his own assistance (as to his own decrees) is due. And this puts men out of a state of nature into that of a commonwealth, by setting up a judge on earth with authority to determine all the controversies and redress the injuries that may happen to any member of the commonwealth; which judge is the legislative or magistrates appointed by it. And wherever there are any number of men, however associated, that have no such decisive power to appeal to, there they are still in the state of nature.

And hence it is evident that absolute monarchy, which by some men is counted for the only government in the world, is indeed inconsistent with civil society, and so can be no form of civil government at all. For the end of civil society being to avoid and remedy those inconveniences of the state of nature which necessarily follow from every man's being judge in his own case, by setting up a known authority, to which everyone of that society may appeal upon any injury received, or controversy that may arise, and which everyone of the society ought to obey, wherever any persons are who have not such an authority to appeal to, for the decision of any difference between them there, those persons are still in the state of nature. And so is every absolute prince in respect of those who are under his *dominion.*

For he being supposed to have all, both legislative and executive, power in himself alone, there is no judge to be found, no appeal lies open to anyone, who may fairly and indifferently, and with authority decide, and from whence relief and redress may by expected of any injury or inconveniency that may be suffered from him, or by his order. So that such a man, however entitled, Czar, or Grand Signior, or how you please, is as much in the state of nature, with all under his dominion, as he is with the rest of mankind. For wherever any two men are, who have no standing rule and common judge to appeal to on earth, for the determination of controversies of right betwixt them, there they are still in the state of nature, and under all the inconveniencies of it, with only this woeful difference to the subject, or rather slave of an absolute prince. That whereas, in the ordinary state of nature, he has a liberty to judge of his right, and according to the best of his power, to maintain it; but whenever his property is invaded by the will and order of his monarch, he has not only no appeal, as those in society ought to have, but, as if he were degraded from the common state of rational creatures, is denied a liberty to judge of, or defend his right, and so is exposed to all the misery and inconveniences that a man can fear from one, who being in the unrestrained state of nature, is yet corrupted with flattery and armed with power.

6. The End of Government

If man in the state of nature be so free as has been said; if he be absolute lord of his own person and possessions; equal to the greatest and subject to no body, why will he part with his freedom? Why will he give up this empire, and subject himself to the dominion and control of any other power? To which 'tis obvious to answer, that though in the state of nature he hath such a right, yet the enjoyment of it is very uncertain and constantly exposed to the invasion of others; for all being kings as much as he, every man his equal, and the greater part no strict observers of equity and justice, the enjoyment of the property he has in this state is very unsafe, very unsecure. This makes him willing to quit this condition which, however free, is full of fears and continual dangers; and 'tis not without reason that he seeks out and is willing to join in society with others who are already united, or have a mind to unite for the mutual preservation of their lives, liberties, and estates, which I call by the general name, property.

The great and chief end therefore, of men's uniting into commonwealths, and putting themselves under government, is the preservation of their property; to which in the state of nature there are many things wanting.

First, There wants an established, settled, known law, received and allowed by common consent to be the standard of right and wrong, and the common measure to decide all controversies between them. For though the law of nature be plain and intelligible to all rational creatures, yet men, being biased by their interest, as well as ignorant for want of study of it, are not apt to allow of it as a law binding to them in the application of it to their particular cases.

Secondly, In the state of nature there wants a known and indifferent judge, with authority to determine all differences according to the established law. For every one in that state being both judge and executioner of the law of nature, men being partial to themselves, passion and revenge is very apt to carry them too far, and with too much heat in their own cases, as well as negligence and unconcernedness, make them too remiss in other men's.

Thirdly, In the state of nature there often wants power to back and support the sentence when right, and to give it due execution. They who by any injustice offended, will seldom fail where they are able by force to make good their injustice. Such resistance many times makes the punishment dangerous, and frequently destructive to those who attempt it.

Thus mankind, notwithstanding all the privileges of the state of nature, being but in an ill condition while they remain in it, are quickly driven into society. Hence it comes to pass, that we seldom find any number of men live any time together in this state. The inconveniences that they are therein exposed to by the irregular and uncertain exercise of the power every man has of punishing the transgressions of others, make them take sanctuary under the established laws of government, and therein seek the preservation of their property. 'Tis this makes them so willingly give up every one his single power of punishing to be exercised by such alone as shall be appointed to it amongst them, and by such rules as the community, or those authorized by them to that purpose, shall agree on. And in this we have the original right and rise of both the legislative and executive power as well as of the governments and societies themselves.

7. The Limits of Government

The great end of men's entering into society being the enjoyment of their properties in peace and safety, and the great instrument and means of that being the laws established in that society, the first and fundamental positive law of all commonwealths is the establishing of the legislative power; as the first and fundamental natural law, which is to govern even the legislative itself, is the preservation of the society, and (as far as will consist with the public good) of every person in it. This legislative is not only the supreme power of the commonwealth, but sacred and unalterable in the hands where the community have once placed it; nor can any edict of anybody else, in what form soever conceived, or by what power soever backed, have the force and obligation of a law which has not its sanction from that legislative which the public has chosen and appointed; for without this the law could not have that which is absolutely necessary to its being a law, the consent of the society, over whom nobody can have a power to make laws but by their own consent and by authority received from them; and therefore all the obedience, which by the most solemn ties anyone can be obliged to pay, ultimately terminates in this supreme power, and is directed by those laws which it enacts. Nor can any oaths to any foreign power whatsoever, or any domestic subordinate power, discharge any member of the society from his obedience to the legislative, acting pursuant to their trust, nor oblige him to any obedience contrary to the laws so enacted or farther than they do allow, it being ridiculous to imagine one can be tied ultimately to obey any power in the society which is not the supreme.

Though the legislative, whether placed in one or more, whether it be always in being or only by intervals, though it be the supreme power in every commonwealth, yet *First,* It is not, nor can possibly be, absolutely arbitrary over the lives and fortunes of the people. For it being but the joint power of every member of the society given up to that person or assembly which is legislator, it can be no more than those persons had in a state of nature before they entered into society, and gave it up to the community. For nobody can transfer to another more power than he has in himself, and nobody has an absolute arbitrary power over himself, or over any other, to destroy his own life, or take away the life or property of another. A man, as has been proved, cannot subject himself to the arbitrary power of another; and having, in the state of nature, no arbitrary power over the life, liberty, or possession of another, but only so much as the law of nature gave him for the preservation of himself and the rest of mankind, this is all he doth, or can give up to the commonwealth, and by it to the legislative power, so that the legislative can have no more than this. Their power in the utmost bounds of it is limited to the public good of the society. It is a power that hath no other end but preservation, and therefore can never have a right to destroy, enslave, or designedly to impoverish the subjects; the obligations of the law of nature cease not in society, but only in many cases are drawn closer, and have, by human laws, known penalties annexed to them to enforce their observation. Thus the law of nature stands as an eternal rule to all men, legislators as well as others. The rules that they make for other men's actions must, as well as their own and other men's actions, be conformable to the law of nature, *i.e.*

to the will of God, of which that is a declaration, and the fundamental law of nature being the preservation of mankind, no human sanction can be good or valid against it.

Secondly, The legislative or supreme authority cannot assume to itself a power to rule by extemporary arbitrary decrees, but is bound to dispense justice and decide the rights of the subject by promulgated standing laws, and known authorized judges. For the law of nature being unwritten, and so nowhere to be found but in the minds of men, they who, through passion or interest, shall miscite or misapply it, cannot so easily be convinced of their mistake where there is no established judge; and so it serves not as it ought, to determine the rights and fence the properties of those that live under it, especially where everyone is judge, interpreter, and executioner of it too, and that in his own case; and he that has right on his side, having ordinarily but his own single strength, hath not force enough to defend himself from injuries or to punish delinquents. To avoid these inconveniencies which disorder men's properties in the state of nature, men unite into societies that they may have the united strength of the whole society to secure and defend their properties, and may have standing rules to bound it by which everyone may know what is his. To this end it is that men give up all their natural power to the society they enter into, and the community put the legislative power into such hands as they think fit, with this trust, that they shall be governed by declared laws, or else their peace, quiet, and property will still be at the same uncertainty as it was in the state of nature.

Absolute arbitrary power, or governing without settled standing laws, can neither of them consist with the ends of society and government, which men would not quit the freedom of the state of nature for, and tie themselves up under, were it not to preserve their lives, liberties, and fortunes, and by stated rules of right and property to secure their peace and quiet. It cannot be supposed that they should intend, had they a power so to do, to give to any one or more an absolute arbitrary power over their persons and estates, and put a force into the magistrate's hand to execute his unlimited will arbitrarily upon them; this were to put themselves into a worse condition than the state of nature, wherein they had a liberty to defend their right against the injuries of others, and were upon equal terms of force to maintain it, whether invaded by a single man or many in combination. Whereas by supposing they have given up themselves to the absolute arbitrary power and will of a legislator, they have disarmed themselves, and armed him to make a prey of them when he pleases; he being in a much worse condition that is exposed to the arbitrary power of one man who has the command of a hundred thousand than he that is exposed to the arbitrary power of a hundred thousand single men, nobody being secure, that his will who has such a command is better than that of other men, though his force be a hundred thousand times stronger. And, therefore, whatever form the commonwealth is under, the ruling power ought to govern by declared and received laws, and not by extemporary dictates and undetermined resolutions, for then mankind will be in a far worse condition than in the state of nature if they shall have armed one or a few men with the joint power of a multitude, to force them to obey at pleasure the exorbitant and unlimited decrees of their sudden thoughts, or unrestrained, and till that moment, unknown wills, without having any measures set down which may guide and justify their actions. For all the power the government has, being only for the good of the society, as it ought not to be arbitrary and at pleasure, so it ought to be exercised by established and promulgated laws, that both the people may know their duty, and be safe and secure within the limits of the law, and the rulers, too, kept within their due bounds, and not to be tempted by the power they have in their hands to employ it to purposes, and by such measures as they would not have known, and own not willingly.

Thirdly, The supreme power cannot take from any man any part of his property without his own consent. For the preservation of property being the end of government, and that for which men enter into society, it necessarily supposes and requires that the people should have property, without which they must be supposed to lose that by entering into society which was the end for which they entered into it; too gross an absurdity for any man to own. Men therefore in society having property, they have such a right to the goods, which by the law of the community are theirs, that nobody hath a right to their substance, or any part of it, from them without their own consent; without this they have no property at all. For I have truly no property in that which another can by right take from me when he pleases against my consent. Hence it is a mistake to think that the supreme or legislative power of any commonwealth can do what it will, and dispose of the estates of the subject arbitrarily, or take any part of them at pleasure. This is not much to be feared in governments where the legislative consists wholly or in part in assemblies which are variable, whose members upon the dissolution of the assembly are subjects under the common laws of their country, equally with the rest. But in governments where the legislative is in one lasting assembly, always in being, or in one man as in absolute monarchies, there is danger still, that they will think themselves to have a distinct interest from the rest of the community, and so will be apt to increase their own riches and power by taking what they think fit from the people. For a man's property is not at all secure, though there be good and equitable laws to set the bounds of it between him and his fellow-subjects, if he who commands those subjects have power to take from any private man what part he pleases of his property, and use and dispose of it as he thinks good.

But government, into whatsoever hands it is put, being as I have before showed, entrusted with this condition, and for this end, that men might have and secure their properties, the prince or senate, however it may have power to make laws for the regulating of property between the subjects one amongst another, yet can never have a power to take to themselves the whole, or any part of the subjects' property, without their own consent; for this would be in effect to leave them no property at all. And to let us see that even absolute power, where it is necessary, is not arbitrary by being absolute, but is still limited by that reason, and confined to those ends which required it in some cases to be absolute, we need look no farther than the common practice of martial discipline. For the preservation of the army, and in it of the whole commonwealth, requires an absolute obedience to the command of every superior officer, and it is justly death to disobey or dispute the most dangerous or unreasonable of them; but yet we see that neither the sergeant that could command a soldier to march up to the mouth of a cannon, or stand in a breach where he is almost sure to perish, can command that soldier to give him one penny of his money; nor the general that can condemn him to death for deserting his post, or not obeying the most desperate orders, cannot yet with all his absolute power of life and death dispose of one farthing of that soldier's estate, or seize one jot of his goods; whom yet he can command anything, and hang for the least disobedience. Because such a blind obedience is necessary to that end for which the commander has his power, *viz.* the preservation of the rest, but the disposing of his goods has nothing to do with it.

'Tis true, governments cannot be supported without great charge, and 'tis fit everyone who enjoys his share of the protection should pay out of his estate his proportion for the maintenance of it. But still it must be with his own consent, *i.e.* the consent of the majority, giving it either by themselves or their representatives chosen by them; for if anyone shall claim a power to lay and levy taxes on the people by his own authority, and without such consent of the people, he thereby invades the fundamental law of property, and subverts the end of government. For what property have I in that which another may be right take when he pleases himself?

Fourthly, The legislative cannot transfer the power of making laws to any other hands, for it being but a delegated power from the people, they who have it cannot pass it over to others. The people alone can appoint the form of the commonwealth, which is by constituting the legislative, and appointing in whose hands that shall be. And when the people have said, We will submit, and be governed by laws made by such men, and in such forms, nobody else can say other men shall make laws for them; nor can they be bound by any laws but such as are enacted by those whom they have chosen and authorized to make laws for them. The power of the legislative being derived from the people by a positive voluntary grant and institution, can be no other than what that positive grant conveyed, which being only to make laws, and not to make legislators, the legislative can have no power to transfer their authority of making laws, and place it in other hands.

These are the bounds which the trust that is put in them by the society and the law of God and nature have set to the legislative power of every commonwealth, in all forms of government.

First, They are to govern by promulgated established laws, not to be varied in particular cases, but to have one rule for rich and poor, for the favourite at Court, and the countryman at plough.

Secondly, These laws also ought to be designed for no other end ultimately but the good of the people.

Thirdly, They must not raise taxes on the property of the people without the consent of the people given by themselves or their deputies. And this properly concerns only such governments where the legislative is always in being, or at least where the people have not reserved any part of the legislative to deputies, to be from time to time chosen by themselves.

Fourthly, The legislative neither must nor can transfer the power of making laws to anybody else, or place it anywhere but where the people have.

8. The Right to Rebel

The reason why men enter into society is the preservation of their property; and the end why they choose and authorize a legislative is that there may be laws made, and rules set, as guards and fences to the properties of all the members of the society, to limit the power and moderate the dominion of every part and member of the society. For since it can never be supposed to be the will of the society that the legislative should have a power to destroy that which every one designs to secure by entering into society, and for which the people submitted themselves to legislators of their own making: whenever the legislators endeavour to take away and destroy the property of the people, or to reduce them to slavery under arbitrary power, they put themselves into a state of war with the people, who are thereupon absolved from any farther obedience, and are left to the common refuge which God hath provided for all men against force and violence. Whensoever therefore the legislative shall transgress this fundamental rule of society, and either by ambition, fear, folly, or corruption, endeavour to grasp themselves, or put into the hands of any other, an absolute power over the lives, liberties, and estates of the people, by this breach of trust they forfeit the power the people had put into their hands for quite contrary ends, and it devolves to the people; who have a right to resume their original liberty, and by the establishment of a new legislative (such as they shall think fit), provide for their own safety and security, which is the end for which they are in society. What I have said here concerning the legislative in general holds true also concerning the supreme executor, who having a double trust put in him, both to have a part in the legislative and the supreme execution of the law, acts against both, when he goes about to set up his own arbitrary will as the law of the society. He acts also contrary to his trust when he employs the force, treasure, and offices of the society to corrupt the representatives and gain them to his purposes, when he openly pre-engages the electors, and prescribes, to their choice, such whom he has, by solicitations, threats, promises, or otherwise, won to his designs, and employs them to bring in such who have promised beforehand what to vote and what to enact. Thus to regulate candidates and electors, and new model the ways of election, what is it but to cut up the government by the roots, and poison the very fountain of public security? For the people having reserved to themselves the choice of their representatives as the fence to their properties, could do it for no other end but that they might always be freely chosen, and so chosen, freely act and advise as the necessity of the commonwealth and the public good should, upon examination and mature debate, be judged to require. This, those who give their votes before they hear the debate, and have weighed the reasons on all sides, are not capable of doing. To prepare such an assembly as this, and endeavour to set up the declared abettors of his own will, for the true representatives of the people, and the law-makers of the society, is certainly as great a breach of trust, and as perfect a declaration of a design to subvert the government, as is possible to be met with. To which, if one shall add rewards and punishments visibly employed to the same end, and all the arts of perverted law made use of to take off and destroy all that stand in the way of such a design, and will not comply and consent to betray the liberties of their country, 'twill be past doubt what is doing. What power they ought to have in the society who thus employ it contrary to the trust went along with it in its first institution, is easy to determine; and one cannot but see that he who has once attempted any such

thing as this cannot any longer be trusted.

To this, perhaps, it will be said, that the people being ignorant and always discontented, to lay the foundation of government in the unsteady opinion and uncertain humour of the people, is to expose it to certain ruin; and no government will be able long to subsist if the people may set up a new legislative whenever they take offence at the old one. To this I answer, quite the contrary. People are not so easily got out of their old forms as some are apt to suggest. They are hardly to be prevailed with to amend the acknowledged faults in the frame they have been accustomed to. And if there be any original defects, or adventitious ones introduced by time or corruption, 'tis not an easy thing to get them changed, even when all the world sees there is an opportunity for it. This slowness and aversion in the people to quit their old constitutions has in the many revolutions [that] have been seen in this kingdom, in this and former ages, still kept us to, or after some interval of fruitless attempts, still brought us back again to our old legislative king, lords and commons; and whatever provocations have made the crown be taken from some of our princes' heads, they never carried the people so far as to place it in another line.

But 'twill be said, this hypothesis lays a ferment for frequent rebellion. To which I answer:

First, No more than any other hypothesis. For when the people are made miserable, and find themselves exposed to the ill usage of arbitrary power; cry up their governors as much as you will for sons of *Jupiter,* let them be sacred and divine, descended or authorized from Heaven; give them out for whom or what you please, the same will happen. The people generally ill treated, and contrary to right, will be ready upon any occasion to ease themselves of a burden that sits heavy upon them. They will wish and seek for the opportunity, which in the change, weakness, and accidents of human affairs, seldom delays long to offer itself. He must have lived but a little while in the world, who has not seen examples of this in his time; and he must have read very little who cannot produce examples of it in all sorts of governments in the world.

Secondly, I answer, such revolutions happen not upon every little mismanagement in public affairs. Great mistakes in the ruling part, many wrong and inconvenient laws, and all the slips of human frailty will be borne by the people without mutiny or murmur. But if a long train of abuses, prevarications, and artifices, all tending the same way, make the design visible to the people, and they cannot but feel what they lie under, and see whither they are going, 'tis not to be wondered that they should then rouse themselves, and endeavour to put the rule into such hands which may secure to them the ends for which government was at first erected, and without which, ancient names and specious forms are so far from being better, that they are much worse than the state of nature or pure anarchy; the inconveniencies being all as great and as near, but the remedy farther off and more difficult.

Thirdly, I answer, That this power in the people of providing for their safety anew by a new legislative when their legislators have acted contrary to their trust by invading their property, is the best fence against rebellion, and the probablest means to hinder it. For rebellion being an opposition, not to persons, but authority, which is founded only in the constitutions and laws of the government; those, whoever they be, who by force break through, and by force justify their violation of them, are truly and properly rebels. For when men, by entering into society and civil government, have excluded force, and introduced laws for the preservation of property, peace, and unity amongst themselves; those who set up force again in opposition to the laws, do *rebellare*—that is, bring back again the state of war, and are properly rebels, which they who are in power, by the pretence they have to authority, the temptation of force they have in their hands, and the flattery of those about them being likeliest to do, the

properest way to prevent the evil is to shew them the danger and injustice of it who are under the greatest temptation to run into it.

In both the forementioned cases, when either the legislative is changed, or the legislators act contrary to the end for which they were constituted, those who are guilty are guilty of rebellion. For if any one by force takes away the established legislative of any society, and the laws by them made, pursuant to their trust, he thereby takes away the umpirage which every one had consented to for a peaceable decision of all their controversies, and a bar to the state of war amongst them. They who remove or change the legislative take away this decisive power, which no body can have but by the appointment and consent of the people; and so destroying the authority which the people did, and no body else can set up, and introducing a power which the people hath not authorized, actually introduce a state of war, which is that of force without authority; and thus by removing the legislative established by the society, in whose decisions the people acquiesced and united as to that of their own will, they untie the knot, and expose the people anew to the state of war. And if those, who by force take away the legislative, are rebels, the legislators themselves, as has been shewn, can be no less esteemed so, when they who were set up for the protection and preservation of the people, their liberties and properties shall by force invade and endeavour to take them away; and so they putting themselves into a state of war with those who made them the protectors and guardians of their peace, are properly, and with the greatest aggravation, *rebellantes*, rebels.

But if they who say it lays a foundation for rebellion mean that it may occasion civil wars or intestine broils to tell the people they are absolved from obedience when illegal attempts are made upon their liberties or properties, and may oppose the unlawful violence of those who were their magistrates when they invade their properties, contrary to the trust put in them; and that, therefore, this doctrine is not to be allowed, being so destructive to the peace of the world; they may as well say, upon the same ground, that honest men may not oppose robbers or pirates, because this may occasion disorder or bloodshed. If any mischief come in such cases, it is not to be charged upon him who defends his own right, but on him that invades his neighbour's. If the innocent honest man must quietly quit all he has for peace sake to him who will lay violent hands upon it, I desire it may be considered what a kind of peace there will be in the world which consists only in violence and rapine, and which is to be maintained only for the benefit of robbers and oppressors. Who would not think it an admirable peace betwixt the mighty and the mean, when the lamb, without resistance, yielded his throat to be torn by the imperious wolf? *Polyphemus*'s den gives us a perfect pattern of such a peace. Such a government wherein *Ulysses* and his companions had nothing to do but quietly to suffer themselves to be devoured. And no doubt, *Ulysses,* who was a prudent man, preached up passive obedience, and exhorted them to a quiet submission by representing to them of what concernment peace was to mankind, and by shewing the inconveniences might happen if they should offer to resist *Polyphemus,* who had now the power over them.

The end of government is the good of mankind; and which is best for mankind, that the people should be always exposed to the boundless will of tyranny, or that the rulers should be sometimes liable to be opposed when they grow exorbitant in the use of their power, and employ it for the destruction, and not the preservation, of the properties of their people?

Nor let any one say that mischief can arise from hence as often as it shall please a busy head or turbulent spirit to desire the alteration of the government. 'Tis true such men may stir whenever they please, but it will be only to their own just ruin and perdition. For till the mischief be grown general, and the ill designs of the rulers become visible, or their attempts sensible to the greater part, the people, who are more disposed to suffer than right themselves by resistance, are not apt to stir. The examples of particular injustice or oppression of here and there an unfortunate man moves them not. But if they universally have a persuasion grounded upon manifest evidence that designs are carrying on against their liberties, and the general course and tendency of things cannot but give them strong suspicions of the evil intention of their governors, who is to be blamed for it? Who can help it if they, who might avoid it, bring themselves into this suspicion? Are the people to be blamed if they have the sense of rational creatures, and can think of things no otherwise than as they find and feel them? And is it not rather their fault who put things in such a posture that they would not have them thought as they are? I grant that the pride, ambition, and turbulency of private men have sometimes caused great disorders in commonwealths, and factions have been fatal to states and kingdoms. But whether the mischief hath oftener begun in the people's wantonness, and a desire to cast off the lawful authority of their rulers, or in the rulers' insolence and endeavours to get and exercise an arbitrary power over their people, whether oppression or disobedience gave the first rise to the disorder, I leave it to impartial history to determine. This I am sure, whoever, either ruler or subject, by force goes about to invade the rights of either prince or people, and lays the foundation for overturning the constitution and frame of any just government, he is guilty of the greatest crime I think a man is capable of, being to answer for all those mischiefs of blood, rapine, and desolation, which the breaking to pieces of governments bring on a country; and he who does it is justly to be esteemed the common enemy and pest of mankind, and is to be treated accordingly.

That subjects or foreigners attempting by force on the properties of any people may be resisted with force is agreed on all hands; but that magistrates doing the same thing may be resisted, hath of late been denied; as if those who had the greatest privileges and advantages by the law had thereby a power to break those laws by which alone they were set in a better place than their brethren; whereas their offence is thereby the greater, both as being ungrateful for the greater share they have by the law, and breaking also that trust which is put into their hands by their brethren.

Whosoever uses force without right, as every one does in society who does it without law, puts himself into a state of war with those against whom he so uses it, and in that state all former ties are cancelled, all other rights cease, and every one has a right to defend himself, and to resist the aggressor.

Here 'tis like the common question will be made, Who shall be judge whether the prince or legislative act contrary to their trust? This, perhaps, ill-affected and factious men may spread amongst the people, when the prince only makes use of his due prerogative. To this I reply, The people shall be judge; for who shall be judge whether his trustee or deputy acts well and according to the trust reposed in him, but he who deputes him and must, by having deputed him, have still a power to discard him when he fails in his trust? If this be reasonable in particular cases of private men, why should it be otherwise in that of the greatest moment, where the welfare of millions is concerned and also where the evil, if not prevented, is greater, and the redress very difficult, dear, and dangerous?

But, farther, this question, (Who shall be judge?) cannot mean that there is no judge at all. For where there is no judicature on earth to decide controversies amongst men, God in Heaven is judge. He alone, 'tis true, is judge of the right. But every man is judge for himself, as in all other cases so in this, whether another hath put himself into a state of war with him, and whether he should appeal to the supreme Judge, as *Jephtha* did.

If a controversy arise betwixt a prince and some of the people in a matter where the law is silent or doubtful, and the thing be of great consequence, I should think the proper umpire, in such a case, should be the body of the people. For in such cases where the prince hath a trust reposed in him, and is dispensed from the common, ordinary rules of the law; there, if any men find themselves aggrieved, and think the prince acts contrary to, or beyond that trust, who so proper to judge as the body of the people (who at first lodged that trust in him) how far they meant it should extend? But if the prince, or whoever they be in the administration, decline that way of determination, the appeal then lies nowhere but to Heaven. Force between either persons, who have no known superior on earth, or which permits no appeal to a judge on earth, being properly a state of war, wherein the appeal lies only to Heaven; and in that state the injured party must judge for himself when he will think fit to make use of that appeal and put himself upon it.

To conclude, The power that every individual gave the society when he entered into it, can never revert to the individuals again, as long as the society lasts, but will always remain in the community; because without this there can be no community, no commonwealth, which is contrary to the original agreement; so also when the society hath placed the legislative in any assembly of men, to continue in them and their successors, with direction and authority for providing such successors, the legislative can never revert to the people whilst that government lasts; because, having provided a legislative with power to continue for ever, they have given up their political power to the legislative, and cannot resume it. But if they have set limits to the duration of their legislative, and made this supreme power in any person or assembly only temporary; or else when, by the miscarriages of those in authority, it is forfeited; upon the forfeiture of their rulers or at the determination of the time set, it reverts to the society, and the people have a right to act as supreme, and continue the legislative in themselves or place it in a new form, or new hands, as they think good.

CHAPTER 16

MONTESQUIEU

T HE seventeenth century was dominated by the struggle for sovereignty between monarchy and parliament. In England, parliamentary supremacy was decisively asserted in the Revolution of 1688. In France, the monarchy was able to overcome all resistance to its power, and after 1614 the Estates General did not meet until 1789—and in 1789 it was too late. The fifty-four years of Louis XIV's personal government (1661–1715) set a standard for royal absolutism in Europe; France was the acknowledged mistress in the arts and letters as well as the first power in population and wealth.

Yet the cost of the glorious rule of *le grand monarque* was immense. In 1685 he revoked the Edict of Nantes, which had granted religious toleration to Protestants a century earlier (1598). Many Protestants were thus forced to leave France. As the Huguenots had been a vigorous element in French trade and industry, their emigration contributed to the growing economic malaise and bankruptcy that threatened France during the latter part of Louis XIV's regime.

Politically, the revocation of the Edict of Nantes was no less disastrous to French clericalism and absolutism, because it was largely through the writings of the Huguenot refugees in England that France—and through the French language the educated classes all over Europe—acquired a direct knowledge of the English Revolution of 1688 and its underlying liberal philosophy. In science, the English influence was felt most directly through the work of Newton; in philosophy and political thought, Locke's name dominated eighteenth-century France. Locke's *Essay Concerning Human Understanding* stressed experience as the sole source of knowledge and thus indirectly opposed a scheme of life that emphasized authority rather than reason and observation. More directly, Locke's *Two Treatises of Government* and *Letters Concerning Toleration* showed the outlines of a new social order in which despotic kingship by divine right and clerical control of thought and education were replaced by political liberalism and intellectual individualism.

Voltaire (1694–1778) spent three years in England, from 1726 to 1729, and his *Letters on the English* (1734) showed the French—and European—reading public a land of freedom and common sense, secular in outlook, tolerant in religion, and respectful of the rule of law. Voltaire was favorably impressed with the rising social prestige of the middle classes in England and with the individual freedom that resulted from wealth earned in trade and commerce. Like most of the French eighteenth-century *philosophes,* Voltaire was satisfied with a political order that secured stability of property and freedom of individual thought and opinion; democratic rule by the people was still an ideal that was not seriously discussed before the latter part of the century.

During the year of Voltaire's return to France, another distinguished French writer, Montesquieu, went to England to see things for himself. Charles-Louis de Secondat, Baron de la Brède et de Montesquieu (1689–1755), came from a noble family of good standing. At one time his family had accepted Protestantism but later abandoned it. Montesquieu received, as was customary at the time, a classical education, and from his Latin studies he derived a deep affection for Stoicism that he retained for the rest of his life. Imbued with the religious tolerance of the Stoics, he wrote, at the age of twenty-two, an essay in which he maintained that the pagan philosophers of antiquity did not deserve eternal damnation. Montesquieu was trained in law and early became associated with the administration of justice in Bordeaux, his parental castle and birthplace being only a few miles from this flourishing city. In 1716 his uncle died and bequeathed to him the office of chief justice. He held that office for only ten years, and then resigned, in order to devote himself entirely to his favorite activity of writing.

By this time Montesquieu had become a European celebrity. In 1721, when he was thirty-two, he had published (anonymously in Geneva) the *Persian Letters,* which had the effect of a literary bombshell in the Parisian *salons.* Through the letters of two imaginary Persian visitors to Paris, Montesquieu showed the reactions of unprejudiced observers to the irrationalities and imperfections of the western world, and the device of two fictional Persians enabled him to comment on taboos that would otherwise be too delicate to handle. The success of the book was increased by the detailed observations of the foreign visitors on the love life of Paris, and the detailed reports that they in turn received from their eunuchs about their harems in Persia. Also, Montesquieu satirized the Roman Catholic Church in a manner that would have been well-nigh impossible without the disguise of the Persians. The pope is described as a magician who makes believe "that three are but one, that the bread one eats is not bread, that the wine one drinks is not wine, and a thousand similar things," and the clergy is characterized as a "society of persons who always take, and never give." In a more serious vein, the statement is made that the "Protestants will become every day richer and stronger, and the Catholics weaker."

The political satire of the *Persian Letters* was thus well couched in the anonymity of the two Persians, the ironical anticlericalism, and the comparative study of erotics in East and West. In 1726 Montesquieu was proposed—at an unusually early age—for membership in the French Academy, but King Louis XV objected. In 1728 he was able to win entry into the ranks of the "immortals" in French letters.

During the same year he set out on his travels, which took him to Austria, Hungary, Italy, Switzerland, Germany, and Holland; from Holland, in the fall of 1729, he went to England, where he stayed until the spring of 1731. As he traveled to England with the Earl of Chesterfield, British Ambassador at the Hague, he was quickly introduced to the most fashionable society in London. He was also presented at court, where he became a favorite of Queen Caroline, who was charmed by his wit and gallantry. Because of his scientific interests (in his younger years Montesquieu had composed papers on natural history, anatomy, and botany) he was elected a member of the Royal Society, then the world's leading scientific society; the close friendships he formed with some of England's foremost scientists he continued throughout the remainder of his life.

Montesquieu made a serious effort to understand English government. He attended both Houses of Parliament, took notes on debates, and met numerous politicians. He also studied the theory of British government and was a great admirer of Locke, whom he called the great instructor of mankind. Montesquieu was fully aware of the corruption of British politics at that time, and he saw other serious shortcomings. Yet his over-all impression was favorable when he compared the social and political conditions of England with those in France.

Like Voltaire, Montesquieu admired the sound common sense of the English aristocracy and middle classes. Political journalism was free and vigorous, and after the cynicism, corruption, and censorship of France the seriousness of English public life captivated him. There was more color and verve in French life, but he believed that the solidity—and often mediocrity—of England was politically more desirable than the dazzling brilliance of the Paris *salons,* in which there was no subject serious enough not to be corroded by cynicism. During his stay in England, Montesquieu made no effort to study the condition of the "lower" classes but confined himself to contacts with the upper classes and distinguished scientists. His picture of England had little relation to her poverty and rotten boroughs, because Montesquieu, like Voltaire, was hardly interested in social problems.

Montesquieu returned to France in 1731, full of ideas and projects for future books. In 1734 he published his *Considerations on the Greatness and Decline of Rome.* Roman history was a convenient starting point for his favorite theories, soon to be developed more fully. Speaking of the capacity of a state to correct its own mistakes and abuses, Montesquieu mentions Rome, Carthage, Athens, and the Italian city-republics; lamenting their shortcomings in self-analysis and self-correction, he says: "The government of England is wiser, because there is a body which examines it continuously and continuously examines itself; its errors never last long, and are often useful because of the spirit of attention they give to the people. In a word, a free government, that is, one that is always agitated, cannot be maintained if it is not capable of correction through its own laws."

Montesquieu's chief work, on which his reputation is founded, is his *Spirit of the Laws* (*De l'ésprit des lois,* 1748). He had been working on it, he said, all his life; in fact, his earlier writings anticipate the main ideas of *The Spirit of the Laws*. The impact of the work was powerful both intellectually and politically. Montesquieu shared with the eighteenth-century French *philosophes*— rational, cosmopolitan humanists—their optimism and faith in human progress through reason; yet the title of the book suggests that Montesquieu, though completely of the Age of Reason, goes beyond it. He is interested in the spirit of the *laws*, not the law.

From the traditional viewpoint, the basic principles of law could be rationally ascertained, and law was characteristically thought of in universal terms. The tendency of the philosophy of natural law was to minimize actual legal differences, treat them as accidental, and as not pertaining to the essence of law. Montesquieu confines, by contrast, the concept of natural law to the state of nature, "before the establishment of society." Once mankind sets up society and government, there are three kinds of law: first, the law of nations, which applies to their mutual intercourse; second, political law, which applies to the relations between government and the governed (constitutional, public, and administrative law); third, civil law, which regulates the relations of citizens among themselves (private law, such as the law of contracts). Montesquieu makes a bow to the traditional viewpoint by saying that "law in general is the human reason, inasmuch as it governs all the inhabitants of the earth; the political and civil laws of each nation ought to be only the particular cases in which human reason is applied." But it is evident that he is interested in the particular applications of law rather than in general law.

Montesquieu outlines his program of combining rationalism (which emphasizes the universal) with the historical method (which emphasizes the uniquely individual) by describing laws as follows: "They should be relative to the climate of each country, to the quality of its soil, to its situation and extent, to the principal occupation of the natives, whether husbandmen, huntsmen, or shepherds: they should have a relation to the degree of liberty which the constitution will bear; to the religion of the inhabitants, to their inclinations, riches, numbers, commerce, manners, and customs." By indicating how laws *ought* to be made, Montesquieu retains his link with the Age of Enlightenment from which he springs. Yet he places his rationalism on the empirical basis of social institutions, history, and environment, in the light of which one cannot produce laws by following mere fancy and imagination, because "laws, in their most general signification, are the necessary relations arising from the nature of things."

This awareness of the toughness of facts gives Montesquieu's work a massive strength that has stood the test of time. Forms of government are therefore, for Montesquieu, complex combinations of physical and environmental factors, on the one hand, and of psychological motivations—ways of life—on the other. His profound remark that the "beautiful system" of the English constitution "was invented first in the woods" showed an amazing historical awareness at a time when constitutions were discussed in the light of first principles of logic and reason. Montesquieu surmised that the origins of English political life had to be searched for in the remote history of the English people rather than in a constitutional charter. Although Montesquieu was anticipated by Aristotle, Polybius, and Bodin (to mention but a few) in the institutional and environmental study of politics, none of his predecessors surpassed him in breadth of interest, detachment of observation, and balance of spirit that sympathetically comprehended the reality of the past as much as the ideal possibilities of the future.

Montesquieu's second key idea is that of the *balanced constitution*, of which the doctrine of the *separation of powers* has become politically the most influential expression. Both concepts are elaborated and illustrated in *The Spirit of the Laws* by references to English government and politics. He characterizes England as a nation "passionately fond of liberty, because this liberty is real," willing to sacrifice its wealth, ease, and interest in defense of its freedom. Obviously alluding to the military adventurism of Louis XIV and the high respect for military virtues in the *ancien régime,* Montesquieu (though of a family that had given a number of professional officers to France) enviously notes that in England military men are regarded "as belonging to a profession which may be useful, but is often dangerous," and that civilians are more esteemed than the military.

The eighteenth century was full of colonial quarrels, particularly between France and England, and Montesquieu was attracted by the intricacies of colonial questions. He observes that English settlers introduced in the colonies their own form of government, and "raised great nations in the forests they were sent to inhabit." At the same time, Montesquieu prophetically foresaw that England, having granted a large measure of self-government to its colonies, would be the first nation to lose them. Similarly, in studying the impact of domestic institutions on foreign policy, Montesquieu thought that English statesmen, "being frequently obliged to justify their conduct before a popular council," would be forced to be "a little more honest" than statesmen who were not accountable to either parliament or public opinion.

The secret of England's freedom lay, for Montesquieu, in her system of government; as a liberal aristocat who favored individual liberty, property, and the ancient privileges of the aristocracy, Montesquieu was impressed by the fact that the English system of government combined within itself the best features of monarchy (in the executive), aristocracy (the House of Lords as the supreme court and as part of the legislative), and democracy (in part of the legislative). Although the forms of state—monarchy, aristocracy, and democracy —were united in English government, the powers of government were separated from one another. There can be no liberty where the executive, legislative, and judicial powers are united in one person or body of persons, because such concentration is bound to result in arbitrary despotism. Montesquieu acutely noted that the English system had an additional check on despotism: the legislative itself was divided into two bodies, the House of Lords, representing the privileges of an hereditary aristocracy, and the House of Commons, representing the popular interests.

Montesquieu holds that the executive power should be in the hands of a monarch, independent of the legislative. He predicted that if the executive power "should be committed to a certain number of persons elected from the legislative body, there would be an end then of liberty." The development of cabinet government was beginning to take place in England when Montesquieu was there, but his picture of the English constitution is more the theory of 1689 than the practice of 1730. Montesquieu's fears were shared, however, by the makers of the Constitution of the United States, and the doctrine of separation of powers has resulted in the exclusion of cabinet ministers from Congress. It has therefore been maintained that the American political system of the twentieth century, in which the independence of executive and legislative from each other is still real, resembles the British constitution of the eighteenth century, in which the Crowns, Lords, and Commons were balanced against one another, rather than that of the twentieth century, in which the House of Commons has become the final arbiter.

Underlying Montesquieu's doctrine of the separation of powers is the unstated premise of the *negative state,* the state that acts primarily as a night watchman maintaining law and order, and protecting the liberty and property of the individual. As long as liberalism was imbued with the philosophy of laissez faire, Montesquieu was one of its apostles. As liberalism—since the early twentieth century—became increasingly oriented toward the positive state, the state of broadened scope and enlarged activity, the doctrine of separation of powers as a philosophy of governmental paralysis and do-nothing lost its erstwhile magic appeal. In the eighteenth century the purpose of the doctrine of separation of powers was to strengthen the popular element of government at the expense of the king. In the nineteenth century Montesquieu's formula was used by conservatives to keep—in the executive branch at least—the power of the monarch intact against demands for full democratic, popular government.

In the final analysis it is not easy to classify Montesquieu's political philosophy. In his explicit beliefs there is a curious mixture of hatred of clericalism and despotism, profound concern for individual liberty, and a strong sense of aristocratic privilege, property, and class. Similarly, the implicit hypotheses of his political theory are complex: his faith in reason, humanity, and progress mark him out as a typical representative of the Age of Enlightenment. At the same time, Montesquieu was institution-minded to the point of venerating the past, and he therefore became suspect with many *philosophes.*

This element in Montesquieu leads straight to Burke, and—by means of considerable distortion—to the romantic, nationalist school of thought. Montesquieu's belief that "nothing must be changed by laws which can be changed by custom and morality" differed strongly from the optimistic faith of the Age of Reason in the possibility of wholesale social change through proper legislation. Yet the peculiar mixture of history and reason, of awareness of the past and concern for the future, of objective observation and desire for reform, has made Montesquieu one of the most influential political writers of the modern age, constantly reinterpreted, constantly rediscovered.

MONTESQUIEU

The Spirit of the Laws *

1. The Social and Physical Foundations of Government

As soon as mankind enter into a state of society they lose the sense of their weakness; equality ceases, and then commences the state of war.

Each particular society begins to feel its strength, whence arises a state of war betwixt different nations. The individuals likewise of each society become sensible of their force; hence the principal advantages of this society they endeavour to convert to their own emolument, which constitutes a state of war betwixt individuals.

These two different kinds of states give rise to human laws. Considered as inhabitants of so great a planet, which necessarily contains a variety of nations, they have laws relative to their mutual intercourse, which is what we call the *law of nations*. As members of a society that must be properly supported, they have laws relative to the governors and the governed, and this we distinguish by the name of *politic law*. They have also another sort of laws, as they stand in relation to each other; by which is understood the *civil law*.

The law of nations is naturally founded on this principle, that different nations ought in time of peace to do one another all the good they can, and in time of war as little injury as possible, without prejudicing their real interests.

The object of war is victory; that of victory is conquest; and that of conquest, preservation. From this and the preceding principle all those rules are derived which constitute the *law of nations*.

All countries have a law of nations, not excepting the Iroquois themselves, though they devour their prisoners; for they send and receive ambassadors, and understand the rights of war and peace. The mischief is, that their law of nations is not founded on true principles.

Besides the law of nations relating to all societies, there is a polity or civil constitution for each particularly considered. No society can subsist without a form of government. "The united strength of individuals," as Gravina well observes, "constitutes what we call the body politic."

The general strength may be in the hands of a single person, or of many. Some think that nature having established paternal authority, the most natural government was that of a single person. But the example of paternal authority proves nothing. For if the power of a father be relative to a single government, that of brothers after the death of a father, and that of cousins german after the decease of brother, refer to a government of many. The political power necessarily comprehends the union of several families.

Better is it to say, that the government most conformable to nature, is that which

---

* From Charles-Louis de Montesquieu, *The Spirit of the Laws* (1748; rev. ed., trans. Thomas Nugent, 1873).

best agrees with the humour and disposition of the people in whose favour it is established.

The strength of individuals cannot be united without a conjunction of all their wills. "The conjunction of those wills," as Gravina again very justly observes, "is what we call the *civil state.*"

Law in general is human reason, inasmuch as it governs all the inhabitants of the earth; the political and civil laws of each nation ought to be only the particular cases in which human reason is applied.

They should be adapted in such a manner to the people for whom they are framed, that it is a great chance if those of one nation suit another.

They should be relative to the nature and principle of each government; whether they form it, as may be said of politic laws; or whether they support it, as in the case of civil institutions.

They should be relative to the climate of each country, to the quality of its soil, to its situation and extent, to the principal occupation of the natives, whether husbandmen, huntsmen, or shepherds; they should have a relation to the degree of liberty which the constitution will bear; to the religion of the inhabitants, to their inclinations, riches, numbers, commerce, manners, and customs. In fine, they have relations to each other, as also to their origin, to the intent of the legislator, and to the order of things on which they are established; in all which different lights they ought to be considered.

This is what I have undertaken to perform in the following work. These relations I shall examine, since all these together constitute what I call the *Spirit of Laws.*

I have not separated the political from the civil institutions: for as I do not pretend to treat of laws, but of their spirit; and as this spirit consists in the various relations which the laws may have to different objects, it is not so much my business to follow the natural order of laws, as that of these relations and objects.

2. Republican Government, and the Laws Relative to Democracy

When the body of the people is possessed of the supreme power, this is called a *democracy.* When the supreme power is lodged in the hands of a part of the people, it is then an *aristocracy.*

In a democracy the people are in some respects the sovereign, and in others the subject.

There can be no exercise of sovereignty but by their suffrages, which are their own will; now the sovereign's will is the sovereign himself. The laws therefore which establish the right of suffrage, are fundamental to this government. And indeed it is as important to regulate in a republic, in what manner, by whom, to whom, and concerning what, suffrages are to be given, as it is in a monarchy to know who is the prince, and after what manner he ought to govern.

Libanius says that at "Athens a stranger, who intermeddled in the assemblies of the people, was punished with death." This is because such a man usurped the rights of sovereignty.

It is an essential point to fix the number of citizens who are to form the public assemblies; otherwise it would be uncertain whether the whole, or only a part of the people, had given their votes. At Sparta the number was fixed to ten thousand. But Rome, designed by Providence to rise from the weakest beginnings to the highest pitch of grandeur; Rome, doomed to experience all the vicissitudes of fortune; Rome, who had sometimes all her inhabitants without her walls, and sometimes all Italy and a considerable part of the world within them: Rome, I say, never fixed the number; and this was one of the principal causes of her ruin.

The people, in whom the supreme power resides, ought to have the management of every thing within their reach: what exceeds their abilities, must be conducted by their ministers.

But they can not properly be said to have

their ministers, without the power of nominating them: it is, therefore, a fundamental maxim in this government, that the people should choose their ministers, that is, their magistrates.

They have occasion, as well as monarchs, and even more so, to be directed by a council or senate. But to have a proper confidence in these, they should have the choosing of the members; whether the election be made by themselves, as at Athens; or by some magistrate deputed for that purpose, as on certain occasions was customary at Rome.

The people are extremely well qualified for choosing those whom they are to intrust with part of their authority. They have only to be determined by things to which they cannot be strangers, and by facts that are obvious to sense. They can tell when a person has fought many battles, and been crowned with success; they are, therefore, very capable of electing a general. They can tell when a judge is assiduous in his office, gives general satisfaction, and has never been charged with bribery: this is sufficient for choosing a prætor. They are struck with the magnificence or riches of a fellow-citizen; no more is requisite for electing an edile. These are facts of which they can have better information in a public forum, than a monarch in his palace. But are they capable of conducting an intricate affair, of seizing and improving the opportunity and critical amount of action? No; this surpasses their abilities.

Should we doubt of the people's natural capacity, in respect to the discernment of merit, we need only cast an eye on the series of surprising elections made by the Athenians and Romans; which no one surely will attribute to hazard.

We know, that though the people of Rome assumed to themselves the right of raising plebeians to public offices, yet they never would exert this power; and though at Athens the magistrates were allowed, by the law of Aristides, to be elected from all the different classes of inhabitants, there never was a case, says Xenophon, that the common people petitioned for employments which could endanger either their security or their glory.

As most citizens have sufficient abilities to choose, though unqualified to be chosen; so the people, though capable of calling others to an account for their administration, are incapable of conducting the administration themselves.

The public business must be carried on with a certain motion, neither too quick nor too slow. But the motion of the people is always either too remiss or too violent. Sometimes with a hundred thousand arms they overturn all before them; and sometimes with a hundred thousand feet they creep like insects.

In a popular state the inhabitants are divided into certain classes. It is in the manner of making this division that great legislators have signalized themselves; and it is on this the duration and prosperity of democracy have ever depended.

Servius Tullius followed the spirit of aristocracy in the distribution of his classes. We find in Livy and in Dionysius Halicarnassus, in what manner he lodged the right of suffrage in the hands of the principal citizens. He had divided the people of Rome into a hundred and ninety-three centuries, which formed six classes; and ranking the rich, who were in smaller numbers, in the first centuries; and those in middling circumstances, who were more numerous, in the next, he flung the indigent multitude into the last; and as each century had but one vote, it was property rather than numbers that decided the elections.

Solon divided the people of Athens into four classes. In this he was directed by the spirit of democracy, his intention not being to fix those who were to choose, but such as were eligible: therefore, leaving to every citizen the right of election, he made the judges eligible from each of those four classes; but the magistrates he ordered to be chosen only out of the first three, consisting of persons of easy fortunes.

As the division of those who have a right of suffrage is a fundamental law in republics, the manner also of giving this suffrage is another fundamental.

The suffrage by *lot* is natural to democracy, as that by *choice* is to aristocracy.

The suffrage by *lot* is a method of electing that offends no one; but animates each citizen with the pleasing hope of serving his country.

Yet as this method is in itself defective, it has been the endeavour of the most eminent legislators to regulate and amend it.

Solon made a law at Athens, that military employments should be conferred by choice; but that senators and judges should be elected by *lot*.

The same legislator ordained that civil magistrates, attended with great expense, should be given by choice; and the others by lot.

In order, however, to amend the suffrage by lot, he made a rule, that none but those who presented themselves should be elected; that the person elected should be examined by judges, and that every one should have a right to accuse him if he were unworthy of the office: this participated at the same time of the suffrage by lot, and of that by choice. When the time of their magistracy was expired, they were obliged to submit to another judgment in regard to their conduct. Persons utterly unqualified, must have been extremely backward in giving in their names to be drawn by lot.

The law which determines the manner of giving suffrage, is likewise fundamental in a democracy. It is a question of some importance, whether the suffrages ought to be public or secret. Cicero observes, that the laws which rendered them secret towards the close of the republic, were the cause of its decline. But as this is differently practised in different republics, I shall offer here my thoughts concerning this subject.

The people's suffrages ought doubtless to be public; and this should be considered as a fundamental law of democracy. The lower class ought to be directed by those of higher rank, and restrained within bounds by the gravity of eminent personages. Hence, by

rendering the suffrages secret in the Roman republic, all was lost; it was no longer possible to direct a populace that sought its own destruction. But when the body of the nobles are to vote in an aristocracy; or in a democracy, the senate; as the business is then only to prevent intrigues, the suffrages cannot be too secret.

Intriguing in a senate is dangerous; dangerous it is also in a body of nobles; but not so in the people, whose nature is to act through passion. In countries where they have no share in the government, we often see them as much inflamed on the account of an actor, as ever they could be for the welfare of the state. The misfortune of a republic is, when intrigues are at an end; which happens when the people are gained by bribery and corruption: in this case they grow indifferent to public affairs, and avarice becomes their predominant passion. Unconcerned about the government, and every thing belonging to it, they quietly wait for their hire.

It is likewise a fundamental law in democracies, that the people should have the sole power to enact laws. And yet there are a thousand occasions on which it is necessary the senate should have a power of decreeing; nay, it is frequently proper to make some trial of a law before it is established. The constitutions of Rome and Athens were excellent. The decrees of the senate had the force of laws for the space of a year; but did not become perpetual till they were ratified by the consent of the people.

3. The Principle of Democracy

There is no great share of probity necessary to support a monarchical or despotic government. The force of laws in one, and the prince's arm in the other, are sufficient to direct and maintain the whole. But in a popular state, one spring more is necessary, namely, *virtue*.

What I have here advanced, is confirmed

by the unanimous testimony of historians, and is extremely agreeable to the nature of things. For it is clear that in a monarchy, where he who commands the execution of the laws, generally thinks himself above them, there is less need of virtue than in a popular government, where the person entrusted with the execution of the laws, is sensible of his being subject to their direction.

Clear it is also, that a monarch, who, through bad advice or indolence, ceases to enforce the execution of the laws, may easily repair the evil; he has only to follow other advice; or to shake off this indolence. But when, in a popular government, there is a suspension of the laws, as this can proceed only from the corruption of the republic, the state is certainly undone.

A very droll spectacle it was in the last century to behold the impotent efforts of the English towards the establishment of democracy. As they who had a share in the direction of public affairs were void of virtue; as their ambition was inflamed by the success of the most daring of their members; as the prevailing parties were successively animated by the spirit of faction, the government was continually changing: the people, amazed at so many revolutions, in vain attempted to erect a commonwealth. At length, when the country had undergone the most violent shocks, they were obliged to have recourse to the very government which they had so wantonly proscribed.

When Sylla thought of restoring Rome to her liberty, this unhappy city was incapable of that blessing. She had only the feeble remains of virtue, which were continually diminishing: instead of being roused out of her lethargy, by Caesar, Tiberius, Caius Claudius, Nero, Domitian, she riveted every day her chains; if she struck some blows, her aim was at the tyrant, but not at the usurpation.

The politic Greeks, who lived under a popular government, knew no other support than virtue. The modern inhabitants of that country are entirely taken up with manufacture, commerce, finances, opulence, and luxury.

When virtue is banished, ambition invades the minds of those who are disposed to receive it, and avarice possesses the whole community. The objects of their desires are changed; what they were fond of before, is become indifferent; they were free, while under the restraint of laws, but they would fain now be free to act against law; and as each citizen is like a slave who has run away from his master, what was a maxim of equity, he calls rigour; what was a rule of action, he styles constraint; and to precaution, he gives the name of fear. Frugality, and not the thirst of gain, now passes for avarice. Formerly the wealth of individuals constituted the public treasure; but now this is become the patrimony of private persons. The members of the commonwealth riot on the public spoils, and its strength is only the power of a few, and the licentiousness of many.

Athens was possessed of the same number of forces, when she triumphed so gloriously, and when with so much infamy she was enslaved. She had twenty thousand citizens, when she defended the Greeks against the Persians, when she contended for empire with Sparta, and invaded Sicily. She had twenty thousand when Demetrius Phalereus numbered them, as slaves are told by the head in a market-place. When Philip attempted to lord it over Greece, and appeared at the gates of Athens, she had even then lost nothing but time. We may see in Demosthenes how difficult it was to awake her: she dreaded Philip, not as the enemy of her liberty, but of her pleasures. This famous city, which had withstood so many defeats, and after having been so often destroyed, had as often risen out of her ashes, was overthrown of Chæronea, and at one blow deprived of all hopes of resource. What does it avail her, that Philip sends back her prisoners, if he does not return her men? It was ever after as easy to triumph over the Athenian forces, as it had been difficult to subdue her virtue.

How was it possible for Carthage to

maintain her ground? When Hannibal, upon his being made prætor, endeavoured to hinder the magistrates from plundering the republic, did not they complain of him to the Romans? Wretches, who would fain be citizens without a city, and beholden for their riches to their very destroyers! Rome soon insisted upon having three hundred of their principal citizens as hostages; she obliged them next to surrender their arms and ships; and then she declared war. From the desperate efforts of this defenceless city, one may judge of what she might have performed in her full vigour, and assisted by virtue.

4. The Principle of Despotic Government

As virtue is necessary in a republic, and in a monarchy honour, so fear is necessary in a despotic government: with regard to virtue, there is no occasion for it, and honour would be extremely dangerous.

Here the immense power of the prince is devolved entirely upon those whom he is pleased to intrust with the administration. Persons capable of setting a value upon themselves, would be likely to create disturbances. Fear must therefore depress their spirits, and extinguish even the least sense of ambition.

A moderate government may, whenever it pleases, and without the least danger, relax its springs. It supports itself by the laws, and by its own internal strength. But when a despotic prince ceases one single moment to lift up his arm, when he cannot instantly demolish those whom he has entrusted with the first employments, all is over: for as fear, the spring of this government, no longer subsists, the people are left without a protector.

It is probably in this sense the Cadis maintained that the Grand Seignior was not obliged to keep his word or oath, when he limited thereby his authority.

It is necessary that the people should be judged by laws, and the great men by the caprice of the prince, that the lives of the lowest subjects should be safe, and the bashaw's head ever in danger. We cannot mention these monstrous governments without horror. The Sophi of Persia, dethroned in our days by Mahomet, the son of Miriveis, saw the constitution subverted before this revolution, because he had been too sparing of blood.

History informs us, that the horrid cruelties of Domitian struck such a terror into the governors, that the people recovered themselves a little under his reign. Thus a torrent overflows one side of a country, and on the other leaves fields untouched, where the eye is refreshed by the prospect of fine meadows.

5. Corruption of the Principles of Democracy

The principle of democracy is corrupted not only when the spirit of equality is extinct, but likewise when they fall into a spirit of extreme equality, and when each citizen would fain be upon a level with those whom he has chosen to command him. Then the people, incapable of bearing the very power they have delegated, want to manage every thing themselves, to debate for the senate, to execute for the magistrate, and to decide for the judges.

When this is the case, virtue can no longer subsist in the republic. The people are desirous of exercising the functions of the magistrates, who cease to be revered. The deliberations of the senate are slighted; all respect is then laid aside for the senators, and consequently for old age. If there is no more respect for old age, there will be none presently for parents; deference to husbands will be likewise thrown off, and submission to masters. This licentiousness will soon become general; and the trouble of command be as fatiguing as that of obedience. Wives, children, slaves will shake off all subjection. No longer will there be any such things as manners, order or virtue.

We find in Xenophon's banquet a very lively description of a republic in which the people abused their equality. Each guest gives in his turn the reason why he is satisfied. "Content I am," says Chamides, "because of my poverty. When I was rich, I was obliged to pay my court to informers, knowing I was more liable to be hurt by them, than capable of doing them harm. The republic constantly demanded some new tax of me; and I could not decline paying. Since I am grown poor, I have acquired authority; nobody threatens me; I rather threaten others. I can go or stay where I please. The rich already rise from their seats and give me the way. I am a king, I was before a slave; I paid taxes to the republic, now it maintains me: I am no longer afraid of losing, but I hope to acquire."

The people fall into this misfortune, when those in whom they confide, desirous of concealing their own corruption, endeavour to corrupt them. To disguise their own ambition, they speak to them only of the grandeur of the state; to conceal their own avarice, they incessantly flatter theirs.

The corruption will increase among the corrupters, and likewise among those who are already corrupted. The people will divide the public money among themselves, and having added the administration of affairs to their indolence, will be for blending their poverty with the amusements of luxury. But with their indolence and luxury, nothing but the public treasure will be able to satisfy their demands.

We must not be surprised to see their suffrages given for money. It is impossible to make great largesses to the people without great extortion: and to compass this, the state must be subverted. The greater the advantages they seem to derive from their liberty, the nearer they approach towards the critical moment of losing it. Petty tyrants arise, who have all the vices of a single tyrant. The small remains of liberty soon become unsupportable; a single tyrant starts up, and the people are stripped

of every thing, even of the profits of their corruption.

Democracy has, therefore, two excesses to avoid; the spirit of inequality, which leads to aristocracy or monarchy; and the spirit of extreme equality, which leads to despotic power, as the latter is completed by conquest.

True it is, that those who corrupted the Greek republics, did not always become tyrants. This was because they had a greater passion for eloquence than for the military art. Besides there reigned an implacable hatred in the breasts of the Greeks against those who subverted a republican government; and for this reason anarchy degenerated into annihilation, instead of being changed into tyranny.

But Syracuse being situated in the midst of a great number of petty states, whose government had been changed from oligarchy to tyranny; and being governed by a senate scarce ever mentioned in history, underwent such miseries as are the consequence of a more than ordinary corruption. This city, ever a prey to licentiousness or oppression, equally labouring under the sudden and alternate succession of liberty and servitude, and notwithstanding her external strength, constantly determined to a revolution by the least foreign power: This city, I say, had in her bosom an immense multitude of people, whose fate it was to have always this cruel alternative, either of choosing a tyrant to govern them, or of acting the tyrant themselves.

6. The Confederate Republic

If a republic be small, it is destroyed by a foreign force; if it be large, it is ruined by an internal imperfection.

To this twofold inconveniency Democracies and Aristocracies are equally liable, whether they be good or bad. The evil is in the very thing itself, and no form can redress it.

It is, therefore, very probable that mankind would have been, at length, obliged to live constantly under the government of a single person, had they not contrived a kind of constitution that has all the internal advantages of a republican, together with the external force of a monarchical, government. I mean a confederate republic.

This form of government is a convention by which several petty states agree to become members of a larger one, which they intend to establish. It is a kind of assemblage of societies, that constitute a new one, capable of increasing by means of farther associations, till they arrive to such a degree of power, as to be able to provide for the security of the whole body.

It was these associations that so long contributed to the prosperity of Greece. By these the Romans attacked the whole globe, and by these alone the whole globe withstood them; for when Rome was arrived to her highest pitch of grandeur, it was the associations beyond the Danube and the Rhine, associations formed by the terror of her arms, that enabled the Barbarians to resist her.

From hence it proceeds that Holland, Germany, and the Swiss Cantons, are considered in Europe as perpetual republics.

The associations of cities were formerly more necessary than in our times. A weak, defenceless town was exposed to greater danger. By conquest it was deprived not only of the executive and legislative power, as at present, but moreover of all human property.

A republic of this kind, able to withstand an external force, may support itself without any internal corruption; the form of this society prevents all manner of inconveniences.

If a single member should attempt to usurp the supreme power, he could not be supposed to have an equal authority and credit in all the confederate states. Were he to have too great an influence over one, this would alarm the rest; were he to subdue a part, that which would still remain free, might oppose him with forces independent of those which he had usurped, and overpower him before he could be settled in his usurpation.

Should a popular insurrection happen in one of the confederate states, the others are able to quell it. Should abuses creep into one part, they are reformed by those that remain sound. The state may be destroyed on one side, and not on the other; the confederacy may be dissolved, and the confederates preserve their sovereignty.

As this government is composed of petty republics, it enjoys the internal happiness of each; and with regard to its external situation, by means of the association, it possesses all the advantages of large monarchies.

7. Meaning of Liberty

There is no word that admits of more various significations, and has made more different impressions on the human mind, than that of *Liberty*. Some have taken it for a facility of deposing a person on whom they had conferred a tyrannical authority; others for the power of choosing a superior whom they are obliged to obey; others for the right of bearing arms, and of being thereby enabled to use violence; others, in fine, for the privilege of being governed by a native of their own country, or by their own laws. A certain nation for a long time thought liberty consisted in the privilege of wearing a long beard. Some have annexed this name to one form of government exclusive of others: those who had a republican taste, applied it to this species of policy; those who liked a monarchical state, gave it to monarchy. Thus they have all applied the name of *liberty* to the government most suitable to their own customs and inclinations; and as in republics the people have not so constant and so present a view of the causes of their misery, and as the magistrates seem to act only in conformity to the laws, hence liberty is generally said to reside in republics, and to be banished from monarchies. In fine, as in democracies the people seem to act almost as they please; this sort of government has been deemed the most free; and the power of the people has been confounded with their liberty.

It is true that in democracies the people seem to act as they please; but political liberty does not consist in an unlimited freedom. In governments, that is, in societies directed by laws, liberty can consist only in the power of doing what we ought to will, and in not being constrained to do what we ought not to will.

We must have continually present to our minds the difference between independence and liberty. Liberty is a right of doing whatever the laws permit; and if a citizen could do what they forbid, he would be no longer possessed of liberty, because all his fellow-citizens would have the same power.

Democratic and aristocratic states are not in their own nature free. Political liberty is to be found only in moderate governments; and even in these, it is not always found. It is there only when there is no abuse of power; but constant experience shows us, that every man invested with power is apt to abuse it, and to carry his authority as far as it will go. Is it not strange, though true, to say, that virtue itself has need of limits?

To prevent this abuse, it is necessary from the very nature of things, power should be a check to power. A government may be so constituted as no man shall be compelled to do things to which the law does not oblige him, nor forced to abstain from things which the law permits.

8. The Constitution of England

In every government there are three sorts of power: the legislative; the executive, in respect to things dependent on the law of nations; and the executive, in regard to matters that depend on the civil law.

By virtue of the first, the prince or magistrate enacts temporary or perpetual laws, and amends or abrogates those that have been already enacted. By the second, he makes peace or war, sends or receives embassies, establishes the public security, and provides against invasions. By the third, he punishes criminals, or determines the disputes that arise between individuals. The latter we shall call the judiciary power, and the other simply the executive power of the state.

The political liberty of the subject is a tranquillity of mind arising from the opinion each person has of his safety. In order to have this liberty, it is requisite the government be so constituted as one man needs not be afraid of another.

When the legislative and executive powers are united in the same person, or in the same body of magistrates, there can be no liberty; because apprehensions may arise, lest the same monarch or senate should enact tyrannical laws, to execute them in a tyrannical manner.

Again there is no liberty, if the judiciary power be not separated from the legislative and executive. Were it joined with the legislative, the life and liberty of the subject would be exposed to arbitrary control; for the judge would be then the legislator. Were it joined to the executive power, the judge might behave with violence and oppression.

There would be an end of everything, were the same man, or the same body, whether of the nobles or of the people, to exercise those three powers, that of enacting laws, that of executing the public resolutions, and of trying the causes of individuals.

Most kingdoms in Europe enjoy a moderate government, because the prince who is invested with the two first powers, leaves the third to his subjects. In Turkey, where these three powers are united in the Sultan's person, the subjects groan under the most dreadful oppression.

9. The Crime of High Treason in Republics

As soon as a republic has compassed the destruction of those who wanted to subvert it, there should be an end of terrors, punishments, and even of rewards.

Great punishments, and consequently great changes, cannot take place without investing some citizens with an exorbitant power. It is, therefore, more advisable in this case to exceed in lenity, than in severity; to banish but few, rather than many; and to leave them their estates, instead of making a vast number of confiscations. Under pretence of avenging the republic's cause, the avengers would establish tyranny. The business is not to destroy the rebel but the rebellion. They ought to return as quick as possible into the usual track of government, in which every one is protected by the laws, and no one injured.

The Greeks set no bounds to the vengeance they took of tyrants, or of those they suspected of tyranny; they put their children to death, nay sometimes five of their nearest relations; and they proscribed an infinite number of families. By such means their republics suffered the most violent shocks: exiles, or the return of the exiled, were always epochs that indicated a change of the constitution.

The Romans had more sense. When Cassius was put to death for having aimed at tyranny, the question was proposed whether his children should undergo the same fate: but they were preserved. "They," says Dionysius Halicarnassus, "who wanted to change this law at the end of the Marsian and civil wars, and to exclude from public offices the children of those who had been proscribed by Sylla, are very much to blame."

10. Religion and Forms of State

When a religion is introduced and fixed in a state, it is commonly such as is most suitable to the plan of government there established; for those who receive it, and those who are the cause of its being received, have scarcely any other idea of policy, than that of the state in which they were born.

When the Christian religion, two centuries ago, became unhappily divided into Catholic and Protestant, the people of the north embraced the Protestant, and those of the south adhered still to the Catholic.

The reason is plain: the people of the north have, and will for ever have, a spirit of liberty and independence, which the people of the south have not; and therefore, a religion which has no visible head, is more agreeable to the independency of the climate, than that which has one.

In the countries themselves, where the Protestant religion became established, the revolutions were made pursuant to the several plans of political government. Luther having great princes on his side, would never have been able to make them relish an ecclesiastical authority that had no exterior pre-eminence; while Calvin, having to do with people who lived under republican governments, or with obscure citizens in monarchies, might very well avoid establishing dignities and preferments.

Each of these two religions was believed to be the most perfect; the Calvinist judging his most conformable to what Christ had said, and the Lutheran to what the Apostles had practised.

11. Religious Toleration

We are here politicians, and not divines; but the divines themselves must allow that there is a great difference between tolerating and approving a religion.

When the legislator has believed it a duty to permit the exercise of many religions, it is necessary that he should enforce also a toleration amongst these religions themselves. It is a principle that every religion which is persecuted, becomes itself persecuting: for as soon as by some accidental turn it arises from persecution, it attacks the religion which persecuted it; not as a religion, but as a tyranny.

It is necessary, then, that the laws require from the several religions, not only that they shall not embroil the state, but that they shall not raise disturbances amongst themselves. A citizen does not fulfil the laws by not disturbing the government; it is requisite that he should not trouble any citizen whomsoever.

CHAPTER 17

ROUSSEAU

THE French Revolution is the dominating event of the eighteenth century, and its impetus is far from being spent even today. Its intellectual preparation ran through three generations, and all significant issues were subjected to critical inquiry and examination. The impact of the debate was intensified by its being carried on in human rather than in national terms, and the universal recognition of France's intellectual leadership in the Age of Reason was a source of her ultimate political leadership, because progressive and democratic forces throughout the world identified themselves with the cause of French freedom.

If the Age of Reason ended, politically, in the Age of Revolution, the fault was not that of philosophers and publicists but of the traditional forces that, by stubbornly resisting mild reform, made radical revolution inevitable. Voltaire and Montesquieu were liberal conservatives of the upper classes, and their purpose was to prevent revolution rather than to promote it; and social revolution was furthest from their thoughts. The England they adored was dominated by a wealthy and vigorous aristocracy. The suffrage was confined to a small number of persons, and Parliament represented primarily the interests of the landowning classes. The political recognition of the English middle classes came in 1832, a century after Voltaire and Montesquieu had visited England, and the acceptance of popular democracy occurred even later.

The whole eighteenth century in France was a race between time and disaster. During the first half of the century, criticism of existing institutions was directed more openly against the church than against the state, although once the principle of ecclesiastical authority was undermined, the issue of political authority was bound to be raised. The social centers of the era were the elegant Parisian *salons,* in which the sparkling wit of the *philosophes* mingled with the charm of beautiful women and the skeptical nonchalance of leisurely aristocrats. The people were still inarticulate; Voltaire spoke of them as *la canaille,* and not a few of the early leaders of the Enlightenment felt the same sentiment toward the masses, whom they met only as untutored servants, workers, or peasants.

Voltaire was little interested in forms of government; a benevolent despot, enlightened enough to protect intellectual liberty and personal property, would have suited his taste best, as he was more interested in the monarch's enlightenment than in his autocratic government. He would rather, he said, "obey a fine lion, much stronger than himself, than two hundred rats of his own species." Though completely unaware of the existence of the social question as a chief driving force of revolution, Voltaire nevertheless opened the way for change by his ruthless and ridiculing attacks on intellectual obscurantism and inequality before the law.

In the second half of the eighteenth century, political criticism and philosophical expression became more daring and outspoken. The monument to that era is the *Encyclopédie* (1751–1772), edited by Diderot and containing contributions from the leading men of the time, d'Alembert, Holbach, Helvétius, Turgot, Haller, Morellet, Quesnay, and, at the beginning, also from Voltaire and Montesquieu. The *Encyclopédie* was originally designed to be mainly a translation of Chambers' *Cyclopaedia*, published in London in 1727, but Diderot desired to produce a work of more original and ambitious scope. The *Encyclopédie* was the first large-scale synthesis of all knowledge, and it represented—more than any other encyclopedia before or after—a whole temper and philosophical outlook.

The *encyclopédistes* belonged to varied schools of thought in science, philosophy, theology, and the arts, yet a collective intellectual denominator soon emerged: naturalism and empiricism in philosophy, deism or agnosticism in theology, utilitarianism in social institutions, constitutionalism in government, and support for industry and commerce in economics. The faith of the *encyclopédistes* was humanitarian, rationalist, and scientific: they believed that nature and society are governed, not by an incomprehensible and arbitrary fate or divine providence, but by an intelligible rational order, and that man's increase of knowledge is the best guide to his happiness and progress.

Despite its novel ideas and emphases, the rational outlook of the Enlightenment was traditional—and the tradition that had sprung from Greece was even older than the rivaling dogmas of church and religion. The historical achievement of the Enlightenment consisted not so much in having discovered the possibilities of reason but in having converted such a large part of the ruling classes of the time to its tenets. There was room for feeling and emotion in this age of rationalism, but they were subordinated to the primacy of reason and stylized in form and expression. The first to attack, not this or that idea or philosophy, but the very foundations of traditional civilization, had to be someone who was not a part of it: Jean Jacques Rousseau (1712–1778).

Before Rousseau appeared on the literary scene in Europe, critics of the existing order had slowly been widening their orbit of interest to include the people in their plans of reform. But "the people" meant primarily the discriminated Third Estate of prosperous and respectable merchants, lawyers, and intellectuals. Rousseau is the first modern writer on politics who was *of* the people: the submerged, inarticulate masses of the *petite bourgeoisie,* the poor artisans and workingmen, the small peasants, the restless and rootless, the *déclassés*, for whom there was no room, and no hope, in the existing order of things.

Rousseau was born of a poor family in Geneva, his French ancestors having migrated there as religious refugees in the sixteenth century. Rousseau's mother died a few days after his birth, and his father, an impecunious watchmaker and more enthusiastic dancing master, was unable to raise Jean Jacques in any coherent fashion. From the age of twelve Rousseau was apprenticed to various masters, but he failed to establish himself in any art or trade. At sixteen he ran away from Geneva, and for the remainder of his life could claim no permanent abode anywhere.

Voltaire and Montesquieu had traveled through Europe in grand style; Rousseau saw much of the Continent through the eyes of a penniless, and at times hunted, vagabond, who did not always know where his next meal would come from and where he would sleep. Poverty made him commit minor thefts and larcenies, change his religion for temporary material advantage, and accept charity from people he detested. He was valet to an Italian aristocrat, secretary to a French diplomat, and a music teacher (with but few pupils) ; he often survived by dint of his own ingenuity and the charity of others, particularly women, who played a large part in his life from his early youth. He never ceased to attract women and to be attracted by them, and he never forgot that they had treated him kindly and recognized his worth long before men began to pay any attention to him.

In 1744 Rousseau went to Paris, having visited it first in 1742. He tried his hand at various schemes, the theater, opera, music, poetry, without making much of a success at anything. Yet his personality opened for him the doors of the best *salons* in Paris, where he met leading Encyclopedists as well as influential women, with several of whom he maintained close ties of friendship. But he never became, nor did he wish to become, a part of the fashionable set of Paris. He had love affairs with society women, but of all his associations with women the one that lasted longest was with Thérèse Levasseur, a servant girl who worked in Rousseau's small hotel in Paris. As he said later in his *Confessions:* "At first I sought to give myself amusement, but I saw I had gone further and had given myself a companion."

Though enjoying, out of vanity, the company of the rich and powerful, he resented being admitted to the exalted society as a matter of personal privilege, and he never shed his plebeian, Puritanical background of a low middle-class family in Geneva. His complex feelings of pleasure and resentment regarding his social standing made it difficult for him to establish lasting human relations, except with Thérèse Levasseur, with whom he lived from his early days in Paris to the end of his life.

In 1749 the Academy of Dijon announced a prize for the best essay on the question : "Has the progress of sciences and arts contributed to corrupt or purify morality ?" In his *Confessions* Rousseau later describes his immediate reaction : "Instantly I saw another universe, and I became another man." He set to work feverishly on the essay and submitted it to the Academy. In 1750 the Academy rewarded it the first prize, and it was published in 1751 under the title *A Discourse on the Moral Effects of the Arts and Sciences.*

Rousseau's thesis was the exact opposite of what was conventionally thought at that time, and he was bold enough to *extol natural man* at the expense of so-called civilized man, for "our minds have been corrupted in proportion as the arts and sciences have improved." The much vaunted politeness, the glory of civilized refinement, is for Rousseau but a "uniform and perfidious veil" under which he sees "jealousy, suspicion, fear, coldness, reserve, hate, and fraud."

In surveying history in support of his cult of natural simplicity, Rousseau is full of enthusiasm for Sparta, a "republic of demi-gods rather than of men," famous for the happy ignorance of its inhabitants, "eternal proof of the vanity of science." By contrast, he denigrates Athens, the center of vice, doomed to perish because of its elegance, luxury, wealth, art, and science: "From Athens we derive those astonishing performances which will serve as models to every corrupt age."

Rousseau sees a direct causal relation between luxury, constantly expanding needs, and the rise of art and science, after which true courage flags and the virtues disappear. Roman history, Rousseau holds, supports this view: as long as Rome was poor and simple she was able to command respect and conquer an empire; after having developed luxury and engulfed the riches of the universe, Rome "fell a prey to peoples who knew not even what riches were." Rousseau inveighs against orators and philosophers as guides to superficiality and perversion. Philosophers consecrate themselves to the destruction of "all that men hold sacred," and Rousseau calls them "charlatans" who sow confusion among men and undermine their simple ideas of patriotism and religion.

Anticipating his own later views on education in *Emile* (1762), Rousseau writes in his first *Discourse* that traditional education is too vocational and too highly specialized, that children remain ignorant of their own language while being taught other languages not spoken anywhere, and that the moral virtues are neglected: "But magnanimity, equity, temperance, humanity and courage will be words of which they know not the meaning." Finally, Rousseau makes the charge that is as timely today as in 1749: "We have physicists, geometricians, chemists, astronomers, poets, musicians, and painters in plenty; but we have no longer a citizen among us."

In 1753 Rousseau competed again in a contest of the Academy of Dijon; the subject was "What is the origin of inequality among men, and is it authorized by natural law?" His first *Discourse* had brought him immediate fame and sensational success. In writing his *Discourse on the Origin of Inequality* (1755), Rousseau felt he no longer needed to shock and captivate his audience by paradoxes and one-sided arguments, and he composed a much more systematic essay, one of the most influential in the history of democratic and socialist thought. He did not win this time, but the second *Discourse* is more important than the first, particularly in relation to the development of Rousseau's political ideas.

Rousseau distinguishes two kinds of inequality. The first is *natural* and consists in differences of age, health, bodily strength, and the qualities of mind and soul. The second is moral or *political inequality,* which owes its existence to social institutions and consists in privileges of wealth, honor, and power. Rousseau finds that natural inequalities are not substantial, that the problem of inequality arises with the formation of society. Nature destined man to live a healthy, simple life and to satisfy his essential needs ("food, a female, and sleep"). By contrast, man in society, or civilized man, has developed varied and unhealthful habits of eating and sleeping, and his mental and physical exhaustion is the result of the pains, anxieties, and torments of civilized living. *Civilization* is thus a *hopeless race to discover remedies for the evils it produces.* The man of nature knows less medicine than civilized man, but the latter brings upon himself more diseases than medicine can cure. Reflection is contrary to nature, and a thinking man, Rousseau says, is "a depraved animal."

This motif ran through the first *Discourse on the Arts and Sciences,* and Rousseau now announces the idea—so contrary to the commonplaces of his time —that human understanding is not the sole domain of reason but is "greatly indebted to passions." In the state of nature, man was guided by two sentiments: self-interest and pity, and having no moral obligations with others, he could not be "good or bad, virtuous or vicious." Rousseau specifically rejects Hobbes' view of the state of nature in which man, not knowing goodness, must therefore be wicked, and he asserts that man's sense of compassion is the original sentiment from which all later virtues flow. Reason and thinking come afterward and isolate man from his fellows, whereas compassion unites him with others. Uncivilized man is always "foolishly ready to obey the first promptings of humanity. It is the populace that flocks together at riots and street-brawls, while the wise man prudently makes off. It is the mob and the market-women who part the combatants, and hinder gentle-folks from cutting one another's throats."

Turning to the origin of inequality in society, Rousseau starts out with a passage that has a distinctly socialist and revolutionary flavor: "The first man who, having enclosed a piece of ground, bethought himself of saying *This is mine,* and found people simple enough to believe him, was the real founder of civil society." The natural voice of compassion was stilled by the usurpations of the rich and the robberies of the poor, and the newborn society thus led to a "horrible state of war." The rich then devised a plan by which they could better enjoy their power and possession without the threat of constant war.

The first step was easy, to obtain agreement among the rich themselves to set up a system of law and government for the maintenance of peace. The second step, "the profoundest plan that ever entered the mind of man," was to employ the forces of the poor for the creation of government, under which all would be protected and their possessions safeguarded: "Such was, or may well have been, the origin of society and law, which bound new fetters on the poor, and gave new powers to the rich; which irretrievably destroyed natural liberty, eternally fixed the law of property and inequality, converted clever usurpation into unalterable right, and, for the advantage of a few ambitious individuals, subjected all mankind to perpetual labor, slavery and wretchedness."

In the long run, however, Rousseau foresees that from extreme inequality of fortunes and conditions spring divisions and dissensions that undermine the fabric of society and government. Despotism arises out of these disorders, but despotism is the "last term of inequality." Popular insurrection deposes the despot, or even puts him to death: "As he was maintained by force alone, it is force alone that overthrows him." This was strong language for the middle of the eighteenth century, when revolution was not thought of as yet and when free expression was curbed by both church and state.

The concluding words of the *Discourse on the Origin of Inequality* made it plain that Rousseau was not referring to hypothetical states of nature or society but to the injustices of contemporary France, "since it is plainly contrary to the laws of nature, however defined, that children should command old men, fools wise men, and that the privileged few should gorge themselves with superfluities, while the starving multitude are in want of the bare necessities of life."

At the time of uttering this ringing challenge, Rousseau did not earn enough to rent a house, much less own one, or to provide enough of the bare necessities for himself and the woman who shared his existence. During most of his life Rousseau lived in houses and cottages that his friends gave him rent-free, and Thérèse Levasseur received more gifts (often rather unashamedly soliciting them from friends) than proud and sensitive Jean Jacques would have cared to know. While he was not of the "starving multitude," he was close enough to its worries, its tragedies and petty cares, to know how poverty could deprave and degrade men and women who were originally good.

In 1755 Rousseau published the *Discourse on Political Economy* in Diderot's *Encyclopédie*. Rousseau's regular assignments for the *Encyclopédie* covered music, and the *Discourse on Political Economy* is less remarkable for its economic observations than for the fact that it is his first constructive approach to a theory of the state, whereas the first two *Discourses* had been mainly critical. The *Discourse on Political Economy* is important in the development of Rousseau's political ideas, inasmuch as it contains the first statement of the concept of the General Will, his most original contribution to political philosophy. Thus, when Rousseau published his most famous work, *The Social Contract*, in 1762, its chief ideas were not the result of a sudden inspiration; they had matured in him over the years and had been partially expressed in his three *Discourses*.

The main concern of *The Social Contract* is the central issue of all political speculation: *political obligation*. "The problem," Rousseau says, "is to find a form of association which will defend and protect with the whole common force the person and goods of each associate, and in which each, while uniting himself with all, may still obey himself alone, and remain as free as before." In the very beginning of the book, Rousseau puts the same question in a more dramatic form: "Man is born free; and everywhere he is in chains."

Like his predecessors, Rousseau uses the conceptions of the state of nature and the social contract that puts an end to it. Rousseau's conception of man's life in the state of nature is not quite so gloomy as that of Hobbes, nor as optimistic as that of Locke. Each man pursues his self-interest in the state of nature until he discovers that his power to preserve himself individually against the threats and hindrances of others is not strong enough. The purpose of the social contract is thus to combine security, which comes from collective association, with liberty, which the individual had before the making of the contract. But the social contract consists in "the total alienation of each associate, together with all his rights, to the whole community."

The total surrender of the individual to the sovereign community is completely contrary to Locke and recalls Hobbes' view of the social contract, in which the individual also surrenders himself completely to the sovereign. But whereas Hobbes' subject is completely submissive to his sovereign, Rousseau rejects this kind of social peace without liberty: "Tranquillity is also found in dungeons; but is that enough to make them desirable places to live in?" To renounce liberty, Rousseau says, is to renounce being a man, for there can be no obligation that is not, to some extent at least, mutual. In Rousseau's social contract man does not surrender completely to a sovereign ruler, but each man gives himself to all, and therefore gives himself to nobody in particular: "As there is no associate over whom he does not acquire the same right as he yields others over himself, he gains an equivalent for everything he loses, and an increase of force for the preservation of what he has."

Rousseau shows in *The Social Contract* a much greater appreciation of civil society, as compared with the state of nature, than he showed in his earlier writings. In the state of nature, Rousseau now says, man is guided by instinct only, whereas in society he is inspired by justice and morality. Man loses through the social contract his natural liberty and an unlimited right to everything he can lay his hands on, but he gains *civil liberty* and property rights in all he possesses. The liberty of the state of nature is no true liberty, because it is merely enslavement to uncontrolled appetites. By contrast, *moral liberty,* which man acquires solely in the civil state, makes him master of himself, because "obedience to a law which we prescribe to ourselves is liberty."

Rousseau's conception of sovereignty differs from both Hobbes' and Locke's. In Hobbes' the people set up a sovereign and transfer all power to him. In Locke's social contract the people set up a limited government for limited purposes, but Locke shuns the conception of sovereignty—popular or monarchical—as a symbol of political absolutism. Rousseau's sovereign is the people, constituted as a political community through the social contract.

Unlike nearly all other major political thinkers, Rousseau considers the *sovereignty of the people inalienable and indivisible.* The people cannot give away, or transfer, to any person or body their ultimate right of self-government, of deciding their own destiny. Whereas Hobbes identified the sovereign with the ruler who exercises sovereignty, Rousseau draws a sharp distinction between sovereignty, which always and wholly resides in the people, and government, which is but a temporary agent (as in Locke's conception) of the sovereign people. Whereas, in Locke, the people transfer the exercise of their supreme authority, legislative, executive, and judicial, to organs of government, Rousseau's concept of inalienable and indivisible sovereignty does not permit the people to transfer their legislative function, the supreme authority in the state. As to the executive and judicial functions, Rousseau realizes that they have to be exercised by special organs of government, but they are completely subordinated to the sovereign people, and there is no hint or suggestion of separation, or balance, of powers.

Rousseau's system of government is unmitigated popular sovereignty, unmodified by competing or balancing powers; this aspect of Rousseau has always strongly appealed to adherents of radical and uncompromising democracy. Rousseau thought that the people of England were mistaken in thinking themselves free; they were actually free only once every few years when electing Members of Parliament. Sovereignty lies in the General Will of the people, and will cannot be represented.

In the *Discourse on Political Economy* Rousseau had already dealt with the problem of the General Will, the key conception in his political philosophy. He sees the body politic "possessed of a will; and this General Will, which tends always to the preservation and welfare of the whole and of every part, and is the source of the laws, constitutes for all the members of the state, in their relation to one another and to it, the rule of what is just or unjust." By introducing the concept of the *General Will,* Rousseau fundamentally alters the mechanistic concept of the state as an instrument (shared by both Hobbes and Locke), and revives the *organic* theory of the state, which goes back to Plato and Aristotle.

Rousseau is keenly aware of the life of groups, which is more than a charter or articles of incorporation. The state is not the only group with a General Will; particular societies and associations, too, have a General Will in relation to their members, though in relation to the state their will is particular, because the General Will of the state is the most comprehensive of all, embracing all members of the community.

Rousseau himself admits, before his critics and commentators made the discovery, that the distinction between the General Will and particular wills is "always very difficult to make." The General Will is not an empirical fact so much as a *moral fact,* and "it is needful only to act justly, to be certain of following the General Will." By establishing the reign of virtue, all particular wills will be brought in conformity with the General Will. The General Will, therefore, is not something that can be legislated against the people from the outside, but is a moral attitude in the heart of the citizens, and "nothing can take the place of morality in the maintenance of government."

The character of the General Will is determined by two elements: first, it *aims at the general good,* and, second, it *must come from all* and *apply to all.* The first refers to the object of the will; the second, to its origin. The Will of All must therefore not be confused with the General Will: "The latter considers only the common interest, while the former takes private interest into account, and is no more than a sum of particular wills." The generality of the will is not so much a matter of numbers as of intrinsic quality and goodness. The people always will the good, but they do not always understand it, particularly when factions make it difficult for the independent citizen to pursue the common good. Nor can the General Will be represented, because representative assemblies tend to develop particular interests of their own, forgetting those of the community. Obviously referring to the direct democracies of Swiss city-republics, Rousseau glowingly describes how "bands of peasants are seen regulating affairs of state under an oak, and always acting wisely," and he prefers the methods of these "happiest people in the world" to the ingenious methods of party government through representation, as practiced in other nations.

Rousseau recognizes that in direct popular government unanimity is, in practice, impossible, and that the vote of the majority binds the minority. The question of how the minority can be free and yet be bound to obey the majority is rejected by Rousseau as wrongly put: when a citizen objects to a proposed law in the popular assembly and finds himself in a minority, he does not thereby lose his freedom, for his minority vote merely proves that he did not recognize the General Will, rather than that the majority, as such, has a right to rule over him. Rousseau cautiously adds that this conception of freedom of the individual "presupposes, indeed, that all the qualities of the General Will still reside in the majority: when they cease to do so, whatever side a man may take, liberty is no longer possible."

Obeying the General Will is thus the expression of the moral freedom of the individual, and if he refuses to obey, he may be compelled to do so: "This means nothing less than that he will be forced to be free." Here Rousseau revives his basic distinction between the apparent liberty of man in the state of nature, which actually is enslavement to selfish appetites, and his moral liberty in civil society, which consists in obeying laws, general in scope and origin, which he, as a member of the body politic, has helped to make. This extreme formulation of Rousseau—that *man can be forced to be free,* that his freedom is not what he thinks it is but what he ought to think it is—could easily be used later by Hegel and the modern worshipers of the state.

Like most democratic theorists of the state, Rousseau was anxious to base political obligation on consent and thus save the idea of individual liberty in the realm of government. Yet he saw beyond the mechanical constructions of liberal political theory, which assumed that the public good would somehow be the final product of all individual private wills and interests. He attributes to the people inalienable sovereignty, but a moral obligation is attached to this precious possession: each citizen must will the general good, because popular sovereignty means the General Will, and self-government is therefore not mere submission to the common good, but its active cultivation: "There can be no patriotism without liberty, no liberty without virtue, no virtue without citizens; create citizens, and you have everything you need; without them, you will have nothing but debased slaves, from the rulers of the state downward."

Debased slaves of totalitarian states have sought to claim Rousseau as an intellectual progenitor of unlimited collectivism and oppressive anti-individualism. True, the organic element in Rousseau's doctrine may be abused, and has been abused, for antidemocratic purposes. Yet the master conception of *The Social Contract* is a community of free men living in a small state in which democracy can be practiced directly by the people, a community of men who see in freedom not only an invitation to personal enjoyment and advantage but also shared responsibility for the welfare of the whole.

Before Rousseau, the classical doctrine of Plato and Aristotle emphasized good government at the expense of self-government. The aim was the good life, not government of the people by the people. The more modern idea of Locke and the liberal school was concerned principally with self-government; it relegated the problem of good government into the background, or it was assumed that good government would naturally result form a combination of public laissez faire and private pursuit of individual advantage. Rousseau is the first modern writer to attempt, not always successfully, to synthesize *good government with self-government* in the key concept of the General Will: the realization of what is best for the community is not enough; it must also be *willed* by the community.

This synthesis explains why Rousseau has been claimed by adherents of the organic theory of the state as well as by followers of liberal democracy, though their conclusions may be antagonistic to each other. The more one is addicted to an extreme view of either the organic or the liberal theory in politics, the easier it is to appropriate only one part of Rousseau. The more one seeks to preserve what is best in the organic theory of the state and to fuse it with liberal democracy, the more one runs into philosophical difficulties that, in the end, resemble those of Rousseau.

Rousseau also saw more clearly than the conventional liberal doctrinaires that the end of government is not confined to the protection of individual liberty but also includes *equality*, because "liberty cannot exist without it." Rousseau reverses in *The Social Contract* the hostility to property that he showed in the first two *Discourses*; here he accepts property as an essential institution of society. But in *The Social Contract* he does not abandon the ideal of economic equality, though the concept of equality should not be taken in a literal sense. No citizen "shall ever be wealthy enough to buy another, and none poor enough to be forced to sell himself." Rousseau realizes that in practice it is difficult to maintain the ideal of equitable distribution of property, but it "is precisely because the force of circumstances tends continually to destroy equality that the force of legislation should always tend to its maintenance."

Whereas Locke failed to see property as a relation of domination of man over man, Rousseau clearly recognized *property* as a form of *private domination* that had to be kept under control by the General Will, the public interest of the community. Rousseau's theory of equitable distribution of property was, however, hardly socialist in the modern sense of the term, because he was not thinking of an industrial society, in which the problem of socialized property chiefly arises, but of communities of small peasants and craftsmen (as in Switzerland), in which individual economic independence and an approximation to the ideal of equal property are feasible. Yet indirectly, this part of Rousseau—the stress on equality—has aided the development of socialist sentiment by sharpening the awareness that political liberty and crass economic inequality are ultimately incompatible if democracy is to survive and expand.

Since the eighteenth century the record of free government everywhere has proved that there can be no reliance on contrivances and institutions alone in the eternal struggle for liberty, and that its survival depends, in the last analysis, on those moral qualities that Rousseau calls the General Will, justice, virtue. The General Will, like individual virtue, cannot be defined in detail; it is an impulse that animates and guides civic action. It receives its ultimate valid definition in the lives of free men rather than in philosophical distinctions.

Rousseau was first vindicated historically by the success of the American Revolution, and the opening words of the Constitution of the United States, "We the people . . . ," were of the spirit of Jean Jacques Rousseau. In the French Revolution, only a few years later, the French nation discovered its communal solidarity in a new birth of individual freedom and popular government. Since then, the message of Rousseau has been carried to all corners of the world, and its vitality and persistent timeliness continue to inspire free men everywhere.

ROUSSEAU

The Social Contract *

1. Man Is Born Free

Man is born free; and everywhere he is in chains. One thinks himself the master of others, and still remains a greater slave than they. How did this change come about? I do not know. What can make it legitimate? That question I think I can answer.

If I took into account only force, and the effects derived from it, I should say: "As long as a people is compelled to obey, and obeys, it does well; as soon as it can shake off the yoke, and shakes it off, it does still better; for, regaining its liberty by the same right as took it away, either it is justified in resuming it, or there was no justification for those who took it away." But the social order is a sacred right which is the basis of all other rights. Nevertheless, this right does not come from nature, and must therefore be founded on conventions. Before coming to that, I have to prove what I have just asserted.

* From Jean Jacques Rousseau, *The Social Contract* (1762, trans. G. D. H. Cole, E. P. Dutton & Company, 1947). By permission.

2. The Right of the Strongest

The strongest is never strong enough to be always the master, unless he transforms strength into right, and obedience into duty. Hence the right of the strongest, which, though to all seeming meant ironically, is really laid down as a fundamental principle. But are we never to have an explanation of this phrase? Force is a physical power, and I fail to see what moral effect it can have. To yield to force is an act of necessity, not of will—at the most, an act of prudence. In what sense can it be a duty?

Suppose for a moment that this so-called "right" exists. I maintain that the sole result is a mass of inexplicable nonsense. For, if force creates right, the effect changes with the cause: every force that is greater than the first succeeds to its right. As soon as it is possible to disobey with impunity, disobedience is legitimate; and, the strongest being always in the right, the only thing that matters is to act so as to become the strongest. But what kind of right is that which perishes when force fails? If we must obey perforce, there is no need to obey because we ought; and if we are not forced to obey, we are under no obligation to do so. Clearly, the word "right" adds nothing to force: in this connection, it means absolutely nothing.

Obey the powers that be. If this means yield to force, it is a good precept, but superfluous: I can answer for its never being violated. All power comes from God, I admit; but so does all sickness: does that mean that we are forbidden to call in the doctor? A brigand surprises me at the edge of a wood: must I not merely surrender my purse on compulsion; but, even if I could withhold it, am I in conscience bound to give it up? For certainly the pistol he holds is also a power.

Let us then admit that force does not create right, and that we are obliged to obey only legitimate powers. In that case, my original question recurs.

3. Slavery

Since no man has a natural authority over his fellow, and force creates no right, we must conclude that conventions form the basis of all legitimate authority among men.

If an individual, says Grotius, can alienate his liberty and make himself the slave of a master, why could not a whole people do the same and make itself subject to a king? There are in this passage plenty of ambiguous words which would need explaining; but let us confine ourselves to the word *alienate*. To alienate is to give or to sell. Now, a man who becomes the slave of another does not give himself; he sells himself, at the least for his subsistence: but for what does a people sell itself? A king is so far from furnishing his subjects with their subsistence that he gets his own only from them; and, according to Rabelais, kings do not live on nothing. Do subjects then give their persons on condition that the king takes their goods also? I fail to see what they have left to preserve.

It will be said that the despot assures his subjects civil tranquillity. Granted; but what do they gain, if the wars his ambition brings down upon them, his insatiable avidity, and the vexatious conduct of his ministers press harder on them than their own dissensions would have done? What do they gain, if the very tranquillity they enjoy is one of their miseries? Tranquillity is found also in dungeons; but is that enough to make them desirable places to live in? The Greeks imprisoned in the cave of the Cyclops lived there very tranquilly, while they were awaiting their turn to be devoured.

To say that a man gives himself gratuitously, is to say what is absurd and inconceivable; such an act is null and illegitimate, from the mere fact that he who does it is out of his mind. To say the same of a whole people is to suppose a people of madmen; and madness creates no right.

Even if each man could alienate himself, he could not alienate his children: they are born men and free; their liberty belongs to them, and no one but they has the right to dispose of it. Before they come to years of discretion, the father can, in their name, lay down conditions for their preservation and well-being, but he cannot give them irrevocably and without conditions: such a gift is contrary to the ends of nature, and exceeds the rights of paternity. It would therefore be necessary, in order to legitimize an arbitrary government, that in every generation the people should be in a position to accept or reject it; but, were this so, the government would be no longer arbitrary.

To renounce liberty is to renounce being a man, to surrender the rights of humanity and even its duties. For him who renounces everything no indemnity is possible. Such a renunciation is incompatible with man's nature; to remove all liberty from his will is to remove all morality from his acts. Finally, it is an empty and contradictory convention that sets up, on the one side, absolute authority, and, on the other, unlimited obedience. Is it not clear that we can be under no obligation to a person from whom we have the right to exact everything? Does not this condition alone, in the absence of equivalence or exchange, in itself involve the nullity of the act? For what right can my slave have against me, when all that he has belongs to me, and, his right being mine, this right of mine against myself is a phrase devoid of meaning?

Grotius and the rest find in war another origin for the so-called right of slavery. The victor having, as they hold, the right of killing the vanquished, the latter can buy back his life at the price of his liberty; and this convention is the more legitimate because it is to the advantage of both parties.

But it is clear that this supposed right to kill the conquered is by no means deducible from the state of war. Men, from the mere fact that, while they are living in their primitive independence, they have no mutual relations stable enough to constitute either the state of peace or the state of war, cannot be naturally enemies. War is constituted by a relation between things, and not between persons; and, as the state of war cannot arise out of simple personal relations, but only out of real relations, private war, or war of man with man, can exist neither in the state of nature, where there is no constant property, nor in the social state, where everything is under the authority of the laws.

Individual combats, duels, and encounters, are acts which cannot constitute a state; while the private wars, authorized by the Establishments of Louis IX, King of France, and suspended by the Peace of God, are abuses of feudalism, in itself an absurd system if ever there was one, and contrary to the principles of natural right and to all good polity.

War then is a relation, not between man and man, but between State and State, and individuals are enemies only accidentally, not as men, nor even as citizens,[1] but as soldiers; not as members of their country, but as its defenders. Finally, each State can have for enemies only other States, and not men; for between things disparate in nature there can be no real relation.

Furthermore, this principle is in conformity with the established rules of all times and the constant practice of all civilized peoples. Declarations of war are intimations less to powers then to their subjects. The foreigner, whether king, individual, or people, who robs, kills, or detains the subjects, without declaring war on the prince, is not an enemy, but a brigand. Even in real war, a just prince, while laying hands, in the enemy's country, on all that belongs to the public, respects the lives and goods of individuals: he respects rights on which his own are founded. The object of the war being the destruction of the hostile State, the other side has a right to kill its defenders, while they are bearing arms, but as soon as they lay them down and surrender, they cease to be enemies or instruments of the enemy, and become once more merely men, whose life no one has any right to take. Sometimes it is possible to kill the State without killing a single one of its members; and war gives no right which is not necessary to the gaining of its object. These principles are not those of Grotius: they are not based on the authority of poets, but derived from the nature of reality and based on reason.

The right of conquest has no foundation other than the right of the strongest. If

---

[1] The Romans, who understood and respected the right of war more than any other nation on earth, carried their scruples on this head so far that a citizen was not allowed to serve as a volunteer without engaging himself expressly against the enemy, and against such and such an enemy by name. A legion in which the younger Cato was seeing his first service under Popilius having been reconstructed, the elder Cato wrote to Popilius that, if he wished his son to continue serving under him, he must administer to him a new military oath, because, the first having been annulled, he was no longer able to bear arms against the enemy. The same Cato wrote to his son telling him to take great care not to go into battle before taking this new oath. I know that the siege of Clusium and other isolated events can be quoted against me; but I am citing laws and customs. The Romans are the people that least often transgressed its laws; and no other people has had such good ones.

war does not give the conqueror the right to massacre the conquered peoples, the right to enslave them cannot be based upon a right which does not exist. No one has a right to kill an enemy except when he cannot make him a slave, and the right to enslave him cannot therefore be derived from the right to kill him. It is accordingly an unfair exchange to make him buy at the price of his liberty his life, over which the victor holds no right. Is it not clear that there is a vicious circle in founding the right of life and death on the right of slavery, and the right of slavery on the right of life and death?

Even if we assume this terrible right to kill everybody, I maintain that a slave made in war, or a conquered people, is under no obligation to a master, except to obey him as far as he is compelled to do so. By taking an equivalent for his life, the victor has not done him a favour; instead of killing him without profit, he has killed him usefully. So far then is he from acquiring over him any authority in addition to that of force, that the state of war continues to subsist between them: their mutual relation is the effect of it, and the usage of the right of war does not imply a treaty of peace. A convention has indeed been made; but this convention, so far from destroying the state of war, presupposes its continuance.

So, from whatever aspect we regard the question, the right of slavery is null and void, not only as being illegitimate, but also because it is absurd and meaningless. The words *slave* and *right* contradict each other, and are mutually exclusive. It will always be equally foolish for a man to say to a man or to a people: "I make with you a convention wholly at your expense and wholly to my advantage; I shall keep it as long as I like, and you will keep it as long as I like."

4. The First Convention of Society

Even if I granted all that I have been refuting, the friends of despotism would be no better off. There will always be a great difference between subduing a multitude and ruling a society. Even if scattered individuals were successively enslaved by one man, however numerous they might be, I still see no more than a master and his slaves, and certainly not a people and its ruler; I see what may be termed an aggregation, but not an association; there is as yet neither public good nor body politic. The man in question, even if he has enslaved half the world, is still only an individual; his interest, apart from that of others, is still a purely private interest. If this same man comes to die, his empire, after him, remains scattered and without unity, as an oak falls and dissolves into a heap of ashes when the fire has consumed it.

A people, says Grotius, can give itself to a king. Then, according to Grotius, a people is a people before it gives itself. The gift is itself a civil act, and implies public deliberation. It would be better, before examining the act by which a people gives itself to a king, to examine that by which it has become a people; for this act, being necessarily prior to the other, is the true foundation of society.

Indeed, if there were no prior convention, where, unless the election were unanimous, would be the obligation on the minority to submit to the choice of the majority? How have a hundred men who wish for a master the right to vote on behalf of ten who do not? The law of majority voting is itself something established by convention, and presupposes unanimity, on one occasion at least.

5. The Social Compact

I suppose men to have reached the point at which the obstacles in the way of their preservation in the state of nature show their power of resistance to be greater than the resources at the disposal of each individual for his maintenance in that state. That primitive condition can then subsist no longer; and the human race would perish unless it changed its manner of existence.

But, as men cannot engender new forces, but only unite and direct existing ones, they have no other means of preserving themselves than the formation, by aggregation, of a sum of forces great enough to overcome the resistance. These they have to bring into play by means of a single motive power, and cause to act in concert.

This sum of forces can arise only where several persons come together: but, as the force and liberty of each man are the chief instruments of his self-preservation, how can he pledge them without harming his own interests, and neglecting the care he owes to himself? This difficulty, in its bearing on my present subject, may be stated in the following terms:

"The problem is to find a form of association which will defend and protect with the whole common force the person and goods of each associate, and in which each, while uniting himself with all, may still obey himself alone, and remain as free as before." This is the fundamental problem of which the *Social Contract* provides the solution.

The clauses of this contract are so determined by the nature of the act that the slightest modification would make them vain and ineffective; so that, although they have perhaps never been formally set forth, they are everywhere the same and everywhere tacitly admitted and recognized, until, on the violation of the social compact, each regains his original rights and resumes his natural liberty, while losing the conventional liberty in favour of which he renounced it.

These clauses, properly understood, may be reduced to one—the total alienation of each associate, together with all his rights, to the whole community; for, in the first place, as each gives himself absolutely, the conditions are the same for all; and, this being so, no one has any interest in making them burdensome to others.

Moreover, the alienation being without reserve, the union is as perfect as it can be, and no associate has anything more to demand: for, if the individuals retained certain rights, as there would be no common

superior to decide between them and the public, each, being on one point his own judge, would ask to be so on all; the state of nature would thus continue, and the association would necessarily become inoperative or tyrannical.

Finally, each man, in giving himself to all, gives himself to nobody; and as there is no associate over which he does not acquire the same right as he yields others over himself, he gains an equivalent for everything he loses, and an increase of force for the preservation of what he has.

If then we discard from the social compact what is not of its essence, we shall find that it reduces itself to the following terms:

"Each of us puts his person and all his power in common under the supreme direction of the general will, and, in our corporate capacity, we receive each member as an indivisible part of the whole."

At once, in place of the individual personality of each contracting party, this act of association creates a moral and collective body, composed of as many members as the assembly contains voters, and receiving from this act its unity, its common identity, its life, and its will. This public person, so formed by the union of all other persons, formerly took the name of *city*,[1]

[1] The real meaning of this word has been almost wholly lost in modern times; most people mistake a town for a city, and a townsman for a citizen. They do not know that houses make a town, but citizens a city. The same mistake long ago cost the Carthaginians dear. I have never read of the title of citizens being given to the subjects of any prince, not even the ancient Macedonians or the English of to-day, though they are nearer liberty than any one else. The French alone everywhere familiarly adopt the name of citizens, because, as can be seen from their dictionaries, they have no idea of its meaning; otherwise they would be guilty in usurping it, of the crime of *lèse-majesté:* among them, the name expresses a virtue, and not a right. When Bodin spoke of our citizens and townsmen, he fell into a bad blunder in taking the one class for the other. M. d'Alembert has avoided the error, and, in his article on Geneva, has clearly distinguished the four orders of men (or even five, counting mere foreigners) who dwell in our town, of which two only compose the Republic. No other French writer, to my knowledge, has understood the real meaning of the word citizen.

and now takes that of *Republic* or *body politic;* it is called by its members *State* when passive, *Sovereign* when active, and *Power* when compared with others like itself. Those who are associated in it take collectively the name of *people,* and severally are called *citizens,* as sharing in the sovereign power, and *subjects,* as being under the laws of the State. But these terms are often confused and taken one for another: it is enough to know how to distinguish them when they are being used with precision.

6. The Sovereign

This formula shows us that the act of association comprises a mutual undertaking between the public and the individuals, and that each individual, in making a contract, as we may say, with himself, is bound in a double capacity; as a member of the Sovereign he is bound to the individuals, and as a member of the State to the Sovereign. But the maxim of civil right, that no one is bound by undertakings made to himself, does not apply in this case; for there is a great difference between incurring an obligation to yourself and incurring one to a whole of which you form a part.

Attention must further be called to the fact that public deliberation, while competent to bind all the subjects to the Sovereign, because of the two different capacities in which each of them may be regarded, cannot, for the opposite reason, bind the Sovereign to itself; and that it is consequently against the nature of the body politic for the Sovereign to impose on itself a law which it cannot infringe. Being able to regard itself in only one capacity, it is in the position of an individual who makes a contract with himself; and this makes it clear that there neither is nor can be any kind of fundamental law binding on the body of the people—not even the social contract itself. This does not mean that the body politic cannot enter into undertakings with others, provided the contract is not infringed by them; for in relation to what is external to it, it becomes a simple being, an individual.

But the body politic or the Sovereign, drawing its being wholly from the sanctity of the contract, can never bind itself, even to an outsider, to do anything derogatory to the original act, for instance, to alienate any part of itself, or to submit to another Sovereign. Violation of the act by which it exists would be self-annihilation; and that which is itself nothing can create nothing.

As soon as this multitude is so united in one body, it is impossible to offend against one of the members without attacking the body, and still more to offend against the body without the members resenting it. Duty and interest therefore equally oblige the two contracting parties to give each other help; and the same men should seek to combine, in their double capacity, all the advantages dependent upon that capacity.

Again, the Sovereign, being formed wholly of the individuals who compose it, neither has nor can have any interest contrary to theirs; and consequently the sovereign power need give no guarantee to its subjects, because it is impossible for the body to wish to hurt all its members. We shall also see later on that it cannot hurt any in particular. The Sovereign, merely by virtue of what it is, is always what it should be.

This, however, is not the case with the relation of the subjects to the Sovereign, which, despite the common interest, would have no security that they would fulfil their undertakings, unless it found means to assure itself of their fidelity.

In fact, each individual, as a man, may have a particular will contrary or dissimilar to the general will which he has as a citizen. His particular interest may speak to him quite differently from the common interest: his absolute and naturally independent existence may make him look upon what he owes to the common cause as a gratuitous contribution, the loss of which will do less harm to others than the payment of it is burdensome to himself; and, regarding the moral person which constitutes the State as a *persona ficta,* because not a man, he may wish to enjoy the rights of citizenship without being ready to fulfil the duties of a subject. The continuance of such an injustice could not but prove the undoing of the body politic.

In order then that the social compact may not be an empty formula, it tacitly includes the undertaking, which alone can give force to the rest, that whoever refuses to obey the general will shall be compelled to do so by the whole body. This means nothing less than that he will be forced to be free; for this is the condition which, by giving each citizen to his country, secures him against all personal dependence. In this lies the key to the working of the political machine; this alone legitimizes civil undertakings, which, without it, would be absurd, tyrannical, and liable to the most frightful abuses.

7. The Civil State

The passage from the state of nature to the civil state produces a very remarkable change in man, by substituting justice for instinct in his conduct, and giving his actions the morality they had formerly lacked. Then only, when the voice of duty takes the place of physical impulses and right of appetite, does man, who so far had considered only himself, find that he is forced to act on different principles, and to consult his reason before listening to his inclinations. Although, in this state, he deprives himself of some advantages which he got from nature, he gains in return others so great, his faculties are so stimulated and developed, his ideas so extended, his feelings so ennobled, and his whole soul so uplifted, that, did not the abuses of this new condition often degrade him below that which he left, he would be bound to bless continually the happy moment which took him from it for ever, and, instead of a stupid and unimaginative animal, made him an intelligent being and a man.

Let us draw up the whole account in terms easily commensurable. What man loses by the social contract is his natural liberty and an unlimited right to everything he tries to get and succeeds in getting; what he gains is civil liberty and the proprietorship of all he possesses. If we are to avoid mistakes in weighing one against the other, we must clearly distinguish natural liberty, which is bounded only by the strength of the individual, from civil liberty, which is limited by the general will; and possession, which is merely the effect of force or the right of the first occupier, from property, which can be founded only on a positive title.

We might, over and above all this, add, to what man acquires in the civil state, moral liberty, which alone makes him truly master of himself; for the mere impulse of appetite is slavery, while obedience to a law which we prescribe to ourselves is liberty. But I have already said too much on this head, and the philosophical meaning of the word liberty does not now concern us.

8. The Inalienability of Sovereignty

The first and most important deduction from the principles we have so far laid down is that the general will alone can direct the State according to the object for which it was instituted, i.e. the common good: for if the clashing of particular interests made the establishment of societies necessary, the agreement of these very interests made it possible. The common element in these different interests is what forms the social tie; and, were there no point of agreement between them all, no society could exist. It is solely on the basis of this common interest that every society should be governed.

I hold then that Sovereignty, being nothing less than the exercise of the general will, can never be alienated, and that the Sovereign, who is no less than a collective being, cannot be represented except by himself:

the power indeed may be transmitted, but not the will.

In reality, if it is not impossible for a particular will to agree on some point with the general will, it is at least impossible for the agreement to be lasting and constant; for the particular will tends, by its very nature, to partiality, while the general will tends to equality. It is even more impossible to have any guarantee of this agreement; for even if it should always exist, it would be the effect not of art, but of chance. The Sovereign may indeed say: "I now will actually what this man wills, or at least what he says he wills;" but it cannot say: "What he wills to-morrow, I too shall will" because it is absurd for the will to bind itself for the future, nor is it incumbent on any will to consent to anything that is not for the good of the being who wills. If then the people promises simply to obey, by that very act it dissolves itself and loses what makes it a people; the moment a master exists, there is no longer a Sovereign, and from that moment the body politic has ceased to exist.

This does not mean that the commands of the rulers cannot pass for general wills, so long as the Sovereign, being free to oppose them, offers no opposition. In such a case, universal silence is taken to imply the consent of the people. This will be explained later on.

9. The Indivisibility of Sovereignty

Sovereignty, for the same reason as makes it inalienable, is indivisible; for will either is, or is not, general; [1] it is the will either of the body of the people, or only of a part of it. In the first case, the will, when declared, is an act of Sovereignty and constitutes law: in the second, it is merely a particular will, or act of magistracy—at the most a decree.

[1] To be general, a will need not always be unanimous; but every vote must be counted: any exclusion is a breach of generality.

But our political theorists, unable to divide Sovereignty in principle, divide it according to its object: into force and will; into legislative power and executive power; into rights of taxation, justice, and war; into internal administration and power of foreign treaty. Sometimes they confuse all these sections, and sometimes they distinguish them; they turn the Sovereign into a fantastic being composed of several connected pieces: it is as if they were making man of several bodies, one with eyes, one with arms, another with feet, and each with nothing besides. We are told that the jugglers of Japan dismember a child before the eyes of the spectators; then they throw all the members into the air one after another, and the child falls down alive and whole. The conjuring tricks of our political theorists are very like that; they first dismember the body politic by an illusion worthy of a fair, and then join it together again we know not how.

This error is due to a lack of exact notions concerning the Sovereign authority, and to taking for parts of it what are only emanations from it. Thus, for example, the acts of declaring war and making peace have been regarded as acts of Sovereignty; but this is not the case, as these acts do not constitute law, but merely the application of a law, a particular act which decides how the law applies, as we shall see clearly when the idea attached to the word "law" has been defined.

If we examined the other divisions in the same manner, we should find that, whenever Sovereignty seems to be divided, there is an illusion: the rights which are taken as being part of Sovereignty are really all subordinate, and always imply supreme wills of which they only sanction the execution.

It would be impossible to estimate the obscurity this lack of exactness has thrown over the decisions of writers who have dealt with political right, when they have used the principles laid down by them to pass judgment on the respective rights of kings and peoples. Every one can see, in Chapters III and IV of the first book of Grotius, how the learned man and his translator, Barbeyrac, entangle and tie themselves up in their own sophistries, for fear of saying too little or too much of what they think, and so offending the interests they have to conciliate. Grotius, a refugee in France, ill content with his own country, and desirous of paying his court to Louis XIII, to whom his book is dedicated, spares no pains to rob the peoples of all their rights and invest kings with them by every conceivable artifice. This would also have been much to the taste of Barbeyrac, who dedicated his translation to George I of England. But unfortunately the expulsion of James II, which he called his "abdication," compelled him to use all reserve, to shuffle and to tergiversate, in order to avoid making William out a usurper. If these two writers had adopted the true principles, all difficulties would have been removed, and they would have been always consistent; but it would have been a sad truth for them to tell, and would have paid court for them to no one save the people. Moreover, truth is no road to fortune, and the people dispenses neither ambassadorships, nor professorships, nor pensions.

10. Infallibility of the General Will

It follows from what has gone before that the general will is always right and tends to the public advantage; but it does not follow that the deliberations of the people are always equally correct. Our will is always for our own good, but we do not always see what that is; the people is never corrupted, but it is often deceived, and on such occasions only does it seem to will what is bad.

There is often a great deal of difference between the will of all and the general will; the latter considers only the common interest, while the former takes private interest into account, and is no more than a sum of particular wills: but take away from these same wills the pluses and minuses that cancel one another,[1] and the general will remains as the sum of the differences.

If, when the people, being furnished with adequate information, held its deliberations, the citizens had no communication one with another, the grand total of the small differences would always give the general will, and the decision would always be good. But when factions arise, and partial associations are formed at the expense of the great association, the will of each of these associations becomes general in relation to its members, while it remains particular in relation to the State: it may then be said that there are no longer as many votes as there are men, but only as many as there are associations. The differences become less numerous and give a less general result. Lastly, when one of these associations is so great as to prevail over all the rest, the result is no longer a sum of small differences, but a single difference; in this case there is no longer a general will, and the opinion which prevails is purely particular.

It is therefore essential, if the general will is to be able to express itself, that there should be no partial society within the State, and that each citizen should think only his own thoughts:[2] which was indeed the sublime and unique system established by the great Lycurgus. But if there are partial societies, it is best to have as many as possible and to prevent them from being unequal, as was done by Solon, Numa, and Servius. These precautions are the only ones

---

[1] "Every interest," says the Marquis d'Argenson, "has different principles. The agreement of two particular interests is formed by opposition to a third." He might have added that the agreement of all interests is formed by opposition to that of each. If there were no different interests, the common interest would be barely felt, as it would encounter no obstacle; all would go on of its own accord, and politics would cease to be an art.

[2] "In fact," says Machiavelli, "there are some divisions that are harmful to a Republic and some that are advantageous. Those which stir up sects and parties are harmful; those attended by neither are advantageous. Since, then, the founder of a Republic cannot help enmities arising, he ought at least to prevent them from growing into sects" (*History of Florence*, Book VII).

that can guarantee that the general will shall be always enlightened, and that the people shall in no way deceive itself.

11. Limits of the Sovereign Power

If the State is a moral person whose life is in the union of its members, and if the most important of its cares is the care for its own preservation, it must have a universal and compelling force, in order to move and dispose each part as may be most advantageous to the whole. As nature gives each man absolute power over all his members, the social compact gives the body politic absolute power over all its members also; and it is this power which, under the direction of the general will, bears, as I have said, the name of Sovereignty.

But, besides the public person, we have to consider the private persons composing it, whose life and liberty are naturally independent of it. We are bound then to distinguish clearly between the respective rights of the citizens and the Sovereign,[1] and between the duties the former have to fulfil as subjects, and the natural rights they should enjoy as men.

Each man alienates, I admit, by the social compact, only such part of his powers, goods, and liberty as it is important for the community to control; but it must also be granted that the Sovereign is sole judge of what is important.

Every service a citizen can render the State he ought to render as soon as the Sovereign demands it; but the Sovereign, for its part, cannot impose upon its subjects any fetters that are useless to the community, nor can it even wish to do so; for no more by the law of reason than by the law of nature can anything occur without a cause.

The undertakings which bind us to the

---

[1] Attentive readers, do not, I pray, be in a hurry to charge me with contradicting myself. The terminology made it unavoidable, considering the poverty of the language; but wait and see.

social body are obligatory only because they are mutual; and their nature is such that in fulfilling them we cannot work for others without working for ourselves. Why is it that the general will is always in the right, and that all continually will the happiness of each one, unless it is because there is not a man who does not think of "each" as meaning him, and consider himself in voting for all? This proves that equality of rights and the idea of justice which such equality creates originate in the preference each man gives to himself, and accordingly in the very nature of man. It proves that the general will, to be really such, must be general in its object as well as its essence; that it must both come from all and apply to all; and that it loses its natural rectitude when it is directed to some particular and determinate object, because in such a case we are judging of something foreign to us, and have no true principle of equity to guide us.

Indeed, as soon as a question of particular fact or right arises on a point not previously regulated by a general convention, the matter becomes contentious. It is a case in which the individuals concerned are one party, and the public the other, but in which I can see neither the law that ought to be followed nor the judge who ought to give the decision. In such a case, it would be absurd to propose to refer the question to an express decision of the general will, which can be only the conclusion reached by one of the parties and in consequence will be, for the other party, merely an external and particular will, inclined on this occasion to injustice and subject to error. Thus, just as a particular will cannot stand for the general will, the general will, in turn, changes its nature, when its object is particular, and, as general, cannot pronounce on a man or a fact. When, for instance, the people of Athens nominated or displaced its rulers, decreed honours to one, and imposed penalties on another, and, by a multitude of particular decrees, exercised all the functions of government indiscriminately, it had in such cases no longer a general will in the strict sense; it was acting no longer as Sovereign, but as magistrate. This will seem contrary to current views; but I must be given time to expound my own.

It should be seen from the foregoing that what makes the will general is less the number of votes than the common interest uniting them; for, under this system, each necessarily submits to the conditions he imposes on others: and this admirable agreement between interest and justice gives to the common deliberations an equitable character which at once vanishes when any particular question is discussed, in the absence of a common interest to unite and identify the ruling of the judge with that of the party.

From whatever side we approach our principle, we reach the same conclusion, that the social compact sets up among the citizens an equality of such a kind, that they all bind themselves to observe the same conditions and should therefore all enjoy the same rights. Thus, from the very nature of the compact, every act of Sovereignty, i.e. every authentic act of the general will, binds or favours all the citizens equally; so that the Sovereign recognizes only the body of the nation, and draws no distinctions between those of whom it is made up. What, then, strictly speaking, is an act of Sovereignty? It is not a convention between a superior and an inferior, but a conviction between the body and each of its members. It is legitimate, because based on the social contract, and equitable, because common to all; useful, because it can have no other object than the general good, and stable, because guaranteed by the public force and the supreme power. So long as the subjects have to submit only to conventions of this sort, they obey no one but their own will; and to ask how far the respective rights of the Sovereign and the citizens extend, is to ask up to what point the latter can enter into undertakings with themselves, each with all, and all with each.

We can see from this that the sovereign power, absolute, sacred, and inviolable as it is, does not and cannot exceed the limits of general conventions, and that every man may dispose at will of such goods and liberty as these conventions leave him; so that the Sovereign never has a right to lay more charges on one subject than on another, because, in that case, the question becomes particular, and ceases to be within its competency.

When these distinctions have once been admitted, it is seen to be so untrue that there is, in the social contract, any real renunciation on the part of the individuals, that the position in which they find themselves as a result of the contract is really preferable to that in which they were before. Instead of a renunciation, they have made an advantageous exchange: instead of an uncertain and precarious way of living they have got one that is better and more secure; instead of natural independence they have got liberty, instead of the power to harm others security for themselves, and instead of their strength, which others might overcome, a right which social union makes invincible. Their very life, which they have devoted to the State, is by it constantly protected; and when they risk it in the State's defence, what more are they doing than giving back what they have received from it? What are they doing that they would not do more often and with greater danger in the state of nature, in which they would inevitably have to fight battles at the peril of their lives in defence of that which is the means of their preservation? All have indeed to fight when their country needs them; but then no one has ever to fight for himself. Do we not gain something by running, on behalf of what gives us our security, only some of the risks we should have to run for ourselves, as soon as we lost it?

12. Law

By the social compact we have given the body politic existence and life; we have now by legislation to give it movement and will. For the original act by which the body is formed and united still in no respect determines what it ought to do for its preservation.

What is well and in conformity with order is so by the nature of things and independently of human conventions. All justice comes from God, who is its sole source; but if we knew how to receive so high an inspiration, we should need neither government nor laws. Doubtless, there is a universal justice emanating from reason alone; but this justice, to be admitted among us, must be mutual. Humanly speaking, in default of natural sanctions, the laws of justice are ineffective among men: they merely make for the good of the wicked and the undoing of the just, when the just man observes them towards everybody and nobody observes them towards him. Conventions and laws are therefore needed to join rights to duties and refer justice to its object. In the state of nature, where everything is common, I owe nothing to him whom I have promised nothing; I recognize as belonging to others only what is of no use to me. In the state of society all rights are fixed by law, and the case becomes different.

But what, after all, is a law? As long as we remain satisfied with attaching purely metaphysical ideas to the word, we shall go on arguing without arriving at an understanding; and when we have defined a law of nature, we shall be no nearer the definition of a law of the State.

I have already said that there can be no general will directed to a particular object. Such an object must be either within or outside the State. If outside, a will which is alien to it cannot be, in relation to it, general; if within, it is part of the State, and in that case there arises a relation between whole and part which makes them two separate beings, of which the part is one, and the whole minus the part the other. But the whole minus a part cannot be the whole; and while this relation persists, there can be no whole, but only two unequal parts; and

it follows that the will of one is no longer in any respect general in relation to the other.

But when the whole people decrees for the whole people, it is considering only itself; and if a relation is then formed, it is between two aspects of the entire object, without there being any division of the whole. In that case the matter about which the decree is made is, like the decreeing will, general. This act is what I call a law.

When I say that the object of laws is always general, I mean that law considers subjects *en masse* and actions in the abstract, and never a particular person or action. Thus the law may indeed decree that there shall be privileges, but cannot confer them on anybody by name. It may set up several classes of citizens, and even lay down the qualifications for membership of these classes, but it cannot nominate such and such persons as belonging to them; it may establish a monarchical government and hereditary succession, but it cannot choose a king, or nominate a royal family. In a word, no function which has a particular object belongs to the legislative power.

On this view, we at once see that it can no longer be asked whose business it is to make laws, since they are acts of the general will; nor whether the prince is above the law, since he is a member of the State; nor whether the law can be unjust, since no one is unjust to himself; nor how we can be both free and subject to the laws, since they are but registers of our wills.

We see further that, as the law unites universality of will with universality of object, what a man, whoever he be, commands of his own motion cannot be a law; and even what the Sovereign commands with regard to a particular matter is no nearer being a law, but is a decree, an act, not of sovereignty, but of magistracy.

I therefore give the name "Republic" to every State that is governed by laws, no matter what the form of its administration may be: for only in such a case does the public interest govern, and the *res publica* rank as a *reality*. Every legitimate government is republican; [1] what government is I will explain later on.

Laws are, properly speaking, only the conditions of civil association. The people, being subject to the laws, ought to be their author: the conditions of the society ought to be regulated solely by those who come together to form it. But how are they to regulate them? Is it to be by common agreement, by a sudden inspiration? Has the body politic an organ to declare its will? Who can give it the foresight to formulate and announce its acts in advance? Or how is it to announce them in the hour of need? How can a blind multitude, which often does not know what it wills, because it rarely knows what is good for it, carry out for itself so great and difficult an enterprise as a system of legislation? Of itself the people wills always the good, but of itself it by no means always sees it. The general will is always in the right, but the judgment which guides it is not always enlightened. It must be got to see objects as they are, and sometimes as they ought to appear to it; it must be shown the good road it is in search of, secured from the seductive influences of individual wills, taught to see times and spaces as a series, and made to weigh the attractions of present and sensible advantages against the danger of distant and hidden evils. The individuals see the good they reject; the public wills the good it does not see. All stand equally in need of guidance. The former must be compelled to bring their wills into conformity with their reason; the latter must be taught to know what it wills. If that is done, public enlightenment leads to the union of understanding and will in the social body: the parts are made to work exactly together, and the whole is raised to its highest power. This makes a legislator necessary.

13. The Legislator

In order to discover the rules of society best suited to nations, a superior intelligence beholding all the passions of men without experiencing any of them would be needed. This intelligence would have to be wholly unrelated to our nature, while knowing it through and through; its happiness would have to be independent of us, and yet ready to occupy itself with ours; and lastly, it would have, in the march of time, to look forward to a distant glory, and, working in one century, to be able to enjoy in the next. [1] It would take gods to give men laws.

What Caligula argued from the facts, Plato, in the dialogue called the *Politicus*, argued in defining the civil or kingly man, on the basis of right. But if great princes are rare, how much more so are great legislators! The former have only to follow the pattern which the latter have to lay down. The legislator is the engineer who invents the machine, the prince merely the mechanic who sets it up and makes it go. "At the birth of societies," says Montesquieu, "the rulers of Republics establish institutions, and afterwards the institutions mould the rulers." [2]

He who dares to undertake the making of a people's institutions ought to feel himself capable, so to speak, of changing human nature, of transforming each individual, who is by himself a complete and solitary whole, into part of a greater whole from which he in a manner receives his life and being; of altering man's constitution for the purpose of strengthening it; and of substituting a partial and moral existence for the physical and independent existence nature has conferred on us all. He must, in a word, take away from man his own resources and give him instead new ones alien to him, and in-

---

[1] I understand by this word, not merely an aristocracy or a democracy, but generally any government directed by the general will, which is the law. To be legitimate, the government must be, not one with the Sovereign, but its minister. In such a case even a monarchy is a Republic.

[1] A people becomes famous only when its legislation begins to decline. We do not know for how many centuries the system of Lycurgus made the Spartans happy before the rest of Greece took any notice of it.

[2] Montesquieu, *The Greatness and Decadence of the Romans*, ch. i.

capable of being made use of without the help of other men. The more completely these natural resources are annihilated, the greater and more lasting are those which he acquires, and the more stable and perfect the new institutions; so that if each citizen is nothing and can do nothing without the rest, and the resources acquired by the whole are equal or superior to the aggregate of the resources of all the individuals, it may be said that legislation is at the highest possible point of perfection.

The legislator occupies in every respect an extraordinary position in the State. If he should do so by reason of his genius, he does so no less by reason of his office, which is neither magistracy, nor Sovereignty. This office, which sets up the Republic, nowhere enters into its constitution; it is an individual and superior function, which has nothing in common with human empire; for if he who holds command over men ought not to have command over the laws, he who has command over the laws ought not any more to have it over men; or else his laws would be the ministers of his passions and would often merely serve to perpetuate his injustices: his private aims would inevitably mar the sanctity of his work.

When Lycurgus gave laws to his country, he began by resigning the throne. It was the custom of most Greek towns to entrust the establishment of their laws to foreigners. The Republics of modern Italy in many cases followed this examples; Geneva did the same and profited by it.[3] Rome, when it was most prosperous, suffered a revival of all the crimes of tyranny, and was brought to the verge of destruction, because it put the legislative authority and the sovereign power into the same hands.

Nevertheless, the decemvirs themselves

[3] Those who know Calvin only as a theologian much underestimate the extent of his genius. The codification of our wise edicts, in which he played a large part, does him no less honour than his *Institute*. Whatever revolution time may bring in our religion, so long as the spirit of patriotism and liberty still lives among us, the memory of this great man will be for ever blessed.

never claimed the right to pass any law merely on their own authority. "Nothing we propose to you," they said to the people, "can pass into law without your consent. Romans, be yourselves the authors of the laws which are to make you happy."

He, therefore, who draws up the laws has, or should have, no right of legislation, and the people cannot, even if it wishes, deprive itself of this incommunicable right, because, according to the fundamental compact, only the general will can bind the individuals, and there can be no assurance that a particular will is in conformity with the general will, until it has been put to the free vote of the people. This I have said already; but it is worth while to repeat it.

Thus in the task of legislation we find together two things which appear to be incompatible: an enterprise too difficult for human powers, and, for its execution, an authority that is no authority.

There is a further difficulty that deserves attention. Wise men, if they try to speak their language to the common herd instead of its own, cannot possibly make themselves understood. There are a thousand kinds of ideas which it is impossible to translate into popular language. Conceptions that are too general and objects that are too remote are equally out of its range: each individual, having no taste for any other plan of government than that which suits his particular interest, finds it difficult to realize the advantages he might hope to draw from the continual privations good laws impose. For a young people to be able to relish sound principles of political theory and follow the fundamental rules of statecraft, the effect would have to become the cause; the social spirit, which should be created by these institutions, would have to preside over their very foundation; and men would have to be before law what they should become by means of law. The legislator therefore, being unable to appeal to either force or reason, must have recourse to an authority of a different order, capable of constraining without violence and persuading without convincing.

This is what has, in all ages, compelled the fathers of nations to have recourse to divine intervention and credit the gods with their own wisdom, in order that the peoples, submitting to the laws of the State as to those of nature, and recognizing the same power in the formation of the city as in that of man, might obey freely, and bear with docility the yoke of the public happiness.

This sublime reason, far above the range of the common herd, is that whose decisions the legislator puts into the mouth of the immortals, in order to constrain by divine authority those whom human prudence could not move.[4] But it is not anybody who can make the gods speak, or get himself believed when he proclaims himself their interpreter. The great soul of the legislator is the only miracle that can prove his mission. Any man may grave tablets of stone, or buy an oracle, or feign secret intercourse with some divinity, or train a bird to whisper in his ear, or find other vulgar ways of imposing on the people. He whose knowledge goes no further may perhaps gather round him a band of fools; but he will never found an empire, and his extravagances will quickly perish with him. Idle tricks form a passing tie; only wisdom can make it lasting. The Judaic law, which still subsists, and that of the child of Ishmael, which, for ten centuries, has ruled half the world, still proclaim the great men who laid them down; and, while the pride of philosophy or the blind spirit of faction sees in them no more than lucky impostures, the true political theorist admires, in the institutions they set up, the great and powerful genius which presides over things made to endure.

We should not, with Warburton, conclude from this that politics and religion have among us a common object, but that,

[4] "In truth," says Machiavelli, "there has never been, in any country, an extraordinary legislator who has not had recourse to God; for otherwise his laws would not have been accepted: there are, in fact, many useful truths of which a wise man may have knowledge without their having in themselves such clear reasons for their being so as to be able to convince others" (*Discourses on Livy*, Bk. V, ch. xi).

in the first periods of nations, the one is used as an instrument for the other.

14. The People

As nature has set bounds to the stature of a well-made man, and, outside those limits, makes nothing but giants or dwarfs, similarly, for the constitution of a State to be at its best, it is possible to fix limits that will make it neither too large for good government, nor too small for self-maintenance. In every body politic there is a maximum strength which it cannot exceed and which it only loses by increasing in size. Every extension of the social tie means its relaxation; and, generally speaking, a small State is stronger in proportion than a great one.

A thousand arguments could be advanced in favour of this principle. First, long distances make administration more difficult, just as a weight becomes heavier at the end of a longer lever. Administration therefore becomes more and more burdensome as the distance grows greater; for, in the first place, each city has its own, which is paid for by the people: each district its own, still paid for by the people: then comes each province, and then the great governments, satrapies, and viceroyalties, always costing more the higher you go, and always at the expense of the unfortunate people. Last of all comes the supreme administration, which eclipses all the rest. All these overcharges are a continual drain upon the subjects; so far from being better governed by all these different orders, they are worse governed than if there were only a single authority over them. In the meantime, there scarce remain resources enough to meet emergencies; and, when recourse must be had to these, the State is always on the eve of destruction.

This is not all; not only has the government less vigour and promptitude for securing the observance of the laws, preventing nuisances, correcting abuses, and guarding against seditious undertakings begun in distant places; the people has less affection for its rulers, whom it never sees, for its country, which, to its eyes, seems like the world, and for its fellow citizens, most of whom are unknown to it. The same laws cannot suit so many diverse provinces with different customs, situated in the most various climates, and incapable of enduring a uniform government. Different laws lead only to trouble and confusion among peoples which, living under the same rulers and in constant communication one with another, intermingle and intermarry, and, coming under the sway of new customs, never know if they can call their very patrimony their own. Talent is buried, virtue unknown, and vice unpunished, among such a multitude of men who do not know one another, gathered together in one place at the seat of the central administration. The leaders, overwhelmed with business, see nothing for themselves; the State is governed by clerks. Finally, the measures which have to be taken to maintain the general authority, which all these distant officials wish to escape or to impose upon, absorb all the energy of the public, so that there is none left for the happiness of the people. There is hardly enough to defend it when need arises, and thus a body which is too big for its constitution gives way and falls crushed under its own weight.

Again, the State must assure itself a safe foundation, if it is to have stability, and to be able to resist the shocks it cannot help experiencing, as well as the efforts it will be forced to make for its maintenance; for all peoples have a kind of centrifugal force that makes them continually act one against another, and tend to aggrandize themselves at their neighbours' expense, like the vortices of Descartes. Thus the weak run the risk of being soon swallowed up; and it is almost impossible for any one to preserve itself except by putting itself in a state of equilibrium with all, so that the pressure is on all sides practically equal.

It may therefore be seen that there are reasons for expansion and reasons for contraction; and it is no small part of the statesman's skill to hit between them the mean that is most favourable to the preservation of the State. It may be said that the reason for expansion, being merely external and relative, ought to be subordinate to the reasons for contraction, which are internal and absolute. A strong and healthy constitution is the first thing to look for; and it is better to count on the vigour which comes of good government than on the resources a great territory furnishes.

It may be added that there have been known States so constituted that the necessity of making conquests entered into their very constitution, and that, in order to maintain themselves, they were forced to expand ceaselessly. It may be that they congratulated themselves greatly on this fortunate necessity, which none the less indicated to them, along with the limits of their greatness, the inevitable moment of their fall.

15. Government in General

I warn the reader that this chapter requires careful reading, and that I am unable to make myself clear to those who refuse to be attentive.

Every free action is produced by the concurrence of two causes; one moral, i.e. the will which determines the act; the other physical, i.e., the power which executes it. When I walk towards an object, it is necessary first that I should will to go there, and, in the second place, that my feet should carry me. If a paralytic wills to run and an active man wills not to, they will both stay where they are. The body politic has the same motive powers; here too force and will are distinguished, will under the name of legislative power and force under that of executive power. Without their concurrence, nothing is, or should be, done.

We have seen that the legislative power belongs to the people, and can belong to it alone. It may, on the other hand, readily be seen, from the principles laid down above, that the executive power cannot belong to the generality as legislature or Sovereign, because it consists wholly of particular acts which fall outside the competency of the law, and consequently of the Sovereign, whose acts must always be laws.

The public force therefore needs an agent of its own to bind it together and set it to work under the direction of the general will, to serve as a means of communication between the State and the Sovereign, and to do for the collective person more or less what the union of soul and body does for man. Here we have what is, in the State, the basis of government, often wrongly confused with the Sovereign, whose minister it is.

What then is government? An intermediate body set up between the subjects and the Sovereign, to secure their mutual correspondence, charged with the execution of the laws and the maintenance of liberty, both civil and political.

The members of this body are called magistrates or *kings*, that is to say *governors*, and the whole body bears the name *prince*.[1] Thus those who hold that the act, by which a people puts itself under a prince, is not a contract, are certainly right. It is simply and solely a commission, an employment, in which the rulers, mere officials of the Sovereign, exercise in their own name the power of which it makes them depositaries. This power it can limit, modify, or recover at pleasure; for the alienation of such a right is incompatible with the nature of the social body, and contrary to the end of association.

I call then *government,* or supreme administration, the legitimate exercise of the executive power, and prince or magistrate the man or the body entrusted with that administration.

In government reside the intermediate forces whose relations make up that of the whole to the whole, or of the Sovereign to the State. This last relation may be represented as that between the extreme terms of a continuous proportion, which has government as its mean proportional. The government gets from the Sovereign the orders it gives the people, and, for the State to be properly balanced, there must, when everything is reckoned in, be equality between the product or power of the government taken in itself, and the product or power of the citizens, who are on the one hand sovereign and on the other subject.

Furthermore, none of these three terms can be altered without the equality being instantly destroyed. If the Sovereign desires to govern, or the magistrate to give laws, or if the subjects refuse to obey, disorder takes the place of regularity, force and will no longer act together, and the State is dissolved and falls into despotism or anarchy. Lastly, as there is only one mean proportional between each relation, there is also only one good government possible for a State. But, as countless events may change the relations of a people, not only may different governments be good for different peoples, but also for the same people at different times.

In attempting to give some idea of the various relations that may hold between these two extreme terms, I shall take as an example the number of a people, which is the most easily expressible.

Suppose the State is composed of ten thousand citizens. The Sovereign can only be considered collectively and as a body; but each member, as being a subject, is regarded as an individual: thus the Sovereign is to the subject as ten thousand to one, i.e. each member of the State has as his share only a ten-thousandth part of the sovereign authority, although he is wholly under its control. If the people numbers a hundred thousand, the condition of the subject undergoes no change, and each equally is under the whole authority of the laws, while his vote, being reduced to one hundred thousandth part, has ten times less influence in drawing them up. The subject therefore remaining always a unit, the relation between him and the Sovereign increases with the number of the citizens. From this

---

[1] Thus at Venice the College, even in the absence of the Doge, is called "Most Serene Prince."

it follows that, the larger the State, the less the liberty.

When I say the relation increases, I mean that it grows more unequal. Thus the greater it is in the geometrical sense, the less relation there is in the ordinary sense of the word. In the former sense, the relation, considered according to quantity, is expressed by the quotient; in the latter, considered according to identity, it is reckoned by similarity.

Now, the less relation the particular wills have to the general will, that is, morals and manners to laws, the more should the repressive force be increased. The government, then, to be good, should be proportionately stronger as the people is more numerous.

On the other hand, as the growth of the State gives the depositaries of the public authority more temptations and chances of abusing their power, the greater the force with which the government ought to be endowed for keeping the people in hand, the greater too should be the force at the disposal of the Sovereign for keeping the government in hand. I am speaking, not of absolute force, but of the relative force of the different parts of the state.

It follows from this double relation that the continuous proportion between the Sovereign, the prince, and the people, is by no means an arbitrary idea, but a necessary consequence of the nature of the body politic. It follows further that, one of the extreme terms, viz. the people, as subject, being fixed and represented by unity, whenever the duplicate ratio increases or diminishes, the simple ratio does the same, and is changed accordingly. From this we see that there is not a single unique and absolute form of government, but as many governments differing in nature as there are States differing in size.

If, ridiculing this system, any one were to say that, in order to find the mean proportional and give form to the body of the government, it is only necessary, according to me, to find the square root of the number of the people, I should answer that I am here taking this number only as an instance; that the relations of which I am speaking are not measured by the number of men alone, but generally by the amount of action, which is a combination of a multitude of causes; and that, further, if, to save words, I borrow for a moment the terms of geometry, I am none the less well aware that moral quantities do not allow of geometrical accuracy.

The government is on a small scale what the body politic which includes it is on a great one. It is a moral person endowed with certain faculties, active like the Sovereign and passive like the State, and capable of being resolved into other similar relations. This accordingly gives rise to a new proportion, within which there is yet another, according to the arrangement of the magistracies, till an indivisible middle term is reached, i.e. a single ruler or supreme magistrate, who may be represented, in the midst of this progression, as the unity between the fractional and the ordinal series.

Without encumbering ourselves with this multiplication of terms, let us rest content with regarding government as a new body within the State, distinct from the people and the Sovereign, and intermediate between them.

There is between these two bodies this essential difference, that the State exists by itself, and the government only through the Sovereign. Thus the dominant will of the prince is, or should be, nothing but the general will or the law; his force is only the public force concentrated in his hands, and, as soon as he tries to base any absolute and independent act on his own authority, the tie that binds the whole together begins to be loosened. If finally the prince should come to have a particular will more active than the will of the Sovereign, and should employ the public force in his hands in obedience to this particular will, there would be, so to speak, two Sovereigns, one rightful and the other actual, the social union would evaporate instantly, and the body politic would be dissolved.

However, in order that the government may have a true existence and a real life distinguishing it from the body of the State, and in order that all its members may be able to act in concert and fulfil the end for which it was set up, it must have a particular personality, a sensibility common to its members, and a force and will of its own making for its preservation. This particular existence implies assemblies, councils, power of deliberation and decision, rights, titles, and privileges belonging exclusively to the prince and making the office of magistrate more honourable in proportion as it is more troublesome. The difficulties lie in the manner of so ordering this subordinate whole within the whole, that it in no way alters the general constitution by affirmation of its own, and always distinguishes the particular force it possesses, which is destined to aid in its preservation, from the public force, which is destined to the preservation of the State; and, in a word, is always ready to sacrifice the government to the people, and never to sacrifice the people to the government.

Furthermore, although the artificial body of the government is the work of another artificial body, and has, we may say, only a borrowed and subordinate life, this does not prevent it from being able to act with more or less vigour or promptitude, or from being, so to speak, in more or less robust health. Finally, without departing directly from the end for which it was instituted, it may deviate more or less from it, according to the manner of its constitution.

From all these differences arise the various relations which the government ought to bear to the body of the State, according to the accidental and particular relations by which the State itself is modified, for often the government that is best in itself will become the most pernicious, if the relations in which it stands have altered according to the defects of the body politic to which it belongs.

16. Democracy

He who makes the law knows better than any one else how it should be executed and interpreted. It seems then impossible to have a better constitution than that in which the executive and legislative powers are united; but this very fact renders the government in certain respects inadequate, because things which should be distinguished are confounded, and the prince and the Sovereign, being the same person, form, so to speak, no more than a government without government.

It is not good for him who makes the laws to execute them, or for the body of the people to turn its attention away from a general standpoint and devote it to particular objects. Nothing is more dangerous than the influence of private interests in public affairs, and the abuse of the laws by the government is a less evil than the corruption of the legislator, which is the inevitable sequel to a particular standpoint. In such a case, the State being altered in substance, all reformation becomes impossible. A people that would never misuse governmental powers would never misuse independence; a people that would always govern well would not need to be governed.

If we take the term in the strict sense, there never has been a real democracy, and there never will be. It is against the natural order for the many to govern and the few to be governed. It is unimaginable that the people should remain continually assembled to devote their time to public affairs, and it is clear that they cannot set up commissions for that purpose without the form of administration being changed.

In fact, I can confidently lay down as a principle that, when the functions of government are shared by several tribunals, the less numerous sooner or later acquire the greatest authority, if only because they are in position to expedite affairs, and power thus naturally comes into their hands.

Besides, how many conditions that are difficult to unite does such a government presuppose! First, a very small State, where the people can readily be got together and where each citizen can with ease know all the rest; secondly, great simplicity of manners, to prevent business from multiplying and raising thorny problems; next, a large measure of equality in rank and fortune, without which equality of rights and authority cannot long subsist; lastly, little or no luxury—for luxury either comes of riches or makes them necessary; it corrupts at once rich and poor, the rich by possession and the poor by covetousness; it sells the country to softness and vanity, and takes away from the State all its citizens, to make them slaves one to another, and one and all to public opinion.

This is why a famous writer has made virtue the fundamental principle of Republics; for all these conditions could not exist without virtue. But, for want of the necessary distinctions, that great thinker was often inexact, and sometimes obscure, and did not see that, the sovereign authority being everywhere the same, the same principle should be found in every well-constituted State, in a greater or less degree, it is true, according to the form of the government.

It may be added that there is no government so subject to civil wars and intestine agitations as democratic or popular government, because there is none which has so strong and continual a tendency to change to another form, or which demands more vigilance and courage for its maintenance as it is. Under such a constitution above all, the citizen should arm himself with strength and constancy, and say, every day of his life, what a virtuous Count Palatine said in the Diet of Poland: "Malo periculosam libertatem quam quietum servitium."

Were there a people of gods, their government would be democratic. So perfect a government is not for men.

17. Deputies or Representatives

As soon as public service ceases to be the chief business of the citizens, and they would rather serve with their money than with their persons, the State is not far from its fall. When it is necessary to march out to war, they pay troops and stay at home: when it is necessary to meet in council, they name deputies and stay at home. By reason of idleness and money, they end by having soldiers to enslave their country and representatives to sell it.

It is through the hustle of commerce and the arts, through the greedy self-interest of profit, and through softness and love of amenities that personal services are replaced by money payments. Men surrender a part of their profits in order to have time to increase them at leisure. Make gifts of money, and you will not be long without chains. The word "finance" is a slavish word, unknown in the city-state. In a country that is truly free, the citizens do everything with their own arms and nothing by means of money; so far from paying to be exempted from their duties, they would even pay for the privilege of fulfilling them themselves. I am far from taking the common view: I hold enforced labour to be less opposed to liberty than taxes.

The better the constitution of a State is, the more do public affairs encroach on private in the minds of the citizens. Private affairs are even of much less importance, because the aggregate of the common happiness furnishes a greater proportion of that of each individual, so that there is less for him to seek in particular cares. In a well-ordered city every man flies to the assemblies: under a bad government no one cares to stir a step to get to them, because no one is interested in what happens there, because it is foreseen that the general will will not prevail, and lastly because domestic cares are all-absorbing. Good laws lead to the making of better ones; bad ones bring about worse. As soon as any man says of the affairs of the State *What does it matter to me?* the State may be given up for lost.

The lukewarmness of patriotism, the activity of private interest, the vastness of States, conquest, and the abuse of government suggested the method of having deputies or representatives of the people in the national assemblies. These are what, in some countries, men have presumed to call the Third Estate. Thus the individual interest of two orders is put first and second; the public interest occupies only the third place.

Sovereignty, for the same reason as makes it inalienable, cannot be represented; it lies essentially in the general will, and will does not admit of representation: it is either the same, or other; there is no intermediate possibility. The deputies of the people, therefore, are not and cannot be its representatives: they are merely its stewards, and can carry through no definitive acts. Every law the people has not ratified in person is null and void—is, in fact, not a law. The people of England regards itself as free; but it is grossly mistaken; it is free only during the election of members of parliament. As soon as they are elected, slavery overtakes it, and it is nothing. The use it makes of the short moments of liberty it enjoys shows indeed that it deserves to lose them.

The idea of representation is modern; it comes to us from feudal government, from that iniquitous and absurd system which degrades humanity and dishonours the name of man. In ancient republics and even in monarchies, the people never had representatives; the word itself was unknown. It is very singular that in Rome, where the tribunes were so sacrosanct, it was never even imagined that they could usurp the functions of the people, and that in the midst of so great a multitude they never attempted to pass on their own authority a single *plebiscitum*. We can, however, form an idea of the difficulties caused sometimes by the people being so numerous, from what happened in the time of the Gracchi, when some of the citizens had to cast their votes from the roofs of buildings.

Where right and liberty are everything, disadvantages count for nothing. Among this wise people everything was given its just value, its lictors were allowed to do what its tribunes would never have dared to attempt; for it had no fear that its lictors would try to represent it.

To explain, however, in what way the tribunes did sometimes represent it, it is enough to conceive how the government represents the Sovereign. Law being purely the declaration of the general will, it is clear that, in the exercise of the legislative power, the people cannot be represented; but in that of the executive power, which is only the force that is applied to give the law effect, it both can and should be represented. We thus see that if we looked closely into the matter we should find that very few nations have any laws. However that may be, it is certain that the tribunes, possessing no executive power, could never represent the Roman people by right of the powers entrusted to them, but only by usurping those of the senate.

In Greece, all that the people had to do, it did for itself; it was constantly assembled in the public square. The Greeks lived in a mild climate; they had no natural greed; slaves did their work for them; their great concern was with liberty. Lacking the same advantages, how can you preserve the same rights? Your severer climates add to your needs; [1] for half the year your public squares are uninhabitable; the flatness of your languages unfits them for being heard in the open air; you sacrifice more for profit than for liberty, and fear slavery less than poverty.

What then? Is liberty maintained only by the help of slavery? It may be so. Extremes meet. Everything that is not in the course of nature has its disadvantages, civil society most of all. There are some unhappy circumstances in which we can only keep our liberty at others' expense, and where the citizen can be perfectly free only when the slave is most a slave. Such was the case with Sparta. As for you, modern peoples, you have no slaves, but you are slaves yourselves; you pay for their liberty with your

---

[1] To adopt in cold countries the luxury and effeminacy of the East is to desire to submit to its chains; it is indeed to bow to them far more inevitably in our case than in theirs.

own. It is in vain that you boast of this preference; I find in it more cowardice than humanity.

I do not mean by all this that it is necessary to have slaves, or that the right of slavery is legitimate: I am merely giving the reason why modern peoples, believing themselves to be free, have representatives, while ancient peoples had none. In any case, the moment a people allows itself to be represented, it is no longer free: it no longer exists.

All things considered, I do not see that it is possible henceforth for the Sovereign to preserve among us the exercise of its rights, unless the city is very small. But if it is very small, it will be conquered? No. I will show later on how the external strength of a great people may be combined with the convenient polity and good order of a small State.

18. Voting

It may be seen that the way in which general business is managed may give a clear enough indication of the actual state of morals and the health of the body politic. The more concert reigns in the assemblies, that is, the nearer opinion approaches unanimity, the greater is the dominance of the general will. On the other hand, long debates, dissensions, and tumult proclaim the ascendancy of particular interests and the decline of the State.

This seems less clear when two or more orders enter into the constitution, as patricians and plebeians did at Rome; for quarrels between these two orders often disturbed the comitia, even in the best days of the Republic. But the exception is rather apparent than real; for then, through the defect that is inherent in the body politic, there were, so to speak, two States in one, and what is not true of the two together is true of either separately. Indeed, even in the most stormy times, the *plebiscita* of the people, when the senate did not inter-fere with them, always went through quietly and by large majorities. The citizens having but one interest, the people had but a single will.

At the other extremity of the circle, unanimity recurs; this is the case when the citizens, having fallen into servitude, have lost both liberty and will. Fear and flattery then change votes into acclamation; deliberation ceases, and only worship or malediction is left. Such was the vile manner in which the senate expressed its views under the emperors. It did so sometimes with absurd precautions. Tacitus observes that, under Otho, the senators, while they heaped curses on Vitellius, contrived at the same time to make a deafening noise, in order that, should he ever become their master, he might not know what each of them had said.

On these various considerations depend the rules by which the methods of counting votes and comparing opinions should be regulated, according as the general will is more or less easy to discover, and the State more or less in its decline.

There is but one law which, from its nature, needs unanimous consent. This is the social compact; for civil association is the most voluntary of all acts. Every man being born free and his own master, no one, under any pretext whatsoever, can make any man subject without his consent. To decide that the son of a slave is born a slave is to decide that he is not born a man.

If then there are opponents when the social compact is made, their opposition does not invalidate the contract, but merely prevents them from being included in it. They are foreigners among citizens. When the State is instituted, residence constitutes consent; to dwell within its territory is to submit to the Sovereign.[1]

Apart from this primitive contract, the

---

[1] This should of course be understood as applying to a free State; for elsewhere family, goods, lack of a refuge, necessity, or violence may detain a man in a country against his will; and then his dwelling there no longer by itself implies his consent to the contract or to its violation.

vote of the majority always binds all the rest. This follows from the contract itself. But it is asked how a man can be both free and forced to conform to wills that are not his own. How are the opponents at once free and subject to laws they have not agreed to?

I retort that the question is wrongly put. The citizen gives his consent to all the laws, including those which are passed in spite of his opposition, and even those which punish him when he dares to break any of them. The constant will of all the members of the State is the general will; by virtue of it they are citizens and free.[2] When in the popular assembly a law is proposed, what the people is asked is not exactly whether it approves or rejects the proposal, but whether it is in conformity with the general will, which is their will. Each man, in giving his vote, states his opinion on that point; and the general will is found by counting votes. When therefore the opinion that is contrary to my own prevails, this proves neither more nor less than that I was mistaken, and that what I thought to be the general will was not so. If my particular opinion had carried the day I should have achieved the opposite of what was my

will; and it is in that case that I should not have been free.

This presupposes, indeed, that all the qualities of the general will still reside in the majority: when they cease to do so, whatever side a man may take, liberty is no longer possible.

In my earlier demonstration of how particular wills are substituted for the general will in public deliberation, I have adequately pointed out the practicable methods of avoiding this abuse; and I shall have more to say of them later on. I have also given the principles for determining the proportional number of votes for declaring that will. A difference of one vote destroys equality; a single opponent destroys unanimity; but between equality and unanimity, there are several grades of unequal division, at each of which this proportion may be fixed in accordance with the condition and the needs of the body politic.

There are two general rules that may serve to regulate this relation. First, the more grave and important the questions discussed, the nearer should the opinion that is to prevail approach unanimity. Secondly, the more the matter in hand calls for speed, the smaller the prescribed difference in the numbers of votes may be allowed to become: where an instant decision has to be reached, a majority of one vote should be enough. The first of these two rules seems more in harmony with the laws, and the second with practical affairs. In any case, it is the combination of them that gives the best proportions for determining the majority necessary.

---

[2] At Genoa, the word "Liberty" may be read over the front of the prisons and on the chains of the galley-slaves. This application of the device is good and just. It is indeed only malefactors of all estates who prevent the citizen from being free. In the country in which all such men were in the galleys, the most perfect liberty would be enjoyed.

CHAPTER 18

BURKE

THE unity of the Atlantic community, far from being a discovery of the twentieth century, has been evolving for three centuries. Its foundation is not the North Atlantic Treaty of 1949 but the English Revolution of 1640, the American Revolution of 1776, and the French Revolution of 1789. The Puritan Revolution of the sixteen-forties and the Glorious Revolution half a century later heralded a new way of life that is still the inspiration of British thought and action today. In politics, parliamentary government supplanted royal absolutism and slowly evolved into popular, democratic government. In economics, commercial and industrial wealth increasingly replaced land as the source of social prestige and influence. In the structure of society, the middle classes gradually became the dominating element, imprinting much of their outlook and morality on the upper and working classes. In religion, the erstwhile conception of a state church and identification of political orthodoxy with religious conformity was first weakened by the toleration of religious dissent and later more completely undermined by the growth of a scientific, humanist, secular philosophy. Locke in the science of society and Newton in the science of physical nature opened up a new world that came to its fullest flowering in the Age of Reason.

The American Revolution was the second act in the drama of democratic revolution. The colonists derived their political heritage from the English experience of 1640 and 1688, and the Revolution was caused by the attempt of the English—doomed to failure from the beginning—to apply to British subjects in North America doctrines and practices of government that had been repudiated through revolution and civil war at home. Moreover, the American Revolution was not only a war of independence but also a conflict between rivaling social classes. The victory of the American Revolution meant the predominance of the middle classes in the development of the new nation, dedicated to the equalitarian ideals of life, liberty, and the pursuit of happiness for all. As in the English revolutions of the seventeenth century, neither extreme radicalism nor ultraconservatism prevailed in the American Revolution. Internally there was less resistance to the revolutionary achievement in the United States than there was to the Puritan successes of the sixteen-forties in England, because even before the Revolution the absence of an aristocracy and the fuller acceptance of religious diversity in America allowed society to develop more freely than was possible in England before the Reform Act of 1832.

The example of the American Revolution was a standing challenge to the established order of Europe, dominated—from France to Siberia—by absolute monarchy, church, and aristocracy. The significance of the English Revolution of 1688 could not be so quickly discerned, because the monarchy continued as the symbol of traditional authority and the landowning classes still controlled both Houses of Parliament until 1832. As for the American Revolution, the absence of monarchy and aristocracy in the new society unmistakably underlined its belief in equality and opportunity. One of the main arguments of the antidemocratic side in the eighteenth century had been the impracticality of the democratic ideal, the insistence that popular government could never work in actuality, that it would quickly degenerate into chaos and anarchy. The sound sense and statesmanship of the American revolutionary leaders quickly turned the revolutionary experiment into a stable order, addressing itself, by its existence and success, to the oppressed everywhere as an invitation to rebellion. In 1824 Prince Metternich, the mouthpiece of European conservatism, said of the United States that "in fostering revolutions wherever they show themselves, in regretting those which have failed, in extending a helping hand to those which seem to prosper, they lend new strength to the apostles of sedition, and reanimate the courage of every conspirator."

The French Revolution, the third act in the drama of modern democratic revolution, began two years after the Constitution of the United States was framed. Peaceful reform would have been possible until the last minute, and the Anglophile, liberal-conservative element was at first in the ascendancy. But the *ancien régime* lacked the most elementary prudence and foresight, and thus made revolution inevitable. The Estates-General met, for the first time since 1614, on May 5, 1789, and on the following day the Third Estate assembled in separate session. The cleavage between the people on the one side, and church and aristocracy on the other, was thereby quickly revealed. Meeting separately, the Third Estate in effect declared itself to be the representative body of the whole nation: the Revolution had started.

No event in modern history so immediately and completely electrified the world as did the French Revolution, particularly after the storming of the Bastille on July 14, 1789. Charles James Fox, the leader of the English Whigs (or Liberals) called it the "greatest event" that had ever happened in the world, and "how much the best!" His remark reveals how, even when politics was mainly the business of a small aristocratic class, attitudes toward foreign countries were largely determined by ideological sympathies. Traditionally, the Tories (or Conservatives) had been the friends of France, although she was England's principal rival for world hegemony, because the *ancien régime* upheld the influence of hierarchy in religion, class in society, and authority in government. Precisely for these reasons the Whigs were anti-French, and also because the Revolution of 1688 was directed against a monarch who was in French pay and in closest sympathy with the French court. But the French Revolution reversed the two traditional attitudes in England. The new anti-French position of the Tories expressed hostility, not to the French people, but to the Jacobin ideals of Liberty, Fraternity, and Equality; similarly, the sudden sympathy of the Whigs, or at least their more radical wing, for France expressed the satisfaction that she had finally done in 1789 what England had accomplished a century before.

In the early stage of the Revolution few understood its long-term impact and significance. Some of the conservative forces in Europe even welcomed the Revolution as a sign of French weakness and decay; they failed to perceive the fresh vitality and vigorous ability of the new democratic leaders, whose aim was to make France not only free but great. The first to raise the issues of the Revolution from the plane of immediate profit and policy to that of principle and philosophy was Edmund Burke (1729–1797), whose *Reflections on the Revolution in France* (1790) was an immediate literary success in England and on the Continent. Moreover, it was a political event of the first order, stemming the flood of sympathy and enthusiasm that until then had been rushing forth from the hearts of the inarticulate masses of Europe, as well as from philosophers and poets who saw in the Revolution the dawn of a new humanity.

Burke's *Reflections* comforted the enemies of the Revolution ("Read it," King George III said to all who came to see him. "It will do you good—do you good! Every gentleman should read it") as much as it antagonized its friends, and it was at once answered by a mass of prorevolutionary books and pamphlets. The most important of those writings is Tom Paine's *Rights of Man* (1791–1792), a fiery answer to the *Reflections,* and—as a defense of French democracy —a worthy successor to his *Common Sense* (1776), one of the trail blazers of the Declaration of Independence.

Burke was born in Dublin in 1729, the son of a successful Irish-Protestant attorney. His mother was a Catholic who did not change her faith, and Burke's Catholic connection (his sister, too, was brought up as a Catholic) provided him with an early education in practical politics. Although Catholics formed the vast majority of the Irish population, they were cruelly oppressed by the ruling Protestant English aristocracy. A special "penal" code was used to exclude Catholics from property, public service, and the professions, reduce them to the state of second-class citizens in their own country, extirpate the Catholic religion, and destroy the sense, and very existence, of Irish nationality. Though Burke came to identify himself ultimately with England, his Irish background and experience always remained a powerful element in his outlook and sympathies.

In 1750 Burke went to London to prepare himself for the legal profession. But his heart was in literature and politics rather than in law, and he preferred the vagaries and uncertainties of the former to the security of the latter, even though his decision cost him his regular allowance from his father.

In 1756 Burke published his first work, *A Vindication of Natural Society.* A short essay, the *Vindication* contains nevertheless most of the key ideas of Burke, developed more exhaustively in his later, and more elaborate, writings. In the preface to the *Vindication* Burke expresses his lack of faith in the capacity of the ordinary person to think things out for himself, and asks, "what would become of the world if the practice of all moral duties, and the foundations of society, rested upon having their reasons made clear and demonstrative to every individual?" His supernatural approach to problems of politics becomes evident in the proposition that "civil government borrows a strength from ecclesiastical," and that in general the "ideas of religion and government are closely connected."

The chief purpose of the *Vindication* becomes evident—to discourage rational inquiry into political institutions as into religion, because the critical spirit of rationalism is bound to challenge, question, attack, and—finally—destroy the civil and religious foundations of society.

Underlying Burke's philosophy in the *Vindication,* published when he was only twenty-seven, is a deep feeling of *pessimism* that nourishes and colors all his thought: "On considering political societies, their origin, their constitution, and their effects, I have sometimes been in a good deal more than doubt whether the Creator did ever really intend man for a state of happiness. He has mixed in his cup a number of natural evils (in spite of the boasts of stoicism they are evils), and every endeavor which the art and policy of mankind has used from the beginning of the world to this day, in order to alleviate or cure them, has only served to introduce new mischiefs, or to aggravate and inflame the old."

Burke approached problems of society in the knowledge that "we owe an implicit reverance to all the institutions of our ancestors," and that we should consider such institutions "with all that modesty" in which a received opinion should be examined.

Burke was even more eager to get into politics than into literature, and he finally entered Parliament at thirty-seven, a comparatively late age in those days. Although he was one of the most brilliant political speakers and writers of his time, he was never able to attain cabinet office; his sincere and impassioned effort to dedicate his life to the English ruling classes did not remove the obstacle of his being a newcomer in English politics. Burke's position was made still more vulnerable by his lifelong financial troubles. He lived above his means, purchased a large estate that he could not pay for, and incurred enormous debts that would have driven him into bankruptcy and disgrace had he not been saved by the generosity of his aristocratic benefactors. Burke's reputation also suffered from speculations, which generally failed, and from his associations with financial adventurers and other persons of doubtful standing. In addition, anti-Catholic bigotry affected his career adversely. His mother was known as a loyal Catholic, he married a Catholic, and he himself was suspected of Catholic sympathies and Jesuit beliefs and practices. In June, 1780, anti-Catholic rioting took place in London for ten days, and Burke's life was openly threatened by the mob.

Burke's *veneration of aristocracy* was not a matter of snobbery but of profound conviction that aristocracy was a part of the divinely ordained scheme of governing society, and he accepted his social inferiority with good cheer. Toward the end of his life he said of himself that he was not "swaddled and rocked and dandled" into a political career: "I possessed not one of the qualities, nor cultivated one of the arts, that recommend men to the favor and protection of the great. I was not made for a minion or a tool. As little did I follow the trade of winning the hearts, by imposing on the understandings of the people. At every step of my progress in life, for in every step was I traversed and opposed, and at every turnpike I met, I was obliged to show my passport, and again and again to prove my sole title to the honor of being useful to my country, by a proof that I was not wholly unacquainted with its laws and the whole system of its interests both abroad and at home; otherwise no rank, no toleration even for me." Although Burke was completely rational in the appraisal of individual members of the aristocracy, especially when they were his political opponents, he never challenged the collective right of the aristocratic class to govern Britain and her empire.

Burke's *Reflections on the Revolution in France* (1790) was the outstanding event in his literary as well as political career. Until the publication of the book, liberal sympathies for the Revolution had been expressed more often and more vigorously than criticisms; the *Reflections* (followed swiftly, in 1791, by *A Letter to a Member of the National Assembly, Thoughts on French Affairs*, and *An Appeal from the Old to the New Whigs*) turned the tables on the liberal sympathizers by enlarging the scope of the debate. What had started out as a discussion of the French Revolution became a searching inquiry into the nature of reform and revolution in general, and out of this inquiry emerged the bible of modern conservatism.

The impact of the *Reflections* was due as much to its subtlety of thought and moral elevation as to its style and language, an arresting mixture of poetry, philosophy, and religious mysticism, all suffused with a penetrating sense of practical wisdom. The French Revolution was, for Burke, not the result of deep-seated historical conflicts and forces, but of wrong doctrines of philosophers who were animated by fanatical atheism, and of vile ambitions of politicians who were driven by opportunist lust for power. Burke is particularly vehement in his denunciation of French philosophers and men of letters—"robbers and assassins: Never before, did a den of bravoes and banditti, assume the garb and tone of an academy of philosophers."

Burke was quick enough to realize that the French Revolution was more than an internal French affair, that it was a "revolution of doctrine and theoretic dogma," and he attacked the state that emerged from it as a "college of armed fanatics, for the propagation of the principles of assassination, robbery, fraud, faction, oppression, and impiety." Wisdom is most terrified by fanaticism, its worst enemy, against which it is the least able to furnish any kind of remedy, and Burke therefore called for a European crusade to crush the revolutionary spirit by force of arms. He was convinced that no monarchy would be safe "as long as this strange, nameless, wild, enthusiastic thing is established in the center of Europe." After England, in concert with other European powers, became involved in war with France, Burke emphasized that the war was directed, not against the French people, but against Jacobin democracy, which could not be shut out by fortresses and territorial limits. In the French Revolution Burke saw a tyranny of the multitude, which is but "a multiplied tyranny."

Against the individualist conception of society of Locke and the French philosophers Burke put forward the *organic theory:* "Society is indeed a contract. Subordinate contracts for objects of mere occasional interest may be dissolved at pleasure—but the state ought not to be considered as nothing better than a partnership agreement in a trade of pepper and coffee, calico or tobacco, or some other such low concern, to be taken up for a little temporary interest, and to be dissolved by the fancy of the parties. It is to be looked on with other reverence; because it is not a partnership in things subservient only to the gross animal existence of a temporary and perishable nature. It is a partnership in all science; a partnership in all art; a partnership in every virtue, and in all perfection. As the ends of such a partnership cannot be obtained in many generations, it becomes a partnership not only between those who are living, but between those who are living, those who are dead and those who are to be born." Because society is the product of a continuous stream of generation cooperating with generation, aiming at the good life in its fullest measure, the burden of proof lies on those "who tear to pieces the whole frame and contexture of their country."

Burke's ideal of statesmanship avoids the extremes of tearing down blindly the existing order and of resisting change at all cost: "A disposition to preserve, and an ability to improve, taken together, would be my standard of a statesman." He sharply distinguishes reform from innovation, which generally derives from a selfish temper and confined views. Whatever innovation, or "hot reformation," can accomplish is bound to be crude, harsh, indigested, mixed with imprudence and injustice, and contrary to human nature and human institutions. *True reform,* which can be brought about only by disinterested statesmen, must be *early* in the interest of government, and *temperate* in the interest of the people, because only temperate reforms are permanent and allow room for growth: "Whenever we improve, it is right to leave room for further improvement."

Every revolution contains some evil, Burke says, as it inevitably destroys part of the moral capital, the good will, of the community, and the moral capital of future generations should be considered as a trust that must not be treated lightly. The English Revolution of 1688 was "a revolution, not made, but prevented," because the nation was on the defensive, seeking to preserve its institutions rather than to subvert or destroy them. The monarchy was continued, and the nation kept "the same ranks, the same orders, the same privileges, the same franchises, the same rules for property, the same subordinations," and, above all, the Revolution was followed by a "happy settlement." Burke contrasts the English Revolution of 1688 with the French Revolution of 1789, in which he sees but destruction, anarchy, and terror.

Burke denies the validity of the central doctrine of democracy: that only the governed have the right to determine who is to govern them, and that all votes count equally. He opposes this democratic method as an "arithmetic" devoid of meaning and thinks of representation in terms of historic interests, such as the Lords, the Commons, the monarchy, the Established Church, rather than in terms of individual citizens. Burke adheres to the medieval idea that man is politically significant, not as an individual citizen, but solely as a member of a group to which he belongs socially or economically. This theory of *corporate representation* was later supported by Hegel and has found its perverted expression more recently in the "corporate state" of the Nazi-Fascist type.

Burke was liberal enough not to desire the oppression of persons of low station, like hairdressers and working tallow chandlers, provided that they stay in their places: "Such descriptions of men ought not to suffer oppression from the state; but the state suffers oppression, if such as they, either individually or collectively, are permitted to rule." Because of his firm conviction that wealth and aristocracy were the repositories of political wisdom and experience, he stubbornly resisted any widening of the suffrage. Under the then existing system of "rotten boroughs," small hamlets were represented in Parliament, whereas large urban communities were not represented at all or grossly underrepresented. This system soon brought England to the brink of revolution, but it was adjudged by Burke to be "adequate to all the purposes for which a representation of the people can be desired or devised." In fact, Burke held that the suffrage ought to be further limited, rather than broadened, if any changes were to be made, because of the "prostitute and daring venality, the corruption of manners, the idleness and profligacy of the lower sort of voters."

Whereas Locke attached to *property* the qualification that it was originally equal, Burke frankly states the doctrine that the "characteristic essence of property, formed out of the combined principles of its acquisition and conservation, is to be *unequal.*" The inequality of property that Burke defended was closely related to his conception of society in which rank and privilege played such a large part. Similarly, Burke fully perceived and approved of political inequality as the concomitant of economic inequality. "Hereditary property and hereditary distinction" wholly composed the House of Lords, and he was pleased that the House of Commons was also made up (in his time) of large property owners.

As to the unpropertied masses, Burke wanted them to be content with *virtual representation,* under which, as he said in a letter to Sir Hercules Langrishe (January 3, 1792), "there is a communion of interests, and a sympathy in feelings and desires between those who act in the name of any description of people, and the people in whose name they act, though the trustees are not actually chosen by them. This is virtual representation. Such a representation I think to be, in many cases, even better than the actual."

Moreover, apart from the direct and explicit support that Burke gave to the sanctity of property and its privileges in government and society, his indirect and implicit support was even more important. What mattered most was that Burke emphasized the values of prescription, inheritance, rank, and distinction, all of which helped to buttress the cause of inequality of property and political rights.

Burke saw society, not in terms of equal individuals, but of unequal groups and historically recognized interests. Property is such an interest, founded on *prescription,* rather than on natural law or abstract reasoning. Aristocracy and monarchy are also institutions based on prescription. Though property is not the only criterion of the privileged classes and interests that Burke deems worthy to rule the nation, he is keenly conscious of the connections between property and the established order based on privilege and rank. The French Revolution was, for Burke, a direct threat to the traditional connection of property and political rule, and he defines Jacobinism as "the revolt of the enterprising talents of a country against its property." The attempt to level inequality never ends in equality, Burke says. Every society has various descriptions of citizens, and "some description must be uppermost." The levelers therefore merely pervert the natural order of society by their abstract schemes that interfere with its proper constitution.

The only time that Burke seems to relinquish his organic conceptions of man and society, when he talks the cold-blooded language of the profit-seeking entrepreneur, is in his discussion of labor, particularly in his *Thoughts and Details on Scarcity* (1795). There is little in this pamphlet that Herbert Spencer could not have wholeheartedly endorsed. Labor, Burke argues, is "a commodity" and as such an article of trade, subject to the fluctuations of supply and demand on the market: "The impossibility of the subsistence of a man, who carries his labor to a market, is totally beside the question in this way of viewing it. The only question is, what is it worth to the buyer?" The poverty of the laboring people, Burke held, was due to their large numbers: "Numbers in their nature imply poverty." Even if all the throats of the rich were cut, the distribution of their wealth would not yield enough bread and cheese for one night's supper of the laboring classes. But, Burke continues, the throats of the rich ought not to be cut, because the rich are the trustees for those who labor, and their accumulated hoards are the banking houses of the poor. All that the rich receive for their office of trusteeship is a "very trifling commission and discount."

If the worker does not earn enough for his subsistence, the state has no right to interfere by guaranteeing minimum wages, and the worker then passes out of the jurisdiction of economic or political laws and becomes an object of mercy and charity. Burke concedes that the duty to practice charity toward the indigent is "imperfect," that is, it cannot be enforced, but he is unwilling to go beyond such voluntary provision for the helpless poor. Whereas Burke rejects the concept of natural law when discussing the Rights of Man, he thinks differently when it comes to the Rights of Commerce: "We, the people, ought to be made sensible, that it is not in breaking the laws of commerce, which are the laws of nature, and consequently the laws of God, that we are to place our hope of softening the divine displeasure to remove any calamity under which we suffer, or which hangs over us."

Burke never composed a systematic treatise of politics, like Hobbes' *Leviathan* or Locke's *Two Treatises of Government*, partly because he was a busy parliamentarian and partly because he needed a concrete issue around which he could develop his general principles. His political ideas cannot be found in one place but have to be gathered from his books, speeches, essays, and letters, although the *Reflections* will always occupy first place. Yet if Burke does not state anywhere a systematic theory of politics, his thought is always cast in forms which do not vary greatly. Above all, Burke distrusts metaphysics and a priori reasoning, and he constantly reiterates the plea that politics is a matter of prudence, expediency, circumstance, utility, experience, history, loyalty, and reverence, and not of abstract speculation: "The science of constructing a commonwealth, or renovating it, or reforming it, is, like every other experimental science, not to be taught *a priori*." Circumstances give to every principle its distinguishing color and discriminating effect: "The circumstances are what render every civil and political scheme beneficial or noxious to mankind." The world of contingency and political combination is always larger than we can imagine in advance, and no lines can be laid down for civil or political wisdom. They are incapable of exact definition.

Politics ought to be adjusted, not to reason, but to human nature, and Burke urges that the practical consequences of any political tenet "go a great way in deciding upon its value. Political problems do not primarily concern truth or falsehood. They relate to good or evil. What in the result is likely to produce evil, is politically false: that which is productive of good, politically true." Burke expresses this purely *utilitarian* and *pragmatic* viewpoint by saying that things that are not practicable are not desirable, and that the consequences of any assumed rights "are of great moment in deciding upon their validity." No universal statement can be made on moral and political subjects, and pure metaphysics does not apply to them. The lines of morality are not like those of mathematics: they admit exceptions and demand modifications, arrived at, not by the process of logic, but by the rules of prudence: "Prudence is not only the first in rank of the virtues political and moral, but she is the director, the regulator, the standard of them all. Metaphysics cannot live without definition; but prudence is cautious how she defines."

In discussing human *liberty* Burke is less interested in the right to freedom than in the aptitude for it. Men are qualified for civil liberty in exact proportion to their self-control, love of justice, sobriety, and soundness of understanding. Society must have a controlling power, and the less of it there is within the minds and hearts of men, the more there must be without: "It is ordained in the eternal constitution of things that men of intemperate minds cannot be free. Their passions forge their fetters." Similarly, Burke refuses to lay down an abstract and general definition of *rights* to which every man is entitled, because they are "a thing to be settled by convention." Government itself is not primarily designed to provide and protect rights but is "a contrivance of human wisdom to provide for human *wants*." The rights of men are their advantages and are in "a sort of *middle*, incapable of definition, but not impossible to be discerned." The balancing of conflicting rights and advantages is a most complex process of compromise, of "adding, subtracting, multiplying, and dividing, morally and not metaphysically or mathematically, true moral denominations."

In appraising the political judgment of Burke it ought to be remembered that he was on the side of the future on three of the principal political issues of his time: Ireland, India, and the American colonies. In all three instances his sympathies were magnanimous, his judgment farsighted, and for these reasons he will always be an abiding inspiration to liberal statesmen. In his attitude toward the French Revolution, Burke (who knew France firsthand from only one visit in 1773) was proved wrong in the light of the future, but he was also wrong from his own viewpoint. France did not degenerate into anarchy, as Burke claimed, and she more than regained her lost military strength and international influence under the impetus of the Revolution. Far from destroying the respect for property, as Burke feared, the French Revolution firmly established a new legal and political order that tenaciously protected the rights of property. Burke profoundly foresaw that the Revolution would end in a military dictatorship; yet it was not the original aims of the Revolution but the military coalition of Europe (including England) against France that paved the way for Napoleon. Moreover, the rule of Napoleon was only an interlude, and the liberating effect of the Revolution proved stronger than the temporary dictatorship.

In comparing the French with the English Revolution, Burke always pointed to the violent and radical character of the first, contrasted with the peaceable and conservative character of the second. Yet the obvious parallel to the French Revolution is not the Bloodless Revolution of 1688, but the very bloody revolution and civil wars of the sixteen-forties, culminating in the execution of Charles I. In cutting off the head of their monarch the French were no more than good disciples of the English, and their Revolution was, at the start, much more peaceful than the Puritan Revolution.

Had there been no military coalition of Europe (for which Burke himself labored with utmost frenzy) against revolutionary France, no invasion of her soil by the Prussians and their allies, it is at least conceivable that France might have worked her passage from royal autocracy to popular government without so much violence and bloodshed. Whereas the English Civil War of the sixteen-forties was wholly the product of irreconcilable domestic forces, the civil strife that developed in France after the outbreak of the Revolution was largely the result of foreign interference, in which the King himself was treacherously implicated.

Above all, Burke failed to see that revolution is not necessarily the result of metaphysical fanaticism but may spring from the soil of experience, the experience of protracted suffering. The breakdown and failure of social and political institutions are just as much a matter of experience as are their growth and development. As Burke himself said, political problems do not primarily concern truth or falsehood, but good or evil, and political principles must be judged by their results. Yet in the matter of the French Revolution, Burke was unwilling to await its consequences because he *knew*, without a shadow of his usual doubt and caution, that the French revolutionaries were no more than a band of robbers and assassins. In the same manner, he also idealized the conditions of prerevolutionary France and its basic institutions, the monarchy, church, and aristocracy. Disregarding the oppressions, humiliations, and frustrations of the French people before the Revolution, Burke was shocked and shaken by the sufferings of Queen Marie Antoinette in a "nation of men of honor, and of cavaliers." Tom Paine's famous reply in the *Rights of Man* to this passage in the *Reflections* is that Burke "pities the plumage, but forgets the dying bird."

Yet, when all is said and done, no reader of Burke, and of his *Reflections* in particular, can escape the impact of a mature, imaginative, and penetrating mind: "The nature of man is intricate; the objects of society are of the greatest possible complexity; and therefore no simple disposition or direction of power can be suitable either to man's nature, or to the quality of his affairs." Bismarck defined politics as the "art of the possible," and this is one of the guiding principles of Burke's approach to politics. Whether or not one accepts the tenets of his political creed, one finds on almost every page of the *Reflections* epigrammatic gems of wisdom and observation that make his thought a permanent inspiration even for those who feel more optimistic about the possibilities of democracy than Burke did.

BURKE

Reflections on the Revolution in France *

1. The French Revolution and the British Constitution

Our oldest reformation is that of Magna Charta. You will see that Sir Edward Coke, that great oracle of our law, and indeed all the great men who follow him, to Blackstone, are industrious to prove the pedigree of our liberties. They endeavour to prove, that the ancient charter, the Magna Charta of King John, was connected with another positive charter from Henry I, and that both the one and the other were nothing more than a reaffirmance of the still more ancient standing law of the kingdom. In the matter of fact, for the greater part, these authors appear to be in the right; perhaps not always; but if the lawyers mistake in some particulars, it proves my position still the more strongly; because it demonstrates the powerful prepossession towards antiquity, with which the minds of all our lawyers and legislators, and of all the people whom they wish to influence, have been

* From Edmund Burke, *Reflections on the Revolution in France* (1790). In form, it is addressed to a French correspondent of Burke.

always filled; and the stationary policy of this kingdom in considering their most sacred rights and franchises as an *inheritance*.

In the famous law of the 3rd of Charles I, called the *Petition of Right*, the parliament says to the king, "Your subjects have *inherited* this freedom," claiming their franchises not on abstract principles "as the rights of men," but as the rights of Englishmen, and as a patrimony derived from their forefathers. Selden, and the other profoundly learned men, who drew this Petition of Right, were as well acquainted, at least, with all the general theories concerning the "rights of men," as any of the discoursers in our pulpits, or on your tribune; full as well as Dr. Price, or as the Abbé Sieyes. But, for reasons worthy of that practical wisdom which superseded their theoretic science, they preferred this positive, recorded, *hereditary* title to all which can be dear to the man and the citizen, to that vague speculative right, which exposed their sure inheritance to be scrambled for and torn to pieces by every wild, litigious spirit.

The same policy pervades all the laws which have since been made for the preservation of our liberties. In the 1st of William and Mary, in the famous statute, called the Declaration of Right, the two Houses utter not a syllable of "a right to frame a government for themselves." You will see, that their whole care was to secure the religion, laws, and liberties, that had been long possessed, and had been lately endangered. "Taking into their most serious consideration the *best* means for making such an establishment, that their religion, laws, and liberties might not be in danger of being again subverted," they auspicate all their proceedings, by stating as some of those *best* means, "in the *first place*" to do "as their *ancestors in like cases have usually* done for vindicating their *ancient* rights and liberties, to *declare*";—and then they pray the king and queen, "that it may be *declared* and enacted, that *all and singular the rights and liberties asserted and declared*, are the true *ancient* and indubitable rights and liberties of the people of this kingdom."

You will observe, that from Magna Charta to the Declaration of Right, it has been the uniform policy of our constitution to claim and assert our liberties, as an *entailed inheritance* derived to us from our forefathers, and to be transmitted to our posterity; as an estate specially belonging to the people of this kingdom, without any reference whatever to any other more general or prior right. By this means our constitution preserves a unity in so great a diversity of its parts. We have an inheritable crown; an inheritable peerage; and a House of Commons and a people inheriting privileges, franchises, and liberties, from a long line of ancestors.

This policy appears to me to be the result of profound reflection; or rather the happy effect of following nature, which is wisdom without reflection, and above it. A spirit of innovation is generally the result of a selfish temper and confined views. People will not look forward to posterity, who never look backward to their ancestors. Be-

sides, the people of England well know, that the idea of inheritance furnishes a sure principle of conservation and a sure principle of transmission; without at all excluding a principle of improvement. It leaves acquisition free; but it secures what it acquires. Whatever advantages are obtained by a state proceeding on these maxims, are locked fast as in a sort of family settlement; grasped as in a kind of mortmain for ever. By a constitutional policy, working after the pattern of nature, we receive, we hold, we transmit our government and our privileges, in the same manner in which we enjoy and transmit our property and our lives. The institutions of policy, the goods of fortune, the gifts of providence, are handed down to us, and from us, in the same course and order. Our political system is placed in a just correspondence and symmetry with the order of the world, and with the mode of existence decreed to a permanent body composed of transitory parts; wherein, by the disposition of a stupendous wisdom, moulding together the great mysterious incorporation of the human race, the whole, at one time, is never old, or middle-aged, or young, but, in a condition of unchangeable constancy, moves on through the varied tenor of perpetual decay, fall, renovation, and progression. Thus, by preserving the method of nature in the conduct of the state, in what we improve, we are never wholly new; in what we retain, we are never wholly obsolete. By adhering in this manner and on those principles to our forefathers, we are guided not by the superstition of antiquarians, but by the spirit of philosophic analogy. In this choice of inheritance we have given to our frame of polity the image of a relation in blood; binding up the constitution of our country with our dearest domestic ties; adopting our fundamental laws into the bosom of our family affections; keeping inseparable, and cherishing with the warmth of all their combined and mutually reflected charities, our state, our hearths, our sepulchres, and our altars.

Through the same plan of a conformity

to nature in our artificial institutions, and by calling in the aid of her unerring and powerful instincts, to fortify the fallible and feeble contrivances of our reason, we have derived several other, and those no small benefits, from considering our liberties in the light of an inheritance. Always acting as if in the presence of canonized forefathers, the spirit of freedom, leading in itself to misrule and excess, is tempered with an awful gravity. This idea of a liberal descent inspires us with a sense of habitual native dignity, which prevents that upstart insolence almost inevitably adhering to and disgracing those who are the first acquirers of any distinction. By this means our liberty becomes a noble freedom. It carries an imposing and majestic aspect. It has a pedigree and illustrating ancestors. It has its bearings, and its ensigns armorial. It has its gallery of portraits; its monumental inscriptions; its records, evidences, and titles. We procure reverence to our civil institutions on the principle upon which nature teaches us to revere individual men; on account of their age, and on account of those from whom they are descended. All your sophisters cannot produce anything better adapted to preserve a rational and manly freedom than the course that we have pursued, who have chosen our nature rather than our speculations, our breasts rather than our inventions, for the great conservatories and magazines of our rights and privileges.

You might, if you pleased, have profited of our example, and have given to your recovered freedom a correspondent dignity. Your privileges, though discontinued, were not lost to memory. Your constitution, it is true, whilst you were out of possession, suffered waste and dilapidation; but you possessed in some parts the walls, and. in all, the foundations, of a noble and venerable castle. You might have repaired those walls; you might have built on those old foundations. Your constitution was suspended before it was perfected; but you had the elements of a constitution very nearly as good as could be wished. In your old states you possessed that variety of parts corresponding with the various descriptions of which your community was happily composed; you had all that combination, and all that opposition of interests, you had that action and counteraction, which, in the natural and in the political world, from the reciprocal struggle of discordant powers, draws out the harmony of the universe. These opposed and conflicting interests, which you considered as so great a blemish in your old and in our present constitution, interpose a salutary check to all precipitate resolutions. They render deliberation a matter not of choice, but of necessity; they make all change a subject of *compromise*, which naturally begets moderation; they produce *temperaments* preventing the sore evil of harsh, crude, unqualified reformations; and rendering all the headlong exertions of arbitrary power, in the few or in the many, for ever impracticable. Through that diversity of members and interests, general liberty had as many securities as there were separate views in the several orders; whilst by pressing down the whole by the weight of a real monarchy, the separate parts would have been prevented from warping, and starting from their allotted places.

You had all these advantages in your ancient states; but you chose to act as if you had never been moulded into civil society, and had everything to begin anew. You began ill, because you began by despising everything that belonged to you. You set up your trade without a cap'tal. If the last generations of your country appeared without much lustre in your eyes, you might have passed them by, and derived your claims from a more early race of ancestors. Under a pious predilection for those ancestors, your imaginations would have realized in them a standard of virtue and wisdom, beyond the vulgar practice of the hour: and you would have risen with the example to whose imitation you aspired. Respecting your forefathers, you would have been taught to respect yourselves. You would not have chosen to consider the French as a people of yesterday, as a nation of low-born servile wretches until the emancipating year of 1789. In order to furnish, at the expense of your honour, an excuse to your apologists here for several enormities of yours, you would not have been content to be represented as a gang of Maroon slaves, suddenly broke loose from the house of bondage, and therefore to be pardoned for your abuse of the liberty to which you were not accustomed, and ill fitted. Would it not, my worthy friend, have been wiser to have you thought, what I, for one, always thought you, a generous and gallant nation, long misled to your disadvantage by your high and romantic sentiments of fidelity, honour, and loyalty; that events had been unfavourable to you, but that you were not enslaved through any illiberal or servile disposition; that in your most devoted submission, you were actuated by a principle of public spirit, and that it was your country you worshipped, in the person of your king? Had you made it to be understood, that in the delusion of this amiable error you had gone farther than your wise ancestors; that you were resolved to resume your ancient privileges, whilst you preserved the spirit of your ancient and your recent loyalty and honour; or if, diffident of yourselves, and not clearly discerning the almost obliterated constitution of your ancestors, you had looked to your neighbours in this land, who had kept alive the ancient principles and models of the old common law of Europe meliorated and adapted to its present state—by following wise examples you would have given new examples of wisdom to the world. You would have rendered the cause of liberty venerable in the eyes of every worthy mind in every nation. You would have shamed despotism from the earth, by showing that freedom was not only reconcilable, but, as when well disciplined it is, auxiliary to law. You would have had an unoppressive but a productive revenue. You would have had a flourishing commerce to feed it. You would have had a free constitution; a potent monarchy; a disciplined army; a reformed and venerated clergy; a mitigated but spirited nobility, to lead your virtue, not to overlay it; you would have had a liberal order of commons, to emulate and to recruit that nobility; you would have had a protected, satisfied, laborious, and obedient people, taught to seek and to recognise the happiness that is to be found by virtue in all conditions; in which consists the true moral equality of mankind, and not in that monstrous fiction, which, by inspiring false ideas and vain expectations into men destined to travel in the obscure walk of laborious life, serves only to aggravate and embitter that real inequality, which it never can remove; and which the order of civil life establishes as much for the benefit of those whom it must leave in a humble state, as those whom it is able to exalt to a condition more splendid, but not more happy. You had a smooth and easy career of felicity and glory laid open to you, beyond anything recorded in the history of the world; but you have shown that difficulty is good for man.

Compute your gains: see what is got by those extravagant and presumptuous speculations which have taught your leaders to despise all their predecessors, and all their contemporaries, and even to despise themselves, until the moment in which they became truly despicable. By following those false lights, France has bought undisguised calamities at a higher price than any nation has purchased the most unequivocal blessings! France has bought poverty by crime! France has not sacrificed her virtue to her interest, but she has abandoned her interest, that she might prostitute her virtue. All other nations have begun the fabric of a new government, or the reformation of an old, by establishing originally, or by enforcing with greater exactness, some rites or other of religion. All other people have laid the foundations of civil freedom in severer manners, and a system of a more austere and masculine morality. France, when she let loose the reins of regal authority, doubled the license of a ferocious dissoluteness in manners, and of an insolent irreligion in opinions and practices; and has extended through all ranks of life, as if she were communicating some privilege, or laying open some secluded benefit, all the unhappy corruptions that usually were the disease of wealth and power. This is one of the new principles of equality in France.

In the calling of the states-general of France, the first thing that struck me, was a great departure from the ancient course. I found the representation for the third estate composed of six hundred persons. They were equal in number to the representatives of both the other orders. If the orders were to act separately, the number would not, beyond the consideration of the expense, be of much moment. But when it became apparent that the three orders were to be melted down into one, the policy and necessary effect of this numerous representation became obvious. A very small desertion from either of the other two orders must throw the power of both into the hands of the third. In fact, the whole power of the state was soon resolved into that body. Its due composition became therefore of infinitely the greater importance.

Judge, Sir, of my surprise, when I found that a very great proportion of the Assembly (a majority, I believe, of the members who attended) was composed of practitioners in the law. It was composed, not of distinguished magistrates, who had given pledges to their country of their science, prudence, and integrity; not of leading advocates, the glory of the bar; not of renowned professors in universities;—but for the far greater part, as it must in such a number, of the inferior, unlearned, mechanical, merely instrumental members of the profession. There were distinguished exceptions; but the general composition was of obscure provincial advocates, of stewards of petty local jurisdictions, country attorneys, notaries, and the whole train of the ministers of municipal litigation, the fomenters and conductors of the petty war of village vexation. From the moment I read the list, I saw distinctly, and very nearly as it has happened, all that was to follow.

The degree of estimation in which any profession is held becomes the standard of the estimation in which the professors hold themselves. Whatever the personal merits of many individual lawyers might have been, and in many it was undoubtedly very considerable, in that military kingdom no part of the profession had been much regarded, except the highest of all, who often united to their professional offices great family splendour, and were invested with great power and authority. These certainly were highly respected, and even with no small degree of awe. The next rank was not much esteemed; the mechanical part was in a very low degree of repute.

Whenever the supreme authority is vested in a body so composed, it must evidently produce the consequences of supreme authority placed in the hands of men not taught habitually to respect themselves; who had no previous fortune in character at stake; who could not be expected to bear with moderation, or to conduct with discretion, a power, which they themselves, more than any others, must be surprised to find in their hands. Who could flatter himself that these men, suddenly, and, as it were, by enchantment, snatched from the humblest rank of subordination, would not be intoxicated with their unprepared greatness? Who could conceive that men, who are habitually meddling, daring, subtle, active, of litigious dispositions and unquiet minds, would easily fall back into their old condition of obscure contention, and laborious, low, and unprofitable chicane? Who could doubt but that, at any expense to the state, of which they understood nothing, they must pursue their private interests which they understood but too well? It was not an event depending on chance, or contingency. It was inevitable; it was necessary; it was planted in the nature of things. They must *join* (if their capacity did not permit them to *lead*) in any project which could procure to them a *litigious constitution;* which could lay open to them those innumerable lucrative jobs, which follow in the train of all great convulsions and revolutions in the

REFLECTIONS ON THE REVOLUTION IN FRANCE 479

state, and particularly in all great and violent permutations of property. Was it to be expected that they would attend to the stability of property, whose existence had always depended upon whatever rendered property questionable, ambiguous, and insecure? Their objects would be enlarged with their elevation, but their disposition and habits, and mode of accomplishing their designs, must remain the same.

Well! but these men were to be tempered and restrained by other descriptions, of more sober and more enlarged understandings. Were they then to be awed by the supereminent authority and awful dignity of a handful of country clowns, who have seats in that Assembly, some of whom are said not to be able to read and write? and by not a greater number of traders, who, though somewhat more instructed, and more conspicuous in the order of society, had never known anything beyond their counting-house. No! both these descriptions were more formed to be overborne and swayed by the intrigues and artifices of lawyers, than to become their counterpoise. With such a dangerous disproportion, the whole must needs be governed by them. To the faculty of law was joined a pretty considerable proportion of the faculty of medicine. This faculty had not, any more than that of the law, possessed in France its just estimation. Its professors, therefore, must have the qualities of men not habituated to sentiments of dignity. But supposing they had ranked as they ought to do, and as with us they do actually, the sides of sick beds are not the academies for forming statesmen and legislators. Then came the dealers in stocks and funds, who must be eager, at any expense, to change their ideal paper wealth for the more solid substance of land. To these were joined men of other descriptions, from whom as little knowledge of, or attention to, the interests of a great state was to be expected, and as little regard to the stability of any institution; men formed to be instruments, not controls. Such in general was the composition of the Tiers État in the National Assembly;

in which was scarcely to be perceived the slightest traces of what we call the natural landed interest of the country.

We know that the British House of Commons, without shutting its doors to any merit in any class, is, by the sure operation of adequate causes, filled with everything illustrious in rank, in descent, in hereditary and in acquired opulence, in cultivated talents, in military, civil, naval, and politic distinction, that the country can afford. But supposing, what hardly can be supposed as a case, that the House of Commons should be composed in the same manner with the Tiers État in France, would this dominion of chicane be borne with patience, or even conceived without horror? God forbid I should insinuate anything derogatory to that profession, which is another priesthood, administrating the rights of sacred justice. But whilst I revere men in the functions which belong to them, and would do as much as one man can do to prevent their exclusion from any, I cannot, to flatter them, give the lie to nature. They are good and useful in the composition; they must be mischievous if they preponderate so as virtually to become the whole. Their very excellence in their peculiar functions may be far from a qualification for others. It cannot escape observation, that when men are too much confined to professional and faculty habits, and as it were inveterate in the recurrent employment of that narrow circle, they are rather disabled than qualified for whatever depends on the knowledge of mankind, on experience in mixed affairs, on a comprehensive, connected view of the various, complicated, external and internal interests, which go to the formation of that multifarious thing called a state.

2. Representation of Property

The Chancellor of France at the opening of the States, said, in a tone of oratorical flourish, that all occupations were honourable. If he meant only, that no honest employment was disgraceful, he would not have gone beyond the truth. But in asserting that anything is honourable, we imply some distinction in its favour. The occupation of a hair-dresser, or of a working tallow-chandler, cannot be a matter of honour to any person—to say nothing of a number of other more servile employments. Such descriptions of men ought not to suffer oppression from the state; but the state suffers oppression, if such as they, either individually or collectively, are permitted to rule. In this you think you are combating prejudice, but you are at war with nature.[1]

I do not, my dear Sir, conceive you to be of that sophistical, captious spirit, or of that uncandid dulness, as to require, for every general observation or sentiment, an explicit detail of the correctives and exceptions, which reason will presume to be included in all the general propositions which come from reasonable men. You do not imagine, that I wish to confine power, authority, and distinction to blood, and names, and titles. No, Sir. There is no qualification for government but virtue and wisdom, actual or presumptive. Wherever they are actually found, they have, in whatever state, condition, profession or trade, the passport of Heaven to human place and honour. Woe

[1] Ecclesiasticus, chap. xxxviii. verses 24, 25. "The wisdom of a learned man cometh by opportunity of leisure: and he that hath little business shall become wise."—"How can he get wisdom that holdeth the plough, and that glorieth in the goad; that driveth oxen; and is occupied in their labours; and whose talk is of bullocks?"
Ver. 27. "So every carpenter and work-master that laboureth night and day," etc.
Ver. 33. "They shall not be sought for in public counsel, nor sit high in the congregation: they shall not sit on the judge's seat, nor understand the sentence of judgment; they cannot declare justice and judgment, and they shall not be found where parables are spoken."
Ver. 34. "But they will maintain the state of the world."
I do not determine whether this book be canonical, as the Gallican church (till lately) has considered it, or apocryphal, as here it is taken. I am sure it contains a great deal of sense and truth.

to the country which would madly and impiously reject the service of the talents and virtues, civil, military, or religious, that are given to grace and to serve it; and would condemn to obscurity everything formed to diffuse lustre and glory around a state! Woe to that country too, that, passing into the opposite extreme, considers a low education, a mean contracted view of things, a sordid, mercenary occupation, as a preferable title to command! Everything ought to be open; but not indifferently to every man. No rotation; no appointment by lot; no mode of election operating in the spirit of sortition, or rotation, can be generally good in a government conversant in extensive objects. Because they have no tendency, direct or indirect, to select the man with a view to the duty, or to accommodate the one to the other. I do not hesitate to say, that the road to eminence and power from obscure condition, ought not to be made too easy, nor a thing too much of course. If rare merit be the rarest of all rare things, it ought to pass through some sort of probation. The temple of honour ought to be seated on an eminence. If it be opened through virtue, let it be remembered too, that virtue is never tried but by some difficulty and some struggle.

Nothing is a due and adequate representation of a state, that does not represent its ability, as well as its property. But as ability is a vigorous and active principle, and as property is sluggish, inert, and timid, it never can be safe from the invasions of ability, unless it be, out of all proportion, predominant in the representation. It must be represented too in great masses of accumulation, or it is not rightly protected. The characteristic essence of property, formed out of the combined principles of its acquisition and conservation, is to be *unequal*. The great masses therefore which excite envy, and tempt rapacity, must be put out of the possibility of danger. Then they form a natural rampart about the lesser properties in all their gradations. The same quantity of property, which is by the natural course of things divided among many, has not the same operation. Its defensive power is weakened as it is diffused. In this diffusion each man's portion is less than what, in the eagerness of his desires, he may flatter himself to obtain by dissipating the accumulations of others. The plunder of the few would indeed give but a share inconceivably small in the distribution to the many. But the many are not capable of making this calculation; and those who lead them to rapine never intend this distribution.

The power of perpetuating our property in our families is one of the most valuable and interesting circumstances belonging to it, and that which tends the most to the perpetuation of society itself. It makes our weakness subservient to our virtue; it grafts benevolence even upon avarice. The possessors of family wealth, and of the distinction which attends hereditary possession (as most concerned in it), are the natural securities for this transmission. With us the House of Peers is formed upon this principle. It is wholly composed of hereditary property and hereditary distinction; and made therefore the third of the legislature; and, in the last event, the sole judge of all property in all its subdivisions. The House of Commons too, though not necessarily, yet in fact, is always so composed, in the far greater part. Let those large proprietors be what they will, and they have their chance of being amongst the best, they are, at the very worst, the ballast in the vessel of the commonwealth. For though hereditary wealth, and the rank which goes with it, are too much idolized by creeping sycophants, and the blind, abject admirers of power, they are too rashly slighted in shallow speculations of the petulant, assuming, short-sighted coxcombs of philosophy. Some decent, regulated pre-eminence, some preference (not exclusive appropriation) given to birth, is neither unnatural, nor unjust, nor impolitic.

It is said, that twenty-four millions ought to prevail over two hundred thousand. True; if the constitution of a kingdom be a problem of arithmetic. This sort of discourse does well enough with the lamp-post for its second: to men who *may* reason calmly, it is ridiculous. The will of the many and their interest must very often differ; and great will be the difference when they make an evil choice. A government of five hundred country attorneys and obscure curates is not good for twenty-four millions of men, though it were chosen by eight-and-forty millions; nor is it the better for being guided by a dozen of persons of quality, who have betrayed their trust in order to obtain that power. At present, you seem in everything to have strayed out of the high road of nature. The property of France does not govern it. Of course property is destroyed, and rational liberty has no existence.

All this violent cry against the nobility I take to be a mere work of art. To be honoured and even privileged by the laws, opinions, and inveterate usages of our country, growing out of the prejudice of ages, has nothing to provoke horror and indignation in any man. Even to be too tenacious of those privileges is not absolutely a crime. The strong struggle in every individual to preserve possession of what he has found to belong to him, and to distinguish him, is one of the securities against injustice and despotism implanted in our nature. It operates as an instinct to secure property, and to preserve communities in a settled state. What is there to shock in this? Nobility is a graceful ornament to the civil order. It is the Corinthian capital of polished society. *Omnes boni nobilitati semper favemus,* was the saying of a wise and good man. It is indeed one sign of a liberal and benevolent mind to incline to it with some sort of partial propensity. He feels no ennobling principle in his own heart, who wishes to level all the artificial institutions which have been adopted for giving a body to opinion, and permanence to fugitive esteem. It is a sour, malignant, envious disposition, without taste for the reality, or for any image or representation of virtue, that sees with joy the unmerited fall of what had long flourished in splendour and in honour. I do not like to see anything destroyed; any void produced in society; any ruin on the face of the land. It was therefore with no disappointment or dissatisfaction that my inquiries and observations did not present to me any incorrigible vices in the noblesse of France, or any abuse which could not be removed by a reform very short of abolition. Your noblesse did not deserve punishment: but to degrade is to punish.

With the National Assembly of France, possession is nothing, law and usage are nothing. I see the National Assembly openly reprobate the doctrine of prescription, which, one of the greatest of their own lawyers tells us, with great truth, is a part of the law of nature. He tells us, that the positive ascertainment of its limits, and its security from invasion, were among the causes for which civil society itself has been instituted. If prescription be once shaken, no species of property is secure, when it once becomes an object large enough to tempt the cupidity of indigent power. I see a practice perfectly correspondent to their contempt of this great fundamental part of natural law. I see the confiscators begin with bishops, and chapters, and monasteries; but I do not see them end there. I see the princes of the blood, who, by the oldest usages of that kingdom, held large landed estates (hardly with the compliment of a debate) deprived of their possessions, and, in lieu of their stable, independent property, reduced to the hope of some precarious, charitable pension, at the pleasure of an assembly, which of course will pay little regard to the rights of pensioners at pleasure, when it despises those of legal proprietors. Flushed with the insolence of their first inglorious victories, and pressed by the distresses caused by their lust of unhallowed lucre, disappointed but not discouraged, they have at length ventured completely to subvert all property of all descriptions throughout the extent of a great kingdom. They have compelled all men, in all transactions of commerce, in the disposal of lands, in civil dealing, and through the whole communion of life, to accept as perfect payment and good and lawful tender, the symbols of their speculations on a projected sale of their plunder. What vestiges of liberty or property have they left? The tenant-right of a cabbage-garden, a year's interest in a hovel, the good-will of an ale-house or a baker's shop, the very shadow of a constructive property, are more ceremoniously treated in our parliament, than with you the oldest and most valuable landed possession, in the hands of the most respectable personages, or than the whole body of the monied and commercial interest of your country. We entertain a high opinion of the legislative authority; but we have never dreamt that parliaments had any right whatever to violate property, to overrule prescription, or to force a currency of their own fiction in the place of that which is real, and recognized by the law of nations. But you, who began with refusing to submit to the most moderate restraints, have ended by establishing an unheard-of despotism. I find the ground upon which your confiscators go is this; that indeed their proceedings could not be supported in a court of justice; but that the rules of prescription cannot bind a legislative assembly. So that this legislative assembly of a free nation sits, not for the security, but for the destruction, of property, and not of property only, but of every rule and maxim which can give it stability, and of those instruments which can alone give it circulation.

In every prosperous community something more is produced than goes to the immediate support of the producer. This surplus forms the income of the landed capitalist. It will be spent by a proprietor who does not labour. But this idleness is itself the spring of labour; this repose the spur to industry. The only concern of the state is, that the capital taken in rent from the land, should be returned again to the industry from whence it came; and that its expenditure should be with the least possible detriment to the morals of those who expend it, and to those of the people to whom it is returned.

Why should the expenditure of a great landed property, which is a dispersion of the surplus product of the soil, appear intolerable to you or to me, when it takes its course through the accumulation of vast libraries, which are the history of the force and weakness of the human mind; through great collections of ancient records, medals, and coins, which attest and explain laws and customs; through paintings and statues, that, by imitating nature, seem to extend the limits of creation; through grand monuments of the dead, which continue the regards and connexions of life beyond the grave; through collections of the specimens of nature, which become a representative assembly of all the classes and families of the world, that by disposition facilitate, and, by exciting curiosity, open the avenues to science? If by great permanent establishments, all these objects of expense are better secured from the inconstant sport of personal caprice and personal extravagance, are they worse than if the same tastes prevailed in scattered individuals? Does not the sweat of the mason and carpenter, who toil in order to partake the sweat of the peasant, flow as pleasantly and as salubriously, in the construction and repair of the majestic edifices of religion, as in the painted booths and sordid sties of vice and luxury; as honourably and as profitably in repairing those sacred works, which grow hoary with innumerable years, as on the momentary receptacles of transient voluptuousness; in opera-houses, and brothels, and gaming-houses, and club-houses, and obelisks in the Champ de Mars? Is the surplus product of the olive and the vine worse employed in the frugal sustenance of persons, whom the fictions of a pious imagination raise to dignity by construing in the service of God, than in pampering the innumerable multitude of those who are degraded by being made useless domestics, subservient to the pride of man? Are the decorations of temples an expenditure less worthy a wise man, than ribbons, and laces, and national cockades, and petit maisons, and petit soupers, and all the innumerable fopperies and follies, in which opulence sports away the burthen of its superfluity?

We tolerate even these; not from love of them, but for fear of worse. We tolerate them; because property and liberty, to a degree, require that toleration. But why proscribe the other, and surely, in every point of view, the more laudable use of estates? Why, through the violation of all property, through an outrage upon every principle of liberty, forcibly carry them from the better to the worse?

With us the king and the lords are several and joint securities for the equality of each district, each province, each city. When did you hear in Great Britain of any province suffering from the inequality of its representation; what district from having no representation at all? Not only our monarchy and our peerage secure the equality on which our unity depends, but it is the spirit of the House of Commons itself. The very inequality of representation, which is so foolishly complained of, is perhaps the very thing which prevents us from thinking or acting as members for districts. Cornwall elects as many members as all Scotland. But is Cornwall better taken care of than Scotland? Few trouble their heads about any of your bases, out of some giddy clubs.

Good order is the foundation of all good things. To be enabled to acquire, the people, without being servile, must be tractable and obedient. The magistrate must have his reverence, the laws their authority. The body of the people must not find the principles of natural subordination by art rooted out of their minds. They must respect that property of which they cannot partake. They must labour to obtain what by labour can be obtained; and when they find, as they commonly do, the success disproportioned to the endeavour, they must be taught their consolation in the final proportions of eternal justice. Of this consolation whoever deprives them, deadens their industry, and strikes at the root of all acquisition as of all conservation. He that does this is the cruel oppressor, the merciless enemy of the poor and wretched; at the same time that by his wicked speculations he exposes the fruits of successful industry, and the accumulations of fortune, to the plunder of the negligent, the disappointed, and the unprosperous.

Too many of the financiers by profession are apt to see nothing in revenue but banks, and circulations, and annuities on lives, and tontines, and perpetual rents, and all the small wares of the ship. In a settled order of the state, these things are not to be slighted, nor is the skill in them to be held of trivial estimation. They are good, but then only good, when they assume the effects of that settled order, and are built upon it. But when men think that these beggarly contrivances may supply a resource for the evils which result from breaking up the foundations of public order, and from causing or suffering the principles of property to be subverted, they will, in the ruin of their country, leave a melancholy and lasting monument of the effect of preposterous politics, and presumptuous, short-sighted, narrow-minded wisdom.

3. Why Government Is Complex

I see that your example is held out to shame us. I know that we are supposed a dull, sluggish race, rendered passive by finding our situation tolerable, and prevented by a mediocrity of freedom from ever attaining to its full perfection. Your leaders in France began by affecting to admire, almost to adore, the British constitution; but as they advanced, they came to look upon it with a sovereign contempt. The friends of your National Assembly amongst us have full as mean an opinion of what was formerly thought the glory of their country. The Revolution Society has discovered that

the English nation is not free. They are convinced that the inequality in our representation is a "defect in our constitution *so gross and palpable,* as to make it excellent chiefly in *form* and *theory.*" [1] That a representation in the legislature of a kingdom is not only the basis of all constitutional liberty in it, but of *"all legitimate government;* that without it a *government* is nothing but an *usurpation;"*—that "when the representation is *partial,* the kingdom possess liberty only *partially;* and if extremely partial, it gives only a *semblance;* and if not only extremely partial, but corruptly chosen, it becomes a *nuisance."* Dr. Price considers this inadequacy of representation as our *fundamental grievance;* and though, as to the corruption of this semblance of representation, he hopes it is not yet arrived to its full perfection of depravity, he fears that "nothing will be done towards gaining for us this *essential blessing,* until some *great abuse of power* again provokes our resentment, or some *great calamity* again alarms our fears, or perhaps till the acquisition of a *pure and equal representation by other countries,* whilst we are *mocked* with the *shadow,* kindles our shame." To this he subjoins a note in these words: "A representation chosen chiefly by the treasury, and a *few* thousands of the *dregs* of the people, who are generally paid for their votes."

You will smile here at the consistency of those democratists, who, when they are not on their guard, treat the humbler part of the community with the greatest contempt, whilst, at the same time, they pretend to make them the depositories of all power. It would require a long discourse to point out to you the many fallacies that lurk in the generality and equivocal nature of the terms "inadequate representation." I shall only say here, in justice to that old-fashioned constitution, under which we have long prospered, that our representation has been found perfectly adequate to all the purposes for which a representation of tne

---

[1] Discourse on the Love of our Country, 3rd edit. p. 39.

people can be desired or devised. I defy the enemies of our constitution to show the contrary. To detail the particulars in which it is found so well to promote its ends, would demand a treatise on our practical constitution. I state here the doctrine of the Revolutionists, only that you and others may see what an opinion these gentlemen entertain of the constitution of their country, and why they seem to think that some great abuse of power, or some great calamity, as giving a chance for the blessing of a constitution according to their ideas, would be much palliated to their feelings; you see *why they* are so much enamoured of your fair and equal representation, which being once obtained, the same effects might follow. You see they consider our House of Commons as only "a semblance," "a form," "a theory," "a shadow," "a mockery," perhaps "a nuisance."

These gentlemen value themselves on being systematic; and not without reason. They must therefore look on this gross and palpable defect of representation, this fundamental grievance (so they call it), as a thing not only vicious in itself, but as rendering our whole government absolutely *illegitimate,* and not at all better than a downright *usurpation.* Another revolution, to get rid of this illegitimate and usurped government, would of course be perfectly justifiable, if not absolutely necessary. Indeed their principle, if you observe it with any attention, goes much further than to an alteration in the election of the House of Commons; for, if popular representation, or choice, is necessary to the *legitimacy* of all government, the House of Lords is, at one stroke, bastardized and corrupted in blood. That house is no representative of the people at all, even in "semblance or in form." The case of the crown is altogether as bad. In vain the crown may endeavour to screen itself against these gentlemen by the authority of the establishment made on the Revolution. The Revolution which is resorted to for a title, on their system, wants a title itself. The Revolution is built, according to their theory, upon a basis not

more solid than our present formalities, as it was made by a House of Lords, not representing any one but themselves; and by a House of Commons exactly such as the present, that is, as they term it, by a mere "shadow and mockery" of representation.

Something they must destroy, or they seem to themselves to exist for no purpose. One set is for destroying the civil power through the ecclesiastical; another, for demolishing the ecclesiastic through the civil. They are aware that the worst consequences might happen to the public in accomplishing this double ruin of church and state; but they are so heated with their theories, that they give more than hints, that this ruin, with all the mischiefs that must lead to it and attend it, and which to themselves appear quite certain, would not be unacceptable to them, or very remote from their wishes. A man amongst them of great authority, and certainly of great talents, speaking of a supposed alliance between church and state, says, "perhaps *we must wait for the fall of the civil powers* before this most unnatural alliance be broken. Calamitous no doubt will that time be. But what convulsion in the political world ought to be a subject of lamentation, if it be attended with so desirable an effect?" You see with what a steady eye these gentlemen are prepared to view the greatest calamities which can befall their country.

It is no wonder therefore, that with these ideas of everything in their constitution and government at home, either in church or state, as illegitimate and usurped, or at best as a vain mockery, they look abroad with an eager and passionate enthusiasm. Whilst they are possessed by these notions, it is vain to talk to them of the practice of their ancestors, the fundamental laws of their country, the fixed form of a constitution, whose merits are confirmed by the solid test of long experience, and an increasing public strength and national prosperity. They despise experience as the wisdom of unlettered men; and as for the rest, they have wrought under ground a mine that will blow up, at one grand explosion, all examples of antiquity, all precedents, charters, and acts of parliament. They have "the rights of men." Against these there can be no prescription; against these no agreement is binding: these admit no temperament and no compromise: anything withheld from their full demand is so much of fraud and injustice. Against these their rights of men let no government look for security in the length of its continuance, or in the justice and lenity of its administration. The objections of these speculatists, if its forms do not quadrate with their theories, are as valid against such an old and beneficent government, as against the most violent tyranny, or the greenest usurpation. They are always at issue with governments, not on a question of abuse, but a question of competency, and a question of title. I have nothing to say to the clumsy subtlety of their political metaphysics. Let them be their amusement in the schools.—"Illa *se jactat in aula—Æolus, et clauso ventorum carcere regnet.*"—But let them not break prison to burst like a *Levanter,* to sweep the earth with their hurricane, and to break up the fountains of the great deep to overwhelm us.

Far am I from denying in theory, full as far is my heart from withholding in practice (if I were of power to give or to withhold), the *real* rights of men. In denying their false claims of right, I do not mean to injure those which are real, and are such as their pretended rights would totally destroy. If civil society be made for the advantage of man, all the advantages for which it is made become his right. It is an institution of beneficence; and law itself is only beneficence acting by a rule. Men have a right to live by that rule; they have a right to do justice, as between their fellows, whether their fellows are in public function or in ordinary occupation. They have a right to the fruits of their industry; and to the means of making their industry fruitful. They have a right to the acquisitions of their parents; to the nourishment and improvement of their offspring; to instruction in life, and to consolation in death.

Whatever each man can separately do, without trespassing upon others, he has a right to do for himself; and he has a right to a fair portion of all which society, with all its combinations of skill and force, can do in his favour. In this partnership all men have equal rights; but not to equal things. He that has but five shillings in the partnership, has as good a right to it, as he that has five hundred pounds has to his larger proportion. But he has not a right to an equal dividend in the product of the joint stock; and as to the share of power, authority, and direction which each individual ought to have in the management of the state, that I must deny to be amongst the direct original rights of man in civil society; for I have in my contemplation the civil social man, and no other. It is a thing to be settled by convention.

If civil society be the offspring of convention, that convention must be its law. That convention must limit and modify all the descriptions of constitution which are formed under it. Every sort of legislative, judicial, or executory power are its creatures. They can have no being in any other state of things; and how can any man claim under the conventions of civil society, rights which do not so much as suppose its existence? rights which are absolutely repugnant to it? One of the first motives to civil society, and which becomes one of its fundamental rules, is, *that no man should be judge in his own cause.* By this each person has at once divested himself of the first fundamental right of uncovenanted man, that is, to judge for himself, and to assert his own cause. He abdicates all right to be his own governor. He inclusively, in a great measure, abandons the right of self-defence, the first law of nature. Men cannot enjoy the rights of an uncivil and of a civil state together. That he may obtain justice, he gives up his right of determining what it is in points the most essential to him. That he may secure some liberty, he makes a surrender in trust of the whole of it.

Government is not made in virtue of natural rights, which may and do exist in total independence of it; and exist in much greater clearness, and in a much greater degree of abstract perfection: but their abstract perfection is their practical defect. By having a right to everything they want everything. Government is a contrivance of human wisdom to provide for human *wants*. Men have a right that these wants should be provided for by this wisdom. Among these wants is to be reckoned the want, out of civil society, of a sufficient restraint upon their passions. Society requires not only that the passions of individuals should be subjected, but that even in the mass and body, as well as in the individuals, the inclinations of men should frequently be thwarted, their will controlled, and their passions brought into subjection. This can only be done *by a power out of themselves;* and not, in the exercise of its function, subject to that will and to those passions which it is its office to bridle and subdue. In this sense the restraints on men, as well as their liberties, are to be reckoned among their rights. But as the liberties and the restrictions vary with times and circumstances, and admit of infinite modifications, they cannot be settled upon any abstract rule; and nothing is so foolish as to discuss them upon that principle.

The moment you abate anything from the full rights of men, each to govern himself, and suffer any artificial, positive limitation upon those rights, from that moment the whole organization of government becomes a consideration of convenience. This it is which makes the constitution of a state, and the due distribution of its powers, a matter of the most delicate and complicated skill. It requires a deep knowledge of human nature and human necessities, and of the things which facilitate or obstruct the various ends, which are to be pursued by the mechanism of civil institutions. The state is to have recruits to its strength, and remedies to its distempers. What is the use of discussing a man's abstract right to food or medicine? The question is upon the method of procuring and administering them. In that deliberation I shall always

advise to call in the aid of the farmer and the physician, rather than the professor of metaphysics.

The science of constructing a commonwealth, or renovating it, or reforming it, is, like every other experimental science, not to be taught *a priori*. Nor is it a short experience that can instruct us in that practical science; because the real effects of moral causes are not always immediate; but that which in the first instance is prejudicial may be excellent in its remoter operation; and its excellence may arise even from the ill effects its produces in the beginning. The reverse also happens: and very plausible schemes, with very pleasing commencements, have often shameful and lamentable conclusions. In states there are often some obscure and almost latent causes, things which appear at first view of little moment, on which a very great part of its prosperity or adversity may most essentially depend. The science of government being therefore so practical in itself, and intended for such practical purposes, a matter which requires experience, and even more experience than any person can gain in his whole life, however sagacious and observing he may be, it is with infinite caution that any man ought to venture upon pulling down an edifice, which has answered in any tolerable degree for ages the common purposes of society, or on building it up again, without having models and patterns of approved utility before his eyes.

These metaphysic rights entering into common life, like rays of light which pierce into a dense medium, are, by the laws of nature, refracted from their straight line. Indeed in the gross and complicated mass of human passions and concerns, the primitive rights of men undergo such a variety of refractions and reflections, that it becomes absurd to talk of them as if they continued in the simplicity of their original direction. The nature of man is intricate; the objects of society are of the greatest possible complexity: and therefore no simple disposition or direction of power can be suitable either to man's nature, or to the quality of his affairs. When I hear the simplicity of contrivance aimed at and boasted of in any new political constitutions, I am at no loss to decide that the artificers are grossly ignorant of their trade, or totally negligent of their duty. The simple governments are fundamentally defective, to say no worse of them. If you were to contemplate society in but one point of view, all these simple modes of polity are infinitely captivating. In effect each would answer its single end much more perfectly than the more complex is able to attain all its complex purposes. But it is better that the whole should be imperfectly and anomalously answered, than that, while some parts are provided for with great exactness, others might be totally neglected, or perhaps materially injured, by the overcare of a favourite member.

The pretended rights of these theorists are all extremes: and in proportion as they are metaphysically true, they are morally and politically false. The rights of men are in a sort of *middle,* incapable of definition, but not impossible to be discerned. The rights of men in governments are their advantages; and these are often in balances between differences of good; in compromises sometimes between good and evil, and sometimes between evil and evil. Political reason is a computing principle; adding, subtracting, multiplying, and dividing, morally and not metaphysically, or mathematically, true moral denominations.

By these theorists the right of the people is almost always sophistically confounded with their power. The body of the community, whenever it can come to act, can meet with no effectual resistance; but till power and right are the same, the whole body of them has no right inconsistent with virtue, and the first of all virtues, prudence. Men have no right to what is not reasonable, and to what is not for their benefit; for though a pleasant writer said, *Liceat perire poetis,* when one of them, in cold blood, is said to have leaped into the flames of a volcanic revolution, *Ardentem frigidus Ætnam insiluit,* I consider such a frolic rather as an unjustifiable poetic licence, than as one of the franchises of Parnassus; and whether he were poet, or divine, or politician, that chose to exercise this kind of right, I think that more wise, because more charitable, thoughts would urge me rather to save the man, than to preserve his brazen slippers as the monuments of his folly.

The kind of anniversary sermons to which a great part of what I write refers, if men are not shamed out of their present course, in commemorating the fact, will cheat many out of the principles, and deprive them of the benefits, of the revolution they commemorate. I confess to you, Sir, I never liked this continual talk of resistance, and revolution, or the practice of making the extreme medicine of the constitution its daily bread. It renders the habit of society dangerously valetudinary; it is taking periodical doses of mercury sublimate, and swallowing down repeated provocatives of cantharides to our love of liberty.

4. Sentiment and Logic in Politics

We are not the converts of Rousseau; we are not the disciples of Voltaire; Helvetius has made no progress amongst us. Atheists are not our preachers; madmen are not our lawgivers. We know that *we* have made no discoveries, and we think that no discoveries are to be made, in morality; nor many in the great principles of government, nor in the ideas of liberty, which were understood long before we were born, altogether as well as they will be after the grave has heaped its mould upon our presumption, and the silent tomb shall have imposed its law on our pert loquacity. In England we have not yet been completely embowelled of our natural entrails; we still feel within us, and we cherish and cultivate, those inbred sentiments which are the faithful guardians, the active monitors of our duty, the true supporters of all liberal and manly morals. We have not been drawn and trussed, in order that we may be filled, like stuffed birds in a museum, with chaff and rags and paltry blurred shreds of paper about the rights of man. We preserve the whole of our feelings still native and entire, unsophisticated by pedantry and infidelity. We have real hearts of flesh and blood beating in our bosoms. We fear God; we look up with awe to kings; with affection to parliaments; with duty to magistrates; with reverence to priests; and with respect to nobility. Why? Because when such ideas are brought before our minds, it is *natural* to be so affected; because all other feelings are false and spurious, and tend to corrupt our minds, to vitiate our primary morals, to render us unfit for rational liberty; and by teaching us a servile, licentious, and abandoned insolence, to be our low sport for a few holidays, to make us perfectly fit for, and justly deserving of, slavery, through the whole course of our lives.

You see, Sir, that in this enlightened age I am bold enough to confess, that we are generally men of untaught feelings; that instead of casting away all our old prejudices, we cherish them to a very considerable degree, and, to take more shame to ourselves, we cherish them because they are prejudices; and the longer they have lasted, and the more generally they have prevailed, the more we cherish them. We are afraid to put men to live and trade each on his own private stock of reason; because we suspect that this stock in each man is small, and that the individuals would do better to avail themselves of the general bank and capital of nations and of ages. Many of our men of speculation, instead of exploding general prejudices, employ their sagacity to discover the latent wisdom which prevails in them. If they find what they seek, and they seldom fail, they think it more wise to continue the prejudice, with the reason involved, than to cast away the coat of prejudice, and to leave nothing but the naked reason; because prejudice, with its reason, has a motive to give action to that reason, and an affection which will give it perma-nence. Prejudice is of ready application in the emergency; it previously engages the mind in a steady course of wisdom and virtue, and does not leave the man hesitating in the moment of decision, sceptical, puzzled, and unresolved. Prejudice renders a man's virtue his habit; and not a series of unconnected acts. Through just prejudice, his duty becomes a part of his nature.

Your literary men, and your politicians, and so do the whole clan of the enlightened among us, essentially differ in these points. They have no respect for the wisdom of others; but they pay it off by a very full measure of confidence in their own. With them it is a sufficient motive to destroy an old scheme of things, because it is an old one. As to the new, they are in no sort of fear with regard to the duration of a building run up in haste; because duration is no object to those who think little or nothing has been done before their time, and who place all their hopes in discovery. They conceive, very systematically, that all things which give perpetuity are mischievous, and therefore they are at inexpiable war with all establishments. They think that government may vary like modes of dress, and with as little ill effect: that there needs no principle of attachment, except a sense of present conveniency, to any constitution of the state. They always speak as if they were of opinion that there is a singular species of compact between them and their magistrates, which binds the magistrate, but which has nothing reciprocal in it, but that the majesty of the people has a right to dissolve it without any reason, but its will. Their attachment to their country itself is only so far as it agrees with some of their fleeting projects; it begins and ends with that scheme of polity which falls in with their momentary opinion.

These doctrines, or rather sentiments, seem prevalent with your new statesmen. But they are wholly different from those on which we have always acted in this country.

5. Religion, Society, Politics

We know, and what is better, we feel inwardly, that religion is the basis of civil society, and the source of all good and of all comfort. In England we are so convinced of this, that there is no rust of superstition, with which the accumulated absurdity of the human mind might have crusted it over in the course of ages, that ninety-nine in a hundred of the people of England would not prefer to impiety. We shall never be such fools as to call in an enemy to the substance of any system to remove its corruptions, to supply its defects, or to perfect its construction. If our religious tenets should ever want a further elucidation, we shall not call on atheism to explain them. We shall not light up our temple from that unhallowed fire. It will be illuminated with other lights. It will be perfumed with other incense, than the infectious stuff which is imported by the smugglers of adulterated metaphysics. If our ecclesiastical establishment should want a revision, it is not avarice or rapacity, public or private, that we shall employ for the audit, or receipt, or application of its consecrated revenue. Violently condemning neither the Greek nor the Armenian, nor, since heats are subsided, the Roman system of religion, we prefer the Protestant; not because we think it has less of the Christian religion in it, but because, in our judgment, it has more. We are Protestants, not from indifference, but from zeal.

We know, and it is our pride to know, that man is by his constitution a religious animal; that atheism is against, not only our reason, but our instincts; and that it cannot prevail long. But if, in the moment of riot, and in a drunken delirium from the hot spirit drawn out of the alembic of hell, which in France is now so furiously boiling, we should uncover our nakedness, by throwing off that Christian religion which has hitherto been our boast and comfort, and one great source of civilization amongst us and amongst many other nations, we are apprehensive (being well aware that the mind will not endure a void) that some uncouth, pernicious, and degrading superstition might take place of it.

For that reason, before we take from our establishment the natural, human means of estimation, and give it up to contempt, as you have done, and in doing it have incurred the penalties you well deserve to suffer, we desire that some other may be presented to us in the place of it. We shall then form our judgment.

On these ideas, instead of quarrelling with establishments, as some do, who have made a philosophy and a religion of their hostility to such institutions, we cleave closely to them. We are resolved to keep an established church, an established monarchy, an established aristocracy, and an established democracy, each in the degree it exists, and in no greater. I shall show you presently how much of each of these we possess.

It has been the misfortune (not, as these gentlemen think it, the glory) of this age, that everything is to be discussed, as if the constitution of our country were to be always a subject rather of altercation, than enjoyment. For this reason, as well as for the satisfaction of those among you (if any such you have among you) who may wish to profit of examples, I venture to trouble you with a few thoughts upon each of these establishments. I do not think they were unwise in ancient Rome, who, when they wished to new-model their laws, set commissioners to examine the best constituted republics within their reach.

First, I beg leave to speak of our church establishment, which is the first of our prejudices, not a prejudice destitute of reason, but involving in it profound and extensive wisdom. I speak of it first. It is first, and last, and midst in our minds. For, taking ground on that religious system, of which we are now in possession, we continue to act on the early received and uniformly continued sense of mankind. That sense not only, like a wise architect, hath built up the august fabric of states, but like a provident proprietor, to preserve the structure from profanation and ruin, as a sacred temple purged from all the impurities of fraud, and violence, and injustice, and tyranny, hath solemnly and for ever consecrated the commonwealth, and all that officiate in it. This consecration is made, that all who administer in the government of men, in which they stand in the person of God Himself, should have high and worthy notions of their function and destination; that their hope should be full of immortality; that they should not look to the paltry pelf of the moment, nor to the temporary and transient praise of the vulgar, but to a solid, permanent exercise, in the permanent part of their nature, and to a permanent fame and glory, in the example they leave as a rich inheritance to the world.

Such sublime principles ought to be infused into persons of exalted situations; and religious establishments provided, that may continually revive and enforce them. Every sort of moral, every sort of civil, every sort of politic institution, aiding the rational and natural ties that connect the human understanding and affections to the divine, are not more than necessary, in order to build up that wonderful structure, Man; whose prerogative it is, to be in a great degree a creature of his own making; and who, when made as he ought to be made, is destined to hold no trivial place in the creation. But whenever man is put over men, as the better nature ought ever to preside, in that case more particularly, he should as nearly as possible be approximated to his perfection.

The consecration of the state, by a state religious establishment, is necessary also to operate with a wholesome awe upon free citizens; because, in order to secure their freedom, they must enjoy some determinate portion of power. To them therefore a religion connected with the state, and with their duty towards it, becomes even more necessary than in such societies, where the people, by the terms of their subjection, are confined to private sentiments, and the management of their own family

concerns. All persons possessing any portion of power ought to be strongly and awfully impressed with an idea that they act in trust: and that they are to account for their conduct in that trust to the one great Master, Author, and Founder of society.

To avoid therefore the evils of inconstancy and versatility, ten thousand times worse than those of obstinacy and the blindest prejudice, we have consecrated the state, that no man should approach to look into its defects or corruptions but with due caution; that he should never dream of beginning its reformation by its subversion; that he should approach to the faults of the state as to the wounds of a father, with pious awe and trembling solicitude. By this wise prejudice we are taught to look with horror on those children of their country, who are prompt rashly to hack that aged parent in pieces, and put him into the kettle of magicians, in hopes that by their poisonous weeds, and wild incantations, they may regenerate the paternal constitution, and renovate their father's life.

Society is indeed a contract. Subordinate contracts for objects of mere occasional interest may be dissolved at pleasure—but the state ought not to be considered as nothing better than a partnership agreement in a trade of pepper and coffee, calico or tobacco, or some other such low concern, to be taken up for a little temporary interest, and to be dissolved by the fancy of the parties. It is to be looked on with other reverence; because it is not a partnership in things subservient only to the gross animal existence of a temporary and perishable nature. It is a partnership in all science; a partnership in all art; a partnership in every virtue, and in all perfection. As the ends of such a partnership cannot be obtained in many generations, it becomes a partnership not only between those who are living, but between those who are living, those who are dead, and those who are to be born. Each contract of each particular state is but a clause in the great primæval contract of eternal society, linking the lower with the higher natures, connecting the visible and invisible world, according to a fixed compact sanctioned by the inviolable oath which holds all physical and all moral natures, each in their appointed place. This law is not subject to the will of those, who by an obligation above them, and infinitely superior, are bound to submit their will to that law. The municipal corporations of that universal kingdom are not morally at liberty at their pleasure, and on their speculations of a contingent improvement, wholly to separate and tear asunder the bands of their subordinate community, and to dissolve it into an unsocial, uncivil, unconnected chaos of elementary principles. It is the first and supreme necessity only, a necessity that is not chosen, but chooses, a necessity paramount to deliberation, that admits no discussion, and demands no evidence, which alone can justify a resort to anarchy. This necessity is no exception to the rule; because this necessity itself is a part too of that moral and physical disposition of things, to which man must be obedient by consent or force: but if that which is only submission to necessity should be made the object of choice, the law is broken, nature is disobeyed, and the rebellious are outlawed, cast forth, and exiled, from this world of reason, and order, and peace, and virtue, and fruitful penitence, into the antagonist world of madness, discord, vice, confusion, and unavailing sorrow.

These, my dear Sir, are, were, and, I think, long will be, the sentiments of not the least learned and reflecting part of this kingdom. They, who are included in this description, form their opinions on such grounds as such persons ought to form them. The less inquiring receive them from an authority, which those whom Providence dooms to live on trust need not be ashamed to rely on. These two sorts of men move in the same direction, though in a different place. They both move with the order of the universe. They all know or feel this great ancient truth: "Quod illi principi et præpotenti Deo qui omnem hunc mundum regit, nihil eorum quæ quidem fiant in terris ac-ceptius quam concilia et cœtus hominum jure sociati quæ civitates appellantur." They take this tenet of the head and heart, not from the great name which it immediately bears, nor from the greater from whence it is derived; but from that which alone can give true weight and sanction to any learned opinion, the common nature and common relation of men. Persuaded that all things ought to be done with reference, and referring all to the point of reference to which all should be directed, they think themselves bound, not only as individuals in the sanctuary of the heart, or as congregated in that personal capacity, to renew the memory of their high origin and caste; but also in their corporate character to perform their national homage to the institutor, and author, and protector of civil society; without which civil society man could not by any possibility arrive at the perfection of which his nature is capable, nor even make a remote and faint approach to it. They conceive that He who gave our nature to be perfected by our virtue, willed also the necessary means of its perfection.—He willed therefore the state —He willed its connexion with the source and original archetype of all perfection. They who are convinced of this His will, which is the law of laws, and the sovereign of sovereigns, cannot think it reprehensible that this our corporate fealty and homage, that this our recognition of a signiory paramount, I had almost said this oblation of the state itself, as a worthy offering on the high altar of universal praise, should be performed as all public, solemn acts are performed, in buildings, in music, in decoration, in speech, in the dignity of persons, according to the customs of mankind, taught by their nature; this is, with modest splendour and unassuming state, with mild majesty and sober pomp. For those purposes they think some part of the wealth of the country is as usefully employed as it can be in fomenting the luxury of individuals. It is the public ornament. It is the public consolation. It nourishes the public hope. The poorest man finds his own importance and dignity in it, whilst the wealth and pride of individuals at every moment makes the man of humble rank and fortune sensible of his inferiority, and degrades and vilifies his condition. It is for the man in humble life, and to raise his nature, and to put him in mind of a state in which the privileges of opulence will cease, when he will be equal by nature, and may be more than equal by virtue, that this portion of the general wealth of his country is employed and sanctified.

The English people are satisfied, that to the great the consolations of religion are as necessary as its instructions. They too are among the unhappy. They feel personal pain, and domestic sorrow. In these they have no privilege, but are subject to pay their full contingent to the contributions levied on mortality. They want this sovereign balm under their gnawing cares and anxieties, which, being less conversant about the limited wants of animal life, range without limit, and are diversified by infinite combinations, in the wild and unbounded regions of imagination. Some charitable dole is wanting to these, our often very unhappy brethren, to fill the gloomy void that reigns in minds which have nothing on earth to hope or fear; something to relieve in the killing languor and over-laboured lassitude of those who have nothing to do; something to excite an appetite to existence in the palled satiety which attends on all pleasures which may be bought, where nature is not left to her own process, where even desire is anticipated, and therefore fruition defeated by meditated schemes and contrivances of delight; and no interval, no obstacles, is interposed between the wish and the accomplishment.

6. Reform and Revolution

The errors and defects of old establishments are visible and palpable. It calls for little ability to point them out; and where absolute power is given, it requires but a word wholly to abolish the vice and the establishment together. The same lazy but restless disposition, which loves sloth and hates quiet, directs the politicians, when they come to work for supplying the place of what they have destroyed. To make everything the reverse of what they have seen is quite as easy as to destroy. No difficulties occur in what has never been tried. Criticism is almost baffled in discovering the defects of what has not existed; and eager enthusiasm and cheating hope have all the wide field of imagination, in which they may expatiate with little or no opposition.

At once to preserve and to reform is quite another thing. When the useful parts of an old establishment are kept, and what is superadded is to be fitted to what is retained, a vigorous mind, steady, persevering attention, various powers of comparison and combination, and the resources of an understanding fruitful in expedients, are to be exercised; they are to be exercised in a continued conflict with the combined force of opposite vices, with the obstinacy that rejects all improvement, and the levity that is fatigued and disgusted with everything of which it is in possession. But you may object—"A process of this kind is slow. It is not fit for an assembly, which glories in performing in a few months the work of ages. Such a mode of reforming, possibly, might take up many years." Without question it might; and it ought. It is one of the excellencies of a method in which time is amongst the assistants, that its operation is slow, and in some cases almost imperceptible. If circumspection and caution are a part of wisdom, when we work only upon inanimate matter, surely they become a part of duty too, when the subject of our demolition and construction is not brick and timber, but sentient beings, by the sudden alteration of whose state, condition, and habits, multitudes may be rendered miserable. But it seems as if it were the prevalent opinion in Paris, that an unfeeling heart, and an undoubting confidence, are the sole qualifications for a perfect legislator.

Far different are my ideas of that high office. The true lawgiver ought to have a heart full of sensibility. He ought to love and respect his kind, and to fear himself. It may be allowed to his temperament to catch his ultimate object with an intuitive glance; but his movements towards it ought to be deliberate. Political arrangement, as it is a work for social ends, is to be only wrought by social means. There mind must conspire with mind. Time is required to produce that union of minds which alone can produce all the good we aim at. Our patience will achieve more than our force. If I might venture to appeal to what is so much out of fashion in Paris, I mean to experience, I should tell you, that in my course I have known, and, according to my measure, have co-operated with great men; and I have never yet seen any plan which has not been mended by the observations of those who were much inferior in understanding to the person who took the lead in the business. By a slow but well-sustained progress, the effect of each step is watched; the good or ill success of the first gives light to us in the second; and so, from light to light, we are conducted with safety through the whole series. We see that the parts or the system do not clash. The evils latent in the most promising contrivances are provided for as they arise. One advantage is as little as possible sacrificed to another. We compensate, we reconcile, we balance. We are enabled to unite into a consistent whole the various anomalies and contending principles that are found in the minds and affairs of men. From hence arises, not an excellence in simplicity, but one far superior, an excellence in composition. Where the great interests of mankind are concerned through a long succession of generations, that succession ought to be admitted into some share in the councils which are so deeply to affect them. If justice requires this, the work itself requires the aid of more minds than one age can furnish. It is from this view of things that the best legislators have been often satisfied with the establishment of some sure, solid, and ruling principle in government; a power like that which some of the philosophers have called a plastic nature; and having fixed the principle, they have left it afterwards to its own operation.

7. Revolution and Military Despotism

It is known, that armies have hitherto yielded a very precarious and uncertain obedience to any senate, or popular authority; and they will least of all yield it to an assembly which is only to have a continuance of two years. The officers must totally lose the characteristic disposition of military men, if they see with perfect submission and due admiration, the dominion of pleaders; especially when they find that they have a new court to pay to an endless succession of those pleaders; whose military policy, and the genius of whose command (if they should have any), must be as uncertain as their duration is transient. In the weakness of one kind of authority, and in the fluctuation of all, the officers of any army will remain for some time mutinous and full of faction, until some popular general, who understands the art of conciliating the soldiery, and who possesses the true spirit of command, shall draw the eyes of all men upon himself. Armies will obey him on his personal account. There is no other way of securing military obedience in this state of things. But the moment in which that event shall happen, the person who really commands the army is your master; the master (that is little) of your king, the master of your assembly, the master of your whole republic.

How came the Assembly by their present power over the army? Chiefly, to be sure, by debauching the soldiers from their officers. They have begun by a most terrible operation. They have touched the central point, about which the particles that compose armies are at repose. They have destroyed the principle of obedience in the great, essential, critical link between the officer and the soldier, just where the chain of military subordination commences and on which the whole of that system depends. The soldier is told he is a citizen, and has the rights of man and citizen. The right of a man, he is told, is to be his own governor, and to be ruled only by those to whom he delegates that self-government. It is very natural he should think that he ought most of all to have his choice where he is to yield the greatest degree of obedience. He will therefore, in all probability, systematically do, what he does at present occasionally; that is, he will exercise at least a negative in the choice of his officers. At present the officers are known at best to be only permissive, and on their good behaviour. In fact, there have been many instances in which they have been cashiered by their corps. Here is a second negative on the choice of the king; a negative as effectual at least as the other of the Assembly. The soldiers know already that it has been a question, not ill received in the National Assembly, whether they ought not to have the direct choice of their officers, or some proportion of them? When such matters are in deliberation it is no extravagant supposition that they will incline to the opinion most favourable to their pretensions. They will not bear to be deemed the army of an imprisoned king, whilst another army in the same country, with whom too they are to feast and confederate, is to be considered as the free army of a free constitution. They will cast their eyes on the other and more permanent army; I mean the municipal. That corps, they will know, does actually elect its own officers. They may not be able to discern the ground of distinction on which they are not to elect a Marquis de la Fayette (or what is his new name?) of their own. If this election of a commander-in-chief be a part of the rights of men, why not of theirs? They see elective justices of peace, elective judges, elective curates, elective bishops, elective municipalities, and elective commanders of the Parisian army. Why should they alone be excluded? Are the brave troops of France the only men in that nation who are not the fit judges of military merit, and of the qualifications necessary for a commander-in-chief? Are they paid by the state, and do they therefore lose the rights of men? They are a part of that nation themselves, and contribute to that pay. And is not the king, is not the National Assembly, and are not all who elect the National Assembly, likewise paid? Instead of seeing all these forfeit their rights by their receiving a salary, they perceive that in all these cases a salary is given for the exercise of those rights. All your resolutions, all your proceedings, all your debates, all the works of your doctors in religion and politics, have industriously been put into their hands; and you expect that they will apply to their own case just as much of your doctrines and examples as suits your pleasure.

Everything depends upon the army in such a government as yours; for you have industriously destroyed all the opinions, and prejudices, and, as far as in you lay, all the instincts which support government. Therefore the moment any difference arises between your National Assembly and any part of the nation, you must have recourse to force. Nothing else is left to you; or rather you have left nothing else to yourselves.

CHAPTER 19

BENTHAM

BURKE'S political philosophy of conservatism, more particularly, his *Reflections on the Revolution in France*, was, with all its literary charm and persuasive poetry, ineffectual in stemming the course of events. Burke, like other writers and statesmen of his time, failed to see that the French Revolution was a symptom of something much more profound: the changing class structure in western Europe. The important fact in Burke's lifetime was not, as he thought, the opposition of rationalism to the traditional order of religion and prescription but a change of another kind, the implications of which largely escaped him: the *Industrial Revolution*.

From the middle of the eighteenth century, England experienced—as the first country in the modern world—a technological and industrial transformation whose impact was revolutionary from the viewpoint of new social ideas and a new material environment. Technologically, the new age was based on coal and iron, to be supplemented later by electricity and steel. Economically, the Industrial Revolution created the factory as its most characteristic institution, which replaced the farm or landed estate as the key unit of production and wealth. Socially, the Industrial Revolution was responsible for three complementary developments: first, the growth of new, and the rapid expansion of old, towns and cities; second, the increase in population, made possible by higher living standards and improved conditions of health; third, the destruction of the existing social hierarchy headed by the landed aristocracy, and its gradual replacement by the manufacturers, financiers, merchants, and professional men as the new dominant social class.

The war with France (1793–1815), fought first with the Revolutionary Government and later with Napoleon, provided the Conservative Government in Britain with a welcome opportunity to repress democratic and radical ideas under the pretext of fighting Jacobinism. The defeat of Napoleon and the revival of the old European order at the Congress of Vienna (1815) seemed to put an end to the nightmare of revolution and democracy. Yet, no sooner had the

Congress of Vienna ended than democratic forces began to stir, until the Continent was swept by a series of revolutions in 1830 and 1848. England was on the brink of revolution in the eighteen-thirties, and although she had led the anti-French coalition, she adopted the basic principles of the French Revolution in the Reform Act of 1832.

The war against France was thus fought in vain, if its main purpose was to protect the old social system from the contagion of radical democracy. The rising middle classes in Britain inevitably developed a new social and political philosophy that was clearly distinct from Burke's adulation of landed aristocracy, as well as from Paine's radicalism and Godwin's anarchy. Burke was too conservative, pessimistic, and traditional, whereas Paine and Godwin were too radical, utopian, and revolutionary. What was needed was a political faith reflecting the outlook of the middle classes, which was essentially empirical, optimistic, willing to innovate, and eager to translate natural science into technology and industry, and political science into government and administration.

The most characteristic expression of this outlook is to be found in the work of Jeremy Bentham (1748–1832), the founder of Utilitarianism, or, as it is also called, Philosophical Radicalism. The influence of his school may be seen in the fact that Benthamism is one of the few political creeds in England named after an individual thinker. Though there is an inclination in some countries (in Spain and Latin America, for example) to identify social philosophies with a particular individual, Benthamism is a rare instance of this kind in British intellectual and political history.

Bentham was born in 1748, only three years after the Jacobite rebellion of 1745 that sought to regain the throne for the Stuarts; he spent most of his life under King George III, who reigned from 1760 to 1820—the last British monarch of autocratic leanings. Bentham died the day before the Reform Bill of 1832 became law. His life thus spanned a long period of transition in British history; while experiencing eighteenth-century autocracy at its worst, he could perceive the firm outlines of nineteenth-century democracy. His life reflects the transformation of his country: Bentham was a Tory until 1808, and he became a radical democrat at the age of sixty, when he was convinced that "the people in power" were against reform, whereas earlier he had assumed that "they only wanted to know what was good in order to embrace it."

Bentham's father and grandfather were well-to-do attorneys, and Bentham was to enter upon the same career. At the comparatively early age of three Bentham was found poring over a big folio volume of Rapin's *History of England;* he read Latin before he was four, French at six, and took to Voltaire for light reading at eight. He entered Oxford at twelve, received his bachelor's degree at fifteen, and then studied the law. He was called to the bar in 1769, but he soon decided that he was more interested in reforming the law than in practicing it. A small annual income of a hundred pounds enabled him to live independently, though modestly; after his father's death in 1792, his financial situation greatly improved, and he was able to live comfortably in his house in London, called "Hermitage." There he spent his life, unmarried, completely devoted to his literary and political activities.

Bentham's house became increasingly the center of international liberalism, and every cause of freedom, from Greece to South America, found in him a warm supporter, always willing to help, encourage, and serve. For Bentham no injustice was too small, no human being unimportant. He was particularly interested in "cases" of little-known victims of political or religious oppression, and political refugees from abroad turned to him as the voice of liberal humanity. Although he did not travel often, his viewpoint was never parochial and nationalistic, and he maintained a vast correspondence with political leaders and heads of state from countries as distant as Russia, Africa, and the Americas.

Above all, Bentham combined, to a rare degree, devotion to general humanitarian causes with the willingness and capacity to do small chores, attend to petty details, and minister to the minutiae of practical action, without vanity, publicity, or quest for glory. His *disinterestedness* and *sympathy* were as much the cause of his world-wide influence as his intellectual zeal and universality of interest. He never sought money or political power, and his kindliness was not confined to human beings but extended to animals. He was opposed—a rarity at that time—to all brutal sports, like fox hunting, bullbaiting, and cockfighting, because, as he said, the question with regard to animals is not, "can they talk, can they reason, but can they suffer?"

Bentham's first book, *Fragment on Government*, was directed against Blackstone, the oracle of English law. The *Fragment* was published in 1776, the year of James Watt's first successful steam engine, the *Declaration of Independence*, and the publication of another milestone of social thought, Adam Smith's *Wealth of Nations*. Bentham published the *Fragment* anonymously, and it was a tribute to the young author that the book was ascribed to leading legal minds of Great Britain, like Lord Mansfield, Lord Camden, and Dunning, until Bentham's father, overcome by paternal pride, revealed the true author. In the *Fragment*, Bentham pragmatically describes the nature of political society in terms of the *habit of obedience*, and not of social contract, natural rights, and other "fictions." He says that the indestructible prerogatives of mankind "have no need to be supported upon the sandy foundation of a fiction," and that the "season of *Fiction* is now over."

In this early work of Bentham there is more than a touch of Burke, because of the constant emphasis that government is not based on metaphysical generalities but on interest and advantage. Where Bentham differed even in his youth from Burke is his insistence that advantage be understood in relation to empirical needs of the individual and society, whereas Burke looked upon interest as the product of historic groups, the individual occupying a subordinate position by comparison. Bentham states that men ought to keep their promises and obey the law because it is in the interest of all to do so, and not because of rules of natural law or abstract reasoning. The question of political obligation, the pivotal problem of politics, is a "question of fact," to be decided by "testimony, observation, and experience." Using strong language in 1776, under the reign of King George III, Bentham argues that subjects should obey "so long as the probable mischiefs of obedience are less than the probable mischiefs of resistance," and that it is the duty of subjects to obey "just as long as it is their *interest*, and no longer."

Bentham's most widely known book is his *Principles of Morals and Legislation* (printed in 1780 and published in 1789). The opening words of the book summarize one of the main assumptions of his outlook: "Nature has placed mankind under the governance of two sovereign masters, *pain* and *pleasure*. It is for them alone to point out what we ought to do, as well as to determine what we shall do. On the one hand the standard of right and wrong, on the other the chain of causes and effects, are fastened to their throne." The principle of *utility*, or the *greatest happiness of the greatest number*, is that quality in an act or object that produces benefit, advantage, pleasure, good, or happiness (assumed by Bentham to be identical), or prevents mischief, pain, evil, or unhappiness. Bentham's lack of sympathy for the organic theory of state and society comes out in his assertion that the "community is a fictitious body," and that the interest of the community is "the sum of the interests of the several members who compose it." There is no notion here of Rousseau's General Will, nor of Burke's view of society as an organic growth, a partnership of past, present, and future generations.

Yet it would be a fatal misunderstanding of Bentham to identify his interest with self interest, and his happiness with happiness of the self only. In the *Principles of Morals and Legislation* Bentham distinguishes self-regarding from extra-regarding pleasures: the former relate to pleasure and happiness of one's self; the latter are an expression of benevolence and relate to happiness of others. Still more explicitly, Bentham states in his *Deontology, or Science of Morality* (1834) that immoral action is "a miscalculation of self-interest," and that it is the purpose of the "intelligent moralist" to show the erroneous estimate that the vicious man makes of pain and pleasure. Similarly, Bentham says in his *Theory of Legislation* (first published in French in 1802 and then in English in 1840) that the charge against Machiavelli does not spring from his having consulted the principle of utility, but from having applied it badly, because "bad faith is bad policy." Far from identifying utility with selfishness, Bentham says in the *Deontology* that the "first law of nature is to wish our own happiness; and the united voices of prudence and efficient benevolence add,—Seek the happiness of others,—seek your own happiness in the happiness of others."

Bentham is fully aware that personal happiness and the happiness of the greatest number are not always identical, and he sees two means by which the gulf between individual selfishness and communal good can be bridged. First, *education* can elevate men's minds so that they will understand that rationally conceived happiness of one's self includes good will, sympathy, and benevolence for others. Because of his strong belief in education—a belief he shares with other reformers—Bentham proposed, well ahead of his time, a system of public education; he was among the principal founders of the University of London. The second means of bridging the gap between individual selfishness and the greatest happiness of the greatest number is the creation of an institutional environment in which man's selfish impulses can be channeled into socially useful purposes, so that it will be contrary to his self-interest to harm others.

Bentham has the typical faith of the reformer that man's behavior is not static and set forever but can be changed through positive acts of *legislation*. Rejecting the "fictions" of natural law and inalienable rights, Bentham strongly believes in the sovereignty of the people, represented in a *one-chamber* legislature; he dismisses the doctrine of checks and balances, or of separation of powers, as concepts designed to prevent the full working of democracy. He pleaded for universal suffrage and republicanism and was one of the main forces working for the political changes finally consummated in the Reform Act of 1832.

Bentham was a strong admirer of the United States, which he considered the only "pure democracy" in existence. "There they are," Bentham said of the United States in the *Plan of Parliamentary Reform* (1817), "living, and (oh horror) flourishing—and so flourishing! flourishing under a government so essentially *illegitimate!* Oh what a reproach, a never-to-be-expunged reproach, to our own Matchless Constitution—matchless in rotten boroughs and sinecures!"

Bentham was too critical to believe that any existing system was perfect or that any formula devised by man could meet all contingencies of real life. He did not invent the idea of utility and the greatest happiness of the greatest number; he merely put these principles to hitherto unknown uses and applications. After the gospel of reverence and veneration enunciated by Burke, Bentham's method of taking nothing for granted, of refusing to accept things just because they had existed for a long time, of exposing every institution to the sole test of its consequences, was like a breath of fresh air. Eighteenth-century England had become smug and complacent, bathing in the adulation and admiration showered on it by leading minds like Voltaire and Montesquieu.

Bentham knew full well that there was no objective standard by which individuals could agree on personal happiness or that of the community, yet he thought that government—and social science—could be advanced by reducing differences of metaphysics into differences of a simpler, and more measurable, order. Problems of utility can more easily be boiled down to issues of fact, Bentham thought, than can problems of fundamental belief. When two parties are at dispute, the failure to bring in the pertinent facts of past experience is the main cause that sets them at variance: "Here, then, we have a plain and open road, perhaps, to present reconcilement: at the worst to an intelligible and explicit issue, that is, to such a ground of difference as may, when thoroughly trodden and explored, be found to lead on to reconcilement at the last. Men, let them but once clearly understand one another, will not be long ere they agree."

To apply Bentham's suggested method to a modern illustration: if a slum clearance project in an industrial city is debated in terms of fundamental issues like free enterprise and socialism, agreement is improbable. If it can be shown what the pertinent facts of the situation are—the cost to the community of existing slums, in terms of increased crime, ill-health, fire hazards, weighed against the cost of putting up better housing with assistance from public funds—the original gap has been considerably narrowed, and agreement will be likelier on this basis than on issues of apparently irreconcilable ultimate values. The progress of social science depends on its ability to *reduce questions of principle to questions of fact,* and Bentham's examination of ideas, acts, and institutions in terms of their practical consequences has been a pioneering contribution to the development of social science and social engineering.

Apart from literary attention, Bentham's early writings brought him the friendship of Lord Shelburne, a distinguished Whig leader, who was Prime Minister for a short time in 1782–1783. Shelburne came to see Bentham at his chambers in Lincoln's Inn, and the acquaintance soon developed into friendship. Bentham stayed with Shelburne at his country house in Bowood, Wiltshire, and there met statesmen and writers, lawyers, and men of affairs. Samuel Romilly, a leading attorney and reformer of the criminal law, came under Bentham's influence, and though Shelburne, Bentham also met Étienne Dumont, a Swiss Protestant minister and political exile from Geneva, who became Bentham's most faithful and devoted literary aide and collaborator.

Bentham had the habit of writing daily a regular quota of pages, but he rarely bothered to put his manuscripts into book form. His published *Works,* eleven volumes of small, double-column print, are only a fraction of his unpublished writings, which comprise over one hundred thousand pages of manuscript, appropriately kept in the library of University College, London. One of its founders, he bequeathed to University College not only all his manuscripts but also his body, because he believed that it should be dissected after his death for scientific purposes. Bentham's skeleton, dressed in his real clothes, and with a wax mask covering his face, can still be seen at University College.

Dumont tirelessly put together Bentham's manuscripts into publishable books. He also corrected and edited some of Bentham's works written in French, later retranslated into English. Owing to Dumont's French editions and translations of Bentham's works, Bentham became the first English name in France, Spain, Latin America, and wherever French was the recognized vehicle of literary intercourse. Through Dumont and Romilly, Bentham also became closely connected with some of the leading French revolutionary leaders, such as Mirabeau, and in August, 1792, the National Assembly conferred on Bentham (and a small group of other foreigners, including Tom Paine, James Madison, and George Washington) the title of Citizen of France.

Bentham's reply to the French Minister of the Interior in accepting French citizenship is typical of his personality and thought. Where other men of more conventional leanings might have accepted honorary French citizenship in a brief note of gratitude, Bentham composed a lengthy letter. Concerning the possible conflict between his British citizenship and the newly conferred French citizenship, Bentham observed that the different forms of the two governments presented no obstacle, because the general good is everywhere the true object of all political action: "Passions and prejudices divide men: great principles unite them." Though a royalist in London, he would gladly be a republican in Paris, and he notes that the British monarch was an Anglican in England, a Presbyterian in Scotland, and a Lutheran in Hanover. Bentham's humanitarian sentiments came out at the end of the letter where he states his opposition to the proscription of political refugees, though he does not share their political views, for "every punishment that is not needed is really a lawless punishment."

Bentham's attitude toward the French Revolution was never in line with prevailing fashions. On the one hand, he was opposed to revolution because he believed in progress through rational and peaceful persuasion (such as he thought possible in England through Parliament) ; on the other hand, he could not be enthusiastic over Burke's incantations of the glories of history because, in the light of Bentham's zeal for reform, history was little more than a record of crime and folly. In any event, Bentham welcomed the opportunities for fresh legislation, unencumbered by tradition and custom, that the French Revolution offered to reformers, and he sent several reform proposals to his French friends and correspondents.

The failure to influence French legislators turned his attention back to English affairs. Among many schemes, Bentham became deeply involved in the project of building a model prison, the Panopticon, a circular building so constructed that the governor of the prison, located in the center, could watch and direct every inmate. Bentham, who abhorred the cruel penalties current in his day, believed that criminals could be re-educated through work and understanding. The Panopticon was to revolutionize the physical layout of prisons as well as the moral approach to the treatment of prisoners. Bentham was engaged on the project for over twenty years and spent a fortune on it. The British Government was at first interested and then withdrew, but finally compensated Bentham for his expenditures. In his own country the Panopticon was to remain an ill-fated design, but in other countries it was more readily used ; in the United States, Joliet Penitentiary (Joliet, Illinois) is an adaptation of Bentham's architectural ideas, as first envisaged in his Panopticon.

Bentham's failure to persuade the rulers of Britain of his reform proposals turned his mind from specific legal and administrative reforms to the more fundamental inquiry into the nature of political organization, the ends of government, and the means of attaining them. Until he was sixty years of age he was never closely allied with either Whigs or Tories, though he had been born and reared a Tory of the Tories. His philanthropic schemes were above party, and Bentham had hoped that the force of logic and reason would be sufficient to bring about social change. Party meant passion, and Bentham distrusted passion. He thought that reason was universally human and nonpartisan. Although this belief may be philosophically right, Bentham failed to see that in politics reason itself is a party, and that it is always opposed by the party of irrationality, custom, and tradition.

Bentham's turn from philanthropy to radical political philosophy was greatly aided by his growing circle of disciples and collaborators, the most important of whom was James Mill, the father of John Stuart Mill. Moreover, after the defeat of Napoleon, democratic and radical ideas could again be expressed more freely in England. When the danger of Jacobinism and Napoleonic imperialism disappeared, it became difficult to brand any deviation from the *status quo* as dangerous and subversive.

In 1824 Bentham founded and financed the *Westminster Review,* the chief organ of Philosophical Radicalism and Utilitarianism, published until 1914 under a series of distinguished editors. In 1827 the foundation stone of University College was laid, Bentham being its chief promoter. Bentham was revolted by the hypocrisy and intellectual stagnation that he noted during his own student days in Oxford, and one of the main purposes of creating a new university in London was to get away from the strong clerical influence that prevailed at both Oxford and Cambridge. When Bentham entered Oxford at the age of twelve, he was forced to sign the Thirty-nine Articles of the Church of England. Other students were wont to subscribe to the Articles as a matter of formality. Not Bentham. He sat down and examined them, one by one. He found that some had no meaning and that others were contrary to reason and Scripture. A few fellow students shared Bentham's apprehensions about signing articles of faith they did not understand or believe in, but Bentham was the one to speak up. He was advised not to substitute his private judgment for the public judgment formed by wise men, and, Bentham said, "I signed: but by the view I found myself forced to take of the whole business, such an impression was made, as will never depart from me but with life."

Bentham never lost the view that the streets in Oxford were "paved with perjury," and if he could not change the two older universities, he was going to start a new university in the heart of London. From a small college with three hundred students, the University of London rapidly developed into the largest university of the British Commonwealth. The example of Bentham's effort in London inspired the establishment of universities and colleges in other cities like Manchester, Leeds, Birmingham, Liverpool, and, in the twentieth century, Reading, Sheffield, Bristol, and Swansea. These newer universities express the educational emancipation of the middle classes following their political emancipation in 1832. They recruit their students from all sections of the population, devote considerable attention to science and technology, and represent the secular, empirical, liberal outlook of the middle classes.

Neither Oxford nor Cambridge had given an important impulse to the scientific revolution of the eighteenth century, nor did the Utilitarians win their way with the aid of a single major supporter from the two older institutions. A large proportion of scientists, inventors, engineers, moral philosophers, and political economists came from Scotland (such as Adam Smith and James Watt, to cite but two of the most outstanding names), and in England the academies of the dissenters (who were excluded from the universities) were the breeding ground of modern physical and social science. London University was more than a new university in which distinctions of religion and social status were not recognized: it was a philosophical program, a bold venture into a new social philosophy. To this day the University of London represents the intellectual forces in England that are the product of industrial economics and democratic politics, and it does not have to live down burdensome traditions of royalism, theology, or political orthodoxy.

In celebrating the bicentennial of Bentham's birthday, the (London) *Times* (February 14, 1948) wrote that "Bentham still exerts a posthumous despotism over English politics, and on the whole it is a benevolent despotism." There is hardly a major reform in British life in the last five generations that does not go back to Bentham. He did a great part of his writing in the field of law, and many reforms of antiquated procedures and methods of evidence, as well as changes in the law of marriage and divorce, property, business, and trade-unions (to mention but a few) were the result of his agitation or that of his disciples. In criminal law, owing to Bentham's and Romilly's efforts, the worst forms of cruel punishment, such as whipping of women, transportation of criminals from England to the colonies, and the pillory, were eliminated, and the supreme penalty of death confined to treason and murder, whereas before Bentham's time there had been over two hundred offenses punishable by death.

In government and administration, Bentham saw the same lack of rational order that he saw in the law. In his *Constitutional Code* (1830–1841), on which he labored during the last eight years of his life but which remained unfinished, he laid down principles of orderly and rational government that were gradually adopted. A public health service, a system of national education, the collection of social and economic statistics (including the periodic taking of the census, the first of which was in 1801), colonial self-government, the proper correlation between central and local government, open competition for entry into the civil service, the organization of government departments in relation to their functional tasks—these are but a few of the major practical reforms of government and administration that Bentham and his group initiated. In the field of working-class activity, labor organizations ceased to be criminal conspiracies after the repeal of the Combination Acts in 1824 and thereafter existed on a legal basis.

Bentham is skeptical with regard to religion because it hinders intellectual progress by supporting belief apart from experience, "its only safe ground." The clergy are, according to Bentham, no more than "the advance-guard of the law," a body of inspectors and moral instructors, and their pay ought to come from the same source as the administration of justice and the police, the clergy being a part of the machinery of "internal security" of the state. Religion also hurts society, Bentham thinks, because it creates animosity against unbelievers and dissenters and subsidizes a standing army of "wonder-workers," the clergy, who deprave the intellect, surround themselves with mystery and superstition, and form an organized "array of human force and fraud." One of Bentham's main criticisms of religion was that it forms an "unholy alliance" with the "sinister interests of the earth." Bentham published one of his books on religion, *Church of Englandism and Its Catechism Examined* (1818), under his own name, and two others under pseudonyms: *The Analysis of Natural Religion on the Temporal Happiness of Mankind* (1822), by "Philip Beauchamp," and *Not Paul, but Jesus* (1823), by "Gamaliel Smith." When the *Analysis of Natural Religion* came out, its publisher, Richard Carlile, was in jail for having committed similar offenses against religion and the established church.

Religious toleration is to a large extent the product of agnostic skepticism rather than of religious fanaticism, and Bentham and his disciples opposed all legal discriminations against dissenters and Roman Catholics. Unitarians were granted toleration in 1813, and Bentham lived to see the emancipation of Roman Catholics in 1829.

Bentham was not interested in the metaphysical or sentimental values of religion, but solely in its utility; from this standpoint he found that religion was useless at best, and positively harmful in its more sinister manifestations. His agnosticism at first impeded the progress of his ideas in England, where religion, particularly in the dissenting churches, has often been in the forefront of liberal reform. Where, as in Continental Europe and South America, religion is generally synonymous with conservatism, and agnosticism with democracy, Bentham was the immediately avowed idol of secularist reformers, rationalists, and democrats.

One of Bentham's richest legacies to the science of government is his awareness that good government is more than a matter of tradition, common sense, and intuition, and that it therefore needs a foundation of preliminary *research* and *investigation*. In the twentieth century, investigation is increasingly becoming a fourth branch of government, without which the traditional three (the legislative, executive, and judicial) cannot properly function. Government has ceased to be a day-to-day affair of simple dimensions, confining itself to the maintenance of law and order, and now requires long-term planning, particularly in relation to national defense and social welfare. Bentham was the first modern writer to apply the investigative approach to problems of public policy, relating social facts to legal and administrative principles, a method that bore rich fruit in its more recent revival by Justice Brandeis and the sociological school of jurisprudence.

Bentham's main contribution to political science was not that he offered a novel principle of political philosophy—the principle of utility was well known to the Sophists in fifth-century Greece, and even the conception of the greatest happiness of the greatest number is no invention of Bentham—but that he steadily applied an *empirical* and *critical method* of investigation to concrete problems of law and government. He justly said of his own work that it was an attempt "to extend the experimental method of reasoning from the physical branch to the moral."

The principle of utility can be criticized for being uninspiring, not imaginative enough, and merely mechanical. Moreover, Bentham's style suffers from excessive Latinity, and his attempts at terminological precision—at times fruitful and suggestive—mar the readability of some of his writings. In general, his prose does not transport his readers into aesthetic ecstasy (he referred, for example, to his constitutionals before breakfast and after dinner as "anti-jentacular and post-prandial circumambulations"). Yet despite such criticisms, to some extent justified, Bentham changed the character of British institutions more than any other man in the nineteenth century.

The heirs of his investigative method, applying factual research to concrete and prosaic problems that affect the life of ordinary men and women, are the *Fabians*. As one looks over the list of publications of the Fabian Society (founded in 1884, and long under the influence of Sidney and Beatrice Webb), one finds little abstract theory but great concern for nursery education, parish councils, community feeding, and full employment. Like Bentham, the Fabian socialists are willing to stake their political fate on a few simple assumptions: first, that facts do matter; second, that there is an intimate relation between facts and social rules and institutions; and, third, that men can be persuaded by reason rather than by force and fraud.

In his economic philosophy Bentham was a pronounced individualist, preferring security of property to equality. But he was not dogmatic, and was ready to abandon laissez faire if in a specific instance a case for governmental intervention could be made on the ground of utility. As a matter of general economic policy, he recognized that government was responsible for public health and education, for "subsistence and defense," and he was well ahead of his time in urging government activity in social welfare, as well as in the building of roads and canals. Bentham also saw that the question of the limitation of individual economic freedom and governmental intervention was not one of pure abstract speculation, but that it could be decided only on the basis of history and environment. He specifically mentions Russia under Peter the Great, in which the scope of spontaneous individual action was "a blank," whereas that of government activity "abundant."

Because Bentham was not committed to any dogma of a priori limitations of public action, and because his ultimate objective was the greatest happiness of the greatest number rather than a particular mechanism to ensure it, it was only a question of time—and changing social and economic circumstances—before Benthamism was directed into the channels of socialism. The second generation of Benthamites, like James Mill, was still committed to the creed of laissez faire. Contrasted with the petty regulation of trade and commerce in the eighteenth century, laissez faire was a liberating and energizing doctrine that seemed to possess the inner evidence of axiomatic truth. Yet the third generation of Benthamism, as characterized by John Stuart Mill, slowly began to perceive that if the state could suppress murder and theft, it could also eliminate, or at least mitigate, economic oppression as an obstacle to personal liberty and happiness. The generation of John Stuart Mill thus formed the link between Benthamism and Fabianism.

BENTHAM

Principles of Morals and Legislation *

1. Of the Principle of Utility

1. Nature has placed mankind under the governance of two sovereign masters, *pain*

---

* From Jeremy Bentham, *An Introduction to the Principles of Morals and Legislation* (1789; rev. ed., 1823).

and *pleasure*. It is for them alone to point out what we ought to do, as well as to determine what we shall do. On the one hand the standard of right and wrong, on the other the chain of causes and effects, are fastened to their throne. They govern us in all we do, in all we say, in all we think;

every effort we can make to throw off our subjection, will serve but to demonstrate and confirm it. In words a man may pretend to abjure their empire: but in reality he will remain subject to it all the while. The *principle of utility* [1] recognizes this subjection, and assumes it for the foundation of that system, the object of which is to rear the fabric of felicity by the hands of reason and of law. Systems which attempt to question it, deal in sounds instead of senses, in caprice instead of reason, in darkness instead of light.

But enough of metaphor and declamation: it is not by such means that moral science is to be improved.

2. The principle of utility is the foundation of the present work: it will be proper therefore at the outset to give an explicit and determinate account of what is meant by it. By the principle [2] of utility is meant

---

[1] Note by the Author, July 1822.

To this denomination has of late been added, or substituted, the *greatest happiness* or *greatest felicity* principle: this for shortness, instead of saying at length *that principle* which states the greatest happiness of all those whose interest is in question, as being the right and proper, and only right and proper and universally desirable, end of human action: of human action in every situation, and in particular in that of a functionary or set of functionaries exercising the powers of Government. The word *utility* does not so clearly point to the ideas of *pleasure* and *pain* as the words *happiness* and *felicity* do: nor does it lead us to the consideration of the *number*, of the interests affected; to the *number*, as being the circumstance, which contributes, in the largest proportion, to the formation of the standard here in question; the *standard of right and wrong*, by which alone the propriety of human conduct, in every situation, can with propriety be tried. This want of a sufficiently manifest connexion between the ideas of *happiness* and *pleasure* on the one hand, and the idea of *utility* on the other, I have every now and then found operating, and with but too much efficiency, as a bar to the acceptance, that might otherwise have been given, to this principle.

[2] The word principle is derived from the Latin principium: which seems to be compounded of the two words *primus,* first, or chief, and *cipium,* a termination which seems to be derived from *capio,* to take, as in *mancipium, municipium;* to which are analogous, *auceps, forceps,* and others. It is a term of very vague and very extensive signification: it is applied to any thing which is conceived to

that principle which approves or disapproves of every action whatsoever, according to the tendency which it appears to have to augment or diminish the happiness of the party whose interest is in question: or, what is the same thing in other words, to promote or to oppose that happiness. I say of every action whatsoever; and therefore not only of every action of a private individual, but of every measure of government.

3. By utility is meant that property in any object, whereby it tends to produce benefit, advantage, pleasure, good, or happiness (all this in the present case comes to the same thing) or (what comes again to the same thing) to prevent the happening of mischief, pain, evil, or unhappiness to the party whose interest is considered: if that party be the community in general, then the happiness of the community: if a particular individual, then the happiness of that individual.

4. The interest of the community is one of the most general expressions that can occur in the phraseology of morals: no wonder that the meaning of it is often lost. When it has a meaning, it is this. The community is a fictitious *body,* composed of the individual persons who are considered as constituting as it were its *members.* The interest of the community then is, what?—the sum of the interests of the several members who compose it.

5. It is in vain to talk of the interest of the community, without understanding what is the interest of the individual. [3] A thing is said to promote the interest, or to be *for* the interest, of an individual, when it tends to add to the sum total of his pleasures: or,

---

serve as a foundation or beginning to any series of operations: in some cases, of physical operations; but of mental operations in the present case.

The principle here in question may be taken for an act of the mind; a sentiment; a sentiment of approbation; a sentiment which, when applied to an action, approves of its utility, as that quality of it by which the measure of approbation or disapprobation bestowed upon it ought to be governed.

[3] Interest is one of those words, which not having any superior *genus,* cannot in the ordinary way be defined.

what comes to the same thing, to diminish the sum total of his pains.

6. An action then may be said to be conformable to the principle of utility, or, for shortness sake, to utility (meaning with respect to the community at large) when the tendency it has to augment the happiness of the community is greater than any it has to diminish it.

7. A measure of government (which is but a particular kind of action, performed by a particular person or persons) may be said to be conformable to or dictated by the principle of utility, when in like manner the tendency which it has to augment the happiness of the community is greater than any which it has to diminish it.

8. When an action, or in particular a measure of government, is supposed by a man to be conformable to the principle of utility, it may be convenient, for the purposes of discourse, to imagine a kind of law or dictate, called a law or dictate of utility; and to speak of the action in question, as being conformable to such law or dictate.

9. A man may be said to be a partizan of the principle of utility, when the approbation or disapprobation he annexes to any action, or to any measure, is determined by and proportioned to the tendency which he conceives it to have to augment or to diminish the happiness of the community: or in other words, to its conformity or unconformity to the laws or dictates of utility.

10. Of an action that is conformable to the principle of utility one may always say either that it is one that ought to be done, or at least that it is not one that ought not to be done. One may say also, that it is right it should be done; at least that it is not wrong it should be done: that it is a right action; at least that it is not a wrong action. When thus interpreted, the words *ought*, and *right* and *wrong*, and others of that stamp, have a meaning: when otherwise, they have none.

11. Has the rectitude of this principle been ever formally contested? It should seem that it had, by those who have not known what they have been meaning. Is it

susceptible of any direct proof? it should seem not: for that which is used to prove every thing else, cannot itself be proved: a chain of proofs must have their commencement somewhere. To give such proof is as impossible as it is needless.

12. Not that there is or ever has been that human creature breathing, however stupid or perverse, who has not on many, perhaps on most occasions of his life, deferred to it. By the natural constitution of the human frame, on most occasions of their lives men in general embrace this principle, without thinking of it: if not for the ordering of their own actions, yet for the trying of their own actions, as well as of those of other men. There have been, at the same time, not many, perhaps, even of the most intelligent, who have been disposed to embrace it purely and without reserve. There are even few who have not taken some occasion or other to quarrel with it, either on account of their not understanding always how to apply it, or on account of some prejudice or other which they were afraid to examine into, or could not bear to part with. For such is the stuff that man is made of: in principle and in practice, in a right track and in a wrong one, the rarest of all human qualities is consistency.

13. When a man attempts to combat the principle of utility, it is with reasons drawn, without his being aware of it, from that very principle itself.[4] His arguments, if they

[4] "The principle of utility (I have heard it said) is a dangerous principle: it is dangerous on certain occasions to consult it." This is as much as to say, what? that it is not consonant to utility, to consult utility: in short, that it is *not* consulting it, to consult it.

Addition by the Author, July 1822.

Not long after the publication of the Fragment on Government, anno 1776, in which, in the character of an all-comprehensive and all-commanding principle, the principle of *utility* was brought to view, one person by whom observation to the above effect was made was *Alexander Wedderburn,* at that time Attorney or Solicitor General, afterwards successively Chief Justice of the Common Pleas, and Chancellor of England, under the successive titles of Lord Loughborough and Earl of Rosslyn. It was made—not indeed in my hearing, but in the hearing of a person by whom it was alprove any thing, prove not that the principle is *wrong*, but that, according to the applications he supposes to be made of it, it is *misapplied*. Is it possible for a man to move the earth? Yes; but he must first find out another earth to stand upon.

14. To disprove the propriety of it by arguments is impossible; but, from the causes that have been mentioned, or from some confused or partial view of it, a man may happen to be disposed not to relish it. Where this is the case, if he thinks the

most immediately communicated to me. So far from being self-contradictory, it was a shrewd and perfectly true one. By that distinguished functionary, the state of the Government was thoroughly understood: by the obscure individual, at that time not so much as supposed to be so: his disquisitions has not been as yet applied, with any thing like a comprehensive view, to the field of Constitutional Law, nor therefore to those features of the English Government, by which the greatest happiness of the ruling *one* with or without that of a favoured few, are now so plainly seen to be the only ends to which the course of it has at any time been directed. The *principle of utility* was an appellative, at that time employed—employed by me, as it had been by others, to designate that which in a more perspicuous and instructive manner, may, as above, be designated by the name of the *greatest happiness principle.* "This principle (said Wedderburn) is a dangerous one." Saying so, he said that which, to a certain extent, is strictly true: a principle, which lays down, as the only *right* and justifiable end of Government, the greatest happiness of the greatest number—how can it be denied, to be a dangerous one? dangerous it unquestionably is, to every government which has for its *actual* end or object, the greatest happiness of a certain *one*, with or without the addition of some comparatively small number of others, whom it is a matter of pleasure or accommodation to him to admit, each of them, to a share in the concern, on the footing of so many junior partners. *Dangerous* it therefore really was, to the interest—the sinister interest—of all those functionaries, himself included, whose interest it was, to maximize delay, vexation, and expense, in judicial and other modes of procedure, for the sake of the profit, extractible out of the expense. In a Government which had for its end in view the greatest happiness of the greatest number, Alexander Wedderburn might have been Attorney General and then Chancellor: but he would not have been Attorney General with £15,000 a year, nor Chancellor, with a peerage with a veto upon all justice, with £25,000 a year, and with 500 sinecures at his disposal, under the name of Ecclesiastical Benefices, besides *et coeteras.*

settling of his opinions on such a subject worth the trouble, let him take the following steps and at length, perhaps, he may come to reconcile himself to it.

I. Let him settle with himself, whether he would wish to discard this principle altogether; if so, let him consider what it is that all his reasonings (in matters of politics especially) can amount to?

II. If he would, let him settle with himself, whether he would judge and act without any principle, or whether there is any other he would judge and act by?

III. If there be, let him examine and satisfy himself whether the principle he thinks he has found is really any separate intelligible principle; or whether it be not a mere principle in words, a kind of phrase, which at bottom expresses neither more nor less than the mere averment of his own unfounded sentiments; that is, what in another person he might be apt to call caprice?

IV. If he is inclined to think that his own approbation or disapprobation, annexed to the idea of an act, without any regard to its consequences, is a sufficient foundation for him to judge and act upon, let him ask himself whether his sentiment is to be a standard of right and wrong, with respect to every other man, or whether every man's sentiment has the same privilege of being a standard to itself?

V. In the first case, let him ask himself whether his principle is not despotical, and hostile to all the rest of human race?

VI. In the second case, whether it is not anarchical, and whether at this rate there are not as many different standards of right and wrong as there are men? and whether even to the sane man, the same thing, which is right to-day, may not (without the least change in its nature) be wrong to-morrow? and whether the same thing is not right and wrong in the same place at the same time? and in either case, whether all argument is not at an end? and whether, when two men have said, "I like this," and "I don't like it," they can (upon such a principle) have any thing more to say?

VII. If he should have said to himself, No:

for that the sentiment which he proposes as a standard must be grounded on reflection, let him say on what particulars the reflection is to turn? if on particulars having relation to the utility of the act, then let him say whether this is not deserting his own principle, and borrowing assistance from that very one in opposition to which he sets it up: or if not on those particulars, on what other particulars?

VIII. If he should be for compounding the matter, and adopting his own principle in part, and the principle of utility in part, let him say how far he will adopt it?

IX. When he has settled with himself where he will stop, then let him ask himself how he justifies to himself the adopting it so far? and why he will not adopt it any farther?

X. Admitting any other principle than the principle of utility to be a right principle, a principle that it is right for a man to pursue; admitting (what is not true) that the word *right* can have a meaning without reference to utility, let him say whether there is any such thing as a *motive* that a man can have to pursue the dictates of it: if there is, let him say what that motive is, and how it is to be distinguished from those which enforce the dictates of utility: if not, then lastly let him say what it is this other principle can be good for?

2. Of Principles Adverse to That of Utility

1. If the principle of utility be a right principle to be governed by, and that in all cases, it follows from what has been just observed, that whatever principle differs from it in any case must necessarily be a wrong one. To prove any other principle, therefore, to be a wrong one, there needs no more than just to show it to be what it is, a principle of which the dictates are in some point or other different from those of the principle of utility: to state it is to confute it.

2. A principle may be different from that of utility in two ways: 1. By being constantly opposed to it: this is the case with a principle which may be termed the principle of *asceticism*.[1] 2. By being sometimes opposed to it, and sometimes not, as it may happen: this is the case with another, which may be termed the principle of *sympathy* and *antipathy*.

3. By the principle of asceticism I mean that principle, which, like the principle of utility, approves or disapproves of any action, according to the tendency which it appears to have to augment or diminish the happiness of the party whose interest is in question; but in an inverse manner: approving of actions in as far as they tend to diminish his happiness; disapproving of them in as far as they tend to augment it.

4. It is evident that any one who reprobates any the least particle of pleasure, as such, from whatever source derived, is *pro tanto* a partizan of the principle of asceticism. It is only upon that principle, and not from the principle of utility, that the most abominable pleasure which the vilest

---

[1] Ascetic is a term that has been sometimes applied to Monks. It comes from a Greek word which signifies *exercise*. The practices by which Monks sought to distinguish themselves from other men were called their Exercises. These exercises consisted in so many contrivances they had for tormenting themselves. By this they thought to ingratiate themselves with the Deity. For the Deity, said they, is a Being of infinite benevolence: now a Being of the most ordinary benevolence is pleased to see others make themselves as happy as they can: therefore to make ourselves as unhappy as we can is the way to please the Deity. If any body asked them, what motive they could find for doing all this? Oh! said they, you are not to imagine that we are punishing ourselves for nothing: we know very well what we are about. You are to know, that for every grain of pain it costs us now, we are to have a hundred grains of pleasure by and by. The case is, that God loves to see us torment ourselves at present: indeed he has as good as told us so. But this is done only to try us, in order just to see how we should behave: which it is plain he could not know, without making the experiment. Now then, from the satisfaction it gives him to see us make ourselves as unhappy as we can make ourselves in this present life, we have a sure proof of the satisfaction it will give him to see us as happy as he can make us in a life to come.

of malefactors ever reaped from his crime would be reprobated, if it stood alone. The case is, that it never does stand alone; but is necessarily followed by such a quantity of pain (or, what comes to the same thing, such a chance for a certain quantity of pain) that the pleasure in comparison of it, is as nothing: and this is the true and sole, but perfectly sufficient, reason for making it a ground for punishment.

5. There are two classes of men of very different complexions, by whom the principle of asceticism appears to have been embraced; the one a set of moralists, the other a set of religionists. Different accordingly have been the motives which appear to have recommended it to the notice of these different parties. Hope, that is the prospect of pleasure, seems to have animated the former: hope, the aliment of philosophic pride: the hope of honour and reputation at the hands of men. Fear, that is the prospect of pain, the latter: fear the offspring of superstitious fancy: the fear of future punishment at the hands of a splenetic and revengeful Deity. I say in this case fear: for of the invisible future, fear is more powerful than hope. These circumstances characterize the two different parties among the partizans of the principle of asceticism; the parties and their motives different, the principle the same.

6. The religious party, however, appear to have carried it farther than the philosophical: they have acted more consistently and less wisely. The philosophical party have scarcely gone farther than to reprobate pleasure: the religious party have frequently gone so far as to make it a matter of merit and of duty to court pain. The philosophical party have hardly gone farther than the making pain a matter of indifference. It is no evil, they have said: they have not said, it is a good. They have not so much as reprobated all pleasure in the lump. They have discarded only what they have called the gross; that is, such as are organical, or of which the origin is easily traced up to such as are organical: they have even cherished and magnified the re-

fined. Yet this, however, not under the name of pleasure: to cleanse itself from the sources of its impure original, it was necessary it should change its name: the honourable, the glorious, the reputable, the becoming, the *honestum*, the *decorum*, it was to be called: in short, any thing but pleasure.

7. From these two sources have flowed the doctrines from which the sentiments of the bulk of mankind have all along received a tincture of this principle; some from the philosophical, some from the religious, some from both. Men of education more frequently from the philosophical, as more suited to the elevation of their sentiments: the vulgar more frequently from the superstitious, as more suited to the narrowness of their intellect, undilated by knowledge: and to the abjectness of their condition, continually open to the attacks of fear. The tinctures, however, derived from the two sources, would naturally intermingle, insomuch that a man would not always know by which of them he was most influenced: and they would often serve to corroborate and enliven one another. It was this conformity that made a kind of alliance between parties of a complexion otherwise so dissimilar: and disposed them to unite upon various occasions against the common enemy, the partizan of the principle of utility, whom they joined in branding with the odious name of Epicurean.

8. The principle of asceticism, however, with whatever warmth it may have been embraced by its partizans as a rule of private conduct, seems not to have been carried to any considerable length, when applied to the business of government. In a few instances it has been carried a little way by the philosophical party: witness the Spartan regimen. Though then, perhaps, it may be considered as having been a measure of security: and an application, though a precipitate and perverse application, of the principle of utility. Scarcely in any instances, to any considerable length, by the religious: for the various monastic orders, and the societies of the Quakers, Dumplers, Moravians, and other religionists, have been free

societies, whose regimen no man has been astricted to without the intervention of his own consent. Whatever merit a man may have thought there would be in making himself miserable, no such notion seems ever to have occurred to any of them, that it may be a merit, much less a duty, to make others miserable: although it should seem, that if a certain quantity of misery were a thing so desirable, it would not matter much whether it were brought by each man upon himself, or by one man upon another. It is true, that from the same source from whence, among the religionists, the attachment to the principle of asceticism took its rise, flowed other doctrines and practices, from which misery in abundance was produced in one man by the instrumentality of another: witness the holy wars, and the persecutions for religion. But the passion for producing misery in these cases proceeded upon some special ground: the exercise of it was confined to persons of particular descriptions: they were tormented, not as men, but as heretics and infidels. To have inflicted the same miseries on their fellow-believers and fellow-secretaries, would have been as blameable in the eyes even of these religionists, as in those of a partizan of the principle of utility. For a man to give himself a certain number of stripes was indeed meritorious: but to give the same number of stripes to another man, not consenting, would have been a sin. We read of saints, who for the good of their souls, and the mortification of their bodies, have voluntarily yielded themselves a prey to vermin: but though many persons of this class have wielded the reins of empire, we read of none who have set themselves to work, and made laws on purpose, with a view of stocking the body politic with the breed of highwaymen, housebreakers, or incendiaries. If at any time they have suffered the nation to be preyed upon by swarms of idle pensioners, or useless placemen, it has rather been from negligence and imbecility, than from any settled plan for oppressing and plundering of the people. If at any time they have sapped the sources of national wealth, by cramping commerce, and driving the inhabitants into emigration, it has been with other views, and in pursuit of other ends. If they have declaimed against the pursuit of pleasure, and the use of wealth, they have commonly stopped at declamation: they have not, like Lycurgus, made express ordinances for the purpose of banishing the precious metals. If they have established idleness by a law, it has been not because idleness, the mother of vice and misery, is itself a virtue, but because idleness (say they) is the road to holiness. If under the notion of fasting, they have joined in the plan of confining their subjects to a diet, thought by some to be of the most nourishing and prolific nature, it has been not for the sake of making them tributaries to the nations by whom that diet was to be supplied, but for the sake of manifesting their own power, and exercising the obedience of the people. If they have established, or suffered to be established, punishments for the breach of celibacy, they have done no more than comply with the petitions of those deluded rigorists, who, dupes to the ambitious and deep-laid policy of their rulers, first laid themselves under that idle obligation by a vow.

9. The principle of asceticism seems originally to have been the reverie of certain hasty speculators, who having perceived, or fancied, that certain pleasures, when reaped in certain circumstances, have, at the long run, been attended with pains more than equivalent to them, took occasion to quarrel with every thing that offered itself under the name of pleasure. Having then got thus far, and having forgot the point which they set out from, they pushed on, and went so much further as to think it meritorious to fall in love with pain. Even this, we see, is at bottom but the principle of utility misapplied.

10. The principle of utility is capable of being consistently pursued; and it is but tautology to say, that the more consistently it is pursued, the better it must ever be for humankind. The principle of asceticism never was, nor ever can be, consistently

pursued by any living creature. Let but one tenth part of the inhabitants of this earth pursue it consistently, and in a day's time they will have turned it into a hell.

11. Among principles adverse to that of utility, that which at this day seems to have most influence in matters of government, is what may be called the principle of sympathy and antipathy. By the principle of sympathy and antipathy, I mean that principle which approves or disapproves of certain actions, not on account of their tending to augment the happiness, nor yet on account of their tending to diminish the happiness of the party whose interest is in question, but merely because a man finds himself disposed to approve or disapprove of them: holding up that approbation or disapprobation as a sufficient reason for itself, and disclaiming the necessity of looking out for any extrinsic ground. Thus far in the general department of morals. and in the particular department of politics, measuring out the quantum (as well as determining the ground) of punishment, by the degree of the disapprobation.

12. It is manifest, that this is rather a principle in name than in reality: it is not a positive principle of itself, so much as a term employed to signify the negation of all principle. What one expects to find in a principle is something that points out some external consideration, as a means of warranting and guiding the internal sentiments of approbation and disapprobation: this expectation is but ill fulfilled by a proposition, which does neither more nor less than hold up each of those sentiments as a ground and standard for itself.

13. In looking over the catalogue of human actions (says a partizan of this principle) in order to determine which of them are to be marked with the seal of disapprobation, you need but to take counsel of your own feelings: whatever you find in yourself a propensity to condemn, is wrong for that very reason. For the same reason it is also meet for punishment: in what proportion it is adverse to utility, or whether it be adverse to utility at all, is a matter that

makes no difference. In that same *proportion* also is it meet for punishment: if you hate much, punish much: if you hate little, punish little: punish as you hate. If you hate not at all, punish not at all: the fine feelings of the soul are not to be overborne and tyrannized by the harsh and rugged dictates of political utility.

14. The various systems that have been formed concerning the standard of right and wrong, may all be reduced to the principle of sympathy and antipathy. One account may serve for all of them. They consist all of them in so many contrivances for avoiding the obligation of appealing to any external standard, and for prevailing upon the reader to accept of the author's sentiment or opinion as a reason for itself. The phrases are different, but the principle is the same.[2]

---

[2] It is curious enough to observe the variety of inventions men have hit upon, and the variety of phrases they have brought forward, in order to conceal from the world, and, if possible, from themselves, this very general and therefore very pardonable self-sufficiency.

1. One man says, he has a thing made on purpose to tell him what is right and what is wrong; and that it is called a *moral sense:* and then he goes to work at his ease, and says, such a thing is right, and such a thing is wrong—why? "because my moral sense tells me it is."

2. Another man comes and alters the phrase: leaving out *moral*, and putting in *common*, in the room of it. He then tells you, that his common sense teaches him what is right and wrong, as surely as the other's moral sense did: meaning by common sense, a sense of some kind or other, which, he says, is possessed by all mankind: the sense of those, whose sense is not the same as the author's being struck out of the account as not worth taking. This contrivance does better than the other; for a moral sense, being a new thing, a man may feel about him a good while without being able to find it out: but common sense is as old as the creation; and there is no man but would be ashamed to be thought not to have as much of it as his neighbours. It has another great advantage: by appearing to share power, it lessens envy: for when a man gets up upon this ground, in order to anathematize those who differ from him, it is not by a *sic volo sic jubeo*, but by a *velitis jubeatis*,

3. Another man comes, and says, that as to a moral sense indeed, he cannot find that he has any such thing: that however he has an *understanding*, which will do quite as well. This understanding, he

15. It is manifest, that the dictates of this principle will frequently coincide with those of utility, though perhaps without intending any such thing. Probably more frequently than not: and hence it is that the business of penal justice is carried on upon that tolerable sort of footing upon which we see it carried on in common at this day. For what more natural or more general ground of hatred to a practice can there be, than the mischievousness of such practice? What all men are exposed to suffer by, all men will be disposed to hate. It is far

yet, however, from being a constant ground: for when a man suffers, it is not always that he knows what it is he suffers by. A man may suffer grievously, for instance, by a new tax, without being able to trace up the cause of his sufferings to the injustice of some neighbour, who has eluded the payment of an old one.

16. The principle of sympathy and antipathy is most apt to err on the side of severity. It is for applying punishment in many cases which deserve none: in many cases which deserve some, it is for applying more

---

says, is the standard of right and wrong: it tells him so and so. All good and wise men understand as he does: if other men's understandings differ in any point from his, so much the worse for them: it is a sure sign they are either defective or corrupt.

4. Another man says, that there is an eternal and immutable Rule of Right: that the rule of right dictates so and so: and then he begins giving you his sentiments upon any thing that comes uppermost: and these sentiments (you are to take for granted) are so many branches of the eternal rule of right.

5. Another man, or perhaps the same man (it's no matter) says, that there are certain practices conformable, and others repugnant, to the Fitness of Things; and then he tells you, at his leisure, what practices are conformable and what repugnant: just as he happens to like a practice or dislike it.

6. A great multitude of people are continually talking of the Law of Nature; and then they go on giving you their sentiments about what is right and what is wrong: and these sentiments, you are to understand, are so many chapters and sections of the Law of Nature.

7. Instead of the phrase, Law of Nature, you have sometimes, Law of Reason, Right Reason, Natural Justice, Natural Equity, Good Order. Any of them will do equally well. This latter is most used in politics. The three last are much more tolerable than the others, because they do not very explicitly claim to be any thing more than phrases: they insist but feebly upon the being looked upon as so many positive standards of themselves, and seem content to be taken, upon occasion, for phrases expressive of the conformity of the thing in question to the proper standard, whatever that may be. On most occasions, however, it will be better to say *utility: utility* is clearer, as referring more explicitly to pain and pleasure.

8. We have one philosopher, who says, there is no harm in any thing in the world but in telling a lie: and that if, for example, you were to murder your own father, this would only be a particular way of saying, he was not your father. Of course,

when this philosopher sees any thing that he does not like, he says, it is a particular way of telling a lie. It is saying, that the act ought to be done, or may be done, when, *in truth*, it ought not to be done.

9. The fairest and openest of them all is that sort of man who speaks out, and says, I am of the number of the Elect: now God himself takes care to inform the Elect what is right: and that with so good effect, and let them strive ever so, they cannot help not only knowing it but practising it. If therefore a man wants to know what is right and what is wrong, he has nothing to do but to come to me.

It is upon the principle of antipathy that such and such acts are often reprobated on the score of their being *unnatural:* the practice of exposing children, established among the Greeks and Romans, was an unnatural practice. Unnatural, when it means any thing, means unfrequent: and there it means something; although nothing to the present purpose. But here it means no such thing: for the frequency of such acts is perhaps the great complaint. It therefore means nothing; nothing, I mean which there is in the act itself. All it can serve to express is, the disposition of the person who is talking of it: the disposition he is in to be angry at the thoughts of it. Does it merit his anger? Very likely it may: but whether it does or not is a question, which, to be answered rightly, can only be answered upon the principle of utility.

Unnatural, is as good a word as moral sense, or common sense; and would be as good a foundation for a system. Such an act is unnatural; that is, repugnant to nature: for I do not like to practice it: and, consequently, do not practice it. It is therefore repugnant to what ought to be the nature of every body else.

The mischief common to all these ways of thinking and arguing (which, in truth, as we have seen, are but one and the same method, couched in different forms of words) is their serving as a cloak, and pretence, and aliment, to despotism: if not a despotism in practice, a despotism however in disposition: which is but too apt, when pretence and than they deserve. There is no incident imaginable, be it ever so trivial, and so remote from mischief, from which this principle may not extract a ground of punishment. Any difference in taste: any difference in opinion: upon one subject as well as

power offer, to show itself in practice. The consequence is, that with intentions very commonly of the purest kind, a man becomes a torment either to himself or his fellow-creatures. If he be of the melancholy cast, he sits in silent grief, bewailing their blindness and depravity: if of the irascible, he declaims with fury and virulence against all who differ from him; blowing up the coals of fanaticism, and branding with the charge of corruption and insincerity, every man who does not think, or profess to think, as he does.

If such a man happens to possess the advantages of style, his book may do a considerable deal of mischief before the nothingness of it is understood. These principles, if such they can be called, it is more frequent to see applied to morals than to politics: but their influence extends itself to both. In politics, as well as morals, a man will be at least equally glad of a pretence for deciding any question in the manner that best pleases him, without the trouble of inquiry. If a man is an infallible judge of what is right and wrong in the actions of private individuals, why not in the measures to be observed by public men in the direction of those actions? accordingly (not to mention other chimeras) I have more than once known the pretended law of nature set up in legislative debates, in opposition to arguments derived from the principle of utility.

"But is it never, then, from any other considerations than those of utility, that we derive our notions of right and wrong?" I do not know: I do not care. Whether a moral sentiment can be originally conceived from any other source than a view of utility, is one question: whether upon examination and reflection it can, in point of fact, be actually persisted in and justified on any other ground, by a person reflecting within himself, is another: whether in point of right it can properly be justified on any other ground, by a person addressing himself to the community, is a third. The two first are questions of speculation: it matters not, comparatively speaking, how they are decided. The last is a question of practice: the decision of it is of as much importance as that of any can be.

"I feel in myself," (say you) "a disposition to approve of such or such an action in a moral view: but this is not owing to any notions I have of its being a useful one to the community. I do not pretend to know whether it be an useful one or not: it may be, for aught I know, a mischievous one." "But is it then," (say I) "a mischievous one? examine: and if you can make yourself sensible that it is so,

upon another. No disagreement so trifling which perseverance and altercation will not render serious. Each becomes in the other's eyes an enemy, and, if laws permit, a criminal.[3] This is one of the circumstances by which the human race is distinguished (not

then, if duty means any thing, that is, moral duty, it is your *duty* at least to abstain from it: and more than that, if it is what lies in your power, and can be done without too great a sacrifice, to endeavour to prevent it. It is not your cherishing the notion of it in your bosom, and giving it the name of virtue, that will excuse you."

"I feel in myself," (say you again) "a disposition to detest such or such an action in a moral view; but this is not owing to any notions I have of its being a mischievous one to the community. I do not pretend to know whether it be a mischievous one or not: it may be not a mischievous one: it may be, for aught I know, an useful one."—"May it indeed," (say I) "an useful one? but let me tell you then, that unless duty, and right and wrong, be just what you please to make them, if it really be not a mischievous one, and any body has a mind to do it, it is no duty of yours, but, on the contrary, it would be very wrong in you, to take upon you to prevent him: detest it within yourself as much as you please; that it may be a very good reason (unless it be also a useful one) for your not doing it yourself: but if you go about, by word or deed, to do any thing to hinder him, or make him suffer for it, it is you, and not he, that have done wrong: it is not your setting yourself to blame his conduct, or branding it with the name of vice, that will make him culpable, or you blameless. Therefore, if you can make yourself content that he shall be of one mind, and you of another, about this matter, and so continue, it is well: but if nothing will serve you, but that you and he must needs be of the same mind, I'll tell you what you have to do: it is for you to get the better of your antipathy, not for him to truckle to it."

[3] King James the First of England had conceived a violent antipathy against Arians: two of whom he burnt. This gratification he procured himself without much difficulty: the notions of the times were favourable to it. He wrote a furious book against Vorstius, for being what was called an Arminian: for Vorstius was at a distance. He also wrote a furious book called "A Counterblast to Tobacco," against the use of that drug, which Sir Walter Raleigh had then lately introduced. Had the notions of the times co-operated with him, he would have burnt the Anabaptist and the smoke of tobacco in the same fire. However, he had the satisfaction of putting Raleigh to death afterwards, though for another crime.

Disputes concerning the comparative excellence of French and Italian music have occasioned very much indeed to its advantage) from the brute creation.

17. It is not, however, by any means unexampled for this principle to err on the side of lenity. A near and perceptible mischief moves antipathy. A remote and imperceptible mischief, though not less real, has no effect. Instances in proof of this will occur in numbers in the course of the work. It would be breaking in upon the order of it to give them here.

18. It may be wondered, perhaps, that in all this while no mention has been made of the *theological* principle; meaning that principle which professes to recur for the standard of right and wrong to the will of God. But the case is, this is not in fact a distinct principle. It is never any thing more or less than one or other of the three beforementioned principles presenting itself under another shape. The *will* of God here meant cannot be his revealed will, as contained in the sacred writings: for that is a system which nobody ever thinks of recurring to at this time of day, for the details of political administration: and even before it can be applied to the details of private conduct, it is universally allowed, by the most eminent divines of all persuasions, to stand in need of pretty ample interpretations; else to what use are the works of those divines? And for the guidance of these

interpretations, it is also allowed, that some other standard must be assumed. The will then which is meant on this occasion, is that which may be called the *presumptive* will: that is to say, that which is presumed to be his will on account of the conformity of its dictates to those of some other principle. What then may be this other principle? it must be one or other of the three mentioned above: for there cannot, as we have seen, be any more. It is plain, therefore, that setting revelation out of the question, no light can ever be thrown upon the standard of right and wrong, by any thing that can be said upon the question, what is God's will. We may be perfectly sure, indeed, that whatever is right is conformable to the will of God: but so far is that from answering the purpose of showing us what is right, that it is necessary to know first whether a thing is right, in order to know from thence whether it be conformable to the will of God.[4]

19. There are two things which are very apt to be confounded, but which it imports us carefully to distinguish:—the motive or cause, which, by operating on the mind of

---

serious bickerings at Paris. One of the parties would not have been sorry (says Mr. D'Alembert) to have brought government into the quarrel. Pretences were sought after and urged. Long before that, a dispute of like nature, and of at least equal warmth, had been kindled at London upon the comparative merits of two composers at London; where riots between the approvers and disapprovers of a new play are, at this day, not unfrequent. The ground of quarrel between the Bigendians and the Littleendians in the fable, was not more frivolous than many an one which has laid empires desolate. In Russia, it is said, there was a time when some thousands of persons lost their lives in a quarrel, in which the government had taken part, about the number of fingers to be used in making the sign of the cross. This was in days of yore: the ministers of Catherine II are better *instructed* than to take any other part in such disputes, than that of preventing the parties concerned from doing one another a mischief.

[4] The principle of theology refers every thing to God's pleasure. But what is God's pleasure? God does not, he confessedly does not now, either speak or write to us. How then are we to know what is his pleasure? By observing what is our own pleasure, and pronouncing it to be his. Accordingly what is called the pleasure of God, is and must necessarily be (revelation apart) neither more nor less than the good pleasure of the person, whoever he be, who is pronouncing what he believes, or pretends, to be God's pleasure. How know you it to be God's pleasure that such or such an act should be abstained from? whence come you even to suppose as much? "Because the engaging in it would, I imagine, be prejudicial upon the whole to the happiness of mankind;" says the partizan of the principal of utility: "Because the commission of it is attended with a gross and sensual, or at least with a trifling and transient satisfaction;" says the partizan of the principle of asceticism: "Because I detest the thought of it; and I cannot, neither ought I to be called upon to tell why;" says he who proceeds upon the principle of antipathy. In the words of one or other of these must that person necessarily answer (revelation apart) who professes to take for his standard the will of God.

an individual, is productive of any act: and the ground or reason which warrants a legislator, or other by-stander, in regarding that act with an eye of approbation. When the act happens, in the particular instance in question, to be productive of effects which we approve of, much more if we happen to observe that the same motive may frequently be productive, in other instances, of the like effects, we are apt to transfer our approbation to the motive itself, and to assume, as the just ground for the approbation we bestow on the act, the circumstance of its originating from that motive. It is in this way that the sentiment of antipathy has often been considered as a just ground of action. Antipathy, for instance, in such or such a case, is the cause of an action which is attended with good effects: but this does not make it a right ground of action in that case, any more than in any other. Still farther. Not only the effects are good, but the agent sees beforehand that they will be so. This may make the action indeed a perfectly right action: but it does not make antipathy a right ground of action. For the same sentiment of antipathy, if implicitly deferred to, may be, and very frequently is, productive of the very worst effects. Antipathy, therefore, can never be a right ground of action. No more, therefore, can resentment, which, as will be seen more particularly hereafter, is but a modification of antipathy. The only right ground of action, that can possibly subsist, is, after all, the consideration of utility, which if it is a right principle of action, and of approbation, in any one case, is so in every other. Other principles in abundance, that is, other motives, may be the reasons why such and such an act *has* been done: that is, the reasons or causes of its being done: but it is this alone that can be the reason why it might or ought to have been done. Antipathy or resentment requires always to be regulated, to prevent its doing mischief: to be regulated by what? always by the principle of utility. The principle of utility neither requires nor admits of any other regulator than itself.

3. Of the Four Sanctions or Sources of Pain and Pleasure

1. It has been shown that the happiness of the individuals, of whom a community is composed, that is their pleasures and their security, is the end and the sole end which the legislator ought to have in view: the sole standard, in conformity to which each individual ought, as far as depends upon the legislator, to be *made* to fashion his behaviour. But whether it be this or any thing else that is to be *done,* there is nothing by which a man can ultimately be *made* to do it, but either pain or pleasure. Having taken a general view of these two grand objects (*viz.,* pleasure, and what comes to the same thing, immunity from pain) in the character of *final* causes; it will be necessary to take a view of pleasure and pain itself, in the character of *efficient* causes or means.

2. There are four distinguishable sources from which pleasure and pain are in use to flow: considered separately, they may be termed the *physical,* the *political,* the *moral,* and the *religious:* and inasmuch as the pleasures and pains belonging to each of them are capable of giving a binding force to any law or rule of conduct, they may all of them be termed *sanctions.*[1]

---

[1] Sanctio, in Latin, was used to signify the *act of binding,* and, by a common grammatical transition, *any thing which serves to bind a man:* to wit, to the observance of such or such a mode of conduct. According to a Latin grammarian, the import of the word is derived by rather a far-fetched process (such as those commonly are, and in a great measure indeed must be, by which intellectual ideas are derived from sensible ones) from the word *sanguis,* blood: because, among the Romans, with a view to inculcate into the people a persuasion that such or such a mode of conduct would be rendered obligatory upon a man by the force of which I call the religious sanction (that is, that he would be made to suffer by the extraordinary interposition of some superior being, if he failed to observe the mode of conduct in question) certain ceremonies were contrived by the priests: in the course of which ceremonies the blood of victims was made use of.

A Sanction then is a source of obligatory powers or *motives:* that is, of *pains* and *pleasures;* which, according as they are connected with such or such

3. If it be in the present life, and from the ordinary course of nature, not purposely modified by the interposition of the will of any human being, nor by any extraordinary interposition of any superior invisible being, that the pleasure or the pain takes place or is expected, it may be said to issue from or to belong to the *physical sanction.*

4. If at the hands of a *particular* person or set of persons in the community, who under names correspondent to that of *judge,* are chosen for the particular purpose of dispensing it, according to the will of the sovereign or supreme ruling power in the state, it may be said to issue from the *political sanction.*

5. If at the hands of such *chance* persons in the community, as the party in question may happen in the course of his life to have concerns with, according to each man's spontaneous disposition, and not according to any settled or concerted rule, it may be said to issue from the *moral* or *popular* sanction.[2]

6. If from the immediate hand of a superior invisible being, either in the present life, or in a future, it may be said to issue from the *religious sanction.*

7. Pleasures or pains which may be expected to issue from the *physical, political,* or *moral* sanctions, must all of them be expected to be experienced, if ever, in the *present* life: those which may be expected to issue from the *religious* sanction, may be expected to be experienced either in the *present* life or in a *future.*

8. Those which can be experienced in the present life, can of course be no others than such as human nature in the course of the present life is susceptible of: and from each

of these sources may flow all the pleasures or pains of which, in the course of the present life, human nature is susceptible. With regard to these then (with which alone we have in this place any concern) those of them which belong to any one of those sanctions, differ not ultimately in kind from those which belong to any one of the other three: the only difference there is among them lies in the circumstances that accompany their production. A suffering which befalls a man in the natural and spontaneous course of things, shall be styled, for instance, a *calamity;* in which case, if it be supposed to befall him through any imprudence of his, it may be styled a punishment issuing from the physical sanction. Now this same suffering, if inflicted by the law, will be what is commonly called a *punishment;* if incurred for want of any friendly assistance, which the misconduct, or supposed misconduct, of the sufferer has occasioned to be withholden, a punishment issuing from the *moral* sanction; if through the immediate interposition of a particular providence, a punishment issuing from the *religious* sanction.

9. A man's goods, or his person, are consumed by fire. If this happened to him by what is called an accident, it was a calamity: if by reason of his own imprudence (for instance, from his neglecting to put his candle out) it may be styled a punishment of the physical sanction: if it happened to him by the sentence of the political magistrate, a punishment belonging to the political sanction; that is, what is commonly called a punishment: if for want of any assistance which his *neighbour* withheld from him out of some dislike to his *moral* character, a punishment of the *moral* sanction: if by an immediate act of *God's* displeasure, manifested an account of some *sin* committed by him, or through any distraction of mind, occasioned by the dread of such pleasure, a punishment of the *religious* sanction.[3]

---

modes of conduct, operate, and are indeed the only things which can operate, as *motives.*

[2] Better termed *popular,* as more directly indicative of its constituent cause; as likewise of its relation to the more common phrase *public opinion,* in French *opinion publique,* the name there given to that tutelary power, of which of late so much is said, and by which so much is done. The latter appellation is however unhappy and inexpressive; since if *opinion* is material, it is only in virtue of the influence it exercises over action, through the medium of the affections and the will.

[3] A suffering conceived to befall a man by the immediate act of God, as above, is often, for shortness' sake, called a *judgment:* instead of saying, a

10. As to such of the pleasures and pains belonging to the religious sanction, as regard a future life, of what kind these may be we cannot know. These lie not open to our observation. During the present life they are matter only of expectation: and, whether that expectation be derived from natural or revealed religion, the particular kind of pleasure or pain, if it be different from all those which lie open to our observation, is what we can have no idea of. The best ideas we can obtain of such pains and pleasures are altogether unliquidated in point of quality. In what other respects our ideas of them *may* be liquidated will be considered in another place.

11. Of these four sanctions the physical is altogether, we may observe, the groundwork of the political and the moral: so is it also of the religious, in as far as the latter bears relation to the present life. It is included in each of those other three. This may operate in any case (that is, any of the pains or pleasures belonging to it may operate) independently of *them:* none of *them* can operate but by means of this. In a word, the powers of nature may operate of themselves; but neither the magistrate, nor men at large, *can* operate, nor is God in the case in question *supposed* to operate, but through the powers of nature.

12. For these four objects, which in their nature have so much in common, it seemed of use to find a common name. It seemed of use, in the first place, for the convenience of giving a name to certain pleasures and pains, for which a name equally characteristic could hardly otherwise have been found: in the second place, for the sake of holding up the efficacy of certain moral forces, the influence of which is apt not to be sufficiently attended to. Does the political sanction exert an influence over the conduct of mankind? The moral, the religious sanctions do so too. In every inch of his career are the operations of the political magistrate liable to be aided or im-

peded by these two foreign powers: who, one or other of them, or both, are sure to be either his rivals or his allies. Does it happen to him to leave them out of his calculations? he will be sure almost to find himself mistaken in the result. Of all this we shall find abundant proofs in the sequel of this work. It behoves him, therefore, to have them continually before his eyes; and that under such a name as exhibits the relation they bear to his own purposes and designs.

4. *Value of a Lot of Pleasure or Pain, How to be Measured*

1. Pleasures then, and the avoidance of pains, are the *ends* which the legislator has in view: it behoves him therefore to understand their *value*. Pleasures and pains are the *instruments* he has to work with: it behoves him therefore to understand their force, which is again, in other words, their value.

2. To a person considered *by himself,* the value of a pleasure or pain considered *by itself,* will be greater or less, according to the four following circumstances:[1]

    I. Its *intensity.*

    II. Its *duration.*

    III. Its *certainty* or *uncertainty.*

    IV. Its *propinquity* or *remoteness.*

3. These are the circumstances which are to be considered in estimating a pleasure or a pain considered each of them by itself. But when the value of any pleasure

---

[1] These circumstances have since been dominated *elements* or *dimensions* of *value* in a pleasure or a pain.

Not long after the publication of the first edition, the following memoriter verses were framed, in the view of lodging more effectually, in the memory, these points, on which the whole fabric of morals and legislation may be seen to rest.

Intense, long, certain, speedy, fruitful, pure—
Such marks in *pleasures* and in *pains* endure.
Such pleasures seek if *private* be thy end:
If it be *public*, wide let them *extend.*
Such *pains* avoid, whichever be thy view:
If pains *must* come, let them *extend* to few.

---

suffering inflicted on him in consequence of a special judgment formed, and resolution thereupon taken, by the Deity.

or pain is considered for the purpose of estimating the tendency of any *act* by which it is produced, there are two other circumstances to be taken into account; these are,

v. Its *fecundity*, or the chance it has of being followed by sensations of the *same* kind: that is, pleasures, if it be a pleasure: pains, if it be a pain.

vi. Its *purity*, or the chance it has of *not* being followed by sensations of the *opposite* kind: that is, pains, if it be a pleasure: pleasures, if it be a pain.

These two last, however, are in strictness scarcely to be deemed properties of the pleasure or the pain itself; they are not, therefore, in strictness to be taken into the account of the value of that pleasure or that pain. They are in strictness to be deemed properties only of the act, or other event, by which such pleasure or pain has been produced; and accordingly are only to be taken into the account of the tendency of such act or such event.

4. To a *number* of persons, with reference to each of whom the value of a pleasure or a pain is considered, it will be greater or less, according to seven circumstances: to wit, the six preceding ones; *viz.*

i. Its *intensity*.

ii. Its *duration*.

iii. Its *certainty* or *uncertainty*.

vi. Its *propinquity* or *remoteness*.

v. Its *fecundity*.

vi. Its *purity*.

And one other; to wit:

vii. Its *extent;* that is, the number of persons to whom it *extends;* or (in other words) who are affected by it.

5. To take an exact account then of the general tendency of any act, by which the interests of a community are affected, proceed as follows. Begin with any one person of those whose interests seem most immediately to be affected by it: and take an account,

i. Of the value of each distinguishable *pleasure* which appears to be produced by it in the *first* instance.

ii. Of the value of each *pain* which ap-

pears to be produced by it in the *first* instance.

iii. Of the value of each pleasure which appears to be produced by it *after* the first. This constitutes the *fecundity* of the first *pleasure* and the *impurity* of the first *pain*.

iv. Of the value of each *pain* which appears to be produced by it after the first. This constitutes the *fecundity* of the first *pain,* and the *impurity* of the first pleasure.

v. Sum up all the values of all the *pleasures* on the one side, and those of all the pains on the other. The balance, if it be on the side of pleasure, will give the *good* tendency of the act upon the whole, with respect to the interests of that *individual* person; if on the side of pain, the *bad* tendency of it upon the whole.

vi. Take an account of the *number* of persons whose interests appear to be concerned; and repeat the above process with respect to each. *Sum up* the numbers expressive of the degrees of *good* tendency, which the act has, with respect to each individual, in regard to whom the tendency of it is *good* upon the whole: do this again with respect to each individual, in regard to whom the tendency of it is *good* upon the whole: do this again with respect to each individual, in regard to whom the tendency of it is *bad* upon the whole. Take the *balance;* which, if on the side of *pleasure,* will give the general *good tendency* of the act, with respect to the total number or community of individuals concerned; if on the side of pain, the general *evil tendency,* with respect to the same community.

6. It is not to be expected that this process should be strictly pursued previously to every moral judgment, or to every legislative or judicial operation. It may, however, be always kept in view: and as near as the process actually pursued on these occasions approaches to it, so near will such process approach to the character of an exact one.

7. The same process is alike applicable to pleasure and pain, in whatever shape they appear: and by whatever denomination they are distinguished: to pleasure, whether it

be called *good* (which is properly the cause or instrument of pleasure) or *profit* (which is distant pleasure, or the cause or instrument of distant pleasure) or *convenience,* or *advantage, benefit, emolument, happiness,* and so forth: to pain, whether it be called *evil* (which corresponds to *good*) or *mischief,* or *inconvenience,* or *disadvantage,* or *loss,* or *unhappiness,* and so forth.

8. Nor is this a novel and unwarranted, any more than it is a useless theory. In all this there is nothing but what the practice of mankind, wheresoever they have a clear view of their own interest, is perfectly conformable to. An article of property, an estate in land, for instance, is valuable. on what account? On account of the pleasures of all kinds which it enables a man to produce, and what comes to the same thing the pains of all kinds which it enables him to avert. But the value of such an article of property is universally understood to rise or fall according to the length or shortness of the time which a man has in it: the certainty or uncertainty of its coming into possession: and the nearness or remoteness of the time at which, if at all, it is to come into possession. As to the *intensity* of the pleasures which a man may derive from it, this is never thought of, because it depends upon the use which each particular person may come to make of it; which cannot be estimated till the particular pleasures he may come to derive from it, or the particular pains he may come to exclude by means of it, are brought to view. For the same reason, neither does he think of the *fecundity* or *purity* of those pleasures.

CHAPTER 20

THE DILEMMA OF DEMOCRACY: LIBERTY AND EQUALITY

EVERY revolution contains a utopian element that inspires its makers and is indispensable to its success. The leaders of the English, American, and French revolutions in the seventeenth and eighteenth centuries looked upon democracy, not as a beginning, but as an end—the culmination of man's age-long struggle for freedom. As long as democracy was a dream, it was impossible to appraise it realistically, and the history of the discussions of democracy from Plato to Burke suffers from a sense of unreality and lack of sufficient experience. Defenders of democracy often saw in it a kind of paradise within the reach of man, whereas its opponents predicted that, if it were ever allowed to exist long enough, it would end in the destruction of society and the moral values that support it.

Various experiences in democracy had failed. The Puritan Revolution was democratic in inspiration, but it was unable to provide a true object lesson of democracy because it quickly turned into dictatorship. The Glorious Revolution of 1688, more successful than the Puritan Revolution in establishing itself as a lasting political regime, was nevertheless liberal-conservative rather than radical-democratic. In the eighteenth century England therefore attracted liberal aristocrats like Montesquieu but had little room for radical democrats like Tom Paine. The latter had to flee his native land to escape political persecution after he had vehemently defended the French Revolution in his controversy with Edmund Burke.

The French Revolution, too, which started with so little violence in 1789, ceased to be an experiment in democracy in 1799, when Napoleon set up a military dictatorship, and shortly thereafter his own brand of monarchy. Napoleon's regime was followed by the even less democratic restoration of the Bourbons, who attempted to go back to the prerevolutionary government of kingship by divine right, in alliance with the clergy and aristocracy. But the Bourbons, who had learned nothing and forgotten nothing, did not retain the throne for long. The Revolution of July, 1830, ousted King Charles X and established a constitutional monarchy in which the middle class was the predominant political and social element. The way was again open for experiments in popular government.

The first major democracy in the modern world is that of the United States; only after its establishment and success could the issue of democracy be brought down from the clouds of subjunctive and hypothetical speculation to the firm ground of positive and empirical observation. The political writer in the nineteenth century first to perceive that democracy was the "irresistible" new form of society and government, and that the United States was the world's key laboratory of democracy, was an aristocratic Frenchman, Alexis de Tocqueville (1805–1859).

Tocqueville's family belonged to the oldest Norman nobility, and one of his ancestors had fought at the Battle of Hastings. Tocqueville's interest in politics came to him naturally. His family had long been active in the magistracy and public administration, and his father was prefect, the highest government authority, in several departments of France. Tocqueville thus had ample opportunity to see the big and little problems of government from the inside. During the Revolution, Tocqueville's maternal grandmother and an aunt were executed, and his parents narrowly escaped the same fate. His father's hair turned white at the age of twenty-one as a result of harassing experiences and imprisonments.

Tocqueville studied the law, as was the tradition of his family, and at the age of twenty-one he embarked on a judicial career. From 1839 to 1848 he was a member of the Chamber of Deputies, where he voted, slightly Left of Center, with the constitutional opposition. In 1849 he was Foreign Minister for a few months. After Louis Napoleon set up his dictatorship, Tocqueville retired from public life, despite the former's repeated attempts to secure his collaboration. Tocqueville was not an outstanding parliamentarian, and he lacked the knack of the practical politician in dealing with people. But the rigorous and uncompromising standards that kept him from being a successful party leader and vote getter also prevented him from participating in the public affairs of a dictatorship. His retirement from active politics gave him time to write a penetrating analysis *The Old Regime and the Revolution* (1856). He broke new ground by emphasizing the elements of continuity in the French Revolution rather than those of sudden change: "The despot fell; but the most substantial portion of his work remained; his administrative system survived his government."

Tocqueville's most famous book, and his most enduring contribution to political thought, is his *Democracy in America* (1835–1840). It is generally conceded to be the greatest work on the United States written by a foreign observer, and it would be difficult to find a work of similar depth and penetration written by an American on his own country. Nothing dates as quickly as books on other countries, yet *Democracy in America* has retained its original freshness and appeal. What is equally astounding is that Tocqueville was able to grasp so much of American civilization after a stay of only nine months, and that the first part of *Democracy in America* was published when the author was barely thirty years old (the second part came out five years later). His ability to forecast the future—which is little different from the ability to interpret the present correctly—is illustrated by the statement that the time would come when North America would be inhabited by one hundred and fifty million people, and that Russia and the United States would each "sway the destinies of half the globe." There is considerable repetition in *Democracy in America,* which detracts from its readability and adds unnecessarily to its length, but its general impact is one of balance, reflection, sympathy, and—perhaps Tocqueville's most appealing quality—fairness.

Shortly after the July Revolution of 1830 introduced constitutional government into France, Tocqueville and a friend, Gustave de Beaumont, decided to visit America; officially, the purpose was to study the prison system in the United States, but in reality Tocqueville was eager to study democracy where he thought it was most firmly established. "I confess," Tocqueville says, "that in America I saw more than America; I sought the image of democracy itself, with its inclinations, its character, its prejudices, and its passions, in order to learn what we have to fear or to hope from its progress."

Tocqueville starts his introduction to *Democracy in America* with the very substance of his book: "Among the novel objects that attracted my attention during my stay in the United States, nothing struck me more forcibly than the general equality of conditions." Whereas students of politics have, in the twentieth century, frequently separated the study of government from the folkways of a people, its way of life, its social, educational, economic, and religious institutions, Tocqueville realized that equality of conditions, the "fundamental fact" of American life, extended "far beyond the political character and the laws of the country, and that it has no less empire over civil society than over the Government; it creates opinions, engenders sentiments, suggests the ordinary practices of life, and modifies whatever it does not produce."

Tocqueville was one of the first European political writers to see that the age of European mastery and leadership in political inventiveness was passing away, and that the United States was destined to be the world's great experiment in democracy. Intellectually, the United States of the early nineteenth century was little more than a province or colony of England, and it was treated as such by most visiting English writers and lecturers. They were amused by the crudities and banalities of American life but failed to see that below the surface a new social and political principle was struggling for recognition and realization. By contrast, Tocqueville perceived that the United States, in the past a dependency of Europe, was going to play an active, independent, and decisive part in the future. What few Americans themselves would believe before the middle of the twentieth century, Tocqueville saw early in the nineteenth: that the United States would cease to be the pupil of Europe and become its teacher, and that the Americanization of the world—not in the sense of imperialist conquest, but of ever-increasing equality of conditions—was inevitable.

Tocqueville understood that the American and French revolutions, like the upheavals in other parts of Europe and the Americas, were not isolated events but parts of a *world revolution:* "It is evident to all alike that a great democratic revolution is going on among us." Tocqueville saw that the French Revolution was not an event but a continuous *process,* and that the Revolution of 1830, which he himself witnessed, was only one act of a drama the end of which he knew he was not to behold. He was convinced that the United States was the most advanced nation in the world revolution of equality, and, he said, "it appears to me beyond a doubt that sooner or later we shall arrive, like the Americans, at an almost complete equality of conditions."

In the preface to the twelfth edition of *Democracy in America* (1848), Tocqueville writes that the principle of popular sovereignty, "enthroned in France but yesterday," had held undivided sway in the United States for sixty years in the most direct, unlimited, and absolute manner. While all the nations of Europe were devastated by war or torn by civil strife, the United States alone remained at peace, guaranteeing the rights of property and avoiding the pitfalls of both anarchy and despotism: "Where else could we find greater cause of hope, or more instructive lessons? Let us look to America, not in order to make a servile copy of the institutions that she has established, but to gain a clearer view of the polity that will be the best for us; let us look there less to find examples than instruction; let us borrow from her the principles, rather than the details, of her laws."

Tocqueville had no illusions about the future of his class. In a letter to Henry Reeve, the translator of *Democracy in America,* Tocqueville says (March 22, 1837) that aristocracy was dead when he was born, and that he could have no affection for it, since "one can be strongly attached only to the living." However, his realization that the age of government by privilege was gone did not lead him to embrace democracy unquestioningly and unhesitatingly. The real alternative was no longer between aristocracy and democracy, he felt. It was between "democracy without poetry and elevation indeed, but with order and morality, and an undisciplined and depraved democracy, subject to sudden frenzies, or to a yoke heavier than any that has galled mankind since the fall of the Roman Empire." Democracy—not only democratic government, but a way of life built on equality—was, Tocqueville saw, the "irresistible future."

What concerned him, however, was the difficulty of *reconciling individuality and liberty with democratic equality.* This is the central theme of *Democracy in America* and the major contribution of Tocqueville to modern political thought. He saw, more clearly than any of his contemporaries, that equality was not an invention of French and American revolutionary agitators, or of clever conspirators who managed to beguile the people and overthrow the established order of state and society. Approaching the issue of equality from an institutional rather than from a purely ideological viewpoint, Tocqueville found that the process of leveling and equalizing had been going on in Europe for seven hundred years, and that "absolute kings were the most efficient levellers of ranks among their subjects." The French and American Revolutions were not, Tocqueville thought, sharp breaks with the past as much as accelerations of trends that had already operated for centuries.

The human (as distinct from the administrative) problem of equality was nearer its solution in democracy than in monarchy and aristocracy, but the central issue of liberty still persisted. Whereas enthusiastic democrats assumed that liberty would cease to be a serious issue in democracy, Tocqueville pointed out that democracy, by the very fact of solving the issue of equality, created new problems of liberty that had not hitherto existed. Democracy demanded a "new science of politics indispensable to a new world," and the experience of the past could not sufficiently illuminate its difficulties, because there was no parallel to it in any age up to the "remotest antiquity."

Tocqueville saw—and his profound insight is still not fully grasped and acted upon in democratic societies—that the threat to liberty is potentially more real and menacing in a democracy than in a monarchy or an aristocracy: "The authority of a king is purely physical, and it controls the actions of the subject without subduing his private will; but the majority possesses a power which is physical and moral at the same time; it acts upon the will as well as upon the actions of men, and it represses not only all contest, but all controversy." Tocqueville saw that democratic despotism would work differently from the classical forms of one-man or class tyranny: "It would be more extensive and more mild; it would degrade men without tormenting them."

Tocqueville emphasizes, in particular, one kind of despotism in a democracy that is not easy to discern because it does not work openly, through political or legal sanctions: the *power of public opinion to suppress unpopular views*. Without being exposed "to the terrors of an auto-da-fé," the individual of unorthodox views may find his political career closed, be ostracized, shunned, spurned, and scorned by his fellow citizens, and abandoned by his friends who are most persuaded of his innocence, "lest they should be shunned in their turn." Nothing disturbed Tocqueville more in his study of democracy than the "quiet and gentle" kind of terror and intimidation that does not destroy, but prevents, existence; that does not tyrannize, but compresses, enervates, extinguishes, and stupefies people "till each nation is reduced to be nothing better than a flock of timid and industrious animals, of which the government is the shepherd."

Tocqueville felt a kind of "religious dread" in contemplating "so irresistible a revolution" as the spread of democracy, and his attitude toward it was never free from ambivalence. He was keenly sensitive to the values of the individual, the unique, the lofty in man, and was distressed by the mediocrity, greed, and triviality in democracies: "When I survey this countless multitude of beings, shaped in each other's likeness, amidst whom nothing rises and nothing falls, the sight of such universal uniformity saddens and chills me, and I am tempted to regret that state of society which has ceased to be." Yet, despite his fears and apprehensions, Tocqueville concludes *Democracy in America* with a note of hope: "A state of equality is perhaps less elevated, but it is more just; and its justice constitutes its greatness and beauty."

Rejecting the view that man is a helpless prisoner of blind and fatal forces —history, race, soil, and climate—Tocqueville asserts man's freedom by virtue of his moral essence: "Providence has not created mankind entirely independent or entirely free. It is true that around every man a fatal circle is traced, beyond which he cannot pass; but within the wide verge of that circle he is powerful and free: as it is with man, so with communities. The nations of our time cannot prevent the conditions of men from becoming equal: but it depends upon themselves whether the principle of equality is to lead them to servitude or freedom, to knowledge or barbarism, to prosperity or to wretchedness."

In November, 1841, Tocqueville wrote a note to himself, entitled "My Instinct, My Opinions," which expresses more strongly—and perhaps more frankly because not meant for publication—his profound apprehension, and even a certain antipathy, with regard to democracy. "Intellectually," Tocqueville says in this note, "I have an inclination for democratic institutions, but I am an aristocrat by instinct—that is to say, I despise and fear the mob. I love passionately liberty, law, and respect for rights, but not democracy. There is the ultimate truth of my soul." As on so many other occasions, Tocqueville insisted that he was neither revolutionary nor conservative, yet "when all is said and done, I hold more by the latter than the former. For I differ from the latter more as to means than as to end, while I differ from the former both as to means and end. Liberty is my first passion. This is the truth."

Tocqueville's intellectual acceptance of democracy was rooted in two feelings: first, that it was irresistible, and that to oppose it with blind, sterile hatred would therefore be futile; second, he was skeptical enough to tolerate democracy without embracing it passionately. In his *Recollections* (written in 1850), Tocqueville says that "what we call necessary institutions are often no more than institutions to which we have grown accustomed."

Tocqueville's acceptance of democracy on the basis of pragmatic skepticism rather than positive faith and affirmation finds a more recent analogy in the late Justice Holmes of the United States Supreme Court. Holmes, a confirmed individualist, often opposed his conservative colleagues on issues involving social experimentation, not because he favored collectivism, but because he was unwilling to share the dogma of the majority of the Court that the laissez-faire philosophy of Herbert Spencer was the last word in human wisdom. Similarly, Tocqueville's attitude toward democracy was hesitant, fearful, and ambivalent, but he was willing to give it a fair chance.

This openness of mind, the attempt to build a political philosophy on empiricism and expediency, without the extremes of revolution and reaction, draws Tocqueville into spiritual kinship with Bodin and Montesquieu. All three belong to the same spiritual family in France, though their backgrounds and ideas differed, and all three have contributed to an intellectual tradition of moderation, conciliation, and antifanaticism. In essence the tradition reflects a temper as much as a body of doctrine—the willingness to accept the second best rather than kill for the absolutely best. In twentieth-century France this tradition of the *politiques*, of Bodin, Montesquieu, and Tocqueville, has come to life again in the Third Force, which, though composed of such divergent elements as secular socialists, Catholic democrats, and laissez-faire republicans, is perhaps the best hope for the survival of French democracy.

One of the most prophetic passages in *Democracy in America* deals with the rise of an *aristocracy of manufacturers* in democratic societies. Tocqueville notes that democracy is favorable to the growth of industry for two reasons: first, there is the emphasis on material welfare for all, rather than for a small aristocratic class, so that the demand for goods is constantly increasing; second, equality of opportunity encourages talent to enter the field of business and industry and to acquire wealth without restrictions of birth, class, and caste. Inevitably, the expansion of manufacturing produces a new type of working class, highly specialized, and employed according to the principle of division of labor. But, while economically efficient, mass production has serious social effects because "in proportion as the workman improves, the man is degraded." The more the worker concentrates his effort and intelligence on a single detail, the more the employer has to survey an extensive whole, so that the mind of the latter is broadened in proportion as that of the former is narrowed. The *employer* resembles more and more the *administrator of a vast empire,* and the worker becomes more and more a brute. Between worker and employer there are frequent relations but "no real partnership." As industry becomes more settled, social relations become more rigid: the worker is continually dependent on the employer "and seems as much born to obey as that other is to command. What is that but aristocracy?"

As an aristocrat of preindustrial background, Tocqueville is keenly sensitive to the differences between the old landed and the new manufacturing aristocracy. In the first, the tie between the landlord and his men was one of shared experience rather than of weekly pay checks. In the age of manufacturing, the employer is not settled among those he employs, and his contact with them is confined to one aspect of life: he asks nothing of them but their labor, and they expect nothing but their wages. Between employer and workers there is thus no permanent tie of habit, duty, custom, or usage, whereas in the old landed aristocracy the master was obliged to protect, aid, and relieve his men, and they to defend and serve him. By contrast, the manufacturing aristocracy first impoverishes the men who serve it and then abandons them to public charity. It has no sense of public responsibility, and its aim is not to govern the population but to use it.

Because of its lack of responsibility the new industrial aristocracy is, Tocqueville predicts, the harshest that ever existed. He advises friends of democracy to "keep their eyes anxiously fixed in this direction; for if ever a permanent inequality of conditions and aristocracy again penetrate into the world, it may be predicted that this is the channel by which they will enter."

But Tocqueville did not think that the *discrepancy between political equality and economic inequality* would be indefinitely accepted by a democratic people. He saw that the first phase of the democratic world revolution, political in nature, would inevitably lead to a second phase, which would be primarily social and economic: "Those who believe that complete equality can be established in a permanent way in the political world without introducing at the same time a certain equality in civil society, seem to me to commit a dangerous error." The July Revolution of 1830 was the last purely political revolution in France,

Tocqueville thought, and he foresaw that the next upheavel would result from economic grievances.

The February Revolution of 1848 was the first in which the industrial working class played a major role, and Tocqueville predicted before the Revolution on what issue the major battles of the future would be fought: "Before long, the political struggle will be restricted to those who have and those who have not; property will form the great field of battle." Only a few weeks before the outbreak of the February Revolution of 1848, Tocqueville said in a speech in the Chamber of Deputies that the passions of the working classes had turned from political to social questions, and that they were forming ideas and opinions destined "not only to upset this or that law, ministry, or even form of government, but society itself, until it totters upon the foundations on which it rests today."

The people are bound to discover, Tocqueville reflects in his *Recollections*, that, having destroyed all other obstacles to equality, the privilege of property remains the only obstacle. Yet he did not think that the people would necessarily use their legislative sovereignty to abolish altogether the institution of property, "the foundation of our social order." He hesitated to predict what specific form popular control of property in a democracy would eventually take because "in matters of social constitution the field of possibilities is much more extensive than men living in their various societies are ready to imagine."

Tocqueville was one of the first political thinkers in the nineteenth century to perceive the long-term pressure of economic inequality on political democracy. He understood, with consummate clarity, the paradoxical relation between democracy and the Industrial Revolution: on the one hand, democracy favors the growth of an industrial economy with its rising living standards for the people; and on the other hand, the process of industrialization creates new problems of inequality that threaten the very foundations of democracy.

Democracy in America, translated into English almost immediately after publication, aroused considerable attention on both sides of the Atlantic. One of the most enthusiastic English reviewers of the work was John Stuart Mill (1806–1873), who compared Tocqueville to Montesquieu and thought that nothing equally profound had yet been written on the subject of democracy. Tocqueville seemed to Mill to have "changed the face of political philosophy" by posing new questions that went to the core of democracy as a system of government and a way of life.

Mill was impressed by the fact that the tendencies which Tocqueville had noted in America—the drive toward equality of conditions with its new problems and pressures—were also gradually permeating England. He shared Tocqueville's concern about the possibility of the tyranny of the majority in democracy, and he added that "it is not from the separate interests, real or imaginary, that minorities are in danger; but from its antipathies of religion, political party, or race." The more perfectly each knows himself the equal of any other individual, "the more helpless he feels against the aggregate mass; and the more incredible it appears to him that the opinions of all the world can possibly be erroneous."

In his *Autobiography*, too, Mill avows how much he owes to Tocqueville, from whom he learned the specific virtues and defects of democracy. In turn,

Tocqueville wrote to Mill that of all reviewers of *Democracy in America* he was the one who best understood the meaning of the work; the two met during Tocqueville's second visit to England in 1835, and their friendly association lasted until Tocqueville's death in 1859.

Mill's *Autobiography* (1873), one of the most fascinating autobiographies of a political philosopher, is remarkable for several reasons. It provides a lifelike, and occasionally intimate, account of the Benthamite circle, Mill's father, James Mill, being the leading disciple of the master. The *Autobiography* also spans an important era of nineteenth-century intellectual history. Mill's interest was not confined to England, and he was particularly conversant with developments in France and the United States. Above all, the *Autobiography* is noteworthy for its account of the intellectual development of Mill himself.

For the generation of Bentham as for that of James Mill democracy was still an objective to aim at, a goal to work for. John Stuart Mill, who belongs to the third generation of Utilitarianism, lived in a world in which middle-class reform had attained a high degree of realization and—gradually shedding the magic of the envisioned future—had begun to reveal its own shortcomings and imperfections. The heyday of middle-class democracy heralded the first dawn of the next phase of social and political development, pointing toward the welfare state and socialism.

Mill typifies in his own life history the evolution of nineteenth-century liberalism. Born and reared as an orthodox and uncontaminated Benthamite, he ended as a "qualified socialist." From a personal viewpoint, moreover, the *Autobiography* is a remarkable record of human endurance. James Mill had definite ideas on how to educate John Stuart from the moment he was born. At the age of three John began to learn Greek, and Latin at the much later age of seven. By that time he had already acquired a solid knowledge of Greek literature and philosophy, including Plato, Herodotus, and Xenophon. He also learned arithmetic and ancient and modern history. When he came to the American war, Mill recalls, he took the side of England, but he was quickly set right by his father who, like all Philosophical Radicals, regarded the United States as the advance guard of democracy and the model of future developments in England.

From his eighth year on, Mill went thoroughly through Latin literature and broadened his knowledge of Greek literature by reading Thucydides, Homer, Euripides, Sophocles, and Polybius. At the same time, he delved into algebra, geometry, the differential calculus, and other portions of high mathematics. He also read books on experimental science and, at the age of twelve, began a course of study in logic, from Aristotle to Hobbes. At thirteen Mill's primary study was political economy, particularly Adam Smith and David Ricardo, the latter being a close friend of Mill's father. At fourteen Mill went to France for a year, spending part of his time with the family of General Sir Samuel Bentham, Jeremy Bentham's brother. Mill fell in love with France, returned there later for prolonged visits, and died in Avignon in 1873.

At the age of seventeen Mill joined the staff of the East India Company as a clerk, became head of his department in 1856, and retired two years later. Most of his immense literary output was accomplished while he held a full-time and absorbing job. In 1865 Mill was asked by a body of voters in Westminster to stand for Parliament. He was convinced that no numerous or influential body of any constituency would wish to be represented by a person of his opinions. He also held the fixed conviction that a candidate should neither incur election expenses nor canvass his constituency. He nevertheless won with a small majority over his Conservative opponent, but he stayed in the House of Commons for only three years. In the election of 1868 he was defeated, but he confesses in his *Autobiography* that he was less surprised by his defeat than by his having been elected the first time.

In his teens Mill wrote and published essays on various political and philosophical topics and contributed to the *Westminster Review*, the official organ of Philosophical Radicalism from its foundation in 1824. In 1834 he published the *System of Logic*, his principal work on philosophy. In 1848 he brought out his *Political Economy*, next to Adam Smith's *Wealth of Nations* the most authoritative work in its field for several generations, and long the most popular textbook in economics in England and the United States.

Yet Mill's claim to enduring fame derives from *On Liberty* (1859); he predicted that of all his writings *On Liberty* was likely to survive longest, and his prediction has come true. Mill says in the *Autobiography* that he wrote *On Liberty* at a time when there may have seemed comparatively little need for it. But he foresaw that illiberal forces in modern industrial society would gain in weight, and he hoped that men would then turn to the teachings of *On Liberty*. Though Mill modestly disclaimed originality other than that which "every thoughtful mind gives to its own mode of conceiving and expressing truths which are common property," *On Liberty* has long been held to be, together with Milton's *Areopagitica*, the finest and most moving essay on liberty in English, perhaps in any language. As time goes on, *On Liberty* grows in stature and meaning because its predictions have come to life more realistically, and more tragically, than seemed possible in the middle of the nineteenth century, when belief in the progress of liberty was well-nigh universal.

Mill explodes the illusion that the evolution of government from tyranny to popular self-rule necessarily solves the problem of liberty. Like Tocqueville, he sees that society may practice a social tyranny more formidable than many kinds of political oppression, because social tyranny leaves fewer means of escape, "penetrating much more deeply into the details of life, and enslaving the soul itself." Protection against political tyranny is therefore not enough; it must be supplemented by protection against the tyranny of prevailing opinion and feeling. Unless *absolute freedom* of opinion and sentiment—scientific, moral, and theological—is guaranteed, a society is not completely free. Mill makes the point, seldom made in the optimistic nineteenth century, that the natural disposition of man is to impose his views, as ruler or fellow citizen, on others, and that want of power is often the cause of toleration of dissent. However, the issue of liberty is one not only of power but of right and obligation, and it makes little difference how numerous the dissentient minority is: "If all mankind minus one, were of one opinion, and only one person were of the contrary opinion, mankind would be no more justified in silencing that one person, than he, if he had the power, would be justified in silencing mankind." Silencing an unorthodox opinion is not only wrong but harmful, because it robs mankind of an opportunity to become acquainted with ideas that may possibly be true, or partly true: "All silencing of discussion is an assumption of infallibility."

Mill recognizes that each individual can grasp no more than some aspects of truth, and that the imperfection of truth is due to the partial knowledge that man is able to attain in his limited experience of the world. Not only is society no infallible judge of truth, but even "ages are no more infallible than individuals." History is full of opinions held by one age to be the ultimate truth and considered by subsequent ages to be false and absurd.

Just as liberty is not complete unless it is absolute, so discussion must be completely unhampered, and free discussion must not be ruled out when "pushed to an extreme," because the arguments for a case are not good unless they are good for an extreme case. Mill is aware of the favorite argument that some opinions must be protected from public discussion and attack because of their usefulness to society, and he retorts that the "usefulness of an opinion is itself a matter of opinion."

Mill does not believe in the "pleasant falsehood" that truth inevitably triumphs over persecution; history "teems with instances of truth put down by persecution." He cites numerous examples of successful persecution in religion in support of his view that "persecution has always succeeded, save where the heretics were too strong a party to be effectually persecuted." The greatest harm of persecution is not done to those who are heretics but to those who are not, because the mental development of the latter is stifled by the fear of heresy. In an atmosphere of cowed conformity and slavish submission there may be a few exceptional great individual thinkers, but not an intellectually active people: "No one can be a great thinker who does not recognize, that as a thinker it is his first duty to follow his intellect to whatever conclusions it may lead."

Mill warns particularly against the blind acceptance of dead formulas as truth, without the challenge of discussion. For its own vitality and survival, truth needs to be "fully, frequently, and fearlessly" discussed, and Mill adds the not unimportant point that the opposing opinion be presented by someone who really believes in it. Only in the constant process of being challenged and assailed can truth grow and establish itself: "Both teachers and learners go to sleep at their post, as soon as there is no enemy in the field."

In summary, says Mill, the necessity of freedom of opinion, and freedom of expression, may be based on three grounds. First, any opinion we silence may be true, and in silencing it we assume our own *infallibility*. Second, though the *silenced opinion* be on the whole erroneous, it may be *partly true*, and because the prevailing opinion on any subject is rarely the complete truth, "it is only by the collision of adverse opinions that the remainder of the truth has any chance of being supplied." Third, even if the prevailing opinion be the *complete truth*, it will inevitably become dogma, prejudice, and formula unless it is exposed to the *challenge of free discussion*.

In his *Autobiography*, Mill says that his father felt himself more indebted for his mental culture to Plato than to any other writer. He shares his father's high esteem for Plato, not because of any sympathy with Plato's specific political or social views, but because of his admiration for the Socratic method, "unsurpassed" in correcting errors and clearing up confusions through relentless exposure of generalities, the "perpetual testing of all general statements by particular instances." Long before instrumentalism made its formal contribution to philosophy, Mill was an instrumentalist in his approach to the problem of truth. He recognized that truth is never finished, certain, and timeless, but that it is always unfinished, tentative, and temporary, subject to new data and experiences; that the quest for truth is an endless road; and that the free debate between opposite viewpoints is more likely to result in an approximation of truth than is the one-sided assertion of dogma and creed, which are beyond dispute. In this concept of truth as a dynamic process of colliding opposites, Mill sacrifices the certainty that is devoid of mental freedom to the uncertainty that is the price of intellectual liberty.

In championing liberty, Mill has a broad goal in mind: the "Greek ideal of self-development." It is the privilege of every human being to use and interpret experience in his own way, and the act of choosing between alternatives brings man's moral faculties into play. A person who acts according to custom and tradition makes no choice, and he who lets others choose his plan of life for him has no need of any faculty other than apelike imitation. Different persons should be permitted to lead different lives; and the plea for *variety* in *On Liberty* is as strong as that for *freedom*. The very progress of industrial civilization creates a uniformity of conditions that makes it difficult for persons to remain individuals, because "they now read the same things, listen to the same things, go to the same places, have their hopes and fears directed to the same objects, have the same rights and liberties, and the same means of asserting them." People who do the same things will easily think the same thoughts, and the pace of standardization of work, play, and, above all, prefabricated opinion (press and radio) has been constantly accelerating in the last hundred years. Because the pressure of industrial society is for greater uniformity, the mere example of nonconformity, "the mere refusal to bend the knee to custom," is in itself a service to the cause of liberty.

Mill reminds those who are willing to repress individual liberty for the sake of a strong state that the worth of a state is no more than the worth of the individuals composing it. The concluding words of *On Liberty* contain a message that is particularly timely in the second half of the twentieth century, when the double threat of permanent war and revolution on a world scale makes it increasingly difficult to preserve the liberal temper and philosophy in politics: "A state which dwarfs its men, in order that they may be more docile instruments in its hands even for beneficial purposes—will find that with small men no great thing can really be accomplished; and that the perfection of machinery to which it has sacrificed everything, will in the end avail it nothing, for want of the vital power which, in order that the machine might work smoothly, it has preferred to banish."

Mill understood that the issue of liberty is closely related to the larger question of social power and organization. Bred as an orthodox Benthamite, his faith in laissez faire was originally stronger than that of Bentham himself; but as time went on, Mill gradually abandoned what was dogmatic in the economic philosophy of laissez faire and adopted a position that was close to that of the Fabian Society, founded only a decade after his death. Had he lived longer, he probably would have been one of its founders. Although in the first edition of his *Political Economy* (1848) his general view of socialism was that it was neither desirable nor practicable, in subsequent editions he revised his attitude. As a utilitarian and pragmatist, Mill was unwilling to commit himself to any economic doctrine without qualifications. He felt that the decision between capitalism and socialism would ultimately be based on one chief consideration: "which of the two systems is consistent with the greatest amount of human liberty and spontaneity." It would be rash to predict that socialism is unable to realize a great part of its aspirations, and the best way to find out, Mill thought, was to give socialists an opportunity of trial.

With regard to individual property, Mill held that the aim of an enlightened social policy should be not to destroy it, but to improve it, and to enable every member of the community to own property. The ultimate form of ownership of the means of production would not be, Mill says in the *Political Economy*, that of capitalist chiefs, with the workers deprived of any voice in the management, but the "association of the laborers themselves on terms of equality, collectively owning the capital with which they carry on their operations, and working under managers elected and removable by themselves."

In 1869 Mill began a book on socialism but did not finish it. *Chapters on Socialism*, published in 1879 by his stepdaughter, contains further important additions to Mill's previously held ideas. Avoiding an extreme position, Mill asserts, on the one hand, that the present system is "not hurrying us into a state of general indigence and slavery from which only socialism can save us." Though the evils and injustices of capitalism are great, they are not increasing but generally decreasing. On the other hand, Mill foresees that individual property is only of provisional existence, though it still has a long term before it, and that the nature of property would change in the course of time. Property denotes in every state of society the largest power of exclusive control over things, "and sometimes, unfortunately, over persons," but these powers vary greatly in accordance with the conceptions of right and justice held in different countries. In his *Autobiography*, Mill sums up most succinctly the problem of socialism as he saw it: how to "unite the greatest individual liberty of action with a common ownership in the raw material of the globe, and an equal participation of all in the benefits of combined labor."

In his analysis of socialist ideas and proposals, Mill curiously disregards Marx and Engels, not even mentioning them, and relies most heavily on Owen, Fourier, Saint-Simon, and Louis Blanc. Mill foresaw that socialism would run into a dead end if it gave up its liberal heritage and embraced the philosophy of the all-powerful state. He was therefore solely interested in French and British socialists, who stressed the cooperative, individualistic, fraternal elements in socialism as a new way of life, and he ignored the doctrines of revolution and dictatorship as propounded by Marx and Engels.

One of the first lessons learned by British socialists after the first stage of socialist reconstruction, inaugurated in 1945, is that the identification of socialism with nationalization is the short road to political suicide, because nationalization is only one aspect of socialism, and not identical with it. The alternative to private ownership of the means of production will be found in other bodies than the state: consumer and producer cooperatives, municipalities, trade-unions, public corporations, and other organizations based on voluntary association rather than on the sovereign authority of the state. Long neglected before 1945, this voluntarist and antistate element in the heritage of British socialism was brought back to life after the first phase of socialist realization revealed the dangerous trend of building socialism by relying too much on the state. By emphasizing again more strongly its cooperative, voluntarist, individualist roots, British socialism is returning to the liberalism of John Stuart Mill.

I. TOCQUEVILLE

Democracy in America *

1. Tyranny of the Majority

I hold it to be an impious and an execrable maxim that, politically speaking, a people has a right to do whatsoever it pleases; and yet I have asserted that all authority originates in the will of the majority. Am I, then, in contradiction with myself?

A general law—which bears the name of Justice—has been made and sanctioned, not only by a majority of this or that people, but by a majority of mankind. The rights of every people are consequently confined within the limits of what is just. A nation may be considered in the light of a jury which is empowered to represent society at large, and to apply the great and general

* From Alexis de Tocqueville, *Democracy in America* (1835–1840; trans. Henry Reeve, 1835–1840).

law of Justice. Ought such a jury, which represents society, to have more power than the society in which the laws it applies originate?

When I refuse to obey an unjust law, I do not contest the right which the majority has of commanding, but I simply appeal from the sovereignty of the people to the sovereignty of mankind. It has been asserted that a people can never entirely outstep the boundaries of justice and of reason in those affairs which are more peculiarly its own; and that consequently full power may fearlessly be given to the majority by which it is represented. But this language is that of a slave.

A majority taken collectively may be regarded as a being whose opinions, and most frequently whose interests, are opposed to those of another being, which is styled a minority. If it be admitted that a man, possessing absolute power, may misuse that power by wronging his adversaries, why should a majority not be liable to the same reproach? Men are not apt to change their characters by agglomeration; nor does their patience in the presence of obstacles increase with the consciousness of their strength.[1] And for these reasons I can never willingly invest any number of my fellow-creatures with that unlimited authority which I should refuse to any one of them.

I do not think that it is possible to combine several principles in the same government, so as at the same time to maintain freedom, and really to oppose them to one another. The form of government which is usually termed *mixed* has always appeared to me to be a mere chimera. Accurately speaking there is no such thing as a mixed government (with the meaning usually given to that word), because in all communities some one principle of action may be discovered, which preponderates over the others. England in the last century, which has been more especially cited as an example of this form of government, was in point of fact an essentially aristocratic state, although it comprised very powerful elements of democracy: for the laws and customs of the country were such, that the aristocracy could not but preponderate in the end, and subject the direction of public affairs to its own will. The error arose from too much attention being paid to the actual struggle which was going on between the nobles and the people, without considering the probable issue of the contest, which was in reality the important point. When a community really has a mixed government, that is to say, when it is equally divided between two adverse principles, it must either pass through a revolution, or fall into complete dissolution.

I am therefore of opinion that some one social power must always be made to predominate over the others; but I think that liberty is endangered when this power is checked by no obstacles which may retard its course, and force it to moderate its own vehemence.

Unlimited power is in itself a bad and dangerous thing; human beings are not competent to exercise it with discretion; and God alone can be omnipotent, because his wisdom and his justice are always equal to his power. But no power upon earth is so worthy of honor for itself, or of reverential obedience to the rights which it represents, that I would consent to admit its uncontrolled and all-predominant authority. When I see that the right and the means of absolute command are conferred on a people or upon a king, upon an aristocracy or a democracy, a monarchy or a republic, I recognize the germ of tyranny, and I journey onwards to a land of more hopeful institutions.

In my opinion the main evil of the present democratic institutions of the United States does not arise, as is often asserted in Europe, from their weakness, but from their overpowering strength; and I am not so much alarmed at the excessive liberty which reigns in that country, as at the very inadequate securities which exist against tyranny.

When an individual or a party is wronged in the United States, to whom can he apply for redress? If to public opinion, public opinion constitutes the majority; if to the legislature, it represents the majority, and implicitly obeys its injunctions; if to the executive power, it is appointed by the majority and remains a passive tool in its hands; the public troops consist of the majority under arms; the jury is the majority invested with the right of hearing judicial cases; and in certain States even the judges are elected by the majority. However iniquitous or absurd the evil of which you com-

---

[1] No one will assert that a people cannot forcibly wrong another people: but parties may be looked upon as lesser nations within a greater one, and they are aliens to each other: if therefore it be admitted that a nation can act tyrannically towards another nation, it cannot be denied that a party may do the same towards another party.

plain may be, you must submit to it as well as you can.[2]

If, on the other hand, a legislative power could be so constituted as to represent the majority without necessarily being the slave of its passions; an executive, so as to re-

[2] A striking instance of the excesses which may be occasioned by the despotism of the majority occurred at Baltimore in the year 1812. At that time the war was very popular in Baltimore. A journal which had taken the other side of the question excited the indignation of the inhabitants by its opposition. The populace assembled, broke the printing presses, and attacked the houses of the newspaper editors. The militia was called out, but no one obeyed the call; and the only means of saving the poor wretches who were threatened by the frenzy of the mob, was to throw them into prison as common malefactors. But even this precaution was ineffectual; the mob collected again during the night; the magistrates again made a vain attempt to call out the militia; the prison was forced, one of the newspaper editors was killed upon the spot, and the others were left for dead: the guilty parties were acquitted by the jury when they were brought to trial.

I said one day to an inhabitant of Pennsylvania, "Be so good as to explain to me how it happens, that in a State founded by Quakers, and celebrated for its toleration, freed Blacks are not allowed to exercise civil rights. They pay the taxes: is it not fair that they should have a vote?"

"You insult us," replied my informant, "if you imagine that our legislators could have committed so gross an act of injustice and intolerance."

"What, then, the Blacks possess the right of voting in this country?"

"Without the slightest doubt."

"How comes it, then, that at the polling-booth this morning I did not perceive a single Negro in the whole meeting?"

"This is not the fault of the law; the Negroes have an undisputed right of voting: but they voluntarily abstain from making their appearance."

"A very pretty piece of modesty on their parts!" rejoined I.

"Why, the truth is, that they are not disinclined to vote, but they are afraid of being maltreated; in this country the law is sometimes unable to maintain its authority without the support of the majority. But in this case the majority entertains very strong prejudices against the Blacks, and the magistrates are unable to protect them in the exercise of their legal privileges."

"What, then, the majority claims the right not only of making the laws, but of breaking the laws it has made?"

tain a certain degree of uncontrolled authority; and a judiciary, so as to remain independent of the two other powers; a government would be formed which would still be democratic, without incurring any risk of tyrannical abuse.

I do not say that tyrannical abuses frequently occur in America at the present day; but I maintain that no sure barrier is established against them, and that the causes which mitigate the government are to be found in the circumstances and the manners of the country more than in its laws.

2. Power of the Majority over Public Opinion

It is in the examination of the display of public opinion in the United States, that we clearly perceive how far the power of the majority surpasses all the powers with which we are acquainted in Europe. Intellectual principles exercise an influence which is so invisible and often so inappreciable, that they baffle the toils of oppression. At the present time the most absolute monarchs in Europe are unable to prevent certain notions, which are opposed to their authority, from circulating in secret throughout their dominions, and even in their courts. Such is not the case in America; as long as the majority is still undecided, discussion is carried on; but as soon as its decision is irrevocably pronounced, a submissive silence is observed; and the friends, as well as the opponents of the measure, unite in assenting to its propriety. The reason of this is perfectly clear: no monarch is so absolute as to combine all the powers of society in his own hands, and to conquer all opposition, with the energy of a majority, which is invested with the right of making and of executing the laws.

The authority of a king is purely physical, and it controls the actions of the subject without subduing his private will; but the majority possesses a power which is physical and moral at the same time; it acts upon the will as well as upon the actions of men, and it represses not only all contest, but all controversy.

I know no country in which there is so little true independence of mind and freedom of discussion as in America. In any constitutional state in Europe every sort of religious and political theory may be advocated and propagated abroad; for there is no country in Europe so subdued by any single authority, as not to contain citizens who are ready to protect the man who raises his voice in the cause of truth, from the consequences of his hardihood. If he is unfortunate enough to live under an absolute government, the people is upon his side; if he inhabits a free country, he may find a shelter behind the authority of the throne, if he require one. The aristocratic part of society supports him in some countries, and the democracy in others. But in a nation where democratic institutions exist, organized like those of the United States, there is but one sole authority, one single element of strength and of success, with nothing beyond it.

In America, the majority arises very formidable barriers to the liberty of opinion: within these barriers an author may write whatever he pleases, but he will repent it if he ever step beyond them. Not that he is exposed to the terrors of an auto-da-fé, but he is tormented by the slights and persecutions of daily obloquy. His political career is closed for ever, since he has offended the only authority which is able to promote his success. Every sort of compensation, even that of celebrity, is refused to him. Before he published his opinions, he imagined that he held them in common with many others; but no sooner has he declared them openly than he is loudly censured by his overbearing opponents, whilst those who think, without having the courage to speak, like him, abandon him in silence. He yields at length, oppressed by the daily efforts he has been making, and he subsides into silence as if he was tormented by remorse for having spoken the truth.

Fetters and headsmen were the coarse instruments which tyranny formerly employed; but the civilization of our age has refined the arts of despotism, which seemed however to have been sufficiently perfected before. The excesses of monarchical power had devised a variety of physical means of oppression; the democratic republics of the present day have rendered it as entirely an affair of the mind, as that will which it is intended to coerce. Under the absolute sway of an individual despot, the body was attacked in order to subdue the soul; and the soul escaped the blows which were directed against it, and rose superior to the attempt; but such is not the course adopted by tyranny in democratic republics; there the body is left free, and the soul is enslaved. The sovereign can no longer say, "You shall think as I do on pain of death": but he says, "You are free to think differently from me, and to retain your life, your property, and all that you possess; but if such be your determination, you are henceforth an alien among your people. You may retain your civil rights, but they will be useless to you, for you will never be chosen by your fellow-citizens, if you solicit their suffrages; and they will affect to scorn you, if you solicit their esteem. You will remain among men, but you will be deprived of the rights of mankind. Your fellow-creatures will shun you like an impure being; and those who are most persuaded of your innocence will abandon you too, lest they should be shunned in their turn. Go in peace! I have given you your life, but it is an existence incomparably worse than death."

Absolute monarchies have thrown an odium upon despotism; let us beware lest democratic republics should restore oppression, and should render it less odious and less degrading in the eyes of the many, by making it still more onerous to the few.

Works have been published in the proudest nations of the Old World, expressly intended to censure the vices and deride the follies of the time: Labruyère inhabited the palace of Louis XIV when he composed his chapter upon the Great, and Molière criticized the courtiers in the very pieces which were acted before the Court. But the ruling power in the United States is not to be made game of; the smallest reproach irritates its sensibility, and the slightest joke which has any foundation in truth renders it indignant; from the style of its language to the more solid virtues of its character, everything must be made the subject of encomium. No writer, whatever be his eminence, can escape from this tribute or adulation to his fellow-citizens. The majority lives in the perpetual practice of self-applause; and there are certain truths which the Americans can only learn from strangers or from experience.

If great writers have not at present existed in America, the reason is very simply given in these facts; there can be no literary genius without freedom of opinion, and freedom of opinion does not exist in America. The Inquisition has never been able to prevent a vast number of antireligious books from circulating in Spain. The empire of the majority succeeds much better in the United States, since it actually removes the wish of publishing them. Unbelievers are to be met with in America, but, to say the truth, there is no public organ of infidelity. Attempts have been made by some governments to protect the morality of nations by prohibiting licentious books. In the United States no one is punished for this sort of works, but no one is induced to write them; not because all the citizens are immaculate in their manners, but because the majority of the community is decent and orderly.

In these cases the advantages derived from the exercise of this power are unquestionable; and I am simply discussing the nature of the power itself. This irresistible authority is a constant fact, and its judicial exercise is an accidental occurrence.

3. Why Democratic Nations Love Equality More than Liberty

The first and most intense passion which is engendered by the equality of conditions is, I need hardly say, the love of that same equality. My readers will therefore not be surprised that I speak of it before all others.

Everybody has remarked, that in our time, and especially in France, this passion for equality is every day gaining ground in the human heart. It has been said a hundred times that our contemporaries are far more ardently and tenaciously attached to equality than to freedom; but, as I do not find that the causes of the fact have been sufficiently analyzed, I shall endeavour to point them out.

It is possible to imagine an extreme point at which freedom and equality would meet and be confounded together. Let us suppose that all the members of the community take a part in the government, and that each one of them has an equal right to take a part in it. As none is different from his fellows, none can exercise a tyrannical power: men will be perfectly free, because they will all be entirely equal; and they will all be perfectly equal, because they will be entirely free. To this ideal state democratic nations tend. Such is the completest form that equality can assume upon earth; but there are a thousand others which, without being equally perfect, are not less cherished by those nations.

The principle of equality may be established in civil society, without prevailing in the political world. Equal rights may exist of indulging in the same pleasures, of entering the same professions, of frequenting the same places—in a word, of living in the same manner and seeking wealth by the same means, although all men do not take an equal share in the government.

A kind of equality may even be established in the political world, though there should be no political freedom there. A man may be the equal of all his countrymen save one, who is the master of all without distinction, and who selects equally from among them all the agents of his power.

Several other combinations might be easily imagined, by which very great equality would be united to institutions more or less free, or even to institutions wholly without freedom.

Although men cannot become absolutely equal unless they be entirely free, and consequently equality, pushed to its furthest extent, may be confounded with freedom, yet there is good reason for distinguishing the one from the other. The taste which men have for liberty, and that which they feel for equality, are, in fact, two different things; and I am not afraid to add, that, among democratic nations, they are two unequal things.

Upon close inspection, it will be seen that there is in every age some peculiar and preponderating fact with which all others are connected; this fact almost always gives birth to some pregnant idea or some ruling passion, which attracts to itself, and bears away in its course, all the feelings and opinions of the time: it is like a great stream, toward which each of the surrounding rivulets seems to flow.

Freedom has appeared in the world at different times and under various forms; it has not been exclusively bound to any social condition, and it is not confined to democracies. Freedom cannot, therefore, form the distinguishing characteristic of democratic ages. The peculiar and preponderating fact which marks those ages as its own is the equality of conditions; the ruling passion of men in those periods is the love of this equality. Ask not what singular charm the men of democratic ages find in being equal, or what special reasons they may have for clinging so tenaciously to equality rather than to the other advantages which society holds out to them: equality is the distinguishing characteristic of the age they live in; that, of itself, is enough to explain that they prefer it to all the rest.

But independently of this reason there are several others, which will at all times

habitually lead men to prefer equality to freedom.

If a people could ever succeed in destroying, or even in diminishing, the equality which prevails in its own body, this could only be accomplished by long and laborious efforts. Its social condition must be modified, its laws abolished, its opinions superseded, its habits changed, its manners corrupted. But political liberty is more easily lost; to neglect to hold it fast, is to allow it to escape.

Men therefore not only cling to equality because it is dear to them; they also adhere to it because they think it will last for ever.

That political freedom may compromise in its excesses the tranquillity, the property, the lives of individuals, is obvious to the narrowest and most unthinking minds. But, on the contrary, none but attentive and clear-sighted men perceive the perils with which equality threatens us, and they commonly avoid pointing them out. They know that the calamities they apprehend are remote, and flatter themselves that they will only fall upon future generations, for which the present generation takes but little thought. The evils which freedom sometimes brings with it are immediate; they are apparent to all, and all are more or less affected by them. The evils which extreme equality may produce are slowly disclosed; they creep gradually into the social frame; they are only seen at intervals, and at the moment at which they become most violent, habit already causes them to be no longer felt.

The advantages which freedom brings are only shown by length of time; and it is always easy to mistake the cause in which they originate. The advantages of equality are instantaneous, and they may constantly be traced from their source.

Political liberty bestows exalted pleasures, from time to time, upon a certain number of citizens. Equality every day confers a number of small enjoyments on every man. The charms of equality are every instant felt, and are within the reach of all: the noblest hearts are not insensible to them, and the most vulgar souls exult in them. The passion which equality engenders must therefore be at once strong and general. Men cannot enjoy political liberty unpurchased by some sacrifices, and they never obtain it without great exertions. But the pleasures of equality are self-proffered: each of the petty incidents of life seems to occasion them, and in order to taste them nothing is required but to live.

Democratic nations are at all times fond of equality, but there are certain epochs at which the passion they entertain for it swells to the height of fury. This occurs at the moment when the old social system, long menaced, completes its own destruction after a last intestine struggle, and when the barriers of rank are at length thrown down. At such times men pounce upon equality as their booty, and they cling to it as to some precious treasure which they fear to lose. The passion for equality penetrates on every side into men's hearts, expands there, and fills them entirely. Tell them not that by this blind surrender of themsleves to an exclusive passion, they risk their dearest interests: they are deaf. Show them not freedom escaping from their grasp, while they are looking another way: they are blind—or rather, they can discern but one sole object to be desired in the universe. .

What I have said is applicable to all democratic nations: what I am about to say concerns the French alone. Among most modern nations, and especially among all those of the continent of Europe, the taste and the idea of freedom only began to exist and to extend itself at the time when social conditions were tending to equality, and as a consequence of that very equality. Absolute kings were the most efficient levellers of ranks among their subjects. Among these nations equality preceded freedom: equality was therefore a fact of some standing, when freedom was still a novelty: the one had already created customs, opinions, and laws belonging to it, when the other, alone and for the first time, came into actual existence. Thus the latter was till only recently an affair of opinion and of taste,

while the former had already crept into the habits of the people, possessed itself of their manners, and given a particular turn to the smallest actions in their lives. Can it be wondered that the men of our own time prefer the one to the other?

I think that democratic communities have a natural taste for freedom: left to themselves, they will seek it, cherish it, and view any privation of it with regret. But for equality, their passion is ardent, insatiable, incessant, invincible: they call for equality in freedom; if they cannot obtain that, they still call for equality in slavery. They will endure poverty, servitude, barbarism—but they will not endure aristocracy.

This is true at all times, and especially true in our own. All men and all powers seeking to cope with this irresistible passion, will be overthrown and destroyed by it. In our age, freedom cannot be established without it, and despotism itself cannot reign without its support.

4. Aristocracy of Manufacturers

I have shown that democracy is favourable to the growth of manufactures, and that it increases without limit the numbers of the manufacturing classes: we shall now see by what side-road manufactures may possibly in their turn bring men back to aristocracy.

It is acknowledged, that when a workman is engaged every day upon the same detail, the whole commodity is produced with greater ease, promptitude, and economy. It is likewise acknowledged, that the cost of the production of manufactured goods is diminished by the extent of the establishment in which they are made, and by the amount of capital employed or of credit. These truths had long been imperfectly discerned, but in our time they have been demonstrated. They have been already applied to many very important kinds of manufactures, and the humblest will gradually be governed by them. I know of nothing in politics which deserves to fix the attention of the legislator more closely than these two new axioms of the science of manufactures.

When a workman is unceasingly and exclusively engaged in the fabrication of one thing, he ultimately does his work with singular dexterity; but at the same time he loses the general faculty of applying his mind to the direction of the work. He every day becomes more adroit and less industrious; so that it may be said of him, that in proportion as the workman improves, the man is degraded. What can be expected of a man who has spent twenty years of his life in making heads for pins? And to what can that mighty human intelligence, which has so often stirred the world, be applied in him, except it be to investigate the best method of making pins' heads? When a workman has spent a considerable portion of his existence in this manner, his thoughts are for ever set upon the object of his daily toil; his body has contracted certain fixed habits, which it can never shake off: in a word, he no longer belongs to himself, but to the calling which he has chosen. It is in vain that laws and manners have been at the pains to level all barriers round such a man, and to open to him on every side a thousand different paths to fortune; a theory of manufactures more powerful than manners and laws binds him to a craft, and frequently to a spot, which he cannot leave: it assigns to him a certain place in society, beyond which he cannot go: in the midst of universal movement, it has rendered him stationary.

In proportion as the principle of the division of labour is more extensively applied, the workman becomes more weak, more narrow-minded and more dependent. The art advances, the artisan recedes. On the other hand, in proportion as it becomes more manifest that the productions of manufactures are by so much the cheaper and better as the manufacture is larger and the amount of capital employed more considerable, wealthy and educated men come for-

ward to embark in manufactures which were heretofore abandoned to poor or ignorant handicraftsmen. The magnitude of the efforts required, and the importance of the results to be obtained, attract them. Thus at the very time at which the science of manufactures lowers the class of workmen, it raises the class of masters.

Whereas the workman concentrates his faculties more and more upon the study of a single detail, the master surveys a more extensive whole, and the mind of the latter is enlarged in proportion as that of the former is narrowed. In a short time the one will require nothing but physical strength without intelligence; the other stands in need of science, and almost of genius, to ensure success. This man resembles more and more the administrator of a vast empire—that man, a brute.

The master and the workman have then here no similarity, and their differences increase every day. They are only connected as the two rings at the extremities of a long chain. Each of them fills the station which is made for him, and out of which he does not get: the one is continually, closely, and necessarily dependant upon the other, and seems as much born to obey as that other is to command. What is this but aristocracy?

As the conditions of men constituting the nation become more and more equal, the demand for manufactured commodities becomes more general and more extensive; and the cheapness which places these objects within the reach of slender fortunes becomes a great element of success. Hence there are every day more men of great opulence and education who devote their wealth and knowledge to manufactures; and who seek, by opening large establishments, and by a strict division of labour, to meet the fresh demands which are made on all sides. Thus, in proportion as the mass of the nation turns to democracy, that particular class which is engaged in manufactures becomes more aristocratic. Men grow more alike in the one—more different in the other; and inequality increases in the less numerous class, in the same ratio in which it decreases in the community.

Hence it would appear, on searching to the bottom, that aristocracy should naturally spring out of the bosom of democracy. But this kind of aristocracy by no means resembles those kinds which preceded it. It will be observed at once, that, as it applies exclusively to manufactures and to some manufacturing callings, it is a monstrous exception in the general aspect of society. The small aristocratic societies which are formed by some manufacturers in the midst of the immense democracy of our age, contain, like the great aristocratic societies of former ages, some men who are very opulent, and a multitude who are wretchedly poor. The poor have few means of escaping from their condition and becoming rich; but the rich are constantly becoming poor, or they give up business when they have realized a fortune. Thus the elements of which the class of the poor is composed, are fixed; but the elements of which the class of the rich is composed are not so. To say the truth, though there are rich men, the class of rich men does not exist; for these rich individuals have no feelings or purposes in common, no mutual traditions or mutual hopes: there are therefore members, but no body.

Not only are the rich not compactly united among themselves, but there is no real bond between them and the poor. Their relative position is not a permanent one; they are constantly drawn together or separated by their interests. The workman is generally dependant on the master, but not on any particular master; these two men meet in the factory, but know not each other elsewhere; and while they come into contact on one point, they stand very wide apart on all others. The manufacturer asks nothing of the workman but his labour; the workman expects nothing from him but his wages. The one contracts no obligation to protect, nor the other to defend; and they are not permanently connected either by habit or by duty.

The aristocracy created by business rarely settles in the midst of the manufacturing population which it directs: the object is not to govern that population, but to use it. An aristocracy thus constituted can have no great hold upon those whom it employs; and even if it succeed in retaining them at one moment, they escape the next: it knows not how to will, and it cannot act.

The territorial aristocracy of former ages was either bound by law, or thought itself bound by usage, to come to the relief of its serving-men, and to succour their distresses. But the manufacturing aristocracy of our age first impoverishes and debases the men who serve it, and then abandons them to be supported by the charity of the public. This is a natural consequence of what has been said before. Between the workman and the master there are frequent relations, but no real partnership.

I am of opinion, upon the whole, that the manufacturing aristocracy which is growing up under our eyes, is one of the harshest which ever existed in the world; but at the same time it is one of the most confined and least dangerous. Nevertheless the friends of democracy should keep their eyes anxiously fixed in this direction; for if ever a permanent inequality of conditions and aristocracy again penetrate into the world, it may be predicted that this is the channel by which they will enter.

5. Equality and Free Institutions

The principle of equality, which makes men independent of each other, gives them a habit and a taste for following, in their private actions, no other guide but their own will. This complete independence, which they constantly enjoy toward their equals and in the intercourse of private life, tends to make them look upon all authority with a jealous eye, and speedily suggests to them the notion and the love of political freedom. Men living at such times have a natural bias to free institutions. Take any one of them at a venture, and search if you can his most deep-seated instincts; you will find that of all governments he will soonest conceive and most highly value that government, whose head he has himself elected, and whose administration he may control.

Of all the political effects produced by the equality of conditions, this love of independence is the first to strike the observing, and to alarm the timid; nor can it be said that their alarm is wholly misplaced, for anarchy has a more formidable aspect in democratic countries than elsewhere. As the citizens have no direct influence on each other, as soon as the supreme power of the nations fails, which kept them all in their several stations, it would seem that disorder must instantly reach its utmost pitch, and that, every man drawing aside in a different direction, the fabric of society must at once crumble away. I am however persuaded that anarchy is not the principal evil which democratic ages have to fear, but the least. For the principle of equality begets two tendencies; the one leads men straight to independence, and may suddenly drive them into anarchy; the other conducts them by a longer, more secret, but more certain road, to servitude. Nations readily discern the former tendency, and are prepared to resist it; they are led away by the latter, without perceiving its drift; hence it is peculiarly important to point it out.

For myself, I am so far from urging as a reproach to the principle of equality that it renders men untractable, that this very circumstance principally calls forth my approbation. I admire to see how it deposits in the mind and heart of man the dim conception and instinctive love of political independence, thus preparing the remedy for the evil which it engenders: it is on this very account that I am attached to it.

6. Centralization of Political Power

As in ages of equality no man is compelled to lend his assistance to his fellowmen, and none has any right to expect much support from them, every one is at once independent and powerless. These two conditions, which must never be either separately considered or confounded together, inspire the citizen of a democratic country with very contrary propensities. His independence fills him with self-reliance and pride among his equals; his debility makes him feel from time to time the want of some outward assistance, which he cannot expect from any of them, because they are all impotent and unsympathizing. In this predicament he naturally turns his eyes to that imposing power which alone rises above the level of universal depression. Of that power his wants and especially his desires continually remind him, until he ultimately views it as the sole and necessary support of his own weakness.[1]

---

[1] In democratic communities nothing but the central power has any stability in its position or any permanence in its undertakings. All the members of society are in ceaseless stir and transformation. Now it is in the nature of all governments to seek constantly to enlarge their sphere of action: hence it is almost impossible that such a government should not ultimately succeed, because it acts with a fixed principle and a constant will, upon men, whose position, whose notions, and whose desires are in continual vacillation.

It frequently happens that the members of the community promote the influence of the central power without intending it. Democratic ages are periods of experiment, innovation, and adventure. At such times there are always a multitude of men engaged in difficult or novel undertakings, which they follow alone, without caring for their fellowmen. Such persons may be ready to admit, as a general principle, that the public authority ought not to interfere in private concerns; but, by an exception to that rule, each of them craves for its assistance in the particular concern on which he is engaged, and seeks to draw upon the influence of the government for his own benefit, though he would restrict it on all other occasions. If a large number of men apply this particular exception to a great variety of different purposes, the sphere of the central power extends insensibly in all directions, although each of them wishes it to be circumscribed.

Thus a democratic government increases its power simply by the fact of its permanence. Time is on its side; every incident befriends it; the passions of individuals unconsciously promote it; and it may be asserted, that the older a democratic community is, the more centralized will its government become.

This may more completely explain what frequently takes place in democratic countries, where the very men who are so impatient of superiors patiently submit to a master, exhibiting at once their pride and their servility.

The hatred which men bear to privilege increases in proportion as privileges become more scarce and less considerable, so that democratic passions would seem to burn most fiercely at the very time when they have least fuel. I have already given the reason of this phenomenon. When all conditions are unequal, no inequality is so great as to offend the eye; whereas the slightest dissimilarity is odious in the midst of general uniformity: the more complete is this uniformity, the more insupportable does the sight of such a difference become. Hence it is natural that the love of equality should constantly increase together with equality itself, and that it should grow by what it feeds upon.

This never-dying, ever-kindling hatred, which sets a democratic people against the smallest privileges, is peculiarly favourable to the gradual concentration of all political rights in the hands of the representative of the state alone. The sovereign, being necessarily and incontestably above all the citizens, excites not their envy, and each of them thinks that he strips his equals of the prerogative which he concedes to the crown.

The man of a democratic age is extremely reluctant to obey his neighbour who is his equal; he refuses to acknowledge in such a person ability superior to his own; he mistrusts his justice, and is jealous of his power; he fears and he contemns him; and he loves continually to remind him of the common dependance in which both of them stand to the same master.

Every central power which follows its natural tendencies courts and encourages the principle of equality; for equality singularly facilitates, extends, and secures the influence of a central power.

In like manner it may be said that every central government worships uniformity: uniformity relieves it from inquiry into an infinite number of small details which must be attended to if rules were to be adapted to men, instead of indiscriminately subjecting men to rules: thus the government likes what the citizens like, and naturally hates what they hate. These common sentiments, which, in democratic nations, constantly unite the sovereign and every member of the community in one and the same conviction, establish a secret and lasting sympathy between them. The faults of the government are pardoned for the sake of its tastes; public confidence is only reluctantly withdrawn in the midst even of its excesses and its errors, and it is restored at the first call. Democratic nations often hate those in whose hands the central power is vested; but they always love that power itself.

Thus, by two separate paths, I have reached the same conclusion. I have shown that the principle of equality suggests to men the notion of a sole, uniform, and strong government; I have now shown that the principle of equality imparts to them a taste for it. To governments of this kind the nations of our age are therefore tending. They are drawn thither by the natural inclination of mind and heart; and in order to reach that result, it is enough that they do not check themselves in their course.

I am of opinion, that, in the democratic ages which are opening upon us, individual independence and local liberties will ever be the produce of artificial contrivance; that centralization will be the natural form of government.[2]

---

[2] A democratic people is not only led by its own tastes to centralize its government, but the passions of all the men by whom it is governed constantly urge it in the same direction. It may easily be foreseen that almost all the able and ambitious members of a democratic community will labour without ceasing to extend the powers of government, because they all hope at some time or other to wield those powers. It is a waste of time to attempt to prove to them that extreme centralization may be injurious to the State, since they are centralizing for their own benefit. Among the public men of democracies there are hardly any but men of great disinterestedness or extreme mediocrity who seek to oppose the centralization of government: the former are scarce, the latter powerless.

7. Democracy and Despotism

I had remarked during my stay in the United States, that a democratic state of society, similar to that of the Americans, might offer singular facilities for the establishment of despotism; and I perceived, upon my return to Europe, how much use had already been made by most of our rulers, of the notions, the sentiments, and the wants engendered by this same social condition, for the purpose of extending the circle of their power. This led me to think that the nations of Christendom would perhaps eventually undergo some sort of oppression like that which hung over several of the nations of the ancient world.

A more accurate examination of the subject, and five years of further meditations, have not diminished my apprehensions, but they have changed the object of them.

No sovereign ever lived in former ages so absolute or so powerful as to undertake to administer by his own agency, and without the assistance of intermediate powers, all the parts of a great empire: none ever attempted to subject all his subjects indiscriminately to strict uniformity of regulation, and personally to tutor and direct every member of the community. The notion of such an undertaking never occurred to the human mind; and if any man had conceived it, the want of information, the imperfection of the administrative system, and above all, the natural obstacles caused by the inequality of conditions, would speedily have checked the execution of so vast a design.

When the Roman emperors were at the height of their power, the different nations of the empire still preserved manners and customs of great diversity; although they were subject to the same monarch, most of the provinces were separately administered; they abounded in powerful and active municipalities; and although the whole government of the empire was centered in the hands of the emperor alone, and he always remained, upon occasions, the supreme arbiter in all matters, yet the details of social life and private occupations lay for the most part beyond his control. The emperors possessed, it is true, an immense and unchecked power, which allowed them to gratify all their whimsical tastes, and to employ for that purpose the whole strength of the State. They frequently abused that power arbitrarily to deprive their subjects of property or of life: their tyranny was extremely onerous to the few, but it did not reach the greater number; it was fixed to some few main objects, and neglected the rest; it was violent, but its range was limited.

But it would seem that if despotism were to be established among the democratic nations of our days, it might assume a different character; it would be more extensive and more mild; it would degrade men without tormenting them. I do not question, that in an age of instruction and equality like our own, sovereigns might more easily succeed in collecting all political power into their own hands, and might interfere more habitually and decidedly within the circle of private interests, than any sovereign of antiquity could ever do. But this same principle of equality which facilitates despotism, tempers its rigour. We have seen how the manners of society become more humane and gentle in proportion as men become more equal and alike. When no member of the community has much power or much wealth, tyranny is, as it were, without opportunities and a field of action. As all fortunes are scanty, the passions of men are naturally circumscribed —their imagination limited, their pleasures simple. This universal moderation moderates the sovereign himself, and checks within certain limits the inordinate stretch of his desires.

Independently of these reasons drawn from the nature of the state of society itself, I might add many others arising from causes beyond my subject; but I shall keep within the limits I have laid down to myself.

Democratic governments may become violent and even cruel at certain periods of extreme effervescence or of great danger;

but these crises will be rare and brief. When I consider the petty passions of our contemporaries, the mildness of their manners, the extent of their education, the purity of their religion, the gentleness of their morality, their regular and industrious habits, and the restraint which they almost all observe in their vices no less than in their virtues, I have no fear that they will meet with tyrants in their rulers, but rather guardians.[1]

I think then that the species of oppression by which democratic nations are menaced is unlike anything which ever before existed in the world: our contemporaries will find no prototype of it in their memories. I am trying myself to choose an expression which will accurately convey the whole of the idea I have formed of it, but in vain; the old words despotism and tyranny are inappropriate: the thing itself is new; and since I cannot name it, I must attempt to define it.

I seek to trace the novel features under which despotism may appear in the world. The first thing that strikes the observation is an innumerable multitude of men all equal and alike, incessantly endeavouring to procure the petty and paltry pleasures with which they glut their lives. Each of them, living apart, is as a stranger to the fate of all the rest—his children and his private friends constitute to him the whole of mankind; as for the rest of his fellow-citizens, he is close to them, but he sees them not;—

he touches them, but he feels them not; he exists but in himself and for himself alone; and if his kindred still remain to him, he may be said at any rate to have lost his country.

Above this race of men stands an immense and tutelary power, which takes upon itself alone to secure their gratifications, and to watch over their fate. That power is absolute, minute, regular, provident, and mild. It would be like the authority of a parent, if, like that authority, its object was to prepare men for manhood; but it seeks on the contrary to keep them in perpetual childhood: it is well content that the people should rejoice, provided they think of nothing but rejoicing. For their happiness such a government willingly labours, but it chooses to be the sole agent and the only arbiter of that happiness: it provides for their security, foresees and supplies their necessities, facilitates their pleasures, manages their principal concerns, directs their industry, regulates the descent of property, and subdivides their inheritances—what remains, but to spare them all the care of thinking and all the trouble of living?

Thus it every day renders the exercise of the free agency of man less useful and less frequent; it circumscribes the will within a narrower range, and gradually robs a man of all the uses of himself. The principle of equality has prepared men for these things: it has predisposed men to endure them, and oftentimes to look on them as benefits.

After having thus successively taken each member of the community in its powerful grasp, and fashioned them at will, the supreme power then extends its arm over the whole community. It covers the surface of society with a net-work of small complicated rules, minute and uniform, through which the most original minds and the most energetic characters cannot penetrate, to rise above the crowd. The will of man is not shattered, but softened, bent, and guided: men are seldom forced by it to act, but they are constantly restrained from acting: such a power does not destroy, but it prevents

---

[1] I have often asked myself what would happen if, amid the relaxation of democratic manners, and as a consequence of the restless spirit of the army, a military government were ever to be founded among any of the nations of the present age. I think that even such a government would not differ very much from the outline I have drawn, and that it would retain none of the fierce characteristics of a military oligarchy. I am persuaded that, in such a case, a sort of fusion would take place between the habits of official men, and those of the military service. The administration would assume something of a military character, and the army some of the usages of the civil administration. The result would be a regular, clear, exact, and absolute system of government: the people would become the reflection of the army, and the community be drilled like a garrison.

existence; it does not tyrannize, but it compresses, enervates, extinguishes, and stupifies a people, till each nation is reduced to be nothing better than a flock of timid and industrious animals, of which the government is the shepherd.

I have always thought that servitude of the regular, quiet, and gentle kind which I have just described, might be combined more easily than is commonly believed with some of the outward forms of freedom; and that it might even establish itself under the wing of the sovereignty of the people.

Our contemporaries are constantly excited by two conflicting passions; they want to be led, and they wish to remain free: as they cannot destroy either one or the other of these contrary propensities, they strive to satisfy them both at once. They devise a sole, tutelary, and all-powerful form of government, but elected by the people. They combine the principle of centralization and that of popular sovereignty; this gives them a respite: they console themselves for being in tutelage by the reflection that they have chosen their own guardians. Every man allows himself to be put in leading-strings, because he sees that it is not a person or a class of persons, but the people at large that holds the end of his chain.

By this system the people shake off their state of dependance just long enough to select their master, and then relapse into it again. A great many persons at the present day are quite contented with this sort of compromise between administrative despotism and the sovereignty of the people; and they think they have done enough for the protection of individual freedom when they have surrendered it to the power of the nation at large. This does not satisfy me: the nature of him I am to obey signifies less to me than the fact of extorted obedience.

I do not however deny that a constitution of this kind appears to me to be infinitely preferable to one, which, after having concentrated all the powers of government, should vest them in the hands of an irresponsible person or body of persons. Of all the forms which democratic despotism could assume, the latter would assuredly be the worst.

When the sovereign is elective, or narrowly watched by a legislature which is really elective and independent, the oppression which he exercises over individuals is sometimes greater, but it is always less degrading; because every man, when he is oppressed and disarmed, may still imagine, that while he yields obedience it is to himself he yields it, and that it is to one of his own inclinations that all the rest give way. In like manner I can understand that when the sovereign represents the nation, and is dependant upon the people, the rights and the power of which every citizen is deprived, not only serve the head of the state, but the state itself; and that private persons derive some return from the sacrifice of their independence which they have made to the public. To create a representation of the people in a very centralized country is, therefore, to diminish the evil which extreme centralization may produce, but not to get rid of it.

I admit that by this means room is left for the intervention of individuals in the more important affairs; but it is not the less suppressed in the smaller and more private ones. It must not be forgotten that it is especially dangerous to enslave men in the minor details of life. For my own part, I should be inclined to think freedom less necessary in great things than in little ones, if it were possible to be secure of the one without possessing the other.

Subjection in minor affairs breaks out every day, and is felt by the whole community indiscriminately. It does not drive men to resistance, but it crosses them at every turn, till they are led to surrender the exercise of their will. Thus their spirit is gradually broken and their character enervated; whereas that obedience, which is exacted on a few important but rare occasions, only exhibits servitude at certain intervals, and throws the burden of it upon a small number of men. It is vain to summon a people, which has been rendered so dependent on the central power, to choose from time to time the representatives of that power; this rare and brief exercise of their free choice, however important it may be, will not prevent them from gradually losing the faculties of thinking, feeling, and acting for themselves, and thus gradually falling below the level of humanity.[2]

I add that they will soon become incapable of exercising the great and only privilege which remains to them. The democratic nations which have introduced freedom into their political constitution, at the very time when they were augmenting the despotism of their administrative constitution, have been led into strange paradoxes. To manage those minor affairs in which good sense is all that is wanted—the people are held to be unequal to the task; but when the government of the country is at stake, the people are invested with immense powers; they are alternately made the playthings of their ruler, and his masters—more than kings, and less than men. After having exhausted all the different modes of election, without finding one to suit their purpose, they are still amazed, and still bent on seeking further; as if the evil they remark did not originate in the constitution of the country far more than in that of the electoral body.

It is, indeed, difficult to conceive how

___

[2] It cannot be absolutely or generally affirmed that the greatest danger of the present age is license or tyranny, anarchy or despotism. Both are equally to be feared; and the one may as easily proceed as the other from the self-same cause, namely, that *general apathy*, which is the consequence of what I have termed Individualism: it is because this apathy exists, that the executive government, having mustered a few troops, is able to commit acts of oppression one day, and the next day a party, which has mustered some thirty men in its ranks, can also commit acts of oppression. Neither one nor the other can found anything to last; and the causes which enable them to succeed easily, prevent them from succeeding long: they rise because nothing opposes them, and they sink because nothing supports them. The proper object therefore of our most strenuous resistance, is far less either anarchy or despotism, than that apathy which may almost indifferently beget either the one or the other.

men who have entirely given up the habit of self-government should succeed in making a proper choice of those by whom they are to be governed; and no one will ever believe that a liberal, wise, and energetic government can spring from the suffrages of a subservient people.

A constitution, which should be republican in its head and ultra-monarchical in all its other parts, has ever appeared to me to be a shortlived monster. The vices of rulers and the ineptitude of the people would speedily bring about its ruin; and the nation, weary of its representatives and of itself, would create freer institutions, or soon return to stretch itself at the feet of a single master.

8. The Coming Era of World Democracy

Before I close for ever the theme that has detained me so long, I would fain take a parting survey of all the various characteristics of modern society, and appreciate at last the general influence to be exercised by the principle of equality upon the fate of mankind; but I am stopped by the difficulty of the task, and in presence of so great an object my sight is troubled, and my reason fails.

The society of the modern world which I have sought to delineate, and which I seek to judge, has but just come into existence. Time has not yet shaped it into perfect form: the great revolution by which it has been created is not yet over; and amid the occurrences of our time, it is almost impossible to discern what will pass away with the revolution itself, and what will survive its close. The world which is rising into existence is still half encumbered by the remains of the world which is waning into decay; and amid the vast perplexity of human affairs, none can say how much of ancient institutions and former manners will remain, or how much will completely disappear.

Although the revolution which is taking place in the social condition, the laws, the opinions and the feelings of men, is still very far from being terminated, yet its results already admit of no comparison with anything that the world has ever before witnessed. I go back from age to age up to the remotest antiquity: but I find no parallel to what is occurring before my eyes: as the past has ceased to throw its light upon the future, the mind of man wanders in obscurity.

Nevertheless, in the midst of a prospect so wide, so novel, and so confused, some of the more prominent characteristics may already be discerned and pointed out. The good things and the evils of life are more equally distributed in the world: great wealth tends to disappear, the number of small fortunes to increase; desires and gratifications are multipled, but extraordinary prosperity and irremediable penury are alike unknown. The sentiment of ambition is universal, but the scope of ambition is seldom vast. Each individual stands apart in solitary weakness; but society at large is active, provident, and powerful: the performances of private persons are insignificant, those of the State immense.

There is little energy of character; but manners are mild, and laws humane. If there be few instances of exalted heroism or of virtues of the highest, brightest, and purest temper, men's habits are regular, violence is rare, and cruelty almost unknown. Human existence becomes longer, and property more secure: life is not adorned with brilliant trophies, but it is extremely easy and tranquil. Few pleasures are either very refined or very coarse; and highly polished manners are as uncommon as great brutality of tastes. Neither men of great learning, nor extremely ignorant communities, are to be met with; genius becomes more rare, information more diffused. The human mind is impelled by the small efforts of all mankind combined together, not by the strenuous activity of certain men. There is less perfection, but more abundance, in all the productions of the arts. The ties of race, of

rank, and of country are relaxed; the great bond of humanity is strengthened.

If I endeavour to find out the most general and the most prominent of all these different characteristics, I shall have occasion to perceive, that what is taking place in men's fortunes manifests itself under a thousand other forms. Almost all extremes are softened or blunted: all that was most prominent is superseded by some mean term, at once less lofty and less low, less brilliant and less obscure, than what before existed in the world.

When I survey this countless multitude of beings, shaped in each other's likeness, amidst whom nothing rises and nothing falls, the sight of such universal uniformity saddens and chills me, and I am tempted to regret that state of society which has ceased to be. When the world was full of men of great importance and extreme insignificance, of great wealth and extreme poverty, of great learning and extreme ignorance, I turned aside from the latter to fix my observation on the former alone, who gratified my sympathies. But I admit that this gratification arose from my own weakness; it is because I am unable to see at once all that is around me, that I am allowed thus to select and separate the objects of my predilection from among so many others. Such is not the case with that Almighty and Eternal Being, whose gaze necessarily includes the whole of created things, and who surveys distinctly, though at once, mankind and man.

We may naturally believe that it is not the singular prosperity of the few, but the greater well-being of all, which is most pleasing in the sight of the Creator and Preserver of men. What appears to me to be man's decline, is to His eye advancement; what afflicts me is acceptable to Him. A state of equality is perhaps less elevated, but is more just; and its justice constitutes its greatness and its beauty. I would strive then to raise myself to this point of the Divine contemplation, and thence to view and to judge the concerns of men.

No man, upon the earth, can as yet affirm absolutely and generally, that the new state of the world is better than its former one; but it is already easy to perceive that this state is different. Some vices and some virtues were so inherent in the constitution of an aristocratic nation, and are so opposite to the character of a modern people, that they can never be infused into it; some good tendencies and some bad propensities which were unknown to the former, are natural to the latter; some ideas suggest themselves spontaneously to the imagination of the one, which are utterly repugnant to the mind of the other. They are like two distinct orders of human beings, each of which has its own merits and defects, its own advantages and its own evils. Care must therefore be taken not to judge the state of society, which is now coming into existence, by notions derived from a state of society which no longer exists; for as these states of society are exceedingly different in their structure, they cannot be submitted to a just or fair comparison.

It would be scarcely more reasonable to require of our own contemporaries the peculiar virtues which originated in the social condition of their forefathers, since that social condition is itself fallen, and has drawn into one promiscuous ruin the good and evil which belonged to it.

But as yet these things are imperfectly understood. I find that a great number of my contemporaries undertake to make a certain selection from among the institutions, the opinions, and the ideas which originated in the aristocratic constitution of society as it was: a portion of these elements they would willingly relinquish, but they would keep the remainder and transplant them into their new world. I apprehend that such men are wasting their time

and their strength in virtuous but unprofitable efforts.

The object is not to retain the peculiar advantages which the inequality of conditions bestows upon mankind, but to secure the new benefits which equality may supply. We have not to seek to make ourselves like our progenitors, but to strive to work out that species of greatness and happiness which is our own.

For myself, who now look back from this extreme limit of my task, and discover from afar, but at once, the various objects which have attracted my more attentive investigation upon my way, I am full of apprehensions and of hopes. I perceive mighty dangers which it is possible to ward off—mighty evils which may be avoided or alleviated; and I cling with a firmer hold to the belief, that for democratic nations to be virtuous and prosperous they require but to will it.

I am aware that many of my contemporaries maintain that nations are never their own masters here below, and that they necessarily obey some insurmountable and unintelligent power, arising from anterior events, from their race, or from the soil and climate of their country. Such principles are false and cowardly; such principles can never produce aught but feeble men and pusillanimous nations. Providence has not created mankind entirely independent or entirely free. It is true that around every man a fatal circle is traced, beyond which he cannot pass; but within the wide verge of that circle he is powerful and free: as it is with man, so with communities. The nations of our time cannot prevent the conditions of men from becoming equal: but it depends upon themselves whether the principle of equality is to lead them to servitude or freedom, to knowledge or barbarism, to prosperity or to wretchedness.

II. MILL

On Liberty *

1. Liberty and Authority

The subject of this Essay is not the so-called Liberty of the Will, so unfortunately opposed to the misnamed doctrine of Philosophical Necessity; but Civil, or Social Liberty: the nature and limits of the power which can be legitimately exercised by society over the individual. A question seldom stated, and hardly ever discussed, in general terms, but which profoundly influences the practical controversies of the age by its latent presence, and is likely soon to make itself recognized as the vital question of the future. It is so far from being new, that, in a certain sense, it has divided mankind, almost from the remotest ages; but in the stage of progress into which the more civilized portions of the species have now entered, it presents itself under new conditions, and requires a different and more fundamental treatment.

The struggle between Liberty and Authority is the most conspicuous feature in the portions of history with which we are earliest familiar, particularly in that of Greece, Rome, and England. But in old times this contest was between subjects, or some classes of subjects, and the Government. By liberty, was meant protection against the tyranny of the political rulers. The rulers were conceived (except in some of the popular governments of Greece) as in a necessarily antagonistic position to the people whom they ruled. They consisted

of a governing One, or a governing tribe or caste, who derived their authority from inheritance or conquest, who, at all events, did not hold it at the pleasure of the governed, and whose supremacy men did not venture, perhaps did not desire, to contest, whatever precautions might be taken against its oppressive exercise. Their power was regarded as necessary, but also as highly dangerous; as a weapon which they would attempt to use against their subjects, no less than against external enemies. To prevent the weaker members of the community from being preyed upon by innumerable vultures, it was needful that there should be an animal of prey stronger than the rest, commissioned to keep them down. But as the king of the vultures would be no less bent upon preying on the flock than any of the minor harpies, it was indispensable to be in a perpetual attitude of defense against his beak and claws. The aim, therefore, of patriots was to set limits to the power which the ruler should be suffered to exercise over the community; and this limitation was what they meant by liberty. It was attempted in two ways. First, by obtaining a recognition of certain immunities, called political liberties or rights, (which it was to be regarded as a breach of duty in the ruler to infringe, and which, if he did infringe, specific resistance, or general rebellion, was held to be justifiable). A second, and generally a later expedient, was the establishment of constitutional checks, (by which the consent of the community, or of a body of some sort, supposed to represent its in-

---

* From John Stuart Mill, *On Liberty* (1859).

terests, was made a necessary condition to some of the more important acts of the governing power). To the first of these modes of limitation, the ruling power, in most European countries, was compelled, more or less, to submit. It was not so with the second; and, to attain this, or when already in some degree possessed, to attain it more completely, became everywhere the principal object of the lovers of liberty. And so long as mankind were content to combat one enemy by another, and to be ruled by a master, on condition of being guaranteed more or less efficaciously against his tyranny, they did not carry their aspirations beyond this point.

A time, however, came, in the progress of human affairs, when men ceased to think it a necessity of nature that their governors should be an independent power, opposed in interest to themselves. It appeared to them much better that the various magistrates of the State should be their tenants or delegates, revocable at their pleasure. In that way alone, it seemed, could they have complete security that the powers of government would never be abused to their disadvantage. By degrees this new demand for elective and temporary rulers became the prominent object of the exertions of the popular party, wherever any such party existed; and superseded, to a considerable extent, the previous efforts to limit the power of rulers. As the struggle proceeded for making the ruling power emanate from the periodical choice of the ruled, some persons began to think that too much importance had been attached to the limitation of the power itself. *That* (it might seem) was a resource against rulers whose interests were habitually opposed to those of the people. What was now wanted was, that the rulers should be identified with the people; that their interest and will should be the interest and will of the nation. The nation did not need to be protected against its own will. There was no fear of tyrannizing over itself. Let the rulers be effectually responsible to it, promptly removable by it, and it could afford to trust them with power of which it could itself dictate the use to be made. Their power was but the nation's own power, concentrated, and in a form convenient for exercise. This mode of thought, or rather perhaps of feeling, was common among the last generation of European liberalism, in the Continental section of which it still apparently predominates. Those who admit any limit to what a government may do, except in the case of such governmnets as they think ought not to exist, stand out as brilliant exceptions among the political thinkers of the Continent. A similar tone of sentiment might by this time have been prevalent in our own country, if the circumstances which for a time encouraged it, had continued unaltered.

But, in political and philosophical theories, as well as in persons, success discloses faults and infirmities which failure might have concealed from observation. The notion, that the people have no need to limit their power over themselves, might seem axiomatic, when popular government was a thing only dreamed about, or read of as having existed at some distant period of the past. Neither was that notion necessarily disturbed by such temporary aberrations as those of the French Revolution, the worst of which were the work of an usurping few, and which, in any case, belonged, not to the permanent working of popular institutions, but to a sudden and convulsive outbreak against monarchical and aristocratic despotism. In time, however, a democratic republic came to occupy a large portion of the earth's surface, and made itself felt as one of the most powerful members of the community of nations; and elective and responsible government became subject to the observations and criticisms which wait upon a great existing fact. It was now perceived that such phrases as "self-government," and "the power of the people over themselves," do not express the true state of the case. The "people" who exercise the power are not always the same people with those over whom it is exercised; and the "self-government" spoken of is not the government of each by himself, but of each by all the rest. The will of the people, moreover, practically means the will of the most numerous or the most active *part* of the people; the majority, or those who succeed in making themselves accepted as the majority; the people, consequently, *may* desire to oppress a part of their number; and precautions are as much needed against this as against any other abuse of power. The limitation, therefore, of the power of government over individuals loses none of its importance when the holders of power are regularly accountable to the community, that is, to the strongest party therein. This view of things, recommending itself equally to the intelligence of thinkers and to the inclination of those important classes in European society to whose real or supposed interests democracy is adverse, has had no difficulty in establishing itself; and in political speculations "the tyranny of the majority" is now generally included among the evils against which society requires to be on its guard.

Like other tyrannies, the tyranny of the majority was at first, and is still vulgarly, held in dread, chiefly as operating through the acts of the public authorities. But reflecting persons perceived that when society is itself the tyrant—society collectively, over the separate individuals who compose it—its means of tyrannizing are not restricted to the acts which it may do by the hands of its political functionaries. Society can and does execute its own mandates: and if it issues wrong mandates instead of right, or any mandates at all in things with which it ought not to meddle, it practices a social tyranny more formidable than many kinds of political oppression, since, though not usually upheld by such extreme penalties, it leaves fewer means of escape, penetrating much more deeply into the details of life, and enslaving the soul itself. Protection, therefore, against the tyranny of the magistrate is not enough: there needs protection also against the tyranny of the prevailing opinion and feeling; against the tendency of society to impose, by other means than civil penalties, its own ideas and practices as rules of conduct on those who dissent from them; to fetter the development, and, if possible, prevent the formation, of any individuality not in harmony with its ways, and compel all characters to fashion themselves upon the model of its own. There is a limit to the legitimate interference of collective opinion with individual independence: and to find that limit, and maintain it against encroachment, is as indispensable to a good condition of human affairs, as protection against political despotism.

But though this proposition is not likely to be contested in general terms, the practical question, where to place the limit—how to make the fitting adjustment between individual independence and social control —is a subject on which nearly everything remains to be done. All that makes existence valuable to any one, depends on the enforcement of restraints upon the actions of other people. Some rules of conduct, therefore, must be imposed, by law in the first place, and by opinion on many things which are not fit subjects for the operation of law. What these rules should be, is the principal question in human affairs; but if we except a few of the most obvious cases, it is one of those which least progress has been made in resolving. No two ages, and scarcely any two countries, have decided it alike; and the decision of one age or country is a wonder to another. Yet the people of any given age and country no more suspect any difficulty in it, than if it were a subject on which mankind had always been agreed. The rules which obtain among themselves appear to them self-evident and self-justifying. This all but universal illusion is one of the examples of the magical influence of custom, which is not only, as the proverb says, a second nature, but is continually mistaken for the first. The effect of custom, in preventing any misgiving respecting the rules of conduct which mankind impose on one another, is all the more complete because the subject is one on which it is not generally considered necessary that reasons should be given, either by one person to others, or by each to himself. People are accustomed to believe, and have been encouraged in the belief by some who aspire to the character of philosophers, that their feelings, on subjects of this nature, are better than reasons, and render reasons unnecessary. The practical principle which guides them to their opinions on the regulation of human conduct, is the feeling in each person's mind that everybody should be required to act as he, and those with whom he sympathizes, would like them to act. No one, indeed, acknowledges to himself that his standard of judgment is his own liking; but an opinion on a point of conduct, not supported by reasons, can only count as one person's preference; and if the reasons, when given are a mere appeal to a similar preference felt by other people, it is still only many people's liking instead of one. To an ordinary man, however, his own preference, thus supported, is not only a perfectly satisfactory reason, but the only one he generally has for any of his notions of morality, taste, or propriety, which are not expressly written in his religious creed; and his chief guide in the interpretation even of that. Men's opinions, accordingly, on what is laudable or blameable, are affected by all the multifarious causes which influence their wishes in regard to the conduct of others, and which are as numerous as those which determine their wishes on any other subject. Sometimes their reason—at other times their prejudices or superstitions: often their social affections, not seldom their antisocial ones, their envy or jealousy, their arrogance or contemptuousness: but most commonly, their desires or fears for themselves—their legitimate or illegitimate self-interest. Wherever there is an ascendant class, a large portion of the morality of the country emanates from its class interests, and its feelings of class superiority. The morality between Spartans and Helots, between planters and negroes, between princes and subjects, between nobles and roturiers, between men and women, has been for the most part the creation of these class interests and feelings: and the sentiments thus generated, react in turn upon the moral feelings of the members of the ascendant class, in their relations among themselves. Where, on the other hand, a class, formerly ascendant, has lost its ascendancy, or where its ascendancy is unpopular, the prevailing moral sentiments frequently bear the impress of an impatient dislike of superiority. Another grand determining principle of the rules of conduct, both in act and forbearance, which have been enforced by law or opinion, has been the servility of mankind towards the supposed preferences or aversions of their temporal masters, or of their gods. This servility, though essentially selfish, is not hypocrisy; it gives rise to perfectly genuine sentiments of abhorrence; it made men burn magicians and heretics. Among so many baser influences, the general and obvious interests of society have of course had a share, and a large one, in the direction of the moral sentiments· less, however, as a matter of reason, and on their own account, than as a consequence of the sympathies and antipathies which grew out of them: and sympathies and antipathies which had little or nothing to do with the interests of society, have made themselves felt in the establishment of moralities with quite as great force.

The likings and dislikings of society, or of some powerful portion of it, are thus the main thing which has practically determined the rules laid down for general observance, under the penalties of law or opinion. And in general, those who have been in advance of society in thought and feeling, have left this condition of things unassailed in principle, however they may have come into conflict with it in some of its details. They have occupied themselves rather in inquiring what things society ought to like or dislike, than in questioning whether its likings or dislikings should be a law to individuals. They preferred endeavoring to alter the feelings of mankind on the particular points on which they were themselves heretical, rather than make common cause in defense of freedom, with heretics generally. The only case in which the higher ground has been taken on principle and maintained with consistency, by any but an individual here and there, is that of religious belief: a case instructive in many ways, and not least so as forming a most striking instance of the fallibility of what is called the moral sense: for the *odium theologicum*, in a sincere bigot, is one of the most unequivocal cases of moral feeling. Those who first broke the yoke of what called itself the Universal Church, were in general as little willing to permit difference of religious opinion as that church itself. But when the heat of the conflict was over, without giving a complete victory to any party, and each church or sect was reduced to limit its hopes to retaining possession of the ground it already occupied; minorities, seeing that they had no chance of becoming majorities, were under the necessity of pleading to those whom they could not convert, for permission to differ. It is accordingly on this battle-field, almost solely, that the rights of the individual against society have been asserted on broad grounds of principle, and the claim of society to exercise authority over dissentients, openly controverted. The great writers to whom the world owes what religious liberty it possesses, have mostly asserted freedom of conscience as an indefeasible right, and denied absolutely that a human being is accountable to others for his religious belief. Yet so natural to mankind is intolerance in whatever they really care about, that religious freedom has hardly anywhere been practically realized, except where religious indifference, which dislikes to have its peace disturbed by theological quarrels, has added its weight to the scale. In the minds of almost all religious persons, even in the most tolerant countries, the duty of toleration is admitted with tacit reserves. One person will bear with dissent in matters of church government, but not of dogma; another can tolerate everybody, short of a Papist or a Unitarian; another, every one who believes in revealed religion; a few extend their charity a little further, but stop at the be-lief in a God and in a future state. Wherever the sentiment of the majority is still genuine and intense, it is found to have abated little of its claim to be obeyed.

The object of this Essay is to assert one very simple principle, as entitled to govern absolutely the dealings of society with the individual in the way of compulsion and control, whether the means used be physical force in the form of legal penalties, or the moral coercion of public opinion. That principle is, that the sole end for which mankind are warranted, individually or collectively, in interfering with the liberty of action of any of their number, is self-protection. That the only purpose for which power can be rightfully exercised over any member of a civilized community, against his will, is to prevent harm to others. His own good, either physical or moral, is not a sufficient warrant. He cannot rightfully be compelled to do or forbear because it will be better for him to do so, because it will make him happier, because, in the opinions of others, to do so would be wise, or even right. These are good reasons for remonstrating with him, or reasoning with him, or persuading him, or entreating him, but not for compelling him, or visiting him with any evil in case he do otherwise. To justify that, the conduct from which it is desired to deter him, must be calculated to produce evil to some one else. The only part of the conduct of any one, for which he is amenable to society, is that which concerns others. In the part which merely concerns himself, his independence is, of right, absolute. Over himself, over his own body and mind, the individual is sovereign.

It is, perhaps, hardly necessary to say that this doctrine is meant to apply only to human beings in the maturity of their faculties. We are not speaking of children, or of young persons below the age which the law may fix as that of manhood or womanhood. Those who are still in a state to require being taken care of by others, must be protected against their own actions as well as against external injury. For the same reason, we may leave out of consideration those backward states of society in which the race itself may be considered as in its nonage. The early difficulties in the way of spontaneous progress are so great, that there is seldom any choice of means for overcoming them; and a ruler full of the spirit of improvement is warranted in the use of any expedients that will attain an end, perhaps otherwise unattainable. Despotism is a legitimate mode of government in dealing with barbarians, provided the end be their improvement, and the means justified by actually effecting that end. Liberty, as a principle, has no application to any state of things anterior to the time when mankind have become capable of being improved by free and equal discussion. Until then, there is nothing for them but implicit obedience to an Akbar or a Charlemagne, if they are so fortunate as to find one. But as soon as mankind have attained the capacity of being guided to their own improvement by conviction or persuasion (a period long since reached in all nations with whom we need here concern ourselves), compulsion, either in the direct form or in that of pains and penalties for non-compliance, is no longer admissible as a means to their own good, and justifiable only for the security of others.

It is proper to state that I forego any advantage which could be derived to my argument from the idea of abstract right, as a thing independent of utility. I regard utility as the ultimate appeal on all ethical questions; but it must be utility in the largest sense, grounded on the permanent interests of man as a progressive being. Those interests, I contend, authorize the subjection of individual spontaneity to external control, only in respect to those actions of each, which concern the interest of other people. If any one does an act hurtful to others, there is a prima facie case for punishing him, by law, or, where legal penalties are not safely applicable, by general disapprobation. There are also many positive acts for the benefit of others, which he may rightfully be compelled to perform; such

as, to give evidence in a court of justice; to bear his fair share in the common defense, or in any other joint work necessary to the interest of the society of which he enjoys the protection; and to perform certain acts of individual beneficence, such as saving a fellow creature's life, or interposing to protect the defenseless against ill-usage, things which whenever it is obviously a man's duty to do, he may rightfully be made responsible to society for not doing. A person may cause evil to others not only by his actions but by his inaction, and in either case he is justly accountable to them for the injury. The latter case, it is true, requires a much more cautious exercise of compulsion than the former. To make any one answerable for doing evil to others, is the rule; to make him answerable for not preventing evil, is, comparatively speaking, the exception. Yet there are many cases clear enough and grave enough to justify that exception. In all things which regard the external relations of the individual, he is *de jure* amenable to those whose interests are concerned, and if need be, to society as their protector. There are often good reasons for not holding him to the responsibility; but these reasons must arise from the special expediencies of the case: either because it is a kind of case in which he is on the whole likely to act better, when left to his own discretion, than when controlled in any way in which society have it in their power to control him; or because the attempt to exercise control would produce other evils, greater than those which it would prevent. When such reasons as these preclude the enforcement of responsibility, the conscience of the agent himself should step into the vacant judgment-seat, and protect those interests of others which have no external protection; judging himself all the more rigidly, because the case does not admit of his being made accountable to the judgment of his fellow creatures.

But there is a sphere of action in which society, as distinguished from the individual, has, if any, only an indirect interest; comprehending all that portion of a person's life and conduct which affects only himself, or if it also affects others, only with their free, voluntary, and undeceived consent and participation. When I say only himself, I mean directly, and in the first instance: for whatever affects himself, may affect others through himself; and the objection which may be grounded on this contingency will receive consideration in the sequel. This, then, is the appropriate region of human liberty. It comprises, first, the inward domain of consciousness; demanding liberty of conscience, in the most comprehensive sense; liberty of thought and feeling; absolute freedom of opinion and sentiment on all subjects, practical or speculative, scientific, moral, or theological. The liberty of expressing and publishing opinions may seem to fall under a different principle, since it belongs to that part of the conduct of an individual which concerns other people; but, being almost of as much importance as the liberty of thought itself, and resting in great part on the same reasons, is practically inseparable from it. Secondly, the principle requires liberty of tastes and pursuits; of framing the plan of our life to suit our own character; of doing as we like, subject to such consequences as may follow: without impediment from our fellow creatures, so long as what we do does not harm them, even though they should think our conduct foolish, perverse, or wrong. Thirdly, from this liberty of each individual, follows the liberty, within the same limits, of combination among individuals; freedom to unite, for any purpose not involving harm to others: the persons combining being supposed to be of full age, and not forced or deceived.

No society in which these liberties are not, on the whole, respected, is free, whatever may be its form of government; and none is completely free in which they do not exist absolute and unqualified. The only freedom which deserves the name, is that of pursuing our own good in our own way, so long as we do not attempt to deprive others of theirs, or impede their efforts to obtain it. Each is the proper guardian of his own health, whether bodily, or mental and spiritual. Mankind are greater gainers by suffering each other to live as seems good to themselves, than by compelling each to live as seems good to the rest.

Though this doctrine is anything but new, and, to some persons, may have the air of a truism, there is no doctrine which stands more directly opposed to the general tendency of existing opinion and practice. Society has expended fully as much effort in the attempt (according to its lights) to compel people to conform to its notions of personal, as of social excellence. The ancient commonwealths thought themselves entitled to practice, and the ancient philosophers countenanced, the regulation of every part of private conduct by public authority, on the ground that the State had a deep interest in the whole bodily and mental discipline of every one of its citizens; a mode of thinking which may have been admissible in small republics surrounded by powerful enemies, in constant peril of being subverted by foreign attack or internal commotion, and to which even a short interval of relaxed energy and self-command might so easily be fatal, that they could not afford to wait for the salutary permanent effects of freedom. In the modern world, the greater size of political communities, and, above all, the separation between spiritual and temporal authority (which placed the direction of men's consciences in other hands than those which controlled their worldly affairs), prevented so great an interference by law in the details of private life; but the engines of moral repression have been wielded more strenuously against divergence from the reigning opinion in self-regarding, than even in social matters; religion, the most powerful of the elements which have entered into the formation of moral feeling, having almost always been governed either by the ambition of a hierarchy, seeking control over every department of human conduct, or by the spirit of Puritanism. And some of those modern reformers who have placed themselves in strongest opposition to the religions of the past, have been no way behind either churches or sects in their assertion of the right of spiritual domination: M. Comte, in particular, whose social system, as unfolded in his *Système de Politique Positive,* aims at establishing (though by moral more than by legal appliances) a despotism of society over the individual, surpassing anything contemplated in the political ideal of the most rigid disciplinarian among the ancient philosophers.

Apart from the peculiar tenets of individual thinkers, there is also in the world at large an increasing inclination to stretch unduly the powers of society over the individual, both by the force of opinion and even by that of legislation: and as the tendency of all the changes taking place in the world is to strengthen society, and diminish the power of the individual, this encroachment is not one of the evils which tend spontaneously to disappear, but, on the contrary, to grow more and more formidable. The disposition of mankind, whether as rulers or as fellow citizens, to impose their own opinions and inclinations as a rule of conduct on others, is so energetically supported by some of the best and by some of the worst feelings incident to human nature, that it is hardly ever kept under restraint by anything but want of power; and as the power is not declining, but growing, unless a strong barrier of moral conviction can be raised against the mischief, we must expect, in the present circumstances of the world, to see it increase.

It will be convenient for the argument, if, instead of at once entering upon the general thesis, we confine ourselves in the first instance to a single branch of it, on which the principle here stated is, if not fully, yet to a certain point, recognized by the current opinions. This one branch is the Liberty of Thought: from which it is impossible to separate the cognate liberty of speaking and of writing. Although these liberties, to some considerable amount, form part of the political morality of all countries which profess religious toleration and free institutions, the grounds, both philosophical and practical, on which they rest, are perhaps not so familiar to the general mind, nor so thoroughly appreciated by many even of the leaders of opinion, as might have been expected. Those grounds, when rightly understood, are of much wider application than to only one division of the subject, and a thorough consideration of this part of the question will be found the best introduction to the remainder. Those to whom nothing which I am about to say will be new, may therefore, I hope, excuse me, if on a subject which for now three centuries has been so often discussed, I venture on one discussion more.

2. Liberty of Thought and Discussion

The time, it is to be hoped, is gone by, when any defense would be necessary of the "liberty of the press" as one of the securities against corrupt or tyrannical government. No argument, we may suppose, can now be needed, against permitting a legislature or an executive, not identified in interest with the people, to prescribe opinions to them, and determine what doctrines or what arguments they shall be allowed to hear. This aspect of the question, besides, has been so often and so triumphantly enforced by preceding writers, that it needs not be specially insisted on in this place. Though the law of England, on the subject of the press, is as servile to this day as it was in the time of the Tudors, there is little danger of its being actually put in force against political discussion, except during some temporary panic, when fear of insurrection drives ministers and judges from their propriety; [1] and, speaking generally,

[1] These words had scarcely been written, when, as if to give them an emphatic contradiction, occurred the Government Press Prosecutions of 1858. That ill-judged interference with the liberty of public discussion has not, however, induced me to alter a single word in the text, nor has it at all weakened my conviction that, moments of panic excepted, the era of pains and penalties for political

it is not, in constitutional countries, to be apprehended, that the government, whether completely responsible to the people or not, will often attempt to control the expression of opinion, except when in doing so it makes itself the organ of the general intolerance of the public. Let us suppose, therefore, that the government is entirely at one with the people, and never thinks of exerting any power of coercion unless in agreement with what it conceives to be their voice. But I deny the right of the people to exercise such coercion, either by themselves or by their government. The power itself is illegitimate. The best government has no more title to it than the worst. It is as noxious, or more noxious, when exerted in accordance with public opinion, than when in opposition to it. If all mankind minus one, were of one opinion, and only one person were of the contrary opinion, mankind would be no more justified in silencing that one person,

_____

discussion has, in our own country, passed away. For, in the first place, the prosecutions were not persisted in; and, in the second, they were never, properly speaking, political prosecutions. The offense charged was not that of criticizing institutions, or the acts or persons of rulers, but of circulating what was deemed an immoral doctrine, the lawfulness of Tyrannicide.

If the arguments of the present chapter are of any validity, there ought to exist the fullest liberty of professing and discussing, as a matter of ethical conviction, any doctrine, however immoral it may be considered. It would, therefore, be irrelevant and out of place to examine here, whether the doctrine of Tyrannicide deserves that title. I shall content myself with saying that the subject has been at all times one of the open questions of morals; that the act of a private citizen in striking down a criminal, who, by raising himself above the law, has placed himself beyond the reach of legal punishment or control, has been accounted by whole nations, and by some of the best and wisest of men, not a crime, but an act of exalted virtue; and that, right or wrong, it is not of the nature of assassination, but of civil war. As such, I hold that the instigation to it, in a specific case, may be a proper subject of punishment, but only if an overt act has followed, and at least a probable connection can be established between the act and the instigation. Even then, it is not a foreign government, but the very government assailed, which alone, in the exercise of self-defense, can legitimately punish attacks directed against its own existence.

than he, if he had the power, would be justified in silencing mankind. Were an opinion a personal possession of no value except to the owner; if to be obstructed in the enjoyment of it were simply a private injury, it would make some difference whether the injury was inflicted only on a few persons or on many. But the peculiar evil of silencing the expression of an opinion is, that it is robbing the human race; posterity as well as the existing generation; those who dissent from the opinion, still more than those who hold it. If the opinion is right, they are deprived of the opportunity of exchanging error for truth: if wrong, they lose, what is almost as great a benefit, the clearer perception and livelier impression of truth, produced by its collusion with error.

It is necessary to consider separately these two hypotheses, each of which has a distinct branch of the argument corresponding to it. We can never be sure that the opinion we are endeavoring to stifle is a false opinion; and if we were sure, stifling it would be an evil still.

First: the opinion which it is attempted to suppress by authority may possibly be true. Those who desire to suppress it, of course deny its truth; but they are not infallible. They have no authority to decide the question for all mankind, and exclude every other person from the means of judging. To refuse a hearing to an opinion, because they are sure that it is false, is to assume that _their_ certainty is the same thing as _absolute_ certainty. All silencing of discussion is an assumption of infallibility. Its condemnation may be allowed to rest on this common argument, not the worse for being common.

Unfortunately for the good sense of mankind, the fact of their fallibility is far from carrying the weight in their practical judgment, which is always allowed to it in theory; for while every one well knows himself to be fallible, few think it necessary to take any precautions against their own fallibility, or admit the supposition that any opinion, of which they feel very certain, may be one of the examples of the error to which they acknowledge themselves to be liable. Absolute princes, or others who are accustomed to unlimited deference, usually feel this complete confidence in their own opinions on nearly all subjects. People more happily situated, who sometimes hear their opinions disputed, and are not wholly unused to be set right when they are wrong, place the same unbounded reliance only on such of their opinions as are shared by all who surround them, or to whom they habitually defer: for in proportion to a man's want of confidence in his own solitary judgment, does he usually repose, with implicit trust, on the infallibility of "the world" in general. And the world, to each individual, means the part of it with which he comes in contact; his party, his sect, his church, his class of society: the man may be called, by comparison, almost liberal and large-minded to whom it means anything so comprehensive as his own country or his own age. Nor is his faith in this collective authority at all shaken by his being aware that other ages, countries, sects, churches, classes, and parties have thought, and even now think, the exact reverse. He devolves upon his own world the responsibility of being in the right against the dissentient worlds of other people; and it never troubles him that mere accident has decided which of these numerous worlds is the object of his reliance, and that the same causes which make him a Churchman in London, would have made him a Buddhist or a Confucian in Pekin. Yet it is as evident in itself, as any amount of argument can make it, that ages are no more infallible than individuals; every age having held many opinions which subsequent ages have deemed not only false but absurd; and it is as certain that many opinions, now general, will be rejected by future ages, as it is that many, once general, are rejected by the present.

The objection likely to be made to this argument would probably take some such form as the following. There is no greater assumption of infallibility in forbidding the propagation of error, than in any other thing which is done by public authority on its own judgment and responsibility. Judgment is given to men that they may use it. Because it may be used erroneously, are men to be told that they ought not to use it at all? To prohibit what they think pernicious, is not claiming exemption from error, but fulfilling the duty incumbent on them, although fallible, of acting on their conscientious conviction. If we were never to act on our opinions, because those opinions may be wrong, we should leave all our interests uncared for, and all our duties unperformed. An objection which applies to all conduct, can be no valid objection to any conduct in particular. It is the duty of governments, and of individuals, to form the truest opinions they can; to form them carefully, and never impose them upon others unless they are quite sure of being right. But when they are sure (such reasoners may say), it is not conscientiousness but cowards to shrink from acting on their opinions, and allow doctrines which they honestly think dangerous to the welfare of mankind, either in this life or in another, to be scattered abroad without restraint, because other people, in less enlightened times, have persecuted opinions now believed to be true. Let us take care, it may be said, not to make the same mistake: but governments and nations have made mistakes in other things, which are not denied to be fit subjects for the exercise of authority: they have laid on bad taxes, made unjust wars. Ought we therefore to lay on no taxes, and, under whatever provocation, make no wars? Men, and governments, must act to the best of their ability. There is no such thing as absolute certainty, but there is assurance sufficient for the purposes of human life. We may, and must, assume our opinion to be true for the guidance of our own conduct: and it is assuming no more when we forbid bad men to pervert society by the propagation of opinions which we regard as false and pernicious.

I answer, that it is assuming very much more. There is the greatest difference between presuming an opinion to be true, because, with every opportunity for contesting it, it has not been refuted, and assuming its truth for the purpose of not permitting its refutation. Complete liberty of contradicting and disproving our opinion, is the very condition which justifies us in assuming its truth for purposes of action; and on no other terms can a being with human faculties have any rational assurance of being right.

When we consider either the history of opinion, or the ordinary conduct of human life, to what is it to be ascribed that the one and the other are no worse than they are? Not certainly to the inherent force of the human understanding; for, on any matter not self-evident, there are ninety-nine persons totally incapable of judging of it, for one who is capable; and the capacity of the hundredth person is only comparative; for the majority of the eminent men of every past generation held many opinions now known to be erroneous, and did or approved numerous things which no one will now justify. Why is it, then, that there is on the whole a preponderance among mankind of rational opinions and rational conduct? If there really is this preponderance —which there must be unless human affairs are, and have always been, in an almost desperate state—it is owing to a quality of the human mind, the source of everything respectable in man either as an intellectual or as a moral being, namely, that his errors are corrigible. He is capable of rectifying his mistakes, by discussion and experience. Not by experience alone. There must be discussion, to show how experience is to be interpreted. Wrong opinions and practices gradually yield to fact and argument: but facts and arguments, to produce any effect on the mind, must be brought before it. Very few facts are able to tell their own story, without comments to bring out their meaning. The whole strength and value, then, of human judgment, depending on the one property, that it can be set right when it is wrong, reliance can be placed on it only when the means of setting it right are

kept constantly at hand. In the case of any person whose judgment is really deserving of confidence, how has it become so? Because he has kept his mind open to criticism of his opinions and conduct. Because it has been his practice to listen to all that could be said against him; to profit by as much of it as was just, and expound to himself, and upon occasion to others, the fallacy of what was fallacious. Because he has felt, that the only way in which a human being can make some approach to knowing the whole of a subject, is by hearing what can be said about it by persons of every variety of opinion, and studying all modes in which it can be looked at by every character of mind. No wise man ever acquired his wisdom in any mode but this; nor is it in the nature of human intellect to become wise in any other manner. The steady habit of correcting and completing his own opinion by collating it with those of others, so far from causing doubt and hesitation in carrying it into practice, is the only stable foundation for a just reliance on it: for, being cognizant of all that can, at least obviously, be said against him, and having taken up his position against all gainsayers —knowing that he has sought for objections and difficulties, instead of avoiding them, and has shut out no light which can be thrown upon the subject from any quarter—he has a right to think his judgment better than that of any person, or any multitude, who have not gone through a similar process.

It is not too much to require that what the wisest of mankind, those who are best entitled to trust their own judgment, find necessary to warrant their relying on it, should be submitted to by that miscellaneous collection of a few wise and many foolish individuals, called the public. The most intolerant of churches, the Roman Catholic Church, even at the canonization of a saint, admits, and listens patiently to, a "devil's advocate." The holiest of men, it appears, cannot be admitted to posthumous honors, until all that the devil could say against him is known and weighed. If even the Newtonian philosophy were not permitted to be questioned, mankind could not feel as complete assurance of its truth as they now do. The beliefs which we have most warrant for, have no safeguard to rest on, but a standing invitation to the whole world to prove them unfounded. If the challenge is not accepted, or is accepted and the attempt fails, we are far enough from certainty still; but we have done the best that the existing state of human reason admits of; we have neglected nothing that could give the truth a chance of reaching us: if the lists are kept open, we may hope that if there be a better truth, it will be found when the human mind is capable of receiving it; and in the meantime we may rely on having attained such approach to truth, as is possible in our own day. This is the amount of certainty attainable by a fallible being, and this the sole way of attaining it.

Strange it is, that men should admit the validity of the arguments for free discussion, but object to their being "pushed to an extreme"; not seeing that unless the reasons are good for an extreme case, they are not good for any case. Strange that they should imagine that they are not assuming infallibility, when they acknowledge that there should be free discussion on all subjects which can possibly be *doubtful,* but think that some particular principle or doctrine should be forbidden to be questioned because it is so *certain,* that is, because *they are certain* that it is certain. To call any proposition certain, while there is any one who would deny its certainty if permitted, but who is not permitted, is to assume that we ourselves, and those who agree with us, are the judges of certainty, and judges without hearing the other side.

In the present age—which has been described as "destitute of faith, but terrified at scepticism"—in which people feel sure, not so much that their opinions are true, as that they should not know what to do without them—the claims of an opinion to be protected from public attack are rested not so much on its truth, as on its importance

to society. There are, it is alleged, certain beliefs, so useful, not to say indispensable to well-being, that it is as much the duty of governments to uphold those beliefs, as to protect any other of the interests of society. In a case of such necessity, and so directly in the line of their duty, something less than infallibility may, it is maintained, warrant, and even bind, governments, to act on their own opinion, confirmed by the general opinion of mankind. It is also often argued, and still oftener thought, that none but bad men would desire to weaken these salutary beliefs; and there can be nothing wrong, it is thought, in restraining bad men, and prohibiting what only such men would wish to practice. This mode of thinking makes the justification of restraints on discussion not a question of the truth of doctrines, but of their usefulness; and flatters itself by that means to escape the responsibility of claiming to be an infallible judge of opinions. But those who thus satisfy themselves, do not perceive that the assumption of infallibility is merely shifted from one point to another. The usefulness of an opinion is itself matter of opinion: as disputable, as open to discussion, and requiring discussion as much, as the opinion itself. There is the same need of an infallible judge of opinions to decide an opinion to be noxious, as to decide it to be false, unless the opinion condemned has full opportunity of defending itself. And it will not do to say that the heretic may be allowed to maintain the utility or harmlessness of his opinion, though forbidden to maintain its truth. The truth of an opinion is part of its utility. If we would know whether or not it is desirable that a proposition should be believed, is it possible to exclude the consideration of whether or not it is true? In the opinion, not of bad men, but of the best men, no belief which is contrary to truth can be really useful: and can you prevent such men from urging that plea, when they are charged with culpability for denying some doctrine which they are told is useful, but which they believe to be false? Those who are on the side of received opinions, never fail to take all possible advantage of this plea; you do not find *them* handling the question of utility as if it could be completely abstracted from that of truth: on the contrary, it is, above all, because their doctrine is the "truth," that the knowledge or the belief of it is held to be so indispensable. There can be no fair discussion of the question of usefulness, when an argument so vital may be employed on one side, but not on the other. And in point of fact, when law or public feeling do not permit the truth of an opinion to be disputed, they are just as little tolerant of a denial of its usefulness. The utmost they allow is an extenuation of its absolute necessity, or of the positive guilt of rejecting it.

In order more fully to illustrate the mischief of denying a hearing to opinions because we, in our own judgment, have condemned them, it will be desirable to fix down the discussion to a concrete case; and I choose, by preference, the cases which are least favorable to me—in which the argument against freedom of opinion, both on the score of truth and on that of utility, is considered the strongest. Let the opinions impugned be the belief in a God and in a future state, or any of the commonly received doctrines of morality. To fight the battle on such ground, gives a great advantage to an unfair antagonist; since he will be sure to say (and many who have no desire to be unfair will say it internally), Are these the doctrines which you do not deem sufficiently certain to be taken under the protection of law? Is the belief in a God one of the opinions, to feel sure of which, you hold to be assuming infallibility? But I must be permitted to observe, that it is not the feeling sure of a doctrine (be it what it may) which I call an assumption of infallibility. It is the undertaking to decide that question *for others*, without allowing them to hear what can be said on the contrary side. And I denounce and reprobate this pretension not the less, if put forth on the side of my most solemn convictions. However positive any one's persuasion may be, not only of the falsity but of the

pernicious consequences—not only of the pernicious consequences, but (to adopt expressions which I altogether condemn) the immorality and impiety of an opinion; yet if, in pursuance of that private judgment, though backed by the public judgment of his country or his contemporaries, he prevents the opinion from being heard in its defense, he assumes infallibility. And so far from the assumption being less objectionable or less dangerous because the opinion is called immoral or impious, this is the case of all others in which it is most fatal. These are exactly the occasions on which the men of one generation commit those dreadful mistakes, which excite the astonishment and horror of posterity. It is among such that we find the instances memorable in history, when the arm of the law has been employed to root out the best men and the noblest doctrines; with deplorable success as to the men, though some of the doctrines have survived to be (as if in mockery) invoked, in defense of similar conduct towards those who dissent from *them,* or from their received interpretation.

Mankind can hardly be too often reminded, that there was once a man named Socrates, between whom and the legal authorities and public opinion of his time, there took place a memorable collision. Born in an age and country abounding in individual greatness, this man has been handed down to us by those who best knew both him and the age, as the most virtuous man in it; while *we* know him as the head and prototype of all subsequent teachers of virtue, the source equally of the lofty inspiration of Plato and the judicious utilitarianism of Aristotle, *"i maëstri di color che sanno,"* the two headsprings of ethical as of all other philosophy. This acknowledged master of all the eminent thinkers who have since lived—whose fame, still growing after more than two thousand years, all but outweighs the whole remainder of the names which make his native city illustrious—was put to death by his countrymen, after a judicial conviction, for impiety and immorality. Impiety, in denying the gods recognized by the State; indeed his accuser asserted (see the *Apologia*) that he believed in no gods at all. Immorality, in being, by his doctrines and instructions, a "corruptor of youth." Of these charges the tribunal, there is every ground for believing, honestly found him guilty, and condemned the man who probably of all then born had deserved best of mankind, to be put to death as a criminal.

To pass from this to the only other instance of judicial iniquity, the mention of which, after the condemnation of Socrates, would not be an anti-climax: the event which took place on Calvary rather more than eighteen hundred years ago. The man who left on the memory of those who witnessed his life and conversation, such an impression of his moral grandeur, that eighteen subsequent centuries have done homage to him as the Almighty in person, was ignominiously put to death, as what? As a blasphemer. Men did not merely mistake their benefactor; they mistook him for the exact contrary of what he was, and treated him as that prodigy of impiety, which they themselves are now held to be, for their treatment of him. The feelings with which mankind now regard these lamentable transactions, especially the later of the two, render them extremely unjust in their judgment of the unhappy actors. These were, to all appearance, not bad men—not worse than men commonly are, but rather the contrary; men who possessed in a full, or somewhat more than a full measure, the religious, moral, and patriotic feelings of their time and people: the very kind of men who, in all times, our own included, have every chance of passing through life blameless and respected. The high-priest who rent his garments when the words were pronounced, which, according to all the ideas of his country, constituted the blackest guilt, was in all probability quite as sincere in his horror and indignation, as the generality of respectable and pious men now are in the religious and moral sentiments they profess; and most of those who now shudder at his conduct, if they had lived in his time, and been born Jews, would have acted precisely as he did. Orthodox Christians who are tempted to think that those who stoned to death the first martyrs must have been worse men than they themselves are, ought to remember that one of those persecutors was Saint Paul.

Let us add one more example, the most striking of all, if the impressiveness of an error is measured by the wisdom and virtue of him who falls into it. If ever any one, possessed of power, had grounds for thinking himself the best and most enlightened among his contemporaries, it was the Emperor Marcus Aurelius. Absolute monarch of the whole civilized world, he preserved through life not only the most unblemished justice, but what was less to be expected from his Stoical breeding, the tenderest heart. The few failings which are attributed to him, were all on the side of indulgence: while his writings, the highest ethical product of the ancient mind, differ scarcely perceptibly, if they differ at all, from the most characteristic teachings of Christ. This man, a better Christian in all but the dogmatic sense of the word, than almost any of the ostensibly Christian sovereigns who have since reigned, persecuted Christianity. Placed at the summit of all the previous attainments of humanity, with an open, unfettered intellect, and a character which led him of himself to embody in his moral writings the Christian ideal, he yet failed to see that Christianity was to be a good and not an evil to the world, with his duties to which he was so deeply penetrated. Existing society he knew to be in a deplorable state. But such as it was, he saw, or thought he saw, that it was held together, and prevented from being worse, by belief and reverence of the received divinities. As a ruler of mankind, he deemed it his duty not to suffer society to fall in pieces; and saw not how, if its existing ties were removed, any others could be formed which could again knit it together. The new religion openly aimed at dissolving these ties: unless, therefore, it was his duty to adopt that religion, it seemed to be his duty to put it down.

Inasmuch then as the theology of Christianity did not appear to him true or of divine origin; inasmuch as this strange history of a crucified God was not credible to him, and a system which purported to rest entirely upon a foundation to him so wholly unbelievable, could not be foreseen by him to be that renovating agency which, after all abatements, it has in fact proved to be; the gentlest and most amiable of philosophers and rulers, under a solemn sense of duty, authorized the persecution of Christianity. To my mind this is one of the most tragical facts in all history. It is a bitter thought, how different a thing the Christianity of the world might have been, if the Christian faith had been adopted as the religion of the empire under the auspices of Marcus Aurelius instead of those of Constantine. But it would be equally unjust to him and false to truth, to deny, that no one plea which can be urged for punishing anti-Christian teaching, was wanting to Marcus Aurelius for punishing, as he did, the propagation of Christianity. No Christian more firmly believes that Atheism is false, and tends to the dissolution of society, than Marcus Aurelius believed the same things of Christianity; he who, of all men then living, might have been thought the most capable of appreciating it. Unless any one who approves of punishment for the promulgation of opinions, flatters himself that he is a wiser and better man than Marcus Aurelius —more deeply versed in the wisdom of his time, more elevated in his intellect above it—more earnest in his search for truth, or more singleminded in his devotion to it when found;—let him abstain from that assumption of the joint infallibility of himself and the multitude, which the great Antoninus made with so unfortunate a result.

Aware of the impossibility of defending the use of punishment for restraining irreligious opinions, by any argument which will not justify Marcus Antoninus, the enemies of religious freedom, when hard pressed, occasionally accept this consequence, and say, with Dr. Johnson, that the persecutors of Christianity were in the right; that persecution is an ordeal through which truth ought to pass, and always passes successfully, legal penalties being, in the end, powerless against truth, though sometimes beneficially effective against mischievous errors. This is a form of the argument for religious intolerance, sufficiently remarkable not to be passed without notice.

A theory which maintains that truth may justifiably be persecuted because persecution cannot possibly do it any harm, cannot be charged with being intentionally hostile to the reception of new truths; but we cannot commend the generosity of its dealing with the persons to whom mankind are indebted for them. To discover to the world something which deeply concerns it, and of which it was previously ignorant; to prove to it that it had been mistaken on some vital point of temporal or spiritual interest, is as important a service as a human being can render to his fellow creatures, and in certain cases, as in those of the early Christians and of the Reformers, those who think with Dr. Johnson believe it to have been the most precious gift which could be bestowed on mankind. That the authors of such splendid benefits should be requited by martyrdom; that their reward should be to be dealt with as the vilest of criminals, is not, upon this theory, a deplorable error and misfortune, for which humanity should mourn in sackcloth and ashes, but the normal and justifiable state of things. The propounder of a new truth, according to this doctrine, should stand, as stood, in the legislation of the Locrians, the proposer of a new law, with a halter round his neck, to be instantly tightened if the public assembly did not, on hearing his reasons, then and there adopt his proposition. People who defend this mode of treating benefactors, cannot be supposed to set much value on the benefit; and I believe this view of the subject is mostly confined to the sort of persons who think that new truths may have been desirable once, but that we have had enough of them now.

But, indeed, the dictum that truth always

triumphs over persecution, is one of those pleasant falsehoods which men repeat after one another till they pass into commonplaces, but which all experience refutes. History teems with instances of truth put down by persecution. If not suppressed for ever, it may be thrown back for centuries. To speak only of religious opinions: the Reformation broke out at least twenty times before Luther, and was put down. Arnold of Brescia was put down. Fra Dolcino was put down. Savonarola was put down. The Albigeois were put down. The Vaudois were put down. The Lollards were put down. The Hussites were put down. Even after the era of Luther, wherever persecution was persisted in, it was successful. In Spain, Italy, Flanders, the Austrian empire, Protestantism was rooted out; and, most likely, would have been so in England, had Queen Mary lived, or Queen Elizabeth died. Persecution has always succeeded, save where the heretics were too strong a party to be effectually persecuted. No reasonable person can doubt that Christianity might have been extirpated in the Roman Empire. It spread, and became predominant, because the persecutions were only occasional, lasting but a short time, and separated by long intervals of almost undisturbed propagandism. It is a piece of idle sentimentality that truth, merely as truth, has any inherent power denied to error, of prevailing against the dungeon and the stake. Men are not more zealous for truth than they often are for error, and a sufficient application of legal or even of social penalities will generally succeed in stopping the propagation of either. The real advantage which truth has, consists in this, that when an opinion is true, it may be extinguished once, twice, or many times, but in the course of ages there will generally be found persons to rediscover it, until some one of its reappearances falls on a time when from favorable circumstances it escapes persecution until it has made such head as to withstand all subsequent attempts to suppress it.

What is boasted of at the present time as the revival of religion, is always, in narrow and uncultivated minds, at least as much the revival of bigotry; and where there is the strong permanent leaven of intolerance in the feelings of a people, which at all times abides in the middle classes of this country, it needs but little to provoke them into actively persecuting those whom they have never ceased to think proper objects of persecution. For it is this—it is the opinions men entertain, and the feelings they cherish, respecting those who disown the beliefs they deem important, which makes this country not a place of mental freedom. For a long time past, the chief mischief of the legal penalties is that they strengthen the social stigma. It is that stigma which is really effective, and so effective is it, that the profession of opinions which are under the ban of society is much less common in England, than is, in many other countries, the avowal of those which incur risk of judicial punishment. In respect to all persons but those whose pecuniary circumstances make them independent of the goodwill of other people, opinion, on this subject, is as efficacious as law; men might as well be imprisoned, as excluded from the means of earning their bread. Those whose bread is already secured, and who desire no favors from men in power, or from bodies of men, or from the public, have nothing to fear from the open avowal of any opinions, but to be ill-thought of and ill-spoken of, and this it ought not to require a very heroic mold to enable them to bear. There is no room for any appeal *ad misericordiam* in behalf of such persons. But though we do not now inflict so much evil on those who think differently from us, as it was formerly our custom to do, it may be that we do ourselves as much evil as ever by our treatment of them. Socrates was put to death, but the Socratic philosophy rose like the sun in heaven, and spread its illumination over the whole intellectual firmament. Christians were cast to the lions, but the Christian church grew up a stately and spreading tree, overtopping the older and less vigorous growths, and stifling them by its shade. Our merely social intolerance kills no one, roots out no opinions, but induces men to disguise them, or to abstain from any active effort for their diffusion. With us, heretical opinions do not perceptibly gain, or even lose, ground in each decade or generation; they never blaze out far and wide, but continue to smolder in the narrow circles of thinking and studious persons among whom they originate, without ever lighting up the general affairs of mankind with either a true or a deceptive light. And thus is kept up a state of things very satisfactory to some minds, because, without the unpleasant process of fining or imprisoning anybody, it maintains all prevailing opinions outwardly undisturbed, while it does not absolutely interdict the exercise of reason by dissentients afflicted with the malady of thought. A convenient plan for having peace in the intellectual world, and keeping all things going on therein very much as they do already. But the price paid for this sort of intellectual pacification, is the sacrifice of the entire moral courage of the human mind. A state of things in which a large portion of the most active and inquiring intellects find it advisable to keep the general principles and grounds of their convictions within their own breasts, and attempt, in what they address to the public, to fit as much as they can of their own conclusions to premises which they have internally renounced, cannot send forth the open, fearless characters, and logical, consistent intellects who once adorned the thinking world. The sort of men who can be looked for under it, are either mere conformers to commonplace, or time-servers for truth, whose arguments on all great subjects are meant for their hearers, and are not those which have convinced themselves. Those who avoid this alternative, do so by narrowing their thoughts and interest to things which can be spoken of without venturing within the region of principles, that is, to small practical matters, which would come right of themselves, if but the minds of mankind were strengthened and enlarged, and which will never be made effectually

right until then: while that which would strengthen and enlarge men's minds, free and daring speculation on the highest subjects, is abandoned.

Those in whose eyes this reticence on the part of heretics is no evil, should consider in the first place, that in consequence of it there is never any fair and thorough discussion of heretical opinions; and that such of them as could not stand such a discussion, though they may be prevented from spreading, do not disappear. But it is not the minds of heretics that are deteriorated most, by the ban placed on all inquiry which does not end in the orthodox conclusions. The greatest harm done is to those who are not heretics, and whose whole mental development is cramped, and their reason cowed, by the fear of heresey. Who can compute what the world loses in the multitude of promising intellects combined with timid characters, who dare not follow out any bold, vigorous, independent train of thought, lest it should land them in something which would admit of being considered irreligious or immoral? Among them we may occasionally see some man of deep conscientiousness, and subtle and refined understanding, who spends a life in sophisticating with an intellect which he cannot silence, and exhausts the resources of ingenuity in attempting to reconcile the promptings of his conscience and reason with orthodoxy, which yet he does not, perhaps, to the end succeed in doing. No one can be a great thinker who does not recognize, that as a thinker it is his first duty to follow his intellect to whatever conclusions it may lead. Truth gains more even by the errors of one who, with due study and preparation, thinks for himself, than by the true opinions of those who only hold them because they do not suffer themselves to think. Not that it is solely, or chiefly, to form great thinkers, that freedom of thinking is required. On the contrary, it is as much and even more indispensable, to enable average human beings to attain the mental stature which they are capable of. There have been, and may again be, great individual thinkers, in a general atmosphere of mental slavery. But there never has been, nor ever will be, in that atmosphere, an intellectually active people. When any people has made a temporary approach to such a character, it has been because the dread of heterodox speculation was for a time suspended. Where there is a tacit convention that principles are not to be disputed; where the discussion of the greatest questions which can occupy humanity is considered to be closed, we cannot hope to find that generally high scale of mental activity which has made some periods of history so remarkable. Never when controversy avoided the subjects which are large and important enough to kindle enthusiasm, was the mind of a people stirred up from its foundations, and the impulse given which raised even persons of the most ordinary intellect to something of the dignity of thinking beings. Of such we have had an example in the condition of Europe during the times immediately following the Reformation; another, though limited to the Continent and to a more cultivated class, in the speculative movement of the latter half of the eighteenth century; and a third, of still briefer duration, in the intellectual fermentation of Germany during the Goethian and Fichtean period. These periods differed widely in the particular opinions which they developed; but were alike in this, that during all three the yoke of authority was broken. In each, an old mental despotism had been thrown off, and no new one had yet taken its place. The impulse given at these three periods has made Europe what it now is. Every single improvement which has taken place either in the human mind or in institutions, may be traced distinctly to one or other of them. Appearances have for some time indicated that all three impulses are wellnigh spent; and we can expect no fresh start, until we again assert our mental freedom.

Let us now pass to the second division of the argument, and dismissing the supposition that any of the received opinions may be false, let us assume them to be true, and examine into the worth of the manner in which they are likely to be held, when their truth is not freely and openly canvassed. However unwillingly a person who has a strong opinion may admit the possibility that his opinion may be false, he ought to be moved by the consideration that however true it may be, if it is not fully, frequently, and fearlessly discussed, it will be held as a dead dogma, not a living truth.

There is a class of persons (happily not quite so numerous as formerly) who think it enough if a person assents undoubtingly to what they think true, though he has no knowledge whatever of the grounds of the opinion, and could not make a tenable defense of it against the most superficial objections. Such persons, if they can once get their creed taught from authority, naturally think that no good, and some harm, comes of its being allowed to be questioned. Where their influence prevails, they make it nearly impossible for the received opinion to be rejected wisely and considerately, though it may still be rejected rashly and ignorantly; for to shut out discussion entirely is seldom possible and, when it once gets in, beliefs not grounded on conviction are apt to give way before the slightest semblance of an argument. Waiving, however, this possibility—assuming that the true opinion abides in the mind, but abides as a prejudice, a belief independent of, and proof against, argument—this is not the way in which truth ought to be held by a rational being. This is not knowing the truth. Truth, thus held, is but one superstition the more accidentally clinging to the words which enunciate a truth.

If the intellect and judgment of mankind ought to be cultivated, a thing which Protestants at least do not deny, on what can these faculties be more appropriately exercised by any one, than on the things which concern him so much that it is considered necessary for him to hold opinions on them? If the cultivation of the understanding consists in one thing more than in another, it is surely in learning the grounds of one's own opinions. Whatever people believe, on subjects on which it is of the first importance to believe rightly, they ought to be able to defend against at least the common objections. But, some one may say, "Let them be *taught* the grounds of their opinions. It does not follow that opinions must be merely parrotted because they are never heard controverted. Persons who learn geometry do not simply commit the theorems to memory, but understand and learn likewise the demonstrations; and it would be absurd to say that they remain ignorant of the grounds of geometrical truths, because they never hear any one deny, and attempt to disprove them." Undoubtedly: and such teaching suffices on a subject like mathematics, where there is nothing at all to be said on the wrong side of the question. The peculiarity of the evidence of mathematical truths is, that all the argument is on one side. There are no objections, and no answers to objections. But on every subject on which difference of opinion is possible, the truth depends on a balance to be struck between two sets of conflicting reasons. Even in natural philosophy, there is always some other explanation possible of the same facts; some geocentric theory instead of heliocentric, some phlogiston instead of oxygen; and it has to be shown why that other theory cannot be the true one: and until this is shown, and until we know how it is shown, we do not understand the grounds of our opinion. But when we turn to subjects infinitely more complicated, to morals, religion, politics, social relations, and the business of life, three-fourths of the arguments for every disputed opinion consist in dispelling the appearances which favor some opinion different from it. The greatest orator, save one, of antiquity, has left it on record that he always studied his adversary's case with as great, if not with still greater, intensity than even his own. What Cicero practiced as the means of forensic success, requires to be imitated by all who study any subject in order to arrive at the truth. He who knows only his own side of the case, knows little of that. His reasons may be good, and no one may have been able to refute them. But if he is equally un-

able to refute the reasons on the opposite side; if he does not so much as know what they are, he has no ground for preferring either opinion. The rational position for him would be suspension of judgment, and unless he contents himself with that, he is either led by authority, or adopts, like the generality of the world, the side to which he feels most inclination. Nor is it enough that he should hear the arguments of adversaries from his own teachers, presented as they state them, and accompanied by what they offer as refutations. That is not the way to do justice to the arguments, or bring them into real contact with his own mind. He must be able to hear them from persons who actually believe them; who defend them in earnest, and do their very utmost for them. He must know them in their most plausible and persuasive form; he must feel the whole force of the difficulty which the true view of the subject has to encounter and dispose of; else he will never really possess himself of the portion of truth which meets and removes that difficulty. Ninety-nine in a hundred of what are called educated men are in this condition; even of those who can argue fluently for their opinions. Their conclusion may be true, but it might be false for anything they know: they have never thrown themselves into the mental position of those who think differently from them, and considered what such persons may have to say; and consequently they do not, in any proper sense of the word, know the doctrine which they themselves profess. They do not know those parts of it which explain and justify the remainder; the considerations which show that a fact which seemingly conflicts with another is reconcilable with it, or that, of two apparently strong reasons, one and not the other ought to be preferred. All that part of the truth which turns the scale, and decides the judgment of a completely informed mind, they are strangers to; nor is it ever really known, but to those who have attended equally and impartially to both sides, and endeavored to see the reasons of both in the strongest light. So essential is this discipline to a real understanding of moral and human subjects, that if opponents of all important truths do not exist, it is indispensable to imagine them, and supply them with the strongest arguments which the most skilful devil's advocate can conjure up.

To abate the force of these considerations, an enemy of free discussion may be supposed to say, that there is no necessity for mankind in general to know and understand all that can be said against or for their opinions by philosophers and theologians. That it is not needful for common men to be able to expose all the misstatements or fallacies of an ingenious opponent. That it is enough if there is always somebody capable of answering them, so that nothing likely to mislead uninstructed persons remains unrefuted. That simple minds, having been taught the obvious grounds of the truths inculcated on them, may trust to authority for the rest, and being aware that they have neither knowledge nor talent to resolve every difficulty which can be raised, may repose in the assurance that all those which have been raised have been or can be answered, by those who are specially trained to the task.

Conceding to this view of the subject the utmost that can be claimed for it by those most easily satisfied with the amount of understanding of truth which ought to accompany the belief of it; even so, the argument for free discussion is no way weakened. For even this doctrine acknowledges that mankind ought to have a rational assurance that all objections have been satisfactorily answered; and how are they to be answered if that which requires to be answered is not spoken? or how can the answer be known to be satisfactory, if the objectors have no opportunity of showing that it is unsatisfactory? If not the public, at least the philosophers and theologians who are to resolve the difficulties, must make themselves familiar with those difficulties in their most puzzling form; and this cannot be accomplished unless they are freely stated, and placed in the most advantageous light which

they admit of. The Catholic Church has its own way of dealing with this embarrassing problem. It makes a broad separation between those who can be permitted to receive its doctrines on conviction, and those who must accept them on trust. Neither, indeed, are allowed any choice as to what they will accept; but the clergy, such at least can be fully confided in, may admissibly and meritoriously make themselves acquainted with the arguments of opponents, in order to answer them, and may, therefore, read heretical books; the laity, not unless by special permission, hard to be obtained. This discipline recognizes a knowledge of the enemy's case as beneficial to the teachers, but finds means, consistent with this, of denying it to the rest of the world: thus giving to the *élite* more mental culture, though not more mental freedom, than it allows to the mass. By this device it succeeds in obtaining the kind of mental superiority which its purposes require; for though culture without freedom never made a large and liberal mind, it can make a clever *nisi prius* advocate of a cause. But in countries professing Protestantism, this resource is denied; since Protestants hold, at least in theory, that the responsibility for the choice of a religion must be borne by each for himself, and cannot be thrown off upon teachers. Besides, in the present state of the world, it is practically impossible that writings which are read by the instructed can be kept from the uninstructed. If the teachers of mankind are to be cognizant of all that they ought to know, everything must be free to be written and published without restraint.

If, however, the mischievous operation of the absence of free discussion, when the received opinions are true, were confined to leaving men ignorant of the grounds of those opinions, it might be thought that this, if an intellectual, is no moral evil, and does not affect the worth of the opinions, regarded in their influence on the character. The fact, however, is, that not only the grounds of the opinion are forgotten in the absence of discussion, but too often the meaning of the opinion itself. The words which convey it, cease to suggest ideas, or suggest only a small portion of those they were originally employed to communicate. Instead of a vivid conception and a living belief, there remain only a few phrases retained by rote; or, if any part, the shell and husk only of the meaning is retained, the finer essence being lost. The great chapter in human history which this fact occupies and fills, cannot be too earnestly studied and meditated on.

It is illustrated in the experience of almost all ethical doctrines and religious creeds. They are all full of meaning and vitality to those who originate them, and to the direct disciples of the originators. Their meaning. continues to be felt in undiminished strength, and is perhaps brought out into even fuller consciousness, so long as the struggle lasts to give the doctrine or creed an ascendancy over other creeds. At last it either prevails, and becomes the general opinion, or its progress stops; it keeps possession of the ground it has gained, but ceases to spread further. When either of these results has become apparent, controversy on the subject flags, and gradually dies away. The doctrine has taken its place, if not as a received opinion, as one of the admitted sects or divisions of opinion: those who hold it have generally inherited, not adopted it; and conversion from one of these doctrines to another, being now an exceptional fact, occupies little place in the thoughts of their professors. Instead of being, as at first, constantly on the alert either to defend themselves against the world, or to bring the world over to them, they have subsided into acquiescence, and neither listen, when they can help it, to arguments against their creed, nor trouble dissentients (if there be such) with arguments in its favor. From this time may usually be dated the decline in the living power of the doctrine. We often hear the teachers of all creeds lamenting the difficulty of keeping up in the minds of believers a lively apprehension of the truth which they nominally recognize, so that it may penetrate the feelings, and acquire a real mastery over the conduct. No such difficulty is complained of while the creed is still fighting for its existence: even the weaker combatants then know and feel what they are fighting for, and the difference between it and other doctrines; and in that period of every creed's existence, not a few persons may be found, who have realized its fundamental principles in all the forms of thought, have weighed and considered them in all their important bearings, and have experienced the full effect on the character, which belief in that creed ought to produce in a mind thoroughly imbued with it. But when it has come to be an hereditary creed, and to be received passively, not actively—when the mind is no longer compelled, in the same degree as at first, to exercise its vital powers on the questions which its belief presents to it, there is a progressive tendency to forget all of the belief except the formularies, or to give it a dull and torpid assent, as if accepting it on trust dispensed with the necessity of realizing it in consciousness, or testing it by personal experience; until it almost ceases to connect itself at all with the inner life of the human being. Then are seen the cases, so frequent in this age of the world as almost to form the majority, in which the creed remains as it were outside the mind, encrusting and petrifying it against all other influences addressed to the higher parts of our nature; manifesting its power by not suffering any fresh and living conviction to get in, but itself doing nothing for the mind or heart, except standing sentinel over them to keep them vacant.

To what an extent doctrines intrinsically fitted to make the deepest impression upon the mind may remain in it as dead beliefs, without being ever realized in the imagination, the feelings, or the understanding, is exemplified by the manner in which the majority of believers hold the doctrines of Christianity. By Christianity I here mean what is accounted such by all churches and sects—the maxims and precepts contained in the New Testament. These are considered sacred, and accepted as laws, by all professing Christians. Yet it is scarcely too much to say that not one Christian in a thousand guides or tests his individual conduct by reference to those laws. The standard to which he does refer it, is the custom of his nation, his class, or his religious profession. He has thus, on the one hand, a collection of ethical maxims, which he believes to have been vouchsafed to him by infallible wisdom as rules for his government; and on the other, a set of everyday judgments and practices, which go a certain length with some of those maxims, not so great a length with others, stand in direct opposition to some, and are, on the whole, a compromise between the Christian creed and the interests and suggestions of worldly life. To the first of these standards he gives his homage; to the other his real allegiance. All Christians believe that the blessed are the poor and humble, and those who are illused by the world; that it is easier for a camel to pass through the eye of a needle than for a rich man to enter the kingdom of heaven; that they should judge not, lest they be judged; that they should swear not at all; that they should love their neighbor as themselves; that if one take their cloak, they should give him their coat also; that they should take no thought for the morrow; that if they would be perfect, they should sell all that they have and give it to the poor. They are not insincere when they say that they believe these things. They do believe them, as people believe what they have always heard lauded and never discussed. But in the sense of that living belief which regulates conduct, they believe these doctrines just up to the point to which it is usual to act upon them. The doctrines in their integrity are serviceable to pelt adversaries with; and it is understood that they are to be put forward (when possible) as the reasons for whatever people do that they think laudable. But any one who reminded them that the maxims require an infinity of things which they never even think of doing, would gain nothing but to be classed among those very unpopular characters who affect to be better

than other people. The doctrines have no hold on ordinary believers—are not a power in their minds. They have an habitual respect for the sound of them, but no feeling which spreads from the words of the things signified, and forces the mind to take *them* in, and make them conform to the formula. Whenever conduct is concerned, they look round for Mr. A and B to direct them how far to go in obeying Christ.

Now we may be well assured that the case was not thus, but far otherwise, with the early Christians. Had it been thus, Christianity never would have expanded from an obscure sect of the despised Hebrews into the religion of the Roman empire. When their enemies said, "See how these Christians love one another" (a remark not likely to be made by anybody now), they assuredly had a much livelier feeling of the meaning of their creed than they have ever had since. And to this cause, probably, it is chiefly owing that Christianity now makes so little progress in extending its domain, and after eighteen centuries, is still nearly confined to Europeans and the descendants of Europeans. Even with the strictly religious, who are much in earnest about their doctrines, and attach a greater amount of meaning to many of them than people in general, it commonly happens that the part which is thus comparatively active in their minds is that which was made by Calvin, or Knox, or some such person much nearer in character to themselves. The sayings of Christ co-exist passively in their minds, producing hardly any effect beyond what is caused by mere listening to words so amiable and bland. There are many reasons, doubtless, why doctrines which are the badge of a sect retain more of their vitality than those common to all recognized sects, and why more pains are taken by teachers to keep their meaning alive; but one reason certainly is, that the peculiar doctrines are more questioned, and have to be oftener defended against open gainsayers. Both teachers and learners go to sleep at their post, as soon as there is no enemy in the field.

The same thing holds true, generally speaking, of all traditional doctrines—those of prudence and knowledge of life, as well as morals or religion. All languages and literatures are full of general observations on life, both as to what it is, and how to conduct oneself in it; observations which everybody knows, which everybody repeats, or hears with acquiescence, which are received as truisms, yet of which most people first truly learn the meaning, when experience, generally of a painful kind, has made it a reality to them. How often, when smarting under some unforeseen misfortune or disappointment, does a person call to mind some proverb or common saying, familiar to him all his life, the meaning of which, if he had ever before felt it as he does now, would have saved him from the calamity. There are indeed reasons for this, other than the absence of discussion: there are many truths of which the full meaning *cannot* be realized, until personal experience has brought it home. But much more of the meaning even of these would have been understood, and what was understood would have been far more deeply impressed on the mind, if the man had been accustomed to hear it argued *pro* and *con* by people who did understand it. The fatal tendency of mankind to leave off thinking about a thing when it is no longer doubtful, is the cause of half their errors. A contemporary author has well spoken of "the deep slumber of a described opinion."

But what! (it may be asked) Is the absence of unanimity an indispensable condition of true knowledge? It is necessary that some part of mankind should persist in error, to enable any to realize the truth? Does a belief cease to be real and vital as soon as it is generally received—and is a proposition never thoroughly understood and felt unless some doubt of it remains? As soon as mankind have unanimously accepted a truth, does the truth perish within them? The highest aim and best result of improved intelligence, it has hitherto been thought, is to unite mankind more and more in the acknowledgment of all impor-tant truths: and does the intelligence only last as long as it has not achieved its object? Do the fruits of conquest perish by the very completeness of the victory?

I affirm no such thing. As mankind improve, the number of doctrines which are no longer disputed or doubted will be constantly on the increase: and the well-being of mankind may almost be measured by the number and gravity of the truths which have reached the point of being uncontested. The cessation, on one question after another, of serious controversy, is one of the necessary incidents of the consolidation of opinion; a consolidation as salutary in the case of true opinions, as it is dangerous and noxious when the opinions are erroneous. But though this gradual narrowing of the bounds of diversity of opinion is necessary in both senses of the term, being at once inevitable and indispensable, we are not therefore obliged to conclude that all its consequences must be beneficial. The loss of so important an aid to the intelligent and living apprehension of a truth, as is afforded by the necessity of explaining it to, or defending it against, opponents, though not sufficient to outweigh, is no trifling drawback from the benefit of its universal recognition. Where this advantage can no longer be had, I confess I should like to see the teachers of mankind endeavoring to provide a substitute for it; some contrivance for making the difficulties of the question as present to the learner's consciousness, as if they were pressed upon him by a dissentient champion, eager for his conversion.

But instead of seeking contrivances for this purpose, they have lost those they formerly had. The Socratic dialectics, so magnificently exemplified in the dialogues of Plato, were a contrivance of this discription. They were essentially a negative discussion of the great questions of philosophy and life, directed with consummate skill to the purpose of convincing any one who had merely adopted the commonplaces of received opinion, that he did not understand the subject—that he as yet attached no definite meaning to the doctrines he professed; in order that, becoming aware of his ignorance, he might be put in the way to attain a stable belief, resting on a clear apprehension both of the meaning of doctrines and of their evidence. The school disputations of the middle ages had a somewhat similar object. They were intended to make sure that the pupil understood his own opinion, and (by necessary correlation) the opinion opposed to it, and could enforce the grounds of the one and confute those of the other. These last-mentioned contests had indeed the incurable defect, that the premises appealed to were taken from authority, not from reason; and, as a discipline to the mind, they were in every respect inferior to the powerful dialectics which formed the intellects of the "Socratici viri": but the modern mind owes far more to both than it is generally willing to admit, and the present modes of education contain nothing which in the smallest degree supplies the place either of the one or of the other. A person who derives all his instruction from teachers or books, even if he escape the besetting temptation of contenting himself with cram, is under no compulsion to hear both sides; accordingly it is far from a frequent accomplishment, even among thinkers, to know both sides; and the weakest part of what everybody says in defense of his opinion, is what he intends as a reply to antagonists. It is the fashion of the present time to disparage negative logic—that which points out weaknesses in theory or errors in practice, without establishing positive truths. Such negative criticism would indeed be poor enough as an ultimate result; but as a means to attaining any positive knowledge or conviction worthy the name, it cannot be valued too highly; and until people are again systematically trained to it, there will be few great thinkers, and a low general average of intellect, in any but the mathematical and physical departments of speculation. On any other subject no one's opinions deserve the name of knowledge, except so far as he has either had forced upon him by others, or gone through of himself, the same

mental process which would have been required of him in carrying on an active controversy with opponents. That, therefore, which when absent, it is so indispensable, but so difficult, to create, how worse than absurd it is to forego, when spontaneously offering itself! If there are any persons who contest a received opinion, or who will do so if law or opinion will let them, let us thank them for it, open our minds to listen to them, and rejoice that there is some one to do for us what we otherwise ought, if we have any regard for either the certainty or the vitality of our convictions, to do with much greater labor for ourselves.

It still remains to speak of one of the principal causes which make diversity of opinion advantageous, and will continue to do so until mankind shall have entered a stage of intellectual advancement which at present seems at an incalculable distance. We have hitherto considered only two possibilities: that the received opinion may be false, and some other opinion, consequently, true; or that, the received opinion being true, a conflict with the opposite error is essential to a clear apprehension and deep feeling of its truth. But there is a commoner case than either of these; when the conflicting doctrines, instead of being one true and the other false, share the truth between them; and the nonconforming opinion is needed to supply the remainder of the truth, of which the received doctrine embodies only a part. Popular opinions, on subjects not palpable to sense, are often true, but seldom or never the whole truth. They are a part of the truth; sometimes a greater, sometimes a smaller part, but exaggerated, distorted, and disjoined from the truths by which they ought to be accompanied and limited. Heretical opinions, on the other hand, are generally some of these suppressed and neglected truths, bursting the bonds which kept them down, and either seeking reconciliation with the truth contained in the common opinion, or fronting it as enemies, and setting themselves up, with similar exclusiveness, as the whole truth. The latter case is hitherto the most frequent, as, in the human mind, one-sidedness has always been the rule, and many-sidedness the exception. Hence, even in revolutions of opinion, one part of the truth usually sets while another rises. Even progress, which ought to superadd, for the most part only substitutes, one partial and incomplete truth for another; improvement consisting chiefly in this, that the new fragment of truth is more wanted, more adapted to the needs of the time, than that which it displaces. Such being the partial character of prevailing opinions, even when resting on a true foundation, every opinion which embodies somewhat of the portion of truth which the common opinion omits, ought to be considered precious, with whatever amount of error and confusion that truth may be blended. No sober judge of human affairs will feel bound to be indignant because those who force on our notice truths which we should otherwise have overlooked, overlook some of those which we see. Rather, he will think that so long as popular truth is one-sided, it is more desirable than otherwise that unpopular truth should have one-sided asserters too; such being usually the most energetic, and the most likely to compel reluctant attention to the fragment of wisdom which they proclaim as if it were the whole.

Thus, in the eighteenth century, when nearly all the instructed, and all those of the uninstructed who were led by them, were lost in admiration of what is called civilization, and of the marvels of modern science, literature, and philosophy, and while greatly overrating the amount of unlikeness between the men of modern and those of ancient times, indulged the belief that the whole of the difference was in their own favor; with what a salutary shock did the paradoxes of Rousseau explode like bombshells in the midst, dislocating the compact mass of one-sided opinion, and forcing its elements to recombine in a better form and with additional ingredients. Not that the current opinions were on the whole farther from the truth than Rous-

seau's were; on the contrary, they were nearer to it; they contained more of positive truth, and very much less of error. Nevertheless there lay in Rousseau's doctrine, and has floated down the stream of opinion along with it, a considerable amount of exactly those truths which the popular opinion wanted; and these are the deposit which was left behind when the flood subsided. The superior worth of simplicity of life, the enervating and demoralizing effect of the trammels and hypocrisies of artificial society, are ideas which have never been entirely absent from cultivated minds since Rousseau wrote; and they will in time produce their due effect, though at present needing to be asserted as much as ever, and to be asserted by deeds, for words, on this subject, have nearly exhausted their power.

In politics, again, it is almost a commonplace, that a party of order or stability, and a party of progress or reform, are both necessary elements of a healthy state of political life; until the one or the other shall have so enlarged its mental grasp as to be a party equally of order and of progress, knowing and distinguishing what is fit to be preserved from what ought to be swept away. Each of these modes of thinking derives its utility from the deficiencies of the other; but it is in a great measure the opposition of the other that keeps each within the limits of reason and sanity. Unless opinions favorable to democracy and to aristocracy, to property and to equality, to co-operation and to competition, to luxury and to abstinence, to sociality and individuality, to liberty and discipline, and all the other standing antagonisms of practical life, are expressed with equal freedom, and enforced and defended with equal talent and energy, there is no chance of both elements obtaining their due; one scale is sure to go up, and the other down. Truth, in the great practical concerns of life, is so much a question of the reconciling and combining of opposites, that very few have minds sufficiently capacious and impartial to make the adjustment with an approach to correctness, and it has to be made by the rough process of a struggle between combatants fighting under hostile banners. On any of the great open questions just enumerated, if either of the two opinions has a better claim than the other, not merely to be tolerated, but to be encouraged and countenanced, it is the one which happens at the particular time and place to be in a minority. That is the opinion which, for the time being, represents the neglected interests, the side of human well-being which is in danger of obtaining less than its share. I am aware that there is not, in this country, any tolerance of differences of opinion on most of these topics. They are adduced to show, by admitted and multiplied examples, the universality of the fact, that only through diversity of opinion is there, in the existing state of human intellect, a chance of fair play to all sides of the truth. When there are persons to be found, who form an exception to the apparent unanimity of the world on any subject, even if the world is in the right, it is always probable that dissentients have something worth hearing to say for themselves, and that truth would lose something by their silence.

It may be objected, "But *some* received principles, especially on the highest and most vital subjects, are more than half-truths. The Christian morality, for instance, is the whole truth on that subject, and if any one teaches a morality which varies from it, he is wholly in error." As this is of all cases the most important in practice, none can be fitter to test the general maxim. But before pronouncing what Christian morality is or is not, it would be desirable to decide what is meant by Christian morality. If it means the morality of the New Testament, I wonder that any one who derives his knowledge of this from the book itself, can suppose that it was announced, or intended, as a complete doctrine of morals. The Gospel always refers to a pre-existing morality, and confines its precepts to the particulars in which that morality was to be corrected, or superseded by a wider and higher; expressing itself, moreover, in terms most general, often impossible to be interpreted literally, and possessing rather the impressiveness of poetry or eloquence than the precision of legislation. To extract from it a body of ethical doctrine, has never been possible without eking it out from the Old Testament, that is, from a system elaborate indeed, but in many respects barbarous, and intended only for a barbarous people. St. Paul, a declared enemy to this Judaical mode of interpreting the doctrine and filling up the scheme of his Master, equally assumes a pre-existing morality, namely that of the Greeks and Romans; and his advice to Christians is in a great measure a system of accommodation to that; even to the extent of giving an apparent sanction to slavery. What is called Christian, but should rather be termed theological, morality, was not the work of Christ or the Apostles, but is of much later origin, having been gradually built up by the Catholic church of the first five centuries, and though not implicitly adopted by moderns and Protestants, has been much less modified by them than might have been expected. For the most part, indeed, they have contented themselves with cutting off the additions which had been made to it in the middle ages, each sect supplying the place by fresh additions, adopted to its own character and tendencies. That mankind owe a great debt to this morality, and to its early teachers, I should be the last person to deny; but I do not scruple to say of it, that it is, in many important points, incomplete and one-sided, and that unless ideas and feelings, not sanctioned by it, had contributed to the formation of European life and character, human affairs would have been in a worse condition than they now are. Christian morality (so called) has all the characters of a reaction; it is, in great part, a protest against Paganism. Its ideal is negative rather than positive; passive rather than active; Innocence rather than Nobleness; Abstinence from Evil, rather than energetic Pursuit of Good: in its precepts (as has been well said) "thou shalt not" predominates unduly over "thou shalt." In its horror of sensuality, it made an idol of asceticism, which has been gradually compromised away into one of legality. It holds out the hope of heaven and the threat of hell, as the appointed and appropriate motives to a virtuous life: in this falling far below the best of the ancients, and doing what lies in it to give to human morality an essentially selfish character, by disconnecting each man's feelings of duty from the interests of his fellow-creatures, except so far as a self-interested inducement is offered to him for consulting them. It is essentially a doctrine of passive obedience; it inculcates submission to all authorities found established; who indeed are not to be actively obeyed when they command what religion forbids, but who are not to be resisted, far less rebelled against, for any amount of wrong to ourselves. And while, in the morality of the best Pagan nations, duty to the State holds even a disproportionate place, infringing on the just liberty of the individual; in purely Christian ethics, that grand department of duty is scarcely noticed or acknowledged. It is in the Koran, not the New Testament, that we read the maxim—"A ruler who appoints any man to an office, when there is in his dominions another man better qualified for it, sins against God and against the State." What little recognition the idea of obligation to the public attains in modern morality, is derived from Greek and Roman sources, not from Christian; as, even in the morality of private life, whatever exists of magnanimity, high-mindedness, personal dignity, even the sense of honor, is derived from the purely human, not the religious part of our education, and never could have grown out of a standard of ethics in which the only worth, professedly recognized, is that of obedience.

I am as far as any one from pretending that these defects are necessarily inherent in the Christian ethics, in every manner in which it can be conceived, or that the many requisites of a complete moral doctrine which it does not contain, do not admit of being reconciled with it. Far less would I insinuate this of the doctrines and precepts of Christ himself. I believe that the sayings of Christ are all, that I can see any evidence of their having been intended to be; that they are irreconcilable with nothing which a comprehensive morality requires; that everything which is excellent in ethics may be brought within them, with no greater violence to their language than has been done to it by all who have attempted to deduce from them any practical system of conduct whatever. But it is quite consistent with this, to believe that they contain, and were meant to contain, only a part of the truth; that many essential elements of the highest morality are among the things which are not provided for, nor intended to be provided for, in the recorded deliverances of the Founder of Christianity, and which have been entirely thrown aside in the system of ethics erected on the basis of those deliverances by the Christian Church. And this being so, I think it a great error to persist in attempting to find in the Christian doctrine that complete rule for our guidance, which its author intended it to sanction and enforce, but only partially to provide. I believe, too, that this narrow theory is becoming a grave practical evil, detracting greatly from the value of the moral training and instruction, which so many well-meaning persons are now at length exerting themselves to promote. I much fear that by attempting to form the mind and feelings on an exclusively religious type, and discarding those secular standards (as for want of a better name they may be called) which heretofore co-existed with and supplemented the Christian ethics, receiving some of its spirit, and infusing into it some of theirs, there will result, and is even now resulting, a low, abject, servile type of character, which, submit itself as it may to what it deems the Supreme Will, is incapable of rising to or sympathizing in the conception of Supreme Goodness. I believe that other ethics than any which can be evolved from exclusively Christian sources, must exist side by side with Christian ethics to produce the moral regeneration of mankind; and that the Christian system is no exception to the rule, that in an imperfect state of the human mind, the interests of truth require a diversity of opinions. It is not necessary that in ceasing to ignore the moral truths not contained in Christianity, men should ignore any of those which it does contain. Such prejudice, or oversight, when it occurs, is altogether an evil; but it is one from which we cannot hope to be always exempt, and must be regarded as the price paid for an inestimable good. The exclusive pretension made by a part of the truth to be the whole, must and ought to be protested against; and if a reactionary impulse should make the protestors unjust in their turn, this one-sidedness, like the other, may be lamented, but must be tolerated. If Christians would teach infidels to be just to Christianity, they should themselves be just to infidelity. It can do truth no service to blink the fact, known to all who have the most ordinary acquaintance with literary history, that a large portion of the noblest and most valuable moral teaching has been the work, not only of men who did not know, but of men who knew and rejected, the Christian faith.

I do not pretend that the most unlimited use of the freedom of enunciating all possible opinions would put an end to the evils of religious or philosophical sectarianism. Every truth which men of narrow capacity are in earnest about, is sure to be asserted, inculcated, and in many ways even acted on, as if no other truth existed in the world, or at all events none that could limit or qualify the first. I acknowledge that the tendency of all opinions to become sectarian is not cured by the freest discussion, but is often heightened and exacerbated thereby; the truth which ought to have been, but was not, seen, being rejected all the more violently because proclaimed by persons regarded as opponents. But it is not on the impassioned partisan, it is on the calmer and more disinterested bystander, that this collision of opinions works its salutary effect. Not the violent conflict between parts of the truth, but the quiet suppression of half

of it, is the formidable evil; there is always hope when people are forced to listen to both sides; it is when they attend only to one that errors harden into prejudices, and truth itself ceases to have the effect of truth, by being exaggerated into falsehood. And since there are few mental attributes more rare than that judicial faculty which can sit in intelligent judgment between two sides of a question, of which only one is represented by an advocate before it, truth has no chance but in proportion as every side of it, every opinion which embodies any fraction of the truth, not only finds advocates, but is so advocated as to be listened to.

We have now recognized the necessity to the mental well-being of mankind (on which all their other well-being depends) of freedom of opinion, and freedom of the expression of opinion, on four distinct grounds; which we will now briefly recapitulate.

First, if any opinion is compelled to silence, that opinion may, for aught we can certainly know, be true. To deny this is to assume our own infallibility.

Secondly, though the silenced opinion be an error, it may, and very commonly does, contain a portion of truth; and since the general or prevailing opinion on any subject is rarely or never the whole truth, it is only by the collision of adverse opinions that the remainder of the truth has any chance of being supplied.

Thirdly, even if the received opinion be not only true, but the whole truth; unless it is suffered to be, and actually is, vigorously and earnestly contested, it will, by most of those who receive it, be held in the manner of a prejudice, with little comprehension or feeling of its rational grounds. And not only this, but, fourthly, the meaning of the doctrine itself will be in danger of being lost, or enfeebled, and deprived of its vital effect on the character and conduct: the dogma becoming a mere formal profession, inefficacious for good, but cumbering the ground, and preventing the growth of any real and heartfelt conviction, from reason or personal experience.

Before quitting the subject of freedom of opinion, it is fit to take some notice of those who say, that the free expression of all opinions should be permitted, on condition that the manner be temperate, and do not pass the bounds of fair discussion. Much might be said on the impossibility of fixing where these supposed bounds are to be placed; for if the test be offense to those whose opinion is attacked, I think experience testifies that this offense is given whenever the attack is telling and powerful, and that every opponent who pushes them hard, and whom they find it difficult to answer, appears to them, if he shows any strong feeling on the subject, an intemperate opponent. But this, though an important consideration in a practical point of view, merges in a more fundamental objection. Undoubtedly the manner of asserting an opinion, even though it be a true one, may be very objectionable, and may justly incur severe censure. But the principal offenses of the kind are such as it is mostly impossible, unless by accidental self-betrayal, to bring home to conviction. The gravest of them is, to argue sophistically, to suppress facts or argument, to misstate the elements of the case, or misrepresent the opposite opinion. But all this, even to the most aggravated degree, is so continually done in perfect good faith, by persons who are not considered, and in many other respects may not deserve to be considered, ignorant or incompetent, that it is rarely possible on adequate grounds conscientiously to stamp the misrepresentation as morally culpable; and still less could law presume to interfere with this kind of controversial misconduct. With regard to what is commonly meant by intemperate discussion, namely invective, sarcasm, personality, and the like, the denunciation of these weapons would deserve more sympathy if it were ever proposed to interdict them equally to both sides; but it is only desired to restrain the employment of them against the prevailing opinion: against the unprevailing they may

not only be used without general disapproval, but will be likely to obtain for him who uses them the praise of honest zeal and righteous indignation. Yet whatever mischief arises from their use, is greatest when they are employed against the comparatively defenseless; and whatever unfair advantage can be derived by any opinion from this mode of asserting it, accrues almost exclusively to received opinions. The worst offense of this kind which can be committed by a polemic, is to stigmatize those who hold the contrary opinion as bad and immoral men. To calumny of this sort, those who hold any unpopular opinion are peculiarly exposed, because they are in general few and uninfluential, and nobody but themselves feels much interested in seeing justice done them; but this weapon is, from the nature of the case, denied to those who attack a prevailing opinion: they can neither use it with safety to themselves, nor, if they could, would it do anything but recoil on their own cause. In general, opinions contrary to those commonly received can only obtain a hearing by studied moderation of language, and the most cautious avoidance of unnecessary offense, from which they hardly ever deviate even in a slight degree without losing ground: while unmeasured vituperation employed on the side of the prevailing opinion, really does deter people from professing contrary opinions, and from listening to those who profess them. For the interest, therefore, of truth and justice, it is far more important to restain this employment of vituperative language than the other; and, for example, if it were necessary to choose, there would be much more need to discourage offensive attacks on infidelity, than on religion. It is, however, obvious that law and authority have no business with restraining either, while opinion ought, in every instance, to determine its verdict by the circumstances of the individual case; condemning every one, on whichever side of the argument he places himself, in whose mode of advocacy either want of candor, or malignity, bigotry, or intolerance of feeling manifest themselves;

but not inferring these vices from the side which a person takes, though it be the contrary side of the question to our own: and giving merited honor to every one, whatever opinion he may hold, who has calmness to see and honesty to state what his opponents and their opinions really are, exaggerating nothing to their discredit, keeping nothing back which tells, or can be supposed to tell, in their favor. This is the real morality of public discussion: and if often violated, I am happy to think that there are many controversialists who to a great extent observe it, and a still greater number who conscientiously strive towards it.

3. Individuality as One of the Elements of Well-being

Such being the reasons which make it imperative that human beings should be free to form opinions, and to express their opinions without reserve; and such the baneful consequences to the intellectual, and through that to the moral nature of man, unless this liberty is either conceded, or asserted in spite of prohibition; let us next examine whether the same reasons do not require that men should be free to act upon their opinions—to carry these out in their lives, without hindrance, either physical or moral, from their fellow men, so long as it is at their own risk and peril. This last proviso is of course indispensable. No one pretends that actions should be as free as opinions. On the contrary, even opinions lose their immunity, when the circumstances in which they are expressed are such as to constitute their expression a positive instigation to some mischievous act. An opinion that corn-dealers are starvers of the poor, or that private property is robbery, ought to be unmolested when simply circulated through the press, but may justly incur punishment when delivered orally to an excited mob assembled before the house of a corn-dealer, or when handed about among the same mob in the form of a placard. Acts, of whatever kind, which, without justifiable cause, do harm to others, may be, and in the more important cases absolutely require to be, controlled by the unfavorable sentiments, and, when needful, by the active interference of mankind. The liberty of the individual must be thus far limited; he must not make himself a nuisance to other people. But if he refrains from molesting others in what concerns them, and merely acts according to his own inclination and judgment in things which concern himself, the same reasons which show that opinion should be free, prove also that he should be allowed, without molestation, to carry his opinions into practice at his own cost. That mankind are not infallible; that their truths, for the most part, are only half-truths; that unity of opinion, unless resulting from the fullest and freest comparison of opposite opinions, is not desirable, and diversity not an evil, but a good, until mankind are much more capable than at present of recognizing all sides of the truth, are principles applicable to men's modes of action, not less than to their opinions. As it is useful that while mankind are imperfect there should be different opinions, so is it that there should be different experiments of living; that free scope should be given to varieties of character, short of injury to others; and that the worth of different modes of life should be proved practically, when any one thinks fit to try them. It is desirable, in short, that in things which do not primarily concern others, individuality should assert itself. Where (not the person's own character) but the traditions or customs of other people are the rule of conduct, there is wanting one of the principal ingredients of human happiness, and quite the chief ingredient of individual and social progress.

In maintaining the principle, the greatest difficulty to be encountered does not lie in the appreciation of means towards an acknowledged end, but in the indifference of persons in general to the end itself. If it were felt that the free development of individuality is one of the leading essentials of well-being; that it is not only a co-ordinate element with all that is designated by the terms civilization, instruction, education, culture, but is itself a necessary part and condition of all those things; there would be no danger that liberty should be undervalued, and the adjustment of the boundaries between it and social control would present no extraordinary difficulty. But the evil is, that individual spontaneity is hardly recognized by the common modes of thinking, as having any intrinsic worth, or deserving any regard on its own account. The majority, being satisfied with the ways of mankind as they now are (for it is they who make them what they are), cannot comprehend why those ways should not be good enough for everybody; and what is more, spontaneity forms no part of the ideal of the majority of moral and social reformers, but is rather looked on with jealousy, as a troublesome and perhaps rebellious obstruction to the general acceptance of what these reformers, in their own judgment, think would be best for mankind. Few persons, out of Germany, even comprehend the meaning of the doctrine which Wilhelm von Humboldt, so eminent both as a savant and as a politician, made the text of a treatise—that "the end of man, or that which is prescribed by the eternal or immutable dictates of reason, and not suggested by vague and transient desires, is the highest and most harmonious development of his powers to a complete and consistent whole"; that, therefore, the object "towards which every human being must ceaselessly direct his efforts, and on which especially those who design to influence their fellow men must ever keep their eyes, is the individuality of power and development"; that for this there are two requisites, "freedom, and variety of situations"; and that from the union of these arise "individual vigor and manifold diversity," which combine themselves in "originality." [1]

---

[1] *The Sphere and Duties of Government,* from the German of Baron Wilhelm von Humboldt, pp. 11–13.

Little, however, as people are accustomed to a doctrine like that of Von Humboldt, and surprising as it may be to them to find so high a value attached to individuality, the question, one must nevertheless think, can only be one of degree. No one's idea of excellence in conduct is that people should do absolutely nothing but copy one another. No one would assert that people ought not to put into their mode of life, and into the conduct of their concerns, any impress whatever of their own judgment, or of their own individual character. On the other hand, it would be absurd to pretend that people ought to live as if nothing whatever had been known in the world before they came into it; as if experience had as yet done nothing towards showing that one mode of existence, or of conduct, is preferable to another. Nobody denies that people should be so taught and trained in youth, as to know and benefit by the ascertained results of human experience. But it is the privilege and proper condition of a human being, arrived at the maturity of his faculties, to use and interpret experience in his own way. It is for him to find out what part of recorded experience is properly applicable to his own circumstances and character. The traditions and customs of other people are, to a certain extent, evidence of what their experience has taught *them;* presumptive evidence, and as such, have a claim to his deference: but, in the first place, their experience may be too narrow; or they may not have interpreted it rightly. Secondly, their interpretation of experience may be correct, but unsuitable to him. Customs are made for customary circumstances, and customary characters; and his circumstances or his character may be uncustomary. Thirdly, though the customs be both good as customs, and suitable to him, yet to conform to custom, merely *as* custom, does not educate or develop in him any of the qualities which are the distinctive endowment of a human being. The human facilities of perception, judgment, discriminative feeling, mental activity, and even moral preference, are exercised only in making a choice. He who does anything because it is the custom, makes no choice. He gains no practice either in discerning or in desiring what is best. The mental and moral, like the muscular powers, are improved only by being used. The faculties are called into no exercise by doing a thing merely because others do it, no more than by believing a thing only because others believe it. If the grounds of an opinion are not conclusive to the person's own reason, his reason cannot be strengthened, but is likely to be weakened, by his adopting it: and if the inducements to an act are not such as are consentaneous to his own feelings and character (where affection, or the rights of others, are not concerned) it is so much done towards rendering his feelings and character inert and torpid, instead of active and energetic.

He who lets the world, or his own portion of it, choose his plan of life for him, has no need of any other faculty than the ape-like one of imitation. He who chooses his plan for himself, employs all his faculties. He must use observation to see, reasoning and judgment to foresee, activity to gather materials for decision, discrimination to decide, and when he has decided, firmness and self-control to hold to his deliberate decision. And these qualities he requires and exercises exactly in proportion as the part of his conduct which he determines according to his own judgment and feelings is a large one. It is possible that he might be guided in some good path, and kept out of harm's way, without any of these things. But what will be his comparative worth as a human being? It really is of importance, not only what men do, but also what manner of men they are that do it. Among the works of man, which human life is rightly employed in perfecting and beautifying, the first in importance surely is man himself. Supposing it were possible to get houses built, corn grown, battles fought, causes tried, and even churches erected and prayers said, by machinery— by automatons in human form—it would be a considerable loss to exchange for these automatons even the men and women who at present inhabit the more civilized parts of the world, and who assuredly are but starved specimens of what nature can and will produce. Human nature is not a machine to be built after a model, and set to do exactly the work prescribed for it, but a tree, which requires to grow and develop itself on all sides, according to the tendency of the inward forces which make it a living thing.

It will probably be conceded that it is desirable people should exercise their understandings, and that an intelligent following of custom, or even occasionally an intelligent deviation from custom, is better than a blind and simply mechanical adhesion to it. To a certain extent it is admitted, that our understanding should be our own: but there is not the same willingness to admit that our desires and impulses should be our own likewise; or that to possess impulses of our own, and of any strength, is anything but a peril and a snare. Yet desires and impulses are as much a part of a perfect human being, as beliefs and restraints: and strong impulses are only perilous when not properly balanced; when one set of aims and inclinations is developed into strength, while others, which ought to co-exist with them, remain weak and inactive. It is not because men's desires are strong that they act ill; it is because their consciences are weak. There is no natural connection between strong impulses and a weak conscience. The natural connection is the other way. To say that one person's desires and feelings are stronger and more various than those of another, is merely to say that he has more of the raw material of human nature, and is therefore capable, perhaps of more evil, but certainly of more good. Strong impulses are but another name for energy. Energy may be turned to bad uses; but more good may always be made of an energetic nature, than of an indolent and impassive one. Those who have most natural feeling, are always those whose cultivated feelings may be made the strongest. The same strong susceptibilities which make the personal impulses vivid and powerful, are also the source from whence are generated the most passionate love of virtue, and the sternest self-control. It is through the cultivation of these, that society both does its duty and protects its interests: not by rejecting the stuff of which heroes are made, because it knows not how to make them. A person whose desires and impulses are his own—are the expression of his own nature, as it has been developed and modified by his own culture—is said to have a character. One whose desires and impulses are not his own, has no character, no more than a steam-engine has a character. If, in addition to being his own, his impulses are strong, and are under the government of a strong will, he has an energetic character. Whoever thinks that individuality of desires and impulses should not be encouraged to unfold itself, must maintain that society has no need of strong natures—is not the better for containing many persons who have much character—and that a high general average of energy is not desirable.

In some early states of society, these forces might be, and were, too much ahead of the power which society then possessed of disciplining and controlling them. There has been a time when the element of spontaneity and individuality was in excess, and the social principle had a hard struggle with it. The difficulty then was, to induce men of strong bodies or minds to pay obedience to any rules which required them to control their impulses. To overcome this difficulty, law and discipline, like the Popes struggling against the Emperors, asserted a power over the whole man, claiming to control all his life in order to control his character—which society had not found any other sufficient means of binding. But society has now fairly got the better of individuality; and the danger which threatens human nature is not the excess, but the deficiency, of personal impulses and preferences. Things are vastly changed, since the passions of those who were strong by station or by personal endowment were in a state of habitual rebellion against laws and ordinances, and required to be rigorously chained up to enable the persons within their reach to enjoy any particle of security. In our times, from the highest class of society down to the lowest, every one lives as under the eye of a hostile and dreaded censorship. Not only in what concerns others, but in what concerns only themselves, the individual or the family do not ask themselves—what do I prefer? or, what would suit my character and disposition? or, what would allow the best and highest in me to have fair play, and enable it to grow and thrive? They ask themselves, what is suitable to my position? what is usually done by persons of my station and pecuniary circumstances? or (worse still) what is usually done by persons of a station and circumstances superior to mine? I do not mean that they choose what is customary, in preference to what suits their own inclination. It does not occur to them to have any inclination, except for what is customary. Thus the mind itself is bowed to the yoke: even in what people do for pleasure, conformity is the first thing thought of; they like in crowds; they exercise choice only among things commonly done: peculiarity of taste, eccentricity of conduct, are shunned equally with crimes: until by dint of not following their own nature, they have no nature to follow: their human capacities are withered and starved: they become incapable of any strong wishes or native pleasures, and are generally without either opinions or feelings of home growth, or properly their own. Now is this, or is it not, the desirable condition of human nature?

It is so, on the Calvinistic theory. According to that, the one great offense of man is self-will. All the good of which humanity is capable, is comprised in obedience. You have no choice; thus you must do, and no otherwise: "whatever is not a duty, is a sin." Human nature being radically corrupt, there is no redemption for any one until human nature is killed within him. To one holding this theory of life, crushing out any of the human faculties, capacities, and susceptibilities, is no evil: man needs no capacity, but that of surrendering himself to the will of God: and if he uses any of his faculties for any other purpose but to do that supposed will more effectually, he is better without them. This is the theory of Calvinism; and it is held, in a mitigated form, by many who do not consider themselves Calvinists; the mitigation consisting in giving a less ascetic interpretation to the alleged will of God; asserting it to be his will that mankind should gratify some of their inclinations; of course not in the manner they themselves prefer, but in the way of obedience, that is, in a way prescribed to them by authority; and, therefore, by the necessary conditions of the case, the same for all.

In some such insidious form there is at present a strong tendency to this narrow theory of life, and to the pinched and hidebound type of human character which it patronizes. Many persons, no doubt, sincerely think that human beings thus cramped and dwarfed, are as their Maker designed them to be; just as many have thought that trees are a much finer thing when clipped into pollards, or cut out into figures of animals, than as nature made them. But if it be any part of religion to believe that man was made by a good Being, it is more consistent with that faith to believe, that this Being gave all human faculties that they might be cultivated and unfolded, not rooted out and consumed, and that he takes delight in every nearer approach made by his creatures to the ideal conception embodied in them, every increase in any of their capabilities of comprehension, of action, or of enjoyment. There is a different type of human excellence from the Calvinistic; a conception of humanity as having its nature bestowed on it for other purposes than merely to be abnegated. "Pagan self-assertion" is one of the elements of human worth, as well as "Christian self-denial." [2] There is a Greek ideal of self-development, which the Platonic and Christian ideal of self-government blends with, but does not

supersede. It may be better to be a John Knox than an Alcibiades, but it is better to be a Pericles than either; nor would a Pericles, if we had one in these days, be without anything good which belonged to John Knox.

It is not by wearing down into uniformity all that is individual in themselves, but by cultivating it and calling it forth, within the limits imposed by the rights and interests of others, that human beings become a noble and beautiful object of contemplation; and as the works partake the character of those who do them, by the same process human life also becomes rich, diversified, and animating, furnishing more abundant aliment to high thoughts and elevating feelings, and strengthening the tie which binds every individual to the race, by making the race infinitely better worth belonging to. In proportion to the development of his individuality, each person becomes more valuable to himself, and is therefore capable of being more valuable to others. There is a greater fullness of life about his own existence, and when there is more life in the units there is more in the mass which is composed of them. As much compression as is necessary to prevent the stronger specimens of human nature from encroaching on the rights of others, cannot be dispensed with; but for this there is ample compensation even in the point of view of human development. The means of development which the individual loses by being prevented from gratifying his inclinations to the injury of others, are chiefly obtained at the expense of the development of other people. And even to himself there is a full equivalent in the better development of the social part of his nature, rendered possible by the restraint put upon the selfish part. To be held to rigid rules of justice for the sake of others, develops the feelings and capacities which have the good of others for their object. But to be restrained in things not affecting their good, by their mere displeasure, develops nothing valuable, except such force of character as may unfold itself in resisting the restraint. If

---

[2] Sterling's *Essays*.

acquiesced in, it dulls and blunts the whole nature. To give any fair plan to the nature of each, it is essential that different persons should be allowed to lead different lives. In proportion as this latitude has been exercised in any age, has that age been noteworthy to posterity. Even despotism does not produce its worst effects, so long as individuality exists under it; and whatever crushes individuality is despotism, by whatever name it may be called, and whether it professes to be enforcing the will of God or the injunctions of men.

Having said that Individuality is the same thing with development, and that it is only the cultivation of individuality which produces, or can produce, well-developed human beings, I might here close the argument: for what more or better can be said of any condition of human affairs, than that it brings human beings themselves nearer to the best thing they can be? or what worse can be said of any obstruction to good, than that it prevents this? Doubtless, however, these considerations will not suffice to convince those who most need convincing; and it is necessary further to show, that these developed human beings are of some use to the undeveloped—to point out to those who do not desire liberty, and would not avail themselves of it, that they may be in some intelligible manner rewarded for allowing other people to make use of it without hindrance.

In the first place, then, I would suggest that they might possibly learn something from them. It will not be denied by anybody, that originality is a valuable element in human affairs. There is always need of persons not only to discover new truths, and point out when what were once truths are true no longer, but also to commence new practices, and set the example of more enlightened conduct, and better taste and sense in human life. This cannot well be gainsaid by anybody who does not believe that the world has already attained perfection in all its ways and practices. It is true that this benefit is not capable of being rendered by everybody alike: there are but few persons, in comparison with the whole of mankind, whose experiments, if adopted by others, would be likely to be any improvement on established practice. But these few are the salt of the earth; without them, human life would become a stagnant pool. Not only is it they who introduce good things which did not before exist; it is they who keep the life in those which already existed. If there were nothing new to be done, would human intellect cease to be necessary? Would it be a reason why those who do the old things should forget why they are done, and do them like cattle, not like human beings? There is only too great a tendency in the best beliefs and practices to degenerate into the mechanical; and unless there were a succession of persons whose ever-recurring originality prevents the grounds of those beliefs and practices from becoming merely traditional, such dead matter would not resist the smallest shock from anything really alive, and there would be no reason why civilization should not die out, as in the Byzantine Empire. Persons of genius, it is true, are, and are always likely to be, a small minority; but in order to have them, it is necessary to preserve the soil in which they grow. Genius can only breathe freely in an *atmosphere* of freedom. Persons of genius are, *ex vi termini, more* individual than any other people—less capable, consequently, of fitting themselves, without hurtful compression, into any of the small number of molds which society provides in order to save its members the trouble of forming their own character. If from timidity they consent to be forced into one of these molds, and to let all that part of themselves which cannot expand under the pressure remain unexpanded, society will be little the better for their genius. If they are of a strong character, and break their fetters, they become a mark for the society which has not succeeded in reducing them to commonplace, to point at with solemn warning as "wild," "erratic," and the like; much as if one should complain of the Niagara river for not flowing smoothly between its banks like a Dutch canal.

I insist thus emphatically on the importance of genius, and the necessity of allowing it to unfold itself freely both in thought and in practice, being well aware that no one will deny the position in theory, but knowing also that almost every one, in reality, is totally indifferent to it. People think genius a fine thing if it enables a man to write an exciting poem, or paint a picture. But in its true sense, that of originality in thought and action, though no one says that it is not a thing to be admired, nearly all, at heart, think that they can do very well without it. Unhappily this is too natural to be wondered at. Originality is the one thing which unoriginal minds cannot feel the use of. They cannot see what it is to do for them: how should they? If they could see what it would do for them, it would not be originality. The first service which originality has to render them, is that of opening their eyes: which being once fully done, they would have a chance of being themselves original. Meanwhile, recollecting that nothing was ever yet done which some one was not the first to do, and that all good things which exist are the fruits of originality, let them be modest enough to believe that there is something still left for it to accomplish, and assure themselves that they are more in need of originality, the less they are conscious of the want.

In sober truth, whatever homage may be professed, or even paid, to real or supposed mental superiority, the general tendency of things throughout the world is to render mediocrity the ascendant power among mankind. In ancient history, in the middle ages, and in a diminishing degree through the long transition from feudality to the present time, the individual was a power in himself; and if he had either great talents or a high social position, he was a considerable power. At present individuals are lost in the crowd. In politics it is almost a triviality to say that public opinion now rules the world. The only power deserving the name is that of masses, and of governments while they make themselves the organ of the tendencies and instincts of masses. This is as true in the moral and social relations of private life as in public transactions. Those whose opinions go by the name of public opinion, are not always the same sort of public: in America they are the whole white population; in England, chiefly the middle class. But they are always a mass, that is to say, collective mediocrity. And what is a still greater novelty, the mass do not now take their opinions from dignitaries in Church or State, from ostensible leaders, or from books. Their thinking is done for them by men much like themselves, addressing them or speaking in their name, on the spur of the moment, through the newspapers. I am not complaining of all this. I do not assert that anything better is compatible, as a general rule, with the present low state of the human mind. But that does not hinder the government of mediocrity from being mediocre government. No government by a democracy or a numerous aristocracy, either in its political acts or in the opinions, qualities, and tone of mind which it fosters, ever did or could rise above mediocrity, except in so far as the sovereign Many have let themselves be guided (which in their best times they always have done) by the counsels and influence of a more highly gifted and instructed One or Few. The initiation of all wise or noble things, comes and must come from individuals; generally at first from some one individual. The honor and glory of the average man is that he is capable of following that initiative; that he can respond internally to wise and noble things, and be led to them with his eyes open. I am not countenancing the sort of "hero-worship" which applauds the strong man of genius for forcibly seizing on the government of the world and making it do his bidding in spite of itself. All he can claim is, freedom to point out the way. The power of compelling others into it, is not only inconsistent with the freedom and development of all the rest, but corrupting to the strong man himself. It does seem, however, that when the opinions of masses of merely average men are everywhere become or becoming the dominant power, the counterpoise and corrective to that tendency would be, the more and more pronounced individuality of those who stand on the higher eminences of thought. It is in these circumstances most especially, that exceptional individuals, instead of being deterred, should be encouraged in acting differently from the mass. In other times there was no advantage in their doing so, unless they acted not only differently, but better. In this age, the mere example of nonconformity, the mere refusal to bend the knee to custom, is itself a service. Precisely because the tyranny of opinion is such as to make eccentricity a reproach, it is desirable, in order to break through that tyranny, that people should be eccentric. Eccentricity has always abounded when and where strength of character has abounded; and the amount

of eccentricity in a society has generally been proportional to the amount of genius, mental vigor, and moral courage which it contained. That so few now dare to be eccentric, marks the chief danger of the time.

The worth of a State, in the long run, is the worth of the individuals composing it; and a State which postpones the interests of *their* mental expansion and elevation, to a little more of administrative skill, or of that semblance of it which practice gives, in the details of business; a State which dwarfs its men, in order that they may be more docile instruments in its hands even for beneficial purposes—will find that with small men no great thing can really be accomplished; and that the perfection of machinery to which it has sacrificed everything, will in the end avail it nothing, for want of the vital power which, in order that the machine might work more smoothly, it has preferred to banish.

CHAPTER 21

THE CULT OF
THE STATE

THE French Revolution accentuated the political and intellectual divisions of Europe. It everywhere made democrats more radical and conservatives more reactionary. In England reform was delayed for a generation, but the war with revolutionary and, later, Napoleonic France could not permanently alter the spread of liberalism, because English liberalism derived its vitality from the twin roots of 1649 and 1689, and not from the French Revolution of 1789. Having made their peace with constitutionalism and parliamentary sovereignty a century before the French Revolution, the English governing classes were more afraid of Napoleon than of Rousseau.

By contrast, on the Continent the philosophy of French individualism and the Rights of Man, more than French power, seemed to threaten the foundations of the established order. Napoleon's armies brought to the masses of the Continent deliverance from social and political oppression by native ruling classes. As time proceeded, however, the French struggle with England for world hegemony turned the whole Continent into a base of operations the cost of which had to be borne by Continental nations. The French objective of conquering England, the last bulwark of resistance to Napoleon, led to the dislocation of the European economy and to the control of the European nations by a regime of tyranny. The principle of liberty, engendered by the French Revolution itself, became the secret weapon that eventually defeated Napoleonic France in 1815.

The Napoleonic wars had a particularly disastrous effect on Germany from which she has not recovered to this day. In England and France, democracy and liberalism had sprung up as native movements against internal oppressors and exploiters. In addition, democracy in both countries, as in the United States, proved successful because it promoted material welfare at home and enhanced national power and prestige abroad. By contrast, the German people first learned

589

of democracy through the invasions of the French revolutionary armies. The enthusiasm for the French Revolution—and later for Napoleon—was sincere and exuberant in many parts of Germany, especially among the middle classes and peasants. If the victorious Napoleonic armies had followed up the annihilation of the feudal order in Germany with the creation of a free German republic, the history of Europe would have taken a new turn, and the Elbe, rather than the Rhine, would have become the frontier of democracy.

As it was, the temporary destruction of feudalism and absolutism in Germany was followed by a French regime of economic and military control in the service of Napoleon's drive for world empire. Whereas the French armies had entered Germany as the torchbearers of liberty and human brotherhood, they left it as the enemies of the German people. The German ruling classes were thus able to discredit "the West"—democracy, liberty, parliamentarism, self-government—in the eyes of the German people by identifying democracy as the symbol of Germany's national enemy. Since that time Germany's tradition of looking upon democracy as her national enemy has been reinforced by her position in World Wars I and II as the leading opponent of the democratic world.

Because the political experience of Germany has been preponderantly authoritarian, its orthodox tradition of political theory has been chiefly, though not wholly, antidemocratic. In this tradition the philosophy of G. W. F. Hegel (1770–1831) towers over the rest in more than one way. Hegel's system encompasses philosophy, metaphysics, religion, art, ethics, history, and politics. In its range alone his work is impressive and of a truly encyclopedic character. His position in Germany was so powerful that even the most ferocious attack against orthodox German philosophy, that of Karl Marx, sprang largely from Hegelian assumptions.

As a student, Hegel's major interest was theology, but he soon gravitated toward philosophy. In 1801 he began to lecture at the University of Jena. In 1806 the French armies defeated Prussia at the decisive battle of Jena, and Hegel saw Napoleon (the "world-soul," as he called him) ride through Jena. During the French Revolution he was an ardent sympathizer of Jacobin radicalism. As Napoleon's star rose, Hegel profoundly admired him for his genius and power. In 1818, three years after the defeat of Napoleon, Hegel was invited to come to the University of Berlin, and he stayed there until his death in 1831. He became the dominant figure at the University, and his influence—like that of Heinrich von Treitschke later in the century—extended over all Germany. In this last phase of his life, Hegel was a devout follower and admirer of the Prussian police state, just as he had previously admired Jacobinism and Napoleon.

The best statement of Hegel's political ideas is to be found in his *Philosophy of Law* (1821). It expresses his conception of freedom, natural and social, which provides the key to an understanding of his political thought. Hegel starts with the assertion that in the physical world nature as it is, is the proper object of knowledge and philosophy. What knowledge has to investigate in nature, Hegel argues, is its "eternal harmony" and "inherent rationality." Proceeding from nature to ethics, Hegel attacks those who believe that the ethical world, actualized in the state, should be approached differently from nature, the physical world. Just as reason becomes "actual" in nature. Hegel says, so it becomes actual in the state. In both instances the observer does not, and cannot, *make* the laws expressing reason but can merely understand them. There is no "chance and caprice" in rationality as it may be apprehended in either the physical world or in the ethical world—the state.

Because some philosophers of the state (Hegel here denounces contemptuously certain German liberal philosophers of his time) have followed the principle that every thinker is authorized "to take his own road," political philosophy has earned for itself all kinds of "scorn and discredit." This has led to the worst kind of scorn, namely, that "everyone is convinced that his mere birthright puts him in a position to pass judgment on philosophy in general and to condemn it." Because philosophy in Germany is "in the service of the state," Hegel accords to the state the right to defend itself against those who "indulge in subjective feeling and particular conviction," from which evil follows "the ruin of public order and the law of the land."

This encouragement to persecute freedom of thought came from Hegel at a time when antiliberal, authoritarian government in Prussia had become more ruthless than ever before. The Prussian absolute state—thus can philosophy debase itself—appeared to Hegel as the historically most perfect realization of political rationality. "What is rational is actual and what is actual is rational"—this most famous of all Hegelian phrases has been interpreted in many ways. Whatever the phrase meant to Hegel himself, its practical impact has been in one direction: to sanctify the existing as the good. Hegel himself might personally have rejected the excessive abuses to which his rationalization of existing institutions lent itself in the hands of others, but the historical effect of Hegel was to strengthen the habit of servility to the existing state and society, which has long characterized German life and thought.

The intimate inner connection between Hegelianism and *militarism* is evident in Hegel's conception that "in duty the individual finds his liberation." This concept of freedom is the product of a society that honors militarism as *the* way of life, as becomes evident in Hegel's further statement that "self-sacrifice" is the "real existence of one's freedom." Such a philosophy is the most effective expression of the militaristic and fascist outlook and succinctly reflects the fascist view that the purpose of man's life is death in the service of the fighting state. Hegel also considers the readiness to sacrifice oneself for the state the "intrinsic worth of courage." The courage of resistance is unknown to him. Whereas Locke sees the indestructible essence of man in his act of resisting, Hegel sees man's fulfillment in obedience. Life, liberty, and the pursuit of happiness are thus the exact opposites of the Hegelian concept of citizenship as *self-sacrifice, duty,* and *discipline.*

If the individual in Hegel's world is nothing, the state is all. In his *Philosophy of History* (published posthumously in 1837), Hegel defines the state as the "realization of Freedom." The state is the actually existing, realized moral life, and "all the worth which the human being possesses—all spiritual reality—he possesses only through the State." The individual has moral value only because he is part of the state, which is the complete actualization of reason. Hegel's state idolatry reaches its peak in his famous phrase that the state is "the Divine Idea as it exists on Earth."

In the Jewish-Christian tradition, the Earthly City can never take the place of the City of God, and no man-made law or institution can therefore command the complete allegiance of man. According to this tradition, man's spiritual reality, based on reason, nature, God, is prior, and superior, to law and the state; the latter are, at best, means of serving the fulfillment of man's moral aspirations. Hegel doubly rejects this Jewish-Christian tradition by regarding the state as the divine idea on earth, the march of God in this world, and by asserting—and here is an important root of modern totalitarianism—that *man derives all spiritual reality from the state*. With all his devout Lutheran theology, Hegel in actuality rejects the most fundamental philosophical principle of Jewish-Christian monotheism: that there is a sphere of conscience in each human being that is exempt from the claims of political authority, and that the state must not fully absorb the spiritual resources and selfhood of the individual.

Because the state is actualized reason and spirit, Hegel says, the law of the state is a manifestation of objective spirit, and "only that which obeys law, is free," for it obeys itself. Hegel rejects the liberal concept of freedom as absence of constraint and calls such freedom formal, subjective, abstracted from its essential objects and aims. Constraints put on the impulses, desires, and passions of the individual are not, Hegel maintains, a limitation of freedom but its indispensable condition, because such compulsion forces man to adjust his behavior to the higher reason of the state. Man's real, substantive freedom (as distinct from mere formal freedom) thus consists in his submitting to, and identifying himself with, the higher rationality of state and law.

Whether man submits voluntarily to the state or has to be constrained, makes little difference, as the Hegelian concept of freedom refers, not to the *mode* of action—free personal choice between existing alternatives, or forcible adaptation of conduct to prescribed rules—but to the *object* of action. If man acts in harmony with the goals of the state, regardless how the harmony is attained, he is free, because his action partakes of the highest form of actualized freedom—the state. On the basis of this assumption, when "the subjective will of man submits to laws, the contradiction between Liberty and Necessity vanishes."

In the democratic tradition of political thought, society means choice and alternative, not submission. According to Hegel, society is a man-made copy of nature with its laws of necessity, in which liberty can be found only by voluntary submission. By contrast, the democratic tradition accepts necessity in physical nature but not in human relations. The reasoning of democrats is that, though one must accept the validity of the law of gravity, one may challenge the validity of any man-made law. Submission to laws of physical nature but defiance of human controls is the distinction that democratic political philosophy carefully draws. Hegel rejects social revolution, just as there is no revolution in nature, whereas democrats, though accepting *evolution* as the only process of change in *nature*, nevertheless accept the possibility, and in some instances even the desirability, of *revolution* as a method of *social change*. In the Hegelian approach to this problem the physical conception of necessity is transferred from the mechanism of nature to the organization of society. The political effects of this transfer are fundamental: just as we are relatively free in nature by knowing, and voluntarily submitting to, the laws of nature, rather than by uselessly trying to change them, we are free in society, the Hegelian argument runs, if we willingly accept the laws imposed upon us.

In both his *Philosophy of Law* and *Philosophy of History* Hegel takes up the question of who ought to determine the laws. He attacks the doctrine that all should participate in the business of the state as a "ridiculous notion." To permit all persons to share in public decisions because affairs of state are the concern of its members is "tantamount to a proposal to put the democratic element without any rational form into the organism of the state." Hegel anticipates the *corporate* organization of the modern fascist state by his emphasis that the individual should be politically articulate only as a member of a social group or class, and not just as a citizen *qua* citizen, as in the liberal democracies.

The fundamental law of the state is the constitution. Hegel opposes the democratic idea of the constitution as an instrument of government, a charter and compact consciously framed for desired ends. The constitution, Hegel says, "should not be regarded as something made, even though it has come into being in time. It must be treated rather as something simply existent in and by itself, as divine therefore, and constant, and so as exalted above the sphere of things that are made." Because the state is "the march of God through the world," the constitution of the state is not something to be tampered with by ordinary mortals.

Going back into the history of the state, Hegel finds that its origin "involves imperious lordship on the one hand, instinctive submission on the other." This *leadership principle*, so characteristic of fascism, is also stressed by Hegel in his discussion of the merits of the different types of constitutions—democracy, aristocracy, and monarchy. The advantage of the monarchical form of government lies in the fact, Hegel argues, that leadership is always clearly present, whereas in aristocracy, and even more in democracy, leaders *may* rise to the top. Because of his preference for monarchy, Hegel rejects the sovereignty of the people, especially if the term implies opposition to the sovereignty of the monarch: "So opposed to the sovereignty of the monarch, the sovereignty of the people is one of the confused notions based on the wild idea of the 'people.' Taken without its monarch and the articulation of the whole which is the indispensable and direct concomitant of monarchy, the people is a formless mass and no longer a state." The democratic doctrine that the people are the state is rejected by Hegel as a "perversity" and a "ruse."

One of the paradoxical phenomena of political philosophy is that those who demand absolute law and order within the state, at the same time propound *anarchy* as the normal, and *desirable*, relation *between states*. On the one hand, Hegel advocates the strong state—on the model of the Prussian police state of the nineteenth century. Yet, when it comes to the question of how states are to live together, Hegel is an enthusiastic anarchist. In fact, he is nihilistic enough to deny that relations between states have anything in common with morality, such as regulates conduct between individuals. There is a pagan note to Hegel's claim that "the nation state is mind in its substantive rationality and immediate actuality and is therefore the absolute power on earth." The whole Stoic-Jewish-Christian tradition which affirms that there is a higher law than the commands of the state—a law of reason, nature, God—is flatly rejected by Hegel. If the state is the absolute power on earth, what happens when several absolutes clash? Hegel cheerfully answers as follows: "If states disagree and their particular wills cannot be harmonized, the matter can only be settled by war."

However, this consequence does not alarm him. On the contrary. Wars are wholesome, he argues, for a number of reasons. First, "corruption in nations would be the product of prolonged, let alone 'perpetual' peace." The trouble with peace, Hegel thinks, is that men stagnate in it. Their idiosyncrasies become more fixed and ossified, and war is desirable to keep the body politic healthy through proper stimulation. In addition, Hegel stresses the salutary impact of war on national unity: "As a result of war, nations are strengthened, but peoples involved in civil strife also acquire peace at home through making war abroad."

Later in the nineteenth century, Bismarck emphasized in his memoirs that war would be the only means to revive and maintain the loyalty of the people, particularly among the working population, who had become infected with the ideas of international socialism. By 1912, the year of the last national election before the outbreak of World War I, the Social Democrats had become the strongest single German party, commanding the allegiance of thirty-five per cent of the German electorate. In the twentieth century, the aggressions of fascist and communist totalitarian dictatorships have corroborated Hegel's conception of war as an instrument of national policy. Totalitarian police states justify repression in the present by promises of grandeur and prosperity in the future; they continually raise political cash (in good will and popular assent) by issuing postdated checks payable in future glory, until aggressive war finally seems the only way out of the accumulated moral debts.

Just as Hegel worships leaders in the life of nations, exempting heroes from the ordinary rules of ethics, so he views the relations between states in terms of leadership. Hegel regards world history, not as a series of unconnected and meaningless events, but as the progressive unfolding of Reason. In each epoch of history one nation is charged by the world spirit with the supreme mission of giving complete effect to the "advance of the self-developing self-consciousness of the world-mind." The nation thus charged by the world spirit is dominant during a whole epoch, and the other nations "are without rights" and "count no longer in world history."

How do we know whom the world spirit appoints from time to time to the office of ruler of the world? Hegel's answer is that the history of the world is "the world's court of judgment." *Victory in war* indicates where the world spirit is taking up residence, and the nation that loses in war thereby proves that the world spirit is no longer in harmony with it.

Because Hegel denies that there is any law or morality governing relations between states, he resorts to war as the means of deciding which of the conflicting nations and values possesses greater excellence. Applying his theory of periodic assignments of *world leadership* to specific nations, Hegel finds that the world spirit has progressively unfolded itself in four major epochs, each representing a principle of its own: first comes the Oriental realm, then the Greek, then the Roman, until the highest principle of the world spirit is reached with the Germans, who represent the "reconciliation of objective truth and freedom."

Though garbed in high-sounding philosophical terms, Hegel's political theory thus contains all essential elements of fascism: racialism, nationalism, the leadership principle, government by authority rather than consent, and, above all, the idolization of power as the supreme test of human values. The last point is perhaps the most important in the whole system of political Hegelianism, and Hegel by no means confined his idealization of power to his later writings. As early as 1802, he wrote in his *Constitution of Germany* that in their idealistic concern for freedom of conscience and political liberty, men are foolish enough to overlook the "truth which lies in power," for power is of the "higher justice of nature and truth" and may therefore forcibly bring men under its sway, in spite of their inner convictions and theories. Even Machiavelli had refrained from identifying power with morality and had held that they were two separate modes of behavior, each possessing its own code of rules, and each independent of the other. Hegel went further than Machiavelli by *identifying power—the state—with morality*. The twin heirs of Hegelianism, totalitarian fascism and communism, have also abandoned old-fashioned ethics, substituting for it Race, State, or Class.

Shortly before Hegel died he wrote a detailed analysis of the *English Reform Bill* (1831). He found that England was behind the "glorious and fortunate" progress of Germany because it lacked the "great sense of princes," and because its monarchical power was too weak and powerless against the "thoughtless mob," which was given too much influence. Hegel predicted that the Reform Bill, if enacted, would amount to revolution rather than reform. He penetratingly observed that in unreformed England new ministries represented the same class interests as the old, but that after the broadening of the suffrage new governments would represent new class interests. Hegel concluded that the enactment of the Reform Bill into law might threaten the stability of the English political system, and that the proposed reforms might degenerate into subversion and revolution, particularly as the English monarchy lacked the power, possessed by other monarchies, to decide political conflicts and prevent them from turning into violence, robbery, and revolution.

The doctrine of democracy as the first step to anarchy is the staple argument of all authoritarian political thinkers, from Plato to present-day opponents of democracy, and Hegel shared the classical authoritarian doctrine that society needs a strong monarchy as a balancing force between contending economic and political interests. Democracy denies that there is any one individual or class that can view conflicts of human values and interests from an olympic height of absolute justice and disinterestedness; it believes that such conflicts can be adjusted peacefully through processes of discussion and persuasion. The antidemocratic theory of politics holds, by contrast, that social conflicts must not be decided by the haphazard and approximate methods of a system in which the "thoughtless mob" is the final source of authority, but only by those who know what absolute justice is. Because they know, they must be obeyed. There is no difference between Hegel's identification of democracy with weakness and the cruder and coarser expressions of the same idea by Treitschke and Hitler. The ultimate assumption of Hegelian political philosophy is victory in war. Yet one of the paradoxes of history is that theories of human conduct and motivation which put victory in war above all other values ultimately lead to military failure.

The expansion of democracy in the nineteenth and twentieth centuries inevitably intensified the antidemocratic reaction of conservative authoritarianism. Starting first in Italy as an antidemocratic and antisocialist movement after World War I, *fascism* is in essence the twentieth-century version of age-old tendencies in politics. Like democracy, it is a universal phenomenon, and it appears in different forms and varieties in accordance with national traditions and circumstances. Like democracy, fascism, or the tendency toward fascism, is firmly entrenched in the ideas and institutions of some countries, and only an ephemeral phenomenon in others.

Unlike the authoritarianism of the seventeenth and eighteenth centuries, fascism is a *postdemocratic* political system and cannot be understood save as a reaction to democracy. Fascism is impossible in countries with no democratic experience at all: in such countries dictatorship may be based on the army, bureaucracy, and church, but it will lack the element of mass enthusiasm and participation characteristic of fascism. Conversely, fascism has never succeeded in a country whose democratic experience has been prolonged and generally shared by the people. Fascism has learned from democracy the value of popular support for national policies, and it seeks to manufacture popular consent by a mixture of propaganda and terror.

In this respect, the difference between fascism and Hegel is clearly evident. Despite the shock of the French Revolution, Hegel still believed that politics was essentially beyond the active interest and participation of the people, and his conception of rule was centered on monarchy, aristocracy, army, and bureaucracy rather than on the totalitarian mass party of the fascist type. The post-Hegelian character of fascism is also expressed in its borrowing from socialism enough anticapitalist slogans and catchwords to attract a part of the working classes.

Another element in fascism that puts it into proper historical perspective in relation to Hegelianism is that fascism can flourish only in countries with at least *some industrial experience*. The connection between fascism and industrialization is twofold: internally, fascist propaganda and terror require a minimum degree of technological development; externally, fascism as a system of *permanent mobilization for war* cannot hope to succeed in the twentieth century without considerable industrial skills and resources.

In its social background, fascism has particularly appealed to two groups: first, a numerically small group of industrialists and landowners who are willing to finance fascist parties in the hope of thereby getting rid of free trade-unions and radical political movements; second, the numerically much more important lower middle classes that dread the prospect of proletarianization and look to fascism for the salvation of their status and prestige in society. Typically, it is the employee rather than the worker who is susceptible to the fascist virus, and the small marginal businessman who is afraid of Big Business and Big Labor. In times of depression, fascism appeals to the unemployed, hopeless, cheerless—the forgotten men of society: by putting them into uniforms, and incorporating them into an organized movement, fascism makes them feel that they "belong," that they are not outcasts, as existing society may seem to consider them.

However, this does not mean that depressions as such lead inevitably to fascism. In the United States, the Great Depression in the early thirties led to the New Deal, and in Scandinavia, it put Social Democratic governments into office. Depressions are always a strain on democratic societies. But the response to the challenge of economic strain may be increased readiness to accept social and economic change, or—and this is the fascist solution—the determination to freeze the existing *status quo* and to resist social and economic change by the use of prisons and concentration camps.

Although their social background is as different from Hegelianism as the twentieth century is from the nineteenth, fascist ideas and principles are closely related to Hegel and the long tradition of antidemocratic thought. There is no Locke, Marx, or Lenin in the theory of fascism; it cannot be gathered from one systematic treatise but must be culled from various sources that express thought and opinion as much as political philosophy. One of the most authoritative brief statements of fascist theory is Mussolini's *Doctrine of Fascism* (1932), which he contributed, with the aid of the Italian philosopher Giovanni Gentile, to the *Italian Encyclopedia* in his capacity as *Duce* of Fascism and of Italy.

Benito Mussolini (1883–1945) started his political career as a journalist; for some time he edited the socialist daily, *Avanti*. When World War I broke out, the majority of the Socialist party favored neutrality. Mussolini, who had previously belonged to the revolutionary, syndicalist wing of the Socialist party, suddenly reversed his stand and favored intervention on the side of the Allies, for which he was expelled from the party in November, 1914. In the same month he started his own paper, *Popolo d'Italia,* later to become the official organ of Italian Fascism. In the first issue of his paper Mussolini explained why he favored intervention: "If the Prussian reaction triumphs in Europe tomorrow, and the destruction of Belgium and the annihilation of France cause the level of European civilization to sink, those who have not attempted to hinder the catastrophe will be traitors and apostates."

In March, 1919, Mussolini and his interventionist friends and associates formed "combat groups" (*Fasci di Combattimento*), the program of which was a mixture of ultrarevolutionary and ultranationalist slogans. At first Mussolini tried to woo the working classes away from the Socialist party (the Communist party, formed in 1921, was not important at the time), but he soon had to admit failure. He then steadily courted political support from the middle classes and financial support from big landowners and industrialists. Realizing the futility of achieving power by legal means, the Fascists began to terrorize opponents, not refraining from arson and assassination. A new feature of Fascist methods emerged in "punitive expeditions" against numerous communities, in which the police allowed the Fascists to terrorize and virtually take over whole towns.

In the national elections of 1921, the Fascists obtained only 35 of 535 seats in Parliament, and Mussolini became more determined than ever to seize the government by force. On October 28, 1922, the Fascists converged on Rome from all parts of Italy, and the following day Mussolini was asked by the King to form a new administration. Mussolini quickly consolidated his power by ruthless persecution of his opponents; the assassination in 1924 of Giacomo Matteotti, a Socialist Deputy, showed that murder was an officially sanctioned weapon of the new regime.

Until 1933 Mussolini was comparatively isolated; but with the advent of the Nazi regime in Germany, a new fascist international was gradually being formed, later joined by Japan and lesser powers. His hatred of democracy and the democratic nations drove Mussolini—all his life anti-German—into the arms of Hitler, and he entered the war on the side of Nazi Germany in June, 1940, when the war, after the defeat of France, seemed to be over. Yet the long years of preparation for war were of no avail, and the military weakness of the Fascist regime became evident from the first operations. Even after Italy surrendered in September, 1943, Mussolini continued to head a German puppet regime in northern Italy. In April, 1945, seeing that all was lost, he sought to escape to Switzerland, where he had spent several years in his youth as a penniless worker and agitator. On his way to the border he was captured by Italian partisans operating behind enemy lines, sentenced to death by an improvised partisan court, and executed. His dead body was publicly hung from a lamppost in Milan —the city in which the Fascist movement was born. Only a few days later, Hitler committed suicide in the Reich Chancellery in Berlin, the building in which he had plotted the conquest of the world by the "master race."

The most characteristic feature of the fascist temper and outlook is *irrationalism*, the distrust of reason, and the stress on the irrational, sentimental, uncontrollable parts of man. Fascism opposes the whole western tradition of rationalism that stems from Greece. The psychological mood of fascism is fanaticism, not skeptical reflection. Because of its basic irrationalism, fascism has "taboo issues" (such as race, the dogma of the party, or the personality of the "leader") that must not be critically discussed. During the Fascist regime in Italy, Mussolini's picture was in all schoolrooms, and it had the caption, "Mussolini is always right."

Fascism denies in principle the basic human equality of the western tradition, and not only accepts *inequality* as a fact but affirms it as an ideal. Though democratic societies do not always live up to their ideal of human equality, they at least accept it as a long-term goal of public policy.

The code of fascist behavior affirms the values of *violence* and the *lie*. Because it distrusts reason and rejects universally valid standards of conduct, fascism does not hesitate to use any means in pursuing its aims. For the same reason, fascism is ready to sacrifice the individual to the state: in the fascist view, the *state* is the *end* and the *individual* the *means*—the exact opposite of the democratic philosophy. "For the Fascist," Mussolini says (and his words express a Hegelian concept in Hegelian terms), "everything is in the State, and nothing human or spiritual exists, much less has value, outside the State." Mussolini therefore also candidly admits that the fascist state is necessarily *totalitarian,* allowing no competing values or social associations besides itself. By contrast, the democratic state is pluralistic: it must recognize the fact that in a free society the loyalty of the individual to the state may conflict with his loyalties to the family, church, or his own conscience as a free person.

The fascist acceptance of inequality and violence naturally results in the theory and practice of government by an *elite:* some men are born to rule, and others to obey. Fascist regimes are undemocratic, not because they always lack the support of the people (in some instances this support may be wholehearted), but because they rule *independently* of popular consent, without a free party system, and without free elections and a free press. The leadership principle is the extreme form of the fascist elite concept, and it fully expresses the irrational character of fascist politics: the leader is considered infallible, endowed with mystical gifts and insight, and he personifies the General Will of the nation. In a conflict of opinion between leader and people, the will of the leader prevails, because his is the General Will, whereas that of the people is only the Will of All.

The fascist emphasis on leadership collides with the simultaneous enforcement of orthodoxy and conformity—the totalitarian uniformity of fascist society. Leaders of fascism like Mussolini and Hitler were formed in nonfascist societies with considerable free competition. The relatively short duration of the main fascist regimes in Italy and Germany has made it impossible for the student of comparative political systems and philosophies to appraise the leadership qualities of a generation born and bred under conditions of fascist uniformity and orthodoxy.

Because fascism is not only a political system but a way of life, it employs *authority* rather than discussion in all spheres of social activity, including the nonpolitical ones. Fascism is typically antifeminist in public life and also supports strong paternal authority in the family, over both wife and children. The father is the "leader of the family." In the schools, discipline is the supreme value inculcated into the minds and hearts of children, and the educational program is little more than a prelude to military training and indoctrination. In industry, authority takes the place of free bargaining between capital and labor. Officially, the fascist state is impartial between capitalists and workers; yet the cemeteries of fascist countries are filled with victimized bodies of trade-unionists rather than bankers and industrialists. Relying on authority and obedience, fascism attracts not only those who want to command but also those who long to obey. In every society there are those who would rather follow and obey than think for themselves and assume responsibilities, and the "escape from freedom" is one of the chief psychological conditions of the spread of fascism.

The *corporate state* is another feature of fascism that expresses its lack of faith in the people: in the corporate system, the economy is organized in state-controlled associations of capital and labor, all working harmoniously for the common good, with the aid and guidance of the dictatorial one-party state. The underlying assumption of corporatism is that man (except for the elite in power) should not be politically articulate in his capacity as a citizen, but as a member of a social or economic group; general political issues are too complicated for him, whereas he is familiar with his work and profession.

In the international field, racialism and imperialism express the two fundamental fascist principles of inequality and violence. Just as within the nation the elite is superior to the rest and may impose its will by violence, so between nations the "elite nation" is considered superior to the others and entitled to rule them by force. As a result, fascism is opposed to international organization and world peace: it "believes neither in the possibility nor in the utility of perpetual peace," Mussolini says, because "war alone brings up to their highest tension all human energies and puts the stamp of nobility upon the peoples who have the courage to meet it." Moreover, fascism is opposed to international organizations for two other reasons: they recognize in some measure the principle of equality among nations, and, second, they seek to institute government by discussion on an international plane. Neither aim is compatible with the fascist theory of politics.

The defeat of the Axis in World War II has by no means removed the threat of fascism. As a political system, fascism may be destroyed for a time. As an attitude of mind, as a psychological temper, as a reflection of personal and social authoritarianism, it can survive political and military defeats. Where democracy is strong, courageous, willing to accept change, there is little danger of fascism.

I. HEGEL

Philosophy of Law *

1. Freedom in Nature and Society

At the present time, the idea that freedom of thought, and of mind generally, evinces itself only in divergence from, indeed in hostility to, what is publicly recognized, might seem to be most firmly rooted in connection with the state, and it is chiefly for this reason that a philosophy of the state might seem essentially to have the

* From G. W. F. Hegel, *Philosophy of Law* (1821; trans. T. M. Knox as *Philosophy of Right*, Oxford University Press, 1942). By permission.

task of discovering and promulgating still another theory, and a special and original one at that. In examining this idea and the activity in conformity with it, we might suppose that no state or constitution had ever existed in the world at all or was even in being at the present time, but that nowadays—and this "nowadays" lasts for ever —we had to start all over again from the beginning, and that the ethical world had just been waiting for such present-day projects, proofs, and investigations. So far as nature is concerned, people grant that it is nature as it is which philosophy has to bring within its ken, that the philosopher's stone lies concealed somewhere within nature itself, that nature is inherently rational and that what knowledge has to investigate and grasp in concepts is this actual reason present in it; not the formations and accidents evident to the superficial observer, but nature's eternal harmony, its harmony however, in the sense of the law and essence immanent within it. The ethical world, on the other hand, the state (i.e. reason as it actualizes itself in the element of self-consciousness), is not allowed to enjoy the good fortune which springs from the fact that it is reason which has achieved power and mastery within that element and which maintains itself and has its home there. The universe of mind is supposed rather to be left to the mercy of chance and caprice, to be God-forsaken, and the result is that if the ethical world is Godless, truth lies outside it, and at the same time, since even so reason is supposed to be in it as well, truth becomes nothing but a problem. But it is this also that is to authorize, nay to oblige, every thinker to take his own road, though not in search of the philosopher's stone, for he is saved this search by the philosophizing of our contemporaries, and everyone nowadays is assured that he has this stone in his grasp as his birthright. Now admittedly it is the case that those who live their lives in the state as it actually exists here and now and find satisfaction there for their knowledge and volition (and of these there are many, more in fact than think or know it, because ultimately this is the position of everybody), or those at any rate who *consciously* find their satisfaction in the state, laugh at these operations and affirmations and regard them as an empty game, sometimes rather funny, sometimes rather serious, now amusing, now dangerous. Thus this restless activity of empty reflection, together with its popularity and the welcome it has received, would be a thing on its own, developing in privacy in its own way, were it not that it is philosophy itself which has earned all kinds of scorn and discredit by its indulgence in this occupation. The worst of these kinds of scorn is this, that, as I said just now, everyone is convinced that his mere birthright puts him in a position to pass judgment on philosophy in general and to condemn it. No other art or science is subjected to this last degree of scorn, to the supposition that we are masters of it without ado.

At the present time, the pettifoggery of caprice has usurped the name of philosophy and succeeded in giving a wide public the opinion that such triflings are philosophy. The result of this is that it has now become almost a disgrace to go on speaking in philosophical terms about the nature of the state, and law-abiding men cannot be blamed if they become impatient so soon as they hear mention of a philosophical science of the state. Still less is it a matter for surprise that governments have at last directed their attention to this kind of philosophy, since, apart from anything else, philosophy with us is not, as it was with the Greeks for instance, pursued in private like an art, but has an existence in the open, in contact with the public, and especially, or even only, in the service of the state. Governments have proved their trust in their scholars who have made philosophy their chosen field by leaving entirely to them the construction and contents of philosophy—though here and there, if you like, it may not have been so much confidence that has been shown as indifference to learning itself, and professorial chairs of philosophy have been retained only as a tradition (in France, for instance, to the best of my knowledge, chairs of metaphysics at least have been allowed to lapse). Their confidence, however, has very often been ill repaid, or alternatively, if you preferred to see indifference, you would have to regard the result, the decay of thorough knowledge, as the penalty of this indifference. Prima facie, superficiality seems to be extremely accommodaing, one might say, at least in relation to public peace and order, because it fails to touch or even to guess at the substance of the things; no action, or at least no police action, would thus have been taken against it in the first instance, had it not been that there still existed in the state a need for a deeper education and insight, a need which the state required philosophical science to satisfy. On the other hand, superficial thinking about the ethical order, about right and duty in general, starts automatically from the maxims which constitute superficiality in this sphere, i.e. from the principles of the Sophists which are so clearly outlined for our information in Plato. What is right these principles locate in subjective aims and opinions, in subjective feeling and particular conviction, and from them there follows the ruin of the inner ethical life and a good conscience, of love and right dealing between private persons, no less than the ruin of public order and the law of the land. The significance which such phenomena must acquire for governments is not likely to suffer any diminution as a result of the pretentiousness which has used that very grant of confidence and the authority of a professorial chair to support the demand that the state should uphold and give scope to what corrupts the ultimate source of achievement, namely universal principles, and so even to the defiance of the state as if such defiance were what it deserved. "If God gives a man an office, he also gives him brains" is an old joke which in these days surely no one will take wholly in earnest.

What is rational is actual and what is actual is rational. On this conviction the plain man like the philosopher takes his stand, and from it philosophy starts in its study of the universe of mind as well as the universe of nature. If reflection, feeling, or whatever form subjective consciousness may take, looks upon the present as something vacuous and looks beyond it with the eyes of superior wisdom, it finds itself in a vacuum, and because it is actual only in the present, it is itself mere vacuity. If on the other hand the Idea passes for "only an Idea," for something represented in an opinion,

philosophy rejects such a view and shows that nothing is actual except the Idea. Once that is granted, the great thing is to apprehend in the show of the temporal and transient the substance which is immanent and the eternal which is present. For since rationality (which is synonomous with the Idea) enters upon external existence simultaneously with its actualization, it emerges with an infinite wealth of forms, shapes and appearances. Around its heart it throws a motley covering with which consciousness is at home to begin with, a covering which the concept has first to penetrate before it can find the inward pulse and feel it still beating in the outward appearances. But the infinite variety of circumstance which is developed in this externality by the light of the essence glinting in it—this endless material and its organization—this is not the subject matter of philosophy.

It is the fact that the ethical order is the system of these specific determinations of the Idea which constitutes its rationality. Hence the ethical order is freedom or the absolute will as what is objective, a circle of necessity whose moments are the ethical powers which regulate the life of individuals. To these powers individuals are related as accidents to substance, and it is in individuals that these powers are represented, have the shape of appearance, and become actualized.

The bond of duty can appear as a restriction only on indeterminate subjectivity or abstract freedom, and on the impulses either of the natural will or of the moral will which determines its indeterminate good arbitrarily. The truth is, however, that in duty the individual finds his liberation; first, liberation from dependence on mere natural impulse and from the depression which as a particular subject he cannot escape in his moral reflections on what ought to be and what might be; secondly, liberation from the indeterminate subjectivity which, never reaching reality or the objective determinacy of action, remains self-enclosed and devoid of actuality. In duty the individual acquires his substantive freedom.

Virtue is the ethical order reflected in the individual character so far as that character is determined by its natural endowment. When virtue displays itself solely as the individual's simple conformity with the duties of the station to which he belongs, it is rectitude.

But when individuals are simply identified with the actual order, ethical life (*das Sittliche*) appears as their general mode of conduct, i.e. as custom (*Sitte*), while the habitual practice of ethical living appears as a second nature which, put in the place of the initial, purely natural will, is the soul of custom permeating it through and through, the significance and the actuality of its existence. It is mind living and present as a world, and the substance of mind thus exists now for the first time as mind.

In this way the ethical substantial order has attained its right, and its right its validity. That is to say, the self-will of the individual has vanished together with his private conscience which had claimed independence and opposed itself to the ethical substance. For, when his character is ethical, he recognizes as the end which moves him to act the universal which is itself unmoved but is disclosed in its specific determinations as rationality actualized. He knows that his own dignity and the whole stability of his particular ends are grounded in this same universal, and it is therein that he actually attains these. Subjectivity is itself the absolute form and existent actuality of the substantial order and the distinction between subject on the one hand and substance on the other, as the object, end, and controlling power of the subject, is the same as, and has vanished directly along with, the distinction between them in form.

The state is the actuality of concrete freedom. But concrete freedom consists in this, that personal individuality and its particular interests not only achieve their complete development and gain explicit recognition for their right (as they do in the sphere of the family and civil society) but, for one thing, they also pass over of their own accord into the interest of the universal, and, for another thing, they know and will the universal; they even recognize it as their own substantive mind; they take it as their end and aim and are active in its pursuit. The result is that the universal does not prevail or achieve completion except along with particular interests and through the co-operation of particular knowing and willing; and individuals likewise do not live as private persons for their own ends alone, but in the very act of willing these they will the universal in the light of the universal and their activity is consciously aimed at none but the universal end. The principle of modern states has prodigious strength and depth because it allows the principle of subjectivity to progress to its culmination in the extreme of self-subsistent personal particularity, and yet at the same time brings it back to the substantive unity and so maintains this unity in the principle of subjectivity itself.

In contrast with the spheres of private rights and private welfare (the family and civil society), the state is from one point of view an external necessity and their higher authority; its nature is such that their laws and interests are subordinate to it and dependent on it. On the other hand, however, it is the end immanent within them, and its strength lies in the unity of its own universal end and aim with the particular interest of individuals, in the fact that individuals have duties to the state in proportion as they have rights against it.

To hold that every single person should share in deliberating and deciding on political matters of general concern on the ground that all individuals are members of the state, that its concerns are their concerns, and that it is their right that what is done should be done with their knowledge and volition, is tantamount to a proposal to put the democratic element without any rational form into the organism of the state, although it is only in virtue of the possession of such a form that the state is an organism at all. This idea comes readily to mind because it does not go beyond the abstraction of "being a member of the state," and it is superficial thinking which clings to abstractions. The rational consideration of a topic, the consciousness of the Idea, is concrete and to that extent coincides with a genuine practical sense. Such a sense is itself nothing but the sense of rationality or the Idea, though it is not to be confused with mere business routine or the horizon of a restricted sphere. The concrete state is the whole, articulated into its particular groups. The member of a state is a member of such a group, i.e. of a social class, and it is only as characterized in this objective way that he comes under consideration when we are dealing with the state. His mere character as universal implies that he is at one and the same time both a private person and also a thinking consciousness, a will which wills the universal. This consciousness and will, however, lose their emptiness and acquire a content and a living actuality only when they are filled with particularity, and particularity means determinacy as particular and a particular class-status; or to put the matter otherwise, abstract individuality is a generic essence, but has its immanent universal actuality as the generic essence next higher in the scale. Hence the single person attains his actual and living destiny for universality only when he becomes a member of a Corporation, a society, &c., and thereby it becomes open to him on the strength of his skill, to enter any class for which he is qualified, the class of civil servants included.

Another presupposition of the idea that all should participate in the business of the state is that everyone is at home in this business—a ridiculous notion, however commonly we may hear it sponsored. Still, in public opinion a field is open to everyone where he can express his purely personal political opinions and make them count.

Since the laws and institutions of the ethical order make up the concept of freedom, they are the substance or universal essence of individuals, who are thus related to them as accidents only. Whether the individual exists or not is all one to the objective ethical order. It alone is permanent and is the power regulating the life of individuals. Thus the ethical order has been represented by mankind as eternal justice, as gods absolutely existent, in contrast with which the empty business of individuals is only a game of see-saw.

Duty is a restriction only on the self-will of subjectivity. It stands in the way only of that abstract good to which subjectivity adheres. When we say: "We want to be free," the primary meaning of the words is simply: "We want abstract freedom," and every institution and every organ of the state passes as a restriction on freedom of that kind. Thus duty is not a restriction on freedom, but only on freedom in the abstract, i.e. on unfreedom. Duty is the attainment of our essence, the winning of positive freedom.

The intrinsic worth of courage as a disposition of mind is to be found in the genuine, absolute, final end, the sovereignty of the state. The work of courage is to actualize this final end, and the means to this end is the sacrifice of personal actuality. This form of experience thus contains the harshness of extreme contradictions: a self-sacrifice which yet is the real existence of one's freedom; the maximum self-subsistence of individuality, yet only as a cog playing its part in the mechanism of an external organization; absolute obedience, renunciation of personal opinions and reasonings, in fact complete *absence* of mind, coupled with the most intense and comprehensive *presence* of mind and decision in the moment of acting; the most hostile and so most personal action against individuals, coupled with an attitude of complete indifference or even liking towards them as individuals.

2. Monarchical versus Popular Government

The state is the actuality of the ethical Idea. It is ethical mind *qua* the substantial will manifest and revealed to itself, knowing and thinking itself, accomplishing what it knows and in so far as it knows it. The state exists immediately in custom, immediately in individual self-consciousness, knowledge, and activity, while self-consciousness in virtue of its sentiment towards the state finds in the state, as its essence and the end and product of its activity, its substantive freedom.

The *Penates* are inward gods, gods of the underworld; the mind of a nation (Athene for instance) is the divine, knowing and willing itself. Family piety is feeling, ethical behavior directed by feeling; political virtue is the willing of the absolute end in terms of thought.

The state is absolutely rational inasmuch as it is the actuality of the substantial will which it possesses in the particular self-consciousness once that consciousness has been raised to consciousness of its universality. This substantial unity is an absolute unmoved end in itself, in which freedom comes into its supreme right. On the other hand this final end has supreme right against the individual, whose supreme duty is to be a member of the state.

If the state is confused with civil society, and if its specific end is laid down as the security and protection of property and personal freedom, then the interest of the individuals as such becomes the ultimate end of their association, and it follows that membership of the state is something optional. But the state's relation to the individual is quite different from this. Since the state is mind objectified, it is only as one of its members that the individual himself has objectivity, genuine individuality, and an ethical life. Unification pure and simple is the true content and aim of the individual, and the individual's destiny is the living of a universal life. His further particular

satisfaction, activity, and mode of conduct have this substantive and universally valid life as their starting point and their result.

Rationality, taken generally and in the abstract, consists in the thoroughgoing unity of the universal and the single. Rationality, concrete in the state, consists (*a*) so far as its content is concerned, in the unity of objective freedom (i.e. freedom of the universal or substantial will) and subjective freedom (i.e. freedom of everyone in his knowing and in his volition of particular ends); and consequently (*b*) so far as its form is concerned, in self-determining action on laws and principles which are thoughts and so universal. This Idea is the absolutely eternal and necessary being of mind.

The state in and by itself is the ethical whole, the actualization of freedom; and it is an absolute end of reason that freedom should be actual. The state is mind on earth and consciously realizing itself there. In nature, on the other hand, mind actualizes itself only as its own other, as mind asleep. Only when it is present in consciousness, when it knows itself as a really existent object, is it the state. In considering freedom, the starting-point must be not individuality, the single self consciousness, but only the essence of self-consciousness; for whether man knows it or not, this essence is externally realized as a self-subsistent power in which single individuals are only moments. The march of God in the world, that is what the state is. The basis of the state is the power of reason actualizing itself as will. In considering the Idea of the state, we must not have our eyes on particular states or on particular institutions. Instead we must consider the Idea, this actual God, by itself. On some principle or other, any state may be shown to be bad, this or that defect may be found in it; and yet, at any rate if one of the mature states of our epoch is in question, it has in it the moments essential to the existence of the state. But since it is easier to find defects than to understand the affirmative, we may readily fall into the mistake of looking at isolated aspects of the state and so forgetting its inward organic life. The state is no ideal work of art; it stands on earth and so in the sphere of caprice, chance, and error, and bad behavior may disfigure it in many respects. But the ugliest of men, or a criminal, or an invalid, or a cripple, is still always a living man. The affirmative, life, subsists despite his defects, and it is this affirmative factor which is our theme here.

We should desire to have in the state nothing except what is an expression of rationality. The state is the world which mind has made for itself; its march, therefore, is on lines that are fixed and absolute. How often we talk of the wisdom of God in nature! But we are not to assume for that reason that the physical world of nature is a loftier thing than the world of mind. As high as mind stands above nature, so high does the state stand above physical life. Man must therefore venerate the state as a secular deity, and observe that if it is difficult to comprehend nature, it is infinitely harder to understand the state. It is a fact of the highest importance that nowadays we have gained a clearcut intuition into the state in general and have been so much engaged in discussing and making constitutions. But by getting so far we have not yet settled everything. In addition, it is necessary to bring to bear on a rational topic the reason underlying intuition, to know what the essence of the matter is and to realize that the obvious is not always the essential.

Another question readily presents itself here: "Who is to frame the constitution?" This question seems clear, but closer inspection shows at once that it is meaningless, for it presupposes that there is no constitution there, but only an agglomeration of atomic individuals. How an agglomeration of individuals could acquire a constitution, whether automatically or by someone's aid, whether as a present or by force or by thought, it would have to be allowed to settle for itself, since with an agglomeration the concept has nothing to do. But if the question presupposes an already existent constitution, then it is not about framing, but only about altering the constitution and the very presupposition of a constitution directly implies that its alteration may come about only by constitutional means. In any case, however, it is absolutely essential that the constitution should not be regarded as something made, even though it has come into being in time. It must be treated rather as something simply existent in and by itself, as divine therefore, and constant, and so as exalted above the sphere of things that are made.

The conception of the monarch is therefore of all conceptions the hardest for ratiocination, i.e. for the method of reflection employed by the Understanding. This method refuses to move beyond isolated categories and hence here again knows only *raisonnement*, finite points of view, and deductive argumentation. Consequently it exhibits the dignity of the monarch as something deduced, not only in its form, but in its essence. The truth is, however, that to be something not deduced but purely self-originating is precisely the conception of monarchy. Akin, then, to this reasoning is the idea of treating the monarch's right as grounded in the authority of God, since it is in its divinity that its unconditional character is contained. We are familiar, however, with the misunderstandings connected with this idea, and it is precisely this "divine" element which it is the task of a philosophic treatment to comprehend.

We may speak of the "sovereignty of the people" in the sense that any people whatever is self-subsistent *vis-à-vis* other peoples, and constitutes a state of its own, like the British people for instance. But the peoples of England, Scotland, or Ireland, or the peoples of Venice, Genoa, Ceylon, &c., are not sovereign peoples at all now that they have ceased to have rulers or supreme governments of their own.

We may also speak of sovereignty in home affairs residing in the people, provided that we are speaking generally about the whole state and meaning only what was shown above, namely, that it is to the state that sovereignty belongs.

The usual sense, however, in which men have recently begun to speak of the "sovereignty of the people" is that it is something opposed to the sovereignty existent in the monarch. So opposed to the sovereignty of the monarch, the sovereignty of the people is one of the confused notions based on the wild idea of the "people." Taken without its monarch and the articulation of the whole which is the indispensable and direct concomitant of monarchy, the people is a formless mass and no longer a state. It lacks every one of those determinate characteristics—sovereignty, government, judges, magistrates, class-divisions, &c., which are to be found only in a whole which is inwardly organized. By the very emergence into a people's life of moments of this kind which have a bearing on an organization, on political life, a people ceases to be that indeterminate abstraction which, when represented in a quite general way, is called the "people."

At the stage at which constitutions are divided, as above mentioned, into democracy, aristocracy, and monarchy, the point of view taken is that of a still substantial unity, abiding in itself, without having yet embarked on its infinite differentiation and the plumbing of its own depths. At that stage, the moment of the final, self-determining, decision of the will does not come on the scene explicitly in its own proper actuality as an organic moment immanent in the state. None the less, even in those comparatively immature constitutional forms, there must always be individuals at the head. Leaders must either be available already, as they are in monarchies of that type, or, as happens in aristocracies, but more particularly in democracies, they may rise to the top, as statesmen or generals, by chance and in accordance with the particular needs of the hour. This must happen since everything done and everything actual is inaugurated and brought to completion by the single decisive act of a leader.

It is often alleged against monarchy that it makes the welfare of the state dependent on chance, for, it is urged, the monarch may be ill educated he may perhaps be unworthy of the highest position in the state, and it is senseless that such a state of affairs should exist because it is supposed to be rational. But all this rests on a presupposition which is nugatory, namely that everything depends on the monarch's *particular* character. In a completely organized state, it is only a question of the culminating point of formal decision (and a natural bulwark against passion). It is wrong therefore to demand objective qualities in a monarch; he has only to say "yes" and dot the "i," because the throne should be such that the significant thing in its holder is not his particular make-up. (Monarchy in this sense is rational because it corresponds with the concept, but since this is hard to grasp, we often fail to notice the rationality of monarchy). Monarchy must be inherently stable and whatever else the monarch may have in addition to this power of final decision is part and parcel of his private character and should be of no consequence. Of course there may be circumstances in which it is this private character alone which has prominence, but in that event the state is either not fully developed, or else is badly constructed. In a well-organized monarchy, the objective aspect belongs to law alone, and the monarch's part is merely to set to the law the subjective "I will."

If we are to grasp the Idea of the monarch, we cannot be content with saying that God has appointed kings to rule over us, since God has made everything, even the worst of things. The point of view of utility does not get us very far either, and it is always possible to point out counter-balancing disadvantages. Still less does it help to regard monarchy as a *positive* right. That I should hold property is necessary, but my

holding of this particular property is contingent; and in the same way, the right
that there must be one man at the head of
affairs seems contingent too if it is treated
as abstract and as posited. This right, however, is inevitably present both as a felt
want and as a requirement of the situation.
Monarchs are not exactly distinguished for
bodily prowess or intellectual gifts, and yet
millions submit to their rule. Now to say
that men allow themselves to be ruled
counter to their own interests, ends, and
intentions is preposterous. Men are not so
stupid. It is their need, it is the inner might
of the Idea, which, even against what they
appear to think, constrains them to obedience and keeps them in that relation.

To define freedom of the press as freedom
to say and write whatever we please is
parallel to the assertion that freedom as
such means freedom to do as we please. Talk
of this kind is due to wholly uneducated,
crude, and superficial ideas. Moreover, it is
in the very nature of the thing that abstract
thinking should nowhere be so stubborn, so
unintelligent, as in this matter of free
speech, because what it is considering is the
most fleeting, the most contingent, and the
most personal side of opinion in its infinite
diversity of content and tergiversation. Beyond the direct incitation to theft, murder,
rebellion, &c., there lies its artfully constructed expression—an expression which
seems in itself quite general and vague,
while all the time it conceals a meaning
anything but vague, or else is compatible
with inferences which are not actually expressed, and it is impossible to determine
whether they rightly follow from it, or
whether they were meant to be inferred
from it. This vagueness of matter and form
precludes laws on these topics from attaining the requisite determinacy of law, and
since the tresspass, wrong, and injury here
are so extremely personal and subjective in
form, judgement on them is reduced equally
to a wholly subjective verdict. Such an injury is directed against the thoughts, opinions, and wills of others, but apart from

that, these form the element in which alone
it is actually anything. But this element is
the sphere of the freedom of others, and it-
therefore depends on them whether the injurious expression of opinion is or is not
actually an effective act.

Laws then may be criticized by exhibiting their indeterminacy as well as by arguing that they leave it open to the speaker
or writer to devise turns of phrase or tricks
of expression, and so evade the laws or
claim that judicial decisions are mere subjective verdicts. Further, however, against
the view that the expression of opinion is
an act with injurious effects, it may be
maintained that it is not an act at all, but
only opining and thinking, or only talking.
And so we have before us a claim that mere
opining and talking is to go unpunished because it is of a purely subjective character
both in form and content, because it does
not mean anything and is of no importance.
And yet in the same breath we have the
claim that this same opining and talking
should be held in high esteem and respect
—the opining because it is personal property and in fact pre-eminently the property
of mind; the talking because it is only this
same property being expressed and used.

But the substance of the matter is and
remains that traducing the honour of anyone, slander, abuse, the contemptuous caricature of government, its ministers, officials, and in particular the person of the
monarch, defiance of the laws, incitement
to rebellion, &c., &c., are all crimes or mis-
demeanours in one or other of their numerous gradations. The rather high degree of
indeterminability which such actions acquire on account of the element in which
they are expressed does not annul this
fundamental character of theirs. Its only
effect is that the subjective field in which
they are committed also determines the
nature and form of the reaction to the offence. It is the field in which the offence was
committed which itself necessitates subjectivity of view, contingency, &c., in the
reaction to the offence, whether the reaction takes the form of punishment proper

or of police action to prevent crimes. Here, as always, abstract thinking sets itself to explain away the fundamental and concrete nature of the thing by concentrating on isolated aspects of its external appearance and on abstractions drawn therefrom.

The sciences, however, are not to be found anywhere in the field of opinion and subjective views, provided of course that they be sciences in other respects. Their exposition is not a matter of clever turns of phrase, allusiveness, half-utterances, and semi-reticences, but consists in the unambiguous, determinate, and open expression of their meaning and purport. It follows that they do not fall under the category of public opinion. Apart from this, however, as I said just now, the element in which views and their expression become actions in the full sense and exist effectively, consists of the intelligence, principles, and opinions of others. Hence this aspect of these actions, i.e. their effectiveness proper and their danger to individuals, society, and the state, depends on the character of the ground on which they fall, just as a spark falling on a heap of gunpowder is more dangerous than if it falls on hard ground where it vanishes without trace. Thus, just as the right of science to express itself depends on and is safeguarded by its subject-matter and content, so an illegitimate expression may also acquire a measure of security, or at least sufferance, in the scorn which it has brought upon itself. An offence of this sort is punishable on its own account too, but part of it may be accounted that kind of nemesis which inner impotence, feeling itself oppressed by the preponderating abilities and virtues of others, is impelled to vent in order to come to itself again in face of such superiority, and to restore some self-consciousness to its own nullity. It was a nemesis of a more harmless type which Roman soldiers vented against their generals when they sang scurrilous songs about them in triumphal processions in order in a way to get even with them for all the hard service and discipline they had undergone, and especially for the omission of their names from the triumphal honours. The former type of nemesis, the bad and hateful type, is deprived of its effect by being treated with scorn, and hence, like the public, which perhaps forms a circle of spectators of scurrility, it is restricted to futile malice and to the self-condemnation which it implicitly contains.

3. Peace and War

War is not to be regarded as an absolute evil and as a purely external accident, which itself therefore has some accidental cause, be it injustices, the passions of nations or the holders of power, &c., or in short, something or other which ought not to be. It is to what is by nature accidental that accidents happen, and the fate whereby they happen is thus a necessity. Here as elsewhere, the point of view from which things seem pure accidents vanishes if we look at them in the light of the concept and philosophy, because philosophy knows accident for a show and sees in it its essence, necessity. It is necessary that the finite—property and life—should be definitely established as accidental, because accidentality is the concept of the finite. From one point of view this necessity appears in the form of the power of nature, and everything is mortal and transient. But in the ethical substance, the state, nature is robbed of this power, and the necessity is exalted to be the work of freedom, to be something ethical. The transience of the finite becomes a willed passing away, and the negativity lying at the roots of the finite becomes the substantive individuality proper to the ethical substance.

War is the state of affairs which deals in earnest with the vanity of temporal goods and concerns—a vanity at other times a common theme of edifying sermonizing. This is what makes it the moment in which the ideality of the particular attains its right and is actualized. War has the higher significance that by its agency, as I have remarked elsewhere, "the ethical health of peoples is preserved in their indifference to the stabilization of finite institutions; just as the blowing of the winds preserves the sea from the foulness which would be the result of a prolonged calm, so also corruption in nations would be the product of prolonged, let alone 'perpetual,' peace." This, however, is said to be only a philosophic idea, or, to use another common expression, a "justification of Providence," and it is maintained that actual wars require some other justification.

The ideality which is in evidence in war, i.e. in an accidental relation of a state to a foreign state, is the same as the ideality in accordance with which the domestic powers of the state are organic moments in a whole. This fact appears in history in various forms, e.g. successful wars have checked domestic unrest and consolidated the power of the state at home. Other phenomena illustrate the same point: e.g. peoples unwilling or afraid to tolerate sovereignty at home have been subjugated from abroad, and they have struggled for their independence with the less glory and success the less they have been able previously to organize the powers of the state in home affairs—their freedom has died from the fear of dying; states whose autonomy has been guaranteed not by their armed forces but in other ways (e.g. by their disproportionate smallness in comparison with their neighbours) have been able to subsist with a constitution of their own which by itself would not have assured peace in either home or foreign affairs.

In peace civil life continually expands; all its departments wall themselves in, and in the long run men stagnate. Their idiosyncrasies become continually more fixed and ossified. But for health the unity of the body is required, and if its parts harden themselves into exclusiveness, that is death. Perpetual peace is often advocated as an ideal towards with humanity should strive. With that end in view, Kant proposed a league of monarchs to adjust differences between states, and the Holy Alliance was meant to be a league of much the same kind. But the state is an individual, and individuality essentially implies negation. Hence even if a number of states make themselves into a family, this group as an individual must engender an opposite and create an enemy. As a result of war, nations are strengthened, but peoples involved in civil strife also acquire peace at home through making wars abroad. To be sure, war produces insecurity of property, but this insecurity of things is nothing but their transience—which is inevitable. We hear plenty of sermons from the pulpit about the insecurity, vanity, and instability of temporal things, but everyone thinks, however much he is moved by what he hears, that he at least will be able to retain his own. But if this insecurity now comes on the scene in the form of hussars with shining sabres and they actualize in real earnest what the preachers have said, then the moving and edifying discourses which foretold all these events turn into curses against the invader. Be that as it may, the fact remains that wars occur when the necessity of the case requires. The seeds burgeon once more, and harangues are silenced by the solemn cycles of history.

States are not private persons but completely autonomous totalities in themselves, and so the relation between them differs from a moral relation and a relation involving private rights. Attempts have often been made to regard the state as a person with the rights of persons and as a moral entity. But the position with private persons is that they are under the jurisdiction of a court which gives effect to what is right in principle. Now a relation between states ought also to be right in principle, but in mundane affairs a principle ought also to have power. Now since there is no power in existence which decides in face of the state what is right in principle and actualizes this decision, it follows that so far as international relations are concerned we can never get beyond an "ought." The relation between states is a relation between autonomous entities which make mutual stipulations but which at the same time are superior to these stipulations.

The nation-state is mind in its substantive rationality and immediate actuality and is therefore the absolute power on earth. It follows that every state is sovereign and autonomous against its neighbours. It is entitled in the first place and without qualification to be sovereign from their point of view, i.e. to be recognized by them as sovereign. At the same time, however, this title is purely formal, and the demand for this recognition of the state, merely on the ground that it is a state, is abstract. Whether a state is in fact something absolute depends on its content, i.e. on its constitution and general situation; and recognition, implying as it does an identity of both form and content, is conditional on the neighbouring state's judgement and will.

If states disagree and their particular wills cannot be harmonized, the matter can only be settled by war. A state through its subjects has widespread connexions and many-sided interests, and these may be readily and considerably injured; but it remains inherently indeterminable which of these injuries is to be regarded as a specific breach of treaty or as an injury to the honour and autonomy of the state. The reason for this is that a state may regard its infinity and honour as at stake in each of its concerns, however minute, and it is all the more inclined to susceptibility to injury the more its strong individuality is impelled as a result of long domestic peace to seek and create a sphere of activity abroad.

Apart from this, the state is in essence mind and therefore cannot be prepared to stop at just taking notice of an injury *after* it has actually occurred. On the contrary, there arises in addition as a cause of strife the *idea* of such an injury as the idea of a danger *threatening* from another state, together with calculations of degrees of probability on this side and that, guessing at intentions, &c., &c.

At one time the opposition between morals and politics, and the demand that the latter should conform to the former, were much canvassed. On this point only a general remark is required here. The welfare of a state has claims to recognition totally different from those of the welfare of the individual. The ethical substance, the state, has its determinate being, i.e. its right, directly embodied in something existent, something not abstract but concrete, and the principle of its conduct and behaviour can only be this concrete existent and not one of the many universal thoughts supposed to be moral commands. When politics is alleged to clash with morals and so to be always wrong, the doctrine propounded rests on superficial ideas about morality, the nature of the state, and the state's relation to the moral point of view.

II. MUSSOLINI

The Doctrine of Fascism *

1. Fundamental Ideas

1. Like every sound political conception, Fascism is both practice and thought; action in which a doctrine is immanent, and a doctrine which, arising out of a given system of historical forces, remains embedded in them and works there from within. Hence it has a form correlative to the contingencies of place and time, but it has also a content of thought which raises it to a formula of truth in the higher level of the history of thought. In the world one does not act spiritually as a human will dominating other wills without a conception of the transient and particular reality under which it is necessary to act, and of the permanent and universal reality in which the first has its being and its life. In order to know men it is necessary to know man; and in order to know man it is necessary to know reality and its laws. There is no concept of the State which is not fundamentally a concept of life: philosophy or intuition, a system of ideas which develops logically or is gathered up into a vision or into a faith, but which is always, at least virtually, an organic conception of the world.

2. Thus Fascism could not be understood in many of its practical manifestations as a party organization, as a system of education, as a discipline, if it were not always looked at in the light of its whole way of conceiving life, a spiritualized way. The world seen through Fascism is not this ma-

terial world which appears on the surface, in which man is an individual separated from all others and standing by himself, and in which he is governed by a natural law that makes him instinctively live a life of selfish and momentary pleasure. The man of Fascism is an individual who is nation and fatherland, which is a moral law, binding together individuals and the generations into a tradition and a mission, suppressing the instinct for a life enclosed within the brief round of pleasure in order to restore within duty a higher life free from the limits of time and space: a life in which the individual, through the denial of himself, through the sacrifice of his own private interests, through death itself, realizes that completely spiritual existence in which his value as a man lies.

3. Therefore it is a spiritualized conception, itself the result of the general reaction of modern times against the flabby materialistic positivism of the nineteenth century. Anti-positivistic, but positive: not sceptical, nor agnostic, nor pessimistic, nor passively optimistic, as are, in general, the doctrines (all negative) that put the centre of life outside man, who with his free will can and must create his own world. Fascism desires an active man, one engaged in activity with all his energies: it desires a man virilely conscious of the difficulties that exist in action and ready to face them. It conceives of life as a struggle, considering that it behoves man to conquer for himself that life truly worthy of him, creating first of all in himself the instrument (physical,

* (1932; trans. Michael Oakeshott, Cambridge University Press, 1939). By permission.

moral, intellectual) in order to construct it. Thus for the single individual, thus for the nation, thus for humanity. Hence the high value of culture in all its forms (art, religion, science), and the enormous importance of education. Hence also the essential value of work, with which man conquers nature and creates the human world (economic, political, moral, intellectual).

4. This positive conception of life is clearly an ethical conception. It covers the whole of reality, not merely the human activity which controls it. No action can be divorced from moral judgement; there is nothing in the world which can be deprived of the value which belongs to everything in its relation to moral ends. Life, therefore, as conceived by the Fascist, is serious, austere, religious: the whole of it is poised in a world supported by the moral and responsible forces of the spirit. The Fascist disdains the "comfortable" life.

5. Fascism is a religious conception in which man is seen in his immanent relationship with a superior law and with an objective Will that transcends the particular individual and raises him to conscious membership of a spiritual society. Whoever has seen in the religious politics of the Fascist regime nothing but mere opportunism has not understood that Fascism besides being a system of government is also, and above all, a system of thought.

6. Fascism is an historical conception, in which man is what he is only in so far as he works with the spiritual process in which he finds himself, in the family or social group, in the nation and in the history in which all nations collaborate. From this follows the great value of tradition, in memories, in language, in customs, in the standards of social life. Outside history man is nothing. Consequently Fascism is opposed to all the individualistic abstractions of a materialistic nature like those of the eighteenth century; and it is opposed to all Jacobin utopias and innovations. It does not consider that "happiness" is possible upon earth, as it appeared to be in the desire of the economic literature of the eight-

eenth century, and hence it rejects all teleological theories according to which mankind would reach a definitive stabilized condition at a certain period in history. This implies putting oneself outside history and life, which is a continual change and coming to be. Politically, Fascism wishes to be a realistic doctrine; practically, it aspires to solve only the problems which arise historically of themselves and that of themselves find or suggest their own solution. To act among men, as to act in the natural world, it is necessary to enter into the process of reality and to master the already operating forces.

7. Against individualism, the Fascist conception is for the State; and it is for the individual in so far as he coincides with the State, which is the conscience and universal will of man in his historical existence. It is opposed to classical Liberalism, which arose from the necessity of reacting against absolutism, and which brought its historical purpose to an end when the State was transformed into the conscience and will of the people. Liberalism denied the State in the interests of the particular individual; Fascism reaffirms the State as the true reality of the individual. And if liberty is to be the attribute of the real man, and not of that abstract puppet envisaged by individualistic Liberalism, Fascism is for liberty. And for the only liberty which can be a real thing, the liberty of the State and of the individual within the State. Therefore, for the Fascist, everything is in the State, and nothing human or spiritual exists, much less has value, outside the State. In this sense Fascism is totalitarian, and the Fascist State, the synthesis and unity of all values, interprets, develops and gives strength to the whole life of the people.

8. Outside the State there can be neither individuals nor groups (political parties, associations, syndicates, classes). Therefore Fascism is opposed to Socialism, which confines the movement of history within the class struggle and ignores the unity of classes established in one economic and moral reality in the State; and analogously it is op-

posed to class syndicalism. Fascism recognizes the real exigencies for which the socialist and syndicalist movement arose, but while recognizing them wishes to bring them under the control of the State and give them a purpose within the corporative system of interests reconciled within the unity of the State.

9. Individuals form classes according to the similarity of their interests, they form syndicates according to differentiated economic activities within these interests; but they form first, and above all, the State, which is not to be thought of numerically as the sum-total of individuals forming the majority of a nation. And consequently Fascism is opposed to Democracy, which equates the nation to the majority, lowering it to the level of that majority; nevertheless it is the purest form of democracy if the nation is conceived, as it should be, qualitatively and not quantitatively, as the most powerful idea (most powerful because most moral, most coherent, most true) which acts within the nation as the conscience and the will of a few, even of One, which ideal tends to become active within the conscience and the will of all—that is to say, of all those who rightly constitute a nation by reason of nature, history or race, and have set out upon the same line of development and spiritual formation as one conscience and one sole will. Not a race,[1] nor a geographically determined region, but as a community historically perpetuating itself, a multitude unified by a single idea, which is the will to existence and to power: consciousness of itself, personality.

10. This higher personality is truly the nation in so far as it is the State. It is not the nation that generates the State, as according to the old naturalistic concept which served as the basis of the political theories of the national States of the nineteenth century. Rather the nation is created by the State, which gives to the people, conscious of its own moral unity, a will and therefore an effective existence. The right of a na-

tion to independence derives not from a literary and ideal consciousness of its own being, still less from a more or less unconscious and inert acceptance of a *de facto* situation, but from an active consciousness, from a political will in action and ready to demonstrate its own rights: that is to say, from a state already coming into being. The State, in fact, as the universal ethical will, is the creator of right.

11. The nation as the State is an ethical reality which exists and lives in so far as it develops. To arrest its development is to kill it. Therefore the State is not only the authority which governs and gives the form of laws and the value of spiritual life to the wills of individuals, but it is also a power that makes its will felt abroad, making it known and respected, in other words, demonstrating the fact of its universality in all the necessary directions of its development. It is consequently organization and expansion, at least virtually. Thus it can be likened to the human will which knows no limits to its development and realizes itself in testing its own limitlessness.

12. The Fascist State, the highest and most powerful form of personality, is a force, but a spiritual force, which takes over all the forms of the moral and intellectual life of man. It cannot therefore confine itself simply to the functions of order and supervision as Liberalism desired. It is not simply a mechanism which limits the sphere of the supposed liberties of the individual. It is the form, the inner standard and the discipline of the whole person; it saturates the will as well as the intelligence. Its principle, the central inspiration of the human personality living in the civil community, pierces into the depths and makes its home in the heart of the man of action as well as of the thinker, of the artist as well as of the scientist: it is the soul of the soul.

13. Fascism, in short, is not only the giver of laws and the founder of institutions, but the educator and promoter of spiritual life. It wants to remake, not the forms of human life, but its content, man, character, faith. And to this end it requires

[1] "Race; it is an emotion, not a reality; ninety-five per cent of it is emotion." Mussolini.

discipline and authority that can enter into the spirits of men and there govern unopposed. Its sign, therefore, is the Lictors' rods, the symbol of unity, of strength and justice.

2. Political and Social Doctrine

1. When in the now distant March of 1919 I summoned to Milan, through the columns of the *Popolo d' Italia,* my surviving supporters who had followed me since the constitution of the Fasces of Revolutionary Action, founded in January 1915, there was no specific doctrinal plan in my mind. I had known and lived through only one doctrine, that of the Socialism of 1903–4 up to the winter of 1914, almost ten years. My experience in this had been that of a follower and of a leader, but not that of a theoretician. My doctrine, even in that period, had been a doctrine of action. An unequivocal Socialism, universally accepted, did not exist after 1905, when the Revisionist Movement began in Germany under Bernstein and there was formed in opposition to that, in the see-saw of tendencies, an extreme revolutionary movement, which in Italy never emerged from the condition of mere words, whilst in Russian Socialism it was the prelude to Bolshevism. Reform, Revolution, Centralization—even the echoes of the terminology are now spent; whilst in the great river of Fascism are to be found the streams which had their source in Sorel, Peguy, in the Lagardelle of the *Mouvement Socialiste* and the groups of Italian Syndicalists, who between 1904 and 1914 brought a note of novelty into Italian Socialism, which by that time had been devitalized and drugged by fornication with Giolitti, in *Pagine Libere* of Olivetti, *La Lupa* of Orano and *Divenire Sociale* of Enrico Leone.

In 1919, at the end of the War, Socialism as a doctrine was already dead: it existed only as hatred, it had still only one possibility, especially in Italy, that of revenge against those who had wished for the War and who should be made to expiate it. The *Popolo d' Italia* expressed it in its subtitle—"The Newspaper of Combatants and Producers." The word "producers" was already the expression of a tendency. Fascism was not given out to the wet nurse of a doctrine elaborated beforehand round a table: it was born of the need for action; it was not a party, but in its first two years it was a movement against all parties. The name which I gave to the organization defined its characteristics. Nevertheless, whoever rereads, in the now crumpled pages of the time, the account of the constituent assembly of the *Fasci italiani di Combattimento* will not find a doctrine, but a series of suggestions, of anticipations, of admonitions, which when freed from the inevitable vein of contingency, were destined later, after a few years, to develop into a series of doctrinal attitudes which made of Fascism a self-sufficient political doctrine able to face all others, both past and present. "If the bourgeoisie," I said at that time, "thinks to find in us a lightning-conductor, it is mistaken. We must go forward in opposition to Labour. . . . We want to accustom the working classes to being under a leader, to convince them also that it is not easy to direct an industry or a commercial undertaking successfully. . . . We shall fight against technical and spiritual retrogression. . . . The successors of the present regime still being undecided, we must not be unwilling to fight for it. We must hasten; when the present regime is superseded, we must be the ones to take its place. The right of succession belongs to us because we pushed the country into the War and we led it to victory. The present method of political representation cannot be sufficient for us, we wish for a direct representation of individual interests. . . . It might be said against this programme that it is a return to the corporations. It doesn't matter! . . . I should like, nevertheless, the Assembly to accept the claims of national syndicalism from the point of view of economics. . . ."

Is it not surprising that from the first day in the Piazza San Sepolcro there should resound the word "Corporation" which was destined in the course of the revolution to signify one of the legislative and social creations at the base of the regime?

2. The years preceding the March on Rome were years during which the necessity of action did not tolerate enquiries or complete elaborations of doctrine. Battles were being fought in the cities and villages. There were discussions, but—and this is more sacred and important—there were deaths. People knew how to die. The doctrine—beautiful, well-formed, divided into chapters and paragraphs and surrounded by a commentary—might be missing; but there was present something more decisive to supplant it—Faith. Nevertheless, he who recalls the past with the aid of books, articles, votes in Parliament, the major and the minor speeches, he who knows how to investigate and weigh evidence, will find that the foundations of the doctrine were laid while the battle was raging. It was precisely in these years that Fascist thought armed itself, refined itself, moving towards one organization of its own. The problems of the individual and the State; the problems of authority and liberty; political and social problems and those more specifically national; the struggle against liberal, democratic, socialist, Masonic, demagogic doctrines was carried on at the same time as the "punitive expeditions." But since the "system" was lacking, adversaries ingenuously denied that Fascism had any power to make a doctrine of its own, while the doctrine rose up, even though tumultuously, at first under the aspect of a violent and dogmatic negation, as happens to all ideas that break new ground, then under the positive aspect of a constructive policy which, during the years 1926, 1927, 1928, was realized in the laws and institutions of the regime.

Fascism is to-day clearly defined not only as a regime but as a doctrine. And I mean by this that Fascism to-day, self-critical as well as critical of other movements, has an unequivocal point of view of its own, a criterion, and hence an aim, in face of all the material and intellectual problems which oppress the people of the world.

3. Above all, Fascism, in so far as it considers and observes the future and the development of humanity quite apart from the political considerations of the moment, believes neither in the possibility nor in the utility of perpetual peace. It thus repudiates the doctrine of Pacifism—born of a renunciation of the struggle and an act of cowardice in the face of sacrifice. War alone brings up to their highest tension all human energies and puts the stamp of nobility upon the peoples who have the courage to meet it. All other trials are substitutes, which never really put a man in front of himself in the alternative of life and death. A doctrine, therefore, which begins with a prejudice in favour of peace is foreign to Fascism; as are foreign to the spirit of Fascism, even though acceptable by reason of the utility which they might have in given political situations, all internationalistic and socialistic systems which, as history proves, can be blown to the winds when emotional, idealistic and practical movements storm the hearts of peoples. Fascism carries over this anti-pacifist spirit even into the lives of individuals. The proud motto of the *Squadrista,* "Me ne frego," written on the bandages of a wound is an act of philosophy which is not only stoical, it is the epitome of a doctrine that is not only political: it is education for combat, the acceptance of the risks which it brings; it is a new way of life for Italy. Thus the Fascist accepts and loves life, he knows nothing of suicide and despises it; he looks on life as duty, ascent, conquest: life which must be noble and full: lived for oneself, but above all for those others near and far away, present and future.

4. The "demographic" policy of the regime follows from these premises. Even the Fascist does in fact love his neighbour, but this "neighbour" is not for him a vague and ill-defined concept; love for one's neighbour does not exclude necessary educational

severities, and still less differentiations and distances. Fascism rejects universal concord, and, since it lives in the community of civilized peoples, it keeps them vigilantly and suspiciously before its eyes, it follows their states of mind and the changes in their interests and its does not let itself be deceived by temporary and fallacious appearances.

5. Such a conception of life makes Fascism the precise negation of that doctrine which formed the basis of the so-called Scientific or Marxian Socialism: the doctrine of historical Materialism according to which the history of human civilizations can be explained only as the struggle of interest between the different social groups and as arising out of change in the means and instruments of production. That economic improvements—discoveries of raw materials, new methods of work, scientific inventions—should have an importance of their own, no one denies, but that they should suffice to explain human history to the exclusion of all other factors is absurd: Fascism believes, now and always, in holiness and in heroism, that is in acts in which no economic motive—remote or immediate—plays a part. With this negation of historical materialism, according to which men would be only by-products of history, who appear and disappear on the surface of the waves while in the depths the real directive forces are at work, there is also denied the immutable and irreparable "class struggle" which is the natural product of this economic conception of history, and above all it is denied that the class struggle can be the primary agent of social changes. Socialism, being thus wounded in these two primary tenets of its doctrine, nothing of it is left save the sentimental aspiration—old as humanity—towards a social order in which the sufferings and the pains of the humblest folk could be alleviated. But here Fascism rejects the concept of an economic "happiness" which would be realized socialistically and almost automatically at a given moment of economic evolution by assuring to all a maximum prosperity. Fascism denies

the possibility of the materialistic conception of "happiness" and leaves it to the economists of the first half of the eighteenth century; it denies, that is, the equation of prosperity with happiness, which would transform men into animals with one sole preoccupation: that of being well-fed and fat, degraded in consequence to a merely physical existence.

6. After Socialism, Fascism attacks the whole complex of democratic ideologies and rejects them both in their theoretical premises and in their applications or practical manifestations. Fascism denies that the majority, through the mere fact of being a majority, can rule human societies; it denies that this majority can govern by means of a periodical consultation; it affirms the irremediable, fruitful and beneficent inequality of men, who cannot be levelled by such a mechanical and extrinsic fact as universal suffrage. By democratic regimes we mean those in which from time to time the people is given the illusion of being sovereign, while true effective sovereignty lies in other, perhaps irresponsible and secret, forces. Democracy is a regime without a king, but with very many kings, perhaps more exclusive, tyrannical and violent than one king even though a tyrant. This explains why Fascism, although before 1922 for reasons of expediency it made a gesture of republicanism, renounced it before the March on Rome, convinced that the question of the political forms of a State is not preeminent to-day, and that studying past and present monarchies, past and present Republics it becomes clear that monarchy and republic are not to be judged *sub specie aeternitatis*, but represent forms in which the political evolution, the history, the tradition, the psychology of a given country are manifested. Now Fascism overcomes the antithesis between monarchy and republic which retarded the movements of democracy, burdening the former with every defect and defending the latter as the regime of perfection. Now it has been seen that there are inherently reactionary and absolutistic republics, and monarchies that wel-

come the most daring political and social innovations.

7. "Reason, Science," said Renan (who was inspired before Fascism existed) in one of his philosophical Meditations, "are products of humanity, but to expect reason directly from the people and through the people is a chimera. It is not necessary for the existence of reason that everybody should know it. In any case, if such an initiation should be made, it would not be made by means of base democracy, which apparently must lead to the extinction of every difficult culture, and every higher discipline. The principle that society exists only for the prosperity and the liberty of the individuals who compose it does not seem to conform with the plans of nature, plans in which the species alone is taken into consideration and the individual seems to be sacrificed. It is strongly to be feared lest the last word of democracy thus understood (I hasten to say that it can also be understood in other ways) would be a social state in which a degenerate mass would have no other care than to enjoy the ignoble pleasures of vulgar men."

Thus far Renan. Fascism rejects in democracy the absurd conventional lie of political equalitarianism clothed in the dress of collective irresponsibility and the myth of happiness and indefinite progress. But if democracy can be understood in other ways, that is, if democracy means not to relegate the people to the periphery of the State, then Fascism could be defined as an "organized, centralized, authoritarian democracy."

8. In face of Liberal doctrines, Fascism takes up an attitude of absolute opposition both in the field of politics and in that of economics. It is not necessary to exaggerate —merely for the purpose of present controversies—the importance of Liberalism in the past century, and to make of that which was one of the numerous doctrines sketched in that century a religion of humanity for all times, present and future. Liberalism flourished for no more than some fifteen years. It was born in 1830, as a reaction against the Holy Alliance that wished to drag Europe back to what it had been before 1789, and it had its year of splendour in 1848 when even Pius IX was a Liberal. Immediately afterwards the decay set in. If 1848 was a year of light and of poetry, 1849 was a year of darkness and of tragedy. The Republic of Rome was destroyed by another Republic, that of France. In the same year Marx launched the gospel of the religion of Socialism with the famous *Communist Manifesto*. In 1851 Napoleon III carried out his unliberal *coup d'état* and ruled over France until 1870, when he was dethroned by a popular revolt, but as a consequence of a military defeat which ranks among the most resounding that history can relate. The victor was Bismarck, who never knew the home of the religion of liberty or who were its prophets. It is symptomatic that a people of high culture like the Germans should have been completely ignorant of the religion of liberty during the whole of the nineteenth century. It was, there, no more than a parenthesis, represented by what has been called the "ridiculous Parliament of Frankfort" which lasted only a season. Germany has achieved her national unity outside the doctrines of Liberalism, against Liberalism, a doctrine which seems foreign to the German soul, a soul essentially monarchical, whilst Liberalism is the historical and logical beginning of anarchism. The stages of German unity are the three wars of 1864, 1866 and 1870, conducted by "Liberals" like Moltke and Bismarck. As for Italian unity, Liberalism has had in it a part absolutely inferior to the share of Mazzini and of Garibaldi, who were not Liberals. Without the intervention of the unliberal Napoleon we should not have gained Lombardy, and without the help of the unliberal Bismarck at Sadowa and Sedan, very probably we should not have gained Venice in 1866; and in 1870 we should not have entered Rome. From 1870–1915 there occurs the period in which the very priests of the new creed had to confess

the twilight of their religion: defeated as it was by decadence in literature, by activism in practice. Activism: that is to say, Nationalism, Futurism, Fascism. The "Liberal" century, after having accumulated an infinity of Gordian knots, tried to untie them by the hecatomb of the World War. Never before has any religion imposed such a cruel sacrifice. Were the gods of Liberalism thirsty for blood? Now Liberalism is about to close the doors of its deserted temples because the peoples feel that its agnosticism in economics, its indifferentism in politics and in morals, would lead, as they have led, the States to certain ruin. In this way one can understand why all the political experiences of the contemporary world are anti-Liberal, and it is supremely ridiculous to wish on that account to class them outside of history; as if history were a hunting ground reserved to Liberalism and its professors, as if Liberalism were the definitive and no longer surpassable message of civilization.

9. But the Fascist repudiations of Socialism, Democracy, Liberalism must not make one think that Fascism wishes to make the world return to what it was before 1789, the year which has been indicated as the year of the beginning of the liberal-democratic age. One does not go backwards. The Fascist doctrine has not chosen De Maistre as its prophet. Monarchical absolutism is a thing of the past and so also is every theocracy. So also feudal privileges and division into impenetrable and isolated castes have had their day. The theory of Fascist authority has nothing to with the police State. A party that governs a nation in a totalitarian way is a new fact in history. References and comparisons are not possible. Fascism takes over from the ruins of Liberal Socialistic democratic doctrines those elements which still have a living value. It preserves those that can be called the established facts of history, it rejects all the rest, that is to say the idea of a doctrine which holds good for all times and all peoples. If it is admitted that the nineteenth century has been the century of Socialism, Liberalism and Democracy, it does not follow that the twentieth must also be the century of Liberalism, Socialism and Democracy. Political doctrines pass; peoples remain. It is to be expected that this century may be that of authority, a century of the "Right," a Fascist century. If the nineteenth was the century of the individual (Liberalism means individualism) it may be expected that this one may be the century of "collectivism" and therefore the century of the State. That a new doctrine should use the still vital elements of other doctrines is perfectly logical. No doctrine is born quite new, shining, never before seen. No doctrine can boast of an absolute "originality." It is bound, even if only historically, to other doctrines that have been, and to develop into other doctrines that will be. Thus the scientific socialism of Marx is bound to the Utopian Socialism of the Fouriers, the Owens and the Saint-Simons; thus the Liberalism of the nineteenth century is connected with the whole "Enlightenment" of the eighteenth century. Thus the doctrines of democracy are bound to the *Encyclopédie*. Every doctrine tends to direct the activity of men towards a determined objective; but the activity of man reacts upon the doctrine, transforms it, adapts it to new necessities or transcends it. The doctrine itself, therefore, must be, not words, but an act of life. Hence, the pragmatic veins in Fascism, its will to power, its will to be, its attitude in the face of the fact of "violence" and of its own courage.

10. The keystone of Fascist doctrine is the conception of the State, of its essence, of its tasks, of its ends. For Fascism the State is an absolute before which individuals and groups are relative. Individuals and groups are "thinkable" in so far as they are within the State. The Liberal State does not direct the interplay and the material and spiritual development of the groups, but limits itself to registering the results; the Fascist State has a consciousness of its own, a will of its own, on this account it is called

an "ethical" State. In 1929, at the first quinquennial assembly of the regime, I said:

For Fascism, the State is not the night-watchman who is concerned only with the personal security of the citizens; nor is it an organization for purely material ends, such as that of guaranteeing a certain degree of prosperity and a relatively peaceful social order, to achieve which a council of administration would be sufficient, nor is it a creation of mere politics with no contact with the material and complex reality of the lives of individuals and the life of peoples. The State, as conceived by Fascism and as it acts, is a spiritual and moral fact because it makes concrete the political, juridical, economic organization of the nation and such an organization is, in its origin and in its development, a manifestation of the spirit. The State is the guarantor of internal and external security, but it is also the guardian and the transmitter of the spirit of the people as it has been elaborated through the centuries in language, custom, faith. The State is not only present, it is also past, and above all future. It is the State which, transcending the brief limit of individual lives, represents the immanent conscience of the nation. The forms in which States express themselves change, but the necessity of the State remains. It is the State which educates citizens for civic virtue, makes them conscious of their mission, calls them to unity; harmonizes their interests in justice; hands on the achievements of thought in the sciences, the arts, in law, in human solidarity; it carries men from the elementary life of the tribe to the highest human expression of power which is Empire; it entrusts to the ages the names of those who died for its integrity or in obedience to its laws; it puts forward as an example and recommends to the generations that are to come the leaders who increased its territory and the men of genius who gave it glory. When the sense of the State declines and the disintegrating and centrifugal tendencies of individuals and groups prevail, national societies move to their decline.

11. From 1929 up to the present day these doctrinal positions have been strengthened by the whole economico-political evolution of the world. It is the State alone that grows in size, in power. It is the State alone that can solve the dramatic contradictions of capitalism. What is called the crisis cannot be overcome except by the State, within the State. Where are the shades of the Jules Simons who, at the dawn of Liberalism, proclaimed that "the State must strive to render itself unnecessary and to prepare for its demise"; of the MacCullochs who, in the second half of the last century, affirmed that the State must abstain from too much governing? And faced with the continual, necessary and inevitable interventions of the State in economic affairs what would the Englishman Bentham now say, according to whom industry should have asked of the State only to be left in peace? Or the German Humboldt, according to whom the "idle" State must be considered the best? It is true that the second generation of Liberal economists was less extremist than the first, and already Smith himself opened, even though cautiously, the door to State intervention in economics. But when one says Liberalism, one says the individual; when one says Fascism, one says the State. But the Fascist State is unique; it is an original creation. It is not reactionary, but revolutionary in that it anticipates the solutions of certain universal problems. These problems are no longer seen in the same light: in the sphere of politics they are removed from party rivalries, from the supreme power of parliament, from the irresponsibility of assemblies; in the sphere of economics they are removed from the sphere of the syndicates' activities—activities that were ever widening their scope and increasing their power both on the workers' side and on the employers'—removed from their struggles and their designs; in the moral sphere they are divorced from ideas of the need for order, discipline and obedience, and lifted into the plane of the moral commandments of the fatherland. Fascism desires the State to be strong, organic and at

the same time founded on a wide popular basis. The Fascist State has also claimed for itself the field of economics and, through the corporative, social and educational institutions which it has created, the meaning of the State reaches out to and includes the farthest off-shoots; and within the State, framed in their respective organizations, there revolve all the political, economic and spiritual forces of the nation. A State founded on millions of individuals who recognize it, feel it, are ready to serve it, is not the tyrannical State of the medieval lord. It has nothing in common with the absolutist States that existed either before or after 1789. In the Fascist State the individual is not suppressed, but rather multiplied, just as in a regiment a soldier is not weakened but multiplied by the number of his comrades. The Fascist State organizes the nation, but it leaves sufficient scope to individuals; it has limited useless or harmful liberties and has preserved those that are essential. It cannot be the individual who decides in this matter, but only the State.

12. The Fascist State does not remain indifferent to the fact of religion in general and to that particular positive religion which is Italian Catholicism. The State has no theology, but it has an ethic. In the Fascist State religion is looked upon as one of the deepest manifestations of the spirit; it is, therefore, not only respected, but defended and protected. The Fascist State does not create a "God" of its own, as Robespierre once, at the height of the Convention's foolishness, wished to do; nor does it vainly seek, like Bolshevism, to expel religion from the minds of men; Fascism respects the God of the ascetics, of the saints, of the heroes, and also God as seen and prayed to by the simple and primitive heart of the people.

13. The Fascist State is a will to power and to government. In it the tradition of Rome is an idea that has force. In the doctrine of Fascism Empire is not only a territorial, military or mercantile expression, but spiritual or moral. One can think of an empire, that is to say a nation that directly or indirectly leads other nations, without needing to conquer a single square kilometre of territory. For Fascism the tendency to Empire, that is to say, to the expansion of nations, is a manifestation of vitality; its opposite, staying at home, is a sign of decadence: peoples who rise or re-rise are imperialist, peoples who die are renunciatory. Fascism is the doctrine that is most fitted to represent the aims, the states of mind, of a people, like the Italian people, rising again after many centuries of abandonment or slavery to foreigners. But Empire calls for discipline, co-ordination of forces, duty and sacrifice; this explains many aspects of the practical working of the regime and the direction of many of the forces of the State and the necessary severity shown to those who would wish to oppose this spontaneous and destined impulse of the Italy of the twentieth century, to oppose it in the name of the superseded ideologies of the nineteenth, repudiated wherever great experiments of political and social transformation have been courageously attempted: especially where, as now, peoples thirst for authority, for leadership, for order. If every age has its own doctrine, it is apparent from a thousand signs that the doctrine of the present age is Fascism. That it is a doctrine of life is shown by the fact that it has resuscitated a faith. That this faith has conquered minds is proved by the fact that Fascism has had its dead and its martyrs.

Fascism henceforward has in the world the universality of all those doctrines which, by fulfilling themselves, have significance in the history of the human spirit.

CHAPTER 22

LIBERALISM— OLD AND NEW

THE cult of the state, whether in the refined form of nineteenth-century Hegelianism or in the crude form of twentieth-century fascism, is essentially linked with militaristic societies. By contrast, the cult of the individual is associated with rationalism and industrialism. The rationalist root of individualism presupposes a basic equality of all men on the ground that every human being is endowed with reason: rationalism stresses the value of the individual rather than that of superindividual, collective, institutional forces that are not rational in origin but the product of custom, sentiment, and belief. Modern industrialism was largely the product of the revolt of the individual against obsolete and obstructionist state regulations of economic life.

The individual element of the pioneering phase of the Industrial Revolution was enhanced by the entrepreneur's personal responsibility and willingness to take risks. The spirit of individualism permeated all spheres of life and thought: agnosticism in religion, empiricism in philosophy, utilitarianism in ethics, laissez faire in economics, antiauthoritarianism in politics, pacifism, anti-imperialism and free trade in international relations, equality for all regardless of sex, class, religion, or race—these expressions of individualism were characteristic of the classical period of liberalism.

Having first experienced the impact of the Industrial Revolution, England developed the earliest and most advanced forms of individualist liberalism. Locke was the first great European liberal in modern times; his philosophy was based on experience, his politics on individual liberty and collective consent, his religion on toleration of diversity. When the factory replaced the village as the dominant social institution in the nineteenth century, when science increasingly challenged the authority of custom and faith, individualism reached its peak in speculative and practical politics.

The most extreme reflection of nineteenth-century individualism is to be found in the encyclopedic system of Herbert Spencer (1820–1903). Both his paternal and maternal ancestors were of a long line of English and French non-conformists, dissenters and rebels, and Spencer traces in his *Autobiography* (1904) his "conspicuous disregard" of political, religious, and social authority to the tradition of independence and dissent so long cherished by his family. Spencer's education was informal, unconventional, and highly deficient in the more traditional studies of literature and history. His father encouraged his interest in science and technology, and Spencer became an engineer. However, he practiced his profession for but a few years, because he became increasingly interested in political economy, sociology, biology, and philosophy. He was a subeditor of *The Economist* from 1848 to 1853, and then ventured into a full-time career as a free-lance author.

As early as 1842 Spencer contributed to the *Nonconformist* a series of letters called *The Proper Sphere of Government*, his first major publication. It contains his political philosophy of extreme individualism and laissez faire, which was little, if at all, modified in his writings of the subsequent sixty years. Spencer expresses in *The Proper Sphere of Government* his belief that "everything in nature has its laws," organic as well as inorganic matter. Man is subject to laws both in his physical and spiritual essence, and "as with man individually, so with man socially." Concerning the evils of society, Spencer postulates a "self-adjusting principle" under which evils rectify themselves, provided that no one interferes with the inherent laws of society.

In discussing the functions of the state, Spencer is concerned with what the state should not do, rather than what it should do. Maintenance of order and administration of justice are the only two proper realms of government activity, and their purpose is "simply to defend the natural rights of man—to protect person and property." The state has no business to promote religion, regulate trade and commerce, encourage colonization, aid the poor, or enforce sanitary laws. Spencer went even so far as to deny the state the right to wage war; but, as he says in his *Autobiography*, his "youthful enthusiasm of two-and twenty" had carried him too far in this respect.

Spencer's next major publication was *Social Statics* (1851). In it he repeats the catalogue of functions the state should not exercise, and he adds the two novel proposals that the state abstain from regulating the currency and that it drop the postal business. Both functions could be carried on more efficiently, Spencer holds, by private competitive enterprise. Like Bentham, Spencer considers the greatest happiness of the greatest number as the ultimate standard of measuring conflicting social policies. Unlike Bentham, who was willing to use the machinery of Parliament and administration for the active promotion of reform and improvement, Spencer firmly believes that active interference with the natural laws of society would do much harm and little good.

Spencer introduced the concept of *evolution* into his political and social speculations and held that the same basic law of growth and evolution pervaded the physical, animal, and human worlds. The *advance from the simple to the complex* is the cardinal principle that Spencer sees exemplified in the origin and development of the earth, its flora and fauna, and, finally, in the evolution of human society. Progress consists essentially in the "transformation of the homogeneous into the heterogeneous." Because it pervades all nature, animate and inanimate, progress is, therefore, "not an accident, but a necessity."

Translating the newly developing concepts of biology into social-science terms, Spencer defines evil as the result of the "non-adaptation of constitution to conditions." The shrub that dwindles in poor soil or dies when removed to a cold climate is no different, in principle, from the suffering of man who is incapable of adapting himself to his environment by means of the faculties he possesses: "Pervading all nature we must see at work a stern discipline, which is a little cruel that it may be very kind." The aged and weak animal is rightly killed by some beast of prey, and such death creates three kinds of happiness: the old animal is spared the suffering of slow and painful starvation, the younger generation can enjoy itself more fully by ridding itself of the burdensome old, and the beasts of prey derive happiness from their activity of killing off the weak and infirm animals. The happiness of humanity is "secured by that same beneficent, though severe discipline, to which the animate creation at large is subject: a discipline which is pitiless in the working out of good: a felicity-pursuing law which never swerves for the avoidance of partial and temporary suffering."

Spencer warns against interference with suffering for sentimental reasons because it distorts the operation of social laws even more grievously. Nature remedies incompetence and ignorance by "inconvenience, suffering, and death." If such penalties seem harsh, Spencer suggests that in reality they produce happiness, because society as a whole benefits from the elimination of the unfit, and the "survival of the fittest" (a phrase coined by Spencer and adopted by Darwin) ensures a constant improvement of the quality of the human race. To relax or suspend the stern discipline of nature slows the progress of society toward the stage in which it will be composed only of those who are well adjusted to their environment, in which the over-all equilibrium between man and his surroundings will be one of static repose. Those who are ill-adapted to their conditions of existence are on trial: "If they are sufficiently complete to live, they *do* live, and it is well they should live. If they are not sufficiently complete to live, they die, and it is best they should die."

Viewing the nature of the state in evolutionary terms, Spencer is little interested in forms of government, such as the traditional distinctions of monarchies, aristocracies, and democracies. The two main forms of state and society, according to Spencer, are the *military state* and the *industrial state*. The military state is the early form of social organization, primitive, barbarian, and geared to permanent readiness for war. The individual is no more than a means to an end set by the state: victory in war. Society is rigidly organized, and every individual occupies the place assigned to him by the exigencies of militarism and authoritarian government. *Status* is the characteristic principle of the military society, and there is little mobility between classes and groups. Spencer defines the military state as one in which "the army is the nation mobilized while the nation is the quiescent army."

Showing unusual foresight long before total war was a reality, Spencer understood the impact of war on society as a whole; although his analysis of the military state refers to an early stage of society, it anticipates with remarkable accuracy the developments of the twentieth century. In the military state, Spencer says, the military chief is likely to be the political leader, and he keenly perceived the inner relations between militarism and despotism. Chauvinism, nationalism, and imperialism are the ideological inspiration of the military state, and the task of its ecclesiastical body is to teach obedience and discipline as primary civic virtues. The economic activities of the industrial classes are subordinated to the military needs of the state, and the purpose of the economy is not to increase personal happiness through greater material welfare but to enhance collective power through successful conquests. There is considerable cooperation in a military state, but it is enforced and involuntary. Because the security of the state is the primary objective of all public action, there is little room for individual liberty, unorthodoxy, or experimentation.

As the military state expands its territory and achieves peace and stability over a long period of time, it gradually evolves into the industrial type of state and society. The latter is in every respect the opposite of the military state. *Contract* rather than status determines the position of the individual in society, as well as his opportunity to move upward or downward. The way of life in the industrial state and society is based on voluntary cooperation, and the tendency is toward the gradual elimination of coercion in all its forms. Spontaneity, diversity, variety, and nonconformity characterize the industrial society with its emphasis on the value of the individual as the supreme end of government. The purpose of the industrial society is to assure the maximum liberty and happiness of its members, whereas the purpose of the military society is to increase its power by rigid regimentation at home and imperialist conquest abroad. In relation to other nations, the industrial society is pacific, eager to exchange the products of labor rather than to acquire wealth by force. Members of the industrial society are therefore antimilitarist, anti-imperialist, cosmopolitan, and humanitarian. Free trade within and between nations is the formula of the industrial society, whereas economic nationalism is the ideal of the military state.

The progress from the military to the industrial society meant for Spencer a simultaneous progressive diminution of government, because government is no more than "proof of still-existing barbarism." The more men learn to cooperate on a peaceful, voluntary, nonexploiting basis, the closer they approximate the ideal of the industrial state and the less they need government, which will eventually wither away. Spencer did not see that modern industrialism itself produced a new kind of predatory ruthlessness, and that the individual can be reduced to the status of a means rather than an end, regardless of whether the idol that devours him is Glory or Wealth. Spencer failed to see in nineteenth-century capitalism the robber-baron type, whose primary virtue was ruthless militancy rather than peaceful cooperation.

Yet when Spencer's idealization of industrialism is allowed for, his insight into the fundamental difference between the military and industrial state is of lasting importance. Around 1900, when the world seemed to be moving in the

direction of expanding world trade and free government, when even the traditional military despotisms of Russia and Germany made their bows to constitutional government, Spencer's distinction between the military and the industrial
state may have appeared little more than an interesting historical hypothesis,
inspired by old-fashioned liberalism. In the second half of the twentieth century,
Spencer's basic distinction throws a great deal of light on the political behavior
of states. The intimate relation between the internal structure of the state and
its foreign aims and policies has been amply demonstrated in this century by
the aggressive wars waged by totalitarian military states against free nations.
Where the production of wealth has been the predominant objective of a nation,
its record as a member of the world community has, on the whole, been less aggressive and rapacious than that of nations whose internal organization has been
thoroughly militarized and regimented for the attainment of power and glory.

Spencer's hypothesis about the nature of the state has therefore little to do
with the controversy of capitalism versus socialism. The basic issue is not, as
Spencer thought, who owns the means of production, but what their social purpose is: more wealth and happiness for the individual members of society (the
ideal of both democratic capitalism and socialism) or greater power of the state
through conquest and expansion (the objective of both fascist capitalism and
totalitarian communism). Spencer thought that private enterprise without interference from the state is the best guarantee of internal and international peace,
and he saw in socialism a return to the preindustrial type of military society. He
did not distinguish between democratic socialism and revolutionary, totalitarian
communism, but used the two concepts interchangeably.

In 1884 Spencer published four essays in the *Contemporary Review,* subsequently assembled in book form under the title, *The Man versus the State.* It
is his most famous work on politics and still the most influential statement of the
philosophy of irreconcilable laissez faire. In the first essay, "The New Tories,"
Spencer attacks the English Liberals for abandoning their historical individualism in favor of social reform and the welfare state. According to Spencer,
English Conservatives, like conservatives generally, are the historical descendants of the principles of militancy and status, whereas the English Liberals, like
liberals generally, stem from industrialism and contract. Spencer also noticed
that economic individualism, abandoned by Liberals, was more and more adopted
by Conservatives, so that the roles of both parties came to be the opposite of
what they had originally been. Spencer thus foresaw that the British Conservatives would become the party of economic individualism and free enterprise,
whereas the Liberals would increasingly accept public control of the economy.

The second essay of *The Man versus the State* is "The Coming Slavery."
In it, Spencer reiterates his belief that the laws of society must not be interfered with by artificial political measures, that it is both futile and harmful to
interfere with the beneficent process of the survival of the fittest, and that interference with natural selection lowers the standards of society as a whole. Spencer
specifically states that all human suffering ought not to be prevented, because
"much of the suffering is curative, and prevention of it is prevention of a remedy."
Spencer stresses the tendency of officialdom and official regulations to increase

in a geometrical ratio to the power of resistance of the regulated citizens. People get more and more accustomed to the idea that the state will take care of them, and thus they lose the spirit of initiative and enterprise. The growth of popular suffrage represents a danger, according to Spencer, inasmuch as the various parties, in order to capture the popular vote, find they have to outbid each other in promises of more social welfare.

Spencer predicted that social-welfare programs would eventually lead to socialization of the means of production, and "all socialism is slavery." Spencer defines a slave as a person who "labors under coercion to satisfy another's desires." Under socialism or communism the individual would be enslaved to the whole community rather than to a particular master, and "it matters not whether his master is a single person or a society." Spencer says that the existence of democratic government would not prevent the despotic character of socialism, and he maintains that officialism will always work differently from the way it may be intended to work. The concentration of great economic power in the hands of the bureaucracy would inevitably lead to political despotism.

Spencer's basic objection to socialism is his feeling that institutional changes cannot abolish the difficulties created by the nature of man, and he attacks the view that "by due skill an ill-working humanity may be framed into well-working institutions. It is a delusion. The defective natures of citizens will show themselves in the bad acting of whatever social structure they are arranged into. There is no political alchemy by which you can get golden conduct out of leaden instincts."

In his third essay, "The Sins of Legislators," Spencer deplores the spread of government activity in social and economic areas. Progress is the result of the desire to "increase personal welfare," and not the product of governmental regulation: "It is not to the State that we owe the multitudinous useful inventions from the spade to the telephone; it was not the State which made possible extended navigation by a developed astronomy; it was not the State which made the discoveries in physics, chemistry, and the rest, which guide modern manufacturers; it was not the State which devised the machinery for producing fabrics of every kind, for transferring men and things from place to place, and for ministering in a thousand ways to our comforts."

Legislators must understand the laws of society before they meddle with them, and Spencer particularly charges legislators with confusing *family ethics* with *state ethics*. In the family, generosity is the guiding principle, and benefits received have little or no relation to merit. In the state, Spencer maintains, the ruling principle ought to be justice, according to which there is a proportioning of benefits to merits, "as throughout the animal world." The intrusion of family ethics into state ethics is a dangerous interference with the laws of nature and society, and is slowly followed by "fatal results." The poverty of the incapable, the sufferings of the imprudent, and the shoulderings aside of the weak by the strong are the decrees of a farseeing benevolence, and Spencer sees his doctrine of society confirmed by Darwin's principle of "natural selection." He defines government as "begotten of aggression and by aggression," and he writes that it continually betrays its aggressive nature, even if it apparently seeks to mitigate suffering, because in the end such relief of suffering is cruelty rather than kindness: "For is it not cruel to increase the sufferings of the better that the sufferings of the worse may be decreased?"

The last essay of *The Man versus the State* is "The Great Political Superstition." In the past, Spencer says, the great political superstition was the divine right of kings. In the present it is the "divine right of parliaments." Spencer attacks the doctrine of sovereignty as propounded by Hobbes and rejects the claim of popular majorities for unlimited authority as being inconsistent with the inalienable rights of the individual. Spencer also rejects the Benthamite doctrine that *individual rights* are created by the state and reverts to the Lockean notion that they *precede the state*. In particular, Spencer emphasizes that "property was well recognized before law existed." The state does not create rights but merely formally sanctions and better defines "those assertions of claims and recognitions of claims which naturally originate from the individual desires of men who have to live in presence of one another." Far from being created by the state, rights stand in inverse relation to it. As the state grows, status and slavery grow with it. The recognition of rights begins when "militancy ceases to be chronic and governmental power declines."

Spencer concludes *The Man versus the State* with the final reminder that government is not a divine institution but a committee of management, and that it has no intrinsic authority beyond the ethical sanction bestowed on it by the free consent of the citizens: "The function of Liberalism in the past was that of putting a limit to the powers of kings. The function of true Liberalism in the future will be that of putting a limit to the powers of parliaments."

Spencer's political ideas hardly changed between 1842, when he published his *Proper Sphere of Government,* and 1903, the year of his death. The constancy of his political thought in the face of a rapidly changing social and economic scene explains why the same ideas that were the last word in radical individualism in the eighteen-forties had become the *ne plus ultra* of orthodox conservatism by 1900. Although Spencer's influence declined in England, it steadily grew in the United States. Just as John Locke dominated American political thought in the eighteenth century by supplying the rationale of government based on consent, Spencer dominated American social philosophy of the latter part of the nineteenth century by supplying the rationale of laissez faire.

The period was one of tremendous industrial expansion in the United States, and Spencer's ideas of laissez faire and the survival of the fittest by natural selection appealed to businessmen and industrial entrepreneurs who themselves had gone through the hard school of ruthless competition, in which no quarter was asked or given. Spencer supplied businessmen with the comforting thought that the survival of the fittest was not only a principle of political or economic conservatism but a universal law that pervaded nature as well as human society. By linking economic laissez faire with progress, Spencer assured the wealthy classes that competitive capitalism was not only in harmony with universal laws but was also in the interest of the general welfare. Business found in Spencer's biological and scientific system a substitute for the lost religious inspiration, and Spencerism became a total view of life rather than a mere social or political theory. With the aid of Spencerism, opposition to social reform appeared no longer as class egotism but as the defense of the true principles of social evolution and progress.

When Spencer visited the United States in 1882, he was immensely impressed by its industrial power, and in his *Autobiography* he records his conviction that "the United States will very soon be by far the most powerful nation in the world." One of Spencer's closest American friends was Andrew Carnegie, the steel magnate, and during his triumphal tour of the country Spencer saw many other successful businessmen and leaders of conservative thought. Yet the restlessness and strain of American life perturbed him, and before he departed for England he declared that the future "has in store a new ideal, differing as much from the present ideal of industrialization as that ideal differs from the past ideal of militancy." His earlier dream that industrialism was the utopia now gave way to the dawning realization that the human cost of industrialism was perhaps higher than he had thought.

Spencerism died as a vitalizing philosophy in the United States after the turn of the century, just as it had died in England a generation earlier. Going first through the experience of the Industrial Revolution, England early showed the reactions to industrialism as a way of life, and popular protest increasingly mounted against the human misery and degradation that industrialism produced together with greater happiness and welfare. Spencerism was a mood that fitted the early phase of ruthless, competitive capitalism of the robber baron type. As soon as that phase had passed in England and, later, in the United States, as soon as the naïve belief in free enterprise as a law of nature was replaced by critical inquiry into its operation as a man-made system, Spencerism lost its vitality and appeal. Yet, though the extreme positions of Spencer's laissez faire were abandoned, much of his thought had imperceptibly permeated the world of liberal capitalism. As long as pecuniary incentives, competition, and individualism are hailed as positive social values, some elements of Spencerism will continue to survive, albeit Spencer's philosophical system as a whole may have outlived its usefulness.

Spencer's appeal to the English Liberals to return to their original individualism remained unheeded, and he correctly foresaw that the Conservatives would become the defenders of economic individualism. In that paradoxical change of parts the Liberals remained the heirs of their tradition of liberty despite their acceptance of more government, and the Conservatives embraced the doctrine of economic liberalism and laissez faire when this doctrine became the socially more conservative one. Spencer failed to see that the issue of more versus less state intervention in economic affairs was essentially one of means and not of objectives, and that laissez faire could be progressive, dynamic, and revolutionary at one time (say, in the eighteenth or early nineteenth century), and conservative, stagnant, and sterile at another time (as in the late nineteenth or twentieth century). The decline of the prestige of economic individualism and laissez faire was not due to anticapitalist propaganda but to the changing economic facts in the last hundred years.

One of the main assumptions of laissez faire was that of harmony and equilibrium: if all individuals pursued their own good, they would thereby, in the end, also promote the general good. The assumption of economic harmony out of competition was later buttressed by the wider generalization, popularized by Spencer and Darwin, that the whole universe was ruled by the law of the survival of the fittest, and that natural selection was not only a theory of evolution but of progress. Interference with the economic activities of individuals by public bodies appeared, in the light of Spencerism, economically unsound as well as an outright obstruction of morals and progress.

The assumptions of laissez faire rested on two unstated social conditions: first, a distribution of wealth and income that, while by no means equal, nevertheless was equitable enough to prevent a widespread sense of acute injustice; second, an economy that was comparatively free from long and severe crises and depressions. As long as both of these conditions existed to a substantial degree, the doctrine of economic individualism was anchored in a substratum of fact from which it could derive nourishment and life. But as capitalism expanded and grew, it undermined the two social conditions on which the acceptance of laissez faire by the public largely rested: the originally substantial equality of wealth and income was increasingly replaced by concentration of capital and—even more significantly—control of business. Monopolies, trusts, and gigantic enterprises created a sense of frustration and protest among the millions whose livelihood and very lives depended on their new masters—the impersonal corporation. As Tocqueville had predicted, the "new aristocracy of manufacturers" was as anxious to exploit the people as the old aristocracy had been, without, however, feeling the same kind of social responsibility toward those who worked for them. The second major change that undermined the general faith in the validity of laissez faire was unemployment. When millions remained out of work for years, when productive resources lay idle, men began to doubt that the economy, left to its own laws and harmonies, actually produced the maximum general good.

Capitalism originally developed as an affirmation of individual rights against the power of the state. As corporate and, later, monopolistic business created vast power aggregates within the structure of capitalism, the threatened individual turned to the state for the protection of his rights against the power of impersonal, bureaucratic entities, in the face of which he felt lost and helpless. True liberalism, from Locke to the present, had always insisted that the state was no more and no less than an instrument of the people: but where eighteenth-century liberalism differed from twentieth-century liberalism was in the belief of the former that once the dominion of the state was removed, the problem of power as such was solved forever. The state would then, in fact, "wither away," and its place would be taken by society as an association of equals, without rulers or ruled. By contrast, liberals of the late nineteenth and twentieth centuries have learned that economic power can impinge as directly on the lives and liberties of the people as political power has done in the past.

Liberals found themselves therefore in the paradoxical position of looking to the state—their historical enemy—for help against the new forms of economic and financial power. In Britain the "People's Budget" of Lloyd George in 1909 introduced large-scale social legislation reflecting the changed outlook of the Liberal party. This new philosophy influenced also the Conservative and Labor parties and set a standard for subsequent social reforms. In the United States there is a direct line from Theodore Roosevelt's Square Deal through Woodrow Wilson's New Freedom to Franklin Delano Roosevelt's New Deal.

All these movements in Britain and the United States have three things in common: first, the belief that every human being is entitled to a minimum of material well-being, such as food, clothing, and decent housing; second, the conviction that expanding living standards are possible with the existing physical resources and scientific knowledge; and, third, the acceptance of the principle that the state has the right and duty to act when private initiative fails. In the twentieth century the expansion of democracy in government through universal suffrage and education has made it possible to use the state in a way that would have been psychologically impossible for eighteenth-century liberals, who knew only government that was undemocratic, and often corrupt and inefficient. For a long time the new liberalism acted more in response to pragmatic needs than to a clearly formulated political theory. Some liberals themselves thought that the acceptance of more public responsibility for social well-being was no more than a temporary lapse from the timeless creed of laissez faire, which described the "normal" conditions of society, whereas reform through parliamentary legislation and public administration was exceptional and "abnormal." The *separation of politics and economics* was one of the most serious legacies of the period of laissez faire, and until they could be reunited, liberalism was bound to continue in a state of doctrinal frustration and *ad hoc* improvisation.

Just as England produced, owing to her peculiar historical circumstances, the most characteristic representative of nineteenth-century economic individualism and laissez faire, Herbert Spencer, she also provided, in response to changing economic conditions, a new approach to political economy and liberalism, most significantly expressed in the work of John Maynard Keynes (1883–1946). Keynes' father was a distinguished economist and philosopher, and his mother was mayor of Cambridge. Keynes was well grounded in mathematics and classics before he entered Cambridge University, where he specialized in philosophy and economics. At the age of twenty-three he passed the Civil Service examination as the second-best candidate. He would have been first, but his worst mark was in economics, though Keynes himself was of the opinion that "the examiners presumably knew less than I did." Keynes worked for two years in the India Office and then returned to Cambridge. During his entire life, his main interests lay in public service, on the one hand, and in teaching economics at Cambridge and editing the *Economic Journal,* on the other. At the Paris Peace Conference in 1919, Keynes was the principal representative of the British Treasury. He resigned because he disagreed with the reparations policy of the Allied Powers, and he wrote a short book, *The Economic Consequences of the Peace* (1919), which made him at once world-famous.

In the years between World Wars I and II, Keynes concentrated on his scholarly activities at Cambridge but did not lose touch with practical affairs. In addition to his heavy duties of writing, editing, and teaching, Keynes found time to serve as chairman of a major insurance company, run an investment company, take an important part in the furthering of the arts, organize a distinguished ballet, and build a new theater. Starting out with no means of his own, he amassed a considerable fortune, most of which he used for the endowment of the arts in Great Britain. During World War II, he served again in the Treasury, and as the war proceeded, he became the chief architect of Britain's long-term financial plans and policies. He rendered his last service to his country by negotiating the American Loan in 1945 and 1946, and he was one of the principal authors of the two new agencies for international monetary and economic cooperation, the International Monetary Fund, and the International Bank for Reconstruction and Development. During World War II, Keynes enthusiastically supported the movement to bring the arts to the people; he became chairman of the Council for the Encouragement of Music and the Arts, and later of the Arts Council. He married a famous dancer, a star member of the former Russian Imperial Ballet. In 1942, Keynes was given a peerage, and some of his speeches in the House of Lords, particularly on the American Loan, made history.

Politically, Keynes never ceased to be a Liberal, although he knew by the middle twenties that the Liberal party would never again be in a position to form a government. In a speech in 1926 (at the Manchester Reform Club, February 9, 1926), Keynes described his political credo as follows: "The political problem of mankind is to combine three things: Economic Efficiency, Social Justice, and Individual Liberty. The first needs criticism, precaution, and technical knowledge; the second an unselfish and enthusiastic spirit which loves the ordinary man; the third, tolerance, breadth, appreciation of the excellencies of variety and independence, which prefers, above everything, to give unhindered opportunity to the exceptional and to the aspiring. The second ingredient is the best possession of the great party of the Proletariat. But the first and third require the qualities of the party which, by its traditions and ancient sympathies, has been the home of Economic Individualism and Social Liberty."

In *The End of Laissez-Faire* (1926; reproduced here in its entirety), Keynes clearly indicated where the new liberalism differed from the old. The very title of his book, *The End of Laissez-Faire*, suggested that Keynes considered the philosophy of laissez faire a thing of the past. He demonstrates the historical and philosophical roots of economic individualism and laissez faire, and traces their long hold on thought and action to their "conformity with the needs and wishes of the business world of the day. They gave full scope to our erstwhile heroes, the great business men." The faith in laissez faire vanished together with the faith in the Captain of Industry, the Master-Individualist, and we "grow more doubtful whether it is he who will lead us into Paradise by the hand."

Yet the rejection of laissez faire did not lead Keynes to accept socialism as an alternative, primarily because socialism seemed to him to be committed to another dogma: that of state control and operation of the economy, just as laissez faire was committed to the dogma of no state interference in the economy. Keynes distinguishes services that are *technically social* from those that are *technically individual*. The state should not meddle in activities that are already performed by individuals, though it could perform them a little better, but do only those things that at present are not done at all. Keynes cites three areas in which government responsibility is desirable: the deliberate control of credit and currency by a central institution; the determination of the scale of savings and investment for the community as a whole; and, last, the formulation of a public policy on the problem of population.

These three areas do not exhaust the list of government responsibilities in economic affairs but indicate the direction in which Keynes' thought was moving. Rejecting the cash nexus and the pecuniary motive as proper foundations of civilized society, Keynes nevertheless came to the conclusion that capitalism, "wisely managed, can probably be made more efficient for attaining economic ends than any alternative system yet in sight, but that in itself it is in many ways extremely objectionable. Our problem is to work out a social organization which shall be as efficient as possible without offending our notions of a satisfactory way of life."

Only three years after publication of *The End of Laissez-Faire* the world was engulfed by an economic crisis, the Great Depression. Perhaps the most serious breakdown of economic life in the last century, it was resolved only by the coming of war in 1939. In 1936 Keynes published his most important contribution to political economy, *The General Theory of Employment, Interest, and Money*. It quickly established itself as a pioneering work in its field, in a class with Adam Smith's *Wealth of Nations* and Karl Marx' *Capital*. The *Wealth of Nations* supplied the thesis of capitalism, *Capital* its antithesis, and the *General Theory* the synthesis, transcending its predecessors in a new approach in which private and public initiative and responsibility merged in the conception of a free society without want.

The classical economists started out with the assumption of full employment and concentrated their analysis on problems of value with regard to the different factors of production. Keynes revolutionized this tradition by making the problem of *full employment* the central issue of economic theory and policy. Since Keynes, the idea has been abandoned, both in doctrine and policy, that full employment is to be expected from the working of automatic economic laws tending to establish by themselves a satisfactory equilibrium, and the conception has been accepted instead that full employment is the result of a deliberate public policy.

The outstanding fault of capitalist society is, according to Keynes, "its failure to provide for full employment and its arbitrary and inequitable distribution of wealth and income." In contemporary conditions, Keynes argues, "the growth of wealth, so far from being dependent on the abstinence of the rich, as is commonly supposed, is more likely to be impeded by it." Yet Keynes by no means opposes economic inequality as such; he holds that "it is better that a man should tyrannize over his bank balance than over his fellow-citizens; and whilst the former is sometimes denounced as being but a means to the latter, sometimes at least it is an alternative." The barbarism and cruelty of totalitarian despotism taught Keynes that political tyranny is generally worse than economic inequality.

Looking beyond the range of government activity as outlined in *The End of Laissez-Faire*, Keynes maintains in his *General Theory* that in principle only experience can show how far the state should go in ensuring full employment by stimulating investment and by increasing the effective purchasing power of the consumers. Specifically, Keynes believes that the state will have to exercise a guiding influence on the scale of consumption through taxation and other means of distributing the national income. In the field of investment, Keynes holds that the traditional methods of relying solely on private initiative have failed, and that "socialization of investment will prove the only means of securing an approximation to full employment."

Beyond this, Keynes sees no necessity for state socialism, and he envisages an economy that, once the goals of investment are set by public policy, will remain essentially in the hands of private enterprise. Keynes considers decentralization and the play of self-interest the two greatest advantages of private enterprise, which is also more efficient than public ownership and operation of the means of production. Far from regarding his proposals for increased government activity in economic affairs, particularly the *socialization of investment,* as the first step in the destruction of capitalism and its replacement by socialism, Keynes is convinced that his conception of a new liberal policy provides the only practicable means of avoiding the total destruction of economic individualism, and of preserving the conditions of the successful functioning of individual enterprise and initiative.

Keynes' impact was immediate in doctrine and policy. In Britain it was soon recognized by all parties that chronic unemployment, so characteristic of the interwar years, must never be allowed again, and during World War II all parties formally committed themselves to policies aiming at full employment. In the United States the New Deal was strongly influenced by the doctrines of Keynes, and President Roosevelt, who personally discussed economic problems with Keynes, was in general sympathy with Keynesian ideas.

Democratic socialists are in agreement with Keynes as far as he goes, yet criticize him for not going far enough. Keynes' policies will cure some of the symptoms, democratic socialists believe, but not the causes of instability and unemployment under capitalism. Marxists have seen in Keynes a typical bourgeois political economist, because his reliance on the state as an impartial agency, promoting the general good, runs counter to one of the fundamental doctrines of Marxism: that the capitalist state is no more than the executive committee of the capitalist class. The capitalist state can therefore, according to Marxists, be no more devoted to the general welfare than can capitalists themselves. By contrast, Keynes' reliance on the state assumes that in a democratic society the public interest can be approximately ascertained through processes of rational inquiry and discussion, and that the state ought, and is able, to formulate public policies that serve the community rather than one particular class or group.

Thus the ultimate assumption of Keynes' new liberalism rests on the same optimistic, rationalist faith that the old liberalism did, and both share with the philosophy of democracy the conviction that men can manage their affairs of government and society by applying thought and intelligence.

I. SPENCER

Laissez Faire

1. The Survival of the Fittest *

Pervading all nature we may see at work a stern discipline, which is a little cruel that it may be very kind. That state of universal warfare maintained throughout the lower creation, to the great perplexity of many worthy people, is at bottom the most merciful provision which the circumstances admit of. It is much better that the ruminant animal, when deprived by age of the vigour which made its existence a pleasure, should be killed by some beast of prey, than that it should linger out a life made painful by infirmities, and eventually die of starvation. By the destruction of all such, not only is existence ended before it becomes burdensome, but room is made for a younger generation capable of the fullest enjoyment; and, moreover, out of the very act of substitution happiness is derived for a tribe of predatory creatures. Note further, that their carnivorous enemies not only remove from herbivorous herds individuals past their prime, but also weed out the sickly, the malformed, and the least fleet or powerful. By the aid of which purifying process, as well as by the fighting, so universal in the pairing season, all vitiation of the race through the multiplication of its inferior samples is prevented; and the maintenance of a constitution completely adapted to surrounding conditions, and therefore most productive of happiness, is ensured.

The development of the higher creation is a progress towards a form of being capable of a happiness undiminished by these drawbacks. It is in the human race that the consummation is to be accomplished. Civilization is the last stage of its accomplishment. And the ideal man is the man in whom all the conditions of that accomplishment are fulfilled. Meanwhile the well-being of existing humanity, and the unfolding of it into this ultimate perfection, are both secured by that same beneficent, though severe discipline, to which the animate creation at large is subject: a discipline which is pitiless in the working out of good: a felicity-pursuing law which never swerves for the avoidance of partial and temporary suffering. The poverty of the incapable, the distresses that come upon the imprudent, the starvation of the idle, and those shoulderings aside of the weak by the strong, which leave so many "in shallows and in miseries," are the decrees of a large, far-seeing benevolence. It seems hard that an unskilfulness which with all his efforts he cannot overcome, should entail hunger upon the artizan. It seems hard that a labourer incapacitated by sickness from competing with his stronger fellows, should have to bear the resulting privations. It seems hard that widows and orphans should be left to struggle for life or death. Nevertheless, when regarded not separately, but in connection with the interests of universal humanity, these harsh fatalities are seen to be full of the highest beneficence—the same beneficence which brings to early graves the children of diseased parents, and singles

---

* From Herbert Spencer, *Social Statics* (1851).

out the low-spirited, the intemperate, and the debilitated as the victims of an epidemic.

There are many very amiable people—people over whom in so far as their feelings are concerned we may fitly rejoice—who have not the nerve to look this matter fairly in the face. Disabled as they are by their sympathies with present suffering, from duly regarding ultimate consequences, they pursue a course which is very injudicious, and in the end even cruel. We do not consider it true kindness in a mother to gratify her child with sweetmeats that are certain to make it ill. We should think it a very foolish sort of benevolence which led a surgeon to let his patient's disease progress to a fatal issue, rather than inflict pain by an operation. Similarly, we must call those spurious philanthropists, who, to prevent present misery, would entail greater misery upon future generations. All defenders of a poor-law must, however, be classed amongst such. That rigorous necessity which, when allowed to act on them, becomes so sharp a spur to the lazy, and so strong a bridle to the random, these paupers' friends would repeal, because of the wailings it here and there produces. Blind to the fact, that under the natural order of things society is constantly excreting its unhealthy, imbecile, slow, vacillating, faithless members, these unthinking, though well-meaning, men advocate an interference which not only stops the purifying process, but even increases the vitiation—absolutely encourages the multiplication of the reckless and incompetent by offering them an unfailing provision, and *dis*courages the multiplication of the competent and provident by heightening the prospective difficulty of maintaining a family. And thus, in their eagerness to prevent the really salutary sufferings that surround us, these sigh-wise and groan-foolish people bequeath to posterity a continually increasing curse.

Returning again to the highest point of view, we find that there is a second and still more injurious mode in which law-enforced charity checks the process of adaptation. To become fit for the social state, man has not only to lose his savageness, but he has to acquire the capacities needful for civilized life. Power of application must be developed; such modification of the intellect as shall qualify it for its new tasks must take place; and, above all, there must be gained the ability to sacrifice a small immediate gratification for a future great one. The state of transition will of course be an unhappy state. Misery inevitably results from incongruity between constitution and conditions. All these evils, which afflict us, and seem to the uninitiated the obvious consequences of this or that removable cause, are unavoidable attendants on the adaptation now in progress. Humanity is being pressed against the inexorable necessities of its new position—is being moulded into harmony with them, and has to bear the resulting unhappiness as best it can. The process *must* be undergone, and the sufferings *must* be endured. No power on earth, no cunningly-devised laws of statesmen, no world-rectifying schemes of the humane, no communist panaceas, no reforms that men ever did broach or ever will broach, can diminish them one jot. Intensified they may be, and are; and in preventing their intensification, the philanthropic will find ample scope for exertion. But there is bound up with the change a *normal* amount of suffering, which cannot be lessened without altering the very laws of life. Every attempt at mitigation of this eventuates in exacerbation of it. All that a poor-law, or any kindred institution can do, is to partially suspend the transition—to take off for awhile, from certain members of society, the painful pressure which is effecting their transformation. At best this is merely to postpone what must ultimately be borne. But it is more than this: it is to undo what has already been done. For the circumstances to which adaptation is taking place cannot be superseded without causing a retrogression—a partial loss of the adaptation previously effected; and as the whole process must some time or other be passed through, the lost ground must be gone over again, and the attendant pain borne afresh. Thus, besides retarding adaptation, a poor-law adds to the distresses inevitably attending it.

At first sight these considerations seem conclusive against *all* relief to the poor—voluntary as well as compulsory; and it is no doubt true that they imply a condemnation of whatever private charity enables the recipients to elude the necessities of our social existence. With this condemnation, however, no rational man will quarrel. That careless squandering of pence which has fostered into perfection a system of organized begging—which has made skilful mendicancy more profitable than ordinary manual labour—which induces the simulation of palsy, epilepsy, cholera, and no end of diseases and deformities—which has called into existence warehouses for the sale and hire of impostor's dresses—which has given to pity-inspiring babes a market value of 9 d. per day— the unthinking benevolence which has generated all this, cannot but be disapproved by every one. Now it is only against this injudicious charity that the foregoing argument tells. To that charity which may be described as helping men to help themselves, it makes no objection—countenances it rather. And in helping men to help themselves, there remains abundant scope for the exercise of a people's sympathies. Accidents will still supply victims on whom generosity may be legitimately expended. Men thrown upon their backs by unforeseen events, men who have failed for want of knowledge inaccessible to them, men ruined by the dishonesty of others, and men in whom hope long delayed has made the heart sick, may, with advantage to all parties, be assisted. Even the prodigal, after severe hardship has branded his memory with the unbending conditions of social life to which he must submit, may properly have another trial afforded him. And, although by these ameliorations the process of adaptation must be remotely interfered with, yet in the majority of cases, it will not be so much retarded in one

direction as it will be advanced in another.

Objectionable as we find a poor-law to be, even under the supposition that it does what it is intended to do—diminish present suffering—how shall we regard it on finding that in reality it does no such thing—cannot do any such thing? Yet, paradoxical as the assertion looks, this is absolutely the fact. Let but the observer cease to contemplate so fixedly one side of the phenomenon—pauperism and its relief, and begin to examine the other side—rates and the *ultimate* contributors of them, and he will discover that to suppose the sum-total of distress diminishable by act-of-parliament bounty is a delusion. A statement of the case in terms of labour and produce will quickly make this clear.

Here, at any specified period, is a given quantity of food and things exchangable for food, in the hands or at the command of the middle and upper classes. A certain portion of this food is needed by these classes themselves, and is consumed by them at the same rate, or very near it, be there scarcity or abundance. Whatever variation occurs in the sum-total of food and its equivalents must therefore affect the remaining portion, not used by these classes for personal sustenance. This remaining portion is given by them to the people in return for their labour, which is partly expended in the production of a further supply of necessaries, and partly in the production of luxuries. Hence, by how much this portion is deficient, by so much must the people come short. Manifestly a re-distribution by legislative or other agency cannot make that sufficient for them which was previously insufficient. It can do nothing but change the parties by whom the insufficiency is felt. If it gives enough to some who else would not have enough, it must inevitably reduce certain others to the condition of not having enough. And thus, to the extent that a poor-law mitigates distress in one place, it unavoidably produces distress in another.

Should there be any to whom this abstract reasoning is unsatisfactory, a concrete statement of the case will, perhaps, remove their doubts. A poors'-rate collector takes from the citizen a sum of money equivalent to bread and clothing for one or more paupers. Had not this sum been so taken, it would either have been used to purchase superfluities, which the citizen now does without, or it would have been paid by him into a bank, and lent by the banker to a manufacturer, merchant, or tradesman; that is, it would ultimately have been given in wages either to the producer of the superfluities or to an operative, paid out of the banker's loan. But this sum having been carried off as poors'-rate, whoever would have received it as wages must now to that extent go without wages. The food which it represented having been taken to sustain a pauper, the artisan to whom that food would have been given in return for work done, must now lack food. And thus, as at first said, the transaction is simply a change of the parties by whom the insufficiency of food is felt.

Nay, the case is even worse. Already it has been pointed out, that by suspending the process of adaptation, a poor-law increases the distress to be borne at some future day; and here we shall find that it also increases the distress to be borne now. For be it remembered, that of the sum taken in any year to support paupers, a large portion would otherwise have gone to support labourers employed in new reproductive works—land-drainage, machine-building, etc. An additional stock of commodities would by-and-by have been produced, and the number of those who go short would consequently have been diminished. Thus the astonishment expressed by some that so much misery should exist, notwithstanding the distribution of fifteen millions a year by endowed charities, benevolent societies, and poor-law unions, is quite uncalled for; seeing that the larger the sum gratuitously administered, the more intense will shortly become the suffering. Manifestly, out of a given population, the greater the number living on the bounty of others, the smaller must be the number living by labour; and

the smaller the number living by labour, the smaller must be the production of food and other necessaries; and the smaller the production of necessaries, the greater must be the distress.

We find, then, that the verdict given by the law of state-duty against a public provision for the indigent is enforced by sundry independent considerations. A critical analysis of the alleged rights, for upholding which a poor-law is defended, shows them to be fictitious. Nor does the plea that a poor-law is a means of distributing compensation for wrongs done to the disinherited people turn out to be valid. The assumption that only by law-administered relief can physical destitution be met, proves to be quite analogous to the assumption that spiritual destitution necessitates a law-administered religion; and consistency requires those who assert the sufficiency of voluntary effort in the one case to assert it in the other also. The substitution of a mechanical charity for charity prompted by the heart is manifestly unfavourable to the growth of men's sympathies, and therefore adverse to the process of adaptation. Legal bounty further retards adaptation by interposing between the people and the conditions to which they must become adapted, so as partially to suspend those conditions. And, to crown all, we find, not only that a poor-law must necessarily fail to diminish popular suffering, but that it must inevitably increase that suffering, both directly by checking the production of commodities, and indirectly by causing a retrogression of character, which painful discipline must at some future day make good.

2. The Coming Slavery *

The kinship of pity to love is shown among other ways in this, that it idealizes its object. Sympathy with one in suffering

* Contemporary Review, XLV (April, 1884). Reprinted in Herbert Spencer, The Man versus the State (1884).

suppresses, for the time being, remembrance of his trangressions. The feeling which vents itself in "poor fellow!" on seeing one in agony, excludes the thought of "bad fellow," which might at another time arise. Naturally, then, if the wretched are unknown or but vaguely known, all the demerits they may have are ignored; and thus it happens that when, as just now, the miseries of the poor are depicted, they are thought of as the miseries of the deserving poor, instead of being thought of, as in large measure they should be, as the miseries of the undeserving poor. Those whose hardships are set forth in pamphlets and proclaimed in sermons and speeches which echo throughout society, are assumed to be all worthy souls, grievously wronged; and none of them are thought of as bearing the penalties of their own misdeeds.

On hailing a cab in a London street, it is surprising how generally the door is officiously opened by one who expects to get something for his trouble. The surprise lessens after counting the many loungers about tavern-doors, or after observing the quickness with which a street-performance, or procession, draws from neighbouring slums and stable-yards a group of idlers. Seeing how numerous they are in every small area, it becomes manifest that tens of thousands of such swarm through London. "They have no work," you say. Say rather that they either refuse work or quickly turn themselves out of it. They are simply good-for-nothings, who in one way or other live on the good-for-somethings—vagrants and sots, criminals and those on the way to crime, youths who are burdens on hard-worked parents, men who appropriate the wages of their wives, fellows who share the gains of prostitutes; and then, less visible and less numerous, there is a corresponding class of women.

Is it natural that happiness should be the lot of such? or is it natural that they should bring unhappiness on themselves and those connected with them? Is it not manifest that there must exist in our midst an immense amount of misery which is a nor-mal result of misconduct, and ought not to be dissociated from it? There is a notion, always more or less prevalent and just now vociferously expressed, that all social suffering is removable, and that it is the duty of somebody or other to remove it. Both these beliefs are false. To separate pain from ill-doing is to fight against the constitution of things, and will be followed by far more pain. Saving men from the natural penalties of dissolute living, eventually necessitates the infliction of artificial penalties in solitary cells, on tread-wheels, and by the lash. I suppose a dictum, on which the current creed and the creed of science are at one, may be considered to have as high an authority as can be found. Well, the command "if any would not work neither should he eat," is simply a Christian enunciation of that universal law of Nature under which life has reached its present height—the law that a creature not energetic enough to maintain itself must die: the sole difference being that the law which in the one case is to be artificially enforced, is, in the other case, a natural necessity. And yet this particular tenet of their religion which science so manifestly justifies, is the one which Christians seem least inclined to accept. The current assumption is that there should be no suffering, and that society is to blame for that which exists.

"But surely we are not without responsibilities, even when the suffering is that of the unworthy?"

If the meaning of the word "we" be so expanded as to include with ourselves our ancestors, and especially our ancestral legislators, I agree. I admit that those who made, and modified, and administered, the old Poor Law, were responsible for producing an appalling amount of demoralization, which it will take more than one generation to remove. I admit, too, the partial responsibility of recent and present lawmakers for regulations which have brought into being a permanent body of tramps, who ramble from union to union; and also their responsibility for maintaining a constant supply of felons by sending back convicts into society under such conditions that they are almost compelled again to commit crimes. Moreover, I admit that the philanthropic are not without their share of responsibility; since, that they may aid the offspring of the unworthy, they disadvantage the offspring of the worthy through burdening their parents by increased local rates. Nay, I even admit that these swarms of good-for-nothings, fostered and multiplied by public and private agencies, have, by sundry mischievous meddlings, been made to suffer more than they would otherwise have suffered. Are these the responsibilities meant? I suspect not.

But now, leaving the question of responsibilities, however conceived, and considering only the evil itself, what shall we say of its treatment? Let me begin with a fact.

A late uncle of mine, the Rev. Thomas Spencer, for some twenty years incumbent of Hinton Charterhouse, near Bath, no sooner entered on his parish duties than he proved himself anxious for the welfare of the poor, by establishing a school, a library, a clothing club, and land-allotments, besides building some model cottages. Moreover, up to 1833 he was a pauper's friend —always for the pauper against the overseer.

There presently came, however, the debates on the Poor Law, which impressed him with the evils of the system then in force. Though an ardent philanthropist he was not a timid sentimentalist. The result was that, immediately the new Poor Law was passed, he proceeded to carry out its provisions in his parish. Almost universal opposition was encountered by him: not the poor only being his opponents, but even the farmers on whom came the burden of heavy poor-rates. For, strange to say, their interests had become apparently identified with the maintenance of this system which taxed them so largely. The explanation is that there had grown up the practice of paying out of the rates a part of the wages of each farm-servant—"make-wages," as the

sum was called. And though the farmers contributed most of the fund from which "make-wages" were paid, yet, since all other ratepayers contributed, the farmers seemed to gain by the arrangement. My uncle, however, not easily deterred, faced all this opposition and enforced the law. The result was that in two years the rates were reduced from £700 a year to £200 a year; while the condition of the parish was greatly improved. "Those who had hitherto loitered at the corners of the streets, or at the doors of the beer-shops, had something else to do, and one after another they obtained employment"; so that out of a population of 800, only 15 had to be sent as incapable paupers to the Bath Union (when that was formed), in place of the 100 who received out-door relief a short time before. If it be said that the £25 telescope which, a few years after, his parishioners presented to my uncle, marked only the gratitude of the ratepayers; then my reply is the fact that when, some years later still, having killed himself by overwork in pursuit of popular welfare, he was taken to Hinton to be buried, the procession which followed him to the grave included not the well-to-do only but the poor.

Several motives have prompted this brief narrative. One is the wish to prove that sympathy with the people and self-sacrificing efforts on their behalf, do not necessarily imply approval of gratuitous aids. Another is the desire to show that benefit may result, not from multiplication of artificial appliances to mitigate distress, but, contrariwise, from diminution of them. And a further purpose I have in view is that of preparing the way for an analogy.

Under another form and in a different sphere, we are now yearly extending a system which is identical in nature with the system of "make-wages" under the old Poor Law. Little as politicians recognize the fact, it is nevertheless demonstrable that these various public appliances for working-class comfort, which they are supplying at the cost of ratepayers, are intrinsically of the same nature as those which, in past times, treated the farmer's man as half-labourer and half-pauper. In either case the worker receives in return for what he does, money wherewith to buy certain of the things he wants; while, to procure the rest of them for him, money is furnished out of a common fund raised by taxes. What matters it whether the things supplied by ratepayers for nothing, instead of by the employer in payment, are of this kind or that kind? the principle is the same. For sums received let us substitute the commodities and benefits purchased; and then see how the matter stands. In old Poor-Law times, the farmer gave for work done the equivalent, say of house-rent, bread, clothes, and fire; while the ratepayers practically supplied the man and his family with their shoes, tea, sugar, candles, a little bacon, &c. The division is, of course, arbitrary; but unquestionably the farmer and the ratepayers furnished these things between them. At the present time the artisan receives from his employer in wages, the equivalent of the consumable commodities he wants; while from the public comes satisfaction for others of his needs and desires. At the cost of ratepayers he has in some cases, and will presently have in more, a house at less than its commercial value; for of course when, as in Liverpool, a municipality spends nearly £200,000 in pulling down and reconstructing low-class dwellings, and is about to spend as much again, the implication is that in some way the ratepayers supply the poor with more accommodation than the rents they pay would otherwise have brought. The artisan further receives from them, in schooling for his children, much more than he pays for; and there is every probability that he will presently receive it from them gratis. The ratepayers also satisfy what desire he may have for books and newspapers, and comfortable places to read them in. In some cases too, as in Manchester, gymnasia for his children of both sexes, as well as recreation grounds, are provided. That is to say, he obtains from a fund raised by local taxes, certain benefits beyond those which the sum received for

his labour enables him to purchase. The sole difference, then, between this system and the old system of "make-wages," is between the kinds of satisfactions obtained; and this difference does not in the least affect the nature of the arrangement.

Moreover, the two are pervaded by substantially the same illusion. In the one case, as in the other, what looks like a gratis benefit is not a gratis benefit. The amount which, under the old Poor Law, the half-pauperized labourer received from the parish to eke out his weekly income, was not really, as it appeared, a bonus; for it was accompanied by a substantially-equivalent decrease of his wages, as was quickly proved when the system was abolished and the wages rose. Just so is it with these seeming boons received by working people in towns. I do not refer only to the fact that they unawares pay in part through the raised rents of their dwellings (when they are not actual ratepayers), but I refer to the fact the wages received by them are, like the wages of the farm-labourer, diminished by these public burdens falling on employers. Read the accounts coming of late from Lancashire concerning the cotton-strike, containing proofs, given by artisans themselves, that the margin of profit is so narrow that the less skilful manufacturers, as well as those with deficient capital, fail, and that the companies of co-operators who compete with them can rarely hold their own; and then consider what is the implication respecting wages. Among the costs of production have to be reckoned taxes, general and local. If, as in our large towns, the local rates now amount to one-third of the rental or more—if the employer has to pay this, not on his private dwelling only, but on his business-premises, factories, warehouses, or the like; it results that the interest on his capital must be diminished by that amount, or the amount must be taken from the wages-fund, or partly one and partly the other. And if competition among capitalists in the same business, and in other businesses, has the effect of so keeping down interest that while some gain, others lose, and not a few are ruined—if capital, not getting adequate interest, flows elsewhere and leaves labour unemployed; then it is manifest that the choice for the artisan under such conditions, lies between diminished amount of work or diminished rate of payment for it. Moreover, for kindred reasons these local burdens raise the costs of the things he consumes. The charges made by distributors, too, are, on the average, determined by the current rates of interest on capital used in distributing businesses; and the extra costs of carrying on such businesses have to be paid for by extra prices. So that as in the past the rural worker lost in one way what he gained in another, so in the present does the urban worker: there being, too, in both cases, the loss entailed on him by the cost of administration and the waste accompanying it.

"But what has all this to do with 'the coming slavery'?" will perhaps be asked. Nothing directly, but a good deal indirectly, as we shall see after yet another preliminary section.

It is said that when railways were first opened in Spain, peasants standing on the tracks were not unfrequently run over; and that the blame fell on the engine-drivers for not stopping: rural experiences having yielded no conception of the momentum of a large mass moving at a high velocity.

The incident is recalled to me on contemplating the ideas of the so-called "practical" politician, into whose mind there enters no thought of such a thing as political momentum, still less of a political momentum which, instead of diminishing or remaining constant, increases. The theory on which he daily proceeds is that the change caused by his measure will stop where he intends it to stop. He contemplates intently the things his act will achieve, but thinks little of the remoter issues of the movement his act sets up, and still less its collateral issues. When, in war-time, "food for powder" was to be provided by encouraging population— when Mr. Pitt said, "Let us make relief in cases where there are a number of children

a matter of right and honour, instead of a ground for opprobrium and contempt;" [1] it was not expected that the poor-rates would be quadrupled in fifty years, that women with many bastards would be preferred as wives to modest women, because of their incomes from the parish, and that hosts of ratepayers would be pulled down into the ranks of pauperism. Legislators who in 1833 voted £20,000 a year to aid in building school-houses, never supposed that the step they then took would lead to forced contributions, local and general, now amounting to £6,000,000; [2] they did not intend to establish the principle that A should be made responsible for educating B's offspring; they did not dream of a compulsion which should deprive poor widows of the help of their elder children; and still less did they dream that their successors, by requiring impoverished parents to apply to Boards of Guardians to pay the fees which School Boards would not remit, would initiate a habit of applying to Boards of Guardians and so cause pauperization. Neither did those who in 1834 passed an Act regulating the labour of women and children in certain factories, imagine that the system they were beginning would end in the restriction and inspection of labour in all kinds of producing establishments where more than fifty people are employed; nor did they conceive that the inspection provided would grow to the extent of requiring that before a "young person" is employed in a factory, authority must be given by a certifying surgeon, who, by personal examination (to which no limit is placed) has satisfied himself that there is no incapacitating disease or bodily infirmity: his verdict determining whether the "young person" shall earn wages or not. Even less, as I say, does the politician who plumes himself on the practicalness of his aims, conceive the indirect results that will follow the direct results of his measures. Thus, to take a case connected with one named above, it was not intended through the system of

[1] Hansard's *Parliamentary History*, 32, p. 710.
[2] *Fortnightly Review*, January, 1884, p. 17.

"payment by results," to do anything more than give teachers an efficient stimulus: it was not supposed that in numerous cases their health would give way under the stimulus; it was not expected that they would be led to adopt a cramming system and to put undue pressure on dull and weak children, often to their great injury; it was not foreseen that in many cases a bodily enfeeblement would be caused which no amount of grammar and geography can compensate for. The licensing of public-houses was simply for maintaining public order: those who devised it never imagined that there would result an organized interest powerfully influencing elections in an unwholesome way. Nor did it occur to the "practical" politicians who provided a compulsory load-line for merchant vessels, that the pressure of ship-owners' interests would habitually cause the putting of the load-line at the very highest limit, and that from precedent to precedent, tending over in the same direction, the load-line would gradually rise in the better class of ships; as from good authority I learn that it has already done. Legislators who, some forty years ago, by Act of Parliament compelled railway-companies to supply cheap locomotion, would have ridiculed the belief, had it been expressed, that eventually their Act would punish the companies which improved the supply; and yet this was the result to companies which began to carry third-class passengers by fast trains, since a penalty to the amount of the passenger-duty was inflicted on them for every third-class passenger so carried. To which instance concerning railways, add a far more striking one disclosed by comparing the railway policies of England and France. The law-makers who provided for the ultimate lapsing of French railways to the State, never conceived the possibility that inferior travelling facilities would result—did not foresee that reluctance to depreciate the value of property eventually coming to the State, would negative the authorization of competing lines, and that in the absence of competing lines locomotion would be relatively costly, slow, and infrequent; for, as Sir Thomas Farrer has shown, the traveller in England has great advantages over the French traveller in the economy, swiftness, and frequency with which his journeys can be made.

But the "practical" politician who, in spite of such experiences repeated generation after generation, goes on thinking only of proximate results, naturally never thinks of results still more remote, still more general, and still more important than those just exemplified. To repeat the metaphor used above—he never asks whether the political momentum set up by his measure, in some cases decreasing but in other cases greatly increasing, will or will not have the same general direction with other such momenta; and whether it may not join them in presently producing an aggregate energy working changes never thought of. Dwelling only on the effects of his particular stream of legislation, and not observing how such other streams already existing, and still other streams which will follow his initiative, pursue the same average course, it never occurs to him that they may presently unite into a voluminous flood utterly changing the face of things. Or to leave figures for a more literal statement, he is unconscious of the truth that he is helping to form a certain type of social organization, and that kindred measures, effecting kindred changes of organization, tend with ever-increasing force to make that type general; until, passing a certain point, the proclivity towards it becomes irresistible. Just as each society aims when possible to produce in other societies a structure akin to its own—just as among the Greeks, the Spartans and the Athenians struggled to spread their respective political institutions, or as, at the time of the French Revolution, the European absolute monarchies aimed to re-establish absolute monarchy in France while the Republic encouraged the formation of other republics; so within every society, each species of structure tends to propagate itself. Just as the system of voluntary co-operation by companies, associations, unions, to achieve business ends and other ends, spreads throughout a community; so does the antagonistic system of compulsory co-operation under State-agencies spread; and the larger becomes its extension the more power of spreading it gets. The question of questions for the politician should ever be—"What type of social structure am I tending to produce?" But this is a question he never entertains.

Here we will entertain it for him. Let us now observe the general course of recent changes, with the accompanying current of ideas, and see whither they are carrying us.

The blank form of a question daily asked is—"We have already done this; why should we not do that?" And the regard for precedent suggested by it, is ever pushing on regulative legislation. Having had brought within their sphere of operation more and more numerous businesses, the Acts restricting hours of employment and dictating the treatment of workers are now to be made applicable to shops. From inspecting lodging-houses to limit the numbers of occupants and enforce sanitary conditions, we have passed to inspecting all houses below a certain rent in which there are members of more than one family, and are now passing to a kindred inspection of all small houses. The buying and working of telegraphs by the State is made a reason for urging that the State should buy and work the railways. Supplying children with food for their minds by public agency is being followed in some cases by supplying food for their bodies; and after the practice has been made gradually more general, we may anticipate that the supply, now proposed to be made gratis in the one case, will eventually be proposed to be made gratis in the other: the argument that good bodies as well as good minds are needful to make good citizens, being logically urged as a reason for the extension.[3] And then, avowedly proceeding on the precedents furnished by the church, the school, and the reading-room, all publicly provided, it is contended that "pleasure, in the sense it is now generally admitted, needs legislating for and organizing at least as much as work."[4]

Not precedent only prompts this spread, but also the necessity which arises for supplementing ineffective measures, and for dealing with the artificial evils continually caused. Failure does not destroy faith in the agencies employed, but merely suggests more stringent use of such agencies or wider ramifications of them. Laws to check intemperance, beginning in early times and coming down to our own times, when further restraints on the sale of intoxicating liquors occupy nights every session, not having done what was expected, there come demands for more thorough-going laws, locally preventing the sale altogether; and here, as in America, these will doubtless be followed by demands that prevention shall be made universal. All the many appliances for "stamping out" epidemic diseases not having succeeded in preventing outbreaks of smallpox, fevers, and the like, a further remedy is applied for in the shape of police-power to search houses for diseased persons, and authority for medical officers to examine any one they think fit, to see whether he or she is suffering from an infectious or contagious malady. Habits of improvidence having for generations been cultivated by the Poor-Law, and the improvident enabled to multiply, the evils produced by compulsory charity are now proposed to be met by compulsory insurance.

The extension of this policy, causing extension of corresponding ideas, fosters everywhere the tacit assumption that Government should step in whenever anything is

---

[3] Verification comes more promptly than I expected. This article has been standing in type since January 30, and in the interval, namely on March

13, the London School Board resolved to apply for authority to use local charitable funds for supplying gratis meals and clothing to indigent children. Presently the definition of "indigent" will be widened; more children will be included, and more funds asked for.

[4] *Fortnightly Review*, January, 1884, p. 21.

not going right. "Surely you would not have this misery continue!" exclaims some one, if you hint a demurrer to much that is now being said and done. Observe what is implied by this exclamation. It takes for granted, first, that all suffering ought to be prevented, which is not true: much suffering is curative, and prevention of it is prevention of a remedy. In the second place, it takes for granted that every evil can be removed: the truth being that, with the existing defects of human nature, many evils can only be thrust out of one place or form into another place or form—often being increased by the change. The exclamation also implies the unhesitating belief, here especially concerning us, that evils of all kinds should be dealt with by the State. There does not occur the inquiry whether there are at work other agencies capable of dealing with evils, and whether the evils in question may not be among those which are best dealt with by these other agencies. And obviously, the more numerous governmental interventions become, the more confirmed does this habit of thought grow, and the more loud and perpetual the demands for intervention.

Every extension of the regulative policy involves an addition to the regulative agents —a further growth of officialism and an increasing power of the organization formed of officials. Take a pair of scales with many shot in the one and a few in the other. Lift shot after shot out of the loaded scale and put it into the unloaded scale. Presently you will produce a balance; and if you go on, the position of the scales will be reversed. Suppose the beam to be unequally divided, and let the lightly loaded scale be at the end of a very long arm; then the transfer of each shot, producing a much greater effect, will far sooner bring about a change of position. I use the figure to illustrate what results from transferring one individual after another from the regulated mass of the community to the regulating structures. The transfer weakens the one and strengthens the other in a far greater degree than is implied by the relative change of num-

bers. A comparatively small body of officials, coherent, having common interests, and acting under central authority, has an immense advantage over an incoherent public which has no settled policy, and can be brought to act unitedly only under strong provocation. Hence an organization of officials, once passing a certain stage of growth, becomes less and less resistible; as we see in the bureaucracies of the Continent.

Not only does the power of resistance of the regulated part decrease in a geometrical ratio as the regulating part increases, but the private interests of many in the regulated part itself, make the change of ratio still more rapid. In every circle conversations show that now, when the passing of competitive examinations renders them eligible for the public service, youths are being educated in such ways that they may pass them and get employment under Government. One consequence is that men who might otherwise reprobate some further growth of officialism, are led to look on it with tolerance, if not favourably, as offering possible careers for those dependent on them and those related to them. Any one who remembers the numbers of upper-class and middle-class families anxious to place their children, will see that no small encouragement to the spread of legislative control is now coming from those who, but for the personal interests thus arising, would be hostile to it.

This pressing desire for careers is enforced by the preference for careers which are thought respectable. "Even if his salary is small, his occupation will be that of a gentleman," thinks the father, who wants to get a Government-clerkship for his son. And this relative dignity of State-servants as compared with those occupied in business increases as the administrative organization becomes a larger and more powerful element in society, and tends more and more to fix the standard of honour. The prevalent ambition with a young Frenchman is to get some small official post in his locality, to rise thence to a place in the local centre of government, and finally to reach some head-office in Paris. And in Russia, where that universality of State-regulation which characterizes the militant type of society has been carried furthest, we see this ambition pushed to its extreme. Says Mr. Wallace, quoting a passage from a play:—"All men, even shopkeepers and cobblers, aim at becoming officers, and the man who has passed his whole life without official rank seems to be not a human being." [5]

These various influences working from above downwards, meet with an increasing response of expectations and solicitations proceeding from below upwards. The hard-worked and over-burdened who form the great majority, and still more the incapables perpetually helped who are ever led to look for more help, are ready supporters of schemes which promise them this or the other benefit by State-agency, and ready believers of those who tell them that such benefits can be given, and ought to be given. They listen with eager faith to all builders of political air-castles, from Oxford graduates down to Irish irreconcilables; and every additional tax-supported appliance for their welfare raises hopes of further ones. Indeed, the more numerous public instrumentalities become, the more is there generated in citizens the notion that everything is to be done for them, and nothing by them. Each generation is made less familiar with the attainment of desired ends by individual actions or private combinations, and more familiar with the attainment of them by governmental agencies; until, eventually, governmental agencies come to be thought of as the only available agencies. This result was well shown in the recent Trades-Unions Congress at Paris. The English delegates, reporting to their constituents, said that between themselves and their foreign colleagues "the point of difference was the extent to which the State should be asked to protect labour"; reference being thus made to the fact, conspicuous in the reports of the proceedings, that the French delegates always invoked

governmental power as the only means of satisfying their wishes.

The diffusion of education has worked, and will work still more, in the same direction. "We must educate our masters," is the well-known saying of a Liberal who opposed the last extension of the franchise. Yes, if the education were worthy to be so called, and were relevant to the political enlightenment needed, much might be hoped from it. But knowing rules of syntax, being able to add up correctly, having geographical information, and a memory stocked with the dates of kings' accessions and generals' victories, no more implies fitness to form political conclusions than acquirement of skill in drawing implies expertness in telegraphing, or than ability to play cricket implies proficiency on the violin. "Surely," rejoins some one, "facility in reading opens the way to political knowledge." Doubtless; but will the way be followed? Table-talk proves that nine out of ten people read what amuses them or interests them rather than what instructs them; and that the last thing they read is something which tells them disagreeable truths or dispels groundless hopes. That popular education results in an extensive reading of publications which foster pleasant illusions rather than of those which insist on hard realities, is beyond question. Says "A Mechanic," writing in the *Pall Mall Gazette* of December 3, 1883:—

> Improved education instils the desire for culture—culture instils the desire for many things as yet quite beyond working men's reach . . . . in the furious competition to which the present age is given up they are utterly impossible to the poorer classes; hence they are discontented with things as they are, and the more educated the more discontented. Hence, too, Mr. Ruskin and Mr. Morris are regarded as true prophets by many of us.

And that the connection of cause and effect here alleged is a real one, we may see clearly enough in the present state of Germany. Being possessed of electoral power, as are

[5] *Russia*, i, 422.

now the mass of those who are thus led to nurture sanguine anticipations of benefits to be obtained by social reorganization, it results that whoever seeks their votes must at least refrain from exposing their mistaken beliefs, even if he does not yield to the temptation to express agreement with them. Every candidate for Parliament is prompted to propose or support some new piece of *ad captandum* legislation. Nay, even the chiefs of parties—these anxious to retain office and those to wrest it from them—severally aim to get adherents by outbidding one another. Each seeks popularity by promising more than his opponent has promised, as we have lately seen. And then, as divisions in Parliament show us, the traditional loyalty to leaders overrides questions concerning the intrinsic propriety of proposed measures. Representatives are unconscientious enough to vote for Bills which they regard as essentially wrong in principle, because party-needs and regard for the next election demand it. And thus a vicious policy is strengthened even by those who see its viciousness.

Meanwhile there goes on out-of-doors an active propaganda to which all these influences are ancillary. Communistic theories, partially indorsed by one Act of Parliament after another, and tacitly if not avowedly favoured by numerous public men seeking supporters, are being advocated more and more vociferously under one or other form by popular leaders, and urged on by organized societies. There is the movement for land-nationalization which, aiming at a system of land-tenure equitable in the abstract, is, as all the world knows, pressed by Mr. George and his friends with avowed disregard for the just claims of existing owners, and as the basis of a scheme going more than half-way to State-communism. And then there is the thorough-going Democratic Federation of Mr. Hyndman and his adherents. We are told by them that "the handful of marauders who now hold possession [of the land] have and can have no right save brute force against the tens of millions whom they wrong." They exclaim

against "the shareholders who have been allowed to lay hands upon (!) our great railway communications." They condemn "above all, the active capitalist class, the loan-mongers, the farmers, the mine exploiters, the contractors, the middlemen, the factory-lords—these, the modern slave drivers" who exact "more and yet more surplus value out of the wage-slaves whom they employ." And they think it "high time" that trade should be "removed from the control of individual greed." [6]

It remains to point out that the tendencies thus variously displayed, are being strengthened by press advocacy, daily more pronounced. Journalists, always chary of saying that which is distasteful to their readers, are some of them going with the stream and adding to its force. Legislative meddlings which they would once have condemned they now pass in silence, if they do not advocate them; and they speak of *laissez-faire* as an exploded doctrine. "People are no longer frightened at the thought of socialism," is the statement which meets us one day. On another day, a town which does not adopt the Free Libraries Act is sneered at as being alarmed by a measure so moderately communistic. And then, along with editorial assertions that this economic evolution is coming and must be accepted, there is prominence given to the contributions of its advocates. Meanwhile those who regard the recent course of legislation as disastrous, and see that its future course is likely to be still more disastrous, are being reduced to silence by the belief that it is useless to reason with people in a state of political intoxication.

See, then, the many concurrent causes which threaten continually to accelerate the transformation now going on. There is that spread of regulation caused by following precedents, which become the more authoritative the further the policy is carried. There is that increasing need for administrative compulsions and restraints, which results from the unforeseen evils and shortcomings

---

[6] *Socialism Made Plain*, Reeves, 185, Fleet Street.

of preceding compulsions and restraints. Moreover, every additional State-interference strengthens the tacit assumption that it is the duty of the State to deal with all evils and secure all benefits. Increasing power of a growing administrative organization is accompanied by decreasing power of the rest of the society to resist its further growth and control. The multiplication of careers opened by a developing bureaucracy, tempts members of the classes regulated by it to favour its extension, as adding to the chances of safe and respectable places for their relatives. The people at large, led to look on benefits received through public agencies as gratis benefits, have their hopes continually excited by the prospects of more. A spreading education, furthering the diffusion of pleasing errors rather than of stern truths, renders such hopes both stronger and more general. Worse still, such hopes are ministered to by candidates for public choice, to augment their chances of success; and leading statesmen, in pursuit of party ends, bid for popular favour by countenancing them. Getting repeated justifications from new laws harmonizing with their doctrines, political enthusiasts and unwise philanthropists push their agitations with growing confidence and success. Journalism, ever responsive to popular opinion, daily strengthens it by giving it voice; while counter-opinion, more and more discouraged, finds little utterance.

Thus influences of various kinds conspire to increase corporate action and decrease individual action. And the change is being on all sides aided by schemers, each of whom thinks only of his pet project and not at all of the general reorganization which his, joined with others such, are working out. It is said that the French Revolution devoured its own children. Here, an analogous castastrophe seems not unlikely. The numerous socialistic changes made by Act of Parliament, joined with the numerous others presently to be made, will by-and-by be all merged in State-socialism—swallowed in the vast wave which they have little by little raised.

"But why is this change described as 'the coming slavery'?" is a question which many will still ask. The reply is simple. All socialism involves slavery.

What is essential to the idea of a slave? We primarily think of him as one who is owned by another. To be more than nominal, however, the ownership must be shown by control of the slave's actions—a control which is habitually for the benefit of the controller. That which fundamentally distinguishes the slave is that he labours under coercion to satisfy another's desires. The relation admits of sundry gradations. Remembering that originally the slave is a prisoner whose life is at the mercy of his captor, it suffices here to note that there is a harsh form of slavery in which, treated as an animal, he has to expend his entire effort for his owner's advantage. Under a system less harsh, though occupied chiefly in working for his owner, he is allowed a short time in which to work for himself, and some ground on which to grow extra food. A further amelioration gives him power to sell the produce of his plot and keep the proceeds. Then we come to the still more moderated form which commonly arises where, having been a free man working on his own land, conquest turns him into what we distinguish as a serf; and he has to give to his owner each year a fixed amount of labour or produce, or both: retaining the rest himself. Finally, in some cases, as in Russia until recently, he is allowed to leave his owner's estate and work or trade for himself elsewhere, under the condition that he shall pay an annual sum. What is it which, in these cases, leads us to qualify our conception of the slavery as more or less severe? Evidently the greater or smaller extent to which effort is compulsorily expended for the benefit of another instead of for self-benefit. If all the slave's labour is for his owner the slavery is heavy, and if but little it is light. Take now a further step. Suppose an owner dies, and his estate with its slaves comes into the hands of trustees; or suppose the estate and everything on it to be bought by a company; is the condition of the slave any the better if the amount of his compulsory labour remains the same? Suppose that for a company we substitute the community; does it make any difference to the slave if the time he has to work for others is as great, and the time left for himself is as small, as before? The essential question is—How much is he compelled to labour for other benefit than his own, and how much can he labour for his own benefit? The degree of his slavery varies according to the ratio between that which he is forced to yield up and that which he is allowed to retain; and it matters not whether his master is a single person or a society. If, without option, he has to labour for the society, and receives from the general stock such portion as the society awards him, he becomes a slave to the society. Socialistic arrangements necessitate an enslavement of this kind; and towards such an enslavement many recent measures, and still more the measures advocated, are carrying us. Let us observe, first, their proximate effects, and then their ultimate effects.

The policy initiated by the Industrial Dwellings Acts admits of development, and will develop. Where municipal bodies turn house-builders, they inevitably lower the values of houses otherwise built, and check the supply of more. Every dictation respecting modes of building and conveniences to be provided, diminishes the builder's profit, and prompts him to use his capital where the profit is not thus diminished. So, too, the owner, already finding that small houses entail much labour and many losses—already subject to troubles of inspection and interference, and to consequent costs, and having his property daily rendered a more undesirable investment, is prompted to sell; and as buyers are for like reasons deterred, he has to sell at a loss. And now these still-multiplying regulations, ending, it may be, as Lord Grey proposes, in one requiring the owner to maintain the salubrity of his houses by evicting dirty tenants, and thus adding to his other responsibilities that of inspector of nuisances, must

further prompt sales and further deter purchasers—so necessitating greater depreciation. What must happen? The multiplication of houses, and especially small houses, being increasingly checked, there must come an increasing demand upon the local authority to make up for the deficient supply. More and more the municipal or kindred body will have to build houses, or to purchase houses rendered unsaleable to private persons in the way shown—houses which, greatly lowered in value as they must become, it will, in many cases, pay to buy rather than to build new ones. Nay, this process must work in a double way; since every entailed increase of local taxation still further depreciates property.[7] And then, when in towns this process has gone so far as to make the local authority the chief owner of houses, there will be a good precedent for publicly providing houses for the rural population, as proposed in the Radical programme,[8] and as urged by the Democratic Federation; which insists on "the compulsory construction of healthy artisans' and agricultural labourers' dwellings in proportion to the population." Manifestly, the tendency of that which has been done, is being done, and is presently to be done, is to approach the socialistic ideal in which the community is sole house-proprietor.

Such, too, must be the effect of the daily-

---

[7] If any one thinks such fears are groundless, let him contemplate the fact that from 1867–8 to 1880–1, our annual local expenditure for the United Kingdom has grown from £36,132,834 to £63,276,283; and that during the same 13 years, the municipal expenditure in England and Wales alone, has grown from 13 millions to 30 millions a year! How the increase of public burdens will join with other causes in bringing about public ownership, is shown by a statement made by Mr. W. Rathbone, M.P., to which my attention has been drawn since the above paragraph was in type. He says, "within my own experience, local taxation in New York has risen from 12s. 6d per cent. to £2 12s. 6d. per cent. on the capital of its citizens —a charge which would more than absorb the whole income of an average English landlord."— *Nineteenth Century*, February, 1883.

[8] *Fortnightly Review*, November, 1883, pp. 619–20.

growing policy on the tenure and utilization of the land. More numerous public benefits, to be achieved by more numerous public agencies, at the cost of augmented public burdens, must increasingly deduct from the returns on land; until, as the depreciation in value becomes greater and greater, the resistance to change of tenure becomes less and less. Already, as every one knows, there is in many places difficulty in obtaining tenants, even at greatly reduced rents; and the land of inferior fertility in some cases lies idle, or when farmed by the owner is often farmed at a loss. Clearly the margin of profit on capital invested in land is not such that taxes, local and general, can be greatly raised to support extended public administrations, without an absorption of it which will prompt owners to sell, and make the best of what reduced price they can get by emigrating and buying land not subject to heavy burdens; as, indeed, some are now doing. This process, carried far, must have the result of throwing inferior land out of cultivation; after which there will be raised more generally the demand made by Mr. Arch, who, addressing the Radical Association of Brighton lately, and, contending that existing landlords do not make their land adequately productive for the public benefit, said "he should like the present Government to pass a Compulsory Cultivation Bill": an applauded proposal which he justified by instancing compulsory vaccination (thus illustrating the influence of precedent). And this demand will be pressed, not only by the need for making the land productive, but also by the need for employing the rural population. After the Government has extended the practice of hiring the unemployed to work on deserted lands, or lands acquired at nominal prices, there will be reached a stage whence there is but a small further step to that arrangement which, in the programme of the Democratic Federation, is to follow nationalization of the land—the "organization of agricultural and industrial armies under State control on co-operative principles."

If any one doubts that such a revolution

may be so reached, facts may be cited showing its likelihood. In Gaul, during the decline of the Roman Empire, "so numerous were the receivers in comparison with the payers, and so enormous the weight of taxation, that the labourer broke down, the plains became deserts, and woods grew where the plough had been." [9] In like manner, when the French Revolution was approaching, the public burdens had become such, that many farms remained uncultivated and many were deserted: one-quarter of the soil was absolutely lying waste; and in some provinces one-half was in heath. Nor have we been without incidents of a kindred nature at home. Besides the facts that under the old Poor Law the rates had in some parishes risen to half the rental, and that in various places farms were lying uncultivated, there is the fact that in one case the rates had absorbed the whole proceeds of the soil.

At Cholesbury, in Buckinghamshire, in 1832, the poor rate "suddenly ceased in consequence of the impossibility to continue its collection, the landlords having given up their rents, the farmers their tenancies, and the clergyman his glebe and his tithes. The clergyman, Mr. Jeston, states that in October, 1832, the parish officers threw up their books, and the poor assembled in a body before his door while he was in bed, asking for advice and food. Partly from his own small means, partly from the charity of neighbours, and partly by rates in aid, imposed on the neighbouring parishes, they were for some time supported." [10]

And the Commissioners add that "the benevolent rector recommends that the whole of the land should be divided among the able-bodied paupers": hoping that after help afforded for two years they might be able to maintain themselves. These facts, giving colour to the prophecy made in Parliament that continuance of the old Poor

---

[9] Lactant. *De M. Persecut.*, cc. 7, 23.

[10] *Report of Commissioners for Inquiry into the Administration and Practical Operation of the Poor Laws*, p. 37. February 20, 1834.

Law for another thirty years would throw the land out of cultivation, clearly show that increase of public burdens may end in forced cultivation under public control.

Then, again, comes State-ownership of railways. Already this exists to a large extent on the Continent. Already we have had here a few years ago loud advocacy of it. And now the cry, which was raised by sundry politicians and publicists, is taken up afresh by the Democratic Federation, which proposes "State-appropriation of railways, with or without compensation." Evidently, pressure from above joined by pressure from below, is likely to effect this change dictated by the policy everywhere spreading; and with it must come many attendant changes. For railway-proprietors, at first owners and workers of railways only, have become masters of numerous businesses directly or indirectly connected with railways; and these will have to be purchased by Government when the railways are purchased. Already exclusive carrier of letters, exclusive transmitter of telegrams, and on the way to become exclusive carrier of parcels, the State will not only be exclusive carrier of passengers, goods, and minerals, but will add to its present various trades many other trades. Even now, besides erecting its naval and military establishments and building harbours, docks, breakwaters, &c., it does the work of shipbuilder, cannon-founder, small-arms maker, manufacturer of ammunition, army-clothier and boot-maker; and when the railways have been appropriated "with or without compensation," as the Democratic Federationists say, it will have to become locomotive-engine-builder, carriage-maker, tarpaulin and grease manufacturer, passenger-vessel owner, coal-miner, stone-quarrier, omnibus proprietor, &c. Meanwhile its local lieutenants, the municipal governments, already in may places suppliers of water, gas-makers, owners and workers of tramways, proprietors of baths, will doubtless have undertaken various other businesses. And when the State, directly or by proxy, has thus come into possession of, or has estab-lished, numerous concerns for wholesale production and for wholesale distribution, there will be good precedents for extending its function to retail distribution: following such an example, say, as is offered by the French Government, which has long been a retail tobacconist.

Evidently then, the changes made, the changes in progress, and the changes urged, are carrying us not only towards State-ownership of land and dwellings and means of communication, all to be administered and worked by State-agents, but towards State-usurpation of all industries; the private forms of which, disadvantaged more and more in competition with the State, which can arrange everything for its own convenience, will more and more die away; just as many voluntary schools have, in presence of Board-schools. And so will be brought about the desired ideal of the socialists.

And now when there has been reached this desired ideal, which "practical" politicians are helping socialists to reach, and which is so tempting on that bright side which socialists contemplate, what must be the accompanying shady side which they do not contemplate? It is a matter of common remark, often made when a marriage is impending, that those possessed by strong hopes habitually dwell on the promised pleasures and think nothing of the accompanying pains. A further exemplification of this truth is supplied by these political enthusiasts and fanatical revolutionists. Impressed with the miseries existing under our present social arrangements, and not regarding these miseries as caused by the ill-working of a human nature but partially adapted to the social state, they imagine them to be forthwith curable by this or that re-arrangement. Yet, even did their plans succeed it could only be by substituting one kind of evil for another. A little deliberate thought would show that under their proposed arrangements, their liberties must be surrendered in proportion as their material welfares were cared for.

For no form of co-operation, small or great, can be carried on without regulation, and an implied submission to the regulating agencies. Even one of their own organizations for effecting social changes yields the proof. It is compelled to have its councils, its local and general officers, its authoritative leaders, who must be obeyed under penalty of confusion and failure. And the experience of those who are loudest in their advocacy of a new social order under the paternal control of a Government, shows that even in private voluntarily-formed societies, the power of the regulative organization becomes great, if not irresistible: often, indeed, causing grumbling and restiveness among those controlled. Trades-unions which carry on a kind of industrial war in defence of workers' interests *versus* employers' interests, find that subordination almost military in its strictness is needful to secure efficient action; for divided councils prove fatal to success. And even in bodies of co-operators, formed for carrying on manufacturing or distributing businesses, and not needing that obedience to leaders which is required where the aims are offensive, it is still found that the administrative agency acquires so great a power that there arise complaints about "the tyranny of organization." Judge then what must happen when, instead of combinations small, local and voluntary, to which men may belong or not as they please, we have a national combination in which each citizen finds himself incorporated, and from which he cannot separate himself without leaving the country. Judge what must under such conditions become the power of a graduated and centralized officialism, holding in its hands the resources of the community, and having behind it whatever amount of force it finds requisite to carry out its decrees and maintain what it calls order. Well may a Prince Bismarck display leanings towards State-socialism.

And then after recognizing, as they must if they think out their scheme, the power possessed by the regulative agency in the new social system so temptingly pictured, let its advocates ask themselves to what end this power must be used. Not dwelling exclusively, as they habitually do, on the material well-being and the mental gratifications to be provided for them by a beneficent administration, let them dwell a little on the price to be paid. The officials cannot create the needful supplies: they can but distribute among individuals that which the individuals have joined to produce. If the public agency is required to provide for them, it must reciprocally require them to furnish the means. There cannot be, as under our existing system, agreement between employer and employed—this the scheme excludes. There must in place of it be command by local authorities over workers, and acceptance by the workers of that which the authorities assign to them. And this, indeed, is the arrangement distinctly, but as it would seem inadvertently, pointed to by the members of the Democratic Federation. For they propose that production should be carried on by "agricultural and industrial *armies* under State-control": apparently not remembering that armies presuppose grades of officers, by whom obedience would have to be insisted upon; since otherwise neither order nor efficient work could be ensured. So that each would stand toward the governing agency in the relation of slave to master.

"But the governing agency would be a master which he and others made and kept constantly in check; and one which therefore would not control him or others more than was needful for the benefit of each and all."

To which reply the first rejoinder is that, even if so, each member of the community as an individual would be a slave to the community as a whole. Such a relation has habitually existed in militant communities, even under quasi-popular forms of government. In ancient Greece the accepted principle was that the citizen belonged neither to himself nor to his family, but belonged to his city—the city being with the Greek equivalent to the community. And this doctrine, proper to a state of constant warfare, is a doctrine which socialism unawares reintroduces into a state intended to be purely industrial. The services of each will belong to the aggregate of all; and for these services, such returns will be given as the authorities think proper. So that even if the administration is of the beneficent kind intended to be secured, slavery, however mild, must be the outcome of the arrangement.

A second rejoinder is that the administration will presently become not of the intended kind, and that the slavery will not be mild. The socialist speculation is vitiated by an assumption like that which vitiates the speculations of the "practical" politician. It is assumed that officialism will work as it is intended to work, which it never does. The machinery of Communism, like existing social machinery, has to be framed out of existing human nature; and the defects of existing human nature will generate in the one the same evils as in the other. The love of power, the selfishness, the injustice, the untruthfulness, which often in comparatively short times bring private organizations to disaster, will inevitably, where their effects accumulate from generation to generation, work evils far greater and less remediable; since, vast and complex and possessed of all the resources, the administrative organization once developed and consolidated, must become irresistible. And if there needs proof that the periodic exercise of electoral power would fail to prevent this, it suffices to instance the French Government, which, purely popular in origin, and subject from time to time to popular judgment, nevertheless tramples on the freedom of citizens to an extent which the English delegates to the late Trades Unions Congress say "is a disgrace to, and an anomaly in, a Republican nation."

The final result would be a revival of despotism. A disciplined army of civil officials, like an army of military officials, gives supreme power to its head—a power which has often led to usurpation, as in mediæval Europe and still more in Japan—nay, has thus so led among our neighbours, within our own times. The recent confessions of M. de Maupas have shown how readily a constitutional head, elected and trusted by the whole people, may, with the aid of a few unscrupulous confederates, paralyze the representative body and make himself autocrat. That those who rose to power in a socialistic organization would not scruple to carry out their aims at all costs, we have good reason for concluding. When we find that shareholders who, sometimes gaining but often losing, have made that railway-system by which national prosperity has been so greatly increased, are spoken of by the council of the Democratic Federation as having "laid hands" on the means of communication, we may infer that those who directed a socialistic administration might interpret with extreme perversity the claims of individuals and classes under their control. And when, further, we find members of this same council urging that the State should take possession of the railways, "with or without compensation," we may suspect that the heads of the ideal society desired would be but little deterred by considerations of equity from pursuing whatever policy they thought needful: a policy which would always be one identified with their own supremacy. It would need but a war with an adjacent society, or some internal discontent demanding forcible suppression, to at once transform a socialistic administration into a grinding tyranny like that of ancient Peru; under which the mass of the people, controlled by grades of officials, and leading lives that were inspected out-of-doors and in-doors, laboured for the support of the organization which regulated them, and were left with but a bare subsistence for themselves. And then would be completely revived, under a different form, that *régime* of status—that system of compulsory co-operation, the decaying tradition of which is represented by the old Toryism, and towards which the new Toryism is carrying us back.

"But we shall be on our guard against all that—we shall take precautions to ward off such disasters," will doubtless say the enthusiasts. Be they "practical" politicians with their new regulative measures, or communists with their schemes for re-organizing labour, the answer is ever the same:— "It is true that plans of kindred nature have, from unforeseen causes and adverse accidents, or the misdeeds of those concerned, been brought to failure; but this time we shall profit by past experiences and succeed." There seems no getting people to accept the truth, which nevertheless is conspicuous enough, that the welfare of a society and the justice of its arrangements are at bottom dependent on the characters of its members; and that improvement in

neither can take place without that improvement in character which results from carrying on peaceful industry under the restraints imposed by an orderly social life. The belief, not only of the socialists but also of those so-called Liberals who are diligently preparing the way for them, is that by due skill an ill-working humanity may be framed into well-working institutions. It is a delusion. The defective natures of citizens will show themselves in the bad acting of whatever social structure they are arranged into. There is no political alchemy by which you can get golden conduct out of leaden instincts.

II. KEYNES

The End of Laissez Faire *

1. The Origins of Individualism

The disposition towards public affairs, which we conveniently sum up as Individualism and *laissez-faire,* drew its sustenance from many different rivulets of thought and springs of feeling. For more than a hundred years our philosophers ruled us, because, by a miracle, they nearly all agreed, or seemed to agree, on this one thing. We do not dance even yet to a new tune. But a change is in the air. We hear but indistinctly what were once the clearest and most distinguishable voices which have ever instructed political mankind. The orchestra of diverse instruments, the chorus of articulate sound, is receding at last into the distance.

* From John Maynard Keynes, *Laissez-Faire and Communism.* Copyright by New Republic, 1926. By permission.

At the end of the seventeenth century the divine right of monarchs gave place to Natural Liberty and to the Compact, and the divine right of the Church to the principle of Toleration, and to the view that a church is "a voluntary society of men," coming together, in a way which is "absolutely free and spontaneous." [1] Fifty years later the divine origin and absolute voice of duty gave place to the calculations of Utility. In the hands of Locke and Hume these doctrines founded Individualism. The Compact presumed rights in the individual; the new ethics, being no more than a scientific study of the consequences of rational self-love, placed the individual at the centre. "The sole trouble Virtue demands," said Hume, "is that of just Calculation, and a steady preference of the greater Happi-

[1] Locke, *A Letter Concerning Toleration.*

ness." [2] These ideas accorded with the practical notions of conservatives and of lawyers. They furnished a satisfactory intellectual foundation to the rights of property and to the liberty of the individual in possession to do what he liked with himself and with his own. This was one of the contributions of the eighteenth century to the air we still breathe.

The purpose of promoting the Individual was to depose the Monarch and the Church; the effect—through the new ethical significance attributed to Contract—was to buttress Property and Prescription. But it was not long before the claims of Society raised themselves anew against the individual. Paley and Bentham accepted utilitarian hedonism [3] from the hands of Hume and his predecessors, but enlarged it into social utility. Rousseau took the Social Contract from Locke and drew out of it the General Will. In each case the transition was made by virtue of the new emphasis laid on Equality. "Locke applies his Social Contract to modify the natural equality of mankind, so far as that phrase implies equality of property or even of privilege, in consideration of general security. In Rousseau's version equality is not only the starting-point but the goal." [4]

Paley and Bentham reached the same destination, but by different routes. Paley avoided an egoistic conclusion to his hedonism by a God from the machine. "Virtue," he says, "is the doing good to mankind, in obedience to the will of God, and for the sake of everlasting happiness"—in this way bringing back I and others to a parity. Ben-

tham reached the same result by pure reason. There is no rational ground, he argued, for preferring the happiness of one individual, even oneself, to that of any other. Hence the greatest happiness of the greatest number is the sole rational object of conduct—taking Utility from Hume, but forgetting that sage man's cynical corollary: " 'Tis not contrary to reason to prefer the destruction of the whole world to the scratching of my finger. 'Tis not contrary to reason for me to choose my total ruin to prevent the least uneasiness of an Indian, or person totally unknown to me. . . . Reason is and ought only to be the slave of the passions, and can never pretend to any other office than to serve and obey them."

Rousseau derived equality from the State of Nature, Paley from the Will of God, Bentham from a mathematical law of Indifference. Equality and altruism had thus entered political philosophy, and from Rousseau and Bentham in conjunction sprang both Democracy and Utilitarian Socialism.

This is the second current—sprung from long-dead controversies, and carried on its way by long-exploded sophistries—which still permeates our atmosphere of thought. But it did not drive out the former current. It mixed with it. The early nineteenth century performed the miraculous union. It harmonised the conservative individualism of Locke, Hume, Johnson, and Burke with the Socialism and democratic egalitarianism of Rousseau, Paley, Bentham, and Godwin. [5]

Nevertheless that age would have been hard put to it to achieve this harmony of opposites if it had not been for the *economists,* who sprang into prominence just at the right moment. The idea of a divine harmony between private advantage and the

---

[2] *An Enquiry Concerning the Principles of Morals,* section lx.

[3] "I omit," says Archdeacon Paley, "much usual declamation upon the dignity and capacity of our nature, the superiority of the soul to the body, of the rational to the animal part of our constitution; upon the worthiness, refinement, and delicacy of some satisfactions, and the meanness, grossness, and sensuality of others: because I hold that pleasures differ in nothing but in continuance and intensity."—*Principles of Moral and Political Philosophy,*—Bk. I, chap. 6.

[4] Leslie Stephen, *English Thought in the Eighteenth Century,* ii, 192.

[5] Godwin carried *laissez-faire* so far that he thought *all* government an evil, in which Bentham almost agreed with him. The doctrine of equality becomes with him one of extreme individualism, verging on anarchy. "The universal exercise of private judgment," he says, "is a doctrine so unspeakably beautiful that the true politician will certainly feel infinite reluctance in admitting the idea of interfering with it".—*Vide* Leslie Stephen, *op. cit.,* ii, 277.

public good is already apparent in Paley. But it was the economists who gave the notion a good scientific basis. Suppose that by the working of natural laws individuals pursuing their own interests with enlightenment in conditions of freedom always tend to promote the general interest at the same time! Our philosophical difficulties are resolved—at least for the practical man, who can then concentrate his efforts on securing the necessary conditions of freedom. To the philosophical doctrine that Government has no right to interfere, and the divine miracle that it has no need to interfere, there is added a scientific proof that its interference is inexpedient. This is the third current of thought, just discoverable in Adam Smith, who was ready in the main to allow the public good to rest on "the natural effort of every individual to better his own condition," but not fully and self-consciously developed until the nineteenth century begins. The principle of *laissez-faire* had arrived to harmonise Individualism and Socialism, and to make at one Hume's Egoism with the Greatest Good of the Greatest Number. The political philosopher could retire in favour of the business man—for the latter could attain the philosopher's *summum bonum* by just pursuing his own private profit.

Yet some other ingredients were needed to complete the pudding. First the corruption and incompetence of eighteenth-century government, many legacies of which survived into the nineteenth. The Individualism of the political philosophers pointed to *laissez-faire*. The divine or scientific harmony (as the case might be) between private interest and public advantage pointed to *laissez-faire*. But above all, the ineptitude of public administrators strongly prejudiced the practical man in favour of *laissez-faire*—a sentiment which has by no means disappeared. Almost everything which the State did in the eighteenth century in excess of its minimum functions was, or seemed, injurious or unsuccessful.

On the other hand, material progress be-

tween 1750 and 1850 came from individual initiative, and owed almost nothing to the directive influence of organised society as a whole. Thus practical experience reinforced *a priori* reasonings. The philosophers and the economists told us that for sundry deep reasons unfettered private enterprise would promote the greatest good of the whole. What could suit the business man better? And could a practical observer, looking about him, deny that the blessings of improvement which distinguished the age he lived in were traceable to the activities of individuals "on the make"? Thus the ground was fertile for a doctrine that, whether on divine, natural, or scientific grounds, State Action should be narrowly confined and economic life left, unregulated so far as may be, to the skill and good sense of individual citizens actuated by the admirable motive of trying to get on in the world.

By the time that the influence of Paley and his like was waning, the innovations of Darwin were shaking the foundations of belief. Nothing could seem more opposed than the old doctrine and the new—the doctrine which looked on the world as the work of the divine Watchmaker and the doctrine which seemed to draw all things out of Chance, Chaos, and Old Time. But at this one point the new ideas bolstered up the old. The economists were teaching that wealth, commerce, and machinery were the children of free competition—that free competition built London. But the Darwinians could go one better than that—free competition had built Man. The human eye was no longer the demonstration of Design, miraculously contriving all things for the best; it was the supreme achievement of Chance, operating under conditions of free competition and *laissez-faire*. The principle of the Survival of the Fittest could be regarded as a vast generalisation of the Ricardian economics. Socialistic interferences became, in the light of this grander synthesis, not merely inexpedient, but impious, as calculated to retard the onward movement of the mighty process by which we ourselves had risen like Aphrodite out of the primeval slime of Ocean.

Therefore I trace the peculiar unity of the everyday political philosophy of the nineteenth century to the success with which it harmonised diversified and warring schools and united all good things to a single end. Hume and Paley, Burke and Rousseau, Godwin and Malthus, Cobbett and Huskisson, Bentham and Coleridge, Darwin and the Bishop of Oxford, were all, it was discovered, preaching practically the same thing—Individualism and *laissez-faire*. This was the Church of England and those her apostles, whilst the company of the economists were there to prove that the least deviation into impiety involved financial ruin.

These reasons and this atmosphere are the explanations, whether we know it or not—and most of us in these degenerate days are largely ignorant in the matter— why we feel such a strong bias in favour of *laissez-faire*, and why State action to regulate the value of money, or the course of investment, or the population, provoke such passionate suspicions in many upright breasts. We have not read these authors; we should consider their arguments preposterous if they were to fall into our hands. Nevertheless we should not I fancy, think as we do, if Hobbes, Locke, Hume, Rousseau, Paley, Adam Smith, Bentham, and Miss Martineau had not thought and written as they did. A study of the history of opinion is a necessary preliminary to the emancipation of the mind. I do not know which makes a man more conservative—to know nothing but the present, or nothing but the past.

2. Laissez Faire and the Economists

I have said that it was the economists who furnished the scientific pretext by which the practical man could solve the contradiction between egoism and socialism which emerged out of the philosophising of the eighteenth century and the decay of revealed religion. But having said this for

shortness' sake, I hasten to qualify it. This is what the economists are *supposed* to have said. No such doctrine is really to be found in the writings of the greatest authorities. It is what the popularisers and the vulgarisers said. It is what the Utilitarians, who admitted Hume's egoism and Bentham's egalitarianism at the same time, were *driven* to believe in, if they were to effect a synthesis.[1] The language of the economists lent itself to the *laissez-faire* interpretation. But the popularity of the doctrine must be laid at the door of the political philosophers of the day, whom it happened to suit, rather than of the political economists.

The maxim *laissez-nous faire* is traditionally attributed to the merchant Legendre addressing Colbert sometime towards the end of the seventeenth century.[2] But there is no doubt that the first writer to use the phrase, and to use it in clear association with the doctrine, is the Marquis d'Argenson about 1751.[3] The Marquis was the first man to wax passionate on the economic advantages of Governments leaving trade alone. To govern better, he said, one must govern less.[4] The true cause of the decline of our manufactures, he declared, is the protection we have given to them.[5]

---

[1] One can sympathise with the view of Coleridge, as summarised by Leslie Stephen, that "the Utilitarians destroyed every element of cohesion, made Society a struggle of selfish interests, and struck at the very roots of all order, patriotism, poetry, and religion."

[2] "Que faut-il faire pour vous aider?" asked Colbert. "Nous laisser faire," answered Legendre.

[3] For the history of the phrase, *vide* Oncken, "Die Maxime Laissez-faire et laissez passer," from whom most of the following quotations are taken. The claims of the Marquis d'Argenson were overlooked until Oncken put them forward, partly because the relevant passages published during his lifetime were anonymous (*Journal Œconomique*, 1751), and partly because his works were not published in full (though probably passed privately from hand to hand during his lifetime) until 1858 (*Mémoires et Journal inédit du Marquis d'Argenson*).

[4] "Pour gouverner mieux, il faudrait gouverner moins."

[5] "On ne peut dire autant de nos fabriques: la vraie cause de leur declin, c'est la protection outrée qu'on leur accorde."

"Laissez faire, telle devrait être la devise de toute puissance publique, depuis que le monde est civilisé." "Detestable principe que celui de ne vouloir notre grandeur que par l'abaissement de nos voisons! Il n'y a que la méchanceté et la malignité du cœur de satisfaites dans ce principe, et l'intérêt y est opposé. Laissez faire, morbleu! Laissez faire!!"

Here we have the economic doctrine of *laissez-faire*, with its most fervent expression in Free Trade, fully clothed. The phrases and the idea must have passed current in Paris from that time on. But they were slow to establish themselves in Literature; and the tradition associating with them the Physiocrats, and particularly de Gournay and Quesnay, finds little support in the writings of this school, though they were, of course, proponents of the essential harmony of social and individual interests. The phrase *laissez-faire* is not to be found in the works of Adam Smith, of Ricardo, or of Malthus. Even the idea is not present in a dogmatic form in any of these authors. Adam Smith, of course, was a Free Trader and an opponent of many eighteenth-century restrictions on trade. But his attitude towards the Navigation Acts and the Usury laws shows that he was not dogmatic. Even his famous passage about "the invisible hand" reflects the philosophy which we associate with Paley rather than the economic dogma of *laissez-faire*. As Sidgwick and Cliff Leslie have pointed out, Adam Smith's advocacy of the "obvious and simple system of natural liberty" is derived from his theistic and optimistic view of the órder of the world, as set forth in his *Theory of Moral Sentiments*, rather than from any proposition of Political Economy proper.[6] The phrase *laissez-faire* was, I think, first brought into popular usage in England by a well-known passage of Dr Franklin's.[7] It is not, indeed, until we come to the later works of Bentham—who was not an econo-

mist at all—that we discover the rule of *laissez-faire*, in the shape in which our grandfathers knew it, adopted into the service of the Utilitarian philosophy. For example, in *A Manual of Political Economy*,[8] he writes: "The general rule is that nothing ought to be done or attempted by government; the motto or watchward of government, on these occasions, ought to be—*Be quiet*. . . . The request which agriculture, manufacturers, and commerce present to governments is as modest and reasonable as that which Diogenes made to Alexander: Stand out of my sunshine."

From this time on it was the political campaign for Free Trade, the influence of the so-called Manchester School and of the Benthamite Utilitarians, the utterances of secondary economic authorities, and the educational stories of Miss Martineau and Mrs Marcet, that fixed *laissez-faire* in the popular mind as the practical conclusion of orthodox Political Economy—with this great difference, that the Malthusian view of Population having been accepted in the meantime by this same school of thought, the optimistic *laissez-faire* of the last half of the eighteenth century gives place to the pessimistic *laissez-faire* of the first half of the nineteenth century.[9]

In Mrs Marcet's *Conversations on Political Economy* (1817) Caroline stands out as long as she can in favour of controlling the expenditure of the rich. But by page 418 she has to admit defeat:

Caroline.—The more I learn upon this subject, the more I feel convinced that the interests of nations, as well as those of individuals, so far from being op-

---

[6] Sidgwick, *Principles of Political Economy*, p. 20.

[7] Bentham uses the expression "*laissez-nous faire*," *Works*, p. 440.

[8] Written in 1793, a chapter published in the *Bibliothèque Britannique* in 1798, and the whole first printed in Bowring's edition of his *Works* (1843).

[9] *Cf.* Sidgwick (*op. cit.*, p. 22): "Even those economists, who adhered in the main to Adam Smith's limitations of the sphere of government, enforced these limitations sadly rather than triumphantly; not as admirers of the social order at present resulting from 'natural liberty,' but as convinced that it is at least preferable to any artificial order that government might be able to substitute for it."

posed to each other, are in the most perfect unison.

Mrs. B.—Liberal and enlarged views will always lead to similar conclusions, and teach us to cherish sentiments of universal benevolence towards each other; hence the superiority of science over mere practical knowledge.

By 1850 the *Easy Lessons for the Use of Young People,* by Archbishop Whately, which the Society for Promoting Christian Knowledge was distributing wholesale, do not admit even of those doubts which Mrs B. allowed Caroline occasionally to entertain.

More harm than good is likely to be done, the little books concludes,

by almost any interference of Government with men's money transactions, whether letting and leasing, or buying and selling of any kind.

True liberty is

that every man should be left free to dispose of his own property, his own time, and strength, and skill, in whatever way he himself may think fit, provided he does no wrong to his neighbours.

In short, the dogma had got hold of the educational machine; it had become a copybook maxim. The Political Philosophy, which the seventeenth and eighteenth centuries had forged in order to throw down Kings and Prelates, had been made milk for babes, and had literally entered the nursery.

Finally, in the works of Bastiat we reach the most extravagant and rhapsodical expression of the Political Economist's religion. In his *Harmonies Economiques,*

I undertake [he says] to demonstrate the Harmony of those laws of Providence which govern human society. What makes these laws harmonious and not discordant is, that all principles, all motives, all springs of action, all interests, co-operate towards a grand final result. . . . And that result is, the indefinite approximation of all classes towards a level, which is always rising; in other words, the *equalisa-*

tion of individuals in the general *amelioration.*

And when, like other priests, he drafts his Credo, it runs as follows:

I believe that He who has arranged the material universe has not withheld His regard from the arrangements of the social world. I believe that He has combined and caused to move in harmony free agents as well as inert molecules. . . . I believe that the invincible social tendency is a constant approximation of men towards a common moral, intellectual, and physical level, with, at the same time, a progressive and indefinite elevation of that level. I believe that all that is necessary to the gradual and peaceful development of humanity is that its tendencies should not be disturbed, nor have the liberty of their movements destroyed.

From the time of John Stuart Mill, economists of authority have been in strong reaction against all such ideas. "Scarcely a single English economist of repute," as Professor Cannan has expressed it, "will join in a frontal attack upon Socialism in general," though, as he also adds, "nearly every economist, whether of repute or not, is always ready to pick holes in most socialistic proposals." [10] Economists no longer have any link with the theological or political philosophies out of which the dogma of Social Harmony was born, and their scientific analysis leads them to no such conclusions.

Cairnes, in the Introductory Lecture on "Political Economy and *Laissez-Faire,*" which he delivered at University College, London, in 1870, was perhaps the first orthodox economist to deliver a frontal attack upon *laissez-faire* in general. "The maxim of *laissez-faire,*" he declared, "has no scientific basis whatever, but is at best a mere handy rule of practice." [11] This, for fifty

---

[10] *Theories of Production and Distribution,* p. 494.

[11] Cairnes well described the "prevailing notion" in the following passage from the same lecture: "The prevailing notion is that P.E. undertakes to show that wealth may be most rapidly

years past, has been the view of all leading economists. Some of the most important work of Alfred Marshall—to take one instance—was directed to the elucidation of the leading cases in which private interest and social interest are *not* harmonious. Nevertheless the guarded and undogmatic attitude of the best economists has not prevailed against the general opinion that an individualistic *laissez-faire* is both what they ought to teach and what in fact they do teach.

3. *The Assumptions of Economic Individualism*

Economists, like other scientists, have chosen the hypothesis from which they set out, and which they offer to beginners, because it is the simplest, and not because it is the nearest to the facts. Partly for this reason, but partly, I admit, because they have been biassed by the traditions of the subject, they have begun by assuming a state of affairs where the ideal distribution of productive resources can be brought about through individuals acting independently by the method of trial and error in such a way that those individuals who move in the right direction will destroy by competition those who move in the wrong direction. This implies that there must be no mercy or protection for those who embark their capital or their labour in the wrong direction. It is a method of bringing the most successful profit-makers to the top

accumulated and most fairly distributed; that is to say, that human well-being may be most effectually promoted, by the simple process of leaving people to themselves; leaving individuals, that is to say, to follow the promptings of self-interest, unrestrained either by the State or by public opinion, so long as they abstain from force and fraud. This is the doctrine commonly known as *laissez-faire*; and accordingly political economy is, I think, very generally regarded as a sort of scientific rendering of this maxim—a vindication of freedom of individual enterprise and of contract as the one and sufficient solution of all industrial problems."

by a ruthless struggle for survival, which selects the most efficient by the bankruptcy of the less efficient. It does not count the cost of the struggle, but looks only to the benefits of the final result which are assumed to be permanent. The object of life being to crop the leaves off the branches up to the greatest possible height, the likeliest way of achieving this end is to leave the giraffes with the longest necks to starve out those whose necks are shorter.

Corresponding to this method of attaining the ideal distribution of the instruments of production between different purposes, there is a similar assumption as to how to attain the ideal distribution of what is available for consumption. In the first place, each individual will discover what amongst the possible objects of consumption *he* wants most by the method of trial and error "at the margin," and in this way not only will each consumer come to distribute his consumption most advantageously, but each object of consumption will find its way into the mouth of the consumer whose relish for it is greatest compared with that of the others, because that consumer will outbid the rest. Thus, if only we leave the giraffes to themselves, (1) the maximum quantity of leaves will be cropped because the giraffes with the longest necks will, by dint of starving out the others, get nearest to the trees; (2) each giraffe will make for the leaves which he finds most succulent amongst those in reach; and (3) the giraffes whose relish for a given leaf is greatest will crane most to reach it. In this way more and juicier leaves will be swallowed, and each individual leaf will reach the throat which thinks it deserves most effort.

This assumption, however, of conditions where unhindered natural selection leads to progress, is only one of the two provisional assumptions which, taken as literal truth, have become the twin buttresses of *laissez-faire*. The other one is the efficacy, and, indeed, the necessity, of the opportunity for unlimited private money-making as an *incentive* to maximum effort. Profit accrues, under *laissez-faire*, to the individual who, whether by skill or good fortune, is found with his productive resources in the right place at the right time. A system which allows the skilful or fortunate individual to reap the whole fruits of this conjuncture evidently offers an immense incentive to the practice of the art of being in the right place at the right time. Thus one of the most powerful of human motives, namely, the love of money, is harnessed to the task of distributing economic resources in the way best calculated to increase wealth.

The parallelism between economic *laissez-faire* and Darwinianism, already briefly noted, is now seen, as Herbert Spencer was foremost to recognise, to be very close indeed. Just as Darwin invoked sexual love, acting through sexual selection, as an adjutant to Natural Selection by competition, to direct evolution along lines which should be desirable as well as effective, so the individualist invokes the love of money, acting through the pursuit of profit, as an adjutant to Natural Selection, to bring about the production on the greatest possible scale of what is most strongly desired as measured by exchange value.

The beauty and the simplicity of such a theory are so great that it is easy to forget that it follows not from the actual facts, but from an incomplete hypothesis introduced for the sake of simplicity. Apart from other objections to be mentioned later, the conclusion that individuals acting independently for their own advantage will produce the greatest aggregate of wealth, depends on a variety of unreal assumptions to the effect that the processes of production and consumption are in no way organic, that there exists a sufficient foreknowledge of conditions and requirements, and that there are adequate opportunities of obtaining this foreknowledge. For economists generally reserve for a later stage of their argument the complications which arise—(1) when the efficient units of production are large relatively to the units of consumption, (2) when overhead costs or joint costs are present, (3) when internal economies tend to the aggregation of production, (4) when the time required for adjustments is long, (5) when ignorance prevails over knowledge, and (6) when monopolies and combinations interfere with equality in bargaining —they reserve, that is to say, for a later stage their analysis of the actual facts. Moreover, many of those who recognise that the simplified hypothesis does not accurately correspond to fact conclude nevertheless that it does represent what is "natural" and therefore ideal. They regard the simplified hypothesis as health, and the further complications as disease.

Yet, besides this question of fact, there are other considerations, familiar enough, which rightly bring into the calculation the cost and character of the competitive struggle itself, and the tendency for wealth to be distributed where it is not appreciated most. If we have the welfare of the giraffes at heart, we must not overlook the sufferings of the shorter necks who are starved out, or the sweet leaves which fall to the ground and are trampled underfoot in the struggle, or the overfeeding of the long-necked ones, or the evil look of anxiety or struggling greediness which overcasts the mild faces of the herd.

But the principles of *laissez-faire* have had other allies besides economic text-books. It must be admitted that they have been confirmed in the minds of sound thinkers and the reasonable public by the poor quality of the opponent proposals—Protectionism on one hand, and Marxian Socialism on the other. Yet these doctrines are both characterised, not only or chiefly by their infringing the general presumption in favour of *laissez-faire,* but by mere logical fallacy. Both are examples of poor thinking, of inability to analyse a process and follow it out to its conclusion. The arguments against them, though reinforced by the principle of *laissez-faire,* do not strictly require it. Of the two, Protectionism is at least plausible, and the forces making for its popularity are nothing to wonder at. But Marxian Socialism must always remain a portent to the historians of Opinion—how a doctrine so illogical and so dull can have exercised so powerful and enduring an influence over the minds of men, and, through them, the events of history. At any rate, the obvious scientific deficiencies of these two schools greatly contributed to the prestige and authority of nineteenth-century *laissez-faire*.

Nor has the most notable divergence into centralised social action on a great scale—the conduct of the late war—encouraged reformers or dispelled old-fashioned prejudices. There is much to be said, it is true, on both sides. War experience in the organisation of socialised production has left some near observers optimistically anxious to repeat it in peace conditions. War socialism unquestionably achieved a production of wealth on a scale far greater than we ever knew in Peace, for though the goods and services delivered were destined for immediate and fruitless extinction, none the less they were wealth. Nevertheless the dissipation of effort was also prodigious, and the atmosphere of waste and not counting the cost was disgusting to any thrifty or provident spirit.

Finally, Individualism and *laissez-faire* could not, in spite of their deep roots in the political and moral philosophies of the late eighteenth and early nineteenth centuries, have secured their lasting hold over the conduct of public affairs, if it had not been for their conformity with the needs and wishes of the business world of the day. They gave full scope to our erstwhile heroes, the great business men. "At least one-half of the best ability in the Western world," Marshall used to say, "is engaged in business." A great part of "the higher imagination" of the age was thus employed. It was on the activities of these men that our hopes of Progress were centred.

Men of this class,

Marshall wrote,[1]

live in constantly shifting visions, fashioned in their own brains, of various routes to their desired end; of the diffi-

culties which Nature will oppose to them on each route, and of the contrivances by which they hope to get the better of her opposition. This imagination gains little credit with the people, because it is not allowed to run riot; its strength is disciplined by a stronger will; and its highest glory is to have attained great ends by means so simple that no one will know, and none but experts will even guess, how a dozen other expedients, each suggesting as much brilliancy to the hasty observer, were set aside in favour of it. The imagination of such a man is employed, like that of the master chessplayer, in forecasting the obstacles which may be opposed to the successful issue of his far-reaching projects, and constantly rejecting brilliant suggestions because he has pictured to himself the counterstrokes to them. His strong nervous force is at the opposite extreme of human nature from that nervous irresponsibility which conceives hasty Utopian schemes, and which is rather to be compared to the bold facility of a weak player, who will speedily solve the most difficult chess problem by taking on himself to move the black men as well as the white.

This is a fine picture of the great Captain of Industry, the Master-Individualist, who serves us in serving himself, just as any other artist does. Yet this one, in his turn, is becoming a tarnished idol. We grow more doubtful whether it is he who will lead us into Paradise by the hand.

These many elements have contributed to the current intellectual bias, the mental make-up, the orthodoxy of the day. The compelling force of many of the original reasons has disappeared, but, as usual, the vitality of the conclusions outlasts them. To suggest social action for the public good to the City of London is like discussing the *Origin of Species* with a Bishop sixty years ago. The first reaction is not intellectual, but moral. An orthodoxy is in question, and the more persuasive the arguments the graver the offence. Nevertheless, venturing into the den of the lethargic monster, at any rate I have traced his claims and pedigree so as to show that he has ruled over us

---

[1] "The Social Possibilities of Economic Chivalry," *Economic Journal* (1907), xvii, p. 9.

rather by hereditary right than by personal merit.

4. The Future Organization of Society

Let us clear from the ground the metaphysical or general principles upon which, from time to time, *laissez-faire* has been founded. It is *not* true that individuals possess a prescriptive "natural liberty" in their economic activities. There is *no* "compact" conferring perpetual rights on those who Have or on those who Acquire. The world is *not* so governed from above that private and social interest always coincide. It is *not* so managed here below that in practice they coincide. It is *not* a correct deduction from the Principles of Economics that enlightened self-interest always operates in the public interest. Nor is it true that self-interest generally *is* enlightened; more often individuals acting separately to promote their own ends are too ignorant or too weak to attain even these. Experience does *not* show that individuals, when they make up a social unit, are always less clear-sighted than when they act separately.

We cannot therefore settle on abstract grounds, but must handle on its merits in detail what Burke termed "one of the finest problems in legislation, namely, to determine what the State ought to take upon itself to direct by the public wisdom, and what it ought to leave, with as little interference as possible, to individual exertion." [1] We have to discriminate between what Bentham, in his forgotten but useful nomenclature, used to term *Agenda* and *Non-Agenda,* and to do this without Bentham's prior presumption that interference is, at the same time, "generally needless" and "generally pernicious." [2] Perhaps the chief task of economists at this hour is to distinguish

afresh the *Agenda* of Government from the *Non-Agenda;* and the companion task of Politics is to devise forms of Government within a Democracy which shall be capable of accomplishing the *Agenda.* I will illustrate what I have in mind by two examples.

(1) I believe that in many cases the ideal size for the unit of control and organisation lies somewhere between the individual and the modern State. I suggest, therefore, that progress lies in the growth and the recognition of semi-autonomous bodies within the State—bodies whose criterion of action within their own field is solely the public good as they understand it, and from whose deliberations motives of private advantage are excluded, though some place it may still be necessary to leave, until the ambit of men's altruism grows wider, to the separate advantage of particular groups, classes, or faculties—bodies which in the ordinary course of affairs are mainly autonomous within their prescribed limitations, but are subject in the last resort to the sovereignty of the democracy expressed through Parliament.

I propose a return, it may be said, towards mediæval conceptions of separate autonomies. But, in England at any rate, corporations are a mode of government which has never ceased to be important and is sympathetic to our institutions. It is easy to give examples, from what already exists, of separate autonomies which have attained or are approaching the mode I designate—the Universities, the Bank of England, the Port of London Authority, even perhaps the Railway Companies. In Germany there are doubtless analogous instances.

But more interesting than these is the trend of Joint Stock Institutions, when they have reached a certain age and size, to approximate to the status of public corporations rather than that of individualistic private enterprise. One of the most interesting and unnoticed developments of recent decades has been the tendency of big enterprise to socialise itself. A point arrives in the growth of a big institution—particularly a big railway or big public utility en-

---

[1] Quoted by M'Culloch in his *Principles of Political Economy.*

[2] Bentham's *Manual of Political Economy,* published posthumously, in Bowring's edition (1843).

terprise, but also a big bank or a big insurance company—at which the owners of the capital, *i.e.* the shareholders, are almost entirely dissociated from the management, with the result that the direct personal interest of the latter in the making of great profit becomes quite secondary. When this stage is reached, the general stability and reputation of the institution are more considered by the management than the maximum of profit for the shareholders. The shareholders must be satisfied by conventionally adequate dividends; but once this is secured, the direct interest of the management often consists in avoiding criticism from the public and from the customers of the concern. This is particularly the case if their great size or semi-monopolistic position renders them conspicuous in the public eye and vulnerable to public attack. The extreme instance, perhaps, of this tendency in the case of an institution, theoretically the unrestricted property of private persons, is the Bank of England. It is almost true to say that there is no class of persons in the Kingdom of whom the Governor of the Bank of England thinks less when he decides on his policy than of his shareholders. Their rights, in excess of their conventional dividend, have already sunk to the neighbourhood of zero. But the same thing is partly true of many other big institutions. They are, as time goes on, socialising themselves.

Not that this is unmixed gain. The same causes promote conservatism and a waning of enterprise. In fact, we already have in these cases many of the faults as well as the advantages of State Socialism. Nevertheless we see here, I think, a natural line of evolution. The battle of Socialism against unlimited private profit is being won in detail hour by hour. In these particular fields—it remains acute elsewhere—this is no longer the pressing problem. There is, for instance, no so-called important political question so really unimportant, so irrelevant to the re-organisation of the economic life of Great Britain, as the Nationalisation of the Railways.

It is true that many big undertakings, particularly Public Utility enterprises and other business requiring a large fixed capital, still need to be semi-socialised. But we must keep our minds flexible regarding the forms of this semi-socialism. We must take full advantage of the natural tendencies of the day, and we must probably prefer semi-autonomous corporations to organs of the Central Government for which Ministers of State are directly responsible.

I criticise doctrinaire State Socialism, not because it seeks to engage men's altruistic impulses in the service of Society, or because it departs from *laissez-faire*, or because it takes away from man's natural liberty to make a million, or because it has courage for bold experiments. All these things I applaud. I criticise it because it misses the significance of what is actually happening; because it is, in fact, little better than a dusty survival of a plan to meet the problems of fifty years ago, based on a misunderstanding of what someone said a hundred years ago. Nineteenth-century State Socialism sprang from Bentham, free competition, etc., and is in some respects a clearer, in some respects a more muddled version of just the same philosophy as underlies nineteenth-century individualism. Both equally laid all their stress on freedom, the one negatively to avoid limitations on existing freedom, the other positively to destroy natural or acquired monopolies. They are different reactions to the same intellectual atmosphere.

(2) I come next to a criterion of *Agenda* which is particularly relevant to what it is urgent and desirable to do in the near future. We must aim at separating those services which are *technically social* from those which are *technically individual*. The most important *Agenda* of the State relate not to those activities which private individuals are already fulfilling, but to those functions which fall outside the sphere of the individual, to those decisions which are made by *no one* if the State does not make them. The important thing for Government is not to do things which individuals are

doing already, and to do them a little better or a little worse; but to do those things which at present are not done at all.

It is not within the scope of my purpose on this occasion to develop practical policies. I limit myself, therefore, to naming some instances of what I mean from amongst those problems about which I happen to have thought most.

Many of the greatest economic evils of our time are the fruits of risk, uncertainty, and ignorance. It is because particular individuals, fortunate in situation or in abilities, are able to take advantage of uncertainty and ignorance, and also because for the same reason big business is often a lottery, that great inequalities of wealth come about; and these same factors are also the cause of the Unemployment of Labour, or the disappointment of reasonable business expectations, and of the impairment of efficiency and production. Yet the cure lies outside the operations of individuals; it may even be to the interest of individuals to aggravate the disease. I believe that the cure for these things is partly to be sought in the deliberate control of the currency and of credit by a central institution, and partly in the collection and dissemination on a great scale of data relating to the business situation, including the full publicity, by law if necessary, of all business facts which it is useful to know. These measures would involve Society in exercising directive intelligence through some appropriate organ of action over many of the inner intricacies of private business, yet it would leave private initiative and enterprise unhindered. Even if these measures prove insufficient, nevertheless they will furnish us with better knowledge than we have now for taking the next step.

My second example relates to Savings and Investment. I believe that some co-ordinated act of intelligent judgment is required as to the scale on which it is desirable that the community as a whole should save, the scale on which these savings should go abroad in the form of foreign investments, and whether the present organisation of the investment market distributes savings along the most nationally productive channels. I do not think that these matters should be left entirely to the chances of private judgment and private profits, as they are at present.

My third example concerns Population. The time has already come when each country needs a considered national policy about what size of Population, whether larger or smaller than at present or the same, is most expedient. And having settled this policy, we must take steps to carry it into operation. The time may arrive a little later when the community as a whole must pay attention to the innate quality as well as to the mere numbers of its future members.

5. The Money Motive

These reflections have been directed towards possible improvements in the technique of modern Capitalism by the agency of collective action. There is nothing in them which is seriously incompatible with what seems to me to be the essential characteristic of Capitalism, namely the dependence upon an intense appeal to the money-making and money-loving instincts of individuals as the main motive force of the economic machine. Nor must I, so near to my end, stray towards other fields. Nevertheless I may do well to remind you, in conclusion, that the fiercest contests and the most deeply felt divisions of opinion are likely to be waged in the coming years not round technical questions, where the arguments on either side are mainly economic, but round those which, for want of better words, may be called psychological or, perhaps, moral.

In Europe, or at least in some parts of Europe—but not, I think, in the United States of America—there is a latent reaction, somewhat widespread, against basing Society to the extent that we do upon fostering, encouraging, and protecting the money-motives of individuals. A preference for arranging our affairs in such a way as to appeal to the money-motive as little as possible, rather than as much as possible, need not be entirely *a priori*, but may be based on the comparison of experiences. Different persons, according to their choice of profession, find the money-motive playing a large or a small part in their daily lives, and historians can tell us about other phases of social organisation in which this motive has played a much smaller part than it does now. Most religions and most philosophies deprecate, to say the least of it, a way of life mainly influenced by considerations of personal money profit. On the other hand, most men to-day reject ascetic notions and do not doubt the real advantages of wealth. Moreover, it seems obvious to them that one cannot do without the money-motive, and that, apart from certain admitted abuses, it does its job well. In the result the average man averts his attention from the problem, and has no clear idea what he really thinks and feels about the whole confounded matter.

Confusion of thought and feeling leads to confusion of speech. Many people, who are really objecting to Capitalism as a way of life, argue as though they were objecting to it on the ground of its inefficiency in attaining its own objects. Contrariwise, devotees of Capitalism are often unduly conservative, and reject reforms in its technique, which might really strengthen and preserve it, for fear that they may prove to be first steps away from Capitalism itself. Nevertheless a time may be coming when we shall get clearer than at present as to when we are talking about Capitalism as an efficient or inefficient technique, and when we are talking about it as desirable or objectionable in itself. For my part, I think that Capitalism, wisely managed, can probably be made more efficient for attaining economic ends than any alternative system yet in sight, but that in itself it is in many ways extremely objectionable. Our problem is to work out a social organisation which shall be as efficient as possible without offending our notions of a satisfactory way of life.

The next step forward must come, not from political agitation or premature experiments, but from thought. We need by an effort of the mind to elucidate our own feelings. At present our sympathy and our judgment are liable to be on different sides, which is a painful and paralysing state of mind. In the field of action reformers will not be successful until they can steadily pursue a clear and definite object with their intellects and their feelings in tune. There is no party in the world at present which appears to me to be pursuing right aims by right methods. Material Poverty provides the incentive to change precisely in situations where there is very little margin for experiments. Material Prosperity removes the incentive just when it might be safe to take a chance. Europe lacks the means, America the will, to make a move. We need a new set of convictions which spring naturally from a candid examination of our own inner feelings in relation to the outside facts.

6. *Full Employment through Public Policy* *

Since the end of the nineteenth century significant progress towards the removal of very great disparities of wealth and income has been achieved through the instrument of direct taxation—income tax and surtax and death duties—expecially in Great Britain. Many people would wish to see this process carried much further, but they are deterred by two considerations; partly by the fear of making skilful evasions too much worth while and also of diminishing unduly the motive towards risk-taking, but mainly, I think, by the belief that the growth of capital depends upon the strength of the motive towards individual saving and that for a large proportion of this growth

* From John Maynard Keynes, *The General Theory of Employment, Interest, and Money.* Copyright by Harcourt, Brace & Company, 1936. By permission.

we are dependent on the savings of the rich out of their superfluity. Our argument does not affect the first of these considerations. But it may considerably modify our attitude towards the second. For we have seen that, up to the point where full employment prevails, the growth of capital depends not at all on a low propensity to consume but is, on the contrary, held back by it; and only in conditions of full employment is a low propensity to consume conducive to the growth of capital. Moreover, experience suggests that in existing conditions saving by institutions and through sinking funds is more than adequate, and that measures for the redistribution of incomes in a way likely to raise the propensity to consume may prove positively favourable to the growth of capital.

The existing confusion of the public mind on the matter is well illustrated by the very common belief that the death duties are responsible for a reduction in the capital wealth of the country. Assuming that the State applies the proceeds of these duties to its ordinary outgoings so that taxes on incomes and consumption are correspondingly reduced or avoided, it is, of course, true that a fiscal policy of heavy death duties has the effect of increasing the community's propensity to consume. But inasmuch as an increase in the habitual propensity to consume will in general (*i.e.* except in conditions of full employment) serve to increase at the same time the inducement to invest, the inference commonly drawn is the exact opposite of the truth.

Thus our argument leads towards the conclusion that in contemporary conditions the growth of wealth, so far from being dependent on the abstinence of the rich, as is commonly supposed, is more likely to be impeded by it. One of the chief social justifications of great inequality of wealth is, therefore, removed. I am not saying that there are no other reasons, unaffected by our theory, capable of justifying some measure of inequality in some circumstances. But it does dispose of the most important

of the reasons why hitherto we have thought it prudent to move carefully. This particularly affects our attitude towards death duties; for there are certain justifications for inequality of incomes which do not apply equally to inequality of inheritances.

For my own part, I believe that there is social and psychological justification for significant inequalities of incomes and wealth, but not for such large disparities as exist to-day. There are valuable human activities which require the motive of money-making and the environment of private wealth-ownership for their full fruition. Moreover, dangerous human proclivities can be canalised into comparatively harmless channels by the existence of opportunities for money-making and private wealth, which, if they cannot be satisfied in this way, may find their outlet in cruelty, the reckless pursuit of personal power and authority, and other forms of self-aggrandisement. It is better that a man should tyrannise over his bank balance than over his fellow-citizens; and whilst the former is sometimes denounced as being but a means to the latter, sometimes at least it is an alternative. But it is not necessary for the stimulation of these activities and the satisfaction of these proclivities that the game should be played for such high stakes as at present. Much lower stakes will serve the purpose equally well, as soon as the players are accustomed to them. The task of transmuting human nature must not be confused with the task of managing it. Though in the ideal commonwealth men may have been taught or inspired or bred to take no interest in the stakes, it may still be wise and prudent statesmanship to allow the game to be played, subject to rules and limitations, so long as the average man, or even a significant section of the community, is in fact strongly addicted to the money-making passion.

There is, however, a second, much more fundamental inference from our argument which has a bearing on the future of inequalities of wealth; namely, our theory of the rate of interest. The justification for a moderately high rate of interest has been found hitherto in the necessity of providing a sufficient inducement to save. But we have shown that the extent of effective saving is necessarily determined by the scale of investment and that the scale of investment is promoted by a *low* rate of interest, provided that we do not attempt to stimulate it in this way beyond the point which corresponds to full employment. Thus it is to our best advantage to reduce the rate of interest to that point relatively to the schedule of the marginal efficiency of capital at which there is full employment.

There can be no doubt that this criterion will lead to a much lower rate of interest than has ruled hitherto; and, so far as one can guess at the schedules of the marginal efficiency of capital corresponding to increasing amounts of capital, the rate of interest is likely to fall steadily, if it should be practicable to maintain conditions of more or less continuous full employment—unless, indeed, there is an excessive change in the aggregate propensity to consume (including the State).

I feel sure that the demand for capital is strictly limited in the sense that it would not be difficult to increase the stock of capital up to a point where its marginal efficiency had fallen to a very low figure. This would not mean that the use of capital instruments would cost almost nothing, but only that the return from them would have to cover little more than their exhaustion by wastage and obsolescence together with some margin to cover risk and the exercise of skill and judgment. In short, the aggregate return from durable goods in the course of their life would, as in the case of short-lived goods, just cover their labour-costs of production *plus* an allowance for risk and the costs of skill and supervision.

Now, though this state of affairs would be quite compatible with some measure of individualism, yet it would mean the euthanasia of the rentier, and, consequently, the euthanasia of the cumulative oppressive power of the capitalist to exploit the scarcity-value of capital. Interest to-day rewards no genuine sacrifice, any more than does the rent of land. The owner of capital can obtain interest because capital is scarce, just as the owner of land can obtain rent because land is scarce. But whilst there may be intrinsic reasons for the scarcity of land, there are no intrinsic reasons for the scarcity of capital. An intrinsic reason for such scarcity, in the sense of a genuine sacrifice which could only be called forth by the offer of a reward in the shape of interest, would not exist, in the long run, except in the event of the individual propensity to consume proving to be of such a character that net saving in conditions of full employment comes to an end before capital has become sufficiently abundant. But even so, it will still be possible for communal saving through the agency of the State to be maintained at a level which will allow the growth of capital up to the point where it ceases to be scarce.

I see, therefore, the rentier aspect of capitalism as a transitional phase which will disappear when it has done its work. And with the disappearance of its rentier aspect much else in it besides will suffer a sea-change. It will be, moreover, a great advantage of the order of events which I am advocating, that the euthanasia of the rentier, of the functionless investor, will be nothing sudden, merely a gradual but prolonged continuance of what we have seen recently in Great Britain, and will need no revolution.

Thus we might aim in practice (there being nothing in this which is unattainable) at an increase in the volume of capital until it ceases to be scarce, so that the functionless investor will no longer receive a bonus; and at a scheme of direct taxation which allows the intelligence and determination and executive skill of the financier, the entrepreneur *et hoc genus omne* (who are certainly so fond of their craft that their labour could be obtained much cheaper than at present), to be harnessed to the service of the community on reasonable terms of reward.

At the same time we must recognise that

only experience can show how far the common will embodied in the policy of the State, ought to be directed to increasing and supplementing the inducement to invest; and how far it is safe to stimulate the average propensity to consume, without forgoing our aim of depriving capital of its scarcity-value within one or two generations. It may turn out that the propensity to consume will be so easily strengthened by the effects of a falling rate of interest, that full employment can be reached with a rate of accumulation little greater than at present. In this event a scheme for the higher taxation of large incomes and inheritances might be open to the objection that it would lead to full employment with a rate of accumulation which was reduced considerably below the current level. I must not be supposed to deny the possibility, or even the probability, of this outcome. For in such matters it is rash to predict how the average man will react to a changed environment. If, however, it should prove easy to secure an approximation to full employment with a rate of accumulation not much greater than at present, an outstanding problem will at least have been solved. And it would remain for separate decision on what scale and by what means it is right and reasonable to call on the living generation to restrict their consumption, so as to establish, in course of time, a state of full investment for their successors.

In some other respects the foregoing theory is moderately conservative in its implications. For whilst it indicates the vital importance of establishing certain central controls in matters which are now left in the main to individual initiative, there are wide fields of activity which are unaffected. The State will have to exercise a guiding influence on the propensity to consume partly through its scheme of taxation, partly by fixing the rate of interest, and partly, perhaps, in others ways. Furthermore, it seems unlikely that the influence of banking policy on the rate of interest will be sufficient by itself to determine an optimum rate of investment. I conceive, therefore, that a some-

what comprehensive socialisation of investment will prove the only means of securing an approximation to full employment; though this need not exclude all manner of compromises and of devices by which public authority will co-operate with private initiative. But beyond this no obvious case is made out for a system of State Socialism which would embrace most of the economic life of the community. It is not the ownership of the instruments of production which it is important for the State to assume. If the State is able to determine the aggregate amount of resources devoted to augmenting the instruments and the basic rate of reward to those who own them, it will have accomplished all that is necessary. Moreover, the necessary measures of socialisation can be introduced gradually and without a break in the general traditions of society.

Our criticism of the accepted classical theory of economics has consisted not so much in finding logical flaws in its analysis as in pointing out that its tacit assumptions are seldom or never satisfied, with the result that it cannot solve the economic problems of the actual world. But if our central controls succeed in establishing an aggregate volume of output corresponding to full employments as nearly as is practicable, the classical theory comes into its own again from this point onwards. If we suppose the volume of output to be given, i.e. to be determined by forces outside the classical scheme of thought, then there is no objection to be raised against the classical analysis of the manner in which private self-interest will determine what in particular is produced, in what proportions the factors of production will be combined to produce it, and how the value of the final product will be distributed between them. Again, if we have dealt otherwise with the problem of thrift, there is no objection to be raised against the modern classical theory as to the degree of consilience between private and public advantage in conditions of perfect and imperfect competition respectively. Thus, apart from the necessity of central controls to bring about an adjustment between the propensity to consume and the inducement to invest, there is no more reason to socialise economic life than there was before.

To put the point concretely, I see no reason to suppose that the existing system seriously misemploys the factors of production which are in use. There are, of course, errors of foresight; but these would not be avoided by centralising decisions. When 9,000,000 men are employed out of 10,000,000 willing and able to work, there is no evidence that the labour of these 9,000,000 men is misdirected. The complaint against the present system is not that these 9,000,000 men ought to be employed on different tasks, but that tasks should be available for the remaining 1,000,000 men. It is in determining the volume, not the direction, of actual employment that the existing system has broken down.

Thus I agree with Gesell that the result of filling in the gaps in the classical theory is not to dispose of the "Manchester System," but to indicate the nature of the environment which the free play of economic forces requires if it is to realise the full potentialities of production. The central controls necessary to ensure full employment will, of course, involve a large extension of the traditional functions of government. Furthermore, the modern classical theory has itself called attention to various conditions in which the free play of economic forces may need to be curbed or guided. But there will still remain a wide field for the exercise of private initiative and responsibility. Within this field the traditional advantages of individualism will still hold good.

Let us stop for a moment to remind ourselves what these advantages are. They are partly advantages of efficiency—the advantages of decentralisation and of the play of self-interest. The advantage to efficiency of the decentralisation of decisions and of individual responsibility is even greater, perhaps, than the nineteenth century supposed; and the reaction against the appeal to self-interest may have gone too far. But, above all, individualism, if it can be purged of its defects and its abuses, is the best safeguard of personal liberty in the sense that, compared with any other system, it greatly widens the field for the exercise of personal choice. It is also the best safeguard of the variety of life, which emerges precisely from this extended field of personal choice, and the loss of which is the greatest of all the losses of the homogeneous or totalitarian state. For this variety preserves the traditions which embody the most secure and successful choices of former generations; it colours the present with the diversification of its fancy; and, being the handmaid of experiment as well as of tradition and of fancy, it is the most powerful instrument to better the future.

Whilst, therefore, the enlargement of the functions of government, involved in the task of adjusting to one another the propensity to consume and the inducement to invest, would seem to a nineteenth-century publicist or to a contemporary American financier to be a terrific encroachment on individualism, I defend it, on the contrary, both as the only practicable means of avoiding the destruction of existing economic forms in their entirety and as the condition of the successful functioning of individual initiative.

For if effective demand is deficient, not only is the public scandal of wasted resources intolerable, but the individual enterpriser who seeks to bring these resources into action is operating with the odds loaded against him. The game of hazard which he plays is furnished with many zeros, so that the players *as a whole* will lose if they have the energy and hope to deal all the cards. Hitherto the increment of the world's wealth has fallen short of the aggregate of positive individual savings; and the difference has been made up by the losses of those whose courage and initiative have not been supplemented by exceptional skill or unusual good fortune. But if effective demand is adequate, average skill and average good fortune will be enough.

The authoritarian state systems of to-day seem to solve the problem of unemployment at the expense of efficiency and of freedom. It is certain that the world will not much longer tolerate the unemployment which, apart from brief intervals of excitement, is associated—and, in my opinion, inevitably associated—with present-day capitalistic individualism. But it may be possible by a right analysis of the problem to cure the disease whilst preserving efficiency and freedom.

I have mentioned in passing that the new system might be more favourable to peace than the old has been. It is worth while to repeat and emphasise that aspect.

War has several causes. Dictators and others such, to whom war offers, in expectation at least, a pleasurable excitement, find it easy to work on the natural bellicosity of their peoples. But, over and above this, facilitating their task of fanning the popular flame, are the economic causes of war, namely, the pressure of population and the competitive struggle for markets. It is the second factor, which probably played a predominant part in the nineteenth century, and might again, that is germane to this discussion.

I have pointed out that, under the system of domestic *laissez-faire* and an international gold standard such as was orthodox in the latter half of the nineteenth century, there was no means open to a government whereby to mitigate economic distress at home except through the competitive struggle for markets. For all measures helpful to a state of chronic or intermittent under-employment were ruled out, except measures to improve the balance of trade on income account.

Thus, whilst economists were accustomed to applaud the prevailing international system as furnishing the fruits of the international division of labour and harmonising at the same time the interests of different nations, there lay concealed a less benign influence; and those statesmen were moved by common sense and a correct apprehension of the true course of events, who believed that if a rich, old country were to neglect the struggle for markets its prosperity would droop and fail. But if nations can learn to provide themselves with full employment by their domestic policy (and, we must add, if they can also attain equilibrium in the trend of their population), there need be no important economic forces calculated to set the interest of one country against that of its neighbours. There would still be room for the international division of labour and for international lending in appropriate conditions. But there would no longer be a pressing motive why one country need force its wares on another or repulse the offerings of its neighbour, not because this was necessary to enable it to pay for what it wished to purchase, but with the express object of upsetting the equilibrium of payments so as to develop a balance of trade in its own favour. International trade would cease to be what it is, namely, a desperate expedient to maintain employment at home by forcing sales on foreign markets and restricting purchases, which, if successful, will merely shift the problem of unemployment to the neighbour which is worsted in the struggle, but a willing and unimpeded exchange of goods and services in conditions of mutual advantage.

Is the fulfilment of these ideas a visionary hope? Have they insufficient roots in the motives which govern the evolution of political society? Are the interests which they will thwart stronger and more obvious than those which they will serve?

I do not attempt an answer in this place. It would need a volume of a different character from this one to indicate even in outline the practical measures in which they might be gradually clothed. But if the ideas are correct—an hypothesis on which the author himself must necessarily base what he writes—it would be a mistake, I predict, to dispute their potency over a period of time. At the present moment people are unusually expectant of a more fundamental diagnosis; more particularly ready to receive it; eager to try it out, if it should be even plausible. But apart from this contemporary mood, the ideas of economists and political philosophers, both when they are right and when they are wrong, are more powerful than is commonly understood. Indeed the world is ruled by little else. Practical men, who believe themselves to be quite exempt from any intellectual influences, are usually the slaves of some defunct economist. Madmen in authority, who hear voices in the air, are distilling their frenzy from some academic scribbler of a few years back. I am sure that the power of vested interests is vastly exaggerated compared with the gradual encroachment of ideas. Not, indeed, immediately, but after a certain interval; for in the field of economic and political philosophy there are not many who are influenced by new theories after they are twenty-five or thirty years of age, so that the ideas which civil servants and politicians and even agitators apply to current events are not likely to be the newest. But, soon or late, it is ideas, not vested interests, which are dangerous for good or evil.

CHAPTER 23

TOTALITARIAN COMMUNISM

I N the nineteenth century, democracy seemed the goal toward which the whole world was inevitably moving. In some countries it was more cheerfully welcomed and more faithfully practiced than in others, but even politically backward states like Russia and Germany had to pay homage to political virtue by gradually broadening, in form, though not always in substance, the range of self-government. In the twentieth century, political hypocrisy, like other expressions of nineteenth-century politeness and formality, is no longer considered obligatory, and the attacks on democracy have been carried on in the open, without the protective façade of apparent concessions to the principle of democracy. In the two decades between World Wars I and II, fascism, merged with the imperial ambitions of Germany, Japan, and Italy, was the main threat to democracy; for a time it was so successful that it was openly hailed even in democratic states as "the wave of the future" by its sympathizers, or by those who felt that democracy was done for in its vain attempt to stem the tide of fascism.

World War II destroyed the military ambitions of the fascist Axis. The strains and stresses of war revealed the hollowness of fascism's claim to have inaugurated a new way of life that combined scientific and industrial efficiency with youthful and dynamic heroism. Yet World War II was hardly over when communism emerged as the new menace of democracy. At the end of World War I, when Russia was the only communist state in the world, and when her industrial and military power seemed to be low, communism was interpreted as a specifically Russian phenomenon without much practical applicability elsewhere. But the defeat of Nazi Germany by the Russian armies in World War II revealed the extent to which the strength of Communist Russia had been underrated. When the war was over, Russia was the dominant military power in

Europe, and she quickly communized Poland, Rumania, Bulgaria, Hungary, and Eastern Germany.

Though the Russian armies were the principal instrument in spreading communism, the force of communist ideology was of vital significance. Whereas fascism did not possess a single creative or constructive idea that went beyond crass national egotism and lust for power, communism—unhampered, in particular, by the deadly burden of fascist racialism—addresses itself to the world as the true heir of the libertarian, equalitarian democratic tradition. Also, whereas fascism proudly proclaimed its "pagan" character in relation to the democratic way of life, which it rejected *in toto*, communism is more "heretical" in terms of the democratic tradition: it accepts the democratic ideals of liberty, equality, and fraternity, and its charge against democracy is not, as is the charge of fascism, that democracy is too faithful to its ideals, but that it has, in fact, betrayed them. Just as in religion paganism has been less dangerous than heresy, because the former rejects truth in its entirety, whereas the latter mingles the true with the false, so communism is, in the long run, more dangerous than fascism, precisely because communism contains important elements of the democratic tradition, distorted and perverted as they may appear in practice.

In Europe, communism has represented itself with considerable success, even in the eyes of many conservatives, as the authentic fighter against social and economic injustice. In Asia, communism is hunger become articulate, longing for faith and action. Whereas the Western democracies taught Asia the right to be happy, without giving it the means to achieve happiness, communism promises the masses of landless, destitute, forgotten Asiatics a new life of equality and abundance. In Europe as in Asia (and tomorrow in Africa and the Americas), communism is more than an idealistic movement of innocent liberal land reformers; yet the existence of serious unsolved agrarian and industrial problems in these countries prepares the proper soil for the growth of communism.

The theory that communism is caused primarily by conspiracy and terror is the product of self-deception in the West, and is potentially deadly in its effects. Men embrace communism, despite its known violence and ruthlessness, when no peaceful ways of social change seem to be left open, when the resources of patience, compromise, and reason appear exhausted. The utopian element in communism appeals particularly to those who are most in need of it, the desperate, despondent, and derelict who seek a new faith. Communism to them is not "scientific Marxism-Leninism" but a religion.

The ideology of communism will remain a potent factor in world politics even if the Soviet Union disappears, for internal or external reasons, as a major world power. Just as revolutionary communism was born long before the Soviet Union came into existence, it may easily outlive her eclipse or demise. The military strength of Russia, China, and other communist states may come and go, but the ideological challenge of communism as a political faith and doctrine will continue.

The greatest single influence in the development of revolutionary communism is Karl Marx (1818–1883). He was born in the Rhineland, which more than any other part of Germany had been strongly permeated with democratic ideas by the French Revolution. Marx attended the University of Berlin for several years, where he studied jurisprudence, philosophy, and history. But he quickly became engaged in political activities and in 1842 joined the staff of the *Rheinische Zeitung*, a democratic newspaper in Cologne. In the following year the paper was suppressed by the Prussian Government, and Marx went to Paris, then the European headquarters of radical movements.

In Paris, Marx met Proudhon, the leading French socialist thinker, Bakunin, the Russian anarchist, and Friedrich Engels (1820–1895), a Rhinelander like Marx, and soon to become his lifelong companion and close collaborator. Engels was the son of a German textile manufacturer with business interests in Germany and England, and he was sent by his father to Manchester in 1842. His *Condition of the Working Class in England* (1844) was a remarkably penetrating study of, squalor, drabness, and poverty in the midst of luxurious wealth, and Engels was the first to draw Marx' attention to England as a laboratory in which industrial capitalism could be most accurately observed.

In 1845 Marx was expelled from France through the intervention of the Prussian Government, and he went to Brussels, another center of political refugees from all over Europe. There Marx composed, with the aid of Engels, the *Communist Manifesto* (1848), the most influential of all his writings, a pamphlet that has made history, inspired devotion and hatred, and divided mankind more profoundly than any other political document. Marx participated in the revolutions of 1848 in France and Germany, and early in 1849 he was expelled again by the Prussian Government, and forbidden to return to his native land.

He went to London in the late summer of 1849, soon followed by Engels. Marx had planned to stay in England for only a few weeks, but he stayed there until his death in 1883. He spent most of his time in the British Museum, digging up obscure sources throwing light on the history and working of industrial capitalism. The first volume of *Das Kapital*, his monumental analysis of the capitalist system, was published in 1867; the second and third volumes appeared posthumously in 1885–1895, edited by Engels.

Marx' writings show little penetration of English *political* ideas and ways of thought, and his lack of insight into the forces and motivations of English politics would have been little better or worse had he stayed in Germany all his life. By contrast, his writings demonstrate a profound knowledge of the English *economic* system, based on detailed and painstaking research. Marx was one of the first social scientists to use neglected government reports and statistical materials as a basic tool of research in the study of social and economic problems. Yet it never occurred to him that the self-analysis of English capitalism, to which he owed the documentary sources of his grand indictment, might eventually evolve into peaceful self-improvement and change.

Marx' analysis of the capitalist system has influenced the making of history even more than the writing of history. Regardless of what one accepts or rejects of Marx' social, economic, political, and philosophical ideas, it is impossible to by-pass him. He said of himself that he was not a "Marxist," and those who insist on all or nothing in relation to his ideas, betray Marx in his own painful and long search for a philosophy that he did not receive ready-made from any master but gathered, and added to his own life experience, from diverse sources: German philosophy, French revolutionary politics, and English economy.

Marx believed that, as he expresses it in one of his earliest writings (*Theses on Feuerbach,* 1845), "in practice man must prove the truth"; thus the easier method of discovering truth through revelation and authority, whether based on Marx or any other god or prophet, is excluded. The *Theses on Feuerbach* were written by Marx when he was only twenty-seven, and his conception of the task of philosophy is clearly indicated by his charge that "the philosophers have only *interpreted* the world; the point however is to *change* it." This activist approach to philosophy is distinctly un-Hegelian, and Marx' life was dedicated to the anti-Hegelian proposition that the actual was far from rational, and that the rational would finally be imposed upon actuality, not by a mystical world spirit, but by the new social class that was the heir of bourgeois science and rationalism: the proletariat.

Marx' philosophy of history and politics has to be gathered from many incidental remarks and comments in his writings and letters, as he never wrote a systematic statement on the basic assumptions of his thought. In the preface to his *Critique of Political Economy* (1859), Marx briefly states his general philosophy of history, based on the thesis that "the anatomy of civil society is to be found in political economy." Pre-Marxian social analysis had emphasized law and politics as the determining factors in society and social change. Marx reverses the scale of importance and considers the "productive forces" of society as the basis, whereas legal relations and forms of government are the "super-structure." Marx puts it in this fashion: "The mode of production of the material means of existence conditions the whole process of social, political, and intellectual life."

One of Marx' most famous sayings is that *men's social existence determines their consciousness,* and not, as had been generally accepted before Marx, that the "consciousness of men determines their existence." What Marx stresses here is that men's ideas are not accidental and haphazard, or freely left to their choice. Thus the legal, political, and religious ideas of a pastoral civilization will fundamentally differ from those of an agricultural, feudal society, and both will have little in common with the social, political, religious, and intellectual outlook of modern capitalist society.

Turning to the question of what causes historical change, Marx renounces the study of monarchs and their relations with court ladies and fellow dynasts, and he is equally dissatisfied with the study of history as a long list of battles and wars. Instead, Marx attempts to find the deeper causes of historical change in forces that go beyond the power of individual rulers and victorious war leaders: "At a certain stage of their development the material productive forces of society come into contradiction with the existing productive relationships, or, what is but a legal expression for these, with the property relationships within which they have moved before. From forms of development of the productive forces these relationships are transformed into their fetters. Then an epoch of social revolution opens. With the change in the economic foundation the whole vast superstructure is more or less rapidly transformed." Thus, when new *productive forces* developed within the *productive relationships* of the feudal system, social revolution was, according to Marx, inevitable, because the productive relationships of the feudal system (property relations, market controls, internal customs and tariffs, monetary instability) did not permit the utilization of the newly developing productive forces of industrial capitalism. What has doomed all historically known economic systems is the fact, according to Marx, that when new productive forces develop, the existing productive relationship stands in the way of their proper utilization. Each system thus becomes eventually wasteful in terms of the potentialities that have developed in its womb but that are not permitted to be born and to grow.

The capitalist system, too, shows the same tendency, according to Marx, and is due to undergo the same fate when the *productive forces* (the capacity to produce) have *outstripped* the *productive relationships* (law of property, production for private profit). The capitalist system as a system of social, economic, and legal relations thus eventually stands in the way of the scientific resources and technological forces that are not permitted to be fully utilized. Only the public ownership of the means of production will, according to Marx, bring into existence a new system of productive relationships (production for common use rather than private profit) that will match the tremendous forces of production actually or potentially existent and known to man.

At a time when capitalism was growing by leaps and bounds and when populations were on the increase in all industrial nations, Marx predicted the failure of the capitalist system to use all available productive forces. The experience since Marx has shown that only in time of war or full-scale preparation for war do capitalist societies produce to the full extent of their capacity. In "normal" times, millions of men are forced to be without work, and machinery rusts in idleness.

In the *Communist Manifesto,* Marx and Engels explain how social change through revolution actually occurs. When the forces of production begin to outstrip the methods of production (or productive relationships), the owners of the means of production do not step aside and thus accelerate the inevitable course of history. Bound by the limitations of their ideology (which, in turn, reflects the existing modes of production), they sincerely believe that the existing system is economically the most efficient, socially the most equitable, and generally in harmony with the laws of nature and the will of whatever god they venerate. It is not a question of the greed of the individual feudal landowner (who obstructs the birth of the more productive capitalist system) or of the selfishness of the individual capitalist (who impedes the nationalization of the means of production). The owners of the means of production will utilize all the instruments of the legal, political, and ideological superstructure to block the growth of the forces that represent the potentially more progressive economic system. For this reason Marx and Engels state early in the *Communist Manifesto* that the "history of all hitherto existing society is the history of class struggles." In the nineteenth century, the bourgeoisie liked to think of itself as conservative, law-abiding, and antirevolutionary—once it had won its class struggle. Yet Marx and Engels remind the bourgeoisie that, historically, it "has played a most revolutionary part."

The end of capitalism will be brought about, according to the *Communist Manifesto,* not by "subversive" conspiracies of professional agitators and revolutionaries, but by the same inexorable laws of social change that destroyed previous systems. Just as feudalism, for example, prepared its own grave by developing these forces—the urban bourgeoisie—which eventually destroyed it, capitalism does the same thing: "The essential condition for the existence and for the sway of the bourgeois class is the formation and augmentation of capital; the condition for capital is wage-labor. Wage-labor rests exclusively on competition between the laborers. The advance of industry, whose involuntary promoter is the bourgeoisie, replaces the isolation of the laborers, due to competition, by their revolutionary combinations, due to association. The development of modern industry, therefore, cuts from under its feet the very foundation on which the bourgeoisie produces and appropriates products. What the bourgeoisie therefore produces, above all, are its own grave-diggers. Its fall and the victory of the proletariat are equally inevitable."

As Marx and Engels look at history, they can find no instance where a major social and economic system has freely abdicated to its successor. Therefore the communists "openly declare that their ends can be attained only by the forcible overthrow of all existing social conditions." This is one of the crucial tenets of Marxist revolutionary communism, and the one that most clearly opposes it irreconcilably to democracy, be it capitalist or socialist democracy.

Marx had no clear-cut theory as to how the political transformation from capitalist to proletarian rule could come about. Though in the *Communist Manifesto* he believed in the need for revolution, he was less dogmatic later. Speaking in 1872 at a public meeting in Amsterdam following the Congress of the International, Marx declared that the means of attaining power for the working class are not everywhere the same: "We know that we must take into consideration the institutions, the habits and customs of different regions, and we do not deny that there are countries like America, England, and—if I knew your institutions better I would perhaps add Holland—where the workers can attain their objective by peaceful means. But such is not the case in all other countries."

Marx never fully pursued the implications of this distinction, and the generally accepted doctrine of communist Marxism is the impossibility of fundamental social and economic change except by class war, violence, and revolution. If Marx had accorded the political factor its due weight, if he had studied the implications of the Reform Act of 1832—a bloodless revolution in which the governing class peacefully ceded its position to the new middle class—he might have foreseen that socialism, too, might be accomplished without violence in countries whose democratic tradition was strong enough to absorb far-reaching social and economic changes without resorting to civil war.

A full recognition of the cultural and political factors in the equation of social change would have amounted to a virtual abandonment, however, of the central position of Marx: that history is the history of class wars, and that ruling classes defend their position to the last, not because of selfish greed, but because their ideological framework, the superstructure of the economic system, compels them to identify their privileged position with that of the whole community. Conversely, the proletariat attacks the capitalist system, and finally overthrows it, according to Marx, not because of some abstract ideals of justice, but because the inevitable evolution of capitalism puts the proletariat in a position of misery and exploitation, while men, knowledge, and resources lie idle.

In Hegel, *war between nations* is the vehicle of historical decision and progress, and the World Spirit assigns to different nations special missions at particular times. In Marx, social change and progress are attained by *war between classes*, and in each historical epoch one particular class is assigned the mission of representing the idea of progress. For Hegel, world history culminates in the German nation, which embodies the finest flowering of freedom and spirit. Hegel thought in dynamic terms until he arrived at the Prussian state. For Marx, history culminates in the proletariat, which embodies the highest social principles of progress and rational ordering of society. Just as Hegel assumed that the process of the fulfillment of spirit and freedom was consummated in Prussianized Germany, Marx assumed that the process of history, the record of class wars, would be consummated in the final victory of the proletariat, after which the dynamics of class war would be followed by the *statics of the classless society.*

No one before Marx saw as clearly as he did the *intimate relationship between private property and power.* In particular, Marx demonstrated that the link between power and property was heightened to its extreme in the capitalist system, inasmuch as its scientific, technological, and managerial forces made possible an accumulation of economic power in the hands of the few, such as would have been impossible before the Industrial Revolution. Yet, realistic as Marx was in his appraisal of *private* property as a system of private government and power of man over man, he was utopian in assuming that property lost the character of power merely by being collectivized. The Marx-Engels doctrine of the "withering away of the state" in the classless society is based on the hypothesis that property in a socialist or communist society ceases to be a system of power when owned by the whole community. Whereas private ownership of the means of production under capitalism, Marx and Engels argue, entails the domination of man over man, public ownership of the means of production under socialism or communism will lead to the "administration of things," so that the state (in its historical meaning as a system of force) would wither away by itself, as there would no longer be any need for it.

The *administration of things* is a matter of technical *knowledge* and not of political *will*. Government as an agency of settling disputes between men by force would be replaced in the classless society by administration as a scientific method of using resources in the best way in accordance with verifiable procedures of science and technology. Locke was the first modern writer to define property as a relationship of man to things, inasmuch as he saw the origin of property in the admixture of human effort to natural resources. Marx's concept of *publicly owned property as a relationship between man and things* closely follows Locke's concept of private property.

The ideal of classical liberalism and that of Marx-Engels have a common utopian element: both assume that human nature can be so improved and perfected by the right kind of institutional changes that government as a mechanism of force becomes superfluous. In the classical doctrine of liberal democracy, the equitable distribution of private property seemed to point to such a state of harmony; in the classical doctrine of Marx-Engels, the transformation of individual work into collective work in the capitalist factory pointed to the practical conclusion that collective ownership of the means of production would assure a basic equality of men that would make government in the traditional sense unnecessary. Both classical democracy and classical Marxism suffer from an excessive optimism with regard to the perfectibility of man, and both wrongly assume that any system of society can be devised that can achieve perfect harmony of interests. Nevertheless, the liberal doctrine of "the less government, the better" and the Marxian doctrine of the "withering away of the state" can be valuable as permanent reminders that the state exists for man, and not man for the state. Whereas a society without force and government is humanly unattainable, the ideal at least of a civilized community should be that of the lowest possible amount of force and compulsion in human relations.

The main difference between the theory of classical democracy and that of Marx-Engels is that the former envisaged a free, harmoniously ordered society as the result of peaceful, gradual growth, whereas Marx-Engels saw in revolution, civil war, and the dictatorship of the proletariat the preparatory stages of peace and harmony. Experience has shown since Marx-Engels that revolution and dictatorship are less likely to induce the state to wither away, or even decrease the use of force and violence, than the slower and more difficult methods of peaceful persuasion and consent. The failure to see the fatal relationship between means and ends is one of the most striking philosophical and practical weaknesses of Marxism, and the one that fundamentally separates it from liberal democracy.

The doctrines of Marx and Engels made a profound impression on social thinkers, reformers, and revolutionaries everywhere. In western Europe and the United States, Marxism was not too successful because the liberal tradition in these countries kept the way open for social reform and progress by peaceful, constitutional means. However, many critics of the injustices and abuses of capitalism accepted a large measure of the Marxian *economic* analysis and indictment of capitalism without embracing Marx' remedy of despair—the revolutionary dictatorship of the proletariat. In western Europe and the United States, the political rights of the people were constantly enlarged through the widening of the franchise at the very time when Marx claimed that a ruling class would never abdicate peacefully. Forward-looking democrats and social reformers felt that, if the political position of the people could be radically improved by constitutional means, social and economic issues would ultimately be solved in the same manner. In France the ideals of the French Revolution, Liberty, Equality, Fraternity, and not the Marxian doctrine of class war and hatred, provided the abiding inspiration for the socialist movement.

In England the firm foundations of parliamentary government, accepted as supreme by all social classes since 1688, made it possible for the working class to use the existing machinery of government for purposes of social reform, just as the middle class had used it earlier for political reform. Whereas the working classes in many countries of continental Europe and elsewhere had to agitate simultaneously for political democracy *and* social democracy, the English workers had the immense benefit of operating within the premises of parliamentary government from the start.

In the United States, Marxian doctrines have found little resonance because the vast opportunities of a new world have generated hope, prosperity, and optimism, which belie the Marxian prognosis of the progressive impoverishment of the masses. Also, Marxism has made little headway in the United States because it has attacked the political foundations of American *democracy* as well as the economic foundations of American *capitalism*.

There were two major countries in the nineteenth century in which the ideas of Marx and Engels became momentous ideological and political forces: Germany and Russia. Despite the façade of the Reichstag, Germany was in fact a political autocracy that did not permit the development of genuine representative government. Philosophically, Marxism may be Hegelianism put upside down (as Marx himself claimed), but Hegel upside down is still Hegel, and the fixed determinism and closed system of Marxism appealed to much that was deeply rooted in the German philosophical tradition. Just as Hegel had asserted that the *state* was an *objective reality*, and its laws, like those of nature, beyond the whim and caprice of the individual, Marx now claimed that the *laws of society* followed an inexorable course, possessing the same *scientific validity* that Hegel had claimed for the laws of the state. By contrast, the liberal philosophical tradition of the West has always rejected the Hegel-Marx conception that human reason can only *understand* the laws of the state or society, and has affirmed the possibility of rational control and creative change of social and political institutions. The experience of free government forms the psychological foundation of the western conceptions of state and society, just as the experience of autocratic government in Germany provides the psychological background for the determinism of Hegel and Marx.

In actual practice, the original extremism of Marxism was gradually transformed into more evolutionary views in the German labor movement, because the Second Reich (1871–1918) provided some measure of legal political activity, supplemented by a considerable amount of paternalistic social-welfare legislation. In phraseology, however, German Marxism continued revolutionary and "scientific," disdainful of the "utopian," that is, ethical and peaceful outlook of western socialists. It is particularly striking that anarchism, the extreme ideal of individualism, never took root in the German labor movement, because Marxism expressed more satisfactorily the need for strong collective action and discipline. In one sense, the political theory of Marx was a form of inverted Prussianism: before the revolution, the Junkers and capitalists sit on top, and rule with an iron hand over the masses of the people. Come the revolution, the roles are reversed: the people control the state through customary authoritarian methods, and the erstwhile oppressors and exploiters are put in their place.

The other major country in which Marx' and Engels' ideas were widely accepted by radical thinkers and political action groups was czarist Russia. In Russia the conditions for the acceptance of Marx were even more favorable than in imperial Germany. Whereas Germany made the pretense of bowing to democracy and parliamentary government, czarism long recoiled from committing itself even to the formalities of liberalism and democracy, on the ground that pretenses, if practiced long enough, might too easily develop into reality. Of all major European states, czarist Russia was first in illiteracy, economic backwardness, religious obscurantism, oppression of minorities, political despotism, and social inequality. Marx' ideas, particularly the prospect of inevitable liberation of the working classes from bondage and oppression through revolutionary action, made a strong impression on Russian radicals, and Russian was the language into which *Das Kapital* was first translated. The Russian censorship permitted the publication of the work on the ground that it would not be read by many because of its difficult style and its strictly scientific method of argumentation.

The spread of Marxist ideas in Russia supplied a new focus of ideology for the disunited anticzarist opposition. It ranged from extreme terrorists, who saw in individual acts of assassination and destruction the road to Russia's liberation, to sentimental populists, who "went to the people," that is, lived and worked with the peasants, hoping that Russia would pass from serfdom to a free and modern peasant community without having to go through the painful process of capitalist industrialization and all its accompanying evils.

In the last quarter of the nineteenth century, industry in Russia made rapid headway, often with the aid of foreign engineers and financiers, and an urban proletariat began to fill the big factory towns. A sense of acute class consciousness developed in the new proletariat, which was without political protection, without hope of social equality, and which was working at a wage level below the bare necessities of life.

The class consciousness of the Russian proletariat was, however, not only a product of oppression and degradation. Because industry came so late to Russia, she skipped the stage of the small workshop and the small factory and adopted the latest methods of technology, which meant large enterprises from the outset. Though the absolute size of the industrial proletariat in Russia was much smaller than that in England, Germany, or the United States, the proportion of workers employed in enterprises of more than one thousand employees was considerably higher in Russia before World War I than even in the United States, not to speak of Germany, France, and England. In cities like Petersburg and Moscow, about half of all industrial workers were concentrated in large factories of more than one thousand employees, a fact that made it easy to awaken in the workers a sense of solidarity and the need for united action.

Because industry was so concentrated in Russia, she lacked a strong intermediary social class between capitalist and worker. In western Europe and the United States, capitalism had largely grown out of already existing middle classes, and their liberal tradition reduced the inevitable tensions between capital and labor. Because such a middle class was largely lacking in Russia, the gulf between employer and employee was well-nigh unbridgeable. Marxism appealed to the rank and file of Russian labor as well as to its leaders, because it seemed an answer to the misery and degradation of the proletariat, inasmuch as the czarist autocracy provided no alternative for revolutionary change.

The man who made of Marxism a political reality in Russia was Vladimir Ilyich Ulyanov, or Lenin, as he later called himself (1870–1924). Lenin came from a middle-class family, both his father and mother having been teachers with progressive views. Their five surviving children became revolutionaries, and Lenin's eldest brother, Alexander, was hanged at the age of nineteen for complicity in an amateurish and abortive plot against Czar Alexander III. Lenin had a typical middle-class education, first attending the secondary school at Simbirsk, and then the law school of the University of Kazan. Because of his early political activities and the circumstances of his brother's execution, Lenin found himself under constant police supervision. However, the czarist police was not nearly so efficient as the later police systems of either Lenin or Stalin, and Lenin managed to maintain political contacts and join illegal groups.

In December, 1895, Lenin was arrested in Petersburg and spent fourteen months in prison. From his prison cell he guided a revolutionary organization he had formed, and he also found the time and means to write letters and pamphlets that he managed to smuggle out of prison. He was able to obtain the books and magazines he needed, and he began in prison to work on *The Development of Capitalism in Russia*. Although in January, 1897, he was sentenced to three years' exile in Siberia, he continued his political and philosophical studies there, received illegal literature, and maintained contacts with illegal revolutionary groups. In 1898 Lenin married Nadezhda Krupskaya, a fellow revolutionary, in his Siberian exile, and their home became the headquarters for the political exiles in that territory. Lenin also found time for recreation, hunting, ice skating, hiking, and chess. His exile provided him with a new name, "Lenin," derived from the river Lena, which flowed through the region of Siberia where he was exiled.

After his release from Siberia in 1900, Lenin went abroad; he spent the next seventeen years with but few interruptions in various European countries, organizing from abroad the illegal revolutionary movement in Russia that was to culminate in the seizure of power in 1917. He returned to Russia after the first Revolution in the spring of 1917, and it was a liberal government that permitted him to return. In seven months he managed to overthrow the Kerensky government, the only free government Russia has known in her entire history.

Lenin's most important theoretical contribution to the theory of Marxism, perhaps his only one, is the doctrine of the *professional revolutionary*, as first developed in *What Is to Be Done?* (1902). Lenin drew a distinction between an organization of workers and an organization of revolutionaries. The former must be essentially trade-union in character, as wide as possible, and as public as political conditions will allow. By contrast, the organization of revolutionaries must consist exclusively of professional revolutionaries, must be small, and "as secret as possible."

Whereas Marx had assumed that the working class would inevitably develop its class consciousness in the daily struggle for its economic existence, Lenin had much less confidence in the ability of the workers to develop politically by their own effort and experience: "Class political consciousness can be brought to the workers *only from without*, that is, only outside of the economic struggle, outside of the sphere of relations between workers and employers." Lenin did not care whether the professional revolutionaries destined to lead the proletariat were of working-class origin or not (he, like Marx and Engels, was middle class), as long as the professional revolutionary did his job well. But because of the difficulties of the work to be done, Lenin insisted that the professional revolutionary must be "no less professionally trained than the police," and, like the police, the organization of professional revolutionaries must be highly centralized and able to supervise and control the open organizations of workers that are legally permitted.

Lenin's views of the extreme concentration of power in the hands of a few leaders of professional revolutionaries led Trotsky in 1904 to assert that Lenin's doctrine of the dictatorship of the proletariat really meant the *dictatorship over the proletariat,* and the struggle of centralism versus democracy became one of the major issues of communist party organization before and after 1917. Trotsky also predicted in 1904 that if Lenin ever took power, "the leonine head of Marx would be the first to fall under the guillotine."

Lenin's most influential political work is *State and Revolution* (1918), written in the late summer of 1917; Lenin was hiding near the Finnish border part of the time, as the Kerensky government had issued an order for his arrest. *State and Revolution* consists of six chapters; as Lenin explains in a postscript (dated December 13, 1917), he planned to add a seventh chapter on the Russian revolutions of 1905 and 1917, but was "interrupted" by the November revolution of 1917, and, as he puts it: "It is more pleasant and useful to go through the 'experience of revolution' than to write about it."

In the literature of Marxism and communism, *State and Revolution* is of immense importance. Where Marx and Engels (in typically nineteenth-century liberal fashion) neglected the factor of *political power*, Lenin, the master strategist of one of the half-dozen great revolutions in history, was keenly interested in the anatomy of the state. Lenin fully accepts the Marxian thesis that the transitional state between capitalism and communism "can be only the revolutionary dictatorship of the proletariat." He denies that capitalism and democracy are compatible, and affirms that under capitalism democracy always remains "a democracy for the minority, only for the possessing classes, only for the rich." Lenin then describes the techniques that the capitalist state employs in order to maintain itself in power. In the words of the *Communist Manifesto,* the "executive of the modern State is but a committee for managing the common affairs of the whole bourgeoisie."

Behind the formalities of *capitalist democracy,* Lenin sees, in effect, the *dictatorship of the bourgeoisie.* He also denies that the transition from capitalism to communism can be accomplished simply, smoothly, and directly, "as the liberal professors and petty-bourgeois opportunists would have us believe. No, development—toward communism—proceeds through the dictatorship of the proletariat; it cannot be otherwise, for the *resistance* of the capitalist exploiters cannot be *broken* by anyone else or in any other way." Whereas Marx had left open the possibility for peaceful social change from capitalism to socialism in politically advanced countries like England, the United States, and the Netherlands, Lenin claims that, by 1917, "this exception made by Marx is no longer valid," because England and the United States had developed bureaucratic institutions "to which everything is subordinated and which trample everything under foot." Far from admitting that both England and the United States had moved steadily in the direction of social reform since Marx, Lenin maintains that both countries had become more repressive, authoritarian, and plutocratic in the meantime. In 1884, Sir William Harcourt, a Liberal leader in the British Parliament, made the statement, "We are all socialists now," indicating the general acceptance of far-reaching social and economic reform by all parties. Yet, according to Lenin, Sir William should have said, "We are all bloodthirsty militaristic capitalists now."

In the transitional stage between capitalism and communism the state will continue to exist, Lenin holds, because machinery for the suppression of the capitalist exploiters will still be required in the dictatorship of the proletariat. But Lenin points out that in this phase the state is already beginning to "wither away," because the task of the majority (the victorious proletariat) in suppressing the minority (the defeated capitalists) is different, in quantitative and qualitative terms, from the previous capitalist state, in which a minority (of capitalists) suppressed the majority (of the exploited). Finally, once communism is fully established, the state becomes "absolutely unnecessary, for there is *no one* to be suppressed—'no one' in the sense of a *class*, in the sense of a systematic struggle against a definite section of the population." With the causes of exploitation of class by class removed, with the abolition of classes, the state will therefore inevitably "wither away." There will be true freedom for all, and "when freedom exists, there will be no state."

Lenin cautiously adds that he leaves the question of length of time, or of "the concrete withering away, quite open." Without indicating the time it will take to transform the "lower phase" of communist society (the dictatorship of the proletariat) into the "higher phase" (the withering away of the state), Lenin describes the conditions of such transformation: "The state will be able to wither away completely when society can apply the rule: 'From each according to his ability, to each according to his needs,' that is, when people have become so accustomed to observing the fundamental rules of social life and when their labor is so productive that they will voluntarily work *according to their ability*." Lenin, like Marx, denies that the vision of a society without a machinery of force and power ("the state") is utopian. Yet Marxism shares with religion, pacifism, and anarchy the faith that man is so perfectible that one day he will no longer need the corrective force of government. In religion, the trouble is the Adam in man; in Marx and Lenin, the Adam is capitalism.

In his *Theses and Report on Bourgeois Democracy and the Dictatorship of the Proletariat*, submitted to the First Congress of the Communist International (March 4, 1919), Lenin—now at the helm of the communist dictatorship—reiterates his belief that there is no "democracy in general" or "dictatorship in general," and that all bourgeois democracies are, in fact, dictatorships of the capitalists over the exploited masses of the people. He vehemently attacks democratic socialists who believe that there is a middle course between capitalist dictatorship and proletarian dictatorship: "All dreams about some third course are merely the reactionary lamentations of the petty bourgeois." In support of his argument, Lenin cites the persecution of communists in even the freest bourgeois democracies, such as Switzerland and the United States, while in Germany working-class leaders like Karl Liebknecht and Rosa Luxemburg had just been murdered: "Nor can it be otherwise as long as capitalism exists, because the development of democracy does not blunt but sharpens the class struggle, which has been brought to the boiling point by the results and influences of the war and its consequences."

In his *Theses on the Fundamental Tasks of the Second Congress of the Communist International* (dated July 4, 1920), Lenin elaborates his belief in the right of the minority to lead, and rule, the majority, even after the dictatorship of the proletariat is established. Just as in *What Is to Be Done?* Lenin had stressed in 1902 that a small minority of professional revolutionaries was necessary to win power for the proletariat, he now stresses the central importance of the minority after power has been conquered. Lenin argues that under the conditions of capitalist domination and its mental enslavement the majority of the workers *cannot* acquire socialist convictions, first, because the capitalists control all mediums of thought and opinion, and, second, because workers in a capitalist society honestly accept many of the prevailing ideas and ideologies, the "superstructure" of capitalism, which is so effective precisely because it operates unconsciously. Lenin therefore says that the majority of the workers will acquire the proper proletarian ideology only after the objective conditions of their lives have been changed, that is, after the communist vanguard of the proletariat has overthrown the capitalist exploiters and the institutions of capitalism. Only a revolutionary change of this kind, Lenin argues, will rid the workers of the "selfishness, disunity, the vices and weaknesses engendered by private property."

Whereas democratic socialists assume that, as was shown in the British General Election of 1945, workers in a liberal capitalist regime can be peacefully converted to socialism, although the mediums of communication are predominantly controlled by capitalist interests, Lenin is more pessimistic. Under capitalism, he maintains, the majority of the workers are incapable of ridding themselves of the capitalist mentality, and only a minority of class-conscious revolutionaries, the communist vanguard of the proletariat, can correctly analyze the situation and map a proper plan of action. The dictatorship of the proletariat is necessary to protect communism from the danger of recrudescent capitalism; the dictatorship over the proletariat by the communist vanguard is necessary until the majority of the workers have rid themselves of the capitalist ideology.

Lenin's justification of dictatorship rests ultimately, like all other apologias of authoritarianism, on the profound conviction that the majority of the people is incapable of understanding and acting "correctly." Possessing the "correct" knowledge of the laws of history and society, communists have the right—and duty—to lead the masses into a new world, though the corrupting influences of the old world may make forcible leadership necessary. In Rousseauan terms, Lenin asserts that *communists,* because of their scientific analysis of society, represent the *General Will of the proletariat,* although the Wills of All in the proletariat may be ignorant or unwilling to admit it because they can only think of their private, individual interests and advantages. The General Will of the proletariat is therefore, for Lenin, not what the majority of the proletarians actually think, but what they would think if they were familiar with the "correct" Marxian analysis of social and economic development.

Because Lenin realizes that communists may not be able to conquer power in open discussion and propaganda, he advises communists to form cells or nuclei in all political, industrial, military, cooperative, educational, and athletic organizations. Such communist cells should be either open or secret, depending on the circumstances of the particular group or organization. The activities of the cells should be closely supervised and coordinated from the center of the communist parties, and the specific psychology of each stratum, group, or profession into which communists have infiltrated should be taken into account.

Even where capitalist democracy seems to be "freest" in the formal and legal sense communists should *combine,* Lenin argues, *legal with illegal work,* legal with illegal organization, because bourgeois governments always prepare for violence against communists, and the guarantees of democratic constitutions cannot be trusted when the rights of communists are at issue. Although he stresses that "illegal work is particularly necessary in the army, the navy and police," he warns against exclusive illegal work by communists and urges them to exhaust at all times the available opportunities of legal work, "forming legal organs of the press and legal organizations under the most varied titles, which may often be changed in the event of necessity." Because communists are engaged in ceaseless war, and class war is a form of ruthless conflict, they should use all possible tactical and strategic means to reach their objective: the revolutionary seizure of power.

These organizational principles of Leninist communism—secrecy, minority leadership, centralized authority, and the use of illegal means—are also characteristic of other organizations, civil and military, that are geared to war.

After the death of Lenin in 1924, his two chief lieutenants, Trotsky and Stalin, struggled for leadership. Trotsky lost, and had to leave the Soviet Union. An exile again, he wandered, as he had done under czarism, from country to country, until he was murdered by a Stalinist agent in Mexico City in the summer of 1940. After the expulsion of Trotsky and his friends from the Politbureau of the Communist party in 1926, Stalin was the sole and undisputed ruler of the Soviet Union. Whereas Lenin had tolerated considerable difference of opinion among communists and had acted with comparative lenience toward noncommunists of the Left provided that they were in broad agreement with his policies, Stalin established a personal regime of one-man rule, which gradually evolved into the traditional Russian pattern of Byzantine adulation and self-abasing hero worship.

Unlike Lenin, Joseph Stalin (1879–1953; his real name was Joseph Vissarionovich Djugashvili) did not come from a middle-class intellectual background. Stalin's father was a poor Georgian shoemaker, and his mother had to work as a washerwoman to supplement the scanty income of the family. Constantly fighting against harsh poverty, Stalin's mother decided to prepare Joseph for a more respected and lucrative career than shoemaking. At the age of nine, Stalin entered the ecclesiastical school at Gori, his birthplace in the Caucasus, and stayed there for five years, attaining an excellent scholastic record. At the age of fifteen he entered the Theological Seminary at Tiflis, capital of the Caucasus. He stayed at the seminary for nearly five years, and his mother's ambition of seeing Joseph become a devout and learned priest almost came true. But Stalin had other plans. Toward the end of his stay at the Theological Seminary he joined a secret Leftist study group within the seminary itself and also participated in a secret organization in Tiflis.

Stalin's revolutionary impulse was awakened not only by the social and economic degradation with which he was so familiar but also by the inferior position of the non-Russian nationalities. Both of Stalin's parents were Georgians who spoke hardly any Russian, and the Georgian peasants were treated little better than serfs by the Russian gentry. Stalin soon went through the conventional course of political education for professional revolutionaries: arrests, imprisonments, and exiles in Siberia. In 1912 Lenin brought Stalin into the Central Committee of the Bolshevik party, and Stalin remained in constant close touch with the party chiefs. Unlike most other principal communist leaders, Stalin stayed in Russia (except for a few hurried visits abroad) throughout the most difficult years of underground activity.

After the overthrow of czarism and the victory of communism in 1917, Stalin quickly moved into the inner leadership of the Communist party, and in 1922 he was made its General Secretary. Endowed with immense administrative ability and ruthless perseverance, Stalin used his position to build up his own machine within the party, even while Lenin was still alive, and soon conducted his first purges to get rid of unreliable, that is, anti-Stalinist, elements. Lenin still thought in Marxian concepts of class and party and made some effort to tolerate noncommunist Left views. Stalin, by contrast, quickly transformed the dictatorship of the proletariat into the personal dictatorship of Joseph Stalin. His two greatest accomplishments are the rapid industrialization of Russia and the victory over Nazi Germany in World War II. The second would have been impossible without the first, and history will tell whether the price paid by the Russian people for those accomplishments was too high.

Under Stalin, unorthodoxy of thought was more severely suppressed than in the worst days of the czars. Das Kapital was published in czarist Russia, as were many other works critical of the existing status quo; the publication of the slightest apology of capitalism, or even the least deviation from the official party line, became an impossibility under the Stalinist regime. As to forcible suppression of opposition activities, exile in Siberia under czarism was a rest cure compared with the slave-labor camps of Stalinism. Though serfdom was abolished in czarist Russia in 1861, Stalin reintroduced slavery for many millions of inmates of the slave-labor camps. Whereas most political exiles survived exile in Siberia under the czarist regime, and not a few were able to escape (as Stalin himself did), the death rate in the Stalinist slave-labor camps has been high, and escapes have been rare.

Stalin's main gift being of a practical and administrative nature, his contribution to the theory of communism contains little that is original. Marx, who had to work out his theories by himself, did not rely on authority, and his method was that of analyzing facts, not of quoting dogmas. Lenin belongs to the first generation of quoters in the history of Marxism. Stalin outdoes Lenin by far, and the fecundity of his citations from undisputed authorities (above all, Marx, Engels, and Lenin) resembles medieval scholastic literature more than twentieth-century political economy.

In his *Foundations of Leninism* (1924), Stalin expounds his conception of communism. He sees the world divided into two camps, "the world front of imperialism, which must be opposed by a common front of the revolutionary movement in all countries." In particular, Stalin affirms that in the contemporary imperialist stage of capitalism "wars cannot be averted," and he urges a *coalition between European communist states and colonial revolutions in Asia*, such as the Soviet Union later practiced with regard to the civil wars in China, Indo-China, Indonesia, and the aggression of Communist North Korea against South Korea in the summer of 1950. In 1924, Stalin considered the communist regime of Soviet Russia as a "base for the overthrow of imperialism in all countries. The revolution is spreading beyond the confines of one country: the period of world revolution has commenced."

In *Problems of Leninism* (1926), Stalin quotes with full approval the following statement by Lenin: "We are living not merely in a state, but in a *system of states;* and it is inconceivable that the Soviet republic should continue to exist for a long period side by side with imperialist states. Ultimately one or the other must conquer." Although Stalin has also occasionally referred, particularly in interviews with foreign newspapermen and politicians, to the possibility of peaceful "co-existence" of capitalism and communism, his view of inevitable conflict has been the one to which he has steadfastly adhered over the years.

The prediction of the inevitable conflict between revolutionary communism and capitalism, fascist or democratic, has also been used by Stalin as an argument for the indefinite duration of his dictatorship and that of the Communist party. According to Marx and Engels, the state was to wither away, once capitalism was completely liquidated. Yet the Russians saw in the nineteen-twenties and -thirties that, although capitalism was totally eliminated through state-owned and state-managed industry and the forcible collectivization of the farmers, the totalitarian police state increased its power and did not show the slightest inclination to wither away.

In his report on the draft constitution of 1936 (the "Stalin Constitution"), Stalin asserted that "the complete victory" of the public ownership of the means of production was a fact, and that "exploitation of men by men has been abolished." Yet the Soviet dictatorship had to go on (as Stalin explained in his report to the Eighteenth Communist Party Congress in 1939) because the Soviet regime was still menaced by *external enemies*. As long as communist states are encircled by capitalist states, the dictatorship of the proletariat as exercised by the communist parties must go on, and the withering away of the state has to be delayed. Until when? Until the whole world, or at least the majority of countries, has turned communist, and "there is no more need to strengthen the army and the state."

Whereas Marx and Engels hoped that the state would wither away after the destruction of capitalism within its borders, Stalin postpones the withering away of the communist totalitarian state into the distant and utopian future when the world has been conquered by communist revolution and formed into one world-state. A communist world-state of the Stalinist type would mean the rule of the whole world by one centralized authority, ultimately by a small group of men within *one* ruling country. But, even if such a communist world-state could be set up, it would still refuse to wither away, for, as the experience of the Stalin-Trotsky controversy and of the Stalin-Tito rift proves, communists, too, may quarrel. The Stalin of such a world-state could then argue that it could not wither away as long as Trotskys and Titos menaced the true communist theory and practice, as interpreted by those who understand it "correctly."

The issue between communism and the noncommunist world is not, as Lenin and Stalin assert, irreconcilable because it affects the fate of capitalism. The progressive socialization of basic industries in Britain and Scandinavia has proved that the means of production may be owned privately or publicly in different countries, or even in the same country, and that such different forms of ownership do not constitute in themselves a source of conflict. *What makes totalitarian communism an issue of peace or war is not its opposition to capitalism, but its determination to impose its philosophy by force of arms.*

At the end of World War II, the eastern European states under Soviet military occupation were turned into communist dictatorships. The most effective argument in defense of such Soviet action was the political immaturity of these states. After all, it was maintained, eastern Europe and the Balkans had never known political democracy, and the real choice lay between their fascist dictatorships before World War II and the communist dictatorships such as the Soviet Union helped to impose after World War II. Yet the naked aggressiveness of totalitarian communism became evident in February, 1948, when the Soviet Union supported the communist plot to destroy the freedom and independence of Czechoslovakia: here was the first instance of the subjugation of a truly democratic state to communist dictatorship by armed force. Also, the aggression of North Korean armies, trained and equipped by the Soviet Union, against South Korea in June, 1950, proved that Stalinist communism had arrived at a stage in which it risked military aggression from the outside to obtain its ends. The Leninist-Stalinist doctrine that revolutionary communism must conquer or die may still come true.

I. MARX and ENGELS

The Communist Manifesto *

A spectre is haunting Europe—the spectre of Communism. All the powers of old Europe have entered into a holy alliance to exorcise this spectre: Pope and Czar, Metternich and Guizot, French Radicals and German police-spies.

Where is the party in opposition that has not been decried as communistic by its opponents in power? Where the Opposition that has not hurled back the branding reproach of Communism, against the more advanced opposition parties, as well as against its reactionary adversaries?

Two things result from this fact:

I. Communism is already acknowledged by all European powers to be itself a power.

II. It is high time that Communists should openly, in the face of the whole world, publish their views, their aims, their tendencies, and meet this nursery tale of the spectre of Communism with a manifesto of the party itself.

To this end, Communists of various nationalities have assembled in London, and sketched the following manifesto, to be published in the English, French, German, Italian, Flemish and Danish languages.

1. Bourgeois and Proletarians

The history of all hitherto existing society is the history of class struggles.

Freeman and slave, patrician and ple-

beian, lord and serf, guild-master and journeyman, in a word, oppressor and oppressed, stood in constant opposition to one another, carried on an uninterrupted, now hidden, now open fight, a fight that each time ended, either in a revolutionary reconstitution of society at large, or in the common ruin of the contending classes.

In the earlier epochs of history, we find almost everywhere a complicated arrangement of society into various orders, a manifold gradation of social rank. In ancient Rome we have patricians, knights, plebeians, slaves; in the Middle Ages, feudal lords, vassals, guild-masters, journeymen, apprentices, serfs; in almost all of these classes, again, subordinate gradations.

The modern bourgeois society that has sprouted from the ruins of feudal society, has not done away with class antagonisms. It has but established new classes, new conditions of oppression, new forms of struggle in place of the old ones.

Our epoch, the epoch of the bourgeoisie, possesses, however, this distinctive feature: It has simplified the class antagonisms. Society as a whole is more and more splitting up into two great hostile camps, into two great classes directly facing each other—bourgeoisie and proletariat.

From the serfs of the Middle Ages sprang the chartered burghers of the earliest towns. From these burgesses the first elements of the bourgeoisie were developed.

The discovery of America, the rounding of the Cape, opened up fresh ground for the rising bourgeoisie. The East-Indian and

---

* (1848; English trans. of 1888, ed. Friedrich Engels.)

Chinese markets, the colonisation of America, trade with the colonies, the increase in the means of exchange and in commodities generally, gave to commerce, to navigation, to industry, an impulse never before known, and thereby, to the revolutionary element in the tottering feudal society, a rapid development.

The feudal system of industry, in which industrial production was monopolised by closed guilds, now no longer sufficed for the growing wants of the new markets. The manufacturing system took its place. The guild-masters were pushed aside by the manufacturing middle class; division of labour between the different corporate guilds vanished in the face of division of labour in each single workshop.

Meantime the markets kept ever growing, the demand ever rising. Even manufacture no longer sufficed. Thereupon, steam and machinery revolutionised industrial production. The place of manufacture was taken by the giant, modern industry, the place of the industrial middle class, by industrial millionaires—the leaders of whole industrial armies, the modern bourgeoisie.

Modern industry has established the world market, for which the discovery of America paved the way. This market has given an immense development to commerce, to navigation, to communication by land. This development has, in its turn, reacted on the extension of industry; and in proportion as industry, commerce, navigation, railways extended, in the same proportion the bourgeoisie developed, increased its capital, and pushed into the background every class handed down from the Middle Ages.

We see, therefore, how the modern bourgeoisie is itself the product of a long course of development, of a series of revolutions in the modes of production and of exchange.

Each step in the development of the bourgeoisie was accompanied by a corresponding political advance of that class. An oppressed class under the sway of the feudal nobility, it became an armed and self-governing association in the mediæval commune; here independent urban republic (as in Italy and Germany), there taxable "third estate" of the monarchy (as in France); afterwards, in the period of manufacture proper, serving either the semi-feudal or the absolute monarchy as a counterpoise against the nobility, and, in fact, cornerstone of the great monarchies in general—the bourgeoisie has at last, since the establishment of modern industry and of the world market, conquered for itself, in the modern representative state, exclusive political sway. The executive of the modern state is but a committee for managing the common affairs of the whole bourgeoisie.

The bourgeoisie has played a most revolutionary rôle in history.

The bourgeoisie, wherever it has got the upper hand, has put an end to all feudal, patriarchal, idyllic relations. It has pitilessly torn asunder the motley feudal ties that bound man to his "natural superiors," and has left no other bond between man and man than naked self-interest, than callous "cash payment." It has drowned the most heavenly ecstasies of religious fervour, of chivalrous enthusiasm, of philistine sentimentalism, in the icy water of egotistical calculation. It has resolved personal worth into exchange value, and in place of the numberless indefeasible chartered freedoms, has set up that single, unconscionable freedom—Free Trade. In one word, for exploitation, veiled by religious and political illusions, it has substituted naked, shameless, direct, brutal exploitation.

The bourgeoisie has stripped of its halo every occupation hitherto honoured and looked up to with reverent awe. It has converted the physician, the lawyer, the priest, the poet, the man of science, into its paid wage-labourers.

The bourgeoisie has torn away from the family its sentimental veil, and has reduced the family relation to a mere money relation.

The bourgeoisie has disclosed how it came to pass that the brutal display of vigour in the Middle Ages, which reactionaries so much admire, found its fitting complement in the most slothful indolence. It has been the first to show what man's activity can bring about. It has accomplished wonders far surpassing Egyptian pyramids, Roman aqueducts, and Gothic cathedrals; it has conducted expeditions that put in the shade all former migrations of nations and crusades.

The bourgeoisie cannot exist without constantly revolutionising the instruments of production, and thereby the relations of production, and with them the whole relations of society. Conservation of the old modes of production in unaltered form, was, on the contrary, the first condition of existence for all earlier industrial classes. Constant revolutionising of production, uninterrupted disturbance of all social conditions, everlasting uncertainty and agitation distinguish the bourgeois epoch from all earlier ones. All fixed, fast-frozen relations, with their train of ancient and venerable prejudices and opinions, are swept away, all new-formed ones become antiquated before they can ossify. All that is solid melts into air, all that is holy is profaned, and man is at last compelled to face with sober senses his real conditions of life and his relations with his kind.

The need of a constantly expanding market for its products chases the bourgeoisie over the whole surface of the globe. It must nestle everywhere, settle everywhere, establish connections everywhere.

The bourgeoisie has through its exploitation of the world market given a cosmopolitan character to production and consumption in every country. To the great chagrin of reactionaries, it has drawn from under the feet of industry the national ground on which it stood. All old-established national industries have been destroyed or are daily being destroyed. They are dislodged by new industries, whose introduction becomes a life and death question for all civilised nations, by industries that no longer work up indigenous raw material, but raw material drawn from the remotest zones; industries whose products are consumed, not only at home, but in every quarter of the globe. In place of the old wants, satisfied by the production of the country, we find new wants, requiring for their satisfaction the products of distant lands and climes. In place of the old local and national seclusion and self-sufficiency, we have intercourse in every direction, universal inter-dependence of nations. And as in material, so also in intellectual production. The intellectual creations of individual nations become common property. National one-sidedness and narrow-mindedness become more and more impossible, and from the numerous national and local literatures there arises a world literature.

The bourgeoisie, by the rapid improvement of all instruments of production, by the immensely facilitated means of communication, draws all nations, even the most barbarian, into civilisation. The cheap prices of its commodities are the heavy artillery with which it batters down all Chinese walls, with which it forces the barbarians' intensely obstinate hatred of foreigners to capitulate. It compels all nations, on pain of extinction, to adopt the bourgeois mode of production; it compels them to introduce what it calls civilisation into their midst, i.e., to become bourgeois themselves. In a word, it creates a world after its own image.

The bourgeoisie has subjected the country to the rule of the towns. It has created enormous cities, has greatly increased the urban population as compared with the rural, and has thus rescued a considerable part of the population from the idiocy of rural life. Just as it has made the country dependent on the towns, so it has made barbarian and semi-barbarian countries dependent on the civilised ones, nations of peasants on nations of bourgeois, the East on the West.

The bourgeoisie keeps more and more doing away with the scattered state of the population, of the means of production, and of property. It has agglomerated population, centralised means of production, and has concentrated property in a few hands. The necessary consequence of this was political centralisation. Independent, or but loosely connected provinces, with separate interests, laws, governments and systems of taxation, became lumped together into one nation, with one government, one code of laws, one national class interest, one frontier and one customs tariff.

The bourgeoisie, during its rule of scarce one hundred years, has created more massive and more colossal productive forces than have all preceding generations together. Subjection of nature's forces to man, machinery, application of chemistry to industry and agriculture, steam-navigation, railways, electric telegraphs, clearing of whole continents for cultivation, canalisation of rivers, whole populations conjured out of the ground—what earlier century had even a presentiment that such productive forces slumbered in the lap of social labour?

We see then that the means of production and of exchange, which served as the foundation for the growth of the bourgeoisie, were generated in feudal society. At a certain stage in the development of these means of production and of exchange, the conditions under which feudal society produced and exchanged, the feudal organisation of agriculture and manufacturing industry, in a word, the feudal relations of property became no longer compatible with the already developed productive forces; they became so many fetters. They had to be burst asunder; they were burst asunder.

Into their place stepped free competition, accompanied by a social and political constitution adapted to it, and by the economic and political sway of the bourgeois class.

A similar movement is going on before our own eyes. Modern bourgeois society with its relations of production, of exchange and of property, a society that has conjured up such gigantic means of production and of exchange, is like the sorcerer who is no longer able to control the powers of the nether world whom he has called up by his spells. For many a decade past the history of industry and commerce is but the history of the revolt of modern productive forces against modern conditions of production, against the property relations that are the conditions for the existence of the bourgeoisie and of its rule. It is enough to mention the commercial crises that by their periodical return put the existence of the entire bourgeois society on trial, each time more threateningly. In these crises a great part not only of the existing products, but also of the previously created productive forces, are periodically destroyed. In these crises there breaks out an epidemic that, in all earlier epochs, would have seemed an absurdity—the epidemic of over-production. Society suddenly finds itself put back into a state of momentary barbarism; it appears as if a famine, a universal war of devastation had cut off the supply of every means of subsistence; industry and commerce seem to be destroyed. And why? Because there is too much civilisation, too much means of subsistence, too much industry, too much commerce. The productive forces at the disposal of society no longer tend to further the development of the conditions of bourgeois property; on the contrary, they have become too powerful for these conditions, by which they are fettered, and no sooner do they overcome these fetters than they bring disorder into the whole of bourgeois society, endanger the existence of bourgeois property. The conditions of bourgeois society are too narrow to comprise the wealth created by them. And how does the bourgeoisie get over these crises? On the one hand by enforced destruction of a mass of productive forces; on the other, by the conquest of new markets, and by the more thorough exploitation of the old ones. That is to say, by paving the way for more extensive and more destructive crises, and by diminishing the means whereby crises are prevented.

The weapons with which the bourgeoisie felled feudalism to the ground are now turned against the bourgeoisie itself.

But not only has the bourgeoisie forged the weapons that bring death to itself; it has also called into existence the men who are to wield those weapons—the modern working class—the proletarians.

In proportion as the bourgeoisie, *i.e.,* capital, is developed, in the same proportion is the proletariat, the modern working class, developed—a class of labourers, who live only so long as they find work, and who find work only so long as their labour increases capital. These labourers, who must sell themselves piecemeal, are a commodity, like every other article of commerce, and are consequently exposed to all the vicissitudes of competition, to all the fluctuations of the market.

Owing to the extensive use of machinery and to division of labour, the work of the proletarians has lost all individual character, and, consequently, all charm for the workman. He becomes an appendage of the machine, and it is only the most simple, most monotonous, and most easily acquired knack, that is required of him. Hence, the cost of production of a workman is restricted, almost entirely, to the means of subsistence that he requires for his maintenance, and for the propagation of his race. But the price of a commodity, and therefore also af labour, is equal to its cost of production. In proportion, therefore, as the repulsiveness of the work increases, the wage decreases. Nay more, in proportion as the use of machinery and division of labour increases, in the same proportion the burden of toil also increases, whether by prolongation of the working hours, by increase of the work exacted in a given time, or by increased speed of the machinery, etc.

Modern industry has converted the little workshop of the patriarchal master into the great factory of the industrial capitalist. Masses of labourers, crowded into the factory, are organised like soldiers. As privates of the industrial army they are placed under the command of a perfect hierarchy of officers and sergeants. Not only are they slaves of the bourgeois class, and of the bourgeois state; they are daily and hourly enslaved by the machine, by the overseer, and, above all, by the individual bourgeois manufacturer himself. The more openly this despotism proclaims gain to be its end and aim, the more petty, the more hateful and the more embittering it is.

The less the skill and exertion of strength implied in manual labour, in other words, the more modern industry develops, the more is the labour of men superseded by that of women. Differences of age and sex have no longer any distinctive social validity for the working class. All are instruments of labour, more or less expensive to use, according to their age and sex.

No sooner has the labourer received his wages in cash, for the moment escaping exploitation by the manufacturer, than he is set upon by the other portions of the bourgeoisie, the landlord, the shopkeeper, the pawnbroker, etc.

The lower strata of the middle class—the small tradespeople, shopkeepers, and retired tradesmen generally, the handicraftsmen and peasants—all these sink gradually into the proletariat, partly because their diminutive capital does not suffice for the scale on which modern industry is carried on, and is swamped in the competition with the large capitalists, partly because their specialised skill is rendered worthless by new methods of production. Thus the proletariat is recruited from all classes of the population.

The proletariat goes through various stages of development. With its birth begins its struggle with the bourgeoisie. At first the contest is carried on by individual labourers, then by the work people of a factory, then by the operatives of one trade, in one locality, against the individual bourgeois who directly exploits them. They direct their attacks not against the bourgeois conditions of production, but against the instruments of production themselves; they destroy imported wares that compete with their labour, they smash machinery to pieces, they set factories ablaze, they seek to restore by force the vanished status of the workman of the Middle Ages.

At this stage the labourers still form an incoherent mass scattered over the whole country, and broken up by their mutual competition. If anywhere they unite to form more compact bodies, this is not yet the consequence of their own active union, but of the union of the bourgeoisie, which class, in order to attain its own political ends, is compelled to set the whole proletariat in motion, and is moreover still able to do so for a time. At this stage, therefore, the proletarians do not fight their enemies, but the enemies of their enemies, the remnants of absolute monarchy, the landowners, the non-industrial bourgeois, the petty bourgeoisie. Thus the whole historical movement is concentrated in the hands of the bourgeoisie; every victory so obtained is a victory for the bourgeoisie.

But with the development of industry the proletariat not only increases in number; it becomes concentrated in greater masses, its strength grows, and it feels that strength more. The various interests and conditions of life within the ranks of the proletariat are more and more equalised, in proportion as machinery obliterates all distinctions of labour and nearly everywhere reduces wages to the same low level. The growing competition among the bourgeois, and the resulting commercial crises, makes the wages of the workers ever more fluctuating. The unceasing improvement of machinery, ever more rapidly developing, makes their livelihood more and more precarious; the collisions between individual workmen and individual bourgeois take more and more the character of collisions between two classes. Thereupon the workers begin to form combinations (trade unions) against the bourgeoisie; they club together in order to keep up the rate of wages; they found permanent associations in order to make provision beforehand for these occasional revolts. Here and there the contest breaks out into riots.

Now and then the workers are victorious, but only for a time. The real fruit of their battles lies, not in the immediate result, but in the ever expanding union of the workers. This union is furthered by the improved means of communication which are created by modern industry, and which place the workers of different localities in contact with one another. It was just this contact that was needed to centralise the numerous local struggles, all of the same character, into one national struggle between classes. But every class struggle is a political struggle. And that union, to attain which the burghers of the Middle Ages, with their miserable highways, required centuries, the modern proletarians, thanks to railways, achieve in a few years.

This organisation of the proletarians into a class, and consequently into a political party, is continually being upset again by the competition between the workers themselves. But it ever rises up again, stronger, firmer, mightier. It compels legislative recognition of particular interests of the workers, by taking advantage of the divisions among the bourgeoisie itself. Thus the ten-hour bill in England was carried.

Altogether, collisions between the classes of the old society further the course of development of the proletariat in many ways. The bourgeoisie finds itself involved in a constant battle. At first with the aristocracy; later on, with those portions of the bourgeoisie itself whose interests have become antagonistic to the progress of industry; at all times with the bourgeoisie of foreign countries. In all these battles it sees itself compelled to appeal to the proletariat, to ask for its help, and thus, to drag it into the political arena. The bourgoisie itself, therefore, supplies the proletariat with its own elements of political and general education, in other words, it furnishes the proletariat with weapons for fighting the bourgeoisie.

Further, as we have already seen, entire sections of the ruling classes are, by the advance of industry, precipitated into the proletariat, or are at least threatened in their conditions of existence. These also supply the proletariat with fresh elements of enlightenment and progress.

Finally, in times when the class struggle nears the decisive hour, the process of dissolution going on within the ruling class, in fact within the whole range of old society, assumes such a violent, glaring character, that a small section of the ruling class cuts itself adrift, and joins the revolutionary class, the class that holds the future in its hands. Just as, therefore, at an earlier period, a section of the nobility went over to the bourgeoisie, so now a portion of the bourgeoisie goes over to the proletariat, and in particular, a portion of the bourgeois ideologists, who have raised themselves to the level of comprehending theoretically the historical movement as a whole.

Of all the classes that stand face to face with the bourgeoisie today, the proletariat alone is a really revolutionary class. The other classes decay and finally disappear in the face of modern industry; the proletariat is its special and essential product.

The lower middle class, the small manufacturer, the shopkeeper, the artisan, the peasant, all these fight against the bourgeoisie, to save from extinction their existence as fractions of the middle class. They are therefore not revolutionary, but conservative. Nay more, they are reactionary, for they try to roll back the wheel of history. If by chance they are revolutionary, they are so only in view of their impending transfer into the proletariat; they thus defend not their present, but their future interests; they desert their own standpoint to adopt that of the proletariat.

The "dangerous class," the social scum (*Lumpenproletariat*), that passively rotting mass thrown off by the lowest layers of old society, may, here and there, be swept into the movement by a proletarian revolution; its conditions of life, however, prepare it far more for the part of a bribed tool of reactionary intrigue.

The social conditions of the old society no longer exist for the proletariat. The proletarian is without property; his relation to his wife and children has no longer anything in common with bourgeois family relations; modern industrial labour, modern subjection to capital, the same in England as in France, in America as in Germany, has stripped him of every trace of national character. Law, morality, religion, are to him so many bourgeois prejudices, behind which lurk in ambush just as many bourgeois interests.

All the preceding classes that got the upper hand, sought to fortify their already acquired status by subjecting society at large to their conditions of appropriation. The proletarians cannot become masters of the productive forces of society, except by abolishing their own previous mode of appropriation, and thereby also every other previous mode of appropriation. They have nothing of their own to secure and to fortify; their mission is to destroy all previous securities for, and insurances of, individual property.

All previous historical movements were movements of minorities, or in the interest of minorities. The proletarian movement is the self-conscious, independent movement of the immense majority, in the interest of the immense majority. The proletariat, the lowest stratum of our present society, cannot stir, cannot raise itself up, without the whole superincumbent strata of official society being sprung into the air.

Though not in substance, yet in form, the struggle of the proletariat with the bourgeoisie is at first a national struggle. The proletariat of each country must, of course, first of all settle matters with its own bourgeoisie.

In depicting the most general phases of the development of the proletariat, we traced the more or less veiled civil war, raging within existing society, up to the point where that war breaks out into open revolution, and where the violent overthrow of the bourgeoisie lays the foundation for the sway of the proletariat.

Hitherto, every form of society has been based, as we have already seen, on the antagonism of oppressing and oppressed classes. But in order to oppress a class, certain conditions must be assured to it under which it can, at least, continue its slavish existence. The serf, in the period of serfdom, raised himself to membership in the commune, just as the petty bourgeois, under the yoke of feudal absolutism, managed to develop into a bourgeois. The modern labourer, on the contrary, instead of rising with the progress of industry, sinks deeper and deeper below the conditions of existence of his own class. He becomes a pauper, and pauperism develops more rapidly than population and wealth. And here it becomes evident, that the bourgeoisie is unfit any longer to be the ruling class in society, and to impose its conditions of existence upon society as an over-riding law. It is unfit to rule because it is incompetent to assure an existence to its slave within his slavery, because it cannot help letting him sink into such a state, that it has to feed him, instead of being fed by him. Society can no longer live under this bourgeoisie, in other words, its existence is no longer compatible with society.

The essential condition for the existence and sway of the bourgeois class, is the formation and augmentation of capital; the condition for capital is wage-labour. Wage-labour rests exclusively on competition between the labourers. The advance of industry, whose involuntary promoter is the bourgeoisie, replaces the isolation of the labourers, due to competition, by their revolutionary combination, due to association. The development of modern industry, therefore, cuts from under its feet the very foundation on which the bourgeoisie produces and appropriates products. What the bourgeoisie therefore produces, above all, are its own grave-diggers. Its fall and the victory of the proletariat are equally inevitable.

2. Proletarians and Communists

In what relation do the Communists stand to the proletarians as a whole?

The Communists do not form a separate party opposed to other working class parties.

They have no interests separate and apart from those of the proletariat as a whole.

They do not set up any sectarian principles of their own, by which to shape and mould the proletarian movement.

The Communists are distinguished from the other working class parties by this only: 1. In the national struggles of the proletarians of the different countries, they point out and bring to the front the common interests of the entire proletariat, independently of all nationality. 2. In the various stages of development which the struggle of the working class against the bourgeoisie has to pass through, they always and everywhere represent the interests of the movement as a whole.

The Communists, therefore, are on the one hand, practically, the most advanced and resolute section of the working class parties of every country, that section which pushes forward all others; on the other hand, theoretically, they have over the great mass of the proletariat the advantage of clearly understanding the line of march, the conditions, and the ultimate general results of the proletarian movement.

The immediate aim of the Communists is the same as that of all the other proletarian parties: Formation of the proletariat into a class, overthrow of bourgeois supremacy, conquest of political power by the proletariat.

The theoretical conclusions of the Communists are in no way based on ideas or principles that have been invented, or discovered, by this or that would-be universal reformer.

They merely express, in general terms, actual relations springing from an existing class struggle, from a historical movement going on under our very eyes. The abolition of existing property relations is not at all a distinctive feature of Communism.

All property relations in the past have continually been subject to historical change consequent upon the change in historical conditions.

The French Revolution, for example, abolished feudal property in favour of bourgeois property.

The distinguishing feature of Communism is not the abolition of property generally, but the abolition of bourgeois property. But modern bourgeois private property is the final and most complete expression of the system of producing and appropriating products that is based on class antagonisms, on the exploitation of the many by the few.

In this sense, the theory of the Communists may be summed up in the single sentence: Abolition of private property.

We Communists have been reproached with the desire of abolishing the right of personally acquiring property as the fruit of a man's own labour, which property is alleged to be the groundwork of all personal freedom, activity and independence.

Hard-won, self-acquired, self-earned property! Do you mean the property of the petty artisan and of the small peasant, a form of property that preceded the bourgeois form? There is no need to abolish that; the development of industry has to a great extent already destroyed it, and is still destroying it daily.

Or do you mean modern bourgeois private property?

But does wage-labour create any property for the labourer? Not a bit. It creates capital, i.e., that kind of property which exploits wage-labour, and which cannot increase except upon condition of begetting a new supply of wage-labour for fresh exploitation. Property, in its present form, is based on the antagonism of capital and wage-labour. Let us examine both sides of this antagonism.

To be a capitalist, is to have not only a purely personal, but a social *status* in production. Capital is a collective product, and only by the united action of many members, nay, in the last resort, only by the united action of all members of society, can it be set in motion.

Capital is therefore not a personal, it is a social, power.

When, therefore, capital is converted into common property, into the property of all members of society, personal property is not thereby transformed into social property. It is only the social character of the property that is changed. It loses its class character.

Let us now take wage-labour.

The average price of wage-labour is the minimum wage, i.e., that quantum of the means of subsistence which is absolutely requisite to keep the labourer in bare existence as a labourer. What, therefore, the wage-labourer appropriates by means of his labour, merely suffices to prolong and reproduce a bare existence. We by no means intend to abolish this personal appropriation of the products of labour, an appropriation that is made for the maintenance and reproduction of human life, and that leaves no surplus wherewith to command the labour of others. All that we want to do away with is the miserable character of this appropriation, under which the labourer lives merely to increase capital, and is allowed to live only insofar as the interest of the ruling class requires it.

In bourgeois society, living labour is but a means to increase accumulated labour. In Communist society, accumulated labour is but a means to widen, to enrich, to promote the existence of the labourer.

In bourgeois society, therefore, the past dominates the present; in Communist society, the present dominates the past. In bourgeois society capital is independent and has individuality, while the living person is dependent and has no individuality.

And the abolition of this state of things is called by the bourgeois, abolition of individuality and freedom! And rightly so. The abolition of bourgeois individuality, bourgeois independence, and bourgeois freedom is undoubtedly aimed at.

By freedom is meant, under the present bourgeois conditions of production, free trade, free selling and buying.

But if selling and buying disappears, free selling and buying disappears also. This talk about free selling and buying, and all the other "brave words" of our bourgeoisie about freedom in general, have a meaning, if any, only in contrast with restricted selling and buying, with the fettered traders of the Middle Ages, but have no meaning when opposed to the Communist abolition of buying and selling, of the bourgeois condition of production, and of the bourgeoisie itself.

You are horrified at our intending to do away with private property. But in your existing society, private property is already done away with for nine-tenths of the population; its existence for the few is solely due to its non-existence in the hands of those nine-tenths. You reproach us, therefore, with intending to do away with a form of property, the necessary condition for whose existence is the non-existence of any property for the immense majority of society.

In a word, you reproach us with intending to do away with your property. Precisely so; that is just what we intend.

From the moment when labour can no longer be converted into capital, money, or rent, into a social power capable of being monopolised, *i.e.*, from the moment when individual property can no longer be transformed into bourgeois property, into capital, from that moment, you say, individuality vanishes.

You must, therefore, confess that by "individual" you mean no other person than the bourgeois, than the middle class owner of property. This person must, indeed, be swept out of the way, and made impossible.

Communism deprives no man of the power to appropriate the products of society; all that it does is to deprive him of the power to subjugate the labour of others by means of such appropriation.

It has been objected, that upon the abolition of private property all work will cease, and universal laziness will overtake us.

According to this, bourgeois society ought long ago to have gone to the dogs through sheer idleness; for those of its members who work, acquire nothing, and those who acquire anything, do not work. The whole of this objection is but another expression of the tautology: There can no longer be any wage-labour when there is no longer any capital.

All objections urged against the Communist mode of producing and appropriating material products, have, in the same way, been urged against the Communist modes of producing and appropriating intellectual products. Just as, to the bourgeois, the disappearance of class property is the disappearance of production itself, so the disappearance of class culture is to him identical with the disappearance of all culture.

That culture, the loss of which he laments, is, for the enormous majority, a mere training to act as a machine.

But don't wrangle with us so long as you apply, to our intended abolition of bourgeois property, the standard of your bourgeois notions of freedom, culture, law, etc. Your very ideas are but the outgrowth of the conditions of your bourgeois production and bourgeois property, just as your jurisprudence is but the will of your class made into a law for all, a will whose essential character and direction are determined by the economic conditions of existence of your class.

The selfish misconception that induces you to transform into eternal laws of nature and of reason, the social forms springing from your present mode of production and form of property—historical relations that rise and disappear in the progress of production—this misconception you share with every ruling class that has preceded you. What you see clearly in the case of ancient property, what you admit in the case of feudal property, you are of course forbidden to admit in the case of your own bourgeois form of property.

Abolition of the family! Even the most radical flare up at this infamous proposal of the Communists.

On what foundation is the present family, the bourgeois family, based? On capital, on private gain. In its completely developed form this family exists only among the bourgeoisie. But this state of things finds its complement in the practical absence of the family among the proletarians, and in public prostitution.

The bourgeois family will vanish as a matter of course when its complement vanishes, and both will vanish with the vanishing of capital.

Do you charge us with wanting to stop the exploitation of children by their parents? To this crime we plead guilty.

But, you will say, we destroy the most hallowed of relations, when we replace home education by social.

And your education! Is not that also social, and determined by the social conditions under which you educate, by the intervention of society, direct or indirect, by means of schools, etc.? The Communists have not invented the intervention of society in education; they do but seek to alter the character of that intervention, and to rescue education from the influence of the ruling class.

The bourgeois claptrap about the family and education, about the hallowed co-relation of parent and child, becomes all the more disgusting, the more, by the action of modern industry, all family ties among the proletarians are torn asunder, and their children transformed into simple articles of commerce and instruments of labour.

But you Communists would introduce community of women, screams the whole bourgeoisie in chorus.

The bourgeois sees in his wife a mere instrument of production. He hears that the instruments of production are to be exploited in common, and, naturally, can come to no other conclusion than that the lot of being common to all will likewise fall to the women.

He has not even a suspicion that the real point aimed at is to do away with the status of women as mere instruments of production.

For the rest, nothing is more ridiculous than the virtuous indignation of our bourgeois at the community of women which, they pretend, is to be openly and officially established by the Communists. The Communists have no need to introduce community of women; it has existed almost from time immemorial.

Our bourgeois, not content with having the wives and daughters of their proletarians

at their disposal, not to speak of common prostitutes, take the greatest pleasure in seducing each other's wives.

Bourgeois marriage is in reality a system of wives in common and thus, at the most, what the Communists might possibly be reproached with is that they desire to introduce, in substitution for a hypocritically concealed, an openly legalised community of women. For the rest, it is self-evident, that the abolition of the present system of production must bring with it the abolition of the community of women springing from that system, *i.e.,* of prostitution both public and private.

The Communists are further reproached with desiring to abolish countries and nationality.

The workingmen have no country. We cannot take from them what they have not got. Since the proletariat must first of all acquire political supremacy, must rise to be the leading class of the nation, must constitute itself *the* nation, it is, so far, itself national, though not in the bourgeois sense of the word.

National differences and antagonisms between peoples are vanishing gradually from day to day, owing to the development of the bourgeoisie, to freedom of commerce, to the world market, to uniformity in the mode of production and in the conditions of life corresponding thereto.

The supremacy of the proletariat will cause them to vanish still faster. United action, of the leading civilised countries at least, is one of the first conditions for the emancipation of the proletariat.

In proportion as the exploitation of one individual by another is put an end to, the exploitation of one nation by another will also be put an end to. In proportion as the antagonism between classes within the nation vanishes, the hostility of one nation to another will come to an end.

The charges against Communism made from a religious, a philosophical, and, generally, from an ideological standpoint, are not deserving of serious examination.

Does it require deep intuition to comprehend that man's ideas, views, and conceptions, in one word, man's consciousness, changes with every change in the conditions of his material existence, in his social relations and in his social life?

What else does the history of ideas prove, than that intellectual production changes its character in proportion as material production is changed? The ruling ideas of each age have ever been the ideas of its ruling class.

When people speak of ideas that revolutionise society, they do but express the fact that within the old society the elements of a new one have been created, and that the dissolution of the old ideas keeps even pace with the dissolution of the old conditions of existence.

When the ancient world was in its last throes, the ancient religions were overcome by Christianity. When Christian ideas succumbed in the 18th century to rationalist ideas, feudal society fought its death-battle with the then revolutionary bourgeoisie. The ideas of religious liberty and freedom of conscience, merely gave expression to the sway of free competition within the domain of knowledge.

"Undoubtedly," it will be said, "religion, moral, philosophical and juridical ideas have been modified in the course of historical development. But religion, morality, philosophy, political science, and law, constantly survived this change."

"There are, besides, eternal truths, such as Freedom, Justice, etc., that are common to all states of society. But Communism abolishes eternal truths, it abolishes all religion, and all morality, instead of constituting them on a new basis; it therefore acts in contradiction to all past historical experience."

What does this accusation reduce itself to? The history of all past society has consisted in the development of class antagonisms, antagonisms that assumed different forms at different epochs.

But whatever form they may have taken, one fact is common to all past ages, viz., the exploitation of one part of society by the other. No wonder, then, that the social consciousness of past ages, despite all the multiplicity and variety it displays, moves within certain common forms, or general ideas, which cannot completely vanish except with the total disappearance of class antagonisms.

The Communist revolution is the most radical rupture with traditional property relations; no wonder that its development involves the most radical rupture with traditional ideas.

But let us have done with the bourgeois objections to Communism.

We have seen above, that the first step in the revolution by the working class, is to raise the proletariat to the position of ruling class, to establish democracy.

The proletariat will use its political supremacy to wrest, by degrees, all capital from the bourgeoisie, to centralise all instruments of production in the hands of the state, i.e., of the proletariat organised as the ruling class; and to increase the total of productive forces as rapidly as possible.

Of course, in the beginning, this cannot be effected except by means of despotic inroads on the rights of property, and on the conditions of bourgeois production; by means of measures, therefore, which appear economically insufficient and untenable, but which, in the course of the movement, outstrip themselves, necessitate further inroads upon the old social order, and are unavoidable as a means of entirely revolutionising the mode of production.

These measures will of course be different in different countries.

Nevertheless in the most advanced countries, the following will be pretty generally applicable.

1. Abolition of property in land and application of all rents of land to public purposes.

2. A heavy progressive or graduated income tax.

3. Abolition of all right of inheritance.

4. Confiscation of the property of all emigrants and rebels.

5. Centralisation of credit in the hands of the state, by means of a national bank with state capital and an exclusive monopoly.

6. Centralisation of the means of communication and transport in the hands of the state.

7. Extension of factories and instruments of production owned by the state; the bringing into cultivation of waste lands, and the improvement of the soil generally in accordance with a common plan.

8. Equal obligation of all to work. Establishment of industrial armies, especially for agriculture.

9. Combination of agriculture with manufacturing industries; gradual abolition of the distinction between town and country, by a more equable distribution of the population over the country.

10. Free education for all children in public schools. Abolition of child factory labour in its present form. Combination of education with industrial production, etc.

When, in the course of development, class distinctions have disappeared, and all production has been concentrated in the hands of a vast association of the whole nation, the public power will lose its political character. Political power, properly so called, is merely the organised power of one class for oppressing another. If the proletariat during its contest with the bourgeoisie is compelled, by the force of circumstances, to organise itself as a class; if, by means of a revolution, it makes itself the ruling class, and, as such sweeps away by force the old conditions of production, then it will, along with these conditions, have swept away the conditions for the existence of class antagonisms, and of classes generally, and will thereby have abolished its own supremacy as a class.

In place of the old bourgeois society, with its classes and class antagonisms, we shall have an association, in which the free development of each is the condition for the free development of all.

3. Socialist and Communist Literature

1. REACTIONARY SOCIALISM

a. Feudal Socialism. Owing to their historical position, it became the vocation of the aristocracies of France and England to write pamphlets against modern bourgeois society. In the French revolution of July, 1830, and in the English reform agitation, these aristocracies again succumbed to the hateful upstart. Thenceforth, a serious political struggle was altogether out of the question. A literary battle alone remained possible. But even in the domain of literature the old cries of the restoration period had become impossible.

In order to arouse sympathy, the aristocracy was obliged to lose sight, apparently, of its own interests, and to formulate its indictment against the bourgeoisie in the interest of the exploited working class alone. Thus the aristocracy took its revenge by singing lampoons against its new master, and whispering in his ears sinister prophecies of coming catastrophe.

In this way arose Feudal Socialism: Half lamentation, half lampoon; half echo of the past, half menace of the future; at times, by its bitter, witty and incisive criticism, striking the bourgeoisie to the very heart's core, but always ludicrous in its effect through total incapacity to comprehend the march of modern history.

The aristocracy, in order to rally the people to them, waved the proletarian almsbag in front for a banner. But the people, as often as it joined them, saw on their hindquarters the old feudal coats of arms, and deserted with loud and irreverent laughter.

One section of the French Legitimists, and "Young England," exhibited this spectacle.

In pointing out that their mode of exploitation was different from that of the bourgeoisie, the feudalists forget that they exploited under circumstances and conditions that were quite different, and that are now antiquated. In showing that, under their rule, the modern proletariat never existed, they forget that the modern bourgeoisie is the necessary offspring of their own form of society.

For the rest, so little do they conceal the reactionary character of their criticism, that their chief accusation against the bourgeoisie amounts to this, that under the bourgeois regime a class is being developed, which is destined to cut up root and branch the old order of society.

What they upbraid the bourgeoisie with is not so much that it creates a proletariat, as that it creates a *revolutionary* proletariat.

In political practice, therefore, they join in all coercive measures against the working class; and in ordinary life, despite their high-falutin phrases, they stoop to pick up the golden apples dropped from the tree of industry, and to barter truth, love, and honour for traffic in wool, beetroot-sugar, and potato spirits.

As the parson has ever gone hand in hand with the landlord, so has Clerical Socialism with Feudal Socialism.

Nothing is easier than to give Christian asceticism a Socialist tinge. Has not Christianity declaimed against private property, against marriage, against the state? Has it not preached in the place of these, charity and poverty, celibacy and mortification of the flesh, monastic life and Mother Church? Christian Socialism is but the holy water with which the priest consecrates the heart-burnings of the aristocrat.

b. Petty Bourgeois Socialism. The feudal aristocracy was not the only class that was ruined by the bourgeoisie, not the only class whose conditions of existence pined and perished in the atmosphere of modern bourgeois society. The mediæval burgesses and the small peasant proprietors were the precursors of the modern bourgeoisie. In those countries which are but little developed, industrially and commercially, these two classes still vegetate side by side with the rising bourgeoisie.

In countries where modern civilisation has become fully developed, a new class of petty bourgeois has been formed, fluctuat-

ing between proletariat and bourgeoisie, and ever renewing itself as a supplementary part of bourgeois society. The individual members of this class, however, are being constantly hurled down into the proletariat by the action of competition, and, as modern industry develops, they even see the moment approaching when they will completely disappear as an independent section of modern society, to be replaced, in manufactures, agriculture and commerce, by overseers, bailiffs and shopmen.

In countries, like France, where the peasants constitute far more than half of the population, it was natural that writers who sided with the proletariat against the bourgeoisie, should use, in their criticism of the bourgeois regime, the standard of the peasant and petty bourgeois, and from the standpoint of these intermediate classes should take up the cudgels for the working class. Thus arose petty bourgeois Socialism. Sismondi was the head of this school, not only in France but also in England.

This school of Socialism dissected with great acuteness the contradictions in the conditions of modern production. It laid bare the hypocritical apologies of economists. It proved, incontrovertibly, the disastrous effects of machinery and division of labour; the concentration of capital and land in a few hands; overproduction and crises; it pointed out the inevitable ruin of the petty bourgeois and peasant, the misery of the proletariat, the anarchy in production, the crying inequalities in the distribution of wealth, the industrial war of extermination between nations, the dissolution of old moral bonds, of the old family relations, of the old nationalities.

In its positive aims, however, this form of Socialism aspires either to restoring the old means of production and of exchange, and with them the old property relations, and the old society, or to cramping the modern means of production and of exchange within the framework of the old property relations that have been, and were bound to be, exploded by those means. In either case, it is both reactionary and utopian.

Its last words are: Corporate guilds for manufacture; patriarchal relations in agriculture.

Ultimately, when stubborn historical facts had dispersed all intoxicating effects of self-deception, this form of Socialism ended in a miserable fit of the blues.

c. German or "True" Socialism. The Socialist and Communist literature of France, a literature that originated under the pressure of a bourgeoisie in power, and that was the expression of the struggle against this power, was introduced into Germany at a time when the bourgeoisie, in that country, had just begun its contest with feudal absolutism.

German philosophers, would-be philosophers, and men of letters eagerly seized on this literature, only forgetting that when these writings immigrated from France into Germany, French social conditions had not immigrated along with them. In contact with German social conditions, this French literature lost all its immediate practical significance, and assumed a purely literary aspect. Thus, to the German philosophers of the 18th century, the demands of the first French Revolution were nothing more than the demands of "Practical Reason" in general, and the utterance of the will of the revolutionary French bourgeoisie signified in their eyes the laws of pure will, of will as it was bound to be, of true human will generally.

The work of the German *literati* consisted solely in bringing the new French ideas into harmony with their ancient philosophical conscience, or rather, in annexing the French ideas without deserting their own philosophic point of view.

This annexation took place in the same way in which a foreign language is appropriated, namely by translation.

It is well known how the monks wrote silly lives of Catholic saints *over* the manuscripts on which the classical works of ancient heathendom had been written. The German *literati* reversed this process with the profane French literature. They wrote their philosophical nonsense beneath the French original. For instance, beneath the French criticism of the economic functions of money, they wrote "alienation of humanity," and beneath the French criticism of the bourgeois state, they wrote, "dethronement of the category of the general," and so forth.

The introduction of these philosophical phrases at the back of the French historical criticisms they dubbed "Philosophy of Action," "True Socialism," "German Science of Socialism," "Philosophical Foundation of Socialism," and so on.

The French Socialist and Communist literature was thus completely emasculated. And, since it ceased in the hands of the German to express the struggle of one class with the other, he felt conscious of having overcome "French one-sidedness" and of representing, not true requirements, but the requirements of truth; not the interests of the proletariat, but the interests of human nature, of man in general, who belongs to no class, has no reality, who exists only in the misty realm of philosophical phantasy.

This German Socialism, which took its school-boy task so seriously and solemnly, and extolled its poor stock-in-trade in such mountebank fashion, meanwhile gradually lost its pedantic innocence.

The fight of the German and especially of the Prussian bourgeoisie against feudal aristocracy and absolute monarchy, in other words, the liberal movement, became more earnest.

By this, the long-wished-for opportunity was offered to "True" Socialism of confronting the political movement with the Socialist demands, of hurling the traditional anathemas against liberalism, against representative government, against bourgeois competition, bourgeois freedom of the press, bourgeois legislation, bourgeois liberty and equality, and of preaching to the masses that they had nothing to gain, and everything to lose, by this bourgeois movement. German Socialism forgot, in the nick of time, that the French criticism, whose silly echo it was, presupposed the existence of modern bourgeois society, with its corresponding economic conditions of existence, and the political constitution adapted thereto, the very things whose attainment was the object of the pending struggle in Germany.

To the absolute governments, with their following of parsons, professors, country squires and officials, it served as a welcome scarecrow against the threatening bourgeoisie.

It was a sweet finish after the bitter pills of floggings and bullets, with which these same governments, just at that time, dosed the risings of the German working class.

While this "True" Socialism thus served the governments as a weapon for fighting the German bourgeoisie, it, at the same time, directly represented a reactionary interest, the interest of the German Philistines. In Germany the petty bourgeois class, a relic of the 16th century, and since then constantly cropping up again under various forms, is the real social basis of the existing state of things.

To preserve this class, is to preserve the existing state of things in Germany. The industrial and political supremacy of the bourgeoisie threatens it with certain destruction—on the one hand, from the concentration of capital; on the other, from the rise of a revolutionary proletariat. "True" Socialism appeared to kill these two birds with one stone. It spread like an epidemic.

The robe of speculative cobwebs, embroidered with flowers of rhetoric, steeped in the dew of sickly sentiment, this transcendental robe in which the German Socialists wrapped their sorry "eternal truths," all skin and bone, served to increase wonderfully the sale of their goods amongst such a public.

And on its part, German Socialism recognised, more and more, its own calling as the bombastic representative of the petty bourgeois Philistine.

It proclaimed the German nation to be the model nation, and the German petty Philistine to be the typical man. To every villainous meanness of this model man it gave a hidden, higher, socialistic interpreta-tion, the exact contrary of his real character. It went to the extreme length of directly opposing the "brutally destructive" tendency of Communism, and of proclaiming its supreme and impartial contempt of all class struggles. With very few exceptions, all the so-called Socialist and Communist publications that now (1847) circulate in Germany belong to the domain of this foul and enervating literature.

2. CONSERVATIVE OR BOURGEOIS SOCIALISM

A part of the bourgeoisie is desirous of redressing social grievances, in order to secure the continued existence of bourgeois society.

To this section belong economists, philanthropists, humanitarians, improvers of the condition of the working class, organisers of charity, members of societies for the prevention of cruelty to animals, temperance fanatics, hole-and-corner reformers of every imaginable kind. This form of Socialism has, moreover, been worked out into complete systems.

We may cite Proudhon's *Philosophy of Poverty* as an example of this form.

The socialistic bourgeois want all the advantages of modern social conditions without the struggles and dangers necessarily resulting therefrom. They desire the existing state of society minus its revolutionary and disintegrating elements. They wish for a bourgeoisie without a proletariat. The bourgeoisie naturally conceives the world in which it is supreme to be the best; and bourgeois Socialism develops this comfortable conception into various more or less complete systems. In requiring the proletariat to carry out such a system, and thereby to march straightway into the social New Jerusalem, it but requires in reality, that the proletariat should remain within the bounds of existing society, but should cast away all its hateful ideas concerning the bourgeoisie.

A second and more practical, but less systematic, form of this Socialism sought to depreciate every revolutionary movement in the eyes of the working class, by showing that no mere political reform, but only a change in the material conditions of existence, in economic relations, could be of any advantage to them. By changes in the material conditions of existence, this form of Socialism, however, by no means understands abolition of the bourgeois relations of production, an abolition that can be effected only by a revolution, but administrative reforms, based on the continued existence of these relations; reforms, therefore, that in no respect affect the relations between capital and labour, but, at the best, lessen the cost, and simplify the administrative work of bourgeois government.

Bourgeois Socialism attains adequate expression, when, and only when, it becomes a mere figure of speech.

Free trade: For the benefit of the working class. Protective duties: For the benefit of the working class. Prison reform: For the benefit of the working class. These are the last words and the only seriously meant words of bourgeois Socialism.

It is summed up in the phrase: the bourgeois are bourgeois—for the benefit of the working class.

3. CRITICAL-UTOPIAN SOCIALISM AND COMMUNISM

We do not here refer to that literature which, in every great modern revolution, has always given voice to the demands of the proletariat, such as the writings of Babeuf and others.

The first direct attempts of the proletariat to attain its own ends—made in times of universal excitement, when feudal society was being overthrown—necessarily failed, owing to the then undeveloped state of the proletariat, as well as to the absence of the economic conditions for its emancipation, conditions that had yet to be produced, and could be produced by the impending bourgeois epoch alone. The revolutionary literature that accompanied these first movements of the proletariat had necessarily a reactionary character. It inculcated universal asceticism and social levelling in its crudest form.

The Socialist and Communist systems properly so called, those of St. Simon, Fourier, Owen and others, spring into existence in the early undeveloped period, described above, of the struggle between proletariat and bourgeoisie (see Section 1. Bourgeois and Proletarians).

The founders of these systems see, indeed, the class antagonisms, as well as the action of the decomposing elements in the prevailing form of society. But the proletariat, as yet in its infancy, offers to them the spectacle of a class without any historical initiative or any independent political movement.

Since the development of class antagonism keeps even pace with the development of industry, the economic situation, as such Socialists find it, does not as yet offer to them the material conditions for the emancipation of the proletariat. They therefore search after a new social science, after new social laws, that are to create these conditions.

Historical action is to yield to their personal inventive action; historically created conditions of emancipation to phantastic ones; and the gradual, spontaneous class organisation of the proletariat to an organisation of society specially contrived by these inventors. Future history resolves itself, in their eyes, into the propaganda and the practical carrying out of their social plans.

In the formation of their plans they are conscious of caring chiefly for the interests of the working class, as being the most suffering class. Only from the point of view of being the most suffering class does the proletariat exist for them.

The undeveloped state of the class struggle, as well as their own surroundings, causes Socialists of this kind to consider themselves far superior to all class antagonisms. They want to improve the condition of every member of society, even that of the most favoured. Hence, they habitually appeal to society at large, without distinction of class; nay, by preference, to the ruling class. For how can people, when once they understand their system, fail to see in it the best possible plan of the best possible state of society?

Hence, they reject all political, and especially all revolutionary action; they wish to attain their ends by peaceful means, and endeavour, by small experiments, necessarily doomed to failure, and by the force of example, to pave the way for the new social gospel.

Such phantastic pictures of future society, painted at a time when the proletariat is still in a very undeveloped state and has but a phantastic conception of its own position, correspond with the first instinctive yearnings of that class for a general reconstruction of society.

But these Socialist and Communist writings contain also a critical element. They attack every principle of existing society. Hence they are full of the most valuable materials for the enlightenment of the working class. The practical measures proposed in them—such as the abolition of the distinction between town and country; abolition of the family, of private gain and of the wage-system; the proclamation of social harmony; the conversion of the functions of the state into a mere superintendence of production—all these proposals point solely to the disappearance of class antagonisms which were, at that time, only just cropping up, and which, in these publications, are recognised in their earliest, indistinct and undefined forms only. These proposals, therefore, are of a purely utopian character.

The significance of Critical-Utopian Socialism and Communism bears an inverse relation to historical development. In proportion as the modern class struggle develops and takes definite shape, this phantastic standing apart from the contest, these phantastic attacks on it, lose all practical value and all theoretical justification. Therefore, although the originators of these systems were, in many respects, revolutionary, their disciples have, in every case, formed mere reactionary sects. They hold fast by the original views of their masters, in opposition to the progressive historical devel-

opment of the proletariat. They, therefore, endeavour, and that consistently, to deaden the class struggle and to reconcile the class antagonisms. They still dream of experimental realisation of their social utopias, of founding isolated *phalanstères,* of establishing "Home Colonies," or setting up a "Little Icaria"—pocket editions of the New Jerusalem—and to realise all these castles in the air, they are compelled to appeal to the feelings and purses of the bourgeois. By degrees they sink into the category of the reactionary conservative Socialists depicted above, differing from these only by more systematic pedantry, and by their fanatical and superstitious belief in the miraculous effects of their social science.

They, therefore, violently oppose all political action on the part of the working class; such action, according to them, can only result from blind unbelief in the new gospel.

The Owenites in England, and the Fourierists in France, respectively, oppose the Chartists and the *Réformistes.*

4. Position of the Communists in Relation to the Various Existing Opposition Parties

Section 2 has made clear the relations of the Communists to the existing working class parties, such as the Chartists in England and the Agrarian Reformers in America.

The Communists fight for the attainment of the immediate aims, for the enforcement of the momentary interests of the working class; but in the movement of the present, they also represent and take care of the future of that movement. In France the Communists ally themselves with the Social-Democrats, against the conservative and radical bourgeoisie, reserving, however, the right to take up a critical position in regard to phrases and illusions traditionally handed down from the great Revolution.

In Switzerland they support the Radicals, without losing sight of the fact that this party consists of antagonistic elements, partly of Democratic Social'sts, in the French sense, partly of radical bourgeois.

In Poland they support the party that insists on an agrarian revolution as the prime condition for national emancipation, that party which fomented the insurrection of Cracow in 1846.

In Germany they fight with the bourgeoisie whenever it acts in a revolutionary way, against the absolute monarchy, the feudal squirearchy, and the petty bourgeoisie.

But they never cease, for a single instant, to instil into the working class the clearest possible recognition of the hostile antagonism between bourgeoisie and proletariat, in order that the German workers may straightway use, as so many weapons against the bourgeoisie, the social and political conditions that the bourgeoisie must necessarily introduce along with its supremacy, and in order that, after the fall of the reactionary classes in Germany, the fight against the bourgeoisie itself may immediately begin.

The Communists turn their attention chiefly to Germany, because that country is on the eve of a bourgeois revolution that is bound to be carried out under more advanced conditions of European civilisation and with a much more developed proletariat than what existed in England in the 17th and in France in the 18th century, and because the bourgeois revolution in Germany will be but the prelude to an immediately following proletarian revolution.

In short, the Communists everywhere support every revolutionary movement against the existing social and political order of things.

In all these movements they bring to the front, as the leading question in each case, the property question, no matter what its degree of development at the time.

Finally, they labour everywhere for the union and agreement of the democratic parties of all countries.

The Communists disdain to conceal their views and aims. They openly declare that their ends can be attained only by the forcible overthrow of all existing social conditions. Let the ruling classes tremble at a Communist revolution. The proletarians have nothing to lose but their chains. They have a world to win.

Workingmen of all countries, unite!

II. LENIN

Strategy of Revolutionary Communism

1. Professional Revolutionaries *

I assert: (1) that no movement can be durable without a stable organisation of

* From V. I. Lenin, *What Is to Be Done?* (1902; in Lenin, *Selected Works*, International Publishers, 1936), II. By permission.

leaders to maintain continuity; (2) that the more widely the masses are spontaneously drawn into the struggle and form the basis of the movement and participate in it, the more necessary is it to have such an organisation, and the more stable must it be (for it is much easier for demagogues to side-track the more backward sections of the masses); (3) that the organisation must consist chiefly of persons engaged in revolutionary activities as a profession; (4) that in a country with an autocratic government, the more we restrict the membership of this organisation to persons who are engaged in revolutionary activities as a profession and who have been professionally trained in the art of combating the political police, the more difficult will it be to catch the organisation, and (5) the *wider* will be the cricle of men and women of the working class or of other classes of society able to join the movement and perform active work in it.

We can never give a mass organisation that degree of secrecy which is essential for the persistent and continuous struggle against the government. But to concentrate all secret functions in the hands of as small a number of professional revolutionaries as possible does not mean that the latter will "do the thinking for all" and that the crowd will not take an active part in the *movement.* On the contrary, the crowd will advance from its ranks increasing numbers of professional revolutionaries, for it will know that it is not enough for a few students and workingmen, waging economic war, to gather together and form a "committee," but that it takes years to train professional revolutionaries; the crowd will "think" not of primitive ways but of training professional revolutionaries. The centralisation of the secret functions of the *organisation* does not mean the centralisation of all the functions of the movement. The active participation of the broad masses in the dissemination of illegal literature will not diminish because a dozen professional revolutionaries centralise the secret part of the work; on the contrary, it will *increase tenfold.* Only in this way will the reading of illegal literature, the contribution to illegal literature and to some extent even the distribution of illegal literature *almost cease to be secret work,* for the police will soon come to realise the folly and futility of

setting the whole judicial and administrative machine into motion to intercept every copy of a publication that is being broadcast in thousands. This applies not only to the press, but to every function of the movement, even to demonstrations. The active and widespread participation of the masses will not suffer; on the contrary, it will benefit by the fact that a "dozen" experienced revolutionaries, no less professionally trained than the police, will centralise all the secret side of the work— prepare leaflets, work out approximate plans and appoint bodies of leaders for each urban district, for each factory district and for each educational institution, etc. (I know that exception will be taken to my "undemocratic" views, but I shall reply to this altogether unintelligent objection later on.) The centralisation of the more secret functions in an organisation of revolutionaries will not diminish, but rather increase the extent and the quality of the activity of a large number of other organisations intended for wide membership and which, therefore, can be as loose and as public as possible, for example, trade unions, workers' circles for self-education and the reading of illegal literature, and socialist and also democratic circles for *all other sections of the population,* etc., etc.

In order to be fully prepared for his task, the working class revolutionary must also become a professional revolutionary. Hence B——v is wrong when he says that as the worker is engaged for eleven and a half hours a day in the factory, therefore, the brunt of all the other revolutionary functions (apart from agitation) *"must necessarily* fall mainly upon the shoulders of an extremely small intellectual force." It need not "necessarily" be so. It is so because we are backward, because we do not recognise our duty to assist every capable worker to become a *professional* agitator, organiser, propagandist, literature distributor, etc. In this respect, we waste our strength in a positively shameful manner; we lack the ability to husband that which should be tended and reared with special care. Look at the Germans: they have a hundred times more forces than we have. But they understand perfectly well that the "average" does not too frequently promote really capable agitators, etc., from its ranks.

Hence they immediately try to place every capable workingman in such conditions as will enable him to develop and apply his abilities to the utmost: he is made a professional agitator, he is encouraged to widen the field of his activity, to spread it from one factory to the whole of his trade, from one locality to the whole country. He acquires experience and dexterity in his profession, his outlook becomes wider, his knowledge increases, he observes the prominent political leaders from other localities and other parties, he strives to rise to their level and combine within himself the knowledge of working class environment and freshness of socialist convictions with professional skill, without which the proletariat *cannot* carry on a stubborn struggle with the excellently trained enemy. Only in this way can men of the stamp of Bebel and Auer be promoted from the ranks of the working class. But what takes place very largely automatically in a politically free country must in Russia be done deliberately and systematically by our organisations. A workingman agitator who is at all talented and "promising" *must not be left* to work eleven hours a day in a factory. We must arrange that he be maintained by the Party, that he may in due time go underground, that he change the place of his activity, otherwise he will not enlarge his experience, he will not widen his outlook, and will not be able to stay in the fight against the gendarmes for at least a few years. As the spontaneous rise of the working class masses becomes wider and deeper, they not only promote from their ranks an increasing number of talented agitators, but also of talented organisers, propagandists and "practical workers" in the best sense of the term (of whom there are so few among our intelligentsia who, in the majority of cases, are somewhat careless and sluggish in their

habits, so characteristic of Russians). When we have detachments of specially trained working class revolutionaries who have gone through long years of preparation (and, of course, revolutionaries "of all arms"), no political police in the world will be able to contend against them, for these detachments of men absolutely devoted and loyal to the revolution will themselves enjoy the absolute confidence and devotion of the broad masses of the workers. The *sin* we commit is that we do not sufficiently "stimulate" the workers to take this path, "common" to them and to the "intellectuals," of professional revolutionary training, and that we too frequently drag them back by our silly speeches about what "can be understood" by the masses of the workers, by the "average workers," etc.

2. *Class Society and the State* *

1. THE STATE AS THE PRODUCT OF THE IR-RECONCILABILITY OF CLASS ANTAGONISMS

What is now happening to Marx's doctrine has, in the course of history, often happened to the doctrines of other revolutionary thinkers and leaders of oppressed classes struggling for emancipation. During the lifetime of great revolutionaries, the oppressing classes have visited relentless persecution on them and received their teaching with the most savage hostility, the most furious hatred, the most ruthless campaign of lies and slanders. After their death, attempts are made to turn them into harmless icons, canonise them, and surround their *names* with a certain halo for the "consolation" of the oppressed classes and with the object of duping them, while at the same time emasculating and vulgarising the *real essence* of their revolutionary theories and blunting their revolutionary edge. At the present time, the bourgeoisie and the opportunists within the labour movement are co-

* From V. I. Lenin, *State and Revolution* (1917; in Lenin, *Selected Works*, International Publishers, 1937), Vol. VII. By permission.

operating in this work of adulterating Marxism. They omit, obliterate, and distort the revolutionary side of its teaching, its revolutionary soul. They push to the foreground and extol what is, or seems, acceptable to the bourgeoisie. All the social-chauvinists are now "Marxists"—joking aside! And more and more do German bourgeois professors, erstwhile specialists in the demolition of Marx, speak now of the "national-German" Marx, who, they aver, has educated the labour unions which are so splendidly organised for conducting the present predatory war!

In such circumstances, the distortion of Marxism being so widespread, it is our first task to *resuscitate* the real teachings of Marx on the state. For this purpose it will be necessary to quote at length from the works of Marx and Engels themselves. Of course, long quotations will make the text cumbersome and in no way help to make it popular reading, but we cannot possibly avoid them. All, or at any rate, all the most essential passages in the works of Marx and Engels on the subject of the state must necessarily be given as fully as possible, in order that the reader may form an independent opinion of all the views of the founders of scientific Socialism and of the development of those views, and in order that their distortions by the present predominant "Kautskyism" may be proved in black and white and rendered plain to all.

Let us begin with the most popular of Engels' works, *Der Ursprung der Familie, des Privateigentums und des Staats*,[1] the sixth edition of which was published in Stuttgart as far back as 1894. We must translate the quotations from the German originals, as the Russian translations, although very numerous, are for the most part either incomplete or very unsatisfactory.

Summarising his historical analysis Engels says:

The state is therefore by no means a power imposed on society from the outside; just as little is it "the reality of the moral idea," "the image and reality of reason," as Hegel asserted. Rather, it is a product of society at a certain stage of development; it is the admission that this society has become entangled in an insoluble contradiction with itself, that it is cleft into irreconcilable antagonisms which it is powerless to dispel. But in order that these antagonisms, classes with conflicting economic interests, may not consume themselves and society in sterile struggle, a power apparently standing above society becomes necessary, whose purpose is to moderate the conflict and keep it within the bounds of "order"; and this power arising out of society, but placing itself above it, and increasingly separating itself from it, is the state.[2]

Here we have, expressed in all its clearness, the basic idea of Marxism on the question of the historical rôle and meaning of the state. The state is the product and the manifestation of the *irreconcilability* of class antagonisms. The state arises when, where, and to the extent that the class antagonisms *cannot* be objectively reconciled. And, conversely, the existence of the state proves that the class antagonisms *are* irreconcilable.

It is precisely on this most important and fundamental point that distortions of Marxism arise along two main lines.

On the one hand, the bourgeois, and particularly the petty-bourgeois, ideologists, compelled under the pressure of indisputable historical facts to admit that the state only exists where there are class antagonisms and the class struggle, "correct" Marx in such a way as to make it appear that the state is an organ for *reconciling* the classes. According to Marx, the state could neither arise nor maintain itself if a reconciliation of classes were possible. But with the petty-bourgeois and philistine professors and publicists, the state—and this frequently on the strength of benevolent references to Marx!

---

[1] Friedrich Engels, *The Origin of the Family, Private Property, and the State,* London and New York, 1933.

[2] *Ibid.*

—becomes a conciliator of the classes. According to Marx, the state is an organ of class *domination,* an organ of *oppression* of one class by another; its aim is the creation of "order" which legalises and perpetuates this oppression by moderating the collisions between the classes. But in the opinion of the petty-bourgeois politicians, order means reconciliation of the classes, and not oppression of one class by another; to moderate collisions does not mean, they say, to deprive the oppressed classes of certain definite means and methods of struggle for overthrowing the oppressors, but to practice reconciliation.

For instance, when, in the Revolution of 1917, the question of the real meaning and rôle of the state arose in all its vastness as a practical question demanding immediate action on a wide mass scale, all the Socialist-Revolutionaries and Mensheviks suddenly and completely sank to the petty-bourgeois theory of "reconciliation" of the classes by the "state." Innumerable resolutions and articles by politicians of both these parties are saturated through and through with this purely petty-bourgeois and philistine theory of "reconciliation." That the state is an organ of domination of a definite class which *cannot* be reconciled with its antipode (the class opposed to it)—this petty-bourgeois democracy is never able to understand. Its attitude towards the state is one of the most telling proofs that our Socialist-Revolutionaries and Mensheviks are not Socialists at all (which we Bolsheviks have always maintained), but petty-bourgeois democrats with a near-Socialist phraseology.

On the other hand, the "Kautskyist" distortion of Marx is far more sublte. "Theoretically," there is no denying that the state is the organ of class domination, or that class antagonisms are irreconcilable. But what is forgotten or glossed over is this: if the state is the product of the irreconcilable character of class antagonisms, if it is a force standing *above* society and "increasingly separating itself from it," then it is clear that the liberation of the oppressed class is impossible not only without a vio-

lent revolution, *but also without the destruction* of the apparatus of state power, which was created by the ruling class and in which this "separation" is embodied. As we shall see later, Marx drew this theoretically self-evident conclusion from a concrete historical analysis of the problems of revolution. And it is exactly this conclusion which Kautsky—as we shall show fully in our subsequent remarks—has "forgotten" and distorted.

2. SPECIAL BODIES OF ARMED MEN, PRISONS, ETC.

Engels continues:

In contrast with the ancient organisation of the *gens,* the first distinguishing characteristic of the state is the grouping of the subjects of the state *on a territorial basis.* . . .

Such a grouping seems "natural" to us, but it came after a prolonged and costly struggle against the old form of tribal or gentilic society.

. . . The second is the establishment of a *public force,* which is no longer absolutely identical with the population organising itself as an armed power. This special public force is necessary, because a self-acting armed organisation of the population has become impossible since the cleavage of society into classes. . . . This public force exists in every state; it consists not merely of armed men, but of material appendages, prisons and repressive institutions of all kinds, of which gentilic society knew nothing. . . .[3]

Engels develops the conception of that "power" which is termed the state—a power arising from society, but placing itself above it and becoming more and more separated from it. What does this power mainly consist of? It consists of special bodies of armed men who have at their disposal prisons, etc.

We are justified in speaking of special bodies of armed men, because the public power peculiar to every state is not "abso-

[3] *Ibid.*

lutely identical" with the armed population, with its "self-acting armed organisation."

Like all the great revolutionary thinkers, Engels tries to draw the attention of the class-conscious workers to that very fact which to prevailing philistinism appears least of all worthy of attention, most common and sanctified by solid, indeed, one might say, petrified prejudices. A standing army and police are the chief instruments of state power. But can this be otherwise?

From the point of view of the vast majority of Europeans at the end of the nineteenth century whom Engels was addressing, and who had neither lived through nor closely observed a single great revolution, this cannot be otherwise. They cannot understand at all what this "self-acting armed organisation of the population" means. To the question, whence arose the need for special bodies of armed men, standing above society and becoming separated from it (police and standing army), the Western European and Russian philistines are inclined to answer with a few phrases borrowed from Spencer or Mikhailovsky, by reference to the complexity of social life, the differentiation of functions, and so forth.

Such a reference seems "scientific" and effectively dulls the senses of the average man, obscuring the most important and basic fact, namely, the break-up of society into irreconcilably antagonistic classes.

Without such a break-up, the "self-acting armed organisation of the population" might have differed from the primitive organisation of a herd of monkeys grasping sticks, or of primitive men, or men united in a tribal form of society, by its complexity, its high technique, and so forth, but would still have been possible.

It is impossible now, because society, in the period of civilisation, is broken up into antagonistic and, indeed, irreconcilably antagonistic classes, which, if armed in a "self-acting" manner, would come into armed struggle with each other. A state is formed, a special power is created in the form of special bodies of armed men, and

every revolution, by shattering the state apparatus, demonstrates to us how the ruling class aims at the restoration of the special bodies of armed men at *its* service, and how the oppressed class tries to create a new organisation of this kind, capable of serving not the exploiters, but the exploited.

In the above observation, Engels raises theoretically the very same question which every great revolution raises practically, palpably, and on a mass scale of action, namely, the question of the relation between special bodies of armed men and the "self-acting armed organisation of the population." We shall see how this is concretely illustrated by the experience of the European and Russian revolutions.

But let us return to Engels' discourse.

He points out that sometimes, for instance, here and there in North America, this public power is weak (he has in mind an exception that is rare in capitalist society, and he speaks about parts of North America in its pre-imperialist days, where the free colonist predominated), but that in general it tends to become stronger:

It [the public power] grows stronger, however, in proportion as the class antagonisms within the state grow sharper, and with the growth in size and population of the adjacent states. We have only to look at our present-day Europe, where class struggle and rivalry in conquest have screwed up the public power to such a pitch that it threatens to devour the whole of society and even the state itself.[4]

This was written as early as the beginning of the 'nineties of last century, Engels' last preface being dated June 16, 1891. The turn towards imperialism, understood to mean complete domination of the trusts, full sway of the large banks, and a colonial policy on a grand scale, and so forth, was only just beginning in France, and was even weaker in North America and in Germany. Since then the "rivalry in conquest" has made gigantic progress—especially as, by the beginning of the second decade of

---

[4] *Ibid.*

the twentieth century, the whole world had been finally divided up between these "rivals in conquest," *i.e.*, between the great predatory powers. Military and naval armaments since then have grown to monstrous proportions, and the predatory war of 1914–1917 for the domination of the world by England or Germany, for the division of the spoils, has brought the "swallowing up" of all the forces of society by the rapacious state power nearer to a complete catastrophe.

As early as 1891 Engels was able to point to "rivalry in conquest" as one of the most important features of the foreign policy of the great powers, but in 1914–1917, when this rivalry, many times intensified, has given birth to an imperialist war, the rascally social-chauvinists cover up their defence of the predatory policy of "their" capitalist classes by phrases about the "defence of the fatherland," or the "defence of the republic and the revolution," etc.!

3. THE STATE AS AN INSTRUMENT FOR THE EXPLOITATION OF THE OPPRESSED CLASS

For the maintenance of a special public force standing above society, taxes and state loans are needed.

Having at their disposal the public force and the right to exact taxes, the officials now stand as organs of society *above* society. The free, voluntary respect which was accorded to the organs of the gentilic form of government does not satisfy them, even if they could have it. . . .

Special laws are enacted regarding the sanctity and the inviolability of the officials. "The shabbiest police servant . . . has more authority" than the representative of the clan, but even the head of the military power of a civilised state "may well envy the least among the chiefs of the clan the unconstrained and uncontested respect which is paid to him." [5]

Here the question regarding the privileged position of the officials as organs of

the state power is clearly stated. The main point is indicated as follows: what is it that places them *above* society? We shall see how this theoretical problem was solved in practice by the Paris Commune in 1871 and how it was slurred over in a reactionary manner by Kautsky in 1912.

As the state arose out of the need to hold class antagonisms is check; but as it, at the same time, arose in the midst of the conflict of these classes, it is, as a rule, the state of the most powerful, economically dominant class, which by virtue thereof becomes also the dominant class politically, and thus acquires new means of holding down and exploiting the oppressed class. . . .

Not only the ancient and feudal states were organs of exploitation of the slaves and serfs, but

the modern representative state is the instrument of the exploitation of wage-labour by capital. By way of exception, however, there are periods when the warring classes so nearly attain equilibrium that the state power, ostensibly appearing as a mediator, assumes for the moment a certain independence in relation to both. . . .[6]

Such were, for instance, the absolute monarchies of the seventeenth and eighteenth centuries, the Bonapartism of the First and Second Empires in France, and the Bismarck régime in Germany.

Such, we may add, is now the Kerensky government in republican Russia after its shift to persecuting the revolutionary proletariat, at a moment when the Soviets, thanks to the leadership of the petty-bourgeois democrats, have *already* become impotent, while the bourgeoisie is *not yet* strong enough to disperse them outright.

In a democratic republic, Engels continues, "wealth wields its power indirectly, but all the more effectively," first, by means of "direct corruption of the officials" (America); second, by means of "the alliance of the government with the stock exchange" (France and America).

---

[5] *Ibid.*

[6] *Ibid.*

At the present time, imperialism and the domination of the banks have "developed" to an unusually fine art both these methods of defending and asserting the omnipotence of wealth in democratic republics of all descriptions. If, for instance, in the very first months of the Russian democratic republic, one might say during the honeymoon of the union of the "Socialists"— Socialist-Revolutionaries and Mensheviks— with the bourgeoisie, Mr. Palchinsky obstructed every measure in the coalition cabinet, restraining the capitalists and their war profiteering, their plundering of the public treasury by means of army contracts; and if, after his resignation, Mr. Palchinsky (replaced, of course, by an exactly similar Palchinsky) was "rewarded" by the capitalists with a "soft" job carrying a salary of 120,-000 rubles per annum, what was this? Direct or indirect bribery? A league of the government with the capitalist syndicates, or "only" friendly relations? What is the rôle played by the Chernovs, Tseretelis, Avksentyevs and Skobelevs? Are they the "direct" or only the indirect allies of the millionaire treasury looters?

The omnipotence of "wealth" is thus more *secure* in a democratic republic, since it does not depend on the poor political shell of capitalism. A democratic republic is the best possible political shell for capitalism, and therefore, once capital has gained control (through the Palchinskys, Chernovs, Tseretelis and Co.) of this very best shell, it establishes its power so securely, so firmly that *no* change, either of persons, or institutions, or parties in the bourgeois republic can shake it.

We must also note that Engels quite definitely regards universal suffrage as a means of bourgeois domination. Universal suffrage, he says, obviously summing up the long experience of German Social-Democracy, is "an index of the maturity of the working class; it cannot, and never will, be anything else but that in the modern state."

The petty-bourgeois democrats, such as our Socialist-Revolutionaries and Mensheviks, and also their twin brothers, the so-cial-chauvinists and opportunists of Western Europe, all expect "more" from universal suffrage. They themselves share, and instil into the minds of the people, the wrong idea that universal suffrage "in the *modern* state" is really capable of expressing the will of the majority of the toilers and of assuring its realisation.

We can here only note this wrong idea, only point out that this perfectly clear, exact and concrete statement by Engels is distorted at every step in the propaganda and agitation of the "official" (*i.e.*, opportunist) Socialist parties. A detailed analysis of all the falseness of this idea, which Engels brushes aside, is given in our further account of the views of Marx and Engels on the "modern" state.

A general summary of his views is given by Engels in the most popular of his works in the following words:

The state, therefore, has not existed from all eternity. There have been societies which managed without it, which had no conception of the state and state power. At a certain stage of economic development, which was necessarily bound up with the cleavage of society into classes, the state became a necessity owing to this cleavage. We are now rapidly approaching a stage in the development of production at which the existence of these classes has not only ceased to be a necessity, but is becoming a positive hindrance to production. They will disappear as inevitably as they arose at an earlier stage. Along with them, the state will inevitably disappear. The society that organises production anew on the basis of a free and equal association of the producers will put the whole state machine where it will then belong: in the museum of antiquities, side by side with the spinning wheel and the bronze axe.[7]

It is not often that we find this passage quoted in the propaganda and agitation literature of contemporary Social-Democracy. But even when we do come across it, it is generally quoted in the same manner as one bows before an icon, *i.e.*, it is done

[7] *Ibid.*

merely to show official respect for Engels, without any attempt to gauge the breadth and depth of revolutionary action presupposed by this relegating of "the whole state machine . . . to the museum of antiquities." In most cases we do not even find an understanding of what Engels calls the state machine.

4. THE "WITHERING AWAY" OF THE STATE AND VIOLENT REVOLUTION

Engels' words regarding the "withering away" of the state enjoy such popularity, they are so often quoted, and they show so clearly the essence of the usual adulteration by means of which Marxism is made to look like opportunism, that we must dwell on them in detail. Let us quote the whole passage from which they are taken.

The proletariat seizes state power, and then transforms the means of production into state property. But in doing this, it puts an end to itself as the proletariat, it puts an end to all class differences and class antagonisms, it puts an end also to the state as the state. Former society, moving in class antagonisms, had need of the state, that is, an organisation of the exploiting class at each period for the maintenance of its external conditions of production; therefore, in particular, for the forcible holding down of the exploited class in the conditions of oppression (slavery, bondage or serfdom, wage-labour) determined by the existing mode of production. The state was the official representative of society as a whole, its embodiment in a visible corporate body; but it was this only in so far as it was the state of that class which itself, in its epoch, represented society as a whole: in ancient times, the state of the slave-owning citizens; in the Middle Ages, of the feudal nobility; in our epoch, of the bourgeoisie. When ultimately it becomes really representative of society as a whole, it makes itself superfluous. As soon as there is no longer any class of society to be held in subjection; as soon as, along with class domination and the struggle for individual existence based on the former anarchy of production, the

collisions and excesses arising from these have also been abolished, there is nothing more to be repressed, and a special repressive force, a state, is no longer necessary. The first act in which the state really comes forward as the representative of society as a whole—the seizure of the means of production in the name of society—is at the same time its last independent act as a state. The interference of a state power in social relations becomes superfluous in one sphere after another, and then becomes dormant of itself. Government over persons is replaced by the administration of things and the direction of the processes of production. The state is not "abolished," *it withers away*. It is from this standpoint that we must appraise the phrase "people's free state"—both its justification at times for agitational purposes, and its ultimate scientific inadequacy—and also the demand of the so-called Anarchists that the state should be abolished overnight.[8]

Without fear of committing an error, it may be said that of this argument by Engels so singularly rich in ideas, only one point has become an integral part of Socialist thought among modern Socialist parties, namely, that, unlike the Anarchist doctrine of the "abolition" of the state, according to Marx the state "withers away." To emasculate Marxism in such a manner is to reduce it to opportunism, for such an "interpretation" only leaves the hazy conception of a slow, even, gradual change, free from leaps and storms, free from revolution. The current popular conception, if one may say so, of the "withering away" of the state undoubtedly means a slurring over, if not a negation, of revolution.

Yet, such an "interpretation" is the crudest distortion of Marxism, which is advantageous only to the bourgeoisie; in point of theory, it is based on a disregard for the most important circumstances and considerations pointed out in the very passage summarising Engels' ideas, which we have just quoted in full.

8 Friedrich Engels, *Anti-Dühring*, London and New York, 1933.

In the first place, Engels at the very outset of his argument says that, in assuming state power, the proletariat by that very act "puts an end to the state as the state." One is "not accustomed" to reflect on what this really means. Generally, it is either ignored altogether, or it is considered as a piece of "Hegelian weakness" on Engels' part. As a matter of fact, however, these words express succinctly the experience of one of the greatest proletarian revolutions —the Paris Commune of 1871, of which we shall speak in greater detail in its proper place. As a matter of fact, Engels speaks here of the destruction of the bourgeois state by the proletarian revolution, while the words about its withering away refer to the remains of *proletarian* statehood *after* the Socialist revolution. The bourgeois state does not "wither away," according to Engels, but is "put an end to" by the proletariat in the course of the revolution. What withers away after the revolution is the proletarian state or semi-state.

Secondly, the state is a "special repressive force." This splendid and extremely profound definition of Engels' is given by him here with complete lucidity. It follows from this that the "special repressive force" of the bourgeoisie for the suppression of the proletariat, of the millions of workers by a handful of the rich, must be replaced by a "special repressive force" of the proletariat for the suppression of the bourgeoisie (the dictatorship of the proletariat). It is just this that constitutes the destruction of "the state as the state." It is just this that constitutes the "act" of "the seizure of the means of production in the name of society." And it is obvious that such a substitution of one (proletarian) "special repressive force" for another (bourgeois) "special repressive force" can in no way take place in the form of a "withering away."

Thirdly, as to the "withering away" or, more expressively and colourfully, as to the state "becoming dormant," Engels refers quite clearly and definitely to the period *after* "the seizure of the means of production [by the state] in the name of society,"

that is, *after* the Socialist revolution. We all know that the political form of the "state" at that time is complete democracy. But it never enters the head of any of the opportunists who shamelessly distort Marx that when Engels speaks here of the state "withering away," or "becoming dormant," he speaks of *democracy*. At first sight this seems very strange. But it is "unintelligible" only to one who has not reflected on the fact that democracy is *also* a state and that, consequently, democracy will *also* disappear when the state disappears. The bourgeois state can only be "put an end to" by a revolution. The state in general, *i.e.,* most complete democracy, can only "wither away."

Fourthly, having formulated his famous proposition that "the state withers away," Engels at once explains concretely that this proposition is directed equally against the opportunists and the Anarchists. In doing this, however, Engels puts in the first place that conclusion from his proposition about the "withering away" of the state which is directed against the opportunists.

One can wager that out of every 10,000 persons who have read or heard about the "withering away" of the state, 9,990 do not know at all, or do not remember, that Engels did not direct his conclusions from this proposition against the Anarchists *alone*. And out of the remaining ten, probably nine do not know the meaning of a "people's free state" nor the reason why an attack on this watchword contains an attack on the opportunists. This is how history is written! This is how a great revolutionary doctrine is imperceptibly adulterated and adapted to current philistinism! The conclusion drawn against the Anarchists has been repeated thousands of times, vulgarised, harangued about in the crudest fashion possible until it has acquired the strength of a prejudice, whereas the conclusion drawn against the opportunists has been hushed up and "forgotten"!

The "people's free state" was a demand in the programme of the German Social-Democrats and their current slogan in the 'seventies. There is no political substance in this slogan other than a pompous middle-class circumlocution of the idea of democracy. In so far as it referred in a lawful manner to a democratic republic, Engels was prepared to "justify" its use "at times" from a propaganda point of view. But this slogan was opportunist, for it not only expressed an exaggerated view of the attractiveness of bourgeois democracy, but also a lack of understanding of the Socialist criticism of every state in general. We are in favour of a democratic republic as the best form of the state for the proletariat under capitalism, but we have no right to forget that wage slavery is the lot of the people even in the most democratic bourgeois republic. Furthermore, every state is a "special repressive force" for the suppression of the oppressed class. Consequently, *no* state is either "free" or a "people's state." Marx and Engels explained this repeatedly to their party comrades in the 'seventies.

Fifthly, in the same work of Engels, from which every one remembers his argument on the "withering away" of the state, there is also a disquisition on the significance of a violent revolution. The historical analysis of its rôle becomes, with Engels, a veritable panegyric on violent revolution. This, of course, "no one remembers"; to talk or even to think of the importance of this idea is not considered good form by contemporary Socialist parties, and in the daily propaganda and agitation among the masses it plays no part whatever. Yet it is indissolubly bound up with the "withering away" of the state in one harmonious whole.

Here is Engels' argument:

... That force, however, plays another rôle (other than that of a diabolical power) in history, a revolutionary rôle; that, in the words of Marx, it is the mid-wife of every old society which is pregnant with the new; that it is the instrument with whose aid social movement forces its way through and shatters the dead, fossilised political forms—of this there is not a word in Herr Dühring. It is only with sighs and groans that he ad-

mits the possibility that force will perhaps be necessary for the overthrow of the economic system of exploitation—unfortunately! because all use of force, forsooth, demoralises the person who uses it. And this in spite of the immense moral and spiritual impetus which has resulted from every victorious revolution! And this in Germany, where a violent collision—which indeed may be forced on the people—would at least have the advantage of wiping out the servility which has permeated the national consciousness as a result of the humiliation of the Thirty Years' War. And this parson's mode of thought—lifeless, insipid and impotent—claims to impose itself on the most revolutionary party which history has known? [9]

How can this panegyric on violent revolution, which Engels insistently brought to the attention of the German Social-Democrats between 1878 and 1894, *i.e.*, right to the time of his death, be combined with the theory of the "withering away" of the state to form one doctrine?

Usually the two views are combined by means of eclecticism, by an unprincipled, sophistic, arbitrary selection (to oblige the powers that be) of either one or the other argument, and in ninety-nine cases out of a hundred (if not more often), it is the idea of the "withering away" that is specially emphasised. Eclecticism is substituted for dialectics—this is the most usual, the most widespread phenomenon to be met with in the official Social-Democratic literature of our day in relation to Marxism. Such a substitution is, of course, nothing new; it may be observed even in the history of classic Greek philosophy. When Marxism is adulterated to become opportunism, the substitution of eclecticism for dialectics is the best method of deceiving the masses; it gives an illusory satisfaction; it seems to take into account all sides of the process, all the tendencies of development, all the contradictory factors and so forth, whereas in reality it offers no consistent and revolu-

[9] *Ibid.*

tionary view of the process of social development at all.

We have already said above and shall show more fully later that the teaching of Marx and Engels regarding the inevitability of a violent revolution refers to the bourgeois state. It *cannot* be replaced by the proletarian state (the dictatorship of the proletariat) through "withering away," but, as a general rule, only through a violent revolution. The panegyric sung in its honour by Engels and fully corresponding to the repeated declarations of Marx (remember the concluding passages of the *Poverty of Philosophy* and the *Communist Manifesto,* with its proud and open declaration of the inevitability of a violent revolution; remember Marx's *Critique of the Gotha Programme* of 1875 in which, almost thirty years later, he mercilessly castigates the opportunist character of that programme) —this praise is by no means a mere "impulse," a mere declamation, or a polemical sally. The necessity of systematically fostering among the masses *this* and just this point of view about violent revolution lies at the root of the *whole* of Marx's and Engels' teaching. The neglect of such propaganda and agitation by both the present predominant social-chauvinist and the Kautskyist currents brings their betrayal of Marx's and Engels' teaching into prominent relief.

The replacement of the bourgeois by the proletarian state is impossible without a violent revolution. The abolition of the proletarian state, *i.e.,* of all states, is only possible through "withering away."

Marx and Engels gave a full and concrete exposition of these views in studying each revolutionary situation separately, in analysing the lessons of the experience of each individual revolution.

3. *Bourgeois Democracy and Proletarian Dictatorship* *

History teaches that not a single oppressed class has ever come into power, or

could come into power, without passing through the period of dictatorship, *i.e.,* the conquest of political power and the violent suppression of the desperate, furious and unscrupulous resistance which the exploiters always put up. The bourgeoisie, whose rule the Socialists who oppose "dictatorship in general" and who bow down before "democracy in general" now defend, achieved power in the advanced countries by means of a number of rebellions, by civil wars, by the violent suppression of kings, feudal barons and slave-owners, and their attempts at restoration. In their books and pamphlets, in the resolutions of their congresses and in their agitational speeches, the Socialists of all countries have explained to the people the class character of these bourgeois revolutions, of this bourgeois dictatorship, a thousand and a million times. Hence, the present defence of bourgeois democracy cloaked in speeches about "democracy in general" and the present howling and shouting against the dictatorship of the proletariat cloaked by cries about "dictatorship in general" are a downright betrayal of socialism, the practical desertion to the side of the bourgeoisie, the denial of the right of the proletariat to make its own, proletarian revolution, and defence of bourgeois reformism at the very historical moment when bourgeois reformism is bankrupt all over the world, and when the war has created a revolutionary situation.

In explaining the class character of bourgeois civilisation, of bourgeois democracy and of bourgeois parliamentarism, all Socialists express the idea which was most scientifically expressed by Marx and Engels when they said that even the most democratic bourgeois republic is nothing more than a machine for the suppression of the working class by the bourgeoisie, of the masses of the toilers by a handful of capi-

* From V. I. Lenin, *Theses and Report on Bourgeois Democracy and the Dictatorship of the Proletariat* (Submitted to the First Congress of the Communist International, March 4, 1919; in Lenin, *Selected Works,* Vol. VII, International Publishers, 1937). By permission.

talists. Every one of the revolutionaries, every one of the Marxists who is now shouting against dictatorship and for democracy has sworn and assured the workers that he recognises this fundamental truth of socialism; but now, when the revolutionary proletariat is in a state of ferment and motion, which are directed towards the destruction of this machine of oppression and towards the achievement of the proletarian dictatorship, these traitors to socialism try to make it appear that the bourgeoisie granted the toilers "pure democracy," that the bourgeoisie has ceased to resist and is prepared to submit to the majority of the toilers, and that no state machine for the suppression of labour by capital exists, or has ever existed, in a democratic republic.

"The right of assembly" may be taken as an example of the demands of "pure democracy." Every class conscious worker who has not broken connections with his class will understand at once that it would be absurd to promise the right of assembly to the exploiters in the period and in the circumstances in which the exploiters are resisting their overthrow and are defending their privileges. Neither in England in 1649 nor in France in 1793 did the bourgeoisie, when it was revolutionary, grant "the right of assembly" to the monarchists and nobles who called for the intervention of foreign troops and who "assembled" for the purpose of organising attempts at restoration. If the modern bourgeoisie, which became reactionary long ago, demands that the proletariat give it guarantees beforehand that it will give "the right of assembly" to the exploiters—irrespective of the resistance the capitalists put up to their expropriation—the proletariat will only laugh at the hypocrisy of the bourgeoisie.

On the other hand, the workers know perfectly well that even in the most democratic bourgeois republics "the right of assembly" is but an empty phrase, because the rich own all the best public and private buildings and sufficient leisure to attend meetings, which are protected by the bour-

geois state apparatus. The proletarians of town and country and the small peasants, *i.e.*, the overwhelming majority of the population, do not enjoy either the first, the second or the third of these privileges. As long as this situation prevails, "equality," *i.e.*, "pure democracy" is a sham. In order to achieve real equality, in order to realise democracy for the toilers in fact, it is first of all necessary to deprive the exploiters of all public and luxurious private buildings, it is first of all necessary to give leisure to the toilers, and to have the freedom of their assemblies protected by the armed workers and not by the sons of the aristocracy or capitalist officers commanding browbeaten soldiers.

Only after this change has taken place will it be possible, without mocking at the workers, the toilers and the poor, to speak of freedom of assembly, of equality. And nobody but the vanguard of the toilers, *viz.*, the proletariat, which overthrows the exploiters, the bourgeoisie, can bring about this change.

"Freedom of the press" is another of the principal slogans of "pure democracy." Here, too, the workers know, and the Socialists of all countries have admitted a million times, that this freedom is a sham as long as the best printing plants and the huge stocks of paper are in the possession of the capitalists, and as long as the press is ruled by capital—which rule manifests itself the more strikingly, more sharply and more cynically, the more democracy and the republican system are developed, as for example in America. In order to achieve real equality and real democracy for the toilers, for the workers and peasants, it is first of all necessary to deprive capital of the opportunity of hiring writers, of buying up publishing houses and bribing newspapers, and it is necessary to overthrow the yoke of capital, to overthrow the exploiters and to suppress their resistance. By "freedom" the capitalists have always meant the freedom of the rich to accumulate profits, and the freedom of the workers to die of starvation. By freedom of the press the capitalists mean the freedom of the rich to bribe the press, freedom to utilise wealth for the purposes of fabricating and manipulating so-called public opinion. Here, too, the champions of "pure democracy" prove in fact to be champions of the filthy and venal system by which the rich control the means for the education of the masses, they prove to be deceivers of the people who, by means of plausible, eloquent and absolutely false phrases, turn the people away from the concrete historical tasks of liberating the press from its bondage to capital. Real freedom and equality will exist under the system which the Communists are building and under which it will be impossible for anyone to enrich himself at another's expense, under which it will be objectively impossible, either directly or indirectly, to subject the press to the power of money, and under which there will be nothing to prevent every toiler (or group of toilers in any number) from having and exercising an equal right to use the public printing plants and public stocks of paper.

The history of the nineteenth and twentieth centuries, even before the war, showed what this notorious "pure democracy" really is under capitalism. The Marxists have always said that the more developed, the "purer" democracy is, the more naked, sharp and ruthless becomes the class struggle, the more "purely" the oppression of capital and the dictatorship of the bourgeoisie stand forth. The Dreyfus case in republican France, the sanguinary shooting down of strikers by mercenaries armed by the capitalists in the free and democratic republic of America—these and thousands of similar facts reveal the truth which the bourgeoisie vainly tries to conceal, viz., that even in the most democratic republics it is the terror and dictatorship of the bourgeoisie which rule and which openly manifest themselves as soon as it begins to seem to the exploiters that the power of capital is tottering.

The main thing the Socialists fail to understand and what constitutes their theoretical shortsightedness, their captivity to bourgeois prejudices and their political treachery to the proletariat, is that in capitalist society, as soon as there is any serious intensification of the class struggle on which it is based, there cannot be any middle course between the dictatorship of the bourgeoisie and the dictatorship of the proletariat. All dreams about some third course are merely the reactionary lamentations of the petty bourgeois. This is confirmed by the experience of more than a hundred years of development of bourgeois democracy and of the labour movement in all the advanced countries, and particularly by the experience of the past five years. It is also confirmed by the whole science of political economy, by the whole content of Marxism, which explains that under any system of commodity production the dictatorship of the bourgeoisie is economically inevitable and that nothing can take the place of the latter except the class that is developed, multiplied, organised and consolidated by the very development of capitalism, viz., the proletarian class.

The other theoretical and political mistake Socialists commit is their failure to understand that for thousands of years, from the embryonic form of the age of antiquity, the forms of democracy underwent inevitable change as one ruling class took the place of another. In the ancient republics of Greece, in the cities of the Middle Ages and in the advanced capitalist countries, democracy has different forms and different degrees of application. It would be very absurd to think that the most profound revolution in the history of mankind, that the first transference of power from the exploiting minority to the exploited majority that has ever occurred in the world, could proceed within the old framework of the old bourgeois parliamentary democracy, that it could proceed without extremely sharp changes, without creating new forms of democracy, new institutions embodying the new conditions for its application, etc.

The dictatorship of the proletariat is similar to the dictatorship of other classes in that, like all dictatorships, it was called forth by the necessity of suppressing the violent resistance of the class that was being deprived of political rule. The fundamental difference between the dictatorship of the proletariat and the dictatorship of other classes—the dictatorship of the landlords in the Middle Ages, the dictatorship of the bourgeoisie in all civilised capitalist countries—is that the dictatorship of the landlords and of the bourgeoisie meant the violent suppression of the resistance of the overwhelming majority of the population, viz., the toilers. The dictatorship of the proletariat, on the contrary, means the violent suppression of the resistance of the exploiters, i.e., the insignificant minority of the population, the landlords and capitalists.

Hence, it follows from this that the dictatorship of the proletariat must inevitably lead, not only to a change in the forms and institutions of democracy, speaking generally, but to such a change as will lead to the extension of the actual enjoyment of democracy to those who are oppressed by capitalism, to the toiling classes, to a degree hitherto unprecedented in world history.

4. Communist Minority Dictatorship and Illegal Work *

The victory of Socialism (as the first stage of Communism) over capitalism requires that the proletariat, as the only really revolutionary class, shall fulfil the three following tasks. First,—overthrow the exploiters, primarily the bourgeoisie as the principal economic and political representatives of the latter; utterly rout them; suppress their resistance; make it utterly impossible for them to attempt to restore the yoke of capital and wage slavery. Second

---

* From V. I. Lenin, *Theses on the Fundamental Tasks of the Second Congress of the Communist International* (July 4, 1920; in Lenin, *Selected Works*, International Publishers, 1938), Vol. X. By permission.

—win over and bring under the leadership of the revolutionary vanguard of the proletariat, of its Communist Party, not only the whole of the proletariat, or the overwhelming, the enormous majority of the latter, but also the whole mass of toilers and those exploited by capital; educate, organise, train and discipline them in the very process of the supremely bold and ruthlessly firm struggle against the exploiters; tear this overwhelming majority of the population in all capitalist countries from its dependence on the bourgeoisie; imbue it by means of its practical experience with confidence in the leading role of the proletariat and of its revolutionary vanguard. Third—neutralise, or render harmless, the inevitable vacillation between the bourgeoisie and the proletariat, between bourgeois democracy and Soviet power, of the class of small proprietors in agriculture, industry and commerce—which is still fairly numerous in nearly all advanced countries, although it comprises the minority of the population—as well as the stratum of intellectuals, office employees, etc., which corresponds to this class.

The first and second tasks are independent tasks, each requiring its own special methods of action toward the exploiters and toward the exploited. The third task emerges from the first two and merely requires the skilful, timely and flexible combination of the first and second types of method in accordance with the concrete circumstances in each separate case of vacillation.

In the concrete situation which has been created by militarism, imperialism, all over the world, and most of all in the most advanced, powerful, most enlightened and free capitalist countries, the strangulation of colonies and weak countries, the world imperialist butchery and the Versailles "Peace" —the very thought of peacefully subordinating the capitalists to the will of the majority of the exploited, of the peaceful, reformist transition to Socialism is not only extreme philistine stupidity, but also downright deception of the workers, the embellishment of capitalist wage slavery, concealment of the truth. The truth is that the bourgeoisie, even the most educated and democratic, now no longer hesitates to resort to any fraud or crime, to massacre millions of workers and peasants in order to save the private ownership of the means of production. Only the violent overthrow of the bourgeoisie, the confiscation of its property, the destruction of the whole of the bourgeois state apparatus from top to bottom—parliamentary, judicial, military, bureaucratic, administrative, municipal, etc., right up to the very wholesale deportation or internment of the most dangerous and stubborn exploiters—putting them under strict surveillance in order to combat inevitable attempts to resist and to restore capitalist slavery—only such measures can ensure the real subordination of the whole class of exploiters.

On the other hand, the common idea prevailing among the old parties and the old leaders of the Second International that the majority of the toilers and the exploited can acquire complete clarity of Socialist consciousness and firm Socialist convictions and character under the conditions of capitalist slavery, under the yoke of the bourgeoisie (which assumes an infinite variety of forms, the more subtle and also more fierce and ruthless the more cultured the given country is) is also the embellishment of capitalism and bourgeois democracy, is also the deception of the workers. As a matter of fact, only after the vanguard of the proletariat, supported by the whole of this, the only revolutionary, class, or the majority of it, overthrows the exploiters, suppresses them, emancipates the exploited from their state of slavery, improves their conditions of life immediately at the expense of the expropriated capitalists, only after this, and in the very process of the acute class struggle, is it possible to educate, train and organise the broadest masses of the toilers and the exploited around the proletariat, and under its influence and guidance, to rid them of the selfishness, disunity, the vices and weaknesses engendered

by private property, and to transform them into a free union of free workers.

The victory over capitalism requires a proper correlation between the leading, Communist, Party, the revolutionary class —the proletariat—and the masses, i.e., all the toilers and exploited. The Communist Party alone, if it is really the vanguard of the revolutionary class, if it really contains all its best representatives, if it consists of fully conscious and loyal Communists who have been educated and hardened by the experience of the persistent revolutionary struggle, if this Party has succeeded in linking itself inseparably with the whole life of its class, and through it, with the whole mass of exploited, and if it has succeeded in completely winning the confidence of this class and this mass— such a Party alone is capable of leading the proletariat in the most ruthless, decisive and final struggle against all the forces of capitalism. On the other hand, only under the leadership of such a Party can the proletariat display the full force of its revolutionary onslaught and neutralise the inevitable apathy and sometimes resistance of the small minority of the aristocracy of labour, the old trade union and co-operative leaders, etc., who have been corrupted by capitalism—only then will it be able to display its whole might, which is immeasurably greater than the proportion of the population it represents owing to the very economic structure of capitalist society. Finally, only after they have been actually emancipated from the yoke of the bourgeoisie and of the bourgeois state apparatus, only after they have obtained the opportunity of organising in their Soviets in a really free (from the exploiters) manner, can the masses, i.e., all the toilers and the exploited, for the first time in history, display all the initiative and energy of tens of millions of people who had been crushed by capitalism. Only when the Soviets have become the sole state apparatus is it possible really to secure the participation in the work of administration of the whole mass of exploited, ninety-nine hundredths of whom even under the most enlightened and free bourgeois democracy were actually debarred from taking part in the work of administration. Only in the Soviets do the masses of exploited really begin to learn, not from booklets, but from their own practical experience, the work of Socialist construction, of creating a new social discipline, a free union of free workers.

The dictatorship of the proletariat is the exercise of the fullest leadership of all the toilers and exploited, who are oppressed, downtrodden, crushed, intimidated, disunited and deceived by the capitalist class, by the only class that has been trained by the whole history of capitalism for such a leading role. Hence, preparation for the dictatorship of the proletariat must be started everywhere and immediately with the following method among others.

In all organisations without exception— unions and associations, primarily proletarian, and also organisations of the non-proletarian, toiling and exploited masses (political, industrial, military, co-operative, educational, sports, etc., etc.), groups or nuclei of Communists should be formed— mainly open groups, but also secret groups, which should be obligatory in every case when their suppression, or the arrest or deportation of their members by the bourgeoisie may be expected—and these nuclei, closely connected with each other and with the Party centre, interchanging their experiences, carrying on work of agitation, propaganda and organisation, adapting themselves to absolutely all spheres of public life, absolutely to all varieties and subdivisions of the toiling masses, must systematically train themselves, and the Party, and the class, and the masses, by means of this diversified work.

In this it is extremely important to work out in a practical manner the various necessary methods of work, on the one hand, in relation to the "leaders" or to the "responsible representatives," who, very often, are

hopelessly corrupted by petty-bourgeois and imperialist prejudices; these "leaders" must be ruthlessly exposed and driven out of the working class movement; and on the other hand, in relation to the masses, who, particularly after the imperialist slaughter, are for the most part inclined to pay heed to and assimilate the doctrine that the leadership of the proletariat is necessary as the only way out of capitalist slavery; we must learn to approach the masses with special patience and caution in order to be able to understand the specific and peculiar features of the psychology of every stratum, profession, etc., of these masses.

In all countries, even the freest, "legal" and "peaceful" in the sense that the class struggle is least acute in them, the time has fully matured when it is absolutely necessary for every Communist Party systematically to combine legal with illegal work, legal with illegal organisation. For in the most enlightened and free countries, those with the most "stable" bourgeois-democratic system, the governments already, notwithstanding their false and hypocritical declarations, systematically resort to secret blacklists of Communists, to endless violations of their own constitutions in order to render semi-secret and secret support to the White Guards and to assassinations of Communists in all countries, to secret preparations for the arrest of Communists, to placing provocateurs among the Communists, etc., etc. Only the most reactionary philistinism, no matter what beautiful, "democratic" and pacifist phrases it may be cloaked in, can deny this fact, or the imperative conclusion that follows from it, viz., that it is necessary, immediately, for all legal Communist Parties to form illegal organisations for the purpose of systematically carrying on illegal work, and of fully preparing for the moment when the bourgeoisie resorts to persecution. Illegal work is particularly necessary in the army, the navy and police; for after the great imperialist butchery all the governments in the world began to fear a people's army which is open to the workers and peasants, and began secretly to resort to all possible methods of forming military units especially picked from the ranks of the bourgeoisie and especially supplied with all technical improvements.

On the other hand, it is also necessary, in all cases without exception, not to restrict oneself to illegal work, but also to carry on legal work, overcoming all obstacles that stand in the way of this, forming legal organs of the press and legal organisations under the most varied titles, which may often be changed in the event of necessity. This is what is now being done by the illegal Communist Parties in Finland, in Hungary, partly in Germany, in Poland, in Latvia, etc. This is what the Industrial Workers of the World in America should do, and this should also be done by all the at present legal Communist Parties when the public prosecutors see fit to take proceedings against them on the basis of the resolutions of the congresses of the Communist International, etc.

The absolute necessity in principle of combining illegal with legal work is determined, not only by the sum total of the specific features of the present period, the period of the eve of the proletarian dictatorship, but also by the necessity of proving to the bourgeoisie that there is not, nor can there be, a sphere or field of work that cannot be won by the Communists; and above all it is determined by the fact that everywhere there are broad strata of the proletariat, and still broader non-proletarian toiling and exploited masses, who still believe in bourgeois-democratic legality and whose awakening is a matter of extreme importance for us.

III. STALIN

Foundations of Leninism *

1. Theory

From this theme I take three questions: (1) the importance of theory for the proletarian movement; (2) criticism of the "theory" of spontaneity; (3) the theory of the proletarian revolution.

1. THE IMPORTANCE OF THEORY

Some think that Leninism is the precedence of practice over theory in the sense

---

* From Joseph Stalin, *Foundations of Leninism* (1924; International Publishers, 1939). By permission.

that its main point is the translation of the Marxian theses into deeds, their "execution"; as for theory, it is alleged that Leninism is rather unconcerned about it. We know that Plekhanov occasionally chaffed Lenin about his "unconcern" for theory, and particularly for philosophy. We also know that theory is not held in great favour by many present-day Leninist practical workers, particularly in view of the overwhelming amount of practical work imposed upon them by present circumstances. I must declare that this more than odd opinion about Lenin and Leninism is quite wrong and bears no relation whatever to the truth; that the attempt of practical workers to brush theory aside runs counter to the whole spirit of Leninism and is fraught with serious dangers to the cause.

Theory is the experience of the working-class movement in all countries taken in its general aspect. Of course, theory becomes aimless if it is not connected with revolutionary practice, just as practice gropes in the dark if its path is not illumined by revolutionary theory. But theory can become a tremendous force in the working-class movement if it is built up in indissoluble connection with revolutionary practice; for it, and it alone, can give the movement confidence, the power of orientation, and an understanding of the inherent connection between surrounding events; for it, and it alone, can help practice to discern not only how and in which direction classes are moving at the present time, but also how and in which direction they will move in the near future. None other than Lenin uttered and repeated scores of times the well-known thesis that:

Without a revolutionary theory there can be no revolutionary movement. (Selected Works, Vol. II, p. 47.)

Lenin, better than anyone else, understood the great importance of theory, particularly for a Party such as ours, in view of the role of vanguard fighter of the international proletariat which has fallen to its lot, and in view of the complicated internal and international situation in which it finds itself. Foreseeing this special role of our Party as far back as 1902, he thought it necessary even then to point out that:

. . . the role of vanguard can be fulfilled only by a party that is guided by the most advanced theory. (Ibid., p. 48.)

It need hardly be proved that now, when Lenin's prediction about the role of our Party has come true, this thesis of Lenin's acquires particular force and particular importance.

2. CRITICISM OF THE "THEORY" OF SPONTANEITY, OR THE ROLE OF THE VANGUARD IN THE MOVEMENT

The "theory" of spontaneity is a theory of opportunism, a theory of worshipping the spontaneity of the labour movement, a theory which actually repudiates the leading role of the vanguard of the working class, of the party of the working class.

The theory of worshipping spontaneity is decidedly opposed to the revolutionary character of the working-class movement; it is opposed to the movement taking the line of struggle against the foundations of capitalism; it stands for the idea of the movement proceeding exclusively along the line of "realizable" demands, of demands "acceptable" to capitalism; it stands entirely for the "line of least resistance." The theory of spontaneity is the ideology of trade unionism.

The theory of worshipping spontaneity is decidedly opposed to lending the spontaneous movement consciousness and system. It is opposed to the idea of the Party marching at the head of the working class, of the Party raising the masses to the level of class consciousness, of the Party leading the movement; it stands for the idea that the class-conscious elements of the movement must not hinder the movement from taking its own course; it stands for the idea that the Party is only to heed the spontaneous movement and follow in its tail. The theory of spontaneity is the theory of belittling the role of the conscious element in the movement, the ideology of *"khvostism"* [1] —the logical basis of *all* opportunism.

In practice this theory, which appeared on the scene even before the first revolution in Russia, led its adherents, the so-called "Economists," to deny the need for an independent workers' party in Russia, to oppose the revolutionary struggle of the working class for the overthrow of tsardom, to preach a purely trade unionist policy in the movement, and, in general, to

[1] *I.e.*, following in the tail; from the Russian word *khvost*, meaning tail.

surrender the labour movement to the hegemony of the liberal bourgeoisie.

The fight of the old *Iskra* and the brilliant criticism of the theory of "khvostism" in Lenin's pamphlet *What Is To Be Done?* not only smashed so-called "Economism," but also created the theoretical foundations for a truly revolutionary movement of the Russian working class.

Without this fight it would have been quite useless even to think of creating an independent workers' party in Russia and of its playing a leading part in the revolution.

3. THE THEORY OF THE PROLETARIAN REVOLUTION

The Leninist theory of the proletarian revolution proceeds from three fundamental theses.

First Thesis: The domination of finance capital in the advanced capitalist countries; the issue of stocks and bonds as the principal operation of finance capital; the export of capital to the sources of raw materials, which is one of the foundations of imperialism; the omnipotence of a financial oligarchy, which is the result of the domination of finance capital—all this reveals the grossly parasitic character of monopolist capitalism, makes the yoke of the capitalist trusts and syndicates a hundred times more burdensome, quickens the revolt of the working class against the foundations of capitalism, and brings the masses to the proletarian revolution as their only salvation. (*Cf.* Lenin, *Imperialism, the Highest Stage of Capitalism.*)

Hence the first conclusion: intensification of the revolutionary crisis within the capitalist countries and growth of the elements of an explosion on the internal, proletarian front in the "mother countries."

Second Thesis: The increase in the export of capital to the colonies and dependent countries; the extension of "spheres of influence" and colonial possessions until they cover the whole globe; the transformation of capitalism into a *world system* of financial enslavement and colonial oppression of the vast majority of the population of the earth by a handful of "advanced" countries—all this has, on the one hand, converted the separate national economies and national territories into links in a single chain called world economy and, on the other hand, split the population of the globe into two camps: a handful of "advanced" capitalist countries which exploit and oppress vast colonies and dependencies, and the vast majority of colonial and dependent countries which are compelled to fight for their liberation from the imperialist yoke. (*Cf. Imperialism.*)

Hence the second conclusion: intensification of the revolutionary crisis in the colonial countries and growth of the elements of revolt against imperialism on the external, colonial front.

Third Thesis: The monopolistic possession of "spheres of influence" and colonies; the uneven development of the different capitalist countries, leading to a frenzied struggle for the redivision of the world between the countries which have already seized territories and those claiming their "share"; imperialist wars as the only method of restoring the disturbed "equilibrium"—all this leads to the aggravation of the third front, the inter-capitalist front, which weakens imperialism and facilitates the amalgamation of the first two fronts against imperialism: the front of the revolutionary proletariat and the front of colonial emancipation. (*Cf. Imperialism.*)

Hence the third conclusion: that under imperialism wars cannot be averted, and that a coalition between the proletarian revolution in Europe and the colonial revolution in the East in a united world front of revolution against the world front of imperialism is inevitable.

Lenin combines all these conclusions into one general conclusion that "*imperialism is the eve of the socialist revolution.*" [2] (*Selected Works,* Vol. V, p. 5.)

The very approach to the question of the proletarian revolution, of the character of

---

[2] My italics.—*J.S.*

the revolution, of its scope, of its depth, the scheme of the revolution in general, changes accordingly.

Formerly, the analysis of the conditions for the proletarian revolution was usually approached from the point of view of the economic state of individual countries. Now, this approach is no longer adequate. Now the matter must be approached from the point of view of the economic state of all or the majority of countries, from the point of view of the state of world economy; for individual countries and individual national economies have ceased to be self-sufficient units, have become links in a single chain called world economy; for the old "cultured" capitalism has evolved into imperialism, and imperialism is a world system of financial enslavement and colonial oppression of the vast majority of the population of the earth by a handful of "advanced" countries.

Formerly, it was the accepted thing to speak of the existence or absence of objective conditions for the proletarian revolution in individual countries, or, to be more precise, in one or another developed country. Now this point of view is no longer adequate. Now we must speak of the existence of objective conditions for the revolution in the entire system of world imperialist economy as an integral unit; the existence within this system of some countries that are not sufficiently developed industrially cannot serve as an insurmountable obstacle to the revolution, *if* the system as a whole, or, more correctly, *because* the system as a whole is already ripe for revolution.

Formerly it was the accepted thing to speak of the proletarian revolution in one or another developed country as of something separate and self-sufficient, facing a separate national front of capital as its opposite. Now this point of view is no longer adequate. Now we must speak of the world proletarian revolution; for the separate national fronts of capital have become links in a single chain called the world front of imperialism, which must be opposed by a common front of the revolutionary movement in all countries.

Formerly, the proletarian revolution was regarded exclusively as the result of the internal development of a given country. Now this point of view is no longer adequate. Now the proletarian revolution must be regarded primarily as the result of the development of the contradictions within the world system of imperialism, as the result of the snapping of the chain of the imperialist world front in one country or another.

Where will the revolution begin? Where, in what country, can the front of capital be pierced first?

Where industry is more developed, where the proletariat constitutes the majority, where there is more culture, where there is more democracy—that was the reply usually given formerly.

No, objects the Leninist theory of revolution; *not necessarily where industry is more developed,* and so forth. The front of capital will be pierced where the chain of imperialism is weakest, for the proletarian revolution is the result of the breaking of the chain of the world imperialist front at its weakest link; and it may turn out that the country which has started the revolution, which has made a breach in the front of capital, is less developed in a capitalist sense than other, more developed, countries, which have, however, remained within the framework of capitalism.

In 1917 the chain of the imperialist world front proved to be weaker in Russia than in the other countries. It was there that the chain gave way and provided an outlet for the proletarian revolution. Why? Because in Russia a great popular revolution was unfolding, and at its head marched the revolutionary proletariat, which had such an important ally as the vast mass of the peasantry who were oppressed and exploited by the landlords. Because the revolution there was opposed by such a hideous representative of imperialism as tsarism, which lacked all moral prestige and was deservedly hated by the whole population. The chain proved to be weaker in Russia, although that country was less developed in a capitalist sense than, say, France or Germany, England or America.

Where will the chain break in the near future? Again, where it is weakest. It is not precluded that the chain may break, say, in India. Why? Because that country has a young, militant, revolutionary proletariat, which has such an ally as the national liberation movement—an undoubtedly powerful and undoubtedly important ally. Because there the revolution is opposed by such a well-known foe as foreign imperialism, which lacks all moral credit and is deservedly hated by the oppressed and exploited masses of India.

It is also quite possible that the chain will break in Germany. Why? Because the factors which are operating, say, in India are beginning to operate in Germany as well; but, of course, the enormous difference in the level of development between India and Germany cannot but leave its impress on the progress and outcome of a revolution in Germany.

That is why Lenin said that:

... The West-European capitalist countries are accomplishing their development towards socialism not by the even "ripening" of socialism, but by the exploitation of some countries by others, by the exploitation of the first of the countries to be vanquished in the imperialist war combined with the exploitation of the whole of the East. On the other hand, precisely as a result of the first imperialist war, the East has been finally drawn into the revolutionary movement, has been drawn into the common maelstrom of the world revolutionary movement. ... (Selected Works, Vol. IX, p. 399.)

Briefly, the chain of the imperialist front must, as a rule, give way where the links are weaker and, at all events, not necessarily where capitalism is more developed, where there is such and such a percentage of proletarians and such and such a percentage of peasants, and so on.

This is why in deciding the question of proletarian revolution statistical calculations of the percentage of the proletarian population in a given country lose the exceptional importance so eagerly attached to them by the pedants of the Second International, who have not understood imperialism and who fear revolution like the plague.

But the overthrow of the power of the bourgeoisie and establishment of the power of the proletariat in one country still does not mean that the complete victory of socialism has been ensured. After consolidating its power and taking the peasantry in tow, the proletariat of the victorious country can and must build up a socialist society. But does this mean that it will thereby achieve the complete and final victory of socialism, i.e., does it mean that with the forces of only one country it can finally consolidate socialism and fully guarantee that country against intervention and, consequently, also against restoration? No, it does not. For this the victory of the revolution in at least several countries is needed. Therefore, the development and support of revolution in other countries is an essential task of the victorious revolution. Therefore, the revolution in the victorious country must regard itself not as a self-sufficient entity but as an aid, as a means of hastening the victory of the proletariat in other countries.

Lenin expressed this thought in a nutshell when he said that the task of the victorious revolution is to do "the utmost possible in one country for the development, support and awakening of the revolution in all countries." (Selected Works, Vol. VII, p. 182.)

These, in general, are the characteristic features of Lenin's theory of proletarian revolution.

2. The Dictatorship of the Proletariat

From this theme I take the three main questions: (1) the dictatorship of the proletariat as the instrument of the proletarian revolution; (2) the dictatorship of the proletariat as the domination of the proletariat over the bourgeoisie; (3) the Soviet power as the state form of the dictatorship of the proletariat.

1. THE DICTATORSHIP OF THE PROLETARIAT AS THE INSTRUMENT OF THE PROLETARIAN REVOLUTION

The question of the proletarian dictatorship is above all a question of the main content of the proletarian revolution. The proletarian revolution, its movement, its scope and its achievements acquire flesh and blood only through the dictatorship of the proletariat. The dictatorship of the proletariat is the instrument of the proletarian revolution, its organ, its most important mainstay, brought into being for the purpose of, firstly, crushing the resistance of the overthrown exploiters and consolidating the achievements of the proletarian revolution, and, secondly, carrying the proletarian revolution to its completion, carrying the revolution to the complete victory of socialism. The revolution can vanquish the bourgeoisie, can overthrow its power, without the dictatorship of the proletariat. But the revolution will be unable to crush the resistance of the bourgeoisie, to maintain its victory and to push forward to the final victory of socialism unless, at a certain stage in its development, it creates a special organ in the form of the dictatorship of the proletariat as its principal mainstay.

"The fundamental question of revolution is the question of power." (*Lenin.*) Does this mean that all that is required is to assume power, to seize it? No, it does not mean that. The seizure of power is only the beginning. For many reasons the bourgeoisie that is overthrown in one country remains for a long time stronger than the proletariat which has overthrown it. Therefore, the whole point is to retain power, to consolidate it, to make it invincible. What is needed to attain this? To attain this it is necessary to carry out at least the three main tasks that confront the dictatorship of the proletariat "on the morrow" of victory:

(a) to break the resistance of the landlords and capitalists who have been overthrown and expropriated by the revolution, to liquidate every attempt on their part to restore the power of capital;

(b) to organize construction in such a way as to rally all the labouring people around the proletariat, and to carry on this work along the lines of preparing for the liquidation, the abolition of classes;

(c) to arm the revolution, to organize the army of the revolution for the struggle against foreign enemies, for the struggle against imperialism.

The dictatorship of the proletariat is needed to carry out, to fulfil these tasks.

The transition from capitalism to communism [says Lenin] represents an entire historical epoch. Until this epoch has terminated, the exploiters will inevitably cherish the hope of restoration, and this *hope* will be converted into *attempts* at restoration. And after their first serious defeat, the overthrown exploiters—who had not expected their overthrow, never believed it possible, never conceded the thought of it—will throw themselves with tenfold energy, with furious passion and hatred grown a hundredfold, into the battle for the recovery of their lost "paradise," on behalf of their families, who had been leading such a sweet and easy life and whom now the "common herd" is condemning to ruin and destitution (or to "common" work). . . . In the train of the capitalist exploiters will be found the broad masses of the petty bourgeoisie, with regard to whom the historical experience of every country for decades testifies that they vacillate and hesitate, one day marching behind the proletariat and the next day taking fright at the difficulties of the revolution; that they become panic-stricken at the first defeat or semi-defeat of the workers, grow nervous, run about aimlessly, snivel, and rush from one camp to the other. (*Selected Works,* Vol. VII, pp. 140–41.)

2. THE DICTATORSHIP OF THE PROLETARIAT AS THE DOMINATION OF THE PROLETARIAT OVER THE BOURGEOISIE

From the foregoing it is evident that the dictatorship of the proletariat is not a mere change of personalities in the government, a change of "cabinet," etc., leaving the old economic and political order intact. The Mensheviks and opportunists of all countries, who fear dictatorship like fire and in their fright substitute the concept "conquest of power" for the concept "dictatorship of the proletariat," usually reduce the meaning of "conquest of power" to a change of "cabinet," to the accession to power of a new ministry made up of people like Scheidemann and Noske, MacDonald and Henderson. It is hardly necessary to explain that these and similar cabinet changes have nothing in common with the dictatorship of the proletariat, with the conquest of real power by the real proletariat. The Mac-Donalds and Scheidemanns in power, while the old bourgeois order is allowed to remain, their so-called governments cannot be anything else than an apparatus serving the bourgeoisie, a screen to hide the ulcers of imperialism, a weapon in the hands of the bourgeoisie against the revolutionary movement of the oppressed and exploited masses. Capital needs such governments as a screen when it finds it inconvenient, unprofitable, difficult to oppress and exploit the masses without the aid of a screen. Of course, the appearance of such governments is a symptom that "over there" (*i.e.*, in the capitalist camp) "all is not quiet at the Shipka Pass" [1]; nevertheless, governments of this kind necessarily remain governments of capital in disguise. The government of a Mac-Donald or a Scheidemann is as far removed from the conquest of power by the proletariat as the sky from the earth. The dictatorship of the proletariat is not a mere change of government, but a new state, with new organs of power, both central and local; it is the state of the proletariat, which has arisen on the ruins of the old state, the state of the bourgeoisie.

In a preface to *The Communist Manifesto* Marx and Engels wrote, quoting from *The Civil War in France:*

> The working class cannot simply lay hold of the ready-made state machine and wield it for its own purpose. (Marx, *Selected Works*, Vol. I, p. 190.)

In a letter to Kugelmann (1871) Marx wrote that the task of the proletarian revolution is

> no longer as before, to transfer the bureaucratic military machine from one hand to another, but to *smash* it, and that is a preliminary condition for every real people's revolution on the Continent. (Marx, *Selected Works*, Vol. II, p. 528.)

Marx's qualifying phrase about the Continent gave the opportunists and Mensheviks of all countries a pretext for proclaiming that Marx had thus conceded the possibility of the peaceful evolution of bourgeois democracy into a proletarian democracy, at least in certain countries outside the European continent (England, America). Marx did in fact concede that possibility, and he had good grounds for conceding it in regard to England and America in the 'seventies of the last century, when monopoly capitalism and imperialism did not yet exist, and when these countries, owing to the special conditions of their development, had as yet no developed militarism and bureaucracy. That was the situation before the appearance of developed imperialism. But later, after a lapse of thirty or forty years, when the situation in these countries had radically changed, when imperialism had developed and had embraced all capitalist countries without exception, when militarism and bureaucracy had appeared in England and America also, when the special conditions for peaceful develop-

---

[1] A Russian saying carried over from the Russo-Turkish War. Heavy fighting was taking place at the Shipka Pass, in which the Russians were suffering severe losses; but Russian Headquarters in their communiques reported: "All quiet at the Shipka Pass."

ment in England and the United States had disappeared—then the qualification in regard to these countries necessarily could no longer hold good.

Today [said Lenin] in 1917, in the epoch of the first great imperialist war, this qualification made by Marx is no longer valid. Both England and America, the greatest and the last representatives —in the whole world—of Anglo-Saxon "liberty," in the sense that militarism and bureaucracy were absent, have slid down entirely into the all-European, filthy, bloody morass of military-bureaucratic institutions to which everything is subordinated and which trample everything underfoot. Today, both in England and in America, the "preliminary condition for every real people's revolution" is the smashing, the *destruction* of the "ready-made state machine" (brought in those countries, between 1914 and 1917, to general "European" imperialist perfection). (*Selected Works,* Vol. VII, p. 37.)

In other words, the law of violent proletarian revolution, the law of the smashing of the bourgeois state machine as a preliminary condition for such a revolution, is an inevitable law of the revolutionary movement in the imperialist countries of the world.

Of course, in the remote future, if the proletariat is victorious in the most important capitalist countries, and if the present capitalist encirclement is replaced by a socialist encirclement, a "peaceful" path of development is quite possible for certain capitalist countries, whose capitalists, in view of the "unfavourable" international situation, will consider it expedient "voluntarily" to make substantial concessions to the proletariat. But this supposition applies only to a remote and possible future. With regard to the immediate future, there is no ground whatsoever for this supposition.

Therefore, Lenin is right in saying:

The proletarian revolution is impossible without the forcible destruction of the bourgeois state machine and the sub-stitution for it of a *new one*. . . . (*Selected Works,* Vol. VII, p. 124.)

3. THE SOVIET POWER AS THE STATE FORM OF THE DICTATORSHIP OF THE PROLETARIAT

The victory of the dictatorship of the proletariat signifies the suppression of the bourgeoisie, the smashing of the bourgeois state machine, and the substitution of proletarian democracy for bourgeois democracy. That is clear. But by means of what organizations can this colossal task be carried out? The old forms of organization of the proletariat, which grew up on the basis of bourgeois parliamentarism, are inadequate for this task—of that there can hardly be any doubt. What then, are the new forms of the organization of the proletariat that are capable of serving as the gravediggers of the bourgeois state machine, that are capable not only of smashing this machine, not only of substituting proletarian democracy for bourgeois democracy, but also of becoming the foundation of the proletarian state power?

This new form of organization of the proletariat is the Soviets.

Wherein lies the strength of the Soviets as compared with the old forms of organization?

In that the Soviets are the most *all-embracing* mass organizations of the proletariat, for they and they alone embrace all workers without exception.

In that the Soviets are the *only* mass organizations which embrace all the oppressed and exploited, workers and peasants, soldiers and sailors, and in which the vanguard of the masses, the proletariat, can, for this reason, most easily and most completely exercise its political leadership of the mass struggle.

In that the Soviets are the *most powerful organs* of the revolutionary struggle of the masses, of the political actions of the masses, of the insurrection of the masses—organs capable of breaking the omnipotence of finance capital and of its political appendages.

3. Strategy and Tactics

From this theme I take six questions: (1) strategy and tactics as the science of leadership in the class struggle of the proletariat; (2) stages of the revolution, and strategy; (3) the flow and ebb of the movement, and tactics; (4) strategic leadership; (5) tactical leadership; (6) reformism and revolutionism.

1. STRATEGY AND TACTICS AS THE SCIENCE OF LEADERSHIP IN THE CLASS STRUGGLE OF THE PROLETARIAT

The period of the domination of the Second International was mainly a period of the formation and training of the proletarian armies amidst conditions of more or less peaceful development. This was the period when parliamentarism was the principal form of class struggle. Questions of great class conflicts, of preparing the proletariat for revolutionary battles, of the ways and means of achieving the dictatorship of the proletariat, did not seem to be on the order of the day at that time. The task was confined to utilizing all paths of legal development for the purpose of forming and training the proletarian armies, to utilizing parliamentarism in conformity with the conditions under which the status of the proletariat was (and as it seemed then, had to remain) that of an Opposition. It need hardly be proved that in such a period and with such a conception of the tasks of the proletariat there could be neither an integral strategy nor any elaborated tactics. There were fragmentary and detached ideas about tactics and strategy, but no tactics or strategy as such.

The mortal sin of the Second International was not that it pursued the tactics of utilizing the parliamentary forms of struggle, but that it overestimated the importance of these forms, that it considered them virtually the only forms; and that when the period of open revolutionary battles set in and the question of extra-parliamentary forms of struggle came to the fore the parties of the Second International turned their backs on these new tasks, refused to shoulder them.

Only in the subsequent period, in the period of direct action by the proletariat, in the period of proletarian revolution, when the question of overthrowing the bourgeoisie became a question of immediate action; when the question of the reserves of the proletariat (strategy) became one of the most burning questions; when all forms of struggle and of organization, parliamentary and extra-parliamentary (tactics) had fully manifested themselves and became well-defined—only in this period could an integral strategy and elaborated tactics for the struggle of the proletariat be drawn up. It was precisely in that period that Lenin brought out into the light of day the brilliant ideas of Marx and Engels on tactics and strategy that had been immured by the opportunists of the Second International. But Lenin did not confine himself to restoring certain tactical propositions of Marx and Engels. He developed them further and supplemented them with new ideas and propositions, combining them all into a system of rules and guiding principles for the leadership of the class struggle of the proletariat. Lenin's pamphlets, such as *What Is To Be Done?; Two Tactics; Imperialism; State and Revolution; The Proletarian Revolution and the Renegade Kautsky; "Left-Wing" Communism,* etc., will undoubtedly always be treasured as priceless contributions to the general store of Marxism, to its revolutionary arsenal. The strategy and tactics of Leninism constitute the science of leadership of the revolutionary struggle of the proletariat.

2. STAGES OF THE REVOLUTION, AND STRATEGY

Strategy is the determination of the direction of the main blow of the proletariat at a given stage of the revolution, the elaboration of a corresponding plan for the disposition of the revolutionary forces (the main and secondary reserves), the fight to carry out this plan throughout the given stage of the revolution.

Our revolution already passed through two stages, and after the October Revolution it has entered a third stage. Our strategy changed accordingly.

First stage. 1903 to February 1917. Objective: to overthrow tsarism and completely wipe out the survivals of mediaevalism. The main force of the revolution: the proletariat. Immediate reserves: the peasantry. Direction of the main blow: the isolation of the liberal-monarchist bourgeoisie, which was striving to win over the peasantry and liquidate the revolution by *compromising* with tsarism. Plan for the disposition of forces: alliance of the working class with the peasantry.

The proletariat must carry to completion the democratic revolution, by allying to itself the mass of the peasantry in order to crush by force the resistance of the autocracy and to paralyse the instability of the bourgeoisie. (Lenin, *Selected Works*, Vol. III, p. 110.)

Second stage. March 1917 to October 1917. Objective: to overthrow imperialism in Russia and to withdraw from the imperialist war. The main force of the revolution: the proletariat. Immediate reserves: the poor peasantry. The proletariat of neighbouring countries as probable reserves. The protracted war and the crisis of imperialism as the favourable factor. Direction of the main blow: isolation of the petty-bourgeois democrats (Mensheviks and Socialist-Revolutionaries), who were striving to win over the toiling masses of the peasantry and to terminate the revolution by *compromising* with imperialism. Plan for the disposition of forces: alliance of the proletariat with the poor peasantry.

The proletariat must accomplish the socialist revolution by allying to itself the mass of the semi-proletarian elements of the population in order to crush by force the resistance of the bourgeoisie and to paralyse the instability of the peasantry and the petty bourgeoisie. (*Ibid.*, p. 111.)

Third stage. Commenced after the October Revolution. Objective: to consolidate the dictatorship of the proletariat in one country, using it as a base for the overthrow of imperialism in all countries. The revolution is spreading beyond the confines of one country; the period of world revolution has commenced. The main forces of the revolution: the dictatorship of the proletariat in one country, the revolutionary movement of the proletariat in all countries. Main reserves: the semi-proletarian and small-peasant masses in the developed countries, the liberation movement in the colonies and dependent countries. Direction of the main blow: isolation of the petty-bourgeois democrats, isolation of the parties of the Second International, which constitute the main support of the policy of *compromise* with imperialism. Plan for the disposition of forces: alliance of the proletarian revolution with the liberation movement in the colonies and the dependent countries.

Strategy deals with the main forces of the revolution and their reserves. It changes with the passing of the revolution from one stage to another, but remains essentially unchanged throughout a given stage.

3. THE FLOW AND EBB OF THE MOVEMENT, AND TACTICS

Tactics are the determination of the line of conduct of the proletariat in the comparatively short period of the flow or ebb of the movement, of the rise or decline of the revolution, the fight to carry out this line by means of replacing old forms of struggle and organization by new ones, old slogans by new ones, by combining these forms, etc. While the object of strategy is to win the war against tsarism, let us say, or against the bourgeoisie, to carry the struggle against tsarism or against the bourgeoisie to its end, tactics concern themselves with less important objects, for they aim not at winning the war as a whole, but at winning a particular engagement, or a particular battle, at carrying through successfully a particular campaign or a particular action corresponding to the concrete circumstances in the given period of rise or decline of the revolution. Tactics are a part of strategy, subordinate to it and serving it.

Tactics change according to flow and ebb. While the strategic plan remained unchanged during the first stage of the revolution (1903 to February 1917) tactics changed several times during that period. In the period from 1903 to 1905 the Party pursued offensive tactics, for the tide of the revolution was rising, the movement was on the upgrade, and tactics had to proceed from this fact. Accordingly, the forms of struggle were revolutionary, corresponding to the requirements of the rising tide of the revolution. Local political strikes, political demonstrations, the general political strike, boycott of the Duma, insurrection, revolutionary fighting slogans—such were the successive forms of the struggle during that period. These changes in the forms of struggle were accompanied by corresponding changes in the forms of organization. Factory committees, revolutionary peasant committees, strike committees, Soviets of workers' deputies, a workers' party operating more or less openly—such were the forms of organization during that period.

In the period from 1907 to 1912 the Party was compelled to resort to tactics of retreat; for we then experienced a decline in the revolutionary movement, the ebb of the revolution, and tactics necessarily had to take this fact into consideration. The forms of struggle, as well as the forms of organization, changed accordingly: Instead of boycott of the Duma there was participation in the Duma; instead of open, direct revolutionary action outside the Duma, there were parliamentary speeches and work in the Duma; instead of general political strikes, there were partial economic strikes, or simply a lull in activities. Of course, the Party had to go underground during that period, while the revolutionary mass organizations were superseded by cultural, educational, cooperative, insurance and other legal organizations.

The same must be said of the second and third stages of the revolution, during which tactics changed dozens of times, whereas the strategical plans remained unchanged.

Tactics deal with the forms of struggle and the forms of organization of the proletariat, with their changes and combinations. During a given stage of the revolution tactics may change several times, depending on the flow and ebb, the rise and decline, of the revolution.

4. STRATEGIC LEADERSHIP

The reserves of the revolution can be:

Direct: (a) the peasantry and in general the intermediate strata of the population within the country; (b) the proletariat of the neighbouring countries; (c) the revolutionary movement in the colonies and dependent countries; (d) the gains and achievements of the dictatorship of the proletariat—part of which the proletariat may give up temporarily, while retaining superiority of forces, in order to buy off a powerful enemy and gain a respite; and

Indirect: (a) the contradictions and conflicts among the nonproletarian classes within the country, which can be utilized by the proletariat to weaken the enemy and to strengthen its own reserves; (b) contradictions, conflicts and wars (the imperialist war, for instance) among the bourgeois states hostile to the proletarian state, which can be utilized by the proletariat in its offensive or in manoeuvring in the event of a forced retreat.

There is no need to speak at length about the reserves of the first category, as their significance is understood by everyone. As for the reserves of the second category, whose significance is not always clear, it must be said that sometimes they are of prime importance for the progress of the revolution. One can hardly deny the enormous importance, for example, of the conflict between the petty-bourgeois democrats (Socialist-Revolutionaries) and the liberal-monarchist bourgeoisie (the Constitutional-Democrats) during and after the first revolution, which undoubtedly played its part in freeing the peasantry from the influence of the bourgeoisie. Still less reason is there for denying the colossal importance of the fact that the principal groups of imperialists were engaged in a deadly war during the period of the October Revolution, when the imperialists, engrossed in war among themselves, were unable to concentrate their forces against the young Soviet power, and the proletariat, for this very reason, was able to get down to the work of organizing its forces and consolidating its power, and to prepare the rout of Kolchak and Denikin. It must be presumed that now, when the contradictions among the imperialist groups are becoming more and more profound, and when a new war among them is becoming inevitable, reserves of this description will assume ever greater importance for the proletariat.

The task of strategic leadership is to make proper use of all these reserves for the achievement of the main object of the revolution at the given stage of its development.

What does making proper use of reserves mean?

It means fulfilling certain necessary conditions, of which the following must be regarded as the principal ones:

First: the concentration of the main forces of the revolution at the enemy's most vulnerable spot at the decisive moment, when the revolution has already become ripe, when the offensive is going full-steam ahead, when insurrection is knocking at the door, and when bringing the reserves up to the vanguard is the decisive condition of success. The Party's strategy during the period from April to October 1917 well illustrates this manner of utilizing reserves. Undoubtedly, the enemy's most vulnerable spot at that time was the war. Undoubtedly, it was on this question, as the fundamental one, that the Party rallied the broadest masses of the population around the proletarian vanguard. The party's strategy during that period was, while training the vanguard for street action by means of manifestations and demonstrations, to bring the reserves up to the vanguard through the medium of the Soviets in the rear and the soldiers' committees at the front. The outcome of the revolution has shown that the reserves were properly utilized.

Here is what Lenin, paraphrasing the well-known theses of Marx and Engels on insurrection, says about this condition of the strategic utilization of the forces of the revolution:

Never *play* with insurrection, but when beginning it firmly realize that you must *go to the end.* You must concentrate a *great superiority of forces* at the decisive point, at the decisive moment, otherwise the enemy, who has the advantage of better preparation and organization, will destroy the insurgents. Once the insurrection has begun, you must act with the greatest *determination,* and by all means, without fail, take the *offensive.* "The defensive is the death of every armed rising." You must try to take the enemy by surprise and seize the moment when his forces are scattered. You must strive for *daily* successes, even if small (one might say hourly, if it is the case of one town), and at all costs retain *"moral ascendancy."* (Lenin, *Collected Works,* Vol. XXI, Russian edition, pp. 319–20.) [1]

Second: the selection of the moment for the decisive blow, of the moment for starting the insurrection, so timed as to coincide with the moment when the crisis has reached its climax, when it is fully apparent that the vanguard is prepared to fight to the end, the reserves are prepared to support the vanguard, and maximum consternation reigns in the ranks of the enemy.

The decisive battle [says Lenin] may be deemed to have fully matured *when* all the class forces hostile to us have become sufficiently entangled, are sufficiently at loggerheads with each other, have sufficiently weakened themselves in a struggle which is beyond their strength; *when* all the vacillating, wavering, unstable, intermediate elements—the petty bourgeoisie and the petty-bourgeois democrats as distinct from the bourgeoisie—have sufficiently exposed themselves be-

---

[1] *Cf.* Lenin and Stalin, *The Russian Revolution* (N.Y., 1938), p. 207.

fore the people, have sufficiently disgraced themselves through their practical bankruptcy; *when* among the proletariat a mass sentiment in favour of supporting the most determined, supremely bold, revolutionary action against the bourgeoisie has arisen and begun vigorously to grow. Then, indeed, revolution is ripe; then, indeed, if we have correctly gauged all the conditions indicated above . . . and if we have chosen the moment rightly, our victory is assured. (*Selected Works*, Vol. X, pp. 137–38.)

The manner in which the October insurrection was carried out may be taken as a model of such strategy.

5. TACTICAL LEADERSHIP

Tactical leadership is a part of strategic leadership, subordinated to the tasks and the requirements of the latter. The task of tactical leadership is to master all forms of struggle and organization of the proletariat and to ensure that they are used properly so as to achieve, with the given alignment of forces, the maximum results necessary to prepare for strategic success.

What does making proper use of the forms of struggle and organization of the proletariat mean?

It means fulfilling certain necessary conditions, of which the following must be regarded as the principal ones:

First: to put in the forefront precisely those forms of struggle and organization which are best suited to the conditions prevailing during the flow or ebb of the movement at a given moment, and which therefore can facilitate and ensure the bringing of the masses to the revolutionary positions, the bringing of the millions to the revolutionary front, and their disposition at the revolutionary front.

The point here is not that the vanguard shall realize the impossibility of preserving the old order of things and the inevitability of its overthrow. The point is that the masses, the millions, shall understand this inevitability and display their readiness to support the vanguard. But the masses can understand this only from their own experience. The task is to enable the vast masses to realize from their own experience the inevitability of the overthrow of the old regime, to promote such methods of struggle and forms of organization as will make it easier for the masses to learn from experience to recognize the correctness of the revolutionary slogans.

The vanguard would have become detached from the working class, and the working class would have lost contact with the masses, if the Party had not decided at the time to participate in the Duma, if it had not decided to concentrate its forces on work in the Duma and to base the struggle on this work, in order to make it easier for the masses to realize from their own experience the futility of the Duma, the falsity of the promises of the Constitutional-Democrats, the impossibility of compromise with tsarism, and the inevitability of an alliance between the peasantry and the working class. Had the masses not gained their experience during the period of the Duma, the exposure of the Constitutional-Democrats and the hegemony of the proletariat would have been impossible.

The danger of the "Otzovist" [2] tactics was that they threatened to detach the vanguard from the millions of its reserves.

The Party would have become detached from the working class, and the working class would have lost its influence among the broad masses of the peasants and soldiers, if the proletariat had followed the "Left" Communists, who called for insurrection in April 1917, when the Mensheviks and the Socialist-Revolutionaries had not yet exposed themselves as advocates of war and imperialism, when the masses had not yet learned from their own experience to recognize the falsity of the speeches of the Mensheviks and the Socialist-Revolutionaries about peace, land and freedom. Had the masses not gained this experience

[2] From the Russian *Otozvat*—to recall; the name given to a group of Bolsheviks who advocated the recall of the Social-Democratic deputies from the Duma.

during the Kerensky period, the Mensheviks and Socialist-Revolutionaries would not have been isolated and the dictatorship of the proletariat would have been impossible. Therefore, the tactics of "patiently explaining" the mistakes of the petty-bourgeois parties and of open struggle in the Soviets were the only correct tactics.

The danger of the tactics of the "Left" Communists was that they threatened to transform the Party from the leader of the proletarian revolution into a handful of inane conspirators with no ground to stand on.

> With the vanguard alone victory cannot be achieved [says Lenin]. To throw the vanguard alone into the decisive battle, before the whole class, before the broad masses have taken up a position either of direct support of the vanguard, or at least of benevolent neutrality towards it . . . would not merely be folly but a crime. And in order that actually the whole class, that actually the broad masses of the toilers and those oppressed by capital may take up such a position, propaganda and agitation alone are not sufficient. For this the masses must have their own political experience. Such is the fundamental law of all great revolutions, now confirmed with amazing force and vividness not only in Russia but also in Germany. It has been necessary, not only for the uncultured, often illiterate, masses of Russia, but also for the highly cultured, entirely literate masses of Germany, to realize from their own painful experience the absolute impotence and spinelessness, the absolute helplessness and servility before the bourgeoisie, the utter vileness of the government of the knights of the Second International, the absolute inevitability of a dictatorship of the extreme reactionaries (Kornilov in Russia, Kapp and Co. in Germany) as the only alternative to a dictatorship of the proletariat, in order to turn resolutely toward communism. (*Selected Works,* Vol. X, p. 136.)

Second: To locate at any given moment that particular link in the chain of processes which, if grasped, will enable us to hold the whole chain and to prepare the conditions for achieving strategic success.

The point here is to single out from all the problems confronting the Party that particular immediate problem, the answer to which constitutes the central point, and the solution of which will ensure the successful solution of the other immediate problems.

6. REFORMISM AND REVOLUTIONISM

What is the difference between revolutionary tactics and reformist tactics?

Some think that Leninism is opposed to reforms, opposed to compromises and to agreements in general. This is absolutely wrong. Bolsheviks know as well as anybody else that in a certain sense "every little helps," that under certain conditions reforms in general, and compromises and agreements in particular, are necessary and useful.

> To carry on a war for the overthrow of the international bourgeoisie [says Lenin], a war which is a hundred times more difficult, protracted and complicated than the most stubborn of ordinary wars between states, and to refuse beforehand to manoeuvre, to utilize the conflict of interests (even though temporary) among one's enemies, to refuse to temporise and compromise with possible (even though transient, unstable, vacillating and conditional) allies—is not this ridiculous in the extreme? Is it not the same as if in the difficult ascent of an unexplored and heretofore inaccessible mountain we were to renounce beforehand the idea that at times we might have to go in zigzags, sometimes retracing our steps, sometimes giving up the course once selected and trying various others? (*Selected Works,* Vol. X, p. 111.)

Obviously, therefore, it is not a matter of reforms or of compromises and agreements, but of the use people make of reforms and compromises.

To a reformist, reforms are everything, while revolutionary work is something incidental, something just to talk about, mere eyewash. That is why, with reformist tactics under the bourgeois regime, reforms are inevitably transformed into an instrument for strengthening that regime, an instrument for disintegrating the revolution.

To a revolutionary, on the contrary, the main thing is revolutionary work and not reforms; to him reforms are by-products of the revolution. That is why, with revolutionary tactics under the bourgeois regime, reforms are naturally transformed into instruments for disintegrating this regime, into instruments for strengthening the revolution, into a base for the further development of the revolutionary movement.

The revolutionary will accept a reform in order to use it as an aid in combining legal work with illegal work, to intensify, under its cover, the illegal work for the revolutionary preparation of the masses for the overthrow of the bourgeoisie.

This is what making revolutionary use of reforms and agreements under the conditions of imperialism means.

The reformist, on the contrary, will accept reforms in order to renounce all illegal work, to thwart the preparation of the masses for the revolution and to rest in the shade of "bestowed" reforms.

This is what reformist tactics mean.

This is the position in regard to reforms and agreements under imperialism.

The situation changes somewhat, however, after the overthrow of imperialism, under the dictatorship of the proletariat. Under certain conditions, in a certain situation, the proletarian power may find itself constrained temporarily to leave the path of the revolutionary reconstruction of the existing order of things and to take the path of its gradual transformation, the "reformist path," as Lenin says in his well-known article "On the Importance of Gold," the path of flanking movements, of reforms and concessions to the non-proletarian classes—in order to disintegrate these classes, to give the revolution a respite, to recuperate and prepare the conditions for a new offensive. It cannot be denied that in a sense this is a reformist path. But it must be borne in mind that there is a fundamental distinction here, which consists in the fact that in this case the reform emanates from the proletarian power, it strengthens the proletarian power, it procures for it a necessary respite; its purpose is to disintegrate, not the revolution, but the non-proletarian classes.

CHAPTER 24

DEMOCRATIC SOCIALISM

V IEWED in historical perspective, capitalism is more than an economic system. Applying rational methods of calculation first to economic practices and institutions, capitalism then increasingly penetrated all other phases of civilization and created a way of life of its own. The growth of modern science and its application in everyday affairs, the emergence of pragmatism in philosophy and individualism in politics, the pre-eminence of civilians over the military, the acceptance of experimentalism in ideas and institutions, the progressive spread of world-mindedness, the utilitarian testing of custom and tradition—these are but a few of the lasting values and attitudes that capitalism has created.

Yet in the very act of solving some of the problems that had given birth to it, capitalism created new problems. Capitalism was the triumphant assertion of individual daring, skill, and enterprise over bureaucratic inertia and ineptitude, and political liberty was greatly strengthened by the new economic individualism. However, as the capitalist economy progressed, the individual form of ownership and work was gradually replaced, owing to technological, financial, and managerial changes, by an economic system in which large-scale enterprise swallowed up the original capitalist owner-worker-manager. *Work* became *collective*, yet *ownership* remained *private*.

Large-scale enterprise, growing inevitably out of the earlier small capitalist enterprises, brought about more than new forms of production and distribution. The spirit of risk taking inherent in individual ownership-management enterprise gave way to bureaucratic routine and quest for security that are characteristic of large-scale organization, whether private or public. The old middle classes of independent entrepreneurs were gradually replaced by the new middle classes of dependent managers, executives, and the lower echelons of the white-collar salariat.

The separation of ownership from management and financial control in the modern corporation greatly facilitated the spread of the capitalist economy, but at the same time it emptied the idea of individual property of much of its original vitality. The peasant will fight and die for his piece of land, the artisan for his home and workshop, but the owner of a few shares of a corporation will hardly exhibit the same enthusiasm and fighting spirit. His connection with the corporation, of which he is legally a part owner, consists in little more than periodic receipts of dividends. Majorities in corporation votes and elections frequently reach margins of as high as ninety-nine per cent. Such percentages resemble more state-managed plebiscites in authoritarian countries than elections in free nations, in which majorities rarely score more than fifty-five or sixty per cent.

Paradoxically, therefore, the more capitalism succeeds, the more it destroys its original institutional and ideological character by "socializing" the framework of society. The first collectivists in capitalism were not its critics, not socialist propagandists, but the most successful capitalist entrepreneurs—men like Andrew Carnegie, John D. Rockefeller, Elbert H. Gary, Edward H. Harriman, Henry Ford—who created vast industrial empires. Like all empires, industrial empires, too, have a tendency to level and flatten out differences, follow routine and precedent, disregard the individual local peculiarity for the sake of the general rule and practice, and, above all, transform personal government into standardized impersonal administration. Large-scale capitalist enterprise thus created the institutional conditions out of which some form of collectivism was bound to develop. Psychologically, there is less difference between large-scale capitalist and large-scale socialized enterprise than between small-scale and large-scale capitalist enterprise.

In addition to institutional socialization, capitalism provided the ideological weapons with which it could be attacked. Rationalism, criticism, utilitarianism, and pragmatism had helped capitalism win its battles against the preceding social-economic system by refusing to accept any institution on the basis of faith and authority. This same spirit of critical rationalism later turned against capitalism itself by refusing to accept private property in the means of production on the basis of unquestioning loyalty and mere legal authority.

The challenge to capitalism was produced by its failures as much as by its successes. The latter would have been sufficient to transform it into some form of socialized system, but the former accelerated this inevitable development. In the first place, *unemployment* is a scourge which has destroyed the belief that the capitalist economy possesses a natural harmony, and that it can provide material welfare for everybody. Secondly, the *contradiction between political freedom and economic dependence* has become increasingly accentuated, and its effect noted by socialists and nonsocialists alike. In the classical period of early capitalism, the late eighteenth and early nineteenth centuries, political liberty and economic independence of the individual were fairly evenly balanced. Since then, political liberty has been greatly expanded through the widening of the suffrage and the removal of many restrictions of age, sex, religion, race, and class. Yet economically the individual has increasingly become more dependent on the giant corporate enterprises that have gradually replaced the small and middle-sized enterprises as the predominant economic and technological unit. The "scissors" between political liberty and economic dependence have thus markedly widened in the last hundred years. Following its own dynamic, political liberty has expanded, while economic independence has simultaneously declined as a result of the predominance of large-scale enterprise in the period of "high" capitalism.

The essence of the problem consists in this: in government, democracy has established the principle that the holders of power must be accountable to the public. The latter is the "boss," the former no more than its agent. Political power in a democracy must not be held for the benefit of the rulers; it is a trust, under which the interest of the people is to be protected. In the economic realm, on the other hand, the dogma of laissez faire has created a constitutional situation that violates the recognized canons of democracy: the owners of capital wield far-reaching power over their employees and the public, without being accountable to the community, without being responsible to those whose lives they determine through vital economic decisions. Whereas in a capitalist democracy political policies are arrived at through processes of consent that begin at the bottom and end at the top, in corporate business economic policies are made from the top to the bottom. The character of modern industrial organization is hierarchical, founded on discipline and obedience. In organizational structure, corporate business resembles more an institution like the army than a parliament. More recently, however, the traditional pattern in industry has been considerably modified and made more democratic by collective bargaining and the influence of the labor movement.

The existence of "industrial absolutism" within the walls of political liberty lies at the basis of the critique of capitalism by socialists and nonsocialists. The notion has been increasingly accepted, not always in clearly formulated ideas or public policies, that the original democratic balance between economic and political liberty must be restored, and that political liberty is doomed unless some way is found to recapture individual economic independence within the conditions of large-scale enterprise. Nonsocialists believe that the evils of monopolistic capitalism can be remedied through antimonopolistic legislation, supplemented more positively by social welfare and security. Socialists believe that more radical changes are necessary, and that the basic economic decisions must be made by the community, not by private owners of the means of production; the basic industries, at least, will therefore have to be directly owned and controlled by the community.

Socialism is not an outside invasion of the citadel of capitalism, but a product of capitalism itself. The struggle between the two is a family affair. Elements of the socialist faith—"one world," peace, equality, social and economic justice—are as old as civilized life. But as an effective political movement, socialism is inseparable from the Industrial Revolution. Without advanced industry and an urban working class there can be no socialist mass organizations. The Industrial Revolution separated man from ownership of the tools of production: first, the self-employing artisan was replaced by the capitalist employer who owned the machines giving work to hundreds and thousands of workers owning nothing but their hands. Second, as modern technology progressed, the proportion of those who owned the instruments of production shrank continually, thus widening the gap between those who own the tools and those who work them. Third, as industry developed, the incidence of capital investment in the process of production rose steadily: greater initial amounts of capital were needed to start business and manufacture. The initial capital outlay needed to produce carts or breed horses is less than that needed to manufacture automobiles, locomotives, or airplanes. Fourth, concentration of capital was accompanied by concentration of control, so that fewer and fewer persons controlled bigger and bigger aggregates of wealth, although ownership—as distinct from control—was spread more widely through the corporate form of business organization.

Where small property has survived as an efficient economic unit, as in agriculture and some branches of industrial servicing and distributing, socialist ideas have made little headway. And where there has been little industrialization, socialism has meant not so much the nationalization of the means of production as the building of an industrial economy on the basis of public ownership. Because initial capital requirements are comparatively heavy at the present stage of technological development, only the state is frequently able, and therefore compelled, to start new industries, or revive old ones. Even an industrially advanced country like Great Britain decided in 1945 to nationalize its basic industries and services, not because the people had become addicted to any a priori dogma of socialist superiority over capitalism, but because they believed that the job of rapidly rebuilding British industry and increasing its productivity demanded resources that only the community as a whole could supply. Similarly, the development of atomic energy in the United States has been from the start controlled, financed, and operated under public auspices, because the government alone is in a position to defray the vast expenditures involved—the highest in industrial history.

Modern anticapitalist movements have appeared in two main forms: revolutionary, totalitarian, Marxist communism aims at the overthrow of capitalism through revolutionary means and believes in the necessity of setting up a dictatorship of the proletariat (through communist parties) until the remnants of capitalist ideology and habits of thought are liquidated. Evolutionary, democratic, liberal socialism, on the other hand, adheres to the strict procedures of *constitutional government* throughout: it seeks power by ballots rather than bullets, and, once in power, it maintains processes of self-government, and subjects itself to the free decision of the people given in free elections.

Revolutionary communism visualizes the transition from capitalist enterprise to public ownership as sudden and complete: there is no payment of compensation for expropriated property, because capitalist property is considered, morally and socially, little better than theft derived from exploitation. By contrast, democratic socialism is slow and piecemeal, evolves (like other transactions of advanced capitalism) on the instalment plan, and has to prove its right to hold power by gaining, and keeping, the freely expressed consent of the majority. In democracies, governments chosen by the majority of the electorate must follow the first law of democratic politics: not to exhaust all opportunities of victory and not to outrage the defeated minority party to the point of humiliation and revolt. In a dictatorship, fascist or communist, opponents are liquidated. In a democracy, opponents must be won over.

Democratic socialism cannot afford to follow dogmas for dogmas' sake but must prove pragmatically, through actual accomplishments, its moral right to apply the principle of public ownership to industries that stand to gain from socialization. As to compensation, democratic socialism does not believe that legitimate expectations of citizens may be violated, and it persists in the belief that expropriation of private property is permissible only after due process and proper compensation. Important as public ownership of the basic industries is to the democratic socialist, he never forgets that it is not a fetish but a means to an end, and that the respect of rights, including legitimate property rights, is the foundation of democracy. Confidence between majority and minority, between government and opposition, is the key to the vitality of democracy, and there can be no confidence where established rights are destroyed by fiat.

If the whole economic system be compared to a basket of eggs, communism burns the basket and scrambles all eggs at once—never to be unscrambled again. Democratic socialism keeps the basket, and cooks only small orders of scrambled eggs at one time, because it believes in Aristotle's wise counsel that "the guest will judge better of a feast than the cook."

Revolutionary communism and democratic socialism are often confused and used as interchangeable concepts because they both seem to agree on one objective: the transfer to public ownership of the means of production. Yet there are two basic differences that irreconcilably separate revolutionary, totalitarian communism from constitutional, democratic socialism. In the first place, the communist is dogmatically committed to the principle of public ownership for *all* forms of property other than personal consumer goods, whereas the socialist is not committed to any a priori dogma of the inherent superiority of public ownership over private. The socialist seeks to establish rational, pragmatic, empirically verifiable *criteria* that qualify an industry *for nationalization:* in one instance the criterion may be a natural monopoly (such as gas and light, water, telephone and telegraph, and other utilities); in another, it may be that of an important industry which has become critically "sick" and which is unlikely to recover under unplanned private enterprise (such as the British coal industry before nationalization); in still another, it may be that of an industry which is too important, in peace and war, to be left under the control of private enterprise although it may be highly efficient and competitive (as in the case of the British steel industry).

The second main difference between communists and socialists is no less important. To the democratic socialist the *freedom of the individual* is so all-important that he puts it *above* everything else, including the *socialization* of the economy. He is a patient person who knows that he may have to wait a long time until he can persuade his fellow citizens that capitalism is inefficient and unjust, and that his proposals are practical and equitable. The communist tells him that it is useless to seek power by persuasion, because all means of communication, education, and propaganda are biased in favor of the capitalist *status quo,* and that the freedom of the press amounts to little in practice if one desires to start a metropolitan newspaper but lacks the four or five million dollars of initial investment. The democratic socialist can only retort that, like other democrats, he has the faith that a reasonable case, reasonably presented, will eventually win the hearts of the people. This faith of democratic socialists may often be overly optimistic, but so is the faith of all democrats.

From the communist viewpoint, the electoral victory of the British Labor party in 1945 was all wrong and should not have happened, according to orthodox Marxism-Leninism: the British press was overwhelmingly in favor of the Conservatives, and the working class therefore was not supposed to have become socialist by mere independence of thought and peaceful political action. According to Lenin, workers under capitalism are mentally enslaved to the capitalist ideology, and they are incapable of being peacefully converted to socialism without changing first the economic structure of society. Because, according to Marx, the conditions of man's life determine his consciousness, workers will think in a socialist manner only *after* capitalism has been destroyed, and not before.

To the communist, every capitalist system, whether democratic or fascist, is a bourgeois dictatorship, and the communist interprets the political institutions of democratic capitalism as sham and hypocrisy that do not affect the reality of dictatorship. Once capitalism—even democratic capitalism—is identified with dictatorship, the communist insistence on violence as the sole means of change is the logical conclusion. The democratic socialist, by contrast, draws a sharp distinction between a capitalist regime that is dictatorial and one that is democratic. Though dictatorial capitalism—fascist or otherwise—cannot be changed peacefully from within, democratic capitalism can. The democratic socialist hopes that, just as *he* puts liberty and respect for law above the organization of the economy, the adherent of democratic capitalism will do likewise.

In practice, *the choice in a democracy will never be between full capitalism and full socialism,* because the genius of democracy consists in tackling issues that are comparatively manageable, and in avoiding, as much as possible, definitive, long-term commitments that are irrevocable. The democratic socialist therefore envisages the transition from a predominantly capitalist economy (a purely capitalist economy has never existed in practice) to a predominantly socialist economy, not as the result of a sudden revolutionary coup that makes the return to capitalism technically and administratively impossible (as in Russia), but as the result of gradual measures, none of which, by itself, irrevocably alters the nature of the whole economy. Whereas communists think in terms of three absolutes—capitalism, revolution, dictatorial communism—socialists think in terms of three *relative* concepts: a predominantly capitalist economy as the starting point, a long process of reform as the period of gradual transition, and a predominantly socialized economy as the probable goal.

The choice between revolutionary, totalitarian communism and evolutionary, democratic socialism is, like other vital choices, not a matter of pure logic. Facts of history limit the range of discretion in social action. Where political democracy has fragile roots, the communist solution of pressing social and economic problems will seem the more natural to those who have never known the experience of free institutions. This fact explains why the transition from monarchical autocracy to communism has been so successful in Russia, Yugoslavia, or Bulgaria, just as the corrupt dictatorship of the Kuomintang in China prepared the road for the communist dictatorship that followed it. Where, however, the tradition of democracy has been deeply embedded in national life and thought, as in Great Britain and Scandinavia, democratic socialism seems the more natural solution of fundamental ills. Sidney Webb and Attlee would be as out of place in Russia or Outer Mongolia, as Lenin and Stalin would be in Westminster.

The gradual transition from *liberal capitalism* to *liberal socialism* in democratic nations like England or Sweden is just as much within the range of foreseeable and probable evolution as was the transition from autocratic czarism to dictatorial communism in a country like Russia. Russia would have experienced an even greater revolution in 1917 if she had turned from autocracy to democracy, rather than exchange one form of autocracy for another. Similarly, Britain could be said to undergo a truly revolutionary change of institutions only if she exchanged her democratic way of life for that of totalitarianism; the change from capitalist democracy to socialist democracy is not so unexpected and quite within the range of predictable developments.

Most nations do not fall into a category of perfect democratic maturity or complete immaturity but generally lie somewhere between the two extremes. Thus, looking at Europe, France or Italy are open cases, and their development toward socialism or communism cannot be easily predicted. In Asia, India seems destined to hold the balance between the forces of freedom and totalitarianism, but it is uncertain whether she will eventually be able to defend herself against communism. In Africa and the Americas, too, there are a number of countries whose institutional experience is neither predominantly democratic nor authoritarian.

The communist objective of world revolution and conquest violates the doctrine of Marx in a fundamental point. According to Marx, the conditions of man's existence determine his consciousness, and social change is therefore not the product of mere will and free choice. Where the conditions of society permit peaceful change from capitalism to socialism, the use of force and revolutionary subversion is, in one sense, un-Marxian. The communist dogma of universal revolution and dictatorship is in harmony with Marx' theory of consciousness only in societies in which the conditions of social and political life have created a general distrust in the possibility of peaceful change, but it is out of harmony in nations whose democratic consciousness is the result of their conditions of existence. Marx himself never fully developed the political implications of his own conception of the relations of political consciousness and ideology to the underlying conditions of existence, although he occasionally referred to England and the United States as two possible exceptions to the universal principle of social change through communist revolution and dictatorship. The communists after Marx have made Marxism more dogmatic on that point than Marx was himself. By insisting on universal revolution and dictatorship, communists in fact proclaim the un-Marxian doctrine that regardless of the historical, cultural, social, economic, and political conditions a uniform consciousness—the creed of communism—can be imposed by sheer force.

Conversely, adherents of the private enterprise system who would like to see the whole world embrace it, also violate elementary good sense and historical experience: whether a society is likely to operate a capitalist economy is not a matter of pure logic and choice but the result of historical environment, cultural heritage, social institutions, and political ideologies. Those who proclaim the defense of private enterprise as the supreme international objective of the democratic nations play into the hands of the communists, because the private enterprise system is desired and practiced by a continually shrinking number of nations, whereas some form of controlled economy is spreading in most countries of the world. The *supreme value of democracy is freedom, not property,* and the democratic world will meet the communist challenge only if it keeps first things first and unites on the issue of freedom as the key issue of human survival. Once the survival of freedom is guaranteed, the question of economic institutions— more or less private or public enterprise—will take care of itself, without wars and hydrogen bombs.

Because democratic socialism is antiauthoritarian, it has not produced any authoritative statement of socialist doctrine accepted by all socialists, as Marx' and Lenin's writings are accepted by communists. There is a mass of socialist thought, but there is no socialist bible similar to Marx' *Communist Manifesto* or Lenin's *State and Revolution.* The leading socialist theoretician between the age of Marx and Engels and the present era is Karl Kautsky (1854–1938).

Kautsky was a native of Prague, then a part of the Austro-Hungarian Empire. At the age of nine he moved to Vienna, and spent most of his life in Austria and Germany. Deeply steeped in Marx' thought, Kautsky met Marx and Engels in London in 1881. After Marx' death, Kautsky visited England again in 1885 and became closely associated with Engels. Following the death of the latter, Kautsky quickly established himself as the leading theoretician of Social Democracy and eventually dominated the thinking of the Second (Socialist) International, just as Marx had dominated the First International (International Workingmen's Association). Kautsky was one of the few socialists in Germany who opposed the war in 1914, whereas the vast majority of the Social Democratic party enthusiastically supported it. After World War I, Kautsky returned to Vienna, but the conquest of Austria by Nazi Germany in the spring of 1938 forced him to flee from Austria. He found refuge in Holland, where he died in the fall of 1938.

Kautsky remained throughout his life an orthodox Marxist in one sense only: he profoundly believed with Marx that the social and economic environment of man was the principal force of historical change, and that capitalism was doomed to disintegrate because of its own contradictions. Yet Kautsky increasingly rejected, as he grew older, revolution and dictatorship as the highway to socialism. In fact, his steadfast adherence to the ideal of democracy for the labor movement caused the communists to hate him bitterly, and in Lenin's writings

Kautsky is attacked more often and more vehemently than any other socialist thinker.

The communist revolution and dictatorship in Russia brought sharp and immediate literary reactions from Kautsky: *Dictatorship of the Proletariat* (1918), *Terrorism and Communism* (1919), *From Democracy to State Slavery* (1921), and, later, *Bolshevism at a Deadlock* (1930). The work that is likely to endure longest is his *Materialist Conception of History* (1927), which, when translated into English, will establish his reputation more securely in the English-speaking countries.

Kautsky was no newcomer to Russian studies: his book on *The Moving Forces of the Russian Revolution* was published in 1906, and its Russian translation contained a preface by Lenin in which he stated that Kautsky was the only western socialist who had a genuine understanding of Russia and her social problems. Yet after the communist revolution in Russia, when Kautsky attacked revolution and dictatorship, Lenin replied in *The Proletarian Revolution and Kautsky the Renegade* (1919). Before Stalin made the term "Trotskyite" the symbol of evil and contempt, Lenin had already coined the term "Kautskyite" as the symbol of treason to Soviet communism. For a long time, being called a Kautskyite in the Soviet Union was equivalent to intellectual—and at times physical—liquidation. Only the invention of Trotskyism as the devil of communism gave Kautsky a respite in communist literature and propaganda.

In his *Terrorism and Communism* Kautsky writes that the "hereditary sin of Bolshevism has been its suppression of democracy through a form of government, namely, the dictatorship, which has no meaning unless it represents the unlimited and despotic power, either of one single person, or of a small organization intimately bound together." Kautsky compares dictatorship to war and adds that it "is as easy to begin a dictatorship as it is to begin war, if one has the State power under control. But when once such steps have been taken, it is difficult at will to stop the one as the other. One has to choose between two alternatives, either to triumph or to end in catastrophe." In conclusion, Kautsky says that he sees only two alternatives, democracy or civil war, and that "wherever Socialism does not appear to be possible on a democratic basis, and where the majority of the people rejects it, its time has not yet fully come."

Kautsky reminds the communists that democracy is not a form of bourgeois domination, because the bourgeoisie originally believed in a suffrage limited by property qualifications, and that the adoption of universal, equal suffrage was the achievement of the working classes. It is up to the working classes to utilize the opportunities offered by universal suffrage: "Democracy, with its universal equal suffrage, is the method to transform the class-struggle out of a hand-to-hand fight into a battle of intelligence, in which one particular class can triumph only if it is intellectually and morally on a level with its opponent. Democracy is the one and only method through which the higher form of life can be realized, and which Socialism declares is the right of civilized men."

Kautsky's last book is *Social Democracy versus Communism*, a collection of essays written during the years 1932–1937, shortly before his death, and published posthumously in 1946. His faith in democracy had to pass, in the meantime, through another test. The victory of Nazism in Germany weakened the confidence of many democrats and seemed to justify the communist thesis that capitalism in decay was bound to lead to fascism, and was, in fact, identical with it. Yet the Nazi experience only strengthened Kautsky's belief in socialism, and in democracy as the only means of attaining it. He conceded that revolutionary methods might be necessary to destroy a regime like that of Nazism, but he reiterated his belief that, once constitutional government was established, socialism must be pursued by strictly democratic means. The transition from capitalism to socialism requires widespread consent, and "a majority of 51 per cent will not suffice." Kautsky adds that "democracy is the shortest, surest and least costly road to Socialism, just as it is the best instrument for the development of the political and social prerequisites for Socialism. Democracy and Socialism are inextricably entwined."

Kautsky compares the communist parties to military organizations. Unlike socialist parties, communist parties "are not organized democratically, but in military fashion. They do not choose their own leaders and slogans but receive them from their high command—in the last instance, from Moscow. The Communists of all countries are its disciplined praetorian guard. *Communism has become for the present rulers of Russia what pan-Slavism was for the tsars, with the exception that the Communists of today are much more obedient to the dictators in Moscow than the pan-Slavists were to the tsars.*"

Kautsky saw therefore no possibility of a "united front" of socialists and communists, such as was proposed by the latter in the middle thirties, when the Soviet Union looked for allies in its defense against Nazi Germany. Far from regarding the Soviet Union as the hope of humanity, he considered its "slave economy" a system based on lies and deception. Whereas, finally, many accepted the claim of the Soviet Union to speak for the workers of the world, Kautsky concludes his *Social Democracy versus Communism* with the warning that the continuance of the communist dictatorship in Russia "constitutes the gravest menace and causes the greatest damage to the struggle of the modern working class for liberation." Moreover, communism contributed to the victory of fascism in several important European countries in two ways: first, by threatening violence and revolution the communists provoked, or at least intensified, the reaction of fascist violence and revolution. Second, by splitting the working-class movement the communists paralyzed the resistance of militant democracy to fascism.

Important as Kautsky was as a socialist theoretician and historian, his impact was limited by the political backwardness of Germany. The failure of democratic socialism in Germany before and after World War I was due, among other things, to the double challenge that the German Social Democratic party had to meet: first, it had to fight for the establishment of a genuine *political* democracy, because the German parties differed not so much on this or that issue of policy but on the issue of democracy itself. Second, the German Social Democrats also struggled, as a socialist movement, for the economic reconstruction of their country along socialist lines. This *two-front war* for simultaneous political and economic democracy proved too great a strain, and the failure of German democratic socialism was sooner or later repeated in other countries in which socialists started out with the handicap of serious political backwardness and authoritarian institutions of government. By contrast, where democracy was widely or universally accepted by all classes of the people, as in England or Scandinavia, Australia or New Zealand, democratic socialism found the most favorable conditions of growth. Only when political democracy was taken for granted could the claims for social and economic democracy be effectively pressed; democratic socialists have never been opposed to political democracy but have merely sought to enlarge and expand democracy from politics and government into the economic and social aspects of human relations.

In the seventeenth century the English were the first people to rebel successfully against political authoritarianism and to establish Parliament as the supreme authority of the nation. Through France, English political ideas of parliamentary sovereignty penetrated continental Europe, and across the seas the new colonial settlements of British origin grew with the heritage of self-government as an inalienable right and liberty. Thus, in the realm of statecraft, parliamentary government has since the seventeenth century been justly considered the most characteristic British contribution to the art and science of politics. Now, in the twentieth century, London may again become the symbol of a world-wide movement aiming at the reconstruction of human relations along new lines—democratic socialism. And in centuries to come the British contribution to democratic socialism in our own age may be compared, in terms of its novelty and universal impact, to the earlier British contributions to democratic politics. England was first in developing socialist ideas because she was first in starting the Industrial Revolution, which created the urban working class, indispensable to the development of a socialist movement. But most important, English socialism had to be democratic from the start, for government by consent was a part of English life.

The founder of British socialism, Robert Owen (1771–1858), built his entire program on *cooperation,* not on class war. Owen did not trust the state to solve economic problems but put his hope in *voluntary associations,* based on the principle of mutual help. Producer and consumer cooperatives, first founded in early nineteenth-century England, were soon followed by trade-unions, and both new institutions were the outgrowth of the Owenite belief in cooperation. The terms "socialist" and "socialism" were first used in the eighteen-twenties in the Owenite *Co-operative Magazine,* and socialism at first literally meant "cooperation." Socialist thought in France (St. Simon, Fourier, Proudhon) and England was originally antistate, even to the point of abolishing the state altogether and substituting society for it. The early socialists completely shared the older liberal doctrine that the *state* was the product of *force,* whereas *society* symbolized the principle of *freedom.*

British and French socialists in the last generation or two have recognized the inevitably important role of the state, not because they have forgotten the earlier socialist individualism and antistatism, but because the structure of industry has changed enormously since the early nineteenth century. The growth of giant corporate enterprises has created a problem of size for which the early cooperative solutions are not always suited. Large-scale capitalism has not only destroyed a large part of small-scale private enterprise but diminished the scope for small-scale cooperative socialism.

Another important source of English socialism is the revolt against the ugliness and squalor of the industrial system. Led by poets like John Ruskin and William Morris, socialists were concerned about the destruction of beauty caused by the rapid and reckless industrialization of England. Work under capitalism became drab and monotonous, and Morris felt intensely that the arts must be brought again into the lives of men and women, and their creative impulses given an opportunity of expression in their daily life and work. Politically, this strand in the fabric of British socialism strengthened its individualistic and antistate tendencies, and some of those who arrived at socialism via the arts came very close to anarchism.

When Marx appeared on the scene, his doctrines found little appeal in England. Despite the fact that Marx lived there for the last thirty-four years of his life, his impact was felt mainly on the European Continent and in Asia and South America. Revolutionary Marxist communism, like revolutionary fascism, attracted in England only a small minority of adherents, who had little significant influence on the nation as a whole.

Shortly after Marx died, the Fabian Society was founded in 1884; it was named after a Roman General, Quintus Fabius Maximus Cunctator—the "Delayer." The early motto of the Fabian Society was: "For the right moment you must wait, as Fabius did; but when the right moment comes you must strike hard, or your waiting will have been vain and fruitless."

No socialist group could be more un-Marxian. Under the leadership of Sidney and Beatrice Webb, Bernard Shaw, H. G. Wells, and, later, Harold J. Laski and G. D. H. Cole, the Fabian Society deliberately set out to convert the governing classes to socialism. The Fabians are the direct descendants of the Benthamites. The latter were interested primarily in legal, constitutional, and political reform, whereas the Fabians—as socialists—are concerned above all with social and economic reform.

The *Fabian Essays* (1889) became for British socialism an abiding source of inspiration. One of the contributors, Sidney Webb, stressed the fact that socialism in England was "but the conscious and explicit assertion of principles of social organization which have been already in great part unconsciously adopted." Webb further defined socialism as "the economic side of the democratic ideal." The Fabian Society for a long time had only a few hundred members, and its number never exceeded a few thousand.

The Fabians confined themselves to "permeating" a numerically small group in modern society—high civil servants, professional men, engineers, technicians, executives, politicians—and left popular propaganda to other socialist organizations. Deliberately choosing the kind of work for which it was best suited, the Fabian Society has always sought to present the case for socialism on the basis of facts rather than emotions. The list of the hundreds and hundreds of Fabian research publications is characterized by its immense practicality; there is little concern for abstract theory. The Fabian Society is rarely to be found in the high intellectual altitudes sniffing the thin air of metaphysics but is "always nosing about in the drains," trying to remedy some immediate and *specific* condition. From its beginning the work of the Fabian Society—decisive for the ultimate success of British socialism—has been based on the gamble that facts do matter, and that men can be peacefully persuaded to apply reason to social problems. In the General Election of 1945, 229 of the 394 Labor M.P.'s were members of the Fabian Society, and more than half of the Government was Fabian. "Permeation" —the characteristic method of Fabianism—bore fruit in the end.

By contrast, only one Communist sat in the House of Commons before 1945. In the General Election of that year the Communists increased their representation by one hundred per cent—from one M.P. to two, of 640. In the General Election of 1950, the British Communists lost both seats in the House of Commons.

Important as the knowledge of the principles of Marxist communism is to Americans, the proper understanding of the main ideas of democratic socialism, particularly as it has developed in Britain, is even more vital. In the last half century the trend all over the world has been toward more public responsibility and collective action. In the United States this tendency found expression in Woodrow Wilson's New Freedom, and in Franklin D. Roosevelt's New Deal. What was, a generation ago, considered in the United States intolerable interference in fields like labor, social security, and education has gradually been accepted by the public as just and inevitable.

If the American economic system, the last island of a sheltered capitalist civilization, is going to develop at all in the direction of more public action and responsibility, Britain—and not Russia—will supply the laboratory in which the American observer will want to see what tests are being made, and why. If the United States were to move toward socialism, it would move slowly, as in England, and not overnight, as in Communist Russia; each step toward socialism would have to be approved by Congress, rather than imposed by a revolutionary militia. The economic problem in Russia was to *build* industry in a highly agrarian and politically inexperienced country. The problem of democratic socialism in the United States, as in Britain, is to *nationalize* the existing key industries in a nation with a high degree of literacy, technical know-how, and democratic experience in politics and government. Furthermore, whereas there was hardly a middle class in Russia in 1917, in the United States, as in Britain, socialism will have to persuade a sufficient proportion of the professional men, managers, technicians, administrators, and scientists that they will fare better under it than under capitalism.

Precisely because the British socialist movement is so liberal, it is impossible to regard any one man or book as the source of truth and dogma. The strength of the British socialist movement has always lain in its ethics rather than its philosophy. Clement R. Attlee (1883———), Prime Minister of the first majority Labor Government in British history, faithfully reflects the character of British socialism. Born into a well-to-do family of a London solicitor, Attlee's early environment was comfortable, conservative, and churchgoing, and he received his education at Haileybury and Oxford. At Oxford, Attlee concentrated on modern history and law, but he was not a conspicuous success as a student or as a leader of student activities. His views were of the orthodox conservative kind in which he was reared, until he started to do social work in the slums of East London in 1905. The contact with poverty transformed Attlee's whole outlook, and he turned to socialism as the way out. "I was not converted by the logic of Karl Marx," Attlee later said of himself; the driving force of his conversion to socialism was his religious sentiment, which was shocked by the misery and degradation of the working people. Not the study of books, but the accumulation of countless daily experiences converted him to socialism. Thus, when he once told a little girl that he had to go home for tea, she told him, "I'm going home to see if there is any tea."

Attlee's association with London's East End did not remain confined to practical social work. From social work he moved into politics, and since 1922 he has represented Limehouse, a working-class constituency, in the House of Commons. His long association with the East End was always a source of profound satisfaction and happiness to Attlee, who worked and lived with the poor for many years. From his daily contacts with people of all kinds he acquired an understanding of their needs and emotional make-up that gave his political outlook a solid foundation of experience. In 1935 Attlee was elected Leader of the Labor party, and ten years later, in the summer of 1945, he became Prime Minister of Great Britain, supported in the House of Commons by a Labor majority of nearly two thirds.

Attlee belonged neither to the Right wing in the Labor party nor to its Left wing but represented the vast dead center, which is always less articulate than either faction of the extreme Right or Left within the party but which nevertheless constitutes the vitality and solidity of the movement. "During all my years in the movement," Attlee writes in *The Labour Party in Perspective* (1937), "what has impressed me most is that its strength depends, not on the brilliance of individuals, but on the quality of the rank and file. It is the self-sacrifice, idealism, and character of the men and women who do the everyday work of the Party up and down the country that makes me hopeful of the future. It is not the theories so much as the lives of those who advocate them which really count in the progress of a great movement."

Attlee's profound faith in the rank and file of the socialist movement differs sharply from Lenin's firm conviction that the majority of the workers in a capitalist society are incapable of thinking and acting correctly, and that they will acquire that capacity only after a minority—a group of communist professional revolutionaries—has destroyed the capitalist system by force. Attlee's stress on the importance of the lives socialists lead, rather than the theories they entertain, is also markedly distinct from Lenin's obsession with the "correctness" of party doctrine. The most opprobrious epithets in communist literature have therefore always been hurled against "deviationists" from the correct party line, such as "Trotskyites," "Bukharinites," or "Zinovievites," whereas shortcomings of character and conduct have been considered less important.

It may sound startling to many European and American socialists that, according to Attlee, "the first place in the influences that built up the Socialist movement must be given to religion. England in the nineteenth century was still a nation of Bible readers. To put the Bible into the hands of an Englishman is to do a very dangerous thing. He will find there material which may send him out as a preacher of some religious, social, or economic doctrine. The large number of religious sects in this country, and the various tenets that many of them hold illustrates this." In many European and Latin American countries, socialism and religion are considered two entirely different worlds, existing in a state of non-belligerent neutrality at best and in a state of open warfare at worst. Pope Pius XI emphasized this fact unequivocally when he warned in his encyclical *Quadragesimo anno* (1931) that "no one can be, at the same time, a sincere Catholic and a true Socialist." England is one of the few countries in which religion has nurtured the socialist faith and has been, as Attlee says, its first influence. He adds that "there are probably more texts from the Bible enunciated from Socialist platforms than from those of all other parties," and that it is "possible in Britain for a parson to declare himself a Communist and for millions of faithful Catholics to support the Labour Party."

Before World War II, Nazi-Fascist propaganda predicted that the choice between communism and fascism was ultimately inevitable, and it simultaneously offered to save the world through the New Order of the Berlin-Rome-Tokyo Axis. Writing in 1937, when that propaganda convinced more than a few, Attlee rejected the alternative between hell and damnation as the only choice: "Avoiding both Fascism and Communism, this country, I believe, can afford to the world an example of how society can adapt itself to new conditions and base itself on new principles without breach of continuity and without violence and intolerance."

The Communist party is, according to Attlee, "not a free agent" but subject to the orders of the Communist International in Moscow. The whole philosophy of communism is based on the "seizure of power by an active minority," and the Communist party "believes in the rule by those who are superior to the ordinary people—in fact, by an intellectual aristocracy."

Attlee also emphasizes the point that the British Labor party, originally a predominantly working-class party, has steadily developed into a national party, and that "many individuals from the better-off classes" have joined the socialist movement because of their realization of the "immoral and unjust basis of capitalism." Neither the Conservative nor the Liberal party in Britain has ever been a class party, and the Labor party continues that tradition. In any event, the institutional mechanism of the two-party system makes it impossible for any party, eager to get into office, to appeal to only one class, section, or region.

The virtual disappearance of the Liberal party in Britain has not meant that Liberalism has declined but that the other two major parties have genuinely accepted the first ideal of Liberalism: complete respect for the individual. In discussing socialist objectives, Attlee writes that "the first point which I desire to make is that the aim of Socialism is to give greater freedom to the individual," and he rejects the concept of the idol state. Shortly after Attlee became Prime Minister in 1945, he explained (in an address before the Trades Union Congress, September 12, 1945) his conception of democracy: "Democracy is not just majority rule, but majority rule with due respect to the rights of minorities. It means that while the will of the majority must prevail there shall be a full opportunity for all points of view to find expression. It means toleration for opposition opinions. Wherever you find suppression of minority opinion, there is no real democracy." This liberal conception of democracy goes back to John Stuart Mill and Locke, not to Marx.

Although it fully accepts and reaffirms the liberal approach to politics and government, British democratic socialism rejects the liberal approach to the *economic* organization of modern industrial society. The older liberal solution of nineteenth-century laissez faire in economics has been rejected by democratic socialists for over a century; but even the more recent economic theory of Keynes and the Keynesians is no substitute for socialism. In what respects Keynes' theory differs from democratic socialism is one of the central issues of G. D. H. Cole's *Socialist Economics* (1950).

Cole (1889–1959) was one of the few modern social philosophers who escaped the bane of creative thought—excessive specialization. He started as a philosopher, and his philosophical training is still reflected in the lucidity and incisiveness of his style and thought. From philosophy, Cole moved on to economics, history, and political theory, always keeping in mind the complexity and intricacy of human relations, and always viewing social issues as issues of human welfare. One of the most prolific writers of his age (his books include numerous novels of mystery and detection), Cole exercised an enormous influence on the generation that grew up between World Wars I and II. Much of Cole's work was done in joint collaboration with his wife, Margaret, and "the Coles" increasingly became an institution in Britain, as "the Webbs" had been a generation earlier. Like the Webbs, the Coles were active in the Fabian Society, G. D. H. Cole serving as its president for many years before and after World War II.

As an economist and a socialist, Cole welcomes the "Keynesian revolution in economic thought" as far as it goes—but it does not go far enough: "Keynesism is after all, in the last analysis, a very elaborate mechanism for *offsetting* rather than curing certain glaring deficiencies in the working of capitalist society." Economic stability cannot be achieved, according to Cole, by Keynesian palliatives alone, and the state—through publicly responsible agencies—will have to own and conduct a large part of the apparatus of production. However, Cole was opposed to complete nationalism of the means of production. The "public sector" of industry "must be large enough to set the tone for the rest, leaving private industry to operate within a framework of public enterprise, rather than the other way around." Moreover, as a liberal democrat, Cole warned against nationalization as the only means of socialization, and stressed particularly cooperative and municipal forms of public enterprise.

After World War II, totalitarian fascism was finished as a military force, and totalitarian communism now took the lead in challenging the free, democratic nations. From the communist viewpoint, the difference between fascist and liberal capitalism is not significant, nor is there much difference between democratic capitalism and democratic socialism: they are all enemies of revolutionary communism, which tolerates no truth other than itself. Militarily and diplomatically, the United States became the chief target of communist international propaganda, yet ideologically the principle target was democratic socialism, particularly as exemplified in Great Britain. A restatement of the main ideas of democratic socialism, particularly in relation to communist onslaughts after World War II, will be found in Lord Lindsay's "The Philosophy of the British Labour Government" (1949), which he contributed to the symposium, *Ideological Differences and World Order* (edited by F. S. C. Northrop).

Lord Lindsay (1879–1952) was Master of Balliol College at Oxford University and one of the leading political philosophers in Great Britain. He joined the Fabian Society as an undergraduate in 1900, and soon took an active part in adult education; his principal concern in political philosophy has been the problem of the *community* and its preservation and strengthening in the complex industrial conditions of the twentieth century. Lindsay sees in socialism the possibility of building a community of free men and women dedicated to joint effort and enjoyment. He holds that "society, if it is to have any meaning, must be a common life; that the common life is something which all members of the society must share, and that the conditions necessary to sharing in it must therefore be at the disposal of everybody." Equality of income is not a prerequisite of the true community: "What is to be insured is the minimum conditions which are necessary for a man or woman to be an active member of a society which is a democratic society and therefore in some true sense a fellowship."

Lindsay is, like Attlee, keenly interested in the religious background of English democracy, particularly the impact of nonconformism on government and administration, and he writes that "the trade unions are the descendants of the Nonconformist congregations, and the Nonconformists were the democratic half of an English society which was aristocratic and Anglican on the top. In political and social matters that dualism has greatly disappeared, or at any rate its contrasts have been greatly softened, but in industry dualism in the nineteenth century took on a new and more intense form."

Yet Lindsay warns against the misconception, widespread among socialists, that the problem of democracy in industry can be simply solved by nationalization. Although nationalization makes *management* responsible to the community through Parliament, the problem of *internal government* in nationalized industry —the relations of management and labor—remains to be solved. Before the actual experience of nationalization this distinction was not clear to socialists themselves, but the experience since 1945 has shown that it is easier to nationalize an industry or service than to solve the problem of its management-labor relations. Socialism cannot be built through the state alone, because "the original ideal experience behind democracy is the working experience of the small democratic community." In the small community there is no gap between "we" and "they" as in the large society, the state. But Lindsay hopes that the common sense and empiricism of British democratic socialism will save it from doctrinaire reliance on the state as the cure-all for its ills and problems, and he stresses that "the partnership in the Labour Party of the cooperative movement is a symbol of their belief that there are other ways than nationalization of making industry democratic."

The experience in Sweden, Denmark, Norway, Israel, and other countries has shown that socialism can be built on cooperative lines in small self-governing communities and associations; in this way the disadvantages of uniformity and centralization inherent in nationalization by the state are avoided. Nationalization is only one form of *socializing* industries and services for the benefit of the community. Its liberal heritage will protect social and economic democracy from the pitfalls of the state, just as in the past it protected political democracy from the same danger. The end of democratic socialism is human freedom; nationalization of industry is a means, and no more, toward this end, and must always remain subordinate to it.

One of the staple arguments against socialism is that it is the first step toward communism, and that a communist is a "socialist in a hurry." The question of whether democratic socialism or intransigent capitalism is a better antidote to communism can be decided by the evidence of experience. Before World War II, communism dominated only one country, Russia, and was influential only in countries that had weak socialist movements. After World War II, communism established its rule in areas of Europe and Asia in which democratic socialist movements had been outlawed or suppressed in fact, as in eastern Europe and China. In western Europe, Communist parties flourished most in countries that, like France and Italy, too hastily reverted to free enterprise. By contrast, Communist parties steadily declined in countries that were governed by wholly or predominantly Socialist governments, such as Sweden, Norway, Denmark, Great Britain, and Israel, or by coalition governments with vigorous Socialist participation, such as Holland, Belgium, Uruguay, and Chile.

The *strength of communism* is in *inverse proportion to that of democratic socialism*. Some nations may continue to practice the system of free enterprise and to reject socialism within their own borders. Yet from the viewpoint of the long-range interests of the free nations—the preservation of freedom and peace in the world—democratic socialism will prove the most powerful ideological opponent of international communism. Capitalism is primarily concerned with political liberty and cares comparatively less about social and economic equality. Communism aims at the latter but ruthlessly opposes and destroys the former. Democratic socialism is the only contemporary challenge to both capitalism and communism, because it seeks to harmonize political freedom with social and economic equality.

So far, democratic socialism has succeeded only in countries like Sweden, Norway, Denmark, New Zealand, Australia, and Britain, which have the strongest traditions of political liberty in the world, coupled with high standards of devotion and integrity in public life. The road to socialist doctrine may be simple, but that to socialist reality is complex: it has been no accident that democratic socialism has grown and governed only in the politically most mature nations, whereas totalitarian communism, like fascism, has taken root primarily in politically less experienced states, whose traditions of political democracy are none too stable and whose standards of government none too high.

If political democracy depends for its success on the thought, effort, good sense, and character of its citizens, a community that desires more than political liberty and seeks to realize democracy in all human relations demands even more.

As Plato saw in the *Republic,* no social or political organization can be better than the quality of the men and women who compose it. The ultimate fate of the vision of democratic socialism will therefore depend on the quality of the lives of those who see in this vision the next stage of free humanity.

I. KAUTSKY

Social Democracy versus Communism *

1. Socialism and Democracy

The interests of the working class require democracy no less than Socialism. Labor can attain to the former sooner than to the latter, for other laboring classes, such as artisans and peasants, as well as many intellectuals, are equally interested in the development of democracy.

In the struggle for democracy and its immediate class interests, necessitating social reforms, the working class is lifted from primitive barbarism to higher forms. The consequences of this struggle create a more fertile ground upon which the enlightened working classes, acting in organized masses, continues to develop its powers by means of free action and movement, thus lifting its development to the highest possible degree and rendering itself capable of pursuing successfully the struggle for the final aims of Socialism.

One may easily admit that democratic methods are not applicable in the struggle against totalitarianism, in fact impossible, and yet make the aim of our fight the restoration of democracy. Much confusion has resulted from the fact that in the discussion

of this question the two points of view have not been clearly defined. Some take the position that democracy, having failed where fascism is in power, must fail also where fascism has been kept from power.

It is self-evident that we cannot fight with the weapons of democracy where such weapons are not available. Some now make the distinction between democratic and revolutionary methods. Some of us are pictured as insisting upon democratic methods, others upon revolutionary methods. The latter are characterized as implying insurrection and the general strike. But this juxtaposition of democratic methods and others is no less erroneous than that of reformists and revolutionists. Our aim is Socialist and revolutionary. Whether we fight for it reformistically or in a revolutionary manner depends not upon our thinking processes, but assumes practical significance only as we view our tactics from the standpoint of a given situation in the state, society and existing class relationships, which we cannot determine at will. This is what determines whether we resort to democratic or "revolutionary" methods of action.

Under the conditions that prevailed in the countries of Continental Europe during the last century, conditions that were characterized by the absence of that measure

* From Karl Kautsky, *Social Democracy versus Communism* (The Rand School Press, 1946). By permission.

of democracy essential to the freedom of movement required by the masses, it was the democrats who were the revolutionists, for they were the ones who fought for democracy with revolutionary methods, because none other were available. At that time the conceptions of democrats and revolutionists were identical.

But it would be ridiculous, with this past period in mind, to consider ourselves obliged to preach a violent political overthrow in countries where democratic institutions have been attained.

There are people who believe that even under a democratic order Labor should utilize the methods of "revolution," insurrection, the general strike, because, in their opinion, such methods will lead to Socialism more quickly than the casting of ballots, and that in the final analysis the opponents of Socialism in the democratic states will yield only to insurrection and the general strike.

In rejecting democracy, they go so far as to believe that a Socialist minority could achieve power by force in a democratic state. And, finally, they assert that Socialists cannot hope to attain an electoral majority even in countries where Labor represents the greatest number as long as the opponents of Socialism retain control over the economic and intellectual instruments of power.

To this we reply: To be sure, the power at the disposal of the opponents of Socialism, the economic dependence of the workers, the influence of the press and the stealing of elections can be brought into play even under democracy. But a Socialist Party which is unable, regardless of these obstacles, to obtain the support of a majority of the people in a democracy will find it even more impossible to obtain such a majority by the use of armed force or the general strike. For in the latter instance the weapons at the disposal of the opponents of Socialism will prove even more effective than under the form of democratic struggle. The road of force and violence requires even

greater sacrifices from Labor than the road of democracy.

On the other hand, the use of force and violence requires the support of a much greater majority of the people if Socialism is to win. A majority of 51 per cent will not suffice.

In a situation in which force is pitted against force, the power at the disposal of the ruling classes comes much more into play than under democracy. To master that power we would require the support of an overwhelming majority of the people. The superiority of numbers is the sole decisive weapon Labor can command in any great decisive contest. To be sure, many workers have not infrequently achieved victory on the barricades or in general strikes, but only when they fought for objectives which were dear not only to the workers but to the great mass of the people as a whole, roused to enthusiasm and support.

Such objectives were always democratic objectives. Yet this alone did not suffice to assure victory in the contest of arms. Such victory required also the weakening of the support accorded to the existing regime by its army and bureaucracy.

Such was the case in the July revolution in Paris (1830), as well as in the uprisings of February and March 1848, and, later, in the general strike in Russia of 1905 and in Germany in 1920.

Both insurrection and general strike have proven quite useless, however, when they were utilized by a minority of the people in efforts to overthrow not a morally bankrupt government but a government supported by a majority of the people. The forcible overthrow of a government possessing not only the power of the state but also the support of a majority of the people is unthinkable. And, as we have already pointed out, any attempt to assert ourselves successfully by force requires not only a majority but an overwhelming majority.

Moreover, the road of force requires greater sacrifices than the road of democracy. It is much easier to prevail upon a person to vote Socialist than it is to move him to give up his job or his life.

Force is, therefore, not a method by which a working class party can advance in a democracy or achieve results that cannot be achieved by democratic methods. Democracy is the shortest, surest and least costly road to Socialism, just as it is the best instrument for the development of the political and social prerequisites for Socialism. Democracy and Socialism are inextricably entwined.

The big exploiters are not unconscious of this fact. Hence, their hatred of democracy and their efforts to destroy it wherever they can. These efforts gain in intensity and violence in proportions as democracy has facilitated the rise of Labor. Is this any reason for Socialists to minimize the value of democracy? What for the moment may appear as the weakness of democracy is in reality the weakness of the working classes. A working class which has not the power to defend democracy, until such time as the relationship of class forces change, is certainly least capable to assert itself against the exploiters by force. Where democracy has been lost, it is the first and most important task of Socialists and Labor to regain it.

It would be nonsensical to contend that Social Democrats are obliged to use democratic methods under all circumstances. Such an obligation we can assume only with respect to those who themselves use only democratic methods. Acts of violence cannot be repelled by ballots, newspaper articles or mass meetings. Nevertheless, in circumstances when Social Democrats are compelled to meet violence with violence they must seek first and foremost to win the support of the majority. This is the essential prerequisite of victory, regardless of whether they apply democratic or other methods. And, furthermore, they must never lose cognizance of the fact that democracy remains always the most valuable instrument Labor can possess.

Where democracy does not exist the most urgent task before Labor and Social Democracy is to establish political freedom. It is quite erroneous to say that the workers must first emancipate themselves economically, and that only then will "true" democracy be possible.

It makes no difference whether or not we choose to regard a strong representative assembly of the people, elected by universal equal suffrage, and coupled with freedom of the press, speech and organization, as mere "formal" democracy. The fact is that without such institutions the workers cannot emancipate themselves economically. To be sure, democratic institutions will change their character when society will be organized on a Socialist basis. Today they are essential instruments of struggle for the working class. Under Socialism they will be only instruments of free social administration. And this will constitute the difference between present day democracy and the democracy of a Socialist society. The fashionable conceptions of "true" and "formal" democracy are mere abstractions.

Some may say that the example of Soviet Russia refutes my conception of democracy. It is argued that in Soviet Russia a proletarian minority succeeded in seizing power by force, something which it could never have attained by democratic methods.

Those who present this argument forget that Czarism was not overthrown by a Bolshevist minority against the majority of the people. Czarism fell because its chief instrument of power—the army— was wrecked and shattered by the arm of German militarism and, in part, turned against the Czar. Moreover, the entire Russian population joined the rebellious troops. Unfortunately, Russia did not possess any class schooled in self-government. As a result, anarchy overwhelmed the country. Amidst this anarchy Bolshevism established itself with the instruments of a new army and bureaucracy.

It would be futile to expect a repetition of anything like this. The state to which these developments gave birth is a distinctly abnormal one. The continued existence of the Bolshevist state is by no means an argument against democracy in a modern state.

There remains now one more argument against democracy to be disposed of—that democracy necessarily implies a weak government. Only the application of extreme pressure will suffice to tackle the monopolists of finance, industry and land ownership, we are told.

This is quite true. The capitalist masters in some countries will stop at nothing to maintain themselves when they are confronted with the danger of expropriation. But this does not necessarily involve the use of military force, the raising of a private army by capital.

Only in a politically backward country does fascism constitute a promising instrument for the exploiters. In the democratic states of Western Europe and in the Anglo-Saxon world the capitalists resort more to economic than military instruments, just as the working class in the great decisive political struggles of the past few decades fought with economic rather than military weapons. The methods pursued by the capitalists are essentially the same as those used by the workers: the strike, the crippling of production. The workers fight by stopping work; the capitalists fight by stopping the circulation of capital. By this means they have succeeded in overthrowing governments which they regard as inimical to their interests.

Only a government which does not stand in superstitious awe before the rights of private property can tackle the resistance of the monopolists of capital. Such a government must not hesitate to confiscate any enterprise which practices passive resistance, and operate it for the social interest.

It is simply impossible from the point of view of sound economics to change the whole of capitalist economy into a Socialist economy at one stroke. There will be many capitalist enterprises which it will be necessary for the time being to continue as such.

And, indeed, it will be to the advantage of the Socialist state to have these enterprises continue functioning without disturbance. But the owners of these enterprises will continue to operate them only when they feel secure against confiscation, and when we assure those of them whose enterprises are to be ultimately socialized a proper measure of compensation.

This very prospect of compensation should move the capitalists in question to refrain from passive resistance, economic sabotage and interference with the new regime. As regards capitalists who will sabotage under any circumstances we need have no compunction about seizing their property in socially necessary means of production. The threat of confiscation will be a most effective weapon to compel their cooperation with the Socialist government.

Economic as well as political considerations will make two things necessary: to reassure those capitalists willing to cooperate against direct confiscation of their property, and the determination to confiscate ruthlessly without compensation any enterprise hostile to the new economy and refusing to adapt itself to it.

But nothing is more erroneous than the assumption that only a dictatorship can show such determination. To be sure, no Socialist governments and certainly no coalition governments have ever been in a position to act with such determination. But it was not democracy that hindered them, but the fact that they did not command a united Socialist majority.

Only such a majority can have not only the courage and will but also the power to break ruthlessly the resistance of the capitalists. Such a majority, as we have already pointed out, can be attained, however, only in democracy.

Considered, therefore, from every point of view democracy facilitates, and in no way retards the emancipation of the working class.

2. The Road to Power

Lately we hear people talking of a dictatorship of the proletariat as a political order under which the working class wields absolute power, without taking into account the level of its development and intelligence. Unlike democracy, we are told, such an order would be a dependable instrument for the building of Socialism, regardless of the element of maturity of the working class.

We need not dwell here on the possibility of establishing such an order in countries where the working class is too weak to establish or defend democracy. I have already emphasized that the working class requires much less power, intelligence and independence to attain democracy and political power through democracy than would be necessary for the establishment and maintenance of its own dictatorship over all other classes of society.

But let us assume, for the sake of argument, that such a dictatorship could be established after the working class will have crushed all its opponents. What would be the consequence?

A dictatorship is a state in which authority is centered in one will, in which any criticism of this will is treated as a major crime. A real dictatorship of the proletariat presupposes, therefore, the existence of a united will in Labor's ranks. Many often assume as a self-evident fact that the working class constitutes a united, homogeneous mass, to be pitted against a homogeneous "reactionary mass." The truth is, however, that the working class is not a self-evident phenomenon or a uniform, homogeneous, "totalitarian" mass, to use a German expression.

It is naive to conceive of the working class as synonymous with the mass of the poor and needy. Marx regarded the proletariat as consisting only of those workers who do not own or control the means of production they must use in order to live, and who are consequently obliged to sell

their labor power. Strictly speaking, the small peasantry or farmers, artisans and petty tradesmen do not belong to the category of the working class, however needy they may be. These elements perceive their salvation not in a Socialist society, but in the rise of prices on commodities they offer for sale. Their ideal is to become bigger peasants or farmers, artisans and businessmen in the society based on private ownership.

On the other hand, the workers themselves are divided into two categories, neither of which owns any means of production. But only under certain specific historical circumstances can they find buyers for their labor power. This becomes possible on a large scale only where capital has acquired control of industry and requires wage labor. Before this development becomes a fact the masses of the propertyless have but one recourse—to beg or steal. This type of proletarian is not necessary to the basis of society. On the contrary, they are an unnecessary burden. They live only upon the alms of the propertied classes or by plundering them. Such workers cannot grasp the ideal of a new, better social order, much less are they fit to fight for it. To the extent to which they are dependent upon the good will of the higher classes they become cringing and sycophantic. Individuals among them, those of stronger character, turn to violent resentment and become criminals. Such elements are easily disposed of by the state.

Due to particularly favorable circumstances, proletarians of this type attained to great political power in ancient Rome, which after prolonged struggles had established a democratic constitution, but a great portion of whose citizens had become impoverished as a result of continued civil wars. Under this condition the urban proletariat obtained the power in the state, but not knowing how to utilize it found nothing better to do than to sell its votes to those who paid the most in bread and circuses, or to sell itself as hired mercenaries to successful and ambitious military leaders.

It was this political and military assistance on the part of the proletariat that made possible the dictatorship of a single individual in Rome, which led to the rise of Caesarism and its development into a state form.

Marx differentiated sharply between the proletariat of this type, which he termed the *Lumpenproletariat,* and the *wage earning proletariat.* It was the latter type that he regarded as capable of developing, in the process of many struggles and through long experience, the requisite power and ability to emancipate itself, and thus move society forward to higher forms.

Hundreds of years of struggle were required before such consciousness became possible, and even then it was confined at the beginning to a small élite, which, perceiving its social power and significance, placed before itself the aim of achieving a fundamental social change.

Under certain circumstances this élite can develop rapidly in numbers, but behind this élite and the *Lumpenproletariat* there remains a mass which Marx well characterized as the "undeveloped figure" of the proletariat. Economically this mass performs the functions of the wage-earning proletariat, but intellectually and culturally it is not much above the level of the *Lumpenproletariat.* It no longer begs for alms but for work, perceiving frequently in the capitalist who employs it not the exploiter who lives upon its labor but the master, the philanthropist, upon whose good will the wage earner subsists. Occasionally, these proletarians begin to glean vaguely the real character of the situation, which in turn, leads them to manifestations of resistance. But they are not capable of continuous, systematic struggle.

Only occasionally are they moved to outbursts of despair, which are followed immediately by dejection and surrender. Higher aims than those of the moment are beyond the scope of the undeveloped proletariat.

This general analysis of the character and composition of the proletariat suffices to reveal its division into three big groups, each with its own mode of thinking, its own capacity for struggle, its own aims and methods.

The development of capitalist industry makes possible the growth of the advanced portion of the proletariat over the other two—the undeveloped proletarians as well as the *Lumpenproletariat.* The World War and the world economic crisis, however, have stimulated the numbers of the last two mentioned groups at the expense not only of the proletarian élite but also of the artisan and small peasant elements. Moreover, the boundaries between the various elements are not sharply drawn. They overlap and vary with the changes in the political and economic situation.

Within the laboring classes themselves there are numerous differentiations of thinking and fighting capacity. These differentiations are partly local in character: city, town and country. There are also the differences of luxury cities and industrial cities: in the first, we find more corrupt servile, reactionary elements among the workers than in the second. Added to these local differentiations are many differentiations of occupation, some of which facilitate the work of education, enlightenment, organization and struggle. Others make it much more difficult. Women have always been more difficult to organize than men. The same is true of workers in isolated occupations, as compared with those in large-scale production.

Thus we have another division in the working class running parallel with the differentiations of the developed and undeveloped workers: that of the organized and unorganized workers. But the two differentiations are not identical. The élite of the workers have never sought to keep aloof from their undeveloped comrades. On the contrary, the elements comprising the labor élite have never tired in their efforts to elevate the whole of the working class. On the other hand, we have seen organizations of workers in certain crafts who, having managed to win very substantial advantages for themselves, have assumed a special character and have sought to exclude outsiders in the manner characteristic of any aristocracy. The unorganized workers are left to their fate. In such instances we find another clear break in the uniformity of the working class. This particular division continued for decades in England, for example, after the collapse of the First International.

In the continental countries of Europe we have had no such situation. In these countries the workers had been compelled to wage a bitter struggle for democracy before they could begin to organize. In that struggle as in all others, the labor élite took the lead. But its aim was one in which the entire working class, as well as the peasants and artisans, were interested, while the intensity of the political movement served to checkmate any manifestations of selfish group-thinking in the trade unions.

In the course of capitalist development, Labor continued to increase, while the workers who owned their means of production increased but slowly and, in some instances, actually decreased. As a general rule, the more developed elements of the working class showed the greatest proportion of increase, i.e. those who influence the less developed elements and stimulate the growth of general class-consciousness as against the influence of craft and other differentiations.

Yet, there are tendencies operating in the opposite direction and giving rise to ever new differentiations in the ranks of Labor.

In addition to those already mentioned there is the category of salaried employees, the so-called white collar workers. Salaried employees as compared with wage earners, perform functions of a mainly capitalist character. The productive capitalist is not merely an exploiter; he performs an important economic function. He organizes and directs enterprises, purchases and assembles the means of production and takes care of the disposal of commodities. The element of profit does not emanate from these activities, but depends rather upon the amount of capital, not upon the quantity of labor,

furnished by the capitalist. Frequently he has to work much harder in a smaller enterprise than in a big one. But what constitutes the prerequisite of profit is the realization of the tasks of productive capital. This realization is not dependent, however, upon the personalities embodied in capitalism. The functions of productive capital are merely transferred to the shoulders of hired help. Such help is required as soon as any given enterprise reaches a certain advanced stage of development.

Where an enterprise develops to the size of a share-holding undertaking, the entire activity of the capitalist is transferred into the hands of hired forces, i.e. of wage earners and other employees, who perform capitalist functions. These elements emanate from circles closer socially to the capitalist, command a higher culture and education and enjoy a bourgeois standard of living.

For a long time this category of employees were considered part of the middle class, enjoying the "protection" of capital as against the workers and the flattery of bourgeois economists and politicians. The more rapid the growth of capitalist enterprises, the wider has been the development of this new middle class, which grew more rapidly in numbers as compared with the old middle class than did the wage earning section of the working class.

More recently, however, it has become apparent that the standard of living of this new middle class has been declining in proportion as higher education has ceased to be a monopoly of a small minority. The more extensive the administrative and commercial apparatus of an enterprise, the more pronounced becomes its hierarchical differentiation. Only a few leading elements reach the top, i.e. the elements who rise above the mass of the commercial and administrative employees. The latter move socially ever closer to the status of simple "wage earners," while those above them develop increasingly the psychology of "masters," to a degree even more pronounced than that displayed by the capitalist. That is why the directors and superintendents of plants and factories are so well paid.

Thus does the majority of the "new middle class" approach ever closer the status of the real working class, enlarging and augmenting its ranks. But within the working class it forms again a separate category, with its own peculiar psychology, standard of living and capacity for struggle, reflecting, in turn, a different approach and policy.

As soon as Labor attains a certain degree of intellectual, political and economic power its begins to exercise an increasing measure of influence upon some sections of the old middle class. Small peasants or farmers, and petty tradesmen find their immediate interests divided between labor and the capitalist class. Their allegiance vacillates at given moments between the two, depending upon the historic circumstances. The farmer and middle class elements in question cannot be characterized as dependable allies of labor, to which circumstance must be ascribed the fact that political development since the French Revolution has been alternating constantly between revolution and counter-revolution, progress and reaction.

Nevertheless, Labor has been acquiring the confidence of these elements in increasing measure, in proportion as these elements themselves have moved closer economically to the status of the working class and as the working class itself has gained in power and influence. On the other hand, the more these elements draw closer to Labor, the more complex and varied does the composition of the working class itself become.

Another differentiation to be mentioned is one that has acquired great significance in recent years: the differentiation between employed and unemployed workers.

Marx showed that chronic unemployment of part of the working class was an inevitable phenomenon of capitalism. But however painful unemployment was in the past for the individual worker, it was, as a rule, a temporary affliction. Since the World War, however, and particularly since the world economic crisis of 1929, unemployment has become a permanent curse for increasing masses of workers. This carries with it the development of a psychology among many workers unfortunately akin to that of the Roman proletariat who, as we have already pointed out, constituted one of the principal roots of the dictatorship of the Caesars.

There are many other differentiations within the respective component parts of the working class, upon which we will not dwell here but examples of which may be cited by anyone familiar with the problem.

But the differentiations already mentioned are the most important and make it impossible for the working class to form a solid, homogeneous mass capable, without the intervention of any other forces, of presenting a united mode of thinking and action. What we see, instead, is a heterogeneous mass, composed of variegated and uneven elements. It was the insight of a Marx that discerned the common interests which, in the long run, must animate all these elements. But the realization of their common tasks and interests depends in turn, upon intensive education and enlightenment.

The development of economic and political class struggles does, indeed, facilitate a closer approach of the various elements of the working class to one another, but this process is being constantly interfered with and vitiated by the influx of ever new elements into the body of the working class. Nor does this influx always imply a strengthening of Labor. It invariably complicates its policy and makes its formulation and application more difficult.

The influence of working class policy gains in strength only in proportion as Labor becomes more united and presents a common front, by which we mean united in more than one sense. It must avoid, first, a zigzag course which leads it into contradictory and unsuccessful experiments. Secondly, it must seek to overcome the many differentiations of craft and local interests, of tradition and capacity for struggle responsible for the temporary or more lasting differentiations in the thinking and aspirations of the respective elements comprising the working class and those closest to it.

Real unity of these various heterogeneous elements can be accomplished only by putting forward great noble objectives and high social ideals. The necessity of such a policy makes the formation of a Labor Party inevitable, sooner or later, wherever a Socialist Party has not already preceded it. Any person who subscribes to the ideals of such a party is to be welcomed into its ranks, but the working class, which can develop its potential powers only as united force, remains the most important, the decisive element of such a party.

As regards the importance of democracy we cannot over-emphasize the fact that higher social perceptions can be attained only through freedom and research. Only under such conditions, through free discussion, can the welfare of Labor be advanced.

3. The "United Front"

Right now one hears louder than ever the demand for a united front which before 1914 existed in almost every country of the world, with the exception of Russia, and which gave the laboring masses a chance to assert themselves successfully. The split in the ranks of the working class was reponsible for the fact that the revolutions of 1918 and 1919 in central Europe did not accomplish the maximum results possible at that time.

On the surface, it appears that the question of the united front involves an effort to bring together two opposing working class tendencies for joint action. Some will ask, "What does this have to do with the character of the dictatorship in Russia? And is not the cessation of fratricidal struggle in the ranks of the working class an urgent necessity?" The workers are fully aware that their power and the achievement of their aim depend upon their unity. They reject anything that threatens unity. They dislike any theoretical conflict which impedes unity of action.

On the other hnad, we must not permit the memory of old conflicts no longer of any immediate significance, to interfere with any process of unification. I, too, recall many splits and conflicts of tendencies in which the followers of the respective camps developed a passionate hatred for each other. And yet, these very same people learned to regard each other later as valuable comrades and friends when the causes of the conflicts had been removed and it had become possible again to work together for common aims through common methods.

I am fully aware of all this, and yet I have no enthusiasm for the efforts being made for the establishment of a "united front."

The very term "united front" gives cause for doubt. Why not "unity" with the Communists? Because the Communists do not want unity. What is proposed is not unity of Social Democratic and Communist workers, under which both would pursue common aims through democratic methods, free discussions, and majority rule, respected by the minority.

To be sure, both the Communist and Socialist Parties regard themselves as working class organizations. Both consist in their overwhelming majority of workers. Many of these work side by side in the same plants and factories. They share the same sufferings and face a common opposition. And yet there are profound differences between them. It is not merely a question of belonging to the same class, but also of the organizations from which the individual workers take their slogans and directions. In the Social Democracy these slogans and directions are given democratically. Its organizations are governed by democracy, as are those of the entire free labor movement. This is not true of all organizations in which workers are active. This is not true, for example, of organizations whose workers are politically regimented and wear a uniform. Such workers follow a military discipline. They receive their slogans from above and they must obey them without question. The attitude of a military organization toward the Social Democracy depends not upon whether such organization is composed of workers but upon the stand taken with respect to the Socialist Party by its high command.

What is true, with certain variations of a military organization is inevitably true also of the Communists. Unlike the Social Democracy, they are not organized democratically, but in military fashion. They do not choose their own leaders and slogans, but receive them from their high command —in the last instance, from Moscow. The Communists of all countries are its disciplined praetorian guard. *Communism has become for the present rulers of Russia what pan-Slavism was for the czars, with the exception that the Communists of today are much more obedient to the dictators in Moscow than the pan-Slavists were to the czars.* Fundamentally, the united front would signify, therefore, not the cooperation of workers acting freely within the labor movement but the cooperation of the democratic Socialist and labor organizations of the world with the strongest dictatorship of the world.

A united front concluded by Social Democrats and Communists in a given country will always be limited by the fact that it rests not upon common interests and ideas but springs from a special situation, which may change overnight. *This is especially true because faithlessness and treachery are part of the substance of dictatorship, that only he becomes a dictator who does not hesitate to destroy his erstwhile comrades whenever they become obstacles in the way of his determination to achieve absolute power.*

The militarized, highly concentrated economy of the Soviet state certainly differs radically from the economy of private capitalism, but it is no less removed from the objective of the emancipation of the working class from all exploitation and enslavement. Before the rise of the Communist dictatorship in Russia, the bourgeois critics of Socialism used to characterize the objective of Socialists as a penitentiary or as a barrack economy. Social Democrats, in turn, repudiated this emphatically. We could not imagine that some day there would arise a group of Socialists claiming to be Marxists who could actually bring such a penitentiary or barrack economy into life, and that instead of being laughed out of court or condemned they would arouse the admiration and approval of some Socialists.

The bloody terror of the regime is hailed by such Socialists as the realization of the Socialist ideal, because, forsooth, there is no place for capitalists in the barrack of Soviet economy, they being permitted to enter it only occasionally as visitors. As such they are invited and received in most friendly manner, guided about with great politeness and asked to express their appreciation of the good food served in the penitentiary.

Those who realize all these facts will perceive that there is, indeed, very little in common between the new ruling aristocracy in Soviet Russia and the free labor movement, very little, indeed, of that community of interests essential for a successful united front between Socialists and Communists.

They differ far too widely in methods and character. Any prolonged cooperation between the two would be based upon a lie. For the Soviet regime, this would be quite acceptable, for falsehood is its outstanding characteristic. The Soviet regime has continuously, without interruption, paraded its slave economy as the emancipation of toiling humanity, but Social Democracy cannot flourish upon a lie, not even when the lie may appear to it to be the truth. Any such situation would lead inevitably to the decline of Socialism and its ultimate destruction.

From the very beginning of their activities, the Bolsheviks have been an element of dissension and weakening in the labor movement. This was inevitable. Such is the effect of dictatorship. The harmonious cooperation of different tendencies in the labor movement is possible only on the basis of democracy. At various times, in devious ways and under manifold guises, the Communists have tried to worm their way into the labor movement, and always with the one objective of either subjecting the organizations of labor to the will of Moscow or of splitting them.

Unity of the working class—yes! But unity only in a free labor movement! No fake unity—no "unity" which leads only to discord and dissension.

Some say we are absolutely opposed to the Communist parties outside but not to the dictatorship in Russia. In reality the reverse is true: cooperation with those Communist groups who are freeing themselves from their dependence on the present rulers of Russia for the purpose of attaining some common goal is possible. This has been proved by experience more than once. On the other hand, those Communists who are ruled by Moscow are implacably hostile to the Socialist parties not because of their Communist objectives, which are shared also by the Communist opposition, but because what the Moscow rulers want is not independently thinking allies but obedient tools.

The enemy that makes impossible any united front resides in Moscow. The conflict between Moscow and the Socialist and Labor parties is not based upon a misunderstanding but is deeply rooted in their respective natures and is just as insoluble as is the contradiction between dictatorship and democracy. One of the most outstanding characteristics of Communists was always their contempt of democracy.

This contempt, adopted by many a Socialist influenced by them, has since brought forth rotten fruit. It weakened the working class, gave permanency to the split which since 1918 has been brought about by the Communists in so many countries, and became one of the primary causes of the many painful defeats democracy has sustained in recent years.

But the consequences of these defeats were so serious for the Soviet State that it saw itself compelled to appeal for help to democracy outside Russia. Its watchword to Communists of all countries was now to take a stand for democracy and for this purpose to form a United Front with the Social Democrats they had hitherto so furiously attacked.[1]

So far as this goes, the situation can be greeted with rejoicing. But our joy is somewhat dampened by the fact that this change of the Communists is not one of principle but is merely one of tactical manoeuvering. They defend democracy only where they are in the opposition. They annihilate it and practice the most cruel subjugation of any form of popular freedom where they are in power.

The ousting of democracy by violent despotism in various great neighbor states of Russia constitutes a serious menace to it. Every one of these despotisms, according to its nature, is pressing for military expansion. Two of them, the German and Japanese, threaten Russia from the East and from the West. But by itself the Russian Army could hardly withstand the pressure from two sides.

Russia needs allies, but they can be found only in the democratic states of the West. There, too, exist elements hostile to democracy. They are Russia's enemies as well. It is not only in the strength of these countries, but in the strength of their democracy, that the Soviet Republic is most keenly interested. This explains the Soviets' sudden interest in democracy, but only there—not at home.

Their aid to democracy must be welcomed by every democratic party. But this help may not be relied on too strongly. It emanates from the foreign policy of the present rulers of Russia and is in direct contrast to its home policy.

More recently Stalin has been obliged to make concessions to democratic ideas. He has granted the Russian people a new Soviet Constitution in place of the previous one, which he himself pronounces "the best democracy in the world."

If any democracy deserves the description of a purely formal one, it is the latest

---

[1] This was written in 1937.

constitution of Stalin. It granted no attribute of real democracy, no freedom of movement for the masses, no liberty of speech, of the press, of meeting, of organizations. Its parliament, not freely elected, is a mere assenting parrot.

How the life of the state really functions under this constitution is clearly demonstrated by the famous political trials which have since been staged by the Soviet Government. But they did not merely disclose the fake character of present day Russian "democracy." The fact that they continue to find their victims in the governing groups demonstrates that the country is in the throes of a vast unrest reaching up into the ruling circles—an unrest which, in spite of most ferocious repression, does not cease.

We may yet expect terrific surprises. Whatever aspect these may bear, they promise to stir the masses into motion and thus to bring real concessions to democracy. If democracy should succeed in deed—actually rather than formally—in gaining ascendancy in Russia, the workers of all lands would be the gainers. Owing to the larger masses which would swell their ranks and the lessened obstacles in their way, their advance would proceed with heightened power and speed.

Then a new era would dawn upon mankind. Its advent depends chiefly on the Communists of Russia. But today it is the duty of Socialists, in all parleys and discussions with Communists, to point out this fact to them, and to explain to them how largely the further advance of the working class parties of the world depends on the granting of real democracy in Russia, what harm they do to Socialism and Labor so long as they deny it in that country.

The reestablishment of a united Socialist and Labor movement is impossible so long as Russia is ruled by a dictatorship seeking to subordinate to itself the working class of the whole world.

A united front will come of itself as soon as this dictatorship has vanished, for without it the Communist parties will be deprived of their life-force. They will speedily disintegrate as soon as slogans and money cease to come from Russia and the iron and golden ring that is holding them together has been removed.

Not the collapse of the dictatorship in Russia but its further continuance in power constitutes the gravest menace and causes the greatest damage to the struggle of the modern working class for liberation.

II. ATTLEE

The Labour Party in Perspective *

1. Sources of British Democratic Socialism

The British Labour Party is an expression of the Socialist movement adapted to British conditions. It is also a political movement of the British people in line of succession to many others. The dominant note of the history of this country is its

* From Clement R. Attlee, *The Labour Party in Perspective* (Victor Gollancz, Ltd., 1937). By permission of Prime Minister Attlee.

continuity. It is our national habit to look for precedents in the past for every step forward which we make. We trace our liberties back to the struggles against kings, barons, and bishops. We trace the growth of political and personal liberty back to Magna Charta and Habeas Corpus. We mark the widening of freedom and its extension from one class to another. The instruments by which that freedom has been achieved differ widely in character. Sometimes it has been a king checking the tyranny of feudal barons. Sometimes it has been nobles and gentry curbing the power of the Crown. Now it has been the Church protecting the people. At another time the people have resisted the pretensions of ecclesiastics.

The battleground of freedom has changed from time to time. The fortresses to be captured have been various. The autocratic power of the king, the dominance in the legislature of the few, have been overthrown. Rights of free speech, freedom of conscience, and the right to take part in government have all been asserted, but at the back of all these contests for political power has been the desire to use that power for economic ends.

The immediate predecessors of the Labour Party were the Liberals. They sought to free the individual from the power of the State. They believed that economic liberty meant political freedom. Realising that British liberty was essentially the liberty of the man of property, they thought that under free competition, and with a wide distribution of individual property, this could be achieved.

The dominant issue throughout the nineteenth century, as it seemed to most thinking men and women, was political liberty. The issue of the twentieth century is economic freedom and social equality. Socialists realised that political and personal liberty must be supplemented by economic liberty. That liberty is not to be obtained individually, but collectively. The change in the scale of industrial operations from a small group of individuals working with simple tools to immense regiments of men and women co-operating in the use of vast machines driven by mechanical power has made it impossible to achieve liberty by an extension of private property to the many. Collective control of the great forces released by modern science is the only way in which to obtain freedom. Collective security is the only form which is possible.

The Labour Party is the inheritor of the achievements of those who fought for liberty in the past. It looks back with sympathy, not only to the political struggles of former days, but to the economic contests. It sees behind the political fight the striving of the workers for their rights. It is determined to preserve the liberties which it has inherited and to add to them. Its aim is the same as that of those who have gone before. It seeks to free the human spirit, but its immediate objectives are those which modern conditions dictate.

It is necessary to bear in mind this historical position of the Labour Party. It is not the creation of a theorist. It does not propagate some theory produced in another country. It is seeking to show the people of Great Britain that the Socialism which it preaches is what the country requires in order in modern conditions to realise to the full the genius of the nation.

For the development of a democratic Socialist movement two things are required: first, the existence of a developed Capitalist system, and second, the emergence of someone who will make a synthesis of the discontents of the wage-earners and relate them to a common cause. For a Socialist movement to develop into a constitutional political party there must be a democratic constitution, with a franchise sufficiently wide to make possible the achievement of political power by the masses.

To understand why the Socialist movement developed in Great Britain on its own distinctive lines, and why the Labour Party came into existence at a particular time, it is necessary to consider the conditions which obtained in the first half of the nineteenth century. The Labour Party is the youngest of the three great British working-class movements. It followed long after the Trade Union and Co-operative movements had become strong. To us this seems normal, but in many countries the organisation of producers and consumers has resulted from the purposeful working of Socialist parties. This order of precedence is the result of many factors which must be examined.

The Capitalist system developed earlier in Great Britain than in other countries, and consequently the organisation of the workers began sooner. In the early years of the nineteenth century the Capitalist system was not fully developed. Industrial units were still comparatively small, and owned by small masters. Industry was not highly integrated. It was a period of transition. In such conditions the interests of particular sections of workers tend to override and obscure in their minds the common concern of the whole class. Advantages may be won for exclusive groups whose skill gives them bargaining power. Differences of status between the workers themselves loom large. The possibilities of individual advancement militate against solidarity.

Nevertheless the evils of Capitalism in the first half of the nineteenth century were so great that there seemed the possibility of a revolution by the workers. A prophet was at hand in Robert Owen, who exposed the nature of Capitalism and pointed to Socialism as the remedy. It might have been expected that at this time a great political Socialist movement would have arisen in this country. There was a period, indeed, in which there seemed the possibility of a violent revolution in Britain, but the moment passed. Revolutionary trade unionism died out. Revolutionary Chartism was, in effect, superseded by other movements, such as the agitation against the Corn Laws, which made a more immediate appeal. The workers of Britain turned to more limited and, as it seemed, more practical objectives. The Trade Union movement, the Co-operative movement, and factory legislation owed much to the inspiration of Owen. They at-

tacked Capitalism from within, and sought either to act as a check on its excesses or to build up a new society within the old. But the impulse for the abolition of the system as a whole died away. Revolution gave place to reform. The British workman politically became a unit in the general body of Liberalism. Organised Labour set itself to extract what it could from Parliament by bringing pressure to bear on both the old parties in the State.

But there was another reason for the slow development of a Socialist movement in this country. We to-day are accustomed to see in political life the domination of the economic issue, and it is an effort for us to realise how throughout the nineteenth century political issues such as franchise reform or Irish Home Rule absorbed the political thought of the workers. Still less are we able in these days to appreciate how important were then considered the quarrels between the various political sects. The nineteenth century, which seems to our young men and women dull, stuffy, and Victorian, was a time when every kind of belief was being challenged and all kinds of struggles were proceeding. It is idle to dismiss these as of no importance because they seem so to us. They were important to the men and women of that time. In this Victorian age there were many prophets preaching various gospels, and this must be borne in mind if one wishes to discover the springs of action of the Labour movement and to appreciate its character. The ideas which called the pioneers to the service of the Socialist movement were very varied. They were not the followers of a single gospel of one prophet. They did not accept one revelation as inspired. It is this which distinguishes the British Socialist movement from many of those on the Continent. Predominantly the parties on the Continent have been built on the writings of Karl Marx. Around his teachings the movement has grown. Different interpretations have been put upon his creed. In some countries other powerful influences have been at work, and the characters of his apostles and the circumstances of the countries to which they belong have necessarily caused differences in the method pursued by particular parties, but they have this in common—that they were formed as definite Socialist movements, inspired by the word revealed to Marx.

In Britain the history of the movement has been entirely different. Widely diffused as his influence has been, the number of those who accepted Marxism as a creed has always been small. The number of those who have entered the Socialist movement as the direct result of his teaching has been but a fraction of the whole. One must seek the inspiration of the majority of British Socialists in other directions.

Leaving aside Owen and the early pioneers, I think that the first place in the influences that built up the Socialist movement must be given to religion. England in the nineteenth century was still a nation of Bible readers. To put the Bible into the hands of an Englishman is to do a very dangerous thing. He will find there material which may send him out as a preacher of some religious, social, or economic doctrine. The large number of religious sects in this country, and the various tenets that many of them hold, illustrate this.

The Bible is full of revolutionary teaching, and it is not surprising that, in a country where thought is free, many men and women have drawn from it the support which they needed for their instinctive revolt against the inhuman conditions which Capitalism brings. I think that probably the majority of those who have built up the Socialist movement in this country have been adherents of the Christian religion— and not merely adherents, but enthusiastic members of some religious body. There are probably more texts from the Bible enunciated from Socialist platforms than from those of all other parties. Not only the adherents of dissenting bodies whose less privileged position inclined them to take a Left Wing line in politics, but also many clergy and laymen of the Established Church, found that the Capitalist system was in-

compatible with Christianity. It is significant that the gap between the end of Owenism and the birth of the Social Democratic Federation is filled by the Christian Socialist movement of Kingsley and Maurice. Here one sees a feature which distinguishes the British movement from most of those abroad. In no other country has Christianity become converted to Socialism to such an extent as in Britain. In no other Socialist movement has Christian thought had such a powerful leavening effect. It is possible in Britain for a parson to declare himself a Communist and for millions of faithful Catholics to support the Labour Party. It may be noted as a factor in building the British Labour movement on broad foundations that so many of the adherents of the Catholic Faith in Britain come from Ireland, where a creed of political and economic revolt has been inculcated into a Catholic population. The British Labour movement owes much to these men and women, who brought over from their own country their hatred of oppression.

The Labour Party necessarily differs from those Continental countries where Socialists found themselves faced by a Church either closely bound up with the State or with property or class interests, and inimical to liberty of thought. Where, as in many countries, the workers in the formative years of the Socialist movement were attached to a dogmatic faith which controlled every phase of their lives, it was natural that the movement of revolt should be anti-clerical. To meet the conditions there was set up a dogmatism equally narrow and exclusive. The divisions between blacks and reds extending into every activity became absolute. Neither side could influence the other any more than can two contending armies entrenched against each other. Such a division undoubtedly gives great driving-force and cohesion to a movement, but it creates such a fissure in the body politic that the result is either stalemate or revolution. Neither can advance nor retreat. In Britain, on the other hand, where political and religious differences do not coincide, there is a constant broadening owing to contact.

There were many other influences at work in the preparation of the ground for the seed of Socialism. The denunciation of industrialists and of Manchester School Economics by Carlyle and Ruskin, and the literature of exposure of social abuses of which Dickens's works are the outstanding example, had their effect. Later the work of those who preached land reform, and especially the campaigns of Henry George, were instrumental in creating a receptivity to Socialist ideas in many minds. From different points of view, humanitarian, artistic, and economic, the flood of criticism of the existing order grew throughout the nineteenth century. It affected the adherents of the old political parties, but it was a long time before a political Socialist movement became really effective.

It naturally follows, however, from the heterogeneity of the sources from which the movement drew its inspiration, that the Labour Party has always comprised people of very various outlooks, and that its note has always been one of comprehensiveness. The natural British tendency to heresy and dissent has prevented the formation of a code of rigid Socialist orthodoxy. Those who have sought to impose one have always failed to make real headway and have remained sects rather than political parties. As in religion, so in politics and economics, the Briton claims the right to think for himself.

A further characteristic of the British movement has been its practicality. It has never consisted of a body of theorists or of revolutionaries who were so absorbed in Utopian dreams that they were unwilling to deal with the actualities of everyday life. From the first, British Socialists have taken their share wherever possible in the responsibility of Government. The British system of local Government has proved to be an excellent training-ground. Long before there were more than a handful of Labour members in Parliament, Socialists had won their way on to local councils and were influencing administration. By showing what could

be done in a small sphere they were able to convert many sceptical workers who would only believe what they saw in being. The work of the Fabian Society in particular inspired many to bring about an immense change in the attitude of local authorities towards social problems. It is hardly realised by many in the movement to-day how much was accomplished by men like Lansbury and Crooks in revolutionising the ideas of the people with regard to Poor Law administration.

Looking back over the past thirty years, the most striking feature in the mentality of the people of this country of all classes has been the change in their attitude to social questions. The assumptions have altered. Propositions indignantly rejected in the nineties have now passed into common acceptance. I can well remember the time when it was assumed that everyone unemployed, was so through his own fault. The fact that to-day unemployment is realised to be in the majority of cases a misfortune due to the maladjustment of the economic machine instead of a failure of character is mainly due to Socialists.

Therefore in judging the work of the Labour Party it is essential to bear in mind not only direct, but indirect, results of its work. Those who count progress only in terms of seats won and of the growth of the numbers of the professed adherents of the Party miss the real significance of what has happened. The outstanding thing is not so much the growth in the strength of the forces which attack the citadel of Capitalism as in the loss of the outworks, the crumbling of the foundations, and the loss of morale of the garrison. The character of Socialist propaganda has changed during the last thirty years because to-day speakers can start their arguments from premises which were denied in the earlier period. The emphasis to-day is less on destruction and more on construction. The task is harder. It is not enough to-day to denounce Capitalism and then leave Socialism to a few general principles. The modern Socialist must be able to show the immediate steps which Socialists will take when they achieve power. The vision of the future has now to be translated into practical action.

2. Faith in Constitutional Government

The Labour Party has deliberately adopted the method of constitutional action and has rejected the tactics of revolution. I have endeavoured [earlier] to show the historical reasons for this. I have traced the growth of the Labour Party from small beginnings to a position in which it challenges the Capitalist parties. Under pressure of that challenge the minor differences between Liberals and Conservatives have practically disappeared. The formation of the National Government marked the end of an epoch. Henceforward the issue that confronts the electors of this country is Socialism versus Capitalism. The Labour Party believes that, when it has obtained the support of a majority of the electors for its policy, it will secure the acquiescence of the greater number of its opponents in the changes which will be brought about.

There are, however, those who claim that Socialism will never be introduced without a violent struggle. They believe that, as soon as it is found that democracy is no longer prepared to be the handmaid of Capitalism, the supporters of the present system will reject it. They think that any attempt to deal with fundamentals will be met by forcible resistance. They think that parliamentary action is only useful as a preparation for an inevitable struggle that will be fought out, not at the ballot-box, but with bayonet and bomb. It is idle to deny that there is this possibility. The last few years have seen the overthrow of democracy in many countries and the development of Fascism, which is only a cloak for Capitalism. It is, however, unwise to argue from the experience of one country to that of another. There is nothing more misleading than to try to apply to all countries a cast-iron theory of historical necessity and to argue that Britain must go the Moscow road unless she follows the example of Berlin or Rome. The theorist at the end of the eighteenth century might equally well have argued that Britain must go the way of France unless she was prepared to align herself with Austria and Prussia. I do not suggest that there is not a possibility of an attempt by reactionaries to seize power by force. I am well aware how slight a hold the principles of democracy have on some of our opponents, but I believe that the vast majority of the people of this country reject such methods, and that an attempt of this kind would be defeated by the loyalty of the mass of the people to the Government.

I believe that a violent struggle in this country would be extremely dangerous to civilisation, which ever side ultimately conquered. British Socialists have always recognised the conflict between classes but have not generally adopted the class war as a theory of society. It is, of course, true that there is a vital conflict in the community between the classes that live by mere ownership and those that live by labour, but it is not nearly so clear-cut and distinct as is sometimes imagined. There are not just two sharply contrasted classes, Capitalists and wage-earners. Between the man who owns nothing but his labour and the man who depends entirely on unearned income there are many grades of people, some of whom are predominantly workers while others are predominantly Capitalists. In this country there are many workers who own some property; there are many Capitalists who do useful service to the community. The method of violent revolution implies the subjugation, if not the extermination, of those classes which are opposed to Socialism. It implies in reality the acceptance of the totalitarian State. I do not accept the totalitarian State as desirable as an end, and I believe that an attempt to achieve it by force brings with it very great evils.

The attempt by one section of the community to dominate all others inevitably means the adoption of terrorism as a weapon. This can be seen in Fascist Italy and Nazi Germany, but it is also evident in Communist Russia. Once the method of terrorism is adopted it is very difficult to abandon it. In theory, the period of terrorism and dictatorship is transitory. In practice, it continues. In Soviet Russia to-day, fifteen years after the cessation of foreign intervention, the method of terrorism continues, as may be seen from the trials of the Trotskyists. However much the leaders of Soviet Russia desire to escape from it, they cannot, because the methods that gained power continue to be employed by those who now seek to attain it. In the totalitarian State a forcible rebellion is the only way to effect change.

In this country there have always been small sections who advocated a forcible revolution, but they have found but little favour with the majority of the people, because such methods are alien to the national temperament. For years there were those who hankered after the romance of the barricades and the rising of the people against their oppressors. The changes in the methods of destruction due to the progress of science have made these dreams further and further from reality.

The Labour Party does not seek to establish a drilled and dragooned community where only one opinion is allowed. On the contrary, it realises that the wealth of a community is its diversity, not its uniformity.

I believe that the people of this country are as unlikely to accept Communism as Fascism. Both systems appeal to the politically immature. Both are distasteful to peoples like the British and French, who have had years of experience of personal freedom and political democracy.

While, as I have stated, the Labour Party has steadily opposed the tactics of revolutionary action and violence, and has always pinned its faith to constitutional action, it has never ignored the possibility that occasions may arise when extra-parliamentary action may become necessary. Its faith in constitutional action inevitably depends on its opponents also adhering to it. As long as the workers have it in their power to achieve their ends by the use of the ballot-box, they have no right to seek to obtain them by other means. If Labour cannot obtain a majority, it must as a minority accept the will of the majority. It may seek to influence that majority, and those to whom it has entrusted power by every lawful means, but to try to enforce its will on a majority by violence is contrary to its democratic faith.

3. The Communist Party

Its members sincerely believe in a method of action which is rejected by the Labour Party. They think that the method of constitutional action is mistaken. It is, of course, an arguable proposition, but it is quite incompatible with whole-hearted support of the Labour Party. The Communist Party, further, is not a free agent. It is subject to the orders of the Comintern. It, therefore, does not admit that the Annual Conference of the Labour Party must be the deciding authority, and that those who have been elected to carry out its decisions must have the necessary authority. Its willingness to enter the Labour Party is, therefore, subject to these two qualifications. It does not believe in the methods of the Labour Party and it does not really accept majority rule. Its whole philosophy is based on the seizure of power by an active minority. Like the I.L.P., it is undemocratic. It believes in rule by those who are superior to ordinary people—in fact, by an ideological aristocracy. I regret the loss to the Labour Party of the services which its members might render, but their very devotion to their particular tenets necessarily makes it impossible for them to work whole-heartedly in the Labour Party.

4. Socialist Objectives

The aim of the Labour Party is the establishment of the Co-operative Commonwealth. Its object, expressed in the Party constitution, is "to secure for the workers by hand or by brain the full fruits of their industry and the most equitable distribution thereof that may be possible, upon the basis of common ownership of the means of production, distribution, and exchange, and the best obtainable system of popular administration and control of each industry or service."

In this chapter I want to explain what is my conception of the kind of society that is there envisaged. I am not going to try to picture a Utopia or to give a detailed sketch of what society will be like under Socialism. However useful such an exercise of the imagination may be, it is out of place in this volume, which has only a limited aim. Further, any picture of a Socialist society is subject to this disability—that it gives a static appearance to something which is of its very nature continually in process of development. There is not some particular state of society on arriving at which one can say, "Finality has been reached." Some future historian will not be able to point to a particular date as that on which the Socialist State was established, in the same way as the United States of America dates from the Declaration of Independence, because Socialists envisage human progress as continuous. The goal which we are striving to reach to-day will only be the starting-point for our successors. Socialism is not an end itself, but only the means of attaining conditions under which the fullest possible life will be available for the human race. Further developments which we cannot contemplate to-day will inevitably follow.

The most that can be done to-day is to show the principles that will be applied in endeavouring to build up a new state of society, to mark clearly the next steps which must be taken, and to indicate the necessary feature which will be displayed in the next stage.

FREEDOM

The first point which I desire to make is that the aim of Socialism is to give greater freedom to the individual. British Social-ists have never made an idol of the State, demanding that individuals should be sacrificed to it. They have never accepted the beehive or the ants' nest as an ideal. They leave that to the advocates of the Corporate State. They have never desired that men and women should be drilled and regimented physically and mentally so that they should be all of one pattern. On the contrary, they appreciate that the wealth of a society is in its variety, not its uniformity. Progress is not towards, but away from the herd. It is no part of the Socialist idea that there should be in every human activity an orthodox pattern to which all must conform.

This is well illustrated by considering the attitude of the Labour Party towards religion. In the Labour Party are found active adherents of many religious creeds, and also men and women who do not conform to any denomination. There has never been any attempt to impose on members of the Party a creed of materialism, any more than there has been any imposition of a religious test. Within the Labour Party everyone is entitled to hold what religious views he will. Where legislation impinges upon religious questions the individual member is accorded complete freedom of action. It is recognised that religion is a sphere which should be left to the individual.

Again, in education, while Socialists have protested against a bias in favour of the existing order being maintained in education, they have not sought to twist education into a means of imposing upon all a rigid orthodoxy. They have such faith in the rightness of their views that they desire the utmost freedom of enquiry and discussion. The action of the Nazi Government in Germany in turning their universities into parrot cages for the repetition of the catchwords of Fascism evokes only contempt. The tendency observable among Communists to try to reduce all history to an economic formula has always been rejected. The conception of proletarian art and literature which must be sharply distinguished from anything hitherto accomplished in those fields is quite alien to true Socialism. It results from a sense of inferiority. British Socialists recognise very clearly the danger that exists in the tyranny of the reformer who wishes to make all men in his own image. The very differences which arise in the Labour movement are an earnest that in the Socialist State of the future there will be constant vigilance to prevent loss of freedom.

State action is advocated by Socialists not for its own sake, but because it is necessary to prevent the oppression of an individual by others, and to secure that liberty of the one does not restrict that of others, or conflict with the common good of society.

Those who attack Socialism on the ground that it will mean the enslavement of the individual belong invariably to the class of people whose possession of property has given them liberty at the expense of the enslavement of others. The possession of property in a Capitalist society has given liberty to a fortunate minority who hardly realise how much its absence means enslavement. The majority of the people of this country are under orders and discipline for the whole of their working day. Freedom is left behind when they "clock in" and only resumed when they go out. Such liberty as they have got as workers has been the fruit of long and bitter struggles by the Trade Unions. But a far greater restriction on liberty than this is imposed on the vast majority of the people of this country by poverty. There is the narrowing of choice in everything. The poor man cannot choose his domicile. He must be prepared at the shortest notice to abandon all his social activities, to leave the niche which he has made for himself in the structure of society, and to remove himself elsewhere, if economic circumstances demand it. This is called "transference." How little would those who so easily recommend this to the workers appreciate being transferred from their pleasant homes in Surrey or Buckinghamshire to Whitechapel or the Black Country. Yet this is an ordinary incident of working-class life. The poor man is restricted in his food, his clothing, his amusements, and his

occupation. The liberty which it is feared Socialism may restrict is the liberty of the few. Moreover, in modern Capitalist society, the power of wealth is such as to affect the lives of the people in thousands of ways. The whole organisation of the country is based on the superior rights of the wealthy. Nothing is sacred to the profit-maker. The beauty and amenities of the country are at his mercy. The life of whole communities may be ruined at his will.

Yet one other vital deprivation of the poor must be mentioned. Leisure, which is the essential thing for the living of a civilised life, is only tardily being recognised as the right of those who work for the community, and is even now miserably insufficient for the majority. Even a fortnight's holiday with pay is exceptional. The result is that for the majority the social heritage of the race is locked up. The two keys, time and money, are not within their reach.

The liberty which Socialists desire is liberty for all. The restrictions which will be imposed will be those only which are essential to secure it. The current misconception of a Socialist society as one in which everyone will be subject to the constant interference of an army of officials is due to the fact that in order to avoid the worst abuses of Capitalism society has had to institute a whole series of services of inspection to check the anti-social actions of those engaged in private enterprise. Factory inspectors are necessary because many employers lack social sense, just as "speed cops" are needed because many motorists lack road sense and a feeling of responsibility to the community. Their presence is not due to the Socialist but the anti-Socialist spirit.

It is true that in the Socialist State people will be deprived of the right of living in idleness at the expense of the community, but this right is in practice denied to the majority already by their economic circumstances. On the other hand, when the community is organised for service instead of profit there will be no such thing as the enforced deprivation of the right to work which is now imposed on nearly two million people in this country at the height of a trade boom, and on many more whenever there is a slump. The denial of the right to work is one of the greatest infringements of liberty imposed under Capitalism, for it deprives the individual of the right of expressing his personality and exercising his functions as a citizen.

My conclusion is that men and women will be more free, not less free, under Socialism. Freedom will be more widely disseminated. There will be no attempt made to impose rigid uniformity. There will be no forcible suppression of adverse opinion. The real change will be that a man will become a citizen, with the rights of a free man during his hours of labour just as in his leisure time. This does not mean that he will have the right to do just as he will. He will have freedom within the necessary restraints which life in a complex society imposes.

SECURITY

One of the most serious charges that can be made against Capitalism is that it fails to give any sense of security to the vast majority of people. There are a few who have, through the possession of property, achieved complete security from the threat of poverty. But they are very few. The overwhelming number of people in every Capitalist country live in constant fear of losing their only means of livelihood through causes entirely outside their own control. Depending as they do entirely upon the sale of their labour, they may at any time find themselves without buyers, owing to a temporary breakdown in some part of the Capitalist machine. Some people have, of course, accumulated savings during the time that they have been at work, but a comparatively short period of unemployment will use up the average working man's savings, and leave him and his family without any means of subsistence except such relief as may be afforded by the State.

The establishment of Socialism will bring about a fundamental alteration in this condition of affairs. A Socialist State cannot afford to allow men to remain idle. As soon, therefore, as there ceases to be a demand for a man's labour in one direction, he will be given some other kind of work to do. He will be certain that as long as he is capable of making a contribution to the national wealth he can be sure of a job, and of sufficient money to keep himself and his family at a reasonable standard of living.

EQUALITY

Socialists do not propose to substitute the domination of society by one privileged class for that of another. They seek to abolish class distinctions altogether. The abolition of classes is fundamental to the Socialist conception of society. Whatever may be the professions of belief in democracy made by supporters of the present system, they do, in fact, think it right and natural that there should be class distinctions. This is the attitude not merely of those at the top, who appear to benefit by the present order, but of the Conservative working man also. As part of the joy of the blessed in the old conception of heaven was the contemplation of the miseries and torture of the damned, so there are people who seem to be unable to derive their satisfaction from their own worth unless they can contrast it with the inferior position of others.

Society to-day is so ordered that there is a struggle between classes, between those who derive their living from the ownership of property and those who are dependent on their labour. This class division is not, however, as clear-cut as some theorists assume. There is much subdivision into grades. Those who are in the higher grades of society would resent being lumped together with small tradesmen and professional men as common members of a single Capitalist class. Similarly, the solidarity of the workers is limited by quite a considerable amount of class distinction, although many old divisions based on pride of craft or of occupation are now disappearing.

Although, on the whole, class distinctions

are less than they were, owing to the breaking down of the barriers of birth, there remains the great factor which divides people into social classes—that is, inequality of wealth. It is not so much the actual possession of wealth which makes for division as access to a certain standard of life which the ownership of money affords.

Socialists do not propose to level down, but to level up. There is no particular virtue in equality in misery and squalor. It is mainly false sentimentality which talks of noble poverty. It is now possible for all to enjoy a reasonably high standard of life. One of the striking features of present-day society is the existence of very low standards of life which are not imposed by the inability of the community to provide better. They are not even necessitated by the demands of the well-to-do for luxuries. They are caused simply by the failure to utilise resources which are available. Without reducing the standards of life of the wealthy, a great advance in the material well-being of the masses is possible, but this is not enough. The existence of wide disparities of wealth, with a consequent segregation of the community into separate classes, is inimical to a true social life. To abolish classes altogether is not so chimerical an undertaking as it would have appeared some years ago. During the past few decades there has been a levelling up of education, culture, and social habits. The gulf which formerly separated the manual worker and the brain worker has narrowed. The dividing-line between classes is far more one of economic circumstances than of cultural differences. Under Socialism the aim will be to utilise the services of all citizens in the way which will be most conducive to the benefit of society and to the individual, and to give to all who render service approximately equal advantages. Equality does not, however, mean identity. Human beings are, of course, unequal, and have diversities of tastes and gifts, but this need not be expressed in wide social inequalities.

No doubt it will be some time before substantial economic equality is achieved, but ultimately it must be. There is no way of measuring the value of the services rendered by those who work in various ways for the community so as to give a greater reward to one rather than to the other. No doubt habit and custom will survive for some time. It is, I think, unlikely that complete uniformity of hours of work will be attained. Some will work longer than others, but have compensating advantages. All will not necessarily have the same amount of purchasing power. The aim, however, of the Socialist State must be equality. This must be the guiding principle applied in its plans of organisation.

DEMOCRACY

I have already stressed the belief of the Labour Party in democracy. In these days, when modern industry and commerce demand the co-operation of a great army of individuals who are entirely unknown to each other, and when, owing to the close integration of world economy, the fortunes of every individual are dependent upon the actions of other people in his own country and abroad to a greater extent than ever before, there is a tendency to regard the problems of politics and economics as too difficult of comprehension for the ordinary man. The average citizen finds himself to be but a cog in a great and complicated machine. He cannot control or even understand it. He is inclined to leave the task to others. Hence has arisen the despairing demand for dictatorship. There seem to be many who have the herd mind. They desire to choose some old bull to follow. Unfortunately, the old bull is generally both stupid and bellicose. There is every indication that he will lead the herd to destruction.

Socialists reject the conception of dictatorship altogether because it is powerless to effect that which they wish. They are not concerned solely with material things. They do not think of human beings as a herd to be fed and watered and kept in security. They think of them as individuals co-operating together to make a fine collective life. For this reason Socialism is a more exacting creed than that of its competitors. It does not demand submission and acquiescence, but active and constant participation in common activities. It demands that every individual shall shoulder his or her responsibilities.

It would no doubt be easier to plan a new organisation of society in which all controlling power would be entrusted to a few super-men by whose orders, through an obedient bureaucracy, the material resources of this country, or even of the world, would be developed, and the activities of all the peoples directed to produce certain results. Provided that there were sufficient faith in the wisdom of those directing affairs, such a society might make rapid material progress, and might endure for a time, but it would be subject to all the dangers and uncertainties which accompany dictatorships, not the least of which is the mental instability which seems almost inevitably to attack dictators. I do not believe that there are human beings who are fit to be entrusted with such absolute power. I believe, too, that such a society would be spiritually very poor. The really fatal objection to any such plan is the absence of all power of changing the régime. Democracy involves the right to change the policy and personnel of those to whom government is confided. Without this right there is no true freedom. Its denial throws all dissenters from the existing order back to violence as the only remedy. The apparent stability of a dictatorship conceals this real weakness. Where the only possibility of change is by violence, the Government is bound to protect itself by intense police activity. It is inevitable that all dictatorships, whether of the Left or the Right, should be policeridden States, with the invariable accompaniments of espionage, delation, and terrorism. The insistence on the maintenance of democracy by the Labour Party against those who advocate dictatorships, whether on the Berlin or Moscow model, is founded upon a deep conviction that any divergence from it involves loss of liberty. Liberty once surrendered is very hard to recapture.

I hold, therefore, that despite the inevitable disadvantages in slowness of action which observance of democratic methods involves, it is necessary to make provision at all stages in the organisation of the Socialist State for the active participation of the citizens and for the exercise of control by them directly over their immediate activities, and indirectly through their representatives over the wider policy of the State. Such control involves the freedom to make mistakes. The idea that the ideal State is one in which no mistakes are made seems to me wrong. Unless there is the liberty to err there is no freedom. Democracy necessarily involves some loss of immediate efficiency, but in the long run makes for its increase. I conceive that in the Socialist State there will be, besides the democratic framework of the State and of industry, a great variety of voluntary societies controlled by the members, wherein all the time a training in democracy will be taking place. There will always be a certain number of people who are unwilling to take responsibility, or whose minds are absorbed in other things, but the success of the Socialist State will depend on the active participation of the greatest possible number in the making of decisions.

It is sometimes suggested that the manager and the technician will be unable to function because of the constant interference of committees of workers or consumers or others. I do not believe this. The genius of the people of this country does not lie in the elaboration of theoretical constitutions but in their practical ability to make them work. The introduction of democracy into industry will give another field for the exercise of this genius. Experience has, I think, shown that, despite the divergence of aim incidental to the Capitalist system, it has been possible in many industries to get wide co-operation between workers and management. I have no doubt that this will be so when the principal bone of contention is removed.

COMMON OWNERSHIP

Land will be owned by the community, not by private individuals, but the citizen will have reasonable security of tenure; in fact, he will be far more secure than are the majority of people at the present day, who are liable to be turned out of their dwellings at the will of a landlord or forced to abandon the homes that they have made through a change in their economic circumstances.

All the major industries will be owned and controlled by the community, but there may well exist for a long time many smaller enterprises which are left to be carried on individually. It is not possible to lay down a hard and fast line on the constitution and management of every industry. There will no doubt be wide diversity in accordance with the requirements of particular undertakings. One may, however, lay down certain essential conditions. The first of these is that the interest of the community as a whole must come before that of any sectional group. The second is that the managers and technicians must be given reasonable freedom if they are to work efficiently, a freedom within the general economic plan; while the third is that the workers must be citizens in industry and not wage slaves. The exact way in which this will be worked out will again depend on the circumstances of particular industries. In the organisation of industry there are to be considered the interests of the community as a whole, the interests of the producers, and the interests of the consumers. Each interest has its particular sphere in which it must be paramount. The organisation of the Labour movement is triple—the Labour Party, the Trade Union movement, and the Co-operative movement. There is, therefore, already in the Labour movement a recognition of these three separate interests, and constant practice in reconciling them. The problems of socialised industry will, therefore, be faced by those who already understand the difficulties and the dangers to be avoided.

There is one great danger that must be avoided—overcentralisation. Great Britain is suffering at the present time from the too great concentration of population and of economic and financial power in London. A Socialist Government will plan for the whole country, but within the general plan there must be local application.

Just as with individuals, so with the country, there is a danger in uniformity. Capitalism is to-day actively engaged in making the whole country uniform. Chain stores, cinemas, and banks, and masses of houses of uniform type, take the place of the distinctive features which gave charm to the countryside. Cheap newspapers and cinemas have the effect of filling people's minds with the same narrow range of ideas. I conceive that under Socialism there will be a wide regional decentralisation, and a deliberate endeavour to allow for each area to express the individuality of the people. In particular there must, of course, be decentralisation in Scotland and Wales. One of the vital problems of the present day is to reconcile the natural claims of nationality with the larger interest of the world as a whole. It may be claimed that in Great Britain the world has been given an example of how three races without losing their national characteristics can combine in a larger unity.

If this success is to continue it must be by giving due weight to the claims of the separate nationalities to preserve their own culture and develop their own national life. True Socialism does not mean an internationalism that ignores the diversities of different peoples, but recognises them and provides for their expression.

COMPENSATION

It is at this point that it is necessary to lay down clearly Labour's point of view on compensation. The Labour Party believes in paying compensation during the period of transition towards the Socialist Commonwealth as part of its conception of the method of change. Confiscation is part of the technique of revolution, not of constitutional action. There are two reasons why it is wise to compensate: the first is ethical, the second practical. During the process of reconstructing the basis of society which must necessarily take some years, it is not equitable to penalise the persons who happen to own the property which comes early in the list of those things which the State determines to acquire. There are those who attach a moral obliquity to the holding of certain kinds of property such as land, mining royalties, or brewery shares, and they desire to punish such property owners. It is not, however, possible to draw these distinctions between various owners. The owner of land may have recently acquired it by giving in exchange the savings of a lifetime of hard work. The owner of some form of property which it is not proposed to take over immediately may have made all his money from owning slum property, but have recently sold the one and acquired the other. Confiscation is a form of taxation differing only from any other tax in the amount taken. The Socialist canon of taxation is to tax according to amount, not according to the source from which that wealth comes, except in so far as it is necessary to distinguish between earned and unearned income. Confiscation is apt to hit the small man as well as the big one whose iniquity bulks large in the eyes of the reformer.

The second reason is one of expediency. It is stupid to arouse unnecessary antagonism. In this country, while the division of wealth is grossly unequal, there are, nevertheless, a mass of workers who own some property. Their interests are with the workers, but if they are deprived unjustly of their reasonable expectations they will feel the injustice acutely. A few cases of gross injustice to individuals will outweigh in the public mind the greater injustice done to the workers collectively. Further, it is of the essence of constitutional change that reasonable expectations should be respected and that the transition to the new order should be as smooth as possible. The violent denunciations of the method of compensation come only from irresponsibles.

Therefore, in all cases where the State finds it necessary to take over private property, reasonable and just compensation will be paid. The redressing of inequalities of wealth must be effected through taxation. The process cannot be combined with nationalisation either equitably or expediently.

INVENTION AND PROGRESS

At the present time inventions almost always bring unmerited sufferings on persons whose livelihood depended on the continuance of things as they had been. Scientific invention, instead of giving increased satisfaction, often means increased insecurity. This does not mean that scientific invention and technical progress are wrong, but that under private enterprise they are used, not for the general good, but for the advantage of a few. Invention and progress are often hindered by vested interests, which prevent the development of new ideas because they threaten the profits of existing undertakings. Under Socialism there will be no need to suppress inventions, because every device for increasing wealth or easing labour will result in the raising of the general standard of life and comfort. A Socialist Government will, therefore, foster research, and give full scope to the application of new inventions. No group of persons will have a vested interest in particular economic processes, and no persons and no districts will be allowed to suffer through a change in industrial activity.

BEAUTY

One of the heaviest indictments against the Capitalist system is that it is destructive of beauty. The widespread ugliness in Britain is the result of putting profits first. Socialists regard economic activities only as the foundation for a full life of the spirit. It is not surprising that so many artists and poets are found in the Socialist ranks. They realise that, until the pressure of material needs is relieved, it is difficult to get people to think of life in terms of beauty. As long as there are wide divergencies of wealth and class divisions in society, false ideals will prevail. One of the greatest tasks for those who are striving to build up a new society is to extend the horizon of the ordinary man and woman. Under present conditions it is often deplorably narrow. It is to be feared that many of those who support the Labour movement do not see much beyond one step upwards in the social scale. Nevertheless, it is something to see thus far, for there are many people in this country who are still pathetically content with the standard to which they have become accustomed. Every step forward means a wider vision. People who do not yet see much beyond, so to speak, the amenities of a London suburb will from that point progress further. There have always been in the ranks of the Socialist movement plenty of people who are discontented with narrow and immediate achievements. I am glad that it should be so, for without continual striving for something better, retrogression is certain.

A Socialist Government, while seeking to increase wealth, and while utilising science and invention to lighten the task of the human race, will not be content with a material success. In planning the new Britain they will think of it, not just as a basis for wealth production, but as the environment in which men and women are to live happily and finely.

NATIONALISM

"National Socialism" is a contradiction in terms. A true Socialist cannot allow his sympathies to be bounded by anything so narrow as a nation, for nationalism is only egotism writ large. It follows that it is impossible for a Socialist Government to pursue a foreign policy that is at variance with its principles. It would be so doing if it attempted to create ideal conditions for the people of its own country at the expense of others. I have already stressed the point that British Socialists do not adhere to an ideological imperialism which would impel them to try to force all other nations into a common mould. Just as, in forming the new social order at home, the ruling principle is not to enforce uniformity but to give individual freedom, so in dealing with external affairs a Socialist Government will recognise the right of each nation to regulate its own affairs according to what it considers desirable, provided that in so doing it does not conflict with the general interests of the human race. In dealing with the other constituents of the British Commonwealth, full effect will be given to this principle. The process whereby the Dominions have become equal partners with the mother country, so that their continued association has become entirely voluntary, must be continued until the commonwealth consists only of free self-governing units. The old idea of class distinctions between the various peoples which are united under the British Crown, distinctions based on colour, race, or history, must give way to equal partnership. Economic exploitation of one territory by another must no longer continue. Equally, in the larger sphere of foreign affairs a Socialist Government will work for the utmost freedom for every nation within the larger unity. Just as a satisfactory social system can only be achieved by the surrender of the absolute right of individuals to do as they please to the interests of the whole community, so, in the world, peace and prosperity can only be secured by the surrender of absolute sovereignty of nations to the common interest of civilisation. It is not by insistence on the absolute rights of nations to do what they will that peace will be secured, but by co-operating in the provision of common services and by the development of common standards. The Socialist looks to the World Co-operative Commonwealth, not as some distant ideal, but as something which must be realised if mankind is not to perish by his own inventions.

I have in this chapter given a brief outline of the kind of Britain and kind of world which I want to see. I have done so, not because I think that I can see very far ahead, or because I think that I can paint in words an attractive picture. This has been done by many others with far more qualifications. I have done it because I want to emphasise two things. The first is that I believe that it is necessary for everyone to think out as clearly as possible what kind of a world he wants and then to consider what is the best way to attain to it. The second is that the Labour Party has its immediate programme, which it intends to carry out whenever it is given power to do so. This programme is directed towards the attainment of some such state of society as I have sketched. It is intended definitely to begin to make those fundamental changes necessary for its realisation. It is based on the principles which I have indicated. I believe that a Socialist Government must have always very clearly before it its ultimate aims and ideals. It must work throughout with the object of attaining them. It must not rest content with minor successes. It must, even when dealing with immediate problems, keep in mind always the goal to which it is tending. It is here that the Labour Party is so different from those parties which believe fundamentally in the retention of a class system of society and in a Capitalist system as the economic foundation of society. They see a form of society in existence which they think to be right although it may require some alterations. Socialists see a society which is wrong and which must be replaced by another. From this its follows that the approach of a Socialist Government to the problems which it has to meet its altogether different from that of its opponents. The latter, accepting things as they are, can be content with patching the old garment. The former must have a definite plan, and must from the start work to make that plan a reality.

THE ENGLAND WE WANT TO SEE

The new order of society will enable millions, who up to now have had to toil in factory and workshop all their lives without any prospect of ever experiencing the good things of life, to get their first opportunity of enjoying some of those luxuries that are now confined exclusively to the well-to-do. Let us consider for a moment the sort of life that we hope will be led by a working man and his family under Socialism.

A great part of the week, under Socialism as under any other system, will inevitably be spent in work. Whether that work is in factory or office, the worker will be able to feel that he is working in his own concern, which belongs to him as a British citizen. He will know that the work he is doing will be of benefit to himself and to every other person in the country. There will be no question of the goods he is producing being destined for destruction as "surplus" because the economic system cannot absorb them. Everything that is made will add to the sum of the country's wealth. He will know, too, that if he continues to work satisfactorily there is no chance of his losing his job. In fact, he will feel that his employment is secure, and that he is contributing to the prosperity of his country. The knowledge that the factory belongs to him will not be confined to a vague and indefinite feeling of ownership. He will, through his union, be able to have a say in its management. If he finds that the conveyor belt is being run too fast, or that the precautions against accidents are not being properly observed, for example, he will be able to take action at once with a view to getting the matter remedied. In a thousand and one ways he will feel the difference between working for a private Capitalist and working for the nation.

Important as will be the change in conditions inside his office or factory, this will only be a part of the profound alteration that Socialism will bring about in his life. It will, as I have said already, give him a far greater degree of leisure than he has known in the past. But leisure is of little use unless it is accompanied by sufficient means to utilise it to the full. The unemployed to-day have "leisure" enough and to spare, but they are deprived of the means of enjoying it. The worker under Socialism, with a forty-hour week and holidays with pay, will be able to use his leisure to the full. New avenues will be opened up to him that to-day are closed through the failure of the Capitalist system to provide a living wage for all.

There are few workers to-day, for example, who can afford to travel. The vast majority have to remain within a short distance of their homes, and never have an opportunity of seeing the world. A reorganised national transport system, providing cheap fares by road or rail for those who want to spend their holidays in visiting other parts of their own country, would revolutionise the average worker's holiday time.

To-day, however, if a working-class family does go into the country for a day, it is, as a rule, simply to travel along road or rail through other people's territory. One of the great changes that will come about in a Socialist Britain will be that large areas of land will be set aside as national parks, in which people will be free to enjoy themselves without being prosecuted for trespassing on private property. In these parks there will be rest-houses, where it will be possible for people to come and stay during their holiday, and camps where they can send their children to get all the benefits of fresh air and sunshine which are denied to the great majority of children living to-day in crowded streets.

Not everyone wants to travel, however, and there are many who may still prefer to stay at home. But they want "home" to be a place that they can be proud of. To-day there are many homes that are simply four walls, and have none of the amenities that they could have if full use were made of all those inventions that science has placed at our disposal. The aim of Socialism will be to see that every family in the country has a house with electric light, and power for cooking, central heating, refrigerator, and plenty of floor-space, one in fact that is well furnished with everything that a modern housewife needs. All this may sound utopian, but if we realise that there are men in the building and allied trades out of work, and being paid by the State for doing nothing, it begins to sound more reasonable.

Finally, there are those who want to develop their own minds further, and secure for themselves the education that they need in order to have a full appreciation of all that is meant in the much misused phrase "culture." To acquire this knowledge costs money. To-day only a limited number of people can afford to educate themselves or their children. A few of the latter, who show exceptional brilliance, may get scholarships, but the vast majority have to be content with what they have learnt at elementary schools. A great extension of educational opportunity both for children and adults would make a profound difference in the lives of numbers of our countrymen. Such an extension is one of the aims of Socialism.

These are just illustrations of the kind of opportunities that Socialism will bring to the average working-class family. There are a hundred others, ranging from a good square meal to a trip to the Continent. All of them may be summed up in a sentence, by saying that we mean to give every man, woman, and child in the country an opportunity to live the fullest life that the resources of our island will allow.

5. Prospects

I do not believe that the only choice before us is the acceptance of Fascism or Communism. I do not think that Britain must follow the Moscow or the Berlin road. Those two roads have certain features in common. They are straight, narrow, and artificial. They drive through the landscape of humanity with little apparent reference to its contours or to the graces of the countryside which have been derived from the past. Those who journey along them attain a very high rate of speed, and they scorn old-fashioned meandering paths. There are many casualties on that account. A high rate of speed may give great pleasure to those who control the machines, but it may mean a vast amount of discomfort to the driven. The real question is, to what place will those who complete the journey arrive? —if, indeed, they do arrive, for there is a great possibility of a terrible catastrophe on the way. One may ask, too, in what kind of condition will those who journey be like when the road has been traversed? One can give no certain answer to these questions, whether one considers the travelers on the Moscow or on the Berlin highways.

I have already set out my objections to the Totalitarian State, whether formed on the Fascist or Communist model, and I will not repeat them here. I do not think that it is desirable as an ideal or necessary as a stage in human development. In my view the Totalitarian State is not an advance in civilisation but a retrogression. It has been adopted by peoples who are politically and socially immature. They have not grasped the fact that the essential condition for an advanced civilisation is toler-ance, and that a society in which men and women of differing views on many subjects can live together in peace and harmony is a higher type than one in which all must conform to a single pattern. The achieve-ment of the Totalitarian State involves the use of force, and its continuance requires the use of the same methods. The one thing indispensable is an all-pervading police service. While this continues there is no freedom, and until it is abolished the ex-periment in Russia will not attract the ma-jority of the British people.

It is, in my view, the strength, not the weakness, of Britain which allows of wide tolerance and freedom, permitting people to disagree on matters of vital importance and yet to continue to live together in friendly intercourse. To exchange this for a society in which everything is subordinated to a ruthless class warfare would be a retrograde step. Avoiding both Fascism and Communism, this country, I believe, can afford to the world an example of how so-ciety can adapt itself to new conditions and base itself on new principles without breach of continuity and without violence and in-tolerance. We have in the past to a great extent avoided the civil wars which have done such a vast amount of harm in other countries. It is, I think, a false reading of history to think that what has happened elsewhere must necessarily happen in this country. It has not been so in the past. It was, I think, characteristic of Britain that, on the only occasion on which there arose a military dictatorship, the dictator was a man who strove continually for tolerance and sought unceasingly to rid himself of the burden of absolute power and to return to the ways of constitutionalism. Cromwell was as English as Mussolini is Italian.

I think that nations tend to follow very closely their national traditions. Italy has frequently been the arena for faction fights and proscriptions. The Fascist methods are nothing new to the descendants of the Guelfs and Ghibellines. Military despotism has been a feature of German history. It is still a question whether or not Russia will return to the autocracy which she has so long endured. It is my faith that Britain will be true to her traditions, and that, despite the profound differences that separate the supporters of Socialism and Capitalism, the changes which are necessary will be brought about without bloodshed and violence. It is the genius of the British people to modify and adapt old institutions to new purposes. I think that the same process which has been followed in the past will be employed in the future for changing the social and economic structure of this country.

I believe that the Labour Party is the in-strument whereby this change will be af-fected. Typically British, the Labour Party has shown its power of adaptation to new conditions and new purposes. At its incep-tion it was a party representing almost en-tirely organised Labour. Its programme was sectional, not national. It has since then de-veloped into a national party, open to all, and has a policy which embraces every phase of national life. In its earlier days it would have been a fair criticism to have said that it could not aspire to power be-cause its appeal was too narrow. It is not true to-day. Increasingly it draws its strength from men and women of all classes of society. Its achievement of power does not depend on an alteration in the quality of its adherents, but in their quantity. It has to convert to its faith many millions of workers who still cling to Capitalism. It has to persuade many members of the classes which depend in the main on their own work for their livelihood that true community of interest is based on fellowship in service, not on participation in profits.

While it is right to face up to the forces that make against the success of the Labour Party, it is not necessary to exaggerate them or to minimise the influences which make for that success. I believe that it is impossible to contend against the tendencies which are making more necessary every day a planned society, and which render it out of the question to continue a class society based on gross inequalities of wealth. Capitalism is manifestly failing. A temporary recovery from depression gives it a short new lease of life, but the next depression is deeper than its predecessor. The increasingly high standards of education of the workers are making the task of the Socialist easier. Developments of mass production are tending to break down barriers of social habit which used to be the strongest supports to class distinctions. The confidence which used to belong to the supporters of the existing order is being steadily sapped. But the future of the Labour Party depends, first and foremost, on the idealism, the devotion, and the intelligence of the rank and file of its adherents. The existence in this country of thousands of men and women who give freely of their time and labour for the cause in which they believe is the thing which has enabled the workers, despite all the advantages of money, education, economic power, and social privilege which belong to their opponents, to create a political party able to contend for power. It is this army of active Socialists which will in due time achieve power and create the Britain

which they desire. The deciding factor, to my mind, will not be leadership or the exact theories which are held to be orthodox Socialism. It will not be the brilliance of particular individuals. The thing which will secure the triumph of Labour will be the demonstration by Socialists in their lives that they have a high ideal and live up to it. People are converted more by what they see Socialists are than by what they hear them say. Here is the responsibility which lies upon everyone in the movement. The daily actions of professing Socialists are either helping or hindering the achievement which all desire.

The thing which does more harm than anything else is the lack of unity among Socialists and the bitterness which is imported into these dissensions. I am no enemy of plain speaking, and I think that it is stupid and dishonest to try to make a superficial unity where there is really profound difference of aim and method, but unnecessary suspicions and personal attacks play into the hands of our enemies.

There remains to be considered the way in which the Labour Party uses power when it has received a mandate from the electors. I am convinced that whenever this mandate has been given, the Labour programme must be carried out with the utmost vigour and resolution. To delay dealing with essentials would be fatal. To show irresolution or cowardice would be to invite defeat. A Labour Government should make it quite plain that it will suffer nothing to hinder it in carrying out the popular will. In all great enterprises it is the first steps that are difficult, and it is the way in which these are taken that makes the difference between success or failure. A Labour Government, not in a spirit of malice or revenge, but with the greatest regard for justice to all, must resolutely set about its task of rebuilding the life of this country on the principles of liberty, equality, and social justice, and of joining with other nations to create a world Commonwealth.

III. COLE

Socialist Economics *

1. The Socialists and the Keynesians

The difference between Keynes and the earlier generations of economists belonging to the classical tradition lies above all in the choice of the central idea round which economic theory is built up. The accepted interpreters of orthodox doctrine right up to Keynes started from the assumption of a natural tendency towards equilibrium at a level that would bring into use every factor of production that was "worth employing" at all, and treated any lapse from such a condition of "full employment" as due to some temporary cause or aberration from this normal state of affairs. It was assumed that there was for every factor of production a "right" price, dependent on its marginal productivity, that would bring the whole of it into use, and that when any factor was not in practice being fully used, the cause must lie either in the fact that its owner was holding out for too high a price, or in some special disturbing force, such as mistaken State intervention or a temporary breakdown of the monetary mechanism of exchange. J. B. Say, in his famous "market theory," had explained long ago that every act of production created, under truly competitive conditions, the demand needed to buy the product at a price that would cover the costs of producing it. On this basis the economists constructed a model economic system which was in perfect equilibrium, the incomes paid out to the factors of pro-

duction just sufficing to clear the market of everything that was produced, at prices which just covered costs at the margin, and gave superior returns to the more efficient factors in proportion to their superior productivity. In this imaginary economic world there was no unemployment, either of human beings or of other factors that could be used in conjunction with human beings. The existence of sub-marginal factors—waste land, obsolete factories and plant, unemployable labour—was regarded as not counting; for such things were not really factors at all. The manifest fact that unemployment did exist, and extended to many factors which could not be thus simply written off as "unemployable" and therefore economically non-existent, was then explained as a consequence of various "frictions" in the smooth working of actual economies, which caused them to deviate from the equilibrium model. This model was usually presented in the first instance as perfectly static, with an endlessly repeated round of productive operations and sales which replenished the coffers of the producers. Technical invention, changes in population, and changes in work-habits (e.g. in hours of labour or in efficiency) were treated as disturbing forces, which were sometimes introduced and taken account of in a second, dynamic model of the economic system. Crises and cyclical fluctuations, about the causes of which there was endless argument, were similarly regarded as disturbing forces of a second order, which needed explaining, but only as deviations

* From G. D. H. Cole, *Socialist Economics* (Victor Gollancz, Ltd., 1950). By permission.

from what ought to happen in a properly functioning economic system.

What Keynes did was to focus attention on the problem of employment, as the central matter in economic theory. He was by no means the first economist to attempt this; but, partly because of his great ability but even more because of the conditions under which he wrote, he was able to persuade his contemporaries to take seriously a number of doctrines which nearly all the professional economists had previously dismissed as the notions of cranks. I have a lively memory, in my young days, of attending lectures at which the economic ideas of J. A. Hobson were denounced and ridiculed, and of having been regarded by not a few of my own pupils as an utterly unsound economist because I tried to teach them, largely under Hobson's influence, economic conceptions which suddenly became respectable when Keynes so ably restated them in an environment of what appeared to be insoluble long-term unemployment. The queues outside the Employment Exchanges, the desolation of the Distressed Areas, the hunger marches, and the immense expenditure on "doles" for doing nothing co-operated with Keynes' expositions—which indeed they also inspired—to bring about a revolution in economic theory as an academic subject, and left the anti-Keynesians fighting, even in the United States, what become more and more evidently a losing battle.

The upshot of Keynes' new theory was to make people see that the "full employment" which the orthodox economists had begun by assuming was not in reality a normal tendency that would assert itself under capitalism in the absence of special disturbing causes, but was, on the contrary, an objective to be aimed at by positive action to bring it about and to maintain it. Keynes showed that, whereas the orthodox economists had been taking for granted that "equilibrium" would mean full employment, there could in fact be equilibrium *at any level,* from full employment to no employment at all. Supply and demand could balance, not only with all the factors of production in use, but equally with many of them out of use: nor was there any natural tendency, when some of the factors had fallen out of use, for them to be brought back into use in the absence of definite measures designed to secure this effect.

The best-known part of this demonstration was that in which Keynes treated of the problem of saving and investment. Until he wrote, it had been common to assume that every act of saving—that is, of abstention from consuming one's whole income—carried with it an equivalent investment in real capital, and thus took off the market enough goods to offset the costs of production and make it profitable to keep the factors of production in recurrent use. Keynes showed —what now seems obvious—that mere abstention from consuming things can create no demand, and that demand will be created on a sufficient scale only if each act of saving is accompanied by the application of an equal sum of money to the purchase of capital goods—that is, by real investment of a corresponding value. But savers, merely by saving, do not in fact bring about any investment at all. The volume of investment depends on the *enterpreneurs,* private or public, who take up money in shares or loans or by using their own savings in a productive way. If there is for any reason a reduced readiness to apply money to the purchase of capital goods, the total demand for labour will be bound to fall off, unless there is a simultaneous and equivalent increase in spending on consumption. This, however, unless it is artificially induced, is most unlikely to happen: indeed, the decrease in demand for capital goods will cause some of the producers of such goods to lose their incomes, and will thus bring about a fall in consumption as well. When this has happened, a new equilibrium between supply and demand may be established at a lower level, with some of the factors of production out of use; nor will there be any necessary tendency for these factors to be reemployed.

But, if equilibrium could exist at *any*

level of employment and production, what became of the beautiful conception of natural forces always making for the best of possible economic worlds, and only thwarted by foolish, even if well meant, interference by Governments, or inflation-loving financiers, or get-rich-quick speculators, or whoever or whatever it was that lurked behind the inconvenient phenomenon of the trade cycle? The entire edifice of *laissez-faire* economic theory collapsed like a house of cards if it had to be admitted that the equilibrium beloved of orthodox economists gave no guarantee of high production or against persistent unemployment. And, when one looked at the facts—the unpleasant facts of the period between the wars—was it not evident that Keynes was in the right? The orthodox economists were, no doubt, still busy explaining that the depression into which the capitalist world had fallen was due to this or that aberration from sound economic behaviour, and that the attempts of Governments to cure the disease by tariffs, work-making, cheap money, and the rest of the expedients they had been driven to were really making the situation a great deal worse. But their lamentations were becoming less and less convincing, the more so because the remedy they seemed most to favour was that of making depression still deeper by deliberate deflation and government "economy" in order to make things better "in the long run." As Keynes exclaimed impatiently, "in the long run we are all dead."

Keynes, then, constructed a new kind of Economics of which the principal lesson was that it was the State's business to maintain a condition of full employment, instead of trusting to the working of "economic laws" to bring such a condition about. It was the State's business, Keynes argued, to ensure that there should be enough demand in the market to clear all that could be produced at prices adequate to cover costs, including normal profits. This should be accepted as a definite responsibility of the Government —of course, with the addition that there should not be too much demand either, only

just enough to hold things steady *and progressive,* in a condition of dynamic equilibrium deliberately brought about by wise economic planning, not naturally happening when nothing was done to induce it.

Once this idea was accepted, there were plenty of ways of acting on it. Public capital expenditure to fill in the gap left by inadequate private investment, or alternately subsidies to business men designed to induce them to take up capital more freely, or, on a different tack, increased consuming power engendered by tax remissions or, alternatively, by actual subsidies to consumption. Monetary inflation Keynes did not urge; but he did agree that the banking system ought to stand ready to create enough credit to finance the requirements of full employment. He wanted monetary policy to become the servant of productive development, not an independent and capricious power whose dictates industry had to obey. He treated the rate of interest, not as a sacred thing to which production had to accommodate itself, but as an instrument that could be regulated by public action to help bring about a lightening of the dead hand of unearned income. Therewith, he played ducks and drakes with the time-honoured notion that an annually balanced budget—or indeed a balanced budget at all—was a *sine qua non* of economic rationality. A budget deficit, that is, the State paying out more than it received in taxes— might be the very best way to maintain employment and production in face of a threatened recession in demand. Keynes knocked down the shibboleths of economic orthodoxy, row upon row, with a consummate skill that even his bitterest opponents had to admire. Within a few years he transformed traditional economics from a jeremiad into a practical programme for making the capitalist system work.

No: that is not quite fair. Keynes had no devotion to the capitalist system as such. Indeed, the entire dispute about Capitalism and Socialism seemed to him to be mainly beside the point. His remedies would serve to render workable either Capitalism or Socialism, or indeed any other system that was compatible with the State's acceptance of the responsibility for ensuring full employment. He made this sound easy—if only the manipulators of public economic policy could be persuaded to behave in a reasonably intelligent fashion.

This new Keynesian Economics deeply affected the thought of Socialists as well as of "progressives" of all sorts who were not Socialists. Keynes made the planning of employment seem so much more important than anything else, at a time when the thoughts of both politicians and economists had become fixed perforce on the disease of unemployment in both its long-term and its cyclical forms. Hitherto, most Socialists had contended that the disease of unemployment was incurable except by socialisation —that is, by the State taking over industry and employing every available person, and at the same time so distributing purchasing power as to ensure that there would be a demand for all that socialised industry could produce. But now it appeared, if Keynes were right, that full employment could be maintained without socialisation, merely by manipulating the correct levers at the centre, in the money and investment markets. There might be a case for socialising this or that industry on other grounds—to prevent monopolistic restriction, or to improve productive efficiency by rationalisation—but not in order to cure unemployment; for that could be done by other, and much less disturbing, methods.

The only economists who were not deeply affected by this revolution in traditional economic thought were the Marxists, who, having a complete and distinct economic theory of their own that had diverged from orthodox theory a century ago and thereafter gone its own way, regarded Keynesism as merely the latest dodge to save Capitalism from itself by invoking the State as its ally. Nothing, the Marxists continued to assert, could save Capitalism from recurrent crises, all leading up to the final crisis in the course of which it would be submerged in world revolution. Some Marxists, indeed,

went so far as to admit that Keynes' nostrums might prove potent enough to stave off capitalist crisis for some time. Professor Varga, the leading theoretician of the Soviet Union, came near to saying this, and was made to eat his words—though he spat some of them out again in the process.

The Socialist economists who were not full-blooded Marxists were in a different case; for most of them had no belief in the inevitability of "Capitalism's Final Crisis." They had been for a long time past calling on the Government to ease unemployment by "public works policy"—that is, by providing useful jobs for workers for whom profit-seeking Capitalism appeared to have no use. They had been contending on this issue with the orthodox economists who argued either that the effect of State action to provide work would be an equivalent diminution in private investment [1] or that, even if extra jobs could be provided, the result would be to throw the economic system out of balance and to lead on to an inflationary crisis.[2] Keynes' new doctrines came as a powerful reinforcement of what they had been saying, and as a great relief to their minds, because they were now able to argue for State action with the grain of traditional economic theory, and not against it as heretics and pariahs foolish enough to be taken in by economic "quacks." Above all, the socialist economists in academic jobs, who had to spend their days teaching students the things that were needed for passing examinations, were immensely reassured, and set to work happily to teach the new Keynesian economics, with a sense that a bridge between the classical tradition and Socialism had been successfully built.

Indeed, it is hardly too much to say that most of the non-Marxist socialist economists swallowed Keynes whole, and became his most fervent disciples. As one who did not, I, in my capacity as a teacher, passed from one discomfort to another. The things I had been arguing, largely on a basis laid by J. A. Hobson, at the risk of spoiling

[1] e.g. the "Treasury Memorandum" of 1929.
[2] e.g. Professor Hayek's earlier writings.

my pupils' examination chances, suddenly became part of the new orthodoxy; and I found myself trying to brake the enthusiasm of students who expected far too much from them. For I continued to believe that, great as was the advance made by Keynes in the techniques of economic manipulation, his conclusions were partly vitiated by his habit of reasoning in terms of global demand and supply, or at any rate of "capital goods" and "consumers' goods" as global divisions of the total product of industry, instead of breaking up the productive system into much smaller and more differentiated groups of real persons and things.

Thus, when Keynes spoke of maintaining total "investment" at an adequate level, I began at once to think of the actual forms of this investment—machines of different sorts, specialised buildings, ships, new mine-sinkings, farm equipment, and so on. And when Keynes spoke of "full employment" I began at once to think of actual men and women, living in particular places and possessing both particular skills, dexterities and aptitudes, and also family attachments and wills to work more or less hard or efficiently. I do not mean that I found other economists ignoring these real factors; but I did find an undue readiness to believe that they were secondary to the main thing—which was to manipulate global demand for investment and consumption goods by making the right budgetary adjustments and accommodating to these the flows of credit out of the banking system, the rates of interest on borrowed money, and the "public works policy" of the State—which last thus appeared not as a prime mover, but rather as one among a number of budgetary devices for keeping economic activity at a high level. I was sceptical about all this, not as doubting its correctness and usefulness up to a point, but as holding that it left many too many of the real factors in the situation out of account.

For, can the State really, by following the Keynesian prescription, maintain full employment without setting inflationary tendencies to work, unless it is in a position to control, broadly, what is to be produced and when, and what is to be charged for it, and also the broad distribution of purchasing power, as well as its global amount? I do not think it can. I am not suggesting that, in order to achieve *and maintain* full employment without inflation, it is necessary for the State to take charge of the entire economy, to fix all prices, or to regulate the whole distribution of incomes among individuals. But I do believe that, in order to achieve the desired result, the State must be in a position to direct investment into particular branches of production, to control the location of industry in order to bring balanced employment to the workers rather than expect them to migrate in large masses in search of work, and to regulate the course of prices and incomes in such a way as to secure a tolerable correspondence between the flow of consumers' goods and services and the demand for them, and at the same time to keep costs at such a level as to enable exporting industries to hold a satisfactory place in the world market.

But I go further than this. Although it would be theoretically possible for the State to exercise all these powers by "controls," without taking any considerable executive functions into its own hands, I cannot conceive of such an arrangement working in practice, except very ill. Control without executive responsibility or financial accountability for the results of the orders given is an instrument that has its uses, and is indeed indispensable if we are to avoid both an excessive concentration of authority and an undue absence of it; but it is an instrument that has grave disadvantages—not least the irritation it is bound to cause among those who have to carry out the orders and to bear the brunt of what ensues.

Take the case of investment. The State can, do doubt, in theory, channel private investment into the forms of development it thinks best; but in practice, if it relies on "controls," it has to do this mainly by forbidding types of investment which it thinks less desirable, or actually disapproves. Even if the effect is not that of reducing the total volume of investment—as it may well be —it is unlikely to be very satisfactory in securing the right balance among the permitted types of investment. In order to achieve this, the State must itself become an investor, and therewith an owner of capital assets: not necessarily the sole owner, but investor and owner on a considerable scale, not only in a limited group of "public service" industries, but over a wide field, covering potentially every major type of capital development. This is apart from the fact—certainly no less important—that "controls" may be quite ineffective in securing a correct total volume of investment at periods when a stimulus, rather than a deterrent, is called for.

Take again the closely related problem of industrial location. The State, if it tries to secure a right distribution and a right local balance of employment openings merely by control, will be in precisely the same difficulty. In this case it can do something—and is actually doing something—by the development of Industrial Trading Estates and New Towns; but that reinforces my point, for such action involves direct public investment, even if plenty of room is left for private capital to operate within the framework of direct public provision.

Or take price regulation. Here, if anywhere, one would expect the control mechanism to be able to work without direct assumption of responsibility by the State. It is, however, notoriously difficult to fix the right prices except for a narrow range of highly standardised goods, most of which are either crude or semi-manufactured foodstuffs or materials. Control can be most easily extended beyond this field by promoting the production of certain "utility" lines of standard qualities and specifications; but this method cannot be extended very far without beginning to impinge on justifiable variety of output, and therewith on consumers' choice. Beyond these limits the State cannot easily tell what prices are fair unless it is itself engaged in production

and in a position to check the private producers' costs by its own experience, either in publicly owned factories or in establishments in which it has at any rate a part interest in ownership and administration.

Finally, take the case of incomes—for the moment not wages but those paid for managerial, professional, and administrative work. If most industries are privately owned and public employment is confined to a narrow group, there will be a strong tendency for private industry to set the standards of payment for such jobs, and for public employments to have to fall in with the capitalist practice. We have seen this occurring already in the case of the new public boards and corporations.

This matters, not only because it is an essential part of socialist policy to reduce differences of earned, as well as of unearned, income, but also because the example of high earnings in the upper ranges of employment naturally sets up, in any society that is moving towards Socialism, a strong pressure all down the scale for higher incomes, beyond what can be afforded without putting inflationary forces in motion. The spectacle of high top salaries leads to demands for high salaries lower down, and also to demands for high wages, not as a reward for high productivity, but as a claim to higher status and a nearer approach to equality.

It is sometimes argued that this need not happen if a very progressive system of taxation on the higher incomes reduces the real inequality of spending power within reasonable bounds. But this view is psychologically incorrect. Rightly or wrongly, men measure relative status in terms of income before, and not after, direct taxation. It is, moreover, an extraordinary and in the long run indefensible process to begin by distributing much more in earned incomes than the recipients are to be allowed to keep, and then to redress undue inequalities by taking back a higher and higher proportion as the income rises. This is a good enough way of dealing with unearned incomes: its extension to earned incomes is a logical absurdity, save as a purely transitional method.

In effect, then, I am arguing that the Keynesian apparatus for maintaining economic equilibrium at a high level will not work in practice unless the State, through some publicly responsible agency—or rather through many such agencies—owns and conducts a large part of the apparatus of production. This does not mean that it is necessary to nationalise everything—heaven forbid! It does mean that the "public sector" of industry must be large enough to set the tone for the rest, leaving private industry to operate within a framework of public enterprise, rather than the other way around. This "public sector" can be itself highly diversified. It can include, besides nationally owned and unified industries and services, state-owned and partly state-owned enterprises in industries still left largely under other forms of ownership. It can include Co-operative Societies, both of consumers and of producers. It can include locally and regionally organised, as well as nationally unified services. It can also have many diverse forms of internal administration, from the Post Office type and the National Board type to various experiments in "workers' control" and industrial democracy. Public enterprise does not and should not mean uniformity: nor should it mean the elimination of competition except where national unification is clearly necessary on grounds of economic efficiency.

The upshot of the argument is that the Keynesian revolution in economic thought is to be welcomed and accepted by Socialists up to a point, but cannot be taken as a substitute for Socialism, or for a socialist economic theory which goes a long way beyond it. Keynesism is after all, in the last analysis, a very elaborate mechanism for *offsetting* rather than curing certain glaring deficiencies in the working of capitalist society. Keynes did not say that he could do away with the inherent instability of Capitalism, with its tendency to engender alternating booms and slumps, with its speculative aberrations, and with its marked preference for monopolistic restriction. He claimed only that he knew how to prevent these tendencies from doing nearly as much harm as they had done in the past. He did not meet even the purely economic case of the Socialists against the capitalist system—much less their whole case, with its large moral and psychological elements.

Accordingly, though Keynesian economics is a great advance on the *laissez-faire*-based economics that preceded it, this advance in no way makes less necessary the formulation of the quite distinct economic theory appropriate to a socialist society. Socialist economists can build on Keynes to a quite considerable extent; and to a still greater extent they can use Keynes as a stick for beating more reactionary economists over the head. But Keynes was no Socialist; he had no deep-seated faith in democracy to drive him on to formulate an economic theory that would meet the needs of a society committed to working out the implications of the democratic attitude in every aspect of social life, including the economic.

IV. LINDSAY

The Philosophy of the British Labour Government *

The British labour movement, like most things British, has always been empirical and very chary about formulating its assumptions. I think its most fundamental assumption is that it represents a policy which, though it may not be clearly formulated, is, all the same, quite clearly distinct from either capitalism on the one hand or Communism on the other. Most of us who have anything to do with the labour movement accept this assumption and would say that what has been wrong with Europe in the last generation is the prevalent assumption that there is no alternative between capitalism on the one hand and Communism or complete and absolute socialism on the other. The Labour party and the Labour Government maintain again and again that what they tend to call social democracy or British socialism is the movement which will satisfy the aspirations of their own working class and the working class of Europe without falling into the extremes of Communism. They will stress at one and the same time its socialist character and its democratic character. They will deny the very common assumption that democratic socialism is a contradiction in terms. They will assert that socialism, as understood in Britain, is the completion of democracy, and will repudiate the Russian claim that Bolshevism is democratic. The faith of the Labour party shows itself in certain quite simple ways: in its insistence

on constitutional methods, its refutation of totalitarianism, its dislike of Communism and the Communist party just because of Communist disregard of constitutional and democratic procedure and of human good faith. The Labour party is indeed more democratically governed than any other of the British political parties. I do not think anybody could be inside the British labour movement without recognizing it to be one of the most democratic movements in the world. There are times when its leaders must think its elaborate democratic machinery and its continual insistence that nothing be done without consultation of the rank and file a great nuisance; yet it is a nuisance which must be borne because of its worth. The Labour Government very largely depends upon the support of the British organized labour movement. That means, in effect, the trade unions and the cooperative party. Its members have all been trained in trade-union branches or "chapels," in cooperative meetings, or in organizations like the Cooperative Women's Guild. They are ordinary men and women managing their own affairs, being accustomed to trust their leaders but to keep leaders in their place. The Labour Parliamentary party in its democratic convictions is only a reflection of the intensely democratic character of the working-class movement on which it depends.

This is my first point: the assumptions of the British Labour Government are the assumptions of the British working-class movement, and these are primarily demo-

* In F. S. C. Northrop (ed.), *Ideological Differences and World Order* (Yale University Press, 1949). By permission.

cratic assumptions. No doubt the British labour movement sometimes wears a superficial coloring of more doctrinaire beliefs, supplied by its intellectuals, sometimes Marxian and sometimes syndicalist. But I do not think these theories supply more than superficial coloring. The labour movement is permeated with working-class theories and assumptions.

It is important to understand the British working-class movement and where it comes from. It is not quite like anything else I know of, and I do not think there is anything quite like it in America. The Webbs, in their book on *Industrial Democracy,* notice the importance of Nonconformity in the history of trade unionism in the early nineteenth century. Where Nonconformity was strong trade unionism was strong, and where it was weak trade unionism was weak. It was the Nonconformist chapels which supplied democratic experience and the leadership of industrial democracy, whether in trade unionism or in cooperation. The British labour movement inherited from this source its intense democracy, its belief in government by persuasion and consent rather than by force, or, more exactly, its preference for negotiation and discussion and argument rather than compulsion, its idealism and its inclination to pacifism. It inherited also from Nonconformity its experience of the power for leadership inherent in the most apparently ordinary people, its concern with and care of what it calls the "rank and file." Nothing is more astonishing to anyone accustomed to British trade unionism than the apparently dictatorial power of some American trade-union leaders.

What has produced the Labour Government is the gradual conversion of the working-class movement to the view that its ideals could not be attained without labour being in office, and without something which, without making very clear to itself what socialism meant, it called socialism. When it was told by clever Fabians or by students of Karl Marx exactly what socialism did mean, it was often content to accept their definition as long as there was no real prospect of the definition being effectively put into practice. But the movement knew what in fact it wanted, what it was accustomed to, and what it believed in. It had used democratic cooperation for over a century to improve the workingman's standard of life, to give him better conditions. It had found that this process was never completely satisfactory because of the power—in its view the completely undemocratic power—of the employing class, and it therefore worked in hope of a time when it should gain power in a labour government and be able to realize its ideals. The Webbs in their history of early trade unionism explained how powerful in that movement are certain quite simple and crude democratic notions not unfamiliar in America: the belief in an abstract equality, according to which everybody is as good as everybody else, a consequent distrust of skill or expert knowledge and a distrust of government by the clever and able. While there is still a good deal of that kind of egalitarianism in the labour movement, trade unionism, though a democracy, is a disciplined democracy. Long and bitter experience has brought home to the trade-union movement that the members have no power apart from their solidarity, and that therefore when all the democratic processes have been observed and there has been dispute and discussion and final voting for all, then all the members must concur in the result of the vote. If the strike is voted by the rank and file, everyone must come out, for divided they fall. Trade unionism in Britain has managed to hold on to both sides; to the right of every member to vote on the question of striking and the duty of every member to acquiesce in the decision of the majority; and the ordinary unionist has little sympathy with the middle-class complaints about trade-union tyranny. Democracy cannot get results without discipline; discipline there must therefore be, and break-away unions and nonunionists are people who will not play the game and who are looked on with disfavor. In so far as the necessity for collective action after democratic decision is concerned the working-class movement has moved some way from the complete liberty of minorities which its origins once suggested.

To say that the British Labour Government rests primarily on the working-class movement is as much as to say that it is not totalitarian. It would never dream for one moment that it was the business of the state to absorb either the trade unions or the cooperative societies. No one in the British labour movement has the smallest desire to worship the state, to think of it as something of value in itself, to set it over against the individual as a higher or more perfect end. Indeed, British labour looks with intense suspicion on such views, even in the mild form in which modern conservatives sometimes promulgate them. If socialism means a belief in the superiority of the state or the collectivity of the community as a whole over against the individual, the British labour movement is not in that sense socialist at all. It could well take for its motto that famous remark by Colonel Raynborough: "The poorest he that is in England has a life to live as the richest he."

There is no trace in the British working-class movement of the belief in the superiority of the state over the individual, or indeed in the superiority of the state over other forms of association. The state is an instrument to be used for the good life of the ordinary man or woman, and the extent to which it has to be used depends on circumstances. The greatly increasing extent to which the present British Labour Government proposes to use the state comes from the special circumstances of modern industrial society.

Now if we connect the Labour Government with working-class movements and trade unions can we find any positive assumption in the history of British trade unionism persisting from its first early days when it was merely a combination to raise wages? There is a famous chapter in the Webbs' *Industrial Democracy,* published

nearly fifty years ago, which suggests a clue. The chapter is entitled "The National Minimum," and begins:

Within a trade, in the absence of any Common Rule, competition between firms leads, as we have seen, to the adoption of practices by which the whole industry is deteriorated. The enforcement of a common minimum standard throughout the trade not only stops the degradation, but in every way conduces to industrial efficiency. Within a community, too, in the absence of regulation, the competition between trades tends to the creation and persistence in certain occupations of conditions of employment injurious to the nation as a whole. The remedy is to extend the conception of the Common Rule from the trade to the whole community, and by prescribing a National Minimum, absolutely to prevent any industry being carried on under conditions detrimental to the public welfare.

The Webbs are summing up an old direction of trade-union action. They have showed how the unions, at first by collective bargaining and afterward by collective bargaining aided by state enforcement, carried out what they call "the policy of the common rule," which is perhaps better described as a rule of minimum conditions of employment. Trade unions in the nineteenth century had gradually more and more enforced, in their respective trades, minimum conditions of work, hours, and pay. They had been struggling all the time against what the Webbs called parasitism. The employer who pays less than the minimum rate or maintains worse than the minimum conditions undercuts the better employer. Hence the necessity of a uniform and enforced rule. The Webbs have shown through most of those illuminating two volumes how this notion of the common rule explains trade-union attitudes and even trade-union defects. They go on, in the chapter from which this passage is quoted to argue that, just as in any one trade, sweating conditions and low wages are parasitic, so the existence of low-paid sweating trade is parasitic in relation to the whole community. It gets more than its share of the market. The Webbs therefore argue that the logical conclusion of this trade-union action is that a standard minimum should be enforced for all trades in the country. This general idea has been adopted more and more since they wrote. Years ago the state established minimum wages in certain industries. It has interfered by the establishment of trade boards in the sweated industries. Above all, by taking over from the trade unions what people call "the great social services" it has done more and more to provide a minimum standard of economic life for the whole population.

I think there is more behind this policy than the Webbs themselves actually saw. They confined themselves to the economic aspects of the matter. But behind these is the more far-reaching and democratic assumption that society, if it is to have any meaning, must be a common life; that the common life is something which all members of the society must share, and that the conditions necessary to sharing in it must therefore be at the disposal of everybody. This is not in the least to say that you cannot have a real society unless all its members have equal incomes or live in exactly the same way. What is to be insured is the minimum conditions which are necessary for a man or woman to be an active member of a society which is a democratic society and therefore in some true sense a fellowship. No one who has the good fortune to belong to an academic society, perhaps the most democratic kind of society which an industrial society affords, can think that it is essential to its fellowship that everybody should have equal incomes. What is important is that the differences between members' incomes are not great enough to matter; or that those who receive the lowest salaries should yet have enough to enjoy with the others the ordinary forms of social life. One of the things most bitterly felt about the long-continued unemployment from which we suffered in the 'thirties was that the unemployed found themselves sud-

denly cut out of society. They had no clothes in which they could decently go to chapel. They had no odd shillings or sixpences to spare for football matches or for drinks. Someone who understood their conditions very well said they felt like ghosts —there, but not really there; in society, but not of it—no doubt partly because of the low economic level at which they were living but chiefly because they did not and could not share the ordinary work and activities of their fellows. If society is to be a reality it must be a common life. If it is to be a common life people must be able to share experiences and activities. They do not need to have equal incomes to do that, but every one of them needs a certain minimum. The early trade unions tried to maintain that certain minimum inside their own trades. But in the complex industrial society of the twentieth century it has been found that that can no longer be done without the intervention of the state.

Such state action is merely an application of fundamental democratic doctrine to the circumstances. If social conditions were such that families enjoyed the necessary minimum of conditions for fellowship, there would be no need for state action at all, as there might be no need for trade unions. The simple agricultural society of New England where Western democracy began had neither trade unions nor that kind of state action, as it needed neither. But in modern times to maintain, or even begin to approach, the essential conditions of a real democratic society enforcement of minimum conditions by the state is indispensable.

In all this there is nothing startlingly socialistic. It would not be going too far to say that something like this doctrine is accepted by all political parties in England. All political parties are behind social insurance. All political parties are behind some national health scheme. All political parties agree that the state has to do something about unemployment. In these matters the differences between political parties are differences of degree. of what each party may be prepared to sacrifice to attain these social-security ends. The trade unions would say that it is they who for over one hundred years have fought for this principle, gradually established it by their own action when they could so establish it, and gradually converted all political parties to it.

Where then does the socialism of the Labour Government and its schemes of nationalization come into this picture, and did not something happen when the trade unions, long committed to the doctrine of the national minimum, became committed to socialism?

To answer this question we must turn to our social history. More than anything else, what helped to put the Labour Government into power was the country's experience of long-term and large-scale unemployment in the early 'thirties. People used to think that unemployment was the fault of the person who got unemployed. It was never easy to grasp the fact that whether there was unemployment or not did not depend only upon the individual, though it was true that the least capable workmen were dismissed first when there was only a little unemployment. But the large-scale unemployment of the early 'thirties was new. There were places I know of in Cumberland and South Wales where practically the whole village or the whole small town was unemployed. Anybody on the spot could see that these men were the victims of something over which they had no control whatever, something with which neither the individuals nor the trade unions could cope. These men and women were the victims of a mysterious thing called the trade cycle. Modern industry, it became clear, works normally with a reserve of labour with which it meets the fluctuations of demand. When demand is low that reserve of labour becomes a body of unemployed, who are to be taken back into work when the demand recovers. Modern industry, as it developed after the first World War, suffered great fluctuations of demand which had terrible results. More and more people came to feel that the results in human suffering were too high a price to pay for the boasted efficiency of this kind of industrial system. No doubt the system may produce great wealth. The men who are employed have a high standard of wages. Indeed, so much wealth did the system produce that the country could provide a standard of life even for the unemployed which was at least bearable. Nevertheless, the effects of long-term unemployment on those who suffer them proved to be so demoralizing that most of the people in the country were determined that such unemployment should not happen again. The economists turned round and expounded schemes by which full employment could be assured. All parties favored such schemes to some extent. But it was generally thought that the Conservative scheme was too cautious and tentative, too wedded to the conditions of the existing system to meet the desperate disease, and that we must combat more drastically the influence of the trade cycle.

The theory of full employment is simple. Instead of starting with existing demands for goods or services and considering how much labour these need, you start with the existing labour force and consider what standard of life can be produced by means of it, given the necessity for imports and raw materials, and so on and so on. But this operation requires a considerable control over investment in capital goods. After the first World War it was thought employers had increased unemployment by a restrictionist policy. If the state were to prevent the fluctuations of the trade cycle and the large-scale unemployment consequent upon them, it would have to control a considerable proportion of capital goods investment, and it could only do that by nationalizing a sufficient proportion of the industries which use most capital goods. Hence the necessity for at least a measure of nationalization.

But full employment clearly involves something more than that. It means using the available labour of the country on a considered plan: giving priority to this industry and withholding it from that. And thus the British working class, committed to a policy of full employment, are committed to planning, which for many people, though not of course for all, is only another name for socialism. They are also committed, though they do not all realize it, to a considerable amount of direction of labour. The problem they have to face, a problem as yet unsolved, is whether planning is compatible with democratic freedom. Anybody can plan and anybody can prevent unemployment if he can order men and women about from this industry to that and determine their relative scale of wages. That might mean a degree of compulsion entirely incompatible with the ideals and traditions of the British Labour party. The problem the party and the government are now facing is whether this problem, the solution of which entails planning, can be solved by persuasion and argument and exhortation and discussion; in short, on democratic principles.

The difficulties of democratic planning can be seen perhaps most interestingly not in the nationalization of industries but in town and country planning. What happens is this. With no conscious control towns spread in haphazard, unsatisfactory, ugly ways. There is a mass of what is called "ribbon development," or building along the roads because that is cheap, and so on; and it is easy to see how the growth of industry and population and the absence of planning make the countryside hideous. It is a simple matter to say: "Let us do this wisely and properly and with order. Let us have architects and men of vision to plan where new towns ought to be and plan them in the most advisable ways." The country then sets up a Minister of Town and Country Planning and he goes ahead to plan new towns. But although everyone knows that if the minister does not plan, there will be a hideous mess, nobody knows exactly where the mess is going to be and everybody hopes it will be somewhere else than near him. And when people are confronted with the conscious choice and decision of a minister that there shall be a new town here or there, all those whose interests are then adversely affected rise in angry protest. They are far less ready to accept even the fairly sensible decision of a responsible minister than the unplanned result which nobody has willed and for which nobody can be made responsible. Things that work out at random, even when results are hateful, seem to many people easier to bear than are the deliberate decisions which do not please everyone. That is why planning needs a great deal of conscious and strong government if it is to make way against a policy of doing nothing and hoping for the best.

The Liberal party was converted by Lord Beveridge to a policy of full employment and was prepared to go some way toward nationalization to secure that end. But while the Liberals perhaps had a prejudice against nationalization, the Labour party had a prejudice for it. The necessities of full employment are not therefore a complete explanation of why the Labour party was converted to socialism, though they had a great deal to do with it.

Let us consider again the experience of trade unionism. Trade unionism has been called by the Webbs "industrial democracy," but that industrial democracy has not produced democratic industrialism. The nature of capitalism has indeed changed, but it has not changed in the direction of democracy. It was originally and still is, in part, a system where the government of industry is in the hands of the owners of capital. By the development of the limited liability company the owners of capital became largely shareholders, who as shareholders, nominally have the final word in the government of a business. But in practice that final word has come to mean very little. The shareholders ordinarily have only nominal control, and businesses are governed by directors, or what is impersonally called "the management." But if the shareholders have little control, the workers organized in their trade unions have no responsibility at all in the management of the business. Professor Whitehead in his *Leadership in a Free Society* has pointed out that the great defect of modern capitalism is that the employers have never regarded their businesses as social groups or societies, and therefore never thought of them as businesses which required government, the members of which had to be persuaded or led to do things. They have thought of their problems as technical problems, questions of the right arrangement and distribution and factors of production, and they have got their workmen to accept these technical solutions by compelling them through the fear of dismissal. The small, old-fashioned family business in England, where the employer knew all his men and their families, was, in spirit, though not in form, far more democratic than the large-scale industries we described.

Industry has therefore been governed oligarchically, or monarchically, and this arbitrary, irresponsible government by employers has stood over against the democratic organization of the employed—the trade unions. The trade unions have been able to insist on certain conditions of employment. They have enforced collective rules of wages, of hours, of conditions, but they have taken and been allowed no responsibility for management. Trade unions have therefore increasingly felt that a modern industrial society is a house divided against itself, a society politically democratic, industrially oligarchic, and they have come to think more and more that this house divided against itself cannot stand. The oligarchy of employers will make political democracy a sham unless the principles of political democracy are transferred to industry. Till that is done the dualism which marks an industrial society will persist.

It has to be remembered that dualism of some kind is a very old feature of English society. The trade unions are the descendants of the Nonconformist congregations, and the Nonconformists were the democratic half of an English society which was aristocratic and Anglican on the top. In political and social matters that dualism has greatly disappeared, or at any rate its contrasts have been greatly softened, but in industry dualism in the nineteenth century took on a new and more intense form.

Industrialism grew up in America in a society which was already largely democratic, where there was an upward movement in society far greater than there ever was in England, and it was therefore natural for American society to think that what mattered in democracy was that any person, whatever his upbringing and whatever the means of his parents, could rise to the top of society. Democratic equality in America was therefore thought of as the right of anyone to become unequal. It is an equal right to inequality.

But in England the democratic ideal formulated itself not as the right for individuals themselves to become employers but as the demand that this dualism of employers and employed, of managers and managed, of governors and governed, should disappear. As the trade unions in England grew and developed and became accepted and respectable, as they have been doing increasingly for the last three quarters of a century, they gradually ceased to be regarded as an irresponsible opposition. Employers came more and more to regard them as an indispensable element in the whole setup of industry. The government in both World Wars negotiated with trade union leaders. More and more things were done through joint committees of employers and employed until finally in the recent war considerable responsibilities of management were placed upon what were called works committees. Some responsibility for production was placed upon the trade unions themselves.

So the old dualism described above began to lose its sharp edges. It was natural therefore for the trade-union movement to think that the ideal to which it was moving was the position in which this contrast was entirely overcome; when the workers would include management in their work and run industry, and industrial democracy would at last produce democratic industrialism and show itself as full-blown socialism. The simplest, though not to my mind the most logical, way of conceiving this result was thought of as nationalization.

If recent bills for nationalization of such fundamental industries as coal mining or transport are examined, it will be seen that what fundamentally has happened is that the state has taken the place of the shareholders. There is a supreme board of directors which has much the same powers and position as a board of directors in any modern big business. The board will represent the interests of the trade unions as well as the interests of the executives, but the new board will be ultimately responsible to the nation as a whole, and will be represented by the minister in Parliament.

This move toward nationalization shows the theoretical development of British socialism. It starts with an intensely democratic society, the working-class movement, the democratic side of British society. It applies its principle to the establishment of common rules and standards in industrial life. Its members retain their strong and fervent democratic spirit, but as businesses grow bigger and trade unions become national bodies, it becomes more and more difficult to retain the democratic spirit in the vastness of our organizations. Nationalization meets some of the difficulties, and it is easy to see how it seems to be the climax of a long democratic development; but closer examination reveals ambiguities which are not yet resolved.

Nationalization as such is the answer to the objection that in capitalism power is in the hands of directors or managers who are responsible to no one. There is much to be said for the view that the existence of such irresponsible power is fundamentally undemocratic. No doubt in very many cases that power is not used without responsibility. Though they cannot be made so to do, the employers may pay attention to the national needs. Nationalizing the Bank of England, for example, has not fundamentally changed its behavior. Nevertheless, regarded institutionally, the government of industry is undemocratic because of its irresponsibility. Nationalization makes management responsible to the community as a whole. The transport system will have to give account to a democratically elected Parliament. Such schemes, however, do not necessarily alter the internal government of an industry or a business. A sharp distinction between those who manage and those who are managed might perfectly well remain under nationalization, and will remain unless something is done about it. And if the labour movement, or the Labour Government, had begun by asking how the internal government of industry could be made democratic, most likely it would not have started with nationalization. It might have ended with it but not have begun with it. Administration would have begun with asking the far more complex question of how the principle of democracy, the combining of efficiency and popular consent, could be applied to a technical business like industry. One of the most persistent ideals of early trade unionism was that of the "self-governing workshop," in which the distinction between the management and the managed had entirely disappeared. Unfortunately experiments made of setting up such work-shops have always, or nearly always, been inefficient. It is interesting to notice that the Russians started with the same idea—that the worker, the ordinary simple worker at the bottom, should run the business—and they have had, in the interest of efficiency, progressively to give up any such notion. This need not mean that the management of business cannot be made in some sense democratic. On the contrary, there have been in recent years in Britain and in the United States many promising attempts to make businesses in some sense democratic societies. But it does mean that the democratization of industry is not a simple but an infinitely complex problem. Experience has shown that there is no single democratic pattern for the management of business, no one way how best to make a business or a plant into a society of men who cooperate, who are driven not by fear of dismissal but by incentives which work because there are trust and understanding and a sense of common purpose.

What I am concerned to point out is that

making a business in itself democratic is not the same problem as making the management of an industry responsible to the community as a whole. Either of these problems could be solved without solving the other. Now that nationalization is beginning to be tried out in England the distinction between these two problems is becoming apparent, but it has never yet been clearly in the minds of the British labour movement before.

There is one sphere at least where the democratic character of the British labour movement and the present Labour Government must be clear to all, and that sphere is its foreign policy and its attitude to imperialism. There have been no differences in the Labour party in regard to the government's attitude to India or Burma. Indian independence has been one of the greatest achievements of the present Labour Government, and that achievement has been possible because of the Labour party's record in the past and because of the confidence which that record has inspired in all parties in India and Burma. Indeed, the difficulty with the Labour Government has been to reconcile its uncompromising idealism with the exigencies of international politics. The party acquiesced in conscription with difficulty and with bad grace. It dislikes the compromises with the ideal solution which practical politics have forced upon it. The World War and Hitler's obvious aggression did much to weaken the persistent pacifism of quite strong elements in the Labour party. The party has in regard to foreign politics the virtues and the weaknesses of democratic idealism, the same virtues and weaknesses which are obvious in American democracy. No one can study the record of the British Labour party in foreign politics without seeing its persistent determination to believe the best of other people, its sometimes pathetic belief that democratic principles, if applied unflinchingly to any people, will solve all problems. Such attitudes have their virtues, as the achievement of Indian independence shows, but they are apt also to produce a woolliness of thought and a

failure to recognize obvious hard facts. Indeed, no party whose philosophy was founded on worship of "the state" and belief in the supreme value of the state and its power could possibly behave in foreign politics as the British Labour party does. The contrast between British Labour democracy and Russian Communism is perhaps nowhere better illustrated than in the Russians' determination to think ill of all foreigners and all foreign nations.

Is there then nothing at all in the view that socialism and democracy are incompatible? Does an indefinite increase in using the powers of the state really raise no difficulties for democracy? Is there nothing in the old connection between democracy and laissez-faire individualism?

I can imagine anyone who has followed the argument of this article saying something like this: This is all very well but it does not somehow work out like that in practice. Whatever may be the underlying motive, in order to carry out these vast schemes of nationalization there has to be set up a great bureaucratic organization whose powers have to be put in the hands not of the people but of officials, and the ordinary man and woman is as powerless in the face of officialdom as he was in the past in the face of his employers.

Socialism may be in theory the final outcome of democratic principles but in practice it is something very different. This objection may be enforced by pointing out that few Western observers would think Russian Communism democratic. Russian Communism claims to be even more democratic than any Western democracy. We should regard this as a complete delusion. Is it possible that British democratic socialism is not also deluded in supposing that it can achieve its ends and yet remain democratic? Plato long ago said of democracy that its insistence on equality had the paradoxical effect of producing tyranny. Does democratic socialism by insisting on industrial democracy produce its opposite in the same paradoxical way?

Why are we forced into this paradox? By

reason of the fallacy which explains many puzzles of democracy—the fallacy that size does not make any difference in principle to the working out of democratic ideals. The original ideal experience behind democracy is the working experience of the small democratic community. Once it is accepted that all are to count, that all equally are to have a voice, that no one has a right to command others, then in the small community all manner of blessed results follow: the community—that is, all the members of it—rule; the distinction between "they" and "we" disappears, as does the distinction between rulers and ruled. "We" are the community; "we" obviously govern in the communal meeting; "we" make decisions about "our" common property. There are some things which "we" the community have in common; other things "we," the single separate selves who make up the community, own separately. In the tiny community, once the distinction between the ruler and the ruled is denied in theory, it can be negated in practice. Democrats have tended to think that this blessed state of affairs, which they have known and enjoyed in the small community, will follow, if the same recipes are used, in any community whatever its size and therefore in the state. But of course this does not happen. Contrivance, thought, constitutional designs, well-planned democratic machinery can do a great deal to reproduce on a large scale the essential features of small-scale democracy. But to think that the practices of a tiny democracy can be realized quite simply in a large-scale democracy is to court disaster. The democratic experience of the tiny community depends on discussion between people who know each other personally and in which all can take a real part. As the community grows in size this ideal experience quickly becomes impossible. A public meeting of all is impossible and a discussion by all even more impossible. Authority has to be delegated. Individuals have to be allowed to do things "in the name of the community." Persons have to be elected to "represent" the community;

their decisions have to be "deemed" to be the decisions of the community, and so on and so on.

The modern democratic state, with a population of many millions, has only the remotest resemblance to its original prototype. If it tries to retain some features of the original experience of the small community, it does so only by leaving others out. It is roughly true that American and English democracy thought that discussion was the essential experience and that their democracy is like primitive democracy in that it is government by discussion; but it is not like it in much else. Discussion *for* us is not the same as discussion *by* us.

Rousseau condemned representative government as a departure from the fundamental simplicity of the public meeting. He approved of the plebiscite or the referendum because it retained the right of each and every member of the community to vote. But that meant dropping the discussion; and a plebiscite has to be arranged by an authoritative person, its questions drawn up, its timing settled by authority; so that it too can easily become an instrument of tyranny. Yet the belief in the referendum as an essentially democratic procedure outlived Napoleon III's demonstration that it need be nothing of the kind and, for all I know, may have outlived Hitler's more convincing demonstrations to the same effect.

Democrats still often speak of successful modern democracy in the language of its simple prototype. They speak of "the voice of the people" as though that could be as simply discovered in their large states as "the sense of the meeting"; of "government by consent" as though the distinction between "we" and "they" could be abolished as completely in a wide-flung nation as it can be in a tiny society; of the people choosing their government as though they selected with a discerning eye the men most fitted to govern them instead of choosing, usually, between candidates selected by the party organizations.

But though the language of modern democrats is often mythical, its use reminds them that the object of their complex modern constitutional machinery is to enable them to capture at least something of the spirit of democracy's original prototype. Myths are useful so long as we remember that they are myths. We are coming to realize that if we are to make large-scale democracy even a tolerable, let alone a good form of government, the ordinary citizen must not act only on those democratic myths but must be realistic about democratic machinery, and think seriously and continually to prevent perversions.

Democratic socialism is still largely in the utopian or myth stage of democracy. It starts, as did early political democracy, in reaction against the denial of democratic equality. Early political democracy was up against the claim of some to rule others as of right, and tended to think that a vigorous repudiation of such antidemocratic claims would be enough to bring real democracy into being. Social democracy starts with the claim of traditional capitalism that the owners of capital may organize and command men in the processes of production. Now that production has got to the stage of complexity in which the organization and discipline, in fact the government of men, has become an essential element in production, the social democrat demands that the government of industry ought to be, like any other government, democratic. So long as it is realized that there is no single pattern of democracy, and that making what government there is in industry democratic is not a charm but a problem, this demand for general social democratic principle seems to me as irresistible as the original claim of political democracy. Only those who are willfully blind can deny the facts of economic power. When there exists power of men over other men, there are political problems, and the thorough-going democrat will insist that the solution of these problems of power must be in principle democratic. The early British socialists found that their solution in what they called "the self-governing workshop" was as democratic and as inadequate to modern conditions as a

modern New England town meeting. Orthodox socialism was as much occupied with the wrongness of the rule of the owner of the means of production as early American political democracy was with the wrongness of the rule of kings.

The belief that once the democratic principle is proclaimed and the autocratic repudiated, industrial democracy will follow by itself is of course seen in its crudest form in Russia. Men who have learned from Marx that economic power counts for far more than political power, and have themselves known nothing about political democracy and had no experience of it, find it easy to believe that once the great and decisive step is taken, once the undemocratic authority of private ownership has gone and public ownership has taken its place, the result is a democracy more perfect than ever existed before. The facts of the NKVD, the dictatorship of Stalin, the autocratic organization of the Communist party—all these are nothing compared with the fact that private economic power has given place to public economic power. To the outsider the social divisions of modern Russia are glaringly evident. But Russia claims to be a classless society because its social divisions are not based on private property in the means of production. Since that old and fatal principle of social division has been abolished, other evils do not matter.

Though it seems fantastic to us in the West to call modern Russia democratic, Russia is now a society in which one great source of undemocratic power has been abolished. That other much worse undemocratic forces are still operating there does not obliterate that fact. If that illuminating and convincing book by Mr. Edward Crankshaw, *Russia and the Russians,* is to be trusted, the ordinary Russian feels that Russia belongs to him, that the achievements of the Five-year Plan and elaborate organization are somehow *his* achievements. The myth, for it is a myth, works to some extent because it has some reality in it. There is bound to be an awakening some day as to how much unreality there is also, as there was an awakening in America to the fallacies of the simple political democratic faith; but in the meantime the myth works, to some extent at least. Meanwhile the British labour movement can learn the danger as well as the achievement of too simple solutions.

The best British statement of what I call the social democratic myth of the simplicity of the problem can be read in the writings of Sir Richard Acland, the founder of the ephemeral but significant Common Wealth party. The democratic idealism of his writings will be apparent to all who read them. They are inspired by it in every sentence. He is determined to overcome the fatal undemocratic distinction between "we" and "they." Sir Richard believes that public ownership will do the trick. He seems to believe that public ownership and such measures as nationalization will enable "us" to own and manage as "we" think best for "our" mutual advantage as truly as the inhabitants of a small Swiss commune may own their forest or pastures.

The leaders of the British Labour party are far too old hands in democratic practice both in trade unions and in national politics to hold a simple faith of this kind. They know what democracy is in practice; they are thoroughly familiar with and de-

voted to democratic procedure. They have far too much democratic common sense to be taken in by the simple mechanical Russian myth. They know there is no single pattern of democratic procedure. Their trade unions have taught them that. The rank and file of the party may perhaps dream the myth that nationalization will of itself make industry democratic, but the Labour Government knows that at best it is only a beginning. The partnership in the Labour party of the cooperative movement is a symbol of their belief that there are other ways than nationalization of making industry democratic. The Labour Government is no doubt continually reproached by its opponents for being doctrinaire. Perhaps some of them are doctrinaires, and yet their program is the program of men who believe in a principle—the application of democracy to industrial production—but who are empiricists in practice and who know that much has to be done, many experiments made, to achieve what they mean by democratic socialism. All successful democratic government is a compromise between public control and efficiency; democratic socialism will be a compromise between public control, efficiency, and private initiative. It will take effort and thought to work it out, and of that the Labour Government must by now be well aware.

CHAPTER 25

THE
WELFARE STATE

T HE very nature of the state implies the concept of welfare. Whatever the form or purpose of the state—be it democratic or totalitarian, republican or monarchical, communist or fascist, capitalist or collectivist—there must be a sufficiently strong feeling throughout the community that its welfare is effectively served by the instrumentalities of government. Even in the era of laissez faire, the state performed more functions of welfare than dogmatic theorists of laissez faire would have liked to admit. Adam Smith, the founder of modern economic science, expressed in his *The Wealth of Nations* (1776) a philosophy which was strongly laissez faire, but not a doctrinaire caricature of laissez faire such as has been perpetrated by many self-styled disciples and followers of Adam Smith in the nineteenth and twentieth centuries. Thus, Smith was always aware that the amassing of wealth was by no means the sole, or main, purpose of human existence. In particular, his famous dictum that *de-fense comes before opulence* is a standing reminder that the first duty of the state is to preserve the liberty of the people against foreign aggression and en-slavement, even if such defense entails heavy financial sacrifice. Secondly, Smith also recognized the duty of the state to protect every member of society against the injustice or oppression of every other member of it. There can be no true welfare in a community that is deprived of law and justice based on fairness and equity, and it is the duty of the state to provide legal security and im-partiality. Thirdly (and perhaps most importantly from the viewpoint of the modern theory of the welfare state), Smith argued that the state has also the duty to erect and maintain public works and public institutions which would be beneficial to society at large, but which no individual, or small number of individuals, would erect or maintain if motivated by the expectation of profit. In addition to being responsible for such basic utilities as roads, harbors, and canals, the state should also properly concern itself, according to Adam Smith, with popular education and some aspects of public health (such as protection against the spreading of epidemics). Finally, while generally opposed to governmental tampering with the price mechanism of the market, Smith nevertheless realized that there were situations in which human needs had precedence over economic laws and interests; for example, if the supply of bread were dominated by a monopoly, the state should be entitled, Smith held, to regulate the price of bread in order to protect the people against unfair exploitation.

In a larger sense, the concept of welfare was implied, not only in this or that specific argument made by the founders of modern economics with their emphasis on laissez faire, but in their outlook as a whole. The classical economists of the eighteenth and early nineteenth centuries sought to put economic analysis and economic policy on a firm basis of rationalism, freed from the irrational burdens of oppressive political control, the paralysis of immemorial custom, and the conflicts of divergent theological systems. The search for an independent science of economics partook of the generally prevailing desire to expand the frontiers of human knowledge on all fronts, but it was also motivated by the ethical consideration that social and economic welfare would thereby be greatly served.

The key conception linking economic analysis with economic policy was that of *utility*, according to which no policy or institution can claim absolute validity for all time and space, but must be judged by its ultimate effects on human happiness. For a long time, the main spokesmen of classical economics assumed, or at least hoped, that human happiness would best be attained by the application of the principles of laissez faire. But the great founders of classical economics, from Adam Smith to John Stuart Mill, did not allow their hopes to become rigid intellectual dogmas. In particular, both Jeremy Bentham and, even more forcefully, John Stuart Mill underwent a remarkable change of outlook. Their early attachment to a relatively extreme position of laissez faire was gradually modified by the impact of nineteenth-century industrialism on the daily lives of the people, and both Bentham and Mill finally adopted a social and political philosophy very closely akin to that of the twentieth-century welfare state. Yet it is important to recall that, in moving away from laissez faire to a more positive conception of the role of the state, Bentham and Mill kept the objective of human happiness clearly in mind, while changing the nature of the means to be employed.

The forces behind the movement of classical western liberalism from laissez faire to the welfare state were economic, political, and psychological. In the eighteenth, or early nineteenth, century, the predominant economic unit in agriculture, commerce, and business was relatively small—frequently operated, managed, and owned by one family. What man then wanted was to be liberated from the ignorance and interference of government dictation; left alone, he felt he could do better economically as well as satisfy his spiritual need for independence and selfhood. The spiritual desire for economic independence thus coincided with the technological reality of an economy in which the most efficient operating unit was relatively small in size. Behind the reasoning of laissez faire in the eighteenth century stood the reality of a society made up largely of independent farmers, artisans, and merchants.

But as industry progressed, culminating in the physical symbol of the factory and in the legal symbol of the business corporation, an increasingly larger proportion of the population became economically dependent, working in mines, factories, offices, and farms of hitherto unknown dimensions. Even many of those who remained nominally independent—the small shopkeeper or small farmer—gradually found themselves dependent on the large enterprises in industry, banking, and insurance. Vast impersonal forces of business cycles, private investment decisions, and governmental fiscal policies determined whether millions of men and women would have jobs or be subjected to the economic misery and spiritual degradation of unemployment, and these forces also determined what their incomes and salaries would be. The helplessness of the individual reached its climax when unforeseen disasters of illness or death hit him or his family. Since private charity was unable to meet such disaster situations, in periods of depression to be found in millions of homes at one and the same time, the state was the one instrumentality left which could help the individual when all the other resources of family and local community proved insufficient. In this sense, the acceptance of the welfare state is a recognition of the technological and *economic* fact that in the economy of the twentieth century most people are wage and salary earners, that is, economically dependent. Seen in the light of economic development, the purpose of the welfare state (as of other institutions, such as labor unions) is to lessen the harmful effects of economic dependence and helplessness which necessarily threaten the individual in the economy of today.

The second driving force behind the evolution of the welfare state is *political.* As more and more people acquired the right to vote, culminating in universal suffrage in most western countries in the twentieth century, the voters discovered that the right to vote entailed not only the political power to choose one's representatives in Parliament or Congress but also vast social and economic powers. In the first stages of widening suffrage, the people were still accustomed to elect their "betters" to public office, and to rely on their choices' guidance and thinking. But as time went on, the masses of the people learned that the vote was a powerful political instrument in improving the traditional living conditions of want and poverty. Whoever promised more voters increased social and economic benefits stood a better chance of election to public office, and whoever lived up to such promises stood an even better chance of re-election. This phenomenon is the fundamental reason behind the growing similarity between the two major parties in Britain and the United States. The Conservative Party in Britain and the Republican Party in the United States, like the Laborites and the Democrats, have increasingly committed themselves to the philosophy and practice of the welfare state; there are many and complex reasons why both parties have done so, but one principal reason is surely the realization that hostility or indifference to a broad program of social and economic security and welfare set up a well-nigh insuperable barrier to political success.

The third force behind the growth of the welfare state is *psychological*. Throughout the whole world—in advanced as well as in underdeveloped countries—people are no longer willing to accept misery and want as unchangeable ordainments of fate and predestination. The decline of the influence of religion has meant that the promise of a better life in the beyond no longer has the same hold on man's imagination as in the past, and even where religious belief is still strong, the feeling has grown that man has a right to the good life here and now, quite independently of the happiness of the soul in the hereafter. In Europe, the desire for a better life, based on economic security and social justice, has been politically expressed, for over a century now, in various movements of social reform, whether socialist or nonsocialist; in the United States, too, protest against economic insecurity and social inequity has found political expression in periodic popular movements from Andrew Jackson's Democracy to the present. The twentieth century, in particular, saw the rise of Theodore Roosevelt's Square Deal, Woodrow Wilson's New Freedom, Franklin D. Roosevelt's New Deal, and Harry S. Truman's Fair Deal. The Republican victory in 1952, instead of leading to a crusade against the New Deal, inaugurated Dwight D. Eisenhower's administration aiming at a middle-of-the-road progressive conservatism. While that philosophy did not go far enough in the opinion of more extreme social reformers, it went much too far in the eyes of the more traditionalist elements in the Republican Party, for whom the Eisenhower outlook was but a "me-too" slightly watered-down version of the New Deal welfare state.

In the underdeveloped countries, the psychological force behind the movements for national independence is partly political in nature, aiming at national independence; but the stirrings in the backward portions of the world are also motivated by the desire for a better material life, for rapid industrialization, and for higher standards of living. Moreover, the world-wide demand for welfare state policies is not based on pure sentiment and psychological force: for the first time in human history, it seems that man has finally arrived at a stage where he has acquired enough knowledge and mastery of nature and its resources to banish harsh poverty from the face of the earth. Before the Industrial Revolution, poverty seemed to be ordained by an inexorable fate, which man might try to propitiate, but which he could not alter. Today, men in advanced as well as in underdeveloped areas increasingly feel that poverty results, not from unchangeable decrees of nature, but from changeable institutions of society.

The main principles of the welfare state are relatively simple: first, the recognition that every member of the community is entitled, solely because he is a human being, to a minimum *standard of living*. Second, the welfare state is committed to a policy of *economic stability and progress,* seeking to eliminate the cycles of violent booms and busts in the economy by public policies whenever private enterprise is unable to prevent by itself the threat of economic instability or decline. Third, the welfare state is committed to *full employment* as one of the top priorities of public policy. The Great Depression of the nineteen thirties showed not only the economic ravages of unemployment, but also the human degradation inflicted upon those who, though able and anxious to work, cannot find jobs for reasons over which they have no control. Adherents of the welfare state believe that free enterprise can be preserved and strengthened by full employment policies without going to the extreme of nationalization. Taxation properly adjusted to periods of prosperity and depression, interest rates determined by governmental decisions according to current and prospective economic needs and conditions, fiscal policies designed to redistribute purchasing power in harmony with the best interests of the nation, investment incentives to private business in times of slack, public works for direct unemployment relief, government credits to builders or buyers of homes —these are but a few of the measures the government can adopt in stabilizing the economy without changing its foundations.

In the field of social security, protection against want, sickness, and old age is not only demanded by humanitarian considerations but can also be justified on economic grounds, since a minimum standard of living guaranteed by social security provides people with a minimum of purchasing power which is indispensable to the operation of industry in prosperity and depression. Collective bargaining between labor and management is another basic contribution toward a more stable and prosperous economy, because higher wages—provided they are based on higher productivity and not on organized extortion—create a bigger market for the products of industry and agriculture. Similarly, an active support program for agriculture, guaranteeing the farmer minimum prices for his products, is of benefit not only to the farmer himself but also to the worker and industrialist, since a prosperous industry depends upon a prosperous agriculture.

In the United States, the Great Depression, starting with the crash on Wall Street in October, 1929, and reaching its peak in 1932, undermined faith in the orthodox philosophy of laissez faire, according to which the disequilibrium of the market would eventually be restored to a new equilibrium without any interference from the outside. When the American economy was shattered to the extent that one out of every four employable persons was without a job, that the farmer could not make a living by selling his produce at reasonable prices, and that more and more businesses went bankrupt or were unable to pay American wages to their employees or earn profits for their shareholders, something had to be done. The New Deal, starting with the first term of President Franklin D. Roosevelt in 1933, was not so much a set of premeditated philosophical principles to be superimposed upon the American people as a series of emergency measures in response to urgent national problems.

The concept of community planning for welfare is not new on the American continent, and in the United States in particular. It may even be argued that the idea of the good life for all was first born in modern history in America, when the settlers came over here from England and the European continent from the seventeenth century on. At first, the vision of the good life was essentially religious and spiritual, the settlers seeking to found a new commonwealth in which everybody could start a new life free from the religious and intellectual dictation and oppression of the Old World. The settlers quickly discovered that the American continent harbored vast resources—unimaginably large by European standards—and the vision of the good life for all began to be transferred from the spiritual to the material plane. Immigrants from all over the world incessantly poured into the United States, in quest of both more human dignity regardless of social or national origin and of a more abundant material existence, freed from the insecurities and scarcities of their former homelands. The frontier was, for a long time, the symbol of abundance for every newcomer in America; but even when the agricultural frontier closed at the end of the nineteenth century, Americans found that the Industrial Revolution, based on immense untapped resources and high technological skill, constantly created new horizons, new frontiers, with an even more generous promise for the good life than the agricultural frontier had ever been able to offer.

Moreover, the idea of public planning for the welfare of the community was in America at all times more than a vague psychological sentiment. The Constitution itself has been called by some the first major act of national planning in the United States, providing not only for the establishment of free, popular government, but also concerning itself with commerce, tariffs, currency, and other economic issues. Very early in the Republic, Alexander Hamilton (not given to any radical leanings) proposed in his *Report on Manufactures* (1791) methods by which the growth of American industry might boat be helped. Shortly thereafter, Jefferson and Jackson —to mention but two in a long list of great American statesmen—provided new ideas and policies in adjusting the growing American economy to the growing American nation. In the field of land policy, public planning accomplished two major objectives: first, the homestead policy of the eighteen sixties, sharply diverting from the older European systems of primogeniture and entail, was designed to ensure an independent farming class in the United States, able to stand on its own feet, and able to meet the responsibilities of citizenship and government. Secondly, the land grant policy in connection with education gave the United States the most democratic, and most advanced, system of higher education in the world.

The Industrial Revolution, spreading with intensified force after the Civil War, raised new problems which were met by positive acts of public policy, although verbal incantations of laissez faire often continued side by side with unabated force. The establishment of the Interstate Commerce Commission, the Federal Trade Commission, and other government agencies from the late eighties on was aimed at regulating business in the public interest. The issue of monopoly (whether in "natural monopolies" such as public utilities or in artificial monopolies of other industries where competition is possible and desirable) and the related issue of bigness increasingly dominated the American political scene, and there were many movements of protest outside the traditional two-party system, from the Populists to the Progressives under "Old Bob" La Follette, which periodically expressed concern lest economic forces get out of hand. Seen therefore in the light of broad historical perspective, the New Deal of the nineteen thirties was but one phase of the reformist tendency in American life, relatively silent and ineffectual in one period but articulate and powerful in another. Compared with the immediately preceding decade of the

Coolidge-Hoover era of relative laissez faire, the New Deal seemed novel, radical, and to some even revolutionary. Compared with the longer background of Theodore Roosevelt's trust-busting, or of Woodrow Wilson's New Freedom, the New Deal seemed much more tame and traditional.

Because the New Deal with its emphasis on the welfare state developed pragmatically in response to immediate needs and emergencies, there is no theoretical Bible of the welfare state, and not even a Karl Marx who can expound its doctrine with universally accepted authority. Yet any student of the welfare state, particularly as it has developed in the United States, will always want to know what President Franklin D. Roosevelt, the main architect of the New Deal, has thought about it. Roosevelt (1882–1945) developed in conflict with his background, upbringing, and immediate social environment. As early as 1912 he supported Woodrow Wilson against his distant cousin, Theodore Roosevelt, and from that time on he was deeply immersed in government and public affairs. From 1928 to 1932 he served as Governor of the State of New York, and the experience of the depression in the Empire State, the first industrial state in the nation, made a deep impact on him. Selected as the presidential candidate by the Democratic Party in 1932, the depth of the depression, Roosevelt was able to carry forty-two states against six won by the Republicans. During the election campaign, Roosevelt attempted to state his philosophy before many audiences throughout the country. On September 23, 1932, he appeared before the Commonwealth Club of San Francisco, a group of distinguished business and professional men, and before them he expounded what is often considered the best systematic statement of his political creed. Roosevelt starts out with the main premise of a liberal, democratic philosophy that government and the economy are to serve man, and not vice versa. He invokes the name of Jefferson in going back to the beginnings of the American nation. Yet in the early part of American history, social conflict was not severe enough to call for too much governmental intervention, because the rich were not too rich, and the poor, not too poor. All this was changed by the coming of the Industrial Revolution in the middle of the nineteenth century.

Unlike social reformers in other lands, Roosevelt did not entertain romantic ideas about the idyllic life prior to the coming of the machine and the devastating effects of the machine. More than any other country in the world, the United States fully accepted, and rightly (Roosevelt argues), the bitter with the sweet. Yet even in the first dynamic phase of American industrial expansion, the role of the government was by no means that of a passive bystander. The growth of the railroads and merchant marine was greatly helped by government assistance, and industry sought, and received, protective tariffs against foreign competition. Even in the heyday of laissez faire, theory did not always square with practice, and each group sought government aid for its own special situation, while still insisting on laissez faire for the others: "Each group has sought protection from the government for its own special interests, without realizing that the function of government must be to favor no small group at the expense of its duty to protect the rights of personal freedom and of private property of all its citizens." With the closing of the frontier at the end of the nineteenth century and the growth of industrial and financial power, the whole problem of opportunity in America arose anew, leading to a virtual stoppage of immigration from foreign countries; and even in the United States itself, Roosevelt says in 1932, "we are now providing a drab living for our own people."

Like Theodore Roosevelt and Woodrow Wilson before him, Roosevelt was particularly perturbed by the concentration of economic power in a few big corporations, and the squeezing out of the little man from business and industry. About six hundred corporations controlled two thirds of American industry, and about ten million small business men divided the remaining third. This imbalance in the American economy, Roosevelt says, "calls for a re-appraisal of values." Important as the exploitation of natural resources is, it is even more imperative to adjust consumption to production, and, above all, to distribute "wealth and products more equitably." Just as strong government has to be tamed and subjected to the national welfare by subjecting it to constitutional procedures, the big corporation, too, must be brought under some sort of constitutional order, reconciling its private interests with those of the whole community. What is needed is "the development of an economic declaration of rights, an economic constitutional order," a task which must be solved by both government and business. Every man has a right not only to life, but also "to make a comfortable living." He may decline to use that right "by sloth or crime." But both government and industry must see to it that everybody be given an opportunity to make a decent living for himself and his family. However, Roosevelt holds that *government should regulate economic activities only as a last resort*, to be undertaken only when private initiative has failed. The main function of government is, not so much to do things that individuals themselves should do, but to maintain a balance, "within which every individual may have a place if he will take it." Finally, Roosevelt expresses his strong faith in the success of American enterprise, optimistic as his faith seemed in the dark days of poverty and depression, because, as he puts it, "failure is not an American habit." Shortly after the address before the Commonwealth Club, Roosevelt was elected President, and in his First Inaugural Address on March 4, 1933, he reiterated his faith in the boundless opportunities of America by coining the since famous phrase that "the only thing we have to fear is fear itself."

Much of the Democratic election campaign of 1932 was directed against President Hoover, under whose administration (1929–1933) the Great Depression started in 1929 and reached its peak in 1932. President Hoover (1874—) was subjected to much attack and not infrequent vituperation and even ridicule by his political opponents, yet he never wavered in his belief that the New Deal welfare state was a dangerous deviation from the American tradition of liberty. Hoover is particularly concerned about the growth of centralized government and a vast bureaucracy administering it. Speaking at Stanford University at a reception in honor of his seventy-fifth birthday (August 10, 1949), Hoover points to the enormous expansion of federal expenditures, yet at the same time reveals the hard fact that about three quarters of such expenditures are related to obligations from former wars and to present national defense. Since the Korean War (1950–1953), government expenditures have risen even more, and the proportion of the expenditures connected with warfare, past, present, or future, has also risen. Moreover, an increasingly larger portion of the population is becoming dependent, directly or indirectly, upon the government, a fact which, according to Hoover, raises serious issues with respect to the whole issue of the relationship of the individual and his government in a free society. The real threat to American freedom is not presented by the few hundred thousand communists in America, but by their fellow travellers and sympathizers, who "are engineering a compromise between free men and these European infections." While most Americans are opposed to collectivism, Hoover feels that high government spending and high taxes are accomplishing the slow collectivization of the American economy: "We have not had a great socialization of property, but we are on the last miles to collectivism through governmental spending of the savings of the people." The concept of the welfare state is thus defined by Hoover as "a disguise for a collectivist state by the route of spending," and like Roosevelt he invokes Jefferson for a conception of individualism, drawing quite different conclusions from Jefferson's views than Roosevelt did in his defense of the welfare state. Individual independence, initiative, and freedom must not be bartered, Hoover concludes, for "a mess of collectivism," and he blames pressure groups and accommodating politicians for much of the trouble caused by the growth of centralized government.

Opposition to the welfare state is also voiced by Roscoe Pound (1870–), one of the most influential jurists of the twentieth century. Teaching law at Harvard from 1910 to 1947, Pound was one of the founders of the "sociological school" in law and jurisprudence, which had a humanizing impact on the theory and practice of both law and government in the United States. In his earlier years, Pound's ideas generally stimulated, and followed, a more liberal and reformist direction; in his later years, particularly as he witnessed the actual operation of the welfare state, he became more conservative. As a student of the Common Law and of legal philosophy, Pound's concern with the welfare state (or "service state," as he prefers to call it) is naturally focused on the possible effects of the ideas and practices of the welfare state on constitutional government as conceived and developed in the American tradition.

Pound concedes that in the complex industrial society of today the state cannot confine its scope of activity to maintaining law and order, but that it must also do many things which the public demands and which private enterprise is unable to do. However, what Pound opposes is, not that the state perform *many* public services without upsetting the traditional legal, political, economic, and social order, but the concept that *all* public services "must and can only be performed by the government—that politically organized society and that alone is to be looked to for everything, and that there is no limit to the services to humanity which it can perform." The latter scheme presupposes "supermen administrators" or an "all-wise majority" omnipotent and omniscient in the whole domain of human welfare. By necessity, Pound argues, such a "superservice state" must develop a vast bureaucracy, and ultimately it may lead to a "totalitarian state," with Marxian communism and political absolutism in its pedigree. Pound deprecates the tendency in the welfare state of developing a new concept of freedom as meaning primarily freedom from want and fear, rather than freedom of self-assertion and self-determination. This corrosion of the traditional concept of liberty by the welfare state is beginning to undermine the American conception of a bill of rights, particularly since the fear of oppression by government is gradually being replaced by a sense of dependence on a benevolent paternalistic state. Moreover, Pound feels that the welfare state is promising too much, and "promissory bills of rights that create expectations of the politically and economically unachievable and weaken faith in constitutions are a step toward the totalitarian state."

The economic aspects of the welfare state are stressed by A. C. Pigou (1877—), next to J. M. Keynes probably the outstanding British economist of the twentieth century. His massive treatise *Economics of Welfare* (1920) is one of the major works of modern economic science, and he has dealt with the problems of economic theory and policy in many writings. In *Socialism versus Capitalism* (1937) Pigou dealt with the economic merits of the problem, leaving the issues of ethical values and political aims largely outside the scope of his discussion. In "Some Aspects of the Welfare State" (1954) Pigou returns to an issue which has increasingly occupied him in his later years. As an economist, Pigou is primarily concerned with economic welfare, which he defines as satisfactions and dissatisfactions derived from economic circumstances, "depending, for a community, partly on the size of its real income, partly on the way in which this was allocated among individuals, and partly on the way in which it was distributed through time." The objective of economic welfare for the people distinguishes the welfare state from the state for which glory, military power, or racial superiority are paramount. However, Pigou rightly warns against the misconception that the welfare state is necessarily democratic, because a police state, too, may aim (among other things, at least) at the economic welfare of the people, although it may use spies and terror in promoting its ends. This often overlooked fact—that the welfare state is not a monopoly of, or much less identical with, the democratic state—helps to explain why the modern fascist regime (as in Nazi Germany or Peronist Argentina) had considerable support among the poorer classes.

Pigou analyzes the operation of the welfare state in the economic field, not as a general problem that can be answered with a flat yes or no, but as a series of specific situations that have to be tackled individually. He starts out with the area of widest agreement: collective needs such as armed forces, police, the judiciary, the machinery of government, and public buildings obviously have to be provided, or at least paid for, by the state. When it comes to the satisfaction of individual needs, the individual person generally ought to know best what he wants and how to get it. Yet even here there are frequent cases when the individual has to be protected against fraud and misrepresentation, as in the advertising (which may be false) of drugs and medicines (which may be harmful). Moreover, this regulatory function of the state need not always be negative, but may also encourage the positive, as in the case of the state supplying school children with free milk and lunches, or selling these items below cost. The case of the monopoly is another instance in which the individual consumer is helpless unless he can mobilize the authority of the state in protecting himself against monopolistic exploitation, or against artificial curtailment of production; the latter may mean higher prices to the consumer, but it may even more seriously affect the national interest in peace and war by deliberately keeping down the productive strength of the nation in the interest of the monopoly.

Concerning the function of the welfare state in redistributing wealth by transferring property from the wealthy to the poor, Pigou notes a very profound change of social thinking in the last century. Whereas at one time being poor was one's fault, if not one's crime, today "other people's poverty is no longer a crime; that is now the fate of other people's wealth!" This view is probably more prevalent in Britain than in the United States, although the first half of Pigou's statement is probably true in most industrial societies today. With regard to the transfer of wealth from the rich to the poor, Pigou argues that the cost has turned out to be smaller than was once supposed. In giving up some luxuries as a result of higher taxation, the wealthy person suffers less than the gain which the poor person receives in satisfying more elementary needs of everyday life.

How much property is to be redistributed by the welfare state in pursuance of its policy of guaranteeing everybody the minimum decencies of life? What is considered a minimum at one time, may be too little at another, and Pigou admits that there is no absolute line which can be mathematically figured out either by an economist or a politician. Yet, as a general line of reasoning, it appears to him that we are moving away from the old concept of the state helping only people who are in *extreme* distress. We no longer wait for the extremity and emergency before we think the state has the duty to help. Nonetheless, there is danger of overstepping the boundary line. Cutting up the cake into too many little pieces, taxing the wealthy too steeply, may weaken their incentive to save, invest, and produce, and the cake may be reduced in size in the end. Contrary to the unqualified enthusiasts of the welfare state, Pigou warns that the welfare state "holds in itself a *cumulative* threat to productivity which is also a threat to its own survival. That threat should be continually and carefully watched. We must not advance too far or too fast."

As time goes on, the realization grows that *the welfare state is not a way of getting something for nothing,* and that *every piece of welfare has to be paid for.* Since taxation in Britain and the United States is reaching a level where there is not much left that can be gotten by "soaking the rich," every increased social benefit must be paid for by increased taxation of the lower-income groups. The problem of the welfare state is becoming less and less one of philosophical principle, and more and more one of actuarial calculation and taxation arithmetic.

In the welfare state, the people agree that a high proportion of their income be spent by the government for certain welfare purposes. Experience shows that people tend to save more easily if they have committed themselves to an insurance policy or a mortgage with fixed monthly payments than if they rely on irregular monthly deposits in a savings account. In the welfare state the situation is similar. The individual hands over to the state the job of saving for him in case of urgent need, such as sickness, old age, or death. If people themselves could save for all such contingencies, much of the welfare state would be unnecessary. But the average person finds it easier to pay higher taxes every month or every year, out of which his social security is ultimately paid, than to save for such eventualities in a personal savings account. There is nothing wrong in admitting this human weakness and entrusting the state with the efficient administration of a comprehensive insurance system, provided it is understood that the costs of such a system have to be borne by taxation, and that therefore the financial principle behind the welfare state is forced personal and communal saving today for the needs of tomorrow rather than a simple transfer of property from the wealthy to the poor.

Is the welfare state compatible with capitalism? When the first basic measures of the welfare state were introduced over twenty years ago in the United States, the prediction was made that the welfare state was the first step to communism, or at least to creeping socialism. Events have disproved that fear. After nearly three decades of the welfare state, adhered to by both Democratic and Republican administrations, the American economy is healthier than ever before, living standards have reached an all-time high, productivity is higher than ever, people live longer and better, and there is more economic equality between the various income groups than in the past. Far from leading to more envy and class conflict, the welfare state has steadily diminished the differences and tensions between the two major American political parties, and revolutionary views and parties have less appeal than ever before. Above all, the welfare state has in no way sapped the spirit of incentive and effort in the American economy; the whip of want and insecurity is not the best guide to progress, and in providing a minimum of social and economic security the welfare state has strengthened the economy as a whole. The performance of the American economy in World War II and in the years since has astounded the whole world, including the communist states; far from being coddled into softness and stagnation by the welfare state, the American economy has demonstrated enormous dynamism, drive, and initiative.

Whereas in the early thirties the welfare state was an issue of partisan politics, bitterly dividing the two major American political parties, there is very little controversy now as far as the basic principles are concerned. Whatever the economic and social consequences of the welfare state are, its long-term political consequences are even more important. Without changing the basic form of government or way of life, the welfare state has strengthened democracy by strengthening the security, self-respect, and freedom of democracy's citizens. The two major nations in the world in which communism poses very little internal danger because of the almost complete absence of class hatred and class war are England and the United States, the two societies which have pioneered in the building up of the welfare state.

I. ROOSEVELT

The Philosophy of the New Deal*

The issue of government has always been whether individual men and women will have to serve some system of government or economics, or whether a system of government or economics exists to serve individual men and women. This question has persistently dominated the discussion of government for many generations. On questions relating to these things men have differed, and for time immemorial it is probable that honest men will continue to differ.

The final word belongs to no man; yet we can still believe in change and in progress. Democracy, as a dear old friend of mine in Indiana, Meredith Nicholson, has called it, is a quest, a never-ending seeking for better things, and in the seeking for these things and the striving for them, there are many roads to follow. But, if we map the course of these roads, we find that there are only two general directions.

When we look about us, we are likely to forget how hard people have worked to win the privilege of government. The growth of the national government of Europe was a struggle for the development of a centralized force in the nation, strong enough to impose peace upon ruling barons. In many instances the victory of the central government, the creation of a strong central government, was a haven of refuge to the individual. The people preferred the master far away to the exploitation and

cruelty of the smaller master near at hand.

But the creators of national government were perforce ruthless men. They were often cruel in their methods, but they did strive steadily toward something that society needed and very much wanted, a strong central State able to keep the peace, to stamp out civil war, to put the unruly nobleman in his place, and to permit the bulk of individuals to live safely. The man of ruthless force had his place in developing a pioneer country, just as he did in fixing the power of the central Government in the development of Nations. Society paid him well for his services and its development. When the development among the Nations of Europe, however, had been completed, ambition and ruthlessness, having served their term, tended to overstep their mark.

There came a growing feeling that Government was conducted for the benefit of a few who thrived unduly at the expense of all. The people sought a balancing—a limiting force. There came gradually, through town councils, trade guilds, national parliaments, by constitution and by popular participation and control, limitations on arbitrary power.

Another factor that tended to limit the power of those who ruled, was the rise of the ethical conception that a ruler bore a responsibility for the welfare of his subjects.

The American colonies were born in this struggle. The American Revolution was a turning point in it. After the Revolution

* From a campaign address by Franklin D. Roosevelt before the Commonwealth Club at San Francisco (September 23, 1932).

the struggle continued and shaped itself in the public life of the country. There were those who because they had seen the confusion which attended the years of war for American independence surrendered to the belief that popular Government was essentially dangerous and essentially unworkable. They were honest people, my friends, and we cannot deny that their experience had warranted some measure of fear. The most brilliant, honest and able exponent of this point of view was Hamilton. He was too impatient of slow-moving methods. Fundamentally he believed that the safety of the republic lay in the autocratic strength of its Government, that the destiny of individuals was to serve that Government, and that fundamentally a great and strong group of central institutions, guided by a small group of able and public spirited citizens, could best direct all Government.

But Mr. Jefferson, in the summer of 1776, after drafting the Declaration of Independence turned his mind to the same problem and took a different view. He did not deceive himself with outward forms. Government to him was a means to an end, not an end in itself; it might be either a refuge and a help or a threat and a danger, depending on the circumstances. We find him carefully analyzing the society for which he was to organize a Government. "We have no paupers. The great mass of our population is of laborers, our rich who cannot live without labor, either manual or professional, being few and of moderate wealth. Most of the laboring class possess property, cultivate their own lands, have families and from the demand for their labor, are enabled to exact from the rich and the competent such prices as enable them to feed abundantly, clothe above mere decency, to labor moderately and raise their families."

These people, he considered, had two sets of rights, those of "personal competency" and those involved in acquiring and possessing property. By "personal competency" he meant the right of free think-

ing, freedom of forming and expressing opinions, and freedom of personal living, each man according to his own lights. To insure the first set of rights, a Government must so order its functions as not to interfere with the individual. But even Jefferson realized that the exercise of the property rights might so interfere with the rights of the individual that the Government, without whose assistance the property rights could not exist, must intervene, not to destroy individualism, but to protect it.

You are familiar with the great political duel which followed; and how Hamilton, and his friends, building toward a dominant centralized power were at length defeated in the great election of 1800, by Mr. Jefferson's party. Out of that duel came the two parties, Republican and Democratic, as we know them today.

So began, in American political life, the new day, the day of the individual against the system, the day in which individualism was made the great watchword of American life. The happiest of economic conditions made that day long and splendid. On the Western frontier, land was substantially free. No one, who did not shirk the task of earning a living, was entirely without opportunity to do so. Depressions could, and did, come and go; but they could not alter the fundamental fact that most of the people lived partly by selling their labor and partly by extracting their livelihood from the soil, so that starvation and dislocation were practically impossible. At the very worst there was always the possibility of climbing into a covered wagon and moving west where the untilled prairies afforded a haven for men to whom the East did not provide a place. So great were our natural resources that we could offer this relief not only to our own people, but to the distressed of all the world; we could invite immigration from Europe, and welcome it with open arms. Traditionally, when a depression came a new section of land was opened in the West; and even our temporary misfortune served our manifest destiny.

It was in the middle of the nineteenth century that a new force was released and a new dream created. The force was what is called the industrial revolution, the advance of steam and machinery and the rise of the forerunners of the modern industrial plant. The dream was the dream of an economic machine, able to raise the standard of living for everyone; to bring luxury within the reach of the humblest; to annihilate distance by steam power and later by electricity, and to release everyone from the drudgery of the heaviest manual toil. It was to be expected that this would necessarily affect Government. Heretofore, Government had merely been called upon to produce conditions within which people could live happily, labor peacefully, and rest secure. Now it was called upon to aid in the consummation of this new dream. There was, however, a shadow over the dream. To be made real, it required use of the talents of men of tremendous will and tremendous ambition, since by no other force could the problems of financing and engineering new developments be brought to a consummation.

So manifest were the advantages of the machine age, however, that the United States fearlessly, cheerfully, and, I think, rightly, accepted the bitter with the sweet. It was thought that no price was too high to pay for the advantages which we could draw from a finished industrial system. The history of the last half century is accordingly in large measure a history of a group of financial Titans, whose methods were not scrutinized with too much care, and who were honored in proportion as they produced the results, irrespective of the means they used. The financiers who pushed the railroads to the Pacific were always ruthless, often wasteful, and frequently corrupt; but they did build railroads, and we have them today. It has been estimated that the American investor paid for the American railway system more than three times over in the process; but

despite this fact the net advantage was to the United States. As long as we had free land; as long as population was growing by leaps and bounds; as long as our industrial plants were insufficient to supply our own needs, society chose to give the ambitious man free play and unlimited reward provided only that he produced the economic plant so much desired.

During this period of expansion, there was equal opportunity for all and the business of Government was not to interfere but to assist in the development of industry. This was done at the request of business men themselves. The tariff was originally imposed for the purpose of "fostering our infant industry," a phrase I think the older among you will remember as a political issue not so long ago. The railroads were subsidized, sometimes by grants of money, oftener by grants of land; some of the most valuable oil lands in the United States were granted to assist the financing of the railroad which pushed through the Southwest. A nascent merchant marine was assisted by grants of money, or by mail subsidies, so that our steam shipping might ply the seven seas. Some of my friends tell me that they do not want the Government in business. With this I agree; but I wonder whether they realize the implications of the past. For while it has been American doctrine that the Government must not go into business in competition with private enterprises, still it has been traditional, particularly in Republican administrations, for business to ask the Government to put at private disposal all kinds of Government assistance. The same man who tells you that he does not want to see the Government interfere in business—and he means it, and has plenty of good reasons for saying so—is the first to go to Washington and ask the Government for a prohibitory tariff on his product. When things get just bad enough, as they did two years ago, he will go with equal speed to the United States Government and ask for a loan; and the Reconstruction Finance Corporation is the outcome of it. Each group has sought protection from the Government for its own special interests, without realizing that the function of Government must be to favor no small group at the expense of its duty to protect the rights of personal freedom and of private property of all its citizens.

In retrospect we can now see that the turn of the tide came with the turn of the century. We were reaching our last frontier; there was no more free land and our industrial combinations had become great uncontrolled and irresponsible units of power within the State. Clear-sighted men saw with fear the danger that opportunity would no longer be equal; that the growing corporation, like the feudal baron of old, might threaten the economic freedom of individuals to earn a living. In that hour, our anti-trust laws were born. The cry was raised against the great corporations. Theodore Roosevelt, the first great Republican Progressive, fought a Presidential campaign on the issue of "trust busting" and talked freely about malefactors of great wealth. If the Government had a policy it was rather to turn the clock back, to destroy the large combinations and to return to the time when every man owned his individual small business.

This was impossible; Theodore Roosevelt, abandoning the idea of "trust busting," was forced to work out a difference between "good" trusts and "bad" trusts. The Supreme Court set forth the famous "rule of reason" by which it seems to have meant that a concentration of industrial power was permissible if the method by which it got its power, and the use it made of that power were reasonable.

Woodrow Wilson, elected in 1912, saw the situation more clearly. Where Jefferson had feared the encroachment of political power on the lives of individuals, Wilson knew that the new power was financial. He saw, in the highly centralized economic system, the despot of the twentieth century, on whom great masses of individuals relied for their safety and their livelihood, and whose irresponsibility and greed (if they were not controlled) would reduce them to starvation and penury. The concentration of financial power had not proceeded so far in 1912 as it has today; but it had grown far enough for Mr. Wilson to realize fully its implications. It is interesting, now, to read his speeches. What is called "radical" today (and I have reason to know whereof I speak) is mild compared to the campaign of Mr. Wilson. "No man can deny," he said, "that the lines of endeavor have more and more narrowed and stiffened; no man who knows anything about the development of industry in this country can have failed to observe that the larger kinds of credit are more and more difficult to obtain unless you obtain them upon terms of uniting your efforts with those who already control the industry of the country, and nobody can fail to observe that every man who tries to set himself up in competition with any process of manufacture which has taken place under the control of large combinations of capital will presently find himself either squeezed out or obliged to sell and allow himself to be absorbed." Had there been no World War—had Mr. Wilson been able to devote eight years to domestic instead of to international affairs—we might have had a wholly different situation at the present time. However, the then distant roar of European cannon, growing ever louder, forced him to abandon the study of this issue. The problem he saw so clearly is left with us as a legacy; and no one of us on either side of the political controversy can deny that it is a matter of grave concern to the Government.

A glance at the situation today only too clearly indicates that equality of opportunity as we have known it no longer exists. Our industrial plant is built; the problem just now is whether under existing conditions it is not overbuilt. Our last frontier has long since been reached, and there is practically no more free land. More than half of our people do not live on the farms or on lands and cannot derive a living by cultivating their own property. There is no safety valve in the form of a Western prairie to which those thrown out of work by the Eastern economic machines can go for a new start. We are not able to invite the immigration from Europe to share our endless plenty. We are now providing a drab living for our own people.

Our system of constantly rising tariffs has at last reacted against us to the point of closing our Canadian frontier on the north, our European markets on the east, many of our Latin-American markets to the south, and a goodly proportion of our Pacific markets on the west, through the retaliatory tariffs of those countries. It has forced many of our great industrial institutions which exported their surplus production to such countries, to establish plants in such countries, within the tariff walls. This has resulted in the reduction of the operation of their American plants, and opportunity for employment.

Just as freedom to farm has ceased, so also the opportunity in business has narrowed. It still is true that men can start small enterprises, trusting to native shrewdness and ability to keep abreast of competitors; but area after area has been preempted altogether by the great corporations, and even in the fields which still have no great concerns, the small man starts under a handicap. The unfeeling statistics of the past three decades show that the independent business man is running a losing race. Perhaps he is forced to the wall; perhaps he cannot command credit; perhaps he is "squeezed out," in Mr. Wilson's words, by highly organized corporate competitors, as your corner grocery man can tell you. Recently a careful study was made of the concentration of business in the United States. It showed that our economic life was dominated by some six hundred odd corporations who controlled two-thirds of American industry. Ten million small business men divided the other third. More striking still, it appeared that if the process of concentration goes on at the same rate, at the end of another cen-

tury we shall have all American industry controlled by a dozen corporations, and run by perhaps a hundred men. But plainly, we are steering a steady course toward economic oligarchy, if we are not there already.

Clearly, all this calls for a reappraisal of values. A mere builder of more industrial plants, a creator of more railroad systems, an organizer of more corporations, is as likely to be a danger as a help. The day of the great promoter or the financial Titan, to whom we granted anything if only he would build, or develop, is over. Our task now is not discovery or exploitation of natural resources, or necessarily producing more goods. It is the soberer, less dramatic business of administering resources and plants already in hand, of seeking to reestablish foreign markets for our surplus production, of meeting the problem of underconsumption, of adjusting production to consumption, of distributing wealth and products more equitably, of adapting existing economic organizations to the service of the people. The day of enlightened administration has come.

Just as in older times the central Government was first a haven of refuge, and then a threat, so now in a closer economic system the central and ambitious financial unit is no longer a servant of national desire, but a danger. I would draw the parallel one step farther. We did not think because national Government had become a threat in the 18th century that therefore we should abandon the principle of national Government. Nor today should we abandon the principle of strong economic units called corporations, merely because their power is susceptible of easy abuse. In other times we dealt with the problem of an unduly ambitious central Government by modifying it gradually into a constitutional democratic Government. So today we are modifying and controlling our economic units.

As I see it, the task of Government in its relation to business is to assist the development of an economic declaration of rights, an economic constitutional order. This is the common task of statesman and business man. It is the minimum requirement of a more permanently safe order of things.

Happily, the times indicate that to create such an order not only is the proper policy of Government, but it is the only line of safety for our economic structures as well. We know, now, that these economic units cannot exist unless prosperity is uniform, that is, unless purchasing power is well distributed throughout every group in the nation. That is why even the most selfish of corporations for its own interest would be glad to see wages restored and unemployment ended and to bring the Western farmer back to his accustomed level of prosperity and to assure a permanent safety to both groups. That is why some enlightened industries themselves endeavor to limit the freedom of action of each man and business group within the industry in the common interest of all; why business men everywhere are asking a form of organization which will bring the scheme of things into balance, even though it may in some measure qualify the freedom of action of individual units within the business.

The exposition need not further be elaborated. It is brief and incomplete, but you will be able to expand it in terms of your own business or occupation without difficulty. I think everyone who has actually entered the economic struggle—which means everyone who was not born to safe wealth—knows in his own experience and his own life that we have now to apply the earlier concepts of American Government to the conditions of today.

The Declaration of Independence discusses the problem of Government in terms of a contract. Government is a relation of give and take, a contract, perforce, if we would follow the thinking out of which it grew. Under such a contract rulers were accorded power, and the people consented to that power on consideration that they be accorded certain rights. The task

of statesmanship has always been the redefinition of these rights in terms of a changing and growing social order. New conditions impose new requirements upon Government and those who conduct Government.

I held, for example, in proceedings before me as Governor, the purpose of which was the removal of the Sheriff of New York, that under modern conditions it was not enough for a public official merely to evade the legal terms of official wrongdoing. He owed a positive duty as well. I said in substance that if he had acquired large sums of money, he was when accused required to explain the sources of such wealth. To that extent this wealth was colored with a public interest. I said that in financial matters, public servants should, even beyond private citizens, be held to a stern and uncompromising rectitude.

I feel that we are coming to a view through the drift of our legislation and our public thinking in the past quarter century that private economic power is, to enlarge an old phrase, a public trust as well. I hold that continued enjoyment of that power by any individual or group must depend upon the fulfillment of that trust. The men who have reached the summit of American business life know this best; happily, many of these urge the binding quality of this greater social contract.

The terms of that contract are as old as the Republic, and as new as the new economic order.

Every man has a right to life; and this means that he has also the right to make a comfortable living. He may by sloth or crime decline to exercise that right; but it may not be denied him. We have no actual famine or dearth; our industrial and agricultural mechanism can produce enough and to spare. Our Government formal and informal, political and economic, owes to everyone an avenue to possess himself of a portion of that plenty sufficient for his needs, through his own work.

Every man has a right to his own property; which means a right to be assured, to the fullest extent attainable, in the safety of his savings. By no other means can men carry the burdens of those parts of life which, in the nature of things, afford no chance of labor; childhood, sickness, old age. In all thought of property, this right is paramount; all other property rights must yield to it. If, in accord with this principle, we must restrict the operations of the speculator, the manipulator, even the financier, I believe we must accept the restriction as needful, not to hamper individualism but to protect it.

These two requirements must be satisfied, in the main, by individuals who claim and hold control of the great industrial and financial combinations which dominate so large a part of our industrial life. They have undertaken to be, not business men, but princes of property. I am not prepared to say that the system which produces them is wrong. I am very clear that they must fearlessly and competently assume the responsibility which goes with the power. So many enlightened business men know this that the statement would be little more than a platitude, were it not for an added implication.

This implication is, briefly, that the responsible heads of finance and industry instead of acting each for himself, must work together to achieve the common end. They must, where necessary, sacrifice this or that private advantage; and in reciprocal self-denial must seek a general advantage. It is here that formal Government—political Government, if you choose—comes in. Whenever in the pursuit of this objective the lone wolf, the unethical competitor, the reckless promoter, the Ishmael or Insull whose hand is against every man's, declines to join in achieving an end recognized as being for the public welfare, and threatens to drag the industry back to a state of anarchy, the Government may properly be asked to apply restraint. Likewise, should the group ever use its collective power contrary to the public welfare, the Government must be swift to enter and protect the public interest.

The Government should assume the function of economic regulation only as a last resort, to be tried only when private initiative, inspired by high responsibility, with such assistance and balance as Government can give, has finally failed. As yet there has been no final failure, because there has been no attempt; and I decline to assume that this nation is unable to meet the situation.

The final term of the high contract was for liberty and the pursuit of happiness. We have learned a great deal of both in the past century. We know that individual liberty and individual happiness mean nothing unless both are ordered in the sense that one man's meat is not another man's poison. We know that the old "rights of personal competency," the right to read, to think, to speak, to choose and live a mode of life, must be respected at all hazards. We know that liberty to do anything which deprives others of those elemental rights is outside the protection of any compact; and that Government in this regard is the maintenance of a balance, within which every individual may have a place if he will take it; in which every individual may find safety if he wishes it; in which every individual may attain such power as his ability permits, consistent with his assuming the accompanying responsibility.

All this is a long, slow task. Nothing is more striking than the simple innocence of the men who insist, whenever an objective is present, on the prompt production of a patent scheme guaranteed to produce a result. Human endeavor is not so simple as that. Government includes the art of formulating a policy, and using the political technique to attain so much of that policy as will receive general support; persuading, leading, sacrificing, teaching always, because the greatest duty of a statesman is to educate. But in the matters of which I have spoken, we are learning rapidly, in a severe school. The lessons so learned must not be forgotten, even in the mental lethargy of a speculative upturn. We must build toward the time when a major depression cannot occur again; and if this means sacrificing the easy profits of inflationist booms, then let them go; and good riddance.

Faith in America, faith in our tradition of personal responsibility, faith in our institutions, faith in ourselves demand that we recognize the new terms of the old social contract. We shall fulfill them, as we

fulfilled the obligation of the apparent Utopia which Jefferson imagined for us in 1776, and which Jefferson, Roosevelt and Wilson sought to bring to realization. We must do so, lest a rising tide of misery, engendered by our common failure, engulf us all. But failure is not an American habit; and in the strength of great hope we must all shoulder our common load.

II. HOOVER

The Welfare State—Road to Collectivism*

The Growth of Governmental Spending

We must wish to maintain a dynamic progressive people. No nation can remain static and survive. But dynamic progress is not made with dynamite. And that dynamite today is the geometrical increase of spending by our governments—federal state, municipal, and local.

Perhaps I can visualize what this growth has been. Twenty years ago, all varieties of government, omitting federal debt service, cost the average family less than $200 annually. Today, also omitting debt service, it costs an average family about $1,300 annually.

This is bad enough. But beyond this is the alarming fact that at this moment executives and legislatures are seriously proposing projects which if enacted would add one-third more annually to our spending. Add to these the debt service and the average family may be paying $1,900 yearly taxes. They may get a little back if they live to over 65 years of age.

It does not seem very generous to set up an "acceptable" standard of living and then make it impossible by taxes.

The Growth of Bureaucracy

No doubt life was simpler about 147 years ago, when our government got well under way. At that time there was less than one government employee, federal, state and local including the paid military, to each 120 of the population. Twenty years ago, there was one government employee to about 40 of the population. Today, there is one government employee to about every 22 of the population. Worse than this, there is today one government employee to about 8 of the working population in the United States.

The Growth of Dependency

Twenty years ago, persons directly or indirectly receiving regular monies from the government—that is, officials, soldiers,

---

* From Herbert Hoover, birthday address at Stanford University (August 10, 1954).

sailors, pensioners, subsidized persons and contractors' employees working exclusively for the government—represented about one person in every 40 of the population.

Today a little more than one person out of every 7 in the population is a regular recipient of government monies. If those of age are all married, they comprise about one-half the voters of the last Presidential election.

Think it over.

In the long run it is the Average Working Citizen who pays by hidden and other taxes. I have made up a little table showing the number of days which this kind of citizen must work on average to pay the taxes.

	Days' Work
Obligations from former wars	11
Defense and Cold War	24
Other federal expenditures	12
State and local expenditures	14
Total thus far	61

But beyond this the seriously proposed further spending now in process will take another 20 days' work from Mr. and Mrs. Average W. Citizen.

Taking out holidays, Sundays, and average vacations, there are about 235 working days in the year. Therefore, this total of 81 days' work a year for taxes will be about one week out of every month.

You might want to work for your family instead of paying for a gigantic bureaucracy.

Think it over.

Confiscation of Savings

To examine what we are doing, we must get away from such sunshine figures as the gross national income. We must reduce our problem to the possible savings of the people after a desirable standard of living. If we adopt the Federal Government's estimate of such a desirable standard, then the actual, and the seriously proposed, national and local government spending will absorb between 75 percent to 85 percent of all the savings of the people. In practice it does not work evenly. The few will have some savings, but the many must reduce their standard of living below the "acceptable" level to pay the tax collector.

And it is out of savings that the people must provide their individual and family security. From savings they must buy their homes, their farms, and their insurance. It is from their savings finding their way into investment that we sustain and stimulate progress in a dynamic productive system.

One end result of the actual and proposed spendings and taxes to meet them is that the Government becomes the major source of credit and capital to the economic system. At best the small business man is starved in the capital he can find. Venture capital to develop new ideas tends to become confined to the large corporations and they grow bigger. There are ample signs of these results already.

Governments do not develop gadgets of improved living.

Another end result is to expose all our independent colleges and other privately supported institutions to the risk of becoming dependent upon the state. Already it is more and more difficult for these institutions to find resources.

Then through politics we will undermine their independence which gives lifting standards and stimulus to government supported institutions.

No nation grows stronger by such subtraction.

Think it over.

Government Borrowing

It is proposed that we can avoid these disasters by more government borrowing. That is a device to load our extravagance and waste on to the next generation. But increasing government debts can carry immediate punishment for that is the road to inflation. There is far more courage in reducing our gigantic national debt than in increasing it. And that is a duty to our children.

Increasing Taxes

And there is no room for this spending and taxes except to cut the standard of living of most of our people below the "acceptable" level. It is easy to say, "Increase corporation taxes." That is an illusion. The bulk of corporation taxes is passed on to the consumer—that is, to every family. It is easy to say, "Increase taxes on the higher personal income brackets." But if all incomes over $8,000 a year were confiscated, it would cover less than 10 percent of these actual and proposed spendings.

The real road before us is to reduce spending and waste and defer some desirable things for a while.

We Cannot Have Everything at Once

There are many absolute necessities and there are many less urgent meritorious and desirable things that every individual family in the nation would like to have but cannot afford. To spend for them, or borrow money for them, would endanger the family home and the family life. So it is with the national family.

So long as we must support the necessary national defense and cold war at a cost of 24 days' work per year to Mr. Average W. Citizen there are many comforting things that should be deferred if we do not wish to continue on this road to ruin of our national family life.

Think it over.

The Back Road to Collectivism

The American mind is troubled by the growth of collectivism throughout the world.

We have a few hundred thousand Communists and their fellow travelers in this country. They cannot destroy the Republic. They are a nuisance and require attention. We also have the doctrinaire socialists who peacefully dream of their utopia.

But there is a considerable group of fuzzy-minded people who are engineering a compromise between free men and these European infections. They fail to realize that our American system has grown away from the systems of Europe for 250 years. They have the foolish notion that a collectivist economy can at the same time preserve personal liberty and constitutional government. That cannot be done.

The steady lowering of the standard of living by this compromised collectivist system under the title "austerity" in England should be a sufficient spectacle for the American people. It aims at an abundant life but it ends in a ration.

Most Americans do not believe in these compromises with collectivism. But they do not realize that through governmental spending and taxes, our nation is blissfully driving down the back road to it at top speed.

In the end these solutions of national problems by spending are always the same —power, more power, more centralization in the hands of the state.

Along this road of spending, the Government either takes over economic life, which is socialism, or dictates institutional and economic life, which is fascism.

We have not had a great socialization of property, but we are on the last miles to collectivism through governmental spending of the savings of the people.

Think it over.

Fooling the People's Thinking

A device of these advocates of gigantic spending is the manipulation of words, phrases, and slogans to convey new meanings different from those we have long understood. These malign distortions drug thinking. They drown it in emotion.

For instance, we see government borrowing and spending transformed into the soft phrase "deficit spending." The slogan of a "welfare state" has emerged as a disguise for a collectivist state by the route of spending. The Founding Fathers would not recognize this distortion of the simple word "welfare" in the Constitution. Certainly Jefferson's idea of the meaning of welfare lies in his statement "To preserve our independence . . . . we must make a choice between economy and liberty or profusion and servitude. . . . . If we can prevent government from wresting the labors of the people under the pretence of caring for them we shall be happy."

Another of these distortions is by those who support such a state and call themselves "liberals." John Morley would not recognize one of them.

Out of these slogans and phrases and new meanings of words come vague promises and misty mirages, such as "security from the cradle to the grave." In action that will frustrate those basic human impulses to production which alone make a dynamic nation.

Think it over.

Where Blame Must Be Placed

It is customary to blame our Administrations or our legislatures for this gigantic increase in spending, these levies on the nation's workdays, and this ride to a dead-end of our unique and successful American system. A large cause of this growing confiscation of the work of the people by our various governments is the multitude of great pressure groups among our own citizens. Also the state and municipal governments pressurize the Federal Government. And within the Federal Government are pressure groups building their own empires.

Aggression of groups and agencies against the savings of the people as a whole is not a process of free men. Special privilege either to business or groups is not liberty.

Many of these groups maintain paid lobbies in Washington or in the State Capitols to press their claims upon the Administrations or the legislatures.

Our representatives must run for election. They can be defeated by these pressure groups. In any event our officials are forced to think in terms of pressure groups, not in terms of need of the whole people.

Perhaps some of my listeners object to somebody else's pressure group. Perhaps you support one of your own. Perhaps some of you do not protest that your leaders are not acting with your authority.

Think it over.

In Conclusion

And finally, may I say that thinking and debate on these questions must not be limited to legislative halls. We should debate them in every school. We should resort to the old cracker barrel debate in every corner grocery. In those places these phrases and slogans can be liquidated by common sense and intellectual integrity.

A splendid storehouse of integrity and freedom has been bequeathed to us by our forefathers. In this day of confusion, of world peril to free men, our high duty is to see that this storehouse is not robbed of its contents.

We dare not see the birthright of posterity to individual independence, initiative, and freedom of choice bartered for a mess of collectivism.

My word to you, my fellow-citizens, on this seventy-fifth birthday is this: The Founding Fathers dedicated the structure of our government "to secure the blessings of liberty to ourselves and our posterity." A century and a half later, we of this generation still inherited this precious blessing. Yet as spendthrifts we are on our way to rob posterity of its inheritance.

The American people have solved many great difficulties in the development of national life. The qualities of self-restraint, of integrity, of conscience and courage still live in our people. It is not too late to summon these qualities into action.

III. POUND

The Welfare State and Constitutional Government *

A Negro who used to do some work for my father had come from the West Indies and was never weary of talking about them. "They has there," he said once, "a drink they calls planter's punch. And, you know, Judge, those planter's punches they creeps up on you surruptitious and clandestyne."

The service state, the state which, instead of preserving peace and order and employing itself with maintaining the general security, takes the whole domain of human welfare for its province and would solve all economic and social ills through its administrative activities, has been creeping up on us in the present century after the manner of "those planter's punches." It was known earlier in Continental Europe. But although some writers in England were calling attention to its possibilities at the end of the last century, it was so at outs with ingrained modes of Anglo-American thought that few tried to put the pieces of evidence together to see what it indicated as to the direction in which we have been moving. In the meantime, since the first world war, it has made exceedingly rapid progress and has covered already a very wide field of individual activity and of official promotion of wide welfare programs on every side.

* From Roscoe Pound, Address before the Economic and Business Foundation and the Service and Professional Clubs at New Castle, Pa. (June 13, 1949).

I say service state rather than welfare state. The term welfare state seems to me a boast. Governments have always held that they were set up to promote and conserve public welfare. This is implicit in the synonym *commonwealth*—the common weal or general welfare personified in the state. So far men have agreed. But when it comes to the question how the common weal or general welfare is to be achieved, they have differed and do differ profoundly. Some think the general welfare is best promoted by a government which maintains order and administers justice, for the rest, leaving men free to do things for themselves in their own way so far as they do not commit aggressions upon others or subject others to unreasonable risk of injury, and act in good faith in their intercourse with others. On the other hand, there have always been those who have believed in a benevolent government which helps men instead of leaving them free to help themselves; who have believed in a paternal ruler or paternal state doing things for his subjects or its citizens to the fullest extent.

Understand, I am not preaching against a service state in itself. The society of today demands services beyond those that the state which only maintained order and repaired injuries could perform. In a complex industrial society it becomes more difficult to do by private initiative many things which the public wishes done and wishes done quickly. Administrative agencies of promoting the general welfare have come to be a necessity and have come to stay. It would be futile to quarrel with the idea of a service state kept in balance with the idea of individual spontaneous initiative characteristic of the American. What one must resist is not state performance of many public services which it can perform without upsetting our legal, political, economic, and social order, but the idea that all public services must and can only be performed by the government—that politically organized society and that alone is to be looked to for everything, and that there is no limit to the services to humanity which it can perform. What I deprecate is carrying to the extreme the idea of regimented cooperation for the general welfare, the exaltation of politically organized society to the position of an absolute ruler. This presupposes supermen administrators or an all-wise majority or plurality, omnicompetent and equal to taking over the whole domain of the general welfare and to determine in detail what it calls for in every situation. The service state in the English-speaking world began by performing a few major additional services beyond maintaining order and administering justice. As it has added more and more it has come to be jealous of public service performed by anyone else.

What is to be the effect of the service state upon American constitutional democracy? The service state as it develops as a superservice state must be *par excellence* a bureau state. From the very nature of administration the bureau state calls for a highly organized official hierarchy. A hierarchy calls for a superman (very likely an *ex officio* superman) at its head. Thus, unless we are vigilant, the service state may lead to a totalitarian state. It has Marxian socialism and absolute government in its pedigree and has grown up along with the totalitarian state in other parts of the world. Liberty—free individual self-assertion, individual initiative and self-help—is looked on with suspicion if not aversion

by the service state, and its advocates seek a "new concept of liberty" as freedom from want and freedom from fear, not freedom of self-assertion, or self-determination. Self-help by the individual, competing with the service rendered by the state, seems an interference with the regime maintained by the government. Spontaneous individual initiative is frowned on as infringing on the domain of state action. The service state easily becomes an omnicompetent state with bureaus of *ex officio* experts and propaganda activities carried on at public expense. If the step to it is gradual, the step from it to an absolute state is easy and may be made quickly.

Bills of rights are a characteristic feature of American constitutions. Beginning with the Virginia Bill of Rights of 1776, enacted immediately after the Declaration of Independence, they have been made a part of all our constitutions, state and federal. Our American bills of rights are prohibitions of governmental action infringing guaranteed rights, that is, guaranteed reasonable expectations involved in life in civilized society. They are laws, part of the constitution as the supreme law of the land, enforceable in legal proceedings in the courts at suit of those whose rights are infringed. They are generically distinct from the declarations of rights on the model of the French Declaration of the Rights of Man which are to be found in constitutions generally outside the English-speaking world. Those are mere preachments, declarations of good intentions or exhortations to governmental authority, legally binding on nobody and unenforceable by anyone whose declared rights are infringed. But the service state is beginning to affect our conception of a bill of rights in America. In a recent proposal for a declaration of rights for a world government we get the Continental note in the very title, but also the note of the service state which is disinclined toward law. There is a declaration of a right of everyone everywhere to claim for himself "release from the bondage of poverty." It is not that he is to be free to free himself from this bondage, but that the state is to free him without his active help in the process. Also he is declared to have a right to claim reward and security according to his needs. But his claim to needs is likely to have few limits and is sure to conflict with claims of others to like needs. Such declarations are not merely preachments, not enforceable or intended to be enforced as law, they are invitations to plundering by rapacious majorities or pluralities.

In a recent book, Professor Corwin has discussed the decadence of fear of oppression by government which has become very marked. Experience of government in seventeenth-century England and experience of government of the colonies from Westminster in the seventeenth and eighteenth centuries had made this fear a dominant consideration in our policy from the beginning till well into the present century. Growth of a feeling of divine right of majorities, akin to that of divine right of kings, has led to an assumption that concern about oppression by government is something we have outgrown. Yet distrust of absolute majority or absolute plurality is as justified in reason and in experience as distrust of the absolute personal ruler. Indeed, the latter may be given pause by fear of an uprising which an intrenched majority need not fear.

It is characteristic of the service state to make lavish promises of satisfying desires which it calls rights. If a constitution promises to every individual "just terms of leisure," those who draft it do not ask themselves whether such provision is a law, a part of the supreme law of the land, or a preachment of policy which no court can enforce and no legislative body can be made to regard. Such preachings enfeeble a whole constitutional structure. As they cannot be enforced, they lend themselves to a doctrine that constitutional provisions are not legally enforceable and may be disregarded at any time in the interest of political policy of the moment. They weaken the constitutional polity we

have built up. Is there wealth enough in the world reachable by taxation imposed by a world government, or even reachable by wholesale confiscation by a world state, to guarantee "just terms of leisure" during life to the whole population of the world or even to four hundred and fifty million Chinese?

Setting forth such things in a constitutional declarations of guaranteed rights makes a farce of constitutions. How can a government release the whole world "from the bondage of poverty?" What organ of government can be made to bring about that enough is produced and is continuously produced to insure plenty for everyone everywhere? How can a court compel legislative or executive or individuals or organizations of individuals to bring this about, or how can executive or legislative compel either or anyone else to do it? Such pronouncements proceed upon a theory which used to be preached by social workers that law is a protest against wrong. Protests against wrong may be very effective in spurring lawmakers to find remedies and enact laws making them effective. But protests themselves lack the quality of enforceability and machinery of enforcement which are demanded for a law in any advanced society. On one occasion Hunt, the agitator, appeared before Lord Ellenborough while sitting at circuit and insistently demanded to be heard. When recognized by the court, Hunt explained that he appeared on behalf of the boy Dogood. On Lord Ellenborough telling him that there was no case of the boy Dogood upon his docket, Hunt exclaimed theatrically: "But, my Lord, am I not in a court of justice?" "No, Mr. Hunt," replied the Chief Justice, "you are in His Majesty's Court of Oyer and Terminer and Jail Delivery to deliver the jail of this county." "Then," said Hunt, "I desire to protest." "Certainly, Mr. Hunt, by all means," said Lord Ellenborough, "Usher, take Mr. Hunt to the corridor and allow him to protest as long and as much as he likes." A law which is simply a protest against wrong is as futile as were the declamations of Hunt in the corridor of Lord Ellenborough's court.

A power to act toward a general equality of satisfaction of wants and a policy of developing such an equality are something very different from a provision in a declaration of rights that a world government guarantees to bring such a policy to fruition. No one can seriously believe that in such time as we can foresee the western world can provide complete social security for the rest of the world, a great part of which is always close to the brink of starvation.

I have spoken at some length of proposals for declarations of rights for a world political organization because the propositions drafted by enthusiastic promoters of a world constitution are followed sometimes in recent proposals for constitution writing in the development of the service state in America. A state which endeavors to relieve its people of want and fear without being able to relieve its individual citizens of the many features of human make-up which lead to poverty and fear is attempting what the colored preacher aptly called unscrewing the inscrutable. How can we expect a state to bring about a complete satisfaction of all the wants of everybody in a world in which we all want the earth, but there are thousands of millions of us and only one earth. Guarantees which are no more than promissory declarations of policy can do no more than deceive. Some years ago, when in one of our states a "modern code" was being urged and propositions for promissory declarations for wide amelioration of human ills were presented, a wise and experienced lawyer suggested that one additional article would make the whole perfect: Be good and you will be happy. Hell is paved with good intentions. An extensive pavement of that material is far from a solid foundation for a politically organized society. The service state is a politically organized society and cannot, as could Baron Munchausen. pull itself up by its own long whiskers.

This does not mean, however, that our nineteenth-century bills of rights cannot be supplemented to meet conditions of the urban industrial society of today. The two new articles in the bill of rights of the New Jersey Constitution of 1947, articles 5 and 19, directed to questions of segregation and discrimination on grounds of race, color, or creed and to rights of organization and collective bargaining, are models of what may be done by constitutional provisions. part of the effective law of the land, enforceable and meant to be enforced, as compared with preachments and promises and wishful declarations of ideal policy.

Promissory bills of rights that create expectations of the politically and economically unachievable and weaken faith in constitutions are a step toward the totalitarian state. The strong selling point of that state is its argument that a strong man, a superman leader, can do what a government hindered by constitutional checks and balances cannot do. When a constitution declares rights as claims to be secured by government which it can't secure, it invites centralization of power in an absolute government which claims ability to secure them. The service state, taking over all functions of public service, operating through bureaus with wide powers and little practical restriction on their powers, through government positions for a large and increasing proportion of the population, and through systematic official propaganda and a system of subsidies to education, science, and research, can easily be taking strides toward an absolute government, although under forms of democracy. Indeed, the extreme advocates of the service state insist that constitutional democracy is a contradition in terms. A democracy must be an unrestricted rule of the majority. The majority must be as absolute a ruler in all things as was the French king of the old regime in France or the Czar in the old regime in Russia. As the seventeenth century argued that a monarchy must in the nature of things be an absolute not a constitutional monarchy, on the same logical grounds it is argued that a democracy must be an absolute not a constitutional democracy.

General welfare service by the state, becoming service for strong aggressive groups or for politically powerful localities at the expense of the public at large, has been the ladder by which absolute rulers have climbed to power and the platform on which they have been able to stay in power. Louis XIV held down France by holding down Paris by distribution of bread at the expense of the provinces. The Spanish absolute monarchy long held itself in power by using the wealth of the New World for service to its subjects at home. Napoleon III used state workshops. Totalitarian Italy used the theory of the service of the corporative state. Totalitarian Russia promises proletariat rule at the expense of the rest of the community. Indeed, in antiquity the Roman emperor held down Italy by extortion of wheat from Egypt.

Since the first world war we have preached a great deal and promised much as to the rights of minorities and of oppressed racial groups. But the lavish promises and administrative absolutism of the super-service state (or shall we say service super-state?), with the absolute ultimate rule of majorities or even of pluralities which they involve, are a menace to the guarantees that a constitution which is a legal document, not merely a frame of government promising welfare services which it cannot be made to perform, is able to give those groups. The attempt to make all men equal in all respects instead of in their political and legal rights and capacities is likely to make them more unequal than nature has done already. Unless we give equality the practical meaning of our American bills of rights, we are likely to be thrown back to a proposition that all men are not born equal but are born equally.

There has been a tendency of men in all history to worship their rulers. In the society of today this takes the form of faith in absolute rule of the majority or,

indeed, of the plurality for the time being. We forget that majority or plurality are only a way out when we cannot get entire agreement. The founders of our polity, with long and bitter experience of absolute rule behind them, sought a government of checks and balances by which absolute rule by anyone was precluded. As Mr. Justice Miller put it, in the centennial year of the American Revolution, the theory of our governments, state and national, is opposed to the deposit of unlimited power anywhere. Today we are told that this doctrine is outmoded. What called for the pronouncement was legislation imposing a tax for subsidy to private manufacturing enterprise. That was regarded as unconstitutional in 1875. But in the service state of today expensive service to some at the cost of others is regarded as a service to the public, as indeed it may be in some cases, and this tempts aggressive groups to obtain legislation providing service to them for which others must pay. A group of this sort easily, in its own mind, identifies itself with the public. Obviously the conception of public service needs to be carefully defined and limited if we are to avoid being led into absolute rule by majority or plurality.

A government which regards itself, under pretext of extending a general welfare service to the public, as entitled to rob Peter to pay Paul, and is free from constitutional restraints upon legislation putting an element or group of the people for the whole, has a bad effect on the morale of the people. If government is a device for benevolent robbery, a would-be Robin Hood of today is not likely to see why his benevolently conceived activities are reprehensible. Based on colonial experience of legislation imposing burdens on some for the benefit of others rather than of the public as a whole, our older constitutions and substantially all constitutions in the nineteenth century forbade special or class legislation. The omission of this provision from recent constitutions is significant. No doubt the restriction in the nineteenth-century constitutions was applied too rigidly and was made to stand in the way of proper welfare legislation. But entire omission points to a feeling that government is intended to be unfair to minorities and that there should be no limit on the ability of organized groups to make their fellow men pay for special service to them.

A service state must be bureaucratic. Bureaus are characteristically zealous to get everything in reach under their control. Would it be a great public service to have a bureau of psychologists to examine us for our aptitudes and assign us, whether we like it or not, to the calling for which

they find us fitted? Before the advent of psychologists such a state was argued for by Greek philosophers. The later Eastern Roman Empire stabilized society by putting and keeping men in callings somewhat in this way. An omnicompetent state postulates omnicompetent bureaus. Why in the perfect all-regulating state allow human energy to be wasted by permitting individuals to engage in futile efforts to employ themselves in callings in which they cannot succeed? Is not that the next move after subsidizing them to persist in these callings in which they are failing and bound to fail?

IV. PIGOU

Economic Aspects of the Welfare State [*]

Anybody wishing to write about the Welfare State must begin with the meaning of words. What is Welfare? Is it something that can belong to a State, a political organisation as such, or is it merely a function—possibly a sum—of the welfares of a number of individuals? To my thinking the answer is clear. Welfare is sometimes belonging to states of mind. Entities like States and Joint Stock Companies cannot partake of it because they cannot have states of mind; though, of course, the individual men and women round whom these entities are built, and, indeed, even insects, can. Thus a society for promoting the welfare of horses or cats, or even for preventing cruelty to bees, would not, even the last, evoke linguistic criticism; but one

* A. C. Pigou, "Some Aspects of the Welfare State," *Diogenes*, No. 7 (Summer 1954). By permission.

for promoting the welfare of Stonehenge or Canterbury Cathedral or of music, as distinct from the makers and enjoyers of music, would be better renamed. Individual consciousness then, and nothing else, is the seat of welfare; and for our purpose we may reasonably confine ourselves to the consciousness of human beings.

Clearly, too, welfare is a thing of two aspects. For a person's state of mind at any time depends partly on his own mental make-up and partly on his external environment. A person with no musical sense will get nothing out of the most admirable concert, and one with an excellent musical sense will get nothing if there is no music to hear. These two elements, subjective and objective, are intimately bound together; the resultant being a function of both together, not a sum of two parts due respectively to the one and the other. Anybody, therefore, concerned with welfare must look to both these aspects of it. To stimulate production of what one may call welfare-goods and pay no heed to people's capacity to use and enjoy them would be wasted effort. No doubt, with goods that satisfy the primary needs for food, clothing, and shelter, nature herself teaches their use without much aid from man. But no sensible philanthropist would provide libraries of good literature for people who cannot and cannot be taught to read.

There are many important aspects of welfare that lie outside an economist's purview, religious experience, domestic harmony—or disharmony—patriotic feeling, appreciation of music and art and fine scenery, the pleasures of physical fitness, athletic achievement. In my book on *The Economics of Welfare* I did not speak of these things, but confined myself to aspects of welfare associated with economic circumstances, and I conceived of economic welfare as satisfactions and dissatisfactions derived from these circumstances, depending, for a community, partly on the size of its real income, partly on the way in which this was allocated among individuals and partly on the way in which it was distributed through time. This way of approach, though a narrow one, is, I still think, convenient. I see no reason for emending it and, as an economist, am not competent to range more widely. Confining myself, therefore, to the economic field, I shall speak of the Welfare State as one that endeavours to promote the economic satisfaction of its citizens—possible conflicts between their interests and other people's being for the present purpose ignored—by stimulating production, improving the allocation of real income and combating large inter-temporal fluctuations.

The Welfare State so conceived stands in sharp contrast with States whose ideal is military power for its own sake, prestige, glory or other such 'glittering prizes'; though this, of course, is not to say that in a fear-dominated world it must not be ready to protect itself against attack.

Again it stands in sharp contrast with a State whose eyes are focused on the interests of particular privileged classes—the monarch and his court, the nobles, the landlords, the dignitaries of the Church. France's *ancien régime* certainly was not a Welfare State; nor can we so label even Athens in its prime; for the slave population, however well treated, were means, not ends. On the other hand, we cannot contrast so sharply a Welfare State with a 'police state'. For a police state may also be a Welfare State genuinely aiming, with its spies and its terrorism, to promote the economic welfare of its people as a whole. We cannot deny this *a priori*. But—*si monumentum quaeris circumspice!*

We have thus by contrasts obtained a rough notion of what a Welfare State is. Before, however, we can usefully investigate its character and implications, a fundamental objection must be faced, which, if valid, would destroy this type of enquiry in the womb. The idea that economic satisfaction should be promoted implies that satisfactions are comparable at least in the sense that one can be greater or less than another, though not necessarily in the sense that one can be greater or less by some specifiable percentage. Now, if we imagine two satisfactions—not two objects yielding satisfaction but two states of satisfaction—presented to the mind of a single person at a given moment it will, I think, be generally agreed that they are comparable. The person to whom they are presented may prefer one to the other or be indifferent between them, and it is reasonable to say in the one case that the preferred satisfaction or, more strictly, prospective satisfaction, is the greater of the two, in the other case that they are equal. Moreover, there is no difficulty in supposing that a man can compare in the same way two satisfactions that he has enjoyed at different times, provided that his memory of them is clear. But as regards satisfactions enjoyed by different people the issue is more difficult. Every mind, it has been said, is inscrutable to every other mind. How is it possible for me or anyone else to decide whether my satisfaction is greater, equal to or less than yours when we are faced with similar, and *a fortiori* with dissimilar situations? And, if this is not possible, how can we support the proposition that a shilling means more— that it yields more satisfaction—to a poor man than to a rich one; a proposition without which the concept of a Welfare State would be robbed of its most significant practical implications?

It must, I think, be granted that as between beings widely dissimilar or accustomed to widely different environments a comparison of satisfactions is not feasible. Does an elephant enjoy a bun more than a polar bear; does a hare dislike—or, if we are huntsmen, perhaps we should say like—being hunted more than a fox does? Was a palaeolithic man painting a reindeer on the walls of his cave happier than a royal academician who has just finished his portrait of 'a prominent businessman'? Such questions are unanswerable, indeed fantastic. But among people *prima facie* similar, growing up in the same general environment, it is reasonable to suppose that their reactions to various economic situations will be roughly similar. Of course, particular individuals will react differently, but representative men in different groups may be expected to react more or less alike. We cannot, of course, prove this to be so, but on the basis of personal experience, discussion and analogy, it seems probable. At all events in practice we always act on that assumption. This is enough to allow our analysis to proceed. It is at all events the best that we can get.

Let us then leave epistemological doubts behind, masked if not disposed of, and pass to a closer study of the Welfare State. To undertake a full and rounded discussion of all its aspects in a paper of this kind would be impracticable. A selection must be made. I single out, therefore, two topics: first, State action to influence, not primarily the total amount of real income

—production in its widest sense—but the direction of it among different sorts of goods and services; secondly, State action to influence the allocation of real income available among persons, more particularly as between well to do and relatively poor people. These topics are, of course, in some measure intertwined. For example, on the one side subsidies designed to stimulate the production or importation of ordinary articles of food indirectly entail a shifting of real income in favour of poor people because these devote a larger proportion of their resources to the purchase of food than richer people do. On the other side, a shift in the allocation of available income in favour of the poor carries with it a shift in the direction of productive resources towards the kinds of goods and services that poor people buy. Nevertheless it will be convenient and make for clarity to treat the two topics separately.

There is general agreement that for certain sorts of goods and services the scale of production *must* be determined by State policy operated through the collection and spending of revenue. These are goods and services that serve collective needs: the Armed Forces, Police, the Judiciary, the provision of public buildings, and so on. It is not necessary that the State should construct battleships in its own shipyards; it may buy them from private firms. But things of this kind must be ordered and paid for out of public funds.

For goods that satisfy individual requirements there is no such necessity. On the contrary, it has often been maintained that, since public officials are unlikely to understand what people want so well as they do themselves, the State ought to leave the choice to them and refrain altogether from interference. But this is crude doctrine and, from the standpoint of the Welfare State, needs substantial qualification.

First, the claim that people know what they want better than officials is certainly not true when they are deceived as to what things offered to them for sale really are.

A big firm buying materials will usually have its own testing department and can protect itself. But the ordinary private customer cannot. It has long been agreed, for example, that the State should defend him by legislation against fraudulent weights and measures, the adulteration of food, and so on. In this country the law now requires the contents of proprietary drugs to be specified and advertisements in which claims are made to cure—as distinct from alleviate—certain at present incurable diseases are forbidden. The fundamental principle is that the ordinary citizen, in spite of the fact that he has more interest in and knowledge of his own wants than any official, nevertheless needs protection against fraud and misrepresentation.

Secondly there is often a wide gap between a person's wants and his needs. No normal child *wants* to be educated, and some parents, looking for his uses as a wage earner, may not want it either. At the other extreme a man may want extremely cocaine, heroin and other such drugs that are bound to do him serious harm. The State forbids the sale of such things to the general public. As to alcoholic drinks and tobacco it really taxes them because they are easy things on which to raise a large revenue; but it has also been argued, at all events as regards alcohol, that checking its consumption by heavy taxes is—for other people's—moral good. An example of positive as distinct from negative intervention is afforded by the British Government's policy of encouraging school-children to drink milk by special subsidies. During the war, of course, through the allocation of materials, priorities, licences, and the refusal to grant licences, very extensive control was exercised by the State, apart altogether from the influence of its own expenditure, on the direction in which productive resources should be employed.

More interesting from the standpoint of the economist is a third consideration. When people decide to spend their money in certain ways it sometimes happens that

their spending yields uncovenanted benefits or inflicts uncovenanted damage on other people whose gains or losses do not enter into the calculations of the spenders. There are many examples of this. The social costs involved in the supply of alcoholic drinks includes the provision of police to control the effects of excess, but these costs do not enter into the price that the purchasers of such drinks have to pay for them. Nor does the damage done to people living near smoking factories and the extra washing bills they have to pay enter into the price of the factory's products. If they did, as, with strict social accounting, they ought to do, the price of those products would be higher, less of them would be demanded and less resources devoted to making them. On the other hand, when a good landlord protects the amenities of the neighbourhood man erects a beautiful instead of an ugly house there is a benefit to others for which he gets no payment. These gaps, positive and negative, between private and public costs were not much in people's minds until fairly recently. Now everybody understands about them. It must be confessed, however, that we seldom know enough to decide in what fields and to what extent the State, on account of them, could usefully interfere with individual freedom of choice. Moreover, even though economists were able to provide a perfect blueprint for beneficial State action, politicians are not philosopher kings and a blueprint might quickly yield place on their desks to the propaganda of competing pressure groups. 'Fancy' finance, like a fancy franchise, whatever its theoretical attractions, has, at all events in a democracy, dim practical prospects.

There remain the well-known disharmonies associated with monopolistic practices which deliberately restrict either directly or by price policy the investment of resources in a monopolist's chosen field. These practices constitute interference by private persons with the consumer's freedom of choice, and action by the State to prevent them is not strictly interference, but, rather, a countering of interference. This is a very old story. The difficulty of devising methods of control that will not at the same time obstruct the economies of production that large-scale combinations and amalgamations sometimes have to offer are well known, and the issue between State control of potential monopolies and State ownership and operation of them is still a live one. It is no part of my plan to debate that issue here. I am concerned only to show that, where monopolistic action is threatened, the thesis that Government should stand aside because private individuals know their own business and their own wants better than officials is undermined. The Welfare State will certainly not stand aside.

I now pass to my second topic, the attitude of the Welfare State to the allocation of real income among various classes of people. Less cumbrously we may say, its attitude to transfers in money or kind from richer to poorer people; though it must be confessed that the concept of transfers is ambiguous until we have decided how much it is 'proper' for people with different incomes to contribute to the general purposes of government—the upkeep of the armed forces and so on. The underlying thesis is that economic welfare as a whole will be promoted if the proportionate share of real income available for the poorer classes was substantially larger than it would be if the State merely kept the ring. The slogan *fair shares,* though a meaningless noise so long as *fair* is undefined, illustrates the benevolent, if muddled, aspirations of many enthusiasts for welfare. These seem at first sight so obviously right that to discuss them is a waste of time. But they were not always deemed obvious. A century and a half ago it was honestly believed by many righteous —shall we say self-righteous—persons that to help poor people in their difficulties was in the long run positively bad for them; that it would only render them idle and thriftless, cause them to produce innumerable offspring for whom they could not

provide, and so on. To prevent mill-owners from employing children for fourteen hours a day was bad for the children because it deprived their parents of the wages they might have earned and so deprived the children of essential food! Alternatively to be poor was one's own fault, a crime fitly punished by suffering.

But now the climate of opinion, at all events in Great Britain, is quite different. Other people's poverty is no longer a crime; that is now the fate of other people's wealth! It is common ground that not only children but men and women too must somehow be saved from excessive toil and protected, at the expense, if need be, of their better-to-do fellows, from the worst severities of economic need. It has come also to be recognised that this can be done at much smaller immediate cost to better-to-do people than was once supposed. For this there are two reasons. First, a given worsening in the economic situation of a reasonably fortunate person will not usually affect him nearly as much when he has become accustomed to it as it does when first imposed. A man with an income of £2,000 a year may suffer a great deal if it is suddenly reduced to £1,000, and that not merely because the process of *becoming* poorer is painful. But, when he has adjusted himself to the new situation he will very likely be nearly, if not quite, as happy as before. Women who before the last war had large households of servants now find making their own beds little hardship, and cooking meals, within limits, may be even interesting. Secondly, whereas for a single person or family to be forced to accept a lower living standard while their friends—and their enemies—are left as before may be very distressing; but, if the whole of their class or group suffer alike, they will scarcely suffer at all. If everybody else is flaunting a pearl necklace and I, being for the purpose of the argument a lady, am not, I am grieved. But, if nobody has a pearl necklace, I shall be equally content with glass beads. Again, if nobody else has a motor car I am quite happy with a bicycle, and, if nobody else has even that, I am still happy with my feet. Yet again, if by the use of some miraculous drug *all* athletes or all animals found that they could run twice as fast as they can today the pleasures of human and animal athletics would be much the same as now. In short, a large part of the economic satisfaction which people derive from substantial incomes depends, not on their income being large absolutely, but upon its being larger, or at least not smaller, than those common in their social entourage. These considerations greatly strengthen the commonsense view that transfers away from better-to-do persons do not hurt the victims much, while the beneficiaries, whose needs are more elementary and less complex, gain from them a great deal.

Even apart, however, from indirect and secondary consequences, which I shall discuss presently, this is not in itself a sufficient defence for the Welfare State. For transfers can be made not merely through the compulsions of government authorities but also alternatively by voluntary action on the part of the well-to-do. Until quite recently it was strongly and widely felt that poor persons could be helped much more effectively by private charity—the squire and ladies bountiful—than by the State. For this view two quite sensible reasons were advanced. First the squire and his ladies could add sympathy to gifts of calves' foot jelly in a way that a public official could not; and the sympathy might to some extent counteract the demoralising effect of the jelly! The administrative machinery of the State and even of local authorities creaks and shudders under a load of red tape. It must proceed by way of general regulations which are often ill-adjusted to particular needs. On the other side is the fact that private charity not only may prove insufficient in the aggregate but also leaves gaps; its effective working depends on the accident of particular needy persons being accessible to particular squires and ladies ready to give them help. So it comes about that after a time the

State, with ever improving administrative machinery, takes over what private effort has pioneered. That is what happened in England with elementary education, first accepted as a voluntary obligation by the churches and from 1870 onwards becoming more and more completely the State's concern. In the same way in this country voluntary hospitals sustained by private subscription showed the way, and presently, under recent legislation, yielded place to the State. Plainly the State has great advantages. But plainly too it will be well advised not to cold-shoulder private benevolence, rather, so far as may be, to walk hand in hand with it. For private benevolence has the heart, for all that the State has the brawn and, more dubiously, the head.

In what circumstances, however, should the State act? That it should intervene to prevent destitution or extreme distress and, if need be, levy taxes and rates on better-to-do persons for that purpose was accepted doctrine long before the concept of the Welfare State was born. But the stress in earlier times was on *extreme* distress. The thought was of salvage operations in exceptional cases. Apart from this it was not the business of the State to interfere with what 'the laws of political economy' had decreed. It must keep the ring; which meant it must defend established—or vested—interests. To attack these even by mildly graduated income tax and death duties was robbery and confiscation. The rights of property were prior to law; the office of law was to sustain them. To suggest that they are the child of law, defensible only so far as they promote the general good, was not only mistaken but immoral. Assisted by the experience and needs of two world-shattering wars we now look back upon these ideas, widespread as they were no more than fifty years ago, with shocked surprise. They have passed into limbo and with their passing the practical issue is no longer whether the State has the right to interfere with the 'natural' distribution of income and wealth, but how far it can do so usefully.

Thus the indirect effects of transfers for the benefit of the poor, to which I have already referred, come into the picture. Alfred Marshall was urgent that the strongest, not merely the highest, motives of human nature should be harnessed to the public good. Among these strongest motives was the desire to earn money for oneself and for one's family. If of the money that well-to-do people earned the State took away too much, or took what it did take through taxes too sharply progressive, would not the victims, or at least a good proportion of them, work less hard and less long and so seriously reduce the size of the national cake? Might they not too be less willing, from what was left to them, to invest in machinery for *manufacturing* cake for other people, not themselves or their children, to enjoy? In short, must there not somewhere be a limiting zone, transfers beyond which in search of improved distribution will cut down production so far that the sum total of economic satisfaction is diminished, not increased? No doubt, if human nature changed and the generality of mankind became as interested in the well-being of strangers and strangers' children as in themselves and children of their own, there would be no risk of this sort of reaction. But, as things are, 'we are neither children nor gods but men in a world of men'. There is no getting away from that.

But here we come upon one of those frustrations with which economists too often meet. We know there must be a limiting zone somewhere and we can describe a number of circumstances and influences upon which its locality partly depends. But it is beyond our powers to determine where at any given time in any given circumstances, in any given country it actually is. We can point out that a number of people are so much interested in their work that they would gladly continue at it for nothing; that transfers to the poor, particularly for education and health, by in-

creasing efficiency and, maybe, the will to work, directly in their measure help production; and other such things. But generalities such as these do not tell us where the limiting zone is; what the reactions on production of particular schemes and scales of taxation will be. Trial will not help, for, unlike physicists and chemists, we cannot make controlled experiments and so cannot isolate the effects of one influence from among the welter of others that are operating at the same time. We can only guess; and, while the guess of an economist is likely to be less bad than other people's, there is no guarantee that, even so, it will not be very bad.

Of course, even if considerable damage to production results from State efforts to improve distribution, economic satisfaction as a whole may still be increased *so long as the damage is not cumulative*. That, as Marshall saw, is where the danger lies. Production, and so real income, falling, the rates of taxation needed to yield a given revenue correspondingly rise. Thus work and investment are discouraged a second time; and yet again a third time and a fourth time. One way of combating this insidious process is by coercion, penalties, appeals to fear; another, often highly effective in war time, less effective in peace, is by appeals to patriotism and a sense of duty; another, which Marshall did not despise, by the award of symbols of honour for good work done. Yet another is direct action by the State to foster productivity, for example by investment in research; or perhaps, as some people believe but others deny, through the supersession in selected industries of private enterprise by State operation; and so on. This is very loose. It cannot be set out in a blue print complete with statistics. It amounts to no more than a warning and a danger signal. The Welfare State holds in itself a *cumulative* threat to productivity, which is also a threat to its own survival. That threat should be continuously and carefully watched. We must not advance too far or too fast. For, if the good is an enemy to the better, the better is also an enemy to the good.

In this discussion I have designedly spoken as though the Welfare State were a closed system and have referred to the outside world only by remarking parenthetically that such a State may need to prepare defences against attack. By this device difficult issues have been shelved. Should a Welfare State in actual life self-containedly build up its own welfare and ignore the distresses of less fortunate parts of the world? How far should it be ready to delay its own advance by making gifts to them? How far should it do this out of pure philanthropy, how far in the hope of reaping ultimate advantage economic or political—there is a well-known, if dubious, slogan that penury is the breeding ground of aggressive revolution—for itself? These are unanswerable questions, not made easier in democratic countries by the fact that governments are trustees for their citizens, many of whom are firmly convinced that

charity begins—and ends—at home. One thing, however, is clear. In the actual world, international tension compels even the most peacefully intentioned governments to large expenditure on the maintenance of armed forces and the development of weapons to which much scientific and technical skill, that might have been used for peaceful purposes, has to be devoted. For example, more than 10 per cent of the annual income of the United Kingdom is now being absorbed in these uses. Defence is a rival to and competitor with the social services. Moreover, the indirect threat to production due to heavy progressive taxation rises more than in proportion to the amount of revenue that has to be raised. To reduce international tension, and therewith the need for armaments and armed forces, is probably the greatest, if also the most difficult, contribution that a statesman could make to the development of the Welfare State.

CHAPTER 26

FREUD

O NE of the main causes of Plato's lasting influence is that his theory of the state is based on a *theory of man*. Although his conception of the nature of man may seem out of date today, in some respects it shows a remarkable understanding of the complexity of human personality. His psychological hypotheses are weakest where his aristocratic, antidemocratic political outlook blocks his objective appraisal of reality, and where the antiscientific, mythical elements in his philosophy are reflected in his views on the nature of man. Yet, despite these psychological imperfections, his political theory gained immensely from his realization that no study of state and society can be fruitful unless it is based on a systematic conception of man's nature and motivations. In particular, Plato's sense of the complexity of social and political issues is anchored in the realization that they cannot be dealt with in isolation, and that they are ultimately human problems, infused with all the contradictory and irrational elements of man's nature and existence. This psychological element in Plato's political theory has always been one of its most suggestive aspects, regardless of whether one follows or rejects the conclusions of political Platonism.

In modern political theory Rousseau was perhaps the last writer who was keenly interested in the totality of man rather than in his political behavior alone. Like Plato, Rousseau was intensely concerned with education as a process of taming man's irrational forces and transmuting them into socially desirable activities from which the state could derive strength and cohesion. After Rousseau, political speculation increasingly abandoned the older tradition of Platonic and medieval thought in which the nature of the state was related to the nature of man. The classical political doctrines since the late eighteenth century generally have assumed an oversimplified rationalistic conception of man without subjecting it carefully to empirical analysis, and have proceeded to build a theory of state and society on the basis of such an assumption. Facts that do not seem to fit into the framework of theory have been dismissed as extraordinary, abnormal, irregular, or contrary to reason. The intellectual failure to account for the causes and existence of irrational, aggressive, and destructive facts in human relations was later reflected in the practical weakness of coping with such tendencies on the larger international scale.

A new dimension of understanding human behavior has been added by the work of Sigmund Freud (1856–1939). Freud started as a practicing physician in Vienna, and his psychological theories evolved out of his experience as a neurologist and psychiatrist, and not from any preconceived ideas. His pioneering contributions to medicine, psychology, and psychiatry are related to his discoveries of the processes and mechanisms of the *unconscious* in man's mind. Whereas pre-Freudian psychology virtually identified mental with conscious processes, Freud maintains (in his *General Introduction to Psychoanalysis*, 1916–1917) that "mental processes are essentially unconscious, and that those which are conscious are merely isolated acts and parts of the whole psychic entity."

Starting his clinical work with the treatment of the repressions and conflicts of neurotics, Freud soon saw that such conflicts were not peculiar to neurotics but were also characteristic of well-adjusted persons, and that neuroses were not diseases in the traditional meaning of the word but ineffective and distorted ways of dealing with psychological stresses and strains. In his *Psychopathology of Everyday Life* (1904), one of his earliest major works, Freud had already shown that the ordinary slips of the tongue, forgetting of familiar names or events, and other faulty actions of normal persons in everyday life were not the product of accident but repressed thoughts of the unconscious that come to the surface despite the attempt to conceal and repress them. The study of the unconscious led Freud to examine the nature of dreams and of wit and humor as expressions of thoughts that cannot be tolerated in the conscious layers of the mind.

Freud's emphasis on the vital role of repressed sexual impulses at first aroused a great deal of opposition. Later that opposition died down when it was understood that the scientific analysis of the unconscious, irrational forces in man has the effect of lessening their damaging effect: the more we progress in understanding the mechanisms and processes of these irrational forces, the more we may eventually succeed in rationally controlling them.

Firmly believing that psychological phenomena are embedded, like all other phenomena of nature, in the stream of causality, Freud pursued the origin of neurotic conflicts in adults to their childhood experiences, repressions, and conflicts. He found striking similarities between the mental processes of neurotics and children, and between these and the mental processes of primitive peoples. Pathological behavior of neurotics is largely and essentially regression to earlier, infantile stages in the development of normal functions, and the myths of primitive peoples show a striking resemblance to the phantasies of some classes of mentally ill in the western world. Particularly as he grew older, Freud became increasingly absorbed in the study of archaeology, ethnology, anthropology, religion, folklore, and mythology, and he drew attention to the remarkable similarities in the mental development of the individual and that of the human race as a whole.

One of Freud's most general works is his *Civilization and Its Discontents* (1930). Freud analyzes modern civilization in terms of two basic types of man's instinctual life: on the one hand, man has an impulse to love and cooperate, and, on the other, man has the impulse to attack and destroy. The first impulse is called by Freud (as by Plato in his *Symposium*) Eros, of which sexual love is only one manifestation. The purpose of the erotic impulse is to tie together, to establish ever greater unities, whereas the purpose of the second, the *death* instinct, is to attack, dissolve, destroy, and, finally, to reduce living things to an inorganic death. Freud shows that civilization owes its existence to the possibility of sublimating love for one's family into the wider friendship and loyalty for the group, society, and, lastly, the state.

Yet the very act of this transformation and sublimation of love creates tensions and frustrations that strengthen the aggressive impulses in man. The progress of civilization is thus a constant struggle between the cooperative and aggressive impulses in man, whose frustrations and conflicts turn into aggressive attitudes toward himself or others.

Writing in 1930, when the world seemed to be relatively safe and stable, Freud says in *Civilization and Its Discontents* that "civilized society is perpetually menaced with disintegration through this primary hostility of men towards one another." Freud argues against the communist thesis that the abolition of private property would eliminate personal and collective aggressions. Without taking sides with regard to the economic desirability of private property, Freud predicted in 1930 that the abolition of private property would not inaugurate a reign of love and cooperation in the Soviet Union. On the contrary, Freud warned that persecution in the Soviet Union would not come to an end once the bourgeois class was liquidated, and he predicted that the Russian Communists would eventually direct their aggressive tendencies against the outside world.

The emotional, "libidinal" ties that bind men together in furthering the progress of civilization are thus constantly menaced by the "natural instinct of aggressiveness in man, the hostility of each one against all and of all against each one." The meaning of the evolution of culture is therefore to be found in the constant struggle between "Eros and Death." Freud refused to prophesy whether aggression and destruction would ultimately triumph over cooperation, and he was perturbed by a new source of tension: men have learned to subdue the forces of nature to such an extent that the extermination of the whole human race has become a distinct possibility, and Freud ascribes to this fact (intensified a thousand times by the subsequent development of the atom and hydrogen bombs) an increased state of unrest, dejection, and apprehension that will lead to still more hostility and aggression.

In 1932 the League of Nations and the International Institute of Intellectual Cooperation asked Albert Einstein, the greatest physicist since Newton, to choose a significant issue of the time, and to discuss it with a person to be selected by him. Einstein chose the problem: "Is there a way of delivering mankind from the menace of war?" as the most important issue of humanity, and he selected Freud as the person most qualified to illuminate its cause and cure. This exchange of letters was published by the League of Nations under the title of *Why War?* in 1933. By that time the establishment of the Nazi regime in Germany had made the question one of tragic timeliness.

Applying again his two basic concepts of erotic and destructive impulses, Freud came to the conclusion that "there is no likelihood of our being able to suppress humanity's aggressive tendencies." The problem of eliminating war, Freud argues, cannot be tackled directly by seeking to abolish the aggressive impulses in man, but must be tackled indirectly by diverting these impulses into channels other than warfare and by strengthening the emotional ties that bring men together in common efforts and enjoyments. Freud also holds that the organization of society along rational principles rather than the traditional pattern of authoritarian leadership would indirectly strengthen the forces of peace. All such indirect methods, however, he is bound to admit, "conjure up an ugly picture of mills that grind so slowly that, before the flour is ready, men are dead of hunger."

Yet, owing to two main facts, Freud is not wholly pessimistic about the possibility of eliminating war: first, man's progressive ability to master intellectually his instinctual life, and, second, "a well-founded dread of the form that future wars will take." Civilization is essentially the process of taming and domesticating man's instincts, and Freud does not know how the next phase of that process will come about. But he ends with the not altogether hopeless note that "meanwhile we may rest on the assurance that whatever makes for cultural development is working also against war."

Freud did most of his life's work in a period of optimistic, rationalistic liberalism. He was one of the few scientists and thinkers of his era who realized how fragile were the foundations of rationalism and optimism, always menaced by the dark and little-known forces of demonic irrationality lurking in the unconscious of man. If the progress of civilization consists in advancing into the frontiers of the unknown, in conquering more and more ignorance and suffering, Freud's contribution to the tradition of scientific humanism is immense. Freud himself resolutely denied that psychoanalysis is in itself a comprehensive philosophy of life, a *Weltanschauung*, and insisted (in the last of his *New Introductory Lectures on Psycho-Analysis,* 1933) that psychoanalysis shares, as a specialized science and branch of psychology, in the general philosophical orientation of all science: "It asserts that there is no other source of knowledge of the universe but the systematic intellectual analysis of carefully verified observations —in fact, what is called research—and that no knowledge can be obtained from revelation, intuition, or divination."

Although Freud well understood that scientific thought is "still in its infancy," and that there are still many problems with which science has been unable to cope, he did not regard reason as an end in itself. In the great tradition of western humanism, he postulated the value of increasing man's happiness and decreasing his suffering as a worth-while practical goal, with reason as the only means to that end.

Whereas Plato saw in vision the supreme act of knowing truth, and in irrational myths the basis of authoritarian leadership, Freud regards verifiable experience as the only source of knowledge, and the rational organization of society —without the Platonic pattern of thought control and aristocratic domination— as the only means to a life of freedom and happiness. Wherever the adversaries of objective science—in fascist, communist, and other states—have gained power, Freud's name is considered dangerous and subversive. Wherever, on the other hand, thought is free and science unfettered, Freud's illumination of the dark recesses of the human mind and his strengthening of the scientific tradition will be honored as a milestone of humanist rationalism.

I. FREUD

Civilization and Its Discontents *

1. The Love Impulse

What are the influences to which the evolution of culture owes its origin, how did it arise and what determined its course?

This task seems too big a one; one may well confess oneself diffident. Here follows what little I have been able to elicit about it.

Once primitive man had made the discovery that it lay in his own hands—speaking literally—to improve his lot on earth by working, it cannot have been a matter of indifference to him whether another man worked with him or against him. The other acquired the value of a fellow-worker, and it was advantageous to live with him. Even earlier, in his ape-like prehistory, man had adopted the habit of forming families: his first helpers were probably the members of his family. One may suppose that the founding of families was in some way connected with the period when the need for genital satisfaction, no longer appearing like an occasional guest who turns up suddenly and then vanishes without letting one hear anything of him for long intervals, had

settled down with each man like a permanent lodger. When this happened, the male acquired a motive for keeping the female, or rather, his sexual objects, near him; while the female, who wanted not to be separated from her helpless young, in their interests, too, had to stay by the stronger male. In this primitive family one essential feature of culture is lacking: the will of the father, the head of it, was unfettered. I have endeavoured in *Totem und Tabu* to show how the way led from this family-life to the succeeding phase of communal existence in the form of a band of brothers. By overpowering the father, the sons had discovered that several men united can be stronger than a single man. The totemic stage of culture is founded upon the restrictions that the band were obliged to impose on one another in order to maintain the new system. These taboos were the first "Right" or law. The life of human beings in common therefore had a twofold foundation, *i.e.* the compulsion to work, created by external necessity, and the power of love, causing the male to wish to keep his sexual object, the female, near him, and the female to keep near her that part of herself which has become detached from her, her child. Eros and Ananke were the parents of human culture,

* From Sigmund Freud, *Civilization and Its Discontents* (Hogarth Press, 1930). By permission.

too. The first result of culture was that a larger number of human beings could then live together in common. And since the two great powers were here co-operating together, one might have expected that further cultural evolution would have proceeded smoothly towards ever greater mastery over the external world, as well as towards greater extension in the numbers of men sharing the life in common. Nor is it easy to understand how this culture can be felt as anything but satisfying by those who partake of it.

Before we go on to enquire where the disturbances in it arise, we will let ourselves digress from the point that love was one of the founders of culture and so fill a gap left in our previous discussion. We said that man, having found by experience that sexual (genital) love afforded him his greatest gratification, so that it became in effect a prototype of all happiness to him, must have been thereby impelled to seek his happiness further along the path of sexual relations, to make genital erotism the central point of his life. We went on to say that in so doing he becomes to a very dangerous degree dependent on a part of the outer world, namely, on his chosen love-object, and this exposes him to most painful sufferings if he is rejected by it or loses it through death or defection. The wise men of all ages have consequently warned us emphatically against this way of life; but in spite of all it retains its attraction for a great number of people.

A small minority are enabled by their constitution nevertheless to find happiness along the path of love; but far-reaching mental transformations of the erotic function are necessary before this is possible. These people make themselves independent of their object's acquiescence by transferring the main value from the fact of being loved to their own act of loving; they protect themselves against loss of it by attaching their love not to individual objects but to all men equally, and they avoid the uncertainties and disappointments of genital love by turning away from its sexual aim and modi-

fying the instinct into an impulse with an *inhibited aim*. The state which they induce in themselves by this process—an unchangeable, undeviating, tender attitude—has little superficial likeness to the stormy vicissitudes of genital love, from which it is nevertheless derived. It seems that Saint Francis of Assisi may have carried this method of using love to produce an inner feeling of happiness as far as anyone; what we are thus characterizing as one of the procedures by which the pleasure-principle fulfils itself has in fact been linked up in many ways with religion; the connection between them may lie in those remote fastnesses of the mind where the distinctions between the ego and objects and between the various objects become matters of indifference. From one ethical standpoint, the deeper motivation of which will later become clear to us, this inclination towards an all-embracing love of others and of the world at large is regarded as the highest state of mind of which man is capable. Even at this early stage in the discussion I will not withhold the two principal objections we have to raise against this view. A love that does not discriminate seems to us to lose some of its own value, since it does an injustice to its object. And secondly, not all men are worthy of love.

The love that instituted the family still retains its power; in its original form it does not stop short of direct sexual satisfaction, and in its modified form as aim-inhibited friendliness it influences our civilization. In both these forms its carries on its task of binding men and women to one another, and it does this with greater intensity than can be achieved through the interest of work in common. The casual and undifferentiated way in which the word "love" is employed by language has its genetic justification. In general usage the relation between a man and a woman whose genital desires have led them to found a family is called love; but the positive attitude of feeling between parents and children, between brothers and sisters in a family, is also called love, although to us this relation merits the description of aim-inhibited love or affection. Love with an inhibited aim was indeed originally full sensual love and in men's unconscious minds is so still. Both of them, the sensual and the aim-inhibited forms, reach out beyond the family and create new bonds with others who before were strangers. Genital love leads to the forming of new families; aim-inhibited love to "friendships," which are valuable culturally because they do not entail many of the limitations of genital love—for instance, its exclusiveness. But the interrelations between love and culture lose their simplicity as development proceeds. On the one hand, love opposes the interests of culture; on the other, culture menaces love with grievous restrictions.

This rift between them seems inevitable; the cause of it is not immediately recognizable. It expresses itself first in a conflict between the family and the larger community to which the individual belongs. We have seen already that one of culture's principal endeavours is to cement men and women together into larger units. But the family will not give up the individual. The closer the attachment between the members of it, the more they often tend to remain aloof from others, and the harder it is for them to enter into the wider circle of the world at large. That form of life in common which is phylogenetically older, and is in childhood its only form, resists being displaced by the type that becomes acquired later with culture. Detachment from the family has become a task that awaits every adolescent, and often society helps him through it with pubertal and initiatory rites. One gets the impression that these difficulties form an integral part of every process of mental evolution—and indeed, at bottom, of every organic development, too.

The next discord is caused by women, who soon become antithetical to cultural trends and spread around them their conservative influence—the women who at the beginning laid the foundations of culture by the appeal of their love. Women represent the interests of the family and sexual life; the work of civilization has become more and more men's business; it confronts them with

ever harder tasks, compels them to sublimations of instinct which women are not easily able to achieve. Since man has not an unlimited amount of mental energy at his disposal, he must accomplish his tasks by distributing his libido to the best advantage. What he employs for cultural purposes he withdraws to a great extent from women and his sexual life; his constant association with men and his dependence on his relations with them even estrange him from his duties as husband and father. Woman finds herself thus forced into the background by the claims of culture and she adopts an inimical attitude towards it.

The tendency of culture to set restrictions upon sexual life is no less evident than its other aim of widening its sphere of operations. Even the earliest phase of it, the totemic, brought in its train the prohibition against incestuous object-choice, perhaps the most maiming wound ever inflicted throughout the ages on the erotic life of man. Further limitations are laid on it by taboos, laws and customs, which touch men as well as women. Various types of culture differ in the lengths to which they carry this; and the material structure of the social fabric also affects the measure of sexual freedom that remains. We have seen that culture obeys the laws of psychological economic necessity in making the restrictions, for it obtains a great part of the mental energy it needs by subtracting it from sexuality. Culture behaves towards sexuality in this respect like a tribe or a section of the population which has gained the upper hand and is exploiting the rest to its own advantage. Fear of a revolt among the oppressed then becomes a motive for even stricter regulations. A high-water mark in this type of development has been reached in our Western European civilization. Psychologically it is fully justified in beginning by censuring any manifestations of the sexual life of children, for there would be no prospect of curbing the sexual desires of adults if the ground had not been prepared for it in childhood. Nevertheless there is no sort of justification for the lengths beyond this to which civilized society goes in actually denying the existence of these manifestations, which are not merely demonstrable but positively glaring. Where sexually mature persons are concerned, object-choice is further narrowed down to the opposite sex and most of the extra-genital forms of satisfaction are interdicted as perversions. The standard which declares itself in these prohibitions is that of a sexual life identical for all; it pays no heed to the disparities in the inborn and acquired sexual constitutions of individuals and cuts off a considerable number of them from sexual enjoyment, thus becoming a cause of grievous injustice. The effect of these restrictive measures might presumably be that all the sexual interest of those who are normal and not constitutionally handicapped could flow without further forfeiture into the channel left open to it. But the only outlet not thus censured, heterosexual genital love, is further circumscribed by the barriers of legitimacy and monogamy. Present-day civilization gives us plainly to understand that sexual relations are permitted only on the basis of a final, indissoluble bond between a man and woman; that sexuality as a source of enjoyment for its own sake is unacceptable to it; and that its intention is to tolerate it only as the hitherto irreplaceable means of multiplying the human race.

This, of course, represents an extreme. Everyone knows that it has proved impossible to put it into execution, even for short periods. Only the weaklings have submitted to such comprehensive interference with their sexual freedom, and stronger natures have done so only under one compensatory condition, of which mention may be made later. Civilized society has seen itself obliged to pass over in silence many transgressions which by its own ordinances it ought to have penalized. This does not justify anyone, however, in leaning towards the other side and assuming that, because it does not achieve all it aims at, such an attitude on the part of society is altogether harmless. The sexual life of civilized man is seriously disabled, whatever we may say; it some-

times makes an impression of being a function in process of becoming atrophied, just as organs like our teeth and our hair seem to be. One is probably right in supposing that the importance of sexuality as a source of pleasurable sensations, *i.e.* as a means of fulfilling the purpose of life, has perceptibly decreased.[1] Sometimes one imagines one perceives that it is not only the oppression of culture, but something in the nature of the function itself, that denies us full satisfaction and urges us in other directions. This may be an error; it is hard to decide.

2. *The Aggressive Impulse*

Psycho-analytic work has shown that these frustrations in respect of sexual life are especially unendurable to the so-called neurotics among us. These persons manufacture substitute-gratifications for themselves in their symptoms, which, however, are either painful in themselves or become the cause of suffering owing to the difficulties they create with the person's environment and society at large. It is easy to understand the latter fact, but the former presents us with a new problem. But culture demands other sacrifices besides that of sexual gratifications.

We have regarded the difficulties in the development of civilization as part of the general difficulty accompanying all evolution, for we have traced them to the inertia of libido, its disinclination to relinquish an old position in favour of a new one. It is much the same thing if we say that the conflict between civilization and sexuality is caused by the circumstance that sexual love is a relationship between two people, in which a third can only be superfluous or dis-

---

[1] There is a short story, which I valued long ago, by a highly sensitive writer, the Englishman, John Galsworthy, who to-day enjoys general recognition; it is called "The Apple Tree." It shows in a very moving and forcible way how there is no longer any place in present-day civilized life for a simple natural love between two human beings.

turbing, whereas civilization is founded on relations between larger groups of persons. When a love-relationship is at its height no room is left for any interest in the surrounding world; the pair of lovers are sufficient unto themselves, do not even need the child they have in common to make them happy. In no other case does Eros so plainly betray the core of his being, his aim of making one out of many; but when he has achieved it in the proverbial way through the love of two human beings, he is not willing to go further.

From all this we might well imagine that a civilized community could consist of pairs of individuals such as this, libidinally satisfied in each other, and linked to all the others by work and common interests. If this were so, culture would not need to levy energy from sexuality. But such a desirable state of things does not exist and never has existed; in actuality culture is not content with such limited ties as these; we see that it endeavours to bind the members of the community to one another by libidinal ties as well, that it makes use of every means and favours every avenue by which powerful identifications can be created among them, and that it exacts a heavy toll of aim-inhibited libido in order to strengthen communities by bonds of friendship between the members. Restrictions upon sexual life are unavoidable if this object is to be attained. But we cannot see the necessity that forces culture along this path and gives rise to its antagonism to sexuality. It must be due to some disturbing influence not yet detected by us.

We may find the clue in one of the so-called ideal standards of civilized society. It runs: "Thou shalt love thy neighbour as thyself." It is world-renowned, undoubtedly older than Christianity which parades it as its proudest profession, yet certainly not very old; in historical times men still knew nothing of it. We will adopt a naïve attitude towards it, as if we were meeting it for the first time. Thereupon we find ourselves unable to suppress a feeling of astonishment, as at something unnatural. Why

should we do this? What good is it to us? Above all, how can we do such a thing? How could it possibly be done? My love seems to me a valuable thing that I have no right to throw away without reflection. It imposes obligations on me which I must be prepared to make sacrifices to fulfil. If I love someone, he must be worthy of it in some way or other. (I am leaving out of account now the use he may be to me, as well as his possible significance to me as a sexual object; neither of these two kinds of relationship between us come into question where the injunction to love my neighbour is concerned.) He will be worthy of it if he is so like me in important respects that I can love myself in him; worthy of it if he is so much more perfect than I that I can love my ideal of myself in him; I must love him if he is the son of my friend, since the pain my friend would feel if anything untoward happened to him would be my pain —I should have to share it. But if he is a stranger to me and cannot attract me by any value he has in himself or any significance he may have already acquired in my emotional life, it will be hard for me to love him. I shall even be doing wrong if I do, for my love is valued as a privilege by all those belonging to me; it is an injustice to them if I put a stranger on a level with them. But if I am to love him (with that kind of universal love) simply because he, too, is a denizen of the earth, like an insect or an earthworm or a grass-snake, then I fear that but a small modicum of love will fall to his lot and it would be impossible for me to give him as much as by all the laws of reason I am entitled to retain for myself. What is the point of an injunction promulgated with such solemnity, if reason does not recommend it to us?

When I look more closely I find still further difficulties. Not merely is this stranger on the whole not worthy of love, but, to be honest, I must confess he has more claim to my hostility, even to my hatred. He does not seem to have the least trace of love for me, does not show me the sligheest consideration. If it will do him any good, he has no hesitation in injuring me, never even asking himself whether the amount of advantage he gains by it bears any proportion to the amount of wrong done to me. What is more, he does not even need to get an advantage from it; if he can merely get a little pleasure out of it, he thinks nothing of jeering at me, insulting me, slandering me, showing his power over me; and the more secure he feels himself, or the more helpless I am, with so much more certainty can I expect this behaviour from him towards me. If he behaved differently, if he showed me consideration and did not molest me, I should in any case, without the aforesaid commandment, be willing to treat him similarly. If the high-sounding ordinance had run, "Love thy neighbour as they neighbour loves thee," I should not take objection to it. And there is a second commandment that seems to me even more incomprehensible, and arouses still stronger opposition in me. It is: "Love thine enemies." When I think it over, however, I am wrong in treating it as a greater imposition. It is at bottom the same thing.[1]

I imagine now I hear a voice gravely adjuring me: "Just because thy neighbour is not worthy of thy love, is probably full of enmity towards thee, thou shouldst love him as thyself." I then perceive the case to be like that of *Credo quia absurdum.*

Now it is, of course, very probable that my neighbour, when he is commanded to love me as himself, will answer exactly as I have done and reject me for the same reasons. I hope he will not have the same objective grounds for doing so, but he will hope so as well. Even so, there are variations in men's behaviour which ethics, disregarding the fact that they are determined, classifies as "good" and "evil." As long as these undeniable variations have not been abolished, conformity to the highest ethical standards constitutes a betrayal of the interests of culture, for it puts a direct premium on wickedness. One is irresistibly reminded here of an incident in the French Chamber when capital punishment was being discussed; the speech of a member who had passionately supported its abolition was being applauded with loud acclamation, when suddenly a voice was heard calling out from the back of the room, *"Que messieurs les assassins commencent!"*

The bit of truth behind all this—one so eagerly denied—is that men are not gentle, friendly creatures wishing for love, who simply defend themselves if they are attacked, but that a powerful measure of desire for aggression has to be reckoned as part of their instinctual endowment. The result is that their neighbour is to them not only a possible helper or sexual object, but also a temptation to them to gratify their aggressiveness on him, to exploit his capacity for work without recompense, to use him sexually without his consent, to seize his possessions, to humiliate him, to cause him pain, to torture and to kill him. *Homo homini lupus;* who has the courage to dispute it in the face of all the evidence in his own life and in history? This aggressive cruelty usually lies in wait for some provocation, or else it steps into the service of some other purpose, the aim of which might as well have been achieved by milder measures. In circumstances that favour it, when those forces in the mind which ordinarily inhibit it cease to operate, it also manifests itself spontaneously and reveals men as savage beasts to whom the thought of sparing their own kind is alien. Anyone who calls to mind the atrocities of the early migrations, of the invasion by the Huns or by the so-called Mongols under Jenghiz Khan and Tamurlane, of the sack of Jerusalem

---

[1] A great poet may permit himself, at least in jest, to give utterance to psychological truths that are heavily censured. Thus Heine: "Mine is the most peaceable disposition. My wishes are a humble dwelling with a thatched roof, but a good bed, good food, milk and butter of the freshest, flowers at my windows, some fine tall trees before my door; and if the good God wants to make me completely happy, he will grant me the joy of seeing some six or seven of my enemies hanging from these trees. With my heart full of deep emotion I shall forgive them before they die all the wrong they did me in their lifetime—true, one must forgive one's enemies, but not until they are brought to execution." (Heine, *Gedanken und Einfälle.*)

by the pious Crusaders, even indeed the horrors of the last world-war, will have to bow his head humbly before the truth of this view of man.

The existence of this tendency to aggression which we can detect in ourselves and rightly presume to be present in others is the factor that disturbs our relations with our neighbours and makes it necessary for culture to institute its high demands. Civilized society is perpetually menaced with disintegration through this primary hostility of men towards one another. Their interests in their common work would not hold them together; the passions of instinct are stronger than reasoned interests. Culture has to call up every possible reinforcement in order to erect barriers against the aggressive instincts of men and hold their manifestations in check by reaction-formations in men's minds. Hence its system of methods by which mankind is to be driven to identifications and aim-inhibited love-relationships; hence the restrictions on sexual life; and hence, too, its ideal command to love one's neighbour as oneself, which is really justified by the fact that nothing is so completely at variance with original human nature as this. With all its striving, this endeavour of culture's has so far not achieved very much. Civilization expects to prevent the worst atrocities of brutal violence by taking upon itself the right to employ violence against criminals, but the law is not able to lay hands on the more discreet and subtle forms in which human aggressions are expressed. The time comes when every one of us has to abandon the illusory anticipations with which in our youth we regarded our fellow-men, and when we realize how much hardship and suffering we have been caused in life through their ill-will. It would be unfair, however, to reproach culture with trying to eliminate all disputes and competition from human concerns. These things are undoubtedly indispensable; but opposition is not necessarily enmity, only it may be misused to make an opening for it.

The Communists believe they have found a way of delivering us from this evil. Man is whole-heartedly good and friendly to his neighbour, they say, but the system of private property has corrupted his nature. The possession of private property gives power to the individual and thence the temptation arises to ill-treat his neighbour; the man who is excluded from the possession of property is obliged to rebel in hostility against the oppressor. If private property were abolished, all valuables held in common and all allowed to share in the enjoyment of them, ill-will and enmity would disappear from among men. Since all needs would be satisfied, none would have any reason to regard another as an enemy; all would willingly undertake the work which is necessary. I have no concern with any economic criticisms of the communistic system; I cannot enquire into whether the abolition of private property is advantageous and expedient.[2] But I am able to recognize that psychologically it is founded on an untenable illusion. By abolishing private property one deprives the human love of aggression of one of its instruments, a strong one undoubtedly, but assuredly not the strongest. It in no way alters the individual differences in power and influence which are turned by aggressiveness to its own use, nor does it change the nature of the instinct in any way. This instinct did not arise as the result of property; it reigned almost supreme in primitive times when possessions were still extremely scanty; it shows itself already in the nursery when possessions have hardly grown out of their original anal shape; it is at the bottom of

[2] Anyone who has been through the misery of poverty in his youth, and has endured the indifference and arrogance of those who have possessions, should be exempt from the suspicion that he has no understanding of or goodwill towards the endeavours made to fight the economic inequality of men and all that it leads to. To be sure, if an attempt is made to base this fight upon an abstract demand for equality for all in the name of justice, there is a very obvious objection to be made, namely, that nature began the injustice by the highly unequal way in which she endows individuals physically and mentally, for which there is no help.

all the relations of affection and love between human beings—possibly with the single exception of that of a mother to her male child. Suppose that personal rights to material goods are done away with, there still remain prerogatives in sexual relationships, which must arouse the strongest rancour and most violent enmity among men and women who are otherwise equal. Let us suppose this were also to be removed by instituting complete liberty in sexual life, so that the family, the germ-life of culture, ceased to exist; one could not, it is true, foresee the new paths on which cultural development might then proceed, but one thing one would be bound to expect, and that is that the ineffaceable feature of human nature would follow wherever it led.

Men clearly do not find it easy to do without satisfaction of this tendency to aggression that is in them; when deprived of satisfaction of it they are ill at ease. There is an advantage, not to be under-valued, in the existence of smaller communities, through which the aggressive instinct can find an outlet in enmity towards those outside the group. It is always possible to unite considerable numbers of men in love towards one another, so long as there are still some remaining as objects for aggressive manifestations. I once interested myself in the peculiar fact that peoples whose territories are adjacent, and are otherwise closely related, are always at feud with and ridiculing each other, as, for instance, the Spaniards and the Portuguese, the North and South Germans, the English and the Scotch, and so on. I gave it the name of "narcissism in respect of minor differences," which does not do much to explain it. One can now see that it is a convenient and relatively harmless form of satisfaction for aggressive tendencies, through which cohesion amongst the members of a group is made easier. The Jewish people, scattered in all directions as they are, have in this way rendered services which deserve recognition to the development of culture in the countries where they settled; but unfortunately not all the massacres of Jews in the Middle Ages sufficed to procure peace and security for their Christian contemporaries. Once the apostle Paul had laid down universal love between all men as the foundation of his Christian community, the inevitable consequence in Christianity was the utmost intolerance towards all who remained outside of it; the Romans, who had not founded their state on love, were not given to lack of religious toleration, although religion was a concern of the state, and the state was permeated through and through with it. Neither was it an unaccountable chance that the dream of a German world-dominion evoked a complementary movement towards anti-semitism; and it is quite intelligible that the attempt to establish a new communistic type of culture in Russia should find psychological support in the persecution of the bourgeois. One only wonders, with some concern, however, how the Soviets will manage when they have exterminated their bourgeois entirely.

If civilization requires such sacrifices, not only of sexuality but also of the aggressive tendencies in mankind, we can better understand why it should be so hard for men to feel happy in it. In actual fact primitive man was better off in this respect, for he knew nothing of any restrictions on his instincts. As a set-off against this, his prospects of enjoying his happiness for any length of time were very slight. Civilized man has exchanged some part of his chances of happiness for a measure of security. We will not forget, however, that in the primal family only the head of it enjoyed this instinctual freedom; the other members lived in slavish thraldom. The antithesis between a minority enjoying cultural advantages and a majority who are robbed of them was therefore most extreme in that primeval period of culture. With regard to the primitive human types living at the present time, careful investigation has revealed that their instinctual life is by no means to be envied on account of its freedom; it is subject to restrictions of a different kind but perhaps even more rigorous than is that of modern civilized man.

In rightly finding fault, as we thus do, with our present state of civilization for so inadequately providing us with what we require to make us happy in life, and for the amount of suffering of a probably avoidable nature it lays us open to—in doing our utmost to lay bare the roots of its deficiencies by our unsparing criticisms, we are undoubtedly exercising our just rights and not showing ourselves enemies of culture. We may expect that in the course of time changes will be carried out in our civilization so that it becomes more satisfying to our needs and no longer open to the reproaches we have made against it. But perhaps we shall also accustom ourselves to the idea that there are certain difficulties inherent in the very nature of culture which will not yield to any efforts at reform. Over and above the obligations of putting restrictions upon our instincts, which we see to be inevitable, we are imminently threatened with the dangers of a state one may call *"la misère psychologique"* of groups. This danger is most menacing where the social forces of cohesion consist predominantly of identifications of the individuals in the group with one another, whilst leading personalities fail to acquire the significance that should fall to them in the process of group-formation.[3] The state of civilization in America at the present day offers a good opportunity for studying this injurious effect of civilization which we have reason to dread. But I will resist the temptation to enter upon a criticism of American culture; I have no desire to give the impression that I would employ American methods myself.

3. The Struggle between Eros and Death

Never before in any of my previous writings have I had the feeling so strongly as I have now that what I am describing is common knowledge, that I am requisitioning

[3] Cf. *Group Psychology and the Analysis of the Ego* (1921). London: Hogarth Press, 1922.

paper and ink, and in due course the labour of compositors and printers, in order to expound things that in themselves are obvious. For this reason, if it should appear that the recognition of a special independent instinct of aggression would entail a modification of the psycho-analytical theory of instincts, I should be glad enough to seize upon the idea.

We shall see that this is not so, that it is merely a matter of coming to closer quarters with a conclusion to which we long ago committed ourselves and following it out to its logical consequences. The whole of analytic theory has evolved gradually enough, but the theory of instincts has groped its way forward under greater difficulties than any other part of it. And yet a theory of instincts was so indispensable for the rest that something had to be adopted in place of it. In my utter perplexity at the beginning, I took as my starting-point the poet-philosopher Schiller's aphorism, that hunger and love make the world go round. Hunger would serve to represent those instincts which aim at preservation of the individual; love seeks for objects; its chief function, which is favoured in every way by nature, is preservation of the species. Thus first arose the contrast between ego instincts and object instincts. For the energy of the latter instincts and exclusively for them I introduced the term libido; an antithesis was thus formed between the ego instincts and the libidinal instincts directed towards objects, *i.e.* love in its widest sense. One of these object instincts, the sadistic, certainly stood out from the rest in that its aim was so very unloving; moreover, it clearly allied itself in many of its aspects with the ego instincts, and its close kinship with instincts of mastery without any libidinal purpose could not be concealed, but these ambiguities could be overcome; in spite of them, sadism plainly belonged to sexual life—the game of cruelty could take the place of the game of love. Neurosis appeared as the outcome of a struggle between the interests of self-preservation and the claims of libido, a struggle in which the ego was victorious, but at the price of great suffering and renunciations.

Every analyst will admit that none of this even now reads like a statement long since recognized as erroneous. All the same, modifications had to be made as our researches advanced from the repressed to the repressing, from the object instincts to the ego. A cardinal point in this advance was the introduction of the concept of narcissism, *i.e.* the idea that libido cathects the ego itself, that its first dwelling-place was in the ego, and that the latter remains to some extent its permanent headquarters. This narcissistic libido turns in the direction of objects, thus becoming object-libido, and can transform itself back into narcissistic libido. The concept of narcissism made it possible to consider the traumatic neuroses, as well as many diseases bordering on the psychoses, and also the latter themselves, from the psycho-analytic angle. It was not necessary to abandon the view that the transference-neuroses are attempts on the part of the ego to guard itself against sexuality, but the concept of the libido was jeopardized. Since the ego-instincts were found to be libidinal as well, it seemed for a time inevitable that libido should become synonymous with instinctual energy in general, as C. G. Jung had previously advocated. Yet there still remained in me a kind of conviction, for which as yet there were no grounds, that the instincts could not all be of the same nature. I made the next step in *Beyond the Pleasure Principle* (1920), when the repetition-compulsion and the conservative character of instinctual life first struck me. On the basis of speculations concerning the origin of life and of biological parallels, I drew the conclusion that, beside the instinct preserving the organic substance and binding it into ever larger units,[1] there must exist another in antithesis to this, which would seek to dissolve these units and reinstate their antecedent inorganic state; that is to say, a death instinct as well as Eros; the phenomena of life would then be explicable from the interplay of the two and their counteracting effects on each other. It was not easy, however, to demonstrate the working of this hypothetical death instinct. The manifestations of Eros were conspicuous and audible enough; one might assume that the death instinct worked silently within the organism towards its disintegration, but that, of course, was no proof. The idea that part of the instinct became directed towards the outer world and then showed itself as an instinct of aggression and destruction carried us a step further. The instinct would thus itself have been pressed into the service of Eros, in that the organism would be destroying something animate or inanimate outside itself instead of itself. Conversely, any cessation of this flow outwards must have the effect of intensifying the self-destruction which in any case would always be going on within. From this example one could then surmise that the two kinds of instincts seldom—perhaps never—appear in isolation, but always mingle with each other in different, very varying proportions, and so make themselves unrecognizable to us. Sadism, long since known to us as a component-instinct of sexuality, would represent a particularly strong admixture of the instinct of destruction into the love impulse; while its counterpart, masochism, would be an alliance between sexuality and the destruction at work within the self, in consequence of which the otherwise imperceptible destructive trend became directly evident and palpable.

The assumption of the existence of a death instinct or a destruction instinct has aroused opposition even in analytical circles; I know that there is a great tendency to ascribe all that is dangerous and hostile in love rather to a fundamental bipolarity in its own nature. The conceptions I have summarized here I first put forward only tentatively, but in the course of time they have won such a hold over me that I can no

---

[1] The contradiction between the tireless tendency of Eros to spread ever further and the general conservative nature of the instincts here becomes very noticeable; it would serve as the starting-point of enquiries into further problems.

longer think in any other way. To my mind they are theoretically far more fruitful than any others it is possible to employ; they provide us with that simplification, without either ignoring or doing violence to the facts, which is what we strive after in scientific work. I know that we have always had before our eyes manifestations of the destruction instinct fused with erotism, directed outwards and inwards in sadism and masochism; but I can no longer understand how we could have overlooked the universality of nonerotic aggression and destruction, and could have omitted to give it its due significance in our interpretation of life. (It is true that the destructive trend that is directed inwards, when it is not erotically tinged, usually eludes our perceptions.) I can remember my own defensive attitude when the idea of an instinct of destruction first made its appearance in psycho-analytical literature and how long it took until I became accessible to it. That others should have shown the same resistance, and still show it, surprises me less. Those who love fairy tales do not like it when people speak of the innate tendencies in mankind towards aggression, destruction and, in addition, cruelty. For God has made them in his own image, with his own perfections; no one wants to be reminded how hard it is to reconcile the undeniable existence—in spite of all the protestations of Christian Science —of evil with his omnipotence and supreme goodness. The devil is, in fact, the best way out in acquittal of God; he can be used to play the same economic rôle of outlet as Jews in the world of Aryan ideals. But even so, one can just as well hold God responsible for the existence of the devil as for the evil he personifies. In view of these difficulties, it is expedient for every man to make humble obeisance on suitable occasions in honour of the high-minded nature of men; it will assist him to become universally beloved and much shall be forgiven unto him on account of it.[2]

The name libido can again be used to denote the manifestations of the power of Eros in contradistinction to the energy of the death instinct.[3] We must confess that it is more difficult for us to detect the latter, and to a great extent we can merely conjecture its existence as a background to Eros, also that it eludes us wherever it is not betrayed by a fusion with Eros. In sadism, where it bends the erotic aim to its own will and yet at the same time gratifies the sexual craving completely, we can obtain the clearest insight into its nature and its relation to Eros. But even where it shows itself without any sexual purpose, even in the blindest frenzy of destructiveness, one cannot ignore the fact that satisfaction of it is accompanied by an extraordinarily intense narcissistic enjoyment, due to the fulfilment it brings to the ego of its oldest omnipotence-wishes. The instinct of destruction, when tempered and harnessed (as it were, inhibited in its aim) and directed towards objects, is compelled to provide the ego with satisfaction of its needs and with power over nature. Since the assumption of its existence is based essentially on theoretical grounds, it must be confessed that it is not entirely proof against theoretical objections. But this is how things appear to us now in the present state of our knowledge; future research and reflection will undoubtedly bring further light which will decide the question.

---

[2] In Goethe's Mephistopheles we have a quite exceptionally striking identification of the principle of evil with the instinct of destruction:

All entities that be
Deserve their end—nonentity.

. . . .

So all that you name sin, destruction—
Wickedness, briefly—proves to be
The native element for me.

As his adversary, the devil himself cites not what is holy and good, but the power in nature working towards the creation and renewal of life —that is, Eros.

From air, from water, germs in thousands,
As from the soil, break forth, break free,
Dry, wet, warm, cold—a pullulation!
Had I not laid on flame a reservation,
Nothing were set apart for me.

[3] Our present point of view can be roughly expressed in the statement that libido participates in every instinctual manifestation, but that not everything in that manifestation is libido.

In all that follows I take up the standpoint that the tendency to aggression is an innate, independent, instinctual disposition in man, and I come back now to the statement that it constitutes the most powerful obstacle to culture. At one point in the course of this discussion the idea took possession of us that culture was a peculiar process passing over human life and we are still under the influence of this idea. We may add to this that the process proves to be in the service of Eros, which aims at binding together single human individuals, then families, then tribes, races, nations, into one great unity, that of humanity. Why this has to be done we do not know; it is simply the work of Eros. These masses of men must be bound to one another libidinally; necessity alone, the advantages of common work, would not hold them together. The natural instinct of aggressiveness in man, the hostility of each one against all and of all against each one, opposes this programme of civilization. This instinct of aggression is the derivative and main representative of the death instinct we have found alongside of Eros, sharing his rule over the earth. And now, it seems to me, the meaning of the evolution of culture is no longer a riddle to us. It must present to us the struggle between Eros and Death, between the instincts of life and the instincts of destruction, as it works itself out in the human species. This struggle is what all life essentially consists of and so the evolution of civilization may be simply described as the struggle of the human species for existence.[4] And it is this battle of the Titans that our nurses and governesses try to compose with their lullaby-song of Heaven!

For various reasons, it is very far from my intention to express any opinion concerning the value of human civilization. I have endeavoured to guard myself against the enthusiastic partiality which believes our civilization to be the most precious thing that we posses or could acquire, and thinks it must inevitably lead us to undreamt-of heights of perfection. I can at any rate listen without taking umbrage to those critics who aver that when one surveys the aims of civilization and the means it employs, one is bound to conclude that the whole thing is not worth the effort and that in the end it can only produce a state of things which no individual will be able to bear. My impartiality is all the easier to me since I know very little about these things and am sure only of one thing, that the judgements of value made by mankind are immediately determined by their desires for happiness; in other words, that those judgements are attempts to prop up their illusions with arguments. I could understand it very well if anyone were to point to the inevitable nature of the process of cultural development and say, for instance, that the tendency to institute restrictions upon sexual life or to carry humanitarian ideals into effect at the cost of natural selection is a developmental trend which it is impossible to avert or divert, and to which it is best for us to submit as though they were natural necessities. I know, too, the objection that can be raised against this: that tendencies such as these, which are believed to have insuperable power behind them, have often in the history of man been thrown aside and replaced by others. My courage fails me, therefore, at the thought of rising up as a prophet before my fellow-men, and I bow to their reproach that I have no consolation to offer them; for at bottom this is what they all demand—the frenzied revolutionary as passionately as the most pious believer.

The fateful question of the human species seems to me to be whether and to what extent the cultural process developed in it will succeed in mastering the derangements of communal life caused by the human instinct of aggression and self-destruction. In this connection, perhaps the phase through which we are at this moment passing deserves special interest. Men have brought their powers of subduing the forces

---

[4] And we may probably add more precisely that its form was necessarily determined after some definite event which still remains to be discovered.

of nature to such a pitch that by using them they could now very easily exterminate one another to the last man. They know this— hence arises a great part of their current unrest, their dejection, their mood of apprehension. And now it may be expected that the other of the two "heavenly forces," eternal Eros, will put forth his strength so as to maintain himself alongside of his equally immortal adversary.

II. EINSTEIN and FREUD

Why War? *

Caputh near Potsdam, 30th July, 1932.
Dear Professor Freud,

The proposal of the League of Nations and its International Institute of Intellectual Co-operation at Paris that I should invite a person, to be chosen by myself, to a frank exchange of views on any problem that I might select affords me a very welcome opportunity of conferring with you upon a question which, as things now are, seems the most insistent of all the problems civilisation has to face. This is the problem: Is there any way of delivering mankind from the menace of war? It is common knowledge that, with the advance of modern science, this issue has come to mean a matter of life and death for civilisation as we know it; nevertheless, for all the zeal displayed, every attempt at its solution has ended in a lamentable breakdown.

I believe, moreover, that those whose duty it is to tackle the problem professionally and practically are growing only too aware of their impotence to deal with it, and have now a very lively desire to learn the views of men who, absorbed in the pursuit of science, can see world-problems in the per-

spective distance lends. As for me, the normal objective of my thought affords no insight into the dark places of human will and feeling. Thus, in the enquiry now proposed, I can do little more than seek to clarify the question at issue and, clearing the ground of the more obvious solutions, enable you to bring the light of your far-reaching knowledge of man's instinctive life to bear upon the problem. There are certain psychological obstacles whose existence a layman in the mental sciences may dimly surmise, but whose interrelations and vagaries he is incompetent to fathom; you, I am convinced, will be able to suggest educative methods, lying more or less outside the scope of politics, which will eliminate these obstacles.

As one immune from nationalist bias, I personally see a simple way of dealing with the superficial (i.e. administrative) aspect of the problem: the setting up, by international consent, of a legislative and judicial body to settle every conflict arising between nations. Each nation would undertake to abide by the orders issued by this legislative body, to invoke its decision in every dispute, to accept its judgments unreservedly and to carry out every measure the tribunal deems necessary for the execution of its decrees.

---

* (International Institute of Intellectual Co-operation, League of Nations, 1933). By permission.

But here, at the outset, I come up against a difficulty; a tribunal is a human institution which, in proportion as the power at its disposal is inadequate to enforce its verdicts, is all the more prone to suffer these to be deflected by extrajudicial pressure. This is a fact with which we have to reckon; law and might inevitably go hand in hand, and juridical decisions approach more nearly the ideal justice demanded by the community (in whose name and interests these verdicts are pronounced) in so far as the community has effective power to compel respect of its juridical ideal. But at present we are far from possessing any supranational organisation competent to render verdicts of incontestable authority and enforce absolute submission to the execution of its verdicts. Thus I am led to my first axiom: the quest of international security involves the unconditional surrender by every nation, in a certain measure, of its liberty of action, its sovereignty that is to say, and it is clear beyond all doubt that no other road can lead to such security.

The ill-success, despite their obvious sincerity, of all the efforts made during the last decade to reach this goal leaves us no room to doubt that strong psychological factors are at work, which paralyse these efforts. Some of these factors are not far to seek. The craving for power which characterises the governing class in every nation is hostile to any limitation of the national sovereignty. This political power-hunger is wont to batten on the activities of another group, whose aspirations are on purely mercenary, economic lines. I have specially in mind that small but determined group, active in every nation, composed of individuals who, indifferent to social considerations and restraints, regard warfare, the manufacture and sale of arms, simply as an occasion to advance their personal interests and enlarge their personal authority.

But recognition of this obvious fact is merely the first step towards an appreciation of the actual state of affairs. Another question follows hard upon it: How is it possible for this small clique to bend the will of the majority, who stand to lose and suffer by a state of war, to the service of their ambitions? (In speaking of the majority, I do not exclude soldiers of every rank who have chosen war as their profession, in the belief that they are serving to defend the highest interests of their race, and that attack is often the best method of defence.) An obvious answer to this question would seem to be that the minority, the ruling class at present, has the schools and press, usually the Church as well, under its thumb. This enables it to organise and sway the emotions of the masses, and make its tool of them.

Yet even this answer does not provide a complete solution. Another question arises from it: How is it these devices succeed so well in rousing men to such wild enthusiasm, even to sacrifice their lives? Only one answer is possible. Because man has within him a lust for hatred and destruction. In normal times this passion exists in a latent state, it emerges only in unusual circumstances; but it is a comparatively easy task to call it into play and raise it to the power of a collective psychosis. Here lies, perhaps, the crux of all the complex of factors we are considering, an enigma that only the expert in the lore of human instincts can resolve.

And so we come to our last question. Is it possible to control man's mental evolution so as to make him proof against the psychoses of hate and destructiveness? Here I am thinking by no means only of the so-called uncultured masses. Experience proves that it is rather the so-called "Intelligentsia" that is most apt to yield to these disastrous collective suggestions, since the intellectual has no direct contact with life in the raw, but encounters it in its easiest, synthetic form—upon the printed page.

To conclude: I have so far been speaking only of wars between nations; what are known as international conflicts. But I am well aware that the aggressive instinct operates under other forms and in other circumstances. (I am thinking of civil wars, for instance, due in earlier days to religious zeal, but nowadays to social factors; or, again, the persecution of racial minorities.) But my insistence on what is the most typical, most cruel and extravagant form of conflict between man and man was deliberate, for here we have the best occasions of discovering ways and means to render all armed conflicts impossible.

I know that in your writings we may find answers, explicit or implied, to all the issues of this urgent and absorbing problem. But it would be of the greatest service to us all were you to present the problem of world peace in the light of your most recent discoveries, for such a presentation well might blaze the trail for new and fruitful modes of action.

Yours very sincerely,

A. Einstein

Vienna, September, 1932.

Dear Professor Einstein,

When I learnt of your intention to invite me to a mutual exchange of views upon a subject which not only interested you personally but seemed deserving, too, of public interest, I cordially assented. I expected you to choose a problem lying on the borderland of the knowable, as it stands to-day, a theme which each of us, physicist and psychologist, might approach from his own angle, to meet at last on common ground, though setting out from different premises. Thus the question which you put me—what is to be done to rid mankind of the war-menace?—took me by surprise. And, next, I was dumbfounded by the thought of my (of *our*, I almost wrote) incompetence; for this struck me as being a matter of practical politics, the statesman's proper study. But then I realised that you did not raise the question in your capacity of scientist or physicist, but as a lover of his fellow men, who responded to the call of the League of Nations much as Fridtjof Nansen, the Polar explorer, took on himself the task of succouring homeless and starving victims of the World War. And, next, I reminded myself that I was not being called on to formulate practical proposals, but,

rather, to explain how this question of preventing wars strikes a psychologist.

But here, too, you have stated the gist of the matter in your letter—and taken the wind out of my sails! Still, I will gladly follow in your wake and content myself with endorsing your conclusions, which, however, I propose to amplify to the best of my knowledge or surmise.

You begin with the relations between Might and Right, and this is assuredly the proper starting-point for our enquiry. But, for the term "might," I would substitute a tougher and more telling word: "violence." In right and violence we have to-day an obvious antinomy. It is easy to prove that one has evolved from the other, and, when we go back to origins and examine primitive conditions, the solution of the problem follows easily enough. I must crave your indulgence if in what follows I speak of well-known, admitted facts as though they were new *data;* the context necessitates this method.

Conflicts of interest between man and man are resolved, in principle, by the recourse to violence. It is the same in the animal kingdom, from which man cannot claim exclusion; nevertheless men are also prone to conflicts of opinion, touching, on occasion, the loftiest peaks of abstract thought, which seem to call for settlement by quite another method. This refinement is, however, a late development. To start with, brute force was the factor which, in small communities, decided points of ownership and the question which man's will was to prevail. Very soon physical force was implemented, then replaced, by the use of various adjuncts; he proved the victor whose weapon was the better, or handled the more skilfully. Now, for the first time, with the coming of weapons, superior brains began to oust brute force, but the object of the conflict remained the same: one party was to be constrained, by the injury done him or impairment of his strength, to retract a claim or a refusal. This end is most effectively gained when the opponent is definitively put out of action—in other words, is killed. This procedure has two advantages; the enemy cannot renew hostilities, and, secondly, his fate deters others from following his example. Moreover, the slaughter of a foe gratified an instinctive craving—a point to which we shall revert hereafter. However, another consideration may be set off against this will to kill: the possibility of using an enemy for servile tasks if his spirit be broken and his life spared. Here violence finds an outlet not in slaughter but in subjugation. Hence springs the practice of giving quarter; but the victor, having from now on to reckon with the craving for revenge that rankles in his victim, forfeits to some extent his personal security.

Thus, under primitive conditions, it is superior force—brute violence, or violence backed by arms—that lords it everywhere. We know that in the course of evolution this state of things was modified, a path was traced that led away from violence to law. But what was this path? Surely it issued from a single verity; that the superiority of one strong man can be overborne by an alliance of many weaklings, that *l'union fait la force*. Brute force is overcome by union, the allied might of scattered units makes good its right against the isolated giant. Thus we may define "right" (i.e. law) as the might of a community. Yet it, too, is nothing else than violence, quick to attack whatever individual stands in its path, and it employs the selfsame methods, follows like ends, with but one difference; it is the communal, not individual violence that has its way. But, for the transition from crude violence to the reign of law, a certain psychological condition must first obtain. The union of the majority must be stable and enduring. If its sole *raison d'être* be the discomfiture of some overweening individual and, after his downfall, it be dissolved, it leads to nothing. Some other man, trusting to his superior power, will seek to reinstate the rule of violence and the cycle will repeat itself unendingly. Thus the union of the people must be permanent and well organised; it must enact rules to meet the risk of possible revolts; must set up machinery ensuring that its rules—the laws—are observed and that such acts of violence as the laws demand are duly carried out. This recognition of a community of interests engenders among the members of the group a sentiment of unity and fraternal solidarity which constitutes its real strength.

So far I have set out what seems to me the kernel of the matter: the suppression of brute force by the transfer of power to a larger combination, founded on the community of sentiments linking up its members. All the rest is mere tautology and glosses. Now the position is simple enough so long as the community consists of a number of equipollent individuals. The laws of such a group can determine to what extent the individual must forfeit his personal freedom, the right of using personal force as an instrument of violence, to ensure the safety of the group. But such a combination is only theoretically possible; in practice the situation is always complicated by the fact that, from the outset, the group includes elements of unequal power, men and women, elders and children, and, very soon, as a result of war and conquest, victors and the vanquished—i.e. masters and slaves—as well. From this time on the common law takes notice of these inequalities of power, laws are made by and for the rulers, giving the servile classes fewer rights. Thenceforward there exist within the state two factors making for legal instability, but legislative evolution, too: first, the attempts by members of the ruling class to set themselves above the law's restrictions and, secondly, the constant struggle of the ruled to extend their rights and see each gain embodied in the code, replacing legal disabilities by equal laws for all. The second of these tendencies will be particularly marked when there takes place a positive mutation of the balance of power within the community, the frequent outcome of certain historical conditions. In such cases the laws may gradually be adjusted to the changed conditions or (as more usually ensues) the ruling class is loath to reckon with the new developments, the result being insurrections and civil wars, a period when law is in abeyance and force once more the arbiter, followed by a new regime of law. There is another factor of constitutional change, which operates in a wholly pacific manner, viz: the cultural evolution of the mass of the community; this factor, however, is of a different order and can only be dealt with later.

Thus we see that, even within the group itself, the exercise of violence cannot be avoided when conflicting interests are at stake. But the common needs and habits of men who live in fellowship under the same sky favour a speedy issue of such conflicts and, this being so, the possibilities of peaceful solutions make steady progress. Yet the most casual glance at world-history will show an unending series of conflicts between one community and another or a group of others, between large and smaller units, between cities, countries, races, tribes, and kingdoms, almost all of which were settled by the ordeal of war. Such wars end either in pillage or in conquest and its fruits, the downfall of the loser. No single all-embracing judgment can be passed on these wars of aggrandisement. Some, like the war between the Mongols and the Turks, have led to unmitigated misery; others, however, have furthered the transition from violence to law, since they brought larger units into being, within whose limits a recourse to violence was banned and a new regime determined all disputes. Thus the Roman conquests brought that boon, the *pax romana,* to the Mediterranean lands. The French kings' lust for aggrandisement created a new France, flourishing in peace and unity. Paradoxical as it sounds, we must admit that warfare well might serve to pave the way to that unbroken peace we so desire, for it is war that brings vast empires into being, within whose frontiers all warfare is proscribed by a strong central power. In practice, however, this end is not attained, for as a rule the fruits of victory are but short-lived, the new-created unit falls asunder once again, generally because there can be no true cohesion between the parts that vi-

olence has welded. Hitherto, moreover, such conquests have only led to aggregations which, for all their magnitude, had limits, and disputes between these units could be resolved only by recourse to arms. For humanity at large the sole result of all these military enterprises was that, instead of frequent not to say incessant little wars, they had now to face great wars which, for all they came less often, were so much the more destructive.

Regarding the world of to-day the same conclusion holds good, and you, too, have reached it, though by a shorter path. There is but one sure way of ending war and that is the establishment, by common consent, of a central control which shall have the last word in every conflict of interests. For this, two things are needed: first, the creation of such a supreme court of judicature; secondly, its investment with adequate executive force. Unless this second requirement be fulfilled, the first is unavailing. Obviously the League of Nations, acting as a Supreme Court, fulfils the first condition; it does not fulfil the second. It has no force at its disposal and can only get it if the members of the new body, its constituent nations, furnish it. And, as things are, this is a forlorn hope. Still we should be taking a very short-sighted view of the League of Nations were we to ignore the fact that here is an experiment the like of which has rarely—never before, perhaps, on such a scale—been attempted in the course of history. It is an attempt to acquire the authority (in other words, coercive influence), which hitherto reposed exclusively on the possession of power, by calling into play certain idealistic attitudes of mind. We have seen that there are two factors of cohesion in a community: violent compulsion and ties of sentiment ("identifications," in technical parlance) between the members of the group. If one of these factors becomes inoperative, the other may still suffice to hold the group together. Obviously such notions as these can only be significant when they are the expression of a deeply rooted sense of unity, shared by all. It is necessary, therefore, to gauge the efficacy of such sentiments. History tells us that, on occasion, they have been effective. For example, the Panhellenic conception, the Greeks' awareness of superiority over their barbarian neighbours, which found expression in the Amphictyonies, the Oracles and Games, was strong enough to humanise the methods of warfare as between Greeks, though inevitably it failed to prevent conflicts between different elements of the Hellenic race or even to deter a city or group of cities from joining forces with their racial foe, the Persians, for the discomfiture of a rival. The solidarity of Christendom in the Renaissance age was no more effective, despite its vast authority, in hindering Christian nations, large and small alike, from calling in the Sultan to their aid. And, in our times, we look in vain for some such unifying notion whose authority would be unquestioned. It is all too clear that the nationalistic ideas, paramount to-day in every country, operate in quite a contrary direction. Some there are who hold that the Bolshevist conceptions may make an end of war, but, as things are, that goal lies very far away and, perhaps, could only be attained after a spell of brutal internecine warfare. Thus it would seem that any effort to replace brute force by the might of an ideal is, under present conditions, doomed to fail. Our logic is at fault if we ignore the fact that right is founded on brute force and even to-day needs violence to maintain it.

I now can comment on another of your statements. You are amazed that it is so easy to infect men with the war-fever, and you surmise that man has in him an active instinct for hatred and destruction, amenable to such stimulations. I entirely agree with you. I believe in the existence of this instinct and have been recently at pains to study its manifestations. In this connexion may I set out a fragment of that knowledge of the instincts, which we psychoanalysts, after so many tentative essays and gropings in the dark, have compassed? We assume that human instincts are of two kinds: those that conserve and unify, which we call "erotic" (in the meaning Plato gives to Eros in his Symposium), or else "sexual" (explicitly extending the popular connotation of "sex"); and, secondly, the instincts to destroy and kill, which we assimilate as the aggressive or destructive instincts. These are, as you perceive, the well-known opposites, Love and Hate, transformed into theoretical entities; they are, perhaps, another aspect of those eternal polarities, attraction and repulsion, which fall within your province. But we must be chary of passing over-hastily to the notions of good and evil. Each of these instincts is every whit as indispensable as its opposite and all the phenomena of life derive from their activity, whether they work in concert or in opposition. It seems that an instinct of either category can operate but rarely in isolation; it is always blended ("alloyed," as we say) with a certain dosage of its opposite, which modifies its aim or even, in certain circumstances, is a prime condition of its attainment. Thus the instinct of self-preservation is certainly of an erotic nature, but to gain its ends this very instinct necessitates aggressive action. In the same way the love-instinct, when directed to a specific object, calls for an admixture of the acquisitive instinct if it is to enter into effective possession of that object. It is the difficulty of isolating the two kinds of instinct in their manifestations that has so long prevented us from recognising them.

If you will travel with me a little further on this road, you will find that human affairs are complicated in yet another way. Only exceptionally does an action follow on the stimulus of a single instinct, which is *per se* a blend of Eros and destructiveness. As a rule several motives of similar composition concur to bring about the act. This fact was duly noted by a colleague of yours, Professor G. C. Lichtenberg, sometime Professor of Physics at Göttingen; he was perhaps even more eminent as a psychologist than as a physical scientist. He evolved the notion of a "Compasscard of Motives" and wrote: "The efficient motives impelling man to act can be classified like the 32 Winds, and described in the same manner; e.g. Food-Food-Fame or Fame-Fame-Food." Thus, when a nation is summoned to engage in war, a whole gamut of human motives may respond to this appeal; high and low motives, some openly avowed, others slurred over. The lust for aggression and destruction is certainly included; the innumerable cruelties of history and man's daily life confirm its prevalence and strength. The stimulation of these destructive impulses by appeals to idealism and the erotic instinct naturally facilitates their release. Musing on the atrocities recorded on history's page, we feel that the ideal motive has often served as a camouflage for the lust of destruction; sometimes, as with the cruelties of the Inquisition, it seems that, while the ideal motives occupied the foreground of consciousness, they drew their strength from the destructive instincts submerged in the unconscious. Both interpretations are feasible.

You are interested, I know, in the prevention of war, not in our theories, and I keep this fact in mind. Yet I would like to dwell a little longer on this destructive instinct which is seldom given the attention that its importance warrants. With the least of speculative efforts we are led to conclude that this instinct functions in every living being, striving to work its ruin and reduce life to its primal state of inert matter. Indeed it might well be called the "death-instinct"; whereas the erotic instincts vouch for the struggle to live on. The death instinct becomes an impulse to destruction when, with the aid of certain organs, it directs its action outwards, against external objects. The living being, that is to say, defends its own existence by destroying foreign bodies. But, in one of its activities, the death instinct is operative *within* the living being and we have sought to trace back a number of normal and pathological phenomena to this *introversion* of the destructive instinct. We have even committed the heresy of explaining the origin of human conscience by some such "turning inward" of the aggressive impulse. Obviously when this internal tendency operates on too large a scale, it is no trivial matter, rather a positively morbid state of things; whereas the diversion of the destructive impulse towards the external world must have beneficial effects. Here is then the biological justification for all those vile, pernicious propensities which we now are combating. We can but own that they are really more akin to nature than this our stand against them, which, in fact, remains to be accounted for.

All this may give you the impression that our theories amount to a species of mythology and a gloomy one at that! But does not every natural science lead ultimately to this—a sort of mythology? Is it otherwise to-day with your physical science?

The upshot of these observations, as bearing on the subject in hand, is that there is no likelihood of our being able to suppress humanity's aggressive tendencies. In some happy corners of the earth, they say, where nature brings forth abundantly whatever man desires, there flourish races whose lives go gently by, unknowing of aggression or constraint. This I can hardly credit; I would like further details about these happy folk. The Bolshevists, too, aspire to do away with human aggressiveness by ensuring the satisfaction of material needs and enforcing equality between man and man. To me this hope seems vain. Meanwhile they busily perfect their armaments, and their hatred of outsiders is not the least of the factors of cohesion amongst themselves. In any case, as you too have observed, complete suppression of man's aggressive tendencies is not in issue; what we may try is to divert it into a channel other than that of warfare.

From our "mythology" of the instincts we may easily deduce a formula for an indirect method of eliminating war. If the propensity for war be due to the destructive instinct, we have always its counter-agent, Eros, to our hand. All that produces ties of sentiment between man and man must serve us as war's antidote. These ties are of two kinds. First, such relations as those towards a beloved object, void though they be of sexual intent. The psychoanalyst need feel no compunction in mentioning "love" in this connexion; religion uses the same language: Love thy neighbour as thyself. A pious injunction easy to enounce, but hard to carry out! The other bond of sentiment is by way of identification. All that brings out the significant resemblances between men calls into play this feeling of community, identification, whereon is founded, in large measure, the whole edifice of human society.

In your strictures on the abuse of authority I find another suggestion for an indirect attack on the war-impulse. That men are divided into leaders and the led is but another manifestation of their inborn and irremediable inequality. The second class constitutes the vast majority; they need a high command to make decisions for them, to which decisions they usually bow without demur. In this context we would point out that men should be at greater pains than heretofore to form a superior class of independent thinkers, unamenable to intimidation and fervent in the quest of truth, whose function it would be to guide the masses dependent on their lead. There is no need to point out how little the rule of politicians and the Church's ban on liberty of thought encourage such a new creation. The ideal conditions would obviously be found in a community where every man subordinated his instinctive life to the dictates of reason. Nothing less than this could bring about so thorough and so durable a union between men, even if this involved the severance of mutual ties of sentiment. But surely such a hope is utterly utopian, as things are. The other indirect methods of preventing war are certainly more feasible, but entail no quick results. They conjure up an ugly picture of mills that grind so slowly that, before the flour is ready, men are dead of hunger.

As you see, little good comes of consulting a theoretician, aloof from worldly contacts. on practical and urgent problems!

Better it were to tackle each successive crisis with means that we have ready to our hands. However, I would like to deal with a question which, though it is not mooted in your letter, interests me greatly. Why do we, you and I and many an other, protest so vehemently against war, instead of just accepting it as another of life's odious importunities? For it seems a natural thing enough, biologically sound and practically unavoidable. I trust you will not be shocked by my raising such a question. For the better conduct of an inquiry it may be well to don a mask of feigned aloofness. The answer to my query may run as follows: Because every man has a right over his own life and war destroys lives that were full of promise; it forces the individual into situations that shame his manhood, obliging him to murder fellow men, against his will; it ravages material amenities, the fruits of human toil, and much besides. Moreover wars, as now conducted, afford no scope for acts of heroism according to the old ideals and, given the high perfection of modern arms, war to-day would mean the sheer extermination of one of the combatants, if not of both. This is so true, so obvious, that we can but wonder why the conduct of war is not banned by general consent. Doubtless either of the points I have just made is open to debate. It may be asked if the community, in its turn, cannot claim a right over the individual lives of its members. Moreover, all forms of war cannot be indiscriminately condemned; so long as there are nations and empires, each prepared callously to exterminate its rival, all alike must be equipped for war. But we will not dwell on any of these problems; they lie outside the debate to which you have invited me. I pass on to another point, the basis, as it strikes me, of our common hatred of war. It is this: we cannot do otherwise than hate it. Pacifists we are, since our organic nature wills us thus to be. Hence it comes easy to us to find arguments that justify our standpoint.

This point, however, calls for elucidation. Here is the way in which I see it. The cultural development of mankind (some, I know, prefer to call it civilisation) has been in progress since immemorial antiquity. To this processus we owe all that is best in our composition, but also much that makes for human suffering. Its origins and causes are obscure, its issue is uncertain, but some of its characteristics are easy to perceive. It well may lead to the extinction of mankind, for it impairs the sexual function in more than one respect, and even to-day the uncivilised races and the backward classes of all nations are multiplying more rapidly than the cultured elements. This process may, perhaps, be likened to the effects of domestication on certain animals—it clearly involves physical changes of structure—but the view that cultural development is an organic process of this order has not yet become generally familiar. The psychic changes which accompany this process of cultural change are striking, and not to be gainsaid. They consist in the progressive rejection of instinctive ends and a scaling down of instinctive reactions. Sensations which delighted our forefathers have become neutral or unbearable to us; and, if our ethical and aesthetic ideals have undergone a change, the causes of this are ultimately organic. On the psychological side two of the most important phenomena of culture are, firstly, a strengthening of the intellect, which tends to master our instinctive life, and, secondly, an introversion of the aggressive impulse, with all its consequent benefits and perils. Now war runs most emphatically counter to the psychic disposition imposed on us by the growth of culture; we are therefore bound to resent war, to find it utterly intolerable. With pacifists like us it is not merely an intellectual and affective repulsion, but a constitutional intolerance, an idiosyncrasy in its most drastic form. And it would seem that the aesthetic ignominies of warfare play almost as large a part in this repugnance as war's atrocities.

How long have we to wait before the rest of men turn pacifist? Impossible to say, and yet perhaps our hope that these two factors—man's cultural disposition and a well-founded dread of the form that future wars will take—may serve to put an end to war in the near future, is not chimerical. But by what ways or by-ways this will come about, we cannot guess. Meanwhile we may rest on the assurance that whatever makes for cultural development is working also against war.

With kindest regards and, should this *exposé* prove a disappointment to you, my sincere regrets,

Yours,
Sigmund Freud

BIBLIOGRAPHICAL NOTES

THE best general history of political theory is Bertrand Russell, *A History of Western Philosophy: And Its Connection with Political and Social Circumstances from the Earliest Times to the Present Day* (New York, 1945). It is the only history of political philosophy written by a distinguished philosopher, and it has three outstanding qualities: first, it is a source of pleasure from a purely literary viewpoint (Russell received the Nobel Prize in literature in 1950) and thus demonstrates that there need be no drudgery in science and philosophy; second, Russell's discussion of political ideas is constantly related to the main issues of general philosophy; third, unlike many writers of histories of political theory who identify themselves in each chapter with the thinker they discuss, Russell writes from a definite and clearly stated point of view. Thus his work has direction and compactness.

The following will also be found useful: Crane Brinton, *Ideas and Men: The Story of Western Thought* (New York, 1950); George Catlin, *The Story of the Political Philosophers* (New York–London, 1939); Thomas I. Cook, *History of Political Philosophy from Plato to Burke* (New York, 1937); J. P. Mayer and others, *Political Thought: The European Tradition* (New York, 1939); and George H. Sabine, *A History of Political Theory*, rev. ed. (New York, 1950).

There is no single collection of the major works of political theory in adequate English translations. The more popular series, such as Everyman's Library, World's Classics, Modern Library, contain a number of classics of political theory in editions of varying quality. More recently, the following series have sought to reprint important source materials in the history of political thought: Blackwell's Political Texts, The Hafner Library of Classics, and The Little Library of Liberal Arts.

Chapter I

Plato

► AGARD, WALTER R., *What Democracy Meant to the Greeks* (Chapel Hill, 1942). Includes a succinct appraisal of Plato (pp. 206–220). For a brief discussion of authoritarian government, see Kurt von Fritz, "Conservative Reaction and One Man Rule in Ancient Greece," *Political Science Quarterly*, LVI, No. 1 (1941), 51–83.

► BARKER, ERNEST, *Greek Political Theory: Plato and His Predecessors*, 2nd ed. (London, 1925). The first four chapters on pre-Platonic political thought (pp. 1–85) are especially valuable, as is the Appendix, "The Later History of Plato's Political Theory" (pp. 383–392). The analysis of the *Republic* forms the core of the book (pp. 145–270).

► BECCARI, ARTURO, *La fondazione delle dottrine politiche in Grecia* (Naples, 1935), and *Il pensiero politico del mondo classico* (Padua, 1941). In the latter work, the author notes the "wonderful renaissance" of Platonic thought, particularly in Nazi Germany and Fascist Italy, and cites the following as the fundamental political ideas of Plato: "the profound significance of myths, the restoration of the ethical character of political life, the necessity of reconciling the individual with the state, the educational function of the state, the training of the ruling class, the critique of oligarchy and democracy as corrupt forms of state, the principle of an organic and hierarchical political system, the necessity of putting at the head of the state men who know how to govern without regard for the outmoded liberty of those who do not, the principle of unity of command, and the high conception of the principle of authority" (p. 68).

See also Arturo Beccari, "L'uomo di stato di Platone," *Rivista internazionale di filo-* *sofia del diritto*, XII (November–December, 1932), 739–750; Rodolfo de Mattei, "Embrioni e anticipazioni della teoria della 'classe politica,'" *Rivista internazionale di filosofia del diritto*, XII (March–April, 1932), 235–244; Marino Gentile, *La politica di Platone* (Padua, 1940); Giovanni Lorenzoni, *La formazione e l'educazione delle classi dirigenti nello Stato di Platone* (Florence, 1927); L. Stefanini, *Platone* (Padua, 1932); Vincenzo Amoruso, "I motivi della Repubblica di Platone," *Gerarchia*, I (April, 1922), 196–204; and Antonio Bruers, "Platone," *Gerarchia*, VIII (May, 1928), 403–405.

► BOSANQUET, BERNARD, *A Companion to Plato's Republic* (New York, 1895). Preceded by an introduction (pp. 1–35), the commentary follows the text of the *Republic* book by book.

► BURCKHARDT, JACOB, *Griechische Kulturgeschichte*, 3 vols. (Leipzig, n.d.). The second volume is on the Greek state and religion.

► CALHOUN, GEORGE M., *Introduction to Greek Legal Science* (Oxford, 1944). Contains considerable material of interest to the student of politics; Chap. III, "Legal Thought in the Aristocracies" (pp. 15–21), and V, "The Athenian Democracy" (pp. 30–49), are particularly relevant.

► CORNFORD, F. M., *Plato's Theory of Knowledge* (London, 1935). Contains translations of Plato's *Theaetetus* and *Sophist*, with running commentaries and an introduction by the translator. See also William D. Ross, *Plato's Theory of Ideas* (Oxford, 1951), and Robert E. Cushman, *Therapeia: Plato's Conception of Philosophy* (Chapel Hill, 1958). For an analysis of the role of mathematical concepts in

Plato's philosophy, see Robert S. Brumbaugh, *Plato's Mathematical Imagination* (Bloomington, 1954), and Anders E. O. Wedberg, *Plato's Philosophy of Mathematics* (Stockholm, 1955).

▶ CROSSMAN, R. H. S., *Plato To-day*, 2nd ed. (London, 1959). Confronts Plato with British democracy, communism, and fascism. Written with verve and insight into modern problems.

▶ DEMOS, RAPHAEL, *The Philosophy of Plato* (New York, 1939). "Man," the fourth and last part (pp. 303–399), is divided into four chapters: "Human Nature"; "Degeneration in the Individual and in the Society"; "The Ideal of Reason"; "Portrait of the Philosopher." Though many interpretive works on Plato deal with his dialogues, which are treated individually, Demos organizes his analysis according to topics; his discussion of Plato's political ideas is therefore drawn from many Platonic sources and thus gains in interest and perspective. Demos arrives at the conclusion that Plato's ideal state "combines the features both of aristocracy and of what we know as democracy." As to the former, the aristocracy "is of the benevolent kind. The rulers will not exploit the masses but will guide them to the fullest realization of their possibilities." As to the democratic aspect, "the state will be democratic in that the energies of the state will be used for the service of the interests, not of the few, but of all" (p. 357).

Demos seems to be insufficiently aware that government *of* the people and *by* the people is indispensable to democracy, and that government *for* the people is perfectly compatible with undemocratic forms of rule. Demos arrives at his position, so similar to that of Plato himself, from the assumption that today reason is "a disintegrating factor," and that since the Reformation the "modern world is broken up into a multiplicity of sects. This is not reason but the chaos in the receptacle" (p. 378). One of the main purposes of the *Republic* was a unified social system, dominated by a hierarchy of values and persons. Modern Pla-

tonists, too, dread the diversity and pluralism of the nonhierarchical and egalitarian society, and yearn for the absolute and universal Good that all men will accept.

▶ DICKINSON, G. LOWES, *Plato and His Dialogues* (London, 1931). Chap. IV is on the *Republic* (pp. 78–170). See also Dickinson's *The Greek View of Life*, 18th ed. (London, 1938), the second chapter of which is "The Greek View of the State" (pp. 69–137). Pericles' funeral address, one of the classical statements on democracy, is reproduced (pp. 121–124). See also A. R. Burns, *Pericles and Athens* (London, 1948).

▶ DODDS, E. R., *The Greeks and the Irrational* (Berkeley, 1951). In probing into the place of irrationality in Greek life and thought, the author explores much territory hitherto unknown or neglected. Chap. VII (pp. 207–235) deals with the irrational, theological, and mystical elements in Plato's thought. Plato's place in the "mystical tradition" (as distinct from the scientific) of classical Greece is also examined in F. M. Cornford, *From Religion to Philosophy* (Harper Torchbooks, 1957), particularly pp. 242–263, and in M. B. Foster, *Mystery and Philosophy* (London, 1957), pp. 31–37.

▶ EHRENBERG, VICTOR, *Aspects of the Ancient World* (Oxford, 1946). Chap. VII (pp. 94–104), "A Totalitarian State," deals with Sparta and shows how "this first and greatest of all authoritarian and totalitarian states" became, after its victory over Athens, "the starting-point and center of political theory. The development, which reached its culmination, though by no means its end, in Plato's imposing and bewildering picture of an ideal State in the *Republic*, led far away from reality." The educational system and communal life of the Spartan ruling class closely resemble those of the guardians in the *Republic*, although they are by no means identical.

▶ FIELD, G. C., *The Philosophy of Plato* (Home University Library, London–New York, 1949). An elementary introduction, useful for the understanding of Plato's political theory in relation to his philosophy, metaphysics, and religion. Field defends

Plato against the charge of antidemocracy.

See also Field's following writings on Plato: *Plato and His Contemporaries*, 2nd ed. (London, 1948), an excellent survey of Plato's life and work against the background of his contemporaries; "Plato's Political Thought and Its Value To-day," *Philosophy*, XVI (July, 1941), 227–241; and "On Misunderstanding Plato," *ibid.*, XIX (April, 1944), 49–62.

► FOSTER, M. B., *The Political Philosophies of Plato and Hegel* (Oxford, 1935). The first two chapters (pp. 1–71) are on Plato and rank among the most brilliant contributions to Platonic studies. Indispensable to an understanding of Plato's political philosophy.

► FREEMAN, KATHLEEN, *The Greek Way: An Anthology* (London, 1947). Translations from Greek verse and prose, representing the "Greek genius for living as well as for thinking."

An excellent anthology of a more literary and philosophical kind is Sir Richard Livingstone (ed.), *The Pageant of Greece* (Oxford, 1923). See also T. R. Glover, *Greek Byways* (Cambridge, 1932), and *The Ancient World* (Cambridge, 1935).

► ———, *The Pre-Socratic Philosophers* (Oxford, 1946), and *Ancilla to the Pre-Socratic Philosophers* (Oxford, 1948). The first is a companion to H. Diels, *Fragmente der Vorsokratiker*, 5th ed. (Berlin, 1934–1938), the foremost collection (in Greek) of pre-Socratic Greek philosophy. The second work by Kathleen Freeman is a complete English translation of the fragments in Diels's collection.

Plato and Aristotle were not, as is often thought, the beginning of Greek philosophy but its peak, or, as some think, the beginning of its decay. One of the main reasons for the pervasive influence of Plato and Aristotle is that their most important writings have been preserved. By contrast, most of the pre-Socratic philosophical writings have either been lost or preserved in small bits and fragments. Thus the *Ancilla to the Pre-Socratic Philosophers*, which contains the complete translation of the fragments in the Diels collection, is only 162 pages long, though referring to ninety sources; in numerous instances, not a single line of important thinkers is preserved.

For a detailed history of pre-Socratic Greek philosophy, see J. Burnet, *Early Greek Philosophy* (London–Edinburgh, 1892), and Theodor Gomperz, *Greek Thinkers* (New York, 1901), Vol. I. A more recent study, brief and lucid, of pre-Socratic philosophy will be found in Léon Robin, *Greek Thought and the Origins of the Scientific Spirit* (trans. from the French, London–New York, 1928), pp. 1–147. Chap. I of F. M. Cornford, *Before and after Socrates* (Cambridge, 1932), is called "Ionian Science before Socrates" (pp. 1–28). See also Milton C. Nahm (ed.), *Selections from Early Greek Philosophy*, 2nd ed. (New York, 1944), for source materials.

Mario Untersteiner, *The Sophists* (translated from the Italian by Kathleen Freeman, Oxford, 1954), is the best introduction to the lives and ideas of the most important sophists, and corrects many traditional misunderstandings and distortions first expressed in Plato's writings. To the sophists we owe the concept, Untersteiner writes, that man has "the right to a human life, human speech, and human thought" (p. xvi).

► FRIEDRICH, CARL J., "Greek Political Heritage and Totalitarianism," *Review of Politics*, II (April, 1940), 218–225. Unlike the nearly universal and one-sided idolizing of Greek political experience that characterizes most writings on the subject, Friedrich warns against the dangers inherent in the basic Greek political attitudes: "So deeply rooted in the state-polis was Greek culture that any glorification of this particular culture-pattern carries within it an exaltation of the state." Friedrich insists that the "crucial issue remains: shall we attach the highest value to the community and its effective secular organization or not?" The great world religions all reject this claim, and Friedrich therefore concludes his analysis with these words: "Let us beware of the heritage of the Greek polis: it is a veritable Trojan horse, smuggled into our Christian civilization" (pp. 224–225).

▶ GROTE, GEORGE, *Plato and the Other Companions of Sokrates,* 3 vols (London, 1865). Despite its age, still one of the best analyses and interpretations of Platonic and Socratic doctrines. Grote's considerable classical scholarship was buttressed by extensive experience in business and government, including ten years as a Member of Parliament, and his comments on the *Republic* (Vol. III, Chaps. XXXIII–XXXV, pp. 27–242) deserve special attention.

Socrates, the central figure in the *Republic,* seems to Grote to have been portrayed by Plato in a distorted fashion. The "real Socrates," as depicted by Plato himself in the *Apology* and other, earlier, dialogues, was a dissenter from the established order, confessing his own ignorance and his inability to teach anything. But in the *Republic,* Plato presents Socrates as "passing to the opposite pole; taking up the orthodox, conservative, point of view," and Socrates "now expects every individual to fall into place, and contract the opinions, prescribed by authority; including among those opinions deliberate ethical and political fictions, such as that about the gold and silver earthborn men. Free-thinking minds, who take views of their own, and enquire into the evidence of these beliefs, become inconvenient and dangerous" (III, 240). Grote's general estimate of the *Republic* was that "we must look upon Plato as a preacher—inculcating a belief which he thinks useful to be diffused; rather than as philosopher, announcing truths of human nature, and laying down a consistent, scientific, theory of Ethics" (*ibid.,* p. 156). See also Vols. II and III of Theodor Gomperz, *Greek Thinkers* (New York, 1905), a classic in the field.

▶ JAEGER, WERNER, *Paideia: The Ideals of Greek Culture,* 3 vols. (New York, 1939–1944). This ambitious work is comprehensive in scope, though lacking in novelty of interpretation. Vols. II and III deal mainly

with Plato, and the *Republic* is analyzed in Vol. II (pp. 198–370).

▶ HAVELOCK, ERIC A., *The Liberal Temper in Greek Politics* (New Haven, 1957). The author of this pioneering work strongly objects to the fact that in most conventional histories of Greek political thought "the naturalists and the materialists, the sophists and the democrats, are treated only as faint and futile voices protesting off-stage," while the undemocratic or antidemocratic views of Plato and Aristotle occupy the center of the stage (p. 19). By contrast, Havelock documents in detail his main thesis that liberalism was a part of the intellectual history of classic Greece, growing outside the walls of Plato's idealism and Aristotle's teleology. Throughout his book Havelock deals fully and fairly with Plato's political thought, presenting many points in a new light.

▶ JEFFERSON, THOMAS, *Writings* (Washington, 1903), Vol. XIV. In a letter to John Adams (July 5, 1814), Jefferson expresses his astonishment about Plato's age-old reputation and arrives at the following conclusion: "Education is chiefly in the hands of persons who, from their profession, have an interest in the reputation and dreams of Plato. They give the tone while at school, and few in their after years have occasion to revise their college opinions. But fashion and authority apart, and bringing Plato to the test of reason, take from him his sophisms, futilities and incomprehensibilities, and what remains: In truth, he is one of the race of genuine sophists, who has escaped the oblivion of his brethren, first, by the elegance of his diction, but chiefly, by the adoption and incorporation of his whimsies into the body of artificial Christianity. His foggy mind is forever presenting the semblances of objects which, half seen through a mist, can be defined neither in form nor dimensions. Yet this, which should have consigned him to early oblivion, really procured him immortality of fame and reverence. The Christian priesthood, finding the doctrines of Christ levelled to every understanding, and too plain to need explanation, saw in the mysticism of Plato materials with which they might build up an artificial system, which might, from its indistinctness, admit everlasting controversy, give employment for their order, and introduce it to profit, power and preeminence" (pp. 148–149).

In a later letter (to William Short, August 4, 1820) Jefferson says that "it is surely time for men to think for themselves, and to throw off the authority of names so artificially magnified" (*ibid.*, XV, 258).

See also Louis B. Wright, "Jefferson and the Classics," *Proceedings of the American Philosophical Society*, LXXXVII (July, 1943), 223–233.

▶ KELSEN, HANS, *What is Justice: Justice, Law, and Politics in the Mirror of Science* (Berkeley and Los Angeles, 1957). Chap. III (pp. 82–109) is on "Platonic Justice." Originally published in *Kant-Studien*, XXXVIII, Nos. 1–2 (1933), 91–117, this is one of the most penetrating studies of Plato and basic to an understanding of his political ideas in the light of his general philosophy and metaphysics. Kelsen writes incisively on the irrational and mystical elements in Plato's philosophy that lead to politically dangerous consequences: "Plato's mysticism, this most complete expression of irrationalism, is the justification of his anti-democratic politics; it is the ideology of every autocracy." Concerning the problem of justice, Kelsen concludes that "rational science can never give an answer to the question concerning the nature of justice, that it cannot solve that problem, but only resolve it. The final position rational science will take in all its different forms is this: there is no such thing as absolute justice, which cannot be defined conceptually. Such an ideal is an illusion. There are only interests and conflicts of interests, which are resolved either by struggle or compromise. In the sphere of rationality, the idea of peace inevitably replaces the ideal of justice" (pp. 116–117 of the original German version, from which this translation is made directly). See also Kelsen's "Platonic Love,"

American Imago, III (April, 1942), 1–112, originally published (in German) in *Imago,* XIX, Nos. 1–2 (1933), 34–98, 225-255. This is the only modern detailed analysis of Plato's homosexuality and its reflection in his philosophical and political ideas.

Contrary to common belief, homosexuality was not widespread in ancient Greece but practiced by only a thin layer of the aristocratic class; the general reaction to boy love was condemnatory and punitive in both social mores and actual penal legislation. Most of those inclined toward homosexuality were married and raised families, and their love of boys was in addition to their normal heterosexual lives; Plato was —even by the standards of these men— more extreme, because he confined himself to an erotic world in which there was no room for marriage or family, or any intimate personal relation with a woman. It was inevitable that the profound conflict with himself and society should pervade all his thinking and writing. Kelsen brilliantly traces the inner relation between Plato's tragic personal life, full of love and affection as well as of guilt and shame, and his schemes for political reform.

A short discussion, "Platonic Love," will also be found in Warner Fite, *The Platonic Legend* (New York, 1934), Chap. VIII (pp. 153–179).

▶ LEON, PHILIP, *Plato* (Nelson's Discussion Books, London–New York, 1939). Chap. I summarizes Plato's life and work (pp. 7–36), IV presents his political philosophy (pp. 75–104), and VI is entitled "Plato and Christ" (pp. 116–141).

▶ LEVINSON, RONALD B., "The *Republic* Revisited," *Yale Review,* XXIX (Autumn, 1939), 153–166. Interprets Plato as "the moralist and poet of the spiritual life" and, though admitting, "without argument or reservation, that Plato was not a democrat," denies that the *Republic* is an "anticipatory confirmation of the contemporary dictatorships." Later, Levinson elaborated his approach in a larger work, *In Defense of Plato* (Cambridge, Mass., 1953). This is the most extensive and detailed defense of

Plato against recent critical writers, particularly Warner Fite, Hans Kelsen, and Karl Popper. For further studies of defense and apology of Plato see John Wild, *Plato's Theory of Man: An Introduction to the Realistic Philosophy of Culture* (Cambridge, Mass., 1946), and *Plato's Modern Enemies and the Theory of Natural Law* (Chicago, 1953); Rupert C. Lodge, *The Philosophy of Plato* (London, 1956); and Paul Friedlaender, *Plato* (New York, 1958).

▶ LIVINGSTONE, R. W. (ed.), *The Legacy of Greece* (Oxford, 1921). One of the best general introductions to Greek civilization, with contributions by Gilbert Murray ("The Value of Greece to the Future of the World"), J. Burnet ("Philosophy"), D'Arcy W. Thompson ("Natural Science"), Arnold Toynbee ("History"), A. E. Zimmern ("Political Thought"), and others on such varied topics as religion, mathematics and astronomy, biology, medicine, literature, and art.

In *The Greek Genius and Its Meaning to Us* (London, 1912), Livingstone interprets Greek genius in terms of the following principal qualities: beauty, freedom, directness, humanism, sanity, and many-sidedness. He stresses that the "main stream of Hellenism" was characterized by these qualities, but that there was a "subordinate current of thought" in Greek life that reflected the absence or even opposite of these qualities, and "the one great extant writer who fully represents" this "unhellenic spirit" is Plato (3rd imp., 1924, p. 182). Livingstone refers particularly to Plato's theories of poetry and love, his hostility to liberty and humanism, and his tendencies toward asceticism and otherworldliness.

In the Introduction to his *Plato: Selected Passages* (London–New York–Toronto, 1940), Livingstone states that the "gravest criticisms against Plato are that he imposes goodness forcibly, that his methods would fail in practice, and that at best they could only produce a mechanical virtue and a static and stereotyped humanity," and that the "authoritarians of all ages are his children—all who from natural pessimism or bitter experience have held that the masses

must be saved from themselves by a governing elite" (p. xxi). Livingstone arrives at this critical view of Plato although he starts his appraisal with the words: "Perhaps no thinker has had as deep and permanent an influence on European thought as Plato, and many people meet him there without recognizing him" (p. vii).

▶ LODGE, RUPERT C., *Plato's Theory of Ethics* (London, 1928). The starting point and main object of inquiry in the *Republic* is the nature of justice. The separation of ethics and politics is a relatively modern phenomenon, unknown to Plato. *Plato's Theory of Ethics* is therefore useful to an understanding of the *Republic*, though it is a work of systematic explanation rather than of critical analysis. For a brief survey of Plato's theories of art, including the role of the artist in society, see Lodge, *Plato's Theory of Art* (London, 1953).

▶ MITCHELL, H., *The Economics of Ancient Greece* (Cambridge, 1940). Has a bibliography (pp. 394–398).

▶ MORE, PAUL ELMER, *Platonism* (Princeton, 1917). Of particular importance is Chap. VI, "The Doctrine of Ideas" (pp. 162–203). In an Appendix (pp. 297–307), the author explains in detail his suggested order of reading Plato.

▶ MUIRHEAD, JOHN H., *The Platonic Tradition in Anglo-Saxon Philosophy* (London–New York, 1931). The subtitle is "Studies in the History of Idealism in England and America."

▶ MURRAY, GILBERT, *Five Stages of Greek Religion* (Thinker's Library, London, 1946). Chap. IV, "The Failure of Nerve" (pp. 123–172), is the most famous of the book. See also Murray's *Greek Studies* (New York, 1946) and *A History of Ancient Greek Literature* (London, 1907). Greek religious conceptions are also discussed in Edwyn Bevan, *Sibyls and Seers* (London, 1928); Kathleen Freeman, *God, Man, and State: Greek Concepts* (London, 1952); Werner Jaeger, *The Theology of the Early Greek Philosophers* (Oxford, 1947); Carl Kerenyi, *The Gods of the Greeks* (Penguin Books, Baltimore, 1958); and Martin P. Nilsson,

Cults, Myths, Oracles, and Politics in Ancient Greece (Lund, 1951).

► MYRES, JOHN L., *The Political Ideas of the Greeks* (New York–Cincinnati, 1927). See also M. Cary and T. J. Haarhoff, *Life and Thought in the Greek and Roman World* (London, 1940), and T. A. Sinclair, *Greek Political Thought* (London, 1951).

► NETTLESHIP, RICHARD LEWIS, *Lectures on the Republic of Plato* (London, 1937). Unlike most commentaries that analyze the *Republic* topically, Nettleship's *Lectures* follows the *Republic* from beginning to end in its own order of themes. For the reader who approaches the *Republic* for the first time, Nettleship's commentary is perhaps the most useful guide, because it follows the text of the *Republic* closely and sympathetically. See also Nettleship's *The Theory of Education in Plato's Republic* (Oxford, 1935) for a brief exposition of Plato's system of education, in many respects the heart of the *Republic*.

A fuller treatment of Plato's educational philosophy will be found in Sir Richard Livingstone, *Plato and Modern Education* (Cambridge–New York, 1944); Rupert C. Lodge, *Plato's Theory of Education* (London, 1947); and Julius Stenzel, *Platon der Erzieher* (Leipzig, 1928). These works present systematic analyses of Plato's educational philosophy based on the *Republic* as well as on several other major dialogues.

► OATES, WHITNEY J., "The Ideal States of Plato and Aristotle," in *The Greek Political Experience: Studies in Honor of William Kelly Prentice* (Princeton, 1941), pp. 187–213. Seeks to demonstrate that Plato and Aristotle "believed fundamentally in the essence of democracy" (p. 193) and were not progenitors of modern totalitarian systems.

► PATER, WALTER, *Plato and Platonism* (Caravan Library, London, 1934). See particularly Chaps. V, "Plato and the Sophists" (pp. 88–110), and IX, "The *Republic*" (pp. 211–240). See also Pater's *Greek Studies* (Caravan Library, London, 1928).

► POPPER, KARL R., *The Open Society and Its Enemies* (Princeton, 1950). Part I,

"The Spell of Plato" (pp. 11–195), is a scathing critique of Plato's political philosophy and its destructive impact on Western civilization. Popper views Plato's proposal to reconstruct the natural harmony of society as follows: "The more we try to return to the heroic age of tribalism, the more surely do we arrive at the Inquisition, at the Secret Police, and at a romanticized gangsterism. Beginning with the suppression of reason and truth, we must end with the most brutal and violent destruction of all that is human. *There is no return to a harmonious state of nature. If we turn back, then we must go the whole way—we must return to the beasts*" (p. 195). For a critical examination, from the viewpoint of logical positivism, of Plato's analogy of government and politics with arts, crafts, and specialized skills, leading to the Platonic justification of rule by the few, see Renford Bambrough, "Plato's Political Analogies," in Peter Laslett (ed.), *Philosophy, Politics, and Society* (Oxford, 1956), pp. 98–115.

► RITTER, CONSTANTIN, *The Essence of Plato's Philosophy* (New York, 1933). A portion of the book deals with Plato's political ideas (pp. 319–356). Ritter was one of Germany's leading authorities on Plato.

► ROBIN, LÉON, "Platon et la science sociale," *Revue de Metaphysique et de Morale*, XXI (March, 1913), 211–255. Defends Plato against the charge of being a utopian and interprets him as the "father of positive sociology."

► RUSCH, ADOLF, "Plato als Erzieher zum deutschen Menschen," in *Humanistische Bildung im nationalsozialistischen Staate* (*Neue Wege zur Antike*, First Series, No. 9, Berlin–Leipzig, 1933), pp. 44–49. Interesting for the ease with which Plato is appropriated for Nazi ideology and the *Führer* ideal, although the author regrets that Plato was not fully aware of the "importance of race" (p. 48). The issue of No. 9 of *Neue Wege zur Antike* contains several other articles that touch, more or less extensively, on Plato. One writer (Benno von Hagen, "Wege zu einem Humanismus im Dritten Reich," *ibid.*, pp. 17–22) claims that the study of Plato must be the center of Greek studies because it is a bridge to the immediate ideas and policies of Nazism, whether it be racial consciousness, the esteem of the warriors, or the exaltation of the leadership principle. Heinrich Härtle, "Nationalsozialistische Philosophie?", *Nationalsozialistische Monatshefte*, XII (September, 1941), 723–731, discusses the relations of Plato and Nazism. The authoritative Nazi view on Socrates and Plato is in Alfred Rosenberg, *Der Mythus des 20. Jahrhunderts*, 26th imp. (Munich, 1934), pp. 50 ff., 78 ff., 284 ff.

► SCHRÖDINGER, ERWIN, *Nature and the Greeks* (Cambridge, 1954). The birth of Greek science, by one of the greatest physicists of the twentieth century.

► SHOREY, PAUL, *Platonism: Ancient and Modern* (Berkeley, 1938). Analyzes the impact of Plato on antiquity, Christianity, the middle ages, the Renaissance, and French and English thought. See also Gilbert Murray, *Hellenism and the Modern World* (London, 1953), and Edwin Hatch, *The Influence of Greek Ideas on Christianity* (Harper Torchbooks, New York, 1957), for treatments of special periods and problems. Comparative analyses between classical Greek and Hebrew styles of thought will be found in Thorleif Boman, *Das hebräische Denken im Vergleich mit dem griechischen* (Goettingen, 1954); M. B. Foster, *Mystery and Philosophy* (London, 1957), Chap. VI (pp. 87–94); and Reinhold Niebuhr, *The Self and the Dramas of History* (New York, 1955), pp. 75–88.

► TAYLOR, ALFRED EDWARD, *Plato: The Man and His Work*, 6th ed. (London, 1949). Chap. I (pp. 1–9) briefly describes Plato's life, and the subsequent chapters analyze his writings. The *Republic* is dealt with in Chap. XI (pp. 263–298). Taylor's *Plato*, generally written from the orthodox viewpoint, ranks as one of the standard works in the field. Accounts of Plato's excursions into practical politics in his earlier years will be found in Gertrude R. Levy, *Plato in Sicily* (London, 1956), and Ludwig Marcuse, *Plato and Dionysius* (New York, 1947).

► ———, *Socrates* (Doubleday Anchor Books, New York, 1957). An excellent brief introduction into the life and thought of Socrates. The best portrait of Socrates appears in the pages of Plato's dialogues *Apology* and *Crito*. See also John D. Montgomery, *The State versus Socrates: A Case Study in Civic Freedom* (Boston, 1954), an anthology of writings on Socrates by many authors, including Friedrich Wilhelm Nietzsche, John Stuart Mill, George Grote, Vilfredo Pareto, A. E. Taylor, Werner Jaeger, Karl R. Popper, Arnold J. Toynbee, and others.

► ———, *Platonism and Its Influence* (Boston, 1924). A volume in the Our Debt to Greece and Rome series. It attempts to indicate "the line of descent by which Platonic ideas have become part of the unconscious inheritance of the educated man of today" (p. 28). More specifically, the author examines the impact of Plato on the subsequent development of science, ethics, and theology. A bibliography is appended (pp. 146–148).

► TOYNBEE, ARNOLD J., *Hellenism: The History of a Civilization* (New York, 1959). The author sees in "man-worship or Humanism" (p. 10) the distinctive mark of Greek civilization. While humanism flourished at other times and places (such as the Italian Renaissance and the French Age of Reason), the Hellenic experiment in Humanism "was the most whole-hearted and uncompromising practice of man-worship that is on record up to date. This is the distinctive mark of Hellenic history, and it raises an interesting question: What was the connexion between the Hellenes' worship of man and Hellenism's rise, achievements, breakdown, and eventual fall? That is the subject of this book" (*ibid.*). The failure of the Greeks to unite politically, the author concludes, rendered the collapse of their civilization inevitable. Today we see again the revival of the Greek worship of idolized local states: "The Modern World must exorcise this demon resolutely if it is to save itself from meeting with its Hellenic predecessor's fate" (p. 253).

► WILAMOWITZ-MOELLENDORFF, ULRICH VON, *Platon*, 2 vols. (Berlin, 1919). The author was one of the greatest classical scholars of the nineteenth and twentieth centuries; the *Republic* is discussed in Vol. I (pp. 389–444) and Vol. II (pp. 179–220) of *Platon*, and the conclusion is that Sparta was obviously the model of the *Republic* (I, 425). In *Der griechische und der Platonische Staatsgedanke* (Berlin, 1919), von Wilamowitz-Moellendorff pleaded for a revival of Plato's political ideals, as he was under the impression that socialism had taken over in Germany and that it tended to degenerate into "wild anarchy" (p. 3). Speaking of Plato's educational system, von Wilamowitz-Moellendorff was struck by the "inter-penetration" of science and militarism in Plato's *Republic*, just as "they got along so well in our old Prussia" (p. 21). See also von Wilamowitz-Moellendorff's *Der Glaube der Hellenen*, 2 vols. (Berlin, 1931–1932), and *Staat und Gesellschaft der Griechen*, in Ulrich von Wilamowitz-Moellendorff, J. Kromayer, and A. Heisenberg, *Staat und Gesellschaft der Griechen und Römer*, 2nd imp. (Leipzig–Berlin, 1923), pp. 1–214. Provocative analyses of Plato as a "founder" rather than a utopian visionary will be found in Kurt Singer, *Plato der Gründer* (Munich, 1927), and Edgar Salin, *Platon und die griechische Utopie* (Munich–Leipzig, 1921).

► WINSPEAR, ALBAN DEWES, *The Genesis of Plato's Thought* (New York, 1940). The only systematic analysis, in English, of Plato's political ideas from a Marxist viewpoint. As Winspear is a good scholar, and not only a good Marxist, his book will be found suggestive, although overdrawn in part. Of related interest, and equally written from a strict Marxian angle, is George Thomson, *Aeschylus and Athens* (London, 1941). Plato's attitude to natural science is discussed in Benjamin Farrington, *Science and Politics in the Ancient World* (New York, 1932), Chaps. VIII (pp. 87–106) and XI (pp. 130–147), and *Greek Science* (London, 1944), Chap. VII (pp. 81–101).

A full discussion of Plato from a Marxist-Stalinist viewpoint will be found in G. F. Aleksandrov, *A History of Western European Philosophy* (trans. from the Russian, New Haven, 1949), pp. 46–55. Marx calls Plato's *Republic* "merely the Athenian idealization of the Egyptian system of castes" (*Capital*, trans. from the 3rd. German ed. by Samuel Moore and Edward Aveling, and ed. by Frederick Engels, New York–London, 1889, p. 361). Marx was keenly interested in the Greek antecedents of philosophical materialism, and his doctoral dissertation, "The Difference Between Democritean and Epicurean Philosophy of Nature" (reprinted in *Marx-Engels Gesamtausgabe*, Frankfort, 1927, Vol. I, Part I, pp. 1–144), contains many references to Plato.

Marxian analyses of Socrates, Democritus, and Epicurus will also be found in Franz Mehring, *Zur Geschichte der Philosophie* (Berlin, 1931), pp. 31–54. Paul W. Junker, *Die Weltanschauung des Marxismus und Platos Staatslehre* (Greifswald, 1925), has an extensive bibliography on the subject of Marxism and Platonism (pp. 111–122). F. M. Cornford, *The Unwritten Philosophy: And Other Essays* (Cambridge, 1950), includes a critical examination, "The Marxist View of Ancient Philosophy" (pp. 117–137).

► ZIMMERN, ALFRED, *The Greek Commonwealth: Politics and Economics in Fifth-Century Athens*, 5th ed. (Oxford, 1931). The best book on the subject. See also André Bonnard, *Greek Civilization*, 2 vols. (New York, 1958–1959); C. M. Bowra, *The Greek Experience* (New York, 1958); John Ferguson, *Moral Values in the Ancient World* (London, 1958); and H. D. F. Kitto, *The Greeks* (Penguin Books, London–Baltimore, 1951).

Chapter 2

Aristotle

▶ BARKER, ERNEST, *The Political Thought of Plato and Aristotle* (London–New York, 1906). Chaps. V–XI (pp. 208–496) deal with Aristotle in a clear and sympathetic manner. An Epilogue ("The Later History of the *Politics*") provides a brief survey of the impact of Aristotle's political ideas on later writers from the Stoics to Hegel. See also Barker's *The Politics of Aristotle* (Oxford, 1946), a translation of Aristotle's *Politics,* with an introduction, notes, and appendixes. The introduction (pp. xi–lxxvi) considers the historical and scientific background, the substance, argument, and vocabulary of the *Politics.*

▶ CHERNISS, HAROLD, *Aristotle's Criticism of Plato and the Academy* (Baltimore, 1944), Vol. I. Purports to "give a complete account and analysis of all that Aristotle says about Plato and about Plato's pupils and associates in the Academy," and is the standard work on the subject. A brief treatment of the relation of Aristotle and Plato will be found in K. V. Gajendragadkar, *Aristotle's Critique of Platonism* (Mysore, 1953), in which the author concludes that Aristotle "remains after all the greatest of the Platonists as also the greatest critic of Plato and his school" (pp. 77–78).

▶ GROTE, GEORGE, *Aristotle,* 2 vols. (London, 1872). Grote died before the work was finished. Neither the *Ethics* nor the *Politics* is specifically dealt with, but most of the other works of Aristotle are carefully analyzed.

▶ HAMBURGER, MAX, *Morals and Law: The Growth of Aristotle's Legal Theory* (New Haven, 1951). Examines Aristotle's concepts of law and justice as set forth, primarily, in his *Ethics, Politics,* and *Rhetoric.* The author holds that Aristotle's legal and political theory went beyond that of his predecessors, including Plato, and that

"it is with Aristotle that modern legal and political science really begins" (p. 182). He concludes as follows: "There is a perfect harmony between Aristotle's ethical, legal, and political theory—the theory of the right mean is the basis; philia, social sympathy, is the life force; equity, fairness, reasonableness, and humaneness the leitmotiv; and well-being, i.e., human happiness and perfection, the supreme end" (p. 183). A diametrically opposed view will be found in Hans Kelsen, "Aristotle's Doctrine of Justice" (in his *What Is Justice: Justice, Law, and Politics in the Mirror of Science,* Berkeley and Los Angeles, 1957, pp. 110–136). Kelsen holds that the Aristotelian principle of giving everyone his due, or "to each his own," is a purely tautological formula, and that "it is so interesting because it shows the unlimited possibility of using this formula to any purpose whatever" (p. 136). See also Walter Siegfried, *Der Rechtsgedanke bei Aristoteles* (Zurich, 1947), for an analysis of Aristotle's legal thought in relation to his general philosophy.

▶ JAEGER, WERNER, *Aristotle: Fundamentals of the History of His Development* (Oxford, 1934). A biography of Aristotle's intellectual development. The last chapter is on "Aristotle's Place in History" (pp. 368–406).

▶ KELSEN, HANS, "The Philosophy of Aristotle and the Hellenic–Macedonian Policy," *Ethics,* XLVIII (October, 1937), 1–64. This essay on Aristotle stresses the inner relation and resemblance between Plato and Aristotle, in philosophy as in political thought, and paints a vivid picture of the background of Aristotle's *Politics.* Kelsen is particularly interested in the impact of Macedonian policy on Aristotle's ideas.

▶ McKEON, RICHARD, "Aristotle's Conception of Moral and Political Philosophy,"

Ethics, LI (April, 1941), 253–290. The author sees the long-term influence of Aristotle not so much in political theory as in types of philosophy, such as pragmatism, functionalism, instrumentalism, and positivism, which are concerned with the relations of causes and effects in knowledge and action.

▶ MURE, G. R. G., *Aristotle* (London, 1932). Part I is called "The Heritage of Aristotle" (pp. 3–68), Part II, "The Philosophy of Aristotle" (pp. 71–230), and Part III, "The Verdict of History" (pp. 233–274), a stimulating survey of the impact of Aristotelianism from antiquity to the modern period. A volume in the Leaders of Philosophy series. See also D. J. Allan, *The Philosophy of Aristotle* (New York, 1952), and Werner Marx, *The Meaning of Aristotle's Ontology* (The Hague, 1954), for general philosophical studies of Aristotle's thought.

▶ NEWMAN, WILLIAM L., *The Politics of Aristotle*, 4 vols. (Oxford, 1887–1902). The first volume is a detailed and scholarly introduction to the *Politics;* the other three volumes contain the Greek text of the *Politics,* with notes and critical comments. Comparing the Aristotelian conception of the state with modern views, the author writes: "We look back to a succession of States which have helped to build up the fabric of European civilization, and the State which has not fought a Salamis, or done great things for religion or law or science, falls, in our view, behind the State which has. We regard the State not as living to itself and dying to itself, but as influencing for good or ill the destinies of mankind. Aristotle, on the contrary, knows nothing of the historical mission of States. He looks to the quality of the life, not to the results achieved—to the intrinsic nobility of the life lived, not to its fruitfulness in consequences" (I, 562–563).

▶ ONCKEN, WILHELM, *Die Staatslehre des Aristoteles,* 2 vols. (Leipzig, 1870–1875). Interprets the political theory of Aristotle as a "political theory of the possessing classes," and affirms that "the *rule of the middle classes* in Aristotle is only another word for the *domination of the possessing classes*" (II, 272). Oncken gives considerable attention to Aristotle's views on monarchy and his relations to Philip and Alexander of Macedon, and stresses the role of monarchy as a protector of the well-to-do. For that reason, Oncken says, the possessing classes, "long tired of democratic disorder," were "from the beginning" pro-Macedonian.

▶ POPPER, KARL R., *The Open Society and Its Enemies* (Princeton, 1950). Chap. XI critically presents several aspects of Aristotelianism (pp. 199–222).

▶ ROBIN, LÉON, *Aristote* (Paris, 1944). A general account of Aristotle's scientific philosophical, and political ideas. The author, a leading French student of Greek thought, concludes his analysis of Aristotle's political theory by doubting whether it is as profound as is commonly assumed. In particular, Robin is surprised that Aristotle saw in the old Greek city-state the normal form of political organization, at the very time when his close personal association with "Macedonian imperialism" should have shown him that the city-state was doomed. Robin concludes that "a somewhat narrow empiricism and a prematurely too broad systematization are the substance of Aristotelian thinking on politics" (p. 283). A succinct account of the *Politics* will also be found in Robin's *Greek Thought and the Origins of the Scientific Spirit* (London–New York, 1928), pp. 268–276. The main criticism there of Aristotle is that he failed to see properly "the great events which were happening or brewing before his eyes in the Greek world. His eyes, like Plato's, were turned on the past, on the small self-centered republic, and he sought its future, blindly, in a reinforcement of that concentration" (p. 276).

▶ ROSS, W. D., *Aristotle,* 2nd ed. (London, 1930). Chap. VIII deals with Aristotle's political thought (pp. 235–269).

▶ STEENBERGHEN, FERNAND VAN, *Aristotle in the West: The Origins of Latin Aristotelianism* (Louvain, 1955). Aims to show "how the union between Aristotelianism and traditional Christian thought came about" (p. 5). The emphasis is on the role of Paris and Oxford Universities in the introduction of Aristotelianism in the thirteenth century. See also Ingemar Duering, *Aristotle in the Ancient Biographical Tradition* (Goeteborg, 1957).

▶ WILAMOWITZ-MOELLENDORF, ULRICH VON, *Aristoteles und Athen*, 2 vols. (Berlin,

1893). A detailed critical analysis of Aristotle and Athens, with particular emphasis on Athenian political institutions. See also Adolf Menzel, *Griechische Soziologie* (Vienna–Leipzig, 1936), containing numerous discussions of Aristotle as one of the founders of political sociology, and Kurt von Fritz, *Aristotle's Constitution of Athens and Related Texts* (New York, 1950).

Chapter 3

Polybius

▶ ABBOTT, EVELYN (ed.), *Hellenica: A Collection of Essays on Greek Poetry, Philosophy, History and Religion* (Oxford and Cambridge, 1880). The essay, "Polybius" (pp. 387–424), is by James Leigh Strachan-Davidson; it provides the background of Polybius' deportation to Rome and critically examines the character of his political and historical views.

▶ CHINARD, GILBERT, "Polybius and the American Constitution," *Journal of the History of Ideas*, I (January, 1940), 38–58. Illuminating on the role and use of Polybius' ideas in the making of the American Constitution. The author gives a brief account of the classical background and education of the revolutionary leaders and then shows specifically, without overstressing his case, to what extent Polybius was a conscious intellectual influence at that time.

▶ FRITZ, KURT VON, *The Theory of the Mixed Constitution in Antiquity: A Critical Analysis of Polybius' Political Ideas* (New York, 1954). Presents, in a masterly fashion, the historical and analytical background of the theory of the mixed constitution, the most influential of Polybius' doctrines in antiquity as well as in the modern age, par-

ticularly in the formative stage of the United States.

▶ GLOVER, T. R., *Springs of Hellas* (Cambridge, 1945). Chap. VI, "Polybius at Rome" (pp. 109–130), is the best short summary of the main events in Polybius' life and his leading political and historical ideas.

▶ SIEGFRIED, WALTER, *Studien zur geschichtlichen Anschauung des Polybios* (Leipzig–Berlin, 1928). Centers on Polybius' philosophy and its relation to other Greek writers. See also Richard Lacqueur, *Polybius* (Leipzig–Berlin, 1913), and Carl Wunderer, *Polybios* (Leipzig, 1927). Two older German studies are Karl Wilhelm Nitzsch, *Polybius: Zur Geschichte antiker Politik und Historiographie* (Kiel, 1842), and W. Markhauser, *Der Geschichtschreiber Polybius, seine Weltanschauung und Staatslehre* (Munich, 1858).

▶ WALBANK, F. W., *A Historical Commentary on Polybius* (Oxford, 1957). The most detailed commentary in English on Polybius' *Histories,* preceded by a detailed bibliography (pp. xiii–xxvii) and a lengthy Introduction on the life and thought of Polybius (pp. 1–37).

Chapter 4

Cicero

► BAILEY, CYRIL (ed.), *The Legacy of Rome* (Oxford, 1923). Contains chapters on empire, administration, communications and commerce, law, family and social life, religion and philosophy, science, literature, art, engineering, and agriculture, written by authorities in their respective fields. Profusely illustrated, this volume is ideally suited as an introduction to Roman thought and civilization. See also R. H. Barrows, *The Romans* (Pelican Books, Harmondsworth, 1949), and Paul MacKendrick, *The Roman Mind at Work* (Anvil Books, Princeton, 1958).

► BARKER, ERNEST, *Church, State, and Study: Essays* (London, 1930). Chap. I (pp. 1–43) is "The Roman Conception of Empire," and Chap. VII (pp. 171–192) "The 'Rule of Law.' "

► BUCKLAND, W. W., and ARNOLD D. MC-NAIR, *Roman Law and Common Law: A Comparison in Outline* (Cambridge, 1936). The authors stress the point that, while the theoretical conceptions of the Roman law and common law are different, "the practical results of the two systems show an astonishing amount of similarity" (p. xviii). Chap. I, "The Sources" (pp. 1–19), is the most relevant to the study of the history of political thought.

► CARLYLE, R. W., and A. J. CARLYLE, *A History of Medieval Political Theory in the West,* 3rd ed. (Edinburgh–London, 1930), Vol. I. The first chapter, "The Political Theory of Cicero" (pp. 1–18), is built around the thesis that there "is no change in political theory so startling in its completeness as the change from the theory of Aristotle to the later philosophical view represented by Cicero and Seneca. Over against Aristotle's view of the natural inequality of human nature we find set out the theory of the natural equality of human nature" (p. 8).

► CAUER, FRIEDRICH, *Ciceros politisches Denken* (Berlin, 1903). A penetrating essay on Cicero's political record and thought. the author stresses the close ties of Cicero with the important business and financial leaders of his time, who "knew how to pursue their class interests ruthlessly, though by legal methods, and claimed those interests to be identical with the highest good of mankind. Cicero was the spokesman of this class morality. He who looks for high-sounding phrases to cover up base intentions, will find an inexhaustible supply in Cicero's writings. As compared with modern thinkers of similar outlook, he has the advantage of fine cultivation and a rich mind. Cicero's connection with high finance runs through his whole political career" (p. 76). Cauer concludes his study as follows: "Only the Greeks have the strength to heal our misdirected thinking, our lifeless feeling. In Cicero we can recognize the symptoms of the disease from which we ourselves suffer" (p. 142). See also Otto Seel, *Cicero: Wort, Staat, Welt* (Stuttgart, 1953), for a more sympathetic and detailed study of Cicero, emphasizing his political ideas.

► CHINARD, GILBERT, "Polybius and the American Constitution," *Journal of the History of Ideas,* I (January, 1940), 38–58. The author points out that "most of the men who made a name for themselves during the revolutionary era were no mean classical scholars. That they read Locke and later Montesquieu cannot be disputed; but at all times they studied and memorized Cicero and some of the Greek historians. It was from Cicero particularly, among the ancients, that they derived their ideals of liberty and government" (p. 40).

► CIACERI, EMANUELE, *Cicerone e i suoi tempi*, 2 vols. (Milan–Rome–Naples, 1926–1930). Stresses the aristocratic, antidemocratic political philosophy of Cicero. See also Maffio Maffii, *Cicerone e il suo dramma politico* (Milan, 1933), and Giuseppe Rensi, *Vite parallele di filosofi: Platone e Cicerone* (Naples, 1934).

► CICERO, MARCUS TULLIUS, *Brutus: On the Nature of the Gods: On Divination: On Duties* (Chicago, 1950). With an excellent "Introduction to the Philosophy of Cicero" (pp. 1–65) by Richard McKeon.

► ———, *On the Commonwealth* (trans., with notes and introduction, by George H. Sabine and Stanley B. Smith, Columbus, Ohio, 1929). Chap. III of the Introduction deals with Cicero's political theory (pp. 39–67), and there is a useful bibliography (pp. 100–102). The text of the *Republic* (called by the translators *On the Commonwealth*) is profusely annotated.

► CONWAY, R. S., "The Originality of Cicero," *Bulletin of the John Rylands Library,* XIV (July, 1930), 361–385. Perhaps overstates the case, but is nevertheless rewarding for its unorthodox approach to the study of Cicero as a political thinker. The author is particularly impressed with Cicero's doctrine of war, according to which the "best state" does not go to war "except in defense of its good faith and safety," and with Cicero's universal outlook and respect for liberty and law. See also Clinton Walker Keyes, "Original Elements in Cicero's Ideal Constitution," *American Journal of Philology*, XLII, No. 4 (1921), 309–323. The main thesis of the article is that the third book of Cicero's *Laws* contains the first outline of a written constitution in political literature, laying down basic rules for the legislative, executive, and judicial functions.

► HALLWARD, B. L., "Cicero Historicus," *Cambridge Historical Journal*, III, No. 3 (1931), 221–237. Cicero had acute political and constitutional judgment: "Indeed, it is doing Cicero less than justice to take his structure at his own estimation as a purely theoretical speculation of political philos-

ophy. He had neither the boldness nor the imagination to produce a Platonic Republic; what he did produce was an interesting commentary on the Roman constitution" (p. 236).

► HASKELL, H. J., *This Was Cicero: Modern Politics in a Roman Toga* (New York, 1942). Fresh, readable, and written with a keen sense of human drama. The author, a newspaperman with a thorough knowledge of politics in Kansas City and Washington, justifies his biography on the ground that it takes into account "factors that have escaped the attention of biographers who were not familiar with politics in action," and his work successfully conveys the political atmosphere in Rome during Cicero's lifetime. Extensive bibliographical notes will be found (pp. 368–406). See also G. C. Richards, *Cicero: A Study* (London, 1935), an account of Cicero's life and thought. The author concludes that "Cicero's position in Rome was one of great influence, because in the total absence of the Press, the Pulpit and the University, he in his single person supplied something of all three" (p. 282). *Eternal Lawyer: A Legal Biography of Cicero*, by (Judge) Robert N. Wilkin (New York, 1947), is a stimulating study of Cicero's career and ideas from the viewpoint of a lawyer with wide interests. The author points out that Cicero "was the first to use the word 'constitution' in its modern sense of public law of the state or law by which government itself was limited," and he stresses Cicero's impact on the makers of the American Constitution (pp. 217 ff.).

► HEINZE, RICHARD, *Vom Geist des Römertums* (Leipzig–Berlin, 1938). A collection of essays on Roman politics, including two chapters on Cicero (pp. 59–170).

► LEE, R. W., *The Elements of Roman Law: With a Translation of the Institutes of Justinian* (London, 1944). The introduction (pp. 1–43) is a general survey of the Roman law, of interest to the student of law as well as the student of political thought. The remainder of the book is a translation of the *Institutes* of Justinian. Thomas Collett Sandars, *The Institutes of Justinian* (London–New York, 1903), contains the text of the *Institutes* in Latin and English, with detailed notes and commentaries. Whereas the *Institutes* are brief and elementary, the extensive code of Justinian is the *Digest*, a translation of which will be found in *The Digest of Justinian* (trans. Charles H. Monro, 2 vols., Cambridge, 1909). The beginning of the first volume contains the sections on the nature and types of law that are of most general interest.

▶ PALLASSE, MAURICE, *Cicéron et les sources de droits* (Annales de l'Université de Lyon, Troisième Série, Droit, Fasc. 8, Paris, 1946). See also L. Laurand, *Cicéron* (Paris, 1933).

▶ RAND, E. K., *Cicero in the Courtroom of St. Thomas Aquinas* (Milwaukee, 1946). A study of Cicero's influence on St. Thomas Aquinas from a general philosophical and literary viewpoint. Cicero was one of the three ancient Latin authors most frequently referred to by St. Thomas Aquinas, the other two being Seneca and Boethius.

▶ ROLFE, JOHN C., *Cicero and His Influence* (Boston, 1923). A volume in the Our Debt to Greece and Rome series, which defends Cicero against his critics, and traces his influence from antiquity to modern times. See also T. Zielinski, *Cicero im Wandel der Jahrhunderte* (Berlin, 1912); Hans Baron, "Cicero and the Roman Civic Spirit in the Middle Ages and Early Renaissance," *The John Rylands Library Bulletin,* 22 (April, 1938), 72–97; Walter Rüegg, *Cicero und der Humanismus* (Zurich, 1946); and Tenney Frank, *Cicero* (Annual Lecture on a Master Mind, in *Proceedings of the British Academy,* London, 1932, pp. 111–134), who summarizes Cicero's influence on the Middle Ages and Renaissance as follows: "To the thinkers of the Middle Ages, who did not have access to the earlier sources, Cicero's philosophical dialogues

were full of illumination and suggestion, and they played a decided role in humanizing philosophy in the fifteenth and sixteenth centuries. Without them the western world would not have been ready to comprehend the libraries of Greek thought that came westward during the renaissance. Even Copernicus confessed that it was from a citation found in Cicero that he formed the idea of the earth's revolutions. Furthermore, these essays are our only source for much of the lost post-Aristotelian work. But apart from our gratitude, the works themselves are of considerable interest because we can discover from them the spirit in which a cultivated Roman of the Republic approached the problems they discuss" (p. 127). An illuminating study, full of interesting historical detail, on Cicero's literary sources of inspiration and his love of books will be found in T. R. Glover, *Springs of Hellas and Other Essays* (Cambridge, 1945), pp. 131–159 ("Cicero among His Books").

▶ SIHLER, E. G., *Cicero of Arpinum: A Political and Literary Biography* (New Haven, 1914). See also Gaston Delayen, *Cicero* (London, 1931), a political biography originally published in French.

▶ SPITZER, S., "Cicero's Stellung zur internationalen Moral," in *Festschrift für Theodor Gomperz* (Vienna, 1902), pp. 208–215.

▶ TAYLOR, HANNIS, *Cicero: A Sketch of His Life and Works* (Chicago, 1918). A comprehensive work, whose usefulness is enhanced by a bibliography (pp. xxxvii–xliv), and an appendix, "The Sayings of Cicero" (pp. 459–603), an anthology of about a thousand extracts selected from Cicero's writings and correspondence. Cicero's correspondence, an unusually rich source for the study of his temper and personality, ranks among the great examples of letter writing in world literature. See also Harold A. K. Hunt, *The Humanism of Cicero* (Melbourne, 1954).

Chapter 5

Slave and Emperor: Two Stoic Philosophers

▶ ARNOLD, E. VERNON, *Roman Stoicism* (Cambridge, 1911). Includes an extensive bibliography (pp. 437–450). The last chapter stresses the profound impact of Stoicism on Christianity (pp. 408–436).

▶ BARKER, ERNEST, *From Alexander to Constantine: Passages and Documents Illustrating the History of Social and Political Ideas 336 B.C.–A.D. 337* (New York, 1956). The best source-book on the political thought of the Hellenistic period, including many less well-known materials.

▶ BARTH, PAUL, *Die Stoa*, 3rd ed. (Stuttgart, 1922). One of the leading German accounts of Stoicism. See also the following: Adolf Bonhöffer, *Epictet und die Stoa* (Stuttgart, 1890), and *Die Ethik des Stoikers Epictet* (Stuttgart, 1894); Werner Luthe, *Die Erkenntnislehre der Stoiker* (Leipzig, 1890); Walter Görlitz, *Marc Aurel: Kaiser und Philosoph* (Leipzig, n.d.); Claus Schrempf, *Weisheit und Weltherrschaft: Kaiser Marc Aurel in seinen Selbstbekenntnissen* (Berlin–Tempelhof, n.d.); and Helfried Hartmann, *Gewissheit und Wahrheit: Der Streit zwischen Stoa und akademischer Skepsis* (Halle, 1927).

▶ DAVIDSON, WILLIAM L., *The Stoic Creed* (Edinburgh, 1907). On the relations of Stoicism and religion, see also the following: James Baldwin Brown, *Stoics and Saints* (New York, 1893); Norman Bentwich, *Hellenism* (Philadelphia, 1943); James Henry Bryant, *The Mutual Influence of Christianity and the Stoic School* (London, 1866); F. W. Farrar, *Seekers after God* (London, 1881); Edwyn Bevan, *Hellenism and Christianity* (London, 1921); Adolf Bonhöffer, *Epiktet und das Neue Testament* (Giessen, 1911); Otto Schmitz, *Der Freiheitsgedanke bei Epiktet und das Freiheitszeugnis des Paulus* (Gütersloh,

1923); and A. Chollet, *La morale stoïcienne en face de la morale chrétienne* (Paris, 1898).

▶ FARQUHARSON, A. S. L., *The Meditations of the Emperor Marcus Antoninus*, 2 vols. (Oxford, 1944). The first volume contains a long introduction, the Greek text and English translation of the *Meditations*, the story of Marcus Aurelius' life, and a detailed commentary on the *Meditations*, book by book, and chapter by chapter. The second volume comments on the Greek text. All in all, this is the most scholarly edition of the *Meditations* and indispensable to the study of Marcus Aurelius and Stoic thought.

▶ HAYWARD, F. H., *Marcus Aurelius: A Saviour of Men* (London, 1935). See also the following biographies: C. Clayton Dove, *Marcus Aurelius Antoninus: His Life and Times* (London, 1930); John C. Joy, *The Emperor Marcus Aurelius: A Study in Ideals* (Dublin, 1913); Henry Dwight Sedgwick, *Marcus Aurelius* (New Haven, 1921); and Paul Barron Watson, *Marcus Aurelius Antoninus* (New York, 1884).

▶ JARRA, EUGENIO, "Marco Aurelio filosofo del diritto," *Rivista internazionale di filosofia del diritto*, XII (July–October, 1932), 489–504.

▶ MURRAY, GILBERT, *The Stoic Philosophy* (Conway Memorial Lecture, New York–London, 1915). One of the outstanding essays in the vast literature on Stoicism. Reprinted in Murray's *Stoic, Christian, and Humanist* (London, 1940), pp. 89–118. See also Margaret E. Reesor, *The Political Theory of the Old and Middle Stoa* (New York, 1951).

▶ OGEREAU, F., *Le système philosophique des stoïciens* (Paris, 1885). See also the following: P. Laffont, *Les opinions politiques et sociales de Marc-Aurel* (Toulouse,

1912); Amand Jagu, *Epictète et Platon* (Paris, 1946); André Cresson, *Marc-Aurel: sa vie, son oeuvre* (Paris, 1942); Guillaume du Vair, *De la sainte philosophie: philosophie morale des stoïques* (Paris, 1946); and *Revue de Théologie et de Philosophie,* XVII, No. 72 (Lausanne, July–September, 1929), the entire issue of which is on Stoicism.

▶ RENAN, ERNEST, *Marcus Aurelius* (trans. Walter G. Hutchinson, Camelot Series, London–Newcastle-on-Tyne, n.d.). One of the finest appreciations of Marcus Aurelius. Speaking of the worship that followed the emperor's death, Renan says: "Never was worship more legitimate, and it remains our own today. Yes, every one of us wears mourning in his heart for Marcus Aurelius, as though he died but yesterday" (p. 242). The main theme of the volume, the seventh and last of Renan's *Origines du Christianisme,* is the development of Christianity under Marcus Aurelius and the relation of Christianity ("the great principle which has effected moral reformation by faith in the supernatural") and of Stoicism ("the finest effort of the lay school of virtue which the world has up till now ever known").

▶ ROSTOVTZEFF, M., *The Social and Economic History of the Hellenistic World,* 3 vols. (Oxford, 1941). Indispensable to an understanding of the background of Sto-

icism and of the whole period of Hellenistic civilization. See also his *Social and Economic History of the Roman Empire* (Oxford, 1926), in the last chapter of which the author examines the problem of decay of ancient civilization, and concludes as follows: "The evolution of the ancient world has a lesson and a warning for us. Our civilization will not last unless it be a civilization not of one class, but of the masses" (pp. 486–487).

▶ STEFANINI, LUIGI, *Il problema morale nell'epicureismo e nello stoicismo,* 3rd ed. (Turin–Milan–Rome, 1934). See also Carlo Terzi, *Il razionalismo morale di Epitteto* (Udine, 1938).

▶ STOCK, ST. GEORGE, *Stoicism* (London, 1908). See also W. W. Capes, *Stoicism* (London, 1880); Charles H. Stanley Davis, *Greek and Roman Stoicism and Some of Its Disciples* (Boston, 1903); Frederick W. Bussell, *Marcus Aurelius and Later Stoics* (New York, 1910); and F. W. H. Myers, *Essays: Classical and Modern* (London, 1921), Chap. III ("Marcus Aurelius Antoninus," pp. 177–223).

▶ WENLEY, ROBERT MARK, *Stoicism and Its Influence* (Boston, 1924). A volume in the series Our Debt to Greece and Rome, providing a brief survey of the influence of Stoicism from antiquity to the nineteenth century.

Chapter 6

St. Augustine

▶ AUGUSTINE, ST., *The City of God* (trans. John Healey, London–New York, 1931). The introduction (pp. vii–lx) by Ernest Barker greatly adds to the value of this abridged reissue of an early seventeenth-century translation of the *City of God.* Concerning the relations between church and state, Barker suggests that this question "hardly enters into St. Augustine's thought,

in the form in which it presented itself to the Middle Ages, or presents itself to us today" (p. xxxi). Granting this premise, Barker nevertheless says that "there is a sense in which the doctrine of the *City of God* is inimical to the State, and even subversive of its existence. St. Augustine shifts the centre of gravity. The men of the ancient world had thought in terms of the

Civitas Romana as the one and only society; they had deified the Roman Emperor as its living incarnation. . . . The ultimate effect of the *City of God* is the elimination of the State: it is the enthronement of the Church . . ." (p. xxxii).

▶ BAYNES, NORMAN H., *The Political Ideas of St. Augustine's De Civitate Dei* (Historical Association Pamphlet, No. 104, London, 1936). The problem of church and state is one of the main themes of this succinct study: "Church and State have their independent spheres of action: true: but through his other-worldly conception of human history it is to the Church that the primacy belongs, and he is mainly concerned with the State as the handmaid of the Church in religious matters" (p. 15). A useful bibliographical note is appended (p. 18).

▶ BEVAN, EDWYN, *Hellenism and Christianity* (London, 1921). Chap. VII ("The Prophet of Personality") is a vivid study of Augustine, "the first modern man," as he is sometimes called, because of his searching self-analysis and psychological insights (pp. 136–144). The whole volume, a collection of essays on the formative period of Christianity and its impact on the Hellenistic world, is rewarding reading. The first chapter, "The East and the West" (pp. 11–38), is now even timelier than when it was first written.

▶ BURLEIGH, JOHN H. S., *The City of God: A Study of St. Augustine's Philosophy* (London, 1949). Interpreting St. Augustine sympathetically from a Protestant viewpoint, the author suggests that "the City of God is none other than the Invisible Church of Wycliffe and Hus, Luther and Calvin" (p. 182).

▶ CAMBRIDGE ECONOMIC HISTORY OF EUROPE. The first volume (ed. J. H. Clapham and Eileen Power, Cambridge, 1941) is *The Agrarian Life of the Middle Ages;* the second volume (ed. M. M. Postan and H. J. Habakkuk, Cambridge, 1952) is *Trade and Industry in the Middle Ages.*

▶ CARLYLE, R. W., and A. J. CARLYLE, *A History of Medieval Political Theory in the West,* 6 vols. (Edinburgh and London, 1903–1936). The most important work, in any language, on medieval political theory. The first volume discusses St. Augustine's doctrine of the state (pp. 164–170), property (pp. 139–142), and slavery (118–121).

▶ COMBES, GUSTAVE, *La doctrine politique de Saint Augustin* (Paris, 1927). One of the leading French works on St. Augustine's political doctrines. See also H.-X. Arquillière, *L'Augustinisme politique* (Paris, 1934), which lists original source materials and critical studies and commentaries, and Étienne Gilson, *Introduction à l'étude de Saint Augustin* (Paris, 1929), which has an extensive bibliography (pp. 309–331). Gilson provides an illuminating philosophical and religious background of St. Augustine's thought, and his book is one of the most useful interpretations of St. Augustine in French. More recent works include Jules Chaix-Ruy, *Saint Augustin: Temps et Histoire* (Paris, 1956); Jean Guitton, *Actualité de Saint Augustin* (Paris, 1955); and Congrès international augustinien, *Augustinus magister,* 3 vols. (Paris, 1954–1955).

▶ COULBORN, RUSHTON (ed.), *Feudalism in History* (Princeton, 1956). Written by leading American scholars in the field, this symposium is a unique contribution to the comparative study of feudalism. In addition to Western Europe, the work deals with Russia, the Byzantine Empire, China, Japan, India, and other areas often neglected.

▶ COULTON, G. G., *Studies in Medieval Thought* (London, 1940). This is the best short introduction to medieval political ideas, by a leading authority on the Middle Ages. Chaps. II and III deal with Augustine and the *City of God* (pp. 24–47). Coulton stresses St. Augustine's acceptance of the state "as a real and necessary factor in human progress since the Fall." The Church "must render unto Caesar the things that are Caesar's. The City of God, being inextricably mixed up with the State—the Churchman being a citizen quite as really as he is a Churchman—therefore the City of God must obey the laws which are promulgated by the Earthly City" (p. 44). See also C. V. Wedgwood, *Velvet Studies* (London, 1946), pp. 74–79 ("The City of God").

► CULLMANN, OSCAR, *The State in the New Testament* (New York, 1956). The author, a leading Protestant theologian in the field of New Testament and early church history, seeks to demonstrate that "the apparent contradictions in the primitive Christian interpretations of the State are in reality not contradictions" (p. 87). The consistency of the New Testament with regard to the state is rooted, the author argues, in the essential Christian tension between the present and the future. A radically different view is presented by Hans Kelsen in his essay on "Justice in the Holy Scriptures," included in his *What Is Justice? Justice, Law, and Politics in the Mirror of Science* (Berkeley and Los Angeles, 1957), pp. 25–81. Kelsen concludes that the Christian theology of justice, based on Paul's teaching, can be summed up as follows: "There is a relative, human, justice which is identical with the positive law, and an absolute, divine, justice which is the secret of faith. Hence, there is in this theology no answer to the question as to what is justice, as a question of human reason referring to an ideal which is not necessarily identical with every positive law and which can be realized in this world" (p. 81). See also Adolf Harnack, *What Is Christianity?* (Harper Torchbooks, New York, 1957), pp. 75–151, for an analysis of the relation of the Gospel to the main political, social, and economic issues of western civilization.

► D'ARCY, M. C. (ed.), *Saint Augustine* (Meridian Books, New York, 1957). A symposium on Augustine's background, life, thought, and impact, written by leading Catholic theologians and philosophers, including Jacques Maritain, Étienne Gilson, Christopher Dawson, and E. I. Watkin. See also Roy W. Battenhouse (ed.), *A Companion to the Study of St. Augustine* (New York, 1955); H. Hohensee, *The Augustinian Concept of Authority* (New York, 1954); and John Joseph O'Meara, *The*

Young Augustine: The Growth of St. Augustine's Mind Up To His Conversion (New York, 1954).

► FIGGIS, JOHN NEVILLE, *The Political Aspects of St. Augustine's "City of God"* (London, 1921). One of the most incisive analyses, in English, of St. Augustine's thought; the last two chapters trace his influence in the Middle Ages and the modern period (pp. 81–117), and the important literature on the *City of God* is briefly summarized in a "Bibliography" (pp. 118–122). Figgis stresses that the conflict between the heavenly and earthly cities is "not primarily between two polities" but represents a deeper antagonism "between the otherworldly and the this-worldly reference to all institutions" (p. 114).

► FRIBERG, HANS DANIEL, *Love and Justice in Political Theory: A Study of Augustine's Definition of the Commonwealth* (Chicago, 1944). A comparison between Cicero's conception of the state in terms of law and justice, and St. Augustine's stress on love as the bond of political organization: "Whereas Cicero denies the existence —at any time, including the future—of an absolutely perfect commonwealth, Augustine recognizes its existence now in full reality in heaven, also now by faith among the believers, and finally in full reality also among them who now believe" (p. 73).

► HEARNSHAW, F. J. C. (ed.), *Medieval Contributions to Modern Civilization* (New York, 1922). A collection of essays, by distinguished authorities, on religion, philosophy, science, art, literature, education, social relations, economics, and politics. The chapter on politics is by J. W. Allen (pp. 225–267), who concludes as follows: "I suggest not merely that any separation of politics from ethics is fatal, but that a society which has lost belief in the validity of its own moral intuitions rests on rotting foundations. I suggest, further, that the idea that government must be directed to a recognized, common, and ultimate end, and refer to a standard of absolute values or be radically purposeless, is perfectly sound. The end, perhaps, need not transcend this world.

It may be possible to find a purpose referring only to this world that will satisfy the soul of man. But I suggest that no such end has yet been found. We can strip from the medieval system of ideas that I have tried to define in outline all that is not essential to it. We can eliminate the Church altogether, and it will still stand logically coherent. It is a question—it is perhaps *the* question—whether we can also eliminate God" (pp. 267–268).

▶ ——— (ed.), *The Social and Political Ideas of Some Great Medieval Thinkers* (London, 1923). Chap. I is an excellent introduction to the main political ideas and issues of the Middle Ages, by Ernest Barker; Chap. II, "St. Augustine and the City of God," is by A. J. Carlyle (pp. 34–52). Concerning the influence of St. Augustine's political theory in his own time and in the Middle Ages, Carlyle says that "so far as it was different from the normal traditions of the Stoic philosophers and of the Christian Fathers it had no importance and no significance, but that so far as it corresponded with these, so far as in his own way and under his own terms he re-stated the traditional view of the Stoics and of the Christian Fathers, it may well be said that St. Augustine had much influence" (pp. 51–52).

▶ LOETSCHER, FREDERICK WILLIAM, "St. Augustine's Conception of the State," *Church History*, IV (March, 1935), 16–42. A sound and systematic analysis of the subject, incorporating much of the best available source material. One of the important points about St. Augustine is "that he developed his theory, as far-reaching in its historical consequences as it is incompatible with modern ideas of religious toleration, that the state, under the guidance of the church, the divinely appointed teacher of revealed truth, must perform a pedagogical and disciplinary function that involves the use of civil power for the conversion of heretics and schismatics or for their adequate punishment if they obstinately persist in their errors" (p. 39), a theory that has given St. Augustine the reputation of being the first defender of the Inquisition.

▶ MORRALL, JOHN B., *Political Thought in Medieval Times* (London, 1958). Provides a brief introduction into the subject, emphasizing the main themes of medieval civilization. See also Gordon Leff, *Medieval Thought from Saint Augustine to Ockham* (Penguin Books, Baltimore, 1958), for a more general survey of medieval philosophy. Chap. II (pp. 32–54) deals with Augustine and his successors.

▶ Moss, H. ST. L. B., *The Birth of the Middle Ages, 395–814* (London, 1935). Part I, "Romans and Barbarians," deals with the period that is fundamental to a full appreciation of St. Augustine (pp. 1–78).

▶ NIEBUHR, REINHOLD, *Christian Realism and Political Problems* (New York, 1953). Chap. IX (pp. 119–146) is on "Augustine's Political Realism" (also reprinted in William Ebenstein, *Political Thought in Perspective* [New York, 1957], pp. 109–124). Niebuhr holds that Augustine is, with regard to basic political problems "a more reliable guide than any known thinker" (p. 146). Augustine helps us, Niebuhr argues, to avoid the pitfalls of the three representative approaches to political problems. The "realists" understand the power of collective self-interest, but not its blindness; the pragmatists perceive the futility of fixed and detailed norms, but do not grasp that love must be the final norm; lastly, modern liberal Christians recognize that love is the supreme norm for man, but often fall into sentimentality by failing to appreciate the persisting power of self-love. Niebuhr stresses that Augustine's thought, avoiding these various pitfalls, is particularly pertinent to the problem of the growing world community today.

▶ POPE, HUGH, *Saint Augustine of Hippo: Essays dealing with his Life and Times and Some Features of His Work* (Westminster, Md., 1949). The first two chapters on Roman Africa and its Christianization (pp. 1–77) are particularly interesting. The third chapter (pp. 78–138) tells the story of St. Augustine's life. The remaining six chapters (pp. 139–361) deal with his thought, stressing particularly his theology.

▶ PREVITÉ-ORTON, C. W., *The Study of Medieval History* (Cambridge, 1937). An Inaugural Lecture, arguing a spirited defense of medieval studies: "Modern civilization, with its thoughts and aptitudes and all that they imply, did not spout forth suddenly in the sixteenth century, charged with imprisoned gases, like a new geyser from a subterranean cavern. It was the natural inheritor of the preceding age, rich with its accumulated gains, and moulded by its experience. In fact, the separation of modern and medieval is, as we all know, largely artificial" (p. 15).

▶ TROELTSCH, ERNST, *Augustin, die christliche Antike und das Mittelalter* (Munich and Berlin, 1915). The best single volume, in German, on Augustine. See also Hermann

Reuter, *Augustinische Studien* (Gotha, 1887), an important starting point of modern Augustinian studies; Otto Schilling, *Die Staats- und Soziallehre des hl. Augustinus* (Freiburg, 1910); Konrad Eckstädt, *Augustins Anschauung vom Staat* (Kirchhain, 1912); and Hans Joachim Diesner, *Studien zur Gesellschaftslehre und sozialen Haltung Augustins* (Halle, 1954). An indispensable work for the study of the social and political doctrines of Christianity is Ernst Troeltsch, *The Social Teaching of the Christian Churches*, 2 vols. (London–New York, 1931). A useful discussion of Christian views on property from Christ to Thomas Aquinas will be found in Konrad Farner, *Christentum und Eigentum* (Bern, 1947).

Chapter 7

John of Salisbury

▶ CARLYLE, R. W., and A. J. CARLYLE, *A History of Medieval Political Theory in the West*, 2nd imp. (Edinburgh–London, 1932), Vol. IV. Chap. II of Part II deals with John of Salisbury's views on the relations of church and state (pp. 330–341). See also *op. cit.* (Edinburgh–London, 1928), Vol. III, Part II, Chap. V, which discusses John of Salisbury's distinction of kingship and tyranny in relation to other medieval doctrines on the subject (pp. 125–146), and G. G. Coulton, *Studies in Medieval Thought* (London, 1940), Chap. VII (pp. 87–95).

▶ LIEBESCHÜTZ, HANS, *Medieval Humanism in the Life and Writings of John of Salisbury* (London, 1950). An original contribution, portraying the life and thought of John of Salisbury against his own medieval background rather than against modern political ideas. A systematic survey of the literature on John in Chap. I (pp. 1–7) adds to the usefulness of the work. See also Johan Huizinga, "John of Salisbury: A Pre-

Gothic Mind," in his *Men and Ideas: History, the Middle Ages, the Renaissance* (Meridian Books, New York, 1959), pp. 159–177.

▶ PIKE, JOSEPH B., *Frivolities of Courtiers and Footprints of Philosophers* (Minneapolis, 1938). A translation of the First, Second, and Third Books, and selections from the Seventh and Eighth Books of John of Salisbury's *Statesman's Book*. It thus supplements the translation of the *Statesman's Book* by John Dickinson (New York, 1928), which contains the Fourth, Fifth, and Sixth Books, and selections from the Seventh and Eighth Books. The Dickinson translation is preceded by a long and excellent introduction (pp. xvii–lxxxii). See also *John of Salisbury's Memoirs of the Papal Court* (trans. from the Latin with Introduction and Notes by Marjorie Chibnall, New York, 1956), and *The Letters of John of Salisbury* (ed. by W. J. Miller and H. E. Butler, revised by C. N. L. Brooke,

New York, 1955), both with lengthy introductory essays on the life and thought of John of Salisbury.

► POOLE, REGINALD LANE, *Illustrations of the History of Medieval Thought and Learning*, 2nd ed. (London, 1920). Chap. VII (pp. 176–197) is on John of Salisbury, and is one of the most useful short summaries of his life and thought. The distinctive mark of John's *Statesman's Book*, Poole says, "is a humanism which seems to remove it from medieval associations" (p. 191). See also Poole's "The Masters of the Schools at Paris and Chartres in John of Salisbury's Time," *English Historical Review*, XXXV (July, 1920), 321–342.

► SCHAARSCHMIDT, C., *Johannes Saresberiensis: Nach Leben und Studien, Schriften und Philosophie* (Leipzig, 1862). One of the first modern, pioneering studies of John of Salisbury. See also Ernst Bernheim, *Mittelalterliche Zeitanschauungen in ihrem Einfluss auf Politik und Geschichsschreibung, Die Zeitanschauungen* (Tubingen, 1918), Vol. I, especially Chap. III (pp. 110–233), on the development of the problem of state and church in the Middle Ages, and Étienne Gilson and Philotheus Böhner, *Die Geschichte der christlichen Philosophie von ihren Anfängen bis Nikolaus von Cues* (Paderborn–Vienna–Zurich, 1937), pp. 341–350, for a brief account of John of Salisbury.

► SPURGEON, CAROLINE F. E. (ed.), *Essays and Studies by Members of the English Association* (Oxford, 1928), Vol. VIII. Chap. II, by Helen Waddell, is on John of Salisbury (pp. 28–51). The author stresses the "critical dispassionate aloofness that sets John solitary in the Middle Ages" (p. 41).

► STUBBS, WILLIAM, *Seventeen Lectures on the Study of Medieval and Modern History* (Oxford, 1886). Chaps. VI and VII

("Learning and Literature at the Court of Henry II") include accounts of John of Salisbury, particularly in relation to contemporary thought and learning (pp. 115–155).

► ULLMANN, WALTER, *Medieval Papalism: The Political Theories of the Medieval Canonists* (London, 1949). A scholarly study of papalist political theories, based on original sources, *Medieval Papalism* is an important and original contribution to a much neglected field. See also Ullmann's article, "The Influence of John of Salisbury on Medieval Italian Jurists," *English Historical Review*, LIX (September, 1944), 384–392, in which he maintains that "recent researches into fourteenth-century jurisprudence have shown that the *Policraticus* was one of the most quoted and perused treatises written by a medieval philosopher" (p. 384).

► WEBB, CLEMENT C. J., *John of Salisbury* (London, 1932). The author sees in John of Salisbury "a typical Englishman. He is a strong 'party man,' yet ready to be, so far as possible, on friendly terms with his opponents; he has an instinctive aversion to extremes, and distaste alike for rhetorical display and *doctrinaire* rigidity; with a constant disposition to seek means of accommodation and even of compromise, if they can be had without abandonment of a few principles which he regards as fundamental" (pp. 176–177). Indispensable as an introduction into the life and work of John of Salisbury.

► WULF, MAURICE DE, *History of Medieval Philosophy*, 2 vols., 3rd ed. (London–New York, 1935–1938). A short discussion of John of Salisbury is in the first volume (pp. 226–232). The *Statesman's Book* is called "the most complete philosophy of the State produced in the first period of the Middle Ages" (p. 231).

Chapter 8

St. Thomas Aquinas

▶ BETTENSON, HENRY (ed.), *Documents of the Christian Church* (New York, 1947). The most easily accessible documentary source book of its kind, containing both official and unofficial statements.

▶ BRACTON, HENRY DE, *On the Laws and Customs of England* (written before 1256). The most systematic expression of the typically medieval doctrine that law derives from custom, that the king, though not subject to man, ought to be subject to "God and to the law, for the law makes the king," and that "there is no king where the will and not the law has dominion" (*On the Laws and Customs of England,* ed. Travers Twiss, London, 1878, I, 39). About two hundred years later, John Fortescue emphasized again the medieval principle that the king "is not able himself to change the laws without the assent of his subjects nor to burden an unwilling people with strange imposts" (*De laudibus legum Angliae* [*In Praise of the Laws of England*], written about 1470, edited and translated, with introduction and notes, by S. B. Chrimes, Cambridge, 1942, p. 25). The concept of the supremacy of law played a major political part in the struggles of Parliament against the Stuarts in the seventeenth century, and Bracton, in particular, was appealed to by Sir Edward Coke, the lawyer and leader of the parliamentary party. Walter Ullmann's *The Medieval Idea of Law* (London, 1946) is focused on the fourteenth century and illuminates hitherto neglected aspects of medieval legal thought and scholarship.

▶ BRENNAN, ROBERT EDWARD, *Thomistic Psychology* (New York, 1941). A "philosophic analysis of the nature of man," with an introduction by Mortimer J. Adler.

▶ CARLYLE, R. W., and A. J. CARLYLE, *A History of Medieval Political Theory in the West,* 2nd ed. (1938), Vol. V. The whole volume is devoted to the political theory of the thirteenth century, including detailed analyses of St. Thomas Aquinas.

▶ CASSIRER, ERNST, *The Myth of the State* (New Haven, 1946). Chaps. VII–IX deal with medieval political philosophy (pp. 78–115).

▶ CHESTERTON, G. K., *St. Thomas Aquinas* (New York, 1933). A vivid and colorful biographical sketch, stressing the rational element in St. Thomas' thought. Chesterton calls him "one of the great liberators of the human intellect" (p. 19), and says that it was "the very life of Thomist teaching that Reason can be trusted; it was the very life of the Lutheran teaching that Reason is utterly untrustworthy" (p. 21). The Protestant Reformation of the sixteenth century was, according to Chesterton, "a belated revolt of the thirteenth-century pessimists" and "a backwash of the old Augustinian Puritanism against the Aristotelian liberality" (p. x).

▶ COPLESTON, F. C., *Aquinas* (Penguin Books, Baltimore, 1955). Chap. V (pp. 192–234) deals with the social and political thought of St. Thomas. Copleston, a leading English Jesuit historian of western ideas, holds that St. Thomas "favored constitutional monarchy" (p. 233). As to the controversial issue of St. Thomas' attitude on tyranny and resistance to tyranny, Copleston argues that according to St. Thomas tyrants "can legitimately be deposed on the ground that they are guilty of abusing their position and power unless, indeed, there is a reason for thinking that rebellion would result in as bad a state of affairs as the one which it was designed to remedy" (p. 232).

▶ D'ARCY, MARTIN C., *Thomas Aquinas* (Boston, 1930). A volume in the Leaders of Philosophy series. The first chapter (pp.

3–31) gives an illuminating account of the historical and philosophical background of the period, with special emphasis on Aristotelianism and scholasticism. The last chapter (pp. 251–275) deals with the impact of Thomism on modern thought, and the author stresses the lack of uniformity in Thomism: "There is a left wing and a right wing of Thomism, there are conservatives and liberals. For this reason one will find no agreement about what are the philosophical weaknesses in St. Thomas which need to be remedied" (p. 271).

▶ D'ENTRÉVES, ALEXANDER PASSERIN, *The Medieval Contribution to Political Thought* (Oxford, 1939). The first, introductory, chapter deals with the general characteristics of medieval political ideas (pp. 1–18). Chap. II is on Thomas Aquinas (pp. 19–43). See also D'Entrèves (ed.), *Aquinas: Selected Political Writings* (Blackwell's Political Texts, Oxford, 1948), pp. vii–xxxiii (introduction).

▶ FARRELL, WALTER, *A Companion to the Summa*, 4 vols. (New York, 1939–1945). A comprehensive work, written from a rigid, literal, and Dominican viewpoint that seeks to interpret recent intellectual and social movements in the light of Thomist principles. Chap. XVIII of the second volume discusses St. Thomas' treatment of the problem of law (pp. 363–389).

▶ GILBY, THOMAS, *The Political Thought of Thomas Aquinas* (Chicago, 1958). The first part gives the intellectual and social background of the whole period in which Thomas Aquinas lived. The second, and much longer, part, traces the philosophical and theological development of St. Thomas, drawn against a broad European canvas. The author, a Dominican teacher and scholar like St. Thomas himself, emphasizes four points in the latter's political thought. First, the acceptance of the Aristotelian view that the state springs from the social appetite of man rather than from his corruption and sin, as had been maintained by St. Augustine and the patristic tradition, later to be resurrected by Martin Luther. Second, the author claims (less convinc-

ingly) that St. Thomas adhered to the Gelasian concept of the twin authorities, spiritual and temporal, each being supreme in its own sphere. Third, St. Thomas upheld the idea of the limited scope of governmental authority; as to tyrannicide, the author concedes that St. Thomas was rather conservative, and "more prim" and "more hesitant" (p. 289) than John of Salisbury, for example. Fourth, St. Thomas stressed that government was more an art than a branch of ethics and science, a point to be developed more fully in modern political thought by Edmund Burke.

▶ GILSON, ÉTIENNE, *The Christian Philosophy of St. Thomas Aquinas* (New York, 1956). An over-all synthesis by one of the leading Thomist philosophers of the twentieth century. Part III (pp. 251–378) deals with the moral, legal, social, and political doctrines of St. Thomas Aquinas. Conceding that for St. Thomas "monarchy is the best form of government" (p. 329), Gilson stresses that this preference does not include absolute monarchy: "The prince or king can only ensure the common good of the people when he is dependent upon them" (*ibid.*). Concerning the general orientation of St. Thomas' thinking, Gilson concludes as follows: "If we grant that a philosophy is not to be defined from the elements it borrows but from the spirit which quickens it, we shall see here neither Platonism nor Aristotelianism, but, above all, Christianity" (p. 378). See also Gilson's *The Philosophy of St. Thomas Aquinas* (St. Louis, Mo., 1939), *Reason and Revelation in the Middle Ages* (New York, 1939), and *The Spirit of Medieval Philosophy* (New York, 1940).

▶ GRABMANN, MARTIN, *Thomas Aquinas: His Personality and Thought* (New York, 1928). The author is the leading modern student of Thomism in Germany. The eighth edition of the (originally German) work contains new materials (*Thomas von Aquin: Persönlichkeit und Gedankenwelt*, Munich, 1949). See also Grabmann's *Mittelalterliches Geistesleben: Abhandlungen zur Geschichte der Scholatik und Mystik*,

2 vols. (Munich, 1926–1936), ranked among the pioneering researches in the field of medieval studies. J. J. Baumann, *Die Staatslehre des h. Thomas von Aquin* (Leipzig, 1873), includes a discussion of St. Thomas' political ideas in relation to the *Kulturkampf,* the struggle between Bismarck and the Roman Catholic Church that was then going on in Germany. Wilhelm Müller, *Der Staat in seinen Beziehungen zur sittlichen Ordnung* (Beiträge zur Geschichte der Philosophie des Mittelalters, ed. Clemens Baeumker, Vol. XIX, No. 1, Munster, 1916) is, unlike Baumann's older study, written from the Roman Catholic viewpoint. Gallus M. Manser, *Das Wesen des Thomismus,* 3rd ed. (Freiburg, 1949), is a work of great erudition, written from the Thomistic viewpoint.

▶ HENLE, ROBERT J., *Saint Thomas and Platonism* (The Hague, 1956). Because of the immense impact of Aristotle on Saint Thomas, the relations between Thomism and Platonism are often neglected or obscured. The author shows in concrete detail the relation of Plato's writings to Thomistic thought.

▶ HUTCHINS, ROBERT M., *St. Thomas and the World State* (Milwaukee, 1949). The author holds that the "existence of a world society, of a family of nations, which popes and Catholic jurists have always asserted, implies, then, world law and world government. The only perfect community today is a world state. It is the only community that is self-sufficing. Every smaller community requires, in the phrase of St. Thomas, the help of another" (p. 40). See also Gerald Francis Benkert, *The Thomistic Conception of an International Society* (The Catholic University of America, *Philosophical Studies,* Vol. 70, Washington, 1942), and Adriano Bernareggi, "La Filosofia del diritto internazionale in S. Tommaso," in *S. Tommaso d'Aquino: pubblicazione commemorativa del sesto centenario della canonizzazione* (Pubblicazioni della Università Cattolica del Sacro Cuore, First Series, Vol. II, Milan, 1923), 193–227.

▶ KILLEEN, SYLVESTER MICHAEL, *The Philosophy of Labor According to Thomas Aquinas* (Washington, 1939). The author admits that St. Thomas justified slavery and serfdom, yet holds that his doctrine "in no way destroyed the dignity of the human person" (p. 69). A more detailed defense of St. Thomas' acceptance of slavery and servitude will be found in Winston Ashley, *The Theory of Natural Slavery According to Aristotle and St. Thomas* (Notre Dame, Ind., 1941): even if servitude is *involuntary,* it "is not *essentially* wrong if (a) it is necessary for the common good of society, and (b) if it does not deprive the subject of his strictly natural rights" (p. 144). At the same time, the author warns that "Christian society must always view with extreme suspicion a system which supposes the perfect virtue of the intelligent, and the low virtue of the poor and simple, a system which naturally aims first at the freedom of the most virtuous, and only secondarily at making a way for the lowest men toward the life of contemplation" (p. 145). See also George V. Dougherty, *The Moral Basis of Social Order According to Saint Thomas* (Washington, 1941); James Henry Hoban, *The Thomistic Concept of Person and Some of Its Social Implications* (Washington, 1939); and Robert G. Brehmer, *The Social Doctrines of the Catholic Church* (New York, 1936).

The two most important official statements of the Roman Catholic Church on social questions are the encyclicals *Rerum novarum (On the Condition of Workers,* 1891) and *Quadragesimo Anno (On Reconstructing Social Order,* 1931). *Rerum novarum* is primarily noteworthy for the fact that the Roman Catholic Church took official cognizance of the problem of labor and capital as early as 1891—about fifty years later than Karl Marx's first writings and about eighty years later than the first French and English socialist discussions, but well ahead of most other churches and governments, which discovered the social problem of capital-labor relations much later.

The stress in *Rerum novarum* is, first, on the principle of private property against the socialist challenge, and, second, on the necessity of ameliorating the lot of workers through social legislation, just wages, the right to form trade-unions, and spiritual renovation under the guidance of the Roman Catholic Church. The acceptance of inequality is expressed in words that remind one more of Herbert Spencer, the apostle of laissez faire economics, than of St. Thomas Aquinas. "There are truly very great and very many natural differences among men. Neither the talents, nor the skill, nor the health, nor the capacities of all are the same, and unequal fortune follows of itself upon necessary inequality in respect to these endowments. And clearly this condition of things is adapted to benefit both individuals and the community; for to carry on its affairs community life requires varied aptitudes and diverse services, and to perform these services men are impelled most by differences in individual property holdings" (*Two Basic Social Encyclicals: On the Condition of Workers, Leo XIII, and Forty Years After on Reconstructing Social Order, Pius XI,* New York, 1943), p. 21.

In the encyclical *Quadragesimo Anno* (1931), the solution of the social problem through the system of "corporatism" is strongly approved. Under corporatism, each industry is organized in separate associations, or "syndicates," of employers and employees, and the officially recognized syndicates enjoy a monopoly of representing employers and employees respectively. Membership in the syndicates is not legally compulsory, but contributions and special taxes to the syndicates are compulsory. The "corporations" are made up of representatives of associations (or "syndicates") of employers and employees, as well as representatives of the state: "Strikes and lockouts are forbidden: if the parties cannot settle their dispute, public authority intervenes" (*op. cit.,* p. 151). The two main advantages of the "corporate system" are listed in *Quadragesimo Anno* as, first, the

collaboration of classes under the authority of the state, and, second, the fact that "socialist organizations and their activities are repressed" (*ibid.*).

In 1931, Fascist Italy was the only country in which "corporatism," as described in *Quadragesimo Anno,* operated—supported by a Fascist one-party dictatorship. The corporate system was later adopted in Portugal under Salazar, in Austria under Dollfuss and Schuschnigg, in Brazil under Vargas, and in Spain under Franco, to mention but a few one-party dictatorships that resembled, to a greater or lesser degree, the original model of Fascist Italy.

Quadragesimo Anno did not confine its censure to socialism ("No one can be at the same time a good Catholic and a true socialist") but also attacked Liberalism by propounding the theory, used by fascists and nazis in identical terms before and after 1931, that "Liberalism is the father of Socialism," and that Bolshevism is the "heir" of the latter (*op. cit.,* p. 169). The "errors" of Liberalism (separation of state and church, public education, freedom of thought and the press, freedom of teaching, rationalism, toleration of wrong ideas, freedom of choosing one's religion) are officially condemned in the *Syllabus of Errors* (1864) of Pope Pius IX (*The Encyclical of Pope Pius IX, given at Rome December 8, 1864, and the Syllabus of Errors Condemned,* 3rd ed., Baltimore, 1870), and in the encyclical *Human Liberty* (1888), the full text of which will be found in *The Great Encyclical Letters of Pope Leo XIII* (New York, 1903), pp. 135–163. The latter also contains Pope Leo XIII's apostolic constitution, *Officiorum ac Munerum (The Prohibition and Censorship of Books,* 1897); it gives a brief history of censorship and prohibition of books since the first century, from which the conclusion is drawn that "the chief care of the Roman Pontiffs has always been to protect civil society from erroneous beliefs and corrupt morals, the twin cause of the decline and ruin of States, which commonly owes its origin and its progress to bad books" (p. 409). The *Prohibition and Censorship* then lists the categories of prohibited books, the conditions of censorship, and the penalties of transgression (pp. 411–421). The *Index of Prohibited Books,* new ed. (Vatican Polyglot Press, 1930), published by order of Pope Pius XI, states that "only those afflicted with that moral pestilence known as liberalism can look on the barriers erected by the legitimate authority against licence in the light of an attack on the free-will of the individual" (p. vii), and that the coercive suppression of the spread of doctrinal errors "in no wise opposes liberty, the exercise of which consists in the choice of those means most apt to obtain eternal salvation" (p. viii).

► LACHANCE, LOUIS, *L'humanisme politique de saint Thomas,* 2 vols. (Paris–Ottawa, 1939). One of the most detailed accounts of the political theory of St. Thomas in any language. See also *Mélanges Thomistes* (publiés par les Dominicains de la Province de France à l'occasion du VI centenaire de la canonisation de saint Thomas d'Aquin, Paris, 1934), a symposium volume with contributions by leading Thomist scholars. An excellent analysis of St. Thomas' social and political ideas will be found in George de Lagarde, *La naissance de l'esprit laique au déclin du moyen âge,* Vol. III, *Secteur social de la scholastique* (Paris, 1942), pp. 69–115. The first volume of this massive inquiry into the birth of the lay spirit in the Middle Ages is entitled *Bilan du XIII*e *siècle* (Paris, 1934). Bernard Roland-Gosselin, *La doctrine politique de saint Thomas d'Aquin* (Paris, 1928), is a useful short summary.

► LEA, H. C., *A History of the Inquisition of the Middle Ages,* 3 vols. (New York, 1887–1888). The standard work on the subject. A penetrating and brief discussion of "Freethought and Inquisition" will be found in G. G. Coulton, *Medieval Panorama* (Cambridge, 1938), Chap. XXXV (pp. 457–476). St. Thomas Aquinas' main discussion of heresy and unbelief is in *Summa Theologica,* II–II, QQ. 10–14. See also

George Quentin Friel, *Punishment in the Philosophy of Saint Thomas Aquinas and among Some Primitive Peoples* (Washington, 1939).

► MCILWAIN, CHARLES HOWARD, *The Growth of Political Theory in the West* (New York, 1932). Contrary to most writers on the subject, McIlwain holds that St. Thomas Aquinas was neither a believer in limited, constitutional monarchy, nor a "Whig" or democrat, but "the greatest of all contemporary exponents of pure monarchy" (p. 333).

► MARGENAU, HENRY, *Thomas and the Physics of 1958: A Confrontation* (Milwaukee, 1958). The author, an American physicist and philosopher of science, examines St. Thomas' views on science in relation to contemporary physics, and finds a harmonious concordance between the two.

► MARITAIN, JACQUES, *St. Thomas Aquinas* (Meridian Books, New York, 1958). Maritain is the outstanding liberal Catholic writer since Lord Acton, and one of the leading modern Thomist philosophers. One of the main propositions of the book is that "St. Thomas wrote not for the thirteenth century but for our time" (p. 103), and that he is "pre-eminently the apostle and teacher of our time" (p. 115). Maritain's estimate of St. Thomas' position is as follows: "It is proper to remember that God in His most exalted works proceeds by way of privileges and exceptions and unique cases. He once sent His only begotten Son on earth, and gave Him a precursor. He once gave the law through Moses—is there anything surprising in that He should once have given His Church a Doctor *par excellence* in philosophical and theological wisdom?" (p. 155). Testimonies of popes on St. Thomas Aquinas and four of the most important official papal pronouncements on Thomism as the official doctrine of the Roman Catholic Church are contained in an appendix (pp. 167–266).

Maritain applies his interpretation of Thomism to modern social and political problems in two books that are most representative of his liberal, democratic, antitotalitarian philosophy: *True Humanism* (New York, 1938), and *Scholasticism and Politics* (New York, 1940). In both books he develops his concept of "personalist democracy," which is opposed both to the "atomistic and mechanistic type of bourgeois individualism, which suppresses the social organic totality" (*Scholasticism and Politics*, p. 82), and to the totalitarian doctrines of communism, nazism, and fascism, which "engulf the person" (*ibid.*). Maritain contrasts "democracy of the individual and humanism of the individual," which "arise from an anthropocentric inspiration," with his own conception of "democracy of the person and humanism of the person," which "spring forth from a theocentric inspiration" (pp. 84–85), and which are based on the idea of man as God's image, the common good, human rights, and concrete liberty. Maritain is particularly concerned about the rights of man: "If the human person is without rights, then rights and, consequently, authority exist nowhere" (p. 111). Maritain is also keenly aware that there can be no rebuilding of society without thoroughgoing social and economic reforms. He interprets socialism as the result, not so much of demands for improved living conditions (which could also be obtained under reformist or paternalist capitalism), but of the struggle for recognition "of an offended and humiliated human dignity" (*True Humanism*, p. 225), which has been distorted by Marxism into class consciousness and class war. Trade-unionism "is at the moment the most considerable and the most promising force of social renovation" (p. 233), though the Christian idea of community is above class, as it is above race and nation: "Yet, precisely because man is at once carnal and spiritual, because every great historic and temporal undertaking has biologico-sociological material foundations, where the very animality of man and a whole irrational capital is at once borne along and exalted, it is natural that, in the transformation of a regime such as the capitalist system, the working classes should furnish this sociological basis: and in

a sense one may speak of their historic mission, may hold that the destiny of humanity depends largely, in actual fact, on their attitude and action" (p. 230).

Concerning the question of property, Maritain recalls the Thomistic doctrine that recognizes, on the one hand, private property, but insists, on the other, that it should serve the good of all. The remedy of the evil of concentration of private property in the hands of the few under capitalism is not, according to Maritain, the abolition of the institution of property but its diffusion and distribution "in ways which can remain very diverse, and which do not exclude, where they are necessary, certain collectivizations" (p. 179). In industry, Maritain is opposed to both state ownership and communism, and prefers cooperative ownership by the workers themselves, because such copartnerships would better protect the freedom of the workers and also provide a better solution of the problem of incentive than is possible under state ownership of industry. Socialist theory in democratic states is likely to move in an analogous direction, stressing socialization (by municipalities, cooperatives, and other associations and corporations) rather than nationalization (by the state). A succinct summary of Maritain's philosophy of "personalist democracy" will be found in his short book, *The Person and the Common Good* (New York, 1947). The basic doctrine of "personalism" is that "the human being is caught between two poles; a material pole, which, in reality, does not concern the true person but rather the shadow of personality or what, in the strict sense, is called *individuality,* and a spiritual pole, which does concern *true personality*" (p. 23). For a detailed analysis of the Thomistic sources of Maritain's philosophy of personalism see Jacques Crotteau, *Les fondements thomistes du personnalisme de Maritain* (Ottawa, 1955).

▶ MURPHY, EDWARD F., *St. Thomas' Political Doctrine and Democracy* (Washington, 1921). Maintains the view that St. Thomas' political ideas "constitute a trove of democratic principle" (p. 269). See also Wilfrid Parsons, "The Medieval Theory of the Tyrant," *Review of Politics*, IV (April, 1942), 129–143.

▶ PEGIS, ANTON C. (ed.), *Basic Writings of Saint Thomas Aquinas*, 2 vols. (New York, 1945). Contains substantial portions of the *Summa Theologica* and the *Summa contra gentiles*, his second most important work. The editor's introduction (pp. xxxv–liii) deals with the background of St. Thomas' thought, particularly in relation to Plato, Aristotle, and Christian theology. The anti-Platonism of St. Thomas receives special consideration.

▶ ——, *Saint Thomas and the Greeks* (Milwaukee, 1939). See also J. L. Stocks, *Aristotelianism* (Boston, 1925), pp. 119–134; Werner Gebauer, *Die Aufnahme der Politik des Aristoteles und die naturrechtliche Begründung des Staates durch Thomas von Aquino* (Stuttgart, 1936); and Georg Freiherr von Hertling, *Historische Beiträge zur Philosophie* (ed. J. A. Endres, Kempten–Munich, 1914), pp. 20–31 ("Zur Geschichte der aristotelischen Politik im Mittelalter").

▶ PIEPER, JOSEF, *The Silence of St. Thomas: Three Essays* (New York, 1957). The third essay on "The Timeliness of Thomism" (pp. 75–108) has some suggestive comparisons between Thomism and contemporary Existentialism.

▶ REDING, MARCEL, *Thomas von Aquin und Karl Marx* (Graz, 1953). The author, a Catholic theologian and moral philosopher, argues that, despite some real differences, there was a deep affinity between St. Thomas and Marx, rooted in the fact that both were "Aristotelians of genius and originality" (p. 5). Aristotle, St. Thomas, and Marx were antimystical, realistic, empirical, and political, and all three emphasized "the orientation of the individual toward the community" (p. 10).

▶ RENARD, GEORGES, *L'institution: fondement d'une rénovation de l'ordre social* (Paris, 1933). A seminal contribution to the institutional approach in the social sciences, written from a Thomistic viewpoint. See also William I. Jennings, "The Institutional Theory," in the symposium by various authors, *Modern Theories of Law* (London, 1933), pp. 68–85, for a general discussion of French institutional theories and their relations to Thomism.

▶ SMITH, GEORGE D. (ed.), *The Teaching of the Catholic Church: A Summary of Catholic Doctrine*, 2 vols. (New York, 1949). A monumental work, with contributions from many distinguished scholars, all members of the clergy. See, in particular, Chap. I, "Faith and Revealed Truth," I, 1–37, and Chap. XX, "The Church on Earth," II, 691–732. There are more references to St. Thomas Aquinas than to any other source of doctrine (see Index, pp. 1313–1314).

▶ STUBBS, WILLIAM, *Seventeen Lectures on the Study of Medieval and Modern History* (Oxford, 1886). Concerning medieval scholastic philosophers, Bishop Stubbs says that they "ticketed every portion of man's moral anatomy, found a rule for every possible choice, a reason and a reward for every virtue, and a punishment for every conceivable crime; they turned generalisations into laws, and deduced from them as laws the very facts from which they had generalised. They benefited mankind by exercising and training subtle wits, and they reduced dialectics, almost, we might say, logic itself, to absurdity. I do not undervalue them, because the great men among them were so great that even such a method did not destroy them: in reading Thomas Aquinas, for instance, one is constantly provoked to say, What could not such a mind have done if it had not been fettered by such a method?" (p. 90). For critical summaries of scholastic philosophy, see also G. G. Coulton, *Studies in Medieval Thought* (London–New York, 1940), pp. 130–150, and Arthur Baumgarten, *Die Geschichte der abendländischen Philosophie* (Geneva, 1945), pp. 138–161. How heresy and free thought continued to exist under scholasticism—albeit under precarious conditions—

is described in J. M. Robertson, *A History of Freethought*, 4th ed. (London, 1936), I, 304–401.

▶ TAYLOR, A. E., *St. Thomas Aquinas as a Philosopher* (Oxford, 1924). St. Thomas is presented as a philosopher who appeared as a most audacious innovator to his contemporaries; in particular, the "substitution of Aristotelianism for Platonism as the basis of a specifically Christian philosophy was a revolution and a rather paradoxical revolution" (p. 10). Aristotle had two main tendencies: one directed toward naturalism, and another deeply embedded in the thought of Plato, and "it is Aristotle the Platonist rather than Aristotle the positivist who influences the thought of Thomas" (p. 25). See also John Frederick Peifer, *The Concept in Thomism* (New York, 1952), and Henri D. Gardeil, *Initiation à la philosophie de saint Thomas d'Aquin*, 2 vols. (Paris, 1952–1953), for general introductions into St. Thomas' philosophy.

▶ TAYLOR, HENRY OSBORN, *The Medieval Mind*, 2 vols. (New York, 1911). Chap. XL in the second volume is on Thomas Aquinas' general philosophy and its relation to medieval thought (pp. 433–483).

▶ WULF, MAURICE DE, *History of Medieval Philosophy*, 2 vols., 3rd ed. (London–New York, 1935–1938). The first volume of this standard work, indispensable for reference purposes, deals with medieval philosophy to the end of the twelfth century, the second with the thirteenth century, including a study of St. Thomas Aquinas (pp. 116–151). Detailed bibliographies greatly enhance the value of the work. Concerning scholasticism—which he accepts enthusiastically—the author makes the point that, when scholastic philosophy is called "a religious philosophy, the qualification is correct if by it is meant that on the one hand revealed doctrine governed the choice of certain special problems, and that on the other hand, dogma served as a regulating principle and as an indirect control of philosophical research. But it ought to be understood that, speaking formally and in strict terms, a philosophy in the degree in which it is distinct from theology, is not susceptible of the adjective Christian, and hence, the expression Christian philosophy is an unsuitable one" (I, 280). To the extent that a philosophy is different from theology, it is not Christian (according to De Wulf), and to the extent that it is not different from theology, it is not philosophy. This extreme (though perhaps logically consistent) position is rejected by another neo-Thomist, Étienne Gilson, who admits the possibility of Christian philosophy in the acceptance of Christian revelation as "an indispensable auxiliary to reason" (*The Spirit of Medieval Philosophy*, p. 37), and in the selection of those philosophical problems that affect the conduct of religious life. See also De Wulf's *Medieval Philosophy: Illustrated from the System of Thomas Aquinas* (Cambridge, Mass., 1922), a short account of St. Thomas' philosophy, including his theory of the state (pp. 117–128), and D. J. Kennedy, *St. Thomas Aquinas and Medieval Philosophy* (New York, 1919), which includes a detailed exposition of the three functions assigned to reason by St. Thomas: "(1) to prepare for faith, (2) to explain the truths of faith, (3) to defend the truths of faith" (pp. 82 ff.). A more critical approach will be found in Philip H. Wicksteed, *The Reactions between Dogma and Philosophy Illustrated from the Works of S. Thomas Aquinas* (Hibbert Lectures, Second Series, London, 1920).

Chapter 9

Dante

▶ Bryce, James, *The Holy Roman Empire,* 7th ed. (New York, 1877). Chap. XV (pp. 239–269) provides a discussion of Dante against the political and intellectual currents of his age.

▶ Burnham, James, *The Machiavellians: Defenders of Freedom* (New York, 1943). Part I is called "Dante: Politics as Wish" (pp. 3–26). Burnham considers *De monarchia* as the prototype of nine tenths of all writing on politics, whose general method consists in concealing the "real meaning" of the argument behind its "formal meaning," the latter being expressed "in terms of the fictional world of religion, metaphysics, miracles, and pseudo-history" (p. 9). Applying this distinction of formal and real meaning to *De monarchia,* Burnham writes: "We think we are debating universal peace, salvation, a unified world government, and the relations between Church and State, when what is really at issue is whether the Florentine Republic is to be run by its own citizens or submitted to the exploitation of a reactionary foreign monarch" (p. 24). Burnham also argues that Dante was a traitor to his country because he supported the imperial cause against Florence, and that "his sociological allegiance was reactionary" (p. 22) because he did not support the cause of the cities, at that time the most progressive elements in politics and culture, but sided with the great nobles and the imperial party, the Ghibellines, who "wanted to stop history short" (*ibid.*). *De monarchia* is, according to Burnham, no more than a "Ghibelline Party Platform," and its "vicious and reactionary" objectives are the "aims of an embittered and incompetent set of traitors" (p. 20). Burnham's severe critique of Dante is provocative, but debunking, too, can go too far.

▶ Church, R. W., *Dante and Other Essays* (London, 1888). The first essay is on Dante (pp. 1–191).

▶ Dante Sexcentenary Lectures, *Rice Institute Pamphlet,* VIII (April, 1921). The most interesting paper is "Dante and the Renaissance," by Albert L. Guérard (pp. 194–215). See also Robert G. Caldwell, "The Political Writings of Dante" (pp. 170–193).

▶ D'entrèves, A. P., *Dante as a Political Thinker* (Oxford, 1952). Interpreting Dante's political thought on the basis of the *Divine Comedy* as well as *De monarchia,* the author finds that there are important discrepancies between the two; specifically, *De monarchia* seems to be "characterized by a temporary forgetfulness, on Dante's side, of the fundamental Christian idea, that from within and not from without, must mankind be redeemed and saved" (p. 51). This viewpoint, the author argues, is recanted by Dante in the *Divine Comedy.* Extensive bibliographical notes (pp. 98–113) enhance the value of this provocative study by a leading authority in the field of Italian thought and letters.

▶ Ercole, Francesco, *Il pensiero politico di Dante,* 2 vols. (Milan, 1927–1928). This collection of penetrating essays on Dante's political ideas, based on *De monarchia* as well as on his other works, has had considerable influence in Italy and other countries. Ercole is particularly illuminating on the genesis of Dante's political philosophy, its Christian-patristic and Aristotelian-Thomistic elements, its relations to the Middle Ages and Renaissance, and its impact on Italian national sentiment. Ercole attributes to Dante a strong nationalism, even in a political and juridical sense, Vol. I, Chaps. I–IV (pp. 11–156). According to Ercole,

Dante was also an Italian imperialist because he believed that the Italians of his day were the direct successors of the Romans, and that therefore the Roman empire would still have to be ruled from Italy. The latter would not only be the seat of empire, but Italians would actually exercise imperial authority over the world: "This means that Dante's solution of the Italian problem resolves itself in a true and proper *primacy of the Italian nation over the world*" (I, 84; see also I, 39–48, and II, 220 ff., 303 ff.).

For nationalist interpretations of Dante and his relation to Italian Fascism, see Michele Barbi, "Nuovi problemi della critica dantesca: L'Italia nell'ideale politico di Dante," *Studi Danteschi*, XXIV (Florence, 1939), 5–37, and Emilio Bodero, "Dante, L'impero e noi," *Nuova Antologia*, CCCLV (May 16, 1931), 188–202. The latter writes that "only today can we understand Dante the Italian and imperialist, because such is the Fascism of Benito Mussolini, Italian and imperialist; only today can we truly recognize in Dante the prophet of our destiny" (p. 198). See also Arrigo Solmi, "La 'Monarchia' di Dante," *Nuova Antologia*, CCCLXXVIII (April 1, 1935), 321–331. For a French view on Dante and Fascism, see Maurice Vallis, "Dante et le fascisme," *Mercure de France*, CCLX (May 15, 1935), 197–202, and "Dante et l'apologie de l'Empire," *ibid.*, CCLXXXVII (November 1, 1938), 586–591. See also Richard Wichterich, "Dante—Machiavelli—Mazzini: Drei Wegbereiter der italienischen Nation," *Deutsches Dante-Jahrbuch*, XX (Weimar, 1938), 182–193. A more cautious interpretation of Dante's views on nationalism and imperialism, and their applicability to Italian problems, will be found in Alessandro Passerin d'Entrèves, *La filosofia politica medioevale* (Turin, 1934), pp. 171–185.

▶ FEDERN, KARL, *Dante and His Time* (New York, 1902). The first part, "The Time," is a detailed narrative of the main political, international, cultural, intellectual, educational, literary, and commercial forces of Dante's age (pp. 3–175). The second part deals with Dante's life and work (pp. 197–297).

▶ GARDNER, EDMUND G., *Dante* (London–Toronto–New York, 1923). Includes a brief exposition of *De monarchia* (pp. 86–95). See also the author's *Dante* (The British Academy, Sixth Annual Lecture on a Master-Mind, London, 1921) for a Liberal interpretation of Dante's political views, linking him with Mazzini (p. 17).

▶ GILSON, ÉTIENNE, *Dante the Philosopher* (New York, 1949). Written from a neo-Thomist viewpoint, this is one of the most brilliant studies of Dante and essential to an understanding of his political philosophy, treated in Part III (pp. 162–224). Gilson is satisfied that Dante was completely loyal to his faith, religion, and church. Yet on the basic issues of the relation of ecclesiastical and temporal powers, and of philosophy and theology, "this alleged Thomist struck a mortal blow at the doctrine of St. Thomas Aquinas" (p. 212).

▶ HASSELL, ULRICH VON, "Die Bedeutung des politischen Gedankens Dantes für die Gegenwart," *Deutsches Dante-Jahrbuch*, XVI (Weimar, 1934), 103–112. The author, German Ambassador in Rome at the time of delivering his address early in 1934, calls Italian Fascism and German Nazism "legitimate children of Dante's political thought" (p. 109), and refers to Dante as a forerunner of Hitler and Mussolini, men "who realize unity and peace in the sense of the great Florentine" (p. 112). See also F. Freiherr von Falkenhausen, "Dante's Staatsidee," *ibid.*, XIX (Weimar, 1937), 47–60, for a similar interpretation.

▶ HENRY, AURELIA, *The De Monarchia of Dante Alighieri* (Boston–New York, 1904). This translation of *De monarchia* contains a long introduction (pp. xvii–li) and numerous notes and cross references of considerable value and usefulness. A translation of *De monarchia* (by Philip H. Wicksteed) will also be found in *The Latin Works of Dante: Translated into English* (Temple Classics, London, 1904), pp. 127–280, accompanied by interpretative comments and explanations. The volume includes Dante's *Letters* (*Epistolae*, pp. 295–368) in an annotated translation; they are one of the principal sources of Dante's political ideas. A convenient edition of the Latin text is Dante, *De monarchia* (the Oxford Text edited by E. Moore, with an introduction on the political theory of Dante, by W. H. V. Reade, Oxford, 1916).

► KELSEN, HANS, *Die Staatslehre des Dante Alighieri* (Vienna–Leipzig, 1905). The first two chapters (pp. 3–38) review the political conditions of the thirteenth century and their reflection in the main political writings of papalists and imperialists. Chaps. III–IX (pp. 38–136) analyze Dante's political ideas, culled from *De monarchia* as well as from *The Divine Comedy*, *The Banquet* (*Il convivio*), and *On Vernacular Language* (*De vulgari eloquentia*). Chap X (pp. 136–148) analyzes the sources of Dante's political thought, particularly in relation to Plato, Aristotle, Cicero, the Scriptures, St. Augustine, St. Thomas Aquinas, and less well-known contemporary publicists. See also Franz Xaver Kraus, *Dante: sein Leben und sein Werk, sein Verhältnis zur Kunst und zur Politik* (Berlin, 1897), and Walter Goetz, *Dante: Gesammelte Aufsätze* (Munich, 1958).

► LENKEITH, NANCY, *Dante and the Legend of Rome* (London, 1952). Dante's humanism, the glorification of the classical culture and heritage, had a decidedly political character: "It was a yearning for a new life which was to be a restoration of the ancient Roman way of being, of an entire civilization which would put to shame the barbarians across the Alps" (p. vii). While Dante was not the first Italian to revive the worship of ancient Rome, "he took the old 'patriotism' of the Italians, their half-poetical half-mythological love of their Roman origins, and attempted to give it a philosophical foundation" (p. 176). For a more detailed analysis of Dante's humanism, see also Augustin Renaudet, *Dante humaniste* (Paris, 1952).

► OZANAM, FRÉDÉRIC, *Dante and Catholic Philosophy in the Thirteenth Century* (New York, 1897). The author, a French scholar, finds that Dante's religious orthodoxy is well established; he calls him the "St. Thomas of poetry" in the Middle Ages (p. 357). An equally sympathetic interpretation will be found in Auguste Valensin, *Le christianisme de Dante* (Paris, 1954). The author, a French Jesuit theologian, warmly defends Dante's religious faith. In this, he follows the official view of the Roman Catholic Church of the last hundred years, as expressed by Pope Benedict XIV in 1914: "Alighierius noster est" ("Dante belongs to us"). Earlier, the Catholic attitude toward Dante was hostile. *De monarchia* was put on the *Index of Forbidden Books* in 1564, and removed from the *Index* only three hundred years later.

A divergent view on Dante's religious thought is expressed by John Jay Chapman, *Dante* (Boston, 1927): "To speak of Dante as a Protestant would be so historically inexact as to be offensive. But Dante represents the spirit that was at the bottom of Protestantism, the impulse of a man to decide the religious question for himself, and to accept as much or as little as he sees fit" (p. 84).

On Dante's relation to the papacy, Chapman writes that neither Luther, Calvin, nor John Knox ever "conceived of such supernal opposition to the Papacy as was Dante's bread and meat for many years. All that those northern reformers wanted was to be let alone. But Dante invades and browbeats the Roman Pontiff. He taught the Italians to hate the Vatican, and his influence it was which, more than any other one thing, led to the triumph of the Risorgimento and the unification of Italy in the last century" (p. 85).

By contrast, Luigi Sturzo, a learned priest and scholar, writes as follows: "For man and Christian the *Divine Comedy* remains the book of art nearest to our spirit and faith" (*Church and State*, New York, 1939, p. 124). See also Francesco Scaduto, *Stato e Chiesa* (Florence, 1882, pp. 51–64) and Michele Barbi, "Nuovi problemi della critica dantesca: Impero e Chiesa," *Studi*

Danteschi, XVI (Florence, 1942), 9–46.

► PAGE, THOMAS NELSON, *Dante and His Influence* (New York, 1922). Dante's political views are mainly discussed in Chap. III (pp. 89–116).

► PAPINI, GIOVANNI, *Dante Vivo* (English trans., New York, 1935). Dante's separation of the political from the religious power "was a first step in progressive anticlericalism: the State ought to be independent of the Church; the State has a right to supervise and direct the Church; the State transfers to itself the greater part of the offices of the Church: the State ignores the Church; the State ought to suppress the Church" (pp. 243–244). It is doubtful whether this kind of logic either proves or disproves Dante's basic position on the issue.

► PIRENNE, HENRI, *Economic and Social History of Medieval Europe* (London, 1936). Describes concisely and accurately the revival and growth of urban life, commerce, and trade in the Middle Ages, and provides the elementary social and economic data for an understanding of Dante's time. One of the best short books in the field.

► ROLBIECKI, JOHN JOSEPH, *The Political Philosophy of Dante Alighieri* (Washington, 1921). Stresses Dante's historical role as an advocate of international institutions for the regulation of the common interests of all mankind. The exposition of Dante's political ideas (pp. 15–150) is followed by a bibliography (pp. 151–156). See also Barbara Barclay Carter, "Dante's Political Conception," *Hibbert Journal*, XXXV (July, 1937), 568–579, and "Dante's Political Ideas," *Review of Politics*, V (July, 1943), 339–355.

► SALVEMINI, GAETANO, "Florence in the Time of Dante," *Speculum*, XI (July, 1936), 317–326. The author, an authority in the field of Italian history, describes Dante as a "chivalrous spirit in a mercantile environment" (p. 323), wholly out of sympathy with its habits and ideals: "He was a broken man and had the bitter pessimism of the broken man. This must have been the state of mind of all those men and women of Dante's generation who, like him, came from the nobility and were unable to adapt themselves to the changed times. With this difference that they did not possess the soul of a Dante" (p. 325). Looking backward, Dante thought he had found the Golden Age of mankind in ancient Rome, "just as William Morris and Ruskin placed the Golden Age in the times of Dante" (p. 326). See also Alfred Doren, "Florenz zur Zeit Dantes," *Deutsches Dante-Jahrbuch*, XVI (New Series, Vol. VII, Weimar, 1934), 87–102, for an account of the social and economic background of Florence in Dante's time. The author writes that Dante's name "suggests originally German descent" (p. 100), and he views sympathetically Dante's opposition to the rising bourgeois civilization and his advocacy of the imperial cause.

► SAYERS, DOROTHY L., *Introductory Papers on Dante* (London, 1954). Attempts to bring Dante to life for the modern reader, on the assumption that he was intended to be read by the common man and woman. The author doubts that *De monarchia* was Dante's "last word on the subject" (p. 211). Specifically, she claims that the two main theses of *De monarchia*—the complete emancipation of philosophy from faith and the establishment of a secular monarchy—were errors, and rectified by Dante himself in the *Divine Comedy*. While the author is primarily interested in Dante as an artist and poet, she has much to say that is relevant to a deeper understanding of Dante's general outlook and philosophy. See also her *Further Papers on Dante* (New York, 1957).

► SCARTAZZINI, G. A., *A Companion to Dante* (London–New York, 1893). A commentary on *De monarchia* is included (pp. 318–340).

► TOYNBEE, PAGET, *Dante Alighieri: His Life and Works*, 4th ed. (New York, 1910). The emphasis is on the political background of Dante's time, particularly in Florence, and on his life and personal characteristics. Dante's Latin works, including *De monarchia,* are briefly analyzed in the last chapter (pp. 231–261). See also C. H. Grand-gent, *Dante* (New York, 1916); Lonsdale Ragg, *Dante and His Italy* (New York, 1907); Paolo Milano (ed.), *The Portable Dante* (The Viking Portable Library, New York, 1948); and Karl Vossler, *Medieval Culture: An Introduction to Dante and His Times,* 2 vols. (New York, 1929).

► WICKSTEED, PHILIP H., *Dante and Aquinas* (London–New York, 1913). In this searching analysis of one of the crucial aspects of Dante's philosophy, the author concludes that "while Dante habitually moved within the circle of scholastic ideas, he did not allow it to confine him when his own thought or his poetic vision broke away from its limitations. In this respect his attitude towards it differed from his attitude towards Christian dogma, which he accepted without question, however grievous a strain it put upon his conscience or his affections" (p. 147). The book also includes illuminating analyses of the relations of medieval thought and Greek philosophy

(pp. 1–26), Neoplatonism (pp. 27–43), and the migration of Aristotle and the trans-formations of Aristotelianism (pp. 44–85). Dante's relation to Virgil, his favorite poet, just as Aristotle was his favorite philoso-pher, is the main subject of J. H. Whitfield, *Dante and Virgil* (Oxford, 1949).

► ZINGARELLI, NICOLA, *La vita, i tempi e le opere di Dante,* 3rd ed., 2 vols. (Milan, 1931). A monumental work, and basic as a source of reference. The *Monarchia* (the author stresses that the correct title is *Monarchia,* and not *De monarchia,* as is the common usage) is examined in Vol. II, Chap. XXV (pp. 679–712). In Dante's con-ception of world monarchy Zingarelli sees "the divine counsel of destining Italy at the head of the world in the temporal rule and government as well as in spiritual guidance" (II, 706). See also Sebastiano Vento, *La filosofia politica di Dante nel "De Monar-chia"* (Turin, 1921), and Gaetano Mar-covaldi, *Aspetti dello spirito di Dante* (Rome, 1955).

Chapter 10

Marsilio of Padua

► ALLEN, J. W., "Marsilio of Padua and Medieval Secularism," in *The Social and Political Ideas of Some Great Medieval Thinkers* (ed. F. J. C. Hearnshaw, London, 1923), pp. 167–191. The author is not sure whether Marsilio "was a Christian in any sense at all, in spite of the display of scriptural texts in the *Defensor.* We all know that the devil himself can quote Scrip-ture" (p. 171). As to the meaning of Mar-silio's concept of the "weightier part" of the citizenry, Allen suggests that normally it would mean the "numerical majority" (p. 182).

► BATTAGLIA, FELICE, *Marsilio da Padova e la filosofia politica del medio evo* (Flor-ence, 1928). In this illuminating and schol-

arly study, one of the best in any language, the author stresses Marsilio's creative con-tribution to the formation of "the new science of society" (p. 261). One of the most rewarding sections of the book deals with the question of Marsilio's doctrine of the "weightier part" (pp. 81–91). Like most Italian writers on Marsilio, Battaglia treats extensively the political ideas and practices of the Italian city-states. A detailed bibli-ography is appended (pp. 263–270). See also the following: Baldassare Labanca, *Marsilio da Padova* (Padua, 1882); An-tonio Cappa-Legora, *La politica di Dante e di Marsilio da Padova* (Rome, 1906); Pasquale Villari, "Marsilio da Padova e il *Defensor Pacis," Nuova Antologia,* CLXIV

(April 1, 1913), 369–379; and Edoardo Ruffini Avondo, "Il *Defensor Pacis* di Marsilio da Padova," *Rivista Storica Italiana,* II (New Series, No. 4, 1924), 113–166. Avondo hails the *Defender of Peace,* together with Dante's *Monarchia* and Machiavelli's *Prince,* as the "highest expression of Italian political science" (p. 113).

► BOASE, T. S. R., *Boniface VIII* (London, 1933). Includes, in the last chapter, a brief account of Boniface's successors, Benedict XI and Clement V.

► BOUTARIC, EDGAR, *La France sous Philippe le Bel* (Paris, 1861). In his discussion of the struggle between France and the papacy in the reign of Philip IV (pp. 88–146), the author tries to be scrupulously fair.

► BRAMPTON, C. KENNETH, "Marsiglio of Padua," *English Historical Review,* XXVII (October, 1922), 501–515. Deals exclusively with Marsilio's life and career.

► CHECCHINI, ALDO, and NORBERTO BOBBIO (eds.), *Marsilio da Padova: studi raccolti nel VI centenario della morte* (Padua, 1942). This symposium emphasizes the Italian background of Marsilio and his groping toward the doctrine of the national state.

► COULTON, G. G., *Studies in Medieval Thought* (London, 1940). Chap. XIV is called "The Lay Revolt" (pp. 181–193). See also his Medieval Panorama (Cambridge, 1938), Chaps. XXXVI, "The Papal Schism" (pp. 477–484), and LII, "The Bursting of the Dykes" (pp. 720–731).

► D'ENTRÈVES, ALEXANDER PASSERIN, *The Medieval Contribution to Political Thought* (London, 1939). Chaps. III and IV are on Marsilio (pp. 44–87). Interprets Marsilio's political theory as a medieval revival of Aristotle's conception of the state. See also the author's *La filosofia politica medioevale* (Turin, 1934), pp. 186–232, and "Rileggendo il *Defensor Pacis,*" *Rivista Storica Italiana,* V (Series IV, Nos. 1–2, 1934), 1–37.

► EMERTON, EPHRAIM, *The Defensor Pacis of Marsiglio of Padua* (Harvard Theological Studies, VIII, Cambridge, Mass., 1920).

At the outset the author writes as follows: "Marsiglio is the herald of a new world, the prophet of a new social order, acutely conscious of his modernness and not afraid to confess it. His book has often been called the most remarkable literary product of the Middle Ages, and I am inclined to accept this verdict" (p. 1). This balanced study is excellent in both exposition and criticism.

► FIGGIS, JOHN NEVILLE, *The Divine Right of Kings* (Cambridge, 1934). Chap. III, "The Holy Roman Empire and the Papacy" (pp. 38–65), gives both the history and theory of the conflict, including brief accounts of Pope Boniface VIII, King Philip IV, and Marsilio of Padua.

► GEWIRTH, ALAN, "John of Jandun and the *Defensor Pacis,*" *Speculum,* XXIII (April, 1948), 267–272. On the basis of a careful comparison of Marsilio's works with those of John of Jandun, the author concludes that "no substantial part of the *Defensor Pacis* was written by John of Jandun. From the external evidence of his close association in friendship and in political activities with Marsilius, it is highly probable that John contributed advice and assistance. But the actual composition and doctrine of the entire treatise are the product of one man, Marsilius of Padua" (p. 272). See also Gewirth's *Marsilius of Padua and Medieval Political Philosophy* (New York, 1951).

► GIERKE, OTTO, *Political Theories of the Middle Age* (trans., with an introduction, by Frederick William Maitland, Cambridge, 1938). Chaps. VI, "The Idea of Popular Sovereignty" (pp. 37–61), and X, "The Beginnings of the Modern State" (pp. 87–100), are particularly pertinent. Maitland's introduction (pp. xii–xlv) is a classic within a classic.

► HENDERSON, ERNEST F. (ed.), *Select Historical Documents of the Middle Ages* (London, 1903). Pope Boniface VIII's two bulls, *Clericis Laicos* (1296) and *Unam Sanctam* (1302), are reprinted (pp. 432–437).

► HOLMES, OLIVER WENDELL, "The Path

of the Law," *Harvard Law Review,* X (No. 8, 1897), 457–478. The definition of the law is given as "the prophecies of what the courts will do in fact, and nothing more pretentious" (pp. 460–461). For Hans Kelsen's view of coercion as an essential element in law, see his *General Theory of Law and State* (Cambridge, Mass., 1945), pp. 18 ff., 122 ff., 391 ff.

► LAGARDE, GEORGES DE, *La naissance de l'esprit laïque au déclin du moyen âge. Vol. II: Marsile de Padoue ou le premier théoricien de l'État laïque* (Saint-Paul-Trois-Châteaux, 1934). Marsilio is seen as the first theoretician of the lay state. The French influences on Marsilio receive special attention. Scholarly and eminently readable. See also Charles Benoist, "L'État italien et la science politique avant Machiavel," *Revue des Deux Mondes,* XXXIX (May 1, 1907), 164–188.

► MCILWAIN, CHARLES HOWARD, *The Growth of Political Thought in the West* (New York, 1932). In his analysis of Marsilio's political ideas (pp. 295–315) the author rejects the accepted democratic interpretation of the doctrine of the "weightier part" of the citizens, and holds that it is "in much closer correspondence with the anti-democratic ideas of Aristotle than with the political conceptions of our modern time" (p. 304). McIlwain calls *The Defender of Peace* "one of the real landmarks" in the development of political thought (p. 313), because it is the first book that "denies to the clergy coercive authority of any kind whatsoever, spiritual or temporal, direct or indirect" (*ibid.*).

► MARSILIO OF PADUA, *The Defender of the Peace* (trans. out of Latin into English by William Marshall, London, 1535). Until the publication of Alan Gewirth's translation in 1956, the Marshall translation was the only one. Published in 1535, at the height of Henry VIII's reign, it is noteworthy for the omission of passages in *The Defender of Peace* that treat of the correction of rulers who abuse their powers. For a study of the influence of Marsilio on

Thomas Starkey, chaplain to Henry VIII, and author of an important political work, the *Dialogue between Cardinal Pole and Thomas Lupset,* see Franklin Le Van Baumer, "Thomas Starkey and Marsilius of Padua," *Politica,* II (November, 1936), 188–205.

► POWICKE, F. M., *The Christian Life in the Middle Ages* (Oxford, 1935). Chap. III is on "Pope Boniface VIII" (pp. 48–73). See also the author's *Ways of Medieval Life and Thought* (London, 1950), Chap. VII: "Reflections on the Medieval State" (pp. 130–148).

► PREVITÉ-ORTON, C. W., *Marsilius of Padua* (Annual Italian Lecture of the British Academy, London, 1935). The best short introduction, in English, to Marsilio's main ideas. The author stresses the impact of republican Padua on Marsilio, and emphasizes the democratic aspects of his political theory. See also Previté-Orton's introduction to his edition of the Latin text of *The Defensor Pacis of Marsilio of Padua* (Cambridge, 1928), pp. ix–xliii; "Marsiglio of Padua," *English Historical Review,* XXXVIII (January, 1923), 1–18; and "The Authors Cited in the *Defensor Pacis,*" in *Essays in History Presented to Reginald Lane Poole* (ed. by H. W. C. Davis, Oxford, 1927), pp. 405–420.

► RIEZLER, SIGMUND, *Die literarischen Widersacher der Päpste zur Zeit Ludwig des Baiers* (Leipzig, 1874). Includes Marsilio of Padua (pp. 30–41, 193–240). The author concludes that Marsilio is the forerunner of a movement that attained its greatest successes in the sixteenth century, "but which has not come to its full completion even in our own days" (p. 298). See also Leopold Stieglitz, *Die Staatstheorie des Marsilius von Padua* (Leipzig–Berlin, 1914); F. von Bezold, "Die Lehre der Volkssouveränität während des Mittelalters," *Historische Zeitschrift,* XXXVI (1876), 313–367; M. Guggenheim, "Marsilius von Padua und die Staatslehre des Aristoteles," *Historische Vierteljahrschrift,* VII, No. 3 (1904), 341–362; Emil Friedberg, "Die mittelalterlichen Lehren über das Verhältnis von Staat und Kirche," *Zeitschrift für Kirchenrecht*, VIII, No. 1 (1869), 69–138 (the analysis of Marsilio is on pp. 110–138); and Heinrich Otto, "Marsilius von Padua und der *Defensor Pacis*," *Historisches Jahrbuch*, XLV (1925), 189–218. Written in defense of the papal position, Otto's essay concludes that Marsilio, significant as his impact was, did not succeed in his ultimate and most important objective, the complete dethroning and lasting paralysis of the papacy (p. 218).

▶ SCHOLZ, RICHARD (ed.), *Marsilius von Padua: Defensor Pacis* (Hanover, 1933). The editor's introduction to the Latin text

of Marsilio's work is primarily devoted to its authorship, sources, and history (pp. v–lxx). See also the following writings by Scholz, one of the leading German authorities on Marsilio: *Die Publizistik zur Zeit Philipps des Schönen und Bonifaz' VIII.* (Stuttgart, 1903), pp. 452–458; "Marsilius von Padua und die Idee der Demokratie," *Zeitschrift für Politik*, I, No. 1 (1908), 61–94; "Marslius von Padua und die Genesis des modernen Staatsbewusstseins" *Historische Zeitschrift*, CLVI, No. 1 (1937), 88–103; and "Marsilius von Padua und Deutschland," in Aldo Checchini and Norberto Bobbio (eds.), *Marsilio da Padova: studi raccolti nel VI centenario della morte* (Padua, 1942), pp. 3–35.

Chapter II

Machiavelli

▶ ACTON, LORD, *The History of Freedom and Other Essays* (London, 1907). Chap. VII (pp. 212–231), on Machiavelli, includes many comments on *The Prince* by famous writers and statesmen. Lord Acton concludes his observations as follows: "Machiavelli is the earliest conscious and articulate exponent of certain living forces in the present world. Religion, progressive enlightenment, the perpetual vigilance of public opinion, have not reduced his empire, or disproved the justice of his conception of mankind. He obtains a new lease of life from causes that are still prevailing, and from doctrines that are apparent in politics, philosophy, and science. Without sparing censure, or employing for comparison the grosser symptoms of the age, we find him near our common level, and perceive that he is not a vanishing type, but a constant and contemporary influence" (p. 231).

▶ ALLEN, J. W., *Political Thought in the Sixteenth Century* (London, 1928). The

second chapter in Part IV (pp. 447–494) is on Machiavelli, whose influence is thus summarized: "Machiavelli's writings form a part of those Renaissance influences which, all through the sixteenth century, made for freedom in thought and the practical toleration of adverse opinion. It is at least in some small degree due to him that political thought assumed, more and more, a practical, common-sense and opportunist character, and turned away from questions it could not answer" (p. 493).

▶ BENOIST, CHARLES, *Le Machiavélisme*, 3 vols. (Paris, 1907–1936). Vol. I is on Machiavellianism before Machiavelli, Vol. II on Machiavelli, and Vol. III on Machiavellianism after Machiavelli. See also the author's "L'influence des idées de Machiavel," in *Recueil des Cours* (Académie de Driot International), IV (1925), 131–306; L. Gautier Vignal, *Machiavel* (Paris, 1929); Augustin Renaudet, *Machiavel: Étude d'histoire des doctrines politiques* (Paris,

1942); Albert Cherel, *La pensée de Machiavel en France* (Paris, 1935); and Charles L. Mayer (Reyam), *Les principes de Machiavel et la politique de la France* (New York, 1943).

▶ BINNS, L. ELLIOTT, *The Decline and Fall of the Medieval Papacy* (London, 1934). Chaps. IX and X (pp. 254–310) are on the Renaissance period.

▶ BURD, L. A., "Florence (II): Machiavelli," in *Cambridge Modern History*, (Cambridge, 1902), Vol. I, Chap. VI (pp. 190–218). See also Chaps. XVI and XVII on the Renaissance (pp. 532–619), and George Clarke Sellery, *The Renaissance: Its Nature and Origins* (Madison, Wis., 1950).

▶ BURNHAM, JAMES, *The Machiavellians* (New York, 1943). Part II (pp. 29–77) is on "Machiavelli: The Science of Power." Burnham says that "Machiavelli divorced politics from ethics only in the same sense that every science must divorce itself from ethics. Scientific descriptions and theories must be based upon the facts, the evidence, not upon the supposed demands of some ethical system" (p. 38). Concerning the attitude to Machiavelli, Burnham observes that "the harsh opinion of Machiavelli has been more widespread in England and the United States than in the nations of Continental Europe. This is no doubt natural, because the distinguishing quality of Anglo-Saxon politics has always been hypocrisy, and hypocrisy must always be at pains to shy away from the truth" (p. 77). Burnham sees in the Machiavellian tradition the true foundation of politics and the science of politics. In addition to Machiavelli, he deals with Mosca, Sorel, Michels, and Pareto. Burnham concludes that democracy as "self-government" or "government by the people" is impossible, and that the theory of democracy as self-government "must be understood as a myth, formula, or derivation" (p. 236).

▶ BUTTERFIELD, HERBERT, *The Statecraft of Machiavelli* (London, 1940). The author sees Machiavelli's main original contribution in his use of history as a method of political analysis, although in practice he is not always scientific in his method, and "when he observes he sees what the ancients have taught him to see, when he examines the facts he may know beforehand the conclusion that he is going to draw from them" (p. 78). The last chapter is an interesting discussion of "Machiavelli and Bolingbroke" (pp. 135–164).

▶ CASSIRER, ERNST, *The Myth of the State* (New Haven, 1946). Chaps. X–XII (pp. 116–162) place Machiavelli in the philosophical and scientific background of his time and interpret his political thought in a fresh and penetrating manner. See also Cassirer's "Some Remarks on the Originality of the Renaissance," *Journal of the History of Ideas*, IV (January, 1943), 49–56. The entire issue is devoted to a symposium on the Renaissance.

▶ CHABOD, FEDERICO, *Machiavelli and the Renaissance* (trans. into English, Cambridge, Mass., 1958). Like most Italian students of Machiavelli, the author emphasizes the context of Italian history and civilization which provide the clue for a proper understanding of Machiavelli's thought. In the same tradition of Italian scholarship, Chabod concentrates on *The Prince* as the core of Machiavelli's ideas, and assigns to *The Discourses* a much less important role than is customary among non-Italian scholars. The author arrives at this relative evaluation of the two works, not only on grounds of intrinsic merit and analysis, but also of chronology: contrary to the commonly held view, according to which *The Discourses* was written much later than *The Prince*, Chabod argues that "it may be regarded as certain that at the time when Machiavelli started work on *The Prince* the first book of *The Discourses* was already largely complete" (p. 31). An extensive bibliography (pp. 201–247) examines the literature on the concept and meaning of the Renaissance.

▶ CHEVALLIER, JEAN-JACQUES, *Les grandes oeuvres politiques de Machiavel à nos jours* (Paris, 1949). Chap. I of Part I (pp. 7–37) is on *The Prince*.

► CROCE, BENEDETTO, *Politics and Morals* (New York, 1945). Defends Machiavelli in the light of Italian politics and traditions: "The art and science of politics, of pure politics, brought to maturity by the Italians, were to him a source of pride" (p. 63). The last chapter is "Historical Pessimism" (pp. 200–204).

► DOWDALL, H. C., "The Word 'State'," *Law Quarterly Review*, XXXIX (January, 1923), 98–125. Examining the origins of the word "state," the author finds that Machiavelli coined the term in the modern sense: "A word was wanted for the kingdom of a king, the duchy of a duke, the county of an *unmittelbar* count, the *dominium* of an independent lord, and the government of a free city—in fact, for every form of government that exercises *imperio sopra gli uomimi*. Machiavelli, by the same stroke, decisively selected, and defined, and proclaimed, the appropriate word; and by explicitly recognizing and naming a general concept suitable for scientific purposes, he rendered possible, and indeed himself founded, the modern science of the State" (pp. 114–115).

► ERCOLE, FRANCESCO, *La politica di Machiavelli* (Rome, 1926). Stresses the element of Italian nationalism in Machiavelli. See also Oreste Ferrara, *Machiavelli* (Milan, 1930); Pietro Lanino, *Niccolò Machiavelli* (Rome, 1921); and Giuseppe Ferrari, *Corso su gli scrittori politici italiani* (Milan, 1929), Chaps. IX–XI (pp. 135–196). For Antimachiavellianism, see Andrea Sorrentino, *Storia dell'antimachiavellismo europeo* (Naples, 1936), and Antonio Panella, *Gli Antimachiavellici* (Florence, 1943).

► FERRERO, GUGLIELMO, "Machiavelli and Machiavellism," *Foreign Affairs*, XVII (April, 1939), 569–577. Asserts that in *The Discourses* there is not a trace of Machiavellianism, and that even *The Prince* contains only a few such passages, "not connected with each other nor with the rest of the argument, which could be either suppressed entirely without mutilating the work or rendered quite inoffensive by disguising their thought in less frank terminology.

Anyone acquainted with the life and character of Machiavelli knows that these fragments of his thought, on which a whole theory of conduct has been erected, are nothing but bad-tempered explosions" (p. 571).

► FIGGIS, JOHN NEVILLE, *Studies of Political Thought from Gerson to Grotius, 1414–1625*, 2nd ed. (Cambridge, 1931). In his appraisal of Machiavelli (pp. 72–93), Figgis stresses the absence of the concept of natural law in Machiavelli and draws suggestive comparisons between Machiavelli and Nietzsche.

► GILBERT, ALLAN H., *Machiavelli's Prince and Its Forerunners* (Durham, N. C., 1938). Advances the thesis—not too convincingly —that *The Prince* is essentially a typical representative of a thousand books written during several centuries preceding Machiavelli, and that "few of the ideas expressed in *The Prince* are altogether novel; most of them are to be found in medieval and renaissance works belonging to the type of books of advice to kings. Possibly a complete reading of the treatises belonging to this class would leave Machiavelli with nothing wholly new" (p. 234). A detailed bibliography is appended (238–247). See also Felix Gilbert, "The Humanist Concept of the Prince and *The Prince* of Machiavelli," *Journal of Modern History*, XI (December, 1939), 449–483, and "Political Thought of the Renaissance and Reformation: A Report on Recent Scholarship," *Huntington Library Quarterly*, IV (July, 1941), 443–468. The latter is a bibliographical article.

► HANCOCK, W. K., "Machiavelli in Modern Dress: An Inquiry into Historical Method," *History*, XX (September, 1935), 97–115. The author sums up his position as follows: "Taught by Machiavelli, we shall try to avoid deluding ourselves about the actualities of historical periods and situations. We shall be alive to the importance of technical capacity in the conduct of policy. We shall not deny that the power and interest of the State is a proper object of statesmanship: we shall on the contrary develop our conception of State-interest in harmony with the developing complexities of community life. So far we keep company with Marchiavelli. But we part company with him when he pushes his theory of interest to the point of denying the existence of a society of states, bound together by obligations of law and morality. At this point we become, without equivocation, Antimachiavellian" (p. 114).

► HEARNSHAW, F. J. C. (ed.), *The Social and Political Ideas of Some Great Thinkers of the Renaissance and the Reformation* (London, 1925). Chap. IV, by the editor, is on Machiavelli (pp. 87–121). The author reaches this conclusion: "I hold that both the conscience of mankind and the verdict of history have declared themselves decisively against Machiavellism. The one says that it is theoretically indefensible, the other that it is practically unsound" (p. 118). Numerous illustrations from history are cited to show that the application of Machiavellian principles does not pay—quite apart from the question of their ethical character.

► KÖNIG, RENÈ, *Niccolò Machiavelli* (Erlenbach–Zurich, 1941). A scholarly and comprehensive examination of Machiavelli's ideas, particularly in relation to the background of the Renaissance, a period of crisis and transition. Includes a bibliography (pp. 348–352).

► LASKI, HAROLD J., *The Dangers of Obedience and Other Essays* (New York, 1930). Chap. IX, "Machiavelli and the Present Time" (pp. 238–263), is a critical study of Machiavelli in the light of political philosophy and historical experience. Machiavelli's doctrine is called a "gospel of death" (p. 262).

► LEWIS, WYNDHAM, *The Lion and the Fox* (New York–London, n.d.). A suggestive study of the impact of Machiavelli on English literature, with particular reference to Shakespeare.

► LODGE, RICHARD, "Machiavelli's *Il Principe*," *Transactions of the Royal Historical Society*, XIII (Fourth Series, 1930), 1–16. This presidential address before the Royal

Historical Society is based on the hypothesis, earlier suggested by Ranke, that "the commentators have misrepresented Machiavelli by taking as general maxims for all princes and all time what he wrote as advice to a particular prince in peculiar and special circumstances and for his guidance to a definite objective" (p. 3).

► MEINECKE, FRIEDRICH, *Machiavellism: The Doctrine of Raison d'État and Its Place in Modern History* (New Haven, 1957). The classic study of the concept and evolution of the reason of state by the foremost German historian of the twentieth century. The introduction (pp. 1–22) analyzes the essence of the reason of state, and Chap. I (pp. 25–48) is on Machiavelli. See also Gerhard Ritter, *The Corrupting Influence of Power* (Hadleigh, Essex, 1952); Chap. II is on Machiavelli as the "Path-Finder of Continental Power Politics" (pp. 17–45). The principal theme of Ritter's book is the contrast between Machiavelli and Thomas More, the "Ideologist of the Island Welfare State" (pp. 46–89), and the historical consequences of this contrast in modern European history (pp. 90–197).

► MEISEL, JAMES H., *The Myth of the Ruling Class: Gaetano Mosca and the "Elite"* (Ann Arbor, 1958). Mosca is the most important modern political writer emphasizing the role of the elite in government and politics. Chap. XIII (pp. 262–285) is on "Machiavelli and the Machiavellians," particularly in relation to the modern elite theory of politics.

► MORLEY, JOHN VISCOUNT, *Politics and History* (London, 1923). A collection of essays, with an interesting paper on Machiavelli (pp. 129–180), written from a Liberal point of view. An appendix, "Notes to Machiavelli" (pp. 305–317), contains bibliographical data and comments. See also Thomas B. Macaulay, *Critical and Historical Essays* (Everyman's Library, London–New York, 1907), Vol. II, Chap. I, "Machiavelli" (pp. 1–37).

► MUIR, D. ERSKINE, *Machiavelli and His Times* (London, 1936). The author sees the clue to Machiavelli's political theory in his "burning indignation at the state of Italy and the decadence of Italians, and a hard ruthless determination to point to the only remedies in which he believed" (p. 251). Attractive illustrations are included in the book.

▶ OLSCHKI, LEONARDO, *Machiavelli the Scientist* (Berkeley, 1945). A brief and illuminating essay, stressing the relation of Machiavelli's ideas to the new scientific tendencies of his time. Olschki characterizes Machiavelli "as one of the greatest exponents of the laical genius of Italy that sought clarity, knowledge, and wisdom as manifestations of a free human judgment and of autonomous intellectual experiences" (p. 56).

▶ PREZZOLINI, GIUSEPPE, *Nicolo Machiavelli the Florentine* (trans. into English, New York, 1928). Impressionistic, and centered on Machiavelli's life.

▶ PULVER, JEFFREY, *Machiavelli: The Man, His Work, and His Times* (London 1937). A bibliography is appended (pp. 307–310).

▶ RIDOLFI, ROBERTO, *Vita di Niccolò Machiavelli* (Rome, 1954). A detailed biography of Machiavelli, stressing his character, life, and career rather than his thought, viewed perceptively and sympathetically by a Florentine historian. For recent Italian studies emphasizing Machiavelli's political ideas, see Giuseppe Prezzolini, *Machiavelli anticristo* (Rome, 1954); Luigi Bottigliero, *Machiavelli* (Milan, 1952); and Carlo Curcio, *Machiavelli nel Risorgimento* (Milan, 1953).

▶ STRAUSS, LEO, *Thoughts on Machiavelli*

(Glencoe, Ill., 1958). Particularly valuable in establishing the unity of Machiavelli's thought in *The Prince* and *The Discourses,* contrary to the traditional view according to which there is a sharp and insoluble contradiction between the two works. In trying to fathom the meaning of Machiavelli's doctrines, the author does not relate Machiavelli to his time and historical environment, but dissects the text of Machiavelli's writings in minute detail, including the frequency of some key concepts (or their absence). Strauss rejects the newer interpretations of Machiavelli as a patriot or scientific student of politics, and accepts the older view of Machiavelli as a "teacher of evil" (p. 9). The symbol of Machiavelli's new philosophy "is the Beast Man as opposed to the God Man: it understands man in the light of the sub-human rather than that of the super-human" (pp. 296–297). Despite its self-imposed limitations of approach, this work is indispensable to the study of Machiavelli.

▶ VILLARI, PASQUALE, *The Life and Times of Niccolo Machiavelli* (New York, 1898). First published in Italian in 1877, this is still one of the main sources of Machiavellian studies, though perhaps too apologetic in tendency. The massive work contains detailed accounts of the background of the whole period as well as of Machiavelli's life and thought. Numerous illustrations are included.

▶ WHITFIELD, JOHN H., *Machiavelli* (Oxford, 1947). Chap. IV (pp. 60–82) of this scholarly and searching work is on *The Prince*. A short bibliography is added (pp. 161–163).

Chapter 12

The Protestant Reformation

▶ ACTON, LORD, *The History of Freedom and Other Essays* (London, 1907). Chap.

IV is called "The Massacre of St. Bartholomew" (pp. 101–149). The royal orders required the public authorities "to collect the Huguenots in some prison or other safe place, where they could be got at by hired bands of volunteer assassins. To screen the King it was desirable that his officers should not superintend the work themselves. Mandelot the Governor of Lyons, having locked the gates of Lyons, and shut up the Huguenots together, took himself out of the way while the Huguenots were butchered" (p. 119). Lord Acton, a devout Catholic, describes the subsequent attempts to white-wash the massacre as follows: "A time came when the Catholics, having long relied on force, were compelled to appeal to opinion. That which had been defiantly acknowl-edged and defended required to be ingeni-ously explained away. The same motive which had justified the murder now prompted the lie. Men shrank from the conviction that the rulers and restorers of their Church had been murderers and abet-ters of murder, and that so much infamy had been coupled with so much zeal. They feared to say that the most monstrous of crimes had been solemnly approved at Rome, lest they should devote the Papacy to the execration of mankind" (p. 148). See also Chap. V, "The Protestant Theory of Persecution" (pp. 150–187), in which Lord Acton deals, in particular, with doctrines and practices of persecution in Lutheranism and Calvinism, and his conclusion is sum-marized in one brief sentence: "Those who —in agreement with the principle of the early Church, that men are free in matters of conscience—condemn all intolerance, will censure Catholics and Protestants alike" (p. 186).

► ALLEN, J. W., *The History of Political Thought in the Sixteenth Century* (London, 1928). Sees the originality of the *Vindiciae* not in the idea of contract, but in the stress on the rights of municipalities, thus fore-shadowing the concept of a federal system; the latter had little impact in France and England but influenced the internal political organization of Holland (pp. 320–331).

► ARMSTRONG, E., "The Political Theory of the Huguenots," *English Historical Review,*

IV (January, 1889), 13–40. Emphasizes the immense practical impact of the *Vindi-ciae,* particularly in England, and less in France.

► BAINTON, ROLAND H., *The Reformation of the Sixteenth Century* (Beacon Paper-backs, Boston, 1956). While stressing the religious ideas and issues in the rise of Prot-estantism, the author gives due attention to its social, economic, and political back-ground. Unlike most other writers, Bainton does not accept the "common generalization that Lutheranism made for totalitarianism and Calvinism for democracy" (p. 233), nor does he favor the view that Protestant-ism and Catholicism can be clearly juxta-posed in terms of their political impact: "Just as the Catholic Church will make a concordat with any regime that allows free-dom to administer the sacraments, free-dom to propagate the faith, freedom to hold property, and freedom for the mon-astic orders, so Protestantism has been will-ing to tolerate any form of government which accords religious liberty to Protes-tantism" (p. 234). Interesting comparisons between Catholic and Protestant attitudes on religious toleration from the fifteenth to the seventeenth centuries will be found in Bainton's *The Travails of Religious Lib-erty* (Harper Torchbooks, New York, 1958) and *The Age of the Reformation* (Anvil Books, Princeton, 1956). E. Harris Harbi-son, *The Age of the Reformation* (Ithaca, 1955) is an excellent brief survey of the period, skillfully relating the new religious movements to the underlying intellectual and social forces throughout Europe.

► BARKER, ERNEST, *Church, State and Study* (London, 1930). Chap. III, "A Hu-guenot Theory of Politics," deals primarily with the *Vindiciae contra tyrannos* (pp. 72–108), and is one of the most instructive analyses of the work. Of special interest is Barker's detailed evidence of the striking similarity between the *Vindiciae* and Locke's *Second Treatise of Government* (pp. 98–99, 106–108). The question of the authorship of the *Vindiciae* is examined by Barker in "The Authorship of the *Vindiciae contra tyrannos,"* Cambridge Historical Journal, III (No. 2, 1930), 164–181. A searching examination of the available facts leads Barker to support the traditional acceptance of Hubert Languet as the author of the *Vindiciae,* whereas the evidence against Duplessis-Mornay seems "absolutely conclusive" (p. 174). In "L'auteur de l'ouvrage *Vindiciae contra tyrannos,"* Revue Historique, CLXVII ('May–June, 1931), 46–59, G. T. van Ysselsteyn defends the hypothesis that the *Vindiciae* is the joint product of Lauguet and Duplessis-Mornay, though he concedes to Languet the original idea and the principal share in its execution. However, van Ysselsteyn makes no reference to Barker's investigation of the issue, and the latter's conclusions still seem more convincing.

▶ ——, *Traditions of Civility* (Cambridge, 1948). Chap. IV, "The Connection of the Renaissance and the Reformation" (pp. 74–123), is an illuminating interpretation of an age "from which we are sprung, and to which we must always return to understand what we are" (p. 123). The essay is admirably suited for a first introduction to the whole subject of Renaissance and Reformation.

▶ BORNKAMM, HEINRICH, *Luther's World of Thought* (St. Louis, 1958). The author, a German church historian and fervent Lutheran, deals not only with Luther's religious doctrines, but also with his political ideas and their impact on German political development. Bornkamm argues that Luther was primarily a religious reformer rather than a political thinker or practical statesman. The main point in Luther's concept of the state is his rejection of the Aristotelian thesis that the state is the product of man's social impulses. Luther follows here—as in so many other issues—the doctrine of Augustine according to which the state is the result of, and remedy for, man's sinfulness. While not denying that the German Protestant rulers used the Lutheran churches as instruments of political absolutism, the author defends Luther on that score by arguing that such developments

ran counter to Luther's intentions and expectations.

▶ CHEVREUL, HENRI, *Hubert Languet* (Paris, 1856). The first twelve chapters of the book deal with Languet's life and career (pp. 1–172). The last chapter, XIII, discusses the *Vindiciae* (pp. 173–204). A list of Languet's works is appended (pp. 205–208).

▶ DEFENCE OF LIBERTY AGAINST TYRANTS, (A Translation of the *Vindiciae contra tyrannos* by Junius Brutus, with an Historical Introduction by Harold J. Laski, London, 1924). Laski's introduction is detailed and penetrating, providing a background of Huguenot political thought as well as a minute analysis of the chief ideas of the *Vindiciae* (pp. 1–60).

▶ ELKAN, ALBERT, *Die Publizistik der Bartholomäusnacht und Mornays Vindiciae contra tyrannos* (Heidelberg, 1905). Disputes Languet's authorship of the *Vindiciae,* which is attributed to Duplessis Mornay. Elkan interprets the *Vindiciae* against the background of Huguenot political literature and calls it "the most typical expression of the Calvinist theory of the state in the second half of the sixteenth century" (p. 171). See also Oskar Scholz, *Huber Languet* (Halle, 1875), and Rudolf Treumann, *Die Monarchomachen* (Leipzig, 1895).

▶ FIGGIS, JOHN NEVILLE, *Studies of Political Thought from Gerson to Grotius, 1414–1625* (Cambridge, 1931). The first part of Lecture III, "Luther and Machiavelli," deals with the impact of Luther on politics (pp. 55–72). For a brief account of the *Vindiciae,* see pp. 134 ff., and *The Divine Right of Kings* (Cambridge, 1934), pp. 113–118.

▶ FOSDICK, HARRY EMERSON (ed.), *Great Voices of the Reformation* (Modern Library Giants, New York, 1954). An anthology of writers of the Reformation, from John Wycliffe to John Wesley, including brief excerpts from less well known sources.

▶ GRISAR, HARTMANN, *Martin Luther: His Life and Work* (St. Louis, 1935). The leading Catholic biography of Luther. See also Jacques Maritain, *Three Reformers: Luther, Descartes, Rousseau* (New York,

1929), for a Catholic interpretation of Luther and his relation to Descartes and Rousseau from the viewpoint of metaphysics and social philosophy.

► HOOGSTRA, JACOB T. (ed.), *American Calvinism: A Survey* (Grand Rapids, 1957). A collection of essays on American Calvinism, treated historically, topically, and regionally. See also Hugh T. Kerr, *What Divides Protestants Today* (Reflection Books, New York, 1958).

► HUNTER, A. MITCHELL, *The Teaching of Calvin: A Modern Interpretation* (London, 1950). Stresses the impact of Calvinism on the rise of modern democracy: "It was principally because Calvin was such an outright uncompromising exponent of essential democracy in Church and State that his influence so quickly eclipsed that of Luther in the extent of its spread and the constructive and directive idealism he infused into the political systems of modern civilization. Calvinism in fact became the most powerful ferment of civic liberty which has ever worked in the world's heart" (p. 304). See also T. F. Torrance, *Calvin's Doctrine of Man* (London, 1949); A. Dakin, *Calvinism* (Philadelphia, 1946); Sir Alfred T. Davies, *John Calvin and the Influence of Protestantism on National Life and Character* (London, 1946); and James Mackinnon, *Calvin and the Reformation* (New York, 1936).

► MACKINNON, JAMES, *Luther and the Reformation,* 4 vols. (New York, 1925–1930). Covers extensively the background, life, thought, and impact of Luther. The best short biography of Luther is Roland H. Bainton, *Here I Stand: A Life of Martin Luther* (New York, 1950). Older, but still useful, is Preserved Smith, *The Life and Letters of Martin Luther* (Boston–New York, 1911). See also Heinrich Boehmer, *Luther and the Reformation in the Light of Modern Research* (London, 1930); Edgar M. Carlson, *The Reinterpretation of Luther* (Philadelphia, 1948); and Robert M. Fife, *The Revolt of Martin Luther* (New York, 1957).

► MCNEILL, JOHN T., *The History and* *Character of Calvinism* (New York, 1954). The first half deals with the origins of Calvinism and the Geneva experiment under Calvin himself; the second half traces the spread of Calvinism to the rest of Europe and North America, and examines the relation of Calvinism to modern issues. With regard to the issue of slavery in the United States, the author writes that, when the civil war came in 1861, "most of the churches upheld the cause espoused by the states in which they were located" (p. 424). See also George L. Mosse, *Calvinism: Authoritarian or Democratic?* (New York, 1957); Charles Davis Cremeans, *The Reception of Calvinistic Thought in England* (Urbana, 1949); R. N. Carew Hunt, *Calvin* (London, 1933); Benjamin B. Warfield, *Calvin and Calvinism* (New York, 1931); William P. Armstrong (ed.), *Calvin and the Reformation* (New York, 1909); and Williston Walker, *John Calvin* (New York, 1906).

► PASCAL, ROY, *The Social Basis of the German Reformation* (London, 1933). Views the Lutheran movement primarily in terms of social and economic conditions in the period of nascent German capitalism. See also Klaus P. Schulz, *Luther und Marx im Spannungsfeld unserer Zeit* (Stuttgart, 1956).

► PLASS, EWALD M. (ed.), *What Luther Says: An Anthology,* 3 vols. (St. Louis, 1959). Presents all aspects of Luther's thought—theological, philosophical, social, political, and economic—in his own words. The entries are in alphabetical order. Since Luther was a prolific writer, and had strong views on many and sundry subjects, this anthology is immensely useful as a quick reference guide to his thought.

► TROELTSCH, ERNST, *The Social Teaching of the Christian Churches,* trans. from the German, 2 vols. (New York, 1931). The second volume of this monumental study by the leading German scholar in the field is devoted to Protestantism. In the treatment of Lutheranism (II, 515–576) Troeltsch brings out the basic authoritarianism in Luther: "All along Luther is opposed to revolutionary schemes which are based on an individualistic point of view, and he is in favor of an authority which controls, conditions, and gradually molds them, even in case of necessity achieving its end by force. In this glorification of authority there were certain resemblances to the doctrine of Machiavelli, which early Lutherans had already noted" (p. 532). Concerning the Lutheran concept of the state, Troeltsch says that it is "the same 'police' and utilitarian idea of State as in Catholicism, only now, in accordance with the circumstances, there is a greater emphasis upon unity of authority" (p. 548).

The discussion of Calvinism (pp. 576–691) starts out with the observation that Calvinism rather than Lutheranism "is the chief force in the Protestant world today" (p. 576). The deeper reason for this lies, according to Troeltsch, in the "active character" of Calvinism, as contrasted with the acquiescence of Lutheranism in existing social and political conditions· "From the political and social point of view the significance of Lutheranism for the modern history of civilization lies in its connection with the reactionary parties" (p. 577). The "Democratic Tendency of Primitive Calvinism" is discussed (pp. 628–630). See also Troeltsch's *Protestantism and Progress: A Historical Study of the Relation of Protestantism to the Modern World* (Beacon Paperbacks, Boston, 1958).

► WARFIELD, BENJAMIN B., *Calvin and Augustine* (Philadelphia, 1956). From Luther onward, Protestant thinkers have felt intense spiritual kinship with Augustine. The author, a distinguished Protestant theologian, states that "it is Augustine who gave us the Reformation" (p. 322).

► WEBER, MAX, *The Protestant Ethic and the Spirit of Capitalism* (London, 1930). Weber, the greatest German sociologist of the twentieth century, attacks the study of capitalism from the religious angle, and stresses the role of Calvinism and Puritanism in the growth of the capitalist spirit. A similar approach will be found in R. H. Tawney, *Religion and the Rise of Capital-*ism (Mentor Books, New York, 1947). Weber's view is challenged by H. M. Robertson in his *Aspects of the Rise of Capitalism: A Criticism of Max Weber and His School* (Cambridge, 1933), in which he tries to prove that capitalism first started in Catholic countries like Italy and France. The answer to Robertson will be found in the work of a Jesuit writer, J. Broderick, *The Economic Morals of the Jesuits: An Answer to Dr. H. M. Robertson* (London, 1934). See also Ralph Barton Perry, *Puritanism and Democracy* (New York, 1944), Chap. XII, "The Economic Virtues" (pp. 297–320), and A. Whitney Griswold, "Three Puritans on Prosperity," *New England Quarterly, VII* (September, 1934), 475–493.

► WEILL, GEORGES, *Les théories sur le pouvoir royal en France pendant les guerres de religion* (Paris, 1891). Stresses the aristocratic element in the *Vindiciae* (pp. 109–121).

► WHALE, J. S., *The Protestant Tradition* (Cambridge, 1955). The first part deals with Luther, Calvin, and the later sectarian movements; the second part takes up the attitudes of the Protestant churches on modern issues, such as religious toleration, church and state, totalitarianism and democracy, and social reform. A brief survey of the history of Protestantism and its relation to modern intellectual and political issues will also be found in W. R. Inge, *Protestantism* (New York, 1935). Henry Townsend, *The Claims of Free Churches* (London, 1949), examines the crucial role of the nonconformist sects and churches in British history: "The idea and experience of freedom which gave birth to the Free Church gave birth also to the Free State" (p. 193). For the impact of Puritanism on Britain and the United States, see also John Brown, *The English Puritans* (Cambridge, 1912); John S. Flynn, *The Influence of Puritanism on the Political and Religious Thought of the English* (London, 1920); and Ralph Barton Perry, *Puritanism and Democracy* (New York, 1944).

► WOLIN, SHELDON S., "Politics and Religion: Luther's Simplistic Imperative," *American Political Science Review*, L (March, 1956), 24–42. The author seeks to resolve the fundamental paradox in Luther's thought: the libertarian implications of his religious doctrines as contrasted with the absolutistic impact of his political writings. Whereas many students of Luther seek to resolve this contradiction in Luther by transforming him into a consistent libertarian or authoritarian in both religion and politics, Wolin argues that there is a common denominator between Luther's religious individualism and his political authoritarianism: his "simplistic imperative," or

the tendency to oversimplify, and, above all, Luther's "failure to appreciate institutions" (p. 40). In religion, this simplistic imperative is shown in Luther's insistence on faith, the purely spiritual relation between man and God, in which churches, laws, ministers, and traditions play a subordinate role. In politics, too, Luther holds the notion that rules and regulations are not important; what matters is the wisdom of the rulers and the unquestioning obedience of the subjects: "In both instances the quest is for personal identification: the believer with his God, the citizen with his government" (p. 42).

Chapter 13

Bodín

▶ ALLEN, J. W., *A History of Political Thought in the Sixteenth Century* (London, 1928). Part III, Chap. VIII, "Jean Bodin" (pp. 394–444), greatly contributes to an understanding of Bodin. The author states that the originality of Bodin's theory of sovereignty consisted essentially "in the fact that he did not connect it specifically and directly with the will of God," and of the various elements that went into Bodin's theory, "the only one that is new is the conception of political society as absolutely and necessarily associated with the existence of the family and of private property and the conception of a consequent limitation of political authority" (p. 423). See also Allen's "Jean Bodin," in F. J. C. Hearnshaw (ed.), *The Social and Political Ideas of Some Great Thinkers of the Sixteenth and Seventeenth Centuries* (London, 1926), Chap. II (pp. 42–62).

▶ BAUDRILLART, HENRI, *J. Bodin et son temps* (Paris, 1853). Part I (pp. 1–110) gives a general survey of sixteenth-century political and economic ideas. Part II (pp.

111–221) tells the story of Bodin's life and work. Part III (pp. 222–512) is an analysis of his *Six Books on the State*. A more recent standard work is Roger Chauviré, *Jean Bodin: auteur de la "République"* (Paris, 1914).

▶ BODIN, JEAN, *De la République* (Collection Le Jardin du Luxembourg, Paris, 1949). A collection of relatively short "fragments" from *Les six livres de la République*, with a brief account of Bodin's career at the end (pp. 103–111). Spelling and punctuation are modernized. *The Six Books of the Commonweal*, the only English translation of the whole work, by Richard Knolles (London, 1606, and edited by Kenneth D. McRae, Cambridge, Mass., 1961), is based on the French and Latin texts of the treatise. See also the translation (in abridged form) by M. J. Tooley (Blackwell's Political Text, New York, 1955).

▶ CARLYLE, R. W. and A. J. CARLYLE, *A History of Medieval Political Theory in the West*, Vol. VI: *Political Theory from 1300 to 1600* (London, 1936). Includes an account of Bodin (pp. 417–429), particularly in relation to the theory of absolute monarchy.

▶ CHEVALLIER, JEAN-JACQUES, *Les grandes oeuvres politiques de Machiavel à nos jours* (Paris, 1949). Stresses the elements of moderation and limitation in Bodin's concept of sovereignty and monarchy (pp. 38–51). Though an essentially descriptive and juristic theory, Bodin's doctrine—even before he gives the reasons for his preference of monarchy—"works already for the King of France" (p. 44).

▶ CHURCH, WILLIAM FARR, *Constitutional Thought in Sixteenth-Century France* (Cambridge, Mass., 1941). Includes a detailed analysis of Bodin in relation to his predecessors and contemporaries (pp. 194–242). Concerning Bodin's influence on his followers, the author writes that "it was not Bodin's thought as a whole which was adopted by his followers but rather certain salient features which were appropriated because of their immediate value or appeal to contemporary writers. And in the process of adoption by others, those portions of Bodin's system undergoing such treatment could but be distorted because of their removal from their original context. Certain important concepts were seized upon, torn from their immediate milieu, and, through association with other ideas, were attributed meanings entirely lacking to Bodin. Such was the fate of his most important contribution, his theory of sovereignty" (p. 244). A detailed bibliography is on pp. 339–350.

▶ DICKINSON, JOHN, "A Working Theory of Sovereignty," *Political Science Quarterly*, XLII (December, 1927), 524–548, and XLIII (March, 1928), 32–63. Defines sovereignty in the legal sense, following Bodin's juristic conception, as "nothing more nor less than a logical postulate or presupposition of any system of order according to law," because if there is to be uniformity of legal rules in a community, "then there must be a single final source of law" that all inferior tribunals and officials recognize as the ultimate authority (p. 525). If competing authorities exist side by side, subject to no common superior, the result is anarchy (p. 526). Dickinson's views are directed against those who confuse the legal concept of sovereignty with the psychological concept of power, as well as against those who, like the pluralists (Harold J. Laski, G. D. H. Cole), deny the usefulness and validity of the doctrine of sovereignty altogether.

The ablest juristic and analytic treatment of the problem of sovereignty will be found in Hans Kelsen's writings: *Das Problem der Souveränität und die Theorie des Völkerrechts*, 2nd ed. (Tubingen, 1920); *Allgemeine Staatslehre* (Berlin, 1925), and *General Theory of Law and State* (Cambridge, Mass., 1945). Dickinson's interpretation of the concept of sovereignty as a logical postulate or presupposition of a system of law is based entirely on Kelsen's view that sovereignty is not a social fact but an hypothesis, the expression of the unity of a legal system.

▶ FIGGIS, J. N., *The Divine Right of Kings* (Cambridge, 1934). For a brief analysis of Bodin, see pp. 126–130; *Studies of Political Thought from Gerson to Grotius, 1414–1625* (Cambridge, 1931), 110 ff.; and "Political Thought in the Sixteenth Century," in *Cambridge Modern History* (Cambridge, 1904), Vol. III, Chap. XXII (pp. 736–769). See also, in the same volume, Chap. I, "The Wars of Religion in France," by A. J. Butler (pp. 1–52).

▶ FOURNOL, E., *Bodin: prédécesseur de Montesquieu* (Paris, 1896). Maintains that it is impossible to judge Bodin's theory of the state according to our familiar standards and in the light of modern ideas. On the one hand, Bodin's doctrine of sovereignty is an energetic and rigorous affirmation of the rights of the state, and on the other hand, Bodin's doctrine of the inviolability of private property puts the individual—or the family—in a strong position; it seems that in his theory "the individual and the state are two separate worlds" (p. 81). Viewed from afar, and in an over-all fashion, "Bodin is a spirit of liberal tendencies whom the contemporary desire for regulating order and his own logical nature have led to the doctrine of absolutism" (p. 112). Fournol also stresses the "spectacle of contemporary anarchy" (*ibid.*) as an influence on Bodin.

▶ GAROSCI, A., *Jean Bodin: politica e diritto nel Rinascimento francese* (Milan, 1934). Useful bibliographical data are on pp. 323–329. See also Guido de Ruggiero, *Rinascimento, Riforma e Controriforma,* 2 vols. (Bari, 1947), especially I, 304–307, and II, 77–82.

▶ GILMORE, MYRON PIPER, *Argument from Roman Law in Political Thought, 1200–1600* (Cambridge, Mass., 1941). Includes an account of Bodin's theory of office (pp. 93–113).

▶ HANCKE, E., *Bodin: Eine Studie über den Begriff der Souverainetät (Untersuchungen zur Deutschen Staats- und Rechtsgeschichte,* ed. Otto Gierke, No. 47, Breslau, 1894). See also Adolf Dock, *Der Souveränetätsbegriff von Bodin bis zu Friedrich dem Grossen* (Strasburg, 1897); Friedrich Meinecke, *Die Idee der Staatsräson* (Munich–Berlin, 1929), pp. 70–80; Ernst Oberfohren, "Jean Bodin und seine Schule: Untersuchungen über die Frühzeit der Universalökonomik," *Weltwirtschaftliches Archiv,* I (April, 1913), 249–285; Hermann Rehm, *Geschichte der Staatrechtswissenschaft* (Freiburg–Leipzig, 1896), pp. 219–231; J. C. Bluntschli, *Geschichte des allgemeinen Staatsrechts und der Politik* (Munich, 1864), pp. 17–46; and Ludwig Gumplowicz, *Geschichte der Staatstheorien* (Innsbruck, 1926), pp. 140–151. For an interpretation of Bodin's doctrine of sovereignty as a political ideology in the service of French monarchical claims, see Hans Kelsen, *Allgemeine Staatslehre* (Berlin, 1925), pp. 113 ff.

▶ LASKI, HAROLD J., *A Grammar of Politics,* 2nd ed. (London, 1930). Chap. II, "Sovereignty" (pp. 44–88), rejects the validity and usefulness of the concept of sovereignty from the viewpoint of legal theory and political philosophy, and seeks to demonstrate that sovereignty does not satisfactorily describe the conduct and goals of the state in its domestic or foreign relations. A more detailed exposition of Laski's theory of pluralism, which replaces the traditional monistic concept of the sovereignty of the state with the concept of associations as the basis of the state, will be found in *Studies in the Problem of Sovereignty* (New Haven, 1917), *Authority in the Modern State* (New Haven, 1919), and *The Foundation of Sovereignty and Other Essays* (New Haven, 1921). Laski's theory of political pluralism stresses individualism and voluntarism: "The will of the State obtains preeminence over the wills of other groups exactly to the point where it is interpreted with sufficient wisdom to obtain general acceptance, and no further. It is a will to some extent competing with other wills, and, Darwin-wise, surviving only by its ability to cope with its environment. Should it venture into dangerous places it pays the penalty of its audacity. It finds its sovereignty by consent transformed into impotence by disagreement. But, it may be objected, in such a view sovereignty means no more than the ability to secure assent. I can only reply to the objection by admitting it. There is no sanction for law other than the human mind. It is sheer illusion to imagine that the authority of the State has any other safeguard than the wills of its members" (*Studies in the Problem of Sovereignty,* p. 14).

See also Jacques Maritain, "The Concept of Sovereignty," *American Political Science Review,* XLIV (June, 1950), 343–357, who fully concurs with Laski, though writing from another philosophical starting point. Maritain, basing his discussion of sovereignty on Bodin, Hobbes, and Rousseau, concludes that the concept of sovereignty be discarded altogether: "The two concepts of Sovereignty and Absolutism have been forged together on the same anvil. They must be scrapped together" (p. 357).

▶ McILWAIN, CHARLES H., "Sovereignty Again," *Economica,* VI (November, 1926), 253–268, reprinted in his *Constitutionalism and the Changing World* (New York, 1939), Chap. II (pp. 26–46). Chap. III, "A Fragment on Sovereignty" (pp. 47–60), is mainly devoted to Bodin. McIlwain hails Bodin as the first author of the theory of the *Rechtsstaat,* the state based on the rule of law, and says that Bodin's analysis "is a sounder foundation on which to build than either the assertions of Hobbes or the negations of the modern Pluralists" (p. 60). The moderate and antidespotic position of Bodin is emphasized by McIlwain in *The Growth of Political Thought in the West* (New York, 1932), pp. 364–394. Concerning the later abuse of Bodin's doctrine of sovereignty for the justification of despotic government, McIlwain writes: "The more liberal parts of Bodin's conception of kingship are a heritage of the middle ages; the development of the absolute monarchy into an arbitrary one is a modern achievement" (p. 388). See also McIlwain's "Sovereignty in the World Today," *Measure,* I (Spring, 1950), 109–117.

▶ MESNARD, PIERRE, *L'essor de la philosophie politique au XVI siècle* (Paris, 1936). Book V, Chap. III (pp. 473–546) is on Bodin's *Six Books of the State.*

▶ MOREAU-REIBEL, JEAN, *Jean Bodin et le droit public comparé* (Paris, 1933). A study of Bodin from the viewpoint of comparative political institutions.

▶ REYNOLDS, BEATRICE, *Proponents of Limited Monarchy in Sixteenth-Century France: Francis Hotman and Jean Bodin* (New York, 1931). The main treatment of Bodin is in Chaps. IV and V (pp. 105–193). A bibliography is appended (pp. 203–208).

▶ SALMON, J. H. M., *The French Religious Wars in English Political Thought* (Oxford, 1959). In the late sixteenth and seventeenth centuries, French political experience and thought had a considerable influence in England, whereas from the eighteenth century onward English political philosophy had a strong appeal in France. Salmon's study shows in detail the impact of French political thought in the late sixteenth and seventeenth centuries on English political theory and practice. In particular, the influence of Bodin on England is analyzed, including his personal links with prominent English publicists and politicians.

▶ SHEPPARD, MAX ADAMS, "Sovereignty at the Crossroads: A Study of Bodin," *Political Science Quarterly,* XLV (December, 1930), 580–603. Stresses the element of the rule of law and fundamental constitutional limitations in Bodin's doctrine of sovereignty.

▶ WEILL, GEORGES, *Les théories sur le pouvoir royal en France pendant les guerres de religion* (Paris, 1891). Chap. VIII is on Bodin (pp. 159–174).

Chapter 14

Hobbes

▶ ALEKSANDROV, G. F., *A History of Western European Philosophy,* 2nd ed. (trans. from the Russian, New Haven, 1949). Hobbes is described as a firm defender of private property, who "regarded the development of society through a prism, which sharply distorted the real position of things. He saw the cause of men's struggle with one another not in the exploitation of man by

man, nor in the private ownership of the means of production, but in the absence of private property. Thus the entire course of the actual development of human society is presented by Hobbes in reverse order" (p. 175). Hobbes "produced the theory that later formed the foundation of innumerable theories of bourgeois governmental structure. This theory fully justified the domination of one section of society over another, of one class over another" (*ibid.*). Hobbes' ideas on state and church were advanced for his time, and he "did much for the development of atheism" (p. 176). Aleksandrov concludes as follows: "The theory developed by Hobbes was progressive and has a tremendous influence on social science in all European countries in the seventeenth and eighteenth centuries" (*ibid.*).

► BOWLE, JOHN, *Hobbes and His Critics* (London, 1951). Hobbes was a highly controversial figure in his own time, and this is the only full account of his contemporary critics—liberal, conservative, religious, and secular. The author not only contributes to a better understanding of Hobbes in the context of his own period, but also shows how some of the main arguments of Hobbes' contemporary critics became the dominant ideas in English political thought from Locke onward.

► CARRITT, E. F., *Morals and Politics* (London, 1935). Chap. III is on Hobbes (pp. 25–39). See also W. R. Sorley, *A History of English Philosophy*, pp. 47–74; R. H. S. Crossman, *Government and the Governed* (London, 1939), pp. 43–69; C. E. Vaughan, *Studies in the History of Political Philosophy before and after Rousseau* (Manchester, 1939), I, 17–61; and J. W. Gough, *The Social Contract* (Oxford, 1936), pp. 100–107).

► CLARK, G. N., *The Seventeenth Century*, 2nd ed. (Oxford, 1947). Of special interest are Chaps. VI, "Comparative Constitutional History" (pp. 82–97), and XIV, "Political Thought" (pp. 208–232).

► DAVIES, GEOFFREY, *The Early Stuarts, 1603–1660* (Oxford History of England, Oxford, 1937). Useful for a better understanding of the background of Hobbes' life and thought. See also Ernest Barker, *Traditions of Civility* (Cambridge, 1948), Chap. VI, *"Oliver Cromwell and the English People"* (pp. 159–192).

► GOOCH, G. P., *Hobbes* (Annual Lecture on a Master Mind, British Academy, London, 1939). Presents Hobbes in the perspec-

tive of English history and his later influence at home and abroad. Gooch concludes that it "is one of the ironies of history that the disciples whom the author of *Leviathan* failed to find in his own country and his own time are crowding the continental stage after the lapse of three hundred years" (p. 42). See also Gooch's *Political Thought in England: From Bacon to Halifax* (Home University Library, London, 1937), Chap. II, "Hobbes" (pp. 35–57).

► HOBBES, THOMAS, *Leviathan* (Blackwell's Political Texts, Oxford, 1946). Contains a long introduction (pp. vii–lxvi) by Michael Oakeshott, which is one of the most original interpretations of Hobbes' political ideas.

► JAMES, DAVID G., *The Life of Reason: Hobbes, Locke, Bolingbroke* (New York, 1949). Chap. I. "The Proud Mind" (pp. 1–62), is on Hobbes. The author sees in the combination of rationalism and materialism in Hobbes a "hopeless contradiction" (p. 268).

► JOUVENEL, BERTRAND DE, *Sovereignty* (Cambridge, 1957). Chap. XIV is on "The Political Consequences of Hobbes" (pp. 231–246). The author rejects the interpretation of Hobbes as a forerunner of totalitarianism: "It is psychologically necessary to successful totalitarianism that each man feels himself a mere part, whereas Hobbesian man feels himself most vividly a whole" (p. 239). Far from being the "father of totalitarianism," Hobbes is "an individualist and progressive, who would like each man to develop his faculties in striving to fulfil his desires, as these are successively aroused. Only, men so employed may do each other harm. The State exists to stop the mischief which the intersection of their appetites may do them" (*ibid.*).

► LAIRD, JOHN, *Hobbes* (London, 1934). In the preface to this volume in the Leaders of Philosophy series, the author calls Hobbes a "psychologist of genius, a notable metaphysician, a political thinker of enduring renown, and a moralist who should be called the father of British ethics in its greatest period, although most of his progeny were anxious to show why and in what ways they could not live down to so disreputable an ancestor" (p. v). Part I is on Hobbes' life and time (pp. 3–81); Part II is on his philosophy, including a long chapter on politics and religion (pp. 85–239); Part III deals with Hobbes' influence (pp. 243–317). A short bibliography is appended (pp. 318–319). See also G. E. C. Catlin, *Thomas Hobbes as Philosopher, Publicist and Man of Letters* (Oxford, 1922); E. L. Woodward, "Thomas Hobbes," in F. J. C. Hearnshaw (ed.), *Social and Political Ideas of Some Great Thinkers of the Sixteenth and Seventeenth Centuries* (London, 1926), Chap. VII (pp. 153–173); and Sterling P. Lamprecht, "Hobbes and Hobbism," *American Political Science Review*, XXXIV (February, 1940), 31–53.

► LANDRY, BERNARD, *Hobbes* (Paris, 1930). The concluding chapter compares Hobbes with Machiavelli, both of whom are held to be "the most famous defenders of a social science which is at once strictly positive and ferociously nationalist" (p. 256). The peace that Hobbes pursues "is not true peace: it is outward tranquillity procured by the police" (p. 272). See also J. Vialatoux, *La cité de Hobbes: théorie de l'état totalitaire* (Paris, 1935), and Jean-Jacques Chevallier, *Les grandes oeuvres politiques de Machiavel à nos jours* (Paris, 1949), pp. 52–69.

► LEVI, ADOLFO, *La filosofia di Tommaso Hobbes* (Milan–Naples, 1929). Part II (pp. 235–419) is on Hobbes' political philosophy.

► MERRIMAN, R. B., *Six Contemporaneous Revolutions* (Glasgow, 1937). Opposing the tendency to regard the Puritan Revolution as an isolated phenomenon in the seventeenth century, the author relates it to five other revolutions on the Continent in the two middle decades of the seventeenth century (Catalonia, Portugal, Naples, France, Holland). In Catalonia, Naples, and France the revolutions failed. In Portugal, national independence was secured. In Holland, the victory of the antimonarchist party proved

impermanent, and "only in England did the principles underlying the revolution really survive, and even there the monarchical constitution was restored" (pp. 30–31).

► PARSONS, TALCOTT, *The Structure of Social Action* (Glencoe, Ill., 1949). In a discussion of "Hobbes and the Problem of Order" Parsons says that "Hobbes' system of social theory is almost a pure case of utilitarianism" (p. 90), and that he "saw the problem with a clarity which has never been surpassed" (p. 93). On "Hobbes and the Utilitarians," see also John Plamenatz, *The English Utilitarians* (Oxford, 1949), pp. 10–16.

► PETERS, RICHARD, *Hobbes* (Penguin Books, Baltimore, 1956). A volume in the "Pelican Philosophy Series." After an introductory chapter on the life of Hobbes in the context of his turbulent era, the author examines the major points of Hobbesian thought on government and politics as well as on logic, psychology, ethics, and religion.

► POLIN, RAYMOND, *Politique et philosophie chez Thomas Hobbes* (Paris, 1953). Emphasizes the philosophical and ethical bases of Hobbes' political thought. Like other French students of Hobbes, the author is impressed by the similarity of the Hobbesian concept of the sovereign will with Rousseau's concept of the "general will." This point is more fully developed in Georges Davy, *Thomas Hobbes et J. J. Rousseau* (Oxford, 1953).

► STEPHEN, LESLIE, *Hobbes* (New York, 1904). One of the best short books on Hobbes. Chap. I (pp. 1–69) is on his life, IV (pp. 173–236) on his political theory. See also George Croom Robertson, *Hobbes* (Edinburgh–London, 1886), and A. E. Taylor, *Hobbes* (London, 1908).

► STRAUSS, LEO, *The Political Philosophy of Hobbes: Its Basis and Its Genesis* (Oxford, 1936, reprinted Chicago, 1952). In this pioneering study, the author seeks to demonstrate that Hobbes' "new moral attitude" precedes his interest in modern science, and that his break with tradition and his original contribution are due rather to that new moral attitude than to his (later) contact with science. Specifically, Strauss argues that however much "Hobbes personally esteemed the aristocracy, and esteemed the specific qualities of the aristocracy, his political philosophy is directed against the aristocratic rules of life in the name of bourgeois rules of life. His morality is the morality of the bourgeois world" (pp. 120–121). The genesis of Hobbes' political philosophy is "nothing other than the progressive supplanting of aristocratic virtue by bourgeois virtue" (p. 126). In an earlier study on Hobbes, Strauss had already written that all the characteristic premises and affirmations of liberalism can be found in Hobbes, and that "the absolutism of Hobbes is nothing but militant liberalism *in statu nascendi,* that is, liberalism in its most radical form. Hobbes is thus the true founder of liberalism, and therefore in looking for a radical critique or justification of liberalism, one has to go back to him" ("Quelques remarques sur la science politique de Hobbes," *Recherches Philosophiques,* II, 1932–1933, p. 610). Strauss emphasizes that Hobbes—though a founder of liberalism—was not a Liberal in the proper sense of the term. For an analysis of Strauss' work on Hobbes, see Michael Oakeshott, "Dr. Leo Strauss on Hobbes," *Politica,* II (June, 1937), 364–379.

▶ TÖNNIES, FERDINAND, *Hobbes: Leben und Lehre* (Stuttgart, 1896). Tönnies was one of the founders of modern sociology, and the leading German authority on Hobbes. See also Richard Hoenigswald, *Hobbes und die Staatsphilosophie* (Munich, 1924); Gustav Louis, *Über den Individualismus des Hobbes* (Halle, 1891); and Z. Lubienski, *Die Grundlagen des ethisch-politischen Systems von Hobbes* (Munich, 1932), which has an extensive bibliography (pp. 275–288).

▶ WARRENDER, HOWARD, *The Political Philosophy of Hobbes: His Theory of Obligation* (Oxford, 1957). Contrary to the traditional interpretation of Hobbes as a positivist sharply opposed to natural law, Warrender argues that Hobbes is "essentially a natural-law philosopher" (p. 323), because his "theory of political society is based upon a theory of duty, and his theory of duty belongs essentially to the natural-law tradition" (p. 322). Although its main conclusions will not be universally accepted, the book is an original and provocative contribution to the study of Hobbes.

Chapter 15

Locke

▶ AARON, R. I., *John Locke* (London–New York, 1937). An excellent volume in the Leaders of Philosophy series; Locke's political, moral, religious, and educational views are examined in Part III (pp. 257–313). A useful bibliography is included (pp. 314–321). See also H. R. Fox Bourne, *The Life of John Locke,* 2 vols. (London, 1876); Lord King, *The Life and Letters of John Locke* (London, 1884), and Thomas Fowler, *Locke* (London, 1880).

▶ ANDERSON, FULTON H., *The Influence of Contemporary Science on Locke's Method and Results* (Toronto, 1923). A brief essay in the University of Toronto Studies.

▶ BASTIDE, CHARLES, *John Locke: ses théories politiques et leur influence en Angleterre* (Paris, 1906). This French standard work examines Locke's political philosophy in the light of his "rationalist and experimental" method: "What Bacon had done for the physical and natural sciences, Locke attempted to do for politics" (p. 253). See also Paul Hazard, *La crise de la conscience européenne, 1680–1715* (Paris, 1935), pp. 245–258, 287–290, 312–316.

▶ CRANSTON, MAURICE, *John Locke: A Biography* (New York, 1957). The definitive biography of Locke, superseding previous accounts of his life. Utilizing a large collection of Locke's personal papers previously inaccessible to scholars, the author presents not only Locke as a man in a new light, but also corrects numerous misconceptions about his intellectual development. Indispensable to the study of Locke and his time.

▶ CROSSMAN, R. H. S., *Government and the Governed*, 4th ed. (London, 1958). Chap. III, "The English Revolution" (pp. 43–80), deals with the background of the age, the contrasting personalities of Hobbes and Locke, and with the latter's political theory. Crossman concludes that "we should not blame Locke for the faults of his successors. In his own day, he was a sane progressive, whose writings tempered the arrogance of the social oligarchy and taught it the discipline of representative institutions. And, if later he was to inspire Burke's conservatism, he inspired Paine and Rousseau —and even Karl Marx as well" (p. 80). See also Willmoore Kendall, *John Locke and the Doctrine of Majority Rule* (Illinois Studies in the Social Sciences, Vol. XXVI, No. 2, Urbana, Ill., 1941).

▶ FECHTNER, EDUARD, *John Locke: ein Bild aus den geistigen Kämpfen Englands im 17. Jahrhundert* (Stuttgart, 1898). A sympathetic account of Locke's life and thought, stressing his concepts of liberty and toleration. See also Robert Reininger, *Locke, Berkeley, Hume* (Munich, 1922), pp. 16–82.

▶ GOUGH, J. W., *John Locke's Political Philosophy* (Oxford, 1950). Eight studies on the following topics: the law of nature; the rights of the individual; government by consent; theory of property; separation of powers and sovereignty; Locke and the Revolution of 1688; political trusteeship; Locke's belief in toleration. Succinct and essential to the study of Locke. Gough's *The Social Contract*, 2nd ed. (Oxford,

1957), traces the development of the social-contract theory from antiquity to the nineteenth century, and has a chapter on Locke (IX, pp. 126–146). See also his introduction to John Locke, *The Second Treatise of Government, and A Letter Concerning Toleration* (Blackwell's Political Texts, Oxford, 1946), pp. vii–xxxvi, and Ernest Barker's introduction to *Social Contract: Essays by Locke, Hume, and Rousseau* (New York, 1948), a considerable portion of which is on Locke (pp. xv–xxvii).

▶ HAMILTON, WALTON H., "Property—According to Locke," *Yale Law Journal*, XLI (April, 1931), 864–880. Protects Locke against his own defenders, especially the zealots who have read into Locke's theory of property more than he himself meant. See also Paschal Larkin, *Property in the Eighteenth Century: with Special Reference to England and Locke* (Dublin, 1930), and Harold J. Laski, *The Rise of European Liberalism* (London, 1936). Laski writes that Locke's state "is nothing so much as a contract between a group of business men who form a limited liability company whose memorandum of association forbids to the directors all those practices of which the Stuarts had, until this time, been guilty" (p. 116). Alberto Bertolino, *Locke Economista* (Siena, 1928), summarizes Locke's economic doctrines in the light of his philosophy and politics.

▶ KRAKOWSKI, EDOUARD, *Les sources mediévales de la philosophie de Locke* (Paris, 1915). Although primarily concerned with the medieval sources of Locke's general philosophy, this work throws some light on generally neglected roots of Locke's political thought. See also A. Telkamp, *Das Verhältnis John Locke's zur Scholastik* (Munster, 1927).

▶ LASKI, HAROLD J., *Political Thought in England: From Locke to Bentham* (London, 1920), pp. 22–61. Laski gives a sympathetic account of Locke's relation to the Revolution of 1688 and his influence on subsequent English thought, as well as his contribution to French and American political ideas and institutions. He emphasizes that Locke was the first English political thinker whose argument was mainly secular, and that Locke rejected a purely legal theory as a sufficient basis of political society. See also J. L. Stocks, *Locke's Contribution to Political Theory* (London, 1933); C. H. Driver, "John Locke," in F. J. C. Hearnshaw (ed.), *The Social and Political Ideas of Some English Thinkers of the Augustan Age* (London, 1928), pp. 66–96; H. R. G. Greaves, "Locke and the Separation of Powers," *Politica,* I (February, 1934), 90–102; Sterling Power Lamprecht, *The Moral and Political Philosophy of John Locke* (New York, 1918); and C. E. Vaughan, *Studies in the History of Political Philosophy before and after Rousseau* (Manchester, 1939), Vol. I, Chap. IV (pp. 130–203). A. H. Maclean, "George Lawson and John Locke," *Cambridge Historical Journal,* IX, No. 1 (1947), 69–77, traces Locke's main political ideas to Lawson, the forgotten author of a liberal treatise on politics, *Politica sacra et civilis,* published in 1660, and concludes that the "most highly characteristic conceptions and arguments of Locke's second treatise *Of Government* had received a formally complete expression in England as early as the year 1660" (p. 77).

► LOCKE, JOHN, *Essays on the Law of Nature* (trans. from the Latin and ed. by W. von Leyden, Oxford, 1954). Contains both the original Latin text and the English translation, published in this volume for the first time. A long introduction (pp. 1–92) by von Leyden gives new information on Locke's early life during which his essays on the law of nature were written, and also relates these early essays to his later chief philosophical and political writings. See also Leo Strauss, "Locke's Doctrine of Natural Law," *American Political Science Review,* LII (June, 1958), 490–501, for a brief appraisal of Locke's concept of natural law in the light of von Leyden's edition of Locke's *Essays on the Law of Nature.*

► LOUGH, JOHN (ed.), *Locke's Travels in France,* 1675–1679 (Cambridge, 1953). Taken from Locke's diaries, letters, and other papers, much of the material in this volume is being published for the first time. Locke's extensive travels in France reveal not only his character and personality, but also contribute to a better understanding of his intellectual growth. For a more detailed study of Locke's intellectual relations with France, see Gabriel D. Bonno, *Les relations intellectuelles de Locke avec la France* (Berkeley, 1955).

► O'CONNOR, D. J., *John Locke* (Penguin Books, Baltimore, 1952). Provides an introduction into the life and thought of Locke in clear and concise language.

► READ, CONYERS (ed.), *The Constitution Reconsidered* (New York, 1938). Contains papers by Charles McIlwain, Gaetano Salvemini, Charles A. Beard, Walton H. Hamilton, and others. R. M. MacIver, "European Doctrines and the Constitution" (pp. 51–61), discusses the influence of Locke. See also Carl Becker, *The Declaration of Independence* (New York, 1922), pp. 24–79, and Edward S. Corwin, *Liberty against Government* (Baton Rouge, 1948), who concludes his analysis of Locke with the statement that "Locke's is the last great name in the tradition of Liberty against Government that is common to our own country and England" (p. 51).

► RUSSELL, BERTRAND, *Philosophy and Politics* (London, 1947). Russell considers empiricism the only philosophy that can be a theoretical justification of democracy: "Locke, who may be regarded, so far as the modern world is concerned, as the founder of empiricism, makes it clear how closely this is connected with his views on liberty and toleration and with his opposition to absolute monarchy" (p. 20). Russell concludes that, "in our own day as in the time of Locke, empiricist Liberalism (which is not incompatible with *democratic socialism*) is the only philosophy that can be adopted by a man who, on the one hand, demands some scientific evidence for his beliefs, and, on the other hand, desires human happiness more than the prevalence of this or that party or creed" (p. 27).

► SIMON, WALTER M., "John Locke: Philosophy and Political Theory," *American*

Political Science Review, XLV (June, 1951), 386–399. Examines the consistency between Locke's general philosophy, particularly his theory of knowledge, and his political theory. Contrary to many other students of Locke who perceive a serious, and perhaps unbridgeable, gap between his general philosophy based on empiricism and his political theory based on natural law, Simon argues that, apart from discrepancies on a few less important points "Locke's major philosophical doctrines find their approximate counterparts in his political theory" (p. 397).

► SORLEY, W. R., A History of English Philosophy (Cambridge, 1937). Chap. VI (pp. 104–131), on Locke, contains a brief account of his life, philosophy, and political thought. The author begins the appraisal of Locke as follows: "John Locke may be regarded as, on the whole, the most important figure in English philosophy. Others excelled him in genius; he had not the comprehensive grasp of Hobbes, or the speculative originality of Berkeley, or the subtlety of Hume; but he was surpassed by none in candour, sagacity, and shrewdness" (p. 104). See also Rupert Lodge, The Great

Thinkers (London, 1949), Chap. VII (pp. 169–205); George Santayana, Some Turns of Thought in Modern Philosophy (Cambridge, 1934), pp. 1–47; Edward Tagart, Locke's Writings and Philosophy (London, 1855); and James McCosh, Locke's Theory of Knowledge (New York, 1884).

► TREVELYAN, GEORGE MACAULAY, The English Revolution, 1688–1689 (London, 1938). Important for the understanding of Locke's background. See also G. N. Clark, The Later Stuarts, 1660–1714 (Oxford, 1934).

► WELDON, T. D., States and Morals (London, 1946). The author of this suggestive book divides all theories of the state into two groups: "Some define it as a kind of organism, others as a kind of machine" (p. 26). Locke falls into the latter category (pp. 122–147).

► YOLTON, JOHN M., John Locke and the Way of Ideas (London, 1956). Analyzes Locke's theory of knowledge and its impact on ethics and religion in the seventeenth and eighteenth centuries. See also Alfred Klemmt, John Locke: Theoretische Philosophie (Meisenheim, 1952), on Locke's general framework of thought.

Chapter 16

Montesquieu

► CABEEN, DAVID C., Montesquieu: A Bibliography (New York, 1947). An annotated bibliography of books and articles (87 pp.).

► CARCASSONNE, E., Montesquieu et le problème de la constitution française au XVIIIe siècle (Paris, 1927). See also Joseph Dedieu, Montesquieu et la tradition politique anglaise en France (Paris, 1909); Adolphe Franck, Réformateurs et publicistes de l'Europe: dix-huitième siècle (Paris, 1893), Book III (pp. 133–283); Emile Faguet, La politique comparée de Montes-

quieu, Rousseau et Voltaire (Paris, 1902); Maxime Leroy, Histoire des idées sociales en France: de Montesquieu à Robespierre (Paris, 1946), Chap. IV (pp. 92–131); "Retour à Montesquieu," Revue Hommes et Mondes, VII (November, 1948), 408–419; Henri Sée, Les idées politiques en France au XVIIIe siècle (Paris, 1920); Léon Brunschvicg, Le progrès de la conscience dans la philosophie occidentale (Paris, 1927), II, 489–501; and Jean-Jacques Chevallier, Les grandes oeuvres politiques de Machiavel à nos jours (Paris,

1949), pp. 100–141. Paul Janet, *Histoire de la science politique*, 2 vols., 4th ed. (Paris, 1913), starts his appraisal of Montesquieu as follows: "The *Spirit of Laws* is, without any doubt, the greatest book of the eighteenth century; in the history of political science, the only work which is comparable (I hardly dare say superior) to it in breadth of plan, wealth of facts, freedom of investigations, and force of principles, is Aristotle's *Politics*" (II, 322).

▶ CATTELAIN, FERNAND, *Étude sur l'influence de Montesquieu dans les constitutions américaines* (Besançon, 1927). See also H. Knust, *Montesquieu und die Verfassungen der Vereinigten Staaten von Amerika* (Munich–Berlin, 1922). Both contain bibliographies.

▶ COLLINS, J. CHURTON, *Voltaire, Montesquieu and Rousseau in England* (London, 1908). The section on Montesquieu's stay in England is on pp. 117–181. In England Montesquieu "perceived and understood what liberty meant, intellectually, morally, politically, socially. He saw it in its ugliness, he saw it in its beauty" (p. 178).

▶ DURKEIM, ÉMILE, *Montesquieu et Rousseau: précurseurs de la sociologie* (Paris, 1953). Durkheim, one of the founders of modern sociology, argues that Montesquieu established for the first time "the fundamental principles of social science" (p. 110). Both the concepts of "social type" and "social law" were first developed by Montesquieu. For a more detailed analysis of Montesquieu's contribution to sociology in general and to political sociology in particular, see also Sergio Cotta, *Montesquieu e la scienza della società* (Turin, 1953).

▶ EHRLICH, EUGEN, "Montesquieu and Sociological Jurisprudence," *Harvard Law Review*, XXIX (April, 1916), 582–600. Analyzes the *Spirit of Laws* as the "first attempt to fashion a sociology of law" (p. 583).

▶ FLETCHER, F. T. H., *Montesquieu and English Politics (1750–1800)* (London, 1939). Unlike most studies on Montesquieu, which stress his indebtedness to England, the author traces the influence of Montes-

quieu on English political thought, particularly in the half century following the publication of the *Spirit of the Laws*. The end of this period is filled with the drama of the French Revolution, and the author notes that Montesquieu was used more by British conservative writers who opposed the French Revolution than by radical and liberal writers.

▶ HOLDSWORTH, W. S., "The Conventions of the Eighteenth Century Constitution," *Iowa Law Review*, XVII (January, 1932), 161–180. In this important study the author points out that the "conventions of the eighteenth century were directed to secure the maintenance of a system of divided powers and of checks and balances. The conventions of the nineteenth and twentieth centuries are directed to secure the political predominance of the House of Commons" (p. 163). King, Lords, and Commons were independent of one another, and it was from this constitution that Montesquieu deduced his view of English politics and of the doctrine of separation of powers. It must therefore be admitted "that there is an element of truth in Montesquieu's analysis. Independent benches of judges did administer a supreme law. The units of government were divided. Each had its independent autonomous powers that it could use freely, subject only to the supreme law administered by the independent benches of judges. The main faults of Montesquieu's theory were that it exaggerated the sharpness of the separation" (p. 165). In conclusion, Holdsworth accepts the view of another conservative writer, Sir Henry Maine, that "the stability and the success of the American Constitution were due in part to the fact that its framers adopted and adapted large parts of the British constitution as it existed between the years 1760 and 1787" (p. 180).

▶ KLEMPERER, VICTOR, *Montesquieu*, 2 vols. (Heidelberg, 1914–1915). Interprets Montesquieu's work as a work of art and poetry. Walter Struck, *Montesquieu als Politiker* (Berlin, 1933), seeks to demonstrate that Montesquieu's contribution to

political science has been vastly overrated, partly because of its practical influence, and partly because of the "silent conspiracy" (p. 325) of French students and biographers of Montesquieu, who have done their best to build him up as a great political thinker for the greater glory of France. The book is useful for the large collection of unfavorable comments on Montesquieu, gathered from many sources. See also Oskar Ewald, *Französische Aufklärungsphilosophie* (Munich, 1924), for an analysis of Montesquieu's thought in relation to the French Enlightenment (pp. 45–53), and Theodor Pietsch, *Über das Verhältnis der politischen Theorie Locke's zu Montesquieu's Lehre von der Theilung der Gewalten* (Breslau, 1887). An interesting case study of Montesquieu's influence on German liberalism will be found in Arthur Fickert, *Montesquieus und Rousseaus Einfluss auf den vormärzlichen Liberalismus Badens* (Leipziger Historische Abhandlungen, Vol. XXXVII, Leipzig, 1914).
► LEVIN, LAWRENCE MEYER, *The Political Doctrine of Montesquieu's Esprit des Lois: Its Classical Background* (New York, 1936). Contains an extensive bibliography (pp. 331–359). See also Gilbert Chinard, "Montesquieu's Historical Pessimism," in *Studies in the History of Culture* (Menasha, Wis., 1942), pp. 161–172, and Franz Neumann's penetrating introduction to the *Spirit of the Laws* (Hafner Library of Classics, New York, 1949).
► MARTIN, KINGSLEY, *French Liberal Thought in the Eighteenth Century*, 2nd ed. (London, 1954). The best general introduction into the political aspects of the Age of Reason. Chap. VI (pp. 147–169) is on Montesquieu. His "constitutional theory was based on Newtonian physics. In his early work he appears to have had a firmer grasp of the organic idea of the State than any other eighteenth-century writer, but his final political theory, in which each power is separate and related to the others only by a system of checks and balances, is entirely mechanical. The whole phraseology and conception is taken from mechanics: the State is a vast piece of engineering in which each

joist is kept in place and made to do its work by an exact calculation of strains and stresses, held in place by a balance here, itself checking another joist, correctly attached and related to its neighbor. Since there is no animating principle, no directing head or organic life, the result would seem to be a motionless equilibrium" (p. 166). See also Harold J. Laski, "The Age of Reason," in F. J. C. Hearnshaw (ed.), *The Social and Political Ideas of Some Great French Thinkers of the Age of Reason* (London, 1930), pp. 9–38, for a brief and brilliant account of the period, and A. J. Grant, "Montesquieu," *ibid.*, pp. 114–135.
► MORGAN, CHARLES, *The Liberty of Thought and the Separation of Powers* (The Zaharoff Lecture for 1948, Oxford, 1948). A reaffirmation of Montesquieu and the doctrine of the separation of powers. Democracy has not solved the issue with which Montesquieu was concerned: "Unchecked power is no less tyranny because someone has voted for it" (p. 17). The concentration of power in the House of Commons, and, more recently, in the hands of the cabinet, alarms Morgan: "By thus flouting every principle of balance for which Montesquieu stood and upon which our own Revolution Settlement was based, we have paved the way that leads from Moscow to Prague and from Prague to London. It is time that Liberty rebuild her barricades" (p. 18). See also Sir Courtenay Ilbert, *Montesquieu* (The Romanes Lecture 1904, Oxford, 1904), who writes on Montesquieu's central doctrine—the relativity of laws—as follows: "His doctrine of the relativity of laws, which is the foundation of enlightened conservatism, and has been used in defense of much conservatism which is not enlightened, is not a sufficient foundation for a constructive system, but was an admirable starting-point for a man whose primary interest lay in observing and comparing different institutions and drawing inferences from their similarities and diversities" (p. 27). The predominantly conservative influence of Montesquieu is more fully analyzed in C. E. Vaughan, *Studies in the History of*

Political Philosophy before and after Rousseau (Manchester, 1939), I, 253–302.

▶ SOREL, ALBERT, *Montesquieu* (Chicago, 1888). Provides, in concise form, a readable and stimulating introduction to Montesquieu's life and work. A fuller account will be found in Louis Vian, *Histoire de Montesquieu: sa vie et ses oeuvres* (Paris, 1878). See also Bernard Groethuysen, *Philosophie de la Révolution française* (Paris, 1956), the first section of which is on Montesquieu (pp. 11–77).

Chapter 17

Rousseau

▶ BOSANQUET, BERNARD, *The Philosophical Theory of the State* (London, 1920). Most of the book deals either with Rousseau directly or with the issues suggested by the problem of the General Will. See also T. H. Green, *Principles of Political Obligation* (London–New York, 1917), pp. 80–92.

▶ BOUCHARD, MARCEL, *L'Académie de Dijon et le premier Discours de Rousseau* (Paris, 1950). The author, Rector of the University of Dijon, describes the background and circumstances of the Academy of Dijon in 1750, from which Rousseau received the first prize for his *Discourse on the Sciences and Arts* in a public contest. It was this award by the Academy of Dijon in 1750 that catapulted Rousseau from obscurity into fame. In addition to new data on Rousseau's early life, the book provides a vivid picture of the Age of Reason in a provincial French town.

▶ CASSIRER, ERNST, *The Question of Jean-Jacques Rousseau* (New York, 1954). One of the most searching philosophical analyses of Rousseau's ethical and political ideas, his views on man and nature, and the originality of his thought.

▶ CHAPMAN, JOHN W., *Rousseau—Totalitarian or Liberal?* (New York, 1956). The author strongly affirms the liberal character of Rousseau's thought. Yet Rousseau's liberalism is closer to modern than to classical liberalism, for "both Rousseau and the modern liberals repudiate the atomism of classical liberal democratic theory" (p. 143).

▶ COBBAN, ALFRED, *Rousseau and the Modern State* (London, 1934). Interprets Rousseau mainly in terms of individualism: "Even when he exalts the community and appears to demand the sacrifice of the individual, it is because a certain voluntary identification of the individual with the community of which he is a member seems to him necessary for his moral well-being. But since he starts from the individual and not from the community he definitely envisages the moral end in terms of individuals, and takes all political and social organizations, right up to the national community itself, as at best means, even if necessary ones" (p. 240). Summarizing Rousseau's position in the history of political thought, Cobban says that the "error of liberal Europe was its attempt to attain its ideal by ignoring the actual, and hard facts have avenged themselves ruthlessly. It was the virtue of Rousseau to have been able to give something like their due to both factors in the social problem, to the individual as well as to the communal aspect of the truth" (p. 251). See also Kingsley Martin, *French Liberal Thought in the Eighteenth Century*, 2nd ed. (London, 1954), pp. 192–219; F. J. C. Hearnshaw, "Rousseau," in the symposium volume edited by himself, *The Social and Political Ideas of Some Great French Thinkers of the Age of Reason*

(London, 1930), pp. 168–193; and J. W. Gough, *The Social Contract,* 2nd ed. (Oxford, 1957), pp. 164–174.

► COLLINS, J. CHURTON, *Voltaire, Montesquieu and Rousseau in England* (London, 1908). Rousseau was a refugee in England between January 1766 and May 1767. Unlike Voltaire and Montesquieu, Rousseau felt thoroughly miserable in England, though treated with kindliness and consideration by his many friends and admirers there. He never learned the English language and developed little understanding for British institutions (pp. 182–271). A full account of Rousseau's stay in England will be found in Louis-John Courtois, *Le séjour de Jean-Jacques Rousseau en Angleterre (1766–1767)* (Lausanne, 1911). The most detailed analysis of Rousseau's impact on eighteenth-century England is Henri Roddier, *J.-J. Rousseau en Angleterre au XVIIIe siècle* (Paris, 1950).

► GLUM, FRIEDRICH, *Jean Jacques Rousseau: Religion und Staat* (Stuttgart, 1956). The author argues that Rousseau's political philosophy "does not belong to the Age of Enlightenment, but is related to the philosophy of Christian natural law before Spinoza and Hobbes, and that he continued the legacy of Plato and Augustine, and even of Thomas Aquinas" (p. 277). Glum calls Rousseau "the last representative of Christian natural law" (*ibid.*). The last chapter of the book surveys the varying interpretations of Rousseau in the principal western countries (pp. 298–411). See also Paul Sakman, *J.-J. Rousseau* (Berlin, 1913); Paul Hensel, *Rousseau* (Leipzig–Berlin, 1919); and F. Eppensteiner, *Rousseaus Einfluss auf die vorrevolutionären Flugschriften und den Ausbruch der Revolution* (Tubingen, 1914).

► GREEN, F. C., *Rousseau and the Idea of Progress* (Oxford, 1950). Rousseau's doctrine of the return to nature does not imply the "crazy notion of reversing the march of civilization," but means that we must "return to the basic human values which are now in danger of being obliterated by the wrong kind of civilization and which are perpetuated by a system of education based on a false idea of what man is and what he needs for his happiness" (p. 17). See also Green's full-length biography of Rousseau, *Jean-Jacques Rousseau: A Critical Study of His Life and Writings* (Cambridge, 1955), one of the best works of its kind in English.

► GROETHUYSEN, BERNARD, *Jean-Jacques Rousseau* (Paris, 1949). Stresses the concept of equality in Rousseau's thought. Whereas in the Christian view equality means essentially equality before suffering and death, for Rousseau it means equality before life. On the impact of Rousseau on the French Revolution, see Groethuysen's *Philosophie de la Révolution française* (Paris, 1956), particularly pp. 171–215. The relation of Rousseau and Napoleon is discussed in F. G. Healey, *Rousseau et Napoléon* (Geneva–Paris, 1957). The author states that "Napoleon first regarded Rousseau as his oracle and master; later, his ambition, his interest, and what he sincerely viewed as the interest of France no longer agreed with Rousseau's ideas, and philosophical speculations ceased to attract Napoleon" (p. 57).

► HENDEL, CHARLES WILLIAM, *Rousseau: Moralist,* 2 vols. (New York, 1934). A philosophical analysis of the evolution of Rousseau's thought. See also Harold Höffding, *Jean Jacques Rousseau and His Philosophy* (New Haven, 1930), and Albert Schinz, *Jean Jacques Rousseau: A Forerunner of Pragmatism* (Chicago, 1909).

► JOSEPHSON, MATTHEW, *Jean Jacques Rousseau* (New York, 1931). A full-length biography, eminently readable, and giving due consideration to both Rouseau's life and thought. A useful bibliography (pp. 535–539) is appended.

► LASKI, HAROLD J., *The Danger of Obedience and Other Essays* (New York, 1930). Chap. VII, "A Portrait of Jean Jacques Rousseau" (pp. 178–206), is an interpretation of Rousseau's main ideas and their impact on modern political theory. His influence was in the direction of both individualism and collectivism, but "the latter aspect has been the more enduring" (pp. 196–197). Laski notes Rousseau's impact on Hegel and Marx, with whom, as with their disciples, "Rousseauism has essentially meant the sacrifice of the individual to an end beyond himself" (p. 197). See also Laski's *Studies in Law and Politics* (London, 1932), Chap. I, "The Age of Reason" pp. 13–37), and Chap. III, "The Socialist Tradition in the French Revolution" (pp. 66–103).

▶ LICHTENBERGER, ANDRÉ, *Le socialisme au XVIIIe siècle* (Paris, 1895). This classic on French socialism in the eighteenth century treats Rousseau and his disciples more extensively than has any other author (Chaps. V–VII, pp. 128–220), and Rousseau is considered the most important precursor of socialism in the eighteenth century. See also the article by the great French socialist leader, Jean Jaurès, on "Les idées politiques et sociales de J.-J. Rousseau," *Revue de Métaphysique et de Morale*, XX, No. 3 (1912), 371–381. The entire issue of the *Revue* is devoted to Rousseau on the occasion of the two-hundredth anniversary of his birth.

▶ MASSON, PIERRE M., *La religion de Jean-Jacques Rousseau*, 3 vols. (Paris, 1916). See also J. Gaberel, *Calvin et Rousseau* (Geneva, 1878); Jacques Maritain, *Jean-Jacques Rousseau et la pensée moderne* (Louvain, 1922); M. A. Bouvier, "Les idées religieuses de J.-J. Rousseau," in J. Braillard and others, *J.-J. Rousseau jugé par les genevois d'aujourd'hui* (Geneva, 1879), pp. 199–261; and Henri Guillemin, "L'homme selon Rousseau," *Annales Jean-Jacques Rousseau*, XXX (1943–1945), 7–26.

▶ MONDOLFO, RODOLFO, *Rousseau e la coscienza moderna* (Florence, 1954). Argues that both modern democracy and socialism are rooted in Rousseau's concepts of natural law, and that his idea of personality transcends individualism and collectivism. See also Paolo Atene, *Gian Giacomo Rousseau: la vita e le opere* (Genua, 1954).

▶ MORLEY, JOHN, *Rousseau*, 2 vols. (London–New York, 1896). A full, and very readable, account of the life and work of Rousseau, who is called the most directly revolutionary of all the speculative precursors of the French Revolution. The *Social Contract* is analyzed in Vol. II, Chap. III (pp. 119–196). See also Morley's *Diderot and the Encyclopedists*, 2 vols. (London–New York, 1897), for a general background of the intellectual movements in Rousseau's time. A brief discussion of Rousseau's relations with the Encyclopedists will be found in Lytton Strachey, *Books and Characters: French and English* (Phoenix Library, London, 1934), pp. 165–175.

▶ MOWAT, R. B., *Jean-Jacques Rousseau* (London, 1938). A full *Life*, written *con amore*, as the author says. See also C. E. Vuilliamy, *Rousseau* (London, 1931), and Francis Gribble, *Rousseau and the Women He Loved* (New York, 1908). The latter, broader than the title suggests, is a full-scale biography, centered around Rousseau's loves and friendships with women.

▶ ROUSSEAU, JEAN JACQUES, *Confessions* (1782–1789). Available in numerous English translations and indispensable to an appreciation of Rousseau's development and thought. The translation of the *Confessions* by J. M. Cohen (Penguin Books, Baltimore, 1953) is recommended.

▶ ————, *The Social Contract, and Discourses* (Everyman's Library, London–New York, 1947). The value of the volume is greatly enhanced by the inclusion of the three *Discourses* on the *Arts and Sciences*, *Origin of Inequality*, and *Political Economy*, because Rousseau's political thought cannot be properly understood from the *Social Contract* alone. The translation by G. D. H. Cole is admirable, and his introduction (pp. v–xli) a model of clarity and insight. Ernest Barker's discussion of Rousseau in his introduction to *Social Contract: Essays by Locke, Hume, and Rousseau* (New York, 1948) is brief but suggestive (pp. xxvii–xliv). J.-J. Rousseau, *Du contrat social* (Collection Oeuvres Immortelles, Geneva, 1947), is a (beautifully printed) edition of the original text, prefaced by an illuminating "Essai sur la politique de Rousseau," by

Bertrand de Jouvenel (pp. 13–160). The edition of *Du contrat social* by Maurice Halbwachs (Bibliothèque Philosophique, Paris, 1943) contains a scholarly introduction by the editor (pp. 5–50), and extensive commentaries following the text of each chapter.

▶ SCHINZ, ALBERT, *La pensée de Jean-Jacques Rousseau* (Paris, 1929). A detailed and scholarly inquiry into Rousseau's thought, emphasizing the tension between Romanticism and Calvinism in his moral and political ideas. See also Olivier Krafft, *La politique de Jean-Jacques Rousseau: aspects méconnus* (Paris, 1958); Jean Starobinski, *Jean-Jacques Rousseau: la transparence et l'obstacle* (Paris, 1958); Maxime Nemo, *L'homme nouveau: Jean-Jacques Rousseau* (Paris, 1957); Pierre Burgelin, *La philosophie de l'existence de Jean-Jacques Rousseau* (Paris, 1952); Jean Guéhenno, *Jean-Jacques*, 3 vols. (Paris, 1948–1952); Daniel Mornet, *Rousseau: l'homme et l'oeuvre* (Paris, 1950); René Gerin, *J.-J. Rousseau* (Paris, 1930); John Charpentier, *Jean-Jacques Rousseau, ou le démocrate par dépit* (Paris, 1931); Joseph Fabre, *Jean-Jacques Rousseau* (Paris, 1912); Emile Faguet, *La politique comparée de Montesquieu, Rousseau et Voltaire* (Paris, 1902); C. Estienne, *Essai sur les oeuvres de J.-J. Rousseau* (Paris, 1858); Maxime Leroy, *Histoire des idées sociales en France de Montesquieu à Robespierre* (Paris, 1946), pp. 132–229; Jean-Jacques Chevallier, *Les grandes oeuvres politiques de Machiavel à nos jours* (Paris, 1949), pp. 142–173; Henri Sée, *Les idées politiques en France au XVIIIe siècle* (Paris, 1920), pp. 105–136; and Adolphe Franck, *Réformateurs et publicistes de l'Europe: dix-huitième siècle* (Paris, 1893), pp. 285–379.

▶ TALMON, J. L., *The Origins of Totalitarian Democracy* (London, 1952). The author's main thesis is that the eighteenth century saw the birth of two contradictory types of democracy: "empirical liberal democracy" and "Messianic totalitarian democracy." Rousseau is considered perhaps the most important single source of totalitarian democracy, particularly by marrying the concept of the general will with that of popular sovereignty (p. 43). For a similar juxtaposition of Rousseau's popular sovereignty and eighteenth-century English liberalism see also Guido de Ruggiero, *The History of European Liberalism* (Beacon Paperbacks, Boston, 1959), particularly the Introduction on "The Eighteenth Century" (pp. 1–90). Ruggiero writes that the attributes of Rousseau's concept of sovereignty "are the exact opposite of the principles of guarantism as derived from the English Constitution" (p. 62).

▶ VAUGHAN, CHARLES E., *The Political Writings of Jean Jacques Rousseau*, 2 vols. (Cambridge, 1915). The most complete collection of all political writings of Rousseau (in French). The introduction in the first volume (pp. 1–117) gives a detailed interpretation of the development of Rousseau's political thought and maintains the thesis that Rousseau, "far from supporting the individualist theory, is its most powerful assailant" (p. 2). See also Vaughan's introduction to his edition of Rousseau's *Contrat Social* (Manchester–London–New York, 1918), pp. xi–lxxii.

▶ VOSSLER, OTTO, *Der Nationalgedanke von Rousseau bis Ranke* (Munich–Berlin, 1937). Chap. II (pp. 21–53) is on Rousseau, who is considered a "conscious, pronounced, proud Genevan nationalist" (p. 50), the "first pioneer of nationalism" (p. 53). See also Franz Pahlmann, *Mensch und Staat bei Rousseau* (Berlin, 1939); and Justus Hashagen, "Zur Deutung Rousseaus," *Historische Zeitschrift*, CXLVIII, No. 2 (1933), 229–247.

▶ WRIGHT, ERNEST HUNTER, *The Meaning of Rousseau* (London, 1929). The central theme of the book is Rousseau's concept of nature, and its four chapters deal with natural man, natural education, natural society, and natural religion. The conclusion reached is that "the natural man is not our first brute forbear, but the last man whom we are travelling on to be" (p. 164). See also Henry V. S. Ogden, "The Antithesis of Nature and Art, and Rousseau's Rejection

Chapter 18

Burke

▶ BARKER, ERNEST, *Essays on Government* (Oxford, 1945). Chaps. VI and VII (pp. 155–235) are illuminating studies on "Burke and His Bristol Constituency," and "Burke and the French Revolution." See also C. E. Vaughan, *Studies in the History of Political Philosophy before and after Rousseau* (Manchester, 1939), II, 1–63.

▶ BRAUNE, FRIEDA, *Edmund Burke in Deutschland* (Heidelberger Abhandlungen zur mittleren und neueren Geschichte, No. 50, Heidelberg, 1917). Traces the contribution of Burke to the growth of German conservatism and political romanticism in the late eighteenth and early nineteenth centuries. Whereas Burke has been hailed in England not only by conservatives but also by liberals and socialists, his influence in Germany—and it was considerable—has been felt mainly in antidemocratic circles. See also Friedrich Meusel, *Edmund Burke und die französische Revolution* (Berlin, 1913); Hans Barth, *Fluten und Dämme* (Zurich, 1943), pp. 39–56; and Otto Vossler, *Der Nationalgedanke von Rousseau bis Ranke* (Munich–Berlin, 1937), pp. 54–76. Vossler calls Burke "the founder of conservative thought" (p. 54). The impact of Burke on German romanticism and conservatism is succinctly presented in Reinhold Aris, *History of Political Thought in Germany, 1789–1815* (London, 1936), pp. 251–265.

▶ BUTLER, GEOFFREY G., *The Tory Tradition: Bolingbroke—Burke—Disraeli—Salisbury* (London, 1914). Chap. II (pp. 30–59) deals with Burke as a principal source of British Conservatism. Burke "must be the

of the Theory of Natural Rights," *American Political Science Review*, XXXII (August, 1938), 643–654.

bible of pure and reformed Conservatism, which alone can oust the misguided if generous proposals of the modern Radicals, and meet and solve the problems which have given those proposals motive force" (p. 59).

▶ COBBAN, ALFRED, *Edmund Burke and the Revolt against the Eighteenth Century* (London, 1929). Chaps. II–IV (pp. 37–132) are devoted to Burke. Cobban emphasizes Burke's originality in relation to the problem of nationality: "He saw, long before most of his contemporaries, the power and rights of that force of national sentiment which eighteenth-century theorists and politicians had conspired to ignore and trample on. The right of a subject nation to freedom just because it *was* a nation was a new idea in political thought. Though the fact had been there for centuries, Burke has the honor of first stating in definite form the theory of nationality" (p. 130).

▶ COPELAND, THOMAS W., *Our Eminent Friend Edmund Burke: Six Essays* (New Haven, 1949). Treats various phases of Burke's life and activities. The most interesting essay is Chap. V, "Burke, Paine, and Jefferson" (pp. 146–182).

▶ FAY, C. R., *Burke and Adam Smith* (Belfast, 1956). Analyzes the personal relations and intellectual affinities between Burke and Adam Smith. An ardent believer in custom, authority, and the organic conception in politics, Burke was an emphatic follower of *laissez-faire* in economics. In fact, Fay writes that Burke's *Thoughts and Details on Scarcity* (1795) was even more effective than Adam Smith's *Wealth of Nations* (1776) in helping Cobden and the

Anti-Corn League Law League "in their fight for free food" (p. 25) in the first half of the nineteenth century.

▶ HAZLITT, WILLIAM, *Political Essays, with Sketches of Public Characters* (London, 1819). Hazlitt, a radical democrat and one of the leading English essayists of the early nineteenth century, devotes two essays to the "Character of Mr. Burke" (pp. 264–269 and pp. 361–377), the first written in 1817 and the second in 1807. Hazlitt concedes that Burke is "the most poetical of our prose writers" (p. 269), but that his theory of government is constructed "not on rational, but on picturesque and fanciful principles; as if a king's crown were a painted gewgaw, to be looked at on gala-days; titles an empty sound to please the ear; and the whole order of society a theatrical procession" (p. 267).

▶ KIRK, RUSSELL, *The Conservative Mind: From Burke to Santayana* (Chicago, 1953). Chap. II (pp. 11–61) is on Burke. The author states that "Burke's ideas provided the defenses of conservatism, on a great scale, that still stand and are not liable to fall in our time" (p. 61). As in the eighteenth century, "our age, too, seems to be groping for certain of the ideas which Burke's inspiration formed into a system of social preservation" (*ibid.*).

▶ LASKI, HAROLD J., *Political Thought in England: from Locke to Bentham* (Home University Library, London, 1937). Chap. VI (pp. 165–215) is on Burke. Laski's conclusion is that "there is hardly a greater figure in the history of political thought in England" (p. 214). Similar, and even more lyrical, expressions are interesting evidence of the hold that the great conservative writer has over a socialist like Laski, and the whole chapter is highly revealing of the political and intellectual climate of England.

▶ MACCUNN, JOHN, *The Political Philosophy of Burke* (London, 1913). A fair and well-balanced analysis of Burke's views on major issues of political philosophy, and one of the most useful works of its kind. In dealing with Burke's attitude on freedom of discussion and religious toleration (Chap.

VII, pp. 104–121), the author says that "no man, it is safe to say, ever discussed politics as he did, none so persistently, none with such eloquence and penetration, none with more determination to go to the root of the matter" (p. 105). This did not prevent Burke from opposing untrammeled freedom in politics and religion: "Few great thinkers, indeed, have gone so far in using incomparable powers of discussion in proving that toleration, as well as discussion, ought to have its limits" (p. 111). See also F. J. C. Hearnshaw, "Edmund Burke," in the work edited by himself, *The Social and Political Ideas of Some Representative Thinkers of the Revolutionary Era* (London, 1931), pp. 72–99; Ivor Brown, *English Political Theory* (London, 1929), pp. 68–87; and R. H. S. Crossman, *Government and the Governed* (London, 1939), pp. 84–86, 117–125. Both Crossman and Brown devote more space to Paine than to Burke in dealing with the English response to the French Revolution, and Crossman calls Paine the "ablest pamphleteer" (p. 117) of the French Revolution.

▶ MAGNUS, PHILIP, *Edmund Burke: A Life* (London, 1939). One of the best modern biographies, with illustrations and contemporary cartoons, and a Select Bibliography (pp. 351–355). The most frequently quoted British statesman, "Burke's political outlook was not shared by all Englishmen, but it was the outlook of the dominant and most characteristic section of the English people. The instinctive political empiricism of the average Englishman now bears for all time the impress of the character and personality of Edmund Burke. It was Burke's genius which first gave shape and direction to what formerly had been little more than an inchoate mass of ideas, floating in the English mind. This was Burke's greatest achievement, and his legacy to his country" (p. 300). See also the following biographies: Robert H. Murray, *Edmund Burke: A Biography* (Oxford, 1931); Bertram Newman, *Edmund Burke* (London, 1927); Thomas Macknight, *History of the Life and Times of Edmund Burke,* 3 vols.

(London, 1858–1860); Sir James Prior, *A Life of Edmund Burke,* 5th ed. (London, 1854, reprinted 1891); and Robert Bisset, *The Life of Edmund Burke,* 2 vols. (London, 1800).

▶ MORLEY, JOHN VISCOUNT, *Burke* (London, 1923). Viscount Morley (1838–1923) was a lifelong Liberal, and—prior to World War I—a member of several Liberal cabinets in Britain. Appraising Burke's place in British history, he concurs with Macaulay, who called him the greatest man in English literature since Milton, and writes as follows: "Opinion is slowly, but without reaction, settling down to the verdict that Burke is one of the abiding names in our history; not because he either saved Europe or destroyed the Whig party, but because he added to the permanent considerations of wise political thought, and to the maxims of wise practice in great affairs, and because he imprints himself upon us with a magnificence and elevation of expression that places him among the highest masters of literature, in one of its highest and most commanding senses" (p. 3). On the other hand, Burke's "passion appears hopelessly fatal to success in the pursuit of Truth, who does not usually reveal herself to followers thus inflamed" (pp. 3–4).

▶ PARKIN, CHARLES, *The Moral Basis of Burke's Political Thought* (Cambridge, 1956). Starting from Burke's own thesis that "the principles of true politics are those of morality enlarged," the author examines the precise nature of Burke's moral principles. He concludes as follows: "The source of moral truth, for Burke, is an eternal moral order which is immanent in the historical process. His morality rests therefore on a religious perception. Man is by constitution a religious animal, and religion must be the foundation of civil society" (p. 131).

▶ ROSSITER, CLINTON, *Conservatism in America* (New York, 1955). Of particular interest is Chap. VI (pp. 213–242), in which the author brilliantly shows the similarities and differences between American and classical conservatism. As to the importance of Burke, Rossiter writes that Burke's *Reflections on the Revolution in France* (1790) "is rightly considered the first and greatest statement of consciously conservative principles" (p. 16).

▶ STANLIS, PETER J., *Edmund Burke and the Natural Law* (Ann Arbor, 1958). The thesis of the work is that "far from being an enemy of natural law, Burke was one of the most eloquent and profound defenders of natural law morality and politics in Western civilization" (p. xi). Emphasizing the religious roots of Burke's thought, the author calls Burke "the foremost modern Christian humanist in politics because he saw the world and the nature of man through the revelations of Christianity and the right reason of natural law" (p. 84). For a more moderate view of linking Burke with the tradition of natural law see Leo Strauss, *Natural Right and History* (Chicago, 1953), pp. 294–323.

▶ STEPHEN, LESLIE, *History of English Thought in the Eighteenth Century,* 2 vols. (London, 1902). The main discussion of Burke is in Vol. II, Chap. IX (pp. 219–252). The author, an emphatic Liberal, begins his analysis of Burke with these words: "No English writer has received, or has deserved, more splendid panegyrics than Burke" (II, 219).

▶ WILSON, WOODROW, "Edmund Burke and the French Revolution," *Century Magazine,* LXII (September, 1901), 784–792. Wilson (then Professor of Jurisprudence and Politics at Princeton University) states first that the Revolution "was the salvation of France, and perhaps of Europe too" (p. 784), but he concludes that Burke "was right, and was himself, when he sought to keep the French infection out of England" (p. 792). See also Annie Marion Osborn, *Rousseau and Burke* (London–New York, 1940), and Jacques Barzun, *Romanticism and the Modern Ego* (Boston, 1943), pp. 41 ff.

▶ YOUNG, G. M., *Burke* (Annual Lecture on a Master Mind, London, 1943). Reprinted in *Proceedings of the British Academy,* XXIX (1943), 19–36. On Burke's fundamental conflict with the philosophy of the French Revolution, Young has this to say: "The Revolution—or say plainly Rousseau—was a challenge not to prescription only, but to the whole body of experience, consideration, and observation on which Burke's natural Politic was built. To this new philosophy, his limitations were meaningless, his co-ordinates were irrelevant: and

Chapter 19

Bentham

▶ ASHTON, T. S., *The Industrial Revolution, 1760–1830* (Home University Library, London–New York, 1948). A well-balanced, brief analysis of the Industrial Revolution and its impact on ideas and institutions, and useful for the understanding of the historical background of Utilitarianism. See also Paul Mantoux, *The Industrial Revolution in the Eighteenth Century* (London, 1928); J. L. Hammond and Barbara Hammond, *The Rise of Modern Industry*, 7th ed. (London, 1947); and E. L. Woodward, *The Age of Reform, 1815–1870* (Oxford, 1938).
▶ ATKINSON, CHARLES MILNER, *Jeremy Bentham: His Life and Work* (London, 1905). The author, a stipendiary magistrate in Leeds, emphasizes the contributions of Bentham to law and jurisprudence. An excellent account of Bentham's earlier years, up to the publication of the *Principles of Morals and Legislation* in 1789, will be found in *The Education of Jeremy Bentham*, by Charles Warren Everett, the foremost American student of Bentham (New York, 1931). Everett also discovered in Bentham's unpublished manuscripts two works, which he edited and published for the first time: *A Commentary on Commentaries* (Oxford, 1928), the original work on Blackstone, of which the *Fragment of Government*, published in 1776, was only a part. Everett's introduction contains, apart from an analysis of the *Commentary*, the first printed story of Bentham's love affair at the age of

man, as Burke saw him, conditioned by the Revolution Settlement and the processes of Party Government, the 400,000 whom he considered to be by leisure and instruction worth calling the people, were no more than a figment of aristocratic self-interest" (pp. 35–36). Written from a strongly conservative and pro-Burkean viewpoint.

twenty-seven. He fell deeply in love with a beautiful girl without money but could not marry her because of his father's strenuous objection (pp. 5–6). The second work, discovered by Everett, is Part II of the *Principles of Morals and Legislation*, it was published, with an introduction by Everett, under the title, *The Limits of Jurisprudence Defined* (New York, 1945).
▶ AYER, A. J., "The Principle of Utility," in George W. Keeton and Georg Schwarzenberger, *Jeremy Bentham and the Law: A Symposium* (London, 1948), pp. 245–259. A philosophical analysis of the principle of utility from the standpoint of logical positivism, by one of its leading British representatives. See also E. F. Carritt, *Ethical and Political Thinking* (Oxford, 1947), pp. 58–69; Wesley C. Mitchell, "Bentham's Felicific Calculus," *Political Science Quarterly*, XXXIII (June, 1918), 161–183; and Bertrand Russell, *Freedom and Organization, 1814–1914* (London, 1949), pp. 103–123, 131–140.
▶ BENTHAM, JEREMY, *A Fragment on Government* and *Introduction to the Principles of Morals and Legislation* (Blackwell's Political Texts, Oxford–New York, 1948). This convenient collection of Bentham's two most important writings on political theory contains a long introduction by the Editor, Wilfrid Harrison (pp. ix–lxvi). Harrison's main criticism of Bentham is as follows: "It is unfortunate that Bentham, a leader of the

attack on natural rights, could not extend his skepticism into the realm of economics. The natural identification of interests, eschewed in the political field, was accepted by him in the field of economics and the way was thus prepared for that separation of politics and economics which was nineteenth-century liberalism's greatest limitation" (pp. lxv–lxvi).

► COHEN, VICTOR, *Bentham* (Fabian Tract No. 211, London, 1927). English socialism, the author says, "owes an inestimable debt of gratitude to the almost mythical exponent of stern individualism" (p. 18). See also Harold J. Laski, "Jeremy Bentham," *New Statesman and Nation*, XXXV (February 21, 1948), 152; William Irvine, "Shaw, the Fabians, and the Utilitarians," *Journal of the History of Ideas*, VIII (April, 1947), 218–231; G. D. H. Cole, *Some Relations between Political and Economic Theory* (London, 1934), pp. 42–58, and *Socialist Economics* (London, 1950), pp. 28 ff.; Kerney M. Adams, "How the Benthamites Became Democrats," *Journal of Social Philosophy and Jurisprudence*, VII (January, 1942), 161–171; Hilda G. Lundin, *The Influence of Jeremy Bentham on English Democratic Development* (University of Iowa Studies in the Social Sciences, Vol. VII, No. 3, Iowa City, 1922); and Alfred T. Williams, *The Concept of Equality in the Writings of Rousseau, Bentham, and Kant* (New York, 1907), pp. 27–39. Guido de Ruggiero, *The History of European Liberalism* (Beacon Paperbacks, Boston, 1959), includes a section on Benthamism and Philosophic Radicalism (pp. 93–108), described as "the French Revolution working at a distance and disguised beneath the features of John Bull" (p. 106).

► DICEY, A. V., *Law and Public Opinion in England during the Nineteenth Century*, 2nd ed. (London, 1914). Lecture VI (pp. 126–210) is "The Period of Benthamism or Individualism" (1825–1870), and Lecture IX (pp. 303–310), "The Debt of Collectivism to Benthamism." Dicey says that the debt of democratic socialism to Benthamism is threefold: a legislative dogma—the principle of utility; a legislative instrument—the active use of parliamentary sovereignty; and a legislative tendency—the constant extension and improvement of the mechanism of government. See also Frederic William Maitland, *Collected Papers* (Cambridge, 1911), I, 112 ff., 146 ff.

► HALÉVY, ELIE, *The Growth of Philosophic Radicalism* (trans. Mary Morris, London, 1928). This is the most illuminating account of the Utilitarians, centered on Bentham. The author, the leading French authority on nineteenth-century England, has the advantage of looking at Utilitarianism from a broad European viewpoint, and he stresses the influence of French thought on Bentham, particularly in his youth. The volume contains the best bibliography of works by, and on, Bentham, compiled by C. W. Everett (pp. 522–546). For an interesting bibliographical study, see also Arnold Muirhead, "A Jeremy Bentham Collection," *The Library* (Fifth Series), I (June, 1946), 6–27.

► KEETON, GEORGE W., and GEORG SCHWARZENBERGER (eds.), *Jeremy Bentham and the Law: A Symposium* (London, 1948). In addition to legal subjects, the symposium also deals with broad political and philosophical issues. See also William Holdsworth, *Some Makers of the English Law* (Cambridge, 1938), pp. 248–256; John Forrest Dillon, "Bentham's Influence in the Reforms of the Nineteenth Century," in *Select Essays in Anglo-American Legal History* (Boston, 1907), I, 492–515; and H. A. Hollond, "Jeremy Bentham," *Cambridge Law Journal*, X (No. 1, 1948), 3–32.

► KRAUS, OSKAR, *Der Machtgedanke und die Friedensidee in der Philosophie der Engländer: Bacon und Bentham* (Leipzig, 1926). Part II is on Bentham as the "father of modern Utilitarianism and pacifism," seeking to vindicate Bentham against his traditional vituperation in German literature. Thus Werner Sombart, *Händler und Helden* (Munich–Leipzig, 1915), calls Bentham's principle of the greatest happiness of the greatest number a "vile (*hundsgemein*) 'ideal'" (p. 19), and represents Bentham as the most typical expression of British commercialism, as contrasted with the heroic spirit of the Germans.

► MILL, JOHN STUART, "Bentham," in *Dissertations and Discussions* (New York, 1882), I, 355–417, reprinted in F. R. Leavis (ed.), *Mill on Bentham and Coleridge* (London, 1950), pp. 39–98. Mill's testimony is particularly valuable, as he knew Bentham personally from early childhood, his father, James Mill, being one of Bentham's closest collaborators and disciples. Mill sees in Bentham, above all, "the great questioner of things established," who broke the yoke of authority by forcing every opinion received on tradition to give an account of itself: "Who, before Bentham (whatever controversies might exist on points of detail), dared to speak disrespectfully, in express terms, of the British Constitution or the English law?" (p. 357). Mill's main criticism of Bentham is want of imagination and failure to appreciate the role of feeling in human conduct: "Knowing so little of human feelings, he knew still less of the influences by which those feelings are formed: all the more subtle workings both of the mind upon itself, and of external things upon the mind, escaped him; and no one, probably, who, in a highly instructed age, ever attempted to give a rule to all human conduct, set out with a more limited conception either of the agencies by which human conduct *is*, or of those by which it *should* be, influenced" (p. 380). In his *Autobiography* (New York, 1924), Mill discusses his views of Bentham and Benthamism in numerous passages (pp. 5, 38–39, 45–50, 54–56, 73–80, 139).

► OGDEN, C. K., *Bentham's Theory of Fictions* (London–New York, 1932). Bentham is one of the founders of semantics, and his work is of direct relevance to the student of politics. The first part consists of Ogden's introduction (pp. ix–clii), the second is a collection of passages from Bentham's writings bearing on semantic problems (pp. 7–150). Ogden's introduction to his edition of Bentham's *Theory of Legislation* (London, 1931) succinctly summarizes the major

points of Bentham's political thought (pp. ix–li). See also Ogden's *Jeremy Bentham: 1832–2032* (London, 1932), containing the Bentham Centenary Lecture, delivered at University College, London, on June 6, 1932, as well as ten appendixes on various topics, including Bentham's views on the United States (pp. 88–93). Despite its brevity, Ogden's *Jeremy Bentham: 1832–2032* is one of the most brilliant appraisals of Bentham.

► PALMER, PAUL A., "Benthamism in England and America," *American Political Science Review*, XXXV (October, 1941), 855–871. Examines the reasons for Bentham's slight influence in the United States. In the opinion of the author, the Lockean tradition of social contract and natural law in the United States formed "an immovable obstacle" (p. 868) to the spread of Benthamism. See also Charles Warren Everett, "Bentham in the United States of America," in George W. Keeton and Georg Schwarzenberger (eds.), *Jeremy Bentham and the Law: A Symposium* (London, 1948), pp. 185–201. In the United States, Everett writes, "it is really only in the last twenty years that the entire climate in which government and courts have functioned has been avowedly utilitarian. The New Deal has been partly collectivist, but wholly Benthamic, for the most part without knowing it" (p. 199).

► PLAMENATZ, JOHN, *The English Utilitarians* (London, 1949). Chap. IV (pp. 59–84) of this thoughtful study, valuable both for its philosophical and historical observations, is on Bentham. John Stuart Mill's essay on *Utilitarianism* is appended (pp. 163–228). See also William L. Davidson, *Political Thought in England: The Utilitarians from Bentham to J. S. Mill* (Home University Library, London, 1935), pp. 7–113; Crane Brinton, *English Political Thought in the Nineteenth Century* (London, 1933), pp. 14–30; John MacCunn, *Six Radical Thinkers* (London, 1907), pp. 3–35; and Thomas Rawson Birks, *Modern Utilitarianism* (London, 1874), pp. 26–32, 107–178.

► STARK, W., "Liberty and Equality: or Jeremy Bentham as an Economist," *Economic Journal,* LI (April, 1941), 56–79, and LVI (December, 1946), 583–608. Bentham, the author says, "stands half-way between capitalism and communism. His aim was the combination of the justice of communism with the efficiency of capitalism: the union of equality in the chances of life with liberty in the pursuits of life" (p. 79). A searching analysis of Bentham's views in relation to economic laissez faire will be found in Jacob Viner, "Bentham and J. S. Mill: The Utilitarian Background," *American Economic Review,* XXXIX (March, 1949), 360–382. See also James Bonar, "In Memoriam Jeremy Bentham," *Economic History,* II (January, 1933), 536–552, and *Philosophy and Political Economy* (London, 1927), pp. 215–236.

► STEPHEN, LESLIE, *The English Utilitarians,* 3 vols. (London, 1900, reprinted, 1950). The first volume of this standard work is on Bentham. A "Note on Bentham's Writings" (pp. 319–326) gives a concise account of Bentham's literary career. The second volume of the *Utilitarians* is on James Mill,

the third on John Stuart Mill. See also David Baumgardt, *Bentham and the Ethics of Today* (Princeton, 1952).

► WALLAS, GRAHAM, *Men and Ideas* (London, 1940). The first two essays are "Bentham" and "Bentham as Political Inventor" (pp. 19–48); they belong to the most penetrating studies of his contributions to the theory and practice of government. In the "history of British political invention by far the greatest name will be that of Bentham, whether as inventor himself, or as having inspired by his suggestions, and by the example of his methods, the inventions of others" (p. 34). Illustrative of Bentham's impact on an early Fabian.

► WILLEY, BASIL, *Nineteenth Century Studies* (London, 1949). Chap. V (pp. 132–140) deals with some aspects of Bentham's ethical and religious views. For different interpretations, see J. M. Robertson, *A History of Freethought in the Nineteenth Century* (London, 1929), pp. 86 ff., 200 ff., and Alfred William Benn, *The History of English Rationalism in the Nineteenth Century* (London–New York, 1906), I, 285–325.

Chapter 20

The Dilemma of Democracy: Liberty and Equality

I. Tocqueville

► BARTH, HANS, *Fluten und Dämme: der philosophische Gedanke in der Politik* (Zurich, 1943). Contains a chapter, "Tocqueville and the Age of Revolutions" (pp. 111–123). See also Helmut Göring, *Tocqueville und die Demokratie* (Munich–Berlin, 1928), and Niklas Peter Barth, *Die Idee der Freiheit und der Demokratie bei Alexis de Tocqueville* (Aarau, 1953).

► LASKI, HAROLD J., "Alexis de Tocqueville and Democracy," in F. J. C. Hearnshaw (ed.), *The Social and Political Ideas*

of Some Representative Thinkers of the Victorian Age (London, 1933), Chap. V (pp. 100–115). Emphasizes Tocqueville as a precursor of Marx: "However different their ways of expression, however antagonistic the purposes they served, Tocqueville would, I suspect, have subscribed to a good deal of what we call the Marxian interpretation of history. Many of his conclusions bear a striking resemblance to those of *The Communist Manifesto;* with, of course, the important difference that what for Marx represented victory for Tocqueville represented defeat" (pp. 113–114).

▶ LEROY, MAXIME, "Alexis de Tocqueville," *Politica*, I (August, 1935), 393–424, reprinted in William Ebenstein, *Political Thought in Perspective* (New York, 1957), pp. 472–500. One of the most trenchant critical analyses of Tocqueville's political ideas. On his liberalism, the author writes as follows: "What kind of liberal was he? He regarded himself as being one according to a particular and original fashion. He was mistaken in this point; for he was one in the conservative spirit as were a number of his liberal friends. Tocqueville does not say liberty without understanding by it liberty and property" (p. 401). Concerning Tocqueville's faith in free associations as a counterweight to the power of the state, Leroy says that they have, like business and labor organizations, developed a concentration of interest and power that may become a threat to individual liberty: "It is no longer the isolated individual, thinking in isolation, according to Tocqueville's wish, who affects society, but coalitions born of democracy. But do not these groups destroy it?" (p. 408). A forceful restatement of some of Tocqueville's main arguments will be found in Bertrand de Jouvenel, *On Power* (New York, 1949).

▶ MARCEL, R. PIERRE, *Essai politique sur Alexis de Tocqueville* (Paris, 1910). See also Antoine Redier, *Comme disait M. de Tocqueville* (Paris, 1925); Jean-Jacques Chevallier, *Les grandes oeuvres politiques de Machiavel à nos jours* (Paris, 1949), pp. 221–249; Emile Faguet, *Politiques et moralistes du dix-neuvième siècle* (Paris, 1900), III, 65–114; and Paul Janet, "Alexis de Tocqueville et la science politique au XIXe siècle," *Revue des Deux Mondes*, XXXIV (July–August, 1861), 101–133.

▶ MATHEW, DAVID, *Acton: The Formative Years* (London, 1946). Chap. VI (pp. 86–98) analyzes the profound influence of Tocqueville on Lord Acton, one of the great liberal thinkers of the nineteenth century.

▶ MAYER, J. P., *Alexis de Tocqueville: A Biographical Essay in Political Science* (New York, 1940). The last chapter, IX, traces Tocqueville's impact on nineteenth- and twentieth-century political thought (pp. 172–191). A bibliography of the more important works is appended (pp. 213–215). See also Mayer's *Political Thought in France from Sieyès to Sorel* (London, 1943), pp. 61–67; Roger Soltau, *French Political Thought in the Nineteenth Century* (New Haven, 1931), pp. 50–56; and William J. Schlaerth (ed.), *Alexis de Tocqueville's Democracy in America: A Symposium* (Fordham University Studies, Burke Society Series, No. 1, New York, 1945).

▶ PIERSON, GEORGE WILSON, *Tocqueville and Beaumont in America* (New York, 1938). The definitive work on the subject. The first eight parts of the book tell the story of Tocqueville's experiences in the United States. Part IX gives a summary of how *Democracy in America* was written, and also analyzes its defects and enduring qualities (pp. 681–777). A detailed bibliography is appended (pp. 825–833). There is an abridged version, *Tocqueville in America* (Anchor Books, New York, 1959).

▶ SCHAPIRO, J. SALWYN, *Liberalism and the Challenge of Fascism: Social Forces in England and France (1815–1870)* (New York, 1949). In his discussion of "Alexis de Tocqueville, Pioneer of Democratic Liberalism in France" (pp. 290–307), the author concludes that Tocqueville was "an example of the tragedy of French liberalism, which since the French Revolution has waged unceasing war on two fronts: against reaction on the right and against revolution on the left" (p. 306). See also Guido de Ruggiero, *The History of European Liberalism* (Beacon Paperbacks, Boston, 1959), pp. 187–198, who calls Tocqueville "perhaps the greatest French writer of the nineteenth century" (p. 187), and James Bryce, *Studies in History and Jurisprudence* (Oxford, 1901), I, 381–429, who describes *Democracy in America* as "one of the few treatises on the philosophy of politics which has risen to the rank of a classic" (p. 381).

▶ SCHEMANN, L. (ed.), *Correspondence entre Alexis de Tocqueville et Arthur de Gobineau, 1843–1859*, 2nd ed. (Paris, 1909). Gobineau's *Inequality of the Human Races*

(1853–1855) is one of the literary foundations of modern racialism, and Tocqueville's correspondence with its author reveals that he was fully aware of the danger of Gobineau's doctrines, which he considered to be the product of materialism and fatalism: "Each of the families which compose the human race may have certain tendencies, certain proper aptitudes born of a thousand different causes. That those tendencies are invincible is something which has never been proved, and which can never be proved, because one would have to know not only the past but also the future. I am sure that if Julius Caesar had had the time, he would have gladly written a book in order to prove that the savages whom he encountered in the island of Great Britain were not of the same human race as the Romans, and whereas the latter were destined by nature to rule the world, the former were only to vegetate in a corner of the globe" (pp. 192–193).

▶ TOCQUEVILLE, ALEXIS DE, *Democracy in America,* 2 vols. (ed. Phillips Bradley, Vintage Books, New York, 1954). See also the following works of Tocqueville: *Recollections* (New York, 1949); *The Old Regime and the French Revolution* (Anchor Books, New York, 1955); *Journeys to England and Ireland* (New Haven, 1958); *The European Revolution and Correspondence with Gobineau* (Anchor Books, New York, 1959); and *Journey to America* (New Haven, 1959).

II. John Stuart Mill

▶ BAIN, ALEXANDER, *John Stuart Mill: A Criticism, with Personal Recollections* (London, 1882). See also W. L. Courtney, *Life of John Stuart Mill* (London, 1889).
▶ BENN, ALFRED WILLIAM, *The History of English Rationalism in the Nineteenth Century,* 2 vols. (London, 1906). Vol. II, Chap. XIV, contains a discussion of *On Liberty* (pp. 188 ff.). See also Ernest Albee, *A History of English Utilitarianism* (London, 1902), Chap. X (pp. 191–267).

▶ BONAR, JAMES, *Philosophy and Political Economy* (London, 1927). Includes a detailed analysis of John Stuart Mill as a political economist (pp. 237–266). See also Jacob Viner, "Bentham and J. S. Mill: The Utilitarian Background," *American Economic Review,* XXXIX (March, 1949), 360–382.
▶ BRITTON, KARL, *John Stuart Mill* (Penguin Books, Baltimore, 1953). Presents the life of Mill and the main aspects of his logic, ethics, and political thought. See also the following: Richard P. Anschutz, *The Philosophy of John Stuart Mill* (Oxford, 1953); Ruth Borchard, *John Stuart Mill: The Man* (London, 1957); Bertrand Russell, *John Stuart Mill* (London, 1955); and John C. Rees, *Mill and His Early Critics* (Leicester, 1956).
▶ DAVIDSON, WILLIAM L., *Political Thought in England: The Utilitarians from Bentham to J. S. Mill* (Home University Library, London, 1935). Chap. X (pp. 216–234) is on Mill. See also Crane Brinton, *English Political Thought in the Nineteenth Century* (London, 1933), pp. 89–103; J. B. Bury, *A History of Freedom of Thought* (Home University Library, London, 1932), pp. 235 ff.; Robert S. Dower, "John Stuart Mill and the Philosophical Radicals," in F. J. C. Hearnshaw (ed.), *The Social and Political Ideas of Some Representative Thinkers of the Age of Reaction and Reconstruction, 1815–1865* (London, 1932), pp. 113–133; Hans Kohn, *Prophets and Peoples: Studies in Nineteenth Century Nationalism* (New York, 1946), pp. 12–42; J. M. Robertson, *Modern Humanists Reconsidered* (London, 1927), pp. 132–165; and R. H. S. Crossman, *Government and the Governed,* 4th ed. (London, 1958), pp. 159–165.
▶ LEVI, ALBERT WILLIAM, *A Study in the Social Philosophy of John Stuart Mill* (Chicago, 1940). See also Charles Larrabee Street, *Individualism and Individuality in the Philosophy of John Stuart Mill* (Milwaukee, 1926); Charles Douglas, *John Stuart Mill: A Study of His Philosophy* (Edinburgh–London, 1895); and Emery

Neff, *Carlyle and Mill* (New York, 1926). The last contains an extensive bibliography (pp. 417–428).

► MacCunn, John, *Six Radical Thinkers* (London, 1907). Chap. II is called "The Utilitarian Optimism of J. S. Mill" (pp. 39–87).

► Mill, John Stuart, "De Tocqueville on Democracy in America," *London Review,* XXVI (July, 1835–January, 1836), 85–129, and *Edinburgh Review,* LXXII (October, 1840–January, 1841), 1–47. In these reviews of the first and second volumes of *Democracy in America,* Mill came out enthusiastically for Tocqueville, comparing him to Montesquieu among French writers. The friendship between Tocqueville and Mill still awaits to be fully explored. For an unpublished correspondence between the two men, see Peter Mayer, "Alexis de Tocqueville and John Stuart Mill," *The Listener* (London, March 16, 1950), 471–472.

► Morley, John, *Critical Miscellanies* (London, 1918), III, 37–92, and *op. cit.* (New York, 1908), IV, 147–170. Morley knew Mill, and his essays on Mill are written with insight and sympathy. See also Lord Acton, "Mill on Liberty," in William Ebenstein, *Political Thought in Perspective* (New York, 1957), pp. 502–523.

► Packe, Michael St. John, *The Life of John Stuart Mill* (New York, 1954). The first full-length biography of Mill, utilizing important new sources previously inaccessible. His relation with Harriet Taylor, so crucial for Mill's personal and intellectual development, is analyzed in detail. See also F. A. Hayek, *John Stuart Mill and Harriet Taylor: Their Friendship and Subsequent Marriage* (Chicago, 1951).

► Plamenatz, John, *The English Utilitarians,* 2nd ed. (Oxford, 1958). Chap. VIII (pp. 122–144) is on Mill. See also R. B.

McCallum's introduction in his edition of Mill's *On Liberty, and Representative Government* (Blackwell's Political Texts, Oxford, 1946), pp. vii–liv; Basil Willey, *Nineteenth Century Studies* (London, 1949), pp. 141–186; Ivor Brown, *English Political Theory* (London, 1929), pp. 118–129; and Robert H. Murray, *English Social and Political Thinkers of the Nineteenth Century* (Cambridge, 1929), I, 376–431.

► Robbins, Lionel, *The Theory of Economic Policy in English Classical Political Economy* (London, 1952). Lecture V is on "The Classical Economists and Socialism: John Stuart Mill" (pp. 142–168).

► Schapiro, J. Salwyn, *Liberalism and the Challenge of Fascism* (New York, 1949). Chap. XI is on "John Stuart Mill: Pioneer of Democratic Liberalism in England" (pp. 256–289). This penetrating essay, which focuses on the significance of Mill in the light of contemporary problems, concludes as follows: "As a consequence of mankind's experience with totalitarianism, Mill's pleas for individual liberty have become more compelling than when they were bold innovations and more persuasive than when they had been accepted platitudes" (p. 289). See also Guido de Ruggiero, *The History of European Liberalism* (Beacon Paperbacks, Boston, 1959), pp. 143 ff.

► Stephen, Leslie, *The English Utilitarians,* 3 vols. (London, 1900; reprinted by the London School of Economics and Political Science, 1950). Vol. III is on John Stuart Mill.

► West, John, *John Stuart Mill* (Fabian Tract No. 168, London, 1913; 3rd reprint, 1933). See also William Irvine, "Shaw, the Fabians, and the Utilitarians," *Journal of the History of Ideas,* VIII (April, 1947), 218–231, which also includes a brief discussion of Mill as the link between Benthamism and Fabianism.

Chapter 21

The Cult of the State

I. Hegel

▶ BOSANQUET, BERNARD, *The Philosophical Theory of the State,* 3rd ed. (London, 1920). The ablest defense of Hegelian political philosophy, centering its analysis on the problem of the "Real Will." Because of its moderation, Bosanquet's book will appear to British and American readers more persuasive than original Hegelianism. An even more moderate expression of Hegelianism, considerably transmuted into, and adapted to, British liberal thought, will be found in Thomas Hill Green, *Principles of Political Obligation,* new imp. (London–New York, 1917). For an interesting comparison and contrast between Hegel and Green with regard to the problem of international order, see D. A. Routh, "The Philosophy of International Relations: T. H. Green *versus* Hegel," *Politica,* III (September, 1938), 223–235.

▶ CARRITT, E. F., *Morals and Politics* (London, 1935). Chap. IX (pp. 105–127) deals with the moral foundations of Hegel's political thought, especially his approach to the problem of political obligation. For a discussion of the two chief exponents of Hegelian political philosophy in England, Green and Bosanquet, see pp. 128–157. John H. Muirhead, *The Platonic Tradition in Anglo-Saxon Philosophy* (London–New York, 1931), provides a brief account of Hegelian influences in England and America (pp. 147–218, 315–323).

▶ DEWEY, JOHN, *German Philosophy and Politics* (New York, 1915). In his discussion of Hegel's political philosophy (pp. 107–120), Dewey emphasizes the elements of nationalism and militarism. See also George Santayana, *Egotism in German Philosophy,* new ed. (London, 1939), Chap. VIII (pp. 70–83). Santayana calls the ser-

vility of Hegel's moral philosophy "simply an apology for the established order of things and for the prejudices of his time and country" (p. 73). Hegel's philosophy sets up an "idol that feeds on blood, the Absolute State" (p. 83). Bertrand Russell, *A History of Western Philosophy* (New York, 1945), examines in Chap. XXII (pp. 730–746) Hegel's political theory in relation to his logic and metaphysics, and arrives at the conclusion that Hegel's doctrine of the state "justifies every internal tyranny and every external aggression" (p. 742).

▶ FINDLAY, JOHN N., *Hegel: A Re-examination* (London, 1958). A systematic presentation and analysis of the major aspects of Hegel's philosophy, written in a spirit of fair criticism and moderate sympathy. Concerning Hegel's political philosophy, the author argues that Hegel described the Prussian state of his time as "the final fruits of the historic development of Spirit" (p. 327), and that Hegel's narrowness of view "is shown, above all, in his carping strictures on the political arrangements of France and England, the two great creative nations of his own time" (*ibid.*). Looking at Hegel's philosophy as a whole, the author calls him "the Aristotle of our post-Renaissance world, our synoptic thinker without peer" (p. 353). Despite Hegel's "later verging towards reaction, he remains the philosopher of Reformation 'inwardness,' of liberal humanism, of perpetual orderly revolution" (p. 354). See also W. T. Stace, *The Philosophy of Hegel: A Systematic Exposition* (New York, 1955), which includes a lucid statement of Hegel's views on state and society (pp. 404–438). Like Findlay, Stace defends Hegel against the charge of being an antiliberal statist and a forerunner of totalitarianism.

▶ FOSTER, M. B., *The Political Philosophies*

of Plato and Hegel (Oxford, 1935). The second part on Hegel is nearly as brilliant as the first on Plato (pp. 72–204). See also Foster's *Die Geschichte als Schicksal des Geistes in der Hegelschen Philosophie* (Tubingen, 1929).

▶ FRIEDRICH, CARL J. (ed.), *The Philosophy of Hegel* (Modern Library, New York, 1953). A collection of portions of Hegel's major writings, including a long Introduction (pp. xiii–lxiv) by the editor.

▶ GLOCKNER, HERMANN, *Hegel*, 2 vols. (Stuttgart, 1929–1940). Glockner's *Hegel-Lexikon*, 4 vols. (Stuttgart, 1935–1939), is a useful reference work. See also Theodor L. Haering, *Hegel: Sein Wollen und sein Werk*, 2 vols. (Leipzig–Berlin, 1929–1938); Willy Moog, *Hegel und die Hegelsche Schule* (Munich, 1930); Gerhardt Giese, *Hegels Staatsidee und der Begriff der Staatserziehung* (Halle-Saale, 1926); Martin Busse, *Hegels Phänomenologie des Geistes und der Staat* (Berlin, 1931); Friedrich Bülow, *Die Entwicklung der Hegelschen Sozialphilosophie* (Leipzig, 1920); Hermann Schmitz, *Hegel als Denker der Individualität* (Meisenheim, 1957); Johannes Flügge, *Die sittlichen Grundlagen des Denkens: Hegels existentielle Erkenntnisgesinnung* (Hamburg, 1953); and Theodor Litt, *Hegel: Versuch einer kritischen Erneuerung* (Heidelberg, 1953).

▶ HELLER, HERMANN, *Hegel und der nationale Machtstaatsgedanke in Deutschland* (Berlin, 1921). See also Karl Löwith, *Von Hegel bis Nietzsche* (Zurich–New York, 1941), pp. 13–17, 283–312, 323–328, 400–405, 447–453; Paul Vogel, *Hegels Gesellschaftsbegriff* (Berlin, 1925); Adam von Trott zu Solz, *Hegels Staatsphilosophie und das Internationale Recht* (Göttingen, 1932); Karl Vorlaender, *Von Machiavelli bis Lenin* (Leipzig, 1926), pp. 195–217; and Julius Löwenstein, *Hegels Staatsidee* (Berlin, 1927).

▶ HOBHOUSE, L. T., *The Metaphysical Theory of the State* (London, 1918). The best critique of Hegelian political philosophy. See especially Chap. III, "The Real Will" (pp. 44–70), and Appendix I,

"Hegel's Theory of the Will" (pp. 138–149). The following controversy about Hegel's "Prussianism" will be found stimulating: T. M. Knox, "Hegel and Prussianism," *Philosophy*, XV (January, 1940), 51–63; E. F. Carritt, "Hegel and Prussianism," *Philosophy*, XV (April, 1940), 190–196; and the final rejoinder by both Knox and Carritt, "Hegel and Prussianism," *Philosophy*, XV (July, 1940), 313–320.

▶ KOLNAI, AUREL, *The War against the West* (New York, 1938). An authoritative study of German antidemocratic thought, based on original sources. A detailed bibliography is appended (pp. 687–701). See also Rohan D'O. Butler, *The Roots of National Socialism, 1783–1933* (New York, 1942), and S. C. Stirk, *The Prussian Spirit: A Survey of German Literature and Politics, 1914–1940* (London, 1941). Reinhold Aris, *History of Political Thought in Germany: From 1789 to 1815* (London, 1936), provides useful background material.

▶ LASKI, HAROLD J., *The State in Theory and Practice* (London, 1935). Chap. I, "The Philosophic Conception of the State" (pp. 15–103), is a detailed critique of this whole tradition in political theory, of which Hegel forms a part. Hegel's philosophy, Laski says, starts by "excluding the major part of the human race from the capacity to be moral beings" (p. 67). Laski sees the main fallacy of the "idealist" ("philosophical" or "metaphysical") theory of the state in its "continuous confusion between the ideal purposes of the state and the actual policy of the government" (p. 69).

▶ LUKACS, GEORG, *Der junge Hegel und die Probleme der kapitalistischen Gesellschaft* (Berlin, 1954). A monumental study of the development of Hegel's early political and philosophical ideas, written from a strictly Marxist viewpoint. The author, a Hungarian "national communist," is probably the most outstanding Marxian student of modern thought in the twentieth century. For a different interpretation of the relations of Hegel and Marx, see Jean Hyppolite, *Etudes sur Marx et Hegel* (Paris, 1955).

► MARCUSE, HERBERT, *Reason and Revolution: Hegel and the Rise of Social Theory*, 2nd ed. (New York, 1955). The most vigorous attempt to present Hegel as a liberal. The author argues that the "progressive ideas of liberalism" (p. 413) in Hegel's political thought are incompatible with fascist totalitarianism, and that German nazism was "anti-Hegelian in all its aims and principles" (pp. 418–419). For a more moderate defense of Hegel against the charges of authoritarianism and totalitarianism, see Eric Weil, *Hegel et l'état* (Paris, 1950).

► MEINECKE, FRIEDRICH, *Machiavellism: The Doctrine of Raison d'État and Its Place in Modern History* (New Haven, 1957). Chap. XIII (pp. 343–369) is on Hegel. In the history of the concept of reason of state, "Machiavelli, Frederick the Great, and Hegel stand out as the three most prominent figures" (p. 366). Writing about Hegel in complete fairness and deep sympathy, Meinecke nevertheless notes his "unfortunate influence on the ideas of German power politics" (p. 368).

► MURE, G. R. G., *An Introduction to Hegel* (Oxford, 1940). Stresses Hegel's conception of logic. Edward Caird, *Hegel* (Edinburgh–London, 1883), is more general and biographical. See also Benedetto Croce, *What Is Living and What Is Dead of the Philosophy of Hegel* (London, 1915), and Iwan Iljin, *Die Philosophie Hegels als kontemplative Gotteslehre* (Bern, 1946).

► POPPER, K. R., *The Open Society and Its Enemies* (Princeton, 1950). Chap. XII, "Hegel and the New Tribalism," (pp. 223–273) contains a pungent point-by-point demonstration of the identity of Hegelianism with "the philosophy of modern totalitarianism" (p. 272). See also T. D. Weldon, *States and Morals* (London, 1946), pp. 86–98; Ernst Cassirer, *The Myth of the State* (New Haven, 1946), pp. 248–276; and Edmond Vermeil, "La pensée politique de Hegel," in Benedetto Croce and others, *Études sur Hegel* (Paris, 1931), pp. 165–234.

► REHFISCH, HANS J. (ed.), *In Tyrannos:*

Four Centuries of Struggle against Tyranny in Germany (London, 1944). Presents the "other side" of German thought and history; on the whole, it admirably achieves its task, although the inclusion of Hegel seems dubious. For useful historical accounts of German liberalism, see Guido de Ruggiero, *The History of European Liberalism* (Beacon Paperbacks, Boston, 1959), pp. 211–274; Rudolf Olden, *The History of Liberty in Germany* (London, 1946); and Leonard Krieger, *The German Idea of Freedom: History of a Political Tradition* (Boston, 1957). Source materials of German libertarian ideas will be found in two anthologies: Federico Federici (ed.), *Der deutsche Liberalismus* (Zurich, 1946), and A. E. Zucker (ed.), *Deutschlands vergessene Freiheit* (Berlin, 1946).

► REYBURN, HUGH A., *The Ethical Theory of Hegel: A Study of the Philosophy of Right* (Oxford, 1921). The last two chapters deal with Hegel's views on the state (pp. 226–268). See also C. E. Vaughan, *Studies in the History of Political Philosophy before and after Rousseau* (Manchester, 1939), II, 143–183, and A. D. Lindsay, "Hegel the German Idealist," in F. J. C. Hearnshaw (ed.), *The Social and Political Ideas of Some Representative Thinkers of the Age of Reaction and Reconstruction, 1815–1865* (London, 1932), pp. 52–67.

► TROELTSCH, ERNST, "The Idea of Natural Law and Humanity in World Politics" (1922), in Otto Gierke, *Natural Law and the Theory of Society, 1500 to 1800* (trans. Ernest Barker, Cambridge, 1934), I, 201–222. This lecture by Troeltsch, one of the most creative German scholars of the twentieth century, and politically a liberal, is a penetrating comparison between German and western thought. Troeltsch points out in what basic respects German thought is opposed to the western tradition, and he suggests that these contrasts are not the product of the last hundred or two hundred years, but go back to the Middle Ages. Troeltsch emphasizes, in particular, the fundamental difference that prevails between the western conception of liberty as absence of constraint and the German view of liberty as voluntary subordination to the state. See also William Ebenstein, *The German Record: A Political Portrait* (New York, 1945), Chap. II, "State and Society in German Politics" (pp. 32–61).

II. Mussolini

▶ ASHTON, E. B., *The Fascist: His State and His Mind* (London, 1937). A general account of fascist theory and its application in economics, government, and international relations. See also Eduard Heimann, *Communism, Fascism, or Democracy?* (New York, 1938), pp. 177–244; Hans Kohn, *Revolutions and Dictatorships* (Cambridge, Mass., 1939), pp. 179–210; Ernest Barker, *Reflections on Government* (London, 1942), pp. 328–398; Walter Lippmann, *The Good Society* (Boston, 1937), pp. 54–66; R. G. Collingwood, *The New Leviathan* (Oxford, 1942), pp. 342–387; Leonard Woolf, *Barbarians Within and Without* (New York, 1939); Dante L. Germino, *The Italian Fascist Party in Power* (Minneapolis, 1959); and William Ebenstein, *Fascist Italy* (New York, 1939), *The Nazi State* (New York, 1943), and *The German Record: A Political Portrait* (New York, 1945).

▶ BORGESE, G. A., "The Intellectual Origins of Fascism," *Social Research*, I (November, 1934), 458–485. One of the best analyses of the literary and philosophical origins of fascism. Borgese's *Goliath: The March of Fascism* (New York, 1938) contains in Part I a lengthy account of the intellectual and historical background of Italian Fascism. For an interesting review of the role of romanticism in the making of fascism, see Peter Quennell, "The Romantic Catastrophe," *Horizon*, I, (May, 1940), 328–345, and (in defense of romanticism) Jacques Barzun, *Romanticism and the Modern Ego* (Boston, 1943).

▶ COBBAN, ALFRED, *Dictatorship: Its History and Theory* (New York, 1939). See also G. P. Gooch, *Dictatorship in Theory*

and Practice (London, 1935); E. E. Kellett, *The Story of Dictatorship* (London, 1937); F. Borkenau, *The Totalitarian Enemy* (London, 1940); E. K. Bramstedt, *Dictatorship and Political Police: The Technique of Control by Fear* (New York, 1945); Hannah Arendt, *The Origins of Totalitarianism*, 2nd ed. (Meridian Books, New York, 1958); Carl J. Friedrich (ed.), *Totalitarianism* (Cambridge, Mass., 1954); and Carl J. Friedrich and Zbigniew K. Brzezinski, *Totalitarian Dictatorship and Autocracy* (Cambridge, Mass., 1956).

▶ DUTT, R. PALME, *Fascism and Social Revolution* (New York, 1934). The most authoritative interpretation of fascism from the orthodox communist viewpoint. The subtitle of the book is "A Study of the Economics and politics of the Extreme Stages of Capitalism in Decay." For other Marxist interpretations of fascism, see Paul Sweezy, *The Theory of Capitalist Development* (New York, 1942), pp. 329–347, and Daniel Guerin, *Fascism and Big Business* (New York, 1939).

▶ FROMM, ERICH, *Escape from Freedom* (New York, 1941). One of the most incisive interpretations of fascism from a psychological viewpoint. Indispensable to an understanding of fascism as a mass movement. A milestone in the empirical study of the psychology of fascism is T. W. Adorno and others, *The Authoritarian Personality* (New York, 1950). Its accomplishments and defects are analyzed in Richard Christie and Marie Jahoda (eds.), *Studies in the Scope and Method of "The Authoritarian Personality"* (Glencoe, 1954). See also Zevedei Barbu, *Democracy and Dictatorship: Their Psychology and Patterns of Life* (Evergreen Books, New York, 1956); Peter Nathan, *The Psychology of Fascism* (London, 1943); R. Osborn, *The Psychology of Reaction* (London, 1938); David Abrahamsen, *Men, Mind, and Power* (New York, 1945); Joost A. M. Meerloo, *The Rape of the Mind* (New York, 1956); William Sargant, *Battle for the Mind* (New York, 1957); Pryn Hopkins, *The Psychology of Social Movements* (New York, 1938); Gardner Murphy

(ed.), *Human Nature and Enduring Peace*
(Third Yearbook of the Society for the
Psychological Study of Social Issues, Bos-
ton–New York, 1945); John Dollard and
Others, *Frustration and Aggression* (New
Haven, 1939); and Lawrence K. Frank,
Society as the Patient (New Brunswick,
1948). For brief analyses of Nazi crimes
see Lord Russell of Liverpool, *The Scourge
of the Swastika: A Short History of Nazi
War Crimes* (Ballantine Books, New York,
1954), and Leo Alexander, "War Crimes
and Their Motivation," *Journal of Criminal
Law and Criminology*, XXXIX (September–October, 1948), 298–326, *ibid.*, XXXIX
(January–February, 1949), 553–564, and
ibid., XL (May–June, 1949), 3–27. The relationship between personality and fascist
ideology is analyzed in Henry V. Dicks,
"Personality Traits and National Socialist
Ideology," *Human Relations,* III (June,
1950), 111–154.

▶ GENTILE, GIOVANNI, "The Philosophic
Basis of Fascism," *Foreign Affairs*, VI (Jan-
uary, 1928), 290–304. A fuller statement by
Gentile, the official philosopher of Italian
Fascism, will be found in his *Origini e
dottrina del fascismo* (Rome, 1929). See
also Lawrence Dennis, *The Coming Ameri-
can Fascism* (New York, 1936), and *The
Dynamics of War and Revolution* (New
York, 1940) for an American approach to
fascism from a profascist viewpoint. Criti-
cal background material will be found in
Raymond Gram Swing, *Forerunners of
American Fascism* (New York, 1935).

▶ KELSEN, HANS, "The Party-Dictator-
ship," *Politica*, II (March, 1936), 19–32.
See also Luigi Sturzo, "The Totalitarian
State," *Social Research,* III (May, 1936),
222–235.

▶ MENZEL, ADOLF, *Der Staatsgedanke des
Faschismus* (Leipzig–Vienna, 1935). See
also J. W. Mannhardt, *Der Faschismus*
(Munich, 1925); Hermann Heller, *Europa
und der Faschismus* (Berlin–Leipzig, 1931);

and Hans Barth, *Fluten und Dämme: Der
philosophische Gedanke in der Politik* (Zurich, 1943), pp. 203–242. A penetrating
analysis of fascism as a mass movement will
be found in Historikus, *Der Faschismus als
Massenbewegung* (Karlsbad, 1934).

▶ RADER, MELVIN, *No Compromise: The
Conflict between Two Worlds* (New York,
1939). A philosophical analysis of the basic
principles of fascism. See also C. E. M.
Joad, *A Guide to the Philosophy of Politics
and Morals* (London, 1938), pp. 605–663;
Bertrand Russell, *In Praise of Idleness and
Other Essays* (London, 1948), pp. 82–108;
and Karl Mannheim, *Ideology and Utopia*
(London–New York, 1940), pp. 119–134.

▶ REICH, WILHELM, *The Mass Psychology
of Fascism* (New York, 1946). Interpreting
fascism from the viewpoint of sexual and
psychological maladjustments, the author
writes that "fascist mysticism is orgastic
longing under the conditions of mystifica-
tion and inhibition of natural sexuality" (p.
xvii). A suggestive book, which tries to
harmonize the "depth psychology of Freud
with the economic theory of Marx" (p.
xix).

▶ SCHAPIRO, J. SALWYN, *Liberalism and
the Challenge of Fascism* (New York,
1949). Chap. XV is entitled "Thomas Carlyle, Prophet of Fascism" (pp. 370–396).
See also H. J. C. Grierson, *Carlyle and
Hitler* (Cambridge, 1933), and Theodor
Heimel, *Carlyle und der Nationalsozialis-
mus* (Würzburg, 1936).

▶ WEST, REBECCA, *The Meaning of Treason* (London, 1949). A subtle psychological
study of the major British fascists who were
tried for treason after World War II, *The
Meaning of Treason* goes a long way in explaining what kind of personality submits
to the fascist ideology in a democratic society. See also Ernest Jones, "The Psychology of Quislingism," *International Journal of Psychoanalysis,* XXII (January,
1941), 1–6.

Chapter 22

Liberalism—Old and New

1. Spencer

▶ ALBEE, ERNEST, *A History of English Utilitarianism* (London–New York, 1902). Chaps. XIII–XV (pp. 268–357) are on Spencer. The author concludes that, "in order to do Mr. Spencer justice, one must regard him as the last great Individualist, in the eighteenth century sense of the word, rather than as the true exponent of Evolutional Ethics" (p. 356).

▶ BARKER, ERNEST, *Political Thought in England, 1848–1914* (Home University Library, London, 1932). Chap. IV (pp. 84–131) is on Spencer—an illuminating interpretation of his political ideas. See also Frederic William Maitland, *Collected Papers* (Cambridge, 1911), I, 247–303; Crane Brinton, *English Political Thought in the Nineteenth Century* (London, 1933), pp. 226–239; F. J. C. Hearnshaw, "Herbert Spencer and the Individualists," in Hearnshaw (ed.), *The Social and Political Ideas of Some Representative Thinkers of the Victorian Age* (London, 1933), pp. 53–83; J. M. Robertson, *Explorations* (London, 1923), pp. 112–140, and *Modern Humanists Reconsidered* (London, 1927), pp. 166–196; and Robert H. Murray, *Studies in the English Social and Political Thinkers of the Nineteenth Century* (Cambridge, 1929), II, 1–47.

▶ DEWEY, JOHN, *Characters and Events*, 2 vols. (New York, 1929). Includes a study of Spencer's philosophy (I, 45–62). See also L. L. Bernard, "Herbert Spencer: The Man and His Age," *South Atlantic Quarterly*, XXI (July, 1922), 241–251.

▶ DUNCAN, DAVID, *Life and Letters of Herbert Spencer*, 2 vols. (New York, 1908). Supplements Spencer's *Autobiography*, 2 vols. (New York, 1904). For a shorter biography, see Hugh Elliot, *Herbert Spencer* (New York, 1917).

▶ ENSOR, R. C. K., *Some Reflections on Herbert Spencer's Doctrine That Progress Is Differentiation* (London, 1946). The Herbert Spencer Lecture, delivered before the University of Oxford, May 28, 1946. Ensor brings out the lasting value of Spencer's doctrine that differentiation is progress, and he shows the dangers in modern civilization resulting from uniformity of mind and outlook, particularly in totalitarian states. Even in democracies, the press, radio, and cinema represent, according to Ensor, dangerous elements of uniformity: "It has been through choruses of enslaved minds that every dictatorship has shouted its way into power" (p. 27).

▶ HOFSTADTER, RICHARD, *Social Darwinism in American Thought*, rev. ed. (Beacon Paperbacks, Boston, 1955). Chap. II, "The Vogue of Spencer" (pp. 31–50), is the best brief analysis of the influence of Spencer's social and political philosophy on American thought. See also Edward L. Youmans, *Herbert Spencer on the Americans, and the Americans on Herbert Spencer* (New York, 1883), containing the text of an interview with Spencer, and a report of the speeches delivered at the farewell banquet given for Spencer before his return to England. Truxtun Beale (ed.), *The Man versus the State* (New York, 1916), contains the full text of *The Man versus the State*, with prefaces to each chapter by distinguished American leaders, such as William Howard Taft, Charles W. Eliot, Elihu Root, Henry Cabot Lodge, Nicholas Murray Butler, E. H. Gary, and others.

▶ MACPHERSON, HECTOR, *Spencer and Spencerism* (New York, 1900). A balanced appraisal of Spencer's social, economic, political, ethical, philosophical, and religious views. See also Josiah Royce, *Herbert Spencer: An Estimate and Review* (New York, 1904); William Henry Hudson, *Herbert Spencer* (London, 1908); and Alfred W. Tillett, *Spencer's Synthetic Philosophy: What It Is All About* (London, 1914).

▶ MENZEL, ADOLF, *Beiträge zur Geschichte der Staatslehre* (Vienna–Leipzig, 1929). Chap. XXIII (pp. 492–518) is on "Herbert Spencer's Theory of the State." See also Otto Gaupp, *Herbert Spencer* (Stuttgart, 1900); K. Gaquoin, *Die Grundlage der Spencerschen Philosophie* (Berlin, 1888); August Stadler, *Herbert Spencer: Spencers Ethik* (Leipzig, 1913); Edward D. Miller, *Spencers Versöhnung des Egoismus und Altruismus* (Berlin, 1899); Felicie Nossig-Prochnik, *zur soziologischen Methodenlehre mit besonderer Rücksicht auf Herbert Spencer* (Bern, 1900); and Carl F. Selle, *Herbert Spencer und Friedrich Nietzsche* (Leipzig, 1902).

▶ NEEDHAM, JOSEPH, *Integrative Levels: A Revaluation of the Idea of Progress* (London, 1937). The Herbert Spencer Lecture, delivered at Oxford, May 27, 1937. Writing from a Marxist viewpoint, the author concludes that Spencer's "wide, and substantially correct, survey of evolution led up only to the anti-climax of middle-class liberal individualism, past which, in spite of himself, he was carried on protesting." Sharing with Spencer the belief in the inevitability of progress, Needham writes as follows: "The higher stages of integration and organization towards which we look have all the authority of evolution behind them. It is no other than Herbert Spencer himself who contributes to this our faith, if faith it be. The devil, as Hippolytus said long ago, may resist the cosmic process. But the last victory will not be his" (p. 59).

▶ RUMNEY, J., *Herbert Spencer's Sociology* (London, 1934). Chap. V. (pp. 130–161) is on "Society, State, Government," and Chap. VI (pp. 162–186) on "Property and Economic Institutions." An extensive bibliography of writings by, and on, Spencer is appended (pp. 311–351).

II. Keynes

▶ BEVERIDGE, WILLIAM H., *Full Employment in a Free Society* (London, 1944). Like Keynes' *General Theory of Employment, Interest, and Money,* Beveridge's *Full Employment in a Free Society* is a pioneering contribution to the solution of the problem of a free society without want and misery, and both works are the products of intellectual leaders of the Liberal party. The underlying principle of *Full Employment in a Free Society* is "to propose for the State only those things which the State alone can do or which it can do better than any local authority or than private citizens either singly or in association, and to leave to these other agencies that which, if they will, they can do as well as or better than the State" (p. 36). Beveridge also emphasizes that his proposals "preserve absolutely all the essential liberties which are more precious than full employment itself. They respect and are designed to preserve many other liberties and institutions which, though not equally essential, are deeply rooted in Britain" (*ibid.*).

▶ DEWEY, JOHN, *Individualism: Old and New* (New York, 1930). A restatement of the more permanent principles of individualism in the light of twentieth-century industrial civilization. See also Dewey's *Liberalism and Social Action* (New York, 1935), *The Public and Its Problems,* new ed. (Chicago, 1946), *Reconstruction in Philosophy,* enlarged ed. (Boston, 1948), and *Problems of Men* (New York, 1946). Appraisals of John Dewey's impact on contemporary social thought will be found in the symposium volume, Sidney Hook (ed.), *John Dewey: Philosopher of Science and Freedom* (New York, 1950).

▶ HAHN, ALBERT L., *The Economics of Illusion: A Critical Analysis of Contemporary Economic Theory and Policy* (New York, 1949). A vigorous critique of Keynes' ideas. See also Henry Hazlitt, *The Failure of the "New Economics": An Analysis of the Keynesian Fallacies* (Princeton–New York, 1959).

▶ HARRIS, SEYMOUR (ed.), *The New Economics: Keynes' Influence on Theory and Public Policy* (New York, 1947). Contains varied appraisals of Keynes' doctrines in relation to classical and Marxian political economy by distinguished American and European economists. Indispensable to an understanding of Keynes' impact on public policy in Britain and the United States. See also A. C. Pigou, *Keynes' General Theory* (London, 1950); Alvin H. Hansen, *A Guide to Keynes* (New York, 1953); Seymour E. Harris, *John Maynard Keynes: Economist and Policy-Maker* (New York, 1955); Kenneth K. Kurihara, *Introduction to Keynesian Dynamics* (New York, 1956); and Joheph A. Schumpeter, *Ten Great Economists* (London, 1952), whose Chap. X is on Keynes (pp. 260–291).

▶ HARROD, R. F., *The Life of John Maynard Keynes* (New York, 1951). The first full-length biography of Keynes' life and work, with particular reference to his economic and political views.

▶ KEYNES, JOHN MAYNARD, *Two Memoirs* (London, 1949). The second memoir is on "My Early Beliefs" (written in 1938), which throws considerable light on Keynes' early intellectual development. See also Keynes' *Essays in Persuasion* (New York, 1932), particularly "Am I a Liberal?" (pp. 323–338), "Liberalism and Labour" (pp. 339–345), and "Economic Possibilities for Our Grandchildren" (pp. 358–373).

▶ KLEIN, LAWRENCE R., *The Keynesian Revolution* (New York, 1947). The last chapter deals with "Keynes and Social Reform" (pp. 165–187), and the author emphasizes the point that the "Keynesian policy is, indeed, a conservative one because it aims to conserve free-enterprise capitalism." The author warns against the danger of fascism as the possible result of laissez faire, fascism being "the worst stage of capitalism. It is the form that our capitalist society will acquire unless we are successful in bringing about Keynesian reforms or a socialist economy. If we let nature take its course, the economic law of motion of capitalism will take us down the same road that

Germany followed so recently" (p. 167).

▶ MACGREGOR, D. H., *Economic Thought and Policy* (Home University Library, London–New York, 1949). Studies the relations of economic thought to public policy, and includes discussions of laissez faire, Keynes, and democratic socialism. An excellent introduction to the subject.

▶ NATIONAL INDUSTRIAL CONFERENCE BOARD, *The Economic Doctrines of John Maynard Keynes* (New York, 1938). Five essays by American economists on theoretical and practical implications of Keynes' doctrines.

▶ POLANYI, KARL, *The Great Transformation* (Beacon Paperbacks, Boston, 1957). A provocative study of the devastating human effects of the market economy, the central institution of the nineteenth century, and of the growing efforts to protect society against the evils of the market economy.

▶ ROBINSON, JOAN, *Introduction to the Theory of Employment* (London, 1937). A simple and brief introduction to the main points of Keynes' theories.

▶ RUGGIERO, GUIDO DE, *The History of European Liberalism* (Beacon Paperbacks, Boston, 1959). The first part of the book deals with the evolution of liberalism in England, France, Germany, and Italy, while the second part inquires into the relations of liberalism and socialism, democracy, religion, and nationalism. A useful bibliography is included (pp. 445–463). See also Maurice Cranston, *Freedom: A New Analysis* (New York, 1953), which contains both a philosophical analysis of the concept of freedom and the historical varieties of liberalism in England, France, Germany, and the United States.

▶ SALTER, ARTHUR, *Personality in Politics* (London, 1947). Chap. X (pp. 138–148) is on "Maynard Keynes: The Artist-Economist." Written from close personal knowledge, this brief essay manages to give an intimate picture of Keynes' personality, life, and thought.

▶ SCHAPIRO, J. SALWYN, *Liberalism and the Challenge of Fascism: Social Forces in England and France (1815–1870)* (New

York, 1949). The last chapter, XVI (pp. 397–403), is on "The Historic Importance of Bourgeois Liberalism," which the author summarizes as follows: "Bourgeois liberalism has long ago ceased to be a factor of importance in England and France. Its shortcomings have been derided by reformers, socialist and nonsocialist. Its contributions have been accepted—and forgotten. Those who still cherish its central doctrine of laissez-faire are regarded as relics of a past that has receded even more in opinion than in time. Yet bourgeois liberalism did perform a historic function the greatness of which merits recognition. It was the fascist threat to parliamentary government and civil liberty, a heritage from bourgeois liberalism, that solidified the English people in the critical year 1940. And it was this same heritage that, in France, inspired the Resistance Movement which led to the creation of the Fourth Republic. In the new

pattern of life and thought that is now emerging, in which socialized democracy is in the foreground, bourgeois liberalism is clearly seen as the background" (p. 403).

▶ SWANSON, ERNST W., and EMERSON P. SCHMIDT, *Economic Stagnation or Progress: A Critique of Recent Doctrines on the Mature Economy, Oversavings, and Deficit Spending* (New York–London, 1946). A sharp critique of Keynes' doctrines.

▶ WOLODIN, W. S., *Keynes: Ein Ideologe des Monopolkapitals* (trans. from the Russian, Berlin, 1955). Official Soviet interpretation of Keynes, in which he appears as a lackey of monopoly capitalism and fascism; the main purpose of his theories is to justify "imperialist reaction and war" (pp. 110 ff.). For a somewhat more restrained Marxist-communist analysis of Keynes, see John Eaton, *Marx Against Keynes* (London, 1951).

Chapter 23

Totalitarian Communism

I. Marx–Engels

▶ BARZUN, JACQUES, *Darwin, Marx, Wagner* (Boston, 1941). Part II (pp. 141–252) deals with Marx as well as with his contemporary and later critics. See also K. Timiryazeff, "Darwin and Marx," in D. Ryazanoff (ed.), *Karl Marx: Man, Thinker, and Revolutionist* (New York, 1927).

▶ BEER, MAX, *The Life and Teaching of Karl Marx* (London, 1925). Concise and readable.

▶ BERLIN, ISAIAH, *Karl Marx*, 2nd ed. (Home University Library, London–New York–Toronto, 1948). One of the most brilliant studies of the life and thought of Marx. A bibliography is appended (pp. 269–273). See also Berlin's "Political Ideals in

the Twentieth Century," *Foreign Affairs*, XXVIII (April, 1950), 351–385.

▶ BERNSTEIN, SAMUEL (ed.), *A Centenary of Marxism* (New York, 1948). Published to commemorate the centenary of the *Communist Manifesto*, this volume represents a special issue of *Science and Society*, XII (Winter, 1948), a leading Marxist quarterly. The first essay is "Marx and Engels on America" (pp. 3–21).

▶ BOBER, MANDELL MORTON, *Karl Marx's Interpretation of History* (Cambridge, Mass., 1927). The author concludes that Marx' interpretation of history is "neither an interpretation nor a philosophy, nor a method of history. It is a canon. It admonishes the student of the history of social manifestations not to neglect the careful study of the economic factors—the forms of economic organization, the class structure, the play of group interests. Such a study will shed light on many historical phenomena; but it will be inadequate to interpret history. Marx' theory is a key that fits many locks but opens few doors" (p. 346). A bibliography is appended (pp. 349–353).

► CARRITT, E. F., *Morals and Politics* (London, 1935). Includes a brief critical analysis of "dialectical materialism" (pp. 170–177). See also J. L. Stocks, *Materialism in Politics* (L. T. Hobhouse Memorial Lectures, No. 7, London, 1937).

► CASSERLEY, J. V. LANGMEAD, *The Bent World: A Christian Examination of East-West Tensions* (New York, 1955). Part I is on "Marxism in Theory and Practice" (pp. 17–62). See also Alexander Miller, *The Christian Significance of Karl Marx* (New York, 1952); Edward Rogers, *A Christian Commentary on Communism* (New York, 1952); and Martin Cyril d'Arcy, *Communism and Christianity* (Penguin Books, Baltimore, 1956). The relations of Islam and Marxism are examined in Mohammed M. Siddiqui, *Marxism or Islam?* (Lahore, 1954), and Abd al-Hakim Khalifa, *Islam and Communism* (Lahore, 1953).

► CHANG, SHERMAN H. M., *The Marxian Theory of the State* (Philadelphia, 1931). Contains a useful bibliography (pp. 201–210).

► COLE, G. D. H., *The Meaning of Marxism* (London, 1948). An excellent introduction to Marxism, this book is not so much a summary of Marx' ideas as a revaluation of his thought in relation to contemporary social and political developments. Cole successfully simplifies some of the complexities of Marx' essential doctrines without doing violence to them. In addition, he analyzes the social changes that have taken place since Marx, and discusses their implications for democratic socialist movements. His discussion of the new class of white-collar workers and their political psychology is particularly noteworthy. Cole's *A History of Socialist Thought*, 4 vols. (New York,

1953–1958), the most scholarly work in the field, covers the period from 1789 to 1931. and deals with all varieties of socialism and Marxism.

► CORNFORTH, MAURICE, *Dialectical Materialism: An Introduction*, 3 vols. (London, 1952–1954). Written from the orthodox Marxist-communist viewpoint. See also his *Science versus Idealism: An Examination of "Pure Empiricism" and Modern Logic* (London, 1946), and *In Defence of Philosophy Against Positivism and Pragmatism* (London, 1950). The author arrives at the conclusion that pragmatism, "particularly in the form which Dewey has given it, is the philosophy of American imperialism. It expresses the outlook and aspirations of American big business in philosophical form" (p. 214).

► CROCE, BENEDETTO, *Historical Materialism and the Economics of Karl Marx* (London, 1914). A critical interpretation by the greatest Italian philosopher of the twentieth century. See also Croce's *Come il Marx fece passare il comunismo dall'utopia alla scienza* (Bari, 1948), a collection of four essays dealing with the Hegelian origins of Marx' thought and his attempt to construct a "scientific" theory of communism.

► DOBB, MAURICE, *Studies in the Development of Capitalism* (London, 1946). The author is one of the leading Marxist economists in England. See also his pamphlet, *Marx as an Economist* (New York, 1945), and *On Economic Theory and Socialism: Collected Papers* (London, 1955).

► EASTMAN, MAX, *Marxism: Is It Science?* (New York, 1940). A vigorous critique of Marxist doctrine. Eastman attacks Marxism mainly on the ground that it is unscientific.

► ENGELS, FRIEDRICH, *On Historical Materialism* (New York, 1940). A brief essay, published first in 1892, and one of the most succinct statements of the meaning of historical materialism. It stresses the English roots of philosophical materialism, especially Bacon, Hobbes, and Locke, the "fathers of the brilliant French school of materialists" that made the eighteenth century a "pre-eminently French century" (p. 8).

► FEDERN, KARL, *The Materialist Interpretation of History* (London, 1939). The subtitle is "A Critical Analysis."

► GRAY, ALEXANDER, *The Socialist Tradition: Moses to Lenin* (London, 1946). One of the few systematic historical treatments of the evolution of socialist thought from the ancients to the moderns; interesting on the Greek, Biblical, and medieval sources of socialist ethics. Chap. XII (pp. 297–351), called "Scientific Socialism," analyzes especially Marx and Engels, and Chap. XVIII (pp. 459–486) is on Lenin. Gray is highly critical of Marx as a thinker and social scientist, and sees in him essentially a prophet and visionary who "has proved the most influential figure of the nineteenth century" (p. 331). As to Lenin, Gray sees his main contribution to Marxism in his theory of the dictatorship of the proletariat. Lenin's peculiar position in the history of socialism is that "somehow he got things done" (p. 484).

► HALDANE, J. B. S., *The Marxist Philosophy and the Sciences* (New York, 1939). Written by a distinguished British scientist, this work analyzes, from a Marxist viewpoint, the application of Marxist principles to mathematics, physics, chemistry, biology, psychology, and sociology. For other treatments of the relations of Marxism to the physical and biological sciences, see Jack Lindsay, *Marxism and Contemporary Science* (London, 1949); Marcel Prenant, *Biology and Marxism* (New York, 1943); N. I. Bukharin and others, *Marxism and Modern Thought* (New York, 1935); and J. D. Bernal, *Marx and Science* (London, 1952), and *The Freedom of Necessity* (London, 1949).

► HOOK, SIDNEY, *Towards the Understanding of Karl Marx* (New York, 1933). An illuminating interpretation of Marx' main ideas and their relation to basic problems of socialist theory. See also Hook's *From Hegel to Marx: Studies in the Intellectual Development of Karl Marx* (New York, 1950), the best work, in English, on the subject.

► ——— (ed.), *The Meaning of Marx* (New York, 1934). This symposium contains "An Introduction to the Study of Marx" by Sherwood Eddy; "The Meaning of Marx" by Sidney Hook; "Why I Am Not a Communist" by Bertrand Russell, John Dewey, and Morris Cohen; and "Communism without Dogma" by Sidney Hook. Stimulating throughout. See also Hook's *Reason, Social Myths, and Democracy* (New York, 1950), *Marx and the Marxists: The Ambiguous Legacy* (Anvil Books, Princeton–New York, 1955), and "What's Left of Karl Marx?" *Saturday Review* (June 6, 1959), 11 ff.

► HUNT, R. N. CAREW, *Marxism: Past and Present* (New York, 1954). One of the best brief introductions into Marx' philosophy of dialectical materialism, his economic and political theories, and the doctrine of the dictatorship of the proletariat. See also H. Stuart Hughes, *Consciousness and Society: The Reorientation of European Social Thought, 1890–1930* (New York, 1958), particularly Chap. III on "The Critique of Marxism" (pp. 67–104).

► JACKSON, T. A., *Dialectics* (New York, 1936). The subtitle of this long treatise is "The Logic of Marxism, and Its Critics: An Essay in Exploration." A much shorter treatment will be found in David Guest, *A Textbook of Dialectical Materialism* (New York, 1939).

► KORSCH, KARL, *Karl Marx* (London, 1938). A volume in the series "Modern Sociologists."

► LANDY, A., *Marxism and the Democratic Tradition* (New York, 1946). Written in popular language, this short work is based on the hypothesis that in the history of modern democracy "the communists have always been the most consistent champions of democracy" (p. 10).

► LASKI, HAROLD J., *Communist Manifesto: Socialist Landmark* (London, 1948). The complete text of the *Communist Manifesto*, together with several prefaces by Marx and Engels, is preceded by a detailed and illuminating introduction (pp. 11–104), written by Laski from a democratic socialist viewpoint. The book was issued by the

Labor party to mark the centenary of the *Communist Manifesto*. See also Laski's *Karl Marx: An Essay* (London, 1921), and *Marx and Today* (London, 1943).

▶ LINDSAY, A. D., *Karl Marx's Capital:An Introductory Essay* (London, 1925). This short volume in the popular series, the World's Manuals, attains its objective admirably. The first chapter (pp. 15–26) gives a brief outline of Marx and Hegel, emphasizing especially the influence of Hegelian dialectic on Marx. Chaps II–IV (pp. 27–108) provide well-balanced introductions to economic determinism, the Marxian labor theory of value, and the meaning of surplus value. The final chapter (pp. 109–125) contains suggestive comparisons between Marx and Rousseau, each the father of a great revolution. This is one of the best first introductions to Marx, particularly his economic and philosophical ideas.

▶ MARX, KARL, and FRIEDRICH ENGELS, *Selected Correspondence* (New York, 1942). Over two hundred letters, written by Marx and Engels to each other or to leading socialist writers and publicists. These letters throw considerable light on the philosophies and personalities of Marx and Engels, and also contain succinctly formulated analyses that frequently make a point more clearly and convincingly than more ponderous treatments in their better-known works.

▶ MAYER, GUSTAV, *Friedrich Engels* (New York, 1936). The standard biography of Engels. Concerning Engels' share in the *Communist Manifesto*, Mayer says that "although it was chiefly Marx who coined the gold, Engels had not been behind him in collecting the ore" (p. 88).

▶ MEHRING, FRANZ, *Karl Marx: The Story of His Life* (New York, 1935). The standard biography. See also Boris Nicolaievsky and Otto Maenchen-Helfen, *Karl Marx: Man and Fighter* (Philadelphia, 1936), and Otto Rühle, *Karl Marx: His Life and Work* (New York, 1929).

▶ MEYER, ALFRED G., *Marxism: The Unity of Theory and Practice* (Cambridge, Mass., 1954). Stresses the human and philosophical aspects of Marx' thought rather than its political or economic doctrines. The most suggestive portion of the book is Chap. II on "Marx as a Radical Critic of Civilization" (pp. 47–73), in which Meyer deals with Marx' concept of "alienation," one of the dominant concepts of contemporary sociology and social psychology; the link between Marx and the Romantics in his critique of industrial civilization is particularly noteworthy and all too often neglected. See also David Braybrooke, "Diagnosis and Remedy in Marx' Doctrine of Alienation," *Social Research*, XXV (Autumn, 1958), 325–345; Reinhold Niebuhr, *The Nature and Destiny of Man*, Vol. I (New York, 1949), pp. 43–53; and Heinrich Popitz, *Der entfremdete Mensch: Zeitkritik und Geschichtsphilosophie des jungen Marx* (Basle, 1953).

▶ PARKES, HENRY BAMFORD, *Marxism: An Autopsy* (Boston, 1939). A trenchant critique of Marxism, which, "owing to the stimulus which it gives to Fascism, must be regarded as a liability rather than an asset to the progressive cause" (p. 6).

▶ POPPER, KARL, *The Open Society and Its Enemies* (Princeton, 1950). The second part is on Hegel and Marx, and the author concentrates on Marx' claim to have formulated a "scientific" theory of society. In the literature on Marx, Popper's work is particularly illuminating, not only because it possesses analytical acumen and philosophical depth but because it places Marx in a tradition of the "enemies of the open society," starting with Plato. Popper's formulation of the concept of the open society is an important contribution to liberal-democratic thought in the twentieth century. See also H. B. Mayo, *Democracy and Marxism* (New York, 1955), for a thoughtful confrontation of the basic tenets of democracy with Marxism.

▶ ROBINSON, JOAN, *An Essay on Marxian Economics* (London, 1942). An analysis of Marxian economics in the light of modern economic theory, particularly Keynes. Short and well written.

▶ RYAZANOFF, D. (ed.), *Karl Marx: Man,*

Thinker, and Revolutionist (New York, 1927). An interesting symposium on Marx, with personal reminiscences by Engels, his daughter Eleanor Marx, and his son-in-law Paul Lafargue, as well as sympathetic studies by Lenin, Mehring, Rosa Luxemburg, and others.

▶ SCHLESINGER, RUDOLF, *Marx: His Time and Ours* (London, 1950). A detailed restatement from an orthodox Marxist viewpoint. The author concludes that "we cannot now refuse the basic Marxist statements any more than a serious physicist can be a non-Newtonian, with the further great difference that, in the field of sociology, more generations must pass before an Einstein appears. He will not come before Marx' work has born all its historical fruits" (pp. 432–433). A bibliography is appended (pp. 434–436).

▶ SCHWARZSCHILD, LEOPOLD, *The Red Prussian: The Life and Legend of Karl Marx* (London, 1948). A highly critical biography, written with verve and fire. The author "debunks" Marx as a man and thinker thoroughly and devastatingly, yet fails to explain why he exercised such a tremendous influence on history.

▶ SÉE, HENRI, *Matérialisme historique et interprétation économique de l'histoire* (Paris, 1927). A brief and balanced appraisal of the economic interpretation of history by a distinguished French economic historian. See also Robert Aron (ed.), *De Marx au marxisme: 1848–1948* (Paris, 1948), a symposium including diverse essays on the evolution of Marxism, and Lucien Laurat, *Le Manifeste Communiste de 1848 et le monde d'aujourd'hui* (Paris, 1948). The relations between Marxism and humanism are examined in Pierre Bigo, *Marxisme et humanisme* (Paris, 1953), and Roger Garaudy, *Humanisme marxiste* (Paris, 1957). For an analysis of Marx' relations to French socialist thought of his time, particularly Proudhon, see W. Pickles, "Marx and Proudhon," *Politica,* III (September, 1938), 236–260.

▶ SWEEZY, PAUL M., *The Theory of Capitalist Development* (New York, 1942).

Chaps. I–XII (pp. 11–236) contain one of the most authoritative recent statements of Marxian political economy, including such basic concepts as value, surplus value, capital accumulation, the law of the falling profit rate, and crises and depressions. Chap. XV (pp. 270–286) analyzes monopoly and its impact on the capitalist economy. See also Sweezy's *Socialism* (New York, 1949), and *The Present as History: Essays and Reviews on Capitalism and Socialism* (New York, 1953).

▶ TROTSKY, LEON, *Karl Marx* (The Living Thoughts Library, New York, 1939). Trotsky's introduction (pp. 1–45) is followed by selected passages from Marx' *Capital* (pp. 48–189). Writing for American readers, and illustrating his theoretical arguments with American materials, Trotsky comes to the conclusion that Marxism has a great future in the United States: "In this, too, America will in a few jumps catch up with Europe and outdistance it. Progressive technique and a progressive social structure will pave their own way in the sphere of doctrine. The best theoreticians of Marxism will appear on American soil. Marx will become the mentor of the advanced American workers" (p. 38). A less optimistic view is expressed by the one-time leader of the Communist Party of the United States, Earl R. Browder, in his *Marx and America* (New York, 1958).

▶ VORLÄNDER, KARL, *Karl Marx: Sein Leben und sein Werk* (Leipzig, 1929). See also Max Adler, *Marx als Denker* (Berlin, 1925); Ferdinand Tönnies, *Marx: Leben und Lehre* (Jena, 1921); Walter Theimer, *Der Marxismus: Lehre, Wirkung, Kritik* (Bern, 1950); Max G. Lange, *Marxismus, Leninismus, Stalinismus: zur Kritik des dialektischen Materialismus* (Stuttgart, 1955); and Rudolf Sannwald, *Marx und die Antike* (Zurich, 1957). The relation of Marx and Hegel is discussed in Siegfried Marck, *Hegelianismus und Marxismus* (Berlin, 1922), and Paul Vogel, *Hegels Gesellschaftsbegriff und seine geschichtliche Fortbildung durch Lorenz Stein, Marx, Engels und Lassalle* (Berlin, 1925).

II. Lenin–Stalin

▶ BERDYAEV, NICOLAS, *The Origin of Russian Communism* (New York, 1937). This stimulating work by an exiled Russian philosopher and religious thinker arrives at the conclusion that "Russian communism is more traditional than is commonly thought and that it is a transformation and deformation of the old Russian messianic idea" (p. 228).

▶ CANTRILL, HADLEY, *The Politics of Despair* (New York, 1958). A pioneering empirical study on the psychology and outlook of Communist voters in France and Italy. See also Gabriel A. Almond, *The Appeals of Communism* (Princeton, 1954), and Morris L. Ernst and David Loth, *Report on the American Communist* (New York, 1952).

▶ CARR, EDWARD HALLETT, *Studies in Revolution* (New York, 1950). The author starts with Saint-Simon and ends with Lenin and Stalin. The book is valuable inasmuch as it emphasizes the relation of Russian communism to the general European revolutionary tradition of the nineteenth century. Yet it overstates its case; Stalin is made to appear as the final link of this tradition, and Stalinism is implied to be the only alternative to liberal democracy. See also Carr's earlier book, *The Soviet Impact on the Western World* (New York, 1947), in which he examines the political, economic, social, international, and ideological influences of Sovietism on the Western world. A succinct summary of "Lenin's Theory of the State" will be found in Carr's *The Bolshevik Revolution, 1917–1923*, Vol. I (London, 1950), pp. 233–249.

▶ CROSSMAN, RICHARD (ed.), *The God That Failed* (Bantam Books, New York, 1954). Six memoirs by former communists and fellow travelers (Arthur Koestler, Ignazio Silone, Richard Wright, André Gide, Louis Fischer, Stephen Spender) on how they embraced the communist faith and why they eventually renounced it. In the literature on communism, this book is of unique value, for it discusses communism in terms of critical personal experiences rather than abstract ideology. Of the six essays, those by Richard Wright, the American writer, and Ignazio Silone, the Italian novelist, are the most moving. In all, this symposium greatly contributes to an understanding of why persons of profoundly religious, ethical, and democratic faith commit themselves to communism as an ideal and hope.

▶ DJILAS, MILOVAN, *The New Class* (Praeger Paperbacks, New York, 1959). Possibly the most important book on communism since the *Communist Manifesto*. The author, a former communist, shows the errors of communist totalitarianism by employing, to a large extent, Marxian concepts and techniques of analysis. See also his *Land Without Justice* (New York, 1958) and *Anatomy of a Moral* (New York, 1959).

▶ EASTMAN, MAX, *Marx and Lenin: The Science of Revolution* (New York, 1927). Comparing Marx with Lenin, the author concludes as follows: "In Marx the Hegelian metaphysician was dominant over the practical scientific thinker; in Lenin the scientific thinker gained the victory. And that victory is the theoretical foundation of Bolshevism. Bolshevism is an unconscious, and therefore incomplete, substitution of a practical science of revolution for that revolutionary philosophy of the universe which Marx created" (p. 168).

▶ FRIEDRICH, CARL J. (ed.), *Totalitarianism* (Cambridge, Mass., 1954). A collection of essays on totalitarianism (mostly of the communist variety) by George F. Kennan, Carl J. Friedrich, H. J. Muller, Harold D. Lasswell, and other leading authorities. See also Carl J. Friedrich and Zbigniew K. Brzezinski, *Totalitarian Dictatorship and Autocracy* (Cambridge, Mass., 1956).

▶ HECKER, JULIUS F., *Moscow Dialogues: Discussions on Red Philosophy* (London, 1933). The relations of communism to philosophy, religion, ethics, and politics, in dialogue form. The viewpoint is that of orthodox communism. See also John Middleton Murry, *The Necessity of Communism* (London, 1932). An illuminating critical exposition and interpretation of Soviet dialectical materialism will be found in I. M. Bochenski, *Der sowjetrussische dialektische Materialismus* (*Diamat*) (Bern, 1950), which also contains a comprehensive bibliography (pp. 185–206).

▶ HILFERDING, RUDOLF, "State Capitalism or Totalitarian State Economy," *Modern Review*, I (June, 1947), 266–271. Maintains that "from a social democratic viewpoint the Bolshevik economy can hardly be called 'socialist,' for to us socialism is indissolubly linked to democracy. According to our concept, socialization of the means of production implies freeing the economy from the rule of one class and vesting it in society as a whole—a society which is democratically self-governed" (p. 270). Much of procommunist apologetics has been based on the proposition that communism, though politically undemocratic, has at least achieved economic democracy. Hilferding demonstrates that no totalitarian economy can be democratic. See also Raymond Aron and others, *The Soviet Economy: A Discussion* (London, 1956), with contributions by Colin Clark, C. A. R. Crosland, Bertrand de Jouvenel, Peter Wiles, and other experts.

▶ HILL, CHRISTOPHER, *Lenin and the Russian Revolution* (London–New York, 1947). A volume in the Teach Yourself History series. See also Ralph Fox, *Lenin: A Biography* (New York, 1931).

▶ HISTORICUS, "Stalin on Revolution," *Foreign Affairs*, XXVII (January, 1949), 175–214. A painstaking piece of research, essential to an understanding of Stalinism. See also G. L. Arnold, "Stalinism," *Political Quarterly*, XXI (October–December, 1950), 338–355; Mark Vishniak, "Lenin's Democracy, and Stalin's," *Foreign Affairs*, XXIV (July, 1946), 610–621; and H. R. Trevor-Roper, "Stalin Would Have Liquidated Marx," *New York Times Magazine* (January 30, 1949), 9 ff.

▶ HUNT, R. N. CAREW, *The Theory and Practice of Communism* (New York, 1950). Part I is entitled "The Marxist Basis"; Part II, "The Development of the European Socialist Movement up to 1914"; and

Part III, "Leninism and Stalinism." An annotated bibliography is appended (pp. 218–227). The interaction of communist ideas and institutions in the Soviet regime is analyzed in Barrington Moore, *Soviet Politics—The Dilemma of Power: The Role of Ideas in Social Change* (Cambridge, Mass., 1950), and Raymond A. Bauer and others, *How the Soviet System Works* (Cambridge, Mass., 1956). An illuminating (and often amusing) volume on the ambiguities of Soviet communist theory and practice is Harry Hodgkinson, *Doubletalk: The Language of Communism* (London, 1955).

▶ KELSEN, HANS, *The Political Theory of Bolshevism: A Critical Analysis* (Berkeley and Los Angeles, 1949). This short book of sixty pages is by all odds the best critical analysis of the political theory of Marx and Engels, and of its later development by Lenin and Stalin. The style is clear and straightforward, the argument balanced and penetrating, and the documentation based largely on the original sources of Marx, Engels, Lenin, and Stalin. A basic tool in the study of the political ideas of communism and democracy.

▶ KOESTLER, ARTHUR, *Darkness at Noon* (Signet Books, New York, 1948). This short novel supplies more insight into the working of totalitarian communism and its terroristic methods than many a ponderous work of nonfiction. The hero of the novel is an old revolutionary whose final fate—imprisonment, abject confession of crimes not committed, and execution—resembles that of the victims of the Moscow treason trials in the nineteen thirties, in which Stalin liquidated most of the remnants of the original leaders of the revolution. See also George Orwell, *1984* (Signet Books, New York, 1950).

▶ LASKI, HAROLD J., *Communism: 1381–1927* (London, 1927). The materialist interpretation of history seems to Laski, "as general doctrine, undeniable." Yet he warns that "there is no justification for the resort to violence until the resources of reason have been exhausted" (p. 180). See, especially, Chap. IV, "The Communist Theory of the State" (pp. 123–182). Laski's conclusion is that the answer to "the new faith" of communism "is not the persecution of those who worship in its sanctuary, but the proof that those who do not share its convictions can scan an horizon not less splendid in the prospect it envisions nor less compelling in the allegiance it invokes" (pp. 250–251). See also Laski's *The Secret Battalion: An Examination of the Communist Attitude to the Labour Party* (London, 1946), a devastating critique of communist methods of political infiltration and deception.

▶ MARCUSE, HERBERT, *Soviet Marxism: A Critical Analysis* (New York, 1958). Examines the relation of Marxist doctrine to Soviet reality, and concludes that Marxist ideology is a decisive part of the Soviet state and society. The author also feels that Soviet Marxism, in spite of its aberrations and distortions, is pushing Soviet society toward more liberalized economic and political practices. Controversial in some of its conclusions, the book is an important contribution to the understanding of Marxism and its relation to communist reality.

▶ POLLÈS, HENRI, *Psychoanalyse du communisme* (Paris, 1949). Written from a militant democratic socialist standpoint. See also Jules Monnerot, *Sociology of Communism* (London, 1953), and Roger Stéphane (ed.), *Questions du communisme* (Paris, 1947).

▶ POSSONY, STEFAN T., *A Century of Conflict: Communist Techniques of World Revolution, 1848–1950* (Chicago, 1953). Emphasizes the strategy and tactics of Marxism and communism rather than pure ideology. See also Harold H. Fisher, *The Communist Revolution: An Outline of Strategy and Tactics* (Stanford, 1955); Franz Borkenau, *European Communism* (New York, 1953); Nathan Leites, *The Operational Code of the Politbureau* (New York, 1951), and *A Study of Bolshevism* (Glencoe, 1953); and Philip Selznick, *The Organizational Weapon* (New York, 1952).

▶ ROSENBERG, ARTHUR, *A History of Bol-*

shevism (London, 1934). The story ends in 1932. See also Franz Borkenau, *World Communism: A History of the Communist International* (New York, 1939), *The Totalitarian Enemy* (London, 1940), and "Marx's Prophecy in the Light of History: Balance Sheet after a Century," *Commentary*, VII (May, 1949), 430–436.

▶ RUSSELL, BERTRAND, *Bolshevism: Practice and Theory* (New York, 1920). This remarkable book, based on a visit to Russia, is one of the few that have stood the test of time, and the author republished it, in an unchanged second edition, in 1949 (London and New York). Russell agreed with the economic objectives of public ownership of industry but disagreed with the political means of ruthlessness employed by communism for the attainment of its ends. Writing in 1920, Russell saw three possibilities of Soviet communist development: "The first is the ultimate defeat of Bolshevism by the forces of capitalism. The second is the victory of the Bolshevists accompanied by a complete loss of their ideals and a regime of Napoleonic imperialism. The third is a prolonged world-war, in which civilization will go under, and all its manifestations (including communism) will be forgotten" (p. 4). See also Russell's "Scylla and Charybdis, or Communism and Fascism," in his *In Praise of Idleness*, 4th imp. (London, 1948), pp. 109–120.

▶ RUSSIAN INSTITUTE, COLUMBIA UNIVERSITY (ed.), *The Anti-Stalin Campaign and International Communism: A Selection of Documents* (New York, 1956). The most important document is the full text of Khrushchev's speech at the Twentieth Congress of the Communist Party of the Soviet Union (February 25, 1956) on the "Cult of the Individual," giving a lengthy (though incomplete) account of the crimes and errors of Stalin (pp. 1–89). The remainder of the volume contains the reactions of communist newspapers and organizations to Khrushchev's sensational speech.

▶ SETON-WATSON, HUGH, *From Lenin to Malenkov: The History of World Communism* (New York, 1953). The author is one of the leading British authorities on Eastern Europe. See also his pamphlet, *Some Myths of Marxism* (Manchester, 1954).

► Shub, David, *Lenin: A Biography* (New York, 1948). One of the most authoritative biographies of Lenin, based on original documentary material. The author, who early in the century participated in the Russian revolutionary movement before coming to the United States in 1908, knew Lenin and other major figures of the time. The book is written from a democratic socialist viewpoint. See also Valeriu Marcu, *Lenin* (New York, 1928), for a more impressionistic account of Lenin's career.

► Simmons, Ernest J. (ed.), *Continuity and Change in Russian and Soviet Thought* (Cambridge, Mass., 1955). Examines to what extent communist ideas continue, or break with, long-term ideas and traditions of pre-communist Russia. The contributors include Isaiah Berlin, Merle Fainsod, Michael Karpovich, Hans Kohn, Herbert Marcuse, Philip E. Moseley, and Ernest J. Simmons.

► Stalin, Joseph, and H. G. Wells, *Marxism vs. Liberalism: An Interview* (Marxist Pamphlets, No. 2, New York, 1945). The full text of an interview Wells had with Stalin in 1934. On the crucial issue of revolution, Stalin told Wells that "you are wrong if you think that the Communists are enamored with violence. They would be very pleased to drop violent methods if the ruling class agreed to give way to the working class. But the experience of history speaks against such an assumption" (p. 21). The text of the interview is also reprinted in *New Statesman and Nation* (October 27, 1934), 601–606.

► Trotsky, Leon, *Stalin: An Appraisal of the Man and His Influence* (New York, 1946). Trotsky concludes his biography of Stalin as follows: " 'L'Etat, c'est moi' (I am the State) is almost a liberal formula by comparison with the actualities of Stalin's totalitarian regime. Louis XIV identified himself only with the State. The Popes of Rome identified themselves with both the State and the Church—but only

during the epoch of temporal power. The totalitarian state goes far beyond Caesaro-Papism, for it has encompassed the entire economy of the country as well. Stalin can justly say, unlike the Sun King, 'La Société, c'est moi' (I am Society)" (p. 421). A list of Trotsky's books and pamphlets in English is included (pp. 477–478). See also Trotsky's *The Stalin School of Falsification* (New York, 1937). Trotsky's most important work is *The History of the Russian Revolution* (three vols. in one, New York, 1937). His most provocative theoretical contribution will be found in *Permanent Revolution* (New York, 1931). *My Life* (New York, 1931) is one of the fascinating autobiographies of world literature. Trotsky's *Lenin* (New York, 1925) is not a formal biography but a collection of memoirs, sketches, and fragments on Lenin.

► Wetter, Gustav A., *Dialectical Materialism: A Historical and Systematic Survey of Philosophy in the Soviet Union* (New York, 1958). The author, an Austrian Jesuit teaching the history of Russian philosophy at the Papal Oriental Institute in Rome, is one of the top experts on Marxism and communism in the Roman Catholic Church. His monumental work is the fruit of many years of study and research. See also his much briefer *Philosophie und Naturwissenschaft in der Sowjetunion* (Hamburg, 1958).

► Wilson, Edmund, *To the Finland Station* (Anchor Books, New York, 1953). The bulk of the book (pp. 111–484) deals with Marx, Engels, Lenin, and Trotsky.

► Wolfe, Bertram D., *Three Who Made a Revolution* (Beacon Press Books, Boston, 1955). The prerevolutionary lives and careers of Lenin, Trotsky, and Stalin.

► Zinner, Paul E. (ed.), *National Communism and Popular Revolt in Eastern Europe* (New York, 1956). A collection of documents covering the background and events of the Hungarian and Polish revolutions in 1956. See also Imre Nagy, *On Communism: In Defense of the New Course* (New York, 1957), a classical exposition of "national communism" by the Prime Minister of Hungary during the Revolution of 1956, and Charles P. Mc-

Chapter 24

Democratic Socialism

▶ ATTLEE, C. R., *The Labour Party in Perspective—and Twelve Years Later* (London, 1949). This reprint of the original edition of 1937 contains a preface by Francis Williams (pp. 9–24), indicating how the policies proposed by Attlee in 1937 were carried out by him after he became Prime Minister in 1954. See also Attlee's autobiography, *As It Happened* (London, 1954), and *Purpose and Policy: Selected Speeches* (London–New York, 1947). For biographical studies of Attlee, see the following: Roy Jenkins, *Mr. Attlee* (London, 1948), an "Interim Biography" by a Labor M.P. with much inside information; Vincent Brome, *Clement Attlee* (London, 1949), a popular "pictorial" biography; J. T. Murphy, *Labour's Big Three: A Biographical Study of Clement Attlee, Herbert Morrison, and Ernest Bevin* (London, 1948); and Patricia Strauss, *Bevin and Co.: The Leaders of British Labour* (New York, 1941), Chap. VII (pp. 89–100). Colm Brogan, *Our New Masters* (London, 1947), contains a chapter on Attlee ("The Mahout," pp. 41–61), as viewed by a highly critical Conservative writer.

▶ BARKER, ERNEST, *Political Thought in England, 1848–1914*, rev. ed. (London, 1928). The last chapter, "Economics and Politics" (pp. 203–247), traces the beginnings of socialist ideas in Britain from the eighteen-eighties on. It analyzes the British reactions to Marx, and briefly describes the birth and growth of Fabianism.

▶ BAROU, N. (ed.), *The Co-Operative Movement in Labour Britain* (London,

1948). Edited for the Fabian Society.

▶ BEER, MAX, *Fifty Years of International Socialism* (London, 1935). This autobiography of a continental socialist, who spent about a quarter of a century in England, contains some penetrating analyses of English politics in general and English socialism in particular. In Chap. XXXIV, "Interview with Lenin" (pp. 144–159), Beer explained to Lenin some of the effects that he observed in revolutionary socialists who had fled from the Continent to England: "Revolutionary exiles, if they live for any length of time in England, turn gradually into reformists; she acts upon them as a derevolutionizing filter. I have met in London former revolutionists and terrorists from Germany and Austria, Communards and Anarcho-Communists from the Latin countries, who had become wise in England. With an air of superior wisdom they held forth on the virtues of 'compromise, statesman-like attitude, sagacity, well-balanced judgment, and preference of expediency to principle,' and all those stock phrases they had heard in lecture-halls, or had read in *The Times* or *The Spectator*" (pp. 152–153).

▶ BLUM, LÉON, *For All Mankind* (New York, 1946). Written by the leader of French socialism and first Socialist Prime Minister of his country, this short book, a moving work of documentary value, discusses the prospects of democratic socialism, particularly in relation to France. Blum spent the period of November, 1940, to December, 1942, in Vichy prisons, and composed *For All Mankind* during his imprisonment. Written during the dark days of World War II, the book never doubts for a moment the ultimate triumph of democracy over fascist totalitarianism. For introductions to the background and evolution of French socialism, see Émile Durkheim, *Le socialisme* (Paris, 1928); Paul Louis, *Histoire du socialisme en France*, 5th ed. (Paris, 1950); Marcel Prélot, *L'évolution politique du socialisme français, 1789–1934* (Paris, 1939); and Maxime Leroy, *Les precurseurs français du socialisme: de Condorcet à Proudhon* (Paris, 1948). The latter is a source book. For the earlier beginnings of French socialism, see William B. Guthrie, *Socialism before the French Revolution* (New York, 1907); Jessica Peixotto, *The French Revolution and Modern French Socialism* (New York, 1901); Harold J. Laski, "The Socialist Tradition in the French Revolution," in F. J. C. Hearnshaw (ed.), *The Social and Political Ideas of Some Representative Thinkers of the Revolutionary Era* (London, 1931), pp. 201–233, reprinted in Laski's *Studies in Law and Politics* (London, 1932), pp. 66–103; and Maxime Leroy, *Histoire des idées sociales en France de Montesquieu à Robespierre*, 2nd ed. (Paris, 1946). For a scathing critique of French socialist policies after World War II, see André Philip, *Le socialisme trahi* (Paris, 1957).

▶ BORKENAU, FRANZ, *Socialism: National or International* (London, 1942). Discusses the struggle of nationalism and internationalism in the various labor movements of the world.

▶ BUBER, MARTIN, *Paths in Utopia* (Beacon Paperbacks, Boston, 1958). The author, holder of the chair of social philosophy at the Hebrew University in Jerusalem, defends the non-Marxist socialism of Owen, Saint-Simon, Fourier, Proudhon, Kropotkin, and Landauer against the Marxist-communist doctrine of class war and dictatorship. Buber attempts to show that socialism based on small associations of freely cooperating individuals is the only realistic approach to the reconstruc-

tion of modern society, and that it is far from being "utopian," as Marx and Engels sarcastically called it, whereas the self-styled "scientific" doctrines of Marx and Lenin are doomed to fail precisely because they violate the true nature of man, his needs for freedom and cooperation. As an example of cooperative socialism based on personal freedom and voluntary association, the author describes in the epilogue the "Kvuza," or Village Commune, in Israel ("An Experiment That Did Not Fail," pp. 139–149). All in all, this book is indispensable to the study of non-Marxist socialism.

▶ COLE, G. D. H., *A History of the Labour Party from 1914* (London, 1948). The best work on the period. The bibliography (pp. 485–500) is greatly enriched by the inclusion of the titles of Labor-party programs, reports, and pamphlets published during the years 1914–1947. See also the following: G. D. H. Cole, *British Working Class Politics, 1832–1914* (London, 1941), and *A Short History of the British Working Class Movement, 1789–1947*, rev. ed. (London, 1948); Max Beer, *A History of British Socialism* (London, 1940); and *Independent Labour Party, 1893–1943: Jubilee Souvenir* (London, 1943). Margaret Cole, *Makers of the Labour Movement* (London, 1948), looks at the development of British socialism through outstanding personalities; the book includes, among others, biographical studies of Tom Paine, Robert Owen, John Stuart Mill, William Morris, James Keir Hardie, Sidney Webb, George Lansbury, and H. G. Wells.

▶ ———, *Socialism in Evolution* (London, 1938). Chap. IV (pp. 133–159), "Marxism in the Western World," is an important critical analysis and modification of basic Marxian doctrines in the light of social and industrial changes since Marx' death. Cole demonstrates, in particular, the impact of the growth of the white-collar workers, the "salariat," as contrasted with the old-type "proletariat" of manual workers in the heavy industries. The failure of continental socialist parties to attract the salariat led to their decline, whereas the British Labor party succeeded in winning the allegiance of the white-collar workers, thus ensuring for itself electoral victories in the General Elections of 1945 and 1950. The other chapters of *Socialism in Evolution* deal with problems of the labor and socialist movements in Europe, particularly western Europe, and throw a good deal of light on the psychology and strategy of English socialism. Cole's *Persons and Periods* (London, 1938) contains two chapters that are especially interesting in the study of English socialism: Chap. VI, "A Study in Legal Repression," and Chap. IX, "Robert Owen and Owenism."

See also the following works by Cole: *Social Theory* (London, 1920); *Guild Socialism Restated* (London, 1920); *Robert Owen* (London, 1925); *Literature and Politics* (London, 1929); *Some Relations between Political and Economic Theory* (London, 1934); *Principles of Economic Planning* (London, 1935); *A Century of Co-operation* (Manchester, 1945); *Socialist Economics* (London, 1950); *Essays in Social Theory* (London, 1950); *Studies in Class Structure* (London, 1955); and *A History of Socialist Thought,* 4 vols. (New York, 1953–1958).

▶ CRIPPS, STAFFORD, *Towards Christian Democracy* (New York, 1946). Like Attlee, Cripps became a socialist largely through his deep religious convictions. He gave up one of the most prominent legal practices to dedicate himself to a career of service in the labor movement and the Government. See also his *Democracy Up-to-Date* (London, 1939). William Dale Morris, *The Christian Origins of Social Revolt* (London, 1949), provides a convenient historical survey of the subject from the Middle Ages to the present, and places modern English socialism in proper perspective. William Temple, *Christianity and the Social Order* (Penguin Special, London–New York, 1942), is a useful illustration of the climate of religious opinion in England. The author, Archbishop of Canterbury, came close to some of the

fundamental positions of British socialism, and his book explains why politically active ministers of religion in Britain will be found more often in the labor movement than in the Conservative Party. Franz Linden, *Sozialismus und Religion: Konfessionssoziologische Untersuchung der Labour Party 1929–1931* (Leipzig, 1932) contains interesting material on religion and the Labor party.

▶ CROSLAND, C. A. R., *The Future of Socialism* (New York, 1957). The most important book on socialism since World War II. The author, a renowned British economist, tones down traditional socialist objectives like nationalization and planning, and stresses social equality and the cultivation of the good life for all. The book concludes as follows: "We do not want to enter the age of abundance, only to find that we have lost the values which might teach us how to enjoy it" (p. 529).

▶ CROSSMAN, R. II. S. (ed.), *New Fabian Essays* (London, 1952). The most interesting essay in this symposium is by Crossman himself, "Towards a Philosophy of Socialism" (pp. 1–32). Stressing the human values of socialism over specific economic or social aims, Crossman concludes that "it is not the pursuit of happiness but the enlargement of freedom which is socialism's highest aim" (p. 29). See also Crossman's pamphlet, *Socialism and the New Despotism* (Fabian Tract No. 298, London, 1956), in which he warns against the dangers of a "new despotism" as a result of excessive nationalization of industry: "In Britain we are faced with the following dilemma. Since the abuses of oligopoly cannot be checked by free competition, the only way to enlarge freedom and achieve a full democracy is to subject the economy to public control. Yet the State bureaucracy itself is one of those concentrations of powers which threaten our freedom. If we increase its authority still further, shall we not be endangering the liberties we are trying to defend?" (p. 13).

▶ DURBIN, E. F. M., *The Politics of*

Democratic Socialism (London, 1940). In the literature on the philosophy of democratic socialism this is one of the enduring works; its stature is likely to grow as time goes on.

▶ GAITSKELL, HUGH, *Socialism and Nationalization* (Fabian Tract No. 300, London, 1956). The Leader of the British Labor Party explains the growing shift of socialist thinking from the concept of nationalization to that of equality. With respect to nationalization, Gaitskell writes that "in the case of management the change, either for good or bad, is not so great as was at one time desired or feared. The nationalized industries cannot be so disinterested in 'profits,' and the larger private firms are not quite so obsessed with them as they were once thought to be" (p. 17). Gaitskell summarizes his argument by saying that "the most vital question is how far greater social and economic equality can be achieved without more nationalization and public ownership" (p. 31). Similar views are also expressed by Gaitskell in his *Recent Developments in British Socialist Thinking* (London, 1956).

▶ GRAY, ALEXANDER, *The Socialist Tradition: Moses to Lenin* (London, 1946). The following portions of this learned and entertainingly written work deal with English socialism: Chap. V (pp. 114–135) on William Godwin; Chap. VIII (pp. 197–217) on Robert Owen; Chap. XI (pp. 257–296), "Early English Socialism"; Chap. XIV, first half (pp. 384–401) on Fabianism; and Chap. XVI (pp. 433–458), "Guild Socialism," particularly on G. D. H. Cole. French socialism is dealt with in Chaps. IV (pp. 76–113), VI–VII (pp. 136–196), and IX–X (pp. 218–256). See also the following: Norman Mackenzie, *Socialism: A Short History* (Hutchinson's University Library, London–New York, 1949); Philip Taft, *Movements for Economic Reform* (New York, 1950); Harry W. Laidler, *Social-Economic Movements: An Historical and Comparative Survey of Socialism, Communism, Co-operation, Utopianism;*

and Other Systems of Reform and Reconstruction (New York, 1946); Werner Sombart, *Sozialismus und soziale Bewegung,* 5th ed. (Jena, 1905); and Georg Adler, *Geschichte des Sozialismus und Kommunismus* (Leipzig, 1920).

▶ HAYEK, FRIEDRICH A., *The Road to Serfdom* (Chicago, 1944). The most popular book against planning. Much of Hayek's argument is based on the thesis that in a planned economy "the worst get to the top," that the rule of law is incompatible with planning, and that the suppression of dissent becomes unavoidable in a planned economy. Hayek reaffirmed his antiplanning position in *Individualism and Economic Order* (Chicago, 1948). In the vast literature of books and pamphlets directed against planning, the following will be found useful: John Jewkes, *Ordeal by Planning* (London, 1948); Walter Lippmann, *The Good Society* (Boston, 1937); G. L. Schwartz, *Why Planning?* (London, 1944); and T. E. Gregory, *The Planned State and the Equalitarian State* (London, 1934). More moderate viewpoints will be found in Lionel Robbins, *The Economic Problem in Peace and War* (London, 1947); Sir Hubert Henderson, *The Uses and Abuses of Economic Planning* (Cambridge, 1947); John Maurice Clark, *Alternative to Serfdom* (New York, 1948); Robert A. Dahl and Charles E. Lindblom, *Politics, Economics, and Welfare* (New York, 1953); and Michael P. Fogarty, *Economic Control* (London, 1955). Hayek's *Road to Serfdom* quickly called forth a stream of books and articles attacking his views; one of the sharpest and most vigorous attacks will be found in Herman Finer, *Road to Reaction* (Boston, 1946).

▶ HEIMANN, EDUARD, *Communism, Fascism, or Democracy?* (New York, 1938). Thought-provoking and stimulating throughout, this work vindicates democracy in general, and socialist democracy in particular, against the challenges of communism and fascism.

► HOBSON, JOHN A., *Towards Social Equality* (L. T. Hobhouse Memorial Lectures, No. 1, London, 1931). See also the following: J. L. Hammond, *The Growth of Common Enjoyment* (L. T. Hobhouse Memorial Lectures, No. 3, London, 1933); Muriel Jaeger, *Liberty versus Equality* (London–New York, 1943); and T. H. Marshall, *Citizenship and Social Class* (Cambridge, 1950). The strongest case for complete economic equality will be found in Bernard Shaw, *The Intelligent Woman's Guide to Socialism and Capitalism* (London, 1928), one of the most brilliant— and amusing—pieces of literature in the whole history of socialism. A well balanced brief analysis of the legal, religious, political, economic, and international aspects of equality is presented in David Thomson, *Equality* (Cambridge, 1949).

► HUTCHISON, KEITH, *The Decline and Fall of British Capitalism* (New York, 1950). Provides the social and economic background for the rise of labor in Britain. Written with insight, knowledge, and perspective. See also G. D. N. Worswick and P. H. Ady (eds.), *The British Economy, 1945–1950* (Oxford, 1952), and Andrew Shonfield, *British Economic Policy Since the War* (Penguin Books, Baltimore, 1958).

► IRVINE, WILLIAM, "Shaw, the Fabians, and the Utilitarians," *Journal of the History of Ideas*, VIII (April, 1947), 218–231. An illuminating study of the relation between Benthamism and Fabianism.

► KAUTSKY, KARL, *Social Democracy versus Communism* (New York, 1946). See also the following: *The Social Revolution* (Chicago, 1905); *The Dictatorship of the Proletariat* (Manchester–London, 1919); *Terrorism and Communism* (London, 1920); *The Labour Revolution* (New York, 1925); *Bolshevism at a Deadlock* (London, 1931); *Die Vorläufer des neueren Sozialismus* (Stuttgart, 1895); *Die materialistische Geschichtsauffassung*, 2 vols. (Berlin, 1927); *Ethik und materialistische Geschichtsauffassung* (Berlin, 1930); and

Aus der Frühzeit des Marxismus: Engels' Briefwechsel mit Kautsky (Prague, 1935).

► LANGE, OSKAR, and FRED M. TAYLOR, *On the Economic Theory of Socialism* (ed. Benjamin E. Lippincott, Minneapolis, 1938). The two essays in this book seek to refute the charge that a socialist economy is not practicable. Specifically, Lange and Taylor turn their attention to leading opponents of socialism among economists, such as Lionel Robbins, F. A. Hayek, and Ludwig von Mises. The main argument of the two authors is that rational allocation of resources is possible under a planned socialist economy. They also emphasize that a socialist economy is not only compatible with democracy but a natural outcome of its basic assumptions. For antisocialist critiques of this position, see F. A. Hayek (ed.), *Collectivist Economic Planning* (London, 1935, 3rd imp., 1947), with essays by Hayek, Pierson, Mises, Halm, and Barone.

► LEVY, A. B., *Private Corporations and Their Control*, 2 vols. (London, 1950). A scholarly and detailed analysis of the economic and legal background of the private corporation as "the powerful instrument of capitalistic enterprise in modern society" (II, 889). A useful bibliography is appended (II, 882–888).

► LEWIS, W. ARTHUR, *The Principles of Economic Planning: A Study for the Fabian Society* (London, 1949). This short book of 128 pages is one of the most original discussions of the major principles involved in economic planning. On the key problem of nationalization the author writes as follows: "Nationalization, then, is frequently desirable. There is no case for nationalizing the whole economy. For nationalization, when all is said, remains a form of monopoly, subject to all the usual disadvantages of monopoly. It is an improvement on private monopoly and desirable in industries that would in any case be monopolistic, but complete nationalization should never be introduced in any industry which is not naturally or desirably monopolistic. The reasons for this are the usual reasons against monopoly; that it breeds inefficiency, stifles initiative and concentrates power" (p. 104).

See also the following: Carl Landaeuer, *Theory of National Economic Planning,* rev. ed. (Berkeley and Los Angeles, 1947); Barbara Wootton, *Freedom under Planning* (Chapel Hill, 1945); James Edward Meade, *Planning and the Price Mechanism* (London, 1948); Oliver Franks, *Central Planning and Control in War and Peace* (London, 1947); E. F. M. Durbin, *Problems of Economic Planning* (London, 1949); W. Friedmann, *The Planned State and the Rule of Law* (Melbourne, 1948); Karl Mannheim, *Freedom, Power, and Democratic Planning* (New York, 1950), and *Man and Society in an Age of Reconstruction* (London, 1940); and Seymour E. Harris, *Economic Planning: The Plans of Fourteen Countries with Analyses of the Plans* (New York, 1949).

▶ MENGER, ANTON, *The Right to the Whole Produce of Labour* (London–New York, 1899). This English translation of an important work by an Austrian economist contains an introduction and bibliography by H. S. Foxwell that are indispensable to the study of early English socialism. The introduction (pp. v–cx) surveys the main figures of English socialist thought in the first half of the nineteenth century. Bibliographical data on early English socialism are supplied by Foxwell (pp. 191–267). Foxwell summarizes his position as follows: "It was a handful of English writers, brought up in the classic country of capitalistic production, and reflecting upon the terrible wreckage of the early pre-regulation period, who laid down the broad lines of thought upon which socialistic criticism of capitalism has ever since proceeded" (p. xxvii).

▶ MISES, LUDWIG VON, *Socialism* (New York, 1935; originally published as *Die Gemeinwirtschaft* in 1922). An important book, because Mises was the first to popularize a few basic arguments against plan-

ning and socialism that later gained wider currency through the books of F. A. Hayek and Walter Lippmann. Socialism is impossible, according to Mises, because of the lack of "economic calculation" in a socialist community. In addition, Mises cites what have become the standard arguments against socialism, from bureaucratic centralization to soulless totalitarianism. In *Human Action: A Treatise on Economics* (New Haven, 1949), Mises reaffirmed his faith in extreme laissez faire; Chap. XXXV, "The Welfare Principle versus the Market Principle" (pp. 829–850), provides a convenient summary of his position. *Socialism* and *Human Action* are perhaps the two most important antisocialist books written primarily from the viewpoint of the economist. In *The Anticapitalist Mentality* (Princeton, 1956) Mises explores the sources of hostility to capitalism, particularly in countries in which the system has worked successfully. Spirited defenses of the capitalist system will also be found in Thomas Wilson, *Capitalism and Economic Progress* (London, 1950); David McCord Wright, *Capitalism* (New York, 1951); and F. A. Hayek (ed.), *Capitalism and the Historians* (Chicago, 1954).

▶ MORRIS, WILLIAM, *Selected Writings,* ed. by G. D. H. Cole (New York, 1934). This Centenary Edition of the Nonesuch Press contains most of Morris' essays and tracts (pp. 475–671).

▶ PIGOU, A. C., *Socialism versus Capitalism* (London, 1937). One of Britain's leading economists deals with such issues as distribution of wealth and income, the allocation of productive resources, unemployment, profit, technical efficiency, and the problem of incentive. He is sympathetic toward the method of "gradualness" in social and economic change, including the nationalization of important industries.

▶ READ, HERBERT, *The Politics of the Unpolitical* (London, 1945). Like William Morris, Read came to socialism via art and poetry, and his socialism, like that of Morris, is a peculiar and unclassifiable blend of intense concern for beauty, individualism, anarchy, and a profound faith that the democratic experience of the human race has only begun—that it must be carried on to previously undreamed-of heights. Read mentions Rousseau, Jefferson, Lincoln, Proudhon, Ruskin, Marx, Morris, and Kropotkin as kindred spirits. In the best Morris tradition, Read invites the reader to take the case of the chair he sits on while reading, and to pursue his social investigations from that point on. Men like Read will rarely found, or join, political parties, but their influence in England has been real, inside and outside the labor movement, because their protest against capitalism has sprung from their consciousness and sufferings as artists and poets, and because they are concerned with people rather than with abstractions. See also Kingsley Amis, *Socialism and the Intellectuals* (Fabian Tract No. 304, London, 1957).

► ROSENBERG, ARTHUR, *Democracy and Socialism: A Contribution to the Political History of the Past 150 Years* (New York, 1939). This work throws a good deal of light on the relations of democracy and socialism from the eighteenth to the twentieth century.

► SCHUMPETER, JOSEPH A., *Capitalism, Socialism, and Democracy,* 3rd ed. (New York–London, 1950). A distinguished economist discusses the causes of the internal disintegration of capitalism and the prospects of democratic socialism in what is likely to become a classic in the literature on socialism. Schumpeter, rather critical of Marxism, is more in sympathy with the British approach.

► SHAW, BERNARD, and OTHERS, *Fabian Essays* (London, 1889). The most famous document on "Fabian Socialism." In addition to Shaw, the contributors are Sidney Webb, Graham Wallas, Sydney Olivier, William Clarke, Annie Besant, and Hubert Bland. It has sold many tens of thousands of copies since its first publication and has never ceased to be a steady seller in the field of socialist literature. For an analysis of Fabianism, see also G. D. H. Cole, *Fabian Socialism* (London, 1943), and *The Fabian Society,* rev. ed. (Fabian Tract No. 258, London, 1949); E. R. Pease, *History of the Fabian Society,* 2nd ed. (London, 1925); Graham Wallas, *Men and Ideas* (London, 1940), pp. 103–107 ("Socialism and the Fabian Society"); the Diamond Jubilee Number of the *Fabian Quarterly* (No. 41, April, 1944), a special issue devoted to the history and prospects of the Fabian Society; and Margaret Cole, "The Fabian Society," *Political Quarterly,* XV (July–September, 1944), 245–256. Margaret Cole (ed.), *The Webbs and Their Work* (London, 1949), is the best introduction to the thought of the two great Fabians, with contributions by Bernard Shaw, Lord Beveridge, G. D. H. Cole, and others. Chap. XVI, "Political Thought and the Webbs" (pp. 251–264), by Leonard Woolf, is an incisive and critical account of the political ideas of the Webbs. Margaret Cole is also the author of a biography, *Beatrice Webb* (New York, 1946). Beatrice Webb has written two books about herself and Sidney Webb that are basic sources for the study of Fabianism and British socialism: *My Apprenticeship* (London, 1926), and *Our Partnership* (London, 1948).

► STREET, ARTHUR, *The Public Corporation in British Experience* (London, 1947). The public corporation, the main organizational form of nationalized industry in Britain, is discussed by the Deputy Chairman of the National Coal Board in Britain. See also the following: William A. Robson (ed.), *Problems of Nationalized Industry* (New York, 1951); Ben W. Lewis, *British Planning and Nationalization* (New York, 1952); Edward Goodman, *Forms of Public Control and Ownership* (London, 1951); Hugh Clegg, *Industrial Democracy and Nationalization* (Oxford, 1951); H. A. Clegg and T. E. Chester, *The Future of Nationalization* (Oxford, 1953); Acton Society Trust, *Management Under Nationalization* (London, 1953); W. Friedmann (ed.), *The*

Public Corporation: A Comparative Symposium (Toronto, 1954); and H. A. Hanson, *Public Enterprise: A Study of Its Organization and Management in Various Countries* (Brussels, 1955).

An important critical examination of the public corporation from a democratic socialist viewpoint will be found in H. R. G. Greaves, "Public Boards and Corporations," *Political Quarterly*, XVI (January–March, 1945), 67–77. Conservative critiques of nationalization and the public corporation will be found in John Baker White, *Nationalization: Chaos or Cure?* (London, 1946); James R. H. Hutchison, *The Great Betrayal* (London, 1950); John Longhurst, *Nationalisation in Practice: The Civil Aviation Experiment* (London, 1950); and R. Kelf-Cohen, *Nationalization in Britain* (New York, 1959).

► STURMTHAL, ADOLF, *The Tragedy of European Labor: 1918–1939* (New York, 1943). An important analysis of the failures of continental European socialism in the period between World Wars I and II. See also Sturmthal's *Unity and Diversity in European Labor* (Glencoe, 1953). Elie Halévy's *Histoire du socialisme européen* (Paris, 1948) and *L'ère des tyrannies: études sur le socialisme et la guerre* (Paris, 1938) will be found useful in the general study of European socialism.

► TAWNEY, R. H., *The British Labor Movement* (New Haven, 1925). See also Tawney's *The Acquisitive Society* (New York, 1921), *Equality* (London, 1931), and *The Western Political Tradition* (Burge Memorial Lecture, London, 1949). A distinguished social and economic historian, Tawney has had an immense influence on the development of socialist thought in Britain, particularly since his style marks him as one of the great prose writers in English literature.

► THOMAS, NORMAN, *A Socialist's Faith* (New York, 1951). By the leader of the American Socialist party. See also Thomas' *Socialism on the Defensive* (New York–London, 1938), *The Choice before Us: Mankind at the Crossroads* (New York,

1934), *As I See It* (New York, 1932), and the following: John Spargo, *Social Democracy Explained* (New York–London, 1918); James MacKaye, *Americanized Socialism: A Yankee View of Capitalism* (New York, 1918); and Morris Hillquist, *Socialism in Theory and Practice* (New York, 1912).

► TRACY, HERBERT (ed.), *The British Labour Party: Its History, Growth, Policy, and Leaders*, 3 vols. (London, 1948). With many contributions by leaders of the Labor party. See also the following: Donald Munro, *Socialism: The British Way* (London, 1948); William Glenvil Hall, *The Labour Party* (Britain in Pictures, London, 1949); Egon Wertheimer, *Portrait of the Labour Party* (London, 1929); Dean E. McHenry, *His Majesty's Opposition: Structure and Problems of the British Labour Party, 1931–1938* (Berkeley, 1940); Hugh Dalton, *Practical Socialism for Britain* (London, 1935); G. E. G. Catlin (ed.), *New Trends in Socialism* (London, 1935); George Lansbury, *My England* (London, 1934); George Orwell, *The Lion and the Unicorn: Socialism and the English Genius* (London, 1941); Richard Acland, *The Forward March* (London, 1941), and *How It Can Be Done* (London, 1944); Francis Williams, *Fifty Years' March: The Rise of the Labour Party* (London, 1950); and R. T. McKenzie, *British Political Parties* (London, 1955), pp. 297–577.

► ULAM, ADAM B., *Philosophical Foundations of English Socialism* (Cambridge, Mass., 1951). Shows, in particular, the impact of philosophical idealism on the early English socialists. See also Socialist Union, *Twentieth Century Socialism* (Penguin Books, Baltimore, 1956).

► WEBB, SIDNEY, and BEATRICE WEBB, *The Decay of Capitalist Civilization*, 3rd ed. (London, 1923). See also *The Consumers' Co-operative Movement* (London, 1921), and *A Constitution for the Socialist Commonwealth of Great Britain* (London, 1920). One of the most important writings of Sidney Webb is *Labour and the New Social Order* (London, 1918), the Labor party program of 1918, which for the first time committed it to socialism. Until that time, the Labor party was not officially socialist.

► WILLIAMS, FRANCIS, *Socialist Britain: Its Background, Its Present, and an Estimate of Its Future* (New York, 1949). A former editor of the *Daily Herald*, the official Labor daily in Britain, Williams also served as public-relations adviser to Prime Minister Attlee, and his book is the result of intimate knowledge of the British labor movement. A detailed and highly critical examination of Labor policies from the Left will be found in Robert A. Brady, *Crisis in Britain: Plans and Achievements of the Labour Government* (Berkeley and Los Angeles, 1950), and A. A. Rogow, *The Labor Government and British Industry, 1945–1951* (Ithaca, 1955). Both focus their attacks on the economic record.

Chapter 25

The Welfare State

► ARNOLD, THURMAN, *The Folklore of Capitalism* (New Haven, 1937). This book, full of wit and irony as well as learning and scholarship, shows that "political government" is not the only, or necessarily the most oppressive, form of government; "economic government," especially as it appears in corporate business and monopolies, also expresses power relations between men. Arnold shows how the folklore and mythology of capitalism transform the realities of economic government into innocent fictions and magic rituals.

► BEARD, CHARLES A., *The Economic Basis of Politics* (New York, 1922). One of Beard's most famous studies; it is particularly significant for its illuminating insights into the American political experience.

► BERLE, A. A., and G. C. MEANS, *The Modern Corporation and Private Property* (New York, 1932). One of the pioneering works in the field of property and its transformation in the age of corporate business. The authors point to the massive concentration of property in the corporate organization of business and industry. A much friendlier attitude toward corporate business is displayed by A. A. Berle in his more recent *The 20th Century Capitalist Revolution* (New York, 1954) and *Power With-*

out Property (New York, 1959). See also George W. Stocking and Myron W. Watkins, *Monopoly and Free Enterprise* (New York, 1951); A. D. H. Kaplan, *Big Enterprise in a Competitive System* (Washington, 1954); Herrymon Maurer, *Great Enterprise: Growth and Behavior of the Big Corporation* (New York, 1955); Walter Adams and Horace M. Gray, *Monopoly in America: The Government as Promoter* (New York, 1955); Walton Hamilton, *The Politics of Industry* (New York, 1957); and *Concentration in American Industry* (Report of the Senate Subcommittee on Antitrust and Monopoly, 85th Congress, 1st Session, Washington, 1957).

► BRANDEIS, LOUIS, *The Curse of Bigness* (New York, 1934). The best selection of Brandeis' papers and statements on social, economic, and political issues. It has also useful bibliographies of books and articles written by, and on, Brandeis. Some of his other important books are: *Other People's Money and How the Bankers Use It* (New York, 1914); *Business—A Profession* (Boston, 1914); *The Social and Economic View of Mr. Justice Brandeis*, ed. by Alfred Lief (New York, 1930). The two most important books on Brandeis are: *Mr. Justice Brandeis*, ed. by Felix Frankfurter (New Haven, 1932), with contributions by

Charles E. Hughes, Max Lerner, Felix Frankfurter, Walton H. Hamilton, and others; and *Brandeis: A Free Man's Life*, by Alpheus T. Mason (New York, 1946). ▶ DE GRAZIA, ALFRED (ed.), *Grass Roots Private Welfare* (New York, 1957). Fifty case studies linked by the common philosophy of solving social problems by voluntary action of the community rather than by compulsory action of the government. See also A. F. C. Bourdillon (ed.), *Voluntary Social Services* (London, 1945), and John G. Turnbull and others, *Economic and Social Security: Public and Private Measures Against Economic Insecurity* (New York, 1957). ▶ DOUGLAS, PAUL H., "Colossus on the Potomac: Causes and Cures of Big Government," *Harper's Magazine*, CCVII (July, 1953), 21–27. Shows that the extension of government is largely the product of war rather than social welfare. ▶ GLUECK, SHELDON (ed.), *The Welfare State and the National Welfare* (Cambridge, Mass., 1952). A symposium of articles hostile to the theory and practice of the welfare state. See also Wilhelm Röpke, *Welfare, Freedom, and Inflation* (London, 1957); Conservative Political Center, *The Future of the Welfare State* (London, 1958); and J. Enoch Powell, "Conservatives and Social Services," *The Political Quarterly*, XXIV (April–June, 1953), 156–166. Critiques of the welfare state from a Left-wing socialist viewpoint will be found in Kingsley Martin, *Socialism and the Welfare State* (London, 1951), and G. D. H. Cole, *Is This Socialism?* (London, 1954). ▶ LEKACHMAN, ROBERT (ed.), *National Policy for Economic Welfare at Home and Abroad* (New York, 1955). A collection of essays by leading American economists on domestic and international aspects of economic and social welfare. ▶ LAUTERBACH, A. T., *Economic Security and Individual Freedom: Can We Have Both?* (Ithaca, 1948). See also I. M. D. Little, *A Critique of Welfare Economics* (Oxford, 1950); D. L. Hobman, *The Welfare State* (London, 1953); William A.

Robson, *The Welfare State* (London, 1957); and Richard M. Titmuss, *Essays on the Welfare State* (London, 1958). ▶ LERNER, MAX, *Ideas Are Weapons* (New York, 1939). This collection of essays has a short paper on "Woodrow Wilson: The New Freedom and the New Deal" (pp. 113–116). Lerner maintains that, despite some differences, "there is a real historical continuity between the New Freedom and the New Deal" (p. 115). ▶ MACIVER, ROBERT M., *The Web of Government* (New York, 1947). In Chap. VI (pp. 114–143), the author probes into "Property and Status" as bases of political authority: "Every system of government sustains a corresponding system of property. To change the one is to change the other" (p. 125). MacIver therefore attacks the Lockean conception of property as a right which exists prior to law and the state. In the discussion of the possibility of economic planning in a democratic society, the author argues for a mixed economy of private and public enterprise: "In the mixed economy there is not the monopoly of power that the socialist economy inevitably entails—monopoly in the sense that now there can be no foci of power outside the political order" (p. 357). MacIver takes up this issue more fully in Chap. XI, "The Transformations of Function," especially in the last section on "functions of economic control" (pp. 340–359). ▶ MADISON, CHARLES A., *Critics and Crusaders: A Century of American Protest* (New York, 1947). A good first introduction into the thinking of the major dissenters in America. The book is divided into the following sections: the "Abolitionists," the "Utopians," the "Anarchists," the "Dissident Economists," the "Militant Liberals," and the "Socialists." There is also a useful bibliography (pp. 539–554). ▶ MERRIAM, CHARLES E., *Public and Private Government* (New Haven, 1944). In these lectures, Merriam summarizes his political thinking and experience on the relationships of public and private government. He demonstrates how political, or public, government is only one of the forms of effective social control and domination, and suggests a broader approach to the whole problem of authority, in which the power and government of social and economic groups are recognized and adequately dealt with.

► NIEBUHR, REINHOLD, *The Children of Light and the Children of Darkness* (New York, 1946). Chap. III (pp. 86–118) is on the relationships of "The Community and Property." Niebuhr rejects both Liberalism and Marxism: "Neither understands property as a form of power which can be used in either its individual or its social form as an instrument of particular interest against the general interest. Liberalism makes this mistake in regard to private property and Marxism makes it in regard to socialized property" (p. 106). Niebuhr admits that, while the logic of history is behind socialization, "a wise community will walk warily and test the effect of each new adventure before further adventures" (p. 117).

► PEACOCK, ALAN T. (ed.), *Income Redistribution and Social Policy* (London, 1954). Chap. VI (pp. 178–267) is on the United States.

► POLANYI, KARL, *The Great Transformation* (Beacon Paperbacks, Boston, 1957). A provocative and challenging inquiry into the disintegration and collapse of the nineteenth-century liberal civilization. The author sees in the doctrine of the "self-regulating market" one of the most fateful assumptions of liberal economics and politics. His interpretation of recent changes emphasizes the rediscovery of society and the reintegration of economics and politics.

► ROOSEVELT, FRANKLIN D., *Selected Speeches, Messages, Press Conferences, and Letters* (edited by Basil Rauch, Rinehart Editions, New York, 1957). The arrangement is chronological. Edwin C. Rozwenc (ed.), *The New Deal: Revolution or Evolution?* (Boston, 1949), is a collection of essays on the New Deal, ranging in the political spectrum from Herbert Hoover to Earl Browder. Richard Hofstadter, *The*

Age of Reform: From Bryan to F. D. R. (New York, 1955), shows the place of the New Deal in the context of the American tradition of reform. Mario Einaudi, *The Roosevelt Revolution* (New York, 1959), shows the place of the New Deal in the context of a world-wide perspective.

► ROWNTREE, B. SEEBOHM, and G. R. LAVERS, *Poverty and the Welfare State* (London, 1951). This detailed social survey of York shows that the proportion of the English working-class population living below the poverty line dropped from 31.1% in 1936 to 2.77% in 1950 (p. 40). Apart from new welfare legislation, the elimination of unemployment was a major factor in reducing poverty.

► VEBLEN, THORSTEIN, *The Engineers and the Price System* (New York, 1921). This short book is probably the best introduction to Veblen's approach to political economy. Veblen's main concern was the growing separation between the business and financial managers on the one hand and the technical experts, the engineers, and workers on the other. Though he was not a socialist, Veblen's critical analysis of American business institutions had a profound influence on American political and economic thought, and his contribution to social science is perhaps the most original the United States has produced in the twentieth century. Unlike Marx, Veblen did not claim to be in communion with the laws of history, and he was not sure what kind of society would develop once absentee ownership and control in industry would be replaced by a new industrial order in which engineers and workers would predominate. See also the following works by Veblen: *The Theory of the Leisure Class* (New York, 1889); *The Instinct of Workmanship and the State of the Industrial Arts* (New York, 1914); *The Higher Learning in America* (New York, 1918); *Absentee Ownership and Business Enterprise in Recent Times: The Case of America* (New York, 1923); and *Essays in Our Changing Order* (New York, 1934). *What Veblen Taught* (edited, with a long introduction, by Wesley C. Mitchell, New

York, 1936) is made up of selections from Veblen's more important writings.

The standard biography is *Thorstein Veblen and His America,* by Joseph Dorfman (New York, 1934). A detailed bibliography of Veblen's writings is given (pp.

519–524). Useful analyses of Veblen are also contained in Max Lerner, *Ideas Are Weapons* (New York, 1939), pp. 117–141, and in Charles A. Madison, *Critics and Crusaders: A Century of American Protest* (New York, 1947), pp. 308–339.

Chapter 26

Freud

▶ ADORNO, T. W., ELSE FRENKEL-BRUNSWIK, DANIEL J. LEVINSON, and R. NEVITT SANFORD, *The Authoritarian Personality* (New York, 1950). This attempt to analyze empirically and measure quantitatively authoritarian attitudes is pioneering in the study of politics. Its research techniques, methods, and findings are analyzed in Richard Christie and Marie Jahoda (eds.), *Studies in the Scope and Method of "The Authoritarian Personality"* (Glencoe, 1954).
▶ ALEXANDER, FRANZ, *The Age of Unreason: A Study of the Irrational Forces in Social Life* (Philadelphia–New York, 1942). Part III contains analyses of the emotional structure of totalitarianism (pp. 264–275) and democracy (pp. 276–293). A useful bibliography is appended (pp. 342–359). For a psychological analysis of the political movements of the Right and Left see also J. C. Flugel, *Man, Morals, and Society* (London, 1945), pp. 281–301; Pryn Hopkins, *The Psychology of Social Movements* (London–New York, 1938); M. Brewster Smith, "Opinions, Personality, and Political Behavior," *American Political Science Review,* LII (March, 1958), 1–26; Herbert McClosky, "Conservatism and Personality," *ibid.* (March, 1958), 27–45; and Henry V. Dicks, "Observations on Contemporary Russian Behavior," *Human Relations,* V (May, 1952), 111–175.
▶ ———, *Fundamentals of Psychoanalysis* (New York, 1948). By one of the leading authorities on psychoanalysis. Each chapter

of the book is followed by a bibliography. For simple presentations of the main theories of psychoanalysis see also Marjorie Brierley, *Trends in Psycho-Analysis* (London, 1951); Clara Thompson, *Psychoanalysis: Evolution and Development* (New York, 1950); Geraldine Coster, *Psychoanalysis for Normal People,* 3rd ed. (London–New York, 1947); and Ruth L. Munroe, *Schools of Psychoanalytic Thought* (New York, 1955).
▶ CHAKOTIN, SERGE, *The Rape of the Masses* (London, 1940). The subtitle is "The Psychology of Totalitarian Political Propaganda." See also Talcott Parsons, "Propaganda and Social Control," *Psychiatry,* V (November, 1942), 551–572.
▶ CRAWSHAY-WILLIAMS, RUPERT, *The Comforts of Unreason* (London, 1947). The subtitle of this stimulating work is "A Study of the Motives behind Irrational Thought."
▶ FESSLER, L., "Psychology of Nationalism," *Psychoanalytic Review,* XXVIII (July, 1941), 372–383. See also Géza Róheim, "The Psychology of Patriotism," *American Imago,* VII (March, 1950), 3–19, and Gertrud M. Kurth, "Hitler's Two Germanies: A Sidelight on Nationalism," in Géza Róheim (ed.), *Psychoanalysis and the Social Sciences* (New York, 1950), II, 293–312.
▶ FODOR, NANDOR, and FRANK GAYNOR (ed.), *Freud: Dictionary of Psychoanalysis* (New York, 1950). Presents, in diction-

ary form, the main concepts of psychoanalysis in quotations from Freud's own writings. Useful for rapid reference.

► FREUD, SIGMUND, *A General Introduction to Psychoanalysis* (New York, 1920), and *New Introductory Lectures on Psycho-Analysis* (New York, 1933). These are the two basic introductory works. See also the following: *The Interpretation of Dreams,* 3rd ed. (New York, 1932); *The Psychopathology of Everyday Life* (New York, 1914); *Three Essays on the Theory of Sexuality* (New York, 1910); *Wit and Its Relation to the Unconscious* (New York, 1916); *Totem and Taboo* (New York, 1918); *Group Psychology and the Analysis of the Ego* (New York, 1922); *The Future of an Illusion* (New York, 1928); and *An Outline of Psycho-Analysis* (New York, 1949). *The Basic Writings of Sigmund Freud* (ed. A. A. Brill, Modern Library, New York, 1938), contains six of Freud's more important works. Freud's *Collected Papers,* 5 vols. (New York, 1959), contains papers contributed to journals and encyclopedias.

► FROMM, ERICH, *Escape from Freedom* (New York, 1941). One of the most successful applications of modified psychoanalytical methods and concepts to the analysis of modern totalitarianism. An extensive and devastatingly critical review of the book from the viewpoint of Freudian psychoanalysis will be found in Otto Fenichel, "Psychoanalytic Remarks on Fromm's Book *Escape from Freedom,*" *Psychoanalytic Review,* XXXI (April, 1944), 133–152. See also Fromm's *Man for Himself: An Inquiry into the Psychology of Ethics* (New York, 1947); *Psychoanalysis and Religion* (New Haven, 1950); *The Sane Society* (New York, 1955); and *Sigmund Freud's Mission: An Analysis of His Personality and Influence* (New York, 1959).

► HOOK, SIDNEY (ed.), *Psychoanalysis, Scientific Method, and Philosophy* (New York, 1959). Examines some of the main presuppositions of psychoanalysis from the viewpoint of scientific philosophy. See also Herbert Feigl (ed.), *The Foundations of Science and the Concepts of Psychology and Psychoanalysis* (Minneapolis, 1956); Lewis S. Feuer, *Psychoanalysis and Ethics* (Springfield, Ill., 1955); Howard L. Philp, *Freud and Religious Belief* (New York, 1956); and Morris Ginsberg, "Psychoanalysis and Ethics," *British Journal of Sociology,* III (December, 1952), 287–304.

► HORNEY, KAREN, *The Neurotic Personality of Our Time* (New York, 1937). One of the leading American psychoanalysts, the author modifies, or at least supplements Freud, by stressing more strongly the cultural and social pressures in the formation of neuroses and conflicts. See also the following of her works: *New Ways in Psychoanalysis* (New York, 1939) and *Our Inner Conflicts* (New York, 1945).

► JONES, ERNEST (ed.), *Social Aspects of Psycho-Analysis* (London, 1924). The most interesting essay is Chap. IV, "Politics" (pp. 128–168), by M. D. Eder. It suggests the potential resources of psychoanalysis that could be employed for a better understanding of politics. See also the following: J. C. Flugel, *Man, Morals, and Society: A Psycho-Analytical Study* (London, 1945); Ranyard West, *Conscience and Society: A Study of the Psychological Prerequisites of Law and Order* (London, 1942); R. E. Money-Kyrle, *Psychoanalysis and Politics* (London, 1951), and "Some Aspects of Political Ethics from the Psycho-Analytical Point of View," *International Journal of Psycho-Analysis,* XXV (Parts 3 and 4, 1944), 166–171; Paul Schilder, "Psychoanalysis of Economics," *Psychoanalytic Review,* XXVII (October, 1940), 401–420; Walter A. Weisskopf, *The Psychology of Economics* (Chicago, 1955); Edward Hitschmann, *Great Men: Psychoanalytic Studies* (New York, 1956); Heinz Hartmann, "Psychoanalysis and Sociology," in Sandor Lorand (ed.), *Psychoanalysis Today* (London, 1948), pp. 326–353; Louis Schneider, *The Freudian Psychology and Veblen's Social Theory* (New York, 1948); and Fritz Redl, "Group Emotion and Leadership," *Psychiatry,* V (November, 1942), 573–596.

▶ ———, *What Is Psychoanalysis?* (London, 1949). Short and lucid introduction by the leading British psychoanalyst. See also the following: *Essays in Applied Psychoanalysis,* 2 vols. (London, 1951); *Collected Papers,* 5th ed. (London, 1948); "The Concept of a Normal Mind," *International Journal of Psycho-Analysis,* XXIII (Part 1, 1942), 1–8; "Evolution and Revolution," *ibid.,* XXII (Parts 3 and 4, 1941), 193–208; and "How Can Civilization Be Saved?" *ibid.,* XXIV (Parts 1 and 2, 1943), 1–7.

▶ ———, *The Life and Work of Sigmund Freud,* 3 vols. (New York, 1953–1957). The most informative biography of Freud by one of his closest friends and collaborators, and likely to remain the standard source for a long time. See also Jones' *Sigmund Freud: Four Centenary Addresses* (New York, 1956).

▶ KELSEN, HANS, "The Conception of State and Social Psychology," *International Journal of Psycho-Analysis,* V (Part 1, 1924), 1–38. Illuminating analysis of various conceptions of the state in social psychology, with particular reference to Freud's group theory.

▶ KLUCKHOHN, CLYDE, and HENRY A. MURRAY (eds.), *Personality in Nature, Society, and Culture* (New York, 1948). A comprehensive source book on the formation of personality with contributions by anthropologists, psychoanalysts, psychiatrists, and sociologists. See also Gordon W. Allport, *Personality: A Psychological Interpretation* (New York, 1937); Silvan S. Tomkins (ed.), *Contemporary Psychopathology* (Cambridge, Mass., 1943); and Ralph Linton, *The Cultural Background of Personality* (New York, 1945).

▶ LASSWELL, HAROLD D., *World Politics and Personal Insecurity* (New York–London, 1935). Lasswell is the first political scientist who has successfully applied psychoanalytical research methods and experience to the empirical study of political processes. See also the following of his books: *Psychopathology and Politics* (Chicago, 1930); *Politics: Who Gets What,*

When, How (New York–London, 1936); *The Analysis of Political Behaviour* (London, 1947); *Power and Personality* (New York, 1948); and, in coauthorship with Abraham Kaplan, *Power and Society: A Framework for Political Inquiry* (New Haven, 1950). *The Political Writings of Harold D. Lasswell* (Glencoe, Ill., 1951), contains reprints of *Psychopathology and Politics; Politics: Who Gets What, When, How;* and a new work, *Democratic Character,* summarizing Lasswell's thought. See also Lasswell's articles: "The Triple Appeal Principle: A Contribution of Psychoanalysis to Political and Social Science," *American Journal of Sociology,* XXXVII (January, 1932), 523–538, and "Psychoanalyse und Sozioanalyse," *Imago,* XIX, No. 3 (1933), 377–383.

▶ LEVY, DAVID M., *New Fields of Psychiatry* (New York, 1947). Contains chapters on industrial, military, and political psychiatry. A bibliography is appended (pp. 162–167).

▶ LEWIN, KURT, *Resolving Social Conflicts: Selected Papers on Group Dynamics* (New York, 1948). Throws a great deal of light on the psychological structure of basic political attitudes and motivations. See also Lewin's *A Dynamic Theory of Personality: Selected Papers* (New York–London, 1935).

▶ LINDNER, ROBERT, *Must You Conform?* (New York, 1956). A collection of essays by an American psychoanalyst; the most interesting essay is on "Political Creed and Character" (pp. 79–119). See also Lindner's *Prescription for Rebellion* (New York, 1952) and *The Fifty-Minute Hour* (Bantam Books, New York, 1956), containing psychoanalytical case studies of fascists and communists.

▶ MacCURDY, J. T., *The Structure of Morale* (Cambridge, 1943). A psychological study of the factors that go into the formation of morale, with specific references to different countries. Chap. VII (pp. 141–151) is called "Dictatorship and Democracy."

▶ MANN, THOMAS, "Freud's Position in the History of Modern Culture," *Psychoanalytic Review,* XXVIII (January, 1941),

92–116. See also Otto Fenichel, "Some Remarks on Freud's Place in the History of Science," *Psychoanalytic Quarterly*, XV (July, 1946), 279–284; Lawrence K. Frank, *Society as the Patient* (New Brunswick, 1948), pp. 162–165 ("Freud's Influence on Western Thinking and Culture"); and Heinz Hartmann, "Psychoanalyse und Weltanschauung," *Psychoanalytische Bewegung*, V, (September–October, 1933), 416–429.

▶ MURPHY, GARDNER (ed.), *Human Nature and Enduring Peace* (Boston–New York, 1945). The contributions deal with problems of war and peace as well as with democracy, fascism, education, and religion. See also the following: Edward Glover, *War, Sadism, and Pacifism* (London, 1933); John Dollard and others, *Frustration and Aggression* (New Haven, 1939); E. F. M. Durbin and John Bowlby, *Personal Aggressiveness and War* (London, 1939); George W Kisker (ed.), *World Tension: The Psychopathology of International Relations* (New York, 1951); T. H. Spear (ed.), *Psychological Factors of Peace and War* (London, 1951); Mark A. May, *A Social Psychology of War and Peace* (New Haven, 1943); Edward Chace Tolman, *Drives toward War* (New York–London, 1942); William A. White, *Thoughts of a Psychiatrist on the War and After* (New York, 1919); and Alix Strachey, *The Unconscious Motives of War: A Psychoanalytical Contribution* (London, 1957).

▶ NATHAN, PETER, *The Psychology of Fascism* (London, 1943). See also David Abrahamsen, *Men, Mind, and Power* (New York, 1945); Ernest Jones, "The Psychology of Quislingism," *International Journal of Psycho-Analysis*, XXII (January, 1941), 1–6; Wilhelm Reich, *The Mass Psychology of Fascism* (New York, 1946); Gustav Bychowski, *Dictators and Disciples: From Caesar to Stalin: A Psychoanalytic Interpretation of History* (New York, 1948); and G. M. Gilbert, *The Psychology of Dictatorship: Based on an Examination of the Leaders of Nazi Germany* (New York, 1950).

▶ NELSON, BENJAMIN (ed.), *Freud and the 20th Century* (Meridian Books, New York, 1957). A collection of essays on various aspects of Freud's influence by distinguished writers, including Alfred Kazin, Gregory Zilboorg, Gardner Murphy, Jacques Maritain, and Reinhold Niebuhr. See also John D. Sutherland (ed.), *Psychoanalysis and Contemporary Thought* (London, 1958), a British symposium celebrating the centenary of Freud's birth.

▶ PSYCHOANALYTISCHE BEWEGUNG, 5 vols. (Vienna, 1929–1933). The entire issue of Vol. III (September–October, 1933) is called "Psychoanalysis of Politics," one of the few symposia of the kind. *Psychoanalytische Bewegung* combined, during the five years of its publication, technical articles with papers on the relations of psychoanalysis to other sciences, including the social studies.

▶ RIEFF, PHILIP, *Freud: The Mind of the Moralist* (New York, 1959). The most successful interpretation and analysis, by a social scientist, of Freud's work, particularly as it bears on questions of ethics, politics, and philosophy. See also Jacob A. Arlow, *The Legacy of Freud* (New York, 1956); Martin Freud, *Sigmund Freud: Man and Father* (New York, 1958); Gregory Zilboorg, *Sigmund Freud: His Exploration of the Mind of Man* (New York, 1951); Herbert Marcuse, *Eros and Civilization: An Inquiry into Freud* (Boston, 1955); Lionel Trilling, *Freud and the Crisis of Our Culture* (Boston, 1955); and Franz Alexander and others, *Freud in der Gegenwart* (Frankfurt, 1957).

▶ RÓHEIM, GÉZA (ed.), *Psychoanalysis and the Social Sciences*, 3 vols. (New York, 1947–1951). Contains interesting contributions on the relations of psychoanalysis and the social sciences, literature, and religion. One of the few systematic collections in this field, showing the practical applicability of psychoanalytical methods to the social studies.

▶ SACHS, HANNS, *Freud: Master and Friend* (London, 1945). The author knew Freud from the early stages of psychoanalysis to his death. See also Walter Hollitscher,

Sigmund Freud: An Introduction (London, 1947), and Max Graf, "Reminiscences of Professor Sigmund Freud," *Psychoanalytic Quarterly*, XI (October, 1942), 465–476. Robert Waelder, *Freud* (Living Thoughts Library, Philadelphia, 1941), is composed of an introduction by Waelder (pp. 1–34) and selections from various writings of Freud.

► SCHILDER, PAUL, *Goals and Desires of Man: A Psychological Survey of Life* (New York, 1942). The author was one of the leading psychoanalysts in Austria and, later, the United States. Several chapters deal with social, economic, and political motivations, processes, and institutions.

► STANTON, ALFRED H., and Stewart E. Perry (eds.), *Personality and Political Crisis: New Perspectives from Social Science and Psychiatry for the Study of War and Politics* (Glencoe, 1951). Among the contributors are Harold D. Lasswell, Talcott Parsons, David Riesman, and David M. Levy. The most successful illustration of applying psychological methods of analysis to political science is David M. Levy's "Anti-Nazis: Criteria of Differentiation" (pp. 151–227).

► WORTIS, JOSEPH, *Soviet Psychiatry* (Baltimore, 1950). Chap. V (pp. 71–102) is entitled "Psychoanalysis and Psychotherapy." Until 1930, psychoanalysis was tolerated in the Soviet Union. After this date it ceased to exist there as an organized scientific activity, and in 1936 the Communist party officially decided that it was incompatible with Marxism-Leninism-Stalinism. Wortis' account includes valuable biblio-

graphical data of Marxist studies of psychoanalysis (pp. 73–75). See also E. Perepel, "The Psychoanalytic Movement in the USSR," *Psychoanalytic Review*, XXVI (April, 1939), 299–300, and Raymond A. Bauer, *The New Man in Soviet Psychology* (Cambridge, Mass., 1952). Brief analyses of Freud in the light of Marxism will also be found in the following: Christopher Caudwell, *Studies in a Dying Culture* (London, 1938), Chap. VII, "Freud: A Study in Bourgeois Psychology" (pp. 158–192); T. A. Jackson, *Dialectics* (New York, 1936), pp. 549–560; Francis Bartlett, "Recent Trends in Psychoanalysis," *Science and Society*, IX (Summer, 1945), 214–231; Judson T. Stone, "The Theory and Practice of Psychoanalysis," *Science and Society*, X (Winter, 1946), 54–79; and Joseph Wortis, "Freud, Horney, Fromm and Others," *Science and Society*, X (Spring, 1946), 176–185. The orthodox Soviet "line" on psychoanalysis is summarized in George Siskind and Henry Martel, "Psychoanalysis: Ideological Instrument of Imperialism," *Political Affairs*, XXIX (December, 1950), 61–74, and D. Fedotov, "The Soviet View of Psychoanalysis," *Monthly Review*, IX (December, 1957), 249–254. For a rejoinder to Fedotov by an American psychoanalyst, see Norman Reider, "A Psychoanalyst Replies," *ibid.*, IX (December, 1957), 254–258. See also "Freud and Pavlov," *Soviet Survey* (London), No. 29 (July–September, 1959), 29–37, for an official Soviet account of a special conference on Freud held by the Academy of Medical Sciences of the USSR.

INDEX